K2695

INTERMEDIATE ACCOUNTING

The Willard J. Graham Series in Accounting

Consulting Editor   ROBERT N. ANTHONY   *Harvard University*

INTERMEDIATE ACCOUNTING

Fifth Edition

GLENN A. WELSCH, Ph.D., C.P.A.
Professor of Accounting

CHARLES T. ZLATKOVICH, Ph.D., C.P.A.
Professor of Accounting

WALTER T. HARRISON, JR., Ph.D., C.P.A.
Assistant Professor of Accounting

all of the
College of Business Administration
The University of Texas at Austin

1979   **RICHARD D. IRWIN, INC.**   Homewood, Illinois   60430
Irwin-Dorsey Limited   Georgetown, Ontario   L7G 4B3

© RICHARD D. IRWIN, INC., 1963, 1968, 1972, 1976, and 1979

ISBN 0-256-02178-3
Library of Congress Catalog Card No. 78–71960

Printed in the United States of America

2 3 4 5 6 7 8 9 0 K 6 5 4 3 2 1 0

LEARNING SYSTEMS COMPANY—
a division of Richard D. Irwin, Inc.—has developed a
PROGRAMMED LEARNING AID
to accompany texts in this subject area.
Copies can be purchased through your bookstore
or by writing PLAIDS.
1818 Ridge Road, Homewood, Illinois 60430.

Preface

This fifth edition of our textbook is primarily designed, as were the four previous editions, for students who have finished a reasonably complete course in the fundamentals of financial accounting. It is equally adaptable to a two-semester sequence or to the needs of schools using the quarter plan. It can also be adapted to shorter courses in which some materials must be omitted.

Accounting theory and concepts are emphasized throughout. Students are provided reasons for the various accounting practices and procedures presented; they learn the important "why" along with the "how" of current accounting practice. This edition continues the comprehensive features which gained wide recognition for the prior editions. Upon completion, the student should be prepared for advanced courses in accounting and for the theory and practice sections of the Uniform CPA Examination. A salient feature of this book is that, rather than avoiding troublesome complexities by omission or oversimplified exposition, it deals with them comprehensively and, where appropriate, alternative viewpoints are presented. Examination of the chapter contents will show that, consistent with the objectives of the book, all important aspects of each topic are considered; this necessarily imposes a comparatively high level of sophistication.

Preferred accounting terminology is used throughout on a consistent basis. Citations and references to pronouncements of the APB, FASB, American Institute of Certified Public Accountants, American Accounting Association, and Securities and Exchange Commission permeate the 25 chapters. A new and useful feature, introduced in the fourth edition, has been expanded and continued as an Appendix after the first chapter. It lists all of the *Accounting Research Bulletins,* (ARBs), *APB Opinions,* and *FASB Statements* up to within two months of publication date. It indicates the title, issue date, and current status of each pronouncement, as well as the *page numbers* on which the document is cited in this book.

To further assist the instructor, the publisher will periodically provide supplementary booklets covering newly issued *FASB Statements.*

Recognizing that students learn much of their accounting during this phase of their study program by solving relevant assignment materials, we have supplied a wealth of questions, short exercises, cases, and problems for each chapter. The questions are designed for class discussion to emphasize definitions and basic relationships. The exercises pinpoint specific issues discussed in the chapter; the comprehensive problems provide an overview of several related topics; and the cases present challenging learning experiences through "open-ended" situations designed for class or group discussion. Approximately 85 percent of these materials from the prior edition have been revised and/or replaced. An appropriate selection of materials from the Uniform CPA Examinations is provided in the assignment material. The unusually wide range of assignment materials of varying levels of difficulty is provided so that selections can be made by the instructor to suit each particular learning situation.

This edition provides a unique variety of supplementary materials to aid the instructor and the student. In addition to the textbook, they include the following:

For the instructor:

1. A comprehensive teacher's manual including several typical assignment schedules, a topical listing and a suggested time schedule for each exercise and problem, and detailed step-by-step computations.
2. An examination booklet classified by chapter.
3. Transparencies for selected assignment materials.

For the student:

4. A study guide that incorporates for each chapter *(a)* study suggestions, *(b)* a summary of important points with illustrations, *(c)* questions for self-evaluation, and *(d)* answers to the questions for self-paced study.
5. A comprehensive *review* practice set designed for use during the early part of the first semester. This practice set is included in the study guide (4 above); transaction narrative, forms, and selected key figures are provided with the practice set. The complete solution is given in the teacher's manual (1 above).
6. A complete set of working papers (forms with selected captions provided) for working each exercise and problem.
7. A list of key solution figures (provided upon request of the instructor).

Chapters are arranged in a teachable and logical sequence and are grouped to facilitate rearrangements to suit individual preferences. Chapters 1 and 2 set the stage for all that follows by presenting an integrated overview of the foundations of accounting theory and the institutional setting in which this foundation is cast. Chapters 3 through 5 present a comprehensive review of the fundamentals of financial accounting and extend somewhat the usual topical coverage of the traditional beginning financial accounting course.

Chapter 6 presents the concepts of future and present value and illustrates some of their primary applications in financial accounting. This location facilitates discussion of the conceptual applications illustrated throughout the chapters that follow (and advanced courses as well). Also, this treatment recognizes the numerous applications of future and present value concepts as required by *APB Opinions, FASB Statements,* and the Uniform CPA Examinations. The introductory coverage of this topic in some elementary accounting textbooks is continued on a higher level of sophistication in this intermediate text.

Chapter 7 discusses effects of changing prices on financial reporting. This chapter considers price level restatement and current replacement cost accounting. In this fifth edition, this discussion was moved up from Chapter 25 because of the pervasiveness of inflation and the resultant widespread concern of the accounting profession, industry, and government over its impact on financial reporting. Also, early study of this important topic provides students with background information that is important to evaluation of many aspects of the historical cost model as discussed and illustrated in the subsequent chapters. However, the chapter has been written so it can be used at any place in the chapter sequence without materially impacting on the chapters that would follow. Chapters 8–12 cover the "current" balance sheet accounts, and Chapters 13–15 cover operational (or fixed) assets.

Chapters 1 through 14 (or 15) are usually viewed as the first course in intermediate accounting. These chapters present a comprehensive treatment of assets and liabilities. Chapters 16 through 18 are devoted to corporations. Long-term investments in equity and debt securities are discussed in Chapters 19 and 20. The five remaining chapters are devoted, in order, to special reporting problems: 21, Pension Costs; 22, Leases; 23, The Statement of Changes in Financial Position; 24, Accounting Changes and Incomplete Records; and 25, Interim Reports, Segment Reporting, and Analysis of Financial Statements. With the exception of Chapter 23, each of these chapters may be omitted in part or in whole, without significantly affecting the continuity of the course.

Certain materials, that sometimes are omitted, have been placed in appendixes at the ends of chapters. The instructor's manual provides a suggested ranking of topics in terms of ease of omission so that the instructor can tailor the course content to individual preferences.

We are indebted to numerous colleagues and students whose comments and suggestions led to valuable improvements in this fifth edition. We appreciate the permission granted by the Financial Accounting Standards Board, the American Accounting Association, and the American Institute of Certified Public Accountants to quote from their various pronouncements. The latter organization also permitted us to make liberal use of materials adapted from the Uniform CPA Examinations. We are indebted to Nationwide Corporation, NCR Corporation, and Peavey Company for permission to reproduce significant portions of their financial reports (end of Chapters 3, 4, and 25).

We are especially appreciative of the contributions of Louis H. Gilles, Jr., Gary L. Cunningham, Melvin C. O'Connor, and Richard E. Czarnecki for their valuable suggestions as to content, arrangement, and assignment materials. We express appreciation to the editorial consultants for their competence in improving the manuscript: Mrs. Harold Scholten, Robert Earl Nelson, Roberta Yankiver Long, Robert Jack Arogeti, and Mary Anne Keely. We wish to acknowledge the valuable suggestions of our colleagues: Allen Bizzell, James W. Deitrick, John Fellingham, Kermit D. Larson, Edward L. Summers, Lawrence A. Tomassini, and David A. Wilson. We also express thanks to the following students at The University of Texas at Austin: I. J. Aarons, Marie Arnold, Elesa Bentsen, Richard G. File, Dawn Renee Greenspan, Elizabeth Henke, Robert W. Jamison, Paul S. Kushel, Edward C. Nathan, Stephanie L. Rocher, Petrea Sandlin, and Kathy Smith. We especially thank Linda Nelson for her excellence in typing and checking the manuscript and for her dedication in performing many other tasks that were essential to completion of this book.

Finally, we express our thanks to numerous users of the prior editions for their valuable suggestions. Suggestions and comments on this fifth edition are invited.

May 1979

GLENN A. WELSCH
CHARLES T. ZLATKOVICH
WALTER T. HARRISON, JR.

Contents

1. **INTRODUCTION, 1**

   Objectives of the Book, 1
   Accounting Defined, 1
   Objectives of External Financial Reporting, 3
     Information Useful in Investment and Credit
         Decisions, 3
     Cash Flow Prospects, 3
     *Information about Enterprise Resources and
         Obligations and Changes in Them, 4*
   Professional Accountants, 4
   Accounting Organizations and Literature, 5
   American Institute of Certified Public Accountants
       (AICPA), 5
   Financial Accounting Standards Board
       (FASB), 7
   Securities and Exchange Commission (SEC), 8
   Persuasion versus Compulsion, 9
   American Accounting Association (AAA), 10
   Income Tax Legislation and Financial
       Accounting, 11
   Concluding Comment, 11
   Appendix—List of Official Pronouncements (with
       page citations), 13

2. **THEORETICAL FOUNDATIONS OF
   FINANCIAL ACCOUNTING AND
   REPORTING, 22**

   Broad Theoretical Structure, 23
   Basic Objectives of Financial Accounting and
       Reporting, 23

Underlying Environmental Assumptions, 26
   Separate-Entity Assumption, 26
   Continuity Assumption, 26
   Unit of Measure Assumption, 27
   Time Period Assumption, 27
Basic Accounting Principles, 28
   Cost Principle, 29
   Revenue Principle, 30
     Revenue Defined, 30
     Measurement of Revenue, 30
     Timing Revenue Recognition, 30
     Service Transactions, 31
     Sales Transactions, 31
   The Matching Principle, 32
   Objectivity Principle, 33
   Consistency Principle, 33
   Financial Reporting Principle, 34
   Modifying (or exception) Principle, 35
     Materiality, 35
     Conservatism, 36
     Industry Peculiarities, 36
Implementing Measurement Principles, 36
   Selection of the Objects, Activities, and Events
       to Be Measured, 37
   Identification and Classification of Attributes,
       37
   Assignment of Quantitative Amounts, 37
   Modifying Measurement Principle, 37
Basic Components of the Accounting Model, 38
Detailed Principles and Procedures, 38
Accounting on the Accrual Basis versus the Cash
   Basis, 39
Conclusion, 40

3. **REVIEW—THE ACCOUNTING MODEL AND INFORMATION PROCESSING, 48**

The Accounting Model, 48
The Accounting Information Processing Cycle, 49
Collection of Raw Economic Data (Phase 1), 49
Transaction Analysis (Phase 2), 52
Journalizing—The Original Data Input (Phase 3), 52
Posting to the Ledger (Phase 4), 52
  Real and Nominal Accounts, 54
  Subsidiary Ledgers and Control Accounts, 54
Prepare a Trial Balance—Unadjusted (Phase 5), 54
Prepare Worksheet (Phase 6), 55
  Worksheet Techniques, 55
  Development of Adjusting Entries, 57
    Prepaid Expense, 57
    Revenue Collected in Advance, 57
    Accrued Expense, 57
  Adjusting Entries for Estimated Items, 58
    Depreciation Expense, 58
    Bad Debt Expense, 58
  Completion of the Worksheet, 59
Prepare Financial Statements (Phase 7), 60
Journalizing and Posting Adjusting Entries (Phase 8), 60
Closing Entries (Phase 9), 60
Post-Closing Trial Balance (Phase 10), 62
Reversing Entries (Phase 11), 62
Information Processing Procedures, 65
Summary of the Information Processing Cycle, 65
Control Accounts and Subsidiary Ledgers, 65
Journals, 65
  Special Journals, 66
    Special Journal for Merchandise Sales on Credit, 67
    Special Journal for Merchandise Purchases on Credit, 68
    Special Journal for Cash Receipts, 69
    Special Journal for Cash Payments, 69
  Reconciling a Subsidiary Ledger, 70
Appendix B—Worksheet for a Manufacturing Company, 70

4. **REVIEW—THE INCOME STATEMENT AND RETAINED EARNINGS, 91**

Concept of Income, 91
  Terminology Problems, 93
Form of Income Statement, 94
  Single-Step Format, 94

Multiple-Step Format, 96
  Manufacturing Situation, 96
  Supporting Expense Schedules, 97
Special Problems Affecting the Income Statement, 97
Disclosure Guidelines, 97
Depreciation, 98
Income Taxes, 98
  Intraperiod Tax Allocation, 98
Earnings Per Share, 100
Extraordinary Items and Prior Period Adjustments, 102
  Reporting Concepts of Net Income, 102
  Extraordinary Items, 104
  Reporting Unusual or Infrequent Items, 105
  Discontinued Operations (disposal) of a Segment of a Business, 105
  Prior Period Adjustments, 106
Accounting Changes and Correction of Errors, 107
  Treatment of Changes in Estimates, 107
  Treatment of Changes in Accounting Principles, 108
  Treatment of Accounting Errors, 108
Statement of Retained Earnings, 109
  Restrictions on Retained Earnings, 109
  Combined Income Statement and Retained Earnings, 110
Actual Financial Statements, 110
Appendix A—Characteristics and Examples of Extraordinary Items, 110
Appendix B—Specimen Statements; 1977–1978 NCR (National Cash Register Corporation), 113

5. **REVIEW—THE BALANCE SHEET AND STATEMENT OF CHANGES IN FINANCIAL POSITION, 134**

Balance Sheet, 134
Characteristics of the Balance Sheet, 134
  Assets Defined, 135
  Liabilities Defined, 135
  Owners' Equity Defined, 135
Measurements (valuations) on the Balance Sheet, 135
Importance of the Balance Sheet, 136
Balance Sheet Format, 136
Classifications in the Balance Sheet, 137
Current Assets, 138
Current Liabilities, 140
Working Capital, 141

Investments and Funds, 141
Operational Assets, 142
   Operational Assets—Tangible, 142
   Operational Assets—Intangible, 142
Other Assets, 142
Deferred Charges, 142
Long-Term Liabilities, 143
Deferred Credits, 143
Owners' Equity, 143
   Capital Stock, 143
   Contributed Capital in Excess of Par or Stated
      Value, 144
   Other Contributed Capital, 144
   Retained Earnings, 144
Unrealized Capital, 145
Statement of Changes in Financial Position, 145
Some Special Reporting Issues, 147
   Terminology, 147
   Comparative Statements, 148
   Rounding of Amounts, 148
   Subsequent Events, 148
   Full Disclosure, 149
   Auditors' Report, 151
Appendix—Specimen Statements, 153

6. **CONCEPTS OF FUTURE AND PRESENT VALUE, 180**

Purpose of the Chapter, 180
Concept of Interest, 181
   Simple versus Compound Interest, 181
   Interest Periods, 182
   Summary of Concepts, 182
Part A—Future Value and Present Value of 1, 182
Future Value of 1, 182
   Calculation of Future Value of 1, 183
   Future Value of a Specified Principal, 184
   Determination of Other Values Related to
      Future Value of 1, 184
   Determination of the Compound Interest Rate,
      184
   Determination of Number of Periods, 185
   An Accounting Application of Future Value of
      1, 185
Present Value of 1, 185
   Computation of Present Value of 1, 186
   An Accounting Application of Present Value
      of 1, 187
Part B—Annuities, 187
Future Value of an Ordinary Annuity, 188
   Use of Table of Future Value of Annuity of 1,
      188

   Determination of Other Values Related to
      Future Value of Annuity, 189
Present Value of an Ordinary Annuity, 190
   Determination of Other Values Related to
      Present Value of Annuity, 191
Annuities Due, 192
   Future Value of Annuity Due, 192
   Present Value of Annuity Due, 194
Using Multiple Table Values, 197
Summary, 199
Table values, 200–207

7. **ACCOUNTING AND REPORTING WHEN PRICES CHANGE, 215**

Price Changes and How They Are Measured, 215
Impact of Inflation on Financial Statements,
   217
Depreciation and Rising Replacement Costs, 217
Piecemeal Accounting Approaches Under
   Conditions of Inflation, 218
**Part A—General Purchasing Power
Restatement of Historical Cost
Amounts, 219**
   Background, 219
Application of General Price Level Index
   Numbers to Restate Financial Statements,
   221
Simplified Illustration of General Price Level
   Restatement, 222
   Application of Conversion Factors, 223
   Computation of the 19D General Purchasing
      Power Gain or Loss on Monetary Items, 223
GPL Restatement of the Balance Sheet, 224
GPL Restatement of the Income Statement, 227
Preparation of Comparative GPL Statements,
   227
   Proof of Restatement, 229
Complex Illustration of General Price Level
   Restatement, 229
**Part B—Current Value Accounting Models,
231**
Current Replacement Cost Disclosure
   Requirement of the SEC, 234
Different Concepts of Capital Maintenance, 234
Differences Between GPL and CRC Accounting
   Models, 234
Relevance of Current Replacement Cost Data,
   235
Holding Gains and Losses on Nonmonetary
   Assets, 235

Current Replacement Cost Accounting
Illustrated, 236
CRC Entries, 237
CRC Financial Statements, 237
*GPL Restatements in CRC Financial
Statements, 237*
Adjustment of the Holding Gain, 242
"Catch-up" Depreciation, 242
Differences Among Historical Cost, General Price
Level, and Current Replacement Cost
Financial Statements, 242
Summary, 244
Appendix—Selected Details of the Securities
and Exchange Commission (SEC or
Commission) Accounting Series Release
(ASR) No. 190, issued March 23, 1976, 244

8. **CASH, SHORT-TERM INVESTMENTS, AND
RECEIVABLES, 264**

Part A—Cash, 264
Composition of Cash, 264
Control of Cash, 265
Control of Cash Receipts, 265
Control of Cash Disbursements, 266
Petty Cash, 266
Cash Overage and Shortage, 267
Reconciliation of Bank with Book Balance, 267
Comprehensive Reconciliation, 269
Part B—Short-Term Investments, 271
Short-Term Investments Defined, 272
Valuation of Short-Term Investments, 272
Lower of Cost or Market, 272
Valuation at Cost, 276
Valuation at Market, 276
Evaluation of the Methods, 277
Identification of Units, 278
Investment Revenue on Short-Term Investments,
278
Comprehensive Illustration Based on Lower of
Cost or Market, 278
Part C—Receivables, 280
Trade Receivables, 280
Accounts Receivable, 280
*Measurement of Bad Debt Expense and
Accounts Receivable, 280*
Accounting for Bad Debt Expense, 281
Evaluation of Methods, 282
Aging Accounts Receivable, 283
Bad Debts Collected, 283
Customers' Credit Balances, 284
Added Facts about Accounts Receivable, 284

Notes Receivable, 284
Provision for Losses on Notes, 286
Discounting of Notes Receivable, 286
*Disclosure of the Contingent Liability on
Discounted Notes, 286*
Dishonored Notes Receivable, 286
Special Receivables, 287
Use of Receivables to Secure Immediate Cash,
287
Assignment, 287
Illustrative Problem, 288
Factoring, 289
Outright Sale of Accounts Receivable, 289
Pledging, 289

9. **LIABILITIES AND INCOME TAXES, 308**

**Part A—Measuring, Recording, and Reporting
Liabilities, 308**
Current Liabilities, 309
Current Liabilities Defined, 309
Accounts Payable, 310
Notes Payable, 310
Interest on Notes Payable, 310
*Interest-Bearing (ordinary) Notes Payable,
311*
*Discounted (noninterest-bearing) Notes
Payable (with no stated interest rate),
311*
*Discounted Note with Interest Based on Face
Amount, 312*
Dividends Payable, 312
Advances and Returnable Deposits, 312
Accrued Liabilities, 313
Deferred Credits, 313
Funds Collected for Third Parties, 314
Payroll Taxes, 314
Federal Income Taxes Withheld, 314
FICA Payroll Taxes, 314
FUTA Payroll Taxes, 315
Tax and Bonus Problems, 316
Long-Term Liabilities, 317
Note Issued for Cash, 317
*Note Issued for Property, Goods, or Services,
317*
Current Maturities of Long-Term Debt, 319
Contingencies and Estimated Liabilities, 319
Loss Contingencies that Must Be Accrued,
319
Loss Contingencies Disclosed Only in Notes,
321
Gain Contingencies, 322
Appropriations and Reserves of Retained
Earnings, 323

Part B—Accounting for Income Taxes, 323
Interperiod Income Tax Allocation, 324
   Timing Differences, 326
   Permanent Differences, 326
   Comprehensive Illustration, 327
   Classification of Deferred Income Taxes, 327
   Changes in Tax Rates, 329
Income Tax Effects of Prior Period Adjustments, 330
Income Tax Loss Carrybacks and Carryforwards, 331
   Accounting for Carrybacks and Carryforwards, 332
   Carryforward Option, 333
The Investment Tax Credit, 334
Intraperiod Income Tax Allocation, 334
Disclosure of Tax Allocation, 337

10. INVENTORIES—GENERAL PROBLEMS, 350

The Nature of Inventories, 350
Classification of Inventories, 350
The Dual Phase of the Inventory Problem, 351
Identification of Goods (Items) that Should Be Included in Inventory, 351
Measurement of Physical Quantities in Inventory, 352
  Periodic Inventory System, 352
  Perpetual Inventory System, 352
Effect of Inventory Errors, 353
Measurement of the Accounting Value of Inventory, 355
Content of Unit Cost, 357
  Freight-In (Freight on Purchases), 358
  Purchase Discounts, 358
Departures from the Cost Principle In Costing Inventory, 358
  Lower of Cost or Market, 358
Accounting Problems in Applying Lower of Cost or Market, 361
  Determination of Overall Inventory Valuation, 361
  Recording Lower of Cost or Market in the Accounts, 361
    Direct Inventory Reduction Method, 362
    Inventory Allowance Method, 362
    Comparison and Evaluation of the Two Methods, 366
Net Realizable Value and Replacement Cost, 366
Inventories Valued above Cost at Selling Price, 367

Relative Sales Value Method, 368
Losses on Purchase Commitments, 368
Appendix—Replacement Cost Disclosure, 369

11. INVENTORIES—FLOW AND MATCHING PROCEDURES, 384

Part A—Inventory Cost Flow Methods, 384
Specific Cost Identification, 385
Average Cost, 386
  Weighted Average Cost, 386
  Moving Average Cost, 386
First-In, First-Out Cost, 387
Last-In, First-Out Cost, 389
  Lifo Inventory Liquidation, 391
  Recording *Lifo* in the Accounts, 392
  Comparison of *Lifo* with *Fifo,* 392
Miscellaneous Inventory Cost Flow Methods, 393
  Next-In, First-Out Method, 394
  Base Stock Method, 394
  Standard Cost Method, 394
  Variable or Direct Cost Method, 395
Selection of a Cost Flow Method, 396
Part B—Complexities in Applying *Lifo,* 396
Initial Adoption of *Lifo,* 397
Application of *Lifo* Inventory Procedures, 398
  Quantity of Goods *Lifo* Method, 398
    Single-Item Approach, 398
    Multiple-Pools Approach, 398
Dollar Value *Lifo* Method, 399
  Applying the Dollar Value *Lifo* Approach, 401
  Inventory Liquidation, 401
  Technological Changes in Inventories, 403
Indexing, 405
Lifo "Reserves," 405
Summary, 406

12. SPECIAL VALUATION PROCEDURES, 417

Part A–1—Estimating Procedures for Inventories, 417
Gross Margin Method, 417
Retail Inventory Method, 420
  Markups and Markdowns, 421
Application of the Retail Inventory Method, 422
  Retail Method, *Fifo* Cost (excluding LCM), 422
  Retail Method, Average Cost (excluding LCM), 423
  Retail Method, Lower of Cost or Market (LCM), 423
  Special Items, 424

Part A–2—Inventories for Long-Term Construction Contracts, 425
Completed Contract Method, 426
Percentage of Completion Method, 426
Evaluation of Methods, 427
Part B—Dollar Value, *Lifo* Retail Method, 430
Application of the Dollar Value, *Lifo* Retail Method, 430
    Changing to Dollar Value *Lifo* Retail—Computation of Base Inventory, 431

13. OPERATIONAL ASSETS: PROPERTY, PLANT AND EQUIPMENT—ACQUISITION, USE, AND RETIREMENT, 446

Capital Expenditures (asset) and Revenue Expenditures (expense), 446
Principles Underlying Accounting for Property, Plant, and Equipment, 447
Tangible Assets Acquired for Cash, 447
Tangible Assets Acquired on Deferred Payment Plan, 448
Tangible Assets Acquired in Exchange for Securities, 449
Tangible Assets Acquired through Exchanges, 449
    Similar versus Dissimilar Assets, 450
    Accounting Procedures for Exchanges, 450
Lump-Sum Purchases of Assets, 452
Make-Ready Costs, 453
Departures from Cost in Accounting for Tangible Operating Assets, 453
    Donated Assets, 453
    Discovery Value, 454
    Writedown of Operational Assets Due to Impairment of Use Value, 455
Assets Constructed for Own Use, 455
    Excess Costs of Construction, 456
Interest during the Construction Period, 456
Expenditures Subsequent to Acquisition, 458
    Repairs and Maintenance, 458
        Ordinary Repairs and Maintenance, 458
    Extraordinary Repairs, 459
    Replacements and Betterments, 459
    Additions, 460
    Rearrangement of Assets, 461
Retirement of Operational Assets, 461
Appendix—Acquisition Costs of Specific Property, 461
    Land, 461
    Buildings, 462

    Machinery, Furniture, Fixtures, and Equipment, 463
    Patterns and Dies, 463
    Returnable Containers, 463
    Leasehold Improvements, 463

14. PROPERTY, PLANT, AND EQUIPMENT— DEPRECIATION AND DEPLETION, 480

Depreciation, 481
    Depreciation and Dividends, 481
    Depreciation and Cash Flow, 481
    Depreciation Is an Estimate, 482
Causes of Depreciation, 482
Factors in Determining Depreciation Expense, 483
Recording Depreciation, 483
Methods of Depreciation, 484
    Straight-Line Method, 484
    Service Hours Method, 485
    Productive Output Method, 486
    Accelerated (reducing charge) Methods, 487
    Sum-of-the-Years'-Digits Method, 487
    Fixed-Percentage-on-Declining-Base Method, 488
    Double-Declining Balance Method, 488
Depreciation Based on Investment Concepts, 489
Fractional Year Depreciation, 489
Special Depreciation Systems, 490
    Inventory (or appraisal) System, 490
    Retirement and Replacement Systems, 491
    Group and Composite Life Systems, 491
Depreciation Policy, 493
Depreciation Disclosures, 494
Changes and Correction of Depreciation, 494
The Investment Tax Credit, 496
Depletion, 497
    Nature of Depletion, 497
Appendix—Annuity and Sinking Fund Methods of Depreciation, 499
Annuity Method of Depreciation, 499
Sinking Fund Method of Depreciation, 500

15. INTANGIBLE ASSETS, 515

Accounting for Intangible Assets, 516
Measuring and Recording Intangible Assets at Acquisition, 516
    Classification of the Cost of Intangible Assets, 516
Amortization of the Cost of Intangible Assets, 516

Disposal of Intangible Assets, 517
Identifiable Intangible Assets, 517
    Patents, 518
    Copyrights, 518
    Franchises, 518
    Trademarks, 519
Unidentifiable Intangible Assets, 519
    Goodwill, 519
        Amortization of Goodwill, 520
        Estimating Goodwill, 520
        Capitalization of Earnings, 521
        Capitalization of Excess Earnings, 521
        *Years' Purchase of Average Excess Earnings,
            522*
        Years' Purchase of Average Earnings, 522
    Present Value Estimation of Goodwill, 522
Deferred Charges, 523
    Organization Costs, 523
    Leaseholds, 524
    Research and Development Costs, 524
Accounting for Exploration Costs, 526
Development Stage Companies, 527
Insurance, 528
    Liability Insurance, 528
    Casualty Insurance, 528
    Coinsurance, 529
    Blanket Policy, 530
    Indemnity under Several Policies, 530
    Accounting for a Casualty Loss, 531
        *Accounting for Casualty Loss Illustrated,
            531*
    Life Insurance, 532
        Cash Surrender and Loan Value, 533
Reporting Intangibles, 534

**16. CORPORATIONS—FORMATION AND
CONTRIBUTED CAPITAL, 550**

Classifications of Corporations, 551
Nature of Capital Stock, 551
Classes of Capital Stock, 552
    Par Value Stock, 553
    Nopar Stock, 553
    Legal Capital, 553
    Common Stock, 554
    Preferred Stock, 554
    Cumulative Preferences on Preferred Stock,
        554
    Participating Preferences on Preferred Stock,
        555
    Asset Preference, 556
    Redemption Preference, 556
    Convertibility Privilege, 556
    Callable Preferred Stock, 556

Accounting for Issuance of Par Value Stock, 557
    Authorization, 557
    Stock Issued for Cash, 557
Accounting for Nopar Capital Stock, 557
Subscriptions, 558
Accounting for Stock Premium and Discount, 560
Special Sales of Stock, 560
    Noncash Sale of Stock, 561
Unrealized Capital Increment, 561
Unrealized Capital Decrement, 562
Assessments on Shareholders, 562
Incorporation of a Going Business, 563

**17. CORPORATIONS—RETAINED EARNINGS
AND CHANGES IN STOCKHOLDERS' EQUITY
AFTER FORMATION, 573**

Part A—Retained Earnings and Dividends, 573
Dividends, 574
    Cash Dividends, 575
    Property Dividends, 576
    Liability Dividends, 576
    Liquidating Dividends, 577
    Stock Dividends, 577
Dividends in Arrears on Preferred Stock, 580
Fractional Share Rights, 581
Dividends and Treasury Stock, 582
Legality of Dividends, 582
Appropriations of Retained Earnings, 583
    Appropriation Related to a Contractual
        Agreement, 584
    Appropriations as an Aspect of Financial
        Planning, 585
    Appropriation for Possible Future Losses, 585
Reporting Retained Earnings, 585
**Part B—Contraction and Expansion of
    Corporate Capital after Formation, 587**
Treasury Stock, 588
Recording and Reporting Treasury Stock
    Transactions, 588
    Cost Method, 589
    Par Value Method, 590
    Recording Treasury Stock—Par Value Method
        for Par Value Stock, 591
Accounting for Nopar Treasury Stock, 592
Treasury Stock Received by Donation, 592
Retirement of Treasury Stock, 592
Restriction of Retained Earnings for Treasury
    Stock, 593
Retirement of Callable and Redeemable Stock,
    594
Convertible Stock, 594

Changing Par Value, 595
Quasi-Reorganizations, 595

18. STOCK RIGHTS AND OPTIONS AND EARNINGS PER SHARE, 613

Part A—Stock Rights and Employee Stock Compensation Plans, 613
Stock Rights, 613
Accounting for Stock Options Issued to
    Employees, 615
  Theoretical Considerations, 616
  Practical Considerations, 617
    Is the Plan Compensatory? 617
  Accounting for Noncompensatory Plans, 617
  Accounting for Compensatory Plans, 617
    When Should the Compensation Cost be
      Measured? 617
    What Is the Total Amount of Compensation
      Cost? 618
    To What Accounting Periods Should the
      Measured Compensation Cost be
      Assigned as Expense? 618
Illustrative Entries for Compensatory Stock
    Option Plans, 619
Part B—Earnings per Share (EPS), 622
Computing EPS with a Simple Capital Structure,
    624
Computing EPS with a Complex Capital Structure,
    626
    Primary Earnings per Share, 627
  Computation of Primary Earnings per Share,
    630
    Fully Diluted Earnings per Share, 630
  Antidilution, 632
  Reporting Earnings per Share, 634

19. LONG-TERM INVESTMENTS IN EQUITY SECURITIES, 644

Recording Long-Term Investments at Date of
    Acquisition, 644
  Special Cost Problems, 645
Accounting and Reporting for Stock Investments
    Subsequent to Acquisition, 646
Part A—Cost, Equity, and Market Value Methods, 647
Cost Method, 647
Equity Method, 650
Market Value Method, 654
Part B—Consolidated Statements, 656
Concept of a Controlling Interest, 656

Acquiring a Controlling Interest, 657
Accounting and Reporting Problems, 657
Combination by Pooling of Interests, 658
    Consolidated Balance Sheet Immediately
      after Acquisition, Pooling of Interests
      Basis, 659
Combination by Purchase, 661
    Consolidated Balance Sheet Immediately
      after Acquisition, Purchase Basis, 661
Preparing Consolidated Statements Subsequent
    to Acquisition, 662
    Consolidated Statements Subsequent to
      Acquisition, Pooling of Interests Basis,
      663
    Consolidated Statements Subsequent to
      Acquisition, Purchase Basis, 664
Part C—Some Special Problems in Accounting for Stock Investments, 668
Stock Dividends Received on Investment
    Shares, 668
Stock Split of Investment Shares, 669
Convertible Securities, 669
Stock Rights on Investment Shares, 670
Illustrative problem, 670
Special-Purpose Funds, 671

20. ACCOUNTING FOR BONDS AS LONG-TERM LIABILITIES AND INVESTMENTS, 684

Nature of Bonds, 684
Classification of Bonds, 685
Financial Market Conditions, 685
Part A—Accounting for Bonds Compared: The Issuer and the Investor, 686
Bond Interest and Prices, 686
  Determination of Bond Prices, 687
Accounting for and Reporting Bonds (Issuer and
    Investor), 688
  Amortization of Discount and Premium, 689
    Straight-Line Amortization, 690
    Interest Method of Amortization, 690
Reporting Bonds on the Financial Statements,
    691
  Reporting by the Issuer, 691
  Reporting by the Investor, 692
Accounting for Semiannual Interest Payments,
    692
Part B—Special Problems in Accounting for Bonds, 693
Bonds Sold and Purchased between Interest
    Dates, 694
  Bonds Sold between Interest Dates at Par, 694

Bonds Sold between Interest Dates at a
Discount or Premium, 695
Accounting When Interest Periods and Fiscal
Periods Do Not Coincide, 696
Bond Issue Costs, 697
Nonconvertible Bonds with Detachable Stock
Warrants, 697
Convertible Bonds, 698
Accounting for the Issuance of Convertible
Bonds, 699
Accounting for Conversion, 699
**Part C—Changes in Obligations Prior to
Maturity, 700**
Early Extinguishment of Debt, 700
Call Provisions, 700
Purchase in the Open Market, 700
Refunding Bonds Payable, 701
Assessing the Income Tax Effects, 703
Classification of Short-Term Obligations
Expected to be Refinanced, 704
Troubled Debt Restructuring, 704
Transfer of Assets and Equity Interests,
706
Transfer of Assets, 706
Transfer of Equity Interest, 706
Modification of Terms of Debt, 707
*Modification When Carrying Amount
Exceeds Cash Payments, 710*
Disclosure Requirements, 711
Appendix—Serial Bonds, 711
Characteristics of Serial Bonds, 711
Determining Selling Price of Serial Bonds, 711
Amortization of Premium and Discount on Serial
Bonds, 711

21. **ACCOUNTING FOR PENSION COSTS, 724**

Pension Plan Fundamentals, 724
A Simplified Pension Plan Example, 725
Past Service Cost Illustrated, 726
APB Opinion No. 8 and Pension Accounting,
727
Actuarial Cost Methods, 727
Illustration of Recording Pension Costs and
Funding, 728
Actuarial Gains and Losses, 732
Maximum and Minimum Limits on Annual Pension
Cost, 734
Pension Plan Disclosures, 735
Effects of ERISA, 736
Disclosure of Unfunded Pension Liabilities,
737

22. **ACCOUNTING FOR LEASES, 748**

Lease Accounting Terminology, 748
Accounting for Operating Leases, 749
*Rent Paid in Advance on Operating Leases,
749*
Capitalization of Leases, 752
Criteria for Capital Leases, 753
Criteria for Capital Leases for Lessees, 753
Criteria for Capital Type Leases by Lessors,
753
Sales Type Leases (Lessor), 754
Direct Financing Leases (Lessor), 754
Lessee Accounting under Capital Leases, 755
Bargain Purchase Options, 757
*Accruals When Fiscal and Lease Dates Do
Not Agree, 759*
Lessor Accounting under Capital Leases, 759
Lessor Accounting under Direct Financing
Leases, 759
Lessor's Implicit Rate, 760
Lessor Accounting under Sales Type Leases,
761
*Residual Value and Investment Tax Credit,
763*
Termination of Lease Agreements, 763
Sale and Leaseback, 764
Financial Statement Disclosure, 765
Classification of Lease Receivables, 766
Appendix—Leveraged Leases, 766
Fundamental Characteristics, 766
Cash Flows under Leveraged Leases, 767

23. **THE STATEMENT OF CHANGES IN
FINANCIAL POSITION, 781**

Basic Characteristics of the Statement of
Changes in Financial Position, 782
Illustration of Cash Flows versus Working
Capital Flows, 783
Criteria for the Statement of Changes in
Financial Position, 786
**Part A—Statement of Changes in Financial
Position, Working Capital Basis, 786**
Approaches to Preparation of the Statement of
Changes in Financial Position, Working
Capital Basis, 788
Fundamentals of the T-Account Approach,
788
Explanation of the Analysis, 789
Fundamentals of the Worksheet Approach,
792
Statement Format, 798

Part B—Statement of Changes in Financial Position, Cash Basis (Or Cash Plus Short-Term Investments), 798
Preparation of the Statement of Changes in Financial Position, Cash Basis, 799
The Worksheet Approach, 800
Comprehensive Illustration, Cash Plus Short-Term Investments, 806

24. **ACCOUNTING CHANGES, ERROR CORRECTION, AND INCOMPLETE RECORDS, 815**

Part A—Accounting Changes and Error Correction, 815
Methods for Recording and Reporting Accounting Changes and Error Corrections, 816
Change in Accounting Principle, 816
Change in Accounting Estimate, 818
Change in Reporting Entity, 819
Correction of Errors, 820
Analytical Procedures for Correcting Errors, 822
Preparing Correcting Entries for Errors, 823
Worksheet Techniques for Correcting Errors, 825
Worksheet to Correct Net Income and Provide Correcting Entries, 826
Worksheets to Recast Financial Statements, 828
Illustrative Problem, 828
Part B—Statements from Single-Entry and Other Incomplete Records, 830
Preparation of Balance Sheet from Single-Entry Records, 830
Computation of Income, 831
Preparation of a Detailed Income Statement from Incomplete Data, 832
Balance Sheet Preparation, 832
Computation of Net Income, 832
Analysis of Revenue and Expenses, 833
Computation of Sales, 833
Computation of Purchases, 834
Computation of Depreciation, 834
Computation of Expenses, 834
Preparation of the Income Statement, 835

Worksheets for Problems from Single-Entry and Other Incomplete Records, 835
Limitations of Single-Entry Recordkeeping, 838

25. **INTERIM REPORTS, SEGMENT REPORTING, AND ANALYSIS OF FINANCIAL STATEMENTS, 851**

Interim Reporting, 851
The Discrete Period and Integral Part Approaches, 851
Segment (or Line of Business) Reporting, 853
Analysis of Financial Statements, 856
Analytical Approaches and Techniques, 856
Examine the Auditors' Report, 856
Analyze the Statement of Accounting Policies, 858
Overall Examination of the Financial Statements, 858
Application of Analytical Techniques, 858
Comparative Statements, 859
Percentage Analysis of Financial Statements, 859
Ratio (Proportionate) Analysis, 861
Ratios That Measure Current Position, 862
Working Capital (Current) Ratio, 862
Acid Test Ratio, 862
Working Capital to Total Assets, 862
Receivable Turnover, 863
Inventory Turnover, 864
Ratios that Measure Equity Position, 865
Equity Ratios, 865
Book Value per Share of Common Stock, 866
Ratios that Measure Operating Results, 867
Profit Margin, 868
Return on Investment, 868
More on Financial Leverage, 869
Investment Turnover, 869
Market Ratios, 869
Use and Interpretation of Ratio Analysis, 870
The Search for Additional Information, 871
Appendix—Actual Financial Statements of Peavey Company, 873

INDEX, 893

1

Introduction

OBJECTIVES OF THE BOOK

Financial accounting represents that branch of accounting which provides financial information primarily for decision makers outside the entity. This financial information is provided to external decision makers primarily via *general-purpose statements* of operating results (i.e., the income statement), financial position (i.e., the balance sheet), and changes in financial position (i.e., statement of changes in financial position), and by notes to the financial statements. Consistent with the broad objective of reporting to external parties, this book concentrates on the application of accounting theory, standards, principles, and procedures to financial accounting problems. The fundamental rationale that underlies the various aspects of financial accounting is stressed. This book is designed especially for accounting majors, regardless of specialized interests in public, industrial, governmental, tax, or social accounting. Another objective is to prepare students for entry into the accounting profession; consequently, current financial accounting practices and trends are emphasized.

The authors presume that the student has completed a course in fundamentals of financial accounting.[1] Satisfactory completion of this text should prepare students for all advanced accounting courses. Emphasis throughout on theory, standards, and principles— the "why" of accounting—enables students to cope with new and complex accounting problems on a conceptual rather than a procedural (or memory) level.

ACCOUNTING DEFINED

Accounting can be broadly defined as an information processing system designed to *capture* and *measure* the economic essence of events that affect an entity and to *report* their economic effects on that entity to decision makers.[2] This definition serves the two basic groups of decision makers—internal decision makers and external decision makers. These two groups require different kinds of information because of their different relationships with the entity.

Internal decision makers are the managers responsible for planning the future of the entity,

---

[1] Refer to books such as G. A. Welsch and R. N. Anthony, *Fundamentals of Financial Accounting,* rev. ed. (Homewood, Ill.: Richard D. Irwin, Inc., 1977).

[2] Another useful definition: Accounting is a service activity. Its function is to provide quantitative information, primarily financial in nature, about economic entities that is intended to be useful in making economic decisions—in making reasoned choices among alternative courses of action. Accounting includes several branches, for example, financial accounting, managerial accounting, and governmental accounting (American Institute of Certified Public Accountants, *Statement of the Accounting Principles Board No. 4,* "Basic Concepts and Accounting Principles Underlying Financial Statements of Business Enterprises" [New York, October 1970], p. 17).

implementing the plans, and controlling operations on a day-to-day basis. Because of their intimate relationship with the entity, they can command whatever financial data they may need at dates of their choice. Furthermore, the information at their disposal generally is not intended to be communicated to outsiders. The process of developing and reporting financial information to internal users is usually called *management accounting,* and the reports are referred to as internal management reports. Because of the confidential nature of internal management reports and their focus on internal decision making, there is no requirement (other than as specified by the management) that they conform to generally accepted accounting principles. Clearly, internal management reports should be structured to conform to the particular decision-making needs of the management.

In contrast, *external* decision makers (i.e., external users of financial information) make distinctly different types of decisions regarding the entity, such as to invest or disinvest, to loan funds, and so on. Among the potential external users are owners, lenders, suppliers, potential investors and creditors, employees, customers, financial analysts and advisors, brokers, underwriters, stock exchanges, lawyers, economists, taxing and regulatory authorities, legislators, financial press and reporting agencies, labor unions, trade associations, business researchers, teachers and students, and the public.[3]

In view of the diverse range of external users of financial data, the accounting profession has developed *general-purpose financial statements* designed to meet their decision-making needs. These statements are developed in a phase of accounting known as *financial accounting.* Financial accounting may be broadly defined as an information processing function. Its purpose is to record transactions and other events affecting the entity and to report their economic impact to external decision makers. External users, because of their detachment from the entity, cannot directly command specific financial information from the entity; therefore, they must

rely on general-purpose financial statements. The accounting profession, in order to serve external users, has developed a network of accounting theory, standards, principles, and procedures designed to assure that external financial reports are (1) relevant—they are designed to serve the decision-making needs of the external users; (2) credible—they are intended to be fair representations of the economic circumstances of the entity; and (3) accurate and free of bias—they must conform to specified standards of accounting and reporting.

The management of an enterprise uses both financial accounting and management accounting reports; however, external users have access only to the financial accounting reports. The same accounting information processing system (generally called the accounting system) accumulates, processes, and reports the information usually contained in the external and the internal financial reports. The external financial statements focus on the entity's assets, liabilities, owners' equity, revenues, expenses, gains, losses, and flow of funds.

Delineation of the objectives of the general-purpose financial statements represents one of the most vexing problems facing the accounting profession. One view holds that a primary objective of financial statements is to report on managers' *stewardship* responsibility to shareholders (reporting on past performance). Another view is that financial statements should provide information that decision makers can use to make *predictions* about future economic consequences accruing from the entity's activities. On a different dimension there is the widespread belief that financial statements should meet the information needs of *sophisticated* decision makers such as pension fund managers and other institutional investors. Others believe that the primary purpose of financial statements should be to meet the information needs of less sophisticated *lay investors* whose access to specific information about an entity is necessarily limited. On these two issues *FASB Statement of Financial Accounting Concepts No. 1* (November 1978) states: "Financial reporting is expected to provide information about an enterprise's financial performance during a period and about how management of an enterprise has dis-

---

[3] Financial Accounting Standards Board, *Statement of Financial Accounting Concepts No. 1, Objectives of Financial Reporting by Business Enterprises* (Stamford, Conn., November 1978), p. 11.

charged its stewardship responsibility to owners." Also, "The information should be comprehensible to those who have a reasonable understanding of business and economic activities and are willing to study the information with reasonable diligence."

OBJECTIVES OF EXTERNAL FINANCIAL REPORTING

Fundamentally, the objective of external financial statements is to communicate the summarized economic effects of completed transactions and certain other events on the financial position and current operations of the entity. Although there are other means of communicating financial information, such as prospectuses (for security offerings), news releases, management "letters," and reports filed with regulatory agencies (such as the Securities and Exchange Commission), the primary means are the periodic financial statements. *General-purpose financial reporting* includes *all information* provided by the accounting system that is reported to external parties, whether included in or reported outside the periodic financial statements.

External financial statements do not focus on specific groups of individuals (such as those listed above), rather they report financial information relevant to (1) investment decisions (by investors), and (2) credit decisions (by creditors). To accomplish these two objectives, two general types of financial statements are used:

1. Those that report the recorded information about the economic resources, obligations, and owners' equity of an entity at a particular point in time. This type is generally referred to as financial position (i.e., the balance sheet).

2. Those that report the recorded financial *changes* in the resources, obligations, and owners' equity resulting from transactions and other events during a specified period of time. This type is generally referred to as changes in financial position (i.e., the income statement and the statement of changes in financial position).

The Financial Accounting Standards Board (FASB) outlined these objectives as follows:

The objectives begin with a broad focus on information that is useful in investment and credit decisions; then narrow that focus to investors' and creditors' primary interest in the prospects of receiving cash from their investments in or loans to business enterprises and the relation of those prospects to the enterprise's prospects; and finally focus on information about an enterprise's economic resources, the claims to those resources, and changes in them, including measures of the enterprise's performance, that is useful in assessing the enterprise's cash flow prospects.[4]

Information Useful in Investment and Credit Decisions

Financial reporting should provide information useful to investors (in making investment decisions) and creditors (in making credit decisions). The terms *investors* and *creditors* include both those who deal directly with the enterprise and those who deal through intermediaries. Financial statements should be unbiased and understandable to the extent reasonably feasible; however, relevant information should not be excluded merely because it is difficult for some to understand or because some particular users choose not to use it.

To meet the needs of investors and creditors, financial statements should provide information about the *(a)* earning power; *(b)* cash inflows and outflows; and *(c)* resources, obligations, and owners' equity of the entity.[5]

Cash Flow Prospects. Investors and creditors, both current and potential, place particular importance on the ability of an enterprise to generate cash in sufficient sums to meet the entity's current and future needs. Investment and credit decisions involve evaluation of present cash (invested or borrowed) and the future cash inflows or outflows that may eventually result. Therefore, the FASB stated that "Financial reporting

---

[4] FASB, *Statement of Financial Accounting Concepts No. 1, "Objectives of Financial Reporting by Business Enterprises"* (Stamford, Conn.), November 1978, p. 15.

[5] Adapted from FASB, *Statement of Financial Accounting Concepts No. 1,* pp. viii and ix. *"Objectives of Financial Reporting by Business Enterprises."* Also in that *Statement,* "For convenience, *financial reporting* is used in place of *general purpose external financial reporting for business enterprises. . . ."*

should provide information to help present and potential investors and creditors and other users in assessing the amounts, timing, and uncertainty of prospective cash receipts from dividends or interest and the proceeds from the sale, redemption, or maturity of securities or loans." Also, that "Information about enterprise earnings based on accrual accounting generally provides a better indication of an enterprise's present and continuing ability to generate favorable cash flows than information limited to the financial effects of cash receipts and payments."[6]

Information about Enterprise Resources and Obligations and Changes in Them. In addition to information about cash flows, the financial statements should report on *(a)* enterprise earnings and *(b)* financial resources. Enterprise earning activities relate to revenues, expenses, gains, and losses accounted for on the accrual basis as opposed to the cash basis (discussed in the next two chapters). Financial reporting should provide information about the economic resources of the enterprise (the assets), its obligations to transfer resources to others (the liabilities), and the sources of owners' equity.

To meet the objectives of financial reporting, the following external financial statements (including notes to the statements) currently are used:

Required statements:

1. Income statement—a periodic statement of the results of operations that reports, for the period just ended, the revenues, expenses, gains, losses, net income, and earnings per share.
2. Balance sheet—a statement of financial position that reports the assets, liabilities, and owners' equity as of the end of the period just ended.
3. Statement of changes in financial position—a statement, for the period just ended, of the inflow of funds, outflow of funds, and net change in funds for the period. This statement measures funds in terms of either cash or working capital.

Other statements generally provided:

4. Statement of retained earnings, or
5. Statement of changes in owners' equity, and
6. Long-term summary of selected financial data.

The chapters to follow explain the collection, analysis, measurement, classification, and recording of the data necessary to develop the above statements and the related additional disclosures by means of notes to those statements.

We stress that the essence of financial accounting is the *measurement* of economic effects and *communication* of the results to external decision makers. The volume of detailed data processing encountered in an accounting system is necessary to achieve the desired result—communication. We strongly emphasize this point because it is easy to become immersed in the system and its procedures and to lose sight of the primary objective—reporting to the decision maker.

PROFESSIONAL ACCOUNTANTS

Accounting has a long and interesting history. Today professional accountants fulfill an important and unique role in society.[7] The professional accountant is usually a *certified public accountant* (CPA). As with lawyers, physicians, and engineers, accountants are engaged in a wide variety of endeavors. The primary endeavors are the following:

1. Public accounting—An independent certified public accountant offers services to the public in a manner similar to a doctor, lawyer, or architect. These services include *(a)* auditing (the attest function), *(b)* tax planning and determination of tax liability, and *(c)* management advisory services (consulting). Certified public accountants in public practice have a unique relationship with their clients as *independent* and impartial reviewers of the financial statements. Although *independent accountants* are

---

[6] FASB, *Statement of Financial Accounting Concepts No. 1,* pp. viii and ix.

[7] A careful distinction should be made between an accountant and a bookkeeper. A bookkeeper is involved in the routine clerical phase of the accounting process, whereas an accountant is competent in transaction analysis, measurement of economic events, systems design, analytical and interpretive processes, financial evaluation, and, indeed, the entire management process.

paid by the client, the independence concept extends their responsibilities to third parties, that is, to users of the financial statements.

The primary service rendered by the independent certified public accountant is the attest function which is achieved as the result of an *audit* of the financial statements, including an auditor's report (see page 162). The auditor's report (1) states the scope of the audit examination of the accounts and (2) expresses the auditor's professional "opinion" as to whether the financial statements are "presented fairly" in accordance with generally accepted accounting principles. The attest function is particularly important to external statement users because it is intended to protect them against outright misrepresentation and bias on the part of the reporting entity. The attest function lends credibility to the financial statements because of the auditor's independence from the client.

2. Industrial accounting—A large number of certified public accountants and certified management accountants (CMA) work in businesses where they serve as accountants, internal auditors, tax specialists, systems experts, controllers, financial vice presidents, and chief executives. In these capacities, their specialized interests typically focus on management, tax, and accounting. As employees, they are not in the role of *independent* certified public accountants.

3. Governmental and nonprofit accounting—Certified public accountants serve at all levels of government and not-for-profit entities: local, state, national, and international. In these capacities they are not in the role of *independent* certified public accountants.

Since this is a financial accounting text, it focuses on generally accepted accounting principles. These are the principles that the *independent* certified public accountant must carefully interpret, apply and enforce, and which private and governmental accountants should follow in their accounting for the affairs of their respective entities.

ACCOUNTING ORGANIZATIONS AND LITERATURE

Because of the importance of external financial reports to investors, creditors, government, and the public at large, there is widespread interest in generally accepted accounting standards and the way in which they are established. In recent years, interest in the response of the accounting profession to its public interest responsibility has increased dramatically. Various aspects of the financial reports of major companies and industries are reported by the news media almost every day.

The development of accounting theory and generally accepted accounting standards has been influenced by the financial community, accounting firms, academicians, individual accountants, federal and state laws, regulatory agencies, and professional accounting organizations.

Primary among the organizations which influence accounting's evolution are the American Institute of Certified Public Accountants, Financial Accounting Standards Board, Securities and Exchange Commission, and the American Accounting Association. These organizations perform an important service in that they interpret and elucidate the objectives, evolution, and complexities of financial accounting.

Similarly, the accounting literature constitutes another integral element in your study of financial accounting. Most of the organizations cited above support publications which are influential since they report the results of research, discuss practical accounting problems, and suggest changes in accounting standards. They are rich sources for discussions of the major issues in accounting. Throughout this book numerous citations from the literature are provided. Early in your study of accounting you should become familiar with the primary accounting publications and use them to expand and enrich your comprehension of the major issues and the relevant alternatives being discussed.

AMERICAN INSTITUTE OF CERTIFIED PUBLIC ACCOUNTANTS (AICPA)

This is the national professional organization of certified public accountants. It is responsive to the needs of CPAs in public practice; consequently, its primary efforts and publications have focused on the practice of public accounting. Its primary publications relating to financial accounting are the following:

1. *The Journal of Accountancy*—a monthly magazine containing pronouncements, articles, and special sections of direct interest to the independent CPA.
2. *Accountants' Index*—an annual publication containing an index of the accounting literature published during the year.
3. *Accounting Trends and Techniques*—an annual publication containing a survey of the characteristics of the annual financial reports of 600 corporations. It presents tabulations, explanations, and illustrations of reporting procedures, policies, terminology, disclosures, and so on.
4. *Accounting Research Studies*—a series of studies that focuses on specific accounting problems. These studies provide background information, discussion of alternative solutions, and often recommendations.
5. *Statements on Auditing Standards*—These periodically issued statements relate to specific auditing standards to be followed by the independent CPA. These statements usually are studied comprehensively in the auditing courses offered at most colleges.
6. Statements that deal with specific accounting principles, standards, and procedures:[8]
   a. *Accounting Research Bulletins*—During the period 1938 through 1959, the AICPA had a *Committee on Accounting Procedure* which was responsible for "narrowing the areas of differences and inconsistencies" in accounting practice. To this end the Committee issued pronouncements dealing with accounting principles and procedures. The first 42 pronouncements were restated and revised as

Accounting Research Bulletin (ARB) No. 43, "Restatement and Revision of Accounting Research Bulletins," June 1953.

From 1953 to 1959, eight additional bulletins were issued; the last *Accounting Research Bulletin* was *No. 51.* In addition, during this period the AICPA Committee on Terminology issued eight terminology bulletins recommending improvements in accounting terminology. These were combined as *Accounting Terminology Bulletin No. 1,* "Review and Resumé, August 1953." Since they have been continued in force, as amended by the Accounting Principles Board (and later by the Financial Accounting Standards Board), they continue to be a part of generally accepted accounting principles.

   b. *Opinions of the Accounting Principles Board*—To provide more emphasis on the formulation of accounting principles, in 1959 the AICPA established the *Accounting Principles Board* (APB) to replace the Committee on Accounting Procedure. The APB designated its pronouncements as *Opinions.* The *Opinions* prescribe specific accounting principles and procedures for designated types of transactions and other events. During its period of existence from 1959 to 1973, the Board issued 31 *Opinions.* In addition, the Board issued four *Statements.* In contrast to the *Opinions,* the *Statements* presented recommendations, rather than requirements, which the Board hoped would be followed with a consequent improvement in financial accounting and reporting to external decision makers.

The *Accounting Research Bulletins (ARBs), Accounting Terminology Bulletins,* and the *Opinions of the Accounting Principles Board* continue in force, as amended; therefore, they frequently are cited in the chapters to follow.[9]

---

[8] The contents of these statements, opinions, and bulletins are listed in the Appendix to this chapter with *page* citations by your authors. Refer to the following sources for details:

a. AICPA Professional Standards, vol. 3, *Accounting—Current Text,* as of July 1, 1978, AICPA.
b. Original Pronouncements—*Opinions of the Accounting Principles Board* (Nos. 1–31 inclusive).

---

[9] AICPA, *APB Accounting Principles,* vols. 1 and 2.

FINANCIAL ACCOUNTING STANDARDS BOARD (FASB)

In the 1960s and early 1970s many complaints arose within and outside the accounting profession, with respect to the institutional arrangements from which accounting standards were established. These complaints criticized *(a)* lack of participation by organizations other than the AICPA, *(b)* "quality" of the opinions, *(c)* failure to develop a "broad statement of the objectives and principles" underlying external financial reports, and *(d)* insufficient output. Consequently, a committee was appointed to "study the issues and problems involved in setting accounting principles, and to make recommendations for improving the process and to make it more responsive to the needs of those who rely on financial statements." The "Wheat" Committee presented its report in March 1972. Basically, the report recommended the following:[10]

1. A Financial Accounting Foundation—composed of nine trustees appointed by the Board of Directors of the AICPA. Responsibilities: to appoint members of the Financial Accounting Standards Board; to appoint a Financial Accounting Standards Advisory Council; to raise funds to support the new structure; and to periodically review and revise the basic structure.
2. A Financial Accounting Standards Board (FASB)—composed of seven full-time members to establish standards of financial accounting and reporting. Four members would be CPAs drawn from public practice. The other three would not need to hold a CPA certificate but should possess extensive experience in the financial reporting field.
3. A Financial Accounting Standards Advisory Council—approximately 35 members. Responsibilities: to work closely with the FASB in an *advisory* capacity; to establish priorities, establish task forces, and react to proposed standards.

4. Research activities—structured with objectives and needs clearly in mind.

The AICPA accepted the recommendations of the Committee. Consequently, the APB was discontinued and the FASB became operational July 1, 1973. The first action of the FASB was a decision that the previous *Accounting Research Bulletins* approved by the APB, and the *Opinions* of the APB (as amended), would continue in force. To date the FASB has issued a number of pronouncements designated as:

1. *Statements of Financial Accounting Standards*—The FASB decided to issue *Statements of Standards* rather than *Opinions* used by the APB. They specify accounting principles and procedures (now called standards) on specific accounting issues. They have the same "force" as the *APB Opinions.*
2. *Interpretations*—These interpret prior *ARBs, APB Opinions,* and *FASB Statements of Financial Accounting Standards.*
3. *Statements of Financial Accounting Concepts*—The purpose of this series, instituted in November 1978, is to set forth fundamental concepts on which financial accounting and reporting standards will be based (see footnote 3).

Prior to issuing a *Statement,* the FASB typically (1) prepares and distributes a *Discussion Memorandum* which provides an exhaustive analysis of the issue under consideration, (2) holds a *public hearing* on the issues, and (3) issues an *exposure draft* of the proposed statement. This process was designed to gain wide participation and full consideration of all relevant aspects of each accounting issue considered. After this process is completed, the FASB then makes a decision *(a)* whether to issue a statement, and *(b)* in case of an issue, the standards of financial accounting and reporting to be prescribed. Most meetings of the FASB have been open to the public since January 1, 1978. The *FASB Statements* and Interpretations are cited throughout this book.

The Appendix at the end of this chapter lists the *ARBs, APB Opinions,* and *FASB Statements*

---

[10] *Establishing Financial Accounting Standards, Report of the Study on Establishment of Accounting Principles, American Institute of Certified Public Accountants,* March 1972, p. 105 (chairman of the Committee, Francis M. Wheat).

issued to date; page citations in this book also are given.

The organization of the Financial Accounting Standards Board significantly changed the role of the American Institute of Certified Public Accountants in the development of accounting standards. Since the 1930s the AICPA has assumed a prominent role in the development of standards, first through the Committee on Accounting Procedure, and then through the Accounting Principles Board. The FASB is independent of the AICPA. However, to continue a strong role, in conjunction with the work of the FASB and the regulatory agencies, the AICPA established the Accounting Standards Division to provide leadership in respect to accounting and reporting issues. Within the Division, the Accounting Standards Executive Committee (AcSEC) is a senior technical committee authorized to speak for the AICPA in the areas of financial accounting and reporting. To this end AcSEC Statements of Position have the objective of influencing the development of accounting standards. In addition, the AICPA maintains leadership in the development of *auditing* standards through the Auditing Standards Executive Committee (AudSEC). This Committee focuses on developing auditing standards and professional ethics and provides continuing education programs for the profession.

SECURITIES AND EXCHANGE COMMISSION (SEC)

A number of governmental regulatory agencies exert a continuing influence on accounting and reporting by businesses. Among these agencies are the Internal Revenue Service, Federal Power Commission, Interstate Commerce Commission, and the Securities and Exchange Commission. The SEC exerts a powerful influence on the development of accounting standards.

Because of the conditions reflected in the securities market at the beginning of the depression of the 1930s, Congress passed the Securities Act of 1933, the Securities Exchange Act of 1934, and the Public Utility Holding Company Act of 1935. The 1934 Act created the Securities and Exchange Commission and gave it broad authority to regulate virtually all aspects of the issuance and sale of securities in interstate commerce, that is, securities sold to the general public, including those listed on the stock exchanges. Congress gave the Commission authority to prescribe external financial reporting requirements for those companies under its jurisdiction. To obtain permission to sell an issue of securities, a company must secure SEC approval of a *prospectus,* which becomes a public record. The prospectus, which is prepared only when there is a new security issuance, reports extensive information about the company, its officers, securities, and financial affairs. The financial portion of the prospectus must be audited by an independent CPA. After receiving permission to sell securities, the company must file with the Commission, as a matter of public record, audited financial statements *each subsequent year* (10–K reports) and unaudited quarterly statements (10–Q reports). The Commission requires more information in the annual financial 10–K reports than is typically included in the "published financial statements" furnished to the shareholders.

The SEC filing and reporting requirements are published as

1. *Regulation S-X*—This is the original document issued by the Commission, as amended and supplemented, which prescribes the reporting requirements, including instructions and forms.
2. *Accounting Series Releases*—These releases are amendments, extensions, and additions to *Regulation S-X.* More than 250 *ASR*s have been issued to date.
3. Special SEC Releases.
4. *Staff Accounting Bulletins (SAB).*

Although the SEC has wide statutory authority to prescribe financial accounting and external reporting requirements for "registered" companies, the Commission generally has relied on the accounting profession to set and enforce accounting standards and to regulate the profession. The working relationship between the SEC and the accounting profession has been a positive one, and accounting regulation has remained largely in the private sector. However, there have been numerous occasions where the SEC has forced the accounting profession to

Appendix—List of Official Pronouncements

This appendix is included to help students *(a)* gain an overview of the official pronouncements, and *(b)* identify appropriate source documents for numerous accounting issues discussed in this book. Further study of these issues in the source documents often is desirable.

Accounting Research Bulletins (ARBs), Accounting Procedures Committee, AICPA (ARBs discontinued in 1959)

ARB No.	Contents	Status, January 1, 1979	Page Citations in this Book
43.	Restatement and Revisions of *Accounting Research Bulletins Nos. 1–42,* June, 1953	Generally continued in force by *APB Opinion No. 6* (as amended)	6, 148, 220, 265, 310, 313, 317, 318, 595
Ch. 1.	Prior Opinions	Amended	588
Ch. 2.	Form of Statements	Amended and partially superseded	148
Ch. 3.	Working Capital	Amended and partially superseded	273
Ch. 4.	Inventory Pricing	Amended	357, 360, 361, 366, 367, 369, 385
Ch. 5.	Intangible Assets	Superseded by *APB Opinions Nos. 16 and 17*	516
Ch. 6.	Contingency Reserves	Superseded by *FASB Statement No. 5*	
Ch. 7.	Capital Accounts	Amended and partially superseded	578, 579, 595
Ch. 8.	Income and Earned Surplus	Superseded by *APB Opinion No. 9*	
Ch. 9.	Depreciation	Amended and partially superseded	454, 455
Ch. 10.	Taxes	Amended and partially superseded	
Ch. 11.	Government Contracts	Amended	
Ch. 12.	Foreign Operations and Foreign Exchange	Amended by *FASB Statement No. 8*	
Ch. 13.	Compensation (Pension Plans)	Amended and partially superseded	616, 617, 619, 620, 622
Ch. 14.	Disclosure of Long-Term Leases in Financial Statements	Superseded by *APB Opinion No. 5*	
Ch. 15.	Unamortized Discount, Issue Cost, and Redemption Premium on Bonds Refunded	Superseded by *APB Opinion No. 26*	
44.	Declining-Balance Depreciation; Revised July 1958	Amended	485, 489
45.	Long-Term Construction-Type Contracts, October 1955	Unchanged	430
46.	Discontinuance of Dating Earned Surplus		

Accounting Research Bulletins (ARBs), Accounting Procedures Committee, AICPA (ARBs discontinued 1959) (continued)

Contents	Status, January 1, 1979	Page Citations in this Book
Accounting for Costs of Pension Plans, September 1956	Superseded by *APB Opinion No. 8*	
Business Combinations, January 1957	Superseded by *APB Opinion No. 16*	
Earnings per Share, April 1958	Superseded by *APB Opinion No. 9*	
Contingencies, October 1958	Superseded by *FASB Statement No. 5*	
Consolidated Financial Statements, August 1959	Amended and partially superseded	6, 656, 657

Accounting Terminology Bulletins, Committee on Terminology, AICPA (Bulletins discontinued in 1959)

Contents	Status, January 1, 1979	Page Citations in this Book
Review and Resume (of the eight original terminology bulletins), June 1953	Partially superseded	6, 109, 147, 481, 552, 573, 583
Proceeds, Revenue, Income, Profit, and Earnings	Amended	417
Book Value	Unchanged	
Cost, Expense, and Loss	Amended	

Accounting Principles Board (APB) Opinions, AICPA (Opinions discontinued in 1973)

Contents	Status, January 1, 1979	Page Citations in this Book
New Depreciation Guidelines and Rules, November 1962	Unchanged	
Accounting for the "Investment Credit," December 1962	Amended	497
Addendum to *Opinion No. 2*—Accounting Principles for Regulated Industries, December 1962	Unchanged	
The Statement of Source and Application of Funds, October 1963	Superseded by *APB Opinion No. 19*	
Accounting for the "Investment Credit" (Amending No. 2), March 1964 . .	Unchanged, but interpreted	497
Reporting of Leases in Financial Statements of Lessee. September 1964	Superseded	

Accounting Principles Board (APB) Opinions, AICPA (Opinions discontinued in 1973) *(continued)*

APB No. Contents	Status, January 1, 1979	Page Citations in this Book
6. Status of *Accounting Research Bulletins,* October 1965	Amended and partially superseded	284, 455, 589, 590, 596
7. Accounting for Leases in Financial Statements of Lessors, May 1966	Superseded	
8. Accounting for the Cost of Pension Plans, November 1966	Unchanged, but interpreted	181, 724, 727, 728, 729, 731, 732, 733, 734, 735, 736, 737, 740, 742, 743, 745
9. Reporting the Results of Operations, December 1966	Amended and partially superseded	100, 102, 103, 104, 106, 107, 109, 555, 581, 585, 586, 622, 650, 820
10. Omnibus Opinion—1966, December 1966	Amended and partially superseded	536, 581, 594
11. Accounting for Income Taxes, December 1967	Amended, partially superseded, and interpreted	98, 100, 323, 324, 326, 327, 329, 330, 332, 333, 334, 335, 337, 342
12. Omnibus Opinion—1967, December 1967	Amended and partially superseded	98, 142, 494, 586, 587, 619
13. Amending Paragraph 6 of *APB Opinion No. 9,* Application to Commercial Banks, March 1969	Unchanged	Beyond scope of this book
14. Accounting for Convertible Debt and Debt Issued with Stock Purchase Warrants, March 1969	Unchanged	697, 698, 699
15. Earnings per Share, May 1969	Amended	100, 101, 102, 622, 624, 627, 628, 629, 630, 631, 634
16. Business Combinations, August 1970	Amended and interpreted	650, 658, 659, 661, 668
17. Intangible Assets, August 1970	Unchanged, but interpreted	516, 517, 519, 520, 523, 541, 545, 653
18. The Equity Method of Accounting for Investments in Common Stock, March 1971	Amended and partially superseded	646, 647, 650, 654
19. Reporting Changes in Financial Position, March 1971	Unchanged	145, 148, 781, 782, 783, 785, 791, 792, 796, 798, 800, 806, 807
20. Accounting Changes, July, 1971	Amended and interpreted	34, 107, 108, 282, 321, 391, 397, 460, 494, 495, 496, 501, 619, 622, 815, 816, 820, 853
21. Interest on Receivables and Payables, August 1971	Unchanged, but interpreted	30, 102, 180, 181, 308, 317, 318, 319, 448, 690, 691, 692, 697, 707, 772
22. Disclosure of Accounting Policies, April 1972	Unchanged	97, 149, 494, 858
23. Accounting for Income Taxes—Special Areas, April, 1972	Amended and interpreted	323
24. Accounting for Income Taxes—Equity Method Investments, April 1972	Unchanged but interpreted	323

Accounting Principles Board (APB) Opinions, AICPA (Opinions discontinued in 1973) *(continued)*

APB No.	Contents	Status January 1, 1979	Page Citations in this Book
25.	Accounting for Stock issued to Employees, October 1972	Unchanged	616, 617, 618, 619, 620, 622
26.	Early Extinguishment of Debt, October 1972	Amended and interpreted	596, 700, 701, 705
27.	Accounting for Lease Transactions by Manufacturer or Dealer Lessors, November 1972	Superseded	
28.	Interim Financial Reporting, May 1973	Partially superseded and interpreted	28, 419, 851, 852, 853
29.	Accounting for Nonmonetary Transactions, May 1973	Unchanged	449, 450, 451, 452, 453, 561, 576, 700, 796
30.	Reporting the Results of Operations, June 1973	Amended and partially superseded	99, 102, 104, 105, 110, 111, 320, 321, 367, 455, 460, 461, 650, 706, 707, 710
31.	Disclosure of Lease Commitments by Lessees, June 1973	Superseded	

Statements of the Accounting Principles Board, Accounting Principles Board (AICPA)

APB No.	Contents	Page Citations in this Book
1.	Statement by the Accounting Principles Board, April 1962	
2.	Disclosure of Supplemental Financial Information by Diversified Companies, September 1967	
3.	Financial Statements Restated for General Price-Level Changes, June 1969	220
4.	Basic Concepts and Accounting Principles Underlying Financial Statements of Business Enterprises, October 1970	1, 34, 39, 93, 94, 134, 135

Financial Accounting Standards Board (FASB), Statements of Financial Accounting *Standards* (1973 to date)

FASB No.	Contents	Status, January 1, 1979	Page Citations in this Book
1.	Disclosure of Foreign Currency, December 1973	Amended by *FASB Statement No. 8*	
2.	Accounting for Research and Development Costs, October 1974	Unchanged, but interpreted	149, 518, 525, 534, 536, 541, 549
3.	Reporting Accounting Changes in Interim Financial Statements, December 1974 (Amend *APB Opinion No. 23*)	Unchanged	

Financial Accounting Standards Board (FASB), Statements of Financial Accounting *Standards* (1973 to date) *(continued)*

FASB No. Contents	Status, January 1, 1979	Page Citations in this Book
4. Reporting Gains and Losses from Extinguishment of Debt, March 1975	Unchanged	700, 701, 704, 714, 715, 796
5. Accounting for Contingencies	Amended, but interpreted	118, 144, 149, 319, 320, 321, 322, 323, 346, 369, 584, 585
6. Classification of Short-Term Obligations Expected to be Refinanced, May 1975	Unchanged, but interpreted	141, 286, 319, 700, 704
7. Accounting and Reporting by Development Stage Enterprises, June 1975	Unchanged, but interpreted	527, 528
8. Accounting for the Translation of Foreign Currency Transactions and Foreign Currency Financial Statements, October 1975		118
9. Accounting for Income Taxes—Oil and Gas Producing Companies (an Amendment of *APB Opinions Nos. 11* and *23*), October 1975	Superseded	323
10. Extension of "Grandfather" Provisions for Business Combinations (an Amendment of *APB Opinion No. 16*), October 1975	Unchanged	
11. Accounting for Contingencies—Transition Method (an Amendment of *FASB Statement No. 5*), December 1975	Unchanged	454, 562
12. Accounting for Certain Marketable Securities, December 1975	Unchanged, but interpreted	145, 272, 273, 274, 275, 276, 277, 291, 366, 562, 647, 648
13. Accounting for Leases, November 1976	Amended, partially superseded, and interpreted (see Exposure Draft section below)	121, 181, 748, 749, 750, 752, 753, 755, 756, 757, 760, 761, 762, 763, 764, 765, 770, 771, 772
14. Financial Reporting for Segments of a Business Enterprise, December 1976	Amended and partially superseded	122, 854
15. Accounting by Debtors and Creditors for Troubled Debt Restructurings, June 1977	Unchanged	596, 700, 701, 704, 705, 706, 707, 710, 711
16. Prior Period Adjustments, June 1977 . . .	Unchanged	102, 106, 107, 108, 109, 330, 520, 585, 586, 820
17. Accounting for Leases—Initial Direct Costs, November 1977	Unchanged	749
18. Financial Reporting for Segments of a Business Enterprise—Interim Financial Statements, November 1977	Unchanged	28, 854
19. Financial Accounting and Reporting by Oil and Gas Producing Companies, December 1977	Partially suspended (see *FASB No. 25* below)	455, 526, 527, 535

Financial Accounting Standards Board (FASB), Statements of Financial Accounting *Standards* (1973 to date) *(continued)*

FASB No. Contents	Status, January 1, 1979	Page Citations in this Book
20. Accounting for Forward Exchange Contracts, December 1977	Unchanged	
21. Suspension of the Reporting of Earnings per Share and Segment Information by Nonpublic Enterprises, April 1978	Unchanged	102, 622, 624, 634, 856
22. Changes in the Provisions of Lease Agreements Resulting from Refundings of Tax-Exempt Debt, June 1978 . . .	Unchanged	764
23. Inception of the Lease, August 1978 . . .	Unchanged	748, 753
24. Reporting Segment Information in Financial Statements that are Presented in Another Enterprise's Financial Report, December 1978	Unchanged	527
25. Suspension of Certain Accounting Requirements for Oil and Gas Companies, February 1979 (amends *FASB No. 19*)	Unchanged	527

Financial Accounting Standards Board (FASB) Statement of Financial Accounting *Concepts* (1978 to present)

FASB No. Contents	Status, January 1, 1979	Page Citations in this Book
1. Objectives of Financial Reporting by Business Enterprises, November 1978	Unchanged	2, 3, 4, 23, 97, 799

Financial Accounting Standards Board (FASB) Interpretations (1973 to date)*

FASB No. Contents	Interpretation of
1. Accounting Changes Related to the Cost of Inventory, June 1974	*APB Opinion No. 20*
2. Imputing Interest on Debt Arrangements Made under the Federal Bankruptcy Act, June 1974	Superseded
3. Accounting for the Cost of Pension Plans Subject to the Employment Retirement Income Security Act of 1974, December 1974	*APB Opinion No. 8*
4. Applicability of *FASB Statement No. 2* to Business Combinations Accounted for by the Purchase Method, February 1975	*FASB Statement No. 2*
5. Applicability of *FASB Statement No. 2* to Development Stage Enterprises, February 1975	*FASB Statement No. 2*
6. Applicability of *FASB Statement No. 2* to Computer Software, February 1975	*FASB Statement No. 2*

Financial Accounting Standards Board (FASB) Interpretations (1973 to date)*(continued)*

FASB No.	Contents	Interpretation of
7.	Applying *FASB Statement No. 7* in Financial Statements of Established Operating Enterprises, October 1975	*FASB Statement No. 7*
8.	Classification of a Short-Term Obligation Repaid Prior to Being Replaced by a Long-Term Security, January 1976	*FASB Statement No. 6*
9.	Applying *APB Opinions No. 16* and *17* when a Savings and Loan Association or a Similar Institution is Acquired in a Business Combination Accounted for by the Purchase Method, February 1976	*APB Opinions 16* and *17*
10.	Application of *FASB Statement No. 12* to Personal Financial Statements, September 1976	*FASB Statement No. 12*
11.	Changes in Market Value after the Balance Sheet Date, September 1976	*FASB Statement No. 12*
12.	Accounting for Previously Established Allowance Accounts, September 1976	*FASB Statement No. 12*
13.	Consolidation of a Parent and its Subsidiaries having Different Balance Sheet Dates, September 1976	*FASB Statement No. 12*
14.	Reasonable Estimation of the Amount of a Loss, September 1976	*FASB Statement No. 5*
15.	Translation of Unamortized Policy Acquisition Costs by a Stock Life Insurance Company, September 1976	*FASB Statement No. 8*
16.	Clarification of Definitions and Accounting for Marketable Equity Securities That Become Nonmarketable, February 1977	*FASB Statement No. 12*
17.	Applying the Lower of Cost or Market Rule in Translated Financial Statements, February 1977	*FASB Statement No. 8*
18.	Accounting for Income Taxes in Interim Periods, March 1977	*APB Opinion No. 28*
19.	Lessee Guarantee of the Residual Value of Leased Property, October 1977	*FASB Statement No. 13*
20.	Reporting Accounting Changes under AICPA Statements of Position, November 1977	*APB Opinion No. 20*
21.	Accounting for Leases in a Business Combination, April 1978	*FASB Statement No. 13*
22.	Applicability of Indefinite Reversal Criteria to Timing Differences, April 1978	*APB Opinions 11* and *23*
23.	Leases of Certain Property Owned by a Governmental Unit or Authority, August 1978	*FASB Statement No. 13*
24.	Leases Involving Only Part of a Building, September 1978	*FASB Statement No. 13*
25.	Accounting for an Unused Investment Tax Credit, September 1978	*APB Opinions No. 2, 4, 11,* and *16*
26.	Accounting for Purchase of a Leased Asset by the Lessee during the Term of the Lease, September 1978	*FASB Statement No. 13*
27.	Accounting for Loss on a Sublease, November 1978	*FASB No. 13* and *APB Opinion No. 30*
28.	Accounting for Stock Appreciation Rights and Other Variable Stock Option or Award Plans, December 1978	*APB Opinions No. 15* and *25*

Financial Accounting Standards Board (FASB) Interpretations (1973 to date) *(continued)*

FASB No.	Contents	Interpretation of
29.	Reporting Tax Benefits Realized on Disposition of Investments in Certain Subsidiaries and Other Investees, February 1979	APB Opinions No. 23 and 25

* Relevant interpretations are included in the text discussion of the related FASB Standard.

Other Pronouncements by Authoritative Entities

Contents	Page Citations in this Book
FASB, *Conceptual Framework for Financial Accounting and Reporting*	23
AAA Committee on Accounting Concepts and Standards—*Accounting and Reporting Standards for Corporate Financial Statements and Preceding Statements and Supplements*	30, 93, 135
SEC, *Accounting Series Release No. 25*	596
SEC, *Accounting Series Release No. 163*	457
SEC, *Accounting Series Release No. 190*, March 1976	40, 220, 234, 244, 245, 246, 369, 370, 371
SEC, *Staff Accounting Bulletin*, Interpretation of ASR No. 190	371
AICPA, *Codification of Statements on Auditing Standards 1977*	34, 148, 149, 151
AICPA, *CPA Handbook*	35
AICPA, *Accounting Trends and Techniques,* 1978	94, 109, 136, 148, 150, 396, 494, 736
AICPA, *Objectives of Financial Statements,* October 1973	000
AICPA. *Accounting Research and Terminology Bulletins, Final Edition,* 1961	140,
AICPA, *Accounting Research Study No 6,* "Reporting the Financial Effects of Price Level Changes," 1963	220
AICPA, *Accounting Research Monograph No. 1*	456
AICPA, *Technical Aids* (CCH, SEC. 4220.01)	596
AICPA, *Accounting Research Bulletin No. 38,* 1949	748
AAA, *Statement of Basic Accounting Theory*	10
AAA, *Statement on Accounting Theory and Theory Acceptance*	10

Financial Accounting Standards Board, (FASB), Exposure Draft of Statements of Financial Accounting Standards

Contents	Status, January 1, 1979	Page Citation in this Book
Capitalization of Interest Cost (FASB), Exposure Draft, December 1978	Exposure	457
Accounting for Certain Service Transactions, Exposure		

Financial Accounting Standards Board, (FASB), Exposure Draft of Statements of Financial Accounting Standards *(continued)*

Contents	Status, January 1, 1979	Page Citation in this Book
Proposed Statement of Accounting Standards on Lessee's Use of the Interest Rate Implicit in the Lease, Proposed Amendment to FASB No. 13, Exposure Draft, November 1978	Exposure	755
Financial Reporting and Changing Prices, December 1978	Exposure	216, 220, 233
Determining Contingent Rentals, Proposed Amendment of FASB Statement No. 13, Exposure Draft, December 1978	Exposure	
Accounting for Sales With Leasebacks, Proposed Amendment of FASB Statement No. 13, Exposure Draft, December 1978	Exposure	
Profit Recognition on Sales-Type Leases of Real Estate, Proposed Amendment of FASB Statement No. 13, Exposure Draft, December 1978	Exposure	
Constant Dollar Accounting, Exposure Draft, March 1979	Exposure	220

2

Theoretical Foundations of Financial Accounting and Reporting

One can approach the study of accounting on a theoretical or procedural basis, or a combination of the two. In this book, consistent with our objectives stated in Chapter 1, we present a combination approach. At this level, the student interested in accounting should learn the basic accounting principles and procedures used to classify, analyze, measure, and record transactions, and to report the summarized results to decision makers. The procedural aspect of financial accounting involves recording accounting entries, maintenance of accounts, and preparation of financial statements. However, of more importance, is a comprehension of the *theoretical foundation* that underlies financial accounting and reporting. This foundation provides the rationale for the procedural aspects of accounting. We emphasize the conceptual foundation throughout this book.

A definition of theory, appropriate for accounting, is "a coherent set of hypothetical, conceptual, and pragmatic principles forming the general frame of reference for a field of inquiry."[1] Accounting theory is man-made. Thus, it changes to respond to the changing so-cial and economic environment within which the accounting function operates.

Accounting theory is in a continuous process of evolution. The organizations discussed in Chapter 1 have been influential in this continuing evolution. Accounting theory, as we know it today, is based upon both inductive and deductive reasoning, economic theory, experience, pragmatism, and general acceptability. Since accounting theory is pragmatic, it cannot be derived from, or proven by, the laws of nature as can be done in mathematics and the natural sciences.

At the present time, there is no single, agreed upon statement of the broad structure of financial accounting theory. However, there does appear to be general agreement with respect to the basic theoretical foundation that underlies financial accounting.

The central purpose of this chapter is to present the theoretical foundation underlying *external financial accounting and reporting* as it is currently practiced. The discussions in this chapter should be studied carefully; however, it is unrealistic to expect complete understanding and knowledge of this foundation at this point in your study. Rather, this chapter is intended to be a reference for study throughout the remaining chapters. As the various concepts, principles, and procedures are discussed in sub-

---

[1] For those who desire to pursue in depth the subject of financial accounting theory, the authors recommend the following: Eldon S. Hendriksen, *Accounting Theory*, 3d ed. (Homewood, Ill.: Richard D. Irwin, Inc., 1977).

sequent chapters, there will be references to this chapter. At these points you should return to this chapter and study the relevant part in depth. If this approach is followed consistently, you will attain a keen understanding of the theoretical foundation upon completion of your study of the remaining chapters.[2]

BROAD THEORETICAL STRUCTURE

In discussing accounting theory, one is confronted with a problem of terminology. Accounting literature makes numerous references to theory, assumptions, concepts, postulates, principles, standards, rules, procedures, and practices. Although each of these terms may be precisely defined, general usage by the profession has served to give them loose and overlapping meanings. To establish a basis for consistent terminology throughout this book, we have designed the broad structure and selected the terminology summarized in Exhibits 2–1 and 2–2. It is *descriptive,* since it describes present accounting, not prescriptive or normative (i.e., what accounting should be in the future). The broad structure of *current* accounting theory and practice is classified into the six basic components shown in the two exhibits.

This frame of reference is easily understood and conforms to current usage. It will serve as a consistent and integrated theoretical structure for the readership of this textbook. Although not complete in every respect, it will serve as a valuable reference when later chapters discuss the rationale for the accounting and reporting treatment accorded the various accounting issues.

Exhibit 2–1 presents the six basic components of the broad structure. The exhibit presents the *basic objectives of accounting* as the highest level in the hierarchy. As we move down the hierarchy, the theoretical focus shifts to the practices of *implementing* principles and proce-

dures (the rules—how it is done). Most of the *ARBs, APB Opinions,* and *FASB Statements* and Interpretations are at this lowest level.

Exhibit 2–2 presents an outline of the six basic components of the broad structure of financial accounting including the specific concepts. The remainder of this chapter will discuss, in order, each of the items listed in Exhibit 2–2.

At this point in your study you should concentrate primarily on the first three components: objectives, environmental assumptions, and basic accounting principles.

BASIC OBJECTIVES OF FINANCIAL ACCOUNTING AND REPORTING

In Chapter 1 the basic objectives of financial accounting were briefly discussed. Recall that the FASB issued its first *Statement of Financial Accounting Concepts* in November 1978. It is the first of a planned series of statements of concepts in the Board's conceptual framework project. Later *Statements* are expected to cover the elements of financial statements and their recognition, measurement, and related matters. The first *Statement* included the following concise list of highlights:[3]

- Financial reporting is not an end in itself but is intended to provide information that is useful in making business and economic decisions.

- The objectives of financial reporting are not immutable—they are affected by the economic, legal, political, and social environment in which financial reporting takes place.

- The objectives are also affected by the characteristics and limitations of the kind of information that financial reporting can provide.
  —The information pertains to business enterprises rather than to industries or the economy as a whole.
  —The information often results from approximate, rather than exact, measures.

---

[2] At the present time the Financial Accounting Standards Board is developing "A Conceptual Framework for Financial Accounting and Reporting." It is anticipated that when this project is completed, comprehensive statements that incorporate the foundations discussed in this chapter will be available. The first phase of this project, *FASB, Statement of Financial Accounting Concepts No. 1,* "Objectives of Financial Reporting by Business Enterprises," November 1978, was discussed in Chapter 1.

---

[3] Adapted from *Statement of Financial Accounting Concepts No. 1,* "Objectives of Financial Reporting by Business Enterprises," November 1978, pp. vii–x.

EXHIBIT 2–1
Hierarchy of a Broad Structure of Financial Accounting and Reporting

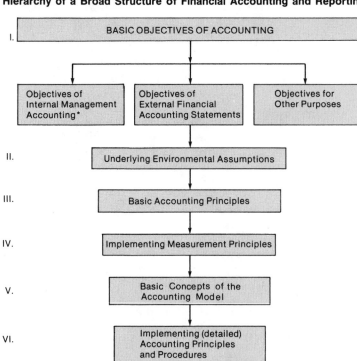

I. BASIC OBJECTIVES OF ACCOUNTING

Objectives of Internal Management Accounting*

Objectives of External Financial Accounting Statements

Objectives for Other Purposes

II. Underlying Environmental Assumptions

III. Basic Accounting Principles

IV. Implementing Measurement Principles

V. Basic Concepts of the Accounting Model

VI. Implementing (detailed) Accounting Principles and Procedures

* Not stressed in this book; see books on management accounting.

—The information largely reflects the financial effects of transactions and events that have already happened.

—The information is but one source of information needed by those who make decisions about business enterprises.

—The information is provided and used at a cost.

· The objectives in this Statement are those of general purpose external financial reporting by business enterprises.

—The objectives stem primarily from the needs of external users who lack the authority to prescribe the information they want and must rely on information management communicates to them.

—The objectives are directed toward the common interests of many users in the ability of an enterprise to generate favorable cash flows but are phrased using investment and credit decisions as a reference to give them

a focus. The objectives are intended to be broad rather than narrow.

—The objectives pertain to financial reporting and are not restricted to financial statements.

· The objectives state that:

—Financial reporting should provide information that is useful to present and potential investors and creditors and other users in making rational investment, credit, and similar decisions. The information should be comprehensible to those who have a reasonable understanding of business and economic activities and are willing to study the information with reasonable diligence.

—Financial reporting should provide information to help present and potential investors and creditors and other users in assessing the amounts, timing, and uncertainty of prospective cash receipts from dividends or interest and the proceeds from the sale, re-

EXHIBIT 2–2
A Broad Structure of Financial Accounting and Reporting

I. Basic Objectives of Accounting.
  1. Objectives of internal management accounting.
  2. Objectives of external financial accounting statements.
  3. Objectives for other purposes (such as reports to government agencies).
II. Underlying Environmental Assumptions.
  1. Separate entity assumption.
  2. Continuity assumption.
  3. Unit of measure assumption.
  4. Time period assumption.
III. Basic Accounting Principles.
  1. Cost principle.
  2. Revenue principle.
  3. Matching principle.
  4. Objectivity principle.
  5. Consistency principle.
  6. Financial reporting principle.
  7. Modifying (or exception) principle.
    a. Materiality.
    b. Conservatism.
    c. Industry peculiarities.
IV. Implementing Measurement Principles.
  1. Selection of the objects, activities, and events to be measured.
  2. Identification and classification of the attributes of each object, activity, and event to be measured.
  3. Assignment of quantitative amounts to the attributes.
    a. Monetary.
    b. Nonmonetary.
  4. Modifying measurement principle.
    a. Uncertainty.
    b. Objectivity.
    c. Limitations of monetary unit.
    d. Cost effectiveness.
V. Basic Concepts of the Accounting Model.
  1. Financial position model: Assets = Liabilities + Owners' Equity.
  2. Results of operations model: Revenues − Expenses = Net Income.
  3. Changes in financial position model: Resource Inflows − Resource Outflows = Net Change in Resources.
VI. Implementing (detailed) Accounting Principles and Procedures.
  1. Those related to determination of net income.
  2. Those related to measurement of assets and liabilities.
  3. Those related to presentation of accounting information.
  4. Those related to how transactions and other events should be recorded, classified, and summarized.
  5. Other accounting procedures.

demption, or maturity of securities or loans. Since investors' and creditors' cash flows are related to enterprise cash flows, financial reporting should provide information to help investors, creditors, and others assess the amounts, timing, and uncertainty of prospective net cash inflows to the related enterprise.

—Financial reporting should provide information about the economic resources of an enterprise, the claims to those resources (obligations of the enterprise to transfer resources to other entities and owners' equity), and the effects of transactions, events, and circumstances that change its resources and claims to those resources.

- "Investors" and "creditors" are used broadly and include not only those who have or contemplate having a claim to enterprise resources but also those who advise or represent them.

- Although investment and credit decisions reflect investors' and creditors' expectations about future enterprise performance, those expectations are commonly based at least partly on evaluations of past enterprise performance.

- The primary focus of financial reporting is information about earnings and its components.

- Information about enterprise earnings based on accrual accounting generally provides a better indication of an enterprise's present and continuing ability to generate favorable cash flows than information limited to the financial effects of cash receipts and payments.

- Financial reporting is expected to provide information about an enterprise's financial performance during a period and about how management of an enterprise has discharged its stewardship responsibility to owners.

- Financial accounting is not designed to measure directly the value of a business enterprise, but the information it provides may be helpful to those who wish to estimate its value.

- Investors, creditors, and others may use reported earnings and information about the elements of financial statements in various ways to assess the prospects for cash flows. They may wish, for example, to evaluate management's performance, estimate "earning power," predict future earnings, assess risk, or to confirm, change, or reject earlier predictions or assessments. Although financial reporting should provide basic information to aid them, they do their own evaluating, estimating, predicting, assessing, confirming, changing, or rejecting.

Management knows more about the enterprise and its affairs than investors, creditors, or other "outsiders" and accordingly can often increase the usefulness of financial information by identifying certain events and circumstances and explaining their financial effects on the enterprise.

UNDERLYING ENVIRONMENTAL ASSUMPTIONS

Since accounting necessarily operates in the "real-world" environment, constraints (or expectations) are imposed on accounting by certain aspects of that environment. Accounting must accept and respond to those constraints because they cannot be changed. Therefore, they may be referred to as the *underlying environmental assumptions*. The four pervasive environmental assumptions are listed in Exhibit 2–2 (Category II) as follows:

1. Separate entity assumption.
2. Continuity assumption.
3. Unit of measure assumption.
4. Time period assumption.

Separate Entity Assumption

Accounting is concerned with specific and separate entities. Thus each enterprise is considered as an *accounting unit* separate and apart from the owner or owners and from other entities. A corporation and the shareholders are separable entities for accounting purposes. Also, partnerships and sole proprietorships are treated as separate and apart from the owners despite the fact that this distinction is not made in the legal sense.

Under the separate entity assumption, the business entity is considered to own all resources committed to its purposes. Therefore, all records and reports are developed from the viewpoint of the particular entity. This viewpoint affects the analysis of transactions, the accumulation and classification of data, and the resultant financial reporting. It provides a basis for clearcut distinction in analyzing transactions between the enterprise and the owners. As an example, the personal residence of an individual owning an unincorporated business is not considered an appropriate item to report for the business, although there is a common owner. In this example the accounting entity makes a distinction that is not made in the legal sense; creditors may look to both the personal residence and the business assets for satisfaction of claims against the business. Accountants would be in an untenable situation from time to time if they did not have this basic concept to rely on in making distinctions between personal and business transactions. Accountants occasionally encounter pressures to overlook this distinction.

Continuity Assumption

The continuity assumption is frequently referred to as the "going concern" assumption. It assumes the business is not expected to liquidate in the foreseeable future. The assumption does not imply that accountancy assumes permanent continuance; rather there is a presumption of stability and continuity for a period of time *sufficient to carry out contemplated operations, contracts, and commitments.* This concept establishes the rationale of accounting on a *nonliquidation basis,* and thus provides the theoretical foundation for many of the valuations and allocations common in accounting. For example, depreciation and amortization procedures rely upon this concept. The estimates of remaining useful life and residual value are based upon continuing use of the asset by the business, rather than upon an expectation of early liquidation of the entity.

This assumption generally underlies the decisions of investors to commit capital to the enterprise. Therefore, accounting for these commitments and the resulting incomes and losses must be based upon the assumption that the enterprise will continue to function in the contemplated manner, performing the business activities consistent with prior objectives including earning a return for the entrepreneur. The concept, as applied to accounting, holds that continuity of business activity is a reasonable expectation. If the particular entity should face serious loss and probable liquidation, conventional accounting based on the continuity assumption would not be appropriate for determining and reporting the true conditions. In such cases *liquidation* accounting is appropriate wherein all valuations immediately are accounted for at estimated realizable amounts.

Accountants recognize that no business entity will continue forever. To satisfy the continuity assumption, it is essential that on the basis of *present facts* it appears that the business will continue so long that its present resources are utilized according to plan without serious loss of capital investment. Only on the basis of this "going concern" assumption can the accounting process remain stable and attain the objective of accurately recording and reporting on the capital commitments, the efficiency of management, and the financial status of the enterprise.

Unit of Measure Assumption

Some unit of exchange is essential to raise the level of commerce above that of barter. Similarly, some unit of measurement is necessary in accounting. With so many diverse assets and equities that must be recorded, analyzed, and reported, there must be a common denominator. Obviously, to be of maximum usefulness, accounting ideally should employ the same unit of measure as is employed by the business community, that is, the monetary unit. Accounting may deal with some data in nonmonetary units; however, the monetary unit predominates. Thus money is the common denominator—the yardstick—in the accounting process.

The unit of measure assumption asserts that accounting will measure and report the results of the economic activities of the entity in terms of money. It recognizes, as does society generally, that the monetary unit is the most effective means of communicating financial information.

Unfortunately, use of a monetary unit for measurement purposes poses a critical problem in accounting. Unlike the yardstick, which is always 36 inches long, the monetary unit (i.e., the dollar) changes in real value or purchasing power. Consequently, when there is inflation or deflation, dollars of different size (i.e., of different real value) are entered in the accounts over a period of time, and dollars of different real value are intermingled in the accounts as if they were of equal purchasing power. Because of this practice it is said that current accounting practice either assumes a "stable monetary unit" or that "changes in the value of money are not significant." However, in view of the relatively recent high rate of inflation, businesses are encouraged to also report operating results and financial position in terms of price level effects. Accounting during periods of inflation and deflation is discussed in Chapter 7.

The unit of measure assumption has exerted a significant impact on the development of accounting. The basic theoretical concepts discussed in the next section of this chapter in part rest upon this assumption.

Time Period Assumption

Although the results of operations of a specific business enterprise cannot be known precisely until the business has completed its life span (i.e., final liquidation), short-term financial reports are necessary because interested parties cannot wait until liquidation for an accounting. Thus the environment—the business community and government—has imposed upon accounting a calendar constraint; that is, the necessity for assigning changes in wealth of a firm to a series of short time periods. These time periods vary; however, the year is the most common interval as a result of established business practice, tradition, and governmental requirements. For example, income tax laws require determination of taxable income on an annual basis. Some firms adhere to the calendar year; however, more and more firms are changing to the fiscal or "natural" business year, the end of which is marked by the lowest point of business activity in each 12-month period. Recently, it has become common for companies to issue *interim* financial statements each quarter which report summary information. Interim financial information "is essential to provide investors and others with timely information as to the progress of the enterprise."[4] Many companies also prepare *internal management* reports on a daily, weekly, or monthly basis.

The time period assumption recognizes the need of the business community, and society in general, for short-term periodic financial statements. This assumption underlies the whole area of *accruals* and *deferrals* that distinguishes accrual basis accounting from cash basis accounting. If there were no need for periodic reports during the life span of a business, accruals and deferrals of revenues and costs would be unnecessary. To illustrate, assume Company X was organized and $100,000 cash was invested in it. Assets were acquired, liabilities incurred, revenues earned, and costs paid for a five-year period, at which time the business was liquidated (everything converted to cash) and the resulting cash of $175,000 was returned to the investors. Assuming no return to the investors during the five-year period, we can report with certainty that the company earned $75,000 cash income. No accruals or deferrals (adjusting entries in the accounts) are necessary to determine the net income for the business. However, if the investors required a financial statement each year, accruals and deferrals for items such as unpaid wages, uncollected revenues, depreciation expense, and prepaid expenses would have to be recorded each period.

The continuity in business operations tends to obscure the results of the short-term "test readings" which accounting renders in the form of periodic financial statements. Many continuous and interrelated streams of data are arbitrarily severed in the preparation of annual financial statements. Despite these difficulties, short-term financial reports are of such significance to decision makers that the accounting process must be designed to produce them. The

time period assumption recognizes this need despite the fact that the true "actual" results for the short term seldom, if ever, can be determined with precision.

BASIC ACCOUNTING PRINCIPLES

In the outline given in Exhibit 2–2, the highest level (Category I) speaks to the objectives of accounting and the next lower level (Category II) focuses on the effects of the environment on accounting. The next lower level (Category III) in Exhibit 2–2 presents the following *basic accounting principles:*

1. Cost principle.
2. Revenue principle.
3. Matching principle.
4. Objectivity principle.
5. Consistency principle.
6. Financial reporting principle.
7. Modifying (or exception) principle.

These principles relate closely to the *historical cost model* that is currently used in accounting. They are operational or implementing principles for attaining the basic objectives and for conforming with the environmental assumptions. These principles have evolved through experience and have been accepted by the accounting profession and the business community on the basis of reasonableness, lack of bias, and relevance.

At this point the student should begin to appreciate the awesome task of meeting the objectives of financial accounting. To repeat from Chapter 1: Accounting can be defined as an information processing system designed to *capture, measure,* and report the economic essence of events that affect the entity. Let us consider the phrase "capture and measure the economic essence of events."

To *capture* the economic essence of events means to understand the economic substance of events. Frequently it is relatively easy to understand what is happening in a set of events; however, the complexity of modern business sometimes makes this phase of accounting particularly challenging. One's understanding of the economic essence of a set of events is determined by that person's frame of reference

---

[4] AICPA, *APB Opinion No. 28,* "Interim Financial Reporting" (New York, May 1973), par. 9. Also see FASB, *Statement of Accounting Standards No. 18,* "Financial Reporting for Segments of a Business Enterprise—Interim Financial Statements" (Stamford, Conn., November 1977). Interim reporting is discussed in Chapter 25.

(i.e., experiences, prejudices, tastes, world view, etc.), and another person's understanding of the essence of the same events may be altogether different because of different frames of reference. Thus, reaching consensus on the economic essence of events often is difficult, even though individuals understand the event.

The *measurement* of the economic essence of events poses an even more formidable problem for the accountant, particularly in the area of *assigning value* to assets, liabilities, and owners' equities. "Values" are inherently future oriented inasmuch as values theoretically are determined on the basis of the present discounted values of *future* cash flows. Thus, even if accountants (and other persons in the business world) can reach consensus as to an understanding of the economic essence of events, the measurement of the economic essence (i.e., the "value") of the event may still be uncertain. Because of this uncertainty, accountants have heretofore been reluctant to present such subjective "values" in accounting reports. Moreover, it is obvious that the opportunity for bias in any accounting model based on "values" introduces the potential for significant legal claims against the accountant, as well as against the entity being reported on.

The third essential element of the accounting process, *reporting,* merits careful consideration because it involves communication of the summarized economic effects on the entity of the events captured and measured.

In summary, the phrase *economic essence* implies the economic nature of accounting measurements. Economics is a behavioral science similar to psychology and sociology and, as we pointed out above, is not susceptible to proof in terms of mathematical or other natural laws. As a result, accounting as the measurement arm of economics operates under the same constraints (plus some others). Therefore, accountants have been forced either to *(a)* lend their names to inherently subjective valuations, or *(b)* construct a scheme of accounting which is more objective in nature. They have very reasonably elected the latter course. This election has forced the development of accounting principles which serve as the theoretical foundation for accounting practice. We now turn our attention to these

accounting principles. Throughout this textbook we refer to "generally accepted accounting principles"—the standards of accounting practice. The basic assumptions and the principles, along with related procedures, comprise generally accepted accounting principles (GAAP).

Cost Principle

The cost principle permeates the entire accounting process. It often is referred to as the "historical cost principle," as opposed to the market value or replacement cost theories. The cost principle holds that *cost* is the appropriate basis for initial accounting recognition (at date of the transaction) of all asset acquisitions, revenues, expenses, liabilities, and owners' equity. It also holds that subsequent to acquisition, cost values are retained throughout the accounting process. The cost principle recognizes the basic subject matter of accounting as *completed exchange transactions* which are to be translated into their financial effect on the entity in terms of the exchange price established at the date of the completed transaction.

In applying the cost principle, the accountant frequently faces a complex problem in *measuring* cost where noncash considerations are involved. In determining cost, the "cash bargained price" is utilized. Where considerations other than cash are involved, the cost measure is the cash equivalent of the consideration given up in the transaction or the cash equivalent of the asset or service acquired, whichever is the more clearly evident. For example, where capital stock is issued to pay for land, the asset is recorded at the market value of the stock or the market value of the land, whichever is the more clearly determinable with greater certainty and objectivity. When both are clearly determinable, the "market value" of the consideration given is preferable.[5] Another problem arises when

---

[5] Unfortunately, the accounting profession uses *fair value, market value, fair market value,* and *current market value* to describe the arm's-length price of an asset used in certain transactions and valuations. We generally use *market value* in this text because it is fully descriptive of the intended meaning. The word "fair" implies that "unfair" values might be used in the accounts, and the modifier "current" is redundant because market value presumes the one prevailing at the relevant time.

noninterest-bearing debt is given for an asset. Cost is the *present value* of the future amount of cash to be paid *(APB Opinion No. 21).* These two problems are discussed in detail in subsequent chapters.

The cost principle holds that, compared with other alternatives, the exchange price derived in an arm's-length transaction is the most useful for accounting and reporting. It is determinable, definite, and objective; it is not a matter of conjecture, opinion, or estimation. It is the basis used by the business community, taxing authorities, and society in general. As a result, users of financial statements know that a substantial portion of the information is based on objectively determined amounts.

To illustrate the importance of these reasons, assume that instead of the cost principle, a "market value principle" is used. This principle would require that at each financial statement date (e.g., each year-end), all of the assets on the balance sheet be stated at their then market value. Annual appraisals and estimates would be necessary for receivables, investments, inventories, plant, equipment, land, patents, liabilities, and so on. The accountants might have one opinion, management another opinion, and both might disagree with outside appraisers (and outside appraisers disagree with one another). The external statement user could place little confidence in these subjective judgments. The question would arise as to what should be included in income. For example, assume a plant that cost $100,000 at the beginning of the year is appraised at $125,000 at year-end. Should the $25,000 increase in reported assets be reflected as income for the year? Critics of the historical cost model counter that the cost principle seriously distorts the financial statements in periods of significant inflation or deflation. Also, many people believe that market value, rather than original cost, better serves the external decision maker. These issues are discussed more fully in Chapter 7.

Revenue Principle

The revenue principle *(a)* defines revenue, *(b)* specifies how revenue should be measured, and *(c)* pinpoints the timing of revenue recognition.

Each of the three facets of the revenue principle presents difficult conceptual and operational problems.

Revenue Defined. Revenue can be defined as "the monetary expression of the aggregate of products or services transferred by an enterprise to its customers during a period of time."[6] The revenue principle holds that revenue should include all changes in the net assets of the firm other than those arising from owners' equity transactions. That is, revenue is the measure of net assets received for *(a)* the sale of goods and services; *(b)* interest, rents, royalties, and so on; *(c)* net gain on the sale of assets other than stock-in-trade; and *(d)* gain from advantageous settlement of liabilities. In applying the broad principle we will see in later chapters that adequate reporting (under the reporting principle) requires that revenue be reported under captions such as operating revenue and extraordinary gains and losses.

Measurement of Revenue. The revenue principle dictates that revenue should be measured as the net cash equivalent price derived in an arm's-length exchange transaction. Thus, revenue is best measured by the net cash exchange value of the product, service, or other asset in the exchange. This concept requires that all discounts be viewed as adjustments made to reach the true cash exchange value (e.g., sales discounts should be deducted from sales revenues), and that in noncash transactions the market value of the consideration given or received, whichever is the more clearly determinable, should determine the revenue measurement.

Timing Revenue Recognition. This subprinciple generally is referred to as the revenue *realization* concept. The basic concept is that revenue is realized, and should be recorded as earned, when *(a)* there has been an exchange transaction involving a transfer of goods or services, and *(b)* the earning process is essentially complete.

The realization concept provides a pragmatic test for timing revenue recognition since it is

---

[6] AAA Committee on Accounting Concepts and Standards, *Accounting and Reporting Standards for Corporate Financial Statements and Preceding Statements and Supplements* (Columbus, Ohio, 1957), p. 5.

characterized more by operational than by strict theoretical content. The primary event for revenue recognition occurs at the point of the sale of goods or services. With respect to merchandise, the point of sale generally is viewed as the time when *ownership* of the goods passes, which ordinarily is when delivery is made. For example, in the case of goods shipped f.o.b. shipping point, ownership passes at the time they are turned over to the shipper (unless specifically agreed otherwise by the parties). In contrast, for goods shipped f.o.b. destination, ownership usually passes at date of delivery to the buyer.

The revenue principle requires *accrual basis accounting* rather than cash basis accounting. For example, completed transactions for the sale of goods or services on credit are recorded and reported (as revenue) in the period in which the sale or service occurred rather than in the period in which the cash is eventually collected. Special applications of the revenue principle in accounting for *service* and *sales* transactions are discussed below.

The revenue principle usually requires that *(a)* revenue from the sale of goods must be recognized when effective ownership to the goods is transferred (usually delivery); *(b)* revenue from services rendered must be recognized when the services are rendered (generally when billable); *(c)* revenue is recognized when assets are made available to others on the basis of use (such as rents, royalties, and interest); and *(d)* revenue is recognized when effective ownership to assets, other than goods and merchandise regularly sold, is transferred. Exceptions to these general conditions for revenue recognition are explained and illustrated in the chapters which follow.

Service Transactions. Accounting for revenue from *service transactions* often poses a special problem because *(a)* services are "intangible" compared with merchandise sold and *(b)* the number and variety of services rendered to the public are increasing. In response to this problem, the *FASB* issued *Accounting for Certain Service Transactions,* (exposure draft), October 1978, which provides specific accounting guidelines.

The pronouncement proposes the basic principle that revenue from service transactions must be recognized on the basis of *performance* because that determines the extent to which the earnings process is complete (or virtually complete). Under this principle, revenue from service transactions should be recognized by applying the

1. Specific performance method—When performance consists of the execution of a specific act, revenue should be recognized when that act takes place. Example—recognition of sales commission revenue when the sale is consummated.
2. Proportional performance method—When performance consists of the execution of more than one separate act, revenue should be recognized on the basis of the proportionate performance of each act (on a systematic or rational basis, such as the ratio of the seller's direct costs to perform to the total estimated direct costs of the transaction). Example—recognition of revenue by a correspondence school that provides lessons, examinations, grading, and evaluations.
3. Completed performance method—When services are performed by completing a series of continuous and directly related acts, such that performance cannot be deemed complete until the final act is executed, revenue should be recognized upon completion of the service. Example—recognition of revenue by a transportation company when the goods are delivered.

In applying each of the above methods, the allocation of expenses related to performance must conform to the matching principle discussed in the next section.

Sales Transactions. Exchange transactions involving the sale of merchandise usually are accounted for using the *sales basis.* Under this basis, sales revenue is recognized when *(a)* there is a completed exchange transaction that transfers effective ownership of the merchandise, *(b)* ultimate collection of the sales price is reasonably certain, and *(c)* the expenses related to the transaction are determinable, with reasonable accuracy, in the period of sale.

Because of special circumstances in applying the *realization concept,* there are four exceptions to the sales basis. The exceptions are as follows:

1. Cash approach—Under this approach revenue is recognized on a cash basis. To illustrate, assume an installment sale of goods for $600 that cost $360 and credit terms of $20 per month for 30 months. There is a potential gross margin of $240 or $8 per installment. Under the cash approach no revenue would be recognized at the date of sale; instead, $8 of gross margin would be recognized as each collection is made. This is also known as the *installment method* of recognizing revenue. This method should be used where the sales basis is not appropriate due to the absence of reasonable assurance that ultimate collection will be made, or where the related expenses cannot yet be determined with a reasonable degree of accuracy. These conditions indicate that the earning process is not essentially completed at time of sale. The installment method has very limited application.

2. Percentage of completion approach—This approach is appropriate for certain long-term construction contracts. Revenue is recognized on the basis of progress of construction, although the earning process is not fully completed until delivery at the completion date. To illustrate, assume a construction company receives a $6,000,000 contract to construct a building that will require three years to build. Assume the estimated construction cost to the contractor is $5,700,000; therefore, a $300,000 profit over the three-year period is expected. At the end of the first year the building is one-third completed. Under this approach, the contractor may recognize $100,000 profit at the end of the first year. Contractors may, at their option, elect to use the percentage of completion approach or apply the revenue principle in the usual way and recognize no revenue until completion of the contract. Both approaches are widely used (see Chapter 12).

3. Production approach—This approach is similar to the percentage of completion approach. It is often applied in the case of cost-plus-fixed-fee contracts. Revenue is recognized as production progresses with a portion of the fixed fee recorded as earned.

4. Cost recovery approach—This approach is sometimes called the *sunk cost* approach. Under this approach all of the related costs incurred (i.e., the sunk costs) are recovered before any gain is recognized. The cost recovery approach should be used for highly speculative transactions where the ultimate outcome is completely unpredictable. For example, an investor may have purchased bonds where the interest was in default for a number of years. The purchase price was at a fraction of the maturity amount of the bonds because of the improbability of final collection. The transaction was highly speculative. Under the cost recovery approach, collections of interest would not be recognized as gain until the original investment was recovered; collections subsequent to this point would be recognized as gain.

The problem of determining when revenue should be recognized is a critical one. The diversity of transactions involving revenue precludes application of a single theoretical concept to all situations; therefore, accountants necessarily have developed the realistic guidelines explained above to determine when revenue should be recognized.

The Matching Principle

The matching principle states that for any period for which income is to be reported, the revenues recognized should be determined according to the revenue principle; then the expenses incurred in generating that revenue should be determined and reported for that period. If revenue is carried over from a prior period or deferred to a future period in accordance with the revenue principle, all identifiable elements of expense related to that revenue likewise should be carried over from the prior period or deferred, as the case may be. This matching of expenses with revenue frequently is a difficult problem. However, careful matching is essential in accounting if there is to be a proper determination of periodic net income.

Many costs are deferred to the future by reporting them as assets because the things to which costs attach aid in the generation of future revenues. Examples are inventories, prepaid expenses, and depreciable assets. Subsequently, as they are used up, they are recorded and reported as periodic expenses to *match* them with the revenues their incurrence served to generate. Their deferral as assets, and their subsequent writeoff as periodic expenses in accordance with the matching principle, is generally based on *cause and effect*. Some are written off as expenses based on physical association (such as inventories and supplies used); some on a time basis (such as rent, interest, insurance, and depreciation), and some because there is no reasonably objective way to measure future benefit (such as advertising, donations to worthy causes, and research and development).

The matching principle requires the use of *accrual basis accounting*, as opposed to cash basis accounting, to record and report expenses. Thus, *adjusting entries* must be used to update expenses for the period. Examples are depreciation expense, supplies used, expired insurance, accrued (i.e., unpaid) expenses such as wages, warranty costs, and estimated bad debt expense. These often require the use of estimates. To illustrate, assume a home appliance is sold for cash during the last month of the current accounting period and it is guaranteed for a period of 12 months from date of sale. The sales revenue will be recognized as earned during the current accounting period. The expense of honoring the warranty also should be recognized in the current accounting period, although the actual warranty cost will not be known until the next year. Therefore, at the end of the current year, the amount of the warranty expense must be estimated, recorded, and reported. In this way the warranty expense is matched with the revenue of the period to which it is related.

Objectivity Principle

This principle asserts that to the fullest extent possible, accounting and reporting should be based on data that are *(a)* objectively determined and *(b)* verifiable. *Objective determination* means that accounting should be based on complete arm's-length exchange transactions in-volving the entity. An arm's-length transaction is characterized by an agreement between two or more parties that have adverse interests—the interest of the seller is a high price, whereas the interest of the buyer is a low price. Accountants recognize that many aspects of accounting are not based on factual data but necessarily involve estimates. For example, depreciation expense is based on *(a)* factual data—the cost of the asset—and *(b)* two estimates—useful life and residual value. The objectivity principle specifies that when estimates are necessary, they should be objectively determined by rational and systematic approaches including consideration of experience and realistic expectations.

Verifiability means that to the fullest extent possible, accounting data should be supported by business documents originating outside the business entity. Events recognized that do not result from transactions (such as periodic depreciation) must be supported by internally prepared documents that can be verified by auditors and others. Thus, verifiability relates to the adequacy of evidence to support the data processed in the accounting system and reported on the financial statements.

Consistency Principle

This principle states that in recording and reporting economic events, there must be consistent application of accounting principles, standards, and procedures from one accounting period to the next. Consistent application in accounting for an entity is essential so that the resulting financial statements for successive periods are reasonably comparable.

Financial reports are more useful when prepared on a consistent basis because trends and other important relations are revealed. Inconsistent application of accounting standards often will materially affect reported income and balance sheet amounts. For example, if a company used *Fifo* one year and *Lifo* the next year for inventory costing, and straight-line depreciation followed by accelerated depreciation, net income and asset amounts reported on the financial statements would become capricious. Inconsistency, if allowed, would open the door to manipulation of financial statements.

The consistency principle does not preclude an entity from changing to a different principle or procedure at any time if it is reasonably clear that it better measures economic reality. *APB Opinion No. 20*, "Accounting Changes" (issued July 1971), specifies the various ways that changes in accounting can be made and the disclosure requirements necessary to adequately explain the related effects. The consistency principle, as implemented by *APB Opinion No. 20*, prevents repetitive and manipulative changes. Accounting changes are discussed in Chapter 24.

The standard opinion given by the independent CPA, as a part of the audited financial statements, specifically recognizes the consistency principle as follows:

> In our opinion the financial statements referred to above present fairly the financial position of X Company as of (at) December 31, 19X, and the results of its operations and the changes in its financial position for the year then ended, in conformity with generally accepted accounting principles applied on a basis *consistent with that of the preceding year*.[7] (Emphasis supplied.)

Financial Reporting Principle

This principle often is called the *full disclosure* (or informative disclosure) principle; however, it is a broader concept. The financial reporting principle maintains that financial statements should be designed and prepared to reasonably assure complete and understandable reporting of all significant information relating to the economic affairs of the accounting entity. The financial statements must be complete in the sense that all information reported is necessary for a "fair" presentation so that a "reasonably prudent investor" would not be misled; that is, sufficient information must be presented to permit a "knowledgeable" user to reach an informed decision. The principle is especially important for unusual events, major changes in expectations, and poststatement findings.

The financial reporting principle pertains to the nature of the statements, information to be

---

[7] AICPA, *Codification of Statements on Auditing Standards*, AU Section 411.02 (New York, 1977).

EXHIBIT 2–3
Financial Reporting Principle
Standards of Financial Statement Presentation

1. Basic financial statements generally required:
    a. Balance sheet—statement of financial position.
    b. Income statement—statement of operations.
    c. Statement of changes in financial position—statement of inflows and outflows of funds.
    d. Supporting schedules essential for full disclosure.
2. Complete balance sheet—include all assets, liabilities, and classes of owners' equity (clearly identified).
3. Complete income statement—include all revenues, expenses, net income, infrequently occurring or unusual items, extraordinary items, and earnings per share (clearly identified).
4. Classification and segregation—separate disclosure of the important components of the financial statements to make the information more useful.
5. Gains and losses—revenues and expenses other than sales of products, merchandise, or services should be separated from other revenues and expenses and the net effects disclosed as gains and losses.
6. Extraordinary items—extraordinary gains and losses (net of tax) should be presented separately from other revenues and expenses in the income statement.
7. Working capital—disclosure of components of working capital (current assets less current liabilities) is presumed to be useful for most enterprises.
8. Offsetting—assets and liabilities in the balance sheet should not be offset unless a legal right of setoff exists.
9. Consolidated statements—when one entity owns more than 50% of the outstanding voting stock of another entity, consolidated statements generally are more meaningful than separate financial statements.
10. Accounting period—basic time period for financial statements is one year; interim financial statements recommended for each quarter.
11. Foreign balances—financial information about foreign operations should be translated into U.S. dollars.
12. Accounting policies—accounting policies should be separately disclosed and explained.
13. Full disclosure—in addition to informative classifications and segregation of information, financial statements should disclose all additional information necessary for fair presentation. Notes and parenthetical information necessary for adequate disclosure are an integral part of the financial statements.

Adapted from: AICPA, *Statement of the Accounting Principles Board No. 4*, "Basic Concepts Underlying Financial Statements of Business Enterprises" (New York, October 1970), pars. 188–201.

shown, classification of information on the statements, parenthetical information in the statements, and explanatory notes included in the statements. *Full disclosure* emphasizes the necessity of including explanatory notes and parenthetical information to supplement the basic amounts reported in the tabular parts of the financial statements.

The standards of financial statement preparation developed by the accounting profession to implement the financial reporting principle are summarized in Exhibit 2–3. Application of these reporting standards will be discussed and illustrated throughout the remaining chapters.

Modifying (or Exception) Principle

A prior discussion established that accounting principles are not principles of nature but are man-made. Further, accounting principles are subject to change when there is a change in the environment in which they operate, or in the related needs of financial statement users. Accounting principles are pragmatic and must be applied to a diverse set of facts and conditions. In view of these considerations, some exceptions to the basic concepts and principles are to be expected. The modifying principle encompasses three fairly specific concepts which have been widely recognized and accepted in accounting as essential to accomplish the broad objectives of accounting. The three concepts that comprise the modifying principle are discussed below.

Materiality. Although accounting rests upon a conceptual foundation, it must be pragmatic. Therefore, the concepts and principles must be applied realistically by taking into account the nature of the economic event—the transaction—in the context of the overall economic environment. Thus, the concept of materiality asserts that although all transactions and other events must be recorded, those involving insignificant economic effects need not be accorded strict theoretical treatment because the economic effect is not *material* enough to affect the decision maker. A less costly and timesaving approach may be used to account for *immaterial amounts*. In applying the modifying (or exception) principle, the accountant must weigh the worth of strict accuracy and compliance with accounting

principles against the cost of strict and detailed recordkeeping. Strict adherence to principles is not required when the usefulness of the financial report is not materially affected.

The accounting profession has not yet been able to precisely define the line between a material and an immaterial amount. Materiality is a question of the effect on the user of the statements. Generally, materiality is measured in relation to the more important financial amounts such as sales dollars, net income, total assets, total liabilities, and owners' equity. The *CPA Handbook* states:

> An item in relation to a financial statement would be considered material only if it would have a significant effect upon an important judgment based on that statement. Whether a particular item is material or significant cannot be determined by consideration only of the item itself. Its relationship to other items and to the surrounding circumstances have to be known before that judgment can be made.[8]

To illustrate, assume X Corporation purchased a pencil sharpener costing $5.98 that has an estimated useful life of three years. The assets on the balance sheet total approximately $100,000, and net income approximates $30,000. Theoretically, the pencil sharpener should be recorded in an asset account and depreciated over three years at approximately $2 per year. Clearly the $5.98 is immaterial in relation to total assets, and the $2 is immaterial to net income. Under the materiality concept the rational accounting approach would be to record the $5.98 as expense in the year of acquisition. No rational decision maker would be influenced by these amounts in this particular situation. Observe that the materiality concept does not permit nonrecording and nonreporting of a transaction; it simply permits a pragmatic approach for handling immaterial amounts.

Some decision makers assume that an amount that is 5% or less of a selected base amount, such as net income, is not material. This tendency should be avoided. The nature of the amount and its relative importance to other important amounts must be considered. For example, because of its size, 5% of revenue of $600 million probably should be considered

[8] AICPA, *CPA Handbook,* vol. II, ch. 17, p. 24.

material. It is important that each accounting entity establish uniform policies for implementing the materiality concept.

Conservatism. The concept of conservatism holds that where acceptable alternatives for an accounting determination are available, the alternative having the *least favorable immediate influence* on owners' equity should be selected. In recognizing assets where two alternative valuations are acceptable, the lower valuation should be selected, and the higher of two alternative liability amounts should be recorded. In recording expenses and revenues where there is reasonable doubt as to the appropriateness of alternative amounts, the one having the least favorable effect on net income should be chosen. Thus, where there is a choice among alternative valuations, accounting seeks to avoid favorable exaggeration by relying on reasonable conservatism. Conservatism in accounting frequently results in an exception from theoretical treatment. For example, "lower of cost or market" as used in costing inventories is a departure from the cost principle.

Although the accounting profession has generally accepted the concept that profits should not be anticipated and that probable losses should be recognized as soon as the amounts are reasonably determinable, overconservatism usually results in misrepresentation. Reliance on conservatism should never be used to avoid the more laborious procedures necessary to attain reasonable accuracy. Many errors in accounting have been committed under the guise of conservatism. A modified view of conservatism currently exerts a significant impact on accounting thought and practices.

It is thought that, when the "correct" amount is not determinable, the users of financial statements usually are better served by understatement rather than overstatement of net income and assets. Accountants must make many accounting decisions based on judgment in selecting alternatives, making estimates, and applying accounting principles. These choices often affect net income, assets, and owners' equity; and they do not have a single answer that can be proven "correct." The concept of conservatism (a better word would be realism) provides a time-tested guideline for making these choices.

Some situations where conservatism is often applied are selection of an estimated useful life and residual value for depreciation purposes, writeoff of an asset of doubtful value, writeoff of an uncollectible account, application of the lower-of-cost-or-market rule in valuing marketable equity securities and inventories, accruing loss contingencies, and using an accelerated depreciation method.

Industry Peculiarities. Because accounting focuses on usefulness, feasibility, and pragmatism, the peculiarities and practices of an industry (such as the utility, railroad, banking, and extractive industries) may warrant certain exceptions to accounting principles and practices. The modifying principle permits special accounting for specific items where there is a clear precedent in the industry based on uniqueness, usefulness, and feasibility. It is appropriate also to note that some differences in accounting occur in response to legal requirements; this is especially true with respect to companies subject to significant and pervasive regulatory controls.

A related exception permits the use of a principle or procedure that is at variance with an official pronouncement if it is deemed necessary to prevent misleading inferences. In such cases the departure must be fully disclosed and the reasons therefor given. This seldom happens, primarily because of the possibility of lawsuits.

IMPLEMENTING MEASUREMENT PRINCIPLES

The information presented in external financial reports results from a wide range of accounting measurements. These measurements necessarily depend upon measurement principles, approaches, and techniques from other disciplines. The implementing measurement principles are those that have special application in accounting. Accounting measurement approaches and techniques generally rest upon the four broad implementing principles listed in Exhibit 2-2 (Category IV):

1. Selection of objects, activities, and events to be measured.
2. Identification and classification of the attributes of each object, activity, and event to be measured.

3. Assignment of quantitative amounts to the attributes.
4. Modifying measurement principle.

Selection of the Objects, Activities, and Events to Be Measured

The first and most fundamental step in measurement is to determine what is to be measured. Fundamentally, accounting measures assets, liabilities, owners' equity, revenues, expenses, gains, losses, and the related resource inflows and outflows. In measuring these broad classifications, *objects* must be selected and measured, such as inventory, plant and equipment, land, receivables, and obligations. Similarly, *activities* such as sales of goods and services, payment of dividends, and sale and issuance of equity securities must be identified for measurement. In addition, selected *events,* other than transactions, often must be measured. Examples of these events are casualty losses, price level changes, depreciation, and certain "unrealized" gains and losses.

Identification and Classification of Attributes

When an object, activity, or event has been selected for measurement, its specific attributes must be identified. For example, if goods held for resale (i.e., inventory) are selected for measurement, attributes such as units, description, condition, cost, net realizable value, replacement cost, and so on, can be measured. For measurement purposes, a *choice* must be made of the *attributes* to be measured that are relevant to the objectives of financial reports. As another example, assume an advertising *activity* is to be measured. Attributes such as description, number of ads, media used, cost, and effectiveness can be considered for measurement, and choices must be made. Measurement of the attributes of depreciation, such as cost basis depreciation, economic depreciation, and types of assets depreciated, are examples of *other events.* Because of relevance, time, and cost, the number of attributes to be measured generally is limited with respect to each object, activity, and other event. The attributes to be measured, to the extent feasible, must be classified to facilitate measurement and data processing. For example, one attribute classification which pervades accounting is the *historical cost* of the object, activity, or event.

Assignment of Quantitative Amounts

Accounting measurements of the selected attributes are for the most part quantitative. Numerical values that can be aggregated are assigned to the attributes of the objects, activities, and other events. For example, numerical values (such as number of units and dollar cost) must be assigned to each asset so that aggregate total asset amounts can be derived. The assignment of quantitative amounts for accounting purposes generally is in monetary terms. However, many numerical accounting measurements are not monetary, such as units of inventory, units sold (number of cars), units produced (tons of steel), trends (e.g., indexes), shares of stock, and the number of employees, plants, and products.

Modifying Measurement Principle

Since accounting measurements are made in an uncertain milieu with limited data available, some adaptation of the basic measurement principle is necessary. This pragmatic aspect of accounting measurement not only affects the measurement process itself but influences accounting principles, procedures, and reports. For example, the inherent difficulty in measuring the "market value" of the numerous "parts" of a large, complex business has been a significant argument for retaining the concept of historical cost as the valuation basis in accounting.

The modifying measurement principle has numerous facets; however, the major aspects are *(a)* uncertainty, *(b)* objectivity, *(c)* limitations of the monetary unit, and *(d)* cost effectiveness. *Uncertainty* arises because many measurements in accounting depend upon predictions. Primarily, these arise from the necessity to allocate values between past and future periods. Examples are depreciation expense, bad debt expense, warranty expense, deferred taxes, amortization of intangibles, and unearned revenue. Higher degrees of uncertainty give rise to more complex measurements.

Because of the importance attached to *objectivity* in accounting and financial reporting (see objectivity principle previously discussed), measurement adaptations are necessary to minimize bias. Moreover, measurements must be based on verifiable and objective evidence. This constraint has had a strong influence on the selection and adaptation of measurement approaches and techniques used in accounting.

The *unit of measure assumption* (previously discussed) imposes a constraint on accounting measurements. There is general agreement that accounting measurements must use the monetary unit, although, over time, it is not a stable measuring unit. The instability of the purchasing power of money as a measurement unit has been the basis for numerous proposals to modify both accounting principles and the selection of measurement approaches and techniques (see Chapter 7).

Cost effectiveness relates the value of information to the cost of measuring and reporting that information. Measurement often is a costly effort; consequently, it must be adapted to meet the constraint of cost effectiveness. This means that some accuracy and completeness in measurement sometimes are sacrificed.

BASIC COMPONENTS OF THE ACCOUNTING MODEL

The accounting process broadly encompasses *(a)* collection of economic data affecting an accounting entity; *(b)* analysis of the economic effects of transactions and other events affecting the entity; *(c)* measuring, recording, and classifying the economic effects; and *(d)* reporting the summarized effects in periodic financial statements. This integrated process is built upon the environmental assumptions, basic accounting principles and measurement principles, and the *accounting model.* This model comprises three submodels which parallel the three financial statements, viz:[9]

9 For a review of these basic concepts, see G. A. Welsch and R. N. Anthony, *Fundamentals of Financial Accounting,* rev. ed. (Homewood, Ill.: Richard D. Irwin, Inc., 1977).

1. Financial position model—This is an economic model, expressed in algebraic format, that reflects the status of the resources (assets), obligations (liabilities), and residual equity (owners' equity) of the entity at specific points in time. Coupled with it, to facilitate data processing, is an arithmetical technique referred to as the debit-credit concept. This model, which reflects the basic content of a balance sheet (more appropriately, a statement of financial position), is

2. Results of operations model—This model is reflected by the income statement or, more appropriately, the statement of operating results. The model is

$$Revenue - Expenses = Net Income$$

3. Changes in financial position model—This model is reflected by the statement of changes in financial position. The model is

$$\left\{ \begin{array}{c} Funds \\ Inflows \end{array} \right\} - \left\{ \begin{array}{c} Funds \\ Outflows \end{array} \right\} = \left\{ \begin{array}{c} Net\ Change \\ in\ Funds \end{array} \right\}$$

The basic accounting model, Assets = Liabilities + Owners' Equity, can be applied using *(a)* historical actual costs (the historical cost model), *(b)* historical costs adjusted for price level changes (the price level model), or *(c)* current values (the current value or replacement cost models). The current value model has numerous variations, some of which are discussed in Chapter 7. It is important to keep in mind that the historical cost model is required by generally accepted accounting principles for the *primary* financial statements; therefore, the chapters to follow focus on that particular model.

DETAILED PRINCIPLES AND PROCEDURES

The environmental assumptions, basic principles, and measurement principles discussed in the preceding paragraphs provide the broad foundation for the *detailed* principles and procedures that have been developed and accepted for financial accounting and reporting purposes. *The detailed principles and procedures prescribe how transactions and other events should be measured, recorded, classified, summarized, and reported.* They are the means of implementing the underlying assumptions and the basic principles. Exhibits 2–1 and 2–2 present six categories of detailed principles and procedures; those relating to the financial reporting principle are summarized in Exhibit 2–3. The detailed principles and procedures are discussed and illustrated throughout the chapters to follow.

The term *generally accepted accounting principles* (often abbreviated as GAAP) is widely used in accounting. Although it is used in several contexts, it generally is used as defined in *APB Statement No. 4* (October 1970), paragraph 138:

> Generally accepted accounting principles therefore is a technical term in financial accounting. Generally accepted accounting principles encompass the conventions, rules, and procedures necessary to define accepted accounting practice at a particular time. The standard of "generally accepted accounting principles" includes not only broad guidelines of general application, but also detailed practices and procedures.

ACCOUNTING ON THE ACCRUAL BASIS VERSUS THE CASH BASIS

In the preceding discussion, we explained that generally accepted accounting principles require the accrual basis for accounting and reporting purposes. Nevertheless, some small businesses use the cash basis because of its simplicity and because the financial reports are constructed only for the owners and perhaps the local banker. However, the banker may well have trouble interpreting them, and they cannot be "certified" by an independent CPA because cash basis does not accord with GAAP.

When cash basis accounting is used, revenue is not recognized when the exchange transaction occurs, but rather only when the cash is collected. Similarly, expenses are not recognized when they are incurred as a result of an exchange transaction, but rather only when the cash payment is made. Therefore, net income (or loss) is essentially a cash concept. Cash basis accounting, since it is not in conformity with generally accepted accounting principles, is only briefly reviewed here to emphasize the characteristics of accrual basis accounting.

Accrual basis accounting is specified by the revenue and matching principles and is implicit in most of the other principles. Under the revenue principle, revenue is considered realized (i.e., earned), and is recognized in the accounts and reports, in the period in which the "revenue" transaction occurs, regardless of the periods in which the related cash is collected. Similarly, under the matching principle, an expense is recognized and matched with the revenue of the period to which it relates, regardless of when the related cash is expended. Therefore, net income determined in accordance with generally accepted accounting principles is not a cash concept.

To illustrate the basic difference between accounting on the accrual basis versus on the cash basis, assume the following summarized data:

	Year 19A	Year 19B	Year 19C
Cash collections for sales:			
On 19A sales	$80,000	$15,000	$ 5,000
On 19B sales		90,000	30,000
Cash payments for expenses:			
On 19A expenses	50,000	7,000	3,000
On 19B expenses	6,000*	50,000	14,000

* Prepayments of 19B expense.

The income statements would reflect the following:

	Year 19A	Year 19B
Cash basis:		
Revenue	$ 80,000	$105,000
Expenses	56,000	57,000
Net income—cash basis	$ 24,000	$ 48,000
Accrual basis:		
Revenue	$100,000	$120,000
Expenses	60,000	70,000
Net income—accrual basis	$ 40,000	$ 50,000

The misstatement of income on the cash basis is material in amount when there is a lag between the exchange transactions and the related cash flow transactions.

CONCLUSION

The discussion of the broad structure of financial accounting and reporting in this chapter is intended to provide a frame of reference for study of subsequent chapters. Rather than presenting these concepts piecemeal throughout the text, the authors have chosen to discuss them in this chapter.

In later chapters we will refer explicitly to one or more of these concepts. Therefore, you should return to this chapter often so that upon completion of the text you will have a keen understanding of the structure of current accounting theory and practice. An in-depth understanding of this foundation will (a) minimize the need to memorize procedures and (b) help to resolve, on a logical basis, complex accounting issues not previously encountered.

We cannot overemphasize the importance of an understanding of the foundation of accounting theory as opposed to a mere memorization of procedures and techniques. The accountant, whether in public practice or in industry, is faced continually with accounting problems that do not fit precisely what may have been encountered or considered previously; somehow many of them do not fit neatly into specific accounting practice and procedures. Consequently, many very practical judgments and decisions must be made by the accountant, and they should be resolved on the basis of sound theoretical analysis. For this approach there must be a logical and internally consistent structure of theoretical support. An accountant must have a deep understanding of the meaning and relevance of accounting theory to function as a professional.

As we have noted in this chapter, only the historical cost model of accounting is generally accepted in the United States. However, there is no guarantee that it will not be modified or replaced in the reasonably near future. In 1976 the SEC (ASR 190) began requiring the largest companies in the United States to disclose, as supplements to the historical cost financial statements, current replacement cost data for inventories and cost of goods sold, operational assets and depreciation. Even though this was an experiment, it appears that accountants may be increasingly called upon to supply data in addition to the objective data on completed transactions which form the basis for the historical cost model. Therefore, in order to provide the users of this text with an understanding of other accounting models, we give extended coverage to these other models in Chapter 7. This coverage is sequenced after thoroughgoing reviews of the historical cost model and present value concepts in Chapters 1–6 because an understanding of the historical cost model facilitates understanding of the alternative models. Similarly, it is sequenced before detailed coverage of individual asset, liability, owners' equity, revenue, and expense topics in Chapters 8–22 in order to facilitate better understanding as well as comparison of the various procedures presented in this text.

QUESTIONS

1. What is the basic objective of accounting and what is the role of external financial reporting in terms of that objective? Refer to Chapter 1.

2. Briefly explain the two types of financial statements that are prepared to assist external decision makers. Refer to Chapter 1.

3. Give the four underlying environmental assumptions and briefly explain each.

4. What is the basic accounting problem created by the unit of measure assumption when there is significant inflation?

5. Explain why the time period assumption causes accruals and deferrals in accounting.

6. Explain the cost principle. Why is it used in preference to a current value model?

7. How is cost measured in noncash transactions?

8. Define the revenue principle and explain each of its three aspects: (a) definition, (b) measurement, and (c) realization.

9. How is revenue measured in transactions involving noncash items (exclude credit situations)?

10. There are four exceptions to the revenue principle: *(a)* cash, *(b)* percentage of completion, *(c)* production, and *(d)* cost recovery. Briefly explain each.

11. Explain the matching principle. What is meant by "the expense should follow the revenue"?

12. Explain why the matching principle usually necessitates the use of adjusting entries. Use depreciation expense and unpaid wages as examples.

13. Relate the matching principle to the revenue and cost principles.

14. Explain the objectivity principle; focus on objectivity and verifiability.

15. Explain the consistency principle. Why is it important to the statement user?

16. Explain the financial reporting principle.

17. Why is a modifying, or exception, principle essential? Briefly explain each of the following: *(a)* materiality, *(b)* conservatism, and *(c)* industry peculiarities.

18. Complete the following:

Example	*Concepts of the Modifying Principle Applied*
a. Banks do not separately report working capital.	_____
b. An asset costs $100,000, the estimated residual value is $400, which was disregarded in computing depreciation.	_____
c. Marketable securities that cost $75,000 were reported on the balance sheet at $62,000, which was the market value at balance sheet date.	_____

19. List and explain the four implementing measurement principles.

20. What are the four basic phases of the accounting process?

21. Give and briefly explain the three basic components of the accounting model.

22. Explain the nature of, and the need for, implementing (detailed) principles and procedures.

23. Briefly explain the technical term "generally accepted accounting principles" as used by the accounting profession.

DECISION CASE 2–1

ABC Corporation, at the end of 19X, reported the following (summarized):

Balance Sheet

Total assets	$400,000
Total liabilities	100,000
Total owners' equity	300,000

Income Statement

Sales revenue	$800,000
Expenses	760,000
Net income	40,000

Required:

a. This problem focuses on the concept of materiality. Define materiality. Do not feel constrained by the definition in the chapter.

b. On the basis of *your definition,* use your best judgment to respond to each of the following examples. For each example make a choice as to materiality, then justify it.

(1) At the end of the accounting year, the amount of accrued wages payable is material if the amount is (check for "yes" response):

___	$ 100	___	$ 10,000
___	500	___	20,000
___	1,000	___	50,000
___	5,000	___	100,000

(2) At the end of the accounting year, unearned revenue (cash has been collected) is material if the amount is (check for "yes" response):

___	$ 100	___	$ 10,000
___	500	___	20,000
___	1,000	___	50,000
___	5,000	___	100,000

(3) At the beginning of the accounting year, an operational asset, with an estimated useful life of five years and no residual value, was purchased. If the cost is not capitalized, it will be expensed as incurred. The amount in this transaction is material if the amount is (check for "yes" response):

___	$ 100	___	$ 10,000
___	500	___	20,000
___	1,000	___	50,000
___	5,000	___	100,000

EXERCISES

Exercise 2-1

Give the generally accepted principle(s) that establishes the dollar valuation in the balance sheet for each of the following items:

a. Accounts receivable.
b. Short-term investments.
c. Inventory.
d. Plant and equipment.
e. Plant site (land).
f. Patent.
g. Unearned rent revenue (rent collected in advance).

Exercise 2-2

Present accounting theory is based on the assumption that the "value of money" is relatively stable. If there is a significant change in the price level or in the purchasing power of the dollar, problems arise in interpreting income data as determined under conventional accounting procedures.

Required:

State and explain briefly the nature of such problems as related to inventories and operational assets. You need not attempt to offer specific solutions to these problems.

(AICPA adapted)

Exercise 2-3

On December 31, 19X, the balance sheet for WT Corporation showed the following (summarized):

Assets

Current assets*		$ 60,000
Operational assets (net)		235,000
Patent		5,000
		$300,000

Liabilities and Stockholders' Equity

Current liabilities		$ 30,000
Long-term liabilities		70,000
Contributed capital	$150,000	
Retained earnings	50,000	200,000
		$300,000

* No cash.

On this date the business (including all assets and liabilities) was sold to John Doe who paid $280,000 cash which included $35,000 for "goodwill." Assume generally accepted accounting principles were followed. Explain in terms of these principles why the selling price was still $45,000 higher than the sum of owners' equity shown on the balance sheet plus the goodwill.

Exercise 2-4

Explain how each of the following items, as reported on B Corporation's balance sheet, violated (if it did) the financial reporting principle.

a. Owners' equity reported only two amounts: capital stock, $100,000; and retained earnings, $80,000. The capital stock has a par value of $100,000 and originally sold for $150,000 cash.
b. Although sales amounted to $900,000 and cost of goods sold, $500,000, the first line on the income statement was revenues, $400,000.
c. No earnings per share amounts were reported.
d. Although current assets amounted to $200,000 and current liabilities, $180,000, the balance sheet reported, under assets, the following single amount: working capital, $20,000.
e. The income statement showed only the following classifications:

> Gross revenues
> Costs
> Net profit

f. There was no comment or explanation of the fact that the company changed its inventory method from *Fifo* to *Lifo*.

(AICPA adapted)

Exercise 2-5

The general manager of Cumberland Manufacturing Company received an income statement from the controller. The statement covered the calendar year. The general manager said to the controller, "This statement indicates that a net income of only $100,000 was earned last year. You know the value of the company is much more than it was this time last year."

"You're probably right," replied the controller. "You see, there are factors in accounting which sometimes keep reported operating results from reflecting the change in market value of the company."

Required:

Present a detailed explanation of the accounting theories and principles to which the controller referred.

(AICPA adapted)

Exercise 2-6

Accountants frequently refer to a concept of "conservatism." Explain what is meant by conservatism in accounting. Discuss the question of the extent to which it is possible to follow accounting procedures which will result in consistently conservative financial statements over a considerable number of years. Give an example of an application of conservatism in accounting.

(AICPA adapted)

Exercise 2–7

In making an audit of a corporation you find certain liabilities, such as taxes, which appear to be overstated. Also some semiobsolete inventory items seem to be undervalued, and the tendency is to expense rather than to capitalize as many items as possible.

In talking with the management about the policies, you are told that "the company has always taken a very conservative view of the business and its future prospects." Management suggests that they do not wish to weaken the company by reporting any more earnings or paying any more dividends than are absolutely necessary, since they do not expect business to continue to be good. They point out that the undervaluation of assets, and so on, does not lose anything for the company and creates reserves for "hard times."

Required:

You are to discuss fully whether the policies followed by the company are appropriate and comment on each of the arguments presented by management.

(AICPA adapted)

Exercise 2–8

What is your understanding of the meaning of *consistency* in the application of accounting principles—for example, as used in the standard form of an independent public accountant's report?

(AICPA adapted)

Exercise 2–9

A financial statement included the following note: "During the current year, plant assets were written down by $2,000,000 because of economic conditions. This resulted in substantial savings to the company. Depreciation and other charges in future years will be lower as a result; this will benefit profits of future years." Appraise this statement in terms of (1) economic soundness and (2) generally accepted accounting principles.

Exercise 2–10

The following summarized data were taken from the records of ZW Company at December 31, 19B, end of the accounting year:

1. Sales: 19B cash sales, $300,000; and 19B credit sales, $110,000.
2. Cash collections during 19B: on 19A credit sales, $30,000; on 19B credit sales, $80,000; and on 19C sales (collected in advance), $20,000.
3. Expenses: 19B cash expenses, $180,000; and 19B credit expenses, $70,000.
4. Cash payments during 19B: for 19A credit expenses, $10,000; for 19B credit expenses, $40,000; and for 19C expenses (paid in advance), $7,000.

Required:

Complete the following statements for 19B as a basis for evaluating the difference between cash and accrual accounting.

	Cash Basis	Accrual Basis
Sales revenue	$_____	$_____
Expenses	_____	_____
Net income	_____	_____

PROBLEMS

Problem 2–1

This problem focuses on the revenue principle. Respond to each of the following:

a. Define revenue in accordance with the revenue principle.
b. What should be the dollar amount of revenue recognized under the revenue principle in the case of (1) sales and services for cash and (2) sales and services rendered in exchange for noncash considerations?
c. When should revenue be recognized in the case of long-term, low down payment sales and when collectibility is very uncertain?
d. When should revenue be recognized for long-term construction contracts?
e. How should revenue be recognized when there is a highly speculative transaction involving potential revenue?

Problem 2–2

X Corporation has been involved in a number of transactions necessitating careful interpretation of the revenue principle. For each of the following 19B transactions (1) specify the amount of revenue that should be recognized during 19B and (2) explain the basis for your determination.

a. Regular credit sales amounted to $600,000, of which two thirds was collected by the end of 19B; the balance will be collected in 19C.

b. Regular services were rendered on credit amounting to $100,000, of which three fourths will be collected in 19C.

c. A special item, that had been repossessed from the first purchaser, was sold again for $5,000. A $1,000 cash down payment was received in 19B; the balance is to be paid on a quarterly basis during 19C and 19D. Repossession again would not be a surprise! The item has a cost of $4,000.

d. On January 1, 19A, the company purchased a $10,000 note. Because it was highly speculative whether the note was collectible, the company was able to acquire it for $1,000 cash. The note specifies 8% simple interest payable each year (disregard interest prior to 19A). The first collection on the note was $1,500 cash on December 31, 19B. Further collections are highly speculative.

Problem 2–3

Appraise each of the following statements for correctness in terms of the appropriate accounting principles and environmental assumptions.

a. Lower of cost or market should be used in costing inventories.

b. The cost principle relates only to the income statement.

c. Revenue should be recognized only when the cash is received.

d. Accruals and deferrals are necessary because of the separate entity assumption.

e. Revenue should be recognized as early as possible and expenses as late as possible.

f. The accounting entity is considered to be separate and apart from the owners.

g. A transaction involving a very small amount does not need to be recorded because of materiality.

h. The monetary unit is not stable over time.

i. Full disclosure requires the use of notes to the financial statements.

Problem 2–4

Cheatum Corporation was experiencing a bad year because they were operating at a loss. In order to minimize the loss, they recorded certain transactions as indicated below. Determine for each transaction what accounting principle was violated (if any) and explain

the nature of the violation. Also, in each instance indicate the correct accounting treatment by giving the correct entry.

a. Goods for resale (inventory) were being acquired for $1 per unit. However, the company located a good deal and acquired 10,000 units for $7,500 cash. They recorded the purchase as follows:

Inventory	10,000	
Cash		7,500
Revenue		2,500

b. At the beginning of the year a new machine costing $24,000 was purchased for cash for use in the business. The estimated useful life was ten years, and the estimated residual value was $4,000. The following depreciation entry was made at the end of the year:

Depreciation expense	1,000	
Accumulated depreciation (based on 20-year life)		1,000

c. A patent was being amortized over a 17-year useful life. The amortization entry made at the end of the current year was

Retained earnings	800	
Patent		800

d. Two delivery trucks were repaired (engine tune-up, new tires, brakes relined, front end realigned) at a cost of $350. The following entry was made:

Operational asset—trucks	350	
Cash		350

e. Although the bad debt loss rate did not change, no adjusting entry was made for the estimate of $1,000.

Problem 2–5

The transactions summarized below were recorded as indicated during the current year. Determine for each transaction what accounting principle was violated (if any) and explain the nature of the violation. Also in each instance indicate how the transaction should have been recorded.

a. The company owns a plant that is located on a river that floods every few years. As a result, the company suffers a flood loss regularly. During the current year the flood was severe causing an uninsured loss of $4,800. The following entry was made for repair of the loss:

Retained earnings	4,800	
Cash		4,800

b. The company originally sold and issued 50,000 shares of $100 par value common stock. During the current year 45,000 of these shares were outstanding and 5,000 were held by the company as treasury stock (they had been repurchased from the shareholders in prior years). Near the end of the current year the board of directors declared and paid a cash dividend of $2 per share. The dividend was recorded as follows:

Retained earnings	100,000	
Cash		90,000
Investment income		10,000

c. The company needed a small structure for temporary storage. A contractor quoted a price of $60,000. The company decided to build it themselves. The cost was $50,000 and construction required three months. The following entry was made:

Operational assets—		
warehouse	60,000	
Cash		50,000
Revenue		10,000

d. To construct the structure in (c) above the company borrowed $50,000 cash from the bank at 10% per annum. The loan was paid at the end of the year, and the following entry was made (12 months' interest):

Note payable	50,000	
Operational assets—		
warehouse	5,000	
Cash		55,000

Problem 2–6

Following is a series of transactions during 19B for RS Corporation. Analyze each and then answer the questions.

a. During 19B the company engaged a local attorney to represent it in a dispute with respect to an accident involving a company vehicle. The attorney presented a bill for services for $1,500. Since the company was short of cash, the attorney agreed to accept 100 shares of RS Corporation common stock (par $10 per share). The last sale of stock was for $17 per share three years earlier. The transaction to record settlement of the attorney's fee is under consideration.
   (1) What accounting principle should govern? Explain.
   (2) When should the fee be recognized as an expense? Explain.
   (3) What amount should be recorded as legal expense? Explain.

b. The corporation sold a large item of equipment which it stocked for sale. The sale was made on December 31, 19B, for $10,000 cash. It is estimated that because of a one-year guarantee on the equipment, during the following year $300 cash will be spent on the warranty. Recognition of the warranty expense is under consideration.
   (1) What accounting principle should govern? Explain.
   (2) When should the warranty expense be recognized? Explain.
   (3) What amount should be recorded as warranty expense in 19B? In 19C? Explain.

c. At December 31, 19B, there was an item in the inventory of goods for sale that cost $200. Because it had become obsolete it was estimated that it could be sold for $50 cash (assume this to be its net realizable value). Accounting for the obsolete item is under consideration.
   (1) What accounting principle should govern? Explain.
   (2) What amount should be used by the company for this item in the December 31, 19B, inventory? Explain.

d. The corporation acquired a special item of equipment that would be used in operations (an operational asset). The supplier's catalog listed the item at $15,000. Since the corporation was short of cash, it exchanged a small parcel of land that it had acquired ten years earlier at a cost of $8,000. The land was assessed for tax purposes at $12,000, and a recent appraisal by an independent appraiser showed a market value of $14,000. Accounting for the equipment is under consideration.
   (1) What accounting principle should govern at the date of acquisition? Explain.
   (2) What amount should be debited to the operational asset account? Explain.
   (3) What accounting principle governs the recognition of depreciation on the asset? Explain.

Problem 2–7

The following summarized data were taken from the records of T Corporation at the end of the annual accounting period, December 31, 19B:

Sales for cash	$246,000
Sales on account	84,000
Cash purchases of merchandise for resale	170,000
Credit purchases of merchandise for resale	40,000
Expenses paid in cash (including any prepayments)	71,000

Accounts receivable:
Balance in the account
on January 1, 19B 23,000
Balance in the account
on December 31, 19B 30,000
Accounts payable:
Balance in the account
on January 1, 19B 14,000
Balance in the account
on December 31, 19B 16,000
Merchandise inventory account:
Beginning inventory,
January 1, 19B 50,000
Ending inventory,
December 31, 19B 60,000
Accrued (unpaid) wages
at December 31, 19B
(none at January 1, 19B) 2,000
Prepaid expenses
at December 31, 19B
(none at January 1, 19B) 3,000
Operational assets—equipment:
Cost when acquired 100,000
Annual depreciation 10,000

Required:

Based on the above data, complete the following income statements for 19B in order to evaluate the difference between cash and accrual basis:

	Cash Basis	Accrual Basis
Sales revenue...............	$_____	$_____
Less expenses:		
Cost of goods sold .... $_____	$_____	
Depreciation expense ...... _____	_____	
Remaining expenses .... _____	_____	
Total expenses .... _____	_____	
Pretax Income	$_____	$_____

Problem 2–8

Appraise each of the following items in financial statements in terms of generally accepted accounting principles. Indicate the principle(s) violated and the violation with respect to each item. Also, in each instance indicate the correct accounting treatment.

a. Inventory (through purchases) was recorded at $8,000 when purchased on credit; terms, 2/10,n/30.

b. The company sustained a $20,000 storm damage loss during the current year. The loss was reported as follows:
   Income statement: extraordinary item—storm loss, $2,000.
   Balance sheet: deferred charge (under assets), $18,000.

c. Accounts receivable of $60,000 included amounts due soon from the company president amounting to $50,000.

d. Usual and ordinary repairs on operational assets were recorded as follows: debit Operational Assets, $8,000; credit Cash, $8,000.

e. Treasury stock (i.e., stock of the company that was sold and subsequently bought back from the shareholders) was reported on the balance sheet as an asset, $25,000.

f. Depreciation expense of $30,000 was deducted directly from Retained Earnings.

g. Income tax expense of $18,000 was deducted directly from Retained Earnings.

Problem 2–9

The general ledger of Enter-tane, Inc., a corporation engaged in the development and production of television programs for commercial sponsorship, contains the following accounts before amortization at the end of the current year:

Account	Balance (debit)
Sealing Wax and Kings	$51,000
The Messenger	36,000
The Desperado	17,500
Shin Bone	8,000
Studio Rearrangement	5,000

An examination of contracts and records revealed the following information:

a. The first two accounts listed above represent the total cost of completed programs that were televised during the accounting period just ended. Under the terms of an existing contract, Sealing Wax and Kings will be rerun during the next accounting period at a fee equal to 50% of the fee for the first televising of the program. The contract for the first run produced $300,000 of revenue. The contract with the sponsor of The Messenger provides that at the sponsor's option, the program can be rerun during the next season at a fee of 75% of the fee on the first televising of the program. There are no present indications that it will be rerun.

b. The balance in The Desperado account is the cost of a new program which has just been completed and is being considered by several companies for commercial sponsorship.

c. The balance in the Shin Bone account represents the cost of a partially completed program for a projected series that has been abandoned.

d. The balance of the Studio Rearrangement account consists of payments made to a firm of engineers which prepared a report relative to the more efficient utilization of existing studio space and equipment.

Required:

1. State the general principle (or principles) of accounting that are applicable to the first *four* accounts.

2. How would you report each of the first *four* accounts in the financial statements of Enter-tane, Inc.? Explain.

3. In what way, if at all, does the Studio Rearrangement account differ from the first four? Explain.

(AICPA adapted)

3

Review—The Accounting Model and Information Processing

The fundamental objective of financial accounting is to provide relevant financial information to external decision makers. The periodic financial statements summarize the economic impacts of a multitude of transactions and other events on an entity. Identification, analysis, recording, and classification of the impacts of transactions and other events require an efficient and usually a sophisticated accounting information processing system. The larger the entity, the greater the number of transactions, and, consequently, the more complex is the information processing system. The information processing system (i.e., the accounting system) must be designed to (1) collect and measure economic data, (2) classify and process the data, and (3) summarize economic effects in financial reports for decision makers. An accounting system must be tailored to the entity's characteristics, such as size, nature of operations, organizational structure, management approaches, and extent of government regulation. However, a fundamental structure, based upon the accounting model, is common to most accounting systems.

We assume in this book that the reader has a sound knowledge of the *fundamentals* of financial accounting. Nevertheless, in this and the next two chapters, we shall review those

fundamentals.[1] The purpose of this chapter is to review and illustrate the *sequential* accounting information processing cycle that is repeated each accounting period.

THE ACCOUNTING MODEL

In Chapter 2 we outlined the fundamental accounting model that underlies most accounting systems. This model is composed of three submodels, each of which represents one basic component of the periodic financial statements designed for external decision makers. The three submodels are as follows:

1. Financial position model (the balance sheet): Assets = Liabilities + Owners' Equity (A = L + OE).
2. Results of operations model (the income statement): Revenues − Expenses = Net Income (R − E = NI).
3. Funds flow model (the statement of changes in financial position): Funds Inflow − Funds Outflow = Net Change in Funds (FI − FO = NCF).

---

[1] For a more comprehensive introductory discussion, see G. A. Welsch and R. N. Anthony, *Fundamentals of Financial Accounting,* rev. ed. (Homewood, Ill.: Richard D. Irwin, Inc., 1977).

Coupled with the accounting model is the debit-credit concept. This is a mathematical technique used to record increases and decreases in specific variables in the model—assets, liabilities, owners' equity, revenues, and expenses.

Fundamentally, all recognized accounting events are recorded in the accounting system in terms of the *financial position model:* A = L + OE. The debit-credit concept is superimposed on this basic model as follows:

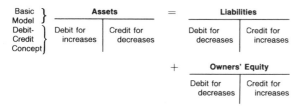

Since investments by owners and revenues *increase* owners' equity and since withdrawals by owners and expenses *decrease* owners' equity, the model can be expanded to include them as follows:

Assets		=	Liabilities	
Debit for increases	Credit for decreases		Debit for decreases	Credit for increases

+	Owners' Equity	
	Debit for de-creases:	Credit for in-creases:
	a. With-drawals by owners.	a. Invest-ments by owners.
	b. Expenses.	b. Revenues.

Observe in the above diagram that although the debits are *always* on the left and the credits are *always* on the right, the increases and decreases are in opposite positions on each side of the equation. That is, debits represent increases to assets and decreases to liabilities and owners' equity, whereas credits represent decreases to assets and increases to liabilities and owners' equity. Expenses are recorded as debits and revenues as credits. This algebraic arrangement forces debits always to equal credits. Thus, the fundamental accounting model always maintains a dual balancing feature, viz:

1. Assets = Liabilities + Owners' Equity.
2. Debits = Credits.

Because of this dual feature, the accounting model is often referred to as a *double-entry system.* The two balancing features add reliability to the output of an accounting system by calling attention to those errors which cause the system to be out of balance.

Whether an accounting system is maintained manually, mechanically, or electronically, each entry is recorded in the basic accounting model. Thus, each entry entered in an accounting system maintains the dual-balancing feature singly and on a cumulative basis. The fundamental information processing approach is reviewed in Exhibit 3–1. In particular, note the following: (1) transaction analysis in terms of the basic accounting model, (2) method of recording the increases and decreases, (3) A = L + OE for each entry and cumulatively, and (4) debits equal credits for each entry and cumulatively.

THE ACCOUNTING INFORMATION PROCESSING CYCLE

The accounting system provides a systematic approach for processing information from the capture of raw economic data that affect the entity to the end result, the periodic financial statements. Therefore, an accounting system incorporates an information processing cycle, often called the accounting cycle, that is repeated each accounting period. This cycle is common to all double-entry accounting systems; however, the larger the enterprise, the more complex its application. The accounting information processing cycle, diagrammed in Exhibit 3–2, reflects the *sequential order* in which specific steps are usually accomplished. Each phase will be discussed and illustrated in order.

COLLECTION OF RAW ECONOMIC DATA (PHASE 1)

The accounting system collects raw economic data about *events* affecting the entity that are to be recorded. Two types of events are recognized in an accounting system: (1) exchange transactions between the entity and one or more outside parties, such as the sale of goods, purchase of assets, sale of securities, and payment of wages; and (2) other events that are not transactions but which exert an economic impact on

EXHIBIT 3–1   Information Inputs in an Accounting System

Typical Transaction	Transaction Analysis	Entry into the Accounting System			Basic Accounting Model (cumulative balances)		
		Accounts	Debit	Credit	A =	L +	OE
1. Service Corporation was organized; owners invested $100,000 cash and received nopar common stock.	Asset increased— cash, $100,000. Owners' equity increased—common stock, $100,000. Liabilities—no effect.	Cash .... Common stock ...	100,000	100,000	+100,000		+100,000
					100,000	–0–	100,000
2. Borrowed $50,000 on a note payable.	Asset increased— cash, $50,000. Liabilities increased— notes payable, $50,000. Owners' equity—no effect.	Cash .... Notes payable	50,000	50,000	+ 50,000	+50,000	
					150,000	50,000	100,000
3. Purchased equipment for use in the business, $40,000; paid cash.	Asset increased— equipment $40,000. Asset decreased— cash, $40,000. Liabilities—no effect. Owners' equity—no effect.	Equipment .... Cash	40,000	40,000	+ 40,000 − 40,000		
					150,000	50,000	100,000
4. Services rendered to clients, $20,000, of which $15,000 was collected in cash.	Assets increased— cash, $15,000; accounts receivable, $5,000. Owners' equity increased—revenue, $20,000. Liabilities—no effect.	Cash .... Accounts receivable .... Service revenue ..	15,000 5,000	20,000	+ 15,000 + 5,000		+ 20,000
					170,000	50,000	120,000
5. Incurred operating expenses, $11,000, of which $8,000 was paid in cash.	Asset decreased— cash, $8,000. Liability increased— accounts payable $3,000. Owners' equity decreased—expense, $11,000.	Expenses .... Cash .... Accounts payable	11,000	8,000 3,000	− 8,000	+ 3,000	− 11,000
					162,000	53,000	109,000
6. Paid $2,000 on accounts payable (5 above).	Asset decreased— cash, $2,000. Liability decreased— accounts payable, $2,000. Owners' equity—no effect.	Accounts payable .... Cash	2,000	2,000	− 2,000	− 2,000	
					160,000	51,000	109,000
7. Depreciation for one year on equipment; estimated life ten years; no residual value (3 above).	Asset decreased— accumulated depreciation, $4,000. Owners' equity decreased—depreciation expense, $4,000. Liabilities—no effect.	Depreciation expense .... Accumulated depreciation, equipment	4,000	4,000	− 4,000		− 4,000
					156,000	51,000	105,000

EXHIBIT 3–2   Diagram of the Accounting Information Processing Cycle

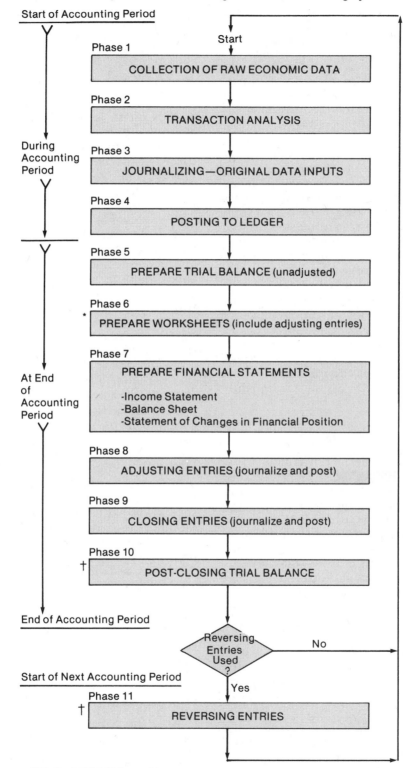

Start of Accounting Period

During Accounting Period

At End of Accounting Period

End of Accounting Period

Start of Next Accounting Period

Start

Phase 1
COLLECTION OF RAW ECONOMIC DATA

Phase 2
TRANSACTION ANALYSIS

Phase 3
JOURNALIZING—ORIGINAL DATA INPUTS

Phase 4
POSTING TO LEDGER

Phase 5
PREPARE TRIAL BALANCE (unadjusted)

Phase 6
* PREPARE WORKSHEETS (include adjusting entries)

Phase 7
PREPARE FINANCIAL STATEMENTS

-Income Statement
-Balance Sheet
-Statement of Changes in Financial Position

Phase 8
ADJUSTING ENTRIES (journalize and post)

Phase 9
CLOSING ENTRIES (journalize and post)

Phase 10
† POST-CLOSING TRIAL BALANCE

Reversing Entries Used ?   No

Yes

Phase 11
† REVERSING ENTRIES

Note: See Exhibit 3–10 for complete summary.
 * Worksheets are optional. If not used, prepare an *adjusted* trial balance after Phase 8 as a basis for preparing the financial statements.
 † Optional.

the enterprise and must be recorded. These events may be external, such as casualties (e.g., floods, fires, hurricanes, etc.) and changes in currency exchange rates. Also, they may be internal, that is, involving the conversion or use of resources such as depreciation of operational assets and amortization of intangibles.[2]

Raw economic data are collected by means of *source documents.* Exchange transactions, since they involve external parties, almost always generate their own source documents—sale invoices, credit bills, freight bills, notes signed by debtors, purchase orders, deposit slips, checks, and so on. For recognized events that are not transactions, the entity itself must prepare the source documents. Examples are depreciation computations, schedules of assets lost due to casualty, amortization schedules, periodic inventory schedules, and issue requisitions. The source documents are an important phase of data collection because *(a)* they provide basic data for transaction analysis (and the resulting journal entry) and *(b)* they constitute a "track record" so that the event and the measurement of its effects on the entity can be subsequently *verified.*

TRANSACTION ANALYSIS (PHASE 2)

Transaction analysis is largely a mental process. It constitutes the study and analysis of each transaction to identify and assess its economic impact on the entity in terms of the accounting model. An analysis is made to measure the economic effect on assets, liabilities, owners' equity, revenues, expenses, fund inflows, fund outflows, and other measurements of interest to the statement users. Transaction analysis is the basis for developing the *accounting entry,* or entries, that must be recorded in the accounting system. Transaction analysis involving complex events often requires a high degree of accounting sophistication since the competence with which it is done ultimately determines the reliability of the periodic financial statements. Effective transaction analysis depends upon sound knowl-

edge of the fundamental theory and structure of accounting discussed in Chapter 2.

JOURNALIZING—THE ORIGINAL DATA INPUT (PHASE 3)

This phase is the initial, or original, input of economic data into an accounting system. The record in which each transaction is first recorded in an accounting system is called the *journal.* This is a chronological record (i.e., by order of date) of each transaction that expresses its economic effects on the entity in terms of the fundamental accounting model (A = L + OE) and in debit-credit format; it directly follows transaction analysis. It records what accounts are increased and decreased and the amount of each change.

Basically, a journal entry lists the date of the transaction, the account(s) debited and the account(s) credited, and their respective amounts. Each entry is recorded so that the integrity of the duality of the system is maintained: A = L + OE and Debits = Credits. Although the journal is not absolutely essential (one could skip it and go directly to the ledger), it is important because it *(a)* maintains a chronological record of the transactions recognized in the system, which is useful for subsequent tracing, and *(b)* shows in one place all aspects of each transaction (i.e., all accounts affected and the amounts).

In an accounting system usually there are two types of journals: (1) the general journal and (2) several special journals. Each special journal is designed to accommodate like-kind transactions. The commonly used special journals are credit sales, credit purchases, cash receipts, cash payments, and the voucher journal. Special journals are discussed and illustrated in Appendix A of this chapter. Most accounting systems use at least a general journal. A general journal will be used in the chapters to follow because of its value for instructional purposes. The general journal format, with a typical entry, is shown in Exhibit 3–3.

POSTING TO THE LEDGER (PHASE 4)

After the initial recording in the journal, the next step is to transfer the information to the ledger. The transfer process, called *posting,* is

---

[2] For convenience in exposition, the term "transactions" will be used broadly to include both transactions and the other events to be recognized.

EXHIBIT 3–3
General Journal and General Ledger Illustrated

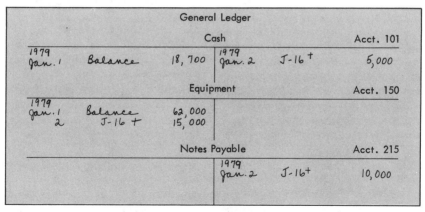

General Journal				
				Page J-16
Date 1979	Accounts and Explanation	Ledger Folio*	Amount Debit	Amount Credit
Jan. 2	Equipment	150	15,000	
	Cash	101		5,000
	Notes payable	215		10,000
	Purchased equipment for use in the business. Paid $5,000 cash and gave a $10,000, one-year, note payable with 9% interest payable at maturity.			

* The figures in this column indicate *(a)* that the amount has been posted to the ledger and *(b)* the account number in the ledger to which posted.

General Ledger					
Cash					Acct. 101
1979 Jan. 1	Balance	18,700	1979 Jan. 2	J-16 †	5,000
Equipment					Acct. 150
1979 Jan. 1	Balance	62,000			
2	J-16 †	15,000			
Notes Payable					Acct. 215
			1979 Jan. 2	J-16†	10,000

† This figure indicates the journal page from which the amount was posted.

done at various times for all transactions. This transfer has the effect of reclassifying the information from a chronological format to an account classification format in the *ledger*. Posting from the journal to the ledger is illustrated in Exhibit 3–3.

Recall that the ledger consists of a large number of separate accounts. There are accounts for each kind of asset (such as cash, accounts receivable, investments, operational assets, and intangible assets), liability (such as accounts payable and bonds payable), owners' equity (such as capital stock and retained earnings), revenue, and expense. Posting amounts from the journal to the ledger results in reclassification of the data into ledger accounts which are compatible with the classifications of information in the financial statements.

Real and Nominal Accounts

The accounts in the ledger often are classified as follows.

1. Real accounts—These are the balance sheet accounts. They are *permanent,* or real, in the sense that they are not closed at the end of the accounting period. They are the asset, liability, and owners' equity accounts. The related contra accounts are also real accounts.
2. Nominal accounts—These are the income statement accounts. They are *temporary,* or nominal, in the sense that they are closed at the end of the accounting period. They are principally the revenue and expense accounts.[3]

An account, either real or nominal, may be "mixed" at a specific time in the sense that its *balance* may contain both a real (i.e., balance sheet) component and a nominal (i.e., income statement) component. To illustrate, assume that on January 1 of the current year, a three-year insurance premium of $600 was paid and debited to a real account, Prepaid Insurance. On December 31 of the current year, of the $600, the nominal component, Insurance Expense, is $200 and the real component, Prepaid Insurance, is $400 (an asset). An adjusting entry on December 31, debiting Insurance Expense and crediting Prepaid Insurance for $200, is necessary to "unmix" the Prepaid Insurance asset account by moving the "nominal" component of $200 to a nominal account, Insurance Expense.

Subsidiary Ledgers and Control Accounts

Most companies use both a *general ledger* and one or more *subsidiary ledgers.* For each subsidiary ledger there is a related *control account* in the general ledger. The control account reflects summary information, whereas the subsidiary ledger reflects the details that support the control account. The general ledger contains the control accounts for all assets, liabilities, owners' equity, revenues, and expenses.

---

[3] Revenue and expense accounts are subaccounts of owners' equity.

Each subsidiary ledger is a device for keeping track of a multitude of details that relate to a particular *control account* in the general ledger. To illustrate, a department store may have 10,000 credit customers. A separate account receivable must be kept for each customer. Rather than 10,000 different accounts receivable in the general ledger, one controlling account, Accounts Receivable Control, should be used. An accounts receivable subsidiary ledger composed of a separate account for each customer should also be maintained. Each credit sale would *(a)* be posted directly to the customer's account in the subsidiary ledger, and *(b)* the total of all credit sales periodically (i.e., daily or weekly) would be posted to the Accounts Receivable Control account in the general ledger. Thus, at any time when posting is complete, the sum of the balances in the customer accounts in the subsidiary ledger would agree with the single balance in the Accounts Receivable Control account.

Subsidiary ledgers often are used for cash (when there are numerous cash accounts), accounts receivable, accounts payable, operational assets, capital stock (a subsidiary ledger for this account is used when a company handles its own stock transfers; it is a record for each shareholder), revenue, and expense. Subsidiary ledgers and control accounts are discussed and illustrated in Appendix A to this chapter.

PREPARE A TRIAL BALANCE— UNADJUSTED (PHASE 5)

At the end of the period, after all of the regular entries for completed transactions have been journalized and posted to the ledger, a trial balance should be prepared. Since this trial balance is prepared *before* the adjusting entries are made, it is often called the *unadjusted trial balance.* A trial balance is simply a list of the accounts in the general ledger and their respective debit or credit balances. A trial balance, prepared after all of the regular entries but before the adjusting entries, serves the following purposes:

1. It verifies that debits equal credits.
2. It provides important information for the development of

a. A worksheet, and
b. The end-of-the-period adjusting entries.

An unadjusted trial balance for Canby Retailers, Inc., is shown in Exhibit 3–4. This trial balance will be used to illustrate the discussions to follow.

EXHIBIT 3–4

CANBY RETAILERS, INC.
Unadjusted Trial Balance
December 31, 1979

Account	Debit	Credit
Cash	$ 55,300	
Short-term notes receivable	20,000	
Accounts receivable	45,000	
Allowance for doubtful accounts		$ 1,000
Inventory of merchandise (periodic system)	75,000	
Prepaid insurance	600	
Interest receivable		
Land	8,000	
Building	160,000	
Accumulated depreciation, building		90,000
Equipment	91,000	
Accumulated depreciation, equipment		27,000
Accounts payable		29,000
Income taxes payable		
Interest payable		
Rent revenue collected in advance		
Bonds payable, 6%		50,000
Common stock, par $10		150,000
Contributed capital in excess of par		20,000
Retained earnings		31,500
Sales revenue		325,200
Interest revenue		500
Rent revenue		1,800
Purchases	130,000	
Freight on purchases	4,000	
Purchase returns		2,000
Selling expenses*	104,000	
General and administrative expenses*	23,600	
Interest expense	2,500	
Extraordinary loss	9,000	
Income tax expense		
Totals	$728,000	$728,000

* These broad categories of expense are used to conserve space. They might well represent control accounts.

PREPARE WORKSHEET (PHASE 6)

As soon as the unadjusted trial balance is available, the following end-of-the-period procedures can be completed:

1. Develop the adjusting entries.
2. Journalize and post the adjusting and closing entries.
3. Prepare an adjusted trial balance.
4. Prepare the financial statements.

These procedures can be completed in the order listed above. Remember that the adjusting entries must be considered before the financial statements can be developed. However, accountants usually insert another step, preparation of two worksheets, viz: (1) one to facilitate development of the adjusting entries, the income statement, and the balance sheet; and (2) one to facilitate preparation of the statement of changes in financial position. These worksheets are simply *facilitating techniques*. They constitute an orderly and systematic approach to completing *(a)* the adjusting and closing entries and *(b)* the financial statements on a timely basis. This is the only reason for using these worksheets (they are not journals, ledgers, or financial statements per se).

A worksheet based on the *unadjusted* trial balance given in Exhibit 3–4 is presented in Exhibit 3–5. This worksheet provides data for the income statement and balance sheet.[4]

Worksheet Techniques

The worksheet shown in Exhibit 3–5 was prepared as follows:

1. Enter the unadjusted trial balance (Exhibit 3–4) on the worksheet using the first pair of amount columns.
2. Develop the adjusting entries and record them in the second pair of columns on the worksheet.

---

[4] If you are not interested in the worksheet technique presented in this chapter, omit the material under the caption "Completion of the Worksheet," page 59. However, mastery of worksheet techniques, especially learning to organize and analyze a mass of data, is almost essential in any accounting or financial capacity from the staff accountant to the chief executive officer.

EXHIBIT 3–5

CANBY RETAILERS, INC.
Worksheet for the Year Ended December 31, 1979

Accounts	Unadjusted Trial Balance Debit	Unadjusted Trial Balance Credit	Adjusting Entries Debit	Adjusting Entries Credit	Adjusted Trial Balance Debit	Adjusted Trial Balance Credit	Income Statement Debit	Income Statement Credit	Retained Earnings Debit	Retained Earnings Credit	Balance Sheet Debit	Balance Sheet Credit
Cash	55,300				55,300						55,300	
Short-term notes receivable	20,000				20,000						20,000	
Accounts receivable	45,000				45,000						45,000	
Allowance for doubtful accounts		1,000		(f) 1,200		2,200						2,200
Interest receivable			(d) 100		100						100	
Inventory (periodic system)	75,000				75,000		75,000	90,000*			90,000	
Prepaid insurance	600			(a) 200	400						400	
Land	8,000				8,000						8,000	
Building	160,000				160,000						160,000	
Accumulated depreciation, building		90,000		(e) 10,000		100,000						100,000
Equipment	91,000				91,000						91,000	
Accumulated depreciation, equipment		27,000		(e) 9,000		36,000						36,000
Accounts payable		29,000				29,000						29,000
Interest payable				(c) 500		500						500
Rent revenue collected in advance				(b) 600		600						600
Bonds payable, 6%		50,000				50,000						50,000
Common stock, par $10		150,000				150,000						150,000
Contributed capital in excess of par		20,000				20,000						20,000
Retained earnings		31,500				31,500				31,500		
Sales revenue		325,200				325,200		325,200				
Interest revenue		500		(d) 100		600		600				
Rent revenue		1,800	(b) 600			1,200		1,200				
Purchases	130,000				130,000		130,000					
Freight on purchases	4,000				4,000		4,000					
Purchase returns		2,000				2,000		2,000				
Selling expenses	104,000		(e) 8,200 (f) 1,200		113,400		113,400					
General and administrative expenses	23,600		(a) 200 (e) 10,800		34,600		34,600					
Interest expense	2,500		(c) 500		3,000		3,000					
Extraordinary loss	9,000				9,000		9,000					
	728,000	728,000	21,600	21,600	748,800	748,800	369,000	419,000				
Income tax expense†			(g) 20,000				20,000					
Income taxes payable				(g) 20,000								20,000
Net income to retained earnings							30,000			30,000		
Retained earnings to balance sheet									61,500			61,500
Totals							419,000	419,000	61,500	61,500	469,800	469,800

* This is only one of several technique for entering the ending inventory on a worksheet.
† ($419,000 − $369,000) .40 = $20,000. There are other ways to reflect income taxes on the worksheet.

3. Extend the unadjusted balances, plus or minus the adjustments, to the Adjusted Trial Balance columns and check for balance.
4. Extend the adjusted amounts to the right, line by line, to the pair of columns under the financial statement on which they should be reported: Income Statement, Retained Earnings (optional), or Balance Sheet.
5. Check each pair of columns for equality of debits and credits.

Development of Adjusting Entries

Because of accrual basis accounting, numerous adjustments must be made to the account balances (as reflected in the unadjusted trial balance) at the end of each accounting period. These adjustments are necessary to restate (i.e., adjust) certain income statement and balance sheet accounts because (1) some accounts have a "mixed" balance which includes both real and nominal components and (2) certain internal and external events have not yet been entered in the accounts. These adjustments may be classified as follows:

Deferred items:

1. Prepaid expense—an expense paid in advance of the period(s) in which it can be properly recognized as an expense on the income statement.
2. Revenue collected in advance—a revenue collected in advance of the period(s) in which it can be properly recognized as realized revenue on the income statement (frequently called unearned revenue and sometimes called deferred revenue).

Accrued items:

3. Accrued expense—an expense incurred but not yet paid; therefore, it must be recorded.
4. Accrued revenue—a revenue earned but not yet collected; therefore, it must be recorded.

Other items:

5. Estimated items.

Prepaid Expense. A prepaid expense occurs when services or supplies were purchased or otherwise acquired but not consumed or used by the end of the accounting period. To illustrate, Canby Retailers on January 1, 1979, paid a three-year insurance premium in advance amounting to $600. At that date, the $600 payment was recorded as a debit to Prepaid Insurance and a credit to Cash. On the unadjusted trial balance of the worksheet, the $600 is reflected as the debit balance of an asset account, Prepaid Insurance. Since $200 of this service was "used" in 1979, there remains a $400 prepaid expense. Therefore, on December 31, 1979, an adjusting entry must be made as follows (the

letter code to the left is used on the worksheet, Exhibit 3–5, for reference in study):

a. December 31, 1979:

Insurance expense (general and administrative expense)	200	
Prepaid insurance		200

The effects of this entry, which are reflected on the worksheet, are (1) to adjust the asset account to $400 on the balance sheet and (2) to record the $200 expense component on the income statement.[5]

Revenue Collected in Advance. Precollected or unearned revenue occurs when a company collects cash for revenues that, at the end of the accounting period, have not yet been fully earned. To illustrate, Canby Retailers, on January 1, 1979, leased to J. R. Jones a small office in their building. At the start they collected $1,800 cash in advance for 18 months rent. At that time, the collection was recorded as a debit to Cash and a credit to Rent Revenue. On December 31, 1979, the $1,800 balance in the Rent Revenue account included $600 unearned rent revenue. Therefore, the following adjusting entry was made (see Exhibit 3–5):

b. December 31, 1979:

Rent revenue	600	
Rent revenue collected in advance*		600

* Often called Unearned Rent Revenue.

This entry leaves $1,200 in the Rent Revenue account and separates as a liability the $600 unearned rent revenue. The $600 is a liability on December 31, 1979, because Canby owes that amount of "occupancy" to Jones. In 1980 the $600 will be transferred to the Rent Revenue account.

Accrued Expense. An accrued expense is one that has been incurred by the end of the accounting period but has not been paid; therefore, it must be recorded. To illustrate, Canby Retailers, Inc., has a liability for bonds payable of $50,000.

---

[5] Sometimes a prepaid expense is initially debited to an expense account instead of an asset account, in which case, an adjusting entry also is required. To illustrate, assume the $600 was initially debited to *Insurance Expense.* The adjusting entry would be debit Prepaid Insurance, $400; credit Insurance Expense, $400. In either case the net effect on the statements is the same.

These bonds require payments of 6% annual interest each October 30. Therefore, on December 31, 1979, accrued (unpaid) interest expense was $50,000 × .06 × 2/12 = $500. This accrued interest must be recognized by the following adjusting entry (see Exhibit 3–5):

c. December 31, 1979:

Interest expense 500
    Interest payable 500

This adjusting entry records (1) the expense for income statement purposes and (2) the liability for balance sheet purposes.

Accrued Revenue. An accrued revenue is one that has been earned by the end of the accounting period but has not yet been collected; therefore, it must be recorded. To illustrate, Canby Retailers, Inc., held short-term notes receivable amounting to $20,000. These notes earn 6% annual interest which is received each November 30. Since interest revenue was earned for the month of December, an adjusting entry must be made as follows (see Exhibit 3–5):

d. December 31, 1979:

Interest receivable 100
    Interest revenue ($20,000 ×
      .06 × 1/12) 100

This entry records (1) an asset (interest receivable) for balance sheet purposes and (2) a revenue (interest revenue) for income statement purposes.

Adjusting Entries for Estimated Items

Some adjusting entries must be based on *estimated amounts* because they depend upon future conditions and events. This means that some revenues and expenses reported for the current period will be determined by estimates. For example, depreciation expense, bad debt expense, and warranty (guarantee) expense must be based on estimates of future useful life, future collectibility, and future expenditures, respectively.

Depreciation Expense. When certain assets, such as a machine, are acquired for use in operating a business (i.e., not for sale), they are "used up" over time through wear and obsolescence.

The amount of this *use cost* is measured each accounting period and recorded as depreciation expense. Depreciation expense is always an estimate because the amount recognized depends upon a known amount, the cost of the asset, and two estimates, useful life and residual (or scrap) value. To illustrate, at the end of 1979 Canby Retailers, Inc., had two assets on which depreciation was computed, viz:

Asset	Computations		Annual Depreciation
Building	$\dfrac{\text{Cost, \$160,000} - \text{Residual Value, \$10,000}}{\text{Estimated Useful Life, 15 Years}}$	=	$10,000
Equipment	$\dfrac{\text{Cost, \$91,000} - \text{Residual Value, \$1,000}}{\text{Estimated Useful Life, Ten Years}}$	=	9,000
Total depreciation expense for the year			$19,000

Based on these computations, an adjusting entry is necessary as follows (see Exhibit 3–5):

e. December 31, 1979:

Depreciation expense (selling) 8,200
Depreciation expense (general
   and administrative) 10,800
    Accumulated depreciation,
      building 10,000
    Accumulated depreciation,
      equipment 9,000

Depreciation expense was debited to two expense accounts because the company follows the policy of *allocating* it to the two categories of expense based upon the proportionate use in each function. This entry (1) records the expense for the income statement and (2) reduces the book value of the building and equipment for balance sheet purposes.

Bad Debt Expense. Sales and services billed on credit almost always cause some losses due to uncollectible accounts receivable (i.e., bad debts). The fact that an account is uncollectible usually is not known for several periods subsequent to the period in which the credit was extended and the sale or service recognized as revenue in accordance with the revenue principle (see Chapter 2). The matching principle (see Chapter 2) requires that all *expenses* associated with sales and service revenue be recognized in the period in which the revenue was recorded. Since the revenues should be recorded as earned in the period the sales were made and the services rendered, and the bad debt loss may not be known for several periods later, an estimation of bad debt expense must be recorded by means of an adjusting entry in the period in which the related revenue was recorded. To illustrate, Canby Retailers, Inc., extended credit on sales during 1979 amounting to $120,000. Experience by the company indicated an expected average bad debt loss rate of 1% of credit sales. Therefore, the following adjusting entry was needed (see Exhibit 3–5):

f. December 31, 1979:

Bad debt expense (selling)	1,200	
Allowance for doubtful accounts .		1,200

The credit is made to an "allowance" account rather than directly to accounts receivable because the identity of specific customers involved is not presently known. Bad debt expense is reported on the income statement, and the allowance account is reported on the balance sheet as a deduction from accounts receivable (i.e., it is a contra asset account). When an account is subsequently determined to be bad, it is written off as a debit to the allowance account and a credit to Accounts Receivable; this write-off will have no effect on expenses or on the net book value of accounts receivable.

Completion of the Worksheet

After the adjusting entries are entered on the worksheet (in the second pair of columns), it is completed by extending each account balance (i.e., the trial balance amount plus or minus any adjustments) to the next columns as illustrated in Exhibit 3–5. Two pairs of the columns shown on this exhibit are not essential: (1) the Adjusted Trial Balance columns, which are used to insure accuracy (i.e., a debits = credits check *after* the adjusting entries), and (2) the Retained Earnings column, which can be merged with the balance sheet. Observe in the extending that debits are extended as debits and credits as credits.

There are three additional aspects of the worksheet that warrant some explanation:

1. Note that the *beginning* inventory amount, $75,000, is extended to the income statement

as a debit and that the *ending* inventory of $90,000 is entered as a credit to the income statement and as a debit to the balance sheet.[6] This procedure results from the company's *periodic inventory system* (see Chapter 10). When a company uses the periodic inventory system, a Purchases account is used and the inventory account is unchanged during the period; thus, it reflects the *beginning inventory* amount. At the end of the accounting period, this balance must be closed and the *ending* inventory amount, determined by physical count and valued at cost, must be recorded. In contrast, when a *perpetual inventory system* is used, purchases and issues are recorded directly in the inventory account on a continuing basis. Therefore, the inventory amount in the trial balance will reflect the ending inventory amount and no closing entries will be needed for it on the worksheet. The inventory balance is extended directly to the Balance Sheet debit column. When the perpetual inventory system is used, there will be no purchases account; however, there will be a Cost of Goods Sold account on the worksheet. The Cost of Goods Sold account is extended directly to the Income Statement debit column as an expense.

2. When all of the amounts have been extended, the difference between the debits and credits under Income Statement will represent *pretax income*. This amount must be determined to compute income tax expense, for which an adjusting entry must be made. To illustrate, for Canby Retailers, Inc., the computation would be as follows, assuming an average 40% income tax rate:

Income Statement column totals (pretax):	
Credit total	$419,000
Debit total	369,000
Pretax income	50,000
Income tax expense ($50,000 × .40)	20,000
Net income	$ 30,000

---

[6] This approach views the two entries for the beginning and ending inventories as *closing* entries (see pages 56 and 62). Another approach is to view them as *adjusting* entries. The technique used on the worksheet for inventories represents only one way; several other ways are widely used. The final result is precisely the same.

The adjusting entry for income taxes would be as follows:

g. December 31, 1979:

Income tax expense	20,000	
Income taxes payable		20,000

3. After the above adjusting entry is made, the extensions can be completed. The amount of net income, $30,000, is entered on the worksheet as a debit to Income Statement and a credit to Retained Earnings. The ending balance of Retained Earnings is then extended to the balance sheet and the last two pairs of columns are summed; in the absence of errors, each pair of columns on the worksheet will balance.

The worksheet can be used as a guide for the remaining phases in the cycle.

A worksheet for a manufacturing company, with explanatory comments, is shown in Appendix B to this chapter.

PREPARE FINANCIAL STATEMENTS (PHASE 7)

The income statement, statement of retained earnings, and balance sheet can be prepared directly from the completed worksheet. An income statement and balance sheet, taken directly from the worksheet (Exhibit 3–5), are presented in Exhibits 3–6 and 3–7, respectively. Financial statements are discussed in more detail in Chapters 4 and 5. A separate worksheet is used to prepare the statement of changes in financial position as illustrated in Chapter 23.

If a worksheet is not used, adjusting entries should be entered directly in the journal and posted to the ledger. Then an *adjusted trial balance,* taken from the ledger, will provide information for these statements.

The statement of changes in financial position requires a separate analysis, usually on a specially designed worksheet similar to those illustrated in Chapter 23.

JOURNALIZING AND POSTING ADJUSTING ENTRIES (PHASE 8)

The adjusting entries should be entered in the general journal and then posted to the general ledger, dated the last day of the accounting period. The adjusting entries *update* the ledger accounts by separating the account balances into their real (i.e., balance sheet) and nominal (i.e., income statement) components. The adjusted nominal accounts are then ready to close. Also, the adjusting entries bring the general ledger accounts into agreement with the financial statements.

If a worksheet, such as Exhibit 3–5, is developed, the adjusting entries can be taken directly from it. They are identical to those illustrated earlier. Note that after the adjusting entries are posted to the general ledger, each account will reflect the account balances shown in Exhibit 3–5 under the caption "Adjusted Trial Balance."

CLOSING ENTRIES (PHASE 9)

Recall that the balance sheet accounts are called *real* or *permanent accounts* in the sense

EXHIBIT 3–6

CANBY RETAILERS, INC.
Income Statement*
For the Year Ended December 31, 1979

Revenues:		
Sales		$325,200
Interest		600
Rent		1,200
Total revenues		327,000
Expenses:		
Cost of goods sold†	$117,000	
Selling	113,400	
General and administrative	34,600	
Interest	3,000	
Total expenses (excluding income taxes)		268,000
Pretax operating income		59,000
Income taxes ($59,000 × .40)		23,600
Income before extraordinary items		35,400
Extraordinary loss	9,000	
Less tax saving ($9,000 × .40)	3,600	5,400
Net Income		$ 30,000

Earnings per share:
Income before extraordinary items
($35,400 ÷ 15,000 shares) $2.36
Extraordinary loss ($5,400 ÷ 15,000 shares) .... (.36)
Net Income ($30,000 ÷ 15,000 shares) 2.00

* This is a single-step income statement; various formats are discussed in Chapter 4.

† Computation of cost of goods sold:

Beginning inventory	$ 75,000
Purchases	130,000
Freight on purchases	4,000
Purchase returns	(2,000)
Total goods available for sale	207,000
Less ending inventory	90,000
Cost of goods sold	$117,000

EXHIBIT 3-7

CANBY RETAILERS, INC.
Balance Sheet*
At December 31, 1979

Assets		
Current Assets:		
Cash		$ 55,300
Notes receivable		20,000
Interest receivable		100
Accounts receivable	$ 45,000	
Allowance for doubtful		
accounts	2,200	42,800
Inventory		90,000
†Prepaid insurance		400
Total Current Assets		208,600
Operational Assets:		
Land		8,000
Building	160,000	
Accumulated depreciation,		
building	100,000	60,000
Equipment	91,000	
Accumulated depreciation,		
equipment	36,000	55,000
Total Operational Assets ...		123,000
Total Assets		$331,600

Liabilities		
Current Liabilities:		
Accounts payable		$ 29,000
Income taxes payable		20,000
Interest payable		500
Rent revenue collected		
in advance		600
Total Current Liabilities		50,100
Long-Term Liabilities:		
Bonds payable, 6%		50,000
Total Liabilities		100,100
Stockholders' Equity		
Contributed Capital:		
Common stock, par $10,		
15,000 shares issued		
and outstanding	$150,000	
Contributed capital		
in excess of par	20,000	
Retained earnings	61,500	
Total Stockholders'		
Equity		231,500
Total Liabilities and		
Stockholders' Equity ..		$331,600

* Balance sheets and appropriate supplementary information are discussed in Chapter 5.

† Conceptually, $200 of this amount should not be reported as a current asset since it will extend two years into the future. When such differences are not material in amount, as in this situation, the conceptual distinction is not necessary (refer to the exception principle, materiality).

that they are not closed out to a zero balance at the end of the accounting period. In contrast, the income statement accounts are called *nominal* or *temporary accounts* because at the end of each accounting period they are closed to a zero balance. The income statement accounts are the *revenue* and *expense* accounts and are *subaccounts* of owners' equity. Revenues increase owners' equity, and expenses decrease owners' equity. These subaccounts are used each period to *classify* and *accumulate* revenue and expense information to facilitate preparation of the income statement. At the end of the period, when they have served this information *classification* and *accumulation* purpose, each account is closed to Income Summary and in turn the net effect of their balances (i.e., net income or net loss) is transferred from Income Summary to Retained Earnings. The transferring process is called closing entries. The purpose is to close the nominal accounts to a zero balance so they will be ready for reuse the next period. A closing entry simply transfers a credit balance to another account as a credit, or it transfers a debit balance to another account as a debit.

Usually a *clearing* or *suspense* account, called Income Summary, is used in the closing process; this account then is closed to Retained Earnings. Sometimes a second clearing account—Cost of Goods Sold—also is used. The clearing accounts are not required; they perform only a facilitating function. Nominal accounts are used the next period to record the revenues and expenses for that period.

The closing entries can be taken directly from

account balances in the *adjusted trial balance,* or, if a worksheet such as the one in Exhibit 3–5 is used, they can be taken directly from the Income Statement columns. To illustrate, the closing entries for Canby Retailers (with an Income Summary account) would be as follows (refer to Exhibit 3–5):[7]

December 31, 1979:

1. To close the revenue accounts to Income Summary:

Sales revenue	325,200	
Interest revenue	600	
Rent revenue	1,200	
Income summary		327,000

2. To close the purchases and beginning inventory accounts and record the ending inventory:[8]

Inventory (December 31, 1979)	90,000	
Purchase returns	2,000	
Income summary	117,000	
Purchases		130,000
Freight on purchases		4,000
Inventory (January 1, 1979)		75,000

3. To close the expense accounts to Income Summary:

---

[7] The closing entries can be grouped in various ways, one of which is illustrated here. Alternatively, a separate closing entry can be made for each nominal account. Obviously, the net effect of the closing process would be the same.

[8] The Cost of Goods Sold account may be used with a periodic inventory system, in which case these accounts are closed to Cost of Goods Sold which is then closed to Income Summary. If a periodic inventory system is used, the inventory accounts may be handled in the adjusting entries, in which case they would not be included in the closing entries. In either approach the *beginning* inventory balance must be closed and the *ending* inventory balance recorded. The net effect is the same. To illustrate, assuming inventory adjusting entries and use of a Cost of Goods Sold account, the above entries would be as follows:

Adjusting entries (inventory):

Cost of goods sold	75,000	
Inventory (beginning)		75,000
Inventory (ending)	90,000	
Cost of goods sold		90,000

Closing entry for purchase accounts:

Purchase returns	2,000	
Cost of goods sold	132,000	
Purchases		130,000
Freight on purchases		4,000
Income summary	117,000	
Cost of goods sold		117,000

Income summary	180,000	
Selling expenses		113,400
General and administrative expenses		34,600
Interest expense		3,000
Extraordinary loss		9,000
Income tax expense		20,000

4. To close Income Summary account to Retained Earnings:

Income summary	30,000	
Retained earnings		30,000

For review purposes, the closing process is diagrammed in T-account form in Exhibit 3–8. Observe that *after the closing process* each income statement (i.e., nominal) account reflects a zero balance; therefore, each is ready to be used again during the next accounting period.

POST-CLOSING TRIAL BALANCE (PHASE 10)

In a preceding paragraph, we defined a trial balance as a listing of the accounts in the general ledger along with their balances. The purposes of a trial balance usually are *(a)* to verify the equality of the debits and credits and *(b)* to have the account balances handy for other uses. We have discussed two different trial balances up to this point: the *unadjusted* trial balance, taken immediately after the current entries are completed for the accounting period but before the adjusting entries, and the *adjusted* trial balance, which reflects the account balances after the adjusting entries. A third trial balance generally is taken after the closing entries have been posted. It is called the *post-closing trial balance* and is used to verify that the debits and credits are equal at the start of the next accounting period. It is usually done on an adding machine (or by computer) rather than by preparing a formal listing.

REVERSING ENTRIES (PHASE 11)

After the adjusting and closing entries are journalized and posted to the general ledger, the accounts are ready for information inputs of the next period. Prior to entering the new information inputs, many companies make *reversing en-*

EXHIBIT 3–8
Closing Process Diagrammed

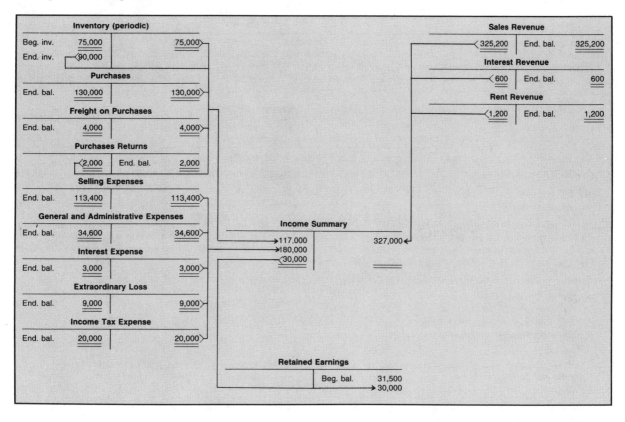

tries. A reversing entry is dated the first day of the next period and simply reverses or "backs out" an adjusting entry that was made at the end of the period just ended. Reversing entries serve only one purpose; that is, to facilitate (or simplify) a subsequent entry. Reversing entries are always optional; the same result is obtained whether or not they are used. If used, only a few of the adjusting entries usually are reversed.

The purpose and application of reversing entries are illustrated in Exhibit 3–9. In the exhibit, a series of entries related to accrued wages is analyzed under two options: (1) with a reversing entry and (2) without a reversing entry. The two options demonstrate the *facilitating* feature of reversing entries and also suggest the kinds of adjusting entries that are candidates for reversal. Although it is impossible to provide rigid

rules for selecting adjusting entries to be reversed, some guidelines can be given.

1. Adjusting entries usually reversed—As a general rule, *only adjusting entries for accrued expenses and accrued (uncollected) revenues* that involve frequent cash flows should be reversed. Examples of accrued expenses are unpaid wages, interest, utilities, and other regularly recurring expenses that require subsequent cash disbursements. Examples of accrued revenues are uncollected interest, rent, and other recurring earned revenues that result in *subsequent* cash collections.

2. Adjusting entries not reversed—As a general rule, adjusting entries for deferred expenses and revenues collected in advance are not

EXHIBIT 3–9
Reversing Entries Illustrated

BOX CORPORATION
Annual Accounting Period Ends December 31, 1979

	With Reversing Entry	*Without Reversing Entry*

a. *Adjusting entry*—The last payroll was paid on December 28, 1979; the next payroll will be on January 4, 1980. Therefore, at December 31, 1979, accrued (unpaid) wages for three days amounted to $15,000. The following adjusting entry is required:

December 31, 1979:	December 31, 1979:
Wage expense. 15,000	Wage expense. 15,000
Wages payable 15,000	Wages payable 15,000

b. *Closing entry*—The revenue and expense accounts are closed to Income Summary.

December 31, 1979:	December 31, 1979:
Income summary* 215,000	Income summary* 215,000
Wage expense 215,000	Wage expense. 215,000

c. At this point the adjusting and closing entries have been journalized and posted to the ledger. The information processing cycle for 1979 has been completed. At this time, January 1, 1980, the accountant must decide what adjusting entries are to be *reversed* (if any). *Question:* Would a reversing entry for accrued wages on January 1, 1980, simplify or facilitate making the next payroll entry on January 4, 1980?

Decision—make a reversing entry, January 1, 1980:	*Decision—no reversing entry to be made.*
Wages payable 15,000	
Wage expense 15,000	
(Note that this reverses the adjusting entry made above on December 31, 1979.)	
Effect: The Wages Payable account now reflects a zero balance; Wage Expense reflects a *credit* balance of $15,000.	Effect: The Wages Payable account continues to reflect a credit balance; Wage Expense reflects a zero balance.

d. *Subsequent payroll entry*—Payment of $36,000 payroll on January 4, 1980. This amount includes the $15,000 liability (wages payable) carried over from December 1979.

January 4, 1980, payroll entry (disregarding payroll taxes):	
Wage expense. 36,000	Wages payable 15,000
Cash. 36,000	Wage expense. 21,000
	Cash 36,000

Did the prior reversing entry simplify this subsequent entry? The answer is yes. The last entry, on the left, required only one debit, and, most importantly, preparation of the January 4 payroll entry did not require reference to the December 31, 1979, adjusting entry. However, after the last entry, under both methods, the Wage Expense account reflects a debit balance of $21,000 and Wages Payable reflects a zero balance. Also, when the payroll processing is computerized, a special routine must be written for the first payment entry which is different from the remaining 51 payroll entries during the year when no reversing entry is made.

* Includes $200,000 wages paid during the period.

reversed. Examples of deferred (i.e., prepaid) expenses are insurance premiums and unused supplies. Examples of revenues collected in advance are precollected rent and magazine subscriptions.

3. Estimated adjusting entries not reversed—Those adjusting entries based on estimates, where there is no subsequent cash inflow or outflow, are not reversed. Examples are depreciation and bad debt expense entries.

Although these general guidelines may be helpful in deciding whether the reversal of a particular adjusting entry would be useful, one must consider *(a)* the original entry, *(b)* the adjusting entry, and *(c)* most importantly, the subsequent entry. The above rules have exceptions and cannot substitute for judgment.

INFORMATION PROCESSING PROCEDURES

Information processing involves the phases or steps used to collect raw economic data, record their economic effects on the entity, classify the information, and, finally, prepare the financial statements and supporting information. In most companies, a large amount of information must be processed daily. This work can be time consuming and costly. Therefore, a well-designed information processing system is needed to provide an efficient flow of information from time of incurrence to the end result, the financial statements. Information processing may be done (1) manually, where the work is performed by hand; (2) mechanically, where the information is processed by sorting equipment, tabulating machines, and so on; and (3) electronically, where electronic computers are used. Typically, an accounting system will use each of these approaches in varying degrees depending upon its complexity.

Consideration of these information approaches is not within the objectives of this book. For instructional purposes, the manual approach is used because the steps are essentially the same regardless of how the processing is done.

SUMMARY OF THE INFORMATION PROCESSING CYCLE

An understanding of the information processing cycle will assist you in comprehending the chapters to follow. Each chapter considers various accounting problems, each of which is related to one or more steps in the cycle. It is especially helpful if you clearly understand how those problems relate to the broad areas of information collection, transaction analysis, recording, classifying, and reporting. The se-

quence of the cycle is both logical and efficient. Exhibit 3–10 lists the major sequential phases of the cycle, summarizes the objective of each, and provides a cross-reference to the chapter.

Appendix A—Control Accounts, Subsidiary Ledgers, and Special Journals

An accounting system usually includes application of the information processing techniques known as special journals, subsidiary ledgers, and control accounts. This Appendix discusses and illustrates these elements of the system.

CONTROL ACCOUNTS AND SUBSIDIARY LEDGERS

The general ledger is the main ledger. It includes an account for each asset, liability, owners' equity, revenue, and expense. To facilitate recordkeeping for accounts that involve a large amount of detail, selected general ledger accounts are designated as *control accounts* to which only summary information is posted. The details related to each control account are maintained in a separate subsidiary ledger (one for each control account). Thus, each control account is supplemented by its specially designated subsidiary ledger. To illustrate, accounts receivable usually is designated as *Accounts Receivable Control* in the general ledger and is supported by a separate *accounts receivable subsidiary ledger* which is composed of individual customer accounts. This arrangement will be illustrated below.

JOURNALS

Both general and special journals are used in most accounting systems. Even when extensive use is made of special journals, a need still exists for a general journal in which to record *(a)* those transactions that do not apply to any of the special journals (Exhibit 3–11), *(b)* nonrepetitive current transactions and *(c)* the adjust-

EXHIBIT 3–10
Summary of the Accounting Information Processing Cycle

Phase (order)	Identification	Objective	Text Page
1	Collection of raw economic data.	To gather inputs to the accounting system. The inputs are supported by source documents as a basis for *(a)* transaction analysis and *(b)* subsequent verification.	49
2	Transaction analysis.	To identify, assess, and measure the economic impact on the enterprise of each transaction recognized. To provide the basis for developing the accounting entry to be made in the journal.	52
3	Journalizing.	To provide a chronological record (i.e., by date) of the entries in the accounting system which reflect the increases and decreases in each account.	52
4	Posting.	To transfer the economic effects from the journal to the ledger; to reclassify and accumulate the economic effects for each asset, liability, owners' equity, revenue, and expense.	52
5	Prepare unadjusted trial balance.	To provide, in a convenient form, a listing of the accounts and their balances in the general ledger after all current entries have been posted. It serves to *(a)* check the debit-credit equality and *(b)* provide data for use in developing the worksheet and the adjusting entries.	54
6*	Prepare worksheets.	To provide an organized and systematic approach at the end of the accounting period for developing *(a)* the adjusting entries, *(b)* the financial statements, and *(c)* the closing entries. One worksheet suffices for the income statement and balance sheet. Another worksheet is needed to develop the statement of changes in financial position.	55
7	Prepare financial statements.	To provide a vehicle for communicating summarized financial information to external decision makers.	60
8	Journalize and post adjusting entries.	To update the general ledger and to separate the "mixed" balances into their real (i.e., balance sheet) and nominal (i.e., income statement) components so the nominal accounts will be ready for the closing process and to bring the general ledger accounts into agreement with the financial statements.	60
9	Journalize and post closing entries.	To close the nominal accounts to retained earnings so they will be ready for reuse during the next period for accumulating and classifying revenues and expenses.	60
10*	Prepare post-closing trial balance.	To verify the debit-credit accuracy of the general ledger after the closing entries are posted.	62
11*	Reversing entries.	To facilitate subsequent entries by reversing certain adjusting entries. They are journalized and posted on the first day of the new period.	62

* Optional.

ing and closing journal entries. Occasionally there will be a complex entry with characteristics that would, in part, qualify for entry in a special journal, and in part in the general journal. Such entries may be entered only in the general journal or, alternatively, "split" between general journal and a special journal.

Special Journals

A special journal serves the same purpose as a general journal except that it is designed to handle *only* one type of transaction because of the large volume of transactions of a particular type. Each special journal, therefore, is designed specifically to simplify the data processing tasks

EXHIBIT 3–11

General Journal				Page J-14
Date 1979	Accounts and Explanation	Ledger Folio	Amounts	
			Debit	Credit
Jan. 2	Equipment - trucks	140	9,000	
	Notes payable	214		9,000
	Purchased truck for use in			
	the business. Gave $9,000,			
	60-day note, interest at 10%			
	per year, payable at maturity.			

involved in journalizing and posting a particular type of transaction. The format of each special journal and the number used depend upon the types of frequent transactions recorded by the entity. Commonly used special journals are the following:

1. Merchandise sales on credit—designed for credit sales entries only.
2. Merchandise purchases on credit—designed for credit purchases only.
3. Cash receipts—designed for all cash receipts (including cash sales).
4. Cash payments—designed for all cash payments (including cash purchases).
5. Voucher system journals (replaces No. 4 when the voucher system is used)—
    a. Voucher register—designed to record vouchers payable only. A voucher payable is prepared for each cash payment regardless of the purpose of the payment.
    b. Check register—designed to record all checks written in payment of vouchers.

Special Journal for Merchandise Sales on Credit. This journal is designed to accommodate entries for credit sales of regular merchandise only. Therefore, it would handle only the following type of entry (cash sales would not be entered in this journal):[9]

---

[9] Terms, 2/10, n/30, mean that if the account is paid within ten days after date of sale, a 2% discount is permitted to encourage early payment. If not paid within the 10-day discount period, the full amount is due at the end of 30 days.

January 2, 1979:

	Correct Method Recorded at Net of Discount	Incorrect Method Recorded at Gross (before Discount)
Accounts receivable	980	1,000
Sales revenue	980	1,000
Credit sale to Adams Company; invoice price, $1,000; terms, 2/10, n/30.		

Credit sales should be recorded at net of discount (rather than at gross amount), as is illustrated above. Theoretically, net of discount is correct; however, because of immateriality they sometimes are recorded at the gross amount (see Chapter 10). Assuming the initial entry was made net of discount, the subsequent collection entry would be as follows:

Case A—Collection within the discount period:

	If Recorded at Net of Discount
Cash	980
Accounts receivable	980

Case B—Collection after the discount period:

Cash	1,000
Accounts receivable	980
Interest revenue	20

Exhibit 3–12 shows a typical special journal for credit sales for a business that has two sales

EXHIBIT 3–12

Special Journal – Merchandise Sales on Credit						Page S-23		
Date 1979	Sales Invoice No.	Accounts Receivable (name)	Terms	Ledger Folio	Receivable and Sale Amount	Dept. Sales		
							Dept. A	Dept. B
Jan. 2	93	Adams Co.	2/10, n/30	112.13	980			
3	94	Sayre Corp.	2/10, n/30	112.80	490			
11	95	Cope & Day Co.	net	112.27	5,734	(Not illustrated — the two totals below would be posted to a sales subsidiary ledger.)		
27	96	XY Mfg. Co.	2/10, n/30	112.91	1,960			
30	97	Miller, J. B.	2/10, n/30	112.42	196			
31	–	Totals	–	–	9,360			
31	–	Posting	–	–	(112/500)			

departments. The general ledger contains an Accounts Receivable Control account. Observe that this special journal provides a convenient format to record all of the relevant data on each credit sale. Also, it can be designed to differentiate sales by department. Clearly, it is easier to enter a credit sale in this format than in the general journal.

The mechanics of posting amounts from the special sales journal to the general and subsidiary ledgers also are simplified. There are two phases of posting a special journal, viz:

1. *Daily posting*—The amount of each credit sale is posted daily to the appropriate individual account in the accounts receivable *subsidiary ledger*. Daily posting is essential so that each customer's account will be up to date when the customer pays. Posting is indicated by entering the account number in the folio column. For example, the number 112.13 entered in the folio column in Exhibit 3–12 is the account number assigned to Adams Company and signifies that $980 was posted as a debit to that account.

2. *Monthly posting*—At the end of each month, the amount column is summed. This total is posted to two accounts in the general ledger; that is, in Exhibit 3–12 the $9,360 was posted (1) as a debit to Account No. 112 (Accounts Receivable Control) and (2) as a credit to Account No. 500 (Sales Revenue Control). The T-accounts shown in Exhibit 3–16 illustrate how these postings are reflected in the general ledger and the subsidiary ledger. Ob-

serve that the two ledgers show the *journal page* from which each amount was posted.

Special Journal for Merchandise Purchases on Credit. In situations where there are numerous credit purchases of merchandise for resale, data processing may be facilitated by using a special journal designed only for this type of transaction, viz:

January 3, 1979:

```
Purchases . . . . . . . . . . . . . . . . . . . . . . . .    990
     Accounts payable (PT Mfg. Co.) . . . . . . .           990
     Purchased merchandise for resale;
     invoice price, $1,000; terms, 1/20, n/30.
```

This transaction, rather than being entered in the general journal, would be entered in the purchases journal as in Exhibit 3–13. In this illustration the purchases are recorded at net of discount, which is the theoretically correct approach. Because of immateriality, purchases sometimes are recorded at their gross amount (see Chapter 8 for discussion of this issue). During the month, each amount would be posted as a credit to the individual creditors' accounts in the *accounts payable subsidiary ledger*.

At the end of the month, the total of the amount column (i.e., $2,760) would be posted to the general ledger as *(a)* a debit to the Purchases account (No. 612)[10] and *(b)* a credit to the Accounts Payable *Control* account (No. 210). These

---

[10] This assumes periodic inventory procedures. Alternatively, if perpetual inventory procedures are used, the debit would be to the Inventory account.

EXHIBIT 3–13

Special Journal-Merchandise Purchases on Credit					Page _P-19_
Date 1979	Purchase Order No.	Account Payable (name)	Terms	Ledger Folio	Amount
Jan. 3	41	P. 2. Mfg. Co.	1/20, n/30	210.61	990
7	42	Able Suppliers, Ltd.	net	210.12	150
31	—	Totals	—	—	2,760
31	—	Posting	—	—	(612/210)

two general ledger accounts are not illustrated in Exhibit 3–16.

Special Journal for Cash Receipts. Since a large volume of transactions for cash receipts is typical, a special cash receipts journal is often used. This special journal is designed to accommodate *all* cash receipts including cash sales. Therefore, it must have a column for *cash debit* and several credit columns. Credit columns are designated for recurring credits, and a Sundry column is used to accommodate infrequent credits. A typical special cash receipts journal is shown in Exhibit 3–14.

During the month, each amount in the Accounts Receivable column is posted as a credit to the individual customer accounts in the *accounts receivable subsidiary ledger*. At the end of the month, *(a)* the individual amounts in the Sundry column are posted as credits to the appropriate general ledger accounts and *(b)* the totals (for Cash, Accounts Receivable, and Sales) are posted to the general ledger as indicated by the folio numbers. The total of the sundry accounts is not posted since the individual amounts have already been posted.

Special Journal for Cash Payments. Because of the large volume of cash disbursements, most companies use a special journal designed to ac-

EXHIBIT 3–14

Special Journal-Cash Receipts		Debits	Credits					Page _CR-19_
Date 1979	Explanation	Cash	Account Title	Ledger Folio	Accounts Receivable	Sundry Accounts	Sales	
Jan. 4	Cash sales	11,200	—				11,200	
7	On acct.	4,490	Sayre Corp.	112.80	4,490			
8	Sale of land	10,000	Land	123		4,000		
			Gain on sale of land	510		6,000		
10	On acct.	1,000	Adams Co.	112.13	1,000			
19	Cash sales	43,600		—			43,600	
20	On acct.	5,734	Cope & Day Co.	112.27	5,734			
31	Totals	116,224		—	11,224	34,000	71,000	
31	Posting	(101)		—	(112)	(NP)*	(500)	

* NP—Not posted as one total because the individual amounts are posted as indicated in the ledge folio column.

EXHIBIT 3–15

Special Journal - Cash Payments								Page _CP-31_
Date 1979	Check No.	Explanation	Credits Cash	Debits				
				Account Name	Ledger Folio	Accounts Payable	Sundry Accounts	Merchandise
Jan. 2	141	Pur. mdse.	3,000	—				3,000
10	142	On acct.	990	P. J. Mfg. Co.	210.61	990		
15	143	Jan. rent	600	Rent exp.	612		600	
16	144	Pur. mdse.	1,810	—				1,810
31	—	Totals	98,400	—		5,820	1,600	34,700
31	—	Posting	(101)	—		(210)	(NP)	(612)

commodate *all* cash payments including cash purchases of merchandise. The special journal must have a column for *cash credits* and a number of debit columns. Debit columns are set up for frequently recurring debits, and a Sundry column is used for infrequent debits. A typical special cash payments journal, with some common entries, is shown in Exhibit 3–15. Posting follows the same procedures explained above for the cash receipts special journal.

Reconciling a Subsidiary Ledger

The sum of all accounts in a subsidiary ledger must agree with the overall balance reflected in the related control account in the general ledger. To assure that this correspondence exists, frequent reconciliations should be made. Clearly, a reconciliation cannot be accomplished unless all posting is complete, both to the control account and to the subsidiary ledger. To illustrate, a reconciliation based upon the information in Exhibit 3–16 for *Accounts Receivable Control* and the *accounts receivable subsidiary ledger* would be as follows:

Reconciliation of Accounts Receivable Subsidiary Ledger (at January 31, 1979)

		Amount
Subsidiary ledger balances:		
112.13	Adams Company	$ 980
112.42	Miller, J. B.	196
112.91	XY Manufacturing Company	1,960
	Total—Agrees with the balance in Accounts Receivable Control	
	($14,360 − $11,224)	$3,136

The above discussion reviewed the concepts underlying special journals, control accounts, and subsidiary ledgers. Their design and use depend upon the characteristics of the company. They do not involve new accounting principles since they are only data processing techniques. The above discussion also emphasized the four primary efficiencies that may result from their use, viz: (1) journalizing is simplified, (2) posting is simplified, (3) subdivision of work is simplified, and (4) a highly trained person is not needed to maintain a special journal or a subsidiary ledger that involves only one type of transaction.[11]

Appendix B—Worksheet for a Manufacturing Company

A worksheet for a manufacturing company is somewhat different from that illustrated in Exhibit 3–5 for a merchandising company. Because of the cost accounting procedures generally used for the manufacturing activity, the worksheet should include a pair of columns for *manufacturing*. All of the manufacturing costs, including the raw materials and work in process

---

[11] Voucher system journals are not discussed since they involve essentially the same procedures as illustrated. The voucher system journals are known as *(a)* the voucher register and *(b)* the check register.

EXHIBIT 3–16
General Ledger and Subsidiary Ledger Illustrated

General Ledger (partial)						
Cash						No. 101
1979 Jan. 1	Balance		18,000	1979 Jan. 31	CP-31	98,400
31		CR-19	116,224			
Accounts Receivable Control						No. 112
1979 Jan. 1	Balance		5,000	1979 Jan. 31	CR-19	11,224
31		S-23	9,360			
Equipment						No. 140
1979 Jan. 2		J-14	9,000			
Notes Payable						No. 214
				1979 Jan. 2	J-14	9,000
Sales Revenue Control						
				1979 Jan. 31	S-23	9,360
				31	CR-19	71,000

Subsidiary Ledger for Accounts Receivable (Acct. No. 112)

Adams Company – Acct. No. 112.13

Date	Folio	Explanation	Debit	Credit	Balance
1979 Jan. 1		Balance			1,000
2	S-23		980		1,980
10	CR-19			1,000	980

Cope & Day Company – Acct. No. 112.27

Date	Folio	Explanation	Debit	Credit	Balance
Jan. 11	S-23		5,734		5,734
20	CR-19			5,734	–0–

Miller, J.B. – Acct. No. 112.42

Date	Folio	Explanation	Debit	Credit	Balance
Jan. 30	S-23		196		196

Sayre Corporation – Acct. No. 112.80

Date	Folio	Explanation	Debit	Credit	Balance
Jan. 1		Balance			4,000
3	S-23		490		4,490
7	CR-19			4,490	–0–

XY Manufacturing Company – Acct. No. 112.91

Date	Folio	Explanation	Debit	Credit	Balance
Jan. 27	S-23		1,960		1,960

EXHIBIT 3–17

DUNCAN MANUFACTURING COMPANY
Worksheet for the Year Ended December 31, 1979

Accounts	Unadjusted Trial Balance		Adjustments		Manufacturing		Income Statement		Balance Sheet	
	Debit	Credit	Debit	Credit	Debit	Credit	Debit	Credit	Debit	Credit
Cash	32,000								32,000	
Inventory, January 1 (periodic system):										
Raw materials	55,000		(d)		55,000	62,000			62,000	
Work in process	76,000		(d)		76,000	81,000			81,000	
Finished goods	54,000		(d)				54,000	52,000	52,000	
Equipment (ten-year life)	300,000								300,000	
Accumulated depreciation—equipment		90,000		(a) 10,000						100,000
Remaining assets	13,000								13,000	
Accounts payable		15,000								15,000
Interest payable				(b) 800						800
Note payable (8% each Nov. 1)		60,000								60,000
Common stock, par $10		200,000								200,000
Retained earnings		74,200								74,200
Sales revenue		474,800						474,800		
Manufacturing costs:										
Raw material purchases	70,000				70,000					
Direct labor	100,000				100,000					
Factory overhead:	75,000		(a) 7,000		82,000					
Distribution expenses	70,000		(a) 2,000				72,000			
General and administrative expenses	65,000		(a) 1,000				66,000			
Interest expense	4,000		(b) 800				4,800			
Cost of goods manufactured						240,000	240,000			
Totals	914,000	914,000	10,800	10,800	383,000	383,000				
Income tax expense			(c) 36,000				36,000			
Income taxes payable				(c) 36,000						36,000
Net income							54,000			54,000
Totals							526,800	526,800	540,000	540,000

(a) To record depreciation.
(b) To record accrued interest.
(c) To record income taxes.
(d) To record ending inventories.

inventories, are extended to the two manufacturing columns. A worksheet for a manufacturing situation is illustrated in Exhibit 3–17. The following six items will be helpful in studying this worksheet:

1. Only representative accounts and adjusting entries are included.

2. There are columns for manufacturing; however, the columns for adjusted trial balance and retained earnings have been omitted to demonstrate these simplifications. They were noted as optional in the chapter.

3. Only three typical adjusting entries are included. Depreciation expense was allocated as follows: factory, 70%; distribution, 20%;

and general, 10%. Interest was accrued for two months.

4. The current cost accounting entries for factory costs were as follows:

Raw material purchases	70,000	
Direct labor	100,000	
Cash		170,000
Factory overhead	75,000	
Various accounts		75,000

5. The ending inventories at December 31, 1979, were as follows:

Raw materials	$62,000
Work in process	81,000
Finished goods	52,000

6. An average corporate income tax rate of 40% is assumed.

A statement of cost of goods manufactured, taken directly from the manufacturing columns in the worksheet, follows:

DUNCAN MANUFACTURING COMPANY
Statement of Cost of Goods Manufactured
For the Year Ended December 31, 1979

Materials:

Beginning inventory	$ 55,000	
Purchases	70,000	
Total materials available	125,000	
Less: Ending inventory	62,000	
Cost of materials issued		$ 63,000
Direct labor		100,000
Factory overhead		82,000
Total factory costs		245,000
Add: Beginning work in process		
inventory		76,000
		321,000
Less: Ending work in process		
inventory		81,000
Cost of goods		
manufactured		$240,000

Observe on the worksheet that cost of goods manufactured ($240,000) was transferred from the Manufacturing columns to the Income Statement columns (a debit since it is to a manufacturing entity what merchandise purchases is to a trading entity). In other respects, the amounts are extended to the last four columns as explained and illustrated in the chapter (Exhibit 3–5).

QUESTIONS

1. Explain why an accounting information processing system must be tailored to the characteristics of the entity.

2. What is the accounting model? Give the three submodels and briefly explain each.

3. Complete the following matrix by entering debit or credit in each cell.

Item	Increase	Decrease
Liabilities		
Revenues		
Assets		
Expenses		
Owners' equity		

4. Explain the dual balancing feature of the fundamental accounting model.

5. Broadly explain the primary purpose of the accounting information processing model.

6. With respect to the collection of raw economic data for the accounting system, why are source documents important? Give some examples of typical source documents.

7. Explain the nature and purpose of transaction analysis.

8. What kind of events are recorded in the accounting system? Explain.

9. What is meant by journalizing? What purpose does it serve?

10. What is meant by posting? What purpose does it serve?

11. Distinguish between real, nominal, and mixed accounts.

12. Classify the following accounts, before the adjusting entries, as real or nominal (explain any assumptions you make):

Accounts Receivable	Prepaid Insurance
Supplies Inventory	Notes Payable
Retained Earnings	Interest Revenue
Patents	Common Stock
Interest Expense	Property Tax Expense

13. Distinguish between the general ledger, control accounts, and subsidiary ledgers. What is the basic purpose of each?

14. Explain the difference between special journals and the general journal.

15. What is a trial balance? What are the two primary purposes of a trial balance? Distinguish between unadjusted, adjusted, and post-closing trial balances.

16. Why is a worksheet a facilitating technique? What does it facilitate?

17. What are the purpose and nature of adjusting entries? Explain why they generally must be made. Explain why the adjusting entries must be considered prior to developing the financial statements.

18. Why are the adjusting entries journalized and posted?

19. What are the purpose and nature of closing entries?

20. What are the purpose and nature of reversing entries? Why are they journalized and posted?

21. X Company owes a $4,000, three-year, 9% note payable. Interest is paid each November 30. Therefore, at the end of the accounting period, December 31, the following adjusting entry was made:

Interest expense   30
    Interest payable   30

Would you recommend using a reversing entry in this situation? Explain.

22. Number the following phases in the accounting information processing cycle to indicate their normal sequence of completion:

_____Journalize and post reversing entries.
_____Posting.
_____Transaction analysis.
_____Collection of raw data.
_____Journalize and post adjusting entries.
_____Journalize and post closing entries.
_____Prepare financial statements.
_____Journalize current transactions.
_____Prepare post-closing trial balance.
_____Prepare worksheets.
_____Prepare unadjusted trial balance.

23. In posting a special journal, there are two phases: daily posting and periodic posting. Explain the purpose and nature of each.

24. What circumstances would suggest the need for special journals? Why?

EXERCISES

Exercise 3–1

1. Develop a diagram that reflects the dual balancing feature of an accounting information processing system.
2. Explain why expenses are increased with a debit and revenues are increased with a credit.
3. Explain the basis for the designation double-entry system.

Exercise 3–2

The following selected transactions were completed during the current year by AB Corporation:

a. AB Corporation sold 50,000 shares of its own common stock, par $1 per share, for $65,000 cash.
b. Borrowed $20,000 cash on a one-year, 9% note payable (interest is paid at maturity date).
c. Purchased real estate for use in the business at a cash cost of $45,000, which consisted of a small building ($35,000) and the lot on which it was located ($10,000).
d. Purchased merchandise for resale at a cash cost of $8,000. Assume periodic inventory system.
e. Purchased merchandise for resale on credit; terms, 2/10, n/30. If paid within ten days, the cash payment would be $490; however, if paid after ten days, the payment would be $500. Since the company takes all discounts, credit purchases are recorded at net. Assume periodic inventory system.
f. Sold merchandise for $12,000; collected 60% in cash and the balance is due in 30 days.
g. Paid the balance due on the purchase in (e) within the ten-day period.

Required:

Enter each of the above transactions in a general journal. Use the letter to the left to indicate the date.

Exercise 3–3

The 11 phases that compose the accounting information processing cycle are listed to the left in scrambled order. To the right is a brief statement of the objective of each phase, also in scrambled order. You are to present two responses.

Required (use separate sheet of paper):

1. In the blanks to the left, number the phases in the usual sequence of completion.
2. In the blanks to the right, use the letters to match each phase with its objective.

Sequence (order) Phases	Matching (with objective)	Objective
_____Journalizing.	_____	a. Verification after closing entries.
_____Journalize and post reversing entries.	_____	b. Communication to decision makers.
_____Transaction analysis.	_____	c. Verification before adjusting entries.
_____Prepare financial statements.	_____	d. Transfer from journal to ledger.
_____Journalize and post closing entries.	_____	e. Based on source documents.
_____Collection of raw data.	_____	f. Update general ledger by separating "mixed" account balances.
_____Posting.		
_____Journalize and post adjusting entries.	_____	g. Assess economic impact of each transaction.
_____Prepare worksheets.	_____	h. Original input into the accounting system.
_____Prepare unadjusted trial balance.	_____	i. To facilitate subsequent entries.
_____Prepare post-closing trial balance.	_____	j. To obtain a zero balance in the revenue and expense accounts.
	_____	k. A logical and systematic technique to aid in completing the end-of-the-period procedures.

Exercise 3–4

BD Corporation completed the three transactions given below:

a. January 1, 19A—sold 10,000 shares of its own unissued common stock, par $1 per share, for $16,000 cash.

b. January 3, 19A—purchased a large machine costing $50,000. Payment was $10,000 cash plus a $15,000, one-year, 10% interest-bearing note payable and a $25,000, three-year, 8% interest-bearing note payable.

c. February 1, 19A—sold two lots that would not be needed for $8,500. Received $3,500 cash down payment and a $5,000, 90-day, 10% interest-bearing note. The two lots had a book value of $6,500.

Required:

1. Give the general journal entry to record each of the three transactions.
2. Set up T-accounts and post the entries in Requirement 1. Use a systematic numbering system for posting purposes.

Exercise 3–5

A clerk for Bea Company prepared the following unadjusted trial balance which the clerk was unable to balance:

Account	Debit	Credit
Cash	$ 35,563	
Accounts receivable	31,000	
Allowance for doubtful accounts	(2,000)	
Inventory		$ 18,000
Equipment	81,500	
Accumulated depreciation		12,000
Accounts payable	18,000	
Notes payable		25,000
Common stock, par $10		80,000
Retained earnings (correct)		14,000
Revenues		75,000
Expenses	60,000	
Totals (out of balance by $63)	$224,063	$224,000

Assume you are examining the accounts and have found the following errors:

a. Equipment purchased for $7,500 at year-end was debited to Expenses.

b. Sales on account for $829 were debited to Accounts Receivable for $892 and credited to Revenues for $829.

c. A $6,000 collection on accounts receivable was debited to Cash and credited to Revenues.

d. The inventory amount is understated by $2,000 (cost of goods sold is included in expenses).

Required:

Prepare a corrected trial balance. Show computations.

Exercise 3–6

Roby Corporation started operations January 1, 1979. It is now December 31, 1979, the end of the annual accounting period. A company clerk who maintained the records prepared the following financial statements at December 31, 1979.

Income Statement

Service revenue	$100,000
Expenses:	
Salaries and wages	30,000
Maintenance	5,000
Service expense	25,000
Other operating	10,000
Total expenses	70,000
Net Income	$ 30,000

Balance Sheet

Assets

Cash	$ 7,500
Note receivable (10%)	1,200
Inventory, supplies	6,000
Equipment	90,000
Other assets	7,300
Total Assets	$112,000

Liabilities

Accounts payable	$ 8,000
Note payable (10%)	24,000
Total Liabilities	32,000

Stockholders' Equity

Capital stock, par $10	50,000
Retained earnings	30,000
Total Stockholders' Equity	80,000
Total Liabilities and Stockholders' Equity	$112,000

The above statements were presented to a local bank to support a loan request. The bank requested that an outside CPA "examine the situation." The CPA identified the following omissions:

a. Service revenue amounting to $5,000 had been collected but not earned at December 31, 1979.
b. At December 31, 1979, wages earned by employees but not yet paid or recorded amounted to $3,000.
c. A count of the inventory of supplies at December 31, 1979, showed $4,000 supplies on hand.
d. The equipment was acquired on January 3, 1979. The estimated residual value was $10,000, and the estimated useful life ten years.
e. The note receivable received from a customer was dated November 1, 1979; the principal plus interest is payable April 30, 1980.
f. The note payable in favor of the local bank was dated June 1, 1979; the principal plus interest is payable May 30, 1980.
g. Assume an average income tax rate of 22% for Roby Corporation and that no income tax has been recorded.

Required: (Round to nearest dollar)

1. Give the adjusting entries (*[a]* through *[g]*) required to correct the accounts for the above omissions.
2. Correct the above statements to reflect the effects of the adjusting entries you made in Requirement 1. Key the entries for identification. Use the following format:

Items	Reported Amounts	Changes from Adjusting Entries (Use + and −)	Correct Amounts
Income Statement:			
Revenues (detail)			
Expenses (detail)			
Pretax income			
Income tax			
Net income			
EPS			
Balance Sheet:			
Assets (detail)			
Liabilities (detail)			
Stockholders' equity (detail)			

3. Reconcile the net change in owners' equity on the income statement with the net change on the balance sheet. Use captions as follows:

	Net Change
Income Statement:	
Total revenues	$
Total expenses	
Increase or decrease in net income	
Balance Sheet:	
Total assets	
Total liabilities	
Increase or decrease in stockholders' equity	

Exercise 3–7

BT Corporation adjusts and closes its accounts each December 31. The following situations require an adjusting entry at the current year-end. You are requested to prepare the adjusting entry in the general journal for each situation. Show computations.

a. A machine is to be depreciated for the full year. It cost $102,000, and the estimated useful life is 15 years, with an estimated residual value of $12,000. Assume straight-line depreciation.
b. Credit sales for the current year amounted to $100,000. The estimated bad debt loss rate on credit sales is ½%.
c. Property taxes for the current year have not been recorded or paid. A statement for the calendar year was received near the end of December for $2,400. The taxes are due and will be paid February 1 in the next year.

d. Supplies costing $800 were purchased for use in the offices during the year and debited to Office Supplies Inventory. The inventories of these supplies on hand were as follows: $100 at the end of the prior year, and $175 at the end of the current year.

e. BT rented an office in its building to an outsider for one year, starting on September 1. Rent for one year amounting to $1,800 was collected at that date. The total amount collected was credited to Rent Revenue.

f. BT received a note receivable from a customer dated November 1 of the current year. It is a $10,000, 9% note, due in one year. At the maturity date, BT will collect the face value of the note plus interest for one year.

Exercise 3–8

For each of the following situations, you are to give, in general journal form, the adjusting entry required at the end of the current annual accounting period, December 31. Show computations.

a. At the end of the year, unpaid and unrecorded wages amounted to $3,000.

b. The company owns a building which is to be depreciated for the full year. It cost $254,000, has an estimated useful life of 20 years, and a residual value of $54,000. Accumulated depreciation at the beginning of the current year was $60,000.

c. The company rented some space in its building to an outsider on August 1 of the current year and collected $2,400 cash, which was rent for one year in advance. Rent Revenue was credited for $2,400 on August 1.

d. The company paid a two-year insurance premium in advance on July 1 of the current year amounting to $1,000. The $1,000 was debited to Prepaid Insurance when paid.

e. Credit sales for the current year amounted to $100,000. The estimated bad debt loss rate is ½% of credit sales.

f. On July 1 of the current year, the company received a $10,000, one-year, 8% note from a customer. At maturity date, the company will collect the face amount of $10,000 plus interest for one year.

Exercise 3–9

Roy Company adjusts and closes its accounts each December 31. Below are two typical situations involving adjusting entries.

a. During the current year, office supplies were purchased for cash, $850. The inventory of office supplies at the end of the prior year was $150. At the end of the current year, the inventory showed $200 unused supplies still on hand. Give the adjusting entry assuming at the time of the purchase that in Case A, $850 was debited to Office Supplies Expense, and in Case B, $850 was debited to Office Supplies Inventory.

b. On June 1, the company collected cash, $2,400, which was for rent collected in advance for the next 12 months. Give the adjusting journal entry assuming at the time of the collection that in Case A, $2,400 was credited to Rent Revenue, and in Case B, $2,400 was credited to Rent Revenue Collected in Advance.

Exercise 3–10

a. On January 1, 19A, the Office Supplies Inventory account showed a balance on hand amounting to $350. During 19A, purchases of office supplies amounted to $800. An inventory of office supplies on hand at December 31, 19A, reflected unused supplies amounting to $425. Give the adjusting journal entry that should be made on December 31, 19A, assuming that in Case A the purchases were debited to the Inventory account, and in Case B the purchases were debited to Office Supplies Expense.

b. On January 1, 19A, the Prepaid Insurance account showed a debit balance of $300, which was for coverage for the three months, January–March. On April 1, 19A, the company took out another policy covering a two-year period from that date. The two-year premium amounting to $3,600 was paid and debited to Prepaid Insurance. Give the adjusting journal entry that should be made on December 31, 19A, to adjust for the entire year.

Exercise 3–11

Write a suitable explanation for each of the following journal entries:

a.	Wage expense	1,400	
	Wages payable		1,400
b.	Warranty (guarantee) expense	950	
	Estimated warranty liability		950
c.	Insurance expense	600	
	Prepaid insurance		600

d.	Interest expense 1,200	
	Interest payable	1,200
e.	Interest receivable 900	
	Interest revenue	900
f.	Rent revenue 750	
	Unearned rent revenue	750
g.	Income summary 5,000	
	Retained earnings	5,000

Exercise 3–12

The adjusted trial balance for TM Company showed the following on December 31, 1979, which is the end of the annual accounting period:

Sales revenue	$82,000
Interest revenue	1,000
Purchases	44,000
Purchase returns	500
Freight-in	1,500
Beginning inventory (periodic)	17,800
Selling expenses	23,000
Administrative expenses	13,000
Interest expense	400
Income tax expense	1,000
Additional data: Ending inventory	19,000

Required:

1. Set up T-accounts for each of the above items; enter the balances and diagram the closing entries. Use both Cost of Goods Sold and Income Summary accounts.
2. Explain the manner in which you handled the inventory amounts. Explain an alternate approach.

Exercise 3–13

At the end of the annual accounting period, Rob Corporation made the following adjusting entries:

December 31, 19B:

a.	Depreciation expense 5,000	
	Accumulated depreciation	5,000
b.	Wage expense 2,000	
	Wages payable	2,000
c.	Bad debt expense 400	
	Allowance for doubtful accounts ..	400
d.	Income tax expense 6,000	
	Income tax payable	6,000

Required:

Journalize the reversing entries that you think would be preferable on January 1, 19C. Explain for

each adjusting entry, the analysis you used to decide whether to reverse it.

Exercise 3–14

At the end of the annual accounting period, AB Corporation made the following adjusting entries:

December 31, 19A:

a.	Property tax expense 800	
	Property taxes payable	800
	(These are paid once each year.)	
b.	Rent receivable 2,000	
	Rent revenue	2,000
	(Rent revenue is collected each month.)	
c.	Patent amortization expense 1,000	
	Patents	1,000
d.	Warranty expense 600	
	Estimated warranty liability	600
e.	Wage expense 2,000	
	Wages payable	2,000

Required:

Journalize the reversing entries that you think should be made on January 1, 19B. Explain, for each adjusting entry, the analysis you used to determine whether to reverse it.

Exercise 3–15

Complete the following tabulations by entering the appropriate amount in each blank space:

1.

	Owners' Equity at Start of Period	Additional Investment by Owner	Withdrawals by Owner	Owners' Equity at End of Period	Net Income (Loss)
a.	$10,000	$2,000	$1,000	$16,400	$____
b.	18,000	3,000	____	22,000	4,700
c.	____	1,200	800	30,000	(2,200)
d.	15,500	600	____	12,950	(2,000)
e.	18,000	____	2,700	22,000	4,700

2.

	Sales	Finished Goods Beginning Inventory	Cost of Goods Manufactured	Finished Goods Ending Inventory	Cost of Goods Sold	Gross Margin	Expenses	Net Income
a.	$____	$15,000	$60,000	$____	$67,000	$23,000	$____	$1,000
b.	80,000	____	48,000	2,000	____	23,000	18,000	____
c.	____	20,000	____	36,000	59,000	18,000	____	8,000

Exercise 3–16 (based on Appendix A)

Dow Company uses special journals for credit sales, credit purchases, cash receipts, and cash payments. For each of the following transactions, you are to indicate the appropriate journal.

Transactions	Appropriate Journal
a. Sold common stock of Dow for cash.	_____
b. Purchased merchandise for resale; terms, 2/10, n/60.	_____
c. Borrowed $5,000 on 8% note.	_____
d. Recorded depreciation expense.	_____
e. Sold merchandise for cash.	_____
f. Purchased merchandise for cash.	_____
g. Purchased equipment for cash.	_____
h. Sold operational asset for cash.	_____
i. Purchased machinery on credit.	_____
j. Collected an account receivable.	_____
k. Paid a note payable.	_____
l. Recorded accrued wages payable.	_____
m. Paid cash dividend on common stock.	_____
n. Recorded estimated bad debt expense.	_____
o. Recorded amortization expense on patent.	_____
p. Sold machinery on credit.	_____

Exercise 3–17 (based on Appendix A)

Brown Retailers use special journals. Following is the special credit sales journal with several representative transactions.

Required:

1. Sum the above special journal and post it to the appropriate accounts in the general ledger and the two subsidiary ledgers. Use control accounts and subsidiary ledgers for sales and accounts receivable; assign systematic numbers to the accounts.
2. Prove the correctness of the two subsidiary ledgers.

Exercise 3–18 (based on Appendix A)

Sorensen Retailers use special journals. Following is a special cash receipts journal with several selected transactions.

						Dept. Sales	
Date	Sales Invoice No.	Account Receivable	Terms	Folio	Amount	A	B
1979:							
Jan. 1	21	Fly Corporation	2/10, n/30		98	40	58
5	22	B. T. Company	2/10, n/30		490	290	200
7	23	Easton Company	2/10, n/30		294	104	190
11	24	Fly Corporation	2/10, n/30		588	288	300
13	25	Wells Company	2/10, n/30		686	300	386
18	26	Fly Corporation	2/10, n/30		147	100	47
21	27	Easton Company	2/10, n/30		784	554	230
28	28	B. T. Company	2/10, n/30		245	200	45
31	29	Wells Company	2/10, n/30		637	407	230

Special Journal—Merchandise Sales on Credit — Page S-9

		Debits		Credits				
Date	Explanation	Cash	Account Title	Folio	Accounts Receivable	Sundry Accounts	Sales
1979:							
Jan. 1	Cash sales	30,000					30,000
2	On account	4,200	Riley Corporation		4,200		
5	Cash sales	10,000					10,000
6	On account	1,240	Brown, Inc.		1,240		
8	Sale of short-term investment	7,000	Short-term investments			4,000	
			Gain on sale of investments			3,000	
11	Cash sales	41,000					41,000
12	Borrowed cash	10,000	Notes payable			10,000	
15	On account	5,500	Watson Company		5,500		
18	Collected interest	600	Interest revenue			600	
31	Cash sales	52,000					52,000

Special Journal—Cash Receipts — Page CR-8

Required:

1. Sum the above special journal and post it to the appropriate accounts in the general ledger and subsidiary ledger. Use control account and subsidiary ledger for accounts receivable. Assign systematic numbers to the accounts. Assume beginning balances of Riley Corporation, $8,400; Brown, Inc., $1,240; and Watson Company, $10,000.
2. Prove the correctness of the subsidiary ledger.

PROBLEMS

Problem 3–1

Below is an intermixture of adjusting and closing (but no reversing) entries. Write a suitable explanation for each of the following end-of-the-period entries:

a.	Sales revenue	50,000	
	Rent revenue	2,000	
	Interest revenue	1,000	
	Sales returns		1,500
	Income summary		51,500
b.	Salary expense	7,000	
	Salaries payable		7,000
c.	Rent revenue	800	
	Unearned rent revenue		800
d.	Income summary	10,000	
	Inventory		10,000
e.	Inventory	12,000	
	Income summary		12,000
f.	Interest receivable	900	
	Interest revenue		900
g.	Supplies expense	400	
	Supplies inventory		400
h.	Income summary	39,000	
	Operating expenses		21,000
	Administrative expenses		16,000
	Interest expense		2,000
i.	Interest expense	750	
	Interest payable		750
j.	Income summary	8,800	
	Retained earnings		8,800
k.	Investment revenue	600	
	Unearned investment revenue		600
l.	Warranty (guarantee) expense	500	
	Estimated warranty liability		500
m.	Income tax expense	3,700	
	Income taxes payable		3,700
n.	Property tax expense	360	
	Property taxes payable		360
o.	Supplies inventory	440	
	Supplies expense		440

Problem 3–2

The following selected transactions were completed during the current year by Ray Corporation:

a. Ray sold 10,000 shares of its own common stock, par $10 per share, for $14 per share and received cash in full.
b. Borrowed $50,000 cash on an 8%, one-year note, interest payable at maturity.
c. Purchased equipment for use in operating the business at a net cash cost of $55,000; paid in full.
d. Purchased merchandise for resale at a cash net cost of $20,500; paid cash. Assume a periodic inventory system.
e. Purchased merchandise for resale on credit terms, 2/10, n/60. The merchandise will cost $9,800 if paid within ten days; after ten days, the payment will be $10,000. The company always takes the discount; therefore, such purchases are recorded at net. Assume periodic inventory system.
f. Sold merchandise for $38,000; collected $30,000 cash, and the balance is due in one month.
g. Paid $12,000 cash for operating expenses.
h. Paid the balance for the merchandise purchased in *(e)* within the ten days.
i. Collected the balance due on the sales in *(f)*.
j. Paid cash for an insurance premium, $600; the premium was for two years' coverage (debit Prepaid Expense).

Required:

1. Enter each of the above transactions in a general journal. Use the letter to the left to indicate the date.
2. Post each entry to appropriate T-accounts (number them consecutively starting with 101).
3. Prepare an unadjusted trial balance.

Problem 3–3

The following selected transactions were completed during the current year by Blue Corporation:

a. At date of organization, sold and issued 50,000 shares of its common stock, par $1 per share, for $80,000 cash.
b. Purchased a plant site for $100,000. The site included a building worth $82,000 and land worth $18,000. Payment was made; $70,000 cash and a $30,000 one-year, 9% note, interest payable at maturity.
c. Borrowed $60,000 cash from the local bank; signed a 9% interest (payable at maturity) note due in six months.

d. Purchased equipment for use in the business for $12,000; paid cash.

e. Purchased goods for resale at a net cost of $80,000; paid $70,000 cash, balance on open account. Assume perpetual inventory system.

f. Sold goods for cash, $62,000.

g. Paid operating expenses, $35,000.

h. Sold goods for cash, $48,000.

i. Purchased goods for cash, $22,000.

j. Paid the $10,000 due from transaction (e).

k. Sold and issued 30,000 shares of its common stock for $50,000.

l. On due date, paid the local bank the note given in entry (c) in the amount of $60,000 plus the interest to maturity date.

m. Purchased a two-year insurance policy on the building and equipment. Paid the two-year premium amounting to $1,400.

Required:

1. Journalize the above transactions in a general journal. Use the letters to the left to indicate dates.

2. Set up T-accounts (number them starting with 101) as needed and post the entries from the journal. Use folio notations.

3. Prepare an unadjusted trial balance.

Problem 3–4

JB Corporation has been in operation since January 1, 19A. It is now December 31, 19B, the end of the annual accounting period. The company has never been audited. The annual statements below were prepared by the company bookkeeper at December 31, 19B (accounts needed in the solution are provided without amounts):

Income Statement

Revenues:	
Service revenue	$250,000
Interest revenue	1,000
Total revenues	251,000
Expenses:	
Salary expense	75,000
Wage expense	60,600
Depreciation expense	
Interest expense	2,400
Other expenses	50,000
Total expenses	188,000
Pretax income	63,000
Income taxes	.
Net Income	$ 63,000
Earnings per share	$3.50

Balance Sheet

Assets

Cash	$ 40,000
Note receivable (10%)	12,000
Interest receivable	
Inventory, supplies	2,000
Prepaid insurance	1,500
Equipment	200,000
Accumulated depreciation	(20,000)
Other assets	85,500
Total Assets	$321,000

Liabilities

Accounts payable	$ 18,000
Wages payable	
Unearned service revenue	
Interest payable	
Income taxes payable	
Notes payable (9%)	40,000
Total Liabilities	58,000

Stockholders' Equity

Capital stock, par $10	180,000
Retained earnings	83,000
Total Stockholders' Equity	263,000
Total Liabilities and Stockholders' Equity	$321,000

An outside accountant was engaged to adjust the statements for any items omitted. As a consequence, the following additional information was developed:

a. No depreciation was reported for 19B. The equipment has a ten-year life and no residual value.

b. Prepaid insurance at the end of 19B was $500. Use Other expenses.

c. Wages unpaid and unrecorded at the end of 19B amounted to $18,000.

d. Interest on the note receivable was last collected at October 30, 19B.

e. The inventory count of supplies at year-end showed $300. Use Other expenses.

f. On December 31, 19B, service revenues collected but unearned amounted to $6,000.

g. Interest on the note payable is paid each August 30.

h. Assume the income tax rate averages 22%.

Required:

1. Prepare adjusting entries for the above in general journal form for December 31, 19B.

2. Restate the above statements after taking into account the adjusting entries made in Requirement 1. Key each adjustment. You need not use additional subclassifications on the statements. Use the following solution format:

Items (list the two statements here)	Reported Amounts	Changes from Adjusting Entries (use + and −)	Correct Amounts

3. Reconcile the net changes on the income statement with the net changes on the balance sheet. Use the following format:

Increase (decrease)

Income Statement:
    Change in total revenues
    Change in total expenses
    Change in net income
Balance Sheet:
    Change in total assets
    Change in total liabilities
    Change in owners' equity

Problem 3–5

RG Company adjusts and closes its books each December 31. It is now December 31, 1979, and the adjusting entries are to be made. You are requested to prepare, in general journal format, the adjusting entry that should be made for each of the following items. Show computations.

a. Credit sales for the year amounted to $200,000. The estimated loss rate on bad debts is ¼%.
b. Unpaid and unrecorded wages at December 31 amounted to $2,100.
c. The company paid a two-year insurance premium in advance on April 1, 1979, amounting to $3,000, which was debited to Prepaid Insurance.
d. The worksheet is being completed, and pretax income has been computed to be $40,000. Assume an average income tax rate of 31.75%.
e. A machine that cost $37,000 is to be depreciated for the full year. The estimated useful life is ten years, and the residual value, $2,000. Assume straightline depreciation.
f. The company rented a warehouse on June 1, 1979, for one year. They had to pay the full amount of rent one year in advance on June 1, amounting to $4,800, which was debited to Rent Expense.
g. The company received a 10% note from a customer with a face amount of $6,000. The note was dated September 1, 1979; the principal plus the interest is payable one year later. Notes Receivable was debited, and Sales credited on September 1, 1979.

h. On December 30, 1979, the property tax bill was received in the amount of $2,000. This amount applied only to 1979 and had not been previously recorded. The taxes are due, and will be paid, on January 15, 1980.
i. On April 1, 1979, the company signed a $30,000, 8% note payable. On that date, Cash was debited and Notes Payable credited for $30,000. The note is payable on March 30, 1980, for the face amount plus interest for one year.
j. The company purchased a patent on January 1, 1979, at a cost of $5,950. On that date, Patent was debited and Cash credited for $5,950. The patent has an estimated useful life of 17 years and no residual value.

Problem 3–6

Mays Company adjusts and closes its accounts each December 31. It is December 31, 1979. You are requested to prepare, in general journal format, the adjusting entry that should be made for each of the following items. Show computations.

a. The company owns a building and the site on which it is situated. The Building account reflects a cost of $267,000; and the Land account, $20,000. The estimated useful life of the building is 20 years, and the residual value, $47,000. Accumulated depreciation to January 1, 1979, was $66,000. Assume straight-line depreciation.
b. Property taxes for the city fiscal year, which ends June 30, 1980, have not been recorded or paid. A tax statement was received near the end of December 1979 for $5,000. The taxes are due, and will be paid, on February 15, 1980. Property tax expense for the city, fiscal year ended June 30, 1979, was $4,800. No property tax expense has been recorded in 1979.
c. The company received a $6,000, 10% note from a customer on June 1, 1979. On that date, Notes Receivable was debited and Sales credited for $6,000. The face of the note plus interest for one year is payable on May 30, 1980.
d. At December 31, 1979, the Supplies Inventory account showed a debit balance of $1,600. An inventory of unused supplies taken at year-end reflected $400.
e. Sales for the year amounted to $1,500,000, of which $300,000 was on credit. The estimated bad debt loss rate, based on credit sales, was ⅓% for the year.
f. On August 1, 1979, the company rented some space in its building to an outsider and collected $4,200 cash rent in advance. This was for the 12 months

starting August 1, 1979, and was credited to Rent Revenue.

g. At December 31, 1979, unrecorded and unpaid salaries amounted to $7,500.

h. On April 1, 1979, the company borrowed $20,000 on a one-year, 9% note. On that date, Cash was debited and Notes Payable credited for $20,000. At maturity the face amount plus interest for one year must be paid.

i. On January 1, 1979, the company purchased, with cash, a patent for use in the business at a cost of $2,550, which was debited to Patent. The patent has an estimated remaining economic life of 15 years and no residual value.

j. The company uses the periodic inventory system whereby the inventory is physically counted, then valued at unit cost at each year-end. The company prefers to consider the inventory amounts as adjusting entries. The beginning inventory amount was $40,000, and the ending inventory (December 31, 1979) was $44,500. You are to give the adjusting entry for each inventory amount assuming a Cost of Goods Sold account is used.

k. The worksheet is being completed; all of the above adjusting entries have been recorded on it. Pretax income has been computed to be $70,000. Assume the average income tax rate is 38%.

Problem 3–7

The following situations relate to the Gray Corporation. The fiscal accounting year ends December 31. The situations relate to the year 1979. Gray Corporation is a manufacturer rather than a retailer. The books are adjusted and closed each December 31.

In each instance, you are to give *only* the adjusting entry (or entries) that would be made on December 31, 1979, incident to adjusting and closing the books and preparation of the annual financial statements. State clearly any assumptions that you make. Give each adjusting entry in general journal format.

a. The company owns a machine that cost $87,000; it was purchased on July 1, 1976. It has an estimated useful life of 15 years and a residual value of $12,000. Straight-line depreciation is used. The machine is still being used.

b. Sales for 1979 amounted to $800,000, including $200,000 credit sales. It is estimated, based on experience of the company, that bad debt losses will be ½% of credit sales.

c. On January 1, 1978, the company purchased a patent that cost $13,600; at that time the estimated useful life remaining was 17 years. The patent is used in operations.

d. At the beginning of 1979, Office Supplies Inventory amounted to $300. During 1979, office supplies amounting to $4,400 were purchased; this amount was debited to Office Supplies Expense. An inventory of office supplies at the end of 1979 showed $250 on the shelves. The January 1 balance of $300 is still reflected in the Office Supplies Inventory account.

e. On July 1, 1979, the company paid a three-year insurance premium amounting to $1,080; this amount was debited to Prepaid Insurance.

f. On October 1, 1979, the company paid rent on some leased office space. The payment of $3,600 cash was for the following 12 months. At the time of payment, Rent Expense was debited for the $3,600.

g. On July 1, 1979, the company borrowed $60,000 from the Sharpstown bank. The loan was for 12 months at 7% interest payable at maturity date.

h. Finished goods inventory on January 1, 1979, was $100,000; and on December 31, 1979, it was $130,000. Assume periodic inventory procedures and that inventory entries are viewed as adjusting entries. Use a Cost of Goods Sold account.

i. The company owned some property (land) that was rented to B. R. Speir on April 1, 1979, for 12 months for $4,200. On April 1 the entire annual rental of $4,200 was credited to Rent Revenue Collected in Advance and Cash was debited.

j. On December 31, 1979, wages earned by employees but not yet paid (nor recorded in the accounts) amounted to $7,000. Disregard payroll taxes.

k. On December 31, 1979, it was discovered that some raw material purchased on the preceding day, although not paid for, was included in the ending inventory. A purchase had not been recorded. The cost was $950. Assume periodic inventory procedures.

l. On September 1, 1979, the company loaned $12,000 to an outside party. The loan was at 9% per annum and was due in six months; interest is to be paid at maturity. Cash was credited for $12,000, and Notes Receivable debited for the same amount on September 1.

m. On January 1, 1979, factory supplies on hand amounted to $100. During 1979, factory supplies costing $2,000 were purchased and debited to Factory Supplies Inventory. At the end of 1979, a physical inventory count revealed that factory supplies on hand amounted to $300.

n. The company purchased a gravel pit on January 1, 1977, at a cost of $24,000; it was estimated that approximately 60,000 tons of gravel could be removed prior to exhaustion. It was also estimated that the company would take five years to exploit this natural resource. Tons of gravel removed were 1977—2,000; 1978—7,000; and 1979—5,000.

o. At the end of 1979, it was found that postage stamps costing $90 were still on hand (in a "postage" box in the office). When the stamps were purchased, Miscellaneous Expense was debited and Cash credited.

p. At the end of 1979, property taxes for 1979 amounting to $2,500 had been assessed on property owned by the company. The taxes are due no later than February 1, 1980. The taxes had not been recorded on the books since payment had not been made.

q. The company borrowed $30,000 from the bank on December 1, 1979. A 60-day note payable was signed that called for 8% interest payable on the due date. As a consequence, on December 1, 1979, Cash was debited and Notes Payable credited for $30,000.

r. On July 1, 1979, the company paid the city a $500 license fee for the next 12 months. On that date, Cash was credited and License Expense debited for $500.

s. On March 1, 1979, the company made a loan to the company president and received a $12,000 note receivable. The loan was due in one year and called for 6% annual interest payable at maturity date.

t. The company owns three "company cars" used by the executives. A six-month maintenance contract on them was signed on October 1, 1979, whereby a local garage agreed to do "all the required maintenance." The payment was made for the following six months in advance. On October 1, 1979, Cash was credited and Maintenance Expense was debited for $1,800.

Problem 3–8

The adjusted trial balance for Dawson Corporation reflected the following on December 31, 1979, end of the annual accounting period:

Cash	$ 27,900	
Accounts receivable	32,000	
Allowance for doubtful accounts		$ 500
Inventory (periodic system)	18,000	
Prepaid insurance	600	
Equipment	100,000	
Accumulated depreciation, equipment		20,000
Accounts payable		13,400
Wages payable		800
Income taxes payable		5,000
Bonds payable		20,000

Common stock, par $10		100,000
Retained earnings		12,400
Sales revenue		126,000
Interest revenue		1,000
Sales returns	3,000	
Purchases	70,000	
Freight-in	2,500	
Purchase returns		900
Operating expenses	28,000	
General expenses (including interest)	13,000	
Income tax expense	5,000	
	$300,000	$300,000

Inventory, December 31, 1979, $23,000.

Required:

1. Set up T-accounts only for the accounts to be closed and Retained Earnings. Enter the balances. Diagram the closing entries. Use both Cost of Goods Sold and Income Summary accounts.
2. Journalize the closing entries to agree with your diagram.
3. Explain the alternate approach when the Cost of Goods Sold account is not used.

Problem 3–9

The summarized adjusted trial balance for Ray Corporation reflected the following on December 31, 1979, end of the annual accounting period:

Cash	$ 60,700	
Inventory (periodic system)	12,000	
Accounts receivable	21,000	
Allowance for doubtful accounts		$ 400
Prepaid insurance	300	
Accounts payable		17,600
Wages payable		1,000
Income taxes payable		2,000
Common stock, par $10		50,000
Retained earnings		17,300
Sales revenue		88,000
Sales returns	2,000	
Purchases	45,000	
Freight-in	1,000	
Purchase returns		700
Operating expenses	18,400	
General expenses (including interest)	14,600	
Income tax expense	2,000	
	$177,000	$177,000

Inventory (ending), December 31, 1979, $18,800.

Required:

1. Set up T-accounts for Retained Earnings and those accounts that are to be closed. Enter the balances.

Diagram the closing entries. Use only the Income Summary account.
2. Journalize the closing entries to agree with your diagram.
3. Explain an alternate approach when the Cost of Goods Sold account is used.

Problem 3–10

The post-closing trial balance of the general ledger of King Corporation at January 1, 1979, reflected the following:

Account No.	Account	Debit	Credit
101	Cash	$28,000	
102	Accounts receivable ...	18,000	
103	Allowance for doubtful accounts ...		$ 400
104	Inventory (periodic)* ...	10,000	
105	Equipment (20-year life; no residual value)	20,000	
106	Accumulated depreciation		6,000
200	Accounts payable		9,000
201	Wages payable		
202	Income taxes payable .		
300	Common stock, par $1 .		50,000
301	Retained earnings		10,600
302	Income summary		
400	Revenues		
500	Operating expenses ...		
501	Purchases		
600	Income tax expense ...		
		$76,000	$76,000

* Ending inventory, $15,000 (at December 31, 1979).

The following is a summary of the transactions during 1979 (use the number to the left to indicate the date):

Date
1. Sold goods, $90,000, of which $20,000 was on credit.
2. Purchased goods, $40,000, of which $10,000 was on credit; assume periodic inventory.
3. Collected accounts receivable, $35,000.
4. Paid accounts payable, $17,000.
5. Paid operating expenses, $23,800.
6. On January 1, 1979, sold common stock of the company, 2,000 shares at par, collected cash in full.
7. On the last day of the year, purchased a new machine at a cost of $12,000; paid cash. Estimated useful life, ten years; residual value, $2,000.

Required:
1. Set up T-accounts in the general ledger for the accounts listed above; they are all you will need. Enter the beginning balances.

2. Journalize each of the above transactions in the general journal.
3. Post the journal entries; use folio notations.
4. Prepare an unadjusted trial balance.
5. Journalize and post the adjusting entries. Accrued (unpaid) wages at year-end amounted to $800. Bad debt expense is estimated to be 1% of credit sales for the period. Assume straight-line depreciation. Assume an average 22% corporate income tax rate.
6. Prepare an adjusted trial balance.
7. Prepare an unclassified income statement and balance sheet.
8. Journalize and post the closing entries (use only the Income Summary account).
9. Prepare a post-closing trial balance.

Problem 3–11

The post-closing trial balance of the general ledger of Dow Corporation at December 31, 1978, reflected the following:

Account No.	Account	Debit	Credit
101	Cash	$ 27,000	
102	Accounts receivable ...	21,000	
103	Allowance for doubtful accounts ...		$ 1,000
104	Inventory (periodic system)*	35,000	
105	Prepaid insurance (20 months remaining)	900	
200	Equipment (20-year estimated life; no residual value) ...	50,000	
201	Accumulated depreciation		22,500
300	Accounts payable		7,500
301	Wages payable		
302	Income taxes payable (for 1978)		4,000
400	Common stock, par $1		80,000
401	Retained earnings		18,900
500	Sales revenue		
600	Purchases		
601	Operating expenses ...		
602	Income tax expense ..		
700	Income summary		
		$133,900	$133,900

* Ending inventory, $45,000 (at December 31, 1979).

The following transactions occurred during 1979 in the order given (use the number at the left to indicate the date):

Date
1. Sold goods for $30,000, of which $10,000 was on credit.

2. Collected $17,000 on accounts receivable.
3. Paid income taxes payable (1978), $4,000.
4. Purchased merchandise, $40,000, of which $8,000 was on credit.
5. Paid accounts payable, $6,000.
6. Sold goods for cash, $72,000.
7. Paid operating expenses, $19,000.
8. On January 1, 1979, sold and issued 1,000 shares of common stock, par $1, for $1,000 cash.
9. Purchased merchandise, $100,000, of which $27,000 was on credit.
10. Sold goods for $98,000, of which $30,000 was on credit.
11. Collected cash on accounts receivable, $26,000.
12. Paid cash on accounts payable, $28,000.
13. Paid various operating expenses in cash, $18,000.

Required:

1. Set up T-accounts in the general ledger for each of the accounts listed in the beginning trial balance and enter the December 31, 1978, balances.
2. Journalize each of the transactions listed above for 1979. Use general journal only.
3. Post the journal entries; use folio notations.
4. Prepare an unadjusted trial balance.
5. Journalize the adjusting entries and post them to the ledger. Assume a bad debt rate of ½% of credit sales for the period and an average 40% corporate income tax rate. At December 31, 1979, accrued wages were $300. Assume straight-line depreciation.
6. Prepare an adjusted trial balance.
7. Prepare an unclassified income statement and balance sheet.
8. Journalize and post the closing entries. Do not use a Cost of Goods Sold account.
9. Prepare a post-closing trial balance.

Problem 3–12

Davis Corporation adjusts and closes its books each December 31. At December 31, 1979, the following unadjusted trial balance has been developed from the general ledger:

Account	Debit	Credit
	Balances (unadjusted)	
Cash	$132,830	
Accounts receivable	34,000	
Allowance for doubtful accounts		$ 5,400
Inventory (periodic system)	62,000	
Prepaid insurance (15 months remaining as of January 1, 1979)	600	
Long-term note receivable (7%)	12,000	
Investment revenue receivable		
Land	27,000	
Building	240,000	
Accumulated depreciation, building		130,000
Equipment	90,000	
Accumulated depreciation, equipment		50,000
Accounts payable		23,000
Salaries payable		
Income taxes payable		
Interest payable		
Unearned rent revenue		
Bonds payable, 5%		120,000
Common stock, par $10		200,000
Contributed capital in excess of par		10,000
Retained earnings		27,900
Sales revenue		290,000
Investment revenue		630
Rent revenue		6,000
Purchases	164,000	
Purchase returns		4,000
Selling expenses	51,000	
General and administrative expenses	35,000	
Interest expense	3,500	
Extraordinary loss (pretax)	15,000	
Income tax expense		
	$866,930	$866,930

Additional data for adjustments and other purposes:

a. Estimated bad debt loss rate is ½% of credit sales. Ten percent of 1979 sales were on credit. Classify as a selling expense.
b. Ending inventory (December 31, 1979), $70,000.
c. Interest on the long-term note receivable was last collected on September 30, 1979.
d. Estimated useful life on the building was 20 years; residual value, $40,000. Allocate 10% to administrative and the balance to selling expenses. Assume straight-line depreciation.
e. Estimated useful life on the equipment was ten years; residual value, zero. Allocate 10% to administrative and the balance to selling expenses. Assume straight-line depreciation.
f. Unrecorded and unpaid sales salaries payable at December 31, 1979, was $7,500.
g. Interest on the bonds payable was paid last on July 31, 1979.
h. On August 1, 1979, the company rented some space in its building to an outsider and collected $6,000 for 12 months rent in advance, which was credited to Rent Revenue.
i. Adjust for expired insurance. Assume selling expense.
j. Assume an average 40% corporate income tax rate on all items including the extraordinary loss.

Required:

1. Enter the above unadjusted trial balance on a worksheet.
2. Enter the adjusting entries on the worksheet and complete it.
3. Prepare an unclassified income statement and balance sheet.
4. Journalize the closing entries. Do not use a Cost of Goods Sold account.

Problem 3–13

Boyd Corporation currently is completing the end-of-the-period accounting process. At December 31, 1979, the following unadjusted trial balance was developed from the general ledger:

Account	Balances (unadjusted) Debit	Balances (unadjusted) Credit
Cash.........................	$ 61,900	
Accounts receivable	38,000	
Allowance for doubtful accounts		$ 2,000
Inventory (periodic system)	80,000	
Sales supplies inventory	900	
Long-term note receivable, 7%	12,000	
Equipment	180,000	
Accumulated depreciation, equipment		64,000
Patent	8,400	
Interest receivable		
Accounts payable		23,000
Interest payable		
Income taxes payable		
Property taxes payable		
Unearned rent revenue		
Mortgage payable, 8%		60,000
Common stock, par $100		100,000
Contributed capital in excess of par		15,000
Retained earnings		32,440
Sales revenue		700,000
Investment revenue		560
Rent revenue		3,000
Purchases	400,000	
Freight-in	7,000	
Purchase returns		2,000
Selling expenses	164,400	
General and administrative expenses	55,000	
Interest expense	4,400	
Income tax expense		
Extraordinary gain (pretax)		10,000
	$1,012,000	$1,012,000

Additional data for adjustments and other purposes:

a. Estimated bad debt loss rate is ¼% of credit sales. Credit sales for the year amounted to $200,000. This is a selling expense.
b. Ending inventory, December 31, 1979, $95,000.
c. Interest on the long-term note receivable was last collected August 31, 1979.
d. Estimated useful life of the equipment is ten years; residual value, $20,000. Allocate 10% to administrative expenses and the balance to selling expenses. Assume straight-line depreciation.
e. Estimated remaining economic life of the patent is 14 years (from January 1, 1979) and no residual value. Assume straight-line amortization to selling expense (used in sales promotion).
f. Interest on the mortgage payable was last paid on November 30, 1979.
g. On June 1, 1979, the company rented some office space to an outsider for one year and collected $3,000 rent in advance for the year; the entire amount was credited to Rent Revenue.
h. On December 31, 1979, received a statement for calendar year 1979 property taxes amounting to $1,300. The amount is due February 15, 1980. Assume it will be paid on that date and that it is a selling expense. None of the amount had been recorded during 1979.
i. Sales supplies on hand at December 31, 1979, amounted to $300 (selling expense).
j. Assume an average 40% corporate income tax rate on all items including the extraordinary gain.

Required:

1. Enter the above unadjusted trial balance on a worksheet.
2. Enter the adjusting entries and complete the worksheet.
3. Prepare an unclassified income statement and balance sheet.
4. Journalize the closing entries. Do not use a Cost of Goods Sold account.

Problem 3–14

At the end of the accounting period, XY Corporation made the following adjusting entries.

December 31, 1979:

a. Depreciation expense 7,000
      Accumulated depreciation 7,000

b. Bad debt expense 1,000
      Allowance for doubtful accounts .. 1,000

c. Insurance expense 600
      Prepaid insurance 600

d.	Supplies expense	2,000	
	Supplies inventory		2,000
e.	Wage expense	5,000	
	Wages payable		5000
f.	Rent receivable	3,000	
	Rent revenue		3,000
g.	Utilities (electric expense)	4,000	
	Estimated utilities payable		4,000
h.	Interest expense	900	
	Interest payable		900

Required:

1. The first four adjusting entries given above generally are not viewed as candidates for reversal on January 1, 1980. Explain why each is generally not a candidate.
2. The last four adjusting entries shown above generally are viewed as candidates for reversal on January 1, 1980. Give the reversing entry for each and explain why it may be desirable to reverse.
3. The last entry may, or may not, be reversed. In either event, the net effect is the same. Assume the next interest payment is March 31, 1980, for $1,200 (interest for the past 12 months). Prepare entries side by side under the headings "With Reversing Entry" and "Without Reversing Entry" and demonstrate that the net effects are the same.

Problem 3–15 (based on Appendix A)

Able Company uses special journals for credit sales and credit purchases of merchandise. Below are listed some selected transactions involving merchandise purchases and sales. Amounts given for credit transactions are before any deduction of discount unless otherwise stated. Sales and purchases on credit are recorded net of discount. Assume periodic inventory.

a. Purchased merchandise for cash, $9,800, from X Corporation.
b. Sold merchandise on credit terms, 2/10, n/30, $1,000, to AD Company.
c. Purchased merchandise, $3,000, terms, 2/10, n/30, from Benson Company.
d. Purchased equipment from Roy Company for use in the business for $10,000; paid cash.
e. Collected for merchandise sold in (b) within ten days.
f. Sold merchandise on credit terms, 2/10, n/30, $2,000, to Z Company.
g. Purchased merchandise for cash, $15,000, from AK Company.
h. Sold merchandise for cash, $41,800, to AD Company.

i. Sold merchandise on credit terms, 2/10, n/30, $4,000, BT Corporation.
j. Purchased merchandise from X Corporation, $1,500; terms, 2/10, n/30.
k. Paid for merchandise purchased in (c) above within the discount period.
l. Sold merchandise to VEE Company, $3,300; terms, 2/10, n/60.
m. Purchased merchandise from Benson Company, $4,000; terms, 2/10, n/30.

Required:

1. Design special journals for (a) credit sales and (b) credit purchases of merchandise similar to those illustrated in the chapter.
2. Enter in the two special journals appropriate transactions from the above list. Enter the remaining entries in the general journal.
3. Set up ledger accounts for Accounts Receivable Control, Accounts Payable Control, Sales Revenue, and Purchases in the general ledger and appropriate subsidiary ledgers for the two control accounts. Use T-account format. Post appropriate amounts to these records. Systematically number the accounts for posting purposes.
4. Prove the accuracy of the accounts receivable and accounts payable records.

Problem 3–16 (based on Appendix A)

Makin Company is a small department store. The accounting system is maintained manually. Control accounts and subsidiary ledgers are used. The following information was selected from the accounting system at January 1, 1979:

Journals	Page No. to Be Used
General journal	J-27
Special journals:	
Mdse. sales on credit	S-13
Mdse. purchases on credit	P-9
Cash receipts	CR-22
Cash payments	CP-34

General Ledger Accounts	Balance Jan. 1, 1979	Account No.
Cash	$ 72,000	101
Accounts receivable	38,000	105
Inventory (periodic system)	45,000	110
Equipment	25,000	204
Accounts payable	21,000	303
Notes payable	10,000	305
Common stock, par $10	100,000	400
Contributed capital in excess of par		401
Retained earnings	49,000	410
Sales revenue		500
Sales returns		501
Purchases		600

Purchase returns	601
Expenses	700

Subsidiary Ledgers

Accounts receivable (No. 105):

Ames, C. P.	7,000	105.1
Graves Company	16,000	105.2
Mason Corporation	5,000	105.3
White Company	10,000	105.4

Accounts payable (No. 303):

Buford Wholesale Company	11,000	303.1
Dawn Suppliers, Inc., ...	7,000	303.2
Paul Wholesale Company	3,000	303.3

The following transactions were completed during January 1979:

Date

1. Purchased merchandise for cash, $18,000.
2. Paid $11,000 owed to Buford Wholesale Company within the discount period.
3. Sold merchandise for cash, $26,000.
4. Purchased a new truck for use in the business; paid cash, $4,200.
5. Sold merchandise to XY Corporation on credit; terms, 2/10, n/60; $9,800 if paid within ten days; otherwise $10,000 (record at net of discount).
6. Paid expenses, $4,500.
7. Purchased merchandise on credit from Sauls Company; terms, 2/10, n/60; $20,000, if paid within ten days; otherwise add 2% charge.
8. Sold merchandise for cash, $37,000.
8. Collected on accounts receivable within the discount period as follows: Ames, $7,000; Graves, $16,000; and White, $10,000.
9. Purchased merchandise for cash, $21,000.
9. Collected in full from XY Corporation for the sale of January 5.
9. Paid accounts payable within the discount period: Dawn, $7,000; and Paul $2,000.
10. Collected accounts receivable from Mason Corporation, $5,000, within the discount period.
10. Returned merchandise purchased from Paul Wholesale Company because its specifications were incorrect; received a credit for $1,000.
14. Paid expenses, $9,600.
15. Sold merchandise for cash, $11,400.
16. Paid balance due to Sauls within the discount period.
19. Borrowed $30,000 cash on a one-year, 8% interest-bearing note.
22. Sold merchandise on credit terms, 2/10, n/30, as follows (net amount): Ames, $6,000; Graves, $13,000; Mason, $9,000; and White, $4,000.
23. A customer returned merchandise, purchased a few days earlier; since the correct size was unavailable, customer was given a cash refund of $175.
24. Collected the balance due from White Company within the discount period.
25. Returned damaged merchandise to a wholesale supplier and received a cash refund of $450.
26. Purchased merchandise on credit from Buford Wholesale Company; terms, 2/10, n/60; net amount, $35,000.
27. Purchased merchandise on credit from Dawn Suppliers, Inc.; terms, 2/10, n/60; net amount, $12,000.
28. Cash sales, $47,000.
29. Sold merchandise on credit to XY Corporation on the usual terms; net amount, $16,500.
30. Collected in full for the credit sale to Mason on January 22.
31. Sold common stock of Makin Company to a new shareholder, 1,000 shares for $20,000 cash.

Required:

1. Set up a general journal and special journals for credit sales, credit purchases, cash receipts, and cash payments, similar to those illustrated in Appendix A. Sales and purchases on credit are recorded at net of discount.
2. Set up T-accounts for the general ledger and two subsidiary ledgers, accounts receivable and accounts payable. Enter the beginning balances in the T-accounts.
3. Journalize the above transactions in the appropriate journals.
4. Post to the subsidiary and general ledgers; use folio numbers.
5. Prepare reconciliation of the subsidiary ledgers.
6. Prepare a trial balance from the general ledger.

Problem 3–17 (based on Appendix B)

Wall Manufacturing Corporation is in the process of completing the end-of-the-period accounting process. It is now December 31, 1979, and the following unadjusted trial balance has been developed from the general ledger:

	Balance (unadjusted)	
Account	*Debit*	*Credit*
Cash	$ 171,300	
Inventory, January 1 (periodic system):		
Raw materials	42,000	
Work in process	60,000	
Finished goods	38,000	
Accounts receivable	18,000	
Allowance for doubtful accounts		$ 450
Factory supplies inventory	6,300	
Plant and equipment	430,000	
Accumulated depreciation		180,000
Remaining assets (not subject to depreciation)	102,000	
Accounts payable		37,000
Wages payable		
Interest payable		
Income taxes payable		

Mortgage payable (9%, each August 31)		40,000
Common stock, par $100		500,000
Retained earnings		42,550
Sales revenue		800,000
Manufacturing costs:		
Raw materials purchases	180,000	
Direct labor	200,000	
Factory overhead	100,000	
Distribution expenses	160,000	
Administrative expenses	90,000	
Interest expense	2,400	
Cost of goods manufactured . . .		
Income tax expense		
	$1,600,000	$1,600,000

Additional data for adjustments and other purposes:

a. Inventories December 31, 1979: raw materials, $45,000; work in process, $54,000; and finished goods, $40,000.

b. Estimated bad debt loss rate is $1/3$% of credit sales. Credit sales for the period were $150,000 (distribution expense).

c. An inventory of factory supplies taken on December 31, 1979, showed unused supplies amounting to $4,800 (factory overhead).

d. Plant and equipment is depreciated over a 20-year life (estimated); residual value is $30,000 (debit Factory Overhead for depreciation).

e. Unrecorded and unpaid administrative wages at December 31, 1979, amounted to $3,500.

f. The most recent interest payment on the mortgage was on August 31, 1979.

g. Assume 40% corporate income tax rate.

Required:

1. Enter the above unadjusted trial balance on a worksheet.
2. Enter the adjusting entries on the worksheet and complete it; assume straight-line depreciation.
3. Prepare a manufacturing statement, single-step income statement, and an unclassified balance sheet.
4. Journalize the closing entries.

4

Review—The Income Statement and Retained Earnings

Periodic financial statements are the means by which the information collected, recorded, and summarized in the accounting system is communicated to external decision makers. The required financial statements are the following:

1. Income statement.
2. Balance sheet (discussed in Chapter 5).
3. Statement of changes in financial position (discussed in Chapters 5 and 23).

The periodic financial statements present primarily *historical* information. They are *general-purpose* statements because they are designed specially to serve several groups of decision makers—investors, creditors, and the public at large. Also, they are summary in nature and are fundamentally related; that is, each statement is interrelated with the other statements. These relationships are illustrated in Exhibit 4–1.

In Exhibit 4–1, the income statement and the statement of changes in financial position are shown as the connecting links between the beginning and ending balance sheets. They are designed to explain to the decision maker the *causes* of the changes in financial position during the current period. The income statement explains the changes from *operations* (i.e., revenues and expenses) and from extraordinary items, whereas the statement of changes in financial position explains the changes in finan-

cial position in terms of *fund* inflows and outflows during the period. The accounting profession regards the three statements as the minimum requirement for reporting to external decision makers.

This chapter discusses the income statement and the statement of retained earnings.

CONCEPT OF INCOME

Income is defined differently by economists and accountants. Many economists define income as the change in real wealth (i.e., command over goods and services) between the beginning and end of a specified period. To state it another way, income is the net increase in real wealth that could be distributed to the owners of a business at the end of the period without reducing the real wealth of the entity from what it was at the start of the period. This concept requires measurement of the wealth at the beginning and end of each period. It provides no specific details for the causes of net income. Conceptually, wealth at each point in time should be measured as the *present value* of all expected future cash flows. Because of the difficulties in applying this concept, other ways of measuring wealth have been suggested, such as the current cash equivalent value.

In contrast, the *accountant* defines net in-

EXHIBIT 4–1
Relationships between Financial Statements

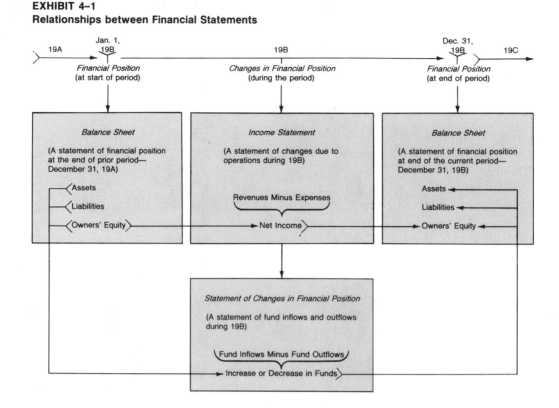

come on the basis of completed transactions that cause revenues and expenses (including certain other gains and losses). Income is defined as the difference between revenues and expenses arising from completed transactions and certain other events (such as depreciation and casualty losses). The economist's concept of income is impractical to apply; it is based upon subjective information and does not provide details required for full disclosure. Consequently, the accounting profession has formulated the *transactions approach* to define and measure net income. The transactions approach is pragmatic, provides details for periodic reporting, focuses on the stewardship function of management, and maintains a relatively high degree of objectivity.

The transactions approach used in accounting collects detailed data on each transaction and records the effects in terms of changes in assets, liabilities, and owners' equity (i.e., in

terms of the basic accounting model). Basically, changes in assets, liabilities, and owners' equity are recognized if they are evidenced by *completed exchange transactions*. Changes in "value" generally are not recognized when they occur if they arise from changes in market valuations or changes in expectations; instead, they are recognized when exchange transactions occur that involve the entity. To illustrate, if an asset is acquired for $1,000 and subsequently increases in value to $1,200, the $200 accretion is not recognized as revenue. Should the asset later be sold for $1,300, a $300 gain would be recognized in the period of sale. The broad structure of accounting discussed in Chapter 2 explicitly requires the transactions approach. Since accounting defines income as the difference between total revenue and total expense, these two concepts require careful definition.

Revenue may be conceptually defined as the inflow of assets or the elimination of liabilities for the aggregate of products or services transferred (i.e., sold) by an enterprise during a specified period.[1] A pragmatic definition is given in *APB Statement No. 4* as follows:

> Revenue is a gross increase in assets or a gross decrease in liabilities recognized and measured in conformity with generally accepted accounting principles that results from those types of profit-directed activities of an enterprise that can change owners' equity. Revenue under present generally accepted accounting principles is derived from three general activities: *(a)* selling products, *(b)* rendering services and permitting others to use enterprise resources, which result in interest, rent, royalties, fees, and the like, and *(c)* disposing of resources other than products— for example, plant and equipment or investments in other entities. Revenue does not include receipt of assets purchased, proceeds of borrowing, investments by owners, or adjustments of revenue of prior periods.[2]

At this point it may be advisable to return to Chapter 2 for a review of the *revenue principle,* with particular attention to when revenue is considered realized.

Expense may be conceptually defined as using or consuming goods and services in the process of obtaining revenues.[3] *APB Statement No. 4* provides a pragmatic definition as follows:

> Expenses are gross decreases in assets or gross increases in liabilities recognized and measured in conformity with generally accepted accounting principles that result from those types of profit-directed activities of an enterprise that can change owners' equity. Important classes of expenses are (1) cost of assets used to produce revenue (for example, cost of goods sold, selling and administrative expenses, and interest expense), (2) expense from nonreciprocal transfers and casualties (for example, taxes, fires and theft), (3) costs of other assets other than prod-

ucts (for example, plant and equipment or investments in other companies), disposed of, (4) costs incurred in unsuccessful efforts, and (5) declines in market prices of inventories held for sale. Expenses do not include repayments of borrowing, expenditures to acquire assets, distributions to owners (including acquisition of treasury stock), or adjustments of expenses of prior periods.[4]

At this point you should return to Chapter 2 and restudy the discussion of the cost principle.

Terminology Problems

The terms revenue, income, earnings, profit, and gain are often used rather loosely. The following distinctions will aid later discussions:

1. Revenue—resources received for goods sold (such as sales revenue) and services provided (such as repair service, rent, and interest revenue).
2. Income—a difference; that is, revenue minus expense.
3. Earnings—another term for income.
4. Profit—another term for income.
5. Gain—a net revenue amount derived from transactions that are indirectly related to normal operations, such as "gain from sale of operational assets." In practice, gains generally are broadly classified as revenue (even though gains are "net" flows).

Similarly, the terms cost, expense, and loss are troublesome; the following distinctions are widely recognized:

1. Cost—the amount of resources given up or commitments incurred to acquire goods and services which, at time of acquisition, are assets, such as, merchandise inventory, prepaid insurance, and operational assets.
2. Expense—the use of assets and services in the creation of revenue; that is, an expired asset. Thus, most costs subsequently become expense. Cost and expense may be the same, as in the case where office supplies are acquired and immediately used. In most instances, expense flows from cost, as in the

---

[1] Adapted from AAA Committee on Accounting Concepts and Standards, *Accounting and Reporting Standards for Corporate Financial Statements and Preceding Statements and Supplements* (Columbus, Ohio, 1957), p. 5.

[2] AICPA, *Statement of the Accounting Principles Board No. 4,* "Basic Concepts and Accounting Principles Underlying Financial Statements of Business Enterprises" (New York, October 1960), pp. 58–60. This definition is conceptually deficient primarily because of circularity; it starts and ends with GAAP.

[3] Adapted from Eldon S. Hendrickson, *Accounting Theory,* 3d ed. (Homewood, Ill.: Richard D. Irwin, Inc., 1977), p. 192.

---

[4] AICPA, *APB Statement No. 4,* pp. 58–60.

case of office supplies acquired and subsequently used over two or more periods.

3. Loss—an unfavorable effect (asset reduction) not directly related to normal operations, such as storm loss, loss on sale of operational assets, and loss due to theft. In practice, losses are broadly classified as expense (even though losses are "net" flows).

FORM OF INCOME STATEMENT

The accounting profession has not specified a particular format that must be used for the income statement because reasonable flexibility to fit various situations is considered more important than a standard format. A complete income statement is required that adequately reports all revenues and expenses. In addition, a number of *ARBs, APB Opinions,* and *FASB Statements* specify certain disclosure requirements that influence income statement presentation. Examples are presentation of extraordinary items, income tax expense, earnings per share, and items that are *either* unusual or occur infrequently.

Two different formats are widely used for the income statement, although there are numerous variations of each. These are generally referred to as the single-step and the multiple-step formats. A recent study of 600 major companies reported that 62% used the single-step and 38% use the multiple-step format.[5]

Single-Step Format

The single-step format focuses on two broad classifications: revenues and expenses. These two classifications are defined in *APB Statement No. 4* (see definitions quoted above). A single-step income statement is illustrated in Exhibit 4–2. Observe the three basic categories: revenues, expenses, and extraordinary items. It is called a single-step statement because there is only one step—income before extraordinary items—involving revenues and expenses. Exhibit 4–2 shows a "pure" single-step format;

---

[5] AICPA, *Accounting Trends and Techniques, 1978* (New York, 1978), p. 237. This is an excellent reference for learning how various companies report the multitude of different items on financial statements.

EXHIBIT 4–2
Single-Step Income Statement

ILLUSTRATIVE COMPANY
Income Statement
For the Year Ended December 31, 19A

Revenues:		
Sales (less returns and allowances of $10,000)		$540,000
Services		130,000
Rent		1,200
Interest and dividends		4,800
Gain on sale of operational assets		6,000
Total revenues		682,000
Expenses:		
*Cost of goods sold	$314,000	
*Distribution	153,500	
*Administrative	73,500	
Depreciation	54,000	
Interest	6,000	
Loss on sale of investments	5,000	
Income taxes	29,500	
Total expenses		635,500
† Income before extraordinary item		46,500
Extraordinary item:		
Loss (specified)	10,000	
Less: Income tax savings	4,800	5,200
Net Income		$ 41,300

Earnings per share of common stock (20,000 shares outstanding):

Income before extraordinary item	$2.33
Extraordinary loss	(.26)
Net Income	$2.07

* These items preferably should be detailed in the statement or separately in the notes to the financial statements or as separate schedules.

† Sometimes captioned "Income from continuing operations."

---

therefore, all revenues are grouped under one classification. This includes gains (other than extraordinary) such as the one illustrated. A gain is distinctly different from the other revenue items illustrated in that it reflects a net difference. That is, the $6,000 gain is the result of a transaction such as:

Cash received from sale of operational asset	$15,000
Less book value of the asset sold	9,000
Gain from sale of operational asset	$ 6,000

In contrast, most other revenues are reported at gross in the sense that the related expenses are deducted separately.

Consistent with the general classification of

revenues, all expenses are also included under one broad category. Included in the expenses is a *loss* which is distinctly different from the other expenses because it is a net difference, as illustrated above for the gain.

There are numerous variations of the single-step format, such as

1. Reporting income taxes separate from expenses (as a separate item immediately preceding income before extraordinary items).
2. Reporting one or more separate captions for certain revenues and expenses (such as *financial items*—interest revenue and interest expense; *other revenues and expenses*—in-

EXHIBIT 4–3
Multiple-Step Income Statement

MELON COMPANY
Income Statement
For the Year Ended December 31, 19A

Sales revenue			$600,000
Less: Sales returns and allowances			18,600
Net sales			581,400
Cost of goods sold:			
Beginning merchandise inventory		$152,000	
Merchandise purchases	$376,500		
Freight-in	1,200		
Cost of purchases	377,700		
Less: Purchase returns and allowances	12,200	365,500	
Total goods available for sale		517,500	
Less: Ending merchandise inventory		159,500	
Cost of goods sold			358,000
Gross margin on sales			223,400
*Operating expenses:			
Distribution expenses		110,000	
General and administrative expenses		43,000	
Total operating expenses			153,000
Income from primary			
operations			70,400
Other revenues:			
Rent	1,200		
Interest and dividends	4,800		
Gain on sale of operational assets	12,000	18,000	
Other expenses:			
Interest	4,500		
Loss on sale of investments	3,500	8,000	10,000
Income before income taxes and			
extraordinary item			80,400
Income taxes			31,166
Income before extraordinary item			49,234
Extraordinary item:			
Loss due to earthquake		10,000	
Less: Income tax saving		3,876	6,124
Net Income			$ 43,110
Earnings per share of common stock (20,000 shares outstanding):			
Income before extraordinary item		$2.46	
Extraordinary loss		(.30)	
Net Income		$2.16	

* These may be detailed on the statement or separately in the notes to the financial statements or as separate schedules.

terest, dividends, gains, and losses; and *other charges and credits*). When one of these three captions is used, usually it is located immediately above the caption, "Income before extraordinary items."

The single-step format enjoys wide use because the broad classifications make it very flexible. Classification problems are minimized, and the presentation is simplified. On the other hand, some accountants feel that more intermediary differences, such as *gross margin on sales,* should be reported for the convenience of the decision maker.

Multiple-Step Format

This format provides multiple classifications, multiple intermediary differences, and somewhat more detail. A "pure" multiple-step format is illustrated in Exhibit 4–3. Observe that the first major difference (between revenue and expense) is gross margin on sales, followed by income from continuing operations, income before taxes and extraordinary items, income before extraordinary items, and finally, net income. There are no broad classifications for revenues and expenses; rather they are reported under several different classifications. Those who prefer the multiple-step format believe that the multiple classifications communicate more effectively to the user. Critics of the multiple-step format cite its relative inflexibility, as evidenced by these common complaints: (1) difficulty in naming and defining appropriate subcategories of revenues and expenses, (2) separation of revenues and expenses into several categories implies a priority that is hard to defend, and (3) the problem of reporting service revenue when there is also sales revenue—inclusion of service revenue and "other" revenues with sales revenue distorts the intermediate amount, gross margin on sales.

Like the single-step format, the multiple-step format has many variations. However, the differences are above the caption, "Income before extraordinary items."

The diversity in income statement formats reflects efforts by entities to tailor the statement to their particular situations and indicates, in part, their conceptions of what should be communicated and how it should be communicated to the user. Income statements for actual companies are presented in the Appendixes to this and the following chapter for your study.

Manufacturing Situation. An income statement of a manufacturing company differs from others in the presentation of manufacturing costs. In a trading company, goods are purchased ready for sale, but a manufacturing company makes its own goods for sale. In the latter case, "Merchandise purchases" is replaced by "Cost of goods manufactured," and a statement of cost of goods manufactured is often prepared as a supporting schedule to the income statement.

If the Melon Company manufactured the goods sold, the cost of goods sold section of the income statement in Exhibit 4–3 would appear as follows:

Cost of goods sold (for a manufacturing firm):		
Finished goods inventory, January 1, 19A	$152,000	
Cost of goods manufactured (see manufacturing schedule) . .	365,500	
Total goods available for sale	517,500	
Less: Finished goods inventory, December 31, 19A	159,500	
Cost of goods sold		$358,000

A supporting schedule of cost of goods manufactured may detail the costs of production as follows:

Manufacturing Schedule

MELON COMPANY
Cost of Goods Manufactured
For the Year Ended December 31, 19A

Raw material:			
Inventory, January 1, 19A		$ 28,000	
Purchases	$196,400		
Less: Purchase returns	800	195,600	
Freight-in		900	
Material available for issue . . .		224,500	
Inventory, December 31, 19A		31,000	
Cost of material issued			$193,500
Direct labor			106,200
Manufacturing expenses (factory overhead):			
Depreciation—buildings		2,200	
Depreciation—machinery		15,100	
Fuel		20,900	

Insurance—buildings and machinery	480	
Indirect labor	16,100	
Repairs—buildings	1,920	
Repairs—machinery	2,800	
Taxes—plant and equipment	1,600	
Total manufacturing expenses		61,100
Goods in process:		
Inventory, January 1, 19A	26,800	
Inventory, December 31, 19A	22,100	
Decrease		4,700
Cost of goods manufactured		$365,500

Supporting Expense Schedules. Frequently, it is desirable to provide detailed information with respect to the summarized amounts shown on an income statement. Generally, this is best done with one or more supplementary schedules. One such schedule was illustrated above for manufacturing costs. A detailed schedule of operating expenses to supplement the income statement given in Exhibit 4–3 could be as follows:

MELON COMPANY
Schedule of Operating Expenses
For the Year Ended December 31, 19A

Operating expenses:		
Distribution expenses:		
Advertising	$32,000	
Salaries	35,000	
Commissions	31,000	
Freight-out	3,000	
Insurance on inventory	1,000	
Other selling expenses	8,000	$110,000
General and administrative expenses:		
Office expenses	4,800	
Office payroll	32,100	
Depreciation of office equipment	1,100	
Rent	2,000	
Bad debt expense	3,000	43,000
Total operating expenses		$153,000

SPECIAL PROBLEMS AFFECTING THE INCOME STATEMENT

Until the 1930s the balance sheet, as a statement of financial position, was viewed by the business community as dominant because the assets and the liabilities were considered the most important indicators of the potential of an enterprise. However, there was a gradual shift to recognition of the ability of the enterprise to generate income and cash as paramount. Consequently, the income statement began to assume a dominant role. Although the importance of cash flow has been largely overlooked in financial reporting, currently it appears to be coming to the forefront.[6]

Because of the importance attached to the income statement for several decades, the accounting profession has refined the concepts and accounting procedures for the measurement and reporting of income. In the remainder of this chapter, we will review the important income reporting issues on which the profession has taken a definite position.

DISCLOSURE GUIDELINES

Recall the discussions of full disclosure under the reporting principle in Chapter 2. This broad principle encompasses all external financial reporting. With respect to the income statement, full disclosure is particularly critical. There is a limit to the extent of disclosure possible in the income statement itself by way of titles, amounts, and parenthetical information. Therefore, the typical income statement includes a number of *notes to the financial statements.* Typically, these notes contain elaborations such as amounts, schedules, and written explanations.

Significantly, *APB Opinion No. 22,* "Disclosure of Accounting Policies" (issued August 1972) par. 8, states that "a description of all significant accounting policies of the reporting entity should be included as an integral part of the financial statements." Examples given are those related to basis of consolidation, depreciation methods, amortization of intangibles, inventory costing, accounting for research and development costs, translation of foreign currencies, recognition of profit on long-term construction contracts, and revenue from leasing transactions.

The primary objective of disclosure notes is the presentation of information that cannot be effectively communicated in another manner.

[6] *FASB, Statement of Financial Accounting Concepts No. 1,* "Objectives of Financial Reporting by Business Enterprises," pp. viii, ix, 15, 17–24.

Therefore, they must be viewed as an integral part of the financial statements. Generally, pronouncements of the profession on reporting specific items specify that they may, or in some cases must, be disclosed in footnotes when it is impractical to adequately present the information in the tabular portions of the statements.

DEPRECIATION

APB Opinion No. 12, paragraph 5, requires that *(a)* the amount of depreciation expense for the period and *(b)* the method or methods of depreciation used, be disclosed either in the financial statements or in the notes thereto. This requirement was instituted because depreciation often is a major noncash expense; therefore, it must be considered in assessing the amount of cash outflow that was needed to meet expenses. Also, since the amount of depreciation expense reported depends upon internal decisions of management rather than on solely external transactions, it is subject to considerable latitude. Statement users need to know both the amount of depreciation expense and the method of its determination in order to evaluate its impact on income, assets, and cash flows.

In manufacturing enterprises, much of the depreciation expense may be included in the ending inventory and cost of goods sold amounts; therefore, reporting depreciation by footnote is characteristic for these kinds of companies.

INCOME TAXES

Income taxes are assessed on profit-making corporations but not on sole proprietorships or partnerships. In contrast, the income of sole proprietorships and partnerships must be reported as income to the owners.[7] In turn, the stockholder must pay income taxes on dividends received; consequently, it is often pointed out that corporate income is subject to double taxation.

Income taxes paid by corporations are viewed as an expense (as opposed to a distribution of profits to the government), and because of their significant amounts, the matching and full disclosure principles must be fully satisfied. To meet these requirements, *APB Opinion No. 11,* prescribed two *separate,* and *distinctly different,* types of income tax allocations. These are usually referred to as:

1. Intraperiod tax allocation—This is an allocation of total income tax expense *within the period* to various components on the financial statements for the current period. This kind of allocation is discussed below (also see Chapter 9).
2. Interperiod tax allocation—This is an allocation of income taxes on certain items *between periods.* It occurs when there are items of revenue and expense on the income statement for the current period that, because of the tax laws, are reported on the income tax return for an earlier or later period. It gives rise to deferred income taxes which appear on the *balance sheet.* This kind of allocation will be discussed in Chapter 9.

At this point, we emphasize that these are different allocations of income taxes, although they are not mutually exclusive. Both types are required since each serves a different reporting purpose.

Intraperiod Tax Allocation[8]

The need for allocation of income tax expense *within the current period* (i.e., intraperiod income tax allocation) is specified in *APB Opinion No. 11* as follows:

> The need for tax allocation *within a period* arises because items included in the determination of taxable income may be presented for accounting purposes as *(a)* extraordinary items, *(b)* adjustments of prior periods (or of the opening balance of retained earnings) or *(c)* as direct entries to other stockholders' equity accounts.[9] (Emphasis supplied.)

---

[7] There are certain exceptions. For example, the income of a corporation that qualifies under Subchapter S, Internal Revenue Code, is taxable income to the owners rather than to the corporation. These are generally referred to as "Subchapter S Corporations."

[8] Intraperiod tax allocation is discussed in this early chapter because it is used in illustrations and problems prior to Chapter 9, where deferred income tax is discussed in detail.

[9] AICPA, *Accounting Principles Board Opinion No. 11,* "Accounting for Income Taxes" (New York, 1967) par. 51.

The concept underlying *intraperiod* tax allocation is that, in accordance with the matching principle, *the income tax consequences should be reported along with the financial effects of the transaction that caused the tax effect.* Thus, total income tax expense for the current period must be allocated to (1) income before extraordinary items, (2) extraordinary items, (3) prior period adjustments (retained earnings), and (4) direct entries to other stockholders' equity accounts to the extent that there are items in each category that affected total income tax expense for the current period. This last category is rare.

Exhibits 4–4 and 4–5 illustrate application of intraperiod tax allocation in two different situations. Note in Exhibit 4–4 that total income tax expense of $49,750 is allocated between income before extraordinary items (a tax of $31,350) and the extraordinary gain (a tax of $18,400). It

would be inappropriate to deduct *total* income tax of $49,750 directly from "income before income taxes" because that would understate income before extraordinary items and overstate income from extraordinary items. A similar distortion would occur if total tax is deducted directly from extraordinary items. Exhibit 4–5 illustrates intraperiod tax allocation where there is an extraordinary loss. Note that the tax saving resulting from the extraordinary loss is deducted from that loss.[10]

---

[10] AICPA, *Accounting Principles Board Opinion No. 30,* "Reporting the Results of Operations" (New York, June 1973), par. 26, states that unusual *or* infrequently occurring items (as opposed to extraordinary items which must be *both* unusual and infrequent) "shall not be reflected on the face of the income statement net of income taxes—or in any manner that may imply that they are extraordinary items." The *Opinion* also states that "amounts of income taxes applicable to discontinued operations and the gain or loss on disposal of the segment should be disclosed on the face of the statement or in related notes."

EXHIBIT 4–4
Intraperiod Tax Allocation—with Extraordinary Gain

Situation

X Corporation accounts for the period reflected the following:

1. Income before income taxes and before extraordinary items, $110,000.
2. Extraordinary gain (specified), $40,000.
3. Income tax expense, $49,750, applicable to all items.

X CORPORATION
Partial Income Statement

Income before income taxes and extraordinary items .		$110,000
Less: Applicable income taxes		31,350
Income before extraordinary items		78,650
Extraordinary items:		
Extraordinary gain (specified)	$40,000	
Less: Applicable income tax	18,400	
Extraordinary gain, net of applicable income tax		21,600
Net Income		$100,250

Computation of intraperiod
tax allocation:
Tax on ordinary income:

			Entry for income taxes:		
$25,000 × 17% =	$ 4,250		Income tax expense	49,750	
$25,000 × 20% =	5,000		Income taxes payable		49,750
$25,000 × 30% =	7,500				
$25,000 × 40% =	10,000				
$10,000 × 46% =	4,600	$31,350			

Tax on extraordinary gain:

$40,000 × 46% =		18,400
Total income tax allocated.		$49,750

Note, these are 1979 rates; they are subject to change by the Congress.

EXHIBIT 4–5
Intraperiod Tax Allocation—with Extraordinary Loss

Situation

Y Corporation accounts for the period reflected the following:

1. Income before income taxes and before extraordinary items, $110,000.
2. Extraordinary loss (specified), $40,000.
3. Income tax expense, $15,250, applicable to all items.

Y CORPORATION
Partial Income Statement

Income before income taxes and extraordinary items		$110,000
Less: Applicable income taxes		31,350
Income before extraordinary items.		78,650
Extraordinary items:		
Extraordinary loss (specified)	$40,000	
Less: Applicable income tax saving	16,100	
Extraordinary loss, net of applicable income tax		23,900
Net Income.		$54,750

Computation of intraperiod tax allocation:		Entry for income taxes:		
Tax on ordinary income:		Income tax expense	15,250	
Per Exhibit 4–4	$31,350	Income taxes payable		15,250
Total tax expense	15,250			
Total income tax allocated to Extraordinary Items	$16,100	(see Ch. 9)		

APB Opinion No. 11, paragraph 52, provides the following guideline for intraperiod income tax allocation:

> The income tax expense attributable to income before extraordinary items is computed by determining the income tax expense related to revenue and expense transactions entering into the determination of such income, without giving effect to the tax consequences of the items excluded from the determination of income before extraordinary items. The income tax expense attributable to other items is determined by the tax consequences of transactions involving these items. If an operating loss exists before extraordinary items, the tax consequences of such loss should be associated with the loss.

Other illustrations of intraperiod income tax allocation are given in Part B of Chapter 9.

EARNINGS PER SHARE

Earnings per share (EPS) is the relationship expressed by dividing *(a)* the portion of reported income available to the holders of common stock by *(b)* the outstanding shares of common stock (i.e., income less the claims of the preferred stock outstanding ÷ average number of shares of common stock outstanding). EPS is not computed for preferred stock.

Reporting earnings per share on corporate financial statements was optional prior to the issuance of *APB Opinion No. 9* in December 1966. In that *Opinion* the Accounting Principles Board stated "that earnings per share data are most useful when furnished in conjunction with a statement of income." The Board *strongly recommended* that earnings per share be disclosed in the statement of income. The *Opinion* also recommended the reporting of per share data amounts for *(a)* income before extraordinary items; *(b)* extraordinary items, if any (less applicable income tax); and *(c)* net income. *APB Opinion No. 15,* issued in May 1969, changed the recommendations to *requirements.* The latter *Opinion* also calls for two presentations of earn-

EXHIBIT 4–6
Calculation of Earnings per Share Under Increasingly Complex Cases

Assumptions	Calculation and Reporting of EPS
Case A: Assumptions: 30,000 common shares outstanding throughout the year; net income for the year, $96,000.	Net income . . . . $96,000 Earnings per common share ($96,000 ÷ 30,000 shares) $3.20

Case B:
Assumptions: 30,000 common shares outstanding throughout the year; income before extraordinary items, $96,000; extraordinary loss less applicable tax saving, $21,000; net income for year, $75,000.
	Income before extraordinary item $96,000
	Extraordinary loss less applicable tax saving 21,000
	Net income $75,000
	Earnings per common share:
	  Income before extraordinary item. $3.20
	  Extraordinary loss. . . . . (.70)
	  Net Income $2.50
	
	  $96,000 ÷ 30,000 shares = $3.20
	  21,000 ÷ 30,000 shares = .70
	  75,000 ÷ 30,000 shares = 2.50

Case C:
Assumptions: 30,000 common shares outstanding from January 1 through April 1, on which date an additional 10,000 common shares were sold; other data as in Case B.
	Income before extraordinary item $96,000
	Extraordinary loss less applicable tax saving 21,000
	Net Income $75,000
	Earnings per common share:
	  Income before extraordinary item. $2.56
	  Extraordinary loss. . . . . (.56)
	  Net Income $2.00
	
	Calculation of weighted average number of shares:
	
	  Dates Months Shares Product
	  Jan. 1–Apr. 1 . . . . 3 30,000 90,000
	  Apr. 1–Dec. 31 . . . . 9 40,000 360,000
	                        12 450,000
	  Average: 450,000 ÷ 12 = 37,500.
	
	  $96,000 ÷ 37,500 shares = $2.56
	  21,000 ÷ 37,500 shares = .56
	  75,000 ÷ 37,500 shares = 2.00

Case D:
Assumptions: 30,000 common shares outstanding from January 1 through April 1, on which date an additional 10,000 common shares were issued as a *stock dividend;* other data as in Case B (no additional shares were sold).
	Income before extraordinary item $96,000
	Extraordinary loss less applicable tax saving 21,000
	Net Income $75,000
	Earnings per common share:
	  Income before extraordinary item. $2.40
	  Extraordinary loss. . . . . (.53)
	  Net Income $1.87
	
	As provided in *APB Opinion No. 15,* when there is a stock dividend, the divisor is the average number of shares outstanding at year-end (including all stock dividends, as if they had been outstanding for the entire year). In this case, this is 30,000 + 10,000 = 40,000.
	
	  $96,000 ÷ 40,000 shares = $2.40
	  21,000 ÷ 40,000 shares = .53
	  75,000 ÷ 40,000 shares = 1.87

ings per share on the income statement: *(a)* primary earnings per share and *(b)* fully diluted earnings per share. These terms are explained and discussed later in this section.

Calculation of Earnings per Share. Earnings per share is discussed in detail in Chapter 18. At this point we will review only the fundamentals. To illustrate the calculation of earnings per share in simple situations, four separate cases are presented in Exhibit 4–6. These cases will provide sufficient background for the discussions prior to Chapter 18.

Case A—This is the simplest case. It involves only common stock with no changes during the year and no extraordinary items on the income statement. In such a situation calculation of earnings per share simply involves dividing net income by the number of shares outstanding, as illustrated in Exhibit 4–6.

Case B—A slight complexity occurs when there is an extraordinary gain or loss on the income statement. In this case, earnings per share amounts would be calculated and reported for *(a)* income before extraordinary items, *(b)* extraordinary items, and *(c)* net income, as illustrated in Exhibit 4–6.

Case C—Another complexity occurs when there is a change during the period in the number of shares outstanding because of the sale of common stock or the purchase of such shares as treasury stock. This complexity requires calculation of the weighted average number of shares outstanding during the year. The weighted average, calculated as illustrated in Exhibit 4–6, is divided into the appropriate income amounts.

Case D—Another complexity arises when there is an increase in the number of shares of common stock outstanding during the period as the result of *(a)* a stock dividend or *(b)* a stock split. In this case, since a stock dividend or stock split is considered retroactive, hence, outstanding for the entire period, the divisor is 40,000 shares, as illustrated in Exhibit 4–6. On this point refer to *APB Opinion No. 15,* par. 48.

Another level of complexity occurs when both common and nonconvertible preferred stock are outstanding. Beyond this situation are those where there are convertible preferred stock or convertible bonds payable (i.e., convertible into common stock). These complexities involve the concepts of common stock equivalents and fully diluted earnings per share. These topics are discussed in Chapter 18.

FASB Statement No. 21, "Suspension of Earnings per Share and Segment Information by Nonpublic Enterprises," April 1978, exempts corporations that are not publicly held from the EPS disclosure requirement.

EXTRAORDINARY ITEMS AND PRIOR PERIOD ADJUSTMENTS

Recall that extraordinary items are reported in a separate category on the income statement *(APB Opinions Nos. 9* and *30),* and prior period adjustments are reported on the statement of retained earnings *(FASB Statement No. 16).* These two types of items have been controversial for a number of years because *(a)* they are difficult to define precisely and *(b)* they reflect different concepts of income.

Reporting Concepts of Net Income

For a number of years, two different reporting concepts of net income have been prominent in accounting practice and literature. These concepts usually are referred to as the *current operating concept* and the *all-inclusive concept.*[11] Fundamentally, they differ with respect to whether unusual and infrequently occurring gains and losses should be included in net income and, consequently, reported on the income statement, or, alternatively, on the statement of retained earnings.

The *current operating concept* holds that in the measurement and reporting of net income, *only* the operating revenues and expenses should be included. Thus, the unusual (or nonoperating) and infrequently occurring losses and gains would be viewed as direct decreases (debits) and increases (credits) to Retained

---

[11] Some synonyms for *current operating* include "earning power," and for *all-inclusive,* "clean surplus" and "historical."

EXHIBIT 4–7
Current Operating and All-Inclusive Concepts Compared

Income Statement

Current Operating Concept		All-Inclusive Concept	
Operating revenues	$980,000	Operating revenues	$980,000
Operating expenses	(880,000)	Operating expenses	(880,000)
		Unusual or infrequently occurring items:	
		Gain—expropriation of plant by foreign government*	30,000
		Loss—earthquake damages	(10,000)
		Gain—damages received in lawsuit	80,000
		Loss—additional assessment of income taxes, prior years	(40,000)
Net Income	$100,000	Net Income	$160,000

Statement of Retained Earnings

Beginning balance	$ 75,000	Beginning balance	$ 75,000
Add net income	100,000	Add net income	160,000
Total	175,000	Total	235,000
Deduct:		Deduct:	
Dividends	(50,000)	Dividends	(50,000)
Unusual or infrequently occurring items:			
Gain—expropriation of plant by foreign government*	30,000		
Loss—earthquake damages	(10,000)		
Gain—damages received in lawsuit	80,000		
Loss—additional assessment of income taxes, prior years	(40,000)		
Ending Balance	$185,000	Ending Balance	$185,000

* Amount reimbursed exceeded book value.

Earnings and reported on the statement of retained earnings.

In contrast, the *all-inclusive concept* holds that in measuring and reporting net income, all operating revenues and expenses *and* all unusual and infrequently occurring gains and losses should be included. Under this concept, the statement of retained earnings, in addition to the beginning and ending balances, would report only the net income, or loss, and dividends declared for the period. The two concepts in their pure form are compared in Exhibit 4–7. This exhibit emphasizes the point at issue— *which* items should be included in net income? Observe that the current operating concept in this case shows a net income of $100,000, com-

pared with $160,000 under the all-inclusive concept.

Historically the AICPA has favored the current operating concept, whereas the AAA has preferred the all-inclusive concept. With the issuance of *Opinion No. 9* in December 1966, the APB took a compromise position which leaned strongly toward the all-inclusive concept. *APB Opinion No. 9* as amended requires that all of the unusual, nonoperating, and infrequently occurring items be included in the computation of net income and reported separately on the income statement, except for a very limited range of items called prior period adjustments. *APB Opinion No. 9* set forth the basic principle as follows:

Net income should reflect all items of profit and loss recognized during the period with the sole exception of the prior period adjustments described below. *Extraordinary items* should, however, be segregated from the results of ordinary operations and shown separately in the income statement, with disclosure of the nature and amounts thereof.

Under this approach, the income statement should disclose the following elements:
Income before extraordinary items
Extraordinary items (less applicable income tax)
Net Income[12]

The *Opinion* specified that the prior period adjustments should be reported on the statement of retained earnings and accounted for as direct debits and credits to Retained Earnings.

Extraordinary Items

Extraordinary items were defined in *APB Opinion No. 9;* however, the definition was imprecise, resulting in wide variation in application. As a consequence, the APB issued *Opinion No. 30* in June 1973. It was hoped that a redefinition of extraordinary items would correct the abuses that resulted from the reporting latitude that developed from application of *APB Opinion No. 9.* The definition of extraordinary items provided by *APB Opinion No. 30* is very restrictive, viz:

Extraordinary items are events and transactions that are distinguished by their unusual nature *and* by the infrequency of their occurrence. Thus, *both* of the following criteria should be met to classify an event or transaction as an extraordinary item:
a. *Unusual nature*—The underlying event or transaction should possess a high degree of abnormality and be of a type clearly unrelated to, or only incidentally related to, the ordinary and typical activities of the entity, taking into account the environment in which the entity operates.
b. *Infrequency of occurrence*—The underlying event or transaction should be of a type that

would not reasonably be expected to recur in the foreseeable future, taking into account the environment in which the entity operates.[13]

Two aspects of the above definitions should be emphasized. First, *both* criteria must be met. Thus, an item that meets *either,* but not both, does not qualify as an extraordinary item. Obviously, there are few extraordinary items. Secondly, in applying the two criteria, the *environment in which the entity operates* is often controlling. For example, earthquake damage usually would be extraordinary—it is certainly unusual and occurs infrequently in most parts of the world. However, if one were to locate a plant on a fault where earthquakes occur regularly, earthquake damage would not be an extraordinary item in that *particular environment;* the damage would be considered "usual or frequent." Thus, whether an event or transaction is extraordinary generally depends not on the type of event but rather *on the environment in which it occurs* (i.e., the situation). This basic point is overlooked in most discussions of extraordinary items; however, it is fully discussed in *Opinion No. 30.* The *Opinion* cites only three different kinds of events that usually would be classified as extraordinary: (1) a major casualty, such as an earthquake; (2) expropriation by a foreign government; and (3) prohibition under a newly enacted law or regulation.

The *Opinion* specifically states that the following *should not* be considered as extraordinary items because they result from customary and continuing business activities:

a. Write-down or write-off of receivables, inventories, equipment leased to others, or other intangible assets.
b. Gains or losses from exchange or translation of foreign currencies, including those related to major devaluations or revaluations.
c. Gains or losses on disposal of a segment of a business.
d. Other gains or losses from sale or abandonment of property, plant, or equipment used in the business.
e. Effects of a strike, including those against competitors and major suppliers.

---

[12] AICPA, *Accounting Principles Board Opinion No. 9,* "Reporting the Results of Operations" (New York, December 1966), pars. 17 and 20.

[13] AICPA, *APB Opinion No. 30,* "Reporting the Results of Operations" (New York, 1973), pars. 19–20.

f. Adjustments of accruals on long-term contracts.

Because of the widespread misunderstanding of extraordinary items, as defined in *Opinion No. 30,* we have included some specific examples in Appendix A to this chapter.[14] Additional examples are given in other chapters where the *APB Opinions* and *FASB Statements* single out a particular item for classification as an extraordinary item.

Reporting Unusual or Infrequent Items

In the discussion above, we referred to items that are *either* unusual or infrequent, but not both. They do not qualify as extraordinary items; however, the prevailing view is that they should be called to the attention of the statement user to fulfill the *full disclosure* requirement. Therefore, *APB Opinion No. 30* requires that they be reported separately on the income statement, viz:

> A material event or transaction that is unusual in nature or occurs infrequently, but not both, and therefore does not meet both criteria for classification as an extraordinary item, should be reported as a separate component of income from continuing operations. The nature and financial effects of each event and transaction should be disclosed on the face of the income statement or alternatively, in notes to the financial statement. Gains and losses of a similar nature should be aggregated. Such items should not be reported on the face of the income statement net of income taxes. . . .[15]

Items that are *either* unusual or infrequent, but not both, may be reported in a manner similar to the following illustration to meet the full disclosure requirement:

Income Statement

Revenues (not detailed)	$990,000
Expenses (not detailed)	878,000
Pretax income from continuing operations	112,000
Unusual or infrequent items (see Note X):	

Loss from disposal of long-term investment	$43,000	
Gain on disposal of machinery	31,000	12,000
Pretax income from operations and unusual or infrequent items		100,000
Income tax on operations and unusual or infrequent items		48,000
Income before extraordinary item		52,000
Extraordinary item:		
Loss due to earthquake damage (less applicable tax saving of $24,461); (see Note Y)		26,500
Net Income		$ 25,500
Earnings per share of common stock (10,000 shares outstanding):		
Income before extraordinary item		$5.20
Extraordinary loss		(2.65)
Net Income		$2.55

Notes to financial statements:
  Note X—details.
  Note Y—details.

Other formats can be devised to display the unusual or infrequent items in ways that meet the spirit of the above quotation from *Opinion No. 30.*

Discontinued Operations (Disposal) of a Segment of a Business

APB Opinion No. 30, "Reporting the Results of Operations," provides guidelines for disposal of a segment of a business that is sold, abandoned, spun off, or otherwise disposed. It requires that any loss or gain on disposal, less the applicable income tax effect, be reported separately as a component of income before extraordinary items. For this purpose the *Opinion* defines *segment of a business* as "a component of an entity whose activities represent a separate major line of business or class of customer." A segment may be a subsidiary, division, department, or other part of the entity provided that its assets, results of operations, and activities can be clearly distinguished physically and operationally, for financial reporting purposes, from the other operations of the entity. The *Opinion* does not apply to the disposal of assets incident to the evolution of the entity's business, such as the disposal of a *part* of a division, subsidiary, or line of business, or the phasing out of product

---

[14] AICPA, "Accounting Interpretations, APB Opinion No. 30," *The Journal of Accountancy,* November 1973, pp. 82–84.

[15] AICPA, *APB Opinion No. 30,* par. 26.

lines, changes in services, the disposal of one or more unrelated assets, or changes due to technological improvements.

To account for the disposal of a segment two dates must be carefully identified. The *measurement* date is the date on which the entity formally commits itself to dispose of a segment. The *disposal date* is the closing date of sale of the assets (i.e., when the segment is transferred) or the date that operations cease if the disposal is by abandonment. The measurement date typically precedes the disposal date; however, they may coincide.

On the *measurement date* an estimate must be made of the *total* loss or gain on disposal of the segment (net of income tax effects). The total estimate must include separate estimates of the gain or loss on (1) the segment assets and (2) segment operations between the measurement and disposal dates. When a loss is estimated it is recorded (accrued) on the measurement date; when a gain is estimated there is no accounting recognition until the actual gain is realized, which ordinarily is the disposal date.

To illustrate reporting of discontinued operations of a segment of an entity, assume Able Corporation unequivocally decided on July 1, 19G, to dispose of Division X, including the right to produce and sell its output, Product A, and that Division X meets the definition of a segment. The disposal date will be March 31, 19H. The fiscal year for Able Corporation ends on December 31. The following relevant information was available:

	Division X	Other Divisions	Total Company
January 1 to June 30, 19G:			
Pretax income (loss)	($10,000)	$100,000	$ 90,000
Income tax @ 40%	4,000*	40,000	36,000
Income (loss) net of tax	(6,000)	60,000	54,000
July 1 to December 31, 19G:			
Pretax income (loss)	($ 5,000)	$120,000	$115,000
Income tax @ 40%	2,000*	48,000	46,000
Income (loss) net of tax	(3,000)	72,000	69,000
Total year	($ 9,000)	$132,000	$123,000

* Tax saving

Able Corporation estimates the loss on disposal of Division X will be $40,000 (on disposal date). This amount includes an additional $2,000 loss from operations in 19H.

The income statement for the year ended December 31, 19G, would report the discontinued operations of Division X (disposal of a segment) as follows:

Able Corporation
Income Statement (partial)
For the Year Ended, December 31, 19G

Income from continuing operations, net of tax ($60,000 + $72,000)		$132,000
Discontinued operations (See Note 4):		
19G operating loss on discontinued division prior to the decision to dispose of the division, net of tax of $4,000	$ 6,000	
Loss estimated on disposal of discontinued division, including a $5,000 operating loss of the discontinued division during 19G after the decision to dispose of it and also including a $2,000 estimated operating loss of the division during the remaining disposal period in 19H (less applicable income tax saving of $18,000)	27,000*	33,000
Income before extraordinary items		99,000
Extraordinary gain, net of tax (Detailed)		10,000
Net income		$109,000

Note 4: On July 1, 19G the Corporation decided to dispose of Division X. For the six months ended June 30, 19G, the operations of Division X incurred a pretax loss of $10,000, as detailed in the income statement under the caption Discontinued Operations. For the six months ended December 31, 19G, Division X operations incurred on additional pretax loss of $5,000, which, in accordance with *APB Opinion No. 30*, was reported as part of the estimated loss on disposal of the Division. Consummation of the disposal is expected early in 19H.

* Computation:

Loss, July 1, 19G to December 31, 19G	$ 5,000
Estimated loss in 19H	2,000
Estimated loss on disposal date	38,000
Total	45,000
Less applicable income tax (40%)	18,000
Total loss on disposal	$27,000

Prior Period Adjustments

Prior period adjustments are accounted for, and reported as, direct charges (or credits) to Retained Earnings. This means that prior period adjustments never flow through the income statement, which suggests that they should be defined very carefully. *APB Opinion No. 9* (December 1966) defined them restrictively by providing four criteria, all of which had to be met for an item to be classified as a prior period adjustment. At that time these criteria served to move the income statement toward the pure all-inclusive concept.

The FASB moved close to the "pure" all-inclusive concept by issuing *Statement No. 16* (June

1977). This *FASB Statement* amended the paragraphs in *APB Opinion No. 9* relating to prior period adjustments. The definition of prior period adjustments was significantly narrowed to include only two items; *FASB Statement No. 16,* paragraph 11, reads:

> Items of profit and loss related to the following shall be accounted for and reported as prior period adjustments and excluded from the determination of net income for the current period:
>
> a) Correction of an error in the financial statements of a prior period and
> b) Adjustments that result from realization of income tax benefits of preacquisition operating loss carryforwards of purchased subsidiaries.

FASB Statement No. 16 requires that all other items of profit and loss recognized during the period be included in the determination of net income for that period.[16] Reporting of prior period adjustments is illustrated in Exhibit 4–8 (also see Chapter 17).

Prior period adjustments usually are recorded in specially designated accounts which are closed to Retained Earnings at the end of the period.

ACCOUNTING CHANGES AND CORRECTION OF ERRORS

Accounting changes and correction of errors are discussed in detail in Chapter 24. However, it is necessary to review them briefly here because a number of specific situations involving them are discussed in several intervening chapters. *APB Opinion No. 20,*[17] as a basis for specifying the accounting and reporting requirements, provides the following classifications:

A. **Accounting Changes:**
1. *Changes in estimates*—The use of estimates (such as in determining depreciation or bad debt expense) is a natural consequence of the accounting process. From time to time, experience and addi-

tional information make it possible for estimates to be improved. For example, an operational asset, after having been used (and depreciated) for 6 years, may realistically be changed from the original 10-year estimated life to a 15-year estimated life. Changes of this type are referred to as "changes in estimates" and are to be distinguished from an error or change in accounting principle.
2. *Changes in accounting principle*—Because of a change in circumstances, or the development of a new accounting principle, a change in the recording and reporting approach for one or more types of transactions may be desirable or necessary. For example, a change in circumstances may make it desirable to change from straight-line depreciation to sum-of-the-years'-digits depreciation. This would be a change in accounting principle, that is, a change from one acceptable principle to another acceptable principle.
3. *Change in the accounting entity* (see Chapter 24).

B. **Correction of Accounting Errors:**
Occasionally an error in the accounting system will be found. If the error is found in the same period in which it was made, the incorrect entry can be changed. However, when an accounting error is found in one period that was made in a *prior period,* correction is more involved. *APB Opinion No. 20* defines the latter type of error as resulting from the use of inappropriate accounting principles (including procedures); and the use of insupportable estimates, mathematical mistakes, oversights, and failure to properly reflect the economic essence of a transaction.

Each of the above items, except change in accounting entity, will be briefly discussed.

Treatment of Changes in Estimates

Revisions of estimates, such as useful lives of depreciable assets, the loss rate for bad debts, and warranty costs, are not considered to be er-

---

[16] The second prior period adjustment listed above—realization of tax benefits from preacquisition loss carryforwards—is beyond the scope of this text; it is discussed in texts devoted primarily to mergers and consolidations.

[17] AICPA, *Accounting Principles Board Opinion No. 20,* "Accounting Changes" (New York, 1971).

rors. Rather, they are identified as *changes in estimates* and are accorded a special kind of treatment. As a company gains more experience in such areas, there is often a sound basis for revising a prior estimate. *APB Opinion No. 20* specifies that in such instances the *prior* accounting results are not to be disturbed. Instead, the new estimate should be used over the remaining periods including the current period. Thus, a change in estimate is made on a *prospective* basis.

To illustrate, assume a machine that cost $24,000 is being depreciated on a straight-line basis over a 10-year estimated useful life with no residual value. Near the end of the seventh year, on the basis of more experience with the machine, it is determined that the total useful life should have been 14 years. Thus, the remaining life is now eight years. This is a change in estimate, and at the end of the current year would not require a correcting entry but only the following *adjusting entry:*

December 31, adjusting entry at end of the current year:

Depreciation expense	1,200	
Accumulated depreciation, machinery		1,200

Computations:

Original cost	$24,000
Accumulated depreciation to date ($24,000 × 6/10)	14,400
Difference—to be depreciated over 8 years remaining life	$ 9,600
Annual depreciation over remaining life: $9,600 ÷ 8 years =	$ 1,200

Treatment of Changes in Accounting Principles

Changes in accounting principles are the result of decisions by the management because a newly selected principle is deemed more appropriate than the principle used to date to measure net income and financial position. When an accounting principle is changed, a "catch-up adjustment" is required to reflect the effect of the changeover.

To illustrate, assume a company had recorded accumulated depreciation of $2,200 on a machine using the straight-line method. A change was made to sum-of-the-years'-digits deprecia-

tion (SYD); the amount of SYD accumulated depreciation would have been $3,400, indicating a "changeover adjustment" of $1,200. The entry to record the change for the period in which the change was made would be as follows:

Change in accounting principle (closed to income summary)	1,200	
Accumulated depreciation		1,200

The $1,200 debit should be reported on the current income statement between the captions "Extraordinary items" and "Net income." At the end of the period of change the usual adjusting entry for depreciation expense would be made using the SYD method (also see Chapter 24).

Treatment of Accounting Errors

Clearly, when an accounting error is identified it should be corrected immediately in a way that will reflect what the results would have been had the error not been committed. Thus, when an error is found that was committed in the *current* period, the accounts should be corrected prior to preparation of the current financial reports. Often this can be best effected by reversing the incorrect entry and reentering the transaction correctly.

When an error is discovered during the current accounting period that was committed during some *prior period,* correction is more complex, especially when two or more past periods are affected. In this kind of situation a *correcting entry* must be made to reflect the correct *current* balances in the *real* accounts (i.e., the balance sheet accounts) and the *nominal* accounts (i.e., the income statement accounts).

Opinion No. 20 states: "The Board concludes that correction of an error in the financial statements of a prior period discovered subsequent to their issuance should be reported as a prior period adjustment." And, as noted above, *FASB Statement No. 16* specifies this as one of the two permissible prior period adjustments. Thus, this type of error requires recognition of a prior period adjustment in the accounts and on the statement of retained earnings.

To illustrate, assume a machine cost $10,000 (with a ten-year estimated useful life and no residual value) when purchased on January 1, 19A. Further, assume that the cost was erroneously debited to an expense account. The error was discovered December 29, 19D. The following correcting entry would be required in 19D, assuming no income tax adjustment:

December 29, 19D:

Machinery	10,000	
Depreciation expense, straight line (for 19D)	1,000	
Accumulated depreciation (19A through 19D)		4,000
Prior period adjustment, error correction		7,000

Any income tax adjustment would be reflected in the amount of the prior period adjustment (see Chapter 24).

The Prior Period Adjustment Error Correction account would be closed directly to Retained Earnings on December 31, 19D. In effect, the adjustment corrects the January 1, 19D (beginning), balance in Retained Earnings.

STATEMENT OF RETAINED EARNINGS

A statement of retained earnings often is presented as a supplement to the income statement and balance sheet because it is needed to comply with the full disclosure requirement. However, many companies present a *statement of owners' equity* instead, which details all changes in owners' equity, including retained earnings. The latter statement is discussed in Chapter 5 (see Exhibit 5–3):[18]

The purpose of the statement of retained earnings is to report all changes in retained earnings during the year, to reconcile the beginning and ending balances of retained earnings, and to provide a connecting link between the income statement and the balance sheet. The ending balance of retained earnings is reported on the balance sheet as one element of owners' equity (see Exhibit 4–1). In accordance with *APB*

Opinion No. 9 and *FASB Statement No. 16*, the major segments of a statement of retained earnings are (1) prior period adjustments, (2) net income or loss for the period, and (3) dividends. An illustrative statement of retained earnings is shown in Exhibit 4–8.

EXHIBIT 4–8
Statement of Retained Earnings Illustrated

ILLUSTRATIVE COMPANY
Statement of Retained Earnings
For the Year Ended December 31, 19C

Retained earnings balance, January 1, 19C	$ 77,400
Prior period adjustments:	
Correction of accounting error from a prior period	(13,000)*
Balance as adjusted	64,400
Add: Net income, 19C (per income statement, Exhibit 4–2)	41,300
	105,700
Deduct: Cash dividends declared in 19C	30,000
Retained Earnings Balance, December 31, 19C (Note 7)	$ 75,700

Notes to financial statements:
Note 7. Retained earnings—Of the $75,700 ending balance in retained earnings, $50,000 is restricted from dividend availability under the terms of the bond indenture. When the bonds are retired, the restriction will be removed.

* If there were income tax effects, they would be reported here, per intraperiod tax allocation.

Restrictions on Retained Earnings

Restrictions on retained earnings limit the availability of retained earnings for dividends to the unrestricted balance. Restrictions may arise because of *legal requirements,* as in the case of treasury stock held (in some states); by *contract,* as in the case of a bond indenture; or by *management decision,* as in the case of "retained earnings appropriated for future plant expansion." When a restriction is removed, the amount then returns to the unrestricted balance. *Accounting Trends and Techniques, 1977* (AICPA), revealed that 73% of the 600 companies surveyed reported restrictions imposed by debt agreements, capital expenditures, treasury stock purchases, or contracts with outside parties. In years past, restrictions sometimes were reported as separate items on the statement of retained earnings (or balance sheet); however, in recent years they generally have been re-

---

[18] Occasionally the obsolete designation "earned surplus" is used instead of retained earnings. On this point AICPA, *Accounting Terminology Bulletin No. 1* (1953), recommended that "the term earned surplus be replaced with terms which indicate the source, such as retained income, retained earnings, accumulated earnings, or earnings retained in the business."

ported in notes to the financial statements, as illustrated in Exhibit 4–8. Retained earnings is discussed in depth in Chapter 17.

Combined Income Statement and Retained Earnings

The income statement and statement of retained earnings may be presented together in the form of a combined statement. The primary advantage is that it brings together related and relevant information for the statement user. The following is a typical format at the bottom of the combined statement:

Net income	$41,300
Retained earnings, January 1, 19C	77,400
Prior period adjustments (Note 6)	(13,000)
Cash dividends during 19C	(30,000)
Retained Earnings, December 31, 19C (Note 7)	$75,700

Notes to financial statements:

Note 6. Prior period adjustments—During the year, the company discovered that an expenditure made in 19A was incorrectly expensed. This error caused net income of that period to be overstated by $13,000.

Note 7. Restrictions—Of the $75,700 ending balance in Retained Earnings, $50,000 is restricted from dividend availability under the terms of the bond indenture. When the bonds are retired, the restriction will be removed.

ACTUAL FINANCIAL STATEMENTS

Throughout this chapter, we have used illustrative examples for instructional purposes. To enable you to gain confidence in understanding financial statements, we have included Appendixes at the end of this and the next chapter which present recent financial statements for two well-known companies. We have selected representative statements that use typical format and terminology. We suggest that you carefully examine these examples and relate them to what you have learned.

Appendix A—Characteristics and Examples of Extraordinary Items*

If it has been determined that the particular event or transaction is not a disposal of a seg-

* Source: Excerpts from "Accounting Interpretations—APB Opinion 30," *Journal of Accountancy,* November 1973, pp. 82–84.

ment of a business, then the criteria for extraordinary items classification should be considered. That is: Does the event or transaction meet *both* criteria of *unusual nature* and *infrequency of occurrence?*

Discussion. Paragraphs 19–22 of *APB Opinion No. 30* discuss the criteria of unusual nature and infrequency of occurrence of events or transactions taking into account the environment in which the entity operates. Paragraph 23 specifies certain gains or losses which should not be reported as extraordinary unless they are the direct result of a major casualty, an expropriation, or a prohibition under a newly enacted law or regulation that clearly meets both criteria for extraordinary classification. Events or transactions which would meet both criteria in the circumstances described are:

A large portion of a tobacco manufacturer's crops are destroyed by a hailstorm. Severe damage from hailstorms in the locality where the manufacturer grows tobacco is rare.

A steel fabricating company sells the only land it owns. The land was acquired ten years ago for future expansion, but shortly thereafter the company abandoned all plans for expansion and held the land for appreciation.

A company sells a block of common stock of a publicly traded company. The block of shares, which represents less than 10% of the publicly held company, is the only security investment the company has ever owned.

An earthquake destroys one of the oil refineries owned by a large multinational oil company.

The following are illustrative of events or transactions which do not meet both criteria in the circumstances described, thus should not be reported as extraordinary items:

A citrus grower's Florida crop is damaged by frost. Frost damage is normally experienced every three or four years. The criterion of infrequency of occurrence taking into account the environment in which the company operates would not be met since the history of losses caused by frost damage provides evidence that such damage may reasonably be expected to recur in the foreseeable future.

A company which operates a chain of warehouses sells the excess land surrounding one of its warehouses. When the company buys property to establish a new warehouse, it usually buys more land than it expects to use for the warehouse with the expectation that the land will appreciate in value. In the past five years, there have been two instances in which the company sold such excess land. The criterion of infrequency of occurrence has not been met since experience indicates that such sales may reasonably be expected to recur in the foreseeable future.

A large diversified company sells a block of shares from its portfolio of securities which it has acquired for investment purposes. This is the first sale from its portfolio of securities. Since the company owns several securities for investment purposes, it should be concluded that sales of such securities are related to its ordinary and typical activities in the environment in which it operates, thus the criterion of unusual nature would not be met.

A textile manufacturer with only one plant moves to another location. It has not relocated a plant in 20 years and has no plans to do so in the foreseeable future. Notwithstanding the infrequency of occurrence of the event as it relates to this particular company, moving from one location to another is an occurrence which is a consequence of customary and continuing business activities, some of which are finding more favorable labor markets, more modern facilities and proximity to customers or suppliers. Therefore, the criterion of unusual nature has not been met and the moving expenses (and related gains and losses) should not be reported as an extraordinary item. Another example of an event which is a consequence of customary and typical business activities (namely financing) is an unsuccessful public registration, the cost of which should not be reported as an extraordinary item. (For additional examples, see paragraph 23 of *APB Opinion No. 30*).

Consolidated
Results of Operations

Revenues
    Net sales . . . .
    Rentals and services . . . .

Costs and expenses
    Cost of products sold . . . .
    Cost of rentals and services . . . .
    Selling, general and administrative . . . .
    Research and development . . . .
    Interest expense . . . .
    Other (income) expenses, net . . . .

Income before income taxes . . . .
    Income taxes. . . . .

Income before minority interests . . . .
    Minority interests in net earnings of subsidiaries . . . .

Income before cumulative effect of changes
    in accounting principles . . . .

    Cumulative effect on prior years of
        changes in accounting principles . . . .

Net income . . . .

Per common share
    Income before changes in accounting principles:
        Primary. . . . .
        Fully diluted . . . .
    Net income including changes in accounting principles:
        Primary. . . . .
        Fully diluted . . . .
    Cash dividends declared:
        Common Stock . . . .
        Preferred Stock . . . .

Year ended December 31

1977	1976	1975 (000 omitted)	1974	1973
$1,625,852	$1,508,202	$1,426,988	$1,292,545	$1,167,006
895,774	804,511	738,619	686,458	649,275
2,521,626	2,312,713	2,165,607	1,979,003	1,816,281
864,651	872,054	792,533	651,868	616,558
543,678	549,870	537,548	465,235	442,321
704,701	614,114	594,985	579,561	539,062
118,096	94,281	84,990	74,200	52,371
58,644	59,570	63,835	55,543	48,207
(37,149)	(50,674)	(32,272)	(20,027)	(24,156)
2,252,621	2,139,215	2,041,619	1,806,380	1,674,363
269,005	173,498	123,988	172,623	141,918
118,100	78,900	53,900	80,900	62,467
150,905	94,598	70,088	91,723	79,451
7,285	4,571	4,148	4,558	7,490
143,620	90,027	65,940	87,165	71,961
—	5,617	6,551	—	—
$ 143,620	$ 95,644	$ 72,491	$ 87,165	$ 71,961
$5.35	$3.53	$2.72	$3.67	$3.10
5.09	3.40	2.65	3.53	3.00
5.35	3.75	2.99	3.67	3.10
5.09	3.60	2.90	3.53	3.00
.80	.72	.72	.72	.48
1.25	1.25	1.25	1.25	1.25

Notes to Consolidated Financial Statements on pages 118 through 123 are an integral part of this statement.
Cost of products sold, cost of rentals and services and selling, general and administrative expense for 1973 through 1976 have been revised to reflect the classification of certain expenses in a manner consistent with that followed for 1977.

Consolidated Financial Position

	December 31	
Assets	**1977**	1976
	(000 omitted)	
Current assets		
Cash and short-term investments...............	**$ 307,279**	$ 310,383
Receivables		
Current accounts.........................	**502,273**	446,783
Installment accounts (including receivables		
due after one year)......................	**92,391**	88,799
	594,664	535,582
Less: Allowance for doubtful accounts	**20,450**	20,721
	574,214	514,861
Inventories		
Finished...............................	**425,107**	369,973
In-process and raw materials	**167,040**	192,161
	592,147	562,134
Deferred income taxes........................	**72,385**	75,530
Prepaid expenses............................	**17,379**	16,635
Total current assets.........................	**1,563,404**	1,479,543
Rental equipment and parts	**662,483**	712,947
Less: Accumulated depreciation	**385,133**	371,668
	277,350	341,279
Property, plant and equipment		
Land.....................................	**25,003**	25,098
Buildings.................................	**252,325**	239,873
Machinery and equipment....................	**486,766**	486,265
	764,094	751,236
Less: Accumulated depreciation	**384,581**	373,844
	379,513	377,392
Deferred income taxes		
and future income tax benefits..................	**43,438**	54,075
Other assets	**77,091**	59,506
Total assets.................................	**$2,340,796**	$2,311,795

Notes to Consolidated Financial Statements on pages 118 through 123 are an integral part of this statement.

Liabilities and shareholders' equity

	December 31	
	1977	1976
	(000 omitted)	
Current liabilities		
Notes payable (principally international)..........	**$ 74,792**	$ 81,478
Current installments on long-term debt	**11,028**	20,212
Accounts payable	**105,026**	94,010
Accrued taxes	**109,005**	107,981
Accrued payroll.............................	**86,599**	76,763
Other accrued liabilities......................	**163,534**	136,672
Customers' deposits and deferred service revenue ...	**148,304**	186,976
Total current liabilities	**698,288**	704,092
Long-term debt (exclusive of installments due within one year)...........................	**514,201**	625,796
International employees' pension and indemnity reserves....................................	**60,901**	53,908
Minority interests	**44,121**	39,151
Shareholders' equity		
Preferred Stock—$1.25 cumulative convertible, $5 par value; authorized—2,000,000 shares; outstanding—297,884 shares in 1977 (312,865 in 1976).........................	**1,490**	1,564
Common Stock—$5 par value; authorized— 40,000,000 shares; outstanding—26,374,374 shares in 1977 (25,989,091 in 1976).............	**399,304**	387,006
Earnings retained for use in the business	**622,491**	500,278
Total shareholders' equity.....................	**1,023,285**	888,848
Total liabilities and shareholders' equity	**$2,340,796**	$2,311,795

Changes in Consolidated Financial Position

	1977
Working capital was provided by:	
Net income	$143,620
Items not requiring current	
outflow of working capital:	
Depreciation...............................	208,432
Net book value of rental equipment sold...........	35,312
Deferred income taxes	
and future income tax benefits	10,637
Increase in international employees'	
pension and indemnity reserves...............	6,993
Other	4,970
Total from operations	409,964
Increase in long-term debt	17,485
Sale of Common Stock	12,224
Other..	13,929
	453,602
Working capital was used for:	
Expenditures for rental equipment and parts	109,211
Expenditures for property, plant and equipment	86,654
Reduction of long-term debt	129,080
Cash dividends to shareholders	21,407
Other..	17,585
	363,937
Increase in working capital	**$ 89,665**
Changes in working capital:	
Cash and short-term investments	$ (3,104)
Accounts receivable..............................	59,353
Inventories....................................	30,013
Deferred income taxes	(3,145)
Prepaid expenses	744
Notes payable	15,870
Payables and accruals	(47,714)
Accrued taxes	(1,024)
Customers' deposits and deferred service revenue	38,672
Increase in working capital	**$ 89,665**

Year ended December 31

1976	1975 (000 omitted)	1974	1973
$ 95,644	$ 72,491	$ 87,165	$ 71,961
178,836	160,812	144,972	145,583
27,925	19,867	14,820	17,644
8,644	504	25,286	10,087
7,059	8,737	3,113	9,622
3,626	(4,866)	2,448	4,556
321,734	257,545	277,804	259,453
18,260	160,803	15,828	26,810
13,405	10,842	17,457	3,894
22,390	5,874	6,247	29,502
375,789	435,064	317,336	319,659
147,684	175,267	141,619	113,337
71,398	96,024	98,335	73,061
56,557	37,496	14,349	25,574
18,488	17,618	17,217	11,400
14,035	—	3,507	22,529
308,162	326,405	275,027	245,901
$ 67,627	$108,659	$ 42,309	$ 73,758
$121,740	$132,153	$ (64,442)	$ 14,016
21,436	(14,534)	55,503	64,383
(43,085)	(134,158)	220,590	80,417
21,788	12,822	14,232	(17,492)
(128)	3,788	(1,518)	(2,822)
34,216	140,059	(156,807)	1,962
(43,409)	24,914	(33,251)	(21,608)
(18,346)	(9,917)	(1,938)	(18,309)
(26,585)	(46,468)	9,940	(26,789)
$ 67,627	$108,659	$ 42,309	$ 73,758

Notes to Consolidated Financial Statements

Note 1 — Summary of Accounting Policies. Accounts of all United States and international subsidiaries and branches are included in the consolidated financial statements. Long-term investments in affiliated companies with 50% or less ownership are accounted for on the equity method.

Short-term investments are carried at cost which approximates market value.

Inventories are stated at the lower of cost or market. Cost is determined principally on a FIFO (first-in, first-out) basis except for United States paper and business forms and supply inventories which are stated on a LIFO (last-in, first-out) basis.

Property, plant and rental equipment is stated at cost. Depreciation is computed primarily on the straight-line method. Any gains or losses realized on disposition of properties are included in income. The estimated useful lives used in computing depreciation for properties are as follows:

	Years
Buildings	20 to 50
Machinery and equipment	4 to 20
Rental equipment and parts	4 to 5

Maintenance and repairs are charged to income. Asset and related reserve amounts are removed from the accounts for retirements or dispositions of property, plant and rental equipment.

Revenue from rental and maintenance contracts is included in income as earned. Profit on installment sales is included in income at the time of sale.

Pension costs are computed on the basis of accepted actuarial methods and include current service costs of all pension plans and the amortization of prior service costs over periods up to 30 years. It is NCR's policy to fund United States pension cost accrued.

The investment tax credit is accounted for under the flow-through method as a reduction in the provision for United States income tax.

Note 2 — Accounting Changes. On January 1, 1976, NCR aligned its foreign-currency translation practice with the requirements of the Financial Accounting Standards Board Statement No. 8 - Accounting for the Translation of Foreign Currency Transactions and Foreign Currency Financial Statements. As a result, the prior practice of translating inventory accounts at current exchange rates was changed to one of translating at rates of exchange (historical) in effect when the inventories were acquired. This change increased 1976 net income by $5,617,000, reflecting the cumulative effect of the accounting change on retained earnings at January 1, 1976. Restatement of years prior to 1976 was not practicable.

On November 28, 1975, NCR aligned its method of accounting for general and unspecified business risks with the requirements of the Financial Accounting Standards Board Statement No. 5 - Accounting for Contingencies, which statement prohibits the maintenance of reserves for general and unspecified business risks. As a result, NCR released its December 31, 1974 international operations reserve of $6,551,000 to 1975 earnings. If this accounting principle change had been applied retroactively, there would have been no effect on earnings in the years 1974 and 1973.

On January 1, 1974, the LIFO valuation method was adopted for United States paper and business forms and supply inventories; this change reduced 1974 net earnings by approximately $4,000,000.

Note 3 — Income Taxes. The provisions for United States and foreign income taxes are comprised of the following amounts:

	Year ended December 31	
	1977	1976
	(000 omitted)	
United States and foreign income taxes:		
Income taxes currently payable	$104,317	$ 90,473
Realized future income tax benefits	36,884	8,644
Tax effect of timing differences	(23,101)	(20,217)
Total provision for income taxes	$118,100	$ 78,900
Foreign income taxes:		
Income taxes currently payable	$ 77,346	$ 68,847
Tax effect of timing differences	(5,194)	(4,488)
	$ 72,152	$ 64,359

Income taxes in 1977 included $3,071,000 ($2,925,000 in 1976) of state taxes on income. The provision for income taxes in 1977 included investment tax credit of $16,799,000 ($6,885,000 in 1976).

Certain revenue and expense items in the Statement of Consolidated Results of Operations are recorded in a year different from the year in which they are recorded for income tax purposes. Thus, several significant differences exist between financial statement income and taxable income. In years prior to 1973, these differences resulted in financial statement loss carryforwards. Accordingly, anticipating that NCR would be profitable in future years and that the charges which resulted in the financial statement loss carryforwards would reduce future taxable income,

NCR recorded anticipated future income tax benefits. NCR has not incurred net operating losses for income tax purposes and, therefore, does not have tax loss carrybacks or carryforwards under definitions of the Internal Revenue Code.

The amount of United States income generated since 1972 has enabled NCR to realize large amounts of the anticipated future income tax benefits: the remaining balance at December 31, 1977, totals $17,191,000 ($54,075,000 at December 31, 1976). Large recurring timing differences, however, have resulted in continued significant cumulative differences between financial statement income and taxable income. The tax effects of these recurring timing differences are reflected in the Statement of Consolidated Financial Position in "Deferred income taxes" (current), and "Deferred income taxes and future income tax benefits" (non-current).

At December 31, 1977, the cumulative amount of undistributed earnings of international subsidiaries was $336,426,000. Since a substantial portion of these earnings has been reinvested, no additional income taxes have been provided other than incremental income taxes applicable to planned remittances.

Note 4 — Long-Term Debt. Consolidated long-term debt was as follows:

	Dates Due	December 31 1977	1976
		(000 omitted)	
Sinking Fund Debentures			
3.375-5.60%	1978-1991	$104,235	$116,737
7.70%	1980-1994	75,299	94,348
9.75%	1986-2000	—	75,000
6.00% Subordinated			
Convertible Debentures	1985-1995	150,000	150,000
9.00% Notes	1985	75,000	75,000
8.25% Note	1978-1996	8,433	8,808
5.25-6.00% Swiss Franc Bonds	1980-1984	23,555	36,703
4.00% U.K. Sterling/Dollar Convertible Guaranteed Loan Stock	1993-1998	10,920	9,900
8.50% U.K. Sterling Guaranteed Loan Stock	1993-1998	10,920	9,900
Lease obligations 4.64-8.13%	1978-2007	37,205	31,207
Mortgages and other		29,662	38,405
		525,229	646,008
Less current installments		11,028	20,212
		$514,201	$625,796

Principal payments required on long-term debt during the next five years are $14,228,000 in 1979, $20,374,000 in 1980, $26,538,000 in 1981, $26,040,000 in 1982 and $18,171,000 in 1983.

The 6.00% Subordinated Convertible Debentures are convertible, unless previously called for redemption, into Common Stock on or before May 1, 1985, at a conversion price of $65 per share.

The 4.00% U.K. Sterling/Dollar Convertible Guaranteed Loan Stock is convertible through December 31, 1980, into shares of Common Stock at the rate of one share of Common Stock, at a conversion price of $70.80, for each £29.50 nominal value of such loan stock surrendered for conversion.

Note 5 — Common Stock and Earnings Retained. Changes in Common Stock and earnings retained were as follows:

	Number of Shares	Common Stock ($5 par)	Earnings Retained for use in the Business
		(000 omitted)	
Balance January 1, 1976	24,033,839	$361,002	$435,606
Acquisition of Data Pathing Incorporated (DPI)	1,358,000	13,284	(12,484)
Net income			95,644
Issue of Common Stock to employees under stock purchase and option plans	506,951	12,185	
Conversion of Preferred Stock	23,015	115	
Exercise of warrants issued in acquisition of DPI	67,286	420	
Cash dividends declared: Common Stock ($.72 per share)			(18,088)
Preferred Stock ($1.25 per share)			(400)
Balance January 1, 1977	25,989,091	387,006	500,278
Net income			143,620
Issue of Common Stock to employees under stock purchase and option plans	370,302	12,224	
Conversion of Preferred Stock	14,981	74	
Cash dividends declared: Common Stock ($.80 per share)			(21,026)
Preferred Stock ($1.25 per share)			(381)
Balance December 31, 1977	26,374,374	$399,304	$622,491

At December 31, 1977, there were 5,689,555 shares of Common Stock reserved for future issuance including 2,307,693 for conversion of the 6% Subordinated Convertible Debentures, 203,390 for conversion of the 4% U.K. Sterling/Dollar Convertible Guaranteed Loan Stock, 2,880,588 for various stock option and stock purchase plans and 297,884 for conversion of Preferred Stock.

Note 6 — Employee Stock Purchase and Option Plans. On April 20, 1977, the shareholders approved the 1977 NCR Employee Stock Purchase Plan. An aggregate of 2,000,000 shares of Common Stock were reserved for purchase during the five-year period of this Plan which commenced August 1, 1977. The purchase price is 85% of the average market price on the last day of each six-month purchase period. Under a similar plan approved by shareholders in 1973 and terminated in 1977, employees purchased 433,038 shares at $24.12 per share in 1976 and 178,872 shares at $28.21 per share in January 1977, and 142,758 at $32.09 per share in July 1977.

On April 21, 1976, the shareholders approved the 1976 Stock Option Plan. A similar plan approved by the shareholders in 1966 expired on February 15, 1976. Under the 1976 Plan, options to purchase shares of Common Stock become exercisable one year after the date granted at the market price on the date of grant, and expire 5 and 10 years after the date of grant for qualified and non-qualified options, respectively. Non-qualified options granted to Officers under the Plan may include stock appreciation rights.

The following table sets forth a summary of activity in options during 1976 and 1977:

	Shares	Price Range
Shares under option		
January 1, 1976...............	401,735	$20.13-$59.06
Options granted (including 186,881 relating to the acquisition of Data Pathing Incorporated)	404,761	6.13- 35.63
Options exercised..............	(148,988)	6.13- 33.56
Options terminated	(46,689)	6.14- 59.06
Shares under option		
January 1, 1977...............	610,819	6.14- 59.06
Options granted...............	233,700	34.87- 44.63
Options exercised..............	(51,707)	6.14- 43.31
Options terminated and surrendered	(33,631)	6.14- 43.31
Shares under option		
December 31, 1977	759,181	6.14- 59.06

At December 31, 1977, there were 96,225 shares of Common Stock reserved for granting future options and options were exercisable to purchase 506,367 shares.

In 1969, the shareholders approved the Executive Restricted Stock Plan. The last award of shares under this Plan was made in January 1970. At December 31, 1977, there were 54,238 shares contingently issued, of which 16,305 were fully paid.

Note 7 — Notes Payable (principally international). Notes payable classified as current liabilities at December 31, 1977, were principally debt instruments with banks with weighted average interest rates of 12.0% (14.2% in 1976). Average aggregate borrowing outstanding during 1977 amounted to $99,200,000 ($105,200,000 in 1976) with a weighted average interest rate of approximately 12.6% (10.8% in 1976). The maximum amount outstanding at any month end during 1977 was $117,200,000 ($123,700,000 in 1976).

Unused lines of credit for short-term financing by NCR and its subsidiaries approximated $311,500,000 at December 31, 1977 ($302,000,000 at December 31, 1976).

At December 31, 1977, certain available lines of credit required the maintenance of average compensating bank balances up to 10% ($8,400,000). In addition, average balances up to 30% ($4,500,000) are required on certain borrowings outstanding at that date.

Note 8 — Leases.

NCR as Lessee:

NCR conducts a part of its marketing and manufacturing operations from leased facilities, the initial lease terms of which vary in length. Many of the leases contain renewal options and escalation clauses.

The following schedule sets forth future minimum lease payments under non-cancellable leases as of December 31, 1977:

Year ending December 31	Capitalized Leases (000 omitted)	Operating Leases (000 omitted)
1978	$ 3,522	$ 22,693
1979	3,490	19,427
1980	3,457	17,371
1981	3,307	15,387
1982	3,098	14,104
After 1982	56,931	114,997
Total minimum payments required	73,805	$203,979
Less imputed interest	36,600	
Present value of net minimum lease payments	$37,205	

Capitalized leases included in property, plant and equipment were as follows:

	As of December 31 (000 omitted) 1977	1976
Land.............................	$ 1,109	$ 1,109
Buildings	22,594	21,854
Machinery and equipment	8,582	8,572
	$32,285	$31,535

Total 1977 rental expense for all operating leases amounted to $37,165,000. Rental expense for the preceding years (1976 through 1973) was $42,915,000, $41,470,000, $32,656,000 and $29,018,000, respectively.

Included under Operating Leases in the table are certain leases entered into prior to December 31, 1976, which will be capitalized in 1978 under Financial Accounting Standards Board Statement No. 13 - Accounting for Leases. Had those leases been capitalized, net property, plant and equipment would have been increased by approximately $45,000,000 at December 31, 1977 ($60,000,000 at December 31, 1976) and liabilities (primarily long-term) would have been increased by approximately $55,000,000 at December 31, 1977 ($69,000,000 at December 31, 1976). Net income for the years ending December 31, 1977 and 1976 would have been decreased by $1,150,000 and $30,000, respectively, had those leases been capitalized.

NCR as Lessor:

NCR offers its customers the option to lease over periods of 1 to 5 years certain equipment it markets. During the life of the lease, the equipment is maintained by NCR and the lessee may elect to purchase or upgrade the equipment.

Note 9 — Pension Plans. NCR and its principal subsidiaries have numerous pension plans covering substantially all United States and international employees. In 1977, $59,931,000 ($44,513,000 in 1976), including amortization of prior service liabilities, was charged to income for payment into United States pension funds and for payment to trusts and insurance companies or the creation of reserves as applicable to international subsidiaries.

The actuarially computed value of vested benefits exceeded the December 31, 1977 market value of the United States pension funds assets and the December 31, 1977 accruals by approximately $113,602,000. The unfunded prior service liability has been actuarially determined to be $190,264,000 as of that date.

Note 10 — Acquisition and Sale. On June 25, 1976, NCR acquired the business and assets of Data Pathing Incorporated ("DPI") in exchange for 1,358,000 shares of Common Stock. This acquisition has been accounted for as a pooling of interests. However, DPI's financial statements were not material and therefore are included in NCR's consolidated financial statements only since date of acquisition.

On August 5, 1976, NCR consummated the sale of a wholly-owned subsidiary, Electronic Communications, Inc. ("ECI"), for $19,000,000 in cash. This resulted in a gain of $2,134,000 which was included in the Statement of Consolidated Results of Operations in "Other (income) expenses, net." NCR sold ECI because its defense-oriented operations were dissimilar to NCR's business.

Note 11 — Replacement Cost Information (Unaudited). The replacement cost of NCR's productive capacity (principally buildings and machinery and equipment) at December 31, 1977, and December 31, 1976, would exceed the amount of the original investment (historical cost) due to effects of inflation on the current cost of these assets. The increased cost would be primarily related to the replacement cost of NCR's Appleton Papers Division's manufacturing facilities. Depreciation expense based on the replacement cost of productive capacity for the years ended December 31, 1977, and December 31, 1976, would be greater than the amount of depreciation expense reported in the results of operations during those periods; however, the effect on total depreciation expense would be offset by the reduction in depreciation charges related to the replacement cost of rental equipment. The replacement cost of NCR's investment in rental equipment and business equipment inventories as of December 31, 1977, and December 31, 1976, would decline due to cost reductions associated with advances in the state of technology which more than compensate for the effects of inflation in the general level of costs of personnel and productive capacity. Paper, business forms and supply inventories at December 31, 1977, and December 31, 1976, which were stated on a LIFO (last-in, first-out) basis would increase on a replacement cost basis. If the costs of inventory sold, exclusive of manufacturing depreciation expense, were adjusted to their replacement cost, the effect on 1977 and 1976 consolidated cost of products sold would not be material. Furthermore, operating cost savings in manpower and utility expenditures which could result from replacement of existing productive capacity with technologically superior equipment were not reflected in the replacement cost amounts. The replacement cost information should not be considered as plans by management to replace productive capacity, rental equipment or inventories. Additional information will be provided in NCR's annual report on Form 10-K filed with the Securities and Exchange Commission.

Note 12 — Industry and Geographic Area Information

Industry Segment Data

NCR operates principally in a Financial Accounting Standard No. 14 segment which includes the developing, manufacturing, marketing, installing and servicing of complete business systems for selected markets worldwide. The remaining part of NCR's business, although closely related, consists of smaller FAS No. 14 segments captioned as "Other" which includes paper manufacturing and sales activities, and another segment involved in the development and manufacture of specialty products utilizing microencapsulation technology. Total revenues include customer revenues as reported in NCR's Statement of Consolidated Results of Operations, and intersegment sales which are transferred at competitive prices.

For the year ending December 31, 1977, depreciation expense for the Business Systems segment was $201,461,000 and capital expenditures were $183,549,000.

	Business Systems	Other	Eliminations	Consolidated
	1977 (000 omitted)			
Revenues — Customer..........................	$2,250,411	$271,215		$2,521,626
Intersegment	—	12,297	$(12,297)	
Total revenues	$2,250,411	$283,512	$(12,297)	$2,521,626
Operating income	$ 279,507	$ 47,270	$ 177	$ 326,954
Interest and non-allocable general corporate expenses ...				57,949
Income before income taxes				$ 269,005
Identifiable assets	$1,897,464	$115,003	$ (1,869)	$2,010,598
Corporate assets				330,198
Total assets				$2,340,796

Geographic Area Data

Transfers between geographic areas are at prices designed to provide a profit after coverage of all manufacturing costs, research and development expenses, and general corporate expenses. Corporate assets are principally cash and marketable securities.

	United States	Great Britain and Continental Europe	Japan, Australia and Far East	Other	Eliminations	Consolidated
	1977 (000 omitted)					
Revenues — Customer.............	$1,271,013	$592,833	$355,032	$302,748		$2,521,626
Intercompany	257,381	34,227	47,725	38,852	$(378,185)	
Total revenues	$1,528,394	$627,060	$402,757	$341,600	$(378,185)	$2,521,626
Operating income.................	$ 206,691	$ 50,939	$ 49,282	$ 48,950	$ (28,908)	$ 326,954
Interest and non-allocable general corporate expenses........						57,949
Income before income taxes........						$ 269,005
Identifiable assets.................	$1,133,732	$462,009	$312,915	$260,302	$(158,360)	$2,010,598
Corporate assets..................						330,198
Total assets...................						$2,340,796

For the year ended December 31, 1976, international customer revenues totaled $1,133,391,000. Related 1976 operating income and identifiable assets (both before eliminations) were $140,362,000 and $941,317,000, respectively. These amounts have been determined on the same basis as the 1977 amounts shown above.

NCR's net investment in international operations was $457,585,000 at December 31, 1977 ($415,991,000 at December 31, 1976). Foreign exchange net losses originating during 1977 totaled $4,430,000; foreign exchange net gains during 1976 were $6,535,000.

Note 13 — Quarterly Data (Unaudited). The quarterly results of operations for 1977 and 1976 are shown below:

	Three Months Ended 1977				Three Months Ended 1976			
	March 31	June 30	September 30	December 31	March 31	June 30	September 30	December 31
	(000 omitted, except per share figures)							
Sales, rentals and services	$515,267	$627,775	$604,245	$774,339	$471,111	$556,252	$569,504	$715,846
Cost of products sold, rentals and services.	$298,568	$346,320	$340,893	$422,548	$291,515	$341,538	$346,065	$442,806
Income before cumulative effect of change in accounting principle	$ 16,609	$ 34,424	$ 33,322	$ 59,265	$ 7,607	$ 18,503	$ 25,049	$ 38,868
Net income.	$ 16,609	$ 34,424	$ 33,322	$ 59,265	$ 13,224	$ 18,503	$ 25,049	$ 38,868
Per common share								
Income before change in accounting principle:								
Primary.	$ .62	$1.29	$1.24	$2.20	$ .31	$ .75	$ .97	$1.50
Fully diluted	.61	1.23	1.18	2.07	.31	.74	.94	1.41
Net income including change in accounting principle:								
Primary.	.62	1.29	1.24	2.20	.54	.75	.96	1.50
Fully diluted	.61	1.23	1.18	2.07	.54	.72	.93	1.41
Dividends paid	.18	.20	.20	.20	.18	.18	.18	.18

Cost of products sold, rentals and services for 1976 have been revised to reflect the classification of certain expenses in a manner consistent with that followed for 1977.

Report of Independent Accountants

To the Shareholders of NCR Corporation

We have examined the consolidated statements of financial position of NCR Corporation and its subsidiaries as of December 31, 1977 and 1976, and the consolidated statements of results of operations and of changes in financial position for each of the five years in the period ended December 31, 1977 (pages 28-39). Our examinations were made in accordance with generally accepted auditing standards and accordingly included such tests of the accounting records and such other auditing procedures as we considered necessary in the circumstances.

As described in Note 2 to the consolidated financial statements, in 1976 the method of accounting for the translation of foreign currency transactions and foreign currency financial statements was aligned with the requirements of Statement No. 8 of the Financial Accounting Standards Board.

In our opinion, the consolidated financial statements examined by us present fairly the financial position of NCR Corporation and its subsidiaries at December 31, 1977 and 1976, and the results of their operations and the changes in their financial position for the two years ended December 31, 1977, in conformity with generally accepted accounting principles consistently applied during the period subsequent to the change, with which we concur, made as of January 1, 1976, referred to in the preceding paragraph. Also, in our opinion, the consolidated statements of results of operations and of changes in financial position for each of the three years in the period ended December 31, 1975, which have been prepared from the applicable statements covered by our opinions in each of those years, present fairly the financial information included therein.

Columbus, Ohio
January 19, 1978

Price Waterhouse Co.

QUESTIONS

1. The income statement is a *general-purpose* statement. What does this mean?

2. Explain briefly how the income statement is a connecting link between the beginning and ending balance sheets.

3. Briefly explain the economist's definition of income. How does the accountant define income as reflected by the completed transactions approach?

4. Define revenue. Compare the conceptual view with the pragmatic definition provided by *APB Statement No. 4.*

5. Define expense. Compare the conceptual view with the pragmatic definition provided by *APB Statement No. 4.*

6. Distinguish between cost, expense, and loss.

7. Briefly explain the two "pure" formats used for income statements. Explain why actual income statements are usually somewhere between these two formats.

8. What is the basic difference between an income statement for a trading company and a manufacturing company?

9. Explain the financial reporting principle, including its full disclosure aspect. (Refer to Chapter 2.)

10. Explain why the total amount of depreciation expense should be disclosed in the financial statement.

11. Briefly distinguish between intraperiod and interperiod tax allocation.

12. Explain why the matching principle requires intraperiod tax allocation.

13. Define earnings per share. Why it is required as an integral part of the income statement? What amounts must be reported on the income statement?

14. Explain the difference between the all-inclusive and the current operating concepts of income.

15. Define an extraordinary item. How should extraordinary items be reported on *(a)* a single-step and *(b)* a multiple-step income statement?

16. How are items that are either unusual or infrequent, but not both, reported on the income statement?

17. Define prior period adjustments. How are prior period adjustments accounted for and reported on the financial statements?

18. What are the four types of changes discussed in *APB Opinion No. 20?* Define what is meant by *(a)* a change due to accounting error and *(b)* a change in estimate.

19. Explain the basic approach in accounting and reporting *(a)* accounting errors and *(b)* changes in estimates.

20. What items are reported on a statement of retained earnings? Explain how it provides a link between the current income statement and the balance sheet.

21. What is meant by restrictions on retained earnings? How are they usually reported?

DECISION CASE 4–1

The president of Round Rock School Supply Company, a wholesaler, presents you with a comparison of distribution costs for two salespersons and wants to know if you think their compensation plan is working to the detriment of the company. The president supplies you with the following data:

	Salesperson	
	McKinney	*Sim*
Gross sales	$247,000	$142,000
Sales returns	17,000	2,000
Cost of goods sold	180,000	100,000
Reimbursed expenses (e.g., entertainment)	5,500	2,100
Other direct charges (e.g., samples distributed)	4,000	450
Commission rate on gross sales dollars	5%	5%

Required:

1. A salesperson's compensation plan encourages one to work to increase the measure of performance to which compensation is related. List the questionable sales practices by a salesperson that might be encouraged by basing commissions on gross sales.

2. *a.* What evidence that the compensation plan may be working to the detriment of the company can be found in the data?

   b. What other information should the president obtain before reaching definite conclusions about this particular situation? Why?

   (AICPA adapted)

DECISION CASE 4–2

J. B. Jacobson opened a small retail cash-and-carry grocery business with an investment of $1,000 cash, $5,000 merchandise, and a lot and building valued at $18,000. Fixtures were obtained by signing a note, payable in equal installments over a 36-month period. Cash is paid for all merchandise purchases, and Jacobson maintains no formal accounting records. When asked how one knew how well one was doing and where one stood, Jacobson made the following statement: "As long as I do not buy or sell anything except merchandise and that remains fairly constant, I can judge my profit or loss by the increase or decrease in my bank balance."

Required:

Evaluate Jacobson's statement in light of the facts known.

DECISION CASE 4–3

Generally accepted accounting principles define income as Revenue minus Expense equals Income. This model requires that revenue and expense be identified and carefully measured. Also, it requires a careful correspondence between revenue and expense.

Required:

1. What principle, or principles, govern identification and measurement of revenues?
2. What principle, or principles, govern identification and measurement of expenses?
3. Identify and explain some of the troublesome problems in applying the principles identified in 1 and 2.
4. What guidelines govern identification and measurement of extraordinary items? Do you agree with these guidelines? Explain.
5. What guidelines govern identification and measurement of prior period adjustments? Do you agree with these guidelines? Explain.
6. What guidelines govern reporting of items that are either unusual or infrequent, but not both? Do you agree with these guidelines? Explain.

EXERCISES

Exercise 4–1

For each of the following transactions, state (1) when revenue and/or expense should be recognized and (2) the amount. Explain the basis for your decision. Assume the accounting period ends December 31, 1979.

a. On December 21, 1979, merchandise was sold for $5,000 cash. The buyer took possession of two thirds of the merchandise on that date. The balance will be picked up on January 3, 1980.

b. Services were rendered to a customer starting on December 27, 1979. The services will be completed around January 8, 1980, at which time $8,000 cash in full will be collected. Assume eight working days are involved of which two were in 1979.

c. During 1979 the company sold ten TV sets and collected $6,000 cash in full. The company gives a one-year guarantee. It is estimated that the average cost per set under the guarantee is $20. Assume by the end of 1979, half of the guarantees on the ten sets have been satisfied.

d. On December 31, 1979, a used truck was sold by the company. The truck had been used in operating the business and had a book value of $300. The sales price was $500, which was payable six months from date of the sale plus 8% interest per annum.

e. On December 27, 1979, the company received an income tax refund of $1,000 after four years of negotiations with the Internal Revenue Service.

Hint: Restudy the revenue, cost, and matching principles in Chapter 2.

Exercise 4–2

For each of the following transactions, state (1) when revenue and/or expense should be recognized and (2) the amount. Explain the basis for your decision. Assume the accounting period ends December 31, 1979.

a. On December 30, 1979, sold $4,000 merchandise; terms, 2/10, n/30.

b. On December 29, 1979, paid $10,000 for advertising in the local paper. The ads related only to a clearance sale that would run from January 1–31, 1980.

c. Performed services each working day for a customer from December 27, 1979, through January 5, 1980. Assume eight working days are involved. Cash collected was $2,000 (in full) on December 27, 1979.

d. Sold a used TV set for $100 on December 28, 1979, and collected $75 cash. The balance is due in six months; however, collection of the balance is very doubtful, and the set will not be worth repossessing again. It is now carried in the inventory of used sets at $60.

e. On December 1, 1979, borrowed $6,000 cash and gave a one-year, 10% note payable for $6,000. Interest is payable at maturity.

126

Hint: Restudy the revenue, cost, and matching principles in Chapter 2.

Exercise 4–3

The following items were taken from the adjusted trial balance of Fast Manufacturing Corporation at December 31, 1979:

Sales	$900,000
Cost of goods manufactured (including depreciation, $52,000)	550,000
Dividends received on investment in stocks	6,500
Finished goods inventory, January 1, 1979	45,000
Interest expense	4,200
Extraordinary item, major fire loss (pretax)	33,000
Distribution expenses	135,300
Common stock, par $10	200,000
Administrative and general expenses	113,000
Interest revenue	2,500
Finished goods inventory, December 31, 1979	51,300
Income taxes; assume an average 40% corporate tax rate	?

Required:

1. Prepare a single-step income statement (include EPS).
2. Prepare a multiple-step income statement (include EPS).
3. Which format do you prefer? Why?

Exercise 4–4

The following items were taken from the adjusted trial balance of Star Trading Corporation on December 31, 1979. Assume an average 40% corporate tax rate on all items (including the casualty loss).

Sales	$640,200
Rent revenue	2,400
Interest revenue	900
Gain on sale of operational assets (assume an ordinary item)	1,000
Distribution expenses	136,000
General and administrative expenses	110,000
Interest expense	1,500
Depreciation for the period	6,000
Extraordinary item: Major casualty loss (pretax)	15,000
Common stock (par $10)	100,000
Cost of goods sold	350,000

Required:

1. Prepare a single-step income statement (include EPS).
2. Prepare a multiple-step income statement (include EPS).
3. Which format do you prefer? Why?

Exercise 4–5

The following pretax amounts were taken from the adjusted trial balance of Dole Corporation on December 31, 1979:

Balance, retained earnings, January 1, 1979	$ 40,000
Sales revenue	291,000
Cost of goods sold	105,000
Distribution expenses	36,000
Administrative expenses	30,000
Extraordinary gain (pretax)	10,000
Prior period adjustment, correction of error from prior period, pretax (a debit)	20,000
Dividends declared	16,000

For problem purposes, assume the corporate income tax rates given in Exhibit 4–4 (including the extraordinary items), and 46% on the prior period adjustment.

Common shares outstanding during the year were 10,000.

Required:

1. Prepare a multiple-step income statement with intraperiod tax allocation and EPS.
2. Prepare a statement of retained earnings with intraperiod tax allocation.
3. Give the entry to record income taxes payable (assume not yet paid).

Exercise 4–6

The following pretax amounts were taken from the adjusted trial balance of Sun Corporation at December 31, 1979:

Dividends declared	$ 30,000
Sales revenue	300,000
Cost of goods sold	110,000
Operating expenses	60,000
Extraordinary loss (pretax)	12,000
Prior period adjustment, correction of error from prior period, pretax (a credit)	10,000
Common stock (par $5)	150,000
Beginning retained earnings, January 1, 1979	40,000

Required:

1. Prepare a complete single-step income statement. For problem purposes, assume the income tax rates given in Exhibit 4–4 (including the extraordinary items) and 46% on the prior period adjustment). Include intraperiod tax allocation and EPS.
2. Prepare a statement of retained earnings.
3. Give the entry to record income taxes payable (assume not yet paid).

Exercise 4–7

The following pretax amounts were taken from the adjusted trial balance of Stoner Corporation at December 31, 1979:

Sales revenue	$250,000
Cost of goods sold	115,000
Operating expenses	80,000
Extraordinary gain (pretax)	12,000
Prior period adjustment, correction of error from prior period, pretax (a debit)	22,000

	Shares
Common stock (par $10):	
Outstanding January 1, 1979	15,000
Sold and issued April 1, 1979	5,000
Sold and issued October 1, 1979	7,000
Outstanding December 31, 1979	27,000

Required:

Prepare a complete single-step income statement. Assume an average 30% corporate tax rate on all items (including the extraordinary item and prior period adjustment). Show computation of earnings per share.

Exercise 4–8

On December 31, 1979, the following pretax amounts were taken from the adjusted trial balance of Garza Corporation:

Sales revenue	$200,000
Cost of goods sold	106,000
Operating expenses	44,000
Extraordinary loss (pretax)	22,000
Prior period adjustment, correction of error from prior period, pretax (a debit)	10,000

Assume an average 40% corporate tax rate on all items.

Common stock (par $10):	
Shares outstanding, January 1, 1979	15,000
Stock dividend, shares issued on July 1, 1979	5,000

Required:

Prepare a single-step income statement. Show computations for earnings per share.

Exercise 4–9

The following pretax amounts were taken from the adjusted trial balance of Deakin Corporation at December 31, 1979:

Sales revenue	$160,000
Service revenue	50,000
Cost of goods sold	100,000

Operating expenses	75,000
Unusual item, gain on sale of major operational asset (pretax)	12,000
Extraordinary item, loss (pretax)	20,000
Prior period adjustment, correction of error from prior period, pretax (a debit)	5,000
Common stock (par $1), 20,000 shares outstanding	

Assume an average 40% corporate tax rate on all items.

Required:

Prepare a single-step income statement that meets the full disclosure requirements with respect to unusual items, extraordinary items, prior period adjustments, intraperiod tax allocation, and earnings per share.

Exercise 4–10

Stokes Company has a machine that cost $40,000 when acquired on January 1, 1974. The estimated useful life was 12 years with a residual value of $4,000. Straight-line depreciation is used. On December 31, 1979, prior to the adjusting entry, it was decided that the machine should have been depreciated over a 20-year useful life and that the residual value should have been $1,000.

Required:

1. Give the adjusting entry at the end of 1979 for depreciation expense. Show computations.
2. Give the correcting entry required at the end of 1979. If none is required, so state and give the reasons.

Exercise 4–11

It is December 31, 1979, and Tye Company is preparing adjusting entries at the end of the year. The company owns two trucks of different types. The following situations confront the company accountant:

Truck No. 1 cost $7,700 on January 1, 1977. It is being depreciated on a straight-line basis over an estimated useful life of ten years with a $700 residual value. At December 31, 1979, it has been determined that the useful life should have been eight years instead of ten, with a revised residual value of $900.

Truck No. 2 cost $4,550 on January 1, 1976. It is being depreciated on a straight-line basis over an estimated useful life of seven years with a $350 residual value. At December 31, 1979, it was discovered that no depreciation had been recorded on this truck for 1976 and 1977.

Required:

1. For each truck, give the correct adjusting entry for depreciation expense at December 31, 1979. Show computations.
2. For each truck, if a correcting entry is required, provide it and show computations. If no correcting entry is needed, give the reasons.

Exercise 4–12

The following pretax amounts were taken from the accounts of Sharp Corporation at December 31, 1979:

Sales revenue	$150,000
Cost of goods sold	85,000
Distribution and administrative expenses	45,000
Extraordinary gain (pretax)	15,000
Prior period adjustment, correction of error from prior period, pretax (a debit)	8,000
Interest expense	600
Cash dividends declared	5,000
Retained earnings balance, January 1, 1979	36,000
Common stock (par $5), 20,000 shares outstanding.	

Assume an average 40% corporate tax rate on all items. Assume the extraordinary gain is subject to tax at the average rate.

Required:

Prepare a combined single-step income statement and statement of retained earnings, including intraperiod income tax allocation and earnings per share. Show computations.

PROBLEMS

Problem 4–1

Below is listed a number of transactions and amounts that are reported on the annual financial statement. For each item, you are to indicate how it usually should be reported. A list of responses is given so you can indicate your response by *code letter*. Enter only one letter for each item. You should comment on doubtful items.

Code	Classification
A.	Balance sheet, appropriately classified.
	Income statement:
B.	Revenue
C.	Expense
D.	Unusual or infrequent, but not both
E.	Extraordinary item
	Statement of retained earnings:
F.	Prior period adjustment (as an addition or deduction)
G.	Addition to retained earnings
H.	Deduction from retained earnings
I.	Note to the financial statement

1. _____ Total amount of cash and credit sales for the period.
2. _____ Allowance for doubtful accounts.
3. _____ Gain on sale of operational asset.
4. _____ Hurricane damages.
5. _____ Payment of $30,000 additional income tax assessment (on prior year's income).
6. _____ Earthquake damages.
7. _____ Distribution expenses.
8. _____ Estimated warranties payable.
9. _____ Gain on disposal of long-term investments in stocks.
10. _____ Net income for the period.
11. _____ Insurance gain on major casualty (fire) — insurance proceeds exceeded the book value of the assets destroyed.
12. _____ Cash dividends declared and paid.
13. _____ Rent collected on office space temporarily leased.
14. _____ Interest paid plus interest accrued on liabilities.
15. _____ Dividends received on stocks held as an investment.
16. _____ Damages paid as a result of a lawsuit by an individual injured while shopping in the store; the litigation covered three years.
17. _____ Loss due to expropriation of a plant in a foreign country.
18. _____ A $10,000 bad debt—the receivable had been outstanding for five years and the party cannot be located.
19. _____ Adjustment due to correction of an error made two years earlier.
20. _____ On December 31 of current year, paid rent expense in advance for the next year.
21. _____ Cost of goods sold.
22. _____ Interest collected from a customer on a ninety day note receivable.
23. _____ Year-end bonus of $50,000 paid to employees for performance during the year.

Problem 4–2

During the current year, 1979, XY Company completed a number of transactions that posed questions as to when revenue and/or expense should be recognized. The end of the accounting period is December

31. For each of the following selected transactions, state when revenue and/or expense should be recognized and give the basis for your decision.

a. Merchandise was sold on credit during 1979. The terms were 25% down payment plus six monthly payments. The collection experience on such sales, although not as good as on regular credit sales (due at end of month of sale), has been quite satisfactory.

b. On December 24, 1979, the company sold a used TV set that had been repossessed and was set up in used goods inventory at $60. The sales price was $110. At the date of sale, $70 cash was collected with the balance due in six months. There is a high probability that collection will not be made and the TV set probably will not be worth repossessing again.

c. During 1979 the company sold 30 TV sets for a total of $6,000 and collected cash in full. The sets are guaranteed for 12 months from date of sale. It is estimated that the guarantee will cost the company, on the average, $15 per set. At year-end, it was estimated that half of the guarantees were still outstanding.

d. On December 14, 1979, received a $20,000 income tax refund from prior years. The negotiations extended over a three-year period.

e. Services were rendered to a customer starting on December 28, 1979, and will be completed January 6, 1980. Cash in full ($5,000) will be collected at date of completion of the services. Assume eight working days.

f. On July 1, 1979, paid a two-year insurance premium in advance, $600.

g. On December 30, 1979, sold merchandise for $5,000; terms, 2/10, n/30.

h. On December 1, 1979, sold a customer merchandise for $1,000. Collected $600 cash and received a $400, 9% note for the remainder, principal plus interest due in three months.

i. On November 15, 1979, the court assessed damages against the company amounting to $25,000 cash. The suit was filed in 1977 as a result of an accident in the company store. Payment will be made on January 10, 1980.

j. On December 23, 1979, purchased merchandise for resale that cost $18,000; terms, 2/10, n/30.

Hint: Restudy the revenue, cost, and matching principles in Chapter 2.

Problem 4–3

During the past year, an independent CPA encountered the following situations that caused serious concern as to proper classification on the financial statements of certain clients. Assume all amounts are material.

a. A client was assessed additional income taxes of $100,000 plus $10,000 interest related to the past three years.

b. A client suffered a major casualty loss (a fire) amounting to $50,000. The client occasionally experiences a fire, but this was the largest such loss ever experienced by the client company.

c. A client company paid $175,000 damages levied by the courts as a result of an injury to a customer, on the company premises, three years earlier.

d. A client sold a large operational asset and reported a gain of $40,000.

e. The major supplier of raw materials to a client company experienced a prolonged strike. As a result, the client company reported a loss of $150,000. This is the first such loss; however, the client has three major suppliers and strikes are not unusual in those industries.

f. A client owns several large blocks of common stock in other corporations. The stock has been held for a number of years and is viewed as a long-term investment. During the past year 20% of the stock was sold to meet an unusual cash demand. Additional sales of the stock are not anticipated.

Required:

1. For each transaction indicate how the financial effects should be classified; that is, classify as (a) ordinary and typical business operations; (b) unusual or infrequent, but not both; (c) extraordinary; or (d) prior period adjustment.

2. Explain the basis for your decision for each situation.

3. Briefly define each of the four categories (listed in Requirement 1) and explain how the effects of each should be reported.

Problem 4–4

The following data were taken from the adjusted trial balance of Super Corporation at December 31, 1979:

Merchandise inventory, January 1, 1979	$ 71,000
Purchases	121,400
Sales	395,000
Purchase returns	3,400
Sales returns	5,000
Common stock (par $10)	200,000
Depreciation expense (70% administrative; 30% distribution)	50,000
Rent revenue	4,000
Interest expense	6,000

Investment revenue	2,500
Distribution expenses (exclusive of depreciation)	105,500
General and administrative expenses (exclusive of depreciation)	46,000
Gain on sale of noncurrent asset (an ordinary gain)	6,000
Loss on sale of long-term investments (ordinary)	3,600
Income tax expense (not including extraordinary item)	?
Extraordinary item: Major loss (pretax)	20,000
Freight paid on purchases	1,000
Merchandise inventory, December 31, 1979	88,000

Assume an average 40% corporate income tax rate on all items (including gains and losses on assets sold and extraordinary items).

Required:

1. Prepare a single-step income statement and a schedule of cost of goods sold to support it. Include an EPS presentation.
2. Prepare a multiple-step income statement including EPS.
3. Explain the relative merits and disadvantages of each format.

Problem 4–5

The following information was taken from the adjusted trial balance of Rose Manufacturing Corporation at December 31, 1979.

Sales	$990,000
Purchases (raw materials)	150,000
Raw materials inventory, January 1, 1979	30,000
Work in process inventory, January 1, 1979	40,000
Finished goods inventory, January 1, 1979	20,000
Sales returns	5,000
Purchase returns	4,000
Freight on purchases	8,000
Distribution expenses	140,000
General and administrative expenses	92,300
Rent revenue	4,000
Investment revenue	3,000
Gain on sale of noncurrent assets, ordinary item (pretax)	6,000
Interest expense	9,000
Extraordinary gain (pretax)	40,000
Loss on sale of long-term investments, ordinary item (pretax)	10,000
Manufacturing expenses:	
Direct labor	230,000
Factory overhead	190,000
Raw materials inventory, December 31, 1979 ..	24,000
Work in process inventory, December 31, 1979	38,000
Finished goods inventory, December 31, 1979..	22,000
Income tax expense	?

Assume an average 40% corporate income tax rate on all items.

Required:

1. Prepare a schedule of cost of goods manufactured to supplement the income statement.
2. Prepare a single-step income statement including EPS. Assume 20,000 shares of common stock outstanding.
3. Prepare a multiple-step income statement including EPS.
4. Discuss the relative merits and disadvantages of each format for the income statement.

Problem 4–6

The following pretax amounts were taken from the adjusted trial balances of Davis Corporation at December 31, 1978, and 1979:

	1979	1978
Sales and service revenue	$200,000	$170,000
Cost of goods sold	80,000	70,000
Operating expenses	67,000	58,000
Extraordinary item, major casualty loss (pretax)	15,000	–0–
Prior period adjustment, correction of error from prior period, pretax (a credit)		10,000
Cash dividends declared	36,000	4,000
Stock dividend (July 1, 1978, see below)		120,000*
Balance, retained earnings, January 1, 1978		160,000

	Shares
Common stock (par $10) shares outstanding:	
January 1, 1978	15,000
Stock dividend, July 1, 1978	5,000
December 31, 1978	20,000
October 1, 1979, sold and issued	10,000
December 31, 1979	30,000
* Amount debited to Retained Earnings.	

Assume an average 40% corporate income tax rate on all items, including the casualty and prior period adjustment.

Required:

1. Prepare a comparative income statement, using single-step format, with columns for 1979 and 1978. Include earnings per share and intraperiod tax allocation. Show computations.
2. Prepare a comparative statement of retained earnings with columns for 1979 and 1978.
3. Give the entry for income taxes at the end of 1978.

Problem 4-7

Dollins Corporation is undergoing the annual audit by the independent CPA at December 31, 1979. During the audit, the following situations were found that needed attention:

a. On December 29, 1977, an asset that cost $3,000 was debited to operating expenses. The asset has a six-year estimated life and no residual value. The company uses straight-line depreciation.

b. Late in 1979 the company constructed a small warehouse using their own employees. The cost was $10,000. However, before the decision to build it themselves was made, they solicited a bid from a contractor; the bid was $15,000. Upon completion of the warehouse, they made the following entry in the accounts:

Warehouse (an operational asset) ..	15,000	
Cash		10,000
Miscellaneous revenue		5,000

c. Prior to recording depreciation expense for 1979, the management decided that a large machine that cost $128,000 should have been depreciated over a useful life of 16 years instead of 20 years. The machine was acquired January 2, 1974. Assume the residual value of $8,000 was not changed. Give the 1979 adjusting entry.

d. During December 1979 the company disposed of an old machine for $6,000 cash. Annual depreciation was $2,000; at the beginning of 1979 the accounts reflected the following:

Machine (cost)	$18,000
Accumulated depreciation	13,000

At date of disposal, the following entry was made:

Cash	6,000	
Machine		6,000

No depreciation was recorded during 1979.

e. A patent that cost $3,400 is being amortized over its legal life of 17 years at $200 per year. At the end of 1978, it had been amortized down to $800. At the end of 1979, it was determined in view of a competitor's patent, that it will have no economic value to the company by the end of 1980. Straight-line amortization is used.

Required:

For each of the above situations, explain what should be done in the accounts. If a journal entry is needed to implement your decision in each case, provide it along with supporting computations.

Problem 4-8

The following pretax amounts were taken from the accounts of Piper Corporation at December 31, 1979:

Sales revenue	$540,000
Cost of goods sold	280,000
Distribution expenses	105,000
Administrative expenses	70,000
Interest revenue	1,000
Interest expense	3,000
Unusual item—gain from sale of noncurrent asset (pretax; an ordinary gain)	19,000
Extraordinary item—loss on major casualty (pretax)	30,000
Balance retained earnings, January 1, 1979	93,000
Cash dividends	15,000
Prior period adjustment, correction of error from prior period, pretax (a debit)	8,000
Common stock (par $1), 50,000 shares outstanding.	
Restriction on retained earnings amounting to $25,000 per indenture agreement on bonds payable.	

Assume an average 45% income tax rate on all items.

Required:

Prepare a combined multiple-step income statement and statement of retained earnings including tax allocation and earnings per share. Show computations.

Problem 4-9

The following amounts were taken from the accounting records of Watson Corporation at December 31, 1979:

Sales revenue	$240,000
Service revenue	60,000
Cost of goods sold	130,000
Distribution and administrative expenses	125,000
Investment revenue	6,000
Interest expense	4,000
Infrequent item—loss on sale of long-term investment (pretax)	10,000
Extraordinary item—earthquake loss (pretax)	27,000
Cash dividends declared	8,000
Prior period adjustment, correction of error from prior period, pretax (a credit)	12,000
Balance retained earnings, January 1, 1979	78,000
Common stock (par $5), 30,000 shares outstanding.	
Restriction on retained earnings, $50,000 per bond payable indenture.	

Assume an average 45% income tax rate on all items.

Required:

Prepare a combined single-step income statement and statement of retained earnings, including tax allocation and earnings per share. Show computations.

Problem 4–10

The following financial statements have come to you for review:

FAST PRODUCTION COMPANY
Profit and Loss Statement
December 31, 1979

Incomes:			
Gross sales		$256,800	
Less: Sales returns		5,120	
Net sales			$251,680
Costs and expenses:			
Cost of goods sold:			
Inventory, January 1		98,500	
Purchases	$132,600		
Less: Purchase returns	2,780	129,820	
		228,320	
Inventory, December 31		102,300	
Cost of goods sold			126,020
Gross profit			125,660
Operating costs:			
Selling		38,000	
General and administrative:			
General	20,000		
Depreciation	8,800		
Bad debts	1,080	29,880	
Total operating costs			67,880
Income from operations			57,780
Other income:			
Interest income			970
Profit			58,750
Less taxes			28,720
Net			$ 30,030

FAST PRODUCTION COMPANY
Earned Surplus Statement
At December 31, 1979

Balance, at start		$267,600
Corrections:		
Additions:		
Depreciation overstated		3,400
Adjusted		271,000
Additions:		
Profit	$30,030	
Gain on sale of land	8,200	38,230
		309,230
Deductions:		
Dividends	30,000	
Loss on sale of machinery	9,650	39,650
Earned Surplus (carried to the balance sheet)		$269,580

Required:

Critically evaluate the above statements. What reporting concept appears to have been applied? Cite items to support your response. List and explain all of the aspects of the above statements that you would change in order to conform to appropriate reporting, terminology, and format.

Problem 4–11

The following income statement and statement of retained earnings were prepared by the bookkeeper for the Lax Corporation:

LAX CORPORATION
Statement of Profit
December 31, 1979

Sales income (net)			$ 85,000
Service income			46,000
Total			131,000
Cost of sales:			
Inventory	$ 34,000		
Purchases (net)	71,000		
Total		105,000	
Inventory		40,000	65,000
Gross profit			66,000
Costs:			
Salaries, wages etc.		36,000	
Depreciation and write-offs		7,000	
Rent		3,000	
Taxes		500	
Utilities		2,100	
Promotion		900	
Sundry		6,700	(55,200)
Special items:			
Gain on asset sold			6,000
Inventory theft			(2,800)
Net Profit			$ 14,000

LAX CORPORATION
Earned Surplus Statement
December 31, 1979

Balance, earned surplus		$27,000
Add: Profit		14,000
Correction of inventory		5,000
Total		46,000
Deduct: Fire loss	$13,000	
Dividends	10,000	
Earned surplus transferred to capital	5,000	28,000
Balance		$18,000

Required:

List each item on the above statements that you believe should be changed and give your recommendations on each with respect to appropriate reporting, terminology, and format.

Problem 4–12

Appendix B to this chapter gives an actual income statement and a balance sheet. Examine them carefully and respond to the following questions (for 1977 only, unless otherwise specified):

a. Are they comparative statements? Why are comparative statements usually presented?

b. Are they consolidated statements? What do you understand this to mean?

c. Is this a trading, financial, or a manufacturing company? Explain.

d. How many different kinds of revenue were reported? How many different kinds of expenses were reported?

e. How were interest expense and interest revenue reported on the income statement?

f. Was the total amount of depreciation expense separately reported on the income statement? If not, where was it presented?

g. Were any unusual or infrequently occurring (but not both) items reported on the income statement in 1976 or 1977?

h. Were any extraordinary items reported in 1976 or 1977 on the income statement? What were they? Were they net of tax?

i. Was there any indication of an accounting change? If so, explain how it was reported and what type of change it was.

j. How many earnings per share amounts were reported? Was there any explanation of the computation of EPS?

k. What "differences" were reported on the income statement? Gross margin? Income from continuing operations? Income before extraordinary items? Net income? Others (list)?

l. What was the profit margin (net income divided by revenue)?

m. Were income taxes allocated in 1977? Explain.

n. What basis was used for valuing inventories?

o. List all unusual features of the income statement. What aspects of it would you criticize? Explain.

p. What amount of working capital was provided from operations in 1977?

q. What was the primary depreciation method used?

r. What amount of the 1977 income tax expense was classified as foreign income taxes?

s. In 1977, what was the total amount of cash dividends declared or paid, on (a) common stock and (b) preferred stock?

t. In 1977, what was the total operating income from foreign activities?

u. What were the total amounts of revenues and net income reported for the first quarter of 1977?

v. Were any prior period adjustments reported in 1976 or 1977? Explain each.

w. Did the auditor's report express any reservations about the financial statements? Explain.

x. Overall, do you believe the balance sheet and the income statement could be improved with respect to format and terminology? Explain each change that you would suggest for consideration.

Problem 4–13

The Appendix to Chapter 5 gives an actual income statement and balance sheet. Examine them carefully and respond to the questions posed in Problem 4–12.

Problem 4–14

Obtain an audited financial statement for the latest year for a company of your choice (from the library or other source) and use it as a basis for responding to each of the questions posed in Problem 4–12.

5

Review—The Balance Sheet and Statement of Changes in Financial Position

The preceding chapter reviewed the income statement and statement of retained earnings. This chapter will review the two remaining statements required by generally accepted accounting principles—the balance sheet and the statement of changes in financial position. The relationships between the required statements were graphically presented in Exhibit 4–1. In this chapter we will discuss the balance sheet, the statement of changes in financial position, and some related reporting issues.

BALANCE SHEET

A balance sheet presents the assets, liabilities, and owners' equity of an enterprise, at a specific date, measured in conformity with generally accepted accounting principles. Because it is a presentation of the current *financial position* of an entity, it is often referred to as the *statement of financial position*. The designation balance sheet was adopted during the period when accounting first evolved; it refers to the fact that it balances in terms of the fundamental accounting model: Assets = Liabilities + Owners' Equity. It is unfortunate that this non-descriptive designation continues to be widely used today. Because of wide usage, we use it in this text, although reluctantly. Titles such as "Statement of Financial Position" or "Statement

of Assets, Liabilities, and Owners' Equity" are to be preferred.

CHARACTERISTICS OF THE BALANCE SHEET

The financial position of an enterprise is represented by the various assets owned, obligations owed, and claims of the owners at a designated date. For example, a balance sheet should be dated "At December 31, 19XX," in contrast with an income statement, which is dated "For the Year Ended December 31, 19XX." *APB Statement No. 4* defines financial position as follows:

> The *financial position* of an enterprise at a particular time comprises its assets, liabilities, and owners' equity and the relationship among them, plus contingencies, commitments, and other financial matters that pertain to the enterprise at that time. The financial position of an enterprise is presented in the *balance sheet* and in notes to the financial statements.[1]

Fundamentally, a balance sheet reports *(a)* a listing of the assets, liabilities, and components of owners' equity; and *(b)* a quantitative measurement (valuation) of each item listed. First,

---

[1] AICPA, *Statement of the Accounting Principles Board No. 4,* "Basic Concepts and Accounting Principles Underlying Financial Statements" (New York, October 1970), pp. 49–50.

let's look at the definitions of the three categories reported.

Assets Defined

Assets can be defined at the conceptual level as follows:

> Assets are economic resources devoted to business purposes within a specific accounting entity; they are aggregates of service-potentials available for or beneficial to expected operations.[2]

Hendricksen observes that this basic definition requires the following characteristics:

1. There must exist some specific right to future benefits or service potentials.
2. The rights must accrue to a specific individual or firm.
3. There must be a legally enforceable claim to the rights or services.[3]

In contrast, *APB Statement No. 4* provides a definition which focuses on current accounting practice, viz:

> *Assets*—economic resources of an enterprise that are recognized and measured in conformity with generally accepted accounting principles. Assets also include certain deferred charges that are not resources but that are recognized and measured in conformity with generally accepted accounting principles.[4]

This definition describes assets in terms of generally accepted accounting principles (GAAP). This approach has been criticized because of its implicit circularity, that is, it defines GAAP and concomitantly relies on GAAP.

Liabilities Defined

Liabilities may be conceptually defined as "obligations to convey assets or perform ser-vices, obligations resulting from past or current transactions and requiring settlement in the future."[5] *APB Statement No. 4* provides the following (circular) definition which reflects current practice:

> *Liabilities*—economic obligations of an enterprise that are recognized and measured in conformity with generally accepted accounting principles. Liabilities also include certain deferred credits that are not obligations but that are recognized and measured in conformity with generally accepted accounting principles.[6]

Owners' Equity Defined

Owners' equity is defined as the amount of the interest of the owners in the enterprise. It is the excess of the assets over the liabilities. It is also referred to as the *residual interest*. The owners' equity section of the balance sheet reports the various *sources* of capital provided by owners, that is, the amount of resources provided by owners (contributed capital) and the amount of internally generated resources retained by the entity (retained earnings).

MEASUREMENTS (VALUATIONS) ON THE BALANCE SHEET

Asset valuations on the balance sheet rarely represent their current market values at the date of the balance sheet. Rather, the assets are reported at their *carrying* or *book value*. Book value is the result of applying the cost and matching principles (with certain exceptions). Generally, it is acquisition cost less accumulated writeoffs to date. Cash is reported at its current value, accounts receivable at expected net realizable value (amount of the receivables less the allowance for doubtful accounts). Inventories and marketable equity securities usually are reported after acquisition at lower of cost or market, and plant and equipment are reported at cost less accumulated depreciation.

---

[2] AAA Committee on Accounting Concepts and Standards, *Accounting and Reporting Standards for Corporate Financial Statements and Preceding Statements and Supplements* (Columbus, Ohio, 1957), p. 3.

[3] Eldon S. Hendricksen, *Accounting Theory*, 3d ed. (Homewood, Ill.: Richard D. Irwin, Inc., 1977), p. 257.

[4] AICPA, *APB Statement No. 4*, pp. 49–50; the statement notes that charges that are not resources include items such as "charges from income tax allocation." See also Chapter 9.

[5] Robert T. Sprouse and Maurice Moonitz, *Accounting Research Study No. 3*, "A Tentative Set of Broad Accounting Principles for Business Enterprise" (New York: AICPA, December 1966), p. 37.

[6] AICPA, *APB Statement No. 4*, pp. 49–50.

Liabilities are reflected on the balance sheet at their carrying or book value. For *current* liabilities, book value commonly is measured as the maturity value of the debt. For *long-term* liabilities, book value is the discounted present value of the future cash outflows. Usually this is the maturity amount plus any unamortized premium or less any unamortized discount (see Chapters 9 and 20).

Since *owners' equity* is a residual amount, it does not report the current market value of the business; rather, it is a measurement of the owners' interest that follows directly from the measurements used for the assets and liabilities, as determined in accordance with generally accepted accounting principles.

Throughout the remaining chapters of this book, we will identify and apply the accounting concepts, standards, and procedures used to derive the measurements that are reported on the financial statements of an enterprise.

IMPORTANCE OF THE BALANCE SHEET

The balance sheet often has been considered less significant to decision makers than the income statement. Nevertheless, sophisticated decision makers consider each part of the overall financial report essential to gaining a balanced view. This includes the income statement, balance sheet, statement of changes in financial position, supporting schedules, notes to the statements, and the auditor's report. To single out one of these parts for exclusive use often results in inadequate information and serious oversights. Similarly, a note may explain the single most important issue with respect to a particular decision. Because of the complexity of most enterprises and the varied economic ramifications, users of financial statements should focus on the totality of the financial statements rather than upon a single amount (such as EPS) or a single report, such as the income statement.

The balance sheet, as a part of the total financial report, is important because it tells, at a specific date, the different assets held, the obligations by type and amount, and the sources and amounts of owners' equity. The balance sheet also provides subclassifications intended to aid

the user. Various balance sheet amounts often are used in conjunction with amounts from other sources (such as the income statement) to analyze relationships, trends, and so on. Examples of such relationships are asset turnover, ratio of debt to owners' equity, earnings per share, and return on investment. Classification of liabilities as long term and short term often aids creditors and others in assessing the ability of the entity to meet its future obligations. All decision makers are interested in these issues as well as the composition of the assets and the capital structure.

Some decision makers believe that the balance sheet has limited usefulness because the assets are not reported at their *current market value*. This is a basic problem facing the accounting profession because it poses critical measurement issues. Criticism is also directed to the fact that some balance sheet amounts (and other reported amounts) involve estimates, such as accumulated depreciation and estimated warranty obligations. Assuming the estimates are realistic, this criticism is not well founded. Of necessity, decision making is surrounded by uncertainty; therefore, accounting necessarily requires extensive use of estimates. Actual historical data provide the decision maker with a base from which to make realistic estimates or predictions.

BALANCE SHEET FORMAT

The reporting principle (see Exhibit 2–3) requires that a full and complete balance sheet be presented as an integral part of the periodic financial report. Although the format of the balance sheet is not specified, one of two different formats is almost always used. The *account form* was used by approximately 64% of the 600 companies reported in the *Accounting Trends and Techniques, 1978* (AICPA). The three major categories may be positioned either horizontally or vertically as shown at top of opposite page.[7]

---

[7] Another, the financial position format, is sometimes used. It is a vertical arrangement that shows noncurrent assets added to, and noncurrent liabilities deducted from, working capital to equal owners' equity.

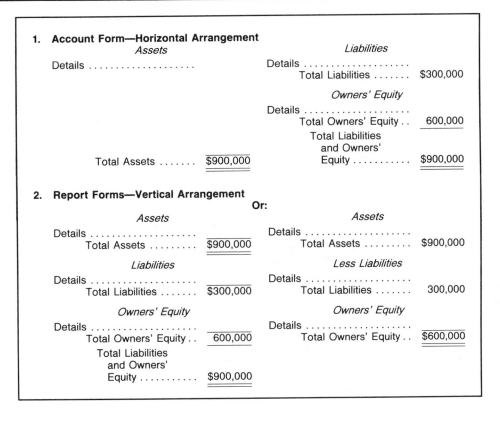

1. **Account Form—Horizontal Arrangement**

Assets	*Liabilities*
Details	Details . . . .
	Total Liabilities $300,000
	Owners' Equity
	Details . . . .
	Total Owners' Equity . . 600,000
	Total Liabilities and Owners'
Total Assets $900,000	Equity $900,000

2. **Report Forms—Vertical Arrangement**

Or:

Assets	*Assets*
Details	Details . . . .
Total Assets $900,000	Total Assets $900,000
Liabilities	*Less Liabilities*
Details	Details . . . .
Total Liabilities $300,000	Total Liabilities 300,000
Owners' Equity	*Owners' Equity*
Details	Details . . . .
Total Owners' Equity . . 600,000	Total Owners' Equity . . $600,000
Total Liabilities and Owners'	
Equity $900,000	

CLASSIFICATIONS IN THE BALANCE SHEET

To help the decision maker in analysis, interpretation, and evaluation of the wide range of financial information reported on a balance sheet, items usually are grouped according to common characteristics. Assets generally are grouped in decreasing order of liquidity (i.e., nearness to cash), the liabilities by time to maturity, and owners' equity in decreasing order of permanency. Classifications of information used in a balance sheet, and the array of items under each classification, are influenced by the industry and characteristics of the enterprise. For example, the balance sheet of a financial institution, such as a bank, will reflect classifications quite different from those for a manufacturing company. Variations in format and classification observed in actual statements generally are designed to comply with the reporting principle, which specifies that reporting must be informative, fair, and not misleading. Therefore, flexibility in format and classifications generally is considered desirable. Nevertheless, there is a reasonable degree of uniformity. The following classifications are representative of current reporting practices:

Assets:
1. Current assets.
2. Investments and funds.
3. Operational (or fixed) assets—tangible.
4. Operational assets—intangible.
5. Other assets.
6. Deferred charges.

Liabilities:
1. Current liabilities (including short-term deferred credits).
2. Long-term liabilities (including long-term deferred credits).

Owners' Equity:
1. Contributed capital:
   a. Capital stock.
   b. Contributed capital in excess of the par or stated value of capital stock.
   c. Other contributed capital.
2. Retained earnings.
3. Unrealized capital losses and gains.

Observe that the above classifications provide for the three major captions—assets, liabilities, and owners' equity. Under each major caption are several subclassifications, the designations of which vary, as explained above. Observe that we have included *deferred credits* in liabilities (some are current, others long term); however, a separate caption, "Deferred Credits," sometimes is reported between long-term liabilities and owners' equity. This poses an inconsistency since the fundamental accounting model represented by the balance sheet (Assets = Liabilities + Owners' Equity) does not include a separate category for deferred credits. Observe that *deferred charges* (i.e., long-term prepaid expenses) are included in the asset category. Since deferred credits are more similar to liabilities than to capital, they are classified as liabilities.

An illustrative balance sheet is shown in Exhibit 5–1 to supplement the following discussions.

CURRENT ASSETS

Current assets are cash and other assets, commonly identified as those which are *reasonably expected* to be realized in cash, or to be sold, or consumed during the *normal operating cycle* of the business or within one year from the balance sheet date, whichever is longer. The normal operating cycle is defined as the average period of time between the expenditure of cash for goods and services and the date that those goods and services are converted back into cash. It is the average length of time from cash expenditure, to inventory, to sale, to accounts receivable, and back to cash. For many businesses, the operating cycle is shorter than one year. However, there are certain businesses, particu-

larly those manufacturing businesses with extended production processes, where the operating cycle extends beyond one year. Examples include shipbuilding, distilleries, and logging.

Current assets usually are presented on the balance sheet in order of decreasing liquidity (i.e., nearness to cash conversion). The major items comprising current assets, in order of liquidity, are cash, short-term investments, receivables, inventories, and prepaid expenses. Items that are not current assets include cash and claims to cash which are restricted for uses other than current operations, long-term investments, receivables which have an extended maturity date, land and natural resources, depreciable assets, and long-term prepayments of expenses.

Although the definition of current assets is reasonably clear-cut, problems are often encountered in implementation. In applying the definition of current assets, the phases "normal operating cycle" and "reasonably expected to be realized in cash" both involve judgment. Consequently, there is a tendency to incorrectly classify certain items as current assets because of the favorable effect on working capital. Recall that working capital is the difference between current assets and current liabilities. For example, marketable securities may be classified as a current or noncurrent asset, depending upon the *stated intention* of management as to the planned holding period. An intention to hold a marketable security beyond the period specified for current assets clearly would require its classification as a noncurrent asset. Thus, a simple change in *intention* of management may alter the classification of the marketable securities. Prepaid expenses is another area where there is considerable variation in classification. A short-term prepayment should be classified as a current asset (i.e., a prepaid expense), whereas a long-term prepayment should be classified as noncurrent (i.e., a deferred charge). Nevertheless, a three-year prepayment of an insurance premium usually is classified as a current asset, a procedure that can be justified only on the basis of the exception principle of immateriality.

In some companies and industries, there is no basis for using a current asset category. For example, financial institutions, such as banks, do not report current assets because it would be

EXHIBIT 5–1

AB CORPORATION
Statement of Financial Position (balance sheet)
At December 31, 1979

Assets

Current Assets:			
Cash			$ 34,000
Short-term investments (current market value,			
$21,000)			20,000
Accounts receivable (trade)		$ 43,100	
Less: Allowance for doubtful accounts		1,300	41,800
Merchandise inventory (*Fifo*, lower of cost or			
market)			120,000
Prepaid expenses:			
Supplies inventory			1,200
Prepaid insurance			3,000
Total Current Assets			220,000
Investments and Funds:			
Investment in bonds of X Corporation (at cost:			
approximate market, $35,000)		30,000	
Investment in stock of Y Corporation (at cost)	$ 77,000		
Less: Allowance to reduce to market value	7,000	70,000	
Plant expansion fund		50,000	
Total Investments and Funds			150,000
Land, Building, and Equipment:			
Land		24,000	
Building	200,000		
Less: Accumulated depreciation (straight line)	80,000	120,000	
Equipment and fixtures	140,000		
Less: Accumulated depreciation (straight line)	56,000	84,000	
Total Land, Building, and Equipment			228,000
Intangible Assets:			
Patent (cost, $17,000, less accumulated amortization,			
$8,000)		9,000	
Franchise (cost, $30,000, less accumulated			
amortization, $14,000)		16,000	
Total Intangible Assets			25,000
Other Assets:			
Land held for future building site			37,000
Deferred Charges:			
Rearrangement costs			8,000
Total Assets			$668,000

Liabilities

Current Liabilities:			
Accounts payable (trade)			$ 43,700
Notes payable			20,000
Rent revenue collected in advance			1,800
Wages payable			2,000
Current payment on long-term note			20,000
Income taxes payable			12,500
Total Current Liabilities			100,000
Long-Term Liabilities:			
Note payable, 9%, due 1980–81	$ 40,000		
Less: 1980 current payment	20,000	$ 20,000	

EXHIBIT 5–1 *(continued)*

Bonds payable, 6%, due 1988 150,000		
Less: Unamortized discount 4,000	146,000	
Total Long-Term Liabilities		166,000
Total Liabilities		266,000

Stockholders' Equity

Contributed Capital:		
Preferred stock, par $10, 6% cumulative, nonparticipating, authorized 20,000 shares, issued and outstanding 5,000 shares	50,000	
Common stock, nopar, authorized 100,000 shares, issued and outstanding 75,000 shares	150,000	
Total Stated Capital	200,000	
Additional contributed capital:		
In excess of par value of preferred stock	40,000	
Total Contributed Capital	240,000	
Retained earnings (Note A)	169,000	
Total Contributed Capital and Retained Earnings	409,000	
Less: Unrealized loss on long-term investment	7,000	
Total Stockholders' Equity		402,000
Total Liabilities and Stockholders' Equity		$668,000

Notes to financial statements:
Note A. Under the terms of the bond indenture, a part of retained earnings, determined by a formula, is restricted from dividend availability. The formula, computed for 1979, restricts retained earnings in the amount of $56,000. This amount will be increased each year as provided by the bond indenture formula. When the bonds are retired, the restriction will be automatically removed.

pointless in view of the nature of their asset structure. Exhibit 5–1 illustrates how current assets should be reported. Observe the parenthetical information provided to satisfy the full disclosure requirement.

CURRENT LIABILITIES

The definition of current liabilities parallels (is dependent upon) the definition of current assets; that is, current liabilities are short-term liabilities "whose liquidation is reasonably expected to require the use of existing resources properly classified as current assets, or the creation of other current liabilities."[8] This definition includes items such as revenue collected in advance, since there is an obligation to "perform or render the revenue activity" within the next year or operating cycle, whichever is longer. Current liabilities include the following short-term items:

1. Accounts payable (trade) for goods and services that enter into the operating cycle of the business.
2. Special payables for nonoperating items and services.
3. Short-term notes payable.
4. Collections in advance for unearned revenue (such as rent revenue collected in advance).
5. Accrued expenses for wages, salaries, commissions, rentals, royalties, income, and other taxes.
6. Other obligations to be paid out of current assets, such as serial maturities of long-term debts.

Items not properly classified as current liabilities include long-term notes, bonds, and obligations that will not be paid out of current assets. For example, a bond issue due during the coming year would not be classified as a current liability if it is to be paid out of a special cash fund classified under the caption "Investments and Funds." Similarly, a currently maturing bond issue that is to be refunded (i.e., paid off by issuing a new series of bonds) should not be

[8] AICPA, *Accounting Research and Terminology Bulletins, Final Edition* (New York, 1961), p. 21.

classified as a current liability as specified in *FASB Statement No. 6.*

WORKING CAPITAL

Working capital is described as current assets minus current liabilities. Because it is an abstract concept, this does not literally define working capital; it simply tells how it is computed. If all of the current assets were converted to cash at their *book value* and all of the current liabilities paid at their book value, working capital would be the amount of cash remaining. Although the concept of working capital is widely used by accountants and security analysts, many investors have problems with it because of the abstraction. They understand cash, as it is definable, is used daily by most people and circulates freely. In contrast, no one ever handles, receives, or pays "working capital" as such. It is for this reason that many investors are more concerned with the amounts of the various items that comprise current assets and current liabilities than with the abstract difference between two opposites. A company may well report an excellent working capital position and at the same time have a serious cash deficiency. For these and other reasons, many accountants believe that cash flow statements are significantly more informative than are working capital statements (see Part B of Chapter 23).

Nevertheless, the amount of working capital and the working capital ratio are viewed as measures of liquidity; that is, the ability of the enterprise to meet its short-term obligations. To illustrate, AB Corporation, Exhibit 5–1, reported the following:

Current assets	$220,000
Current liabilities	100,000
Difference—working capital	$120,000
Working capital ratio: $220,000 ÷ $100,000 =	2.2

The working capital is $120,000, and the working capital (or current) ratio is 2.2. The ratio indicates that at book value the current assets are 2.2 times the current liabilities, or that for each $1 of current liabilities there is $2.20 in current assets. Because of the use of working capital as an index of liquidity, the independent

auditor sometimes encounters attempts to misclassify some noncurrent assets as current and some current liabilities as noncurrent in order to report a better working capital position than actually exists.

Offsetting of current assets and liabilities is improper because this practice avoids full disclosure and would permit a business to show a more favorable current ratio than actually exists. For example, if AB Corporation were to offset a current liability of $50,000 against current assets, the current ratio would show $170,000 ÷ $50,000 = 3.4 instead of the correct ratio of 2.2.

Offsetting is permissible only when a legal right of offset exists. Thus, it would be proper to offset a $5,000 overdraft in one account with a bank against another account reflecting $8,000 on deposit in that same bank. Offsetting the two amounts referred to in the preceding paragraph for AB Corporation is unacceptable.

INVESTMENTS AND FUNDS

This caption is often labeled "Investments." It includes noncurrent assets (other than the operating assets, other assets, and deferred charges) acquired for their financial or investment advantage, and funds set aside for future purposes. The long-term items reported under this caption include the following:

1. Long-term investments in securities, such as stocks, bonds, and long-term notes.
2. Investments in subsidiaries, including long-term advances.
3. Long-term investments in tangible assets, such as land and buildings, which are not used in current operations.
4. Funds set aside for long-term future use, such as bond sinking funds (to retire bonds payable), expansion funds, stock retirement funds, and long-term savings deposits.
5. Cash surrender value of life insurance policies carried by the company.

The important distinctions are that *(a)* the items are nonoperational and *(b)* management plans long-term retention of them. The single fact that an investment is currently marketable neither prevents nor requires its inclusion under this caption (see above discussion of current assets). Exhibit 5–1 illustrates typical reporting of this category of assets.

OPERATIONAL ASSETS

Operational assets are defined as those assets used in carrying out the operations of the entity. Operational assets are carefully distinguished from stock in trade (i.e., inventories of raw materials, work in process, finished goods, merchandise, and supplies). Historically, operational assets have been labeled as *fixed assets* because of their relative permanence or long-term nature. Operational assets are subclassified as follows:

1. Tangible—Those assets characterized by physical existence, such as land, buildings, machinery, equipment, furniture, fixtures, tools, containers, and natural resources.
2. Intangible—Those assets that have no physical existence but instead have value because of the rights which ownership confers. Examples are patents, copyrights, trademarks, brand names, leaseholds, formulas, processes, and goodwill.

Operational Assets—Tangible

This group of operational assets is separately reported on the balance sheet under various captions depending upon the type of business. Manufacturing enterprises generally use captions such as *property, plant, and equipment;* and other enterprises use captions such as *property and equipment,* or simply *property.* Companies seldom use the older caption, *fixed assets.*

Tangible operational assets include items that are *(a)* not subject to depreciation (land) and *(b)* depreciable items, such as buildings, machinery, and fixtures. Land should be reported separately from depreciable assets.

APB Opinion No. 12 requires that the balance sheet, or the notes thereto, report *(a)* balances of major classes of depreciable assets by nature or function; *(b)* accumulated depreciation, either by major classes of depreciable assets or in total; and *(c)* a general description of the methods used in computing depreciation for the major classes of operational assets. The term "reserve for depreciation" should not be used to refer to accumulated depreciation because no "reserve" exists. Exhibit 5–1 illustrates appropriate reporting of tangible operational assets.

Operational Assets—Intangible

This asset classification is separately reported on the balance sheet under the title *intangible assets.* Major items should be separately listed, and the accumulated amount of *amortization* also should be disclosed. Seldom is the contra account, accumulated amortization, separately listed; this practice contrasts with the usual treatment given tangible operational assets (see Exhibit 5–1). Although deferred charges are "intangible," they differ from Operational Assets—Intangible in that the latter represent *exclusive rights* while deferred charges do not (they are long-term prepaid expenses).

OTHER ASSETS

"Other assets" are those items which cannot be reasonably categorized under the usual asset classifications. Examples include cash in closed banks and idle operational assets (such as an idle plant). Items should be analyzed carefully before being reported as other assets because often there is a logical basis for classifying them elsewhere. Items such as deferred strike losses and flood losses intended to be written off in time are sometimes reported as other assets. This treatment is insupportable inasmuch as there is no element of future benefit associated with such losses; hence, there is no asset value. They should be included on the income statement as losses.

DEFERRED CHARGES

Deferred charges represent debit balances derived from expenditures which have an expected benefit to be realized over more than one future period. Hence, they are carried forward to be matched with future revenues. The everyday meaning of deferred is *delayed,* and charge is synonymous with *debit;* hence, these "delayed debits" have been held for matching against future revenues. Deferred charges are distinguished from prepaid expenses on the basis of the *time* over which they will be amortized; that is, they involve a longer period of time than do prepaid expenses. The latter must meet the requirements of the definition of current assets. The following accounts typify those found under the "Deferred Charges" caption: Machinery Rearrangement Costs, Taxes (especially in connection with tax deferments, such as discussed in Chapter 9), Organization Costs (alternatively shown under "Intangibles"), Pension Costs Paid in Advance, and Insurance Prepayments (long-term prepayments not properly classified as a current asset), and certain start-up costs.

LONG-TERM LIABILITIES

A long-term liability is an obligation that will not require the use of current assets for payment during the upcoming operating cycle or during the next year, whichever is longer. All liabilities not appropriately classified as current liabilities are reported under this caption. Typical long-term liabilities are bonds payable, long-term notes payable, long-term lease obligations, and the noncurrent portion of deferred income taxes.

Bonds payable should be reported at their par value (face amount) plus any unamortized premium, or less any unamortized discount. To illustrate:

Bonds sold at par:

Long-term liabilities	$100,000

Bonds sold at a discount:

Long-Term Liabilities:
Bonds payable, 7½%, due 19X	$100,000	
Less: Unamortized bond discount	7,000	$ 93,000

Bonds sold at a premium:

Long-Term Liabilities:
Bonds payable, 9%, due 19X	$100,000	
Add: Unamortized bond premium	7,000	$107,000

DEFERRED CREDITS

Occasionally a company will include the caption "Deferred Credits," between long-term liabilities and owners' equity. Typical deferred credits are long-term deferred income taxes, deferred revenues (i.e., revenues collected in advance), and deferred investment tax credits. Use of this caption generally is discouraged because such items are liabilities, contra assets, or owners' equity. Practically all companies report them under the liability captions. More detailed discussion of deferred credits appears in Chapter 9 (also refer to footnote 4 of this chapter).

OWNERS' EQUITY

Owners' equity represents the residual financial interests in a business. It is the difference between total assets and total liabilities. For a sole proprietorship, it usually is called proprietor's equity (or capital); for a partnership, partners' equity (or capital); and for a corporation, stockholders' or shareholders' equity. Because of certain legal implications (refer to the discussion of legal capital in Chapter 16), rather than any theoretical meaning, owners' equity is subclassified to reflect sources. Therefore, for a corporation, the following sources commonly are reported:

1. Contributed capital:
   a. Capital stock.
   b. Contributed capital in excess of the par or stated value of the capital stock.
   c. Other contributed capital.
2. Retained earnings.
3. Unrealized losses and gains.

Capital Stock

This caption reports the *source* of owners' equity as represented by the stated or legal capital of the corporation. Legal capital is specified by state law and in the Articles of Incorporation (i.e., the Charter) of the company. This source is the amount of legal capital *provided by the stockholders.* Each class of stock, common and preferred, must be reported at the par, or stated amount; or in the case of nopar stock, the total amount paid in (these matters vary depending upon the law of the state of incorporation). Details of each class of capital stock should be set out separately, including the title of each issue; number of shares authorized, issued, outstanding, and subscribed; conversion features; callability; preferences; and any other special features.

Contributed Capital in Excess of Par or Stated Value

This is sometimes called *additional paid-in capital.* It reports the amounts received by the corporation in excess of the par or stated value of the capital stock outstanding. These amounts usually arise when the corporation sells its stock at a premium (sometimes called premium on capital stock), or issues stock dividends. These topics are discussed in detail in Chapters 16–18.

Other Contributed Capital

This is another source of contributed capital. It arises from such transactions as treasury stock, and retirements and conversion of stock (see Chapter 17).

Retained Earnings

Retained earnings (formerly called earned surplus) is the corporation's accumulated earnings, less accumulated losses, and dividends to date. It reports the amount of resources (from undistributed earnings) that the corporation has retained for use in operations and for growth. In most corporations, over the long term, retained earnings is the major *source* of owners' equity. In the long term, most corporations distribute dividends to the stockholders amounting to less than 50% of the earnings, thus establishing a continuing source of internally generated funds. Indirectly, retained earnings represent additional investments by the stockholders since they have foregone dividends equal to the cumulative balance of retained earnings. A negative balance in retained earnings is usually called a *deficit.*

Not infrequently, a portion of the total amount of retained earnings is *restricted* or *appropriated.* This means that during the pe-

riod of restriction, the specified amount is not available for dividends. For example, AB Corporation (Exhibit 5–1) has total retained earnings of $169,000; however, $56,000 of that amount is restricted for a specific period of time. After the restriction is removed, the $56,000 again becomes available for dividends, subject to subsequent declaration by the board of directors of the corporation. A restriction may result from a *legal requirement,* as in the case where state law (in which the corporation is organized) imposes a restriction equal to the cost of any treasury stock held. Such laws are designed to protect the creditors of the corporation. Or, a restriction may be *contractual,* as in the case where the bond indenture carries such a stipulation. This situation is illustrated in Exhibit 5–1. Finally, the board of directors may exercise its *discretion* and decide to "appropriate" a portion of retained earnings, as in the case of "retained earnings appropriated for future plant expansion."

Restrictions or appropriations may be reflected in either of two ways. A few companies make an entry in the accounts to reflect the restriction or appropriation. For example, the $56,000 restriction on retained earnings reported by AB Corporation (Exhibit 5–1) could be recorded and reported as follows:

Entry in the accounts:

Retained earnings	56,000	
Retained earnings restricted by bond indenture		56,000

Reporting on the balance sheet then could be as follows:

Retained earnings, unappropriated .	$113,000	
Retained earnings, restricted by bond indenture	56,000	
Total retained earnings		$169,000

In recent years, the above approach has practically disappeared. Instead, no formal entry is made in the accounts. Restrictions and appropriations are usually disclosed in the notes to the financial statements, as illustrated in Exhibit 5–1. *FASB Statement No. 5,* paragraph 15, states: "Costs and losses shall not be charged to an appropriation of retained earnings and no part of the appropriation shall be transferred to income." Accounting for, and reporting of, retained earnings is discussed in detail in Chapter 17.

UNREALIZED CAPITAL

This component of owners' equity has seldom been used in the past because of some unsettled accounting issues related to market valuations. However, the recent issuance of *FASB Statement No. 12* (December 31, 1975) caused it to be used more often because the *Statement* requires recognition of the "unrealized loss and loss recovery" resulting from the application of the concept of lower of cost or market to long-term equity investments in capital stock (not bonds) accounted for on the cost basis. *Statement No. 12* requires accounting for and reporting the accumulated unrealized loss separately as an *unrealized element of owners' equity* (i.e., a reduction in owners' equity as shown in Exhibit 5–1). This topic is discussed in detail in Chapter 19.

Unrealized capital has been used in some situations to accommodate a "gain" arising from the writing up of operational assets (see Chapter 13). This discussion is not intended to imply that write-ups of assets to market value are currently in accordance with generally accepted accounting principles. However, there are a few exceptions, as explained in Chapters 7, 8, 13, and 19.

STATEMENT OF CHANGES IN FINANCIAL POSITION

Since the issuance of *APB Opinion No. 19* (effective September 30, 1971), a statement of changes in financial position, in addition to the income statement and balance sheet, must be included in the annual financial report. Although it evolved from the old funds statement (which was optional), it is significantly different in a number of respects. The statement of changes in financial position reports the *financing* and *investing* activities of a business enterprise during a specified period.

It is a *change statement,* as diagrammed in Exhibit 4–1, because the financing and investing activities explain the causes of the changes between the beginning and ending balance sheets,

other than those changes explained by the income statement (which is also a change statement). Thus, it is dated the same as the income statement, "For the Year Ended (date)." Exhibit 5–2 presents a statement (cash basis) specially designed for instructional purposes. Other statements of changes in financial position (on both cash and working capital bases) are shown in the appendixes to this chapter and Chapter 4.

The financing activities are represented as *inflows of funds* into the enterprise, primarily from *(a)* operations (i.e., revenues less expenses), *(b)* issuance of capital stock, *(c)* borrowing, and *(d)* sale of assets owned by the entity (such as investments and operational assets). The investing activities are *outflows of funds* from the enterprise, primarily for *(a)* acquisition of assets (such as investments and operational assets), *(b)* retirement of debt, and *(c)* payment of dividends. Thus, the statement reports all inflows and outflows of funds.

For purposes of the statement of changes in financial position, funds usually are defined (i.e., measured) as either (1) cash equivalents (cash plus short-term investments) or (2) working capital (current assets minus current liabilities). Consequently, when a statement of changes in financial position is used, the user should be alert to identify which of these two significantly different measures of funds was used in its preparation. *APB Opinion No. 19* permits either measure but requires that the identity be specified.

The statement of changes in financial position also must be based on an *all-resources concept.* This means that *all* significant financing and investing activities must be incorporated in it regardless of whether cash or working capital was directly affected. The word *all* is particularly important because it requires that direct exchanges (i.e., trades) be included even though neither cash nor working capital was affected. Examples of direct exchanges are the acquisition of property and paying for it by issuing capital stock, the conversion of bonds payable to common stock, and the trading of one asset, such as a tract of land, for a machine. In direct exchanges, there often is neither an inflow nor outflow of either cash or working capital. Nevertheless, transactions of this type must be included

EXHIBIT 5–2

EXAMPLE CORPORATION
Statement of Changes in Financial Position—Cash Basis
For the Year Ended December 31, 1979

Sources of cash (inflow of funds):
From operations:

Revenues (accrual basis)	$850,000	
Add (deduct) adjustments to convert to cash basis:		
Increase in accounts receivable (trade)	(10,000)	
Cash generated from revenues		$840,000
Expenses (accrual basis)	740,000	
Add (deduct) adjustments to convert to cash basis:		
Depreciation expense	(30,000)	
Amortization of intangibles	(1,000)	
Inventory increase	28,000	
Accounts payable decrease (trade)	12,000	
Income taxes payable increase	(14,000)	
Loss on sale of operational assets	(5,000)	
Cash disbursed for expenses		730,000
Total cash generated by operations		110,000
From extraordinary item net of income tax		20,000
From other sources:		
Sale of preferred stock	45,000	
Sale of operational assets	25,000	
Common stock issued to retire convertible bonds (Note A)	100,000	
Total cash generated from other sources		170,000
Total cash generated from all sources		300,000

Uses of cash (outflow of funds):

Payment of cash dividends	40,000	
Payment of long-term note payable	50,000	
Acquisition of operational assets	120,000	
Purchase of long-term investment, stock of X Corporation	30,000	
Retirement of 5%, convertible bonds payable (Note A)	100,000	
Total cash expended for all purposes		340,000
Net increase (decrease) in cash during the period		$ (40,000)

Notes to financial statements:
Note A. All of the outstanding 5% convertible bonds payable were tendered to the company for conversion to nopar common stock in accordance with the conversion provision in the bond indenture. Conversion required the issuance of 10,000 shares of nopar common stock; no cash was paid or received incidental to the conversion.

"as if" funds equal to the market value actually flowed in and out. This type of transaction is illustrated in Exhibit 5–2, which assumes that at the start of the period the company had outstanding 5% convertible bonds payable with a maturity amount of $100,000. The bonds carried a conversion agreement which permitted the bondholders to turn them in during 1979 or 1980 and receive, in return, a specified number of shares of the nopar common stock of the company. During 1979, all of the bondholders tendered their bonds and received the requisite number of shares of stock. Thus, debt was retired by the issuance of common stock (a direct exchange of noncash items). Although no cash flowed in either direction, the transaction is reported on the statement of changes in financial position "as if" cash was received for the stock and was then immediately disbursed to retire the bonds. Therefore, the noncash exchange is reflected both as a source of cash and a use of cash, supplemented with an explanatory note to assure full disclosure. Without the all-re-sources requirement, direct exchanges would not be reported in the statement, thereby omitting significant financing and investing activities.

Observe in Exhibit 5–2 that cash flows related to operations are shown separately for revenues and expenses. In contrast, the statement usually is designed to start with the difference, net income, and then report "adjustments" to derive "total cash generated by operations." The approach illustrated in Exhibit 5–2 is favored for instructional purposes (and often for communication purposes) because it does not imply that depreciation and amortization are sources of cash; rather, it emphasizes that they are adjustments to derive total cash outflows required for the expenses. Also, in this format, the cash effects of revenues and expenses are reported separately. The net effect is the same regardless of the approach used.

The statement of changes in financial position is not difficult to understand and interpret, especially when prepared on a cash equivalent basis as in Exhibit 5–2. However, the adjustments in the section "from operations" sometimes are not readily understood. Exhibit 5–2 reports that sales recognized, on an accrual basis, amounted to $850,000; however, since $10,000 of that amount was not collected by the end of the year, the cash inflow from sales was $840,000. Alternatively, had accounts receivables *decreased,* the $10,000 would have been added, giving a cash inflow from sales of $860,000. In a similar manner, total expenses, determined on an accrual basis, must be adjusted to a cash basis. Depreciation expense and amortization expense must be *deducted* from expenses since they were included in total expense but did not require cash expenditures. The inventory increase is added since additional cash (above cost of goods sold) was expended for this increase. Similarly, the *decrease* in accounts payable required the expenditure of additional cash above the amount of expenses recognized on the accrual basis. The increase in income taxes payable means that less cash ($14,000) was expended for this item than the amount of income tax expense reported. The loss on sale of operational assets, although included in total ex-penses, does not represent cash. The amount of cash from the sale of operational assets is reported under "Other sources" as $25,000.[9]

Preparation and interpretation of the statement of changes in financial position on both the cash equivalent and the working capital bases are discussed in detail in Chapter 23.

SOME SPECIAL REPORTING ISSUES

We will conclude the review of information processing and the financial statements with a brief discussion of several special reporting issues that are commonly encountered.

Terminology

As in all professions, accounting has its own jargon. Often the same word or phrase is used to mean different things. We commented on some of these terminology problems in Chapter 2—concepts, assumptions, principles, standards, and procedures. In preparing reports, accountants should refrain, as much as possible, from using vague, undefined, and complex terminology. Generally less technical terms can be used to better convey the message. Captions in statements and titles of amounts reported should be carefully selected, particularly since the statements will be used by a wide range of decision makers. From time to time pronouncements such as the *ARBs, APB Opinions,* and *FASB Statements* specifically recommend improved terminology.

For example, some years ago, the term "reserve" was used by accountants to refer to *(a)* a contra asset account, such as "reserve for depreciation" for accumulated depreciation; *(b)* an estimated liability, such as "reserve for warranties" for estimated warranty liability; and *(c)* an appropriation of retained earnings, such as "reserve for future expansion." *Accounting Terminology Bulletin No. 1* recommended that the term be restricted to the latter usage. However, many accountants do not use it even in that context.

---

[9] The entry to record the disposal of the operational assets was

Cash (sales price)	25,000	
Loss on sale of operational assets	5,000	
Operational assets (book value)		30,000

Similarly, the terminology bulletin recommended use of the terms *retained earnings* instead of earned surplus and *net income* instead of net profit. *APB Opinion No. 19* recommended use of the title, *statement of changes in financial position,* instead of the older title, funds flow statement. Confusion of the terms cost and expense, and revenues and income, discussed in Chapter 4, are other examples of careless terminology. Throughout later chapters we will often discuss preferred terminology since effective communication is a primary objective of accounting.

Comparative Statements

To evaluate the financial potentials of an enterprise, one should assemble comparable financial information for two or more periods. For prediction purposes, trends are much more revealing than information for only one period. In recognition of this fact, *ARB No. 43* states:

> The presentation of comparative financial statements in annual and other reports enhances the usefulness of such reports and brings out more clearly the nature and trends of current changes affecting the enterprise. Such presentation emphasizes the fact that statements for a series of periods are far more significant than those for a single period and that the accounts for one period are but an installment of what is essentially a continuous history.[10]

Comparative statements for the current and prior year are now considered essential to meet the full disclosure requirement. The actual statements shown in the Appendixes at the end of Chapters 4 and 5 display comparative amounts. In addition to comparative statements, many companies present a special tabulation of especially relevant financial items for time spans of 5 to 20 or more years. Items often included are total revenues, income before extraordinary items, net income, depreciation expense, earnings per share, dividends, total assets, total owners' equity, number of shares outstanding, and average stock price. These long-term summaries are particularly useful in trend analysis.

Rounding of Amounts

All major companies round amounts in their financial statements. According to AICPA, *Accounting Trends and Techniques, 1978* (New York, 1978), of the 600 companies surveyed, 31% rounded to the nearest dollar, 63% to the nearest thousand dollars, and 6% to the nearest million dollars; none reported cents. Amounts not rounded often suggest to the casual reader greater precision than actually exists.

Subsequent Events

Certain important events or transactions which occur subsequent to the balance sheet date but prior to the actual issuance of the financial statements (ordinarily one to three months) and which have a material effect on the financial statements are called *subsequent events.* Subsequent events must be reported because they involve important information that could influence the statement users' interpretation and evaluation of the potentials of the enterprise. Auditing standards define these events and specify that they must be either (1) reflected in the statements or (2) disclosed in notes to the statements, depending upon their nature.[11]

The effects of subsequent events should be reflected directly *in the statements* if they *(a)* provide additional evidence about conditions *that existed at balance sheet date, (b)* affect estimates inherent in the process of preparing the financial statements, and *(c)* require adjustments to the financial statements resulting from the estimates. An example would be a material loss on an uncollectible receivable because of a customer's deteriorating financial condition. The deteriorating financial condition presumably was occurring at balance sheet date, but recent information made it more evident.

Subsequent events should be *disclosed only in notes* to the statements if they *(a)* result from conditions that did not exist at balance sheet

---

[10] AICPA, *Accounting Research Bulletin No. 43,* "Restatement and Revision of Accounting Research Bulletins" (New York, 1953), chap. 2, sec. A.

[11] AICPA, *Codification of Statements on Auditing Standards,* AU Sec. 560 (New York, 1973).

date, (b) arose subsequent to the balance sheet date, and (c) do not merit adjustment to the current financial statements. Examples listed in *Codification of Statements on Auditing Standards* AU Sec. 560.06, are sale of a bond or capital stock issue, litigation based on an event subsequent to the balance sheet date, inventory losses due to casualty, and losses caused by a condition that arose subsequent to balance sheet date (such as a fire or flood). The fire or flood did not "exist" at the balance sheet date.

This topic is considered in depth in auditing texts and courses.

FASB Statement No. 5, "Accounting for Contingencies," issued in March 1975, defines *loss contingencies* and *gain contingencies.* It also specifies the conditions under which contingencies must be either (a) accrued and reported in the financial statements or (b) disclosed in notes to the statements. This subject is discussed in detail in Chapter 9.

Full Disclosure

Full disclosure is a particularly important aspect of the *reporting principle* discussed in Chapter 2. Full disclosure requires complete and understandable reporting of all significant information relating to the economic affairs of the enterprise so that the financial statements will not be misleading. Full disclosure requires, in addition to the financial information reported in the body of the financial statements, additional information in notes to the financial statements, supporting schedules, cross-references, contra items, and parenthetical explanations. The accountant must exercise judgment in deciding the way in which each significant event or transaction should be reported to meet the full disclosure requirement.

Notes to the financial statements are a singularly important part of the financial report because a note is often the only feasible way to adequately explain and elaborate on certain critical events and situations. A particular note may refer to a single amount on one of the three basic statements or to several amounts on two or more of them, or to a situation that is not directly reflected on any of them. The guideline for deciding when a note is required, other than

when specifically required, is largely judgmental within the framework of complete reporting. Notes typically are a combination of narrative elaboration, additional amounts, and supplementary tables.

A number of *APB Opinions* and *FASB Statements* specifically require certain disclosures in the notes to the financial statements. For example, *FASB Statement of Accounting Standards No. 2,* "Accounting for Research and Development Costs" (October 1974), states:

> A government-regulated enterprise that defers research and development costs for financial accounting purposes in accordance with Addendum to APB Opinion No. 2, "Accounting for the Investment Credit," shall disclose the following additional information about its research and development costs:
> a. Accounting policy, including basis for amortization.
> b. Total research and development costs incurred each period for which an income statement is presented and the amount of those costs that has been capitalized or deferred in each period.

Moreover, *APB Opinion No. 22,* "Disclosure of Accounting Policies" (April 1972), specifically requires that information about *important* accounting policies adopted by the enterprise, including their identification and description, must be disclosed "in a separate *Summary of Significant Accounting Policies* preceding the notes to the financial statements or as the initial note." At a minimum, the summary should include policies that involve (a) a selection from existing acceptable alternatives, (b) principles and methods peculiar to the industry, and (c) unusual or innovative applications of generally accepted accounting principles.

The actual statements presented in the Appendixes to Chapters 4 and 5 include typical notes.

Supporting schedules may be incorporated into the notes or presented separately. Supporting schedules are typical for large and complex companies, and in situations where a particular item involves a number of complex changes during the period. We mentioned in Chapter 4 that when there have been numerous changes in owners' equity, the statement of retained earn-

EXHIBIT 5-3
Consolidated Statement of Shareholders' Equity

STRUTHERS WELLS CORPORATION
November Fiscal Year-End

	$1.25 Cumulative Preferred Stock	Common Stock	Additional Paid-In Capital	Retained Earnings (deficit)	Unrealized Loss on Noncurrent Marketable Equity Securities	$1.25 Cumulative Preferred Stock in Treasury	Total
Balance—December 1, 197F	$2,063,325	$2,195,669	$8,045,940	$(4,806,966)		$(23,311)	$ 7,474,657
Cash distribution paid on $1.25 cumulative preferred stock			(100,561)				(100,561)
148 shares of $1.25 cumulative preferred stock acquired for Treasury						(1,628)	(1,628)
Adjustment to carrying value of subsidiary distributed to shareholders			10,094				10,094
Issuance of 6,130 shares under employment agreement		6,130	33,409				39,539
Purchase and retirement of 237,036 shares of common stock		(237,036)	(1,896,288)				(2,133,324)
Issuance of 1,000 shares on exercise of stock option		1,000	3,630				4,630
Dividend on common stock			(98,288)				(98,288)
Net income				3,117,618			3,117,618
Balance—November 30, 197G	$2,063,325	$1,965,763	$5,997,936	$(1,689,348)		$(24,939)	$ 8,312,737
Cash distribution paid on $1.25 cumulative preferred stock			(74,958)	(25,142)			(100,100)
1,716 shares of $1.25 cumulative preferred stock acquired for Treasury						(29,205)	(29,205)
Adjustment to carrying value of subsidiary distributed to shareholders			(13,750)				(13,750)
Issuance of 10,000 shares under employment agreement		10,000	66,625				76,625
Issuance of 18,000 shares on exercise of stock options		18,000	64,040				82,040
Dividends on common stock			(298,765)	(149,532)			(448,297)
Writedown of investments in noncurrent marketable equity securities					(67,521)		(67,521)
3% stock dividend paid December 31, 197H		58,666	366,663	(434,504)			(9,175)
Net income				3,162,135			3,162,135
Balance—November 30, 197H	$2,063,325	$2,052,429	$6,107,791	$ 863,609	$(67,521)	$(54,144)	$10,965,489

Notes to financial statements:

Note 9 (in part): Shareholders' Equity:

Stock Dividend—On October 20, 197H, the Board of Directors declared a 3% common stock dividend payable to stockholders of record on December 31, 197H. At November 30, 197H, the Company has given effect to the common stock dividend by capitalizing $425,329 of retained earnings, representing the fair value on the declaration date of 58,666 shares of common stock to be issued. In addition, cash to be paid in lieu of fractional shares ($9,175) has been accrued and charged to retained earnings.

Source: AICPA, Accounting Trends and Techniques, 1977, (New York, 1977), p. 304.

ings often is replaced with a more comprehensive schedule. As an example, Exhibit 5–3 presents an actual supplementary schedule, *statement of stockholders' equity,* that often is used to disclose the detailed changes and balances of all elements of owners' equity.

Parenthetical notes are widely used to disclose information such as the method of inventory costing, for example, Inventory (*Fifo;* applied on lower-of-cost-or-market basis). *Contra items,* such as accumulated depreciation and allowance for doubtful accounts, are reported as separate line deductions or parenthetically. *Cross-references* may provide expeditious and useful disclosures, as in the case of mortgaged assets. Assets pledged as security for a loan may be identified parenthetically, and the related liability is cross-referenced to the pledged assets. Examples of these types of disclosures are shown in Exhibit 5–1, and the actual financial statements at the end of Chapters 4 and 5.

Auditors' Report

The auditors' report is also called the accountants' report and the independent accountants' report. It usually follows the financial statements and the notes; however, many believe that it should be the first item because of its importance to statement users and the heavy responsibility auditors assume in expressing their opinion on the financial statements. The independent auditors' primary function is to express an *opinion* on the financial statements. While the auditors have sole responsibility for their opinion expressed in the auditors' report, the primary responsibility for the statements and the supporting notes rests with the management of the enterprise. The statements are those of the management; the auditors affirm or disaffirm them in the *opinion.*

The auditors' report includes (1) a *scope* paragraph and (2) an *opinion* paragraph. The standard format of the auditors' report is as follows:

(Scope paragraph)

We have examined the balance sheet of X Company as of (at) December 31, 19XX, and the related statements of income, retained earnings and changes in financial position for the year

then ended. Our examination was made in accordance with generally accepted auditing standards and, accordingly, included such tests of the accounting records and such other auditing procedures as we considered necessary in the circumstances.

(Opinion paragraph)

In our opinion, the financial statements referred to above present fairly the financial position of X Company as of (at) December 31, 19XX, and the results of its operations and the changes in its financial position for the year then ended, in conformity with generally accepted accounting principles applied on a basis consistent with that of the preceding year.[12]

There are seven key elements in the auditors' report that have special significance:

1. Date.
2. Salutation.
3. Identification of the statements examined.
4. Statement of scope of the examination.
5. Opinion introduction.
6. Reference to fair presentation in conformity with generally accepted accounting principles.
7. Reference to consistency.[13]

Upon completion of the audit, the auditors are required to draft the opinion paragraph to clearly communicate their judgment by giving one of the following:

1. Unqualified opinion—An unqualified opinion is given when the CPA has formed the opinion that the statements (1) "fairly present" results of operations, financial position, and changes in financial position; (2) conform to generally accepted accounting principles, applied on a consistent basis; and (3) full disclosure requirements are met so that the statements are not misleading.
2. Qualified opinion—A qualified opinion is given when there is an "exception" or "subject to" clause because all of the key requirements for an unqualified opinion are not fully met. A qualified opinion must clearly explain the reason for the "exception" or

---

[12] AICPA, *Codification of Statements on Auditing Standards* (New York, 1977), AU Sec. 509.07.

[13] AICPA, *The Auditor's Report—Its Meaning and Significance* (New York, 1967), p. 2.

"subject to" and its effect on the financial statements.

3. Adverse opinion—An adverse opinion is given when the financial statements do not "fairly present" (see above). Also, material exceptions require an adverse opinion on the statements as a whole.

4. Disclaimer of opinion—When the auditors have not been able to obtain sufficient competent evidential matter to form an opinion, auditors must state they are unable to express an opinion (i.e., they issue a disclaimer). Auditors must explain the reasons for not giving an opinion.

A comprehensive discussion of the responsibilities of independent auditors is beyond the scope of this book. The above summary is provided to indicate the importance of auditors' representations when an opinion is provided on whether the representations of the management in the financial statements fairly present, to all users of the statements, the company's financial position, statement of income, and changes in financial position. It is reasonable, therefore, to suggest that the auditors' report should be read prior to spending much time on the financial statements. If it is other than unqualified, one should proceed with extreme caution.

**NATIONWIDE
CORPORATION**

CONSOLIDATED STATEMENTS OF INCOME
Years ended December 31, 1977 and 1976
(000's omitted except for per share amounts)

	1977	1976
Premiums and other revenue:		
Premiums:		
Life and other considerations	$162,119	153,541
Annuity and deposit administration	79,978	55,109
	242,097	208,650
Accident and health	152,626	143,463
Other insurance	16,044	13,148
	410,767	365,261
Net investment income (after deducting expenses of $9,491 in 1977 and $10,363 in 1976)	84,071	71,705
Financial services and other	16,415	14,832
Total income	511,253	451,798
Benefits and expenses:		
Insurance benefits:		
Life and annuities:		
Death and other benefits	83,613	79,281
Increase in future policy benefits	122,046	94,822
	205,659	174,103
Accident and health:		
Benefits	107,850	102,634
Increase in future policy benefits	6,301	3,502
	114,151	106,136
Other insurance	13,913	11,985
Policyholder dividends	28,845	25,945
Amortization of deferred life policy acquisition costs .	18,141	17,239
Other operating costs and expenses	82,795	78,563
Minority interests	2,779	2,293
Total expenses	466,283	416,264
Income before income taxes, equity in (losses) of affiliates, realized investment (losses) and extraordinary item	44.970	35,534
Income tax expense (note 3):		
Current	14,452	12,034
Deferred	1,891	1,358
	16,343	13,392
Equity in (losses) of affiliates	(596)	(190)
Income before realized investment (losses) and extraordinary item	28,031	21,952
Realized investment (losses) less applicable taxes*	(575)	(174)
Income before extraordinary item	27,456	21,778
Extraordinary item-tax benefit from use of prior years' capital loss carryforward (note 4)	863	—
Net income	$ 28,319	21,778
Per common share:		
Operations	$ 2.74	2.15
Realized investment (losses)	(.06)	(.02)
Extraordinary item	.09	—
	$ 2.77	2.13

*Unrealized appreciation, net of taxes, of marketable equity securities has not been reflected in the statements of income. The unrealized appreciation (depreciation) aggregated $(6,121) in 1977, and $10,874 in 1976.

See accompanying notes to consolidated financial statements.

NATIONWIDE CORPORATION

CONSOLIDATED BALANCE SHEETS
December 31, 1977 and 1976
(000's omitted)

	1977	1976
Assets		
Investments:		
Bonds and notes, at amortized cost (market $650,475 in 1977; $526,749 in 1976)	$ 683,186	547,594
Preferred stocks, at cost (market $40,754 in 1977; $29,866 in 1976)	42,620	31,956
Preferred stocks, at market (cost $21,122 in 1977; $13,183 in 1976)	17,898	10,496
Common stocks, at market (cost $78,677 in 1977; $65,227 in 1976)	84,477	79,273
Mortgage loans on real estate, net of allowance of $150 in 1977 ($559 — 1976)	352,669	352,586
Real estate, at cost less accumulated depreciation of $1,355 ($4,245 — 1976) and allowances of $2,738 ($2,055 — 1976)	22,419	53,114
Policy loans	85,513	77,528
Other loans and investments, at cost	13,078	11,940
Total investments	1.301,860	1,164,487
Cash	14,811	13,686
Investments in affiliates, at equity	1,076	1,672
Accounts receivable, less allowances of $1,752 ($1,929 — 1976)	19,980	17,138
Deferred policy acquisition costs	194,208	180,553
Property and equipment, at cost less accumulated depreciation of $2,512 ($2,188 — 1976)	3,427	3,520
Other assets	26,198	23,708
Assets held in Separate Accounts	162,558	141,936
Excess of investments in consolidated subsidiaries over fair value of net assets	25,716	25,779
	$1,749,834	1,572,479

See accompanying notes to consolidated financial statements.

	1977	1976
Liabilities and Shareholders' Equity		
Future policy benefits	S 989,417	860,938
Policy and contract claims	91,190	74,085
Policyholders' dividend accumulations	103,033	95,331
Other policyholders' funds	32,521	29,733
	1,216,161	1,060,087
Accrued income taxes:		
Current	4,776	3,555
Deferred, including $1,193 applicable to unrealized		
investment gains in 1977 ($3,091 in 1976)	31,883	33,926
	36,659	37,481
Mortgage payable	—	19,964
Other liabilities	31,618	30,080
Liabilities related to Separate Accounts	162,558	141,936
Minority interests	20,183	18,207
Total liabilities	1,467,179	1,307,755
Shareholders' equity (notes 6, 7 and 8):		
Preferred and Preference shares, no par value.		
Authorized 3,000,000 shares, none issued	—	—
Common shares:		
Class A, $2.50 par value. Authorized 15,000,000		
shares, issued 4,726,437 (4,725,437 in 1976)	11,816	11,814
Class B, $.50 par value. Authorized 10,000,000		
shares; issued 5,506,593	2,753	2,753
	14,569	14,567
Capital in excess of par value	84,690	84,604
Unrealized investment gains, net	620	6,798
Retained earnings	182,806	158,785
	282,685	264,754
Less 2,000 Class A shares in treasury, at cost	30	30
Total shareholders' equity	282,655	264,724
	$1,749,834	1,572,479

CONSOLIDATED STATEMENTS OF SHAREHOLDERS' EQUITY
Years ended December 31, 1977 and 1976
(000's omitted)

1977	Common shares (Class A and B)	Capital in excess of par value	Unrealized investment gains (losses), net	Retained earnings
Balance, beginning of year	$14,567	84,604	6,798	158,785
Net income	—	—	—	28,319
Unrealized investment (losses), net	—	—	(6,178)	—
Dividends to shareholders ($.42 per share)	—	—	—	(4,298)
Employee stock options and other	2	86	—	—
Balance, end of year	$14,569	84,690	620	182,806

NATIONWIDE CORPORATION

STATEMENTS OF CHANGES IN FINANCIAL POSITION
Years ended December 31, 1977 and 1976
(000's omitted)

Funds provided:
  From operations:
      Net income excluding extraordinary item ....

      Charges (credits) to income not requiring funds:
          Increase in future policy benefits, claims
              and other policyholder funds ....
          Amortization of deferred life policy acquisition costs ....
          Increase (decrease) in deferred income taxes ....
          Increase (decrease) in accounts payable and other liabilities ....
          Realized investment losses due to valuation allowances and
              permanent impairments ....
          Other, net ....
          Equity in earnings of affiliates ....
                          Funds provided by operations ....
  Extraordinary item ....
  Cumulative effect of change in accounting did not provide or use funds ....
  Investments sold or matured, including mortgage loan principal receipts* ....
  Proceeds from sale of real estate to parent ....
  Proceeds from borrowed money ....
  Other, net ....
  Decrease in cash ....

Funds applied:
  Investments purchased*..
  Additions to deferred life policy acquisition costs ....
  Policy loans, net ....
  Repayment of borrowed money ....
  Dividends to shareholders ....
  Other, net ....
  Increase in cash ....

*Excluding short-term investments.

See accompanying notes to consolidated financial statements.

1976	Common shares (Class A and B)	Capital in excess of par value	Unrealized investment gains (losses), net	Retained earnings
Balance, beginning of year	14,567	84,604	(4,258)	140,588
Net income	—	—	—	21,778
Unrealized investment gains, net	—	—	11,056	—
Dividends to shareholders ($.35 per share)	—	—	—	(3,581)
Balance, end of year	$14,567	84,604	6,798	158,785

Consolidated		Combined Life Insurance Subsidiaries		National Casualty Company— Other Insurance Operations		Combined Financial Service Subsidiaries	
1977	1976	1977	1976	1977	1976	1977	1976
$ 27,456	21,778	26,280	20,605	1,150	1,560	1,622	1,631
156,074	115,187	145,218	108,188	11,340	6,877	—	—
18,141	17,239	18,148	17,248	—	—	—	—
283	1,358	(1)	1,084	(331)	(634)	—	—
2,306	4,545	1,880	5,240	363	(1,244)	(43)	639
1,444	1,238	1,640	1,238	—	—	—	—
(2,835)	(564)	(2,181)	1,123	(2,600)	(2,800)	(936)	(178)
596	190	—	—	596	190	—	—
203,465	160,971	190,984	154,726	10,518	3,949	643	2,092
863	—	863	—	—	—	—	—
124,539	59,129	116,298	53,920	8,047	5,209	—	—
—	—	194	2,722	—	—	—	—
300	—	—	—	—	—	300	—
—	2,012	—	—	20	1,184	403	—
—	—	—	—	—	763	118	2
$329,167	222,112	308,339	211,368	18,585	11,105	1,464	2,094
261,934	175,679	244,738	164,314	17,723	10,705	4	660
31,043	29,331	31,043	29,331	—	—	—	—
7,985	6,784	7,977	6,772	—	—	76	103
20,040	6,575	19,964	6,472	—	—	1,384	1,153
4,298	3,581	3,379	3,008	600	400	—	178
2,742	—	939	435	—	—	—	—
1,125	162	299	1,036	262	—	—	—
$329,167	222,112	308,339	211,368	18,585	11,105	1,464	2,094

NOTE: The consolidated amounts will not necessarily equal the sum of the groups due to parent company and inter-company eliminations.

NATIONWIDE CORPORATION AND SUBSIDIARIES

NOTES
To Consolidated Financial Statements

December 31, 1977 and 1976

(1) Summary of Significant Accounting Policies

The consolidated financial statements include the accounts of the Corporation and all significant subsidiaries. The financial statements of the life insurance subsidiaries and other financial service subsidiaries are also presented on a combined basis. All material intercompany accounts and transactions have been eliminated in consolidation.

Investments are carried on the basis indicated in the accompanying balance sheets. Unrealized gains and losses, less the applicable Federal income tax effect, are credited or charged to shareholders' equity. Realized gains or losses on the sale of investments, which are determined on the basis of specific security identification, less the related Federal income tax effect, have been included in net income. Estimates for permanent impairment and valuation allowances are included in realized gains or losses on investments.

The excess of cost over market of bonds and applicable preferred stocks was $34,577,000 at December 31, 1977. No provision has been made for possible losses resulting from the decline in current market value as it is the intention to hold the securities to maturity, where applicable, or until such time as disposition would not result in a material loss.

(a) Insurance Accounting

The statutory financial statements of the life and casualty insurance subsidiaries have been adjusted to conform to generally accepted accounting principles. The significant adjustments and accounting policies are as follows:

Life Insurance Subsidiaries

Premium income is generally reported as earned when collected except for certain accident and health contracts where premiums are earned on a monthly pro rata basis. Benefits and expenses are associated with premium income so as to result in recognition of profits over the life of the contracts. This association is accomplished by means of the provision for liabilities for future benefits and the amortization of policy acquisition costs.

The costs of acquiring new business, principally commissions, certain expenses of the policy issue and underwriting department and certain variable agency expenses have been deferred. These deferred acquisition costs are being amortized with interest over the premium paying period of the related policies in proportion to the ratio of actual annual premium revenue to the total premium revenue anticipated. Such anticipated premium revenue was estimated using the same assumptions as were used for computing liabilities for future policy benefits.

Future policy benefits have been calculated using a net level premium method based on estimates of mortality, investment yields, and withdrawals which were used or which were being experienced at the time the policies were issued, rather than the assumptions prescribed by state regulatory authorities. See note 2 for the more material assumptions pertinent thereto.

Participating business represents approximately 72% of the ordinary life insurance in force, 79% of the number of policies in force and 78% of premium revenue (72%, 81% and 79%, respectively, in 1976). The provision for policy-holder dividends is based on current dividend scales. Future dividends are provided for ratably in future policy benefits based on dividend scales in effect at the time the policies were issued. Dividend scales are approved by the Boards of Directors.

Property and Casualty Subsidiary

Premiums earned by this subsidiary principally relate to accident and health insurance, with the remainder consisting of reinsurance of primarily property and casualty coverages. Insurance premiums are recognized as revenues ratably over the terms of the policies. Unearned premiums are computed on both a monthly and daily pro rata basis, and are stated after deduction for reinsurance placed with other insurers.

The accrual for losses is based upon aggregate case basis estimates for reported losses, estimates of unreported losses based upon past experience, estimates received relating to assumed reinsurance, and deduction of amounts for reinsurance placed with reinsurers. Additionally, an accrual for loss adjustment expenses is estimated to provide for future expenses to be incurred in settlement of the claims provided for in the accrual for losses.

(b) Income Taxes

Provision for Federal income taxes is based upon separate Federal income tax returns for life subsidiaries and a consolidated income tax return for the Corporation and all other subsidiaries. In this regard the includable subsidiaries pay to the Corporation the amount which would have been payable on a separate return basis, and the Corporation pays the tax due on a consolidated basis. Investment credits, which are not material, are credited to income taxes in the year realized.

The Corporation has filed an election permitting the exclusion from taxation of dividends paid to the Corporation by life insurance subsidiaries. The Corporation and its subsidiaries follow the practice of providing for deferred income taxes in transactions that represent timing differences between financial and tax reporting.

(c) Excess of Investments in Consolidated Subsidiaries Over Fair Value of Net Assets

Such excess as arose prior to November 1, 1970 is not being amortized as there is considered to be no diminution in the value of the assets or businesses acquired. Subsequent to such date the Corporation undertook to acquire additional interest in subsidiaries. The equity acquired, adjusted for purchase accounting where appropriate, in excess of the cash paid for the additional interests, has been applied as a reduction of the amounts previously recorded. Amortization of these intangibles, where appropriate, is not material to the results of operations.

(d) Pension Plan

The Corporation is a participant, together with other affiliated companies, in a pension plan covering substantially all employees. Plan contributions are invested in group annuity contracts. Pension costs are computed on the entry age normal method with frozen initial liability. The Corporation charges as expense each year normal cost plus the amount required to amortize unfunded liabilities in fifteen years. The Corporation funds pension costs accrued.

(e) Earnings Per Share

The earnings per share was computed on 10,230,530 shares (10,230,030 in 1976), the average number of Class A and Class B shares combined. There is no material dilution of earnings per share as a result of outstanding stock options.

(f) Reclassifications

Certain reclassifications have been made in the 1976 financial statements to conform to the 1977 presentation.

(2) Future Policy Benefits

The actuarial assumptions for individual life policies which have been made in the adjustment of statutory future policy benefits to the basis of generally accepted accounting principles, and which are believed to adequately provide for the possibility of adverse deviations from expected experience, are:

Withdrawals: Withdrawal rates for individual life policies are based on individual company experience with due consideration given to issue age, type of coverage and policy duration.

Interest: Rates for each company were determined considering (among other things) the company's investment experience. Rates for 1966-1972 issues range from 6% to $6^{1}/_{2}\%$ (graded on a 5 year step-rated basis to 4% or $4^{1}/_{2}\%$ no later than the end of the 20th policy year), except that West Coast Life for years of issue 1966-1972 has used a level rate (for all durations) of 4% or $4^{1}/_{2}\%$. Such rates were also used in 1973, except for Nationwide Life which used 7% graded to 4%-5%. The rates used subsequent to 1973 ranged from $6^{1}/_{2}\%$-7% graded to 4%-5%. Rates for earlier years of issue were generally lower than those used for the issues of 1966-1972.

Mortality: Mortality rates used for each company in the computations of policy reserves are based on published mortality tables modified as necessary to conform to each company's expected experience.

(3) Federal Income Taxes

The life insurance subsidiaries are taxable under the Life Insurance Company Income Tax Act of 1959, which has permitted certain accumulations in retained earnings, aggregating $19,629,000 at December 31, 1977, which would be subject to income taxes to such companies upon distribution to shareholders. The companies do not contemplate any such distributions, and accordingly have made no provision for income taxes on such amount.

The amounts and sources of deferred Federal income taxes, computed at the normal rate, are:

	1977	1976
	(000's omitted)	
Deferred policy acquisition costs and policy liabilities	$ 5,420	$ 4,300
Additional net level reserve deductions	2,146	2,507
Special life insurance company deductions and exclusions	(2,496)	(2,065)
Dividends subject to statutory limitations	(2,096)	(2,523)
Expenses not currently deductible	(330)	(108)
Other	(753)	(753)
Total	$ 1,891	$ 1,358

Total Federal income tax expense is less than the amount computed by applying the normal tax to income before taxes. The reasons for this difference are:

	1977	1976
Computed tax rate	48%	48%
Tax-exempt interest and dividends received	(8)	(6)
Special life insurance deductions and exclusions	(7)	(7)
Minority interest adjustment and other	3	3
Effective rate	36%	38%

(4) Sale of Building and Extraordinary Item

In 1977 West Coast Life Insurance Company sold its home office building and realized a gain for financial statement and tax return purposes. As a result of the sale, West Coast Life was able to use its $2,877,000 capital loss carryforward which resulted in a tax reduction of $863,000 which is shown as an extraordinary item in the accompanying financial statements.

(5) Accounting Change
In connection with a program for strengthening long-term disability reserves, National Casualty Company increased accident and health benefits $2,411,000.

The reserve increase was partially offset by that company changing its method of calculating these reserves in 1977 to recognize the time value of money (discounting) at an assumed interest rate of 4%. The discounting increased the company's income before the cumulative effect of the accounting change by $993,000 and net income by $1,745,000. This change, reduced by the consolidated income tax effect, is not significant to consolidated net income.

(6) Preferred and Common Shares
(a) Preferred Shares
The Corporation has authorized 2,000,000 shares of Preferred Stock without par value and 1,000,000 shares of Preference Stock without par value, none of which are issued. The Preferred and Preference shares shall have cumulative dividend rights and may be issued in series upon terms which, except for voting rights, are to be set by the Board of Directors. The holders of Preferred Stock shall be entitled to one vote for each share held and shall vote with Class A common shareholders as a class unless the Preferred Stock is convertible into Class B common shares in which event such holder shall vote with Class B common shareholders as a class. The holders of Preference Stock would not be entitled to vote except in specific situations.

(b) Common Shares
The Class A and Class B (all of the Class B are owned by Nationwide Mutual and Nationwide Mutual Fire Insurance Companies) common shareholders have the following rights: (1) corporate action requiring shareholder approval, except the election of directors, must be approved by the holders of a majority of each class of shares; (2) each class of shareholders is entitled to elect one-half of the members of the Board of Directors except that the number to be elected by the Class B shareholders is subject to reduction as the proportion of Class B shares to total shares outstanding is reduced; (3) the Class B common shares, under certain circumstances, are convertible into Class A common shares, for which 5,506,593 shares of Class A are reserved; and (4) in the event of liquidation, dissolution or winding up

of the Corporation, after the payment of its debts, the holders of the Class A common shares are first entitled to a distribution equivalent to $2.50 per share, then the holders of the Class B common shares are entitled to $2.50 per share and thereafter the remaining assets are to be distributed on a pro rata basis.

(7) Retained Earnings and Dividend Restrictions
Participating Insurance
Participating insurance constitutes 80% of the ordinary life insurance in force of Nationwide Life Insurance Company (88% owned) which is included in the consolidated and combined life financial statements. In accordance with the requirements of the New York statutes, Nationwide Life has agreed with the Superintendent of Insurance of that state that so long as participating policies and contracts are held by residents of New York, no profits on participating policies and contracts in excess of the larger of (a) ten percent of such profits or (b) fifty cents per year per thousand dollars of participating life insurance in force, exclusive of group term, at the year-end shall inure to the benefit of the shareholders. Such New York statutes further provide that so long as such agreement is in effect, such excess of profits shall be exhibited as "participating policyholders' surplus" in annual statements filed with the Superintendent and shall be used only for the payment or apportionment of dividends to participating policyholders at least to the extent required by statute or for the purpose of making up any loss on participating policies.

In the opinion of counsel for the Company, with the concurring opinion of New York counsel as to New York law, the ultimate ownership of the entire surplus, however classified, of the Company resides in the shareholders, subject to the usual requirements under state laws and regulations that certain deposits, reserves and minimum surplus be maintained for the protection of the policyholders until all policy contracts are discharged.

Based on the opinions of counsel with respect to the ownership of its surplus, the Company is of the opinion that the earnings attributable to participating policies in excess of the amounts paid as dividends to policyholders belong to the shareholders rather than the policyholders, and such earnings are so treated by the Company.

The amount of shareholders' equity other than capital shares included in the financial statements of the combined life insurance companies pertaining to Nationwide Life Insurance Company at December 31, 1977 and 1976 was $154,364,000 and $138,196,000, respectively. The amount thereof not available for dividends due to the New York restriction and to adjustments relating to generally accepted accounting principles was approximately

$142,289,000 and $130,850,000, respectively ($125,130,000 and $115,070,000 applicable to the Corporation).

Retained Earnings

The undistributed income of the insurance subsidiaries included in retained earnings includes adjustments of net assets from statutory to a generally accepted accounting basis which amounts, together with the previously described amounts relating to Nationwide Life Insurance Company, are not available for distribution to the parent company and are therefore considered to be restricted. Any dividends paid by the insurance subsidiaries are subject to the applicable requirements of regulatory authorities.

After giving effect to the aforementioned matters, the amount of the Corporation's retained earnings which was restricted at December 31, 1977 was $135,500,000.

(8) Stock Options

Under a qualified stock option plan 243,960 Class A common shares have been reserved for issuance to employees of the Corporation and its subsidiaries. Options are exercisable under specified conditions during a five year period from the date of grant. At December 31, 1977 options for 65,334 shares were exercisable and 174,960 shares remained available for the granting of additional options.

Information as of December 31, 1977 with respect to options under the plan is as follows:

	1977		1976	
	Average price	Number of shares	Average price	Number of shares
Outstanding at beginning of year	$10.98	88,500	$11.47	81,500
Granted	—	—	8.94	17,500
Exercised	7.31	(1,000)	—	—
Expired	18.72	(18,500)	11.38	(10,500)
Outstanding at end of year	$ 8.95	69,000	$10.98	88,500

(9) Pension Plan

Net assets of the pension plans of the Corporation and its subsidiaries exceeded the actuarially computed value of the vested benefits as of the most recent valuation date. Pension costs charged to operations during the years 1977 and 1976 were approximately $2,941,000 and $2,671,000, respectively.

The plans were amended in 1976 to comply with provisions of the Employee Retirement Income Security Act of 1974 and for other changes. During 1977, certain actuarial assumptions relating to participants' salaries and social security covered earnings were revised. These changes had no material effect on net income of the respective years.

(10) Realized and Unrealized Investment Gains (Losses)

Realized investment gains (losses), net, were comprised of the following:

	1977	1976
	(000's omitted)	
Valuation allowances and permanent impairments	$ (1,444)	(1,238)
Realized gains	869	1,064
	$ (575)	(174)

At December 31, 1977, net unrealized gains were $1,718,000, before providing for deferred income taxes, composed of $13,601,000 of unrealized gains and $11,883,000 of unrealized losses, and are included as an addition to shareholders' equity, net of deferred income taxes and the interest of minority shareholders.

(11) Contingencies

The Corporation and its subsidiaries are defendants in several lawsuits. In the opinion of management, the effects, if any, of such lawsuits are not expected to be material to the consolidated financial position or related results of operations.

(12) Transactions With Affiliates

The Corporation and certain consolidated subsidiaries share home office, other facilities and equipment and certain common management and administrative services with affiliates.

(13) Quarterly Operating Results (Unaudited)

Selected quarterly financial data for the years ended December 31, 1977 and 1976 were as follows:

(000's omitted except for per share information)

	1977 Quarter ended			
	March 31,	June 30,	Sept. 30,	Dec. 31,
Total income	$117,447	126,002	127,328	140,476
Income before tax and realized gains (losses)	$ 11,068	10,638	11,141	12,123
Income from operations	6,591	6,667	6,995	7,778
Realized investment gains (losses), less applicable taxes	(195)	170	350	(900)
Extraordinary item	—	—	863	—
Net income	$ 6,396	6,837	8,208	6,878
Per common share:				
Operations	$ .65	.64	.69	.76
Realized investment gains (losses)	(.02)	.02	.03	(.09)
Extraordinary item	—	—	.09	—
Net income	$ .63	.66	.81	.67

(000's omitted except for per share information)

1976
Quarter ended

	March 31,	June 30,	Sept. 30,	Dec. 31,
Total income	$100,999	105,659	115,781	129,359
Income before tax and realized gains (losses)	$ 8,186	9,159	10,144	8,045
Income from operations	4,887	5,853	6,754	4,458
Realized investment gains (losses), less applicable taxes	226	(401)	(184)	185
Net income	$ 5,113	5,452	6,570	4,643
Per common share: Operations	$ .48	.57	.66	.44
Realized investment gains (losses)	.02	(.04)	(.02)	.02
Net income	$ .50	.53	.64	.46

(14) Segment Information

Nationwide Corporation is a holding company principally engaged through its subsidiaries in the business of life, health and casualty insurance and financial services. The following is a summary of information about the Corporation's operations in different business segments for the year ended December 31, 1977 (000's omitted).

	Premiums and other revenue	Income from operations	Identifiable assets excluding investments in consolidated subsidiaries
Combined Life Insurance Subsidiaries	$424,196	42,944	1,603,290
National Casualty Company	70,361	1,282	100,059
Combined Financial Service Subsidiaries	15,403	3,361	6,643
Parent company	6,079	3,908	17,143
Consolidation adjustments	(4,786)	(6,525)	22,699
Consolidated	$511,253	44,970	1,749,834

PEAT, MARWICK, MITCHELL & CO.
CERTIFIED PUBLIC ACCOUNTANTS
100 EAST BROAD STREET
COLUMBUS, OHIO 43215

The Board of Directors and the Shareholders of Nationwide Corporation:

We have examined the accompanying consolidated financial statements of Nationwide Corporation and the financial statements of the combined life insurance subsidiaries, the combined financial service subsidiaries, and National Casualty Company as of December 31, 1977 and 1976 and for the years then ended. Our examinations were made in accordance with generally accepted auditing standards, and accordingly included such tests of the accounting records and such other auditing procedures as we considered necessary in the circumstances.

Participating insurance and the related surplus of a major life insurance subsidiary are discussed in note 7. The subsidiary and the Corporation and their counsel are of the opinion that the ultimate ownership of the participating surplus in excess of contemplated equitable policyholder dividends belongs to the shareholders. The accompanying financial statements are presented on such basis.

In our opinion, the accompanying consolidated balance sheets of Nationwide Corporation, the balance sheets of the combined life insurance subsidiaries, the combined financial service subsidiaries, and National Casualty Company and the applicable related statements of income, shareholders' equity and changes in financial position present fairly the financial position of Nationwide Corporation and its subsidiaries, the respective combined companies and National Casualty Company at December 31, 1977 and 1976 and the applicable results of operations and changes in financial position for the years then ended, in conformity with generally accepted accounting principles consistently applied during the period except for the change in 1977, with which we concur, in the method of calculating long-term disability loss reserves of National Casualty Company as described in note 5 to the financial statements.

PEAT, MARWICK, MITCHELL & CO.

March 3, 1978

NATIONWIDE CORPORATION

EARNINGS, DIVIDENDS AND MARKET INFORMATION

		Operating Income Per Share	Net Income Per Share	Dividends Declared Per Share	Market Price of Shares* High Bid	Low Bid
First Quarter	— 1977....	$ .65	$ .63	$.105	11¹₂	9½
Second Quarter	— 1977....	.64	.66	.105	13	10¼
Third Quarter	— 1977....	.69	.81	.105	13³₈	11½
Fourth Quarter	— 1977....	.76	.67	.105	12¹₂	10⅜
Calendar	— 1977....	$2.74	$2.77	$.42		
First Quarter	— 1976....	$ .48	$ .50	$ —	$ 9⅝	$ 7
Second Quarter	— 1976....	.57	.53	.175	8¾	7
Third Quarter	— 1976....	.66	.64	—	10½	8½
Fourth Quarter	— 1976....	.44	.46	.175	9¾	8⅝
Calendar	— 1976....	$2.15	$2.13	$.35		

Earning per share based on 10,230,500 shares outstanding

*Nationwide Corporation Class A common shares are traded in the Over-the-Counter market. The market price quotations were furnished by the National Quotation Bureau, Inc.

STATISTICAL SUMMARY
(000's omitted)

SUBSIDIARY COMPANIES COMBINED*	1977	1976	1975	1974	1973
Shareholders' equity (consolidated)	$ 282,655	$ 264,724	$ 235,471	$ 218,015	$ 215,127
Assets	1,709,993	1,534,992	1,341,557	1,194,469	1,125,688
Life insurance in force	15,067,239	14,164,803	13,567,284	12,974,403	11,923,721
Individual life sales	1,597,180	1,623,984	1,522,939	1,383,057	1,418,493
Group life sales	862,113	664,852	834,276	682,733	598,865
Total life sales	2,459,293	2,288,836	2,357,215	2,065,790	2,017,358
Individual life premiums	121,920	115,558	107,079	100,773	92,147
Group life premiums	40,199	37,983	38,086	35,185	40,288
Individual health premiums	47,656	43,761	37,611	35,070	33,165
Group health premiums	104,970	99,702	96,362	86,546	82,559
Individual annuity considerations	39,126	17,005	1,849	1,136	1,228
Group annuity considerations	40,852	38,104	11,754	8,845	10,125
Other insurance premiums	16,044	13,148	10,930	9,154	8,574
Total premiums and other considerations	410,767	365,261	303,671	276,709	268,086
Mutual fund sales	19,067	15,505	12,225	13,892	19,473
Financial services fees and related income	15,403	13,816	11,825	11,465	10,373
Ratio of investment income to mean assets — Life companies	7.17%	6.92%	6.68%	6.57%	6.24%

*Includes all subsidiary companies owned as of 12/31/77

QUESTIONS

1. What is a balance sheet? Why is it dated differently than an income statement and a statement of changes in financial position?

2. Define assets.

3. Define liabilities.

4. Explain, in general terms, why the balance sheet is important to the decision maker.

5. Explain why the balance sheet does not report the current market value of a business.

6. Contrast the two balance sheet formats.

7. Define current assets and current liabilities emphasizing their interrelationship.

8. Define working capital. What is the current ratio?

9. Distinguish between short-term investments and the investments classified as investments and funds. Under what conditions could an investment be moved from current assets to investments and funds and vice versa?

10. What are operational assets? Distinguish between tangible and intangible operational assets.

11. Why is it often necessary to use a caption "Other Assets"? Give two examples of items that might be reported under this classification.

12. Explain a deferred charge and contrast it with a prepaid expense.

13. Distinguish between current and noncurrent liabilities. Under what conditions would a noncurrent liability amount be reclassified as a current liability?

14. What is a deferred credit? Explain why this classification, reported on a balance sheet between liabilities and owners' equity, is difficult to defend conceptually.

15. What is owners' equity? What are the main components of owners' equity?

16. What is a restriction on retained earnings? How are restrictions reported?

17. What is the purpose of the statement of changes in financial position? What is meant by the all-resources concept?

18. Distinguish between a statement of changes in financial position prepared on (a) a cash equivalent basis and (b) a working capital basis.

19. Explain the position of the accounting profession with respect to use of the terms reserves, surplus, and net profit. Why is care in selection of terminology used in financial statements important?

20. What are comparative statements? Why are they important?

21. What is meant by subsequent events? Why are they reported? How are they reported?

22. In general, why are notes in the financial statements important? How does the accountant determine when a note should be included?

23. What is the auditors' report? Basically, what does it include? Why is it especially important to the statement user?

24. Are the financial statements the representations of the management of the enterprise, the independent accountant, or both? Explain.

DECISION CASE 5–1

A. McDougald & Sons is a family corporation operating a chain of seven retail clothing stores in the Southwest. The total owners' equity of $5 million (all shares are outstanding) is owned by A. McDougald (president and founder) and eight members of the McDougald family. Except for accounts payable, modest amounts of short-term bank credit, and the usual short-term liabilities, the entire resources of the enterprise came from contributed capital and retained earnings. The general reputation of the company is excellent, and there have never been complaints about slowness in paying its liabilities. The family now has an opportunity to undertake a profitable expansion from seven to ten stores and estimates that upwards of $2,500,000 will be required for the purpose. It will be necessary to borrow this sum, and the issuance of five- to eight-year mortgage notes is contemplated.

Because the business is closely held and has never borrowed to an extent that made issuance of financial statements to outsiders necessary, the only persons who have seen the corporation's statements are members of the family, a few top employees, and some governmental officials, chiefly tax agents. When A. McDougald was told by a prospective lender that detailed financial statements for the past five years and audited statements for the most recent year as a basis for considering the loan would have to be provided, McDougald's initial reaction was to "hit the ceiling." After consideration, however, McDougald became willing to have the audit made and to release balance sheets as of the end of the most recent five years. McDougald was, as yet, unwilling to release statements of income and changes in financial position, and a majority of the other owners agreed with this stand.

Required:

1. If these five balance sheets are quite detailed, what can prospective lenders ascertain from them?
2. In your opinion would the five balance sheets give enough information to warrant granting a $2,500,000 secured intermediate-term loan? Explain the basis for your response.
3. If you were the lending officer of the prospective creditor and sought a compromise in the form of getting some added financial facts without receiving the other statements, what added information would be most useful to you?

EXERCISES

Exercise 5–1

Below left is a list of several different items from a typical balance sheet for a corporation. Below right is a list of brief statements of the valuations usually reported on the balance sheet for the different items.

Required:

Use the code letters to the right to indicate, for each balance sheet item listed, the *usual* valuation reported on the balance sheet. Comment on any doubtful items. Some code letters may be used more than once or not at all.

Balance Sheet Items	Valuations Usually Reported
1.____Accounts receivable (trade).	a. Amount payable when due (usually no interest because short-term).
2.____Short-term investments.	b. Lower of cost or market.
3.____Merchandise inventory.	c. Original cost when acquired.
4.____Long-term investment in bonds of another company (purchased at a discount).	d. Market value at date of the balance sheet whether it is above or below cost.
5.____Plant site (in use).	e. Original cost less accumulated amortization over estimated economic life.
6.____Plant and equipment (in use).	f. Par value of the issued shares.
7.____Patent (in use).	g. Face amount of the obligation plus unamortized premium.
8.____Accounts payable (trade).	h. Realizable value expected.
9.____Bonds payable (sold at a premium).	i. Principal of the asset less unamortized discount.
10.____Common stock (par $10 per share).	j. Cost when acquired less accumulated depreciation.
11.____Contributed capital in excess of par.	k. Accumulated income less accumulated losses and dividends.
12.____Retained earnings.	
13.____Land (future plant site).	

14.____Idle plant (awaiting disposal).
15.____Natural resource.

l. Excess of issue price over par or stated value.
m. No valuation reported (explain).
n. Expected net disposal proceeds.
o. Cost less accumulated depletion.
p. None of the above (when this response is used, explain the valuation usually used).

Exercise 5–2

Following are listed, in scrambled order, the major and minor captions for a balance sheet and a statement of changes in financial position (cash equivalent basis). Terminology given in the chapter is used.

1. Owners' equity.
2. Sources of cash (inflows).
3. Contributed capital.
4. Add (deduct) adjustments to revenue to derive cash basis.
5. Retained earnings.
6. Expenses (accrual basis).
7. Current liabilities.
8. From extraordinary items (net of tax).
9. Uses of cash.
10. Unrealized capital.
11. Assets.
12. Total cash expended for all purposes.
13. Operational assets—tangible.
14. Cash generated from revenues.
15. Total cash generated from other sources.
16. Long-term liabilities.
17. Total assets.
18. Current assets.
19. Capital stock.
20. Cash from other sources.
21. Other assets.
22. From operations (cash inflow).
23. Revenues (accrual basis).
24. Contributed capital in excess of par.
25. Deferred charges.
26. Total cash generated by operations.
27. Total cash generated from all sources.
28. Liabilities.
29. Investments and funds.
30. Net increase (decrease) in cash.
31. Operational assets—intangible.
32. Cash disbursed for expenses.
33. Total liabilities.
34. Total liabilities and owners' equity.
35. Total owners' equity.
36. Add (deduct) adjustments to expenses to derive cash basis.

Required:

Set up two captions: *(a)* Balance Sheet and *(b)* Statement of Changes in Financial Position. For each caption, list the numbers given above in the order that they normally would be reported on the statements (do not renumber). Example:

a. Balance Sheet: 11, 18, and so on.
b. Statement of Changes in Financial Position: 2, 22, and so on.

Comment on any doubtful items.

Exercise 5–3

Indicate the best answer for each of the following (explain any qualifications):

1. Working capital means
   a. Excess of current assets over current liabilities.
   b. Current assets.
   c. Capital contributed by stockholders.
   d. Capital contributed by stockholders plus retained earnings.
2. The distinction between current and noncurrent assets and liabilities is based primarily upon
   a. One year; no exceptions.
   b. One year or operating cycle, whichever is shorter.
   c. One year or operating cycle, whichever is longer.
   d. Operating cycle; no exceptions.
3. Under generally accepted accounting principles, unexpired insurance is a
   a. Noncurrent asset.
   b. Deferred charge.
   c. Prepaid expense.
   d. Short-term investment.
4. Which of the following is not a current asset?
   a. Office supplies inventory.
   b. Short-term investment.
   c. Petty cash (undeposited cash).
   d. Cash surrender value of life insurance policies.
5. Which of the following is not a current liability?
   a. Accrued interest on notes payable.
   b. Accrued interest on bonds payable.
   c. Rent revenue collected in advance.
   d. Premium on bonds payable (unamortized).
6. A deficit is synonymous with
   a. A net loss for the current period.
   b. A cash overdraft at the bank.
   c. Negative working capital at the end of the period.
   d. A debit balance in retained earnings at the end of the period.

7. A balance sheet is an expression of the model
   a. Assets = Liabilities + Owners' Equity.
   b. Assets = Liabilities − Owners' Equity.
   c. Assets + Liabilities = Owners' Equity.
   d. Working Capital + Operational Assets − Long-Term Liabilities = Contributed Capital.
8. Acceptable usage of the term *reserve* is reflected by
   a. Deduction from an asset to reflect accumulated depreciation.
   b. Description of a known liability for which the amount is estimated.
   c. Restriction on retained earnings.
   d. Deduction on the income statement for an expected loss.
9. Which terminology essentially is synonymous with "balance sheet"?
   a. Operating statement.
   b. Statement of changes in financial position.
   c. Statement of financial value of the business.
   d. Statement of resources, obligations, and residual equity.
10. The "operating cycle concept"
   a. Causes the distinction between current and noncurrent items to depend upon whether they will affect cash within one year.
   b. Permits some assets to be classed as current even though they are more than one year removed from becoming cash.
   c. Is becoming obsolete.
   d. Affects the income statement but not the balance sheet.

Exercise 5–4

A typical balance sheet has the following captions:

A. Current assets.
B. Investments and funds.
C. Operational assets (land, buildings, and equipment).
D. Intangible assets.
E. Other assets.
F. Deferred charges.
G. Current liabilities.
H. Long-term liabilities.
I. Capital stock.
J. Additional contributed capital.
K. Retained earnings

Indicate by use of the above letters (use capitals and print) how each of the following items would be classified. When an item is a contra amount (i.e., a deduction) in a caption, place a minus before the lettered response.

1. Accounts payable (trade).
2. Bonds payable (due in ten years).

3. Accumulated depreciation.
4. Investment in stock of X Company (long term).
5. Plant site (in use).
6. Restriction on retained earnings.
7. Office supplies inventory.
8. Loan to company president (collection not expected for two years).
9. Accumulated income less accumulated dividends.
10. Bond discount unamortized (on bonds payable).
11. Bond sinking fund (to retire long-term bonds).
12. Prepaid insurance.
13. Accounts receivable (trade).
14. Short-term investment.
15. Allowance for doubtful accounts.
16. Building (in use).
17. Common stock (par $10).
18. Interest revenue earned but not collected.
19. Patent.
20. Land (speculative).

Exercise 5–5

Typical balance sheet captions are listed in Exercise 5–4. Indicate, by use of the letters given there (use capitals and print), how each of the following items would be classified. When an item is a contra amount (i.e., a deduction) in a caption, place a minus before the lettered response.

1. Short-term investments.
2. Premium unamortized (on bonds payable).
3. Bonds payable (long term).
4. Cash dividends payable (within six months).
5. Rent revenue collected in advance.
6. Accumulated depreciation.
7. Premium on common stock issued.
8. Idle plant held for final disposal.
9. Deferred costs being amortized over five years.
10. Inventory of supplies.
11. Preferred stock.
12. Discount unamortized on long-term investment in bonds of another company.
13. Installment payment due in six months on long-term note payable.
14. Accrued interest on note payable.
15. Rent revenue receivable.
16. Allowance for doubtful accounts.
17. Investment in bonds of another company (long term).
18. Undeposited cash (for making change).
19. Accounts receivable (trade).
20. Deficit.

Exercise 5–6

The following balance sheet has come to your attention:

BX CORPORATION
Balance Sheet Statement
For Year Ended December 31, 1979

Assets

Liquid Assets:			
Cash		$ 31,000	
Receivables	$ 29,000		
Less: Reserve for bad debts	700	28,300	
Inventories		42,000	
			$101,300
Investments and Funds:			
Petty cash fund		200	
Sinking fund		70,000	
			70,200
Permanent Assets:			
Land and building	140,000		
Less: Reserve for depreciation	9,000	131,000	
Equipment	84,000		
Less: Reserve for depreciation	29,000	55,000	
			186,000
Deferred Charges:			
Prepaid expenses		2,700	
Accrued sinking fund income (interest)		600	
			3,300
Total			$360,800

Obligations

Short Term:			
Accrued interest on mortgage payable		$ 700	
Accounts payable		36,500	
Reserve for income taxes	$ 13,000		
Less: U.S. government bonds	8,000	5,000	
			$ 42,200
Long Term:			
Mortgage payable*			74,000

Net Worth

Capital stock		150,000	
Earned surplus		52,400	
Reserve for contingencies		66,400	
		268,800	
Less: Treasury stock		24,200	
			244,600
Total			$360,800

* The mortgage payable matures April 18, 1980, and is funded by the sinking fund.

Required:

Constructively criticize the above balance sheet. Set up your responses in the following format:

Specific Criticism (list)	Explanation of Criticism	Recommended Treatment
1.		
Etc.		

Exercise 5–7

The following trial balance was prepared by Stanley, Incorporated, as of December 31, 1979. The adjusting entries for 1979 have been made except for any specifically noted below.

Cash	$ 9,000	
Accounts receivable	15,000	
Inventories	12,000	
Equipment	22,400	
Land	6,400	
Building	7,600	
Deferred charges	1,100	
Accounts payable		$ 5,500
Note payable—9%		8,000
Capital stock (par $10)		38,500
Earned surplus		21,500
	$73,500	$73,500

You ascertain that certain errors and omissions are reflected in the above, including the following:

1. The $15,000 balance in accounts receivable represents the entire amount owed to the company; of this sum, $12,400 is from trade customers, and 5% of that amount is estimated to be uncollectible. The remaining sum owed to the company represents a long-term advance to its president.
2. Inventories include $2,000 of goods incorrectly inventoried at double their cost (i.e., at $4,000). No correction has been recorded. Office supplies on hand of $500 are also included in the balance of inventories.
3. When the equipment and building were purchased new on January 1, 1974, they had, respectively, estimated lives of 10 and 25 years. They have been depreciated by the straight-line method on the assumption of zero residual values, and depreciation has been credited directly to the asset accounts.
4. The balance of the Land account includes a $1,000 payment made as a deposit of earnest money on the purchase of an adjoining tract. The option to buy it has not yet been exercised and probably will not be exercised during the coming year.
5. The interest-bearing note matures March 31, 1980, having been drawn July 1, 1979. Interest on it has been ignored.
6. Common stock shares outstanding, 3,500.

Required:

Prepare a correct classified balance sheet using preferred terminology. Use whichever form is specified by your instructor; if not specified, use the format you prefer. Show computation of retained earnings reported on the balance sheet.

Exercise 5–8

The ledger of Mite Manufacturing Company reflects obsolete terminology, but you find its books have been, on the whole, accurately kept. After the most recent closing of the books at December 31, 1979, the following accounts were submitted to you for the preparation of a balance sheet:

Accounts payable	$33,200
Accounts receivable	9,500
Accrued expenses (credit)	800
Bonds payable—7%	25,000
Capital stock ($100 par)	70,000
Cash	13,000
Earned surplus	xx,xxx
Factory equipment	31,200
Finished goods	12,100
Investments	13,000
Office equipment	9,500
Raw materials	9,600
Reserve for bad debts	500
Reserve for depreciation	9,000
Rent paid in advance (a debit)	3,000
Sinking fund	7,835
Land	15,000
Note receivable	6,600
Work in process	18,300

You ascertain that two thirds of the depreciation relates to factory and one third to office equipment. Of the balance in the Investments account, $4,000 will be converted to cash during the coming year; the remainder represents a long-term investment. Rent paid in advance is for the next year. The land was acquired as a future plant site. The note receivable was signed by the company president on October 1, 1979, and is due in 1981 when the principal amount ($6,600) plus 10% interest per annum will be paid to the company. The sinking fund is being accumulated to retire the bonds at maturity.

Required:

1. Prepare a classified balance sheet using preferred terminology.
2. Compute (a) the amount of working capital and (b) the current ratio.

Exercise 5–9

Baker Corporation is preparing the balance sheet at December 31, 1979. The following items are at issue:

a. Note payable, long-term, $60,000. This note will be paid in installments. The first installment of $20,000 will be paid August 1, 1980.

b. Bonds payable, 6%, $200,000; at December 31, 1979, unamortized premium amounted to $6,000.

c. Bond sinking fund, $40,000; this fund is being accumulated to retire the bonds at maturity. There is a restriction on retained earnings required by the bond indenture equal to the balance in the bond sinking fund.

d. Rent revenue collected in advance for the first quarter of 1980, $6,000.

e. After the balance sheet date, but prior to issuance of the 1979 balance sheet, one third of the merchandise inventory was destroyed by flood (date, January 13, 1980); estimated loss, $150,000.

Required:

Show, by illustration, how each of these items should be reported on the December 31, 1979, balance sheet.

Exercise 5–10

Based upon the following information, prepare the stockholders' equity section of the balance sheet for Bay Corporation at December 31, 1979.

Retained earnings, unappropriated	$ 80,000
Preferred stock, par $10, authorized 20,000 shares	150,000
Restriction on retained earnings as required by a special contract	20,000
Cash received above par of preferred stock	15,000
Common stock, nopar, 60,000 shares issued (100,000 shares authorized)	200,000

Exercise 5–11

The records of Marple Corporation provided the following selected data on December 31, 1979:

Preferred stock, par $10, 100,000 shares authorized	$400,000
Common stock, nopar 200,000 shares authorized of which 150,000 is outstanding	600,000
Premium on preferred stock	80,000
Earned surplus (free) at start of year	40,000
Reserves at end of 1979 for:	
Bad debts	11,000
Depreciation	90,000
Patent amortization	6,000
Warranty obligations	14,000
Income tax obligations	31,000
Future plant expansion	100,000
Retirement of bonds payable (required by the bond indenture)	50,000

Net income for 1979	45,000
Dividends declared and paid in 1979	30,000
Bond sinking fund	50,000

Required:

1. Prepare the stockholders' equity section of the balance sheet using preferred terminology and format.

2. If any of the above items are omitted from the stockholders' equity section, explain how they should be reported.

Exercise 5–12

The following adjusted trial balance was prepared by Davis Corporation at December 31, 1979:

Debit

Cost of goods sold	$272,000
Distribution and administrative expenses	130,000
Income tax expense	41,500
Cash	39,000
Short-term investments	12,000
Accounts receivable	70,000
Merchandise inventory*	70,000
Office supplies inventory	2,000
Investment in bonds of X Corporation (long-term), cost (market value $35,000)	33,000
Land (plant site in use)	10,000
Plant and equipment	120,000
Franchise (less amortization)	8,000
Rearrangement costs†	15,000
Idle equipment held for disposal	7,500
Dividends paid during 1979	40,000
	$870,000

Credit

Sales revenue	$520,000
Accumulated depreciation, plant and equipment	40,000
Accounts payable	50,000
Income taxes payable	11,000
Bonds payable	50,000
Allowance for doubtful accounts	3,000
Premium on bonds payable (unamortized)	1,000
Common stock, par $10 (authorized 50,000 shares)	150,000
Excess of issue price over par of common stock	18,000
Retained earnings, balance January 1, 1979	27,000
	$870,000

* Perpetual inventory system.
† Amortization period three years; this is the unamortized balance.

Required:

1. Prepare a single-step income statement.
2. Prepare a classified balance sheet.

Exercise 5–13

The following statement has just been prepared by Condor Corporation:

CONDOR CORPORATION
Statement of Changes in Financial Position
For the Year Ended December 31, 1979

Sources of funds:

From operations:		
Revenues	$260,000	
Decrease in trade accounts receivable	8,000	
Total funds from revenues		$268,000
Expenses	220,000	
Add (deduct) adjustments to convert to cash basis:		
Depreciation	(17,000)	
Amortization of patent ...	(1,000)	
Inventory increase	7,000	
Accounts payable decrease	2,000	
Income taxes payable increase	(1,000)	
Loss on sale of machinery	(4,000)	
Total funds for expenses.....		206,000
Funds generated by operations		62,000
From other sources:		
Sale of machinery	12,000	
Long-term note payable	25,000	
Issuance of capital stock for future plant site (Note A)	30,000	
Total funds from other sources		67,000
Total funds generated during the year		129,000
Uses of funds:		
Retirement of mortgage note	20,000	
Cash dividends	24,000	
Purchase of long-term investment (stock, X Corporation)	15,000	
Acquisition of machinery (operational asset)	11,000	

Acquisition of land for future plant site (Note A)	30,000	
Total funds used during the year		100,000
Net increase (decrease) in cash and short-term investments during the year		$ 29,000

Required:

1. How are funds measured in this statement? Explain.
2. What was the net income for the year? How much did cash increase from operations? How did management generate more cash from operations than profit?
3. Explain the transaction "sale of machinery." Note that it is referred to twice.
4. Write Note A with respect to the future plant site. Note that it is referred to twice.
5. Explain why depreciation expense and amortization of patent were deducted from total expenses. Why was the inventory change added to expenses?
6. Some changes in terminology are needed. Identify them and suggest preferable terminology.

PROBLEMS

Problem 5–1

Below left is a list of typical items from a balance sheet for a corporation. Below right is a list of brief statements of *valuations* usually reported on a balance sheet for different items.

Required:

Use the code letters to the right to indicate, for each balance sheet item listed, the *usual* valuation reported on the balance sheet. Provide explanatory comments for each doubtful item. Some code letters may be used more than once or not at all.

Balance Sheet Items	*Valuations Usually Reported*
1.____ Cash.	a. Total amount paid in by stockholders when issued.
2.____ Short-term investments.	b. Face amount collectible at maturity.
3.____ Accounts receivable (trade).	c. Lower of cost or market.
4.____ Notes receivable (short-term).	d. Cost to acquire the asset.
5.____ Merchandise inventory.	e. Excess of issue price over par value of stock.
6.____ Prepaid expenses (such as prepaid insurance).	f. Accumulated income less accumulated dividends.
	g. Cost to acquire less amortization to date.

7._____Long-term investment in bonds of another company (purchased at a premium).

8._____Long-term investment in stock of another company (less than 20% of the outstanding shares).

9._____Plant site (in use).

10._____Plant equipment (in use).

11._____Patent (used in operations).

12._____Deferred charge.

13._____Accounts payable (trade).

14._____Income taxes payable.

15._____Notes payable (short-term).

16._____Bonds payable (sold at a discount).

17._____Common stock (no-par).

18._____Preferred stock (par $10 per share).

19._____Contributed capital in excess of par.

20._____Retained earnings.

21._____Land held for speculation.

22._____Land held for a future plant site.

23._____Damaged merchandise (goods held for sale).

h. Estimated net realizable value (amount billed less estimated loss due to uncollectibility).

i. Par value of shares issued.

j. Cost less expired or used portion.

k. Cost at date of investment.

l. Replacement cost.

m. Cost at date of investment plus unamortized premium.

n. Current market value.

o. Amount payable when due (short-term).

p. Face amount of the obligation less unamortized discount.

q. Cost to acquire less accumulated depreciation.

r. Market value at the date of the balance sheet whether it is above or below cost.

s. No valuation reported (explain).

t. None of the above (when this response is used, explain the valuation usually used).

Problem 5–2

Typical balance sheet classifications are as follows:

A. Current assets.
B. Investments and funds.
C. Operational assets (tangible).
D. Intangible assets.
E. Other assets.
F. Deferred charges.
G. Current liabilities.
H. Long-term liabilities.
I. Capital stock.
J. Additional contributed capital.
K. Retained earnings.

Indicate by use of the above letters (use capitals and print), how each of the following items would be classified. When it is a contra item (i.e., a deduction) in a caption, place a minus sign before it. Comment on doubtful items; and if an item is not reported on the balance sheet, write *none*.

1. Cash.
2. Cash set aside to meet long-term purchase commitment.

3. Land (used as plant site).
4. Accrued salaries.
5. Investment in subsidiary (long term; not a controlling interest).
6. Inventory of damaged goods.
7. Idle plant being held for disposal.
8. Investment in bonds of another company.
9. Cash surrender value of life insurance policy.
10. Goodwill.
11. Natural resource (timber tract).
12. Allowance for doubtful accounts.
13. Stock subscriptions receivable (no plans to collect in near future).
14. Organization costs.
15. Discount on bonds payable.
16. Service revenue collected in advance.
17. Accrued interest payable.
18. Accumulated amortization on patent.
19. Prepaid rent expense.
20. Short-term investment (common stock).
21. Rent revenue collected but not earned.
22. Net of accumulated earnings and dividends.
23. Trade accounts payable.
24. Current maturity of long-term debt.
25. Land (held for speculation).
26. Notes payable (short term).
27. Special cash fund accumulated to build plant five years hence.
28. Bonds issued—to be paid within six months out of bond sinking fund.
29. Long-term investment in rental building.
30. Copyright.
31. Accumulated depreciation.
32. Deferred plant rearrangement costs.
33. Franchise.
34. Revenue earned but not collected.
35. Premium on bonds payable (unamortized).
36. Common stock (at par value).
37. Petty cash fund.
38. Deficit.
39. Contributed capital in excess of par.
40. Earnings retained in the business.

(AICPA adapted)

Problem 5–3

The president of Raby Manufacturing Company is a personal friend of yours and she tells you the company has never had an audit and is contemplating having one principally because it is suspected that the financial statements are not well prepared. As an example the president hands you the following balance sheet for review:

RABY MANUFACTURING CO., INC.
Balance Sheet
For the Year Ended December 31, 1979

Resources

Liquid Assets:

Cash in banks	$12,000	
Receivables from various sources net of reserve for bad debts	5,000	
Inventories	6,000	
Cash for daily use	500	
Total	23,500	

Permanent Assets:

Treasury stock	5,000	
Fixed assets (net)	26,000	
Grand Total	$54,500	

Obligations and Net Worth

Short-Term:

Trade payables	$ 3,000	
Salaries accrued	1,000	
Total	4,000	

Long-Term:

Mortgage	7,000	

Net Worth:

Capital stock	$30,000	
Earned surplus	13,500	
Total	43,500	
Grand Total	$54,500	

Required:

1. List and explain your criticisms of the above balance sheet.
2. Using the above data, prepare a classified balance sheet that meets your specifications. Where amounts needed are missing, use assumed, but realistic, amounts. *Hint:* Treasury stock is a reduction of stockholders' equity since it is the company's own stock reacquired by purchase. Total assets is $49,500.

Problem 5–4

The most recent balance sheet of Thomas Corporation appears below:

THOMAS CORPORATION
Balance Sheet
For the Year Ended December 31, 1979

Assets

Current:

Cash	$ 5,000	
Marketable securities	10,000	

Accounts receivable	30,000	
Merchandise	25,000	
Supplies	5,000	
Stock of Company W (not a controlling interest)	17,000	$ 92,000

Investments:

Cash surrender value of life insurance	20,000	
Treasury stock (2,500 shares)	25,000	45,000

Tangible:

Buildings and land	$56,000		
Less: Reserve for depreciation	10,000	46,000	
Equipment	15,000		
Less: Reserve for depreciation	10,000	5,000	51,000

Deferred:

Prepaid expenses	2,000	
Discount on bonds payable	10,000	12,000
Total		$200,000

Liabilities and Capital

Current:

Accounts payable	$16,000	
Reserve for income taxes	17,000	
Customers' accounts with credit balance	100	$ 33,100

Long-Term (interest paid at year-end):

Bonds payable	45,000	
Mortgage	12,000	57,000
Reserve for bad debts		900

Capital:

Capital stock, authorized 10,000 shares, par $10 . . .	75,000	
Earned surplus	25,000	
Capital surplus	9,000	109,000
Total		$200,000

Required:

1. List and explain your criticisms of the above balance sheet.
2. Prepare a correct classified balance sheet. *Hint:* The capital stock was sold above par. Deduct treasury stock from shareholders' equity.

Problem 5–5

The balance sheet shown below, which was submitted to you for review, has been prepared for inclusion in the published annual report of the XYZ Company for the year ended December 31, 1979:

XYZ COMPANY
Balance Sheet
December 31, 1979

Assets

Current Assets:		
Cash		$ 1,900,000
Accounts receivable	$3,900,000	
Less: Reserve for bad debts	50,000	3,850,000
Inventories—at the lower of cost (determined by the		
first-in, first-out method) or market		3,500,000
Total Current Assets		9,250,000
Fixed Assets:		
Land—at cost	200,000	
Buildings, machinery and		
fixtures—at cost $4,200,000		
Less: Reserves for depreciation . . . 1,490,000	2,710,000	2,910,000
Deferred Charges and Other Assets:		
Cash surrender value of life insurance	15,000	
Unamortized discount on first-mortgage note	42,000	
Prepaid expenses	40,000	97,000
Total Assets		$12,257,000

Liabilities

Current Liabilities:		
Notes payable to bank		$ 750,000
Current maturities of first-mortgage note		600,000
Accounts payable—trade		1,900,000
Reserve for income taxes for the year ended		
December 31, 1979		700,000
Accrued expenses		550,000
		4,500,000
Funded Debt:		
4% first-mortgage note payable in quarterly		
installments of $150,000	$4,200,000	
Less: Current maturities	600,000	3,600,000
Reserves:		
Reserve for damages	50,000	
Reserve for possible future inventory losses	300,000	
Reserve for contingencies	500,000	
Reserve for additional federal income taxes	100,000	950,000
Capital:		
Capital stock—authorized, issued and outstanding		
100,000 shares of $10 par value	1,000,000	
Capital surplus	300,000	
Earned surplus	1,907,000	3,207,000
Total Liabilities		$12,257,000

Additional data:

1. Reserve for damages was set up by a charge against current fiscal year's income to cover damages possibly payable by the company as a defendant in a lawsuit in progress at the balance sheet date. Suit was subsequently settled for $50,000 prior to issuance of the statement.

2. Reserve for possible future inventory losses was set up in prior years, by action of board of directors, by charges against earned surplus. No change occurred in the account during the current fiscal year.

3. Reserve for contingencies was set up by charges against earned surplus over a period of several years by the board of directors to provide for a

possible future recession in general business conditions.

4. Reserve for federal income taxes was set up in a prior year and relates to additional taxes which the Internal Revenue Service contended that the company owed. The company has good evidence that settlement will be effected for the $100,000.

5. Capital surplus consists of the difference between the par value of $10 per share of capital stock and the price at which the stock was actually issued.

Required:

State what changes in classification or terminology you would advocate in the presentation of this balance sheet to make it conform with generally accepted accounting principles and with preferred terminology. State your reasons for your suggested changes.

(AICPA adapted)

Problem 5–6

The adjusted trial balance for Wallis Corporation, and other related data, at December 31, 1979, are given below in scrambled order. Although the company uses obsolete terminology, the amounts are correct (but certain amounts may have to be reported separately). Assume perpetual inventory.

Additional data:

a. Market value of the short-term marketable securities is $46,000.

b. Merchandise inventory is based on *Fifo,* lower of cost or market.

c. Goodwill is being amortized (i.e., written off) over a 20-year period. The amortization for 1979 has already been recorded (as a direct credit to the Goodwill account). Amortization of other intangibles is recorded in this manner except for the patent (a contra account is used for it).

d. Reserve for income taxes represents the estimated taxes payable at the end of 1979. Reserve for estimated damages was recorded by debiting Retained Earnings during 1978. The $10,000 was the estimated amount of damages that would have to be paid as a result of a damage suit against the company. At December 31, 1979, the appeal was still pending. The $10,000 is an appropriation, or restriction, placed on retained earnings by management.

e. Operating expenses as given include interest expense, and revenues include interest and investment revenues.

f. The cash advance from customer was for a special order that will not be completed and shipped until

March 1980; the sales price has not been definitely established since it will be based upon cost (no revenue should be recognized for 1979).

Debit

Cash	$ 36,600
Land (used for building site)	29,000
Cost of goods sold	110,500
Short-term securities (stock of S Company)	42,000
Goodwill (unamortized cost)	12,000
Merchandise inventory	30,000
Office supplies inventory	1,000
Patent	7,000
Operating expenses	42,000
Income tax expense	17,500
Bond discount (unamortized)	7,500
Prepaid insurance	900
Building (at cost)	150,000
Land (held for speculation)	31,000
Accrued interest receivable	300
Accounts receivable (trade)	17,700
Note receivable, 10% (long-term investment)	20,000
Cash surrender value of life insurance policy	9,000
Deferred store rearrangement costs (assume a deferred charge)	6,000
Dividends paid during 1979	15,000
Prior period adjustment (correction of error from prior year—no tax effect)	16,000
	$601,000

Credit

Reserve for bad debts	$ 1,100
Accounts payable (trade)	15,000
Revenues	210,000
Reserve for income taxes	7,500
Note payable (short-term)	12,000
Common stock, par $10, authorized 50,000 shares	100,000
Reserve for depreciation, building	90,000
Retained earnings, January 1, 1979	38,000
Accrued wages	2,100
Reserve for estimated damages	10,000
Premium on common stock	15,000
Reserve for patent amortization	4,000
Cash advance from customer	3,000
Accrued property taxes	1,300
Note payable (long-term)	16,000
Rent revenue collected in advance	1,000
Bonds payable, 6% ($25,000 due June 1, 1980)	75,000
	$601,000

Required:

1. Prepare a single-step income statement and a separate statement of retained earnings.

2. Prepare a classified balance sheet including appro-

priate disclosures. Use preferred terminology and format.

Problem 5–7

The adjusted trial balance for Dawson Manufacturing Corporation at December 31, 1979, is given below in scrambled order. Debits and credits are not indicated. All amounts are correct. Assume a normal balance situation in each account. Assume a perpetual inventory system.

Work in process inventory	$ 24,000
Accrued interest on notes payable	1,000
Accrued interest receivable	1,200
Accrued income on short-term investments	1,000
Common stock, nopar, authorized 20,000 shares, issued 10,000	150,000
Cash in bank	40,000
Trademarks (unamortized cost)	1,400
Land held for speculation	17,000
Supplies inventory	600
Goodwill (unamortized cost)	20,000
Raw material inventory	13,000
Bond sinking fund	10,000
Accrued property taxes	1,200
Accounts receivable (trade)	19,000
Accrued wages	2,300
Mortgage payable (due in three years)	10,000
Building	130,000
Prepaid rent expense	1,700
Organization expenses (unamortized cost— assume deferred charge)	7,800
Deposits (cash collected from customers on sales orders to be delivered next quarter; no revenue yet recognized)	1,000
Long-term investment in bonds of K Corporation (at cost)	60,000
Patents (unamortized cost)	12,000
Reserve for bond sinking fund*	10,000
Reserve for depreciation, office equipment	1,600
Reserve for depreciation, building	5,000
Premium on preferred stock	8,000
Cash on hand for change	400
Preferred stock, par $100, authorized 5,000 shares, 5% noncumulative	60,000
Precollected rent income	900
Finished goods inventory	42,000
Note receivable (short-term)	4,000
Bonds payable, 6%, (due in 15 years)	50,000
Accounts payable (trade)	11,000
Reserve for bad debts	1,400
Notes payable (short-term)	7,000
Office equipment	25,000
Land (used as building site)	8,000
Short-term investments (at cost)	15,500

Retained earnings, unappropriated (balance January 1, 1979)	13,200
Cash dividends paid during 1979	20,000
Revenues during 1979	400,000
Cost of goods sold for 1979	210,000
Expenses for 1979 (including income taxes)	90,000
Income taxes payable	40,000

* This is a restriction on retained earnings required by the bond indenture equal to the bond sinking fund which is being accumulated to retire the bonds.

Additional information:

Inventories are based on *Fifo,* lower of cost or market.

Required:

1. Prepare a single-step income statement; use preferred terminology. To compute earnings per share, deduct $3,000 of net income as an allocation to preferred stock.
2. Prepare a classified balance sheet; use preferred terminology and format. Comment on any items you consider doubtful with respect to classification.
3. Assume that between December 31, 1979, and issuance of the financial statements, a flood damaged the finished goods inventory in an amount estimated to be $17,000. Prepare an appropriate disclosure note to the balance sheet.

Problem 5–8

WT Corporation has just prepared the annual financial statements dated December 31, 1979. The stockholders' equity section of the balance sheet was as follows:

Stockholders' Equity

Contributed Capital:	
Preferred stock, par $10, 5%, nonparticipating, cumulative; authorized 100,000 shares, issued and outstanding 60,000 shares (of which 3,000 are held as treasury stock)	$ 600,000
Common stock, nopar; authorized 500,000 shares, issued and outstanding 200,000 shares	1,249,000
Contributed capital in excess of par, preferred stock	115,000
Total Contributed Capital	1,964,000
Retained earnings	102,000
Total	2,066,000
Less: Treasury stock (preferred stock, 3,000 shares), at cost	38,000
Total Stockholders' Equity	$2,028,000

During 1979 the following transactions and data affected stockholders' equity in various ways:

a. Prior period adjustment:
Accounting errors made
in prior periods
(net of tax), a debit .... $ 15,000
b. Sold capital stock
(January 3, 1979):
(1) Preferred stock,
10,000 shares at $12 .... $120,000
(2) Common stock,
6,000 shares at $7.50 45,000
c. Treasury stock acquired,
2,000 shares of
preferred at $13
per share 26,000
d. Shares issued for
common stock dividend
on common stock,
40,000 shares at $7
(debited to retained
earnings).............................. 280,000
e. Net income reported 165,000
f. Cash dividends:
(1) Preferred stock
(rounded) 28,000
(2) Common stock 50,000
g. On December 31, 1979,
the board of directors
voted to approve
appropriation of
$200,000 of retained
earnings for "Reserve
for Future Expansion."

Required:

Based upon the above information prepare a statement to provide full disclosure of the changes in stockholders' equity for WT Corporation during 1979. The statement, to supplement the balance sheet, should be set up as follows:

a. Caption:

WT CORPORATION
Statement of Stockholders' Equity—1979
(in thousands [deductions in parentheses])

b. List the Items *(a)* through *(g)*, given above, to the left (start with the January 1, 1979, balance and end with the December 31, 1979, items) and set up nine column headings as follows:

Preferred Stock—Par $10:
1. Shares
2. Amount

Treasury Stock, Preferred:
3. Shares
4. Cost

Common Stock, Nopar:
5. Shares
6. Amount

Contributed Capital in Excess of Par:
7. Amount

Retained Earnings:
8. Amount

Total:
9. Amount

Note. The beginning balances intentionally are not given. You must derive them from the data given.

Problem 5–9

The following statement has just been prepared by Dyer Corporation:

DYER CORPORATION
Statement of Changes in Financial Position
For the Year Ended December 31, 19x

Sources of funds:		
From operations:		
Revenues	$630,000	
Add (deduct) to con-		
vert to cash basis:		
Accounts receivable		
decrease	15,000	
Total funds		
from revenues		$645,000
Expenses	550,000	
Add (deduct) to con-		
vert to cash basis:		
Depreciation	(30,000)	
Inventory increase	17,000	
Accounts payable increase .	(11,000)	
Income taxes payable		
decrease	4,000	
Loss on sale of long-		
term investment	(3,000)	
Total funds required		
for expenses		527,000
Funds generated by		
operations		118,000
From other sources:		
Sale of long-term		
investment	21,000	
Disposal of land (Note A)	50,000	
Sale of unissued common		
stock	15,000	
Long-term note payable......	20,000	
Total funds from		
other sources		106,000
Total funds		
generated		224,000
Uses of funds:		
Dividends	40,000	
Acquisition of machinery		
(Note A)	50,000	
Payment on bonds payable	100,000	
Total funds used		190,000

Increase in cash and short-term investments during the year	$ 34,000

Required:

1. How are funds measured in this statement? Explain.
2. What was net income for the year? How much cash was generated from operations? Explain how management generated more cash than profits.
3. What was the primary source of funds? What was the primary use of funds? What sources and uses would you rely upon for predictions of funds flow in this company? Explain.
4. Explain the long-term investment transaction. Why is it reflected in two places?
5. Write Note A with respect to the machinery and land.
6. Explain why the accounts receivable decrease was added to revenues.
7. Explain the reason for the addition or deduction of each adjustment to total expenses.
8. Some changes in terminology would be helpful. Identify them and suggest preferable terminology.

Problem 5–10

The following information was taken from the records of Reedy Corporation for the year ended December 31, 1979:

Net income (revenues, $600,000— expenses, $530,000)	$70,000
Depreciation expense	12,000*
Accounts receivable increase	3,000
Accounts payable decrease	4,000
Purchase of operational assets (cash)	28,000
Merchandise inventory increase	7,000
Cash dividends paid	20,000
Loss on sale of operational asset (cash, $18,000—book value, $20,000)	2,000
Sold unissued common stock (cash)	25,000
Acquired future plant site; payment by issuance of 5,000 shares of common stock (market value)	24,000
Payment on bonds payable	25,000
Borrowed on long-term mortgage note	30,000

   * Included in the $530,000 expenses.

Required:

1. Use the above information to prepare a statement of changes in financial position, cash plus short-term investments basis.
2. Write the disclosure note with respect to the future plant site.

Problem 5–11

The Appendix to this chapter gives an actual income statement, balance sheet, and statement of changes in financial position. Examine them carefully and respond to the following questions. Respond for the latest year (1977) unless directed otherwise.

a. Are they comparative statements? What is the primary benefit of comparative statements?

b. Are they consolidated statements? What do you understand this to mean?

c. What different subclassifications were used for assets? for liabilities? for shareholders' equity? Explain variations from those suggested in the chapter.

d. During 1977, what was the change in real estate investments?

e. How did the company value its investments in common stocks?

f. How much did deferred policy acquisition costs change during 1977? Explain this item.

g. What was the percent of the allowance for doubtful accounts to total accounts receivable?

h. How were operational assets labeled and valued? Explain. What was the ratio of accumulated depreciation to cost on each category of total operational assets?

i. What was the amount of unamortized goodwill at the end of 1977?

j. What percents of accrued income taxes was current and noncurrent in 1977?

k. Was any unamortized bond premium or discount reported? If yes, how was it reported? Do you agree with the method of reporting? Explain.

l. Were there any convertible debt securities? What were the terms of conversion?

m. How many different classes of stock were there? What was the par value per share of each? For each class, how many shares were (1) authorized, (2) issued, (3) held as treasury stock, and (4) outstanding?

n. Were there any restrictions on retained earnings? How were they reported?

o. What percent of total assets were provided by (1) creditors and (2) owners?

p. Was the statement of changes in financial position prepared on a working capital basis or a cash equivalent basis? How was this made known in the statement?

q. What percent of total fund inflows came from (1) operations, (2) extraordinary items, and (3) other sources?

r. What was the scope of the independent auditors' examination? What kind of opinion did the auditor give? Explain.

s. Overall, do you believe the income statement and balance sheet could be improved with respect to format and terminology? Explain each change that you would recommend for consideration.

Problem 5–12

Appendix B to Chapter 4 gives an actual income statement, balance sheet, and statement of changes in financial position. Examine them carefully and respond to the questions posed in Problem 5–11. Respond for the latest year (1977) unless directed otherwise.

Problem 5–13

Obtain an audited financial statement for the latest year for a company of your choice (from the library or other source) and use it as a basis for responding to each of the questions posed in Problem 5–11.

Problem 5–14 (review of Chapters 3, 4, and 5)

On January 1, 1979, Hays Company had the following trial balance:

Account No.	Account	Debit	Credit
101	Cash	$ 96,000	
102	Accounts receivable	45,000	
103	Allowance for doubtful accounts		$ 670
104	Office supplies inventory	800	
105	Inventory (periodic system)*	60,000	
106	Short-term investments		
107	Investment revenue receivable		
108	Fund to construct future plant	30,000	
109	Machinery	120,000	
110	Accumulated depreciation, machinery		72,000
111	Land (future plant site)	15,000	
112	Patent	4,000	
113	Other assets	55,000	
201	Accounts payable		35,000
202	Interest payable		
203	Income taxes payable (1978)		12,330
204	Long-term mortgage note		
301	Common stock (par $10)		150,000
302	Contributed capital in excess of par		30,000
303	Retained earnings		125,800
400	Income summary		
500	Sales revenue		
501	Investment revenue		
600	Purchases		
601	Freight on purchases		
602	Purchase returns		
700	Selling expenses		
701	General and administrative expenses		
702	Interest expense		
703	Depreciation expense		

704	Income tax expense		
801	Extraordinary items		
802	Prior period adjustments		
		$425,800	$425,800

* Depending on the worksheet technique used, an additional account for the ending inventory could be used.

1979 entries (use numbers to left for date notations):

1. Paid 1978 income taxes payable on March 3, 1979, in full.
2. Purchases .... $350,000 (of which $50,000 was on credit)
   Purchase returns .... 1,000 (on account)
   Freight on purchases .... 2,000 (cash)
3. The following selling expenses were incurred and paid during 1979:
   Advertising .... $ 10,000
   Salaries 130,000
   Other selling 15,000
4. The following general and administrative expenses were incurred and paid during 1979:
   Salaries $100,000
   Office supplies (purchased) .... 500 (debit Account No. 104)
   Rent expense 24,000
5. An 8% mortgage note was dated and signed on March 1, 1979, for $75,000; this amount of cash was received. Interest will be paid annually on this date.
6. A short-term bond investment was acquired for cash on June 1, 1979, at par, $20,000. Interest at 6% is payable annually on June 1.
7. Suffered severe flood loss amounting to $40,000. Assume an extraordinary item and credit cash because this was spent to restore the damages.
8. Correction of accounting error in prior period resulting from understated billing for credit sales to a customer. Received $30,000 cash on this date (during 1979). Assume an income tax effect of $12,000.
9. At December 31, 1979, interest on the building fund amounting to $1,500 was added to the fund balance.
10. Cash collections on accounts receivable, $85,000.
11. Cash payments on accounts payable, $65,000.
12. Cash paid for dividends amounting to $2 per share (debit retained earnings).
13. Sales were $700,000 of which 15% was on credit.

Required:

1. Set up a general journal and T-accounts (with account numbers). Enter beginning balances in the ledger accounts. All of the ledger accounts needed are listed in the above trial balance.
2. Journalize and post the current entries. Use posting notations.
3. Set up a worksheet with a minimum of eight columns (or more if you prefer). Develop the unadjusted trial balance from the ledger and enter it

into the first two money columns of the work-sheet.

4. Enter the following adjusting entries on the work-sheet and complete it (label the adjusting entries with the letters to the left).

 a. Bad debt expense is 1% of total credit sales (debit Selling Expense).

 b. Office supplies inventory at December 31, 1979, was determined by count to be $600.

 c. Accrue the short-term investment revenue at 6% per year.

 d. The machinery had an estimated life of ten years, no residual value; assume straight-line depreciation and a full year's depreciation for 1979.

 e. On January 1, 1979, the patent had eight years remaining life; assume straight-line amortization. Record amortization as general and administrative expenses.

 f. Accrue interest on the mortgage note.

 g. Assume an average income tax rate of 40% on all items.

 h. The ending inventory was $70,000.

5. Prepare a single-step income statement and statement of retained earnings.

6. Prepare a classified balance sheet.

7. Journalize and post the adjusting entries.

8. Journalize and post the closing entries.

9. Prepare a post-closing trial balance.

10. Which adjusting entries would you reverse?

6

Concepts of Future and Present Value

PURPOSE OF THE CHAPTER

This chapter focuses on the time value of money, commonly called interest. *It is the cost of using money over time.* Outflows for the time value of money are identified as interest expense, whereas inflows for the time value of money are identified as interest revenue. Entities at various times make decisions that involve either *(a)* receiving funds, goods, or services currently with a promise to make payments over one or more future periods; or *(b)* disbursing funds as an investment to obtain returns over one or more future periods. In both situations the time value of money is fundamental to the decision-making process and in subsequently measuring and reporting the financial effects of earlier decisions. Federal and sometimes other laws require that the *true annual* rate of interest be specified on most installment contracts and consumer loans. This often requires application of future and present value concepts.

Because of the time value of money (aside from inflation or deflation), a dollar has a different value today (often referred to as time zero) than at future or past dates. Therefore, dollar inflows and outflows that occur at significantly different dates cannot simply be aggregated in a meaningful way; rather they must be restated at a common date to reflect the time value of money by applying the concepts of present and/or future value. Restatement for the interest fac-

tor is essential in many situations, such as *(a)* when preparing information inputs for decision making (e.g., capital budgeting) and *(b)* for accounting measurement and reporting. Therefore, the accountant's knowledge necessarily must include an understanding of the concepts discussed in this chapter. Discussion of these concepts is presented early in this book because of their widespread use in accounting measurements, recording, and reporting, as discussed and illustrated in later chapters. Some applications of future and present value concepts in accounting are as follows:

1. Notes receivable and payable—Measuring and reporting those notes that either carry no stated rate of interest or a rate of interest that is not realistic in comparison with the "going" rates (required by *APB Opinion No. 21*).
2. Assets—Measuring and reporting assets acquired with long-term debt when the interest rate is unspecified (as in a so-called noninterest-bearing note) or unrealistic (required by *APB Opinion No. 21*).
3. Premium and discount on certain receivables and payables—Measuring the amortization of bond premium and discount for both long-term investments in bonds and bonds payable (required by *APB Opinion No. 21*).

4. Leases—Measuring and reporting long-term leases (required by *FASB Statement No. 13*).

5. Pensions—Measuring and reporting numerous aspects of pension plans (required by *APB Opinion No. 8*).

6. Installment contracts—Measuring and reporting the effects of assets acquired or sold on long-term installment terms (required by *APB Opinion No. 21*).

7. Sinking funds—Measuring and reporting resources (funds) set aside for specific uses in the future (required by GAAP).

8. Depreciation—Measuring depreciation expense when the sinking fund or annuity methods are used.

9. Capital additions—Evaluation of the probable economic effects of alternative investments in capital assets.

10. Business combinations—Measuring and reporting such items as receivables, debts, and accruals in a business combination by purchase.

11. Goodwill—Estimating the "value" of goodwill.

12. Future commitments of goods and/or services—Measuring and reporting future commitments to furnish or receive goods or services when the interest rate is unspecified or unrealistic (required by GAAP).

The purpose of this chapter is to present the concepts of future and present value in a way that emphasizes their application in the accounting process—measuring, recording, and reporting. The basic concepts are presented and illustrated in a way that builds a solid foundation for their applications in subsequent chapters (and in more advanced accounting courses) where *specific accounting applications* are discussed and illustrated. The use of prepared tables, which are available from many sources, is emphasized. Part A discusses the future and present values of 1, and Part B discusses annuities.

CONCEPT OF INTEREST

Interest (i.e., the time value of money) represents the excess of resources (usually cash) received or paid over the amount of resources lent or borrowed at a different date. To illustrate, assume Entity A loaned Entity B $6,000 cash for one year with the stipulation that $6,600 cash would be repaid. The time value of money for this contract would be as follows:

Beginning of year, amount of resources committed	$6,000
End of year, amount of resources returned	6,600
Difference—time value of money per contract	$ 600
Analysis:	
Actual interest in dollars $600	
Actual interest as a rate ($600 ÷ $6,000) 10%	

Simple versus Compound Interest

In the above example the interest was based on the principal amount ($6,000), which would be the usual case in a loan covering one period only. When a loan covers two or more periods, interest may be computed on either a simple or a compound interest basis. *Simple interest* is computed only on the principal amount. For example, assume the above loan contract was for two years with specified simple interest of 10% per year on the principal amount of $6,000. The amount of interest for the two-year period would be $600 × 2 = $1,200 (i.e., the simple interest amount). In contrast, *compound interest* is computed on the principal amount plus all interest that has accumulated on the principal. For example, assume the above loan contract was for two years with specified compound interest of 10% per year. The amount of compound interest would be computed as follows for Entity A:

	Interest	Basis for Interest	Resource Flows
Year 1:			
Principal (resource committed)		$6,000	$6,000
Interest ($6,000 × .10)	$ 600		
Year 2:			
Amount subject to interest . . .		6,600	
Interest ($6,600 × .10)	660		
Total interest (resource inflow)			1,260
Total resource inflow			$7,260

Clearly, when a choice is available, at a given interest rate an investor would prefer compound interest. In the above example the investor would receive \$60 (i.e., \$1,260 − \$1,200) more interest on a compound interest basis than on a simple interest basis. In contrast, the borrower would have to pay \$60 more interest. Simple interest usually is applicable to short-term receivables and payables, and compound interest often is used for long-term contracts.

Interest Periods

Contracts which call for compound interest usually specify the interest rate on an *annual* basis. The interest periods—those intervals at which interest is accrued and added to the principal—may or may not be as much as one year apart. For example, a contract may call for "interest at 8% compounded annually," or for "interest at 8% compounded semiannually." In the first instance the rate is 8% for one interest period of a year; in the second instance the rate is 4% for each interest period of six months. If interest of 8% is compounded quarterly, the rate per period (quarter) is 2%, and there would be four interest periods per year. If an annual rate is stated and there is no mention of the frequency of compounding, interest is assumed to be compounded annually.[1]

Summary of Concepts

Future and present value involve four basic concepts. These four concepts, discussed in the order listed below, may be briefly identified as:

Part A—Values of 1:

1. *Future value of 1*—the future value of \$1 at the end of n periods at i compound interest rate.

$$f = (1 + i)^n \text{ (Table 6–1, page 200)}$$

2. *Present value of 1*—the present value of \$1 due n periods hence, discounted at i compound interest rate.

$$p = \frac{1}{(1 + i)^n} \text{ (Table 6–2, page 202)}$$

Part B—Annuities:

3. *Future value of annuity of 1*—the future value of n periodic contributions (rents) of \$1 each plus accumulated compound interest at i rate.

$$F_o = \frac{(1 + i)^n - 1}{i} \text{ (Table 6–3, page 204)}$$

4. *Present value of annuity of 1*—the present value of n periodic contributions (rents) of \$1 each to be received, or paid, each period discounted at i compound interest rate. Stated another way: The amount that must be invested today at i compound interest rate in order to receive n periodic receipts in the future of \$1 each.[2]

$$P_o = \frac{1 - \dfrac{1}{(1 + i)^n}}{i} \text{ (Table 6–4, page 206)}$$

PART A—FUTURE VALUE AND PRESENT VALUE OF 1

In order to understand these two concepts, a clear distinction between "future value" and "present value" is essential. Fundamentally, the difference is in the time assumption. "Future value" is a concept that looks *forward* from present dollars to future dollars, whereas "present value" is a concept that looks *back* from future dollars to present dollars. This distinction is graphically displayed at the top of the next page. Note in particular the time direction indicated by the arrows.

FUTURE VALUE OF 1

The concept of future value of 1 (the symbol used herein is f) is often called compound interest. The future value is the principal at the start plus accumulated compound interest. For example, \$1,000 deposited on January 1, 1979, in a

---

[1] Throughout this chapter and in the problem materials, short-term periods and even interest rates usually are used to facilitate comprehension. Also, amounts usually are rounded to the nearest dollar for convenience.

[2] As indicated by the subscript *"o"* these are for *ordinary* annuities, not annuities due. Also, the notations used vary considerably. *FV* and *PV* often are used as abbreviations for future and present value, respectively.

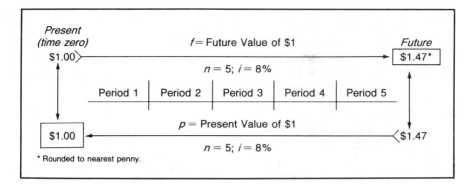

savings account at 8% interest per year would amount (accumulate) to $1,469 at the end of the fifth year (December 31, 1983) assuming annual compounding. The increase of $469 would be accumulated compound interest during the five years.

Calculation of Future Value of 1

It is convenient and customary to use a base figure of 1 in compound interest calculations. In the United States it would be natural to think of 1 as one dollar. The figure 1 could just as readily stand for one peso or one of some other unit of currency.

We can determine, by any of several related methods, how much an investment of $1 would be worth in the future if invested for a specified number of periods at a specified compounding rate per period. To illustrate, assume $1 is invested for five years at 8% compounded annually. The total principal and compound interest at the end of the five years may be determined by any of the following methods:

1. *By successive interest computations*—Multiply the principal ($1) by the interest rate (.08) and add the $0.08 interest thus obtained for the

first period, and the sum ($1.08) is the amount at the end of the first period. This amount becomes the interest-bearing principal for the second period. This sum is principal plus interest $(1 + i)$, which may then be used as the multiplier in each succeeding period to secure the compound amount. Exhibit 6–1 uses this multiplier to secure the future value at the end of each of the five periods.

2. *By formula*—Substitute into a formula which states that for n interest periods at i rate of interest the future value of 1 is $f = (1 + i)^n$. Substituting, we would say $1 invested at 8% annual compound interest for 5 years = ($1 + .08)^5$, or $1.47 (see Table 6–1). Fifth-power multiplication is a laborious process and would be more so where the exponent is large. If a calculator is not available, one could employ logarithms to simplify the calculations.

3. *By table*—Standard tables showing the various future and present values may be obtained from numerous sources. Partial tables are presented in this chapter for your convenience. Table 6–1 is based on the formula $f = (1 + i)^n$; therefore it presents the future value of 1 values (for a limited number of periods and interest rates). Reference to Table 6–1, down the 8% column

EXHIBIT 6–1

	By Successive Computations			By Formula
Period	Balance at Start of Period	× Multiplier (1 + i)	= Amount at End of Period	Alternate Computation at End $(1 + i)^n$
1	$1	1.08	$1.08	$(1.08)^1 = $1.08
2	1.08	1.08	1.1664	$(1.08)^2 = $ 1.1664
3	1.1664	1.08	1.25971	$(1.08)^3 = $ 1.25971
4	1.25971	1.08	1.36049	$(1.08)^4 = $ 1.36049
5	1.36049	1.08	1.46933	$(1.08)^5 = $ 1.46933

and across on the five-period line, shows the future value of 1 to be 1.46933 (i.e., $1.47, as computed in Exhibit 6–1). Obviously, tables facilitate computation of future and present values. However, a word of caution is in order. Observe that Table 6–1 is entitled *Future Value of 1* and the underlying formula is $f = (1 + i)^n$. The heading of the table (including the formula on which it is based) must be considered carefully since it is very easy to take an amount from the wrong table. Also, not infrequently tables show values carried to only two, three, or four decimal places. When the table value is to be applied to a large amount, rounding to this extent can cause a material error in the resulting amount computed. Observe that the tables presented in this chapter are carried to five places.

Future Value of a Specified Principal

Since the standard tables are based on $1 (as in Table 6–1), amounts other than $1 are simply multiplied by the appropriate table value. To illustrate, assume a company deposits $10,000 cash in a fund (or a savings account) that will earn 8% compounded annually for six years. How much will be in the fund at the end of the sixth year from the deposit date? We can readily compute this future value by referring to Table 6–1, Future Value of 1, as follows: $10,000 × $f_{n=6; \, i=8\%}$; that is, $10,000 × 1.58687 = $15,869. The interest revenue earned over the six years would be $5,869.

As another example, assume another company deposits $50,000 cash in a building fund which will be needed at the end of ten years and that the fund will earn 8% interest per annum compounded semiannually. Since the interest periods are one-half year, there are 20 interest periods and the compound interest rate is 4% per period. By reference to Table 6–1, the computation of the future value is $50,000 × $f_{n=20; \, i=4\%}$; that is, $50,000 × 2.19112 = $109,556. Interest revenue earned over the ten-year period would be $59,556.

Determination of Other Values Related to Future Value of 1

In each of the two examples given above, *three* values were provided. To restate the first

example: *(a)* principal, $10,000; *(b)* interest rate, 8%; and *(c)* periods, 6. A fourth value, the future amount $15,869, was computed. Obviously, if *any* three of these four values are known, the other one can be derived. Thus, there are three types of problems that may be encountered:

1. To determine the future value (discussed above—compound amount of a specified principal).
2. To determine the required interest rate (discussed below—determination of the compound interest rate).
3. To determine the required number of interest periods (discussed below—determination of the number of periods).

Determination of the Compound Interest Rate

If the future value to which a given principal sum will accumulate (or is desired to accumulate) is known, and the number of periods is known, the required rate of compound interest can be calculated.

As an example, assume it is desired *(a)* to invest $5,000, *(b)* at interest compounded annually for ten years, and *(c)* to accumulate $10,795. What rate of interest is required? To find the required rate the following steps may be taken:

1. $10,795 ÷ $5,000 = 2.159, the future value to which 1 would accumulate at the unknown interest rate by the end of the ten-year period.
2. Referring to a future value of 1 table (Table 6–1) and reading across the ten-period line, we find the future value 2.15892 under the 8% column; thus 8% is the required interest rate.

Sometimes it is necessary to interpolate to derive the required rate. Suppose once again $5,000 is to be invested for ten years. In this case it is desired to accumulate $11,000. Here the rate of increase is the same as if $1 had grown to $2.20 (i.e., $11,000 ÷ $5,000). Referring to the ten-period line, we find the value under 8% is 2.15892; under the next higher rate, 9%, it is 2.36736. Therefore, the rate is between 8% and 9%—somewhat closer to the former—not quite one fifth of the way between them. We can conclude that the required interest rate must be about 8¼%. Or more precisely, by interpolation:[3]

$$8\% = 2.15892$$
$$? = 2.20 \quad \rightarrow 2.20 - 2.15892 = .04108$$
$$9\% = 2.36736 \quad \rightarrow 2.36736 - 2.15892 = .20844$$

$$8\% + \left[\left(\frac{.04108}{.20844} \right) \times (9\% - 8\%) \right] = \underline{8.19} + \%$$

Determination of Number of Periods

If the future value to which a given sum will accumulate is known, and if the interest rate is known, the required number of periods can be calculated. To use the above example again, assume the following is known: *(a)* investment, $5,000, *(b)* accumulation desired, $10,795; and *(c)* the desired interest rate, 8%. To compute the required number of interest periods, the following steps may be taken:

1. $10,795 ÷ $5,000 = 2.159, the future value 1 would accumulate at 8% for the unknown number of interest periods.
2. Referring to future value of 1 table (Table 6–1) and reading down the 8% column, we find 2.159 (rounded) on the ten-year line; thus the required number of interest periods is ten.

An Accounting Application of Future Value of 1

Sonora Corporation, in order to assure funds for a planned future expansion, deposited $50,000 cash in a plant expansion fund on January 1, 1979. The bank, serving as trustee, will pay 7% interest compounded annually. The funds will be needed on January 1, 1982.

Required:

1. Compute the fund balance at December 31, 1981.
2. Prepare an accumulation table for the fund.

---

[3] Linear interpolation was illustrated. A more precise answer can be obtained by using a calculator and the following procedure:

$$\$5,000 \ (1 + i)^{10} = \$11,000$$
$$(1 + i)^{10} = \$11,000 ÷ \$5,000$$
$$(1 + i) = (2.2)^{1/10}$$
$$i = 8.20374\%$$

3. Give the accounting entries for the entire period including withdrawal on January 1, 1982.

Solution:

1. Fund balance at December 31, 1981:

   $50,000 × $f_{n=3;\ i=7\%}$ =
   $50,000 × 1.22504 (Table 6–1) = $61,252

2. Accumulation table, plant expansion fund:

Date	Interest Revenue	Fund Balance
1/1/79 deposit ..		$50,000
12/31/79	$50,000 × .07 = $3,500	53,500
12/31/80	53,500 × .07 = 3,745	57,245
12/31/81	57,245 × .07 = 4,007	61,252

3. Entries:

   1/1/79 deposit of cash:

Plant expansion fund	50,000	
Cash		50,000

   Each December 31 interest revenue earned:

	12/31/79	12/31/80	12/31/81
Plant expansion fund	3,500	3,745	4,007
Investment revenue ...	3,500	3,745	4,007

   1/1/82 withdrawal of fund:

Cash	61,252	
Plant expansion fund		61,252

PRESENT VALUE OF 1

Present value is the present, or time zero, value of a sum of future dollars discounted back from a specified future date to the present date at a given rate of compound interest. Present value involves compound discounting; thus it can be described as the inverse of the future value of 1 concept.

Since a future value is discounted, the present value will always be less than the future value. For example, $1 discounted at 8% per annum for one year has a present value of $0.9259, and discounted for two years it has a present value of $0.8573. The symbol usually used for present value of 1 is p.

We have seen that $1 invested at i interest rate per period has a future value of $(1 + i)^n$ dollars. It follows that $(1 + i)^n$ dollars has a present value that is less than $(1 + i)^n$ due to an inverse or reciprocal relationship. To illustrate, assume $1, an interest rate of 8%, and 1 period, as shown in the drawing at bottom of this page. The reciprocal relationship between the future value of 1 and the present value of 1 provides a symbolic expression of the computation of present value amounts, viz:

$$\text{Future Value of 1, } f = (1 + i)^n$$

Therefore, the reciprocal relationship is

$$\text{Present Value of 1, } p = \frac{1}{(1 + i)^n}$$

This is the formula for computation of all present value of 1 amounts.

Computation of Present Value of 1

Present value of 1 amounts can be laboriously computed by compound discounting inversely to that shown on Exhibit 6–1 for future amounts. Also, present value amounts can be computed by dividing the values given in Table 6–1, Future value of 1, into 1.00. For example, $p_{n=5; i=8\%}$ can be computed as follows: $1.00 \div 1.46933$ (Table 6–1) $= .68058$ (verifiable in Table 6–2). However, a much more convenient approach is to use a standard table that discounts $1 for various "$n$" and "$i$" values. A *present value of 1* table for various interest rates and periods is shown as Table 6–2. (Carefully observe the table heading and the underlying formula.) Each value in this table is a reciprocal of the corresponding value in the future value of 1 table.

An Accounting Application of Present Value of 1

To compute the present value of a future amount, the appropriate present value amount from Table 6–2 is multiplied by the specified future amount. To illustrate, assume Blue Corporation acquired a new machine on January 1, 1979. Because of a shortage of cash, the vendor agreed to let Blue Corporation pay for the machine three years after purchase, that is, on December 31, 1981. The amount to be paid at that date is $50,000, which includes all interest charges. Assume the going compound interest rate is 8% per year. Question: Taking into account the interest, what was the cost of the machine, when acquired, in conformity with the cost principle? We must compute the present value of the future amount of $50,000 as follows: $50,000 \times p_{n=3; i=8\%} = $50,000 \times .79383$ (from Table 6–2) $= $39,692. A *debt schedule* for this situation would be as follows:

Date	Interest Expense Incurred	Liability Balance
1/1/79		$39,692
12/31/79	$39,692 × .08 = $3,175	42,867
12/31/80	42,867 × .08 = 3,429	46,296
12/31/81	46,296 × .08 = 3,704	50,000

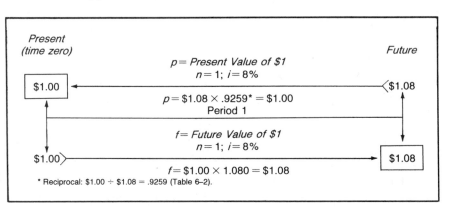

Present (time zero) — Future

p = Present Value of $1
n = 1; i = 8%

$1.00 ← $1.08

p = $1.08 × .9259* = $1.00
Period 1

f = Future Value of $1
n = 1; i = 8%

$1.00 → $1.08

f = $1.00 × 1.080 = $1.08
* Reciprocal: $1.00 ÷ $1.08 = .9259 (Table 6–2).

It follows that the sequence of entries for this situation would be the following:[4]

1/1/79 acquisition of the machine:

```
Machine .......................... 39,692
    Liability ......................           39,692
```

Each December 31, to record interest expense incurred:

	12/31/79	12/31/80	12/31/81
Interest expense	3,175	3,429	3,704
Liability	3,175	3,429	3,704

12/31/81 payment of the liability:

---

[4] Alternatively, these entries could be made as follows with the same ultimate results:

January 1, 1979:

```
Machine ........................................... 39,692
Discount on liability* ............................. 10,308
    Liability ...................................           50,000
```
* This is sometimes called deferred interest expense; it is a contra liability account.

Each December 31:

	12/31/79	12/31/80	12/31/81
Interest expense	3,175	3,429	3,704
Discount on liability	3,175	3,429	3,704

December 31, 1981:

```
Liability ........................................... 50,000
    Cash ...........................................           50,000
```

```
Liability ........................... 50,000
    Cash ..........................          50,000
```

The required interest rate or the required time period can be computed for present value of 1 as illustrated above for future value of 1.

PART B—ANNUITIES

Annuities are identical to the future value of 1 and present value of 1 concepts except for one addition, the concept of an *annuity*. The term annuity means a series of payments, or receipts, of *equal amounts* for a series of *equal time periods* at a constant interest rate. There is one equal amount (often called a rent) for each equal time period. In contrast, future value of 1 and present value of 1 involve a single amount only at the beginning (present) or at a future specified date. The monthly payments on an auto loan, for example, constitute an annuity; there is an equal cash payment each month by one party and an equal cash receipt each month by the other party. In annuity formulas, tables, and discussions, *"n" refers to the number of rents,* not to the number of interest periods. The future and present value of an annuity is graphically displayed on a *time scale* at the bottom of this page.

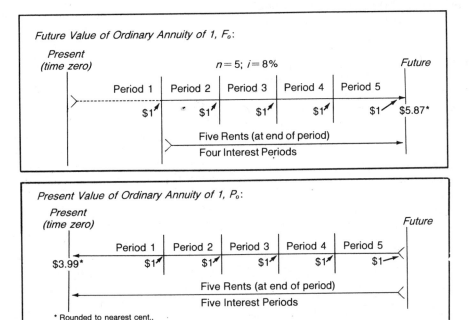

In the above illustration observe that there are five *equal* rents—one in each period (since $n = 5$)—and the rents are at the *end* of each period. The *future value of ordinary annuity of 1* is a future concept, and the future value of the five rents of $1 is $5.87. The future value will always be greater than the sum of the rents by the amount of the compound interest accumulation. Since the rents for an *ordinary* annuity are assumed to be on the *last day of each period,* observe that for the future value of an annuity of 1, the future amount is calculated at the date of the last rent; thus, the last payment coincides with the end of the annuity term. This means that since there is no interest after the last rent, there is one more rent than *interest* periods. The illustration above involves five rents ($n = 5$); however, the future value annuity earns interest for only four periods ($j = 4$), or, $n = 5$ & $j = 4$. In contrast, in the present value illustration, it is $n = 5$ & $j = 5$. These effects are a consequence of the end-of-the-period assumption for the rents in ordinary annuities.[5]

The *present value of annuity of 1* is a present (i.e., time zero) concept. As shown in the above illustration, the present value of the five rents of $1 each is $3.99. The present value will always be *less* than the sum of the rents by the amount of the compound interest discounting. Note that the present value of an ordinary annuity of 1, as shown above, is assumed to be at the *beginning* of the first period (i.e., time zero) and the rents are assumed to be at the end of each period. This means that there is the same number of interest discount periods as rents.

While the term annuity may imply equal *annual* rents to some, we should note that equal rents over any series of equal time intervals, such as monthly, quarterly, semiannually, or annually, constitute an annuity.

FUTURE VALUE OF AN ORDINARY ANNUITY

The *future value of an annuity* is the *future* sum of all its rents plus the compound interest

on each. Consider a simple example. Suppose you deposit $100 per year for four years (periods) in a fund which earns compound interest at 6% per annum. At the date of the last deposit, the first rent will have earned compound interest for three years, the second for two years, the third for one year. On this ordinary annuity there will be no interest accumulation on the fourth rent since we are computing the future value on the date of deposit of this rent. Applying principles we learned in Part A on future value of 1, the accumulation at the *date of the last deposit* will consist of the following:

Date of Deposit— End of	Future Value at End of Year 4 of Each Deposit
Year 1	$100 × (1.06)^3 = $119.10
Year 2	100 × (1.06)^2 = 112.36
Year 3	100 × (1.06)^1 = 106.00
Year 4	100 100.00
Future value of ordinary annuity.......	$437.46

The symbol used to denote the future value of an ordinary annuity of 1 is F_o. The formula to compute the future value of an ordinary annuity of 1 is based upon the formula for a future value of 1 (Table 6–1), since the amount of an annuity of 1, as illustrated above, is the sum of a series of computations of the future value of 1. Therefore, the formula is

$$F_o = \frac{(1 + i)^n - 1}{i}$$

Notice in the heading of Table 6–3 that this is the indicated formula for those table values. Observe that the notation *"n"* refers to the number of *periodic rents* and *not* to the number of interest periods; *"i"* refers to the interest rate per period (and not to the annual rate except when the periods are one year in length). The values given in Table 6–3 are at the *date of the last rent* (i.e., the rents are at the end of each period); therefore, they are for *ordinary* annuities, as is indicated in the title of the table.

Use of Table of Future Value of Annuity of 1

Tables of future value of annuity of 1 are commonly used to calculate the future value of a

---

[5] In contrast to ordinary annuities, annuities due (see footnotes 10 and 11) assume the rents are at the beginning of each period. Annuities due are discussed in a subsequent section of this chapter.

series of rents at a specific rate of compound interest. In most situations the following are known: (1) the amount of the equal rents; (2) the number of rents, *"n"*; and (3) the constant interest rate per period, *"i."* To determine the future value in a specific situation, the appropriate value from Table 6–3 is multiplied by the amount of the periodic rent.

To illustrate an accounting application, assume Hill Corporation plans to expand its office building three years from now. To assure sufficient cash for this purpose the company has decided to set up a building fund by making three equal annual contributions of $60,000 cash on each December 31, starting in 1979. The funds will be needed on December 31, 1981, the date of the last deposit. The fund will be deposited with a trustee and will earn 7% per year compounded annually.

Required:

1. What will be the balance of the fund on December 31, 1981; that is, immediately after the last deposit?
2. Prepare a fund accumulation table for this situation.
3. Prepare the accounting entries for the entire period.

Solution:

1. Balance in the fund on December 31, 1981 (ordinary annuity basis):

   $60,000 \times F_{o_{n=3;\ i=7\%}}$ =
   $60,000 \times 3.21490$ (Table 6–3) = $192,894

2. Accumulation table—building fund, through December 31, 1981:

Date	Cash Deposits	Interest Revenue Earned	Fund Increases	Fund Balance
12/31/79 ...	$60,000		$60,000	$ 60,000
12/31/80 ...		$ 60,000 × .07 = $4,200	4,200	64,200
12/31/80 ...	60,000		60,000	124,200
12/31/81 ...		124,200 × .07 = 8,694	8,694	132,894
12/31/81 ...	60,000		60,000	192,894*

* Balance on date of last deposit (i.e., an ordinary annuity). Assumes that interest is credited to the fund each December 31.

3. Required journal entries:

   Deposits in the fund:

	12/31/79	12/31/80	12/31/81
Building fund ...	60,000	60,000	60,000
Cash	60,000	60,000	60,000

Interest revenue earned on the fund:

	12/31/80	12/31/81
Building fund	4,200	8,694
Interest revenue	4,200	8,694

Determination of Other Values Related to Future Value of Annuity

In the immediately preceding example, *three* values were given: (1) periodic rents, $60,000; (2) number of periodic rents, 3; and (3) the periodic interest rate, 7%. A fourth value, the future accumulation in a building fund, $192,894, was computed. Obviously, if any three of these four values are known, the other one can be derived. Thus, as was illustrated with respect to the future value of 1, there are four types of potential problems involving the future value of an annuity of 1, viz:

1. To determine the future value of a number of periodic rents (discussed immediately above).
2. To determine the required interest rate.[6]
   Example (based on above data):
   Given:
   a. Periodic rents, $60,000.
   b. Number of rents, 3.
   c. Future accumulation desired, $192,894.
   To derive the required interest rate:
   a. $192,894 ÷ $60,000 = 3.2149 (table value for 3 rents at unknown interest rate).
   b. Reference to Table 6–3, *line* for 3 rents indicates the required interest rate to be 7%.
3. To determine the required number of periodic rents.
   Example (based on above data):
   Given:
   a. Periodic rents, $60,000.
   b. Future accumulation desired, $192,894.

---

[6] In the following examples, the data used above, with one "given" changed in each instance, are used in order to demonstrate the correctness of the answer and the method of the computational approach.

c. Interest rate, 7% per period.

To derive the required number of rents:

a. $192,894 ÷ $60,000 = 3.2149 (table value for 1 at 7% for unknown number of rents).

b. Reference to Table 6–3, *column* for 7% interest indicates the required number of rents to be 3.

4. To determine the required amount of each rent.

Example (based on above data):

Given:

a. Number of rents, 3.

b. Interest rate per period, 7%.

c. Future accumulation desired, $192,894.

To derive the required amount of each rent:

a. Reference to Table 6–3, *column* for 7% and *line* for 3 rents, gives the value 3.2149.

b. $192,894 ÷ 3.2149 = $60,000 (the required amount of each periodic rent).

PRESENT VALUE OF AN ORDINARY ANNUITY

The *present value of an annuity* is the equivalent value *now* (i.e., at time zero) of a series of future dollars (i.e., equal periodic rents) discounted back from a series of specific future dates to the present date at a specified constant rate of compound interest per period (i.e., compound discounting). Since it involves compound discounting instead of compound interest, it can be described as the converse of the future value of an annuity explained above. For example, $1 (the equal periodic rent) due at the *end* of each of three periods in the future (total sum due $3), when discounted back at 8% compound interest, has a present value of $2.58. Alternatively, $2.58 deposited today at 8% compound interest per period would pay back $1 at the end of each of the three future periods. Significantly, it should be noted that the rents in the present value of an *ordinary* annuity are assumed to be at the *end* of each period; hence, in contrast to the future value of an ordinary annuity of 1, there is

the same number of interest periods as rents. That is, $n = 3$ & $j = 3$ (see page 188).[7]

The symbol often used to denote the present value of an ordinary annuity of 1 is P_o. As before, "n" indicates the number of periodic *rents*, and "i" the rate of discounting each period. Table 6–4 gives the present values of ordinary annuities of 1 for a number of periods and interest rates. Observe the heading of the statement and the underlying formula:

$$P_o = \frac{1 - \dfrac{1}{(1+i)^n}}{i}$$

The present values in Table 6–4 are for *ordinary* annuities; therefore, those values are at the *beginning of the period* of the first rent (see page 206). To illustrate a typical accounting application, assume Delphi Corporation is negotiating the purchase of a certain natural resource. It is estimated that the resource will produce a net cash inflow of $200,000 per year for the next three years. Assume that the inflow will be at the end of each year and that the "going" rate of compound interest is 8% per year. *Question:* What is the maximum amount that should be paid today (i.e., at the present time) for the natural resource assuming complete exhaustion at the end of three years and no residual value?

Solution:

This requires computation of the present value of the three future equal rents as follows:

$200,000 × P_{o_{n=3;\ i=8\%}}$ =
$200,000 × 2.5771$ (Table 6–4) = $\underline{\$515,420}$[8]

---

[7] In both instances an *ordinary* annuity is assumed; annuities due are discussed in the next section.

[8] As with the future value of an ordinary annuity, the *present value* of an ordinary annuity is simply the sum of the present values of the individual rents:

Date of Rent	Amount of Rent		Present Value of $1 (Table 6–2)		Present Value of Each Rent
End of Year 1	$200,000	×	$1/(1.08)^1 = .92593$	=	$185,186
End of Year 2	200,000	×	$1/(1.08)^2 = .85734$	=	171,468
End of Year 3	200,000	×	$1/(1.08)^3 = .79383$	=	158,766
Present value of ordinary annuity (at start of Year 1)					$515,420

If purchased at this price, the acquisition entry would be as follows:

Natural resource (identified) 515,420
    Cash (and/or debt)   515,420

Determination of Other Values Related to Present Value of Annuity

In the immediately preceding example, *three* values were given: (1) the periodic rent or contribution, r; (2) the number of periodic contributions, n; and (3) the periodic discounting rate, i. A fourth value, the present value, P($515,420$), was computed. Obviously, if *any* three of these four values are known, the other one can be derived, using the table. Thus, as illustrated for the future value of an annuity of 1, there are four types of potential problems related to the present value of an annuity, viz:

1. To determine the present value of a series of future rents (discussed and illustrated immediately above).
2. To determine the required interest rate.
   Example (based on above data):
   Given:
      a. Periodic rents, $200,000.
      b. Number of periodic rents, 3.
      c. Present value of the future rents, $515,420.
   To derive the required interest rate:
      a. $515,420 ÷ $200,000 = 2.5771 (approximate table value for 3 rents at unknown interest rate).
      b. Reference to Table 6–4, *line* for 3 rents, indicates the required interest rate to be 8%.
3. To determine the required number of periodic rents.
   Example (based on above data):
   Given:
      a. Periodic rents, $200,000.
      b. Interest rate, 8%.
      c. Present value of the future rents, $515,420.
   To derive the required number of periodic rents:
      a. $515,420 ÷ $200,000 = 2.5771 (approximate table value at 8% at the required number of rents).

      b. Reference to Table 6–4, *column* for 8%, indicates that 3 periodic rents are required.
4. To determine the required amount of each rent.
   Example (based on above data):
   Given:
      a. Number of periodic rents, 3.
      b. Interest rate per period, 8%.
      c. Present value of the future rents, $515,420.
   To derive the required amount of each rent:
      a. Table 6–4 value at 8%, 3 rents = 2.5771.
      b. $515,420 ÷ 2.5771 = $200,000 (the periodic rent).

To illustrate an accounting application to derive the required rent for the present value of annuity, assume Voss Corporation purchased a plant asset resulting in the incurrence of a $50,000 debt on January 1, 1979. The liability is to be paid in three equal installments on each December 31, starting at the end of 1979. The interest rate is 9 percent, and each equal installment is to include both interest and principal.

Required:

1. Compute the required amount of each equal annual installment.
2. Prepare a debt amortization schedule for this situation.
3. Give the journal entries for the period of the debt.

Solution:

1. $50,000 ÷ $P_{o_{n=3;\ i=9\%}}$ =
   $50,000 ÷ 2.53129 (Table 6–4) = $19,753 (the periodic rent)

2. A debt amortization schedule is a decumulation table that shows the reduction of the debt from $50,000 to zero over the three-year period. The debt amortization schedule showing interest expense and reduction of principal each period would be as follows:

Debt Amortization Schedule

Date	Cash Payment	Interest Expense	Payment on Principal	Unpaid Principal
1/1/79				$50,000
12/31/79 . . .	$19,753 [a]	$4,500 [b]	$15,253 [c]	34,747 [d]
12/31/80 . . .	19,753	3,127	16,626	18,121
12/31/81 . . .	19,753	1,632*	18,121	–0–

[a] Computed above.   * Adjusted for rounding error.
Successive computations:
[b] $50,000 × .09 = $4,500.
[c] $19,753 − $4,500 = $15,253.
[d] $50,000 − $15,253 = $34,747.

3. Journal entries:

1/1/79 to record the debt:

Plant asset 50,000
    Liability 50,000

Each December 31 to record payment (per above schedule):

	12/31/79	12/31/80	12/31/81
Interest expense . .	4,500	3,127	1,632
Liability	15,253	16,626	18,121
Cash	19,753	19,753	19,753

ANNUITIES DUE

Discussion of annuities to this point has been confined to *ordinary annuities* since they represent the more or less "normal" situation encountered. Recall that with respect to ordinary annui-

ties, specific assumptions were noted in the preceding discussions relative to the *timing* of the rents and the interest periods. *Annuities due* involve different assumptions with respect to the timing of rents. The timing distinction is that for ordinary annuities, the rents are assumed to be paid or received at the *end* of each period; in contrast, for annuities due, the rents are assumed to be paid or received at the *beginning* of each period.

Future Value of Annuity Due

In the case of the future value of an ordinary annuity, the future amount is calculated as of the date of the last rent since the rents are assumed to be at the end of each period. In contrast, the future value of an *annuity due is calculated for one interest period after the date of the last rent* since the rents are assumed to be at the beginning of each period. The contrast between the two timing assumptions is graphically shown at the bottom of this page:[9]

[9] The subscript *"o"* is an ordinary annuity and *"d"* an annuity due. The terms "ordinary" and "due" were coined by mathematicians; many accountants prefer more descriptive terminology:

1. Instead of "ordinary"—"end-of-the-period annuities," or "annuities in arrears."
2. Instead/ of "due"—"beginning-of-the-period annuities," or "annuities in advance."

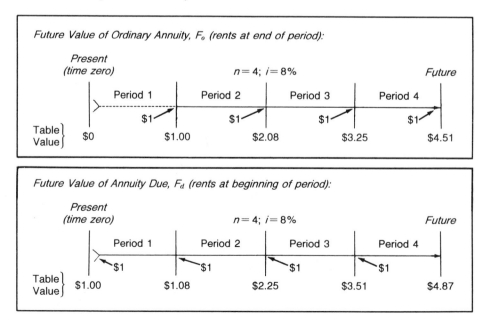

Future Value of Ordinary Annuity, F_o (rents at end of period):

Future Value of Annuity Due, F_d (rents at beginning of period):

The basic differences reflected in the immediately preceding diagrams are shown immediately below.

	Characteristic	Type of Future Value Annuity	
		F_o—Ordinary	F_d—Due
1.	Timing of each rent.	End of each period	Beginning of each period
2.	Number of rents.	Four ⎫	Four ⎫
3.	Number of interest periods.	Three ⎬ $(n = 4 \& j = 3)$	Four ⎬ $(n = 4 \& j = 4)$
4.	Point in time of the future value	On date of last rent	One interest period after the last rent

The differences reflected in (1), (3), and (4), by definition are due solely to the different timing assumptions for the rents. An understanding of the difference between an ordinary annuity and an annuity due is important in solving annuity problems. Care must be exercised to select the one that fits the specific situation.

Ordinary annuity tables are found in various sources more often than annuity due tables. In situations where only an ordinary annuity table is available and an annuity *due* amount is needed, the conversion is simple and straightforward. Conversion from an ordinary annuity to an annuity due amount can be accomplished easily in either of two ways, viz:

1. Multiply the future value of ordinary annuity amount by $(1 + i)$. That is, $F_d = F_o \times (1 + i)$. For example, the *annuity due* amounts shown in the graphic illustration on the previous page were computed as follows:

Interest	Rents	Amount of Future Value of Ordinary Annuity (Table 6–3)	×	Multiplier $(1 + i)$	=	Future Value of Annuity Due
8%	1	1.00000	×	(1.08)	=	1.08000
8%	2	2.08000	×	(1.08)	=	2.24640
8%	3	3.24640	×	(1.08)	=	3.50611
8%	4	4.50611	×	(1.08)	=	4.86660

2. Read the amount from the future value of an ordinary annuity table for *one greater* rent than the number of rents specified in the annuity due problem, then *subtract* the numeral 1 from it.[10] This has the effect of

adding interest to the ordinary annuity amount for one period to derive the annuity due amount. To illustrate, for $n = 4$; $i = 8\%$:

From Table 6–3 (FV of ordinary annuity), $n = 5$; $i = 8\%$	5.86660
Subtract the numeral 1	−1.00000
Difference—FV of annuity due, $n = 4$; $i = 8\%$	4.86660

In applying the concepts of future and present value, it is generally helpful to graphically analyze the situation, or problem, in a manner similar to the graphic illustrations in this chapter. This initial step will indicate the appropriate future or present value concept to apply. Two examples are given below with explanation of the solution approaches. These illustrate different situations requiring computation óf the future value of ordinary annuity and future value of annuity due.

Situation A: On January 1, 1979, Dawson Corporation entered into a contract with a foreign company that required Dawson to pay $50,000 cash on December 31, 1981. Dawson was to deposit three equal annual dollar amounts in a Swiss bank starting December 31, 1979, so that the $50,000 would be available on December 31, 1981. On that date the bank would pay the foreign company in full. The bank agreed to add 6% annual compound interest to the fund each December 31.

Required:

1. Diagram the annuity required by the agreement to establish the debt payment fund with the bank.
2. What kind of annuity is indicated? Explain.
3. Compute the amount of the equal annual payments.

Solution:

1. Diagram of the ordinary annuity ($n = 3$; $i = 6\%$) is shown at top of the next page.

---

[10] Frequently expressed as $(n + 1 \text{ rents}) - 1$. This method, as well as the one above, serves to increase the number of interest periods by 1 for an annuity due and maintains the same number of rents.

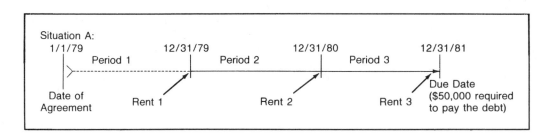

2. Since the rents are at the end of the period, this is the future value of an *ordinary* annuity; that is, the future value is at the date of the last rent.

3. $\text{Rent} = \dfrac{\text{Future value}}{F_{o_{n=3;\ i=6\%}}} = \dfrac{\$50,000}{3.1836(\text{Table } 6\text{–}3)}$
$= \underline{\$15,705}$

Situation B: On January 1, 1979, Cotter Corporation decided to create a plant expansion fund by making three annual deposits of $60,000 each on January 1, 1979, 1980, and 1981. The fund will be held by a trustee who will increase the fund on a 7% annual compound interest basis. The fund will be needed on December 31, 1981.

Required:

1. Diagram the annuity created in this situation.
2. What kind of annuity is indicated? Explain.
3. Compute the balance in the fund on December 31, 1981, and prepare a fund accumulation table.

Solution:

1. Diagram of the annuity due ($n = 3$; $i = 7\%$) is shown at bottom of this page.
2. Since the rents are at the beginning of each period, this is an annuity *due;* the amount desired in the fund is at one interest period after the last rent. Since the rents build a

future amount, it is a *future value of annuity due of 1.*

3. Fund balance at December 31, 1981:

Conversion:

$F_{d_{n=3;i=7\%}} = 3.2149 \text{ (Table } 6\text{–}3) \times 1.07$
$= 3.43994$
$\text{Fund balance} = \$60,000 \times 3.43994$
$= \underline{\$206,396}$

The fund accumulation table for this future value of annuity due, $n = 3$; $i = 7\%$ would be as follows:

Date	Cash Deposits	Interest Revenue Earned	Fund Increases	Fund Balance
1/1/79	$60,000		$60,000	$ 60,000
12/31/79 ..		$ 60,000 × .07 = $ 4,200	4,200	64,200
1/1/80	60,000		60,000	124,200
12/31/80 ..		124,200 × .07 = 8,694	8,694	132,894
1/1/81	60,000		60,000	192,894
12/31/81 ..		192,894 × .07 = 13,502*	13,502	206,396

* Round $1 to come out even.

This accumulation table, prepared on an annuity due basis, may be compared with a similar set of facts, on an ordinary annuity basis, illustrated on page 189. Compare the timing difference for the rents and the resultant effects on the interest accumulations and fund balances.

Present Value of Annuity Due

In the case of present value of an *ordinary annuity,* the rents are assumed to be at the end

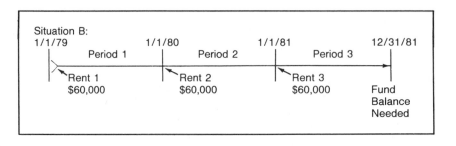

of the period; therefore, the discount is calculated as of one period back from each rent. In contrast, the present value of an *annuity due* assumes the rents are at the beginning of each period; therefore, there is no discounting of the first rent. The contrast between the two timing assumptions for present value of an annuity is graphically shown at the bottom of this page. The diagram below shows that for the *present value of an ordinary annuity,* the rents are at the end of each period. There is the same number of interest discount periods as rents; that is, $n = 4$ & $j = 4$ (see page 187).

In contrast, the *present value of an annuity due* has rents at the beginning of each period. There is one less interest discount period than rents; in total it is $n = 4$ & $j = 3$.

Often an ordinary annuity table is available but not an annuity due table. In such situations the present value of an ordinary annuity may be converted to the present value of an annuity due by using either of the two approaches discussed on page 193, viz:

1. Multiply the present value ordinary annuity by $(1 + i)$. For example, the present value of an annuity due of 1 for $n = 4$; $i = 6\%$ is 3.46511 from Table 6–4 × 1.06 = 3.67301.
2. Read the present value of an ordinary annuity of 1 table for *one less* than the number of rents specified in the annuity due problem,

then *add* the numeral 1 to it.[11] To illustrate for $n = 4$; $i = 6\%$:

From Table 6–4 (present value of ordinary annuity) $n = 3$; $i = 6\%$	2.67301
Add the numeral 1	1.00000
Summation—present value of annuity due, $n = 4$; $i = 6\%$	3.67301

Two situations presented below, with solutions, illustrate the different situations where the present value of an ordinary annuity and present value of an annuity due are applied. Careful attention to the timing of the rents is necessary in order to determine which type of annuity should be applied to each situation or problem.

Situation C: On January 1, 1979, Brown Corporation owed a $30,000 debt which was due. The creditor agreed to let Brown pay the debt in four equal annual payments on December 31, 1979, 1980, 1981, and 1982. Interest at 8% per year is payable on the unpaid principal. Each equal payment includes interest and principal.

Required:

1. Diagram the annuity represented by the required annual payments.

---

[11] Frequently expressed as $(n - 1$ rents$) + 1$. Either method serves to reduce the discount period by one for an annuity due and maintains the same number of rents.

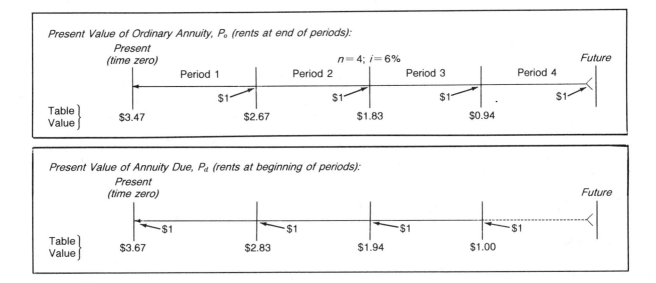

Present Value of Ordinary Annuity, P_o (rents at end of periods):

Present (time zero) — $n = 4$; $i = 6\%$ — Future

Period 1 | Period 2 | Period 3 | Period 4

$1 | $1 | $1 | $1

Table Value: $3.47 | $2.67 | $1.83 | $0.94

Present Value of Annuity Due, P_d (rents at beginning of periods):

Present (time zero) — Future

$1 | $1 | $1 | $1

Table Value: $3.67 | $2.83 | $1.94 | $1.00

2. What kind of annuity is represented? Explain.
3. Compute the amount of the equal annual payments on the debt.

Solution:

1. Diagram of the ordinary annuity ($n = 4$; $i = 8\%$) is shown at bottom of this page.
2. Since the payments are to be made at the end of each period, this is an ordinary annuity, and the present value (i.e., the principal of the debt) is at the beginning of the first period.
3. The amount of each equal annual payment is computed as follows:

$$\text{Rent} = \frac{\text{Present Value}}{P_{o_{n=4;\,i=8\%}}} = \frac{\$30,000}{3.31213 \text{ (Table 6–4)}}$$
$$= \$9,058$$

Situation D: John Doe was seriously injured while working for X Corporation. On January 1, 1979, an agreement was reached whereby X Corporation would deposit $100,000 with the City Bank as trustee for the benefit of Doe. The bank agreed to pay 6% compound interest per year on the unused principal while making five equal annual payments to Doe from the principal plus interest earned. The payments are to be made on each January 1, starting immediately, until the fund (principal plus all interest accumulations) is fully expended.

Required:

1. Diagram the annuity represented by the payments.
2. What kind of annuity is represented? Explain.
3. Compute the amount of each equal annual payment to Doe.

Solution:

1. Diagram of the annuity due ($n = 5$; $i = 6\%$) is shown at bottom of this page.
2. Since the rents are at the beginning of the period (the first one starts immediately), this is an annuity due. Since the $100,000 is deposited at the beginning, that amount represents the present value of the annuity due, on which the amount of the equal rents is based. The computation is as follows:

3. $\text{Rent} = \dfrac{\text{Present Value}}{P_{d_{n=5;\,i=6\%}}} = \dfrac{\$100,000}{4.46510^*} = \underline{\underline{\$22,396.}}$

* Conversion:
From Table 6–4, $4.21236 \times 1.06 = 4.46510$.

In summary, another useful way to view the distinction between an ordinary annuity and an annuity due is to focus on the date the annuity amount is needed. Annuities can be shifted from an ordinary annuity to an annuity due (or vice versa) simply by shifting the date when the desired value is needed.

The *future value* of an ordinary annuity is

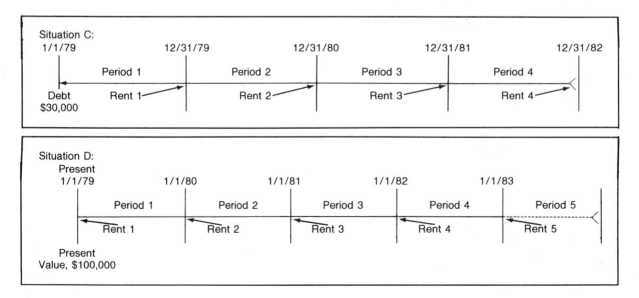

Periods	9%	10%	11%	12%	15%	18%	20%
1	1.09000	1.10000	1.11000	1.12000	1.15000	1.18000	1.20000
2	1.18810	1.21000	1.23210	1.25440	1.32250	1.39240	1.44000
3	1.29503	1.33100	1.36763	1.40493	1.52088	1.64303	1.72800
4	1.41158	1.46410	1.51807	1.57352	1.74901	1.93878	2.07360
5	1.53862	1.61051	1.68506	1.76234	2.01136	2.28776	2.48832
6	1.67710	1.77156	1.87041	1.97382	2.31306	2.69955	2.98598
7	1.82804	1.94872	2.07616	2.21068	2.66002	3.18547	3.58318
8	1.99256	2.14359	2.30454	2.47596	3.05902	3.75886	4.29982
9	2.17189	2.35795	2.55804	2.77308	3.51788	4.43545	5.15978
10	2.36736	2.59374	2.83942	3.10585	4.04556	5.23384	6.19174
11	2.58043	2.85312	3.15176	3.47855	4.65239	6.17593	7.43008
12	2.81266	3.13843	3.49845	3.89598	5.35025	7.28759	8.91610
13	3.06580	3.45227	3.88328	4.36349	6.15279	8.59936	10.69932
14	3.34173	3.79750	4.31044	4.88711	7.07571	10.14724	12.83918
15	3.64248	4.17725	4.78459	5.47357	8.13706	11.97375	15.40702
16	3.97031	4.59497	5.31089	6.13039	9.35762	14.12902	18.48843
17	4.32763	5.05447	5.89509	6.86604	10.76126	16.67225	22.18611
18	4.71712	5.55992	6.54355	7.68997	12.37545	19.67325	26.62333
19	5.14166	6.11591	7.26334	8.61276	14.23177	23.21444	31.94800
20	5.60441	6.72750	8.06231	9.64629	16.36654	27.39303	38.33760
21	6.10881	7.40025	8.94917	10.80385	18.82152	32.32378	46.00512
22	6.65860	8.14027	9.93357	12.10031	21.64475	38.14206	55.20614
23	7.25787	8.95430	11.02627	13.55235	24.89146	45.00763	66.24737
24	7.91108	9.84973	12.23916	15.17863	28.62518	53.10901	79.49685
25	8.62308	10.83471	13.58546	17.00006	32.91895	62.66863	95.39622

TABLE 6–2

Present Value of 1, $p = \dfrac{1}{(1+i)^n}$

Periods	2%	2½%	3%	4%	5%	6%	7%	8%
1	.98039	.97561	.97087	.96154	.95238	.94340	.93458	.92593
2	.96117	.95181	.94260	.92456	.90703	.89000	.87344	.85734
3	.94232	.92860	.91514	.88900	.86384	.83962	.81630	.79383
4	.92385	.90595	.88849	.85480	.82270	.79209	.76290	.73503
5	.90573	.88385	.86261	.82193	.78353	.74726	.71299	.68058
6	.88797	.86230	.83748	.79031	.74622	.70496	.66634	.63017
7	.87056	.84127	.81309	.75992	.71068	.66506	.62275	.58349
8	.85349	.82075	.78941	.73069	.67684	.62741	.58201	.54027
9	.83676	.80073	.76642	.70259	.64461	.59190	.54393	.50025
10	.82035	.78120	.74409	.67556	.61391	.55839	.50835	.46319
11	.80426	.76214	.72242	.64958	.58468	.52679	.47509	.42888
12	.78849	.74356	.70138	.62460	.55684	.49697	.44401	.39711
13	.77303	.72542	.68095	.60057	.53032	.46884	.41496	.36770
14	.75788	.70773	.66112	.57748	.50507	.44230	.38782	.34046
15	.74301	.69047	.64186	.55526	.48102	.41727	.36245	.31524
16	.72845	.67362	.62317	.53391	.45811	.39365	.33873	.29189
17	.71416	.65720	.60502	.51337	.43630	.37136	.31657	.27027
18	.70016	.64117	.58739	.49363	.41552	.35034	.29586	.25025
19	.68643	.62553	.57029	.47464	.39573	.33051	.27651	.23171
20	.67297	.61027	.55368	.45639	.37689	.31180	.25842	.21455
21	.65978	.59539	.53755	.43883	.35894	.29416	.24151	.19866
22	.64684	.58086	.52189	.42196	.34185	.27751	.22571	.18394
23	.63416	.56670	.50669	.40573	.32557	.26180	.21095	.17032
24	.62172	.55288	.49193	.39012	.31007	.24698	.19715	.15770
25	.60953	.53939	.47761	.37512	.29530	.23300	.18425	.14602

Periods	9%	10%	11%	12%	15%	18%	20%
1	.91743	.90909	.90090	.89286	.86957	.84746	.83333
2	.84168	.82645	.81162	.79719	.75614	.71818	.69444
3	.77218	.75131	.73119	.71178	.65752	.60863	.57870
4	.70843	.68301	.65873	.63552	.57175	.51579	.48225
5	.64993	.62092	.59345	.56743	.49718	.43711	.40188
6	.59627	.56447	.53464	.50663	.43233	.37043	.33490
7	.54703	.51316	.48166	.45235	.37594	.31393	.27908
8	.50187	.46651	.43393	.40388	.32690	.26604	.23257
9	.46043	.42410	.39092	.36061	.28426	.22546	.19381
10	.42241	.38554	.35218	.32197	.24718	.19106	.16151
11	.38753	.35049	.31728	.28748	.21494	.16192	.13459
12	.35553	.31863	.28584	.25668	.18691	.13722	.11216
13	.32618	.28966	.25751	.22917	.16253	.11629	.09346
14	.29925	.26333	.23199	.20462	.14133	.09855	.07789
15	.27454	.23939	.20900	.18270	.12289	.08352	.06491
16	.25187	.21763	.18829	.16312	.10686	.07078	.05409
17	.23107	.19784	.16963	.14564	.09293	.05998	.04507
18	.21199	.17986	.15282	.13004	.08081	.05083	.03756
19	.19449	.16351	.13768	.11611	.07027	.04308	.03130
20	.17843	.14864	.12403	.10367	.06110	.03651	.02608
21	.16370	.13513	.11174	.09256	.05313	.03094	.02174
22	.15018	.12285	.10067	.08264	.04620	.02622	.01811
23	.13778	.11168	.09069	.07379	.04017	.02222	.01509
24	.12640	.10153	.08170	.06588	.03493	.01883	.01258
25	.11597	.09230	.07361	.05882	.03038	.01596	.01048

TABLE 6–3

Future Value of Annuity of 1 (ordinary), $F_o = \dfrac{(1+i)^n - 1}{i}$

Periodic Rents (n)	2%	2½%	3%	4%	5%	6%	7%	8%
1	1.00000	1.00000	1.00000	1.00000	1.00000	1.00000	1.00000	1.00000
2	2.02000	2.02500	2.03000	2.04000	2.05000	2.06000	2.07000	2.08000
3	3.06040	3.07563	3.09090	3.12160	3.15250	3.18360	3.21490	3.24640
4	4.12161	4.15252	4.18363	4.24646	4.31013	4.37462	4.43994	4.50611
5	5.20404	5.25633	5.30914	5.41632	5.52563	5.63709	5.75074	5.86660
6	6.30812	6.38774	6.46841	6.63298	6.80191	6.97532	7.15329	7.33593
7	7.43428	7.54743	7.66246	7.89829	8.14201	8.39384	8.65402	8.92280
8	8.58297	8.73612	8.89234	9.21423	9.54911	9.89747	10.25980	10.63663
9	9.75463	9.95452	10.15911	10.58280	11.02656	11.49132	11.97799	12.48756
10	10.94972	11.20338	11.46388	12.00611	12.57789	13.18079	13.81645	14.48656
11	12.16872	12.48347	12.80780	13.48635	14.20679	14.97164	15.78360	16.64549
12	13.41209	13.79555	14.19203	15.02581	15.91713	16.86994	17.88845	18.97713
13	14.68033	15.14044	15.61779	16.62684	17.71298	18.88214	20.14064	21.49530
14	15.97394	16.51895	17.08632	18.29191	19.59863	21.01507	22.55049	24.21492
15	17.29342	17.93193	18.59891	20.02359	21.57856	23.27597	25.12902	27.15211
16	18.63929	19.38022	20.15688	21.82453	23.65749	25.67253	27.88805	30.32428
17	20.01207	20.86473	21.76159	23.69751	25.84037	28.21288	30.84022	33.75023
18	21.41231	22.38635	23.41444	25.64541	28.13238	30.90565	33.99903	37.45024
19	22.84056	23.94601	25.11687	27.67123	30.53900	33.75999	37.37896	41.44626
20	24.29737	25.54466	26.87037	29.77808	33.06595	36.78559	40.99549	45.76196
21	25.78332	27.18327	28.67649	31.96920	35.71925	39.99273	44.86518	50.42292
22	27.29898	28.86286	30.53678	34.24797	38.50521	43.39229	49.00574	55.45676
23	28.84496	30.58443	32.45288	36.61789	41.43048	46.99583	53.43614	60.89330
24	30.42186	32.34904	34.42647	39.08260	44.50200	50.81558	58.17667	66.76476
25	32.03030	34.15776	36.45926	41.64591	47.72710	54.86451	63.24904	73.10594

Periodic Rents (n)	9%	10%	11%	12%	15%	18%	20%
1	1.00000	1.00000	1.00000	1.00000	1.00000	1.00000	1.00000
2	2.09000	2.10000	2.11000	2.12000	2.15000	2.18000	2.20000
3	3.27810	3.31000	3.34210	3.37440	3.47250	3.57240	3.64000
4	4.57313	4.64100	4.70973	4.77933	4.99338	5.21543	5.36800
5	5.98471	6.10510	6.22780	6.35285	6.74238	7.15421	7.44160
6	7.52333	7.71561	7.91286	8.11519	8.75374	9.44197	9.92992
7	9.20043	9.48717	9.78327	10.08901	11.06680	12.14152	12.91590
8	11.02847	11.43589	11.85943	12.29969	13.72682	15.32700	16.49908
9	13.02104	13.57948	14.16397	14.77566	16.78584	19.08585	20.79890
10	15.19293	15.93742	16.72201	17.54874	20.30372	23.52131	25.95868
11	17.56029	18.53117	19.56143	20.65458	24.34928	28.75514	32.15042
12	20.14072	21.38428	22.71319	24.13313	29.00167	34.93107	39.58050
13	22.95338	24.52271	26.21164	28.02911	34.35192	42.21866	48.49660
14	26.01919	27.97498	30.09492	32.39260	40.50471	50.81802	59.19592
15	29.36092	31.77248	34.40536	37.27971	47.58041	60.96527	72.03511
16	33.00340	35.94973	39.18995	42.75328	55.71747	72.93901	87.44213
17	36.97370	40.54470	44.50084	48.88367	65.07509	87.06804	105.93056
18	41.30134	45.59917	50.39594	55.74971	75.83636	103.74028	128.11667
19	46.01846	51.15909	56.93949	63.43968	88.21181	123.41353	154.74000
20	51.16012	57.27500	64.20283	72.05244	102.44358	146.62797	186.68800
21	56.76453	64.00250	72.26514	81.69874	118.81012	174.02100	225.02560
22	62.87334	71.40275	81.21431	92.50258	137.63164	206.34479	271.03072
23	69.53194	79.54302	91.14788	104.60289	159.27638	244.48685	326.23686
24	76.78981	88.49733	102.17415	118.15524	184.16784	289.49448	392.48424
25	84.70090	98.34706	114.41331	133.33387	212.79302	342.60349	471.98108

TABLE 6–4

Present Value of Annuity of 1 (ordinary), $P_o = \dfrac{1 - \dfrac{1}{(1+i)^n}}{i}$

Periodic Rents (n)	2%	2½%	3%	4%	5%	6%	7%	8%
1	.98039	.97561	.97087	.96154	.95238	.94340	.93458	.92593
2	1.94156	1.92742	1.91347	1.88609	1.85941	1.83339	1.80802	1.78326
3	2.88388	2.85602	2.82861	2.77509	2.72325	2.67301	2.62432	2.57710
4	3.80773	3.76197	3.71710	3.62990	3.54595	3.46511	3.38721	3.31213
5	4.71346	4.64583	4.57971	4.45182	4.32948	4.21236	4.10020	3.99271
6	5.60143	5.50813	5.41719	5.24214	5.07569	4.91732	4.76654	4.62288
7	6.47199	6.34939	6.23028	6.00205	5.78637	5.58238	5.38929	5.20637
8	7.32548	7.17014	7.01969	6.73274	6.46321	6.20979	5.97130	5.74664
9	8.16224	7.97087	7.78611	7.43533	7.10782	6.80169	6.51523	6.24689
10	8.98259	8.75206	8.53020	8.11090	7.72173	7.36009	7.02358	6.71008
11	9.78685	9.51421	9.25262	8.76048	8.30641	7.88687	7.49867	7.13896
12	10.57534	10.25776	9.95400	9.38507	8.86325	8.38384	7.94269	7.53608
13	11.34837	10.98318	10.63496	9.98565	9.39357	8.85268	8.35765	7.90378
14	12.10625	11.69091	11.29607	10.56312	9.89864	9.29498	8.74547	8.24424
15	12.84926	12.38138	11.93794	11.11839	10.37966	9.71225	9.10791	8.55948
16	13.57771	13.05500	12.56110	11.65230	10.83777	10.10590	9.44665	8.85137
17	14.29187	13.71220	13.16612	12.16567	11.27407	10.47726	9.76322	9.12164
18	14.99203	14.35336	13.75351	12.65930	11.68959	10.82760	10.05909	9.37189
19	15.67846	14.97889	14.32380	13.13394	12.08532	11.15812	10.33560	9.60360
20	16.35143	15.58916	14.87747	13.59033	12.46221	11.46992	10.59401	9.81815
21	17.01121	16.18455	15.41502	14.02916	12.82115	11.76408	10.83553	10.01680
22	17.65805	16.76541	15.93692	14.45112	13.16300	12.04158	11.06124	10.20074
23	18.29220	17.33211	16.44361	14.85684	13.48857	12.30338	11.27219	10.37106
24	18.91393	17.88499	16.93554	15.24696	13.79864	12.55036	11.46933	10.52876
25	19.52346	18.42438	17.41315	15.62208	14.09394	12.78336	11.65358	10.67478

Periodic Rents (n)	9%	10%	11%	12%	15%	18%	20%
1	.91743	.90909	.90090	.89286	.86957	.84746	.83333
2	1.75911	1.73554	1.71252	1.69005	1.62571	1.56564	1.52778
3	2.53129	2.48685	2.44371	2.40183	2.28323	2.17427	2.10648
4	3.23972	3.16987	3.10245	3.03735	2.85498	2.69006	2.58873
5	3.88965	3.79079	3.69590	3.60478	3.35216	3.12717	2.99061
6	4.48592	4.35526	4.23054	4.11141	3.78448	3.49760	3.32551
7	5.03295	4.86842	4.71220	4.56376	4.16042	3.81153	3.60459
8	5.53482	5.33493	5.14612	4.96764	4.48732	4.07757	3.83716
9	5.99525	5.75902	5.53705	5.32825	4.77158	4.30302	4.03097
10	6.41766	6.14457	5.88923	5.65022	5.01877	4.49409	4.19247
11	6.80519	6.49506	6.20652	5.93770	5.23371	4.65601	4.32706
12	7.16073	6.81369	6.49236	6.19437	5.42062	4.79322	4.43922
13	7.48690	7.10336	6.74987	6.42355	5.58315	4.90951	4.53268
14	7.78615	7.36669	6.98187	6.62817	5.72448	5.00806	4.61057
15	8.06069	7.60608	7.19087	6.81086	5.84737	5.09158	4.67547
16	8.31256	7.82371	7.37916	6.97399	5.95423	5.16235	4.72956
17	8.54363	8.02155	7.54879	7.11963	6.04716	5.22233	4.77463
18	8.75563	8.20141	7.70162	7.24967	6.12797	5.27316	4.81219
19	8.95011	8.36492	7.83929	7.36578	6.19823	5.31624	4.84350
20	9.12855	8.51356	7.96333	7.46944	6.25933	5.35275	4.86958
21	9.29224	8.64869	8.07507	7.56200	6.31246	5.38368	4.89132
22	9.44243	8.77154	8.17574	7.64465	6.35866	5.40990	4.90943
23	9.58021	8.88322	5.26643	7.71843	6.39884	5.43212	4.92453
24	9.70661	8.98474	8.34814	7.78432	6.43377	5.45095	4.93710
25	9.82258	9.07704	8.42174	7.84314	6.46415	5.46691	4.94759

QUESTIONS

1. Explain what is meant by the time value of money.

2. Fundamentally what is the difference between simple interest and compound interest?

3. Briefly explain each of the following:
   a. Future value of 1.
   b. Present value of 1.
   c. Future value of annuity of 1.
   d. Present value of annuity of 1.

4. Explain what is meant by the future value of 1. Relate it to the present value of 1.

5. If the table value for a future value of 1 is known, how may it be converted to the table value for present value of 1?

6. Define an annuity in general terms. Explain rents and relate them to time periods and interest rates.

7. The table for future value of an annuity provides the value 3.09 (rounded) at 3% for three periods; explain the meaning of this table value.

8. What is meant by the present value of an annuity? Contrast it with the future value of an annuity.

9. Explain the fundamental difference between (a) future value of an ordinary annuity and (b) future value of an annuity due.

10. Explain the fundamental difference between (a) present value of an ordinary annuity and (b) present value of an annuity due.

EXERCISES (round solutions to nearest dollar)

PART A
Exercises 6–1 to 6–10

Exercise 6–1

AB Company plans to deposit $60,000 today into a special building fund which will be needed at the end of six years. They are looking for a financial institution (as trustee) that will pay them 8% interest on the fund balance.

Required:

How much will the fund total assuming (show computations):

Case A—Annual compounding?
Case B—Semiannual compounding?
Case C—Quarterly compounding?

Exercise 6–2

May Company, at the present date, has $40,000 which will be deposited in a savings account until needed. It is anticipated that $80,000 will be needed at the end of nine years to expand some manufacturing facilities. What approximate rate of interest would be required to accumulate the $80,000 assuming compounding on an annual basis? Show computations; no need to interpolate.

Exercise 6–3

Dawson Corporation is planning an addition to its office building as soon as adequate funds can be accumulated. The corporation has estimated that the addition will cost approximately $150,000. At the present time $100,000 cash is on hand that will not be needed in the near future. A local savings institution will pay 7% interest (compounded annually). How many periods would be required to accumulate the $150,000? Show computations; no need to interpolate.

Exercise 6–4

South Company has on hand $100,000 cash that will not be needed in the near future. However, the company will expand operations within the next three to five years. The company has decided to establish a savings account locally which will earn 6% interest compounded annually. The interest will be added to the fund each year. Assuming the deposit of $100,000 is made on January 1, 1980, (a) compute the balance that will be in the fund at the end of the third year and (b) prepare an accumulation table for the fund.

Exercise 6–5

Samson Company will need $200,000 cash to renovate an old plant five years from now. Assume a financial institution will increase a fund at 8% interest. Compute the amount of cash that must be deposited now to meet the future need assuming (show computations):

Case A—Annual compounding?
Case B—Semiannual compounding?
Case C—Quarterly compounding?

Exercise 6–6

Baker Company, on January 1, 1979, has a contract whereby the company is due to receive $50,000 cash on December 31, 1984. The company is short of cash and desires to discount (sell) this claim. Baker is willing to accept a 12% annual discount. Under these conditions how much cash would Baker receive on January 1, 1979?

Exercise 6–7

On January 1, 1979, Fawn Corporation signed a $200,000 noninterest-bearing note which is due on December 31, 1983. According to the agreement Fawn has the option to pay the $200,000 at maturity date or to pay the obligation in full on January 1, 1979, on a 6% compound interest discount basis. What would be the single amount of cash required on January 1, 1979, to settle the debt in full? Show computations. Assume this debt was incurred to purchase an operational asset. What should be recorded as the cost of the asset? Explain.

Exercise 6–8

Stone Corporation plans a plant expansion which will require approximately $300,000 at December 31, 1981. Since they have some idle cash on hand now, January 1, 1979, they desire to know how much they would have to invest as a lump sum now to accumulate the required amount, assuming 7% annual compound interest is added to the fund each December 31.

Required:
1. Compute the amount that must be invested on January 1, 1979.
2. Prepare an accumulation table for the plant expansion fund.

Exercise 6–9

Rollins Company purchased some additional equipment that was needed because of a new contract. The equipment was purchased on January 1, 1979. Because the contract would require two years to complete and Rollins was short of cash, the vendor agreed to accept a down payment of $10,000 and a two-year non-interest-bearing note for $45,000 (this amount includes all interest charges) due December 31, 1980. Assume a 10% annual rate of interest.

Required:
1. Compute the cost of the equipment. Show computations.
2. Give the entry at date of acquisition of the equipment.
3. Prepare a debt amortization schedule.

Exercise 6–10

B. Smith has a small child. Smith has decided to set up a fund to provide for the child's college education. A local financial institution will handle the fund and increase it each year on a 6% annual compound interest basis. Smith desires to make a single deposit on January 1, 1979, and specifies that the fund must have a $40,000 balance at the end of the 16th year. What amount of cash must be deposited on January 1, 1979? Show computations. Set up an accumulation table to cover the first three years.

PART B
Exercises 6–11 to 6–20

Exercise 6–11

Bowie Company desires to accumulate a plant expansion fund over the next few years. The company will make equal annual contributions to the fund starting on December 31, 1979. The fund will be increased by the trustee by 8% annual interest. What will be the balance in the fund immediately after the last deposit assuming

1. Five annual contributions of $5,000 each and annual compounding?
2. Ten semiannual contributions of $2,500 each and semiannual compounding?
3. Twenty quarterly contributions of $1,250 each and quarterly compounding?

Exercise 6–12

Marks Corporation has decided to accumulate a debt retirement fund by making three equal annual deposits of $22,000 on each December 31, starting at the end of 1979. Assume the fund will accumulate annual compound interest at 7% per year which will be added to the fund balance.

Required:
1. What will be the balance in the fund on December 31, 1981 (immediately after the last deposit)?
2. Prepare an accumulation table for this fund.
3. Prepare the journal entries for the period January 1, 1979, through December 31, 1981.

Exercise 6–13

Wells Corporation plans to establish a debt retirement fund, beginning December 31, 1979, amounting to $8,750, by making end-of-the-period contributions of $2,000 to a trustee each December 31, so that the desired amount will be available on December 31,

1982, the date of the last rent. Compute the required interest rate that must be earned by the fund on an annual compound basis to satisfy these requirements. Show your computations.

Exercise 6–14

Mabry Corporation has decided to create a plant expansion fund by making equal annual deposits of $3,000 on each December 31. Interest at 7% compounded annually will be added to the fund balance. The company wants to know how many deposits will be required to build a fund of $75,390 immediately after the last deposit. Show your computations.

Exercise 6–15

Ross Company desires to accumulate a fund to retire a debt of $100,000. The debt is due on January 1, 1986. Equal annual contributions will be made to the fund by Ross on each December 31, starting in 1979 and ending in 1985. The fund will be increased each year by 5% annual compound interest. Compute the amount of the equal contributions at each year-end.

Exercise 6–16

Brown Company is considering purchasing a large used machine that is in excellent mechanical condition. The company plans to keep the machine for ten years, at which time the residual value will be zero. An analysis of the capacity of the machine and the costs of operating it (including materials used in production) provided an estimate that the machine would increase aftertax net cash inflow by approximately $10,000 per year.

Required:
1. Compute the approximate amount that Brown should be willing to pay now for the machine assuming a target earnings rate of 10% per year. Assume also that the revenue is realized at each year-end. Show your computations.
2. What price should be paid assuming a $2,000 residual value?

Exercise 6–17

On January 1, 1979, Richards Corporation purchased a machine at a cost of $60,000. They paid $26,791 cash and incurred a debt for the difference. This debt is to be paid off in equal annual installments

of $6,000 payable each December 31. The interest rate on the unpaid balance each period is 9% per annum. How many equal payments must be made at each year-end? Show your computations.

Exercise 6–18

Complete the following table assuming $n = 7$; $i = 9\%$:

	Concept	Symbol	Formula	"Value" Based on $1	Source
1.	Future value of 1.	___	___	___	___
2.	Present value of 1.	___	___	___	___
3.	Future value of ordinary annuity of 1.	___	___	___	___
4.	Present value of ordinary annuity of 1.	___	___	___	___
5.	Future value of annuity due of 1.	___	___	___	___
6.	Present value of annuity due of 1.	___	___	___	___

Exercise 6–19

On January 1, 1979, Wallis Company decided to create an expansion fund by making equal annual deposits of $66,000. The fund is required on December 31, 1983. Interest at 6% compounded annually will be added to the fund. Five deposits are planned. Two alternative dates are under consideration, viz:

Alternative A—Make the annual deposits on each December 31 starting in 1979.

Alternative B—Make the annual deposits on each January 1 starting in 1979.

Required:
Complete the following table:

Alternative	Type of Annuity	Balance in the Fund at End of 1983	
		Computations	Amount
A			
B			

Exercise 6–20

High Company agreed on January 1, 1979, to deposit $120,000 cash with a trustee. The trustee will increase the fund on a 5% compound interest basis on the fund balance each successive year. The trustee is required to pay out the fund in ten equal annual installments to a former employee of High so that the fund is completely exhausted at the end of that time. Two alternative payment dates are under consideration, viz:

Alternative A—Make the annual payments to the former employee each December 31 starting in 1979.

Alternative B—Make the annual payments to the former employee each January 1 starting in 1979.

Required:

Complete the following table:

		Amount of the Equal Annual Payments	
Alternative	Type of Annuity	Computations	Amount
A			
B			

PROBLEMS (round solutions to nearest dollar)

PART A
Problems 6–1 to 6–7

Problem 6–1

Duncan Company plans to deposit $30,000 in a special fund on January 1, 1979, for future use as needed. The fund will accumulate 8% interest per year.

Required:

1. Complete the following table by entering, into each cell, the balance in the fund:

	Number of Years	
Compounding Assumption	2	4
Annual		
Semiannual		
Quarterly		

2. Prepare an accumulation table based on the first cell (annual only).

3. Give journal entries for the fund based on the first cell (annual only).

Problem 6–2

1. On January 1, 19A, an investor deposited $7,000 into a savings account that would accumulate at 7% annual compound interest for three years. Compute the balance that would be in the savings account at the end of the third year. Prepare an accumulation table for this situation.
2. On January 1, 19A, another investor deposited $7,000 into a savings account that would accumulate to $8,337 at the end of three years assuming annual compound interest. Compute the interest rate that would be necessary. Show computations. Prepare an accumulation table for this situation.
3. On January 1, 19A, another investor deposited $7,000 into a savings account that would accumulate to $9,381 assuming 5% annual compound interest. Compute the number of periods that would be necessary. Show computations. Prepare an accumulation table for this situation.

Problem 6–3

1. An investor planned to deposit $40,000 into a savings account that would accumulate to $42,400 at the end of Year 1. Assume the deposit was made at the beginning of Year 1. What would be the balance in the fund at the end of the fifth year? The tenth year? The 20th year? Show computations.
2. Another investor planned to deposit $50,000 into a savings account that would accumulate to $89,542 at the end of the tenth year. What rate of annual compound interest would have to be earned on the fund to meet these specifications? Show computations.
3. Another investor planned to deposit $10,000 at annual compound interest. The investor desires to accumulate $20,000 over a ten-year period. What rate of interest would be required to meet these specifications? Show computations. Interpolation is required.

Problem 6–4

Daly Corporation decided to place $100,000 into a special expansion fund for use in the future as needed. The fund will accumulate at 6% annual compound interest. The fund will be established on March 1, 1979, and the interest will be added to the fund balance on an annual compound interest basis.

Required:

1. Compute the balance that will be in the fund at the end of three years, five years, and ten years, respectively.
2. Prepare an accumulation table for three years.
3. Give the journal entries for Daly Corporation for the first three years. Disregard adjusting and closing entries.
4. What adjusting entry would be made on December 31, 1979, assuming this is the end of the accounting period for Daly Corporation?

Problem 6–5

XY Company anticipates that it will need $200,000 cash for an expansion in the next few years. Assume an annual interest rate of 8%. The company desires to make a single contribution now, January 1, 1979, so that the $200,000 will be available when needed.

Required:

1. Complete the following table by entering into each cell the amount that must be deposited now to meet the above specifications:

	Number of Years	
Compounding Assumption	2	3
Annual		
Semiannual		

2. Prepare an accumulation table based on the first cell.
3. Give journal entries for the fund based on the first cell.

Problem 6–6

Sord Construction Company has just won a bid on a major contract. The contract will require the purchase of new equipment costing approximately $200,000. The vendor, X Company, requires $50,000 cash down payment and will accept a two-year, $150,000, noninterest-bearing note (assume an interest rate on this type of note to be 9% per annum). The $150,000 includes all interest charges.

Required:

1. Compute the cost of the equipment on January 1, 1979. Show computations.
2. Give the entry by Sord on date of purchase to record the equipment and the related financing.
3. Prepare a debt amortization schedule for the note

that reflects the annual interest expense and the principal.
4. Give journal entries by Sord each year while the note is outstanding and for final payment of the note.
5. Assume that Sord is short of cash on the date of the purchase. To raise cash for the down payment, Sord is considering the sale (discounting) of a $70,000 receivable owed to them by John Doe that is due on December 31, 1981 (i.e., three years hence). The receivable is evidenced by a noninterest-bearing note. Sord has located an individual that will buy this future claim at a 12% compound annual discount. Compute the amount that Sord would receive on January 1, 1979, the date of the sale of the future claim against John Doe. Show computations.

Problem 6–7

Goode Company is trying to "clean up" some of its debts. On January 1, 1979, the company has savings accounts as follows:

Date Established	Amount Deposited (a single deposit for each)	Annual Compound Interest Rate
1/1/68	$20,000	4%
1/1/74	90,000	5

The outstanding debts to be paid off are as follows:

Due Date	Type of Note	Face of Note
12/31/81	Noninterest bearing	$ 60,000
12/31/88	Noninterest bearing	200,000

Required:

1. Compute the amount of cash that can be obtained from the two savings accounts on January 1, 1979.
2. Compute the amount for which the two debts can be settled on January 1, 1979, assuming a going rate of interest of 9%.
3. How much cash, in addition to the cash available from the savings accounts, will be needed to settle the two debts on January 1, 1979?

PART B
Problems 6–8 to 6–17

Problem 6–8

Abell Corporation is contemplating the accumulation of a special fund to be used for expanding sales activities into the western part of the country. It is January 1, 1979, and the fund will be needed at the beginning of 1982, according to present plans. The fund will earn 6% interest compounded annually. The company is considering two plans for accumulating the fund by December 31, 1981, viz:

Plan A—Make three annual deposits of $50,000 each, starting on December 31, 1979.

Plan B—Make three annual deposits of $50,000 each, starting on January 1, 1979.

Required:

1. What kind of annuity is involved for each plan? Compute the balance that will be in the special fund on December 31, 1981, under each plan. Show computations.
2. Prepare an accumulation table for each plan.
3. Tabulate the entries for each plan. Set up a tabulation with the following captions:

	Fund,	Cash,	Interest Revenue,
Date	Debit	Credit	Credit

4. Explain why the fund has a different balance under each plan.

Problem 6–9

Evans Corporation desires to build a special debt retirement fund amounting to $50,000. A trustee has agreed to handle the fund and to increase it on a 5% annual compound interest basis. Evans will make equal annual contributions of $11,600 at the end of each year, starting on December 31, 1979. Assume an ordinary annuity situation.

Required:

1. Determine the number of contributions that Evans must make to meet these specifications. Show computations.
2. Prepare an accumulation table for the fund.
3. Give the journal entries during the period the fund is being accumulated.

Problem 6–10

Virginia Company agreed with its president, J. Smith, to set up a fund with a trustee that will pay Smith $50,000 per year for the three years following retirement. Smith will retire on January 1, 1979, and the equal annual payments are to be made by the trustee each December 31 starting in 1979. The trustee will add to the fund 6% annual compound interest on the fund balance each year-end. The fund is to have a zero balance on December 31, 1981, the date of the last payment.

Required:

1. Compute the single sum that must be deposited

with the trustee on January 1, 1979, to meet these specifications.
2. Prepare a decumulation table through December 31, 1981. Set up table captions as follows: Date, Cash Payments, Interest Revenue Earned, Fund Decreases, and Fund Balance.

Problem 6–11

Fast Construction Company can purchase a used crane which will be needed on a new job that will continue for approximately three years. It is January 1, 1979, and the crane is needed immediately. Because of a shortage of cash, Fast has asked the vendor for credit terms with no down payment. The vendor charges 12% annual compound interest. The crane can be purchased under these terms by making three payments of $8,000 each on December 31, 1979, 1980, and 1981.

Required:

1. What should be the cash price of the crane on January 1, 1979?
2. Give the entry to record the purchase of the crane on the credit terms.
3. Prepare a debt amortization schedule using the following format:

	Cash	Interest	Reduction	Liability
Date	Payment	Expense	of Principal	Balance

Problem 6–12

Perky Student is considering the purchase of a Super Sail Boat which has a cash price of $6,500. Terms can be arranged for a $2,000 cash down payment and payment of the remaining $4,500, plus interest at 11% per annum, in three equal annual payments. Assume purchase on January 1, 1979, and payments on each December 31 thereafter.

Required:

1. Compute the amount of each annual payment assuming annual compound interest.
2. What did the boat cost? What was the interest amount?
3. Prepare a debt amortization schedule using the following format:

	Cash	Interest	Reduction	Liability
Date	Payment	Expense	of Principal	Balance

Problem 6–13

Jones has an industrious daughter, Lois, who is 15 years old today. For her birthday Jones invests $20,000 toward her college education. Jones stipulates that Lois may withdraw four equal annual amounts from the fund, the first withdrawal to be made on her 18th birthday. The savings and loan association in which Jones placed the investment will add to the fund annual compound interest at the rate of 7% at the end of each year.

Requird:

Compute the amount of each of the four withdrawals by Lois which will completely deplete the fund on the date of the final withdrawal. *Hint:* Diagram the problem situation.

Problem 6–14

WT Company rents a warehouse for an annual rental of $2,000. They have some idle cash and have approached the owner with a proposal to pay three years' rent in advance. The owner has agreed to a compound discount rate of 10%.

Required:

1. Assume it is January 1, 1979, and that the three rents are due on January 1, 1979, 1980, and 1981. Compute the amount that WT Company would have to pay as a single sum on January 1, 1979. What kind of annuity is this? Explain.
2. Assume it is January 1, 1979, and that the three rents are due on December 31, 1979, 1980, and 1981. Compute the amount that WT Company would have to pay as a single sum on January 1, 1979. What kind of annuity is this? Explain.
3. Explain why the single sums to be paid as computed under Requirements 1 and 2 are different.

Problem 6–15

On January 1, 1979, Vee Company signed a three-year contract to rent some space that they needed immediately. The lease provided that Vee could pay annual rentals of $17,000 on each January 1, beginning in 1979, or, alternatively, they can pay rent in advance at a 7% annual compound discount.

Required:

1. What single sum would have to be paid by Vee on January 1, 1979, for the 1979, 1980, and 1981 annual rentals?
2. Assume it is January 1, 1979, and the three rents are due on December 31, 1979, 1980, and 1981. Compute the single sum Vee would have to pay on January 1, 1979.
3. Analyze the difference in the results between Requirements 1 and 2.

Problem 6–16

On January 1, 1979, Sun Company owes an $80,000 debt which is now due. Since the company is short of cash, they have reached an agreement with the creditor whereby the debt and interest are to be paid in equal annual installments on January 1, 1979, 1980, and 1981. Interest is 9% annual compounding.

Required:

1. What kind of annuity is this? Explain.
2. Compute the amount of the equal annual payments.
3. Prepare a debt amortization schedule, using the following format:

Date	Cash Payment	Interest Expense	Reduction of Principal	Liability Balance
1/1/79				$80,000

Problem 6–17

Don Corporation is negotiating to purchase a plant from another company that will complement Don's operations. They have just completed a careful study of the plant and have developed the following estimates:

Expected net cash revenues:	
Years 1–5 (per year)	$50,000
Years 6–10 (per year)	40,000
Year 11	30,000
Year 12	10,000
Expected net residual value at end of Year 12	3,000

Required:

1. Compute the amount that Don should be willing to pay for the plant assuming an 11% return on the investment. Assume all amounts are at year-end and are given net of income taxes.
2. Assume the down payment is $150,000. Don can pay this, and the bank will lend Don the balance at 9% per annum payable in equal annual payments (including interest and principal) over five years. The payments will be at each year-end, starting one year after the date of purchase. Compute the amount of the equal annual payments on the loan. Compute the total interest that will be paid.
3. Give the entries (or entry) to record the purchase in Requirement 1 and the loan in Requirement 2 using the amounts you computed.
4. Give entries at the end of Year 1 to record (a) net revenue, (b) interest expense, and (c) the loan payment.

7

Accounting and Reporting When Prices Change*

Each of us is aware that prices of most things we buy have been rising sharply. While this fact may have unpleasant personal consequences, the purpose of this chapter is to analyze the accounting consequences and to describe various proposals designed to cope with them.

When the unit of measure assumption was discussed in Chapter 2, it was noted that the conventional accounting model, based on historical cost, either assumed a stable monetary unit or assumed that changes in the value of money were not material. During some periods in the history of the U.S. economy such assumptions were valid. In recent years, however, for the vast majority of businesses and other entities, changing prices have become quite important in accounting and financial reporting, as will be shown in the section "Impact of Inflation on Financial Statements."

PRICE CHANGES AND HOW THEY ARE MEASURED

Since the early years of the Great Depression of the 1930s, prices of virtually all goods and services in the United States (and in most of the world) have been rising almost without interruption. Stated another way, the general purchasing power of the dollar (and other monetary units) has been falling almost continuously.

General purchasing power is the power of the monetary unit to purchase real goods and services. When there is an increase in general prices (i.e., the general purchasing power of the monetary unit decreases), the condition is referred to as *inflation*. When there is a general decline in prices (i.e., when the general purchasing power of the monetary unit rises), that condition is called *deflation*. Because inflation has been so pervasive, our discussions, illustrations, and assignment material will be primarily in the context of rising prices; however, the concepts discussed apply to deflation as well.

Because the dollar is used as the unit of measure or common denominator to express many diverse kinds of assets and liabilities, and because each business entity is likely to own many kinds of assets and have diverse types of liabilities, and also because statement users are interested in making interfirm and interperiod comparisons, it is logical and, perhaps, necessary

---

* This chapter, which discusses possible accounting responses to changing prices, appears early in the text because moderate or severe inflation can vitiate some of the information content of conventionally prepared financial statements. Students can gain a better appreciation of both the strengths and weaknesses of conventional historical cost accounting by early coverage of this material. Some professors may prefer to cover this material later or even to omit it. The chapter can be included in a course at almost any point without difficulty.

that measures be devised to express the degree of change in the prices of assets and the purchasing power represented by various claims. Measurement of these effects often requires the use of price index numbers.

A price index has been defined as "a series of measurements, expressed as percentages, of the relationship between the average price of a group of goods and services at a succession of dates and the average price of a similar group of goods and services at a common date. The components of the series are price index numbers. A price index does not, however, measure the movement of the individual component prices, some of which move in one direction, and some in the opposite direction."[1] There are several index numbers which purport to measure general changes in prices in the United States. The three most widely known measures of general price changes in the United States are the Gross National Product Implicit Price Deflator (GNP Deflator), the Consumer Price Index, and the Wholesale Price Index. The GNP Deflator was preferred as a measure of price changes for producing general price level (GPL) statements in a series of authoritative but nonbinding pronouncements issued earlier by the APB and FASB.[2] However, in an exposure draft of its latest pronouncement relating to GPL statements, the FASB has expressed a preference for the Consumer Price Index (for All Urban Consumers). Highlights of this proposal are presented on page 220. The two general price level indices move roughly in parallel as shown at the bottom of this page. Thus, when there is a sharp rise or persistent upward movement of prices, all will show increases, but not exactly the same relative change because they use different weights and are based upon different market baskets of goods.

Bear in mind that a general price index is an average or composite of many prices; thus, it measures the trend of its particular group of prices over time. Not all prices affecting the index change at the same rate; during inflation some will rise faster than others, and while the overall index is rising, some prices included in the set may be falling. For example, consider price declines in calculators and other electronic devices in recent years even though prices in general have risen.

The GNP Deflator was preferred as the basis for preparing GPL statements in three earlier studies published by authoritative segments of the accounting profession. In the latest document on this topic the FASB has expressed a preference for use of the Consumer Price Index for All Urban Consumers (see footnote 5). Because of the emphasis on these two measures, it is pertinent to indicate the extent to which prices have changed according to them. The government (and others who prepare index numbers) change the *base year* of their indicators from time to time. Moving the base year forward periodically serves to make current quotations more modern and relevant to the experience of current users of the index number;

[1] AICPA, *Accounting Research Study No. 6,* "Reporting the Financial Effects of Price-Level Changes" (New York, 1963), p. 63.

[2] *FASB, Exposure Draft,* "Financial Reporting and Changing Prices" (Stamford, Conn., December 1974).

Year	GNP Annual Average*	CPI	Year	GNP Annual Average	GNP Rate of Inflation	CPI	CPI Rate of Inflation
1930	33.1		1970	91.4		116.3	
1935	28.6		1971	96.0	5.0	121.3	4.3
1940	29.5		1972	100.0	4.2	125.3	3.3
1945	40.1		1973	106.0	6.0	133.1	6.2
1950	53.6	72.1	1974	116.4	9.8	147.7	11.0
1955	61.0	80.2	1975	127.3	9.4	161.2	9.1
1960	68.7	88.7	1976	133.8	5.1	170.5	5.8
1965	74.3	94.5	1977	141.6	5.8	181.5	6.5
1967		100.0	1978†	153.6	8.5	197.7‡	8.9

* The index values given above for 1930–1971 are expressed in terms of the 1972 base year (as 100.0) and are based on the rates of change reflected in the GNP Implicit Price Deflator values given when the base year was 1958.
† Third quarter.
‡ July 1978.

however, it serves to camouflage the extent to which inflation has occurred. For many years, 1958 was the base year of the GNP Deflator; it was assigned a value of 100 and earlier and later prices were expressed relative to 1958 prices. Recently the GNP index was changed so that 1972 became the base year. The Consumer Price Index (CPI), which is currently based on 1967, has similarly experienced a series of revisions.

In the tabulation at the bottom of page 216 observe that the GNP uses 1972 as a base and the CPI uses 1967.

IMPACT OF INFLATION ON FINANCIAL STATEMENTS

The impact of inflation on financial reports, prepared in accordance with the conventional historical cost accounting model, varies considerably from one entity and one period to the next, depending upon a number of factors. The financial statements of businesses which are *capital intensive* (i.e., they commit a relatively large proportion of their resources to investment in operational assets) are likely to be affected by inflation more than those whose capital is largely committed to short-term assets. At the same time, businesses which borrow heavily on a long-term basis (and this is likely to include the capital intensive ones) are in a better position to gain from inflation (as a result of holding payables) than those which do not. Also, some businesses can serve their customers with little or no investment in inventory, while others must make large investments in inventory which may have a low turnover. The latter types of businesses are affected by inflation more than the former.

During a period of inflation, the conventional historical cost accounting model reflects a matching of dollars of different "size" or purchasing power on the income statement. Revenues are usually expressed in current dollars, but some of the expenses matched against them may not be current because they are from very old transactions. For example, depreciation and similar cost expirations may reflect cost levels which prevailed years earlier when the dollar had a vastly different purchasing power. Depending on the inventory flow method in use,

cost of goods sold may represent an amount in current dollars or it may not. If there is a relatively high correspondence between the volume of purchases and the volume of sales, and if selling prices are based on current costs, use of *Lifo* will tend to give a reasonable matching of current costs against current revenues.[3] The conventional historical cost model ignores the fact that an entity which maintains large balances of cash and receivables during periods of inflation loses purchasing power as a result, while one that is heavily in debt gains because it has borrowed dollars with greater *buying* power than the ones it will use to repay the debt. Conventional historical cost accounting defers all gains (or losses) from holding an asset until it is sold; no recognition is given to the price level effect on that gain (or loss).

When there has been marked inflation and comparative statements for two or more successive periods are prepared on a conventional basis, they can be quite misleading. Suppose, for example, the sales amount on the current income statement is 15% higher than it was on the income statement of four years ago. If prices of the company's product and general prices have risen 50% in the interval, there has been a material decline in *physical volume* of goods sold. On a common dollar (i.e., price level restated) basis the change in volume would have been evident. Historical cost financial statements also obscure the comparability of financial statements of two or more entities whose accounts consist of items that were bought in different years.

DEPRECIATION AND RISING REPLACEMENT COSTS

The purpose of depreciation accounting, as traditionally viewed, is to allocate the acquisition cost of depreciable property over its economic useful life. Other things being equal, reflecting depreciation results in "sheltering" an amount of assets equal to the recorded depreciation (on the depreciable assets), thereby facili-

---

[3] At the same time, use of *Lifo* during a period of sustained inflation will ultimately result in an unrealistically low balance sheet valuation of inventories. Also, it does not "correct" for the low (old) depreciation costs included (by allocation) in manufactured inventories.

tating their replacement if the replacement cost is the same as the original cost. Since depreciation is an expense, it is included in pricing decisions of products and services sold by the entity. Therefore, the management of an entity must be concerned with the adequacy of depreciation charges in *(a)* asset replacement and *(b)* current pricing policy. Because the historical cost basis permits depreciation expense to be based only on historical cost, extensive attention is being accorded some form of price level accounting or market value accounting (both discussed later in this chapter), because under conditions of inflation they would afford means of recording depreciation expense that *(a)* in total may approximate replacement costs and *(b)* is appropriate to realistic financing policy.

Illustrated simply, suppose Jones bought a new automobile in 1975 and put it into service as a taxi in a small town. Jones and a hired driver comprise the entire staff of the enterprise. All expenses except depreciation of the cab are incurred on a cash basis; as a consequence, except for depreciation, the excess of receipts over payments can be regarded by Jones as pretax income. Because the cab cost $4,100 and is expected to sell for $600 after five years of use, Jones decided to set aside $700 each year to replace the cab. The $700 depreciation expense is deducted on the tax return. Each year Jones spends the cash receipts from the business, less the $700 cash set aside, for living expenses and income taxes. By 1979 the cheapest comparably equipped car had risen in cost to $6,800, and it likely would cost $7,400 if Jones replaced the cab on schedule in 1980. Where will Jones get the extra $3,300 (i.e., $7,400 − $600 − $3,500) that will be needed? The $3,500 set aside plus the $600 trade-in allowance will not buy even the smallest comparably equipped compact car by 1980; besides such a vehicle would be unsuitable for use in the enterprise. It appears logical to conclude that Jones has overstated the income from the enterprise by $3,300. Moreover, Jones paid income taxes on what amounts to both income and a return of capital. Finally, Jones has not priced the taxi services on the basis of economic reality if the additional cost of replacing the taxi was disregarded.

One may ask whether this example is relevant to a large corporation. The answer is yes. Profitable corporations often pay taxes at rates exceeding 40% on most of their income and, in addition, their shareholders pay another income tax on cash dividends when received. Therefore, to the extent that what is taxed as income is really a return of capital, the problem exists. Corporations have essentially the same asset replacement and pricing problems as Jones. In an era of sustained inflation, a hotel chain, a factory, or a local business which does not include in its pricing of products and services an amount sufficient to cover the future replacement cost of facilities now in use will be unable to maintain its present scope of operations when the existing facilities must be replaced unless it is willing and able *(a)* to incur added debt or *(b)* obtain additional equity capital and perhaps to dilute the equity of existing owners. The adoption of either price level or market value accounting will not solve the capital replacement and pricing problems of an entity, but it will add more economic realism to financial reports on which these decisions, in part, are made.

PIECEMEAL ACCOUNTING APPROACHES UNDER CONDITIONS OF INFLATION

One piecemeal accounting approach to cope with inflation effects focuses on *inventories.* The *Lifo* inventory method has been cited as a means of achieving a closer matching of current expenses against current revenues when prices are changing. This is true only to the extent that there is correspondence between the physical volume of goods purchased and sold during the period. Also, if prices double after *Lifo* is adopted (as they did between 1959 and 1976) and physical volume remains constant, the inventory value reported on the balance sheet would be about half the inventory cost. Thus, this piecemeal solution is totally inadequate because *(a)* it does not attain better reporting on the financial statements (particularly the balance sheet), and *(b)* it deals with only one problem on the income statement—cost of goods sold.

Another accounting approach focuses on *depreciation* and similar cost allocations. The use of accelerated depreciation in the accounts and reports has been cited as a means of solving the problem of *understatement* of depreciation during inflation. Accelerated depreciation is effective only when property, plant, and equipment items subject to depreciation are relatively new because the compensating effect generally occurs during the first half of the useful lives of the assets. Over the total useful life of an asset, the aggregate amount of the depreciation cannot exceed what it would be under straight-line or any other allowed alternative. This piecemeal solution is singularly deficient because it *(a)* deals only with the short run, *(b)* focuses only on one aspect of the problem—depreciable assets, and *(c)* tends to cause arbitrarily determined effects.

Still another piecemeal accounting approach which produces a balance sheet impact, but does not affect reported income, is the technique of appropriating retained earnings for the excess of replacement cost over the book value of the assets to notify statement users that management is cognizant of inflationary effects on asset replacement and that dividends must be restricted. This implies that there are no adequate means of coping with the price level problem within the purview of the historical cost model. This piecemeal approach is deficient in that it ignores the income statement and simply discloses the excess replacement cost.

Another piecemeal approach, not accorded general acceptability, is the proposal that an additional expense be reported in the income statement to compensate for the understatement of depreciation, cost of goods sold, and other expenses likely to be too low because of inflation during the period. The proposal has a number of difficulties. First, no guidelines exist for the determination of such "excess" expenses; second, it does not appropriately reflect the balance sheet impact; and, third, it does not deal with the broader problem of inflationary impacts.

These piecemeal approaches are subject to numerous objections. They ignore replacement cost. In some situations they may attain a reasonable short-run result for a specific item (from a standpoint of counteracting the effects of inflation) on one financial statement, but they either ignore or worsen the reporting on another statement. They make it difficult to compute the traditional rates of return for the entity (partly because of the lack of consistency between the balance sheet and income statement). They may lull many users of the financial statements into a false sense of security that the inflation problem is adequately accounted for and reported by the entity or that it is not a serious problem. Finally, they do not deal in a systematic and comprehensive manner with inflationary effects. Therefore, they run the risk of causing inconsistent measurements of assets, liabilities, and income. The two major models that deal with the price level problem *comprehensively* are discussed and illustrated in—

Part A—General Purchasing Power (price level) Restatement of Historical Cost Amounts (on the financial statements)

Part B—Current Value Accounting Models

PART A—GENERAL PURCHASING POWER RESTATEMENT OF HISTORICAL COST AMOUNTS

Fundamentally, the *general* purchasing power or *general* price level approach uses a selected index, such as the Consumer Price Index, to *restate on a current basis* those elements of the financial statements which are out of date in terms of the recent price levels. This general explanation requires demonstration of its application. Therefore, after a review of the background of the general price level approach, the application steps will be explained. This will be followed by a simple example and then a more complex illustration. For brevity we will refer to General Price Level Restatement as GPL Restatement; Current Replacement Cost as CRC; and Historical Cost as HC.

Background

Dr. Henry W. Sweeney introduced the GPL approach in a series of articles in *The Accounting Review* in the 1920s and 1930s. The concept and its application were presented in his book *Stabilized Accounting* which first appeared in 1936 and was republished as an accounting classic in 1964. Sweeney's thinking was heavily influenced by experience and practice in Germany following World War I when that nation experienced drastic and devastating inflation. Although academicians were aware of the techniques involved in GPL restatement (also called general purchasing power or price level approach), they were largely ignored by the world of accounting practice. The first significant attention by practitioners to the deficiencies of historical cost based accounting during periods when prices change rapidly was in 1947 and 1948 when the AICPA's Committee on Accounting Procedure[4] reaffirmed the profession's basic position that historical cost should continue to be the basis of financial statement preparation. At the same time the Committee said:

> In considering depreciation in connection with product costs, prices, and business policies, management must take into consideration the likelihood that replacement costs of plant assets then in use would greatly exceed their historical costs.
>
> Periodic appropriation of net income or retained earnings in contemplation of replacement of plant at higher costs was a proper managerial action.

The APB studied the problem of accounting during inflationary conditions and published *Accounting Research Study No. 6, "Reporting the Financial Effects of Price-Level Changes,"* in 1963 and *APB Statement No. 3, "Financial Statements Restated for General-Price Level Changes,"* in 1969. Both documents recommended experimentation with GPL restatement of conventional historical cost based statements using the GNP Deflator and the techniques described below. Neither publication had the force and effect of an *APB Opinion.* Consequently, very little voluntary experimentation with GPL statements resulted.

Shortly after the FASB was organized, there was a resurgence of inflation, with the result that in late 1974 the FASB issued an exposure draft of a proposed statement of accounting standards on price level accounting. The proposed FASB statement would have *required* essentially the same action as called for on a voluntary basis in the 1963 and 1969 APB publications.[5] Continuing its study of reporting the effects of inflation the FASB issued a draft of a proposed Standard "Financial Reporting and Changing Prices," (December, 1978) and a supplement "Constant Dollar Accounting" (March, 1979). The two proposed documents would require the following minimum supplementary disclosures of effects of inflation on certain entities:

a. EITHER (1) *Supplementary* information on (a) income from continuing operations on a *current cost* basis (covered in Part B of this chapter) and on (b) holding gains and losses net of inflation.

OR (2) Supplementary information on income from continuing operations based on GPL restatement of the historical cost amounts.

b. The amount of the purchasing power gain or loss on net monetary items. These disclosure requirements would supplement the traditional historical cost financial statements. Also, they would only be required of publicly held corporations with (a) inventories and property, plant, and equipment (gross of depreciation) of $125 million or more and also (b) total assets amounting to $1 billion or more. As we have indicated above, the proposal would require the use of the Consumer Price Index, for measuring general inflation.

The principal alternative to GPL restatement of financial statements is "market value" measurements for specific statement elements. Market value received important official support in March 1976 when the SEC issued *Accounting Series Release No. 190.* This release required (with some exceptions) approximately 1,000 of the largest companies filing reports with the SEC to disclose by notes in their 1977 (and subsequent) SEC reports the estimated current costs of replacing inventories and productive assets. Disclosure of the amounts of cost of goods sold and depreciation computed on a replacement

---

[4] The Committee, as predecessor to the APB and FASB, was responsible for issuing *Accounting Research Bulletins;* many of these bulletins *(ARBs)* are still effective and have the same status as *APB Opinions* and *FASB Statements.*

[5] The proposed statement was later withdrawn and never became effective. Neither the business community nor the SEC showed much enthusiasm for it.

cost basis also was required. This topic is discussed in Part B and the Appendix of this chapter.

APPLICATION OF GENERAL PRICE LEVEL INDEX NUMBERS TO RESTATE FINANCIAL STATEMENTS

The GPL procedures described and illustrated in the next several pages are those that were prescribed in the 1974 *proposed* FASB Statement discussed above. We have chosen to follow the 1974 GPL framework instead of the 1978 exposure draft because the former embodies a comprehensive approach to the preparation of a complete set of GPL financial statements. By contrast, the 1978 document merely requires the disclosure of selected items. These selected items can be extracted from the complete set of GPL financial statements discussed and illustrated in this chapter. Implementation of GPL restatement of financial statements involves the following steps:

1. Obtain the complete set of financial statements prepared under current GAAP.
2. Select the appropriate index to use and obtain the index numbers for each period covering the life of the *oldest* item on the financial statements. The FASB recommended use of the Consumer Price Index for All Urban Consumers.
3. Each statement item is classified as either monetary or nonmonetary. *Monetary items* are defined as cash and claims to cash that are fixed in terms of numbers of dollars regardless of change in prices. Thus, cash, receivables, and most liabilities are monetary items. All other items are classified as *nonmonetary* items. Thus, such items as inventories, operational assets, and common stock equity are nonmonetary items. Exhibit 7–1 presents more details on the classification of items as monetary or nonmonetary.
4. Restate each *nonmonetary* item in terms of its current general purchasing power for financial statement purposes. This involves multiplication of the amount to be restated by a *conversion fraction,* the denominator of which is the index number that prevailed when the amount was first entered into the

EXHIBIT 7–1

Classification of Items as Monetary or Nonmonetary

	Monetary	Nonmonetary
Cash on hand and in banks [a]	x	
Marketable securities:		
Stocks (nonmonetary because prices can change)		x
Bonds (expected to be held to maturity)	x	
Bonds (expected to be sold before maturity)		x
Receivables	x	
Allowance for doubtful accounts	x	
Inventories [b]		x
Prepaid expenses		x
Property, plant, and equipment		x
Accumulated depreciation		x
Cash surrender value of life insurance	x	
Deferred charges (including income taxes)		x
Intangibles		x
Accounts and notes payable, accrued expenses payable	x	
Advances received on sales contracts [c]		x
Bonds payable and other long-term debt	x	
Unamortized premium or discount on debt	x	
Obligations under warranties		x
Preferred stock [d]		x
Common stockholders' equity		x

[a] All claims are assumed to be payable in U.S. dollars unless specifically stated otherwise.

[b] An exception would be inventories produced under fixed price contracts accounted for at the contract price. Such inventories would be monetary.

[c] This obligation will be satisfied by delivery of goods or services that are nonmonetary because their prices can fluctuate.

[d] Preferred stock carried at an amount equal to its fixed liquidation or redemption price is monetary because the claim of the preferred shareholders on assets of the entity is in a fixed number of dollars. In other instances preferred stock would be nonmonetary.

accounts and the numerator is the current year index number (i.e., at the date of the restatement). To illustrate, assume land was acquired for $22,000 when the Consumer Price Index number was 110; and on the date the financial statements are being prepared it is 132. The land would be restated for the price level change as follows: $22,000 × (132 ÷ 110) = $26,400. Alternatively, the arithmetic could be rearranged to first compute a *conversion percent* (i.e., 132 ÷ 110 = 120%) which is then multiplied by the amount to be restated (i.e., $22,000 × 120% = $26,400).[6] Significantly, the monetary items are not restated on the financial statements because the number of dollars they will command (assets) or demand (liabilities) is fixed (i.e., they do not change as a result of changes in the general price level).

5. Compute the *general purchasing power gain or loss* (sometimes called GPL *gain or loss*) on the monetary items. No gain or loss is computed on the nonmonetary items. GPL gains and losses are computed *only* on monetary items because the number of dollars to satisfy them is fixed—they are constant in amount, although these dollars do change in real value. The change in their real value is the general purchasing power gain or loss. To compute the general purchasing power gain or loss, the monetary items are restated in the computation (but not on the GPL financial statements). The difference between the GPL restated amount and the reported historical cost is the GPL gain or loss. In contrast, for *nonmonetary* items, because of their characteristics, a change in prices also changes the number of dollars they command. Thus, no GPL gain or loss is computed on nonmonetary items in the GPL restatement. Nonmonetary items are not included in the computation of GPL gains or losses;

---

[6] The fraction procedure, since it shows directly the two price index numbers used, has the advantage of reminding whoever performs the restatement or those interested in the computational details of the specific values used. The conversion percent procedure saves computational time if the same index factors are used more than once and it directly reflects the percentage price change involved. Since the difference is merely arithmetical, and the results are the same, both are widely used.

however, they are restated on the GPL financial statements, as indicated in Step 4 above. The GPL gain and loss effects of holding *monetary items* may be summarized as follows:

Item	General Price Level Rising		General Price Level Falling	
	Gain	Loss	Gain	Loss
Monetary assets		✓	✓	
Monetary liabilities	✓			✓

SIMPLIFIED ILLUSTRATION OF GENERAL PRICE LEVEL RESTATEMENT

To illustrate all aspects of the accounting process, including GPL restatement, this example will include the following:

1. Beginning trial balance (dated December 31, 19C) for XY Company (given in the first two columns of Exhibit 7–2).
2. Transactions for 19D including GPL index data:
   a. Sold merchandise at an approximately uniform rate throughout the year for cash and on credit, $400,000.
   b. Bought merchandise at an approximately uniform rate throughout the year on credit, cost $290,000 (assume periodic inventory system).
   c. Payments on current liabilities, $340,000.
   d. Declared and paid a $12,000 cash dividend at year-end.
   e. Various expenses paid at an approximately uniform rate throughout the year, $55,000.
   f. Depreciation expense on fixtures, $20,000. The fixtures, acquired on January 1, 19A, when the prevailing GPL index was at 116, have an estimated ten-year life and zero residual value. The future plant site also was acquired on this date.
   g. Income tax expense of $20,000 was accrued uniformly throughout the year.
   h. Ending inventory, $105,000.
   i. Relevant GPL index data:

	GPL Index Numbers	Conversion Factor	
		Fraction	Percent
January 1, 19A	116	159.5/116 =	137.5
December 31, 19C	145	159.5/145 =	110.0
December 31, 19D	159.5	159.5/159.5 =	100.0
Average for 19D	151.9	159.5/151.9 =	105.0

3. Worksheet for 19D to derive traditional cost basis income statement and balance sheet (Exhibit 7–2).
4. Application of conversion factors (i.e., the GPL Index numbers) to compute the general purchasing power gain or loss on monetary items (Exhibit 7–3).

5. Application of conversion factors (i.e., the GPL index numbers) to convert traditional cost basis statements to a GPL restated basis (Exhibit 7–4 and 7–5).

Application of Conversion Factors

The preceding summary of steps to develop restated GPL financial statements indicated that cost basis amounts are restated (by using the appropriate GPL index numbers) for two purposes, viz:

1. To compute the GPL gain or loss on *monetary items*.
2. To develop GPL restated financial statements by restating the *nonmonetary items*.

EXHIBIT 7–2

XY COMPANY
Worksheet to Develop Income Statement and Balance Sheet—Traditional Historical Cost Basis
Year Ended December 31, 19D

Account	Balances December 31, 19C		19D Transactions and Adjustments		Income Statement—19D		Balance Sheet, December 31, 19D	
	Debit	Credit	Debit	Credit	Debit	Credit	Debit	Credit
Cash and receivables	145,000		(a) 400,000	(c) 340,000 (d) 12,000 (e) 55,000			138,000	
Inventory	90,000				90,000	105,000*	105,000	
Future plant site	50,000						50,000	
Fixtures	200,000						200,000	
Accumulated depreciation		60,000		(f) 20,000				80,000
Current payables including taxes		60,000	(c) 340,000	(b) 290,000 (g) 20,000				30,000
Long-term note payable		50,000						50,000
Common stock, par $10		300,000						300,000
Retained earnings		15,000	(d) 12,000		30,000†			33,000
Sales				(a) 400,000		400,000		
Purchases			(b) 290,000		290,000			
Expenses (except depreciation and income taxes)			(e) 55,000		55,000			
Depreciation expense			(f) 20,000		20,000			
Income tax expense			(g) 20,000		20,000			
	485,000	485,000	1,137,000	1,137,000	505,000	505,000	493,000	493,000

* Ending inventory.
† Net income transferred to retained earnings ($15,000 − $12,000 + $30,000 = $33,000).

EXHIBIT 7-3

XY COMPANY
Calculation of General Purchasing Power (price level) Gain or Loss
Year Ended December 31, 19D

Monetary Items	Cost Basis Amount (per books)	Conversion Factor	GPL Restated at December 31, 19D
Net monetary items at December 31, 19C:			
Cash and receivables	$145,000		
Current payables, including income taxes	(60,000)		
Long-term note payable	(50,000)		
Net monetary assets	35,000 (a)	159.5/145 = 110%	$ 38,500 (b)
Add source of net monetary assets during 19D:			
Sales	400,000	159.5/151.9 = 105%	420,000
Total monetary assets	$435,000		458,500 (c)
Deduct uses of monetary assets during 19D:			
Purchases	$290,000	159.5/151.9 = 105%	304,500
Operating expenses (except depreciation since it is not a monetary item)	55,000	159.5/151.9 = 105%	57,750
Income taxes	20,000	159.5/151.9 = 105%	21,000
Dividends paid at year-end	12,000	159.5/159.5 = 100%	12,000
Total uses	$377,000		395,250 (d)
Net monetary assets restated at December 31, 19D ($458,500 − $395,250)			63,250
Net monetary assets at December 31, 19D, not restated:			
Cash and receivables	$138,000		
Current payables including taxes	(30,000)		
Mortgage payable	(50,000)		
Actual net monetary assets	$ 58,000		58,000†
General purchasing power loss in 19D on monetary items			$ 5,250 (e)

* The notations (a) through (e) refer to the explanation starting below.
† This amount can be calculated directly as $435,000 − $377,000 = $58,000, or detailed as reflected here.

Computation of the 19D General Purchasing Power Gain or Loss on Monetary Items

Computation of the general purchasing power gain or loss on *monetary items* (Step 5, page 222) involves a series of substeps. Description of the substeps below is tied to data set forth in Exhibit 7–2 and illustrated in Exhibit 7–3.

a. Determine the excess of the *monetary assets* over the *monetary liabilities* (or vice versa) at the *start* of the period for which statements are being prepared. At the start of the period (January 1, 19D) there was an excess of *net monetary assets* of $35,000 as shown in Exhibit 7–3.

b. Restate the net of monetary assets per (a) to its end-of-the-period purchasing power equivalent. In the illustration, since the GPL index increased from 145 to 159.5, or 10% (i.e., 159.5 ÷ 145 = 110%), during the year the net monetary asset amount is restated as $35,000 × (159.5 ÷ 145) = $38,500 as shown in Exhibit 7–3.

c. Identify those transactions during the period which *increased monetary assets;* restate them to amounts they would have been had they occurred at the end of the period and add the restated amount to the restated amount derived in (b). In the illustration, since sales for the year of $400,000 were at an approximately uniform rate during the year, this amount is restated as $400,000 × (159.5 ÷ 151.9) = $420,000 as shown in Exhibit 7–3.

d. Identify those transactions which *used monetary assets* during the period; restate them to end-of-the-period equivalents. In the example, purchases and two types of expenses plus dividends required cash outlays of $377,000. Because these transactions occurred at different times during the year, they are not restated by the same conversion factor. Since the transactions for purchases, operating expenses, and income taxes were at an approximately uniform rate, the restatement fraction is the same as that used for sales (i.e., 159.5 ÷ 151.9) as reflected in Exhibit 7–3. Dividends were paid at year-end; therefore, no restatement of that amount is needed. The actual total of monetary assets ($435,000) is not directly restated; rather, the restated total is the sum of the individual restatements. The restated total uses of monetary assets ($395,250) is subtracted from the restated total monetary assets ($458,500) to derive the restated net monetary assets of $63,250; this is the amount of monetary assets in excess of monetary liabilities on a restated basis at the end of the period (December 31, 19D).

e. The difference between the ending balance of the net monetary assets *restated* ($63,250) and the *actual* net monetary assets not restated ($58,000) is the GPL gain or loss. If the restated amount is greater, there is a GPL loss, as in Exhibit 7–3 (a $5,250 loss). If the restated amount is less, there is a GPL gain. For example, if the net monetary assets over liabilities had been $10,000 less, or $53,250, and the ending net monetary assets over liabilities had been the same $58,000, a GPL gain of $4,750 would have been indicated.

GPL RESTATEMENT OF THE BALANCE SHEET

When steps in the application of the GPL approach were summarized, it was pointed out that *only nonmonetary items* are restated in terms of their current general purchasing power on the financial statements. As to balance sheet items, this means taking the end-of-the-period index value as a numerator and the index value which prevailed when the nonmonetary item was first recorded in the accounts as a denominator and multiplying this fraction by the historical cost (book carrying amount) of each nonmonetary item. For example, the future plant site was acquired on January 1, 19A, when the index was 116. To determine the purchasing power equivalent of the HC of that asset at the end of 19D, when the index is at 159.5, the restatement would be $50,000 × (159.5 ÷ 116) = $68,750. As to ending inventory, under a *Fifo* flow assumption, the inventory came from purchases made during the period, so the inventory needs an upward adjustment only by the amount corresponding to the time between purchases and the end-of-the-period index value. Since purchases were assumed to have occurred evenly over the period and since the average index number for the period was 151.9 (as compared with the ending index number of 159.5), the ending inventory restatement would be $105,000 × (159.5 ÷ 151.9) = $110,250. Use of the average index number of the period (i.e., 151.9) as the denominator in the conversion ratio implicitly assumes that ending inventory is made up of units that were acquired evenly during the year. If the company has a high inventory turnover, it should use an average index number for the actual period over which ending inventory was acquired, such as the last half, or perhaps the last quarter of the year. If the company had been using *Lifo* for some period of time, the degree of inventory restatement would have been much larger because the lag would be much longer.

Recall that *monetary* items on the GPL financial statements *are not restated* because the amounts of cash, receivables, and payables are fixed; they do not change in dollar amount because of a change in the price level. As to common stock equity, the lump-sum restated amount is shown because separate historical cost figures for capital stock, contributed capital in excess of par, and retained earnings generally would not have much significance. The view is that attempting to preserve such a separation on GPL restated statements would be meaningless from a legal standpoint.

EXHIBIT 7–4

XY COMPANY
Restatement of Balance Sheet—GPL Basis
December 31, 19D

Assets	Cost Basis Amount	Conversion Factor	GPL Restated Amount
Cash and receivables	$138,000	Monetary	$138,000
Inventory	105,000	159.5/151.9 = 105%	110,250
Future plant site	50,000	159.5/116 = 137.5%	68,750
Fixtures	200,000	159.5/116 = 137.5%	275,000
Less: Accumulated depreciation	(80,000)	159.5/116 = 137.5%	(110,000)
Total Assets	$413,000		$482,000
Liabilities			
Current payables, including taxes	$ 30,000	Monetary	$ 30,000
Long-term payable	50,000	Monetary	50,000
Total Liabilities	80,000		80,000
Stockholders' Equity			
Common stock	300,000		
Retained earnings	33,000		
Total Stockholders' Equity	333,000		402,000*
Total Liabilities and Stockholders' Equity	$413,000		$482,000

* This is a balancing figure; Total Assets Restated, $482,000 − Total Liabilities, $80,000 = Stockholders' Equity Restated, $402,000. A way to prove the clerical accuracy of the balancing figure is presented in the "Proof of Restatement" section of this chapter.

EXHIBIT 7–5

XY COMPANY
Restatement of Income Statement—GPL Basis
Year Ended December 31, 19D

	Cost Basis Amount	Conversion Factor	GPL Restated Amount
Sales	$400,000	159.5/151.9 = 105%	$420,000
Inventory, January 1, 19D	90,000	159.5/145 = 110%	99,000
Purchases	290,000	159.5/151.9 = 105%	304,500
Goods available	380,000		403,500
Inventory, December 31, 19D	105,000	159.5/151.9 = 105%	110,250
Cost of goods sold	275,000		293,250
Gross margin	125,000		126,750
Expenses*	55,000	159.5/151.9 = 105%	57,750
Depreciation expense	20,000	159.5/116 = 137.5%	27,500
Total operating expense	75,000		85,250
Income before taxes	50,000		41,500
Income taxes	20,000	159.5/151.9 = 105%	21,000
Net Income	$ 30,000		20,500
General purchasing power loss			5,250
Net Income Restated			$ 15,250

* Excluding depreciation and income taxes. Depreciation is restated from the price level at acquisition date (116) because the $20,000 is in those "old" dollars.

EXHIBIT 7–6

XY COMPANY
Data for Comparative Balance Sheet—GPL Restatement of Prior Year, 19C
For Comparative Statement, 19C and 19D
(stated in terms of 19D price level)

Assets	19C Cost Basis Amount	Conversion Factor	GPL Restated Amount (to 19D price level)
Cash and receivables	$145,000	159.5/145 = 110%	$159,500
Inventory	90,000	159.5/145 = 110%	99,000
Future plant site	50,000	159.5/116 = 137.5%	68,750
Fixtures	200,000	159.5/116 = 137.5%	275,000
Less: Accumulated depreciation	(60,000)	159.5/116 = 137.5%	(82,500)
Total Assets	$425,000		$519,750
Liabilities			
Current payables, including taxes	$ 60,000	159.5/145 = 110%	$ 66,000
Mortgage note payable	50,000	159.5/145 = 110%	55,000
Total Liabilities	110,000		121,000
Stockholders' Equity			
Common stock	300,000		
Retained earnings	15,000		
Total Stockholders' Equity	315,000		398,750*
Total Liabilities and Stockholders' Equity	$425,000		$519,750

* This is a balancing figure:

Total Assets Restated, $519,750—Total Liabilities Restated, $121,000 = Stockholders' Equity Restated, $398,750.

The restated 19D balance sheet for XY Company is shown in Exhibit 7–4.

GPL RESTATEMENT OF THE INCOME STATEMENT

The revenue and expense items which affect monetary items on an essentially current basis (such as sales, purchases, and expenses, but not depreciation and similar long-term nonmonetary items) require restatement only to the extent average prices for the period lag the level of prices at the end of the period. Thus, in the example, 19D sales would be restated upward by 5% (i.e., 159.5 ÷ 151.9 = 105%).

Depreciation expense is restated by relating it to the GPL restatement of the assets involved. To illustrate, in the example for XY Company the fixtures cost $200,000 and were depreciated on a cost basis of 10% or $20,000 for 19D. The $200,000 asset cost is restated to $275,000 by ap-

plication of the conversion factor (i.e., 159.5/116). Thus, restated depreciation expense is $20,000 × (159.5/116) = $27,500.

Cost of goods sold is derived as beginning inventory plus purchases minus ending inventory. Restatement of this amount requires restatement of each of these three component amounts. To illustrate, for XY Company the beginning inventory was assumed to have been acquired at the end of 19C when the price level was 145; hence, it is restated as $90,000 × (159.5/145) = $99,000. Both purchases and ending inventory are subject to a 105 conversion factor (i.e., 159.5/151.9), as explained above.

The restated 19D income statement for XY Company is shown in Exhibit 7–5.

PREPARATION OF COMPARATIVE GPL STATEMENTS

The preceding discussion and illustrations focused on the development of GPL restatement

EXHIBIT 7–7

AB COMPANY
Worksheet to Develop Income Statement and Balance Sheet—Historical Cost Basis
For year Ended December 31, 19F

Account	Dec. 31, 19E Balances		19F Transactions and Adjustments		19F Income Statement		Dec. 31, 19F Balance Sheet	
Cash	36,000		(f) 115,000	(e) 12,000 (g) 80,000 (h) 10,000 (i) 20,000			29,000	
Receivables	24,000		(a) 120,000	(f) 115,000			29,000	
Inventory	20,000				20,000	25,000*	25,000	
Building	100,000						100,000	
Accumulated depreciation, building		20,000		(c) 4,000				24,000
Fixtures	40,000		(i) 20,000				60,000	
Accumulated depreciation, fixtures		20,000		(d) 4,000				24,000
Accounts payable		35,000	(g) 80,000	(b) 85,000				40,000
Income taxes payable				(j) 10,000				10,000
Capital stock		100,000						100,000
Retained earnings		45,000	(h) 10,000		10,000†			45,000
Sales				(a) 120,000		120,000		
Purchases			(b) 85,000		85,000			
Depreciation expense, building			(c) 4,000		4,000			
Depreciation expense, fixtures			(d) 4,000		4,000			
General expenses			(e) 12,000		12,000			
Income tax expense			(j) 10,000		10,000			
	220,000	220,000	460,000	460,000	145,000	145,000	243,000	243,000

* Ending inventory, $25,000.

† Net income transferred to retained earnings.

Transactions during 19F (summarized):
- (a) Sales of $30,000 were made each quarter (assume all on credit).
- (b) Purchases of $20,000 were made each of the first three quarters and $25,000 the last quarter (assume all on credit).
- (c) The building is depreciated 4% per year with no residual value; when bought in 19A, the price index was 127. The conversion factor is 159/127, or 125.2%.
- (d) Fixtures are depreciated 10% per year with no residual value; when the original fixtures were bought in 19B, the price index was 138. The conversion factor is 159/138 or 115.2%.
- (e) General expenses of $3,000 were paid each quarter.
- (f) Collections on receivables, $115,000.
- (g) Payments on accounts payable, $80,000.
- (h) At midyear, a $10,000 cash dividend was paid (index value at the time, 153).
- (i) New fixtures costing $20,000 were bought at year-end.
- (j) Income taxes in the amount of $2,500 were accrued each quarter.

for the current year (i.e., 19D for XY Company). An additional problem is posed when *comparative* GPL statements are needed, which is the usual situation. The problem arises because GPL statements, as reported for the *prior* year, are no longer appropriate on a current dollar basis; they must be restated again, but on the current year GPL basis. The restatement procedures are similar to those discussed above.

To illustrate, assume comparative statements are required at the end of 19D for XY Company. The balance sheet reported at the end of the prior year, December 31, 19C, on a GPL basis, was as follows:

XY COMPANY
Restated Balance Sheet—GPL Basis
At December 31, 19C

Assets

Cash and receivables	$145,000
Inventory	90,000
Future plant site	62,500
Fixtures	250,000
Accumulated depreciation	(75,000)
	$472,500

Liabilities and Stockholders' Equity

Current payables	$ 60,000
Long-term note payable	50,000
Stockholders' equity	362,500
	$472,500

EXHIBIT 7–8

AB COMPANY					
Restatement Schedule of Quarterly Revenues and Expenses					
For Year Ended December 31, 19F					

	First Quarter	Second Quarter	Third Quarter	Fourth Quarter	Year Total
Conversion—fraction	159/150	159/153	159/155.9	159/159	
—percent	106	103.9	102	100	
Sales	$30,000	$30,000	$30,000	$30,000	$120,000
GPL restated sales	31,800	31,170	30,600	30,000	123,570
Purchases	20,000	20,000	20,000	25,000	85,000
GPL restated purchases	21,200	20,780	20,400	25,000	87,380
General expenses	3,000	3,000	3,000	3,000	12,000
GPL restated general expenses	3,180	3,117	3,060	3,000	12,357
Income tax	2,500	2,500	2,500	2,500	10,000
GPL restated income tax	2,650	2,598	2,550	2,500	10,298

EXHIBIT 7–9

AB COMPANY			
Calculation of GPL Gain or Loss			
For Year Ended December 31, 19F			

	Cost Basis Amount (per books)	Conversion Factor	GPL Restated at Dec. 31, 19F
Net monetary assets at December 31, 19E:			
Cash	$ 36,000		
Receivables	24,000		
Accounts payable	(35,000)		
Net	25,000	159/147 = 108.2%	$ 27,050
Add: Sources of net monetary assets during 19F:			
Sales	120,000	*	123,570
Subtotal	145,000		150,620
Deduct: Uses of net monetary assets during 19F:			
Purchases	85,000	*	87,380
General expenses (except depreciation)	12,000	*	12,357
Income tax expense	10,000	*	10,298
Dividends paid at midyear	10,000	159/153 = 103.9%	10,390
Fixtures purchased	20,000	159/159 = 100%	20,000
Total uses	137,000		140,425
Net monetary assets at December 31, 19F, restated ($150,620 − $140,425)			10,195
Net monetary assets at December 31, 19F, not restated:			
Cash	29,000		
Receivables	29,000		
Accounts payable	(40,000)		
Income taxes payable	(10,000)		
Total	$ 8,000		8,000
Purchasing power loss in 19F on monetary items			$ 2,195

* See Exhibit 7–8.

EXHIBIT 7–10

AB COMPANY
Restatement of Balance Sheet—GPL Basis
At December 31, 19F

	Cost Basis Amount	Conversion Factor	GPL Restated Amount
Cash	$ 29,000		$ 29,000
Receivables	29,000		29,000
Inventory	25,000	(a)	25,000
Building (b)	100,000	159/127 = 125.2%	125,200
Accumulated depreciation, building	(24,000)	159/127 = 125.2%	(30,048)
Fixtures	60,000	(c)	66,080
Accumulated depreciation, fixtures	(24,000)	159/138 = 115.2%	(27,648)
	$195,000		$216,584
Accounts payable	40,000		40,000
Income taxes payable	10,000		10,000
Capital stock	100,000		
Retained earnings	45,000		
Total stockholders' equity			166,584
	$195,000		$216,584

(a) Since the ending inventory was entirely from purchases during the fourth quarter, no price level restatement on the statement should be made. This is because the year-end value is the same as the average index value for the fourth quarter.

(b) The index was 127 when the building was acquired.

(c) Old asset acquired for $40,000 in 19B when index was 138; therefore, restatement is as follows:

$40,000 × $159/138$ (i.e., 115.2) =	$46,080
New asset acquired for $20,000 on December 31, 19F; therefore, no restatement needed	20,000
Total GPL restated amount	$66,080

EXHIBIT 7–11

AB COMPANY
Restatement of Income Statement—GPL Basis
For Year Ended December 31, 19F

	Cost Basis Amount	Conversion Factor	GPL Restated Amount
Sales	$120,000	(a)	$123,570
Inventory, January 1, 19F	20,000	159/147 = 108.2%	21,640
Purchases	85,000	(a)	87,380
Goods available for sale	105,000		109,020
Inventory, December 31, 19F	25,000	(b)	25,000
Cost of goods sold	80,000		84,020
Gross margin	40,000		39,550
General expenses	12,000	(a)	12,357
Depreciation expense, building	4,000	159/127 = 125.2% (b)	5,008
Depreciation expense, fixtures	4,000	159/138 = 115.2% (b)	4,608
Total expenses	20,000		21,973
Income before taxes	20,000		17,577
Income tax	(10,000)	(a)	(10,298)
Purchasing power loss	—	(c)	(2,195)
Net Income	$ 10,000		$ 5,084

(a) See Exhibit 7–8.

(b) See GPL restated balance sheet Exhibit 7–10.

(c) See Exhibit 7–9.

EXHIBIT 7–12

AB COMPANY
Data for Comparative Balance Sheet—GPL Restatement of Prior Year (19E)
At December 31, 19E, and 19F
(stated in terms of December 31, 19F, price level)

	Cost Basis Amount	Conversion Factor	GPL Restated Amount
Cash	$ 36,000	159/147 = 108.2%	$ 38,952
Receivables	24,000	159/147 = 108.2%	25,968
Inventory	20,000	159/147 = 108.2%	21,640
Building	100,000	159/127 = 125.2%	125,200
Accumulated depreciation, building	(20,000)	159/127 = 125.2%	(25,040)
Fixtures	40,000	159/138 = 115.2%	46,080
Accumulated depreciation, fixtures	(20,000)	159/138 = 115.2%	(23,040)
	$180,000		$209,760
Accounts payable	35,000	159/147 = 108.2%	$ 37,870
Stockholders' equity	145,000		171,890*
	$180,000		$209,760

* Balancing amount. For profit check, see Exhibit 7–13.

EXHIBIT 7–13

AB COMPANY
Proof of GPL Restatement
December 31, 19F

December 31, 19E, stockholders' equity at December 31, 19F, GPL (Exhibit 7–12)	$171,890
Add: Net income, including GPL gain or loss (Exhibit 7–11)	5,084
Total	176,974
Deduct: Dividends adjusted to GPL basis (Exhibit 7–9)	10,390
December 31, 19F, stockholders' equity at December 31, 19F, GPL (Exhibit 7–10)	$166,584

Since this balance sheet is no longer relevant to current purchasing power, at December 31, 19D, the 19C cost basis statement must again be restated using 19D conversion factors as reflected in Exhibit 7–6.[7] The GPL restated amounts shown in Exhibits 7–4 and 7–6 would be reported in juxtaposition on the 19D comparative GPL balance sheets.

Preparation of a comparative income statement would require the same approach. Since 19C revenue and expense data were not provided for XY Company, development of the comparative income statement is not illustrated at this point. However, the basic procedure which would be followed can easily be described. Assume sales for 19C on a historical cost basis were $340,000 and had been restated to $350,000 on the 19C GPL statement because the year-end index number was almost 3% higher than the average index value for 19C. Now assume the year-end index number for 19D is 10% higher (i.e., 19C index = 145; 19D index = 159.5) than the year-end value prevailing at 19C year-end. Consequently, the original $350,000 sales amount would be restated again to $385,000 (i.e., $350,000 × 159.5/145) when the 19C amounts are restated to 19D year-end equivalent purchasing power. Consider another item, depreciation ex-

---

[7] The 19D restatement of 19C GPL financial statements for comparative purposes can also be accomplished by "rolling forward" the 19C GPL restated financial statements by 10% since (a) the 19C statements are already price level restated to 19C indexed values and (b) the general level of prices rose by 10% during 19D.

pense. On the 19C price level statement, this expense would have been $25,000 (i.e., $20,000 × 145/116). The $25,000 would be again restated upward by 10% (i.e., 159.5 ÷ 145 = 110) for the 19D comparative income statement to $27,500, which is the same amount as on the 19D GPL statement (because straight-line depreciation was used).

Proof of Restatement

When comparative balance sheets are prepared as illustrated above, a proof of the accuracy of the GPL restatement process can be developed as follows:

December 31, 19C, stockholders' equity at December 31, 19D, GPL (Exhibit 7–6)	$398,750
Add: Net income including GPL gain or loss (Exhibit 7–5)	15,250
Total	414,000
Deduct: Dividends adjusted to GPL basis (Exhibit 7–3)	12,000
December 31, 19D, stockholders' equity at December 31, 19D, GPL (Exhibit 7–4)	$402,000

COMPLEX ILLUSTRATION OF GENERAL PRICE LEVEL RESTATEMENT

This illustration is more realistic than the preceding one because revenue and expense data are given on a quarterly rather than on an annual basis. It also involves the acquisition of operational assets and payment of a dividend during the year. If the price level data are released on a quarterly basis, quarterly application is realistic. This illustration describes the development of GPL statements for AB Company for the year ended December 31, 19F. The assumed data are as follows:

1. Relevant GPL index numbers (see also transactions [c] and [d] in Exhibit 7–7).

	GPL Index Number
December 31, 19E (when beginning inventory was acquired and when cash, accounts receivable, and accounts payable arose)	147

Quarterly averages:	
First quarter, 19F	150
Second quarter, 19F	153
Third quarter, 19F	155.9
Fourth quarter, at December 31, 19F	159

The year-end value is assumed to be the same as the average for the fourth quarter. As noted in Exhibit 7–7, the index was at 127 when the building was acquired (see footnote (c)) and at 138 when the original fixtures were bought (see footnote (d)).

2. Trial balance, cost basis, December 31, 19E: As reflected on Exhibit 7–7.

3. Transactions for 19F: As reflected at the bottom of Exhibit 7–7.

4. Additional information: Assume a *Fifo* basis for inventory (therefore, the ending inventory was from purchases made during the fourth quarter). Sales, purchases, general expenses, and income tax expense are restated from historical cost amounts to GPL amounts on a quarterly basis.

Based on these data, development of GPL statements for 19F is illustrated as follows:

1. *Exhibit* 7–7—Worksheet to develop traditional cost basis income statement and balance sheet for 19F.

2. *Exhibit* 7–8—GPL restatement of quarterly revenues and expenses. Completion of this schedule requires application of the 19D *quarterly* conversion factors to the cost basis amounts. The annual total for each revenue and expense is transferred to the restated annual income statement.

3. *Exhibit* 7–9—Calculation of GPL gain or loss on monetary items. The GPL loss of $2,195 is carried to the income statement.

4. *Exhibit* 7–10—GPL restatement of 19F balance sheet. Observe that only the nonmonetary amounts are restated and that restated stockholders' equity is a balancing figure.

5. *Exhibit* 7–11—GPL restatement of 19F income statement.

6. *Exhibit* 7–12—Data for comparative balance sheet—restatement of 19E balance sheet at 19F price level.

7. *Exhibit* 7–13—Proof of restatement—December 31, 19F.

' The above discussions and exhibits illustrated the development of financial statements restated on a GPL basis and explained the underlying concepts and basic computational procedures. They encompassed the proposed FASB Statement and should provide an adequate understanding of the problems and their proposed resolution. GPL financial statements do not report the "current replacement cost (CRC)" or market value of the specific items on the financial statements, except by coincidence. The next Part of this chapter discusses the problems and procedures of substituting *current values* for the values reported in historical cost based financial statements.

PART B—CURRENT VALUE ACCOUNTING MODELS

Part A of the chapter discussed general price level (GPL) restatement of financial statements. This approach for reporting the effects of changes in the general price level does not involve introduction of GPL values into the accounting records; the historical cost accounting model is retained. The results of that model are simply restated in terms of current dollars. In contrast, Part B discusses *current value* accounting models. These models introduce current values into the accounting records as well as into the financial statements.

There are two basic categories of current value accounting models, one based on current "exit" value (or selling price), the other on current "entry" value (or replacement cost). Both exit value and entry value accounting models have strong advocates and, because of the recent high rates of inflation, both are being examined along with general price level restatement as possible alternatives or supplements to historical cost accounting.

Accounting models based on current entry or exit value represent fundamental departures from the historical cost accounting model since they substitute *current* values in place of *historical* values for the various financial statement amounts. In contrast, general price level restatement (discussed in the first part of this chapter) is not a fundamental departure from historical cost accounting. Rather, the historical amounts are simply restated in terms of current dollars.

The current exit value accounting models do not have support as widespread as general price level restatement or the current entry value accounting models because most exit value accounting models ignore the sales event in the recognition of revenue. That is, in most exit value accounting models, revenue or gain is recognized as soon as the market value (selling price) of an asset exceeds historical cost. Because most accountants regard the sales event as critical to revenue recognition, exit value accounting models are mentioned only briefly in this chapter.

Therefore, the remainder of this chapter discusses current entry value accounting. Recent reporting requirements of the Securities and Exchange Commission (SEC) and the FASB have accorded a measure of general acceptability to the current entry value (i.e., current replacement cost) concept. As noted in Part A of this chapter, the FASB's proposed Statement, "Financial Reporting and Changing Prices," (December 1978) would, if adopted, require supplementary disclosures of *either* GPL restated historical cost *or* current replacement cost data for selected items of financial information. While the proposed requirements do not encompass a complete set of financial statements, a rich understanding of the replacement cost model is essential for compliance with the proposed requirements. Accordingly, this part of the chapter discusses and illustrates the replacement cost model, including the preparation of a set of replacement cost financial statements. Thus, we provide the context for the proposed disclosures.[8]

---

[8] The model we present can be used to generate the data proposed by the FASB. For example, the FASB replacement cost disclosures would require that the effect of general inflation on the cost of assets be separated from the effect of specific changes in the replacement costs of those assets. This feature is included in the model we present. Also, *both* replacement cost models provide for reporting the purchasing power gain or loss on monetary items, as discussed and illustrated in Part A of this chapter. The only substantive difference between the two models is that the FASB disclosures require current cost depreciation to be computed on the average replacement cost of the depreciable assets during the current period, whereas the model presented in this chapter computes depreciation based on end-of-period replacement cost.

CURRENT REPLACEMENT COST DISCLOSURE REQUIREMENTS OF THE SEC

In March 1976 the Securities and Exchange Commission (SEC) issued *Accounting Series Release (ASR) No. 190* in which it required certain companies to report CRC data as *supplements* (e.g., in notes) to the traditional historical cost financial statements which are included in annual 10-K reports filed with the SEC. The rule applied to registered companies that have "inventories and gross property, plant and equipment which aggregate more than $100 million and which comprise more than 10% of total assets." In particular, CRC data are required for inventories and cost of goods sold, productive capacity (i.e., operational assets), and depreciation expense.

ASR No. 190 defines replacement cost as "the lowest amount that would have to be paid in the normal course of business to obtain a new asset of equivalent operating or productive capability." It lists four principal methods of estimating CRC: indexing using specific (versus general) price indexes, direct pricing, unit pricing, and functional pricing. These terms are defined in the Appendix to this chapter. The Appendix also presents a number of pertinent citations from *ASR No. 190* and the related Staff Accounting Bulletins. (Also see Chapter 10 and the related Appendix.)

To facilitate the discussion, the following abbreviations will be used: HC = historical cost, GPL = general price level, and CRC = current replacement cost.

DIFFERENT CONCEPTS OF CAPITAL MAINTENANCE

Two different concepts of capital maintenance underlie the various replacement cost accounting models. The FASB endorsed the *financial capital* concept, which holds that capital is maintained when the *money value* of net assets remains constant. A key implication of this concept is that holding gains or losses on assets (explained in a later section of this chapter) are included as an element of income because they contribute to the maintenance of financial capital. By contrast, the *physical capital* concept holds that capital is maintained when the net assets remain sufficient to produce a *fixed quantity* (as opposed to *money value*) of goods and services. The model we present in this chapter is based on the financial capital concept.

DIFFERENCES BETWEEN GPL AND CRC ACCOUNTING MODELS

As discussed in the first part of this chapter, GPL restatement employs a general price index which is the composite of the price changes of many different items. By contrast, the CRC accounting model employs the current replacement cost of the productive capacity of the entity.

An actual example will demonstrate the difference between GPL restatement and CRC accounting. During recent years prices in general have risen. Consequently, GPL restatement would produce GPL asset and expense restatements which exceed HC amounts. Therefore, GPL restated income would generally be less than HC income. In some high-technology industries, such as computers and pocket calculators, the CRC of inventories is actually *less* than historical cost. Therefore, even though the CRC of the operational assets of these companies exceeds historical cost, which would make CRC depreciation expense greater than HC depreciation expense, the reduction in CRC of inventory has so great an impact on income (through cost of goods sold) that CRC income exceeds HC income.[9] For these companies, CRC income exceeds HC income and HC income exceeds GPL restated income. Thus, for these companies, GPL income and CRC income are very different indeed. The question which naturally arises in this context is: Which is the measure of "true" in-

---

[9] This was the case for IBM in 1977. For details, see *Forbes,* June 12, 1978, p. 108.

come: CRC income, HC income, GPL restated income, or some other income measure?

RELEVANCE OF CURRENT REPLACEMENT COST DATA

Proponents of CRC accounting believe that CRC data provide better answers than HC or GPL data to two related questions which are considered particularly important to investment and management decisions:

The income question: How much can the entity distribute to its owners without impairing the financial capability of the entity to operate at the same level of activity in the future?

The financial position question: How much will it cost the entity to replace worn-out assets that are necessary to continue operations at the same level of activity in the future?

To respond to the *income* question, the CRC income statement matches the current replacement costs of assets consumed (principally cost of goods sold and depreciation expense) against current revenues. CRC income thus "provides for the replacement of" inventory and operational assets in the sense that 100% of the reported CRC income of the period could be distributed to owners without impairing the financial capability of the company to continue the same level of operating activity.

To respond to the *financial position* question, the CRC balance sheet reports inventory and operational assets at the current cost of replacing the productive capacity of the entity at the end of the period.

Historical cost and GPL restatement would probably provide answers to these two questions which differ from the CRC answer because HC and GPL incomes and asset values would not (or would only coincidentally) be equal to CRC income and asset values. The accounting literature does not provide a clear-cut basis for deciding which model is "best." However, the measurement of *distributable income* is frequently mentioned as one criterion for assessing the relative merit of an accounting model. Other factors to consider are the cost of obtaining the data required by the model and users' understanding and acceptance of the information output of the model.

HOLDING GAINS AND LOSSES ON NONMONETARY ASSETS

By measuring expenses for the period and assets held at the end of the period at current replacement cost, the CRC model identifies "holding" gains and losses on assets. Holding gains and losses are *unrealized* changes in the replacement cost of nonmonetary assets.[10] Holding gains and losses are of two types: fictional and real.[11] *Fictional* holding gains and losses result from changes in replacement cost which are due to changes in the general price level. *Real* holding gains and losses are changes in replacement cost aside from the general price level change. Two examples will illustrate these definitions:

Example 1, a real holding gain—Suppose a company paid $5,000 for inventory on January 1, 19A, when the GPL was 100. One month later the replacement cost of the inventory was $5,150 and the GPL index was 101. The diagram below shows the *real* and *fictional* holding gains.

	$50 *Fictional* Holding Gain	$100 *Real* Holding Gain	
$5,000		$5,050 ($5,000 × 101/100)	$5,150
HC		GPL Restated Cost	CRC

Example 2, a real holding loss—Assume the same facts as in Example 1, except that the CRC of the inventory is $5,030. The diagram below shows the *fictional* holding gain and the *real* holding loss.

---

[10] Other titles given to holding gains are *cost savings* and *capital maintenance adjustments.*

[11] Edwards and Bell popularized the terminology "fictional" and "real." See Edgar O. Edwards and Philip W. Bell, *The Theory and Measurement of Business Income* (Berkeley, Calif.: University of California Press, 1961), p. 124.

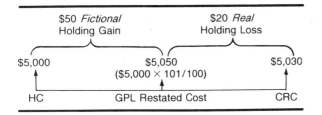

Using Example 1 above, the entries to record the transactions and the CRC change related to the inventory would be as follows:

January 1, 19A—Acquisition of inventory (assume a perpetual inventory system):

Inventory........................	5,000	
Cash (or accounts payable)........		5,000

January 31, 19A—Writeup of inventory to CRC and recognition of holding gain on inventory:

Inventory ($5,150 − $5,000)..........	150	
Holding gain on inventory.........		150

February 2, 19A—Sale of inventory (assume sales price of $8,000):

Cash (or accounts receivable).........	8,000	
Sales revenue.................		8,000
Cost of goods sold ($5,000 + $150).....	5,150	
Inventory		5,150

The inventory would be reported at CRC of $5,150 on the CRC balance sheet at January 31, 19A. The CRC income statement for January 19A would report the $100 *real* holding gain on inventory.[12] CRC accounting would *not* report the $50 fictional holding gain on the inventory since that only represents "keeping up with inflation" and indicates no "real" increment in value.[13]

The January 31 entry above shows that recog-

nition of the holding gain is necessary for reporting inventory at CRC because the holding gain on inventory is credited to write inventory up to a higher CRC. It also facilitates reporting cost of goods sold at CRC of $5,150 (when the inventory is sold), as well as the real element of the holding gain, on the income statement.

In this example the CRC income statement for February would report gross margin of $2,850 (i.e., $8,000 − $5,150), whereas the HC income statement for February would report gross margin at $3,000 (i.e., $8,000 − $5,000). The following diagram shows the differences between CRC and HC accounting for the above facts:

	HC	CRC
Balance Sheet, January 31, 19A:		
Inventory	$5,000	$5,150
Income Statement for January 19A:		
Holding gain—real	–0–	$ 100
Income Statement for February 19A:		
Sales............................	$8,000	$8,000
Cost of goods sold.................	5,000	5,150
Gross margin on sales	$3,000	$2,850

The holding gains and losses on *nonmonetary* assets (discussed above) must not be confused with the purchasing power gains and losses on *monetary* items discussed in the first part of this chapter. The two concepts are fundamentally different. The former pertains only to nonmonetary assets, and the latter pertains only to monetary items. The particular CRC model (there are several different CRC models) presented in this chapter reports both real holding gains and losses on *nonmonetary* assets and purchasing power gains and losses on *monetary* items, so it is important not to confuse them.

CURRENT REPLACEMENT COST ACCOUNTING ILLUSTRATED

Current replacement cost financial statements and entries will now be illustrated for a simplified set of facts. The data are used to compare HC, GPL, and CRC models. The GPL and CRC models are *not* a full-fledged part of generally accepted accounting principles. However, the comparative illustration provides a valuable

---

[12] Some authors recommend reporting holding gains and losses as separate elements of owners' equity on the balance sheet rather than on the income statement. This issue is not resolved. Regardless of where holding gains and losses are reported, the effect on *total* owners' equity is the same.

[13] *Recording* the full holding gain (i.e., both real and fictional elements) and only *reporting* the *real* holding gain is probably confusing to many readers. The means of accomplishing this are shown in the detailed illustration of CRC accounting at the end of this chapter (see note [b] of Exhibit 7–16).

learning experience because it *(a)* affords a basis for understanding a major issue facing the accounting profession today and *(b)* facilitates assessment of the strengths and weaknesses of each model.

The purposes of the illustration are to

1. Show how CRC data are entered in the accounts. GPL restatement is different from CRC accounting in this respect because under GPL restatement the effects of price changes are shown only in the statements; there are no book entries in GPL restatement.
2. Contrast HC, GPL, and CRC financial statements.
3. Indicate how GPL restatement affects CRC financial statements.

Before the illustration, each purpose is discussed.

CRC Entries. For each asset for which CRC exceeds the replacement cost on the last statement date (or in the case of a new asset, if CRC exceeds historical cost), a CRC entry is made which debits the specific asset account and credits a holding gain. Another CRC entry is made to record additional CRC depreciation on the CRC writeup; Depreciation Expense is debited, and Accumulated Depreciation is credited. In the event replacement cost has fallen, the initial CRC entry debits a holding loss and credits the asset account; the second CRC entry records a reduction in total depreciation expense.

CRC Financial Statements. HC, GPL, and CRC financial statements are presented in comparative columnar format to facilitate study. Operational assets are used to demonstrate the differences in asset carrying values and depreciation expense for HC, GPL, and CRC models (see Exhibit 7–17 for a direct comparison of the three models).

GPL Restatements in CRC Financial Statements. It is necessary to use GPL restatements in CRC financial statements for three reasons: (1) to compute the purchasing power gain or loss on *monetary* items (exactly as done in the GPL model), (2) to separate real and fictional holding gains and losses on *nonmonetary* assets, and (3) to attain interperiod comparability of the financial statements. To illustrate this last point, assume that a company presented CRC financial statements for 19A. The CRC statements for 19A would be stated in dollars of current purchasing power for 19A. The CRC financial statements for 19B would be stated in dollars of current purchasing power for 19B. Assuming inflation during 19B, the 19A and 19B statements are not directly comparable because each dollar on the 19A statements is individually worth more than each dollar on the 19B statements. For this reason the 19A statements must be restated again to 19B dollars to make the 19A and 19B statements comparable. This restating also is done to attain interperiod comparability in GPL financial statements (as demonstrated in Part A of this chapter).[14]

It is assumed in the illustration that CRC data are available at minimal additional cost and can be estimated with reasonable objectivity. These assumptions may be unrealistic for many companies; however, they are used for expository purposes to avoid measurement problems which would obscure the basic concepts underlying the CRC model.

The illustrative company is a laundry (i.e., a service operation), to avoid the computational burden associated with inventories. The laundry has one class of nonmonetary assets, machinery. This situation will provide a realistic view of CRC depreciation and operational assets, which are the kinds of items for which historical cost data are least meaningful during periods of inflation. Thus, while the fact situation in the illustration is grossly oversimplified, it captures the major concept of the CRC model.

Exhibit 7–14 presents *(a)* HC balance sheets for D&B Laundries at December 31, 19A (when the machines were purchased new), and at December 31, 19B, and December 31, 19C; and *(b)* HC income statements for 19B and 19C.

Since the CRC financial statements are constructed from the HC statements, it is critical for the reader to carefully examine the histori-

---

[14] CRC accounting also facilitates interfirm comparisons within a period, since under CRC accounting, assets are stated at *current* replacement cost. Therefore, the dollars reflected in account balances on the CRC financial statements are all current, hence, comparable from firm to firm. The GPL restatements do not "cause" the interfirm comparability. However, as long as financial statements reflect *current* dollars, whether on a CRC or a GPL restated basis, they are comparable both across periods as well as across firms.

cal cost financial statements and additional data in Exhibit 7–14. In particular, note that the December 31, 19B, balance sheet follows from the December 31, 19A, balance sheet plus the 19B income statement. For example, 19B net cash receipts were $2,000 (i.e., $10,000 − $8,000 from the 19B income statement). This $2,000 increase plus beginning cash of $2,500 equals the cash balance of $4,500 at December 31, 19B. Also, beginning owners' equity of $2,500 plus HC income of $1,000 for 19B equals owners' equity of $3,500 at December 31, 19B. The same procedures are followed for 19C. It will be necessary throughout the remainder of the chapter to refer back to the basic data presented in Exhibit 7–14.

Exhibit 7–15 presents GPL financial state-

ments, along with the computation of the purchasing power gain or loss on monetary items, and a proof of the correctness of ending owners' equity for 19B and 19C. The 19B statements reflect December 31, 19B, dollars; and the 19C statements reflect December 31, 19C, dollars. Therefore, the final portion of Exhibit 7–15 presents comparative GPL statements for 19B and 19C, in which the 19B statements are restated to 19C dollars for comparative statement purposes. While Exhibit 7–15 affords a review of Part A of this chapter, it is not the focal point of this part of the chapter. Rather, it is used as an intermediate step for purposes of illustrating the similarities and differences between GPL restatement and CRC accounting.

EXHIBIT 7–14
Historical Cost Data—D&B Laundries

D&B LAUNDRIES Income Statements—Historical Cost Years Ended December 31, 19B and 19C			D&B LAUNDRIES Balance Sheets—Historical Cost December 31,19A–19C			
	19B	19C		19A	19B	19C
Service revenue	$10,000	$12,000	Cash	$2,500	$4,500	$6,900
Expenses:			Machinery	4,000	4,000	4,000
Depreciation	(1,000)	(1,000)	Accumulated			
Other	(8,000)	(9,600)	depreciation	(–0–)	(1,000)	(2,000)
HC Income	$ 1,000	$ 1,400		$6,500	$7,500	$8,900
			Current liabilities	$1,500	$1,500	$1,500
			Long-term			
			liabilities	2,500	2,500	2,500
			Owners' equity	2,500	3,500	4,900
				$6,500	$7,500	$8,900

Additional data:

1. All service revenue is collected in cash from coin-operated machines at year-end.*
2. All cash expenses (i.e., other than depreciation) are paid at year-end.*
3. Short-term and long-term liability balances do not change.
4. Machinery, acquired at the end of 19A, is depreciated on a straight-line basis over four years with no estimated residual value.
5. The general level of prices (GPL) increases by 6% per year during 19B and 19C; therefore, the GPL index numbers are January 1, 19B—100; December 31, 19B—106; and December 31, 19C—112.36.
6. The current replacement cost of machinery increases by 10% during 19B and 19C (i.e., the specific CRC index numbers for the machinery of D&B Laundries are 100 at January 1, 19B; 110 at December 31, 19B; and 121 at December 31, 19C).

* We realize that no business collects all revenues and pays all cash expenses at year-end. Instead, the revenues and expenses occur throughout the year. Thus, it may appear to some readers that some form of *average* replacement cost for the year should be used on the income statement. This may not be the case, however. The literature on CRC is not sufficiently developed to have resolved the issue of whether averages or year-end values of replacement cost for expenses should be reported on the income statement. This issue is more complex than it may appear. For instance, to those readers who may feel that *average* replacement cost should be matched against the revenue of a period, we would point out that "current" replacement cost could be construed to mean "current as of the date of the financial statements," presumably the *end* of the accounting period. Therefore, it is not clear to the authors that average rather than year-end replacement cost should be matched against revenue for the period since price changes may occur between the "average date" and year-end. We cannot adequately explore this issue within the space constraints of this chapter. Therefore, we make the unrealistic assumption that all revenues and all expenses occur at year-end. This avoids the conceptual problem discussed above. It also avoids the computational burden of using average CRC and general price level data on the income statement and year-end data on the balance sheet. Our presentation captures the central concept of current replacement cost accounting, the unrealistic assumptions notwithstanding.

EXHIBIT 7–15
GPL Financial Statements—D&B Laundries

D&B LAUNDRIES
Income Statement—GPL
Year Ended December 31, 19B

Service revenue		$10,000
Expenses:		
Depreciation ($1,000 × 106/100)	(1,060)	
Other	(8,000)	
Operating income		940
General purchasing power gain on monetary items		90 [a]
GPL Income		$ 1,030

D&B LAUNDRIES
Balance Sheet—GPL
December 31, 19B

Cash		$4,500
Machinery ($4,000 × 106/100)		4,240
Accumulated depreciation ($1,000 × 106/100)		(1,060)
		$7,680
Current liabilities		$1,500
Long-term liabilities		2,500
Owners' equity		3,680 [b]
		$7,680

[a] General purchasing power gain on monetary items computed as follows:

Net *restated monetary liabilities* on 1/1/19B, ($1,500 + $2,500 − $2,500 = $1,500) from 19A HC balance sheet	$1,500 × 106/100 = $1,590	
Less HC *net monetary liabilities* on 1/1/19B		1,500
General purchasing power gain		$ 90

Note: Since all cash revenues and cash expenses occurred at year-end, these transactions had no purchasing power effects during the year. As a result, the only purchasing power effect related to beginning monetary items.

[b] Proof of correctness of GPL restated ending owners' equity for 19B:

Beginning owners' equity ($2,500) restated for the general rise in prices (i.e., multiplied by 106/100) equals beginning owners' equity restated in end-of-the-period dollars ($2,650). Beginning owners' equity stated in end-of-the-period dollars ($2,650) plus 19B GPL income ($1,030) equals ending GPL restated owners' equity ($3,680).

D&B LAUNDRIES
Income Statement—GPL
Year Ended December 31, 19C

Service revenue		$12,000
Expenses:		
Depreciation ($1,000 × 112.36/100)	(1,124)	
Other	(9,600)	
Operating income		1,276
General purchasing power loss on monetary items		(30) [c]
GPL Income		$ 1,246

D&B LAUNDRIES
Balance Sheet—GPL
December 31, 19C

Cash		$6,900
Machinery ($4,000 × 112.36/100)		4,494
Accumulated depreciation ($2,000 × 112.36/100)		(2,247)
		$9,147
Current liabilities		$1,500
Long-term liabilities		2,500
Owners' equity		5,147 [d]
		$9,147

[c] $500 × 112.36/106 = $530 − $500 = general purchasing power loss of $30.

[d]
$3,680 (from 19B GPL balance sheet above) × 112.36/106	$3,901
Add GPL income for 19C	1,246
Ending owners' equity	$5,147

D&B LAUNDRIES
Comparative Income Statements—GPL
Years Ended December 31, 19B and 19C

	19B Restated in 19C Dollars		19C from Above
Service revenue	$10,000 × 112.36/106 =	$10,600	$12,000
Expenses:			
Depreciation	(1,060) × 112.36/106 =	(1,124)	(1,124)
Other	(8,000) × 112.36/106 =	(8,480)	(9,600)
Operating income		996	1,276
General purchasing power gain (loss) on monetary items	90 × 112.36/106 =	95	(30)
GPL Income		$ 1,091	$ 1,246

D&B LAUNDRIES
Comparative Balance Sheets—GPL
December 31, 19B and 19C

	19B Restated in 19C Dollars		19C from Above
Cash	$4,500 × 112.36/106 =	$4,770	$6,900
Machinery	4,240 × 112.36/106 =	4,494	4,494
Accumulated depreciation	(1,060) × 112.36/106 =	(1,124)	(2,247)
		$8,140	$9,147
Current liabilities	1,500 × 112.36/106 =	$1,590	$1,500
Long-term liabilities	2,500 × 112.36/106 =	2,650	2,500
Owners' equity	3,680 × 112.36/106 =	3,900	5,147
		$8,140	$9,147

Exhibit 7–16 presents CRC financial statements.[15] The primary features of CRC financial statements are the following:

1. A CRC income statement is similar to a GPL income statement in that current dollars of expense are matched with current dollars of revenue. Thus, the expenses and revenues are comparable, unlike the matching in the historical cost model (when the GPL changes). In the CRC income statement, however, CRC depreciation is the current cost of replacing the specific productive capacity (which expired during the period) of the D&B Laundries rather than GPL restated depreciation.

2. The CRC income statement also reports the real holding gain from the specific rise in the replacement cost of D&B Laundries' operational assets. Only "real" holding gains (i.e., those in excess of the general rate of inflation) are reported. Computation of the real holding gain is shown in the exhibit.

3. The CRC income statement reports the general purchasing power gain or loss from holding *monetary* items during an inflationary period. This is the same gain or loss reported in the GPL statements, so it can simply be taken from the GPL income statements in Exhibit 7–15.

---

[15] The CRC accounting model underlying the CRC financial statements is adapted from William J. Bruns, Jr., and Richard F. Vancil, *A Primer on Replacement Cost Accounting* (New Jersey: Thomas Horton & Daughters, 1976).

EXHIBIT 7–16
CRC Financial Statements and Entries—D&B Laundries

D&B LAUNDRIES
Income Statement—CRC
Year Ended December 31, 19B

Service revenue	$10,000
Expenses:	
Depreciation ($1,000 × 110/100)	(1,100)
Other	(8,000)
Operating income	900
General purchasing power gain on monetary items (Exhibit 7–15)	90
Real holding gain on nonmonetary assets—machinery	160 [a]
CRC Income	$ 1,150

D&B LAUNDRIES
Balance Sheet—CRC
December 31, 19B

Cash	$4,500
Machinery ($4,000 × 110/100)	4,400
Accumulated depreciation ($1,000 × 110/100)	(1,100)
	$7,800
Current liabilities	$1,500
Long-term liabilities	2,500
Owners' equity	3,800 [b]
	$7,800

[a] Rise in replacement cost of undepreciated machinery (i.e., total holding gain) during 19B ($4,000 × .10) $400
Less: Rise in replacement cost due to general inflation (i.e., fictional holding gain during 19B ($4,000 × .06) 240
Real holding gain on machinery [$4,000 × (.10 − .06)] during 19B (Note: Real holding gains are computed on beginning-of-the-period undepreciated replacement cost, i.e., $4,000 − $0) $160

[b] Proof of correctness of ending CRC owners' equity for 19B:
Beginning 19B owners' equity—HC, restated in 12/31/19B dollars ($2,500 × 106/100) $2,650
Add CRC income for 19B 1,150
CRC owners' equity at end of 19B (includes $240 fictional holding gain on machinery in addition to the $160 real holding gain in CRC income) $3,800

The 19B $3,800 ending balance in owners' equity contains both the real and fictional holding gains on machinery (see footnote 13). The real holding gain ($160) is included above in CRC income for 19B. The fictional (i.e., GPL) holding gain ($240) is included, along with the purchasing power gain on monetary items, in the $150 restatement of beginning owners' equity ($2,500) to its year-end equivalent ($2,650), as shown below:

Fictional (i.e., GPL) holding gain on nonmonetary asset—machinery (see note [a] above) $240
Less purchasing power gain on monetary liabilities—see Exhibit 7–15 and note that monetary liabilities exceed monetary assets .... (90)
Restatement of beginning owners' equity ($2,650 − $2,500) $150

In summary, the GPL restatement of assets minus the GPL restatement of liabilities equals the GPL restatement of owners' equity.

Journal entries required to adjust the HC account balances to a CRC basis:

1. To record total holding gain on machinery for 19B:

Machinery ($4,000 × .10) 400
Holding gain on machinery 400

EXHIBIT 7–16 *(continued)*

This entry includes the fictional component of the holding gain ($240 in note [a] above). This is consistent with the way general price changes are recognized in the GPL model, that is, via restatement of the HC amounts rather than by formal journal entries to the GPL effect.

2. To record 19B depreciation of the CRC increment (in addition to $1,000 of regular depreciation on historical cost):

Depreciation expense ($400 ÷ 4) 100
    Accumulated depreciation 100

D&B LAUNDRIES
Income Statement—CRC
Year Ended December 31, 19C

Service revenue	$12,000
Expenses:	
Depreciation ($1,000 ×121/100)	(1,210)
Other	(9,600)
Operating income	1,190
General purchasing power loss on monetary	
items (Exhibit 7–15)	(30)
Real holding gain on nonmonetary assets—	
machinery	132 [c]
CRC Income	$ 1,292

D&B LAUNDRIES
Balance Sheet—CRC
December 31, 19C

Cash	$6,900
Machinery ($4,000 × 121/100)	4,840
Accumulated depreciation ($2,000 × 121/100) . .	(2,420)
	$9,320
Current liabilities	$1,500
Long-term liabilities	2,500
Owners' equity	5,320 [d]
	$9,320

[c] Rise in replacement cost of undepreciated machinery (i.e., total holding gain) during 19C [($4,400 − $1,100) × .10] during 19C $330
    Less: Rise in replacement cost due to general inflation (i.e., fictional holding gain) ($3,300 × .06) during 19C . . . . (198)
    Real holding gain on machinery [$3,300 × (.10 − .06)] during 19C $132

Note: Real holding gains on nonmonetary assets are computed on beginning-of-the-period undepreciated replacement cost (i.e., $4,400 − $1,100).
[d] Beginning 19C owners' equity from CRC balance sheet at 12/31/19B above, restated in 12/31/19C dollars ($3,800 × 112.36/106) $4,028
    Add CRC income for 19C 1,292
    CRC owners' equity at end of 19C (includes $198 fictional holding gain on machinery, in addition to the $132 real holding gain in CRC income). . . . $5,320

Journal entries required to adjust HC account balances to a CRC basis:

3. To record total holding gain on machinery for 19C:

Machinery ($4,400 × .10) 440
    Holding gain on machinery 440

4. To record 19C depreciation on the CRC increment (in addition to $1,000 of regular depreciation on historical cost):

Depreciation expense [($400 ÷ 4) +
  ($440 ÷ 4)] 210
Holding gain on machinery (explained
  in the text discussion following
  this exhibit) 110
    Accumulated depreciation 320

D&B LAUNDRIES
Comparative Income Statements—CRC
Years Ended December 31, 19B, and 19C

	19B Restated in 19C Dollars		19C from Above
Service revenue	$10,000 × 112.36/106 = $10,600		$12,000
Expenses:			
Depreciation	(1,100) × 112.36/106 = (1,166)		(1,210)
Other	(8,000) × 112.36/106 = (8,480)		(9,600)
Operating income		954	1,190
General purchasing power gain (loss) on monetary items	90 × 112.36/106 =	95	(30)
Real holding gain on non-monetary asset—machinery	160 × 112.36/106 =	170	132
CRC Income		$ 1,219	$ 1,292

D&B LAUNDRIES
Comparative Balance Sheets—CRC
December 31, 19B, and 19C

	19B Restated in 19C Dollars		19C from Above
Cash	$4,500 × 112.36/106 = $4,770		$6,900
Machinery	4,400 × 112.36/106 = 4,664		4,840
Accumulated depreciation	(1,100) × 112.36/106 = (1,166)		(2,420)
		$8,268	$9,320
Current liabilities	1,500 × 112.36/106 = $1,590		$1,500
Long-term liabilities	2,500 × 112.36/106 = 2,650		2,500
Owners' equity	3,800 × 112.36/106 = 4,028		5,320
		$8,268	$9,320

4. The CRC balance sheet reports the operational assets of D&B Laundries at the specific cost of replacing the productive capacity of the entity.

The CRC depreciation entry for 19C in Exhibit 7–16 is perhaps the most difficult aspect of CRC accounting to understand. Concentrate initially on the debit to depreciation expense. Since the initial cost of the machinery was $4,000 and since the compound rise in replacement cost over two years is 21% (i.e., 10% during 19B, then 10% during 19C), CRC depreciation for 19C is HC depreciation, $1,000, plus an additional 21%, or $1,210 total. The $210 debit to depreciation expense restates HC depreciation to CRC depreciation.

The $320 credit to accumulated depreciation can be explained as follows. The CRC of the machinery on December 31, 19C, is $4,840 (i.e., ($4,000 × 121/100), and the four-year machine is now two years old. Therefore, CRC accumulated depreciation must be $2,420 (i.e., half of CRC of $4,840) at December 31, 19C. Total depreciation recorded prior to the 19C entry is $2,100 (i.e., $1,000 of HC depreciation for each of 19B and 19C plus $100 of additional CRC depreciation for 19B). Therefore, CRC accumulated depreciation at the end of 19C ($2,420) minus previously recorded CRC depreciation ($2,100) equals $320.

The $110 is debited to the holding gain account for two related reasons: (1) to adjust the total holding gain for 19C from the $440 recorded to the correct balance ($330, as shown in note [c] of Exhibit 7–16) and (2) to record "catch-up" depreciation.

Adjustment of the Holding Gain. Holding gains accrue on *net* assets held, not on gross assets. In note *(c)* of Exhibit 7–16 the holding gain for 19C was based on *net* replacement cost of $3,300 (i.e., $4,400 − $1,100) at January 1, 19C. Holding gains cannot accrue on depreciated portions of assets since what is depreciated is gone. Therefore, since a $440 holding gain is recorded for 19C, when the carrying value of the machinery is restated to its CRC at December 31, 19C (see entry 3 in Exhibit 7–16), it is necessary to reduce the holding gain to a "net of depreciation" basis. The $110 debit to holding gain (in entry 4) reduces the holding gain to $330.

"Catch-up" Depreciation. Catch-up depreciation represents the portion of the 19C asset restatement which is expired because it pertains to prior periods. Bear in mind that the machinery is two years old, or half used up at the end of 19C. The $440 CRC increment to machinery for 19C ignores depreciation because it is additional (replacement) *cost*. Therefore, it is necessary to record two years' use (for 19B and 19C) of the 19C replacement cost adjustment of $440. The 19C year's use, or $110 (i.e., one fourth of $440), is included in the 19C replacement cost depreciation entry for $210 (as shown in the computation of the $210 in entry 4, Exhibit 7–16). The 19B use of the 19C replacement cost adjustment (i.e., ¼ of $440 = $110) is the "catch-up" depreciation and is recorded in CRC accounting by debiting the holding gain account, as in entry 4, Exhibit 7–16.

Exhibit 7–17 presents 19B–19C comparative income statements and balance sheets under the HC, GPL, and CRC models. The amounts are taken from Exhibits 7–14, 7–15, and 7–16.

DIFFERENCES AMONG HISTORICAL COST, GENERAL PRICE LEVEL, AND CURRENT REPLACEMENT COST FINANCIAL STATEMENTS

The following discussion is based on Exhibit 7–17 (years 19B and 19C). The HC financial statements for 19B and 19C are *not* comparable because the 19B statements are stated in 19B dollars and the 19C statements are stated in 19C dollars. By contrast, both GPL and CRC financial statements are comparable between years because these statements reflect 19C dollars for both years.

Likewise, HC depreciation expense for 19C is not comparable with 19C revenue because depreciation is stated in 19B dollars (the machinery was new on January 1, 19B), whereas 19C revenue is stated in 19C dollars. In contrast, on the GPL and CRC financial statements, depreciation expense and revenue are comparable because the GPL and CRC depreciation expense for 19C and the revenue for 19C reflect 19C dollars.

Perhaps the most important difference among HC, GPL, and CRC amounts is the depre-

EXHIBIT 7–17
Comparative HC, GPL, and CRC Financial Statements of D&B Laundries for 19B and 19C

D&B LAUNDRIES
Comparative Income Statements
Years Ended December 31, 19B and 19C

	Historical Cost		General Price Level		Current Replacement Cost	
	19B	19C	19B	19C	19B	19C
Service revenue	$10,000	$12,000	$10,600	$12,000	$10,600	$12,000
Expenses:						
Depreciation	(1,000)	(1,000)	(1,124)	(1,124)	(1,166)	(1,210)
Other	(8,000)	(9,600)	(8,480)	(9,600)	(8,480)	(9,600)
Operating income	1,000	1,400	996	1,276	954	1,190
General purchasing power gain (loss) on monetary items			95	(30)	95	(30)
Real holding gain on non-monetary assets—machinery					170	132
Income	$ 1,000	$ 1,400	$ 1,091	$ 1,246	$ 1,219	$ 1,292

D&B LAUNDRIES
Comparative Balance Sheets
December 31, 19B, and 19C

	Historical Cost		General Price Level		Current Replacement Cost	
	19B	19C	19B	19C	19B	19C
Cash	$ 4,500	$ 6,900	$ 4,770	$ 6,900	$ 4,770	$ 6,900
Machinery	4,000	4,000	4,494	4,494	4,664	4,840
Accumulated depreciation	(1,000)	(2,000)	(1,124)	(2,247)	(1,166)	(2,420)
	$ 7,500	$ 8,900	$ 8,140	$ 9,147	$ 8,268	$ 9,320
Current liabilities	$ 1,500	$ 1,500	$ 1,590	$ 1,500	$ 1,590	$ 1,500
Long-term liabilities	2,500	2,500	2,650	2,500	2,650	2,500
Owners' equity	3,500	4,900	3,900	5,147	4,028	5,320
	$ 7,500	$ 8,900	$ 8,140	$ 9,147	$ 8,268	$ 9,320

Note: Comparison of the concepts of HC, GPL, and CRC can be effective without detailed concern with Exhibits 7–15 and 7–16.

ciation expense. GPL depreciation reflects HC depreciation restated in current dollars. As such, it is not bound to reflect depreciation in the economic utility of the machinery. CRC depreciation is intended to serve this purpose. Proponents of CRC accounting argue on this basis that the resulting CRC operating income is the "best" measure of *distributable* income.

The HC income statement ignores both the purchasing power gain or loss on monetary items and the real holding gain on nonmonetary assets—machinery. In contrast, the GPL income statement reports the purchasing power gain or loss on monetary items but ignores the real holding gain on nonmonetary assets—machinery. Importantly, the CRC income statement reports both of these kinds of gains and losses.

Note that for both years, in this particular example, the CRC income statements report the *highest income* but the *lowest operating income.* Therefore, while CRC distributable (i.e., operating) income is the lowest of the three, CRC total real wealth increment (i.e., income) is the highest. Again, proponents of CRC accounting would point out the alleged value of knowing both realized and unrealized components of income for decision making. For instance, if dividend payments were based upon distributable income (refer to the income question posed at the outset of Part B), D&B Laundries would likely pay less in cash dividends if the company utilized CRC accounting. In this way they would reduce the risk of inadvertently distributing permanent capital to their stockholders.

On the balance sheets of D&B Laundries, total assets and owners' equity are reported at the highest amounts under CRC. The principal reason for this situation is that the CRC of machinery increased during 19B and 19C at annual rates (10%) in *excess* of the annual increase in the general price level (6%). The CRC balance sheets reflect operational assets at the cost that D&B Laundries could expect to incur currently to replace them with assets of equivalent productive capacity. Had CRC increased at a rate *less* than the GPL rate opposite results generally would prevail.

SUMMARY

The tone of this discussion suggests that current replacement cost accounting measures up reasonably well against both historical cost accounting and general price level restatement. It is easy to make such a case in a textbook because real-world complexities such as measuring current replacement cost can be avoided. But the 1,000 or so companies subject to the CRC requirement of the SEC cannot avoid these complexities.

It should also be noted that the SEC does not require, nor does GAAP permit, a *comprehensive* application of CRC accounting as illustrated in this chapter. The Appendix indicates that the SEC requires a *piecemeal* approach to *disclosing* CRC data. The same is true of the FASB's proposed approach. Nevertheless, an understanding of CRC accounting is incomplete without a basic understanding of the model as discussed and illustrated in this chapter. This understanding is essential for an evaluation of the various alternative accounting models.

In the final analysis, the test of any model (in any discipline) is the quality of the predictions the model helps to generate. In the past the historical cost accounting model appears to have yielded predictions of business outcomes which have been sufficiently accurate to cause retention of the HC accounting model. Only time will tell whether the users of financial statements continue to have enough confidence in its results for predictive purposes to retain HC accounting. This chapter has discussed the most frequently mentioned supplements or alternatives to the HC model—GPL restatement and CRC accounting.

Appendix—Selected Details of the Securities and Exchange Commission (SEC or Commission) Accounting Series Release (ASR) No. 190, Issued March 23, 1976

ASR No. 190 states:

> The new rule as adopted requires registrants [i.e., companies whose stock is registered with the SEC] who have inventories and gross property, plant and equipment which aggregate more than $100 million and which comprise more than 10% of total assets to disclose the *estimated current replacement cost of inventories and productive capacity at the end of each fiscal year for which a balance sheet is required and the approximate amount of cost of sales and depreciation based on replacement cost for the two most recent full fiscal years.* In addition, registrants are required to disclose the methods used in determining these amounts and to furnish any additional information of which management is aware and believes is necessary to prevent the information from being misleading. This information may be presented either in a footnote to the financial statements or in a separate section of the financial statements following the notes. In either place, the information may be designated as "unaudited."

> In requiring these data, the Commission is aware that it is requiring companies to make disclosures of costs which cannot be calculated with precision. They must be estimated on the basis of numerous assumptions which may vary

over time and from company to company and through the use of techniques which are not so fully developed that they can be standardized at the present time, if ever. This is because estimates of current replacement cost must be made within the framework of each registrant's economic situation and because there are difficult conceptual and empirical judgments which must be made in the light of different specific factual circumstances in developing the data. Nevertheless, the Commission believes that such data are important and useful to investors and are not otherwise obtainable. It feels that imprecision, if properly explained, will not make the data misleading. The Commission encourages registrants to supplement the required disclosures with information which management believes will be helpful to investors in understanding the impact of price changes and other current economic conditions on reported results (Emphasis supplied.)

In a separate Staff Accounting Bulletin, the staff of the SEC defined two key terms:

> For purposes of this rule, *replacement cost* is the lowest amount that would have to be paid in the normal course of business to obtain a new asset of equivalent operating or productive capability. In the case of depreciable, depletable or amortizable assets, replacement cost (new) and depreciated replacement cost should be distinguished. Replacement cost (new) is the total estimated current cost of replacing total productive capacity at the end of the year while depreciated replacement cost is the replacement cost (new) adjusted for the already expired service potential of such assets. (Emphasis supplied.)

> *Productive capacity* is a measurement of a company's ability to produce and distribute. The productive capacity of a manufacturer would be measured by the number of units it can presently produce and distribute within a particular time frame; in the case of a telephone company, for example, it would be a measurement of the number of telephone calls it can presently complete within a certain time frame. (Emphasis supplied.)

ASR No. 190 also noted that

> The Commission's judgment that delay [in the requirement that CRC data be disclosed] is not appropriate is based on a number of factors. First, it believes that under current economic conditions, data about the impact of changes in the prices of specific goods and services on business firms is of great significance to investors in developing an understanding of the current operations of any firm. While the current [as of spring 1976] general rate of inflation has been reduced from 1974 levels, it is still at a level such that unsupplemented historical cost based data do not adequately reflect current business economics. Further, in an inflationary economy specific costs and prices which may affect a business change more rapidly than the general price level. These factors make the impact of delay more severe than would be the case in a time of price stability.

The SEC also bore in mind the cost of implementing its CRC disclosure requirements, as noted in the following quote from *ASR No. 190:*

> The Commission has carefully considered the cost of implementation and weighed it against the need of investors for replacement cost information. It has concluded that in the case of companies of large size which generally have the largest public investor interest, the data are of such importance that the benefits of disclosure clearly outweigh the costs of data preparation. In the case of smaller companies where the cost burden is proportionately greater and the extent of public investor interest is proportionately less, the balance between economic costs and benefits is less clear. Accordingly, the Commission has determined initially to exempt from the rule companies whose inventories and gross property, plant and equipment aggregate less than $100 million. While it urges such companies to make appropriate disclosure of the effect of specific price changes and inflation in general on their operations, it is not at this time requiring them to make the specific disclosure required by this rule. As experience is gained with the costs of implementing the rule and the benefit of the information to investors, the Commission will consider the desirability of eliminating or amending the exemption.

> In addition, the Commission has concluded that companies whose inventories and gross properties comprise less than 10% of total assets need not make the disclosure since in the case of such companies the effects of such disclosure on financial statements would generally be immaterial.

And,

> . . . the adopted rule permits the disclosures either in the footnotes or in a separate section of

the financial statements [included in annual 10-K reports filed with the SEC] which follows the notes and is appropriately labeled.

Companies are allowed to use the method of estimating CRC which management believes is most appropriate in the economic circumstances of the company. In a separate Staff Accounting Bulletin, the SEC recommended four ways of estimating current replacement costs:

Indexing provides a valid measurement of replacement cost provided the index is adjusted for technological change or if the asset type has not had technological change. Indexing should be applied to homogeneous asset groups on a vintaged basis and should not be applied to used asset purchases.

Direct pricing applies to assets or groups of assets whereby direct labor and material prices are determined from purchase orders, invoices, engineering estimates, price lists, manufacturers' quotes, internally published labor and material prices, and other direct price sources.

Unit pricing is a structured variation of direct pricing whereby a building, inventory lot, or other type of asset is directly priced based upon labor, material, and overhead estimates, then divided into a unit measure (e.g., replacement cost per square foot of building, replacement cost per unit of inventory, etc.).

Functional pricing is generally used to determine the replacement cost for a processing function rather than for a specific asset or asset group. Functional pricing can be applied to a heterogeneous group of assets. Functional pricing often combines the techniques of indexing, direct pricing, and unit pricing. It measures the cost of productive capacity based on the number of units which can be produced within a particular time period. For example, a meat packing plant with a replacement cost of $5,000,000 has the capacity to process 500 head of cattle per day, resulting in the functional replacement cost of $10,000 per head of cattle per day. Functional pricing may involve the usage of information such as:

- Engineering studies.
- Recently built processing facilities.
- Design specifications for processing plants.
- Major equipment suppliers.
- Manufacturers' quotes.
- Internal estimates for installation and/or modifications.
- Trade association studies.

Functional pricing takes into consideration and adjusts for technological change, but one major consideration is additional adjustments for economics of scale. (Emphasis supplied.)

Other specific provisions of the SEC current replacement cost disclosure requirements include the following:

1. The rule does not apply to land, work in process inventory, or intangible assets.
2. Replacement cost should be based on the entity's normal approach to replacement of capacity.
3. Replacement cost should be disclosed for inventory and productive capacity assets which will *not* be specifically replaced if capacity will nevertheless be maintained.
4. Replacement costs are required instead of *reproduction* costs because the former consider the effects of changes in technology whereas the latter do not. In particular, replacement costs should take into account the technology which is current as of the reporting period, rather than the expected technology as of the expected date of actual replacement.
5. Replacement cost includes the cost of environmental protection devices.
6. Companies should not give explicit recognition to operating economies inherent in the use of better technology from replacement capacity (i.e., operational, or fixed, assets) because such economies are prospective. However, companies can report cost savings for inventories when such cost savings are reasonably assured, either by netting such cost savings against replacement cost and separate disclosure or by separate disclosure only.
7. Point estimates of CRC are not required. Ranges of estimated CRC are permitted if reasons therefor are given.
8. *Lifo* is an acceptable way to estimate cost of goods sold, and *Fifo* is an acceptable way to estimate ending inventory *if they approximate CRC* of cost of goods sold and ending inventory, respectively.
9. CRC for cost of goods sold and depreciation expense should be based on average CRC for the period, and CRC for ending inven-

tory and productive capacity should be based on CRC at the balance sheet date.

10. CRC for depreciation should be computed using the straight-line method.

QUESTIONS

PART A

1. What is the price phenomenon known as *inflation?* What is the opposite condition called?

2. What indices measure changes in the general purchasing power of the U.S. dollar? What index has been preferred for preparation of GPL adjusted financial statements?

3. In general terms, how much have prices changed in the United States between 1950 and 1977? Why may it be inaccurate to say that prices have changed as much as the percentage of rise in the GPL index between these dates?

4. "When prices are going up, they all go up; when they drop, they all drop." Comment on this statement.

5. Among sales, cost of goods sold, salaries, and depreciation expense, during an era of rapidly changing prices, which would be on the most current cost basis under the conventional historical cost model and which would be on the least current cost basis? Give reasons for your response.

6. When prices are changing rapidly, why are financial statements prepared on the historical cost basis likely to be deficient in some respects?

7. When prices are rising and depreciation expense is computed on the conventional historical cost basis, what is likely to be true insofar as replacement of the depreciable assets is concerned?

8. Several "piecemeal" procedures have been employed or proposed to cope with the inadequacies of historical cost basis accounting under conditions of rapidly changing prices. Briefly describe them. Indicate which ones are acceptable in the framework of generally accepted accounting principles.

9. Under the GPL restatement approach, financial statement items are classified as monetary or nonmonetary. Briefly, by which criteria can these two categories be distinguished?

10. Indicate, with explanations where necessary, whether the following items are monetary or nonmonetary: *(a)* stocks held as investments, *(b)* bonds held as investments, *(c)* deposits in domestic banks, *(d)* deposits in foreign banks, *(e)* allowance for doubtful accounts, *(f)* machinery and equipment, *(g)* accounts payable, *(h)* preferred stock, *(i)* retained earnings, and *(j)* deferred credit related to income taxes.

11. During its most recent fiscal period, XY Company had a larger balance of cash and receivables than liabilities; general prices rose steadily. Would this condition give rise to a GPL gain or loss?

12. If prices rise steadily over an extended period of time, indicate whether the following items would give rise to a general purchasing power gain, a general purchasing power loss, or neither general purchasing power gain nor loss:
   a. Maintaining a balance in a checking account.
   b. Owing bonds payable.
   c. Owning land.
   d. Amortizing goodwill.
   e. Holding common treasury stock.

13. If data are available on a quarterly basis rather than on an annual basis, how would this alter the preparation of price level restated statements at the end of a year?

14. The valuation basis used in conventional historical cost financial statements is
   a. Market value.
   b. Original cost
   c. Replacement cost.
   d. A mixture of costs and values.
   e. None of the above.
   (AICPA adapted)

PART B

15. What are the advantages and disadvantages of current replacement cost accounting in relation to general price level restatement?

16. What are two ways in which general price level restatements can be incorporated into current replacement cost accounting financial statements?

17. Why are holding gains and losses on nonmonetary assets in current replacement cost accounting defined in relation to the GPL?

18. How does the recognition of holding gains and losses on nonmonetary assets under CRC accounting affect the ability of an entity to "manipulate

its earnings" by selling selected assets which have increased or decreased in value?

19. *a.* Which companies are required by the SEC's *Accounting Series Release No. 190* (March 1976) to disclose current replacement cost data?
   b. Which replacement cost data must be disclosed?
   c. Are the replacement cost data substitutes for, or supplements to, the basic historical cost financial statements?
   d. In which document is current replacement cost data disclosed?

20. Name and briefly describe four recommended ways of estimating current replacement cost (based on the Appendix).

DECISION CASE 7–1

In this situation, restated price level statements, as supplements to the conventional cost basis statements are presented (inflation has been near double-digit rates). Knowing that you have accounting training, a friend, who owns common stock in several companies, drops their latest annual reports before you with a look that hovers between dismay and bewilderment.

Your friend begins, "I used to think that I understood a little about these reports, but now that the companies have all gone to this price level accounting, the only things clear to me are the nice pictures of company employees and products!" Upon your inquiry, it develops that the following points bother your friend most of all:

a. Most of the companies reported higher net income on their conventional cost basis statements than on their GPL statements, while at the same time the latter statements showed the assets to be larger in amount.
b. Some of the companies reported general purchasing power gains concurrent with operating gains; others reported general purchasing power losses concurrent with operating gains; yet all of the companies were subject to the same degree of inflation.
c. The comparative statements, prepared on a restated GPL basis, showed that even the amount of cash reported for last year had changed. Your friend wonders whether the companies discovered overages or shortages of cash or are somehow "juggling the figures."
d. Your friend realizes that the prices of most things are rising and wonders whether the increased val-

ues of certain assets on the restated GPL statements represent what the items are worth. At the same time, your friend noticed that some assets are carried at identical amounts on both sets of statements.

Required:

1. Explain the specifics that are confusing your friend in such a way that a sophisticated layperson (who is not an accountant) can understand them.
2. To cope with inflation (or deflation), aside from GPL statements, what alternative accounting techniques could be used? Describe them briefly and cite some of their pros and cons.
3. What is your assessment of the usefulness of GPL restated financial statements? Give reasons for your answer.

EXERCISES

PART A
Exercises 7–1 to 7–9

Note: Unless instructed otherwise, round all GPL conversion ratios to $\frac{1}{10}$ percent, e.g., 106.3% or 1.063.

Exercise 7–1

Select the best answer in each of the following. Items are independent of one another except where indicated to the contrary. Give the basis, including computations, for your choice.

The following information is applicable to Items 1 through 4:

Equipment purchased for $120,000 on January 1, 19A, when the price index was 100, was sold on December 31, 19C, at a price of $85,000. The equipment originally was expected to last six years with no residual value and was depreciated on a straight-line basis. The price index at the end of 19A was 125; 19B, 150; and 19C, 175.

1. GPL financial statements prepared at the end of 19A would include
   a. Equipment, $150,000; accumulated depreciation, $25,000; and a gain, $30,000.
   b. Equipment, $150,000; accumulated depreciation, $25,000; and no gain or loss.
   c. Equipment, $150,000; accumulated depreciation, $20,000; and a gain, $30,000.
   d. Equipment, $120,000; accumulated depreciation, $20,000; and a gain, $30,000.
   e. None of the above.
2. GPL comparative statements prepared at the end

of 19B would show the 19A financial statements' amount for equipment (net of accumulated depreciation) at
   a. $150,000.
   b. $125,000.
   c. $100,000.
   d. $80,000.
   e. None of the above.
3. GPL financial statements prepared at the end of 19B should include depreciation expense of
   a. $35,000.
   b. $30,000.
   c. $25,000.
   d. $20,000.
   e. None of the above.
4. The GPL income statement prepared at the end of 19C should include
   a. A gain of $35,000.
   b. A gain of $25,000.
   c. No gain or loss.
   d. A loss of $5,000.
   e. None of the above.
5. If land were purchased at a cost of $20,000 in January 19A when the GPL index was 120 and sold in December 19F when the index was 150, the selling price that would result in no economic gain or loss would be
   a. $30,000.
   b. $24,000.
   c. $20,000.
   d. $16,000.
   e. None of the above.
6. If land were purchased in 19A for $100,000 when the GPL index was 100 and sold at the end of 19G for $160,000 when the index was 170, the general price level statement of income for 19G would show
   a. A price level gain of $70,000 and a loss on sale of land of $10,000.
   b. A gain on sale of land of $60,000.
   c. A price level loss of $10,000.
   d. A loss on sale of land of $10,000.
   e. None of the above.
7. If the base year is 19A (when the GPL index = 100) and land is purchased for $50,000 in 19C when the general price index is 108.5, the cost of the land restated to 19A general purchasing power (rounded to the nearest whole dollar) would be
   a. $54,250.
   b. $50,000.
   c. $46,083.
   d. $45,750.
   e. None of the above.
8. Assume the same facts as in Item 7. The cost of the land restated to December 31, 19G, general pur-

chasing power when the GPL index was 119.2 (rounded to the nearest whole dollar) would be
   a. $59,600.
   b. $54,931.
   c. $46,083.
   d. $45,512.
   e. None of the above.

(AICPA adapted)

Exercise 7–2

Select the best answer in each of the following. Give the basis for your response.

1. In preparing price level financial statements, a nonmonetary item would be
   a. Accounts payable in cash.
   b. Long-term bonds payable.
   c. Accounts receivable.
   d. Allowance for doubtful accounts.
   e. None of the above.
2. In preparing GPL financial statements, monetary items consist of
   a. Cash items plus all receivables with a fixed maturity date.
   b. Cash, other assets expected to be converted into cash and current liabilities.
   c. Assets and liabilities whose amounts are fixed by contract or otherwise in terms of dollars, regardless of price level changes.
   d. Assets and liabilities classed as current on the balance sheet.
   e. None of the above.
3. An accountant who recommends the restatement of financial statements for GPL changes should not support this recommendation by stating that
   a. Purchasing power gains and losses should be recognized.
   b. Historical dollars are not comparable to present-day dollars.
   c. The conversion of asset costs to a common dollar basis is a useful extension of the original cost basis of asset valuation.
   d. Assets should be valued at their replacement cost.
4. When GPL balance sheets are prepared, they should be presented in terms of
   a. The general purchasing power of the dollar at the latest balance sheet date.
   b. The general purchasing power of the dollar in the base period.
   c. The average general purchasing power of the dollar for the latest fiscal period.
   d. The general purchasing power of the dollar at the time the financial statements are issued.
   e. None of the above.

5. During a period of deflation, an entity usually would have the greatest gain in general purchasing power by holding
   a. Cash.
   b. Plant and equipment.
   c. Accounts payable.
   d. Mortgages payable.
   e. None of the above.
6. The GPL restatement of historical dollar financial statements to reflect GPL changes reports assets at
   a. Lower cost or market.
   b. Current appraisal values.
   c. Costs adjusted for purchasing power changes.
   d. Current replacement cost.
   e. None of the above.
7. An unacceptable practice for reporting GPL information is
   a. The inclusion of general purchasing power gains and losses on monetary items in the price level income statement.
   b. The inclusion of extraordinary gains and losses in the GPL income statement.
   c. The use of charts, ratios, and narrative information.
   d. The use of specific price indices to restate inventories, plant, and equipment.
   e. None of the above.

(AICPA adapted)

Exercise 7–3

Doris Company is preparing financial statements on the purchasing power basis. Selected data are as follows:

1. Price index data:

   January 1, 19A 114
   December 31, 19A 120
   June 30, 19B 126
   December 31, 19D 168
   Average for 19E 174
   December 31, 19E 180

2. Property, plant, and equipment acquisition and depreciation data:
   a. Land acquired January 1, 19A, at a cost of $80,000.
   b. Building acquired December 31, 19A, at a cost of $120,000; by year-end, 19D and 19E, respectively, accumulated depreciation on the building amounted to $44,000 and $48,000.
   c. Equipment costing $168,000 was acquired June 30, 19B; by December 31, 19D, accumulated depreciation amounted to $109,200; depreciation recorded for 19E was $8,400.

   d. New equipment added during 19E at a time when the index was at an average value for the year cost $58,000; depreciation recorded on this new equipment for 19E amounted to $4,350.
3. Monetary items: At the start of 19E, total monetary assets amounted to $112,000 while total monetary liabilities amounted to $180,000. At the end of 19E, total monetary assets amounted to $120,000 while total monetary liabilities were $190,000.

Required:

Use the numbers below for identification and compute the amounts for each numbered item. Round conversion ratios to five decimal places.

A. On the GPL balance sheet as of December 31, 19E, carrying values for each would be
   1. Land.
   2. Building (gross amount).
   3. Accumulated depreciation—building.
   4. Original equipment (gross amount).
   5. New equipment (gross amount).
   6. Accumulated depreciation on equipment (original).
   7. Accumulated depreciation on equipment (new).
   8. Total monetary assets.
   9. Total monetary liabilities.
B. On the GPL income statement for the year ended December 31, 19E, amounts reported would be
   10. Depreciation expense (original equipment).
   11. Depreciation expense (new equipment).
   12. Depreciation expense (building).
   13. Sales (if sales of $310,000 were made evenly throughout 19E).
C. If, as of December 31, 19E, comparative balance sheets were being prepared on a GPL basis and the amounts related to the December 31, 19D, balance sheet were being restated, the amounts would be
   14. Land.
   15. Equipment (gross amount).
   16. Building (gross amount).
   17. Accumulated depreciation—building.
   18. Monetary assets.
   19. Monetary liabilities.

Exercise 7–4

Some items on conventional cost basis financial statements are expressed in current period dollars (or nearly so), while other items are normally expressed in dollars of prior periods.

Required:

1. Name the principal balance sheet items which likely would not be expressed in current period dollars. If any part of your answer depends on the accounting procedures employed, explain.
2. Name the principal items in the income statement which likely would not be expressed in current period dollars (or nearly so). If any part of your answer depends on the accounting procedures used, explain.
3. Name the principal items in the statement of changes in financial position which likely would not be expressed in current period dollars. If any part of your answer depends on the accounting procedures used, explain.

(AICPA adapted)

Exercise 7–5

T Company is completing its fifth year of operations (19E). Comparative balance sheets (historical cost basis) at year-end 19D and 19E are as follows:

	December 31	
	19D	*19E*
Cash and receivables	$250,000	$325,000
Inventories	187,500	162,500
Future plant site	62,500	62,500
Fixtures	210,000	270,000
Accumulated depreciation	(50,000)	(74,000)
	$660,000	$746,000
Current liabilities	$ 75,000	$137,500
Long-term liabilities	150,000	125,000
Capital stock	400,000	400,000
Retained earnings	35,000	83,500
	$660,000	$746,000

The income statement (historical cost basis) for the year ended December 31, 19E, follows.

Sales		$1,000,000
Cost of goods sold:		
Beginning inventory	$187,500	
Purchases	625,000	
Goods available	812,500	
Ending inventory	162,500	
Cost of goods sold		650,000
Gross margin		350,000
Expenses:		
Operating expenses except depreciation	120,000	
Depreciation	24,000	144,000
Income before taxes		206,000
Income taxes		87,500
Net income		$ 118,500

A dividend of $70,000 was paid at year-end. At midyear added fixtures costing $60,000 were bought. The annual rate of depreciation on fixtures is 10% of cost. Inventories are on a *Fifo* basis. When the original fixtures and the future plant site were acquired during the first year of operations, the relevant price index was at 126. Other price index data and conversion factors are as follows:

	Index	Conversion Factor %
December 31, 19E	163.8	100
December 31, 19D	150	109.2
Average for 19E	157.5	104

Assume the beginning inventory was acquired at 19D year-end prices. Purchases, sales, operating expenses, and income taxes occurred or accrued ratably throughout the year.

Required:

1. Prepare a GPL balance sheet as of December 31, 19E, and a GPL income statement for 19E. Determine the GPL (purchasing power) gain or loss and present a separate schedule detailing its computation.
2. Indicate the gross and net carrying values of the fixtures and of the future plant site for a GPL balance sheet as of December 31, 19D.

Exercise 7–6

The items reflected in the trial balance below were acquired when the relevant price index was 105.

Cash	$27,235	
Land	79,500	
Liability		$ 2,570
Capital stock		100,000
Retained earnings		4,165

The following transactions took place during the first quarter of the current fiscal year:

Date	Index	Data
Oct. 1	110	Purchased machinery costing $9,600 on account.
15	120	Paid for machinery purchased on October 1.
31	135	Billed customers for services rendered, $8,000.
Nov. 15	140	Paid $1,230 of the initial liability balance.
30	145	Collected half of the billed revenue.
Dec. 10	150	Paid general expense of $5,700.
31	160	Recorded three months' depreciation on machinery, which has a five-year life with no scrap value.

Required:

1. Enter the initial balances, and then record the transactions for the first quarter directly into ledger accounts; also include, in parentheses, the GPL index number prevailing when each transaction occurred.
2. As of the close of the quarter, prepare both balance sheets and income statements on both conventional cost basis and price level basis using the general index number procedures illustrated in the chapter. Show calculation of the GPL (purchasing power) gain or loss. Since no average index value for the period is given, it will be necessary to apply to each transaction, a specific conversion factor or fraction. For example, if a $360 transaction occurred when the index was 120, in December 31 terms, this would convert to $360 × 160/120 = $480. Round all calculations to the nearest dollar.
3. Prove the correctness of ending GPL owners' equity.

Exercise 7–7

An investor bought land for $90,000 in 19A when the index measuring general purchasing power of the dollar was 110. Assuming a gain on sale of the land is taxable at a capital gains rate of 25%, at what price would the land have to be sold on each of the following dates for the investor to maintain the equivalent purchasing power after taxes? In each instance the index number on the date of sale was as follows:

Date of sale		Index
a.	October 1, 19B	121
b.	May 1, 19C	129
c.	July 1, 19D	143
d.	December 1, 19E	154

Round answers to nearest dollar.

Exercise 7–8

Marx Corporation is completing its fifth year of operations (19E). Comparative balance sheets on a historical cost basis prepared at the end of 19D and 19E were as follows:

	December 31	
	19D	*19E*
Cash	$ (4,400)	$ 2,500
Accounts receivable	13,000	15,000
Inventory	18,000	20,000
Furniture and fixtures	6,000	8,000
Accumulated depreciation	(2,200)	(3,000)
	$30,400	$42,500

Accounts payable	$ 4,400	$ 7,000
Capital stock	20,000	20,000
Retained earnings	6,000	15,500
	$30,400	$42,500

The income statement for 19E on a historical cost basis was as below:

Sales		$82,000
Cost of goods sold:		
Beginning inventory	$18,000	
Purchases	43,600	
Goods available	61,600	
Ending inventory	20,000	41,600
Gross margin		40,400
Expenses:		
Depreciation	800	
Salaries	16,000	
Other (including taxes)	10,100	26,900
Net income		13,500
Dividends		4,000
Transferred to retained earnings		$ 9,500

Half of the dividends were paid at midyear, the other half at year-end. Additional fixtures were acquired at the start of the year. Fixtures are depreciated on the assumptions of a ten-year life, and zero residual value under the straight-line method. Expenses were paid uniformly during the year. Purchases and sales occurred uniformly during the year. The ending inventory is assumed to be acquired at year-end prices; the beginning inventory was acquired at year-end prices of the prior year.

When the original fixtures, costing $6,000, were bought May 1, 19A, the price index was at 112. Other price index data are as follows:

	Index
December 31, 19E	154
December 31, 19D	140
Average for 19E and midyear value	146.67

Required:

1. Prepare comparative GPL restated statements as of December 31, 19E, and December 31, 19D, using the statements given and the index number data. Determine the GPL gain or loss and present a separate schedule detailing its computation.
2. Prove the correctness of your GPL statements and computations and present the proof in a separate schedule.

Exercise 7–9

1. The valuation basis used in conventional HC financial statements is

a. Market value.
b. Original cost.
c. Replacement cost.
d. A mixture of costs and values.
e. None of the above.

2. When preparing general price level financial statements, it would not be appropriate to use
   a. Cost or market, whichever is lower, in the valuation of inventories.
   b. Replacement cost in the valuation of plant assets.
   c. The historical cost basis in reporting income tax expense.
   d. The actual amounts payable in reporting liabilities on the balance sheet.
   e. Any of the above.

3. For comparison purposes, general price level financial statements of earlier periods should be restated to the general purchasing power dollars of
   a. The beginning of the base period.
   b. An average for the current period.
   c. The beginning of the current period.
   d. The end of the current period.
   e. None of the above.

4. Gains and losses on nonmonetary assets usually are reported in historical dollar financial statements when the items are sold. Gains and losses on the sale of nonmonetary assets should be reported in general price level financial statements
   a. In the same period, but the amount will probably differ.
   b. In the same period and the same amount.
   c. Over the life of the nonmonetary asset.
   d. Partly over the life of the nonmonetary asset and the remainder when the asset is sold.
   e. None of the above.

5. A practice for presenting general price level restated information which is not acceptable is the
   a. Use of charts, ratios, and narrative information.
   b. Use of specific price indices to restate inventories, plant, and equipment.
   c. Inclusion of general price level gains and losses on monetary items in the general price level adjusted statement of income.
   d. Inclusion of extraordinary gains and losses in the general price level adjusted statement of income.

6. For purposes of restating financial statements for changes in the general level of prices, monetary items consist of
   a. Assets and liabilities whose amounts are fixed by contract or otherwise in terms of dollars regardless of price level changes.
   b. Assets and liabilities which are classified as current on the balance sheet.
   c. Cash items plus all receivables with a fixed maturity date.
   d. Cash, other assets expected to be converted into cash, and current liabilities.

7. Following are four observations regarding the amounts reported in financial statements that have been restated for general price level changes. Which observation is valid?
   a. The amount obtained by restating an asset's cost for general price level changes usually approximates its current market value.
   b. The amounts restated for general price level changes are not departures from historical cost.
   c. When inventory increases and prices are rising, last-in, first-out (Lifo) inventory accounting has the same effect on financial statements as amounts restated for general price level changes.
   d. When inventory remains constant and prices are rising, Lifo inventory accounting has the same effect on financial statements as amounts restated for general price level changes.

Items 8, 9, and 10 are based on the following information:

The following schedule lists the general price level index at the end of each of the five indicated years:

197A	100
197B	110
197C	115
197D	120
197E	140

8. In December 197D, the Meetu Corporation purchased land for $300,000. The land was held until December 197E, when it was sold for $400,000. The general price level statement of income for the year ended December 31, 197E, should include how much gain or loss on this sale?
   a. $20,000 loss.
   b. $20,000 general price level loss.
   c. $50,000 gain.
   d. $100,000 gain.

9. On January 1, 197B, the Silver Company purchased equipment for $300,000. The equipment was being depreciated over an estimated life of ten years on the straight-line method, with no estimated residual value. On December 31, 197E, the equipment was sold for $200,000. The general price level statement of income prepared for the year ended December 31, 197E, should include how much gain or loss from this sale?

a. $10,600 loss.
b. $16,000 gain.
c. $20,000 gain.
d. $52,000 loss.

10. An analysis of the Gallant Corporation's "Machinery and Equipment" account as of December 31, 197E, follows:

Machinery and equipment:

Acquired in December 197B	$400,000
Acquired in December 197D	100,000
Balance	$500,000

Accumulated Depreciation:

On equipment acquired in December 197B	$160,000
On equipment acquired in December 197D	20,000
Balance	$180,000

A general price level balance sheet prepared as of December 31, 197E, should include machinery and equipment net of accumulated depreciation of

a. $284,848.
b. $360,000.
c. $398,788.
d. $448,000.

(AICPA adapted)

PART B
Exercises 7–10 to 7–15

Exercise 7–10

The controller of the Robinson Company is discussing a comment you made in the course of presenting your audit report.

". . . and frankly," L. Fisher continued, "I agree that we, too, are responsible for finding ways to produce more relevant financial statements which are as reliable as the ones we now produce.

"For example, suppose the company acquired a finished item for inventory for $40 when the general price level index was 110. And, later, the item was sold for $75 when the general price level index was 121 and the current replacement cost was $54. We could calculate a 'holding gain.' "

Required:

1. Explain to what extent and how current values already are used *within* generally accepted accounting principles to value inventories.
2. Calculate in good form the amount of the holding gain in Fisher's example.
3. Why is the use of current replacement cost for *both*

inventories and cost of goods sold preferred by some accounting authorities to the generally accepted use of *Fifo* or *Lifo?*

(AICPA adapted)

Exercise 7–11

X Trucking Company transfers freight from its home office in Cleveland, Tennessee, to cities throughout the United States. Thus, it is a service-oriented enterprise and has no merchandise inventory. On January 1, 19A, the historical cost balance sheet of X Trucking Company was as follows:

X TRUCKING COMPANY
Balance Sheet
January 1, 19A

Assets

Cash and receivables	$12,000
Trucks	80,000
Accumulated depreciation	(–0–)
	$92,000

Liabilities and Owners' Equity

Current liabilities	$10,000
Long-term liabilities	30,000
Owners' equity	52,000
	$92,000

Assume for simplicity that all revenues and all expenses occur at year-end. The trucks are new on January 1, 19A, are expected to remain in service for five years, and will be depreciated on a straight-line basis with no estimated residual value. GPL indexes were 100 at January 1, 19A, and 108 at December 31, 19A. Current replacement cost of the trucks at December 31, 19A, was $88,000.

Historical cost transactions for 19A include the following:

1. Payment of the $10,000 beginning balance of current liabilities.
2. Service revenue of $100,000, of which $70,000 is collected in cash.
3. Depreciation of $16,000.
4. Other expenses of $75,000, of which $35,000 is unpaid at December 31, 19A. The $35,000 of liabilities are "current."

Required:

1. Prepare the historical cost journal entries to record the above transactions.
2. Prepare the historical cost balance sheet at December 31, 19A, and the historical cost income statement for the year then ended.
3. Prepare the current replacement cost journal entries for 19A.

Exercise 7–12

Refer to the basic facts of Exercise 7–11.

Required:

1. Prepare the current replacement cost balance sheet of X Trucking Company at December 31, 19A.
2. Prepare the CRC income statement of X Trucking Company for the year ended December 31, 19A.
3. Prove the correctness of CRC owners' equity at December 31, 19A.

Exercise 7–13

Refer to Exercise 7–11. The only change in the data is that the replacement cost of trucks is $85,000 instead of $88,000 on December 31, 19A.

Required:

1. Prepare the 19A current replacement cost journal entries of X Trucking Company.
2. Prepare the CRC balance sheet of X Trucking Company at December 31, 19A, in comparative form with the CRC balance sheet on January 1, 19A. For this requirement assume that the January 1, 19A, historical cost balance sheet approximates current replacement cost on that date.
3. Prove the correctness of CRC owners' equity at December 31, 19A. That is, compute CRC income and reconcile beginning and ending CRC owners' equity.
4. Describe the procedure that would be used to restate the CRC income statement for the year preceding 19A on a basis comparable with the CRC income statement for 19A.

Exercise 7–14 (based on the Appendix)

Note: Exercise 7–14 contains questions over material which is only indirectly covered in the chapter.

Raft Builders International purchased all of the shares of P Corporation (it will be a subsidiary) on January 1, 19A, at a cost of $100,000. P Corporation had cash and receivables of $10,000, finished goods inventory $50,000, building $25,000 with accumulated depreciation $10,000, land $10,000, and goodwill $15,000. The purchased company had no liabilities at the time of the acquisition, and the GPL index was 109.

It is now December 31, 19A, and the GPL index is 119.9. The December 31, 19A, balance sheet data of the purchased company are as follows, with historical cost and current replacement cost data in comparative form:

P CORPORATION
Balance Sheet—HC and CRC
December 31, 19A

	Historical Cost	Current Replacement Cost
Cash and receivables	$ 15,000	$ 15,000
Finished goods inventory	65,000	75,000
Building	25,000	30,000
Accumulated depreciation—building	(11,000)	(13,200)
Land	10,000	30,000
Total Assets	$104,000	$136,800
Liabilities	$ 25,000	$ 25,000
Owners' equity	79,000	111,800
Total Equities	$104,000	$136,800

Required:

1. The $15,000 of purchased goodwill would be reflected by Raft Builders because they paid for it. If the current replacement cost (CRC) of the goodwill could be estimated, would Raft Builders report the CRC of the goodwill under the CRC disclosure rules of *ASR No. 190?* Assume that the above balance sheet was prepared by the subsidiary to satisfy the CRC disclosure rules of *ASR No. 190* of the SEC.
2. Which item on the balance sheet is reported incorrectly? Why?
3. Does the fact that CRC data are presented for the building mean that the building will be specifically replaced?
4. Which inventory method might P Corporation have used to estimate the CRC of ending inventory? How does this method approximate CRC of ending inventory?

Exercise 7–15

Osgood Bosworth, Inc., is a manufacturing company with a significant investment in machinery and equipment. In recent years historical cost income has increased dramatically as company products have found increasing consumer acceptance. Bosworth has paid dividends equal to 70% of historical cost income for the past ten years. Therefore, as income has increased, dividends have risen; and as a result shareholders are delighted with their investment in Bosworth. Until the last two years, inflation was a relatively low 2–4% per year. However, during each of the past two years, the general price index rose by 10%. Two years from now, Bosworth machinery will be ten years old and fully depreciated; as a result it will be replaced at an estimated cost of 300% of the cost (not depreciated cost) of its existing machinery and equipment. Replacement costs are expected to rise by 15% during each of the next two years. Income (historical cost basis) and straight-line depreciation (also on a historical cost basis) for the year just ended (today is December 31, end of the current fiscal year) were $100,000 and $120,000, respectively.

Required:

Ignoring inventories, income taxes, and the purchasing power effect on the monetary items of Bosworth, prepare a schedule to reveal to Bosworth management the extent, if any, to which dividends for the current year represent a return of permanent capital rather than a distribution of earnings. Assume that CRC operating income (i.e., distributable income) is the appropriate measure of "true" income.

PROBLEMS

Note: Unless directed otherwise, round all GPL and CRC conversion ratios to $\frac{1}{10}$ percent, e.g., 106.3% or 1.063.

PART A
Problems 7–1 to 7–10

Problem 7–1

Clara Company is preparing financial statements on a GPL basis. Selected data are as follows:
1. GPL index numbers:

Date	Index
January 1, 19A	90
December 31, 19A	95
June 30, 19B	100
December 31, 19B	106
December 31, 19D	145
Average for 19E	150
December 31, 19E	155

2. From historical cost statements—property, plant, and equipment acquisition and depreciation data:
  a. Land acquired January 1, 19A, at a cost of $45,000.
  b. Building acquired December 31, 19A, at a cost of $380,000; by year-end 19D and 19E, respectively, Accumulated Depreciation—Building account reflected balances of $22,800 and $30,400.
  c. Fixtures costing $77,000 were acquired June 30, 19B; on these accumulated depreciation re-

corded by year-end 19D and 19E amounted to $19,250 and $26,950.
  d. Additional fixtures were bought in midyear 19E for $30,000 when the index was 150; by year-end depreciation recorded on the newest fixtures amounted to $2,250.
3. Monetary assets: At the start of 19E, total monetary assets were $87,000 and total monetary liabilities were $31,900. At the end of 19E, total monetary assets were $96,400 and total monetary liabilities were $33,800.

Required:

Use the numbers given below for identification and compute the amounts that would appear on GPL financial statements. Round conversion ratios to five decimal places.
A. On the GPL balance sheet as of December 31, 19E, the carrying values would be
  1. Land.
  2. Building (gross amount).
  3. Old fixtures (gross amount).
  4. New fixtures (gross amount).
  5. Accumulated depreciation—building.
  6. Accumulated depreciation—old fixtures.
  7. Accumulated depreciation—new fixtures.
  8. Total monetary assets.
  9. Total monetary liabilities.
B. On the GPL income statement for the year ended December 31, 19E, amounts reported would be
  10. Depreciation expense (building).
  11. Depreciation expense (new fixtures).
  12. Depreciation expense (old fixtures).
  13. Purchases (assume purchases of $285,000 were made evenly throughout 19E).
  14. GPL gain or loss (based solely on starting and ending monetary items).
C. If, as of December 31, 19E, comparative balance sheets were being prepared on a GPL basis and amounts related to the December 31, 19D, balance sheet were being restated, the restated amounts would be
  15. Land.
  16. Fixtures (gross amount).
  17. Monetary assets.
  18. Monetary liabilities.
  19. Building (gross amount).
  20. Accumulated depreciation—fixtures.

Problem 7–2

Barden Corporation, a manufacturer with large investments in plant and equipment, began operations in 1940. The company's history has been one of expansion in sales, production, and physical facilities. Recently, some concern has been expressed that the conventional historical cost financial statements do not provide sufficient information for decisions by investors. After consideration of proposals for various types of supplementary financial statements to be included in the 1979 annual report, management has decided to present a balance sheet as of December 31, 1979, and a statement of income and retained earnings for 1979, both restated for changes in the general price level.

Required:

1. On what basis can it be contended that Barden's conventional statements should be restated for changes in the general price level?
2. Distinguish between financial statements restated for general price level changes and current market value financial statements.
3. Distinguish between monetary and nonmonetary assets and liabilities as the terms are used in general price level restatement. Give examples of each.
4. Outline the procedures Barden should follow in preparing the proposed supplementary statements.
5. Indicate the major similarities and differences between the proposed supplementary statements and the corresponding conventional historical cost statements.
6. Assuming that in the future Barden will want to present comparative supplementary statements, can the 1979 supplementary statements be presented in 1980 without adjustment? Explain.

(AICPA adapted)

Problem 7–3

CTZ Company prepared the following comparative balance sheets (historical cost basis) at the close of its fourth year of operations (19D):

	December 31	
	19C	19D
Cash	$ 30,000	$ 41,400
Receivables	74,000	99,000
Inventory	25,000	39,000
Land	100,000	100,000
Building	320,000	320,000
Accumulated depreciation—building	(38,400)	(51,200)
Fixtures	90,000	120,000
Accumulated depreciation—fixtures	(40,500)	(58,500)
Total	$560,100	$609,700

Current liabilities	$ 55,000	$ 80,000
Bonds payable	45,000	45,000
Common stock	250,000	250,000
Retained earnings	210,100	234,700
Total	$560,100	$609,700

The income statement (historical cost basis) for 19D was as follows:

Sales		$950,000
Cost of goods sold:		
Beginning inventory	$ 25,000	
Purchases	584,000	
Goods available	609,000	
Ending inventory	39,000	
Cost of goods sold		570,000
Gross margin		380,000
Expenses:		
Operating expenses	125,000	
Depreciation—building	12,800	
Depreciation—fixtures	18,000	
Salaries	100,000	255,800
Income before taxes		124,200
Income tax		49,600
Net Income		$ 74,600

A $50,000 dividend was paid at year-end. Fixtures costing $30,000 were bought on January 2, 19D. Fixtures are depreciated 15% per annum on cost. Inventories are on a *Fifo* basis; assume the ending inventory was acquired at the average level of prices prevailing during 19D. When the land, buildings, and original fixtures were acquired, the GPL was 112.5. Other price index data are as follows:

	GPL Index	Conversion Factor %
December 31, 19D	135	100
December 31, 19C	125	108
Average for 19D	129.8	104

The beginning inventory was acquired at 19C year-end prices. Purchases, sales, operating expenses (which include interest), salaries, and income taxes accrued evenly throughout 19D. The building is depreciated over a 25-year life; no residual value, straight-line basis.

Required (round amounts to nearest dollar):

1. Prepare a price level balance sheet as of December 31, 19D, and a price level income statement for 19D; show computation of the GPL gain or loss for the year.
2. Indicate the gross and net carrying values of land, fixtures, and building for a GPL balance sheet as of December 31, 19C.

Problem 7–4

Eugenia Company prepared the following comparative balance sheets (historical cost basis) at the close of its tenth year of operations (19J):

	December 31	
	19I	*19J*
Cash	$ 75,000	$101,000
Receivables	215,000	195,000
Inventory	135,000	127,000
Land	150,000	150,000
Building	240,000	240,000
Accumulated depreciation—		
building	(56,000)	(64,000)
Machinery	225,000	280,000
Accumulated depreciation—		
machinery	(115,000)	(137,500)
Total	$869,000	$891,500
Current liabilities	$124,000	$137,000
Long-term liabilities	75,000	81,000
Bonds payable	60,000	60,000
Common stock	350,000	350,000
Retained earnings	260,000	263,500
Total	$869,000	$891,500

The land was bought in 19A when the GPL index was 104. The building was acquired early in 19C when the GPL index was 107; it has an estimated 30-year life and no residual value and is depreciated on a straight-line basis. Machinery is depreciated 10% per annum on cost with no residual value. The first machine was bought in 19B when the GPL index was 106 at a cost of $50,000; a second machine was acquired for $100,000 in 19D when the index was 108.5; a third machine was bought in 19H when the index was 117. A full year's depreciation is taken in the year of acquisition unless the purchase is at year-end. At year-end 19J machinery costing $55,000 was acquired.

On January 2, 19J, an $85,000 dividend was declared and paid. Assume the beginning inventory was acquired when the GPL index was 107; the ending inventory should be converted on the assumption the index was 125 when it was bought.

Sales, operating expenses, income taxes, and purchases occurred ratably during 19J. Relevant GPL index data (aside from that already given) are as follows:

	GPL Index
December 31, 19J	127
December 31, 19I	121
Average for 19J	125

The income statement (historical cost basis) for the year 19J was as follows:

Sales		$1,275,000
Cost of goods sold:		
Inventory, January 1	$135,000	
Purchases	850,000	
Goods available	985,000	
Inventory, December 31	127,000	
Cost of goods sold		858,000
Gross margin		417,000
Expenses:		
Operating expenses	210,000	
Depreciation, building	8,000	
Depreciation, machinery	22,500	240,500
Income before taxes		176,500
Income tax		88,000
Net Income		$ 88,500

Required (round amounts to nearest dollar):

1. Prepare an income statement for 19J and a balance sheet as of December 31, 19J, on a GPL restated basis. Show computations of the general purchasing power gain or loss.
2. Prove the correctness of ending price level restated owners' equity at December 31, 19J.

Problem 7–5

When items in the following trial balance were acquired, the GPL index was 150.

Cash	$ 7,500	
Equipment	10,000	
Accumulated depreciation		$2,000
Liability		1,900
Capital stock		8,000
Retained earnings		5,600

Transactions during the first half of the current fiscal year follow. GPL index values prevailing at the time are indicated parenthetically.

Jan. 10 A payment of $800 on the liability balance is made (160).
Feb. 15 Revenue for services is billed to customers, $2,500 (175).
Mar. 1 Four fifths of the revenue billed is collected (180).
Apr. 20 Land is purchased for $8,000 cash (190).
May 5 General expenses are paid, $500 (185).
June 30 Recorded six months' depreciation on the equipment which has a ten-year life and no residual value (200).

The index at June 30 was 200.

Required:

1. Enter the initial balances, then record the six months' transactions directly in ledger accounts;

also enter the date and the GPL index number parenthetically.

2. At the close of the six-month period, prepare both conventional and price level balance sheets and income statements using general index number procedures illustrated in the chapter. Calculate the general purchasing power gain or loss. Since no average for the six-month period is given, it will be necessary to apply, to each transaction and balance, a specific conversion factor. For example, if a $660 transaction occurred when the price index was 165, in June 30 terms (when the index was 200), the restatement would be calculated as $660 × 200/165 = $800. Round all calculations to nearest dollar.

Problem 7–6

Published financial statements of United States companies are currently prepared on a stable dollar assumption even though the general purchasing power of the dollar has declined considerably because of inflation in recent years. To account for this changing value of the dollar, many accountants suggest that financial statements should be restated for general price level changes. Three independent, unrelated statements regarding general price level restated financial statements follow. Each statement contains some fallacious reasoning.

Statement I:

The accounting profession has not seriously considered price level restated financial statements before because the rate of inflation usually has been so small from year to year that the restatements would have been immaterial in amount. Price level restated financial statements represent a departure from the historical cost basis of accounting. Financial statements should be prepared from facts, not estimates.

Statement II:

If financial statements were restated for general price level changes, depreciation charges in the earnings statement would permit the recovery of dollars of current purchasing power and thereby equal the cost of new assets to replace the old ones. General price level restated data would yield statements of financial position amounts closely approximating current values. Furthermore, management can make better decisions if general price level restated financial statements are published.

Statement III:

When restating financial data for general price level changes, a distinction must be made between monetary and nonmonetary assets and liabilities, which, under the historical cost basis of accounting, have been identified as "current" and "noncurrent." When using the historical cost basis of accounting, no purchasing power gain or loss is recognized in the accounting process, but when financial statements are restated for general price level changes, a purchasing power gain or loss will be recognized on monetary and nonmonetary items.

Required:

Evaluate each of the independent statements and identify the areas of fallacious reasoning in each and explain why the reasoning is incorrect. Complete your discussion of each statement before proceeding to the next statement.

(AICPA adapted)

Problem 7–7

Novo Company's balance sheets (historical cost basis) at December 31, 19B, and 19C were as follows:

	December 31	
	19B	*19C*
Cash	$ 8,000	$ 7,600
Accounts receivable	19,000	31,000
Inventory	20,000	18,000
Equipment	21,000	29,400
Accumulated depreciation	(11,000)	(17,400)
	$57,000	$68,600
Accounts payable	$24,000	$29,000
Capital stock	25,000	30,000
Retained earnings	8,000	9,600
	$57,000	$68,600

The income statement (historical cost basis) for the year ended December 31, 19C, was as follows:

Sales		$80,000
Beginning inventory	$20,000	
Purchases	42,000	
Goods available	62,000	
Ending inventory	18,000	
Cost of goods sold		44,000
Gross margin		36,000
Expenses:		
Salaries	15,000	
Other (including income tax)	9,000	
Depreciation	6,400	30,400
Net Income		$ 5,600

Original equipment was acquired January 1, 19A, and was not augmented until January 1, 19C. Equipment is being depreciated over a six-year life by the sum-of-the-years' digits method with an assumed zero residual value. When the first equipment was acquired, the GPL index was at 96.

The company uses the *Lifo* inventory method; the beginning inventory for 19C is below the level at which the company began operations January 1, 19A. Salaries and other expenses were incurred evenly over the year, and purchases and sales occurred evenly over the year. The additional capital stock was sold on June 30, 19C. Dividends were paid at midyear and year-end in equal amounts of $2,000 per payment.

GPL price index data are as follows:

	GPL Index
December 31, 19B	120
Midyear 19C and average	126
December 31, 19C	132

Required:

1. Using the conventional statements and the index data given, prepare a comparative GPL restated balance sheet and 19C income statement. Determine the GPL purchasing power gain or loss for 19C and present a separate schedule detailing its computation.
2. Prove the correctness of the GPL restated statements and present the proof in a separate schedule.

Problem 7–8

Select the best answer in each of the following. Justify your choices.

1. The Chalk Company reported sales of $2,000,000 in 19B and $3,000,000 in 19C made evenly throughout each year. The general price level index during 19A remained constant at 100, and at the end of 19B and 19C it was 102 and 104, respectively. What should Chalk report as sales for 19C, restated for general price level changes?
   a. $3,000,000.
   b. $3,029,126.
   c. $3,058,821.
   d. $3,120,000.
2. On January 2, 19C, the Mannix Corporation mortgaged one of its properties as collateral for a $1,000,000, 7%, five-year loan. During 19C, the general price level increased evenly, resulting in a 5% rise for the year.

   In preparing a balance sheet expressing financial position in terms of the general price level at the end of 19C, at what amount should Mannix report its mortgage note payable?

   a. $950,000.
   b. $1,000,000.
   c. $1,025,000.
   d. $1,050,000.

3. A company was formed on January 1, 19B. Selected balances from the historical dollar balance sheet at December 31, 19B, were as follows:

Accounts receivable	$ 70,000
Accounts payable	60,000
Long-term debt	110,000
Common stock	100,000

   At what amounts should these selected accounts be shown in a general price level balance sheet at December 31, 19B, if the general price level index was 100 at December 31, 19A, and 110 at December 31, 19B?

	Accounts Receivable	Accounts Payable	Long-term Debt	Common stock
a.	$70,000	$60,000	$110,000	$100,000
b.	70,000	60,000	110,000	110,000
c.	70,000	60,000	121,000	110,000
d.	77,000	66,000	121,000	110,000

4. The historical dollar balance sheet of the Rhuda Company showed the original cost of depreciable assets as $5,000,000 at December 31, 19A, and $6,000,000 at December 31, 19B. These assets' costs are being depreciated on a straight-line basis over a ten-year period with no residual value. Acquisitions of $1,000,000 were made on January 1, 19B. A full year's depreciation was taken in the year of acquisition.

   Rhuda presents general price level financial statements as supplemental information to their historical dollar financial statements. The December 31, 19A depreciable assets balance (before accumulated depreciation) restated to reflect December 31, 19B, purchasing power was $5,800,000. What amount of depreciation expense should be shown in the general price level income statement for 19B if the general price level index was 100 at December 31, 19A, and 110 at December 31, 19B?
   a. $600,000.
   b. $660,000.
   c. $670,000.
   d. $690,000.

5. If a constant unit of measure during a period of inflation is used, the general purchasing power of the dollar in which some expenses are measured (for assets systematically allocated among several accounting periods) may differ significantly from the general purchasing power of the dollar in which revenue is measured. Which of the following accounting procedures minimizes this effect?

a. Allowance method of accounting for bad debts.
b. Income tax allocation.
c. Accelerated depreciation.
d. Valuing inventory at the lower of cost or market.

6. Replacement cost can be determined by all but which of the following?
   a. Entry values.
   b. Input values.
   c. A general index such as the GNP Deflator.
   d. Expected discounted cash flow to be derived from the item being valued.

7. Land was purchased for $20,000 when an appropriate price index was at 115. When the index was at 138, the land was sold for $25,000. Ignoring taxes on the transaction, the landowner, for having bought and sold the land, is economically
   a. Worse off.
   b. Better off.
   c. In the same position.

   (AICPA adapted except for 6 and 7)

Problem 7–9

Skadden, Inc., a retailer, was organized during 19A. Skadden's management has decided to supplement its December 31, 19D, historical dollar financial statements with general price level financial statements. The following trial balance (historical dollars) and additional information have been furnished:

SKADDEN, INC.
Trial Balance
December 31, 19D

	Debit	Credit
Cash and receivables (net)	$ 540,000	
Short-term investments (common stock)	400,000	
Inventory	440,000	
Equipment	650,000	
Accumulated depreciation—equipment		$ 164,000
Accounts payable		300,000
6% first-mortgage bonds, due 19V		500,000
Common stock, $10 par		1,000,000
Retained earnings, December 31, 19C	46,000	
Sales		1,900,000
Cost of goods sold	1,508,000	
Depreciation	65,000	
Other operating expenses and interest	215,000	
	$3,864,000	$3,864,000

a. Monetary assets (cash and receivables) exceeded monetary liabilities (accounts payable and bonds payable) by $445,000 at December 31, 19C.
b. Purchases ($1,840,000 in 19D) and sales are made uniformly throughout the year.
c. Depreciation is computed on a straight-line basis, with a full year's depreciation being taken in the year of acquisition and none in the year of retirement. The depreciation rate is 10%, and no residual value is anticipated. Acquisitions and retirements have been made fairly evenly over each year, and the retirements in 19D consisted of assets purchased during 19B which were scrapped. An analysis of the equipment account reveals the following:

Year	Beginning Balance	Additions	Retirements	Ending Balance
19B	—	$550,000	—	$550,000
19C	$550,000	10,000	—	560,000
19D	560,000	150,000	$60,000	650,000

d. The bonds were issued in 19B, and the short-term investment shares of common stock were purchased fairly evenly over 19D. Other operating expenses and interest are assumed to be incurred evenly throughout the year.
e. Assume that Gross National Product Implicit Price Deflators (1958 = 100) were as follows:

Annual Averages	Index	Quarterly Averages	Index
19A	113.9	19C, 4th	123.5
19B	116.8	19D, 1st	124.9
19C	121.8	2d	126.1
19D	126.7	3d	127.3
		4th	128.5

Required:

1. Prepare a schedule to convert the Equipment account balance at December 31, 19D, from historical cost to GPL restated dollars.
2. Prepare a schedule to analyze in historical dollars the Equipment—Accumulated Depreciation account for the year 19D.
3. Prepare a schedule to analyze in general price level dollars the Equipment—Accumulated Depreciation account for the year 19D.
4. Prepare a schedule to compute Skadden's general price level gain or loss on its net holdings of monetary assets for 19D (ignore income tax implications). The schedule should give consideration to appropriate items on or related to the balance sheet and the income statement.

(AICPA adapted)

Problem 7-10

For questions 1-4 below, use the following general price level data:

Date	GPL Index
12/31/19A	165
3/31/19B	171
6/30/19B	175
9/30/19B	180
12/31/19B	186
3/31/19C	190
6/30/19C	194
9/30/19C	198
12/31/19C	201

1. On January 1, 19B, P Corporation had as its only asset $7,000 in cash (no liabilities). On March 31, 19B, P Corporation paid $5,000 for a machine which will have a ten-year life and no residual value. On September 30, 19B, P Corporation purchased merchandise inventory on account for $1,000. At an even rate during the three months ended December 31, 19B, P Corporation paid off the $1,000 on the inventory and sold half the inventory for $650 cash. If these are the only transactions P Corporation entered into during 19B, the company will report for 19B a purchasing power gain or loss on monetary items of
   a. Loss of $365.
   b. Loss of $426.
   c. Gain of $365.
   d. Gain of $429.
2. On its December 31, 19B, GPL balance sheet, P Corporation will report cash of
   a. $1,650.
   b. $2,080.
   c. $1,285.
   d. $2,904.
3. Assume that P Corporation's January 1, 19B, owners' equity consisted of capital stock of $7,000. On its GPL income statement for the year ended December 31, 19B, P Corporation will report net income (loss)—*ignoring the purchasing power gain or loss on monetary items*—of
   a. $(276).
   b. $(264).
   c. $(255).
   d. $253.
4. You are in the process of preparing the 19C, GPL financial statements (assume that you have been given the necessary transaction data involving revenues and expenses for 19C). In particular, you are now "rolling forward" the January 1, 19C, historical cost balance sheet in order to obtain the January 1, 19C, GPL owners' equity balance stated in terms of December 31, 19C, dollars—as a test on the accuracy of your other GPL restatements. Assuming that the beginning cash balance arose on the beginning date, the correct January 1, 19C, owners' equity stated in December 31, 19C, dollars would be
   a. $7,197.
   b. $7,322.
   c. $7,777.
   d. $7,975.
   e. None of the above.
5. Which of the following items is a nonmonetary item?
   a. Marketable securities—bonds to be held to maturity.
   b. Accounts receivable.
   c. Accounts payable.
   d. Preferred equity stated at liquidation value.
   e. Unearned revenue.
6. Under GPL restatement, purchasing power gains are earned during inflation on
   a. Net monetary assets.
   b. Net monetary liabilities.
   c. Nonmonetary assets.
   d. Nonmonetary liabilities.

PROBLEMS

PART B
Problems 7-11 to 7-13

Note: Problem 7-11 contains questions over theoretical material which is only indirectly covered in the chapter.

Problem 7-11

Part A

In this chapter "real" holding gains and losses on nonmonetary assets are presented as elements of income (i.e., on the income statement). This issue has not been resolved, and many accountants favor reporting holding gains and losses as a direct element of owners' equity, thereby bypassing the income statement.

Required:

List and discuss arguments for reporting holding gains and losses on nonmonetary assets on the income statement versus reporting holding gains and losses as separate elements of owners' equity on the balance sheet. List and discuss arguments for reporting holding gains and losses on nonmonetary assets as separate elements of owners' equity on the balance sheet.

Part B

In this chapter, year-end replacement cost data were used throughout for revenues and expenses. On the other hand, the SEC requires companies to report average annual CRC data for depreciation and cost of goods sold.

Required:

List and discuss arguments for using average replacement cost data for expenses versus using year-end replacement cost data for expenses. List and discuss arguments for using year-end replacement cost data for expenses.

Problem 7–12

IMB Corporation presents two-year comparative historical cost financial statements in its annual report. The historical cost statements for 19B and 19C were as follows:

IMB CORPORATION
Income Statements
Years Ended December 31, 19B and 19C

	19B	19C
Service revenue	$100,000	$108,000
Expenses:		
Depreciation	(18,000)	(18,000)
Other	(72,000)	(78,000)
Income	$ 10,000	$ 12,000

IMB CORPORATION
Balance Sheets
December 31, 19B and 19C

	19B	19C
Cash	$ 65,000	$ 95,000
Operational assets	108,000	108,000
Accumulated depreciation	(18,000)	(36,000)
	$155,000	$167,000
Liabilities	$ 70,000	$ 70,000
Owners' equity	85,000	97,000
	$155,000	$167,000

The December 31, 19A, historical cost balance sheet data for IMB Corporation were cash, $145,000; operational assets, $60,000; accumulated depreciation, $60,000; liabilities, $70,000; and owners' equity, $75,000.

Additional data

1. Operational assets were purchased new on January 1, 19B. They are expected to remain in service for six years, with no estimated residual value. Straight-line depreciation is used.
2. Assume that all service revenue and all "other" expenses are for cash and occur at year-end.
3. The GPL increased by 5% during 19B and 6% during 19C. That is, GPL index values were 100 at the end of 19A, 105 at the end of 19B, and 111.3 at the end of 19C.
4. The replacement cost of operational assets increased 8% during 19B and 10% during 19C. That is, the CRC index of IMB Corporation operational assets was 100 at the end of 19A, 108 at the end of 19B, and 118.8 at the end of 19C.

Required (round amounts to nearest dollar):

1. Prepare HC and CRC journal entries for all transactions, including adjusting entries but *not* closing entries, of IMB Corporation for 19B and 19C.
2. Prepare comparative CRC balance sheets and income statements of IMB Corporation for 19B and 19C. Show all computations.
3. Based on the CRC financial statements, which year presents the more favorable impression of IMB's operations? Support your conclusion, particularly with respect to the relevant comparisons between 19B and 19C.

Problem 7–13

Refer to the basic data of problem 7–12. Assume all facts are the same except for additional data Items 3 and 4. In place of the GPL and CRC data given there, substitute the following:

	General Price Level	Current Replacement Cost of Operational Assets
December 31, 19A	127.00	$108,000
December 31, 19B	134.62	118,800
December 31, 19C	145.39	123,552

Required (round amounts to nearest dollar):

1. Prepare the historical cost and current replacement cost journal entries for all transactions, including adjusting but *not* closing entries, of IMB Corporation for 19B and 19C.
2. Prepare comparative current replacement cost balance sheets and income statements of IMB Corporation for 19B and 19C. Show all computations.
3. Based on the CRC financial statements, which year presents the more favorable impression of IMB's operations? Be able to support your conclusions, particularly with respect to the relevant comparisons between 19B and 19C.

8

Cash, Short-Term Investments, and Receivables

This chapter discusses cash and near-cash items, often called quick assets. The three most liquid assets are cash, short-term investments, and current receivables (including short-term notes receivable). Their interchangeability and other similarities make it desirable to discuss them in a single integrated chapter. Planning, control, and accounting for this particular group of current assets involve common problems, concepts, and procedures. To facilitate discussion the chapter is divided into three parts: Part A—Cash, Part B—Short-Term Investments, and Part C—Receivables.

PART A—CASH

Money is the medium of exchange and is used to express most of the measurements in accounting. Because of its pervasive use by society, the concept of cash is understood by nearly everyone; however, accounting for and reporting cash inflows and outflows presents some special problems. This part examines accounting for cash, including its control; reporting cash flows is discussed in Chapter 23, The Statement of Changes in Financial Position.

COMPOSITION OF CASH

Two primary characteristics of cash are (1) its availability as a medium of exchange and (2) its use as a measurement in accounting for the other items. Although its purchasing power may change, accountants make no effort to revalue cash for such changes.[1]

Cash includes coins, currency, and certain types of formal negotiable instruments, such as checks, which are accepted by banks for deposit; but it excludes some items commonly intermingled with cash. Postage stamps should be reported as supplies; while IOUs from officers, owners, or employees should be classified as special receivables, not as cash. Formal *negotiable* instruments (i.e., transferable by endorsement) which are due on demand are properly classified as cash. Thus, bank drafts, cashier's checks, money orders, certified checks, and ordinary checks constitute cash for accounting purposes. Balances on deposit in commercial banks should be considered as cash if subject to immediate use. Balances in savings accounts generally should be classed as short-term investments.

A company may agree to maintain *compensating balances* on deposit with a bank that extends credit to the company. Under such ar-

---

[1] This statement applies to cash balances which are already expressed in terms of domestic dollars. Foreign currency balances must be translated to current dollar equivalents; thus, the dollar value of a foreign deposit will fluctuate as international exchange rates vary. Another aspect of "revaluation" of cash involves general price level restatements discussed in Chapter 7.

rangements the borrower agrees, in effect, not to withdraw the entire balance of a loan or line of credit. The practical effect is to raise interest rates since the sum borrowed cannot be used in its entirety, thus creating a nonspendable portion of a checking account. Existence of such an arrangement must be disclosed; otherwise statement readers are entitled to assume the entire cash balance is available to meet currently maturing debts and expenses.

Current assets were discussed in Chapter 5. The AICPA Committee on Accounting Procedure, in *Accounting Research Bulletin No. 43*, stated:

> Even though not actually set aside in special accounts, funds that are clearly to be used in the near future for the liquidation of long-term debts, payments to sinking funds, or for similar purposes should also, under this concept, be excluded from current assets. However, where such funds are considered to offset maturing debt which has properly been set up as a current liability, they may be included within the current asset classification.[2]

Petty cash funds (discussed below) and cash held by branches or divisions should be included in cash because such funds ordinarily are used to meet current operating expenses and to liquidate current liabilities.

Checks which have not been mailed or otherwise delivered to the payees by the end of the accounting period should not be deducted from the cash balance. Entries already made to record the checks should be changed before preparing the financial statements. An overdraft in a bank account should be shown as a current liability. However, if a depositor has overdrawn one account with Bank A but has positive balances in other accounts in that bank, it is appropriate to offset and report the net asset or liability on the balance sheet because the single bank is in a position to protect both accounts. It is incorrect to offset an overdraft in Bank A against a balance on deposit in Bank B because the positive account is open to withdrawal without knowledge by the other bank. Although amounts in-

vested in certificates of deposit (CDs) are often reported along with the amount of cash in checking accounts, it is preferable to report the CD balance separately or parenthetically as a short-term investment.

CONTROL OF CASH

The control of cash is critical in many businesses because *(a)* it is usually in short supply, or in some cases there is idle cash; *(b)* it is easy to conceal and transport; and *(c)* it is desired by everyone.

The control of cash involves careful planning of cash needs and control of expenditures, careful recordkeeping to assure that all cash is properly accounted for, and short-term control reports. Thus, control of cash generally requires the following:

1. A detailed cash budget that specifies planned cash inflows and outflows (not considered in this book).
2. Detailed cash control reports for internal management use *(a)* to assure that cash is controlled as planned and *(b)* as a basis for revising cash plans.
3. A system of internal control that incorporates careful delegation of authority for handling cash receipts, cash payments, and the related recordkeeping.
4. Detailed accounting for all cash receipts and cash disbursements including assurances that there are no unauthorized uses of cash receipts or improper cash disbursements. Chapter 3, Appendix A, discussed and illustrated the use of control and subsidiary accounts and special journals. These are important procedures to use in attaining adequate control of cash.
5. Adequate disclosure of cash inflows and outflows in the external financial statements provided to stockholders and others. This subject is discussed in Chapter 23, The Statement of Changes in Financial Position, Cash Basis.

Control of Cash Receipts

Cash inflows in most businesses come from numerous sources; therefore, the detailed proce-

---

[2] AICPA, *Accounting Research Bulletin No. 43*, "Restatement and Revision of Accounting Research Bulletins" (New York, 1961), p. 21.

dures that should be used to attain adequate control are varied. However, the following procedures are important in all situations:

1. Assign cash-handling and cash-recording responsibilities and develop a system so there is a continuous and uninterrupted flow of cash from initial receipt to deposit in an authorized bank account. This requires *(a)* immediate counting of all cash received, *(b)* immediate recording of all cash received, and *(c)* timely deposit of all cash received.
2. Maintain separation of all responsibilities for the cash-handling and cash-recording functions. In this manner an effective system of internal checks is implemented.
3. Assure continuous and close supervision of all cash-handling and cash-recording functions, including daily cash reports for internal use.

Control of Cash Disbursements

The cash outflows in most businesses are for many purposes. Many of the cash defalcations happen in the disbursements process because they are relatively easy to conceal unless there is an effective system to control cash payments. In such situations, one or more of the fundamentals of internal control is missing. Although each control system should be tailored to the situation, there are several fundamentals that are indispensable; these are as follows:

1. Make all cash disbursements by check. An exception can be made for small, miscellaneous payments by use of a petty cash system.
2. Establish a petty cash system with tight controls and close supervision.
3. Prepare checks and sign them only when supported by adequate documentation and verification.
4. Separate responsibilities for cash disbursement documentation, check writing, check signing, check mailing, and recordkeeping.
5. Supervise continuously and closely all cash disbursement and recordkeeping functions including periodic internal reports.

Petty Cash

The term petty cash, or *imprest cash,* refers to a systematic approach often used for making

small expenditures which would be too costly and time consuming to make by check. Examples of such payments are for the daily paper delivered to the office, express shipments, local taxi fares, special postage charges on delivery, and minor office supplies. A petty cash system operates as follows:

1. A reliable employee is designated as the petty cash custodian. This person receives a single amount of cash for specified petty cash purposes, disburses the funds as needed, receives adequate documentation for each disbursement, maintains a running record of the cash on hand, and periodically reports the total amount spent supported by the documentation received for each disbursement. The record maintained, in addition to the documentation, often is referred to as the petty cash book.
2. When the amount of petty cash held by the custodian runs low, a request for a resupply, supported by the documentation of prior expenditures, is submitted to the designated supervisor of company cash.
3. The initial amount to establish the petty cash fund, and subsequent resupply to the custodian, are provided by separate checks, made payable to petty cash, and processed in the normal manner.
4. Accounting—the initial check establishing the petty cash fund is recorded as a debit to Petty Cash and a credit to Cash. Checks to resupply the fund are recorded by debiting the expense accounts (or other accounts) for the expenditures reported by the custodian and by crediting Cash.
5. There should be close supervision and surprise audits of petty cash on hand and supporting documentation for expenditures.

To illustrate operation of a petty cash fund, assume one is established in the amount of $100 and employee X is designated as the custodian. At the end of the first two weeks, the custodian requests a resupply of the $87 spent, supported by adequate documentation that reflected the following: postage, $18.50; office supplies bought, $23.60; taxi fares (local), $31.00; meals for employees, $10.00; and daily paper, $3.90. The indicated entries would be as follows:

To establish the petty cash fund:

Petty cash	100.00	
Cash		100.00

To replenish the fund (at end of second week):

Postage expense	18.50	
Office supplies expense	23.60	
Administrative expense	44.90	
Cash		87.00

The effect of the last entry is to replenish the amount of petty cash held by the custodian to $100, which is the amount already reflected in the Petty Cash account.

CASH OVERAGE AND SHORTAGE

Cash is susceptible to theft, and it is inevitable that errors will be made in counting cash; therefore, cash overages and shortages must be expected. Cash overages and shortages, usually determined on a daily basis, should be recorded in an account entitled Cash Overages and Shortages with an offset to the regular Cash account. A debit balance in this account represents an operating expense, and a credit represents a miscellaneous revenue. In the absence of theft, cash overages and shortages tend to balance out to zero over a period of time. In contrast, theft, when discovered, should be recorded as a credit to the regular Cash account and as a debit to (a) a receivable if recovery is expected from the individual involved or an insurance or bonding company, or (b) a loss account on the presumption that recovery is improbable.

RECONCILIATION OF BANK WITH BOOK BALANCE

At the end of each month, the ending cash balance on deposit reported in the bank statement should be reconciled with the ending cash balance as reflected in all of the cash accounts (including petty cash) of the business. Reconciliation of bank with book balances serves two important purposes: (1) establishes a measure of control—it serves to check the accuracy of the records of both the bank and the company, and (2) facilitates accounting entries—it provides information for entries in the books of the company for items reflected on the bank statement

that have not been recorded by the company (e.g., a bank service charge).

Reconciliation of the ending bank balance with the ending balance of the Cash accounts requires an analysis of the *monthly bank statement* and the cash records maintained by the company. Generally there will be a difference between the *bank* and *book* cash balances for the following reasons:

A. Items already recorded as cash receipts in the books of the company but not yet added to the bank balance on the bank statement.

    Examples:

    1. Deposits in transit—receipts deposited in the bank by the company but not yet reported by the bank on the current bank statement.

    2. Cash on hand including petty cash (i.e., cash not on deposit).

B. Amounts already added to the bank balance but not recorded in the company books.

    Examples:

    1. Interest allowed the depositor by the bank but not yet recorded in the company books.

    2. Collections (and deposits) of notes and drafts by the bank for the depositor but not yet recorded in the company books.

C. Amounts already recorded as cash disbursements in the company books but not deducted by the bank from the bank balance.

    Example:

    1. Outstanding checks—checks written and properly recorded in the company books but not yet cleared through the bank.

D. Amounts already subtracted from the bank balance but not yet recorded in the company books:

    Example:

    1. Bank service charge.

It is possible to reconcile the ending bank and book cash balances by working from the bank balance to the book balance, or the opposite, or to reconcile both the book balance and bank bal-

EXHIBIT 8–1

Bank Reconciliation (true balance method)			
July 31, 19X			
Bank Balance		*Book Balance*	
Ending balance per bank	$4,355	Ending balance per books	$6,200
Add:		Deduct:	
Deposit in transit		NSF check charged back	(40)
($11,500–$9,400)	2,100	Unrecorded service charge	(5)
Deduct:			
Outstanding checks			
($12,300–$12,000)	(300)		
True cash balance, ending	$6,155		$6,155

ance to a common amount known as the correct or *true cash balance.* The "true cash balance" method is generally used.[3] The method is illustrated in Exhibit 8–1 based on the following data:

Suppose X Company began business with a $7,000 deposit in a bank and deposited all its receipts and made all its disbursements by check. During the first month if its deposits amounted to $11,500 and its checks drawn amounted to $12,300, its ledger account Cash in Bank would appear as below:

Company Books in July:

Cash in Bank

July 1 balance	7,000	Checks in July	12,300
Deposits in July	11,500	July 31 balance	6,200
	18,500		18,500
August 1 balance	6,200		

In addition, assume the following:

a. Only $9,400 of the deposits reached the bank.
b. Only $12,000 of the checks cleared the bank.

---

[3] The "true cash balance" method is preferable for the following reasons:

a. The reconciliation naturally falls into two parts (books and bank); the "book" part of the reconciliation provides the entries necessary to correct the company's Cash account to the true cash balance.
b. It is understandable. After the correctness of each item has been verified, the reconciliation merely involves placing such items under the appropriate part as an addition or deduction.
c. The reconciliation can be used as a schedule supporting the cash balance reported on the balance sheet; the last line on the reconciliation is reported on the balance sheet.

c. The bank charged back a $40 customer check deposited late in the month because of insufficient funds in the customer's bank account (i.e., a "hot" check from a customer).
d. The bank charged a $5 service charge.
e. The company had not reflected either the $40 NSF item or the $5 bank charge. (NSF means "insufficient funds" in the bank to cover the amount of the "hot" check.)

Because of these differences between the book and bank accounts, there would be a need to reconcile the $6,200 book balance to the $4,355 bank balance (below). The bank's record with X Company would appear as a liability on the bank's books as follows:

Bank Books in July:

X Company

Checks in July	12,000	July 1 balance	7,000
NSF check	40	July deposits	9,400
Service charge	5		
July 31 balance	4,355		
	16,400		16,400
		August 1 balance	4,355

As just noted, there are three ways to reconcile bank and book balances; however, reconciling the bank balance and the book balance to a common amount known as the correct or *true balance* is preferable and is illustrated in Exhibit 8–1.

Entries from the "book balance" portion of the bank reconciliation necessary to reflect the items not previously recorded on the company's records and to adjust the Cash account to the true cash balance would be as follows:

```
Expense—bank charges .....................    5
Account receivable (NSF, customer) ..........   40
    Cash ................................          45
```

If there is little likelihood of collecting the $40 NSF customer's check, it would be more appropriate to debit the Allowance for Doubtful Accounts.

COMPREHENSIVE RECONCILIATION

A comprehensive bank reconciliation (often referred to as a "Proof of Cash") starts with the bank reconciliation of the preceding period and ties it in with the bank and book differences (separately for receipts and payments of the current period) and ends with the reconciliation for the current period. Its format reconciles all amounts to a set of "true balances" (i.e., amounts which would exist if neither the bank nor the depositor made any errors nor had any items recorded which the other did not similarly record).

To illustrate for X Company, the bank's statement for the month of August in summarized form appears below:

BANK Z STATEMENT

```
Balance carried forward
    from July ....................          $  4,355
Deposits:
  August 1 (from X Company
    deposit in transit on July
    31) .........................   $ 2,100
  August 2–31 (from X
    Company) ....................    13,120
  Note collected (on or near
    August 31) ..................     1,050
        Total receipts ..............               16,270
Bank charges:
  Checks (drawn in July
    but cleared in August)..........      300
  Checks (drawn in Au-
    gust and cleared in
    August) ....................     14,670
  Service charge .................        8
        Total charges ..............               (14,978)
Balance, August 31 ..............               $  5,647
```

The ledger accounts of the depositor and of the bank for the month of August follow:

Company Books for August:

Cash in Bank

August 1 balance	6,200	Entry at left, NSF plus bank charges	45
Deposits in August	14,400	Checks in August	15,250
		August 31 balance	5,305
	20,600		20,600
September 1 balance	5,305		

Bank Books for August:

X Company

Checks in August	14,970	August 1 balance	4,355
Service charge	8	Deposits in August	15,220
August 31 balance	5,647	Note collected for	
	20,625	company	1,050
			20,625
		September 1 balance	5,647

The company would determine its outstanding checks by matching checks returned with the bank statement with the record of checks drawn (check register); however, the determination can also be made as follows:

```
Checks outstanding July 31 ..................   $   300
Checks drawn in August .....................     15,250
Total checks which could clear ...............     15,550
Checks cleared in August ....................     14,970
Checks outstanding August 31 ...............   $   580
```

Deposits in transit at August 31 would be determined by matching deposit slips returned by the bank with duplicates prepared by the company; however, the determination can also be made as follows:

```
Deposits in transit July 31 ...................   $ 2,100
Deposits in August ..........................     14,400
Total deposits which could clear ..............     16,500
Deposits cleared in August ...................     15,220
Deposits in transit August 31 ................   $ 1,280
```

The comprehensive reconciliation for August would appear as shown in Exhibit 8–2.

Steps in the preparation of the comprehensive reconciliations are as follows:

1. First column—Enter the "bank" and "book" data directly from the last column of a similar reconciliation for the *preceding period* (usually a month).

EXHIBIT 8–2
Comprehensive Bank Reconciliation

	(1) July 31 Balance	+	(2) August Receipts	−	(3) August Payments	=	(4) August 31 Balance
Bank:							
Balances per bank	$4,355		$16,270		$14,978		$5,647
Deposits in transit:							
July 31	2,100		(2,100)				
August 31			1,280				1,280
Outstanding checks:							
July 31	(300)				(300)		
August 31					580		(580)
True cash balances, ending	$6,155		$15,450		$15,258		$6,347
Books:							
Balances per books	$6,200		$14,400		$15,295		$5,305
Unrecorded service charges:							
July 31	(5)				(5)		
August 31					8		(8)
NSF check returned	(40)				(40)		
Note collected for company			1,050				1,050
True cash balances, ending	$6,155		$15,450		$15,258		$6,347

2. Bank section, top line—Enter the total receipts and the total payments recorded by the bank; and in the fourth column, enter the resultant ending balance.
3. Bank section, fourth column—Enter items recorded by the company and not recorded by the bank (normally this will consist principally of outstanding deposits and checks at the close of the period).
4. Bank section extensions from first column—Bring across into the receipts and payments columns the items listed in the first column which were reconciled last month (normally these will be subtractions because they were recognized as receipts or payments one month late).
5. Bank section extensions (leftward) from fourth column—"Back in" from the fourth column (August 31 Balance) items to be reconciled at the end of the current month. (Normally these will be additions because they were not recognized in the month they should have been.)
6. Bank section, true cash balance—Complete the bank portion by vertically footing the

columns to arrive at true receipts and payments and the true ending bank balance.
7. Book section, top line—Enter total receipts and payments recorded in the company books with the resultant ending book balance in the fourth column. (This is the counterpart of [2] above.)
8. Book section extensions from first column—Bring across into the receipts and payments column the items listed in the first column which were reconciled last month (normally subtracted because of their recognition as receipts or payments one month late).
9. Book section extensions (leftward) from fourth column—"Back in" from the fourth column (August 31 Balance) items to be reconciled at the end of the current month. (This corresponds to [5] above.)
10. Book section, true cash balance—Complete the book portion by vertically footing the columns to arrive at true receipts and payments and the true ending book balance.
11. Tests for accuracy:
    a. The top and bottom lines of each section

when crossfooted should reflect balances as shown on the bank statement and in the company's ledger account Cash.

b. Total receipts and total payments when footed vertically should reflect agreement between "bank" and "book" amounts.

c. The final *balances* of "true cash" should reflect agreement between "bank" and "book" amounts.

Although the addition or subtraction of items in the inner columns (receipts and payments) is quite logical, a mechanical rule may assist when one is becoming familiar with this form of reconciliation. All items in the beginning or ending balance columns must, of course, be reflected in one of the inner columns. If an item is added in an outer column and appears in an *adjacent* inner column, its sign changes (i.e., it is subtracted in the inner column). On the other hand, if an item in one of the balance columns does not appear in an *adjacent* inner column, it retains the same sign as it had in the balance column.

Returning for a moment to the details of Exhibit 8–2, if the company is preparing financial statements as of August 31 it should record the $8 August service charge and the collection of the $1,050 proceeds from the note (assume that $50 is interest) as August transactions so that the books and financial statements as of August 31 reflect the ending cash balance of $6,347. If statements are not being prepared as of August 31, delay of recording these items until September is unimportant. The entries should be recorded as follows:

Expense—bank charges	8	
Cash		8
Cash	1,050	
Note receivable		1,000
Interest revenue		50

Comprehensive reconciliation affords several advantages over the type of reconciliation presented on page 268. It arrays both the bank and book data in detail so irregularities and errors can be quickly spotted. This is especially important where there is more than one checking ac-

count and interaccount transfers have occurred. If there is an interaccount deposit reflected on one reconciliation for which no interaccount check appears on the other, an irregularity is quite possible. All data, including receipts and payments, are reflected on a "true balance" basis.

PART B—SHORT-TERM INVESTMENTS

Investments usually are classified for balance sheet purposes as either short-term investments (sometimes called marketable or temporary securities) or long-term investments (sometimes simply called investments or permanent investments). This distinction is entirely one of accounting and not of law and arises out of the nature of the asset held and the purpose or intent of management in making the investment. Investment purposes may be outlined as follows:

A. Short-term investments.
  1. Funds invested in marketable securities to produce revenue that would otherwise not be earned on seasonal excesses of cash.

B. Long-term investments. (Discussed in Chapters 19 and 20).
  1. Stocks of other companies (investees) held to achieve control over their operations and policies (i.e., a controlling interest).
  2. Securities of other entities (not held for control) and advances to such entities.
  3. Funds earmarked for designated purposes such as retirement of a bond issue, plant expansion or replacement, or payment of noncurrent debt.
  4. Cash surrender value of life insurance on company executives.
  5. Assets other than investment securities held to produce nonoperating revenue or for future use or sale. Such properties are not used in regular business operations currently but may have been so used in the past or may be intended for such use in the future. Alternatively, they are sometimes reported under "Other Assets" if they do not produce current revenue.

SHORT-TERM INVESTMENTS DEFINED

Short-term investments are reported on the balance sheet under the "Current Assets" caption. To be classified as a current asset, a short-term investment should meet the following two-fold test:

1. The security must be readily marketable. It must be regularly traded on a security exchange or in some other established market.[4]
2. The company's management does not intend to keep the security beyond the current operating cycle or one year, whichever is longer. This criterion has proven somewhat troublesome to auditors in practice. "Intentions" are elusive and can change from one fiscal period to the next.

VALUATION OF SHORT-TERM INVESTMENTS

Short-term investments are recorded initially at cost in accordance with the cost principle. Subsequent to acquisition they may be accounted for at

1. Lower of cost or market (LCM).
2. Cost.
3. Market.

Lower of Cost or Market

FASB Statement No. 12, "Accounting for Certain Marketable Securities," requires that investments in marketable *equity* securities be valued at each balance sheet date on a lower-of-cost-or-market basis.[5] Application of this statement to long-term investments in marketable equity securities will be discussed in Chapter 19; therefore, this chapter will focus only on *short-term* investments. Equity securities, as used in *Statement No. 12,* encompass all capital stock (including warrants, rights, and stock op-

tions) except preferred stock that, by its terms, must be redeemed either at the option of the issuer or the investor. Equity securities do not include debt securities such as bonds and other debt instruments.

FASB Statement No. 12 specifies: "The carrying amount of a marketable equity securities portfolio shall be the lower of its aggregate cost or market value, determined at balance sheet date. The amount by which aggregate cost of the portfolio exceeds market value shall be accounted for as the valuation allowance."

In applying the concept of lower of cost or market (LCM), *FASB Statement No. 12* distinguishes between realized and unrealized gains and losses. A *realized gain or loss* is defined as the difference between the net proceeds from the sale of a marketable equity security and its cost. Net unrealized gain or loss on a portfolio of marketable equity securities is the difference between their cost and market value on an *aggregate portfolio basis* at a given date.

To illustrate, suppose the portfolio of short-term securities of Merian Company consists of the following individual securities at the close of the first fiscal year, 19A (or that in the preceding period their market value exceeded their cost):

Short-Term Marketable Security	End of the Year, 19A		
	Aggregate Cost	Aggregate Market	Unit LCM
Equity securities:			
Apex common stock, 50 shares	$ 5,200	$ 4,800	$ 4,800
Caldor preferred stock, nonredeemable, par $100, 100 shares	11,000	11,250	11,000
Total portfolio of short-term *equity* securities	16,200	16,050	15,800
Debt securities:			
Baker 8% bonds, $10,000 maturity value	9,700	9,600	9,600
Total portfolio of all short-term securities	$25,900	$25,650	$25,400

Two questions arise immediately concerning the appropriate valuation of the above short-term investments:

1. What valuation represents *market* for comparison with *cost* in applying the lower-of-cost-or-market rule (i.e., should the above

---

[4] FASB Interpretation No. 16, "Clarification of Definitions and Accounting for Marketable Equity Securities that Become Nonmarketable," (February 1977) provides detailed rules pertaining to one aspect of *marketability.*

[5] The provisions of *FASB Statement No. 12* do not apply to industries having specialized practices with respect to marketable securities, including such financial organizations as insurance companies, investment companies, mutual funds, and securities dealers.

"Aggregate Market" column total be used or should the above "Unit Market" column total be used to compare with the "Aggregate Cost" column total)?

2. How does the lower-of-cost-or-market rule apply to short-term *equity* securities and to short-term *debt* securities?

In response to the first question regarding which way to measure *market* (for comparison with cost) in applying the LCM rule, *FASB Statement No. 12* specifies "aggregate market." Thus, for Merian Company the portfolio of *equity* securities would involve comparison of the aggregate market of $16,050 (not $15,800) with aggregate cost of $16,200. Alternatively, if the debt securities (bonds) are included in the total portfolio for LCM application, the aggregate market total of $25,650 would be compared with the aggregate cost total of $25,900. In either instance the "aggregate market" valuation is a better valuation than the "unit market" valuation because Merian Company would realize the former amount if the entire portfolio were converted to cash as of the statement date.[6] It was probably for this reason that *FASB Statement No. 12* clearly specified "the lower of its aggregate cost or market value."

Turning to the second question as to which short-term securities should be accounted for using the lower-of-cost-or-market rule, *FASB Statement No. 12* specifically limited the standard to only *equity* securities. It leaves open the valuation of *debt* securities held as short-term investments. Thus, for Merian Company, the *Statement* strictly interpreted applies only to the Apex and Caldor shares. Under this interpretation, these shares would constitute a separate portfolio of equity securities and the Baker bonds would constitute another separate short-term investment portfolio. This application would require that the equity security portfolio be accounted for under the LCM rule and the debt security portfolio be accounted for *at cost* (rather than at LCM) in accordance with the provisions of Chapter 3, *ARB No. 43*, which states:

In the case of marketable securities where market value is less than cost by a *substantial amount* and it is evident that the decline in market value is *not due to a mere temporary condition*, the amount to be included as a current asset should not exceed the market value. (Emphasis supplied.)

ARB No. 43 did not, however, deal with the question of whether a writeup of a previous writedown might be permissible to reflect a recovery in the market. In contrast, *FASB Statement No. 12* requires such a writeup (but not above cost) for securities valued under the LCM rule.

As a result of the situation described immediately above, current practice reflects two ways of accounting for short-term debt securities held as investments:

1. Include both equity and debt securities in one overall short-term investment portfolio valued under the LCM rule.
2. Value the equity securities as one separate portfolio at *LCM* and value the debt securities as another portfolio at *cost*.

Although *FASB Statement No. 12* addresses only marketable equity securities, logic and consistency call for application of the same valuation procedures to marketable debt securities held as short-term investments. Any marketable security, equity or debt, is bought for the same purposes: to employ idle cash to earn a short-term return. In the case of bonds classified as short-term investments, there is little likelihood that they would ever be held to maturity date. Furthermore, the significance of short-term investments is the total amount of cash that would have been realized from disposal of both the equity and debt securities at balance sheet date. Both types of securities must meet the same test for classification as a current asset. These facts make valuing the short-term debt securities at unamortized cost (i.e., the cost method) irrelevant.

A literal interpretation of *Statement No. 12* would require separate valuation of equity and debt securities held as short-term investments. By its silence about debt securities, the *Statement* appears to *permit* valuation of both debt and equity securities as one short-term invest-

---

[6] Some disposal costs may be incurred, but traditionally consideration of these has been deferred until they are actually incurred at disposal date of the security.

ment portfolio under the LCM rule. Although current practice on this issue is somewhat diverse, combining debt and equity securities in one overall portfolio for LCM valuation appears to be widely accepted. Accordingly, in this text the more logical view of combining them is illustrated and will be assumed unless specifically stated otherwise.

Returning to the illustration of Merian Company, assuming both equity and debt securities are valued as one short-term investment portfolio, the company would recognize the decline in market value at the end of the 19A fiscal year as follows:

December 31, 19A—To record LCM on short-term investment portfolio:

Unrealized loss on short-term investments
($25,900 − $25,650) 250
    Allowance to reduce short-term
      investments to market 250

The unrealized loss account is closed to Income Summary and is reported on the income statement as a "financial" item. The allowance account, as a contra account to short-term investments, should be reported either as a deduction from short-term investments (at cost) or presented in a one-line format as follows:

Current Assets:
   Short-term investments, at market value
    (cost $25,900) $25,650

Notes to the statements also could be used to disclose the cost amount and the amount of the unrealized loss recognized. The unrealized loss is not a deduction for *income tax purposes;* cost of the securities is used for measurement of the taxable gain or loss.[7]

In the above entry to record the LCM effect, the debit was to an *unrealized loss* (the terminology used in *FASB Statement No. 12*) and the loss was recognized as a deduction from income of the period in which the market prices dropped.[8] Recoveries in the market value of a portfolio of short-term investments result in an increase in income (as illustrated below). The amount of the market recovery is credited to an *unrealized gain* (also the terminology used in *FASB Statement No. 12*). The amount of "recoveries" (i.e., unrealized gains) recorded cannot exceed the previous unrealized losses recognized on the same portfolio. Notwithstanding a balance in the allowance account, *FASB Statement No. 12* requires that the *realized* gain or loss on the disposal of a short-term investment, accounted for under the LCM rule, be measured as the difference between the *original cost* (not the LCM value) and the sales price of the security. To illustrate, assume Merian Company, on April 5, 19B, sold the 50 shares of Apex stock for $4,950 and incurred disposal costs of $125. The required entry would be as follows:

April 5, 19B—To record sale of short-term investment:

Cash ($4,950 − $125) 4,825
Loss (realized) on sale of short-term
  investments 375
    Short-term investments, Apex common
      stock (original cost) 5,200

Observe that the above entry did not reduce the prior balance in the allowance account. The *Statement* specifies that the balance in the allowance account is restated *only* at the end of each fiscal year.

At the end of the next fiscal year, subsequent to a writedown of a short-term investment portfolio to LCM, the *amount needed* in the allowance account may increase or decrease depending on a new LCM computation based on the securities held at the end of that fiscal year. To illustrate, assume that on September 1, 19B, Merian Company purchased (as a short-term investment) 50 shares of Davis common stock, no-par, at $101 per share. In addition, acquisition costs of $50 were incurred. The entry to record the purchase would be as follows:

---

[7] Any taxable gain or loss ordinarily would be recognized when the security is sold and would be measured by comparing the net sales proceeds with the original cost. Paragraph 22 of *FASB Statement No. 12* provides that recognition of unrealized gains or losses on marketable securities shall be considered as a timing difference for income tax allocation purposes (see Chapter 9).

[8] You will find in studying Chapter 19 that "unrealized losses" related to *long-term investments* are not reported in the income statement but rather are reported as a contra account (deduction) to owners' equity. Subsequent recoveries, up to original cost, are recorded as a reduction of the contra account.

September 1, 19B—To record the purchase of a short-term investment:

Short-term investments, Davis common
   stock, nopar (50 × $101) + $50 5,100
     Cash 5,100

Now assume that there were no additional transactions during 19B that affected the short-term investment portfolio and that the December 31, 19B, market values are: Caldor preferred stock, 108½; Baker 8% bonds, 98; and Davis common stock, 101.[9] Assuming both the equity and debt short-term securities held at the end of 19B are included as one portfolio, the LCM schedule would be as follows:

Short-Term Marketable Security	Cost	Market
Caldor preferred stock, nonredeemable, par $100, 100 shares	$11,000	$10,850
Baker 8% bonds, $10,000 maturity value	9,700	9,800
Davis common stock, nopar, 50 shares	5,100	5,050
Total aggregate market of short-term investment portfolio	$25,800	$25,700

Aggregate market at the end of 19B is less than aggregate cost by $100 (i.e., $25,800 − $25,700). Therefore, the balance in the allowance account must be reduced from the prior 19A balance of $250 to the required balance of $100 (i.e., a reduction of $150) as shown in the following entry:

December 31, 19B—To adjust the balance in the allowance account on the basis of the security portfolio at the end of the year:

Allowance to reduce short-term
   investments to market 150
   Recovery of unrealized loss
     on short-term investments* 150

  * Some accountants prefer the terminology "Unrealized Gain on Short-Term Investments" because an "Unrealized Loss" was reported on the income statement earlier, and this is in the nature of a "market gain" in the current period. Both titles appear to be widely used.

---

  [9] The typical method of quoting bond prices was reflected. They are quoted as a percent of par, and the typical corporate bond is in units of $1,000 (see Chapter 20). Shares of stock are quoted at the number of dollars per share; for example, a quotation of 108½ means $108.50 per share.

If aggregate market had dropped during 19B to the extent that the $250 credit balance in the allowance account is inadequate, the account would have been increased (credited). In contrast, if market had equaled or exceeded cost, the allowance account would be reduced to zero and the resulting unrealized credit reflected in the income statement in 19B. In no event, however, under the LCM rule can the unrealized recovery or gains exceed the previously recorded unrealized loss.

FASB Statement No. 12 requires that when marketable equity securities are transferred between the short-term and long-term investment portfolios in either direction, the transfer must be effected at their lower-of-cost-or-market value at the time of the transfer. When market is below cost, market value becomes the new cost basis and the difference is accounted for as a realized loss and included in the determination of income in the period of transfer.[10]

Disclosure requirements specified by *FASB Statement No. 12* are the following:

a. As of the date of each balance sheet presented, aggregate cost and market value (each segregated between current and noncurrent portfolios when a classified balance sheet is presented) with identification as to which is the carrying amount.

b. As of the date of the latest balance sheet presented, the following, segregated between current and noncurrent portfolios when a classified balance sheet is presented:
   i. Gross unrealized gains representing the excess of market value over cost for all marketable equity securities in the portfolio having such an excess.
   ii. Gross unrealized losses representing the excess of cost over market value for all marketable equity securities in the portfolio having such an excess.

c. For each period for which an income statement is presented:
   i. Net realized gain or loss included in the determination of net income.
   ii. The basis on which cost was determined in computing realized gain or loss (i.e., average cost or other method used).

---

  [10] Further discussion of this point and illustrative entries are presented in Chapter 19.

iii. The change in the valuation allowance(s) that has been included in the equity section of the balance sheet during the period and, when a classified balance sheet is presented, the amount of such change included in the determination of net income.

Accounting for *long-term* investments in equity securities is discussed in Chapter 19 and for debt securities in Chapter 20.

Valuation at Cost

Since *FASB Statement No. 12,* when strictly applied, does not apply to *debt securities* held as short-term investments, such securities can be accounted for at *cost* rather than being included in a single portfolio along with short-term investments in equity securities as discussed and illustrated on pages 273–75. If accounted for as a separate portfolio, short-term investments in debt securities are recorded at cost at acquisition date and are subsequently carried at that value unless market value subsequently becomes less than cost (1) by a substantial amount and (2) the market decline is not due to a mere temporary condition (refer to the quotation from *ARB No. 43* on page 273). Subsequent to such a writedown, which would be rare, recoveries in market value are not recognized in the accounts (as is done under the LCM rule) because the reduced carrying value is viewed as "cost" for future accounting purposes. For income tax purposes, such losses and write-downs are not recognized, and the basis of the debt security continues to be its original cost.

When a debt security is acquired as a short-term investment, accrued interest from the last interest date to the date of acquisition must be recognized. To illustrate, assume that on September 1, 19A, X Company purchased (as a short-term investment) five $1,000 bonds (9% annual interest payable each June 30) of Y Company at 101¼ plus the two months' accrued interest, and that acquisition costs of $50 were incurred. The required entry would be the following:

September 1, 19B—To record purchase of bond investment:

Short-term investments, Y Company bonds [($5,000 × 1.0125) + $50]	5,112.50	
Interest revenue* ($5,000 × 9% × ²⁄₁₂)	75.00	
Cash ($5,062.50 + $50 + $75)		5,187.50

Short-term investments, Y Company bonds [($5,000 × 1.0125) + $50]   5,112.50
Interest revenue* ($5,000 × 9% × $2/12$)   75.00
  Cash ($5,062.50 + $50 + $75)   5,187.50

* Alternatively, this debit could be to Interest Receivable; after the subsequent entry is made to record receipt of the interest for six months, the net effect would be the same. If the annual fiscal period ends prior to the next interest date, Interest Receivable should be debited.

Valuation at Market

In accounting for short-term investments after acquisition date, the cost method basically retains original cost. The LCM method reduces the original cost valuation to market (when the latter is lower) and, if the market recovers, increases the valuation (but not in excess of original cost). These changes in value result in the reporting of *unrealized* losses and gains. In contrast, the *market value method* revalues the investment portfolio at the end of each period at market (regardless of cost), which results in "holding" gains and losses, depending on the direction of the change in market prices.

With inflation being a continuing phenomenon and with attendant continuing disparity between the cost of many assets and their current replacement values, there have been strong arguments from many quarters to supplement the conventional cost basis financial statements with some kind of *restated* statements or to supplement them with selected data from the statements discussed in Chapter 7. There are often significant differences in the reported values on cost basis financial statements compared with statements prepared to reflect the effects of price changes. In the case of short-term investments, however, the differences are likely to be relatively small because of the comparatively short holding period. Nonetheless, there are many proponents of market valuation of investment securities, even when market is *higher* than original cost.

Accounting and reporting marketable securities on the basis of *market value* rather than cost poses two problems: (1) determination of the appropriate market value of the securities at the end of each period and (2) the method of recognizing the resulting market gain or loss (often called holding gains or losses). In accordance with present GAAP, the revenue realization principle does not permit the recognition of holding gains (except as specified in *FASB Statement No. 12*, i.e., to the extent of previously recognized holding losses); however, holding losses are recognized by using the LCM approach.

To illustrate the issue of recognizing holding gains on short-term investments, assume a short-term investment in common stock is acquired at a cost of $10,000 at the beginning of 19A. Assume the market value of the stock at the end of 19A is $11,000. Assuming accounting on the basis of market value, the indicated entries would be as follows:

At date of acquisition (record at cost):

Investments, short term	10,000	
Cash		10,000

At end of period (market $11,000), to record market gain:

Investments, short term	1,000	
Unrealized market gain on investments (or		
market gain on investments)		1,000

Some accountants feel strongly that the market gain of $1,000 should be reflected on the income statement for 19A. Others feel equally strong that the market gain should be reported on the balance sheet at the end of 19A as unrealized capital and that a gain should be recognized on the income statement only when the investment is sold. Of course, this latter approach inconsistently reports the investment on the balance sheet at market value but reports net income on the basis of cost. To illustrate the two views, assume the investment is sold during 19B for $11,500. The indicated entry would be as follows:

a. Assuming market gain was considered as *realized* and reported on the income statement in 19A:

Cash	11,500	
Investments, short term		11,000
Gain on sale of investments		
(closed to Income Summary)		500

b. Assuming the market gain was considered as *unrealized* and reported as a separate element of owner's equity in 19A:

Cash	11,500	
Unrealized market gain on		
investments	1,000	
Investments, short term		11,000
Gain on sale of investment		1,500

A balance in the Unrealized Market Gain on Investments account (if used) would be classified on the balance sheet under Owners' Equity as "Unrealized capital."

The market value method is not considered GAAP at the present time except for certain financial institutions such as mutual funds and insurance companies. As a special industry exception to GAAP, the method is used; however, the issue of how to report the *holding* gains and losses is not settled. Both methods discussed above can be observed in practice.[11]

Evaluation of the Methods

The LCM method is criticized because it is inconsistent. When market values drop and aggregate market is below aggregate cost, LCM correctly reflects the realizable value of a portfolio of marketable securities; but when aggregate market exceeds aggregate cost, it does not, resulting in an understatement of asset value and of income relative to a market value measure. In successive periods marketable securities may be valued at cost, at market, and then again at cost. Its lack of conformity with income tax requirements requires interperiod tax allocation.

The chief objection to the *cost method* for short-term investments is that an overstatement of asset values and income results when market value drops below cost. Identical securities are reported at different costs simply because they were acquired at different times. When investments are carried at cost, it is possible to manipulate income by selecting which units are sold if there are two different lots of the same security. Another opportunity for manipulation exists because securities can be sold just before the close of a period and replaced immediately after the start of the next period. Some advantages of cost are its objectivity, the fact that it

---

[11] Recall that *FASB Statement No. 12 requires* that LCM unrealized losses and gains *(a)* on short-term investments be reported on the income statement and *(b)* on long-term investments be reported under owners' equity.

parallels the valuation basis used for most other assets, and its conformity with income tax requirements.

The use of the *market value method,* is criticized because market values are not always readily determinable. Sometimes the market for a security is "thin," and it is rarely traded.[12] Market value is not viewed by some as a very relevant figure until actual sale of a security becomes imminent. Market values generally cannot be used for income tax purposes. On the other hand, market value has the advantages that *(a)* it eliminates the inconsistencies cited above against lower of cost or market and *(b)* it assigns to each period gains or losses that occurred during the period rather than postponing recognition until the time of sale, as occurs under the cost method. Reporting short-term investments at market informs statement users of the real value of the asset that management substituted for cash. Finally, it is difficult to manipulate income when securities are valued at market. On balance, the market value approach appears preferable, but it is not GAAP except for certain financial institutions.

IDENTIFICATION OF UNITS

When short-term investments are sold, or otherwise disposed of, a question frequently is posed in respect to identification of unit cost. For example, assume three purchases of stock in XY Corporation as follows: purchase No. 1, 200 shares @ $80; purchase No. 2, 300 shares @ $100; and purchase No. 3, 100 shares @ $110. Now assume 100 shares are sold at $120. What is cost? For accounting purposes, *specific identification* of the particular shares sold is preferable; however, in cases where such identification is not feasible, *Fifo* or *average cost* flow may be assumed; the former appears to be more generally used. The Internal Revenue Service requires specific identification for tax purposes; and when it cannot be applied, *Fifo* must be used.

---

[12] In the unlikely event that an investor's holdings of securities were so extensive that liquidation of the entire holdings at once would materially affect the market price, the use of market values is subject to some caution if not criticism.

INVESTMENT REVENUE ON SHORT-TERM INVESTMENTS

Investment revenue from short-term investments in *capital stock* of other companies is recorded upon notification of the declaration of a cash dividend. Stock dividends received on such stock do not represent revenue; rather they serve to reduce the cost per share of the investment. Cash dividends on capital stock (common or preferred) held as an investment are not accrued prior to declaration.

Bonds purchased at a price above par are acquired at a premium; and if acquired below par, at a discount. In the case of short-term investments in bonds, the investment account is debited at cost and premium or discount accounts are not used. Premium or discount on a short-term bond investment is not amortized because, by definition, the investment will be converted to cash in the near future and the disposal date and price are unknown. This is in contrast to the accounting for bonds held as a long-term investment where amortization of premium and discount is required (see Chapter 20). Interest receivable on short-term investments in bonds is accrued at the end of the accounting period by means of an adjusting entry.

COMPREHENSIVE ILLUSTRATION BASED ON LOWER OF COST OR MARKET

This part is concluded with a brief but comprehensive illustration of accounting for short-term investments over a one-year period by a company whose operating cycle extends beyond one year.

As of the close of 19A the company's portfolio of marketable securities was as follows:

Marketable Security	End of 19A	
	Cost	Market
DEF Company 8% bonds (interest dates April 1 and October 1, $6,000 maturity value)	$ 6,300	$ 5,900
GHI Corporation common stock, nopar (100 shares)	8,700	8,875
Aggregate portfolio total	$15,000	$14,775

EXHIBIT 8–3
Accounting for Short-Term Investments*

February 1, 19B—Sold half of the DEF bonds for net proceeds of $3,050. (Accrued interest revenue, $3,000 × .08 × $\frac{4}{12}$ = $80; credit to investment account, ½ of $6,300 = $3,150).	Cash .... Loss on sale of short-term investment .... Investments, short-term (DEF bonds) .... Interest revenue	3,050 180	3,150 80
March 1, 19B—Collected quarterly dividend of $90 on GHI stock (declared earlier during the current period).	Cash .... Dividend revenue	90	90
April 1, 19B—Collected semiannual interest on DEF bonds ($3,000 × .08 × $\frac{6}{12}$ = $120).	Cash .... Interest revenue	120	120
June 1, 19B—Collected quarterly dividend of $90 on GHI stock (declared earlier during the current period).	Cash .... Dividend revenue	90	90
August 15, 19B—Bought 40 shares of JKL common stock at 87¾ plus brokerage fees of $90 for cash [(40 × $87.75) + $90 = $3,600].	Investments, short-term (JKL stock) .... Cash	3,600	3,600
September 1, 19B—Collected quarterly dividend of $90 on GHI stock (declared earlier during the current period).	Cash .... Dividend revenue	90	90
September 15, 19B—Sold 60 shares of GHI stock at 95 and incurred selling costs of $120 [(60 × $95) − $120 = $5,580; credit to investment account, $\frac{6}{10}$ of $8,700 = $5,220].	Cash .... Gain on sale of short-term investments .... Investments, short-term (GHI stock)	5,580	360 5,220
October 1, 19B—Collected semiannual interest on DEF bonds ($3,000 × .08 × $\frac{6}{12}$ = $120).	Cash .... Interest revenue	120	120
November 1, 19B—Paid $7,800 for MNO Company bonds including accrued interest. These 9%, $8,000 par bonds pay interest each February 1 and August 1 ($8,000 × .09 × $\frac{3}{12}$ = $180).	Investments, short-term (MNO bonds) .... Interest revenue .... Cash	7,620 180	7,800
November 5, 19B—Collected quarterly dividend of $25 on JKL stock (declared earlier during the current period).	Cash .... Dividend revenue	25	25
December 1, 19B—Collected quarterly dividend of $36 on remaining GHI shares (declared earlier during the current period).	Cash .... Dividend revenue	36	36
December 31, 19B—Accrued interest on DEF and MNO bonds [($3,000 × .08 × $\frac{3}{12}$) + ($8,000 × .09 × $\frac{5}{12}$) = $360].	Interest receivable .... Interest revenue	360	360

* All of the transactions presented relate to *short-term investments*, and specific securities held would be reported on the balance sheet under that caption rather than by the name of the issuer. If the investments are sufficiently numerous, a controlling account for Short-Term Investments would be established and supported by a subsidiary ledger. Also, both equity and debt securities are assumed to be included in one portfolio.

After the reversing entries on January 1, 19B, the company's ledger accounts reflected a $120 debit balance in Interest Revenue and a $225 credit balance in the account, Allowance to Reduce Short-Term Investments to Market. Transactions and related entries for short-term investments during 19B were as shown in Exhibit 8–3, assuming both equity and debt securities are included in a single short-term investment portfolio for LCM purposes.

At year-end, original costs and market values of securities held are as follows:

Investment	Amount Held	Unit Market Price	At End of 19B Cost	At End of 19B Market
DEF bonds	$3,000	100½	$ 3,150	$ 3,015
GHI stock	40 shares	88	3,480	3,520
JKL stock	40 shares	91	3,600	3,640
MNO bonds	$8,000	94¼	7,620	7,540
Aggregate portfolio total			$17,850	$17,715

Since there is a difference between cost and market of $135, aggregate market being lower, and since at the close of the preceding period the difference was $225, the allowance account should be reduced as follows:

December 31, 19B:

Allowance to reduce short-term investments to market ($225 − $135)	90	
Recovery of unrealized loss on short-term investments		90

Closing entries would be required as follows:

December 31, 19B:

Interest revenue*	380	
Dividend revenue	331	
Gain on sale of short-term investments	360	
Recovery of unrealized loss on short-term investments	90	
Loss on sale of short-term investments		180
Income summary		981

* Includes $120 reversal from prior year on DEF bonds.

If shares of stock are purchased between the dividend *declaration* date and the date of *record* (see Chapter 17), the amount of declared dividends applicable to the shares purchased should be debited to Dividends Receivable (or Dividend Revenue) because that portion of the cash paid is not a part of the cost of the stock investment. When the dividend subsequently is collected, the credit should be to Dividends Receivable (or Dividend Revenue).

PART C—RECEIVABLES

This part focuses on classification, measurement (valuation), and accounting for receivables. Broadly, the term *receivables* encompasses an entity's claims for money, goods, or services from other entities. Largely, receivables consist of amounts due from customers and clients aris-

ing from normal operations; however, receivables from other sources are sometimes encountered. Discussion of receivables is structured as follows:

1. Trade receivables:
   a. Accounts receivable.
   b. Notes receivable.
2. Special receivables.
3. Receivables used to secure immediate cash.

TRADE RECEIVABLES

Trade receivables usually mark the first point in the sequence of merchandising and service transactions. The amounts recorded as trade receivables are established by exchange credit transactions. The two principal classes of trade receivables are accounts receivable and notes receivable.

ACCOUNTS RECEIVABLE

The term *accounts receivable* is commonly used to designate trade debtors' accounts. Other receivables are separately designated and recorded as special receivables. Legitimate objection may be raised against the unqualified title "Accounts Receivable." Strictly speaking, any claim for which no written statement of the obligation has been received by the creditor, as opposed to a note receivable, is an account receivable. The careless use of a title so broadly inclusive is not sufficiently descriptive to convey the true nature of the various assets included. It is preferable to employ more descriptive titles for the various classes of accounts receivable, such as "Accounts Receivable—Trade Debtors" for accounts due for regular sales to customers. Such usage conveys to statement users the true nature of these assets. Ordinarily accounts receivable are classified under the "Current Assets" caption on the balance sheet; yet there are some special accounts receivable which should not be classified as current assets.

Measurement of Bad Debt Expense and Accounts Receivable. Valuation of accounts receivable poses the problem of estimating the amount which actually will be realized from collection of the accounts.[13] When credit is extended on a continuing basis, there are some inevitable losses due to uncollectibility. These losses are considered a normal expense of business. In accordance with the matching principle, this expense should be matched with the revenue of the period in which the sales and service transactions occurred, rather than in later periods when the specific accounts receivable are found to be uncollectible. Since bad accounts cannot be known in advance (otherwise no receivable would have been created), the bad debt expense must be estimated in advance. It should be recorded in the accounts and reported on the current financial statements.

Some small entities use a "specific chargeoff method" whereby losses from uncollectible receivables are deferred until it becomes positively known that a particular account is bad. At that time, Accounts Receivable is credited for the uncollectible balance and Bad Debt Expense is debited. While this procedure has the advantage of greater certainty and is permitted for income tax purposes (as is the allowance method), it is subject to criticism on two major counts: (1) Receivables are overstated; there is no allowance to deduct even though it is virtually certain that not all receivables will be collected. (2) The period in which the writeoff occurs is often later than the period in which the receivable was created; this results in incorrect matching—one of the costs of extending credit is bad debt losses, and the loss or expense should be recognized in the period when the revenue was recognized. For these reasons the "chargeoff" method cannot be characterized as GAAP.

The Accounts Receivable account should reflect the amount billed (net of any cash discount); and a special valuation, or contra asset account, Allowance for Doubtful Accounts (or Allowance for Bad Debts), should be used to record the estimated bad debts.

Two methods are commonly used to estimate the adjustment to the Allowance for Doubtful Accounts; each method has two adaptations as follows:

1. By estimating bad debt expense:
   a. Based on experience the average percentage relationship between actual bad debt losses and *net credit sales* is ascertained. This percentage, adjusted for anticipated conditions, is then applied to the actual net credit sales of the period to determine both the current expense and concurrent addition to the Allowance for Doubtful Accounts.
   b. Use the same procedure as in *(a)* except the percentage of bad debts to total sales (i.e., cash sales plus credit sales) is used.
2. By estimating the net value of the current receivables:
   a. Determine from experience the average percentage relationship between uncollectible accounts receivable and outstanding accounts receivable. This percentage, adjusted for expected conditions, is then applied each period to the ending balance in accounts receivable. The balance in the allowance account is then adjusted so that its balance equals the total amount of the estimated uncollectible accounts.
   b. Age the accounts receivable; and from the aging analysis and other available information, estimate the total uncollectible accounts. The balance in the allowance account is then adjusted so that its balance equals the total amount of the estimated uncollectible accounts.

The use of any of these approaches to estimate bad debts must recognize changes in credit policy, changes in economic conditions, and any other external factors which might have a bearing upon the ability of customers to pay their debts. After a method is selected, it should be subjected to a more or less continuous review on the part of the accountant and the officers of the company so that rates used can be revised or the approach changed to attain reliable results.

Accounting for Bad Debt Expense. The two methods of measuring bad debt expense out-

---

[13] Receivables arising from sales and services should be recorded at net of any trade discounts; see Chapter 10 for a complete discussion of accounting for cash discounts on receivables.

lined above affect the way in which the amount is determined for the adjusting entry to record estimated bad debt expense at the end of the period. In the first approach, the amount calculated on the basis of sales becomes the adjustment amount without regard to any prior balance in the allowance. In contrast, in the second approach, the *allowance* account is adjusted *to* the estimated balance needed; in other words, any existing balance in the allowance is taken into consideration to compute the adjustment amount.

To illustrate accounting for bad debt expense and uncollectible receivables, assume the following data for X Company:

Beginning balances:	
Accounts receivable (debit)	$100,000
Allowance for doubtful accounts (credit)	2,000
Transactions during the period:	
Credit sales	500,000
Cash sales	700,000
Collections on accounts receivable	420,000
Prior accounts written off as uncollectible during the period	2,500

The indicated entries relating to bad debts are as follows:

To write off the uncollectible accounts:

Allowance for doubtful accounts	2,500	
Accounts receivable (specific accounts)		2,500

The writeoff of uncollectible accounts as bad normally would occur during the period and would precede the end-of-the-period adjusting entries. In some cases, such as after a large writeoff or when currently created receivables are written off before the end of the period, the allowance account may have a temporary debit balance prior to the adjusting entry ($500 in this example). The two different methods for estimating the amount for the adjusting entry for bad debt expense are implemented as follows:

Method 1—Adjustment of the allowance by estimating bad debt expense: Assume experience has indicated that 1% of credit sales normally will not be collected and that this pattern is expected to continue.

Bad debt expense ($500,000 × 1%)	5,000	
Allowance for doubtful accounts		5,000

After posting this entry, the allowance account will reflect a credit balance of $4,500 and the ending balance in accounts receivable will be $100,000 + $500,000 − $420,000 − $2,500 = $177,500.

Method 2—Adjustment of allowance by estimating the net value of the current receivables: Assume it is estimated that 1.1% of the ending balance of accounts receivable eventually will be uncollectible.

Bad debt expense	2,453	
Allowance for doubtful accounts		2,453

Computation:
To adjust to the desired credit balance as follows:

Desired balance [1.1% of ($100,000 + $500,000 − $420,000 − $2,500)]	$1,953
Debit balance in allowance before adjustment	500
Amount of credit needed	$2,453

In the preceding illustration, the $2,500 writeoff of receivables during the current period had the effect of causing the allowance account to have a debit balance of $500 before the end-of-the-period adjustment. This does not necessarily indicate that past estimates of bad debt losses were too low. It is possible that the $2,500 writeoff includes some receivables created during the same period. If the allowance account should have a debit balance soon after making the end-of-the-period adjustment, an inadequate provision for bad debts is probably indicated. When it is determined that bad debt estimates have been too low or too high, current and future rates should be adjusted accordingly. This would be accounted for as a *change in accounting estimate* as prescribed in *APB Opinion No. 20,* "Accounting Changes" (see Chapters 4 and 24).

Evaluation of Methods

Both methods of estimating bad debts are acceptable under generally accepted accounting principles. Each method has certain strengths and weaknesses. The first method discussed, *estimation of bad debt expense,* based on credit sales, is generally preferable because it accords with the matching principle by measuring current bad debt expense in relationship to the revenues of the current period that caused the bad accounts. Thus, it focuses on matching current expense with current revenue and emphasizes

EXHIBIT 8–4
Aging Schedule for Accounts Receivable (at December 31, 19X)

Customer	Receivable Balance Dec. 31, 19X	Not Past Due	Past Due		
			1–30 Days	31–60 Days	Over 60 Days
Davis	$ 500	$ 400	$ 100		
Evans	900	900			
Field	1,650		1,350	$ 300	
Harris	90			30	$ 60
King	800	700	60	40	
Zilch	250	250			
Total	$32,500	$26,000	$4,200	$2,000	$300

the income statement rather than the balance sheet. The use of credit sales instead of total sales as the basis of the adjustment is preferable because cash sales cannot cause credit losses.

The second method discussed, *estimation of net value of present receivables,* is essentially an evaluation of the net realizable value of all accounts receivable reflected in the accounts at the end of the current period. It only incidentally measures bad debt expense. It suffers from the probability that the bad debt expense reported on the income statement for the period may not be related to the credit sales of the current period, which would violate the matching principle. It favors the balance sheet over the income statement. In applying this method, aging the accounts receivable (discussed below) at the end of each period is preferable to the use of a simple estimate as illustrated above.

Aging Accounts Receivable. Aging accounts receivables involves an analysis of each individual account to determine the amounts not yet due, moderately past due, and considerably past due. Classification of amounts by age (i.e., length of time uncollected) is deemed important because experience indicates that the older an account, the higher the probability of uncollectibility. Aging requires the preparation of an *aging schedule* similar to the illustration in Exhibit 8–4. In the absence of specific identification of collections, as related to several entries in an account, *Fifo* order is used in the aging schedule.

Upon completion of the aging schedule, each

past-due amount should be reviewed by credit department personnel to determine its probable collectibility. Sometimes such a procedure is prohibitively time consuming; therefore, a general approach often used is to develop estimated loss percentages for each *age category* based on loss experience of the company. This approach to the aging schedule is shown in Exhibit 8–5.

Based on the computation in Exhibit 8–5, at December 31, 19X, the allowance for doubtful accounts would be adjusted *to* a credit balance of $1,246.

Bad Debts Collected. When an amount is collected from a customer whose account was previously written off as uncollectible, the customer's account should be recharged with the amount actually collected and the allowance

EXHIBIT 8–5
Estimating Allowance for Doubtful Accounts, Aging Approach (at December 31, 19X)

Status	Total Balances	Loss Experience Percentage	Estimated Amount to Be Lost
Not due	$26,000	1%	$ 260
1–30 days past due	4,200	8	336
31–60 days past due	2,000	25	500
Over 60 days past due	300	50	150
	$32,500		$1,246

account should be credited for the same amount. This entry will cause the debtor's account to reflect a detailed record of the credit and related collections and will correct the allowance account. Such information may be useful in future dealings with the customer. The collection then is recorded as a debit to Cash and a credit to Accounts Receivable.

Customers' Credit Balances. When individual customers' accounts have material credit balances (from prepayments or overpayments), separate disclosure as liabilities is preferable; "Credit Balance of Customers' Accounts" is a suitable liability account title.

Added Facts about Accounts Receivable

Accounts Receivable is normally a controlling account, and detailed records of customer transactions and balances are carried in subsidiary records for each customer. Accounts Receivable balances reported on the statements should not reflect charges for containers if these charges will be canceled when the containers are returned. Sales to affiliated companies give rise to current accounts receivable and are not normally reported separately.[14] On the other hand, advances to affiliates are usually regarded as long term and would normally be reported as "Investments and Funds" instead of under "Current Assets."

Chapter 5 indicated that "Current Assets" includes all receivables identified with the normal operating cycle. Installment and certain other receivables are current even when not due within 12 months, provided they arise from operating cycle transactions.

When amounts charged to customers on sales contracts include interest, finance, and other related charges which are actually earned with the passage of time, they should be accounted for as specified in *APB Opinion No. 6:* "Unearned discounts (other than cash or quantity discounts and the like), finance charges and interest included in the face amount of receivables should be shown as a deduction from the related receivables."

Special allowance accounts are sometimes provided for discounts expected to be taken by customers, for anticipated sales returns and allowances, for freight charges to be deducted by customers, and the like. Where provided, such accounts have the effect of reducing income for the period in which they are established and of lowering the net reported value of receivables. While a good theoretical case can be made for such procedures, since the amounts provided tend to be about the same from one period to the next, and since the effects on income and receivables carrying values often are not material, most entities do not employ such refinements.

NOTES RECEIVABLE

Notes receivable include trade notes receivable, which arise from regular operations, and special notes receivable, which are classed as either current or noncurrent assets, depending upon their maturity dates and their relation to the operating cycle. Short-term trade notes receivable are the most common. Trade notes and special notes should be accounted for and reported separately.

Notes receivable represent unconditional written promises to pay the payee or holder of the note (i.e., a holder in due course) a specified sum. The payee ordinarily would be in possession of the note unless it has been endorsed to a subsequent holder in due course. Not all notes are negotiable (i.e., transferable by endorsement); hence, separate classification of negotiable and nonnegotiable notes is desirable. Requisites for negotiability are a matter of law.

Notes may be designated as *(a)* interest bearing or *(b)* noninterest bearing (discounted notes); theoretically, however, all commercial notes are interest bearing. Interest-bearing notes require payment of the *face* amount of the note at maturity plus interest. In contrast, a noninterest-bearing note includes the interest in the face amount. Thus the present value of an interest-bearing note is the same as its maturity amount (i.e., its face value, provided the discount rate used corresponds to the interest rate of the note). In

---

[14] Such receivables would normally be eliminated against the corresponding payables when consolidated balance sheets are prepared. (See Chapter 19.)

contrast, the present value (at any discount rate) of a noninterest-bearing note is less than its maturity amount.

Trade notes receivable should be recorded in the accounts and reported at their present value (refer to Chapter 6). Since an interest-bearing note that specifies the going rate of interest will have a current present value that is the same as its face amount, it is recorded at the face amount when received.[15] However, when a note is noninterest-bearing or when the specified interest rate on an interest-bearing note is different from the going rate, the computed present value and the maturity amounts will be different. In these two situations the current present value should be computed and reported as discussed and illustrated in Chapter 9 in respect to notes payable.

For purposes of this chapter a note receivable under two different assumptions (Case A, interest bearing; and Case B, noninterest bearing) will be illustrated.

Assume K Company sold merchandise for $2,000 on April 1, 19A, on credit and received a note receivable due in one year. The going rate of interest is 9%, and the accounting period ends on December 31. Assume two different situations, viz:

Case A—Interest-bearing note, face amount $2,000. Payable at maturity, face amount plus interest at 9%, $180; total, $2,180.

Case B—Noninterest-bearing (i.e., discounted) note, face amount, $2,180, which includes 9% interest on the net amount of the sales price (rather than on the face amount of the note). The amount of the sale can be verified as $2,180 ÷ 1.09 = $2,000.[16]

The entries for each separate case are as follows:

	Case A Interest-Bearing Note	Case B Noninterest-Bearing (discounted) Note
April 1, 19A—to record note and sale:		
Notes receivable	2,000	2,180
Unearned discount on notes receivable*		180
Sales revenue	2,000	2,000

* Alternative title, Unearned interest revenue or Discount on notes receivable.

	Case A	Case B
December 31, 19A—adjusting entry at end of accounting period:		
Interest receivable ($2,000 × 9% × 9/12)	135	
Unearned discount on notes receivable		135
Interest revenue..........	135	135
March 31, 19B—collection of note (assuming no reversing entry on January 1, 19B):		
Cash	2,180	2,180
Unearned discount on notes receivable		45
Interest receivable	135	
Interest revenue..........	45	45
Notes receivable	2,000	2,180

On the December 31, 19A, balance sheet, the balance in "Unearned discount on notes receivable" should be deducted from "Notes receivable" to reflect the amortized value of the note.[17]

Though not all of the documents reported under the caption "Notes receivable" technically are notes, the distinctions between them are seldom deemed vital enough to warrant the use of separate accounts for each type. For example, bills of exchange and trade acceptances usually are included in notes receivable. Drafts, trade acceptances, and other bills of exchange are written orders drawn by one party on a second party to pay a third party an amount of money under specified conditions.

The Notes Receivable account should include only commercial paper with trade debtors which is related to the operating cycle and not past due. All other notes, including those between the entity and its officers, employees, or

[15] This can be demonstrated readily by using the appropriate table values given in Chapter 6 to discount from maturity to the present (a) the maturity amount and (b) the interest payments required. These two discounted amounts when summed will always equal the face amount of the interest-bearing note.

[16] See Chapter 9, Part A on liabilities for discussion of notes payable (which are parallel to notes receivable), including the situation where the interest rate is applied to the face amount of the note.

[17] Alternatively, the noninterest-bearing note could have been recorded net of the discount (i.e., at $2,000) and the discount amortization entered in the note account so that the balance would be $2,180 at maturity date. The results are precisely the same.

stockholders, should be reported separately. Notes of affiliated companies also should be shown separately.

Balance sheet classification of notes receivable may be either current or noncurrent, depending upon collection expectations.

Provision for Losses on Notes. Provision for uncollectible notes from trade customers generally are included in the credit balance in Allowance for Doubtful Accounts.

Discounting of Notes Receivable. If a note receivable is sold (and endorsed) to another payee before maturity, the original payee receives cash before maturity, but may become *contingently liable* for payment of the note. The sale of a note receivable is generally called discounting a note receivable, and the existence of a contingent liability depends upon whether the note was endorsed with or without recourse. Since the bank or other endorsee normally is unwilling to accept the note without recourse, most notes create a contingent liability when discounted (i.e., sold to a third party).

The interest cost of discounting a note receivable is computed as follows:

$$\left\{ \begin{array}{l} \text{Interest Cost} \\ \text{(or discount)} \end{array} \right\} = \left\{ \begin{array}{l} \text{Maturity Value} \\ \text{of the Note} \end{array} \right\} \times \left\{ \begin{array}{l} \text{Discount} \\ \text{Rate} \end{array} \right\} \times \left\{ \begin{array}{l} \text{Time to Be Held} \\ \text{by the New Payee} \end{array} \right\}$$

To illustrate, assume Company X has a 90-day, 10% interest-bearing note receivable, face amount, $3,000. It is discounted at the bank at 9% after being held 30 days from issue date. The proceeds and interest cost would be calculated as follows:

Maturity amount:		
Face amount	$3,000	
Interest to maturity		
($3,000 × 10% × 3/12)	75	
Total maturity amount		$3,075.00
Interest cost (discount based on		
maturity amount)		
($3,075 × 9% × 2/12)		46.13
Proceeds (cash received		
upon discounting)		$3,028.87

Company X, the endorser, would record the discounting transaction in either of the following ways:

	Interest Expense and Revenue Recognized Separately	Interest Expense and Revenue Recognized at Net
Cash	3,028.87	3,028.87
Interest expense	46.13	
Notes receivable	3,000.00	3,000.00
Interest revenue	75.00	28.87

Some prefer the first entry because it separately recognizes the expense and revenue elements. Also, some accountants prefer to credit Notes Receivable Discounted for the face amount of the note; this account is a contra account to Notes Receivable. It is one method of recording the contingent liability (also see Chapter 9).[18]

Disclosure of the Contingent Liability on Discounted Notes. Reporting contingencies, as specified in *FASB Statement No. 5,* is discussed and illustrated in Chapter 9. When a note receivable is discounted, the transfer by endorsement with recourse creates a contingent liability for the endorser, as defined in *FASB Statement No. 5.* The contingent liability usually is disclosed by a note to the financial statements such as the following: "The company is contingently liable for discounted notes receivable amounting to $3,000. There is no reason to expect default." Other methods sometimes used are as follows:

1. Current Assets:		
Notes receivable (contingent		
liability for notes receivable		
discounted, $3,000)		$7,000
2. Current Assets:		
Notes receivable	$10,000	
Less: Notes receivable		
discounted	3,000	7,000

Dishonored Notes Receivable. When a note receivable is not paid or renewed at maturity, it is said to be dishonored. The accounting procedure for a dishonored note depends on whether the note was discounted. If a discounted note is dishonored, ordinarily it will be necessary for the original payee to pay it (unless the payee endorsed it without recourse).

---

[18] A less conventional, though theoretically defensible, recording of the transaction would be as follows:

Cash	3,028.87	
Interest revenue (for 1 month)		25.00
Gain on discount of notes		
($28.87–$25.00)		3.87
Notes receivable		3,000.00

Often the refinements in recording discounted notes involve amounts (such as the $3.87) which are not material.

To illustrate, assume the $3,000 interest-bearing note discounted by Company X was defaulted by the maker. Company X paid the bank the face amount of the note plus interest and a protest fee of $15. Company X would record the default as follows:

Special receivable—dishonored note 3,090
    Cash ($3,000 + $75 + $15) 3,090

On the other hand, if this same note had not been discounted, upon dishonor the required entry by Company X would have been as follows:

Special receivable—dishonored note 3,075
    Notes receivable 3,000
    Interest revenue 75
  To charge dishonored note to account
  of maker including accrued interest
  to maturity date.

After dishonor, interest accrues on the face amount plus accrued interest and any protest fees at the *legal* rate of interest. However, if the note is uncollectible, the total claim should be written off as a bad debt.

Balance sheet presentation of dishonored notes should list a special receivable with adequate provision for the uncollectibility expectations. Footnote disclosure is necessary for large notes in default.

SPECIAL RECEIVABLES

Receivables, other than trade receivables, generally are classified as special receivables. They may be represented by open accounts or notes and may be current or noncurrent. Some of the usual types of special receivables are as follows:

1. Deposits made to other parties to cover potential damages, and deposits made to guarantee performance of a contract or payment of an expense.
2. Prepayments to others on contingent purchases and expense contracts.
3. Claims against trade creditors for damaged, lost, or returned goods.
4. Claims against common carriers for lost or damaged goods.
5. Claims against the government for rebates.
6. Claims against customers for return of containers (no deposit).
7. Advances to subsidiaries.
8. Advances to officers and employees.
9. Dividends receivable (cash and property dividends declared but not yet paid by the issuing corporation).
10. Unexpended balances of working funds in the hands of agents.
11. Claims against insurance companies for losses sustained.
12. Claims in litigation.
13. Unpaid stock subscriptions (subscriptions receivable).

Special receivables that are related to the operating cycle or are collectible within one year (whichever is the longer) should be appropriately designated and reported in the current asset section of the balance sheet. Other special receivables normally are reported on the balance sheet under a noncurrent caption such as "Other Assets."[19]

Special receivables should be valued as to collectibility, and a special allowance for doubtful accounts in this category should be established if warranted.

USE OF RECEIVABLES TO SECURE IMMEDIATE CASH

Companies frequently utilize receivables to secure immediate cash prior to the regular collection date. The common methods of obtaining immediate cash on receivables are (1) discounting of notes receivable (discussed above), (2) assignment of accounts receivable, (3) factoring of accounts receivable, (4) outright sale of accounts receivable, and (5) pledging accounts receivable. While detailed contractual arrangements vary, the following brief description generally typifies these transactions and their accounting.

Assignment

Accounts receivable financing frequently involves the assignment to a financing institution

---

[19] "Advances to subsidiaries" (Item 7) would normally be reported under "Investments and Funds." Usually most of the receivables listed above are properly classified as current assets.

of receivables arising on open-account sales. Frequently, these assignments are made on a "with recourse, nonnotification" basis. "With recourse" means that accounts becoming excessively delinquent or uncollectible must be repurchased by the seller or replaced with other accounts receivable of equivalent value. "Nonnotification" means debtors are not informed of the assignment and hence remit to the seller in the usual way. As the seller collects on the receivables assigned, the cash is remitted to the finance company.

The cash advanced by the financial institution may range from 70% to 95% of the amount in the accounts. Annual interest rates charged may range as high as 18% to 20% when risks are great, especially when assignment is on a nonrecourse basis, or when the low dollar amount per account causes high costs.

Assignment of receivables with recourse is akin to the discounting of notes receivable, and the accounting procedure is essentially parallel. An illustrative problem is presented to demon-strate the essential accounting for the assignment of accounts receivable.

Illustrative Problem. W Company assigned $40,000 of its trade receivables to Z Finance Company under a contract, supported by a promissory note, whereby the latter agreed to advance 85% of their amount to W Company.

Debtors remit directly to W since the assignment was "with recourse, nonnotification." The series of transactions and related entries are shown in Exhibit 8–6.

On January 31, the balance sheet would reflect the following:

W COMPANY

Current Assets:		
Accounts receivable (assumed)		$150,000
Accounts receivable assigned ($40,000 − $30,500)	$9,500	
Less: Note payable on assigned accounts ($34,000 − $29,700)	4,300	
Equity in accounts receivable assigned		5,200
Total accounts receivable . . .		$155,200

EXHIBIT 8–6
Assignment of Accounts Receivable

	Transaction	*Entries on W's Books*		
a.	Jan. 2: Assigned $40,000 accounts receivable; advance received, 85%; gave note payable.	Accounts receivable assigned . . . . Accounts receivable	40,000	40,000
		Cash ($40,000 × 85%) . . . . Notes payable (Z Finance Co.)	34,000	34,000
b.	Jan. 3–30: Collected $30,000 of assigned accounts less cash discounts $300. In addition, sales returns were $500.	Cash . . . . Sales discounts . . . . Sales returns . . . . Accounts receivable assigned	29,700 300 500	30,500
c.	Jan. 31: Remitted collections to finance company plus $350 interest.	Interest expense . . . . Notes payable (Z Finance Co.) . . . . Cash	350 29,700	30,050
d.	Feb. 1–27: Collected balance of assigned accounts except $200 written off as uncollectible.	Cash . . . . Allowance for doubtful accounts . . . . . . Accounts receivable assigned	9,300 200	9,500
e.	Feb. 28: Remitted balance due to finance company ($34,000 − $29,700 = $4,300) plus $100 interest.	Interest expense . . . . Notes payable (Z Finance Co.) . . . . Cash	100 4,300	4,400

Note: If the collections are remitted directly to the finance company (not deposited by W Company into their own bank account), entries *(b)* and *(c)* and *(d)* and *(e)*, respectively, would be combined into two entries.

The details of a contract, such as the one illustrated above, will determine the appropriate accounting entries.

Factoring

Accounts receivable may be sold on a *without recourse* basis to factors.[20] Customers whose accounts are sold are instructed to pay directly to the factor who assumes the functions of billing, collecting, and so on.

Under a factoring contract, the factor controls the granting of credit by the client. As the latter sells to customers, copies of the sales invoices and supporting documents are sent to the factor. The client usually obtains cash immediately upon transferring the invoices. Gross amounts of the invoices less any sales discounts and allowances and less the factor's commission and a margin or reserve (factor's margin or reserve) to cover expected returns and claims is the measure of cash available. Interest (above the factor's commission) is charged only on cash drawn *prior* to the average due date of the factored invoices. Available money not drawn plus the amount reserved becomes available without interest cost on the average due date.

In addition to interest, factors charge commissions to compensate for their credit and collection services and the credit losses they must bear. Since cash needs are often seasonal, proportions of available cash drawn usually will vary throughout the term of the factoring contract.

Outright Sale of Accounts Receivable

Occasionally accounts receivable are sold outright to a third party, usually without recourse. Outright sale often involves a high discount rate, varying from 15% to 50%, depending upon the circumstances. Outright sale occurs most frequently when a business is in serious financial difficulty. No unique accounting problems are involved; Cash is debited, the receivables sold and the related amount of the allow-

ance for doubtful accounts are closed out; and the difference is recorded as finance expense.

Pledging

Loans are sometimes obtained from banks and other lenders by pledging accounts receivable as security. The borrower continues to collect the receivables and usually is required to apply all or a large percent of collections as made to reduction of the loan. This method of lending on receivables is sometimes used because commercial banks may lack express or implied powers to buy accounts receivable. The fact that portions of the receivables have been pledged should be disclosed by balance sheet notes or parenthetical notations. Accounting by the borrower is similar to that illustrated above for assignment.

QUESTIONS

PART A

1. Define cash in the accounting sense.

2. In what circumstances, if any, is it permissible to offset a bank overdraft against a positive balance in another bank account?

3. If you were called upon to establish a petty cash system that would be particularly effective from the standpoint of internal control, what important features would you incorporate into it?

4. Where (if at all) do items (a) through (g) belong in the following reconciliation?

Balance per bank statement, June 30 ...	$x,xxx.xx
Additions	
Deductions	
June 30 true balance	$9,600.00
Balance per our ledger, June 30	$x,xxx.xx
Additions	
Deductions	
June 30 true balance	$9,600.00

   a. Note collected by bank for the depositor on June 29; notification was received July 2 when the June 30 bank statement was received.
   b. Checks drawn in June which had not cleared bank by June 30.
   c. Check of a depositor with a similar name which was returned with checks accompany-

---

[20] Factors are financing organizations which buy trade receivables. Factoring is encountered in many industries but is especially widespread in the textile industry.

ing June 30 bank statement and which was charged to our account.

d. Bank service charge for which notification was received upon receipt of bank statement.

e. Deposit mailed June 30 which reached bank July 1 (not yet on the bank statement).

f. Notification of charge for imprinting our name on blank checks was received with the June 30 bank statement.

g. Upon refooting cash receipts journal, we discovered that one receipt was omitted in arriving at the total which was posted to the Cash account in the ledger.

5. Briefly describe a "comprehensive" bank reconciliation. What advantage does the comprehensive reconciliation afford over a conventional bank reconciliation which covers a single point in time?

6. Define the following items associated with *cash:*
   a. Compensating balance.
   b. NSF check.
   c. CD.

PART B

7. What criteria must a security meet to qualify as a short-term investment?

8. What is properly included in the cost of short-term investments?

9. In what ways, if any, does the accounting for investments in bonds differ if the securities are held as long-term investments instead of as short-term investments?

10. An investor bought 100 shares of PQ Company stock in January for $6,700 and another 100 in March for $7,000. In October, the investor sold 150 of the shares at 77. What is the amount of the gain or loss? Discuss briefly.

11. The account, Allowance to Reduce Short-Term Investments in Equity Securities to Market, may properly be debited or credited. Under what circumstances would this account be credited? Debited? What is the maximum amount it can be debited?

PART C

12. Briefly describe the basic approaches to estimating the allowance for doubtful accounts in connection with trade receivables. Evaluate each approach as to the financial statement which the approach emphasizes.

13. It sometimes happens that a receivable which has been written off as uncollectible is subsequently collected. Describe the accounting procedures in such an event.

14. How should customer accounts with credit balances be reported in the financial statements?

15. T Company received a $1,000, 8% note from a customer which will mature in three months. After holding it one month, the note was discounted by T at the bank at 9%. Compute T's proceeds.

16. How should special receivables be reported on the balance sheet?

17. In relation to accounts receivable, what is the meaning of each of the following terms?
    a. Assignment.
    b. Factoring.
    c. Pledging.

DECISION CASE 8–1

The president of the D'Anna Company, a manufacturer, is concerned about valuation of the company's material investment in marketable securities; she wants to value them at closing prices traded on the New York and American Stock Exchanges at year-end. The closing prices were substantially in excess of acquisition cost.

She stated ". . . the thousands of transactions in shares of open-end investment trusts (mutual funds) at prices reflecting current market prices of their portfolios are evidence that most people view these value changes as equivalent to realization. Indeed, the cost of the investment is an incredibly low figure to present."

As D'Anna's independent auditor, you explained that some transactions, events, and changes in valuation are not recognized for accounting purposes under generally accepted accounting principles.

Required:

1. List the various types of transactions, events, and changes in valuation that are *not* recognized for accounting purposes under GAAP.

2. a. What should be considered in selecting the method of revenue recognition that is most appropriate for a particular situation. Do *not* list methods of revenue recognition.

   b. Discuss the appropriateness of D'Anna Company's proposal to recognize as revenue the excess of closing prices listed by the stock exchanges over the cost of the investment.

(AICPA adapted)

DECISION CASE 8–2

PART A

FASB Statement No. 12 generally became effective for financial statements covering annual and interim periods ending on or after December 31, 1975. There were some exceptions as to the effective date, one of which pertained to paragraph 10. Provisions of this paragraph (quoted below) did not apply to transfers of securities between current and noncurrent classifications made as of or before December 31, 1975.

> If there is a change in the classification of a marketable equity security between current and noncurrent, the security shall be transferred between the corresponding portfolios at the lower of its cost or market value at date of transfer. If market value is less than cost, the market value shall become the new cost basis, and the difference shall be accounted for as if it were a realized loss and included in the determination of net income.

The following note to financial statements appeared in the annual report of Norton Simon, Inc., for the fiscal year ended June 30, 1976:

> Marketable equity securities included in short-term investments at June 30, 1975, had a cost of $34,168,000. At June 30, 1975, short-term investments were stated generally at lower of cost or market. Marketable equity securities, with a gross unrealized loss of approximately $10,-000,000 at June 30, 1975, were transferred at cost from short-term to long-term investments as of December 31, 1975, in accordance with provisions of *Statement No. 12* of The Financial Accounting Standards Board. Realized losses on marketable equity securities amounted to $400,000 in 1976 and $3,228,000 in 1975. During 1975, the valuation allowance for marketable equity securities was reduced $5,339,000 as a result of realized losses and changes in market value of investments.

Required:

1. Assuming the securities transferred to long-term investments had not changed in value between June 30, 1975, and January 2, 1976, what would have been the differential effect of the December 31, 1975, transfer relative to a January 1976 transfer?
2. Assuming the securities had not been transferred and that their value on June 30, 1976, was the same as at June 30, 1975, how would the note to the financial statements have been modified?

PART B

Notes to the financial statements relating to marketable securities included in current assets of Stauffer Chemical Company in the annual report for the year ended December 31, 1976, included the following:

Marketable Securities

	(in thousands)	
	1976	1975
Marketable securities—at cost .	$102,596	$33,370
Approximate gross unrealized losses	(1,309)	(3,296)
Approximate gross unrealized gains	654	12
Valuation allowances	(655)	(3,284)
Marketable securities—at market	$101,941	$30,086
Valuation allowance decrease included in income	$ 2,629	$ 882
Realized net loss (specific identification method)	$ 14	$ 223

Required:

Comment on this note and the disclosure it provides.

EXERCISES

PART A
Exercises 8–1 to 8–7

Exercise 8–1

What treatment should be accorded the following items held by ABC Company as of December 31?

1. Checks payable to ABC Company in the amount of $350 dated early January of the following year.
2. A customer check payable to ABC Company for $50, included in its December 20 deposit, was returned by the bank stamped "NSF." No entry has yet been made to reflect the return.
3. A $20,000 CD on which interest accrued to December 31 has just been recorded by debiting Interest Receivable and crediting Interest Revenue. The chief accountant proposes to report the $20,000 as "Cash in Bank."
4. ABC operates a $200 petty cash fund. As of December 31 the fund cashier reports expense vouchers covering various expenses in the amount of $167.20 and cash of $31.80.
5. Postage stamps valued at $30 are found in the cash

drawer. The chief accountant proposes to report them as "Cash."

6. A cashier's check in the amount of $200 payable to ABC Company is in the cash drawer; it is dated December 29. The chief accountant proposes to report it as part of "Cash."
7. Three checks totaling $465 payable to vendors who have sold merchandise to ABC Company on account dated December 31 are still on hand unmailed after the last mail pickup. They have been entered as payments in the check register and ledger.
8. At December 30, ABC Company had left a note which matures December 31 with its bank for collection. The note is for $2,000 and bears interest at 9%, having run for three months. As yet, ABC has not heard from the bank as to the outcome of its collection efforts but is confident of a favorable outcome because of the extremely high credit rating of the maker of the note.

Exercise 8–2

Indicate the amount (and how derived) at which each of the following independent cases could be properly reported as ordinary Cash:

a. Balance in general checking account, Bank H, $5,000; overdraft in special checking account, Bank H, $800; IOU held from company president for $400, received six weeks ago in settlement of advance to the president.
b. Balance in Bank P, $20,000; refundable deposit with state treasurer to guarantee performance of highway contract in progress, $10,000; balance in Banco de Sur America, $2,000 (foreign and restricted).
c. Cash on hand, $500; cash in Bank C, $9,000; cash held by salespersons as advances on expense accounts, $800; postage stamps on hand received from mail-order customers, $50.
d. Balance in checking account, $10,000; demand certificates of deposits, $5,000; deposit with bond sinking fund trustee, $15,000; cash on hand, $1,000.
e. Negotiable instruments in cash drawer on December 31:

(Relates to Exercise 8–2) From	Date of Check
Customer W	Dec. 29
Customer X	Dec. 30
Customer Y	Dec. 24
Customer Z (postdated)	Jan. 2
J. T. Brown	Dec. 29

Exercise 8–3

As a part of their newly designed internal control system, the Jay Corporation established a petty cash fund. Operations for the first month were as follows:

a. Wrote a check for $500 on August 1 and turned the cash over to the custodian.
b. Summary of the petty cash expenditures:

	Aug. 1–15	Aug. 16–31
Postage	$ 40	$ 58
Supplies used	220	190
Delivery expense	98	178
Miscellaneous expenses	35	40
Totals	$393	$466

c. Fund replenished on August 16.
d. Fund replenished on August 31 and increased by $200.

Required:

Give all entries indicated through August.

Exercise 8–4

Burns Company, as a matter of policy, deposits all receipts and makes all payments by check. The following data were taken from the cash records of the company:

Reconciliation at May 31

Balance per bank	$6,000
Add: Outstanding deposits	1,200
	7,200
Deduct: Outstanding checks	1,400
Balance per books	$5,800

June Results

	Per Bank	Per Books
Balance, June 30	$ 3,090	$ 4,200
June deposits	10,600	12,300
June checks	14,500	13,900
June note collected	1,000	—
June bank charges	10	—

Other Data	
On past-due account	$500
In payment of $1,000 invoice of December 23	700
Previously deposited and returned; insufficient funds	300
In full payment of account	400
American Express travelers check	100

Required (for June):

1. Compute the deposits in transit and outstanding checks as of June 30.
2. Reconcile the bank account as of June 30.
3. Give any entries indicated for the books.

Exercise 8–5

Reconciliation of Myron Company's bank account at May 31 was as follows:

Balance per bank statement	$12,500
Deposits outstanding	1,500
Checks outstanding	150*
True cash balance	$13,850
Balance per books	$13,864
Unrecorded service charge	14*
True cash balance	$13,850

    * Denotes deduction.

June data are as follows:

	Bank	Books
Checks recorded	$11,500	$11,800
Deposits recorded	10,100	11,000
Service charges recorded	12	14
Collection by bank ($800 note plus interest)	820	—
NSF check returned with June 30 statement (will be redeposited; assumed to be good)	50	—
Balances June 30	11,858	13,050

Required:

1. Compute deposits in transit and checks outstanding at June 30.
2. Prepare a reconciliation for June.
3. Prepare entries needed at June 30.

Exercise 8–6

Kay Company's cash transactions were made through its accounts at First National Bank. On April 30 the company reconciled its bank and book balances as follows:

Balance per bank statement		$7,900
Deduct outstanding checks:		
No. 698	$ 30	
No. 699	80	
No. 702	25	135
		7,765
Add:		
Deposits in transit	150	
April service charge	3	
May Company check charged to our account	40	193
April 30 book balance		$7,958

In summary form, the Cash account on Kay Company's books for May is as below:

Cash			
April 30, balance	7,958	April service charge	3
May collections	14,210	Checks drawn	13,812

At May 31 the following checks were outstanding: No. 702, $25; No. 735, $100; No. 738, $60; and No. 740, $20. The May 31 receipts amounting to $420 were mailed to the bank at the close of business that day. The May service charge of $5 was recorded by the bank only. The $40 item shown on the April 30 reconciliation was corrected by the bank during May. May receipts and payments for Kay Company's account recorded by the bank were $13,980 and $13,747 respectively. From the foregoing, the correct ending bank balance can be derived.

Required:

Prepare a comprehensive reconciliation for May.

Exercise 8–7

Dilson Company deposits all its receipts in the bank and makes all disbursements by check. Its February 28 bank reconciliation was as follows:

Balance per bank		$5,414
Add:		
Deposits in transit	$170	
Unrecorded bank service charge	6	176
		5,590
Deduct: Outstanding checks		390
Balance per books		$5,200

March data are as follows:

	Per Bank	Per Books
Balance, March 31	$6,024	$3,994
March deposits reflected	4,760	4,900
March checks reflected	6,170*	6,100
Note collected (including $20 interest)	2,020	—
Service charge recorded	—	6

    * Includes a check drawn by Wilson Company for $150.

Required:

1. Determine the apparent deposits in transit and checks as of March 31.
2. Prepare a comprehensive reconciliation for March.
3. If March 31 were the end of Dilson's fiscal year, what entries would be needed on its books? Draft them.

Exercise 8–8

At January 1, the short-term investments of Church Company were as follows:

Number Held	Description	Par Value Each	Total Cost
8	Bonds, Day Company, 5% per annum (paid each April 1 and October 1)*	$1,000	$7,800
100	Shares, Knight Company common stock	50	8,300

* Assume accrued interest reversed January 1.

Market value was in excess of cost at January 1.

The transactions below relate to the above short-term investments and those bought and sold during the year. All transactions are cash.

Feb. 2 Received $150 dividend from Knight Company.
Mar. 1 Sold four (4) Day Company bonds for a total consideration (including accrued interest) of $4,100.
Apr. 1 Collected semiannual interest on Day Company bonds.
May 1 Bought three bonds of King, Ltd. These 4%, $1,000 bonds pay interest each March 1 and September 1. Total consideration paid, $3,050.
June 1 For $4,200 total consideration sold the remaining Day Company bonds.
Aug. 2 Received $150 dividend from Knight Company.
Sept. 1 Collected semiannual interest on King, Ltd., bonds.
Dec. 31 Adjust and close books; recognize all accruals. At January 1, as stated, market value of marketable securities exceeded cost. However, at December 31, market prices on a per security basis were as follows:

	Market Price
Knight Company common shares	72½
King, Ltd., bonds	102*

* Does not include accrued interest.

Required:

Journalize the foregoing transactions. At year-end make adjusting and closing entries. The stock is to be valued as one portfolio at lower of cost or market, and the bonds are to be valued as a separate portfolio at cost.

Exercise 8–9

Case A. At December 31, 19A, the portfolio of short-term investments of Metz Company was comprised of the following items:

Description	Quantity	Cost	Unit Market Prices
Hygro Corp. bonds, 7%, $1,000	5	$5,200	101½
Damon common stock	50 shares	2,300	40⅝
Martin common stock	100 shares	2,100	24

Assuming lower of cost or market is applied to all short-term investments as a single portfolio:

a. At what value should the aggregate of short-term investments be reported on the December 31, 19A, balance sheet of Metz Company? Show computations.

b. One year later, the short-term investment portfolio of Metz consisted of the following:

Description	Quantity	Cost	Unit Market Prices
Damon common stock	20 shares	$ 920	37¼
Martin common stock	30 shares	630	23
Dries Corporation bonds, 8%, $1,000	4	4,040	100½

During 19B, Metz had sold the 30 Damon shares at a gain of $200 and the 70 Martin shares at a gain of $140. At what value should the aggregate of short-term investments be reported on the December 31, 19B, balance sheet of Metz Company assuming lower of cost or market for all securities? Show computations.

Case B. Davis Company bought, as a short-term investment, seven of the $1,000 bonds of Massengill Corporation on April 1, 19A, at 102 plus accrued interest. These 9% bonds pay interest semiannually each May 1 and November 1. On December 1, 19A, four (4) of the bonds were sold at 101¼ plus accrued interest. Davis Company adjusts and closes books on December 31.

a. Journalize all events (except closing entries) relating to the bonds for 19A assuming the cost method.

b. If the bonds had been bought as a long-term or permanent investment, what added information would have been needed and why?

Exercise 8–10

Prepare journal entries to record the following transactions (use the cost method) relating to 9% bonds of Dee Corporation purchased as a short-term investment. These bonds pay interest each May 1 and November 1.

Aug. 1 Cash of $39,800 is disbursed for $40,000 par value bonds including interest.
Nov. 1 Collected interest.

Dec. 31 Adjust and close books for the year. The market value of the bonds is 98 excluding interest (a "mere temporary" condition).

Jan. 1 Make any desirable reversing entries.

Feb. 1 Sold half of the bonds, receiving a check for $19,600 including accrued interest.

May   1 Collected interest.

Exercise 8–11

In November 19A, Q Corporation acquired the following short-term investments in marketable equity securities:

Company L—500 shares common stock (nopar) at $60 per share.

Company M—300 shares preferred stock (par $10, nonredeemable) at $20 per share.

Additional data:

Dec. 31, 19A Market values: L stock, $52; and M stock, $24.

Mar. 2, 19B Received cash dividends per share as follows: L stock, $1.00; and M stock, $0.50.

Oct. 1, 19B Sold 100 of the Company M shares at $25 per share.

Dec. 31, 19B Market values: L stock, $56; and M stock, $27.

Required:

1. Give all entries indicated for Q Corporation for the above short-term investments in marketable equity securities (LCM method) assuming no other short-term investments.

2. Show how the investments and related gains and losses would be reflected on the financial statements for Q Corporation for 19A and 19B.

Exercise 8–12

Select the best answer in each of the following; justify your choices.

1. Which of the following transactions would increase a company's positive current ratio?
   a. Receive a stock dividend on a short-term investment.
   b. Borrow money on a short-term note.
   c. Sell a short-term investment at a loss.
   d. Sell a short-term investment at a gain.

2. Davis Company owns some shares of stock which its management would like very much to sell. There is, however, serious question about the company's ability to sell the stock quickly at other than a sacrifice price. If the investment is valued at cost, it should be classified as a
   a. Current asset.
   b. Long-term investment.

   c. Contra item under capital.
   d. Deferred charge.

3. The test of marketability must be met before an investment in securities owned can be properly classified as
   a. Debentures.
   b. Treasury stock.
   c. Long-term investments.
   d. Current assets.

4. How should the premium or discount on bonds purchased as a short-term investment be reported in published financial statements?
   a. As expense or revenue in the period the bonds are purchased.
   b. As an integral part of the cost of the asset acquired (investment) and amortized over a period of not less than 60 months.
   c. As an integral part of the cost of the asset acquired (investment) until such time as the investment is sold.
   d. As an integral part of the cost of the asset acquired (investment) and amortized over the period the bonds are expected to be held.

5. Marketable securities held to finance future construction of additional plants should be classified on the balance sheet as
   a. Current assets.
   b. Property, plant, and equipment.
   c. Intangible assets.
   d. Investments and funds.

(all except No. 1, AICPA adapted)

PART C
Exercises 8–13 to 8–21

Exercise 8–13

When examining the accounts of Horan Company, you ascertain that balances relating to both receivables and payables are included in a single controlling account (called Receivables), which has a $48,100 debit balance. An analysis of the details of this account revealed the following:

	Debit	Credit
Accounts receivable—customers	$80,000	
Accounts receivable—officers	4,000	
Debit balances—creditors	900	
Expense advances to salespersons ..	2,000	
Capital stock subscriptions receivable	9,200	
Accounts payable for merchandise ..		$38,500
Unpaid salaries		6,600
Credit balances in customer accounts		2,000
Payments received in advance for shipments not yet made		900

Required:

1. Give entry to reflect correct treatment of the above items and to reclassify items which do not belong in the Receivables account.
2. How should the items be reported on Horan Company's balance sheet?

Exercise 8–14

When examining the accounts of Healy Company, you ascertain that balances relating to both receivables and payables are included in a single controlling account (called Receivables), which has a $49,300 debit balance. An analysis of the details of this account revealed the following:

	Debit	Credit
Accounts receivable—customers	$80,000	
Accounts receivable—officers	5,000	
Debit balances—creditors	1,100	
Expense advances to salespersons ..	2,500	
Capital stock subscriptions receivable	9,200	
Accounts payable for merchandise ..		$39,200
Unpaid salaries		7,100
Credit balances in customer accounts		1,300
Payments received from customers in advance for shipments not yet made		900

Required:

1. Give entry to reflect correct treatment of the above items and to reclassify items which do not belong in the Receivables account.
2. How should the items be reported on Healy Company's balance sheet?

Exercise 8–15

An analysis of the Receivables control account (debit balance, $102,900) of Elba Corporation at December 31 revealed the following:

a.	Accounts from regular sales (current)	$80,000
b.	Accounts known to be uncollectible	2,500
c.	Dishonored notes charged back to customers' accounts	8,000
d.	Credit balances in customer accounts	600
e.	Past due accounts of customers	6,000
f.	Due from employees	7,000

The Allowance for Doubtful Accounts is adjusted each December 31. Its balance before adjustment on December 31 was a $1,600 debit. It was estimated that losses on receivables at December 31 would average as follows:

Item	Loss %
a	1
c	20
e	5

Required:

1. Give journal entries *(a)* to reclassify items which do not belong in the Receivables account and *(b)* to reflect bad debt expense.
2. Indicate proper reporting on Elba Corporation's December 31 balance sheet. Assume all amounts to be material.

Exercise 8–16

The following data are available concerning a company whose fiscal year is the calendar year:

Sales (of which $80,000 are on credit)	$100,000
Accounts receivable, January 1	60,000
Accounts receivable, December 31	70,000
Allowance for doubtful accounts, January 1	2,000 (credit)
Allowance for doubtful accounts, December 31*	1,000 (debit)

*Before making year-end adjusting entry for bad debt expense.

Required:

1. Assuming there were no recoveries of doubtful accounts which had been previously charged off as uncollectible, what was the amount of receivables charged off as uncollectible during the year?
2. What was the amount of cash inflow from receivables during the year?
3. Give the year-end adjusting entry for bad debts under each of the following independent assumptions:
   a. Bad debt expense estimated to be 4% of credit sales.
   b. Bad debt expense estimated to be 3% of total sales.
   c. Bad debts allowance estimated to be 5% of uncollected receivables at December 31.
   d. Bad debts allowance estimated on basis of aging; the estimate is
      (1) On receivables less than 60 days old ($20,000), 1%.
      (2) On receivables 60 to 120 days old ($40,000), 3½%.
      (3) On remaining receivables, 6%.

Exercise 8–17

Temple Company has been in business three years and is being audited for the first time. Concerning accounts receivable, the auditor ascertained that the company has been charging off receivables as they finally proved uncollectible and treating them as expenses at the time of writeoff. (Stated another way, receivables were valued at 100 cents on the dollar.)

It is determined that receivables losses have approximated (and can be expected to continue to approximate) 2% of net sales. Until this first audit, the company's sales and receivable writeoff experience was as below:

Year of Sales	Amount of Sales	Accounts Written Off in—		
		19A	19B	19C
19A	$600,000	$3,000	$7,500	$1,000
19B	750,000	—	3,500	6,500
19C	850,000	—	—	4,000

Required:

1. Indicate the amount by which net income was understated or overstated (ignoring income tax effects) each year under the company's policy. Assume for purpose of this requirement that the old policy was also used in arriving at the above amounts for 19C.
2. If Temple Company were to switch to a more acceptable basis of accounting for bad debts, assuming books were still open for 19C, what entry should be made at year-end, 19C?

Exercise 8–18

Fuschia Company accepted an interest-bearing note receivable for $4,000 from a customer whose account receivable had become due. In respect to the note, give the indicated journal entry for each of the following independent events; show computations. (Use 30-day months, not days, for interest computations.)

1. Received the note, which matures in four months and bears interest at 9%.
2. Discounted the above note after two months at 10% interest. Make the entry under the two methods of recording.
3. The customer paid the note at maturity.
4. The customer defaulted on the note, and Fuschia Company paid the holder including a $15 protest fee.

Exercise 8–19

On November 1, 19A, Bard Company received from two customers two notes for merchandise sold to them. Each note was in settlement for a sale of goods for $8,000. Customer A gave a three-month 7% interest-

bearing note. Customer B gave a three-month, noninterest-bearing note with an implied interest rate of 7% (i.e., 7% interest on the sales price was included in the face of the note).

Required:

1. Give all entries (including adjusting and closing entries) pertaining to the two notes on Bard Company's books from date of receipt through time of payment, assuming the company adjusts and closes its books at December 31, 19A.
2. Show how the notes should be reflected on the December 31, 19A, balance sheet.

Exercise 8–20

A, Inc., assigned $60,000 of its receivables to Z Finance Company. The contract provided that Z would advance 80% of their gross value. A's debtors continued to remit directly to it; the cash, less finance charges, is then remitted to the finance company.

During the first month, customers owing $41,000 remitted $39,400 to A, Inc., thereby taking advantage of $600 cash discounts. Sales returns totaled $1,000. The finance charge paid after the first month was $350.

During the second month, remaining receivables were collected in full except for $400 written off as uncollectible. Final settlement was effected with the finance company, including payment of $150 added interest.

Required:

Give the journal entries needed to record the above assignment of accounts receivable. Closing entries are not necessary.

Exercise 8–21

Determine the best answer in each of the following questions. Write question numbers and answers alongside on the solution you submit.

1. Which of the following methods of determining bad debt expense does not match expense and revenue?
   a. Charging bad debts with a percentage of sales under the allowance method.
   b. Charging bad debts with a percentage of accounts receivable under the allowance method.
   c. Charging bad debts with an amount derived from aging the accounts receivable under the allowance method.
   d. Charging bad debts as accounts are written off as uncollectible.

The following data pertain to Items 2 through 6:

RETAIL ESTABLISHMENT, INC.
Balance Sheets

	December 31	
Assets	19B	19A
Current Assets:		
Cash	$ 150,000	$100,000
Marketable securities	40,000	
Accounts receivable—net .	420,000	290,000
Merchandise inventory	330,000	210,000
Prepaid expenses	50,000	25,000
	990,000	625,000
Land, buildings, and fixtures..............	565,000	300,000
Less: Accumulated depreciation	55,000	25,000
	510,000	275,000
	$1,500,000	$900,000

Equities		
Current Liabilities:		
Accounts payable	$ 265,000	$220,000
Accrued expenses	70,000	65,000
Dividends payable	35,000	—
	370,000	285,000
Notes payable—due 19E	250,000	
Stockholders' Equity:		
Common stock...........	600,000	450,000
Retained earnings	280,000	165,000
	880,000	615,000
	$1,500,000	$900,000

RETAIL ESTABLISHMENT, INC.
Income Statements

	Year Ended December 31	
	19B	19A
Net sales—including service charges	$3,200,000	$2,000,000
Cost of goods sold	2,500,000	1,600,000
Gross profit	700,000	400,000
Expenses—including income taxes	500,000	260,000
Net Income	$ 200,000	$ 140,000

Additional information available included the following:

Although Retail Establishment will report all changes in financial position, management has adopted a format emphasizing the flow of cash.

All accounts receivable and accounts payable relate to trade merchandise. Cash discounts are not allowed to customers, but a service charge is added to an account for late payment. Accounts payable are recorded net and always are paid to take all of the discount allowed. The Allowance for Doubtful Accounts at the end of 19B was the same as at the end of 19A; no receivables were charged against the Allowance during 19B.

The proceeds from the note payable were used to finance a new store building. Capital stock was sold to provide additional working capital.

2. Cash collected during 19B from accounts receivable amounted to
  a. $3,200,000.
  b. $3,070,000.
  c. $2,920,000.
  d. $2,780,000.
  e. None of the above or not determinable from the above facts.

3. Cash payments during 19B on accounts payable to suppliers amounted to
  a. $2,575,000.
  b. $2,500,000.
  c. $2,455,000.
  d. $2,335,000.
  e. None of the above or not determinable from the above facts.

4. Cash dividend payments during 19B amounted to
  a. $120,000.
  b. $115,000.
  c. $85,000.
  d. $35,000.
  e. None of the above or not determinable from the above facts.

5. Cash receipts during 19B which were not provided by operations totaled
  a. $400,000.
  b. $250,000.
  c. $150,000.
  d. $70,000.
  e. None of the above or not determinable from the above facts.

6. Cash payments for assets during 19B which were not reflected in operations totaled
  a. $305,000.
  b. $265,000.
  c. $185,000.
  d. $40,000.
  e. None of the above or not determinable from the above facts.

7. The advantage of relating a company's bad debt experience to its accounts receivable is that this approach
  a. Gives a reasonably correct statement of receivables in the balance sheet.

b. Relates bad debts expense to the period of sale.

c. Is the only generally accepted method for valuing accounts receivable.

d. Makes estimates of uncollectible accounts unnecessary.

8. Park Company's account balances at December 31, 19A, for Accounts Receivable and the related Allowance for Uncollectible Accounts are $600,000 and $800, respectively. From an aging of accounts receivable, it is estimated that $8,100 of the December 31 receivables will be uncollectible. The net realizable value of accounts receivable would be

a. $600,000.

b. $599,200.

c. $592,700.

d. $591,900.

e. None of the above.

9. Which of the following statements is not valid in determining balance sheet disclosure of accounts receivable?

a. Accounts receivable should be identified on the balance sheet as "pledged" if they are used as security for a loan even though the loan is shown on the same balance sheet as a liability.

b. That portion of installment accounts receivable from customers which falls due more than 12 months from the balance sheet date usually would be excluded from the current assets.

c. Allowances may be deducted from the accounts receivable for discounts, returns, and adjustments to be made in the future on accounts shown in the current balance sheet.

10. During 19A Larry Company, which uses the allowance method of accounting for uncollectible accounts, had charges to Doubtful Accounts Expense of $80,000 and wrote off as uncollectible accounts receivable of $55,000. These transactions decreased working capital by

a. $80,000.

b. $55,000.

c. $25,000.

d. $0.

e. None of the above.

11. On a balance sheet, what is the preferable presentation of notes or accounts receivable from officers, employees, or affiliated companies?

a. As trade notes and accounts receivable if they otherwise qualify as current assets.

b. As assets but separately from other receivables.

c. As offsets to capital.

d. By notes or footnotes.

(AICPA adapted)

PROBLEMS

PART A
Problems 8–1 to 8–6

Problem 8–1

The cash records for Van Company provided the following data for the month of March:

	March 1	March 31
Balances per bank statement ...	$15,400.09	$14,360.09
Balances per company books ...	14,175.00	13,399.00

Relevant items:

a.	Outstanding checks March 31 (verified as correct)	$1,450
b.	Deposits in transit March 31 (verified as correct)	950
c.	Interest earned on bank balance (reported on bank statement)	18
d.	NSF check (customer check returned with bank statement)	50
e.	Service charge by bank (reported on bank statement)	7
f.	Error in deposit of cash sales (deposit slip showed overage, corrected by bank)	10
g.	Bank error (check for $10.98 cleared at $10.89)	
h.	Note collected by bank for us (including $40 interest).............................	1,040
i.	Deduction for church (per signed bank deduction form)	20
j.	Cash on hand	500

Required:

1. Prepare a bank reconciliation in good form showing correct balance for the March 31 balance sheet. *Hint:* Be alert for a cash overage or shortage.

2. Prepare necessary entries at March 31.

Problem 8–2

The records pertaining to cash for High Company provided the following data for May:

Bank statement:

a.	Balance, May 31	$34,500
b.	Service charges for May	5
c.	NSF check returned with May statement; customer gave this check, will redeposit next week, assumed to be good	50
d.	Note receivable ($5,000) collected for High by the bank and added to balance ..	5,200

e. Error from previous month in interest collected on another note receivable; bank credited High account in May for the amount to correct the error (the May bank statement was first notification of the collection) 100

Books:

f. Balance, May 31 30,700
g. Cash on hand 400
h. Deposit in transit..................... 3,700
i. Outstanding checks at May 31 2,665

Required:

1. Prepare a bank reconciliation in good form. Assume all amounts provided above are correct. *Hint:* Be alert for a cash overage or shortage.
2. Give required entries for May 31.

Problem 8–3

Tetzlaff Corporation began doing business with Fidelity Bank on October 1. On that date, the true cash balance was $4,000. All cash transactions are cleared through the bank account. Subsequent transactions during October and November relating to the Tetzlaff and Fidelity accounts are summarized below:

	Tetzlaff Company Books	Fidelity Bank Books
October deposits	$7,360	$7,110
October checks	6,290	6,130
October service charge	—	10
October 31 balance	5,070	4,970
November deposits (regular)	8,220	8,280
November checks	9,410	9,220
November service charge	—	15
Note collected by bank (includes $15 interest)		1,015
October service charge (recorded during November)	10	—
November 30 balance	3,870	5,030

Required:

1. On the basis of the foregoing data, prepare a comprehensive bank reconciliation for November.
2. Assuming November 30 is the end of Tetzlaff's fiscal year, give entries that would be required by the bank reconciliation.

Problem 8–4

You are examining the records of a client whose internal control is weak. Part of your work includes reconciliation of cash for December 19A. You have determined that the client's reconciliation as of No-

vember 30, 19A, is correct. The following information is available to you:

Client's Reconciliation, November 30, 19A

Cash per general ledger	$2,631.74
Less: Cash on hand	210.89
	2,420.85
Less: Bank service charge for November	9.00
	2,411.85
Add: Outstanding checks	991.00
Balance per bank	$3,402.85

Cash receipts are summarized weekly; the cash receipts books for December appear below:

Dec.		
1	Balance from Nov. 30	$ 2,631.74
8	Received on accounts	25,774.80
15	Received on accounts	27,447.56
22	Received on accounts	4,659.82
29	Received on accounts	5,886.85
		$65,300.77

The cash payments recorded for December were as follows:

Dec.		
1	November service charge	$ 9.00
3	Checks	5,236.50
5	Checks	3,645.21
8	Checks	16,394.89
10	Checks	15,873.42
12	Checks	4,848.89
19	Checks	3,622.83
22	Checks	3,692.09
31	Checks	7,657.70
Balance—December 31	....	4,311.24
		$65,300.77

Cash on hand December 31 amounted to $100. The transactions per the December bank statement, which are correctly recorded by the bank, show that deposits amounted to $62,870.92; checks paid amounted to $57,952.03; service charges for the month were $10; and a charge of $100 was made against the account because of the return unpaid of a customer's check (not included in the $57,952.03). Neither the service charge nor the returned check was recorded on the client's books. The total of outstanding checks as of December 31 was found to be $4,110.50.

Required:

Prepare a comprehensive bank reconciliation for December. *Hint:* Verify all footings and be alert for errors and/or shortages.

(AICPA adapted)

Problem 8–5

In connection with an audit of cash of Distributors, Inc., as of December 31, 19A, the following information has been obtained:

a. Balance per bank:

11/30/19A	$ 185,700
12/31/19A	193,674

b. Balance per books:

11/30/19A	154,826
12/31/19A	167,598

c. Receipts for the month of December 19A:

Per bank	1,350,450
Per books	2,335,445

d. Outstanding checks:

11/30/19A	63,524
12/31/19A	75,046

e. Dishonored checks are recorded as a reduction of cash receipts. Dishonored checks which are later redeposited are then recorded as a regular cash receipt. Dishonored checks returned by the bank and recorded by Distributors, Inc., amounted to $6,250 during the month of December 19A; according to the books, $5,000 were redeposited. Dishonored checks reported on the bank statement but not in the books until the following months amounted to $250 at November 30, 19A, and $2,300 at December 31, 19A.

f. On December 31, 19A, a $2,323 check of ABC Company was charged to Distributors, Inc., account by the bank in error.

g. Proceeds of a note of the Able Company collected by the bank on December 10, 19A, were not entered on the books:

Principal	$2,000
Interest	20
	2,020
Less: Collection charge	5
	$2,015

h. The company has hypothecated (assigned) its accounts receivable with the bank under an agreement whereby the bank lends the company 80% on the hypothecated accounts receivable. Accounting for and collection of the accounts are performed by the company, and adjustments of the loan are made from daily sales reports and daily deposits.

    The bank credits the Distributors, Inc., account and increases the amount of the loan for 80% of the reported sales. The loan agreement states specifically that the sales report must be accepted by the bank before Distributors, Inc., is credited. Sales reports are forwarded by Distributors, Inc., to the bank on the first day following the date of sales.

    The bank allocates each deposit 80% to the payment of the loan and 20% to the Distributors, Inc., account.

    Thus, only 80% of each day's sales and 20% of each collection are entered on the bank statement.

    The Distributors, Inc., accountant records the hypothecation of new accounts receivable (80% of sales) as a debit to Cash and a credit to the bank loan as of the date of sales. One hundred percent of the collections on accounts receivable is recorded as a cash receipt; 80% of the collections is recorded in the cash disbursements book as a payment on the loan.

    In connection with the hypothecation, the following facts were determined:

(1) Included in the deposits in transit is cash from the hypothecation of accounts receivable. Sales were $40,500 on November 30, 19A, and $42,250 on December 31, 19A. The balance of the deposit in transit at December 31, 19A, was made up from collections of $32,110 which were entered on the books in the manner indicated above.

(2) Collections on accounts receivable deposited in December, other than deposits in transit, totaled $1,200,000.

(3) Sales for December totaled $1,450,000.

(4) Interest on the bank loan for the month of December, charged by the bank but not recorded on the books, amounted to $6,140.

Required:

1. Prepare bank reconciliations as of November 30, 19A, and December 31, 19A, and reconciliations of cash receipts and disbursements per bank with cash receipts and disbursements per books for the month of December 19A. (Assume that you have satisfied yourself as to the propriety of the above information.) Show computations where applicable.

2. Prepare adjusting journal entries as required to correct the Cash account at December 31, 19A.

                      (AICPA adapted)

Problem 8–6

Trask Company began doing business with First Bank on February 1 at which time its true cash balance was $6,000. All the company's cash transactions are cleared through the bank account. Subsequent transactions during February and March relating to Trask Company and its dealings with First Bank are summarized on the following page:

	Trask Company Books	First Bank Books
February deposits	$4,180	$3,870
February checks	4,375	4,210
February service charge	—	5
February 28 balance	5,805	5,655
March deposits (regular)	5,280	5,385
March checks	5,415	5,380
March service charge	—	10
Note collected by bank in March (includes interest of $20)	—	520
February service charge (recorded in March)	5	—
March 31 balance	5,665	6,170

Required:

1. On the basis of the foregoing data, prepare a comprehensive reconciliation for March.
2. Prepare journal entries to bring Trask Company's books up to date as of March 31.

PART B
Problems 8–7 to 8–13

Problem 8–7

On January 1, 19A, Scott Company acquired the following short-term investments in marketable equity securities (top of next column):

Company	Stock	Number of Shares	Cost per Share
T	Common (nopar)	1,000	$20
U	Common (par $10)	600	15
V	Preferred (par $20, nonconvertible)	400	30

Data subsequent to the acquisition are as follows:

Dec. 31, 19A Market values: T stock, $16; U stock, $15; and V stock, $34.
Feb. 10, 19B Cash dividends received per share: T stock, $1.50; U stock, $1.00; and V stock, $0.50.
Nov. 1, 19B Sold the shares of V stock at $38 per share.
Dec. 31, 19B Market values: T stock, $18; U stock, $17; and V stock, $33.

Required:

1. Give all entries indicated for Scott Company for 19A and 19B. Use LCM and assume there was no balance in the allowance account on January 1, 19A.
2. Show how the income statement and balance sheet for Scott Company would reflect the short-term investments for 19A and 19B.

Problem 8–8

The exhibit below purports to set forth the effects of the indicated accounting for investments on the

		19A Statements			19B Statements		
(Relates to Problem 8–8) Items		Current Assets	Net Income	Liabilities	Current Assets	Net Income	Owners' Equity
1.	At year-end 19A, accrued interest on bonds (cost method) held as short-term investments was ignored. All investments were sold during 19B.	—	—	0	0	0	—
2.	Marketable equity securities were valued at cost ($10,000) at year-end 19A when market was $9,500; and at market ($8,600) when cost was $8,000 at the end of 19B (use LCM).	+	+	0	—	0	+
3.	Brooks had bought marketable securities at the end of 19A but had not paid for them, and no entry for their purchase was made until 19B. They were sold for a gain properly recorded during 19B.	—	—	—	0	0	+
4.	Shares of stock which had been properly carried as short-term investments (cost method) when initially bought were reclassified to long-term investments during 19B when their market value was below cost. (At end of 19A cost exceeded market.) The transfer was recorded at cost.	0	0	0	0	0	0
5.	Late in 19A Brooks Company issued a note to an officer in exchange for Brooks shares the officer had acquired under option. They are still classified as a short-term investment at year-end 19B.	0	0	+	0	0	0

Brooks Department Store. Where the indicated accounting would make a statement element too high, a "+" is used; for too low, a "−" is used; if there is no effect (item is correct), a "0" is used. There are, however, some mistakes in the exhibit. You are to indicate the number of mistakes on each line and identify the mistakes. Ignore income tax aspects. Each case is independent. Marketable securities are short-term investments in the first three instances.

Problem 8–9

Walsh Manufacturing Company's short-term investment portfolio was recorded at the following costs at December 31, 19A; (there was no 19A balance in the allowance account):

	Cost
AB Company, nine 8% bonds (face, $9,000; interest dates 3/1 and 9/1)	$9,300
BC Corporation common, nopar (50 shares)	1,800
CD Corporation, 4% preferred, 150 shares (par, $40)	8,000

Transactions relating to the securities during 19B were as follows:

Jan. 25 Received semiannual dividend check on CD shares.

Mar. 1 Collected semiannual interest on AB bonds.

Apr. 15 Sold 30 shares of BC Corporation stock for $1,020.

May 1 Sold six of the AB bonds for a total consideration (including accrued interest) of $6,350.

June 20 Purchased 50 shares of EF Corporation, common, at 47 plus $30 brokerage fees.

July 25 Received semiannual dividend check on CD shares.

Sept. 1 Collected semiannual interest on AB bonds.

Oct. 1 Purchased a $1,000, 9% bond of DE, Inc., for total consideration of $1,100. Interest payment dates on this bond are February 1 and August 1.

Nov. 17 Sold remaining BC Corporation shares for $700.

Dec. 2 Received $60 dividend check from EF Corporation.

31 Preparatory to adjusting and closing the books for the year, the following data as to market values of securities held were obtained:

Security	Market
AB bonds (ex-interest)	103
CD preferred	54
DE, Inc., bond (ex-interest)	104
EF common	45

Required:

Journalize the foregoing transactions; adjust and close the books at December 31, 19B. Value the total portfolio of securities (including the bonds) at lower of cost or market by means of an Allowance to Reduce Short-Term Investments to LCM account.

Hint: Do not overlook reversal of accrued interest adjustment on AB bonds on January 1, 19B.

Problem 8–10

DEF Manufacturing Company has followed the practice of valuing all of its short-term investments in marketable securities as one portfolio at the lower of cost or market. At December 31, 19B, its account, Short-Term Investment in Marketable Securities, had a balance of $40,000, and the account, Allowance to Reduce Investments from Cost to Market, had a balance of $2,000. Analysis disclosed that on December 31, 19A, the facts relating to the securities were as follows:

Security	Cost	Market	Allowance Required
X Company bonds	$20,000	$19,000	$1,000
Y Company bonds	10,000	9,000	1,000
Z Company bonds	20,000	20,300	0
	$50,000		$2,000

During 19B, the Y Company bonds were sold for $9,200; the difference between the $9,200 and the cost of $10,000 was charged to "Loss on Sale of Securities." The market price of the bonds on December 31, 19B, was X Company bonds, $19,200; and Z Company bonds, $20,400.

Required:

1. What justification is there for the use of the lower of cost or market in valuing short-term investments in marketable securities?

2. Did DEF Company properly apply this rule on December 31, 19A? Explain, including any alternative methods of application.

3. Are there any additional entries necessary for DEF Company at December 31, 19B, to reflect the facts on the balance sheet and income statement in accordance with generally accepted accounting principles? Explain.

(AICPA adapted)

Problem 8–11

Winans Company bought its first short-term investments in 19A and still held them at December 31 of that year, when they had the following values:

Security	Amount	Cost	Market
AB common stock ..	50 shares	$ 4,000	$ 3,725
CD 8% bonds	$6,000 maturity value	6,400	6,500
		$10,400	$10,225

Cash revenue from these investments was correctly accounted for by the company bookkeeper during 19A and 19B, except that *(a)* no accrual of revenue was reflected at year-end 19A and *(b)* the investments were not accounted for as a single portfolio at LCM, as intended by management.

On July 1, 19B, all of the AB shares were sold for $3,700, and the transaction was recorded by the bookkeeper as follows:

Cash	3,700	
Miscellaneous expense	100	
Loss on sale of securities	200	
AB common stock		4,000

The debit to Miscellaneous Expense represents $100 of selling costs incurred in disposing of the shares.

On August 1, 19B, half of the CD bonds were sold for $3,350, and the transaction was recorded by the bookkeeper as follows:

Cash	3,350	
Miscellaneous expense	50	
Gain on sale of securities		200
CD bonds		3,200

The entry to Miscellaneous Expense reflects selling costs.

The CD bonds regularly pay interest each May 1 and November 1. Quarterly dividends of $40 were collected on the AB common shares on March 15 as well as on June 15. On December 1, 19B, the company bought $5,000 par bonds of EF Corporation for $5,350. These bonds pay 9% interest per annum on February 1 and August 1, and their purchase was recorded as follows:

EF Bonds	5,300	
Miscellaneous expense	50	
Cash		5,350

The debit to Miscellaneous Expense represents the expense of buying the bonds. The bookkeeper resigned early in December and had not been replaced by year-end, but there were no securities transactions after the December 1 bond purchase.

Required:

1. Draft entries to correct the accounts as of January 1, 19B, assuming both equity and debt securities are included in the short-term investment portfolio for LCM purposes.
2. Draft entries to correct the errors in the accounts for Year 19B. As of December 31, 19B, the CD bonds were quoted at 108 and the EF bonds were quoted at 102.
3. Prepare adjusting and closing entries as of December 31, 19B.

Problem 8–12

Check the best answer in each of the following and provide the basis (including computations where appropriate) to support your choice.

1. The June bank statement of Lucas Company showed a June 30 ending balance of $187,387. During June, the bank charged back NSF (i.e., insufficient funds) checks totaling $3,056, of which $1,856 had been redeposited by June 30. Deposits in transit on June 30 were $20,400. Outstanding checks on June 30 were $60,645, including a $10,000 check which the bank had certified on June 28. On June 14 the bank charged Lucas' account for a $2,300 item which should have been charged against the account of Luby Company; the bank did not detect the error. During June the bank collected foreign items for Lucas; the proceeds were $8,684, and bank charges for this service were $19. On June 30 the adjusted cash in bank of Lucas Company is
   a. $149,442.
   b. $159,442.
   c. $147,142.
   d. $158,242.
   e. None of the above.
2. Which of the following items should never be included in the current section of the balance sheet?
   a. Premium paid on short-term bond investment.
   b. Receivable from customer not collectible during coming year.
   c. Deferred income taxes resulting from interperiod income tax allocation.
   d. Funded serial bonds.
3. The test of marketability must be met before securities owned can be properly classified as
   a. Pledged securities.
   b. Common stock.
   c. Bonds payable.
   d. None of the above.
4. How is the premium or discount on bonds purchased as a short-term investment generally reported in published financial statements?
   a. As an integral part of the cost of the asset acquired (investment) and amortized over a period of not less than 12 months.
   b. As an integral part of the cost of the asset acquired (investment) until such time as the investment is sold.
   c. As expense or revenue at the time the bonds are purchased.
   d. As an integral part of the cost of the asset acquired (investment) and amortized over the period the bonds are expected to be held.

5. Postage stamps and IOUs found in cash drawers should be reported as
   a. Prepaid expense and receivables.
   b. Cash, because they represent the equivalent of money.
   c. Petty cash.
   d. Investments.

6. George Company maintains two checking accounts. A special checking account is used for the weekly payroll only, and the general checking account is used for all other disbursements. Each week, a check for the aggregate amount of the payrolls is drawn on the general account and deposited in the Payroll account. Individual checks are drawn on the Payroll account. The company maintains a $5,000 minimum balance in the Payroll account. On a monthly bank reconciliation, the Payroll account should
   a. Show a zero balance per the bank statement.
   b. Show a $5,000 balance per the bank statement.
   c. Reconcile to $5,000.
   d. Be reconciled jointly with the general account in a single reconciliation.

7. Which of the following is a current asset?
   a. Cash surrender value of a life insurance policy of which the company is the beneficiary.
   b. Investment in marketable securities for the purpose of continuing control of the issuing company.
   c. Cash designated for the purchase of tangible operational assets.
   d. Trade installment receivables normally collectible in 18 months.

8. Which of the following should not be considered as a current asset?
   a. Installment notes receivable due over 18 months in accordance with normal trade practice.
   b. Prepaid property taxes.
   c. Marketable securities purchased as a short-term investment with cash provided by current operations.
   d. Cash surrender value of a life insurance policy carried by a corporation, the beneficiary, on its president.

(AICPA adapted)

Problem 8–13

This is a *research problem* which requires that certain library materials be consulted. There is no specific, single answer because the answer can differ according to (a) the companies selected and (b) the date on which it is solved.

Required:

1. Determine the stocks which comprise the Dow Jones Industrial Average and list them in your solution.

2. Select any five of the stocks from Requirement 1 and assume that the company for which you are accounting acquired a portfolio of 100 shares of common stock in each of the five companies selected. Assume that the cost to your company was the per share price as of the close of business on January 2 of the current year. (If January 2 was not a trading day on which the market was open, use the first trading day following January 2.) For each value so determined, assume 1% brokerage and other acquisition costs.

3. As of the date the problem is assigned, ascertain the market value of the portfolio of five stocks. If, for some reason, this date is not feasible, use the next preceding date for which the required information is available.

4. Array the cost and market figures in a schedule and determine the proper balance sheet carrying value of the portfolio based on the assumption the stocks are held as temporary investments.

5. On the assumption that at the close of the preceding period Allowance to Reduce Short-Term Investments to Market had a balance of $800, indicate the required adjusting entry as of the date you ascertain market values in Requirement 3. For purpose of this requirement assume (a) that the securities which accounted for the $800 allowance have been sold, (b) that the portfolio now consists only of the five stocks chosen in Requirement 2, and (c) this date is the end of the fiscal year for your company.

PART C
Problems 8–14 to 8–18

Problem 8–14

Records for Hill Trading Company concerning their receivables and recent sales history provided the following:

Cash sales for the period	$1,200,000
Credit sales for the period	900,000
Balance in trade receivables, start of period	180,000
Balance in trade receivables, end of period	200,000
Balance in allowance for doubtful accounts, start of period	3,000 (credit)
Accounts written off as uncollectible during period	5,000

Recently Hill's management has become concerned about various estimates used in their accounting process, including those relating to receivables and bad debts. The company is reviewing the various alternatives with a view to selecting the most appropriate approach and related estimates.

Assume the following simplified estimates:

1. Bad debt expense approximates ⅗% of credit sales.
2. Bad debt expense approximates ¼% of net sales (cash plus credit sales).
3. Four percent of the uncollected receivables àt year-end will be bad at any one time.
4. Aging of the accounts at the end of the period indicated that three fourths of them would incur a 3% loss while the other one fourth would incur an 8% loss.

Required:

Four different approaches are being considered. Identify and briefly explain and give the advantages of each approach. After each explanation, give the adjusting entry based on the period data available.

Problem 8–15

The Installment Jewelry Company has been in business for five years but has never had an audit of its financial statements. Engaged to make an audit for 19E, you find that the company's balance sheet carries no allowance for doubtful accounts; instead, uncollectible accounts have been expensed as written off with recoveries credited to income as collected. The company's policy is to write off at December 31 of each year those accounts on which no collections have been received for three months. The installment contracts generally provide for uniform monthly collections over a time span of two years from date of sale.

Upon your recommendation the company agrees to revise its accounts for 19E in order to account for bad debts on the allowance basis. The allowance is to be based on a percentage of sales which is derived from the experience of prior years.

Statistics for the past five years are as follows:

Year	Credit Sales	Accounts Written Off and Year of Sale			Recoveries and Year of Sale
19A......	$100,000	(19A) $ 550			
19B......	250,000	(19A) 1,500	(19B) $1,000		(19A) $100
19C......	300,000	(19A) 500	(19B) 4,000	(19C) $1,300	(19B) 400
19D......	325,000	(19B) 1,200	(19C) 4,500	(19D) 1,500	(19C) 500
19E......	275,000	(19C) 2,700	(19D) 5,000	(19E) 1,400	(19D) 600

Accounts receivable at December 31, 19E, were as follows:

19D sales......................	$ 15,000
19E sales......................	135,000
	$150,000

Required:

Prepare the adjusting journal entry or entries with appropriate explanations to set up the Allowance for Doubtful Accounts. (Support each item with organized computations; income tax implications should be ignored. The books have been adjusted but not closed at December 31, 19E.)

(AICPA adapted)

Problem 8–16

Brandt Company sold a building and the land on which it is located on January 1, 19A, receiving, as its consideration, a $150,000 note receivable maturing in three years without interest. The sale was recorded as follows by Brandt Company:

Note receivable	150,000	
Accumulated depreciation—		
building	100,000	
Building......................		150,000
Land		60,000
Gain on sale of building		40,000

It has been determined that 7% is a reasonable interest rate to impute to the note. You are recommending adjusting and correcting entries as of December 31, 19A (end of Brandt Company's fiscal year). The books have not been adjusted or closed for 19A.

Required:

1. Give an entry to correct the sale entry and the adjustment for interest as of December 31, 19A. (Round to nearest dollar.)
2. Give entry to recognize interest earned at December 31, 19B.
3. Make entries at end of 19C to (a) recognize interest earned and (b) record collection of the note.
4. Aside from the correction in Requirement 1 for interest, do you see any other problem in the sale entry as originally made? Explain.

Problem 8–17

Lestor Company has experienced a critical cash flow problem as a result of collection problems with certain customers. Consequently, it has become involved in a number of transactions relating to its notes receivable. The following transactions occurred during a period ending December 31 (end of the accounting period):

May   1   Received an $8,000, 90-day, 9% interest-bearing note from E. M. Smith, a customer, in settlement of an account receivable for that amount.

June 1   Received a $12,000, six-month, 9% interest-bearing note from M. Johnson, a customer, in settlement of an account receivable for that amount.

Aug. 1   Discounted the Johnson note at the bank at 10%.
      2   Smith defaulted on the $8,000 note.

Sept. 1   Received a one-year, noninterest-bearing note from D. Karnes, a customer, in settlement of a $5,000 account receivable. The face of the note was $5,400, and the going rate of interest was 8% (on the net amount of the receivable).

Oct. 1   Received a $20,000, 90-day note from R. M. Cates, a customer. The note was in payment for goods Cates purchased and was interest bearing at 10%.
      1   Collected the defaulted Smith note plus accrued interest to September 30 (10% per annum on the total amount due for two months).

Dec. 1   Johnson defaulted on the $12,000 note. Lestor Company paid the bank the total amount due plus a $25 protest fee.
      30   Collected Cates note in full. Collected from Johnson in full including interest on the full amount at 10% since default date.
      31   Accrued interest on outstanding notes.

Required:

1. Give the entry to record each of the above transactions. Show computations.
2. Show how the outstanding notes at December 31 would be reported on the balance sheet.

Problem 8–18

Doe Company finances some of its current operations by assigning accounts receivable to a finance company. On July 1, 19A, it assigned, with recourse, accounts amounting to $50,000, the finance company advancing 80% of the accounts assigned (20% of the total to be withheld until the finance company has made full recovery), less a commission charge of ½% of the total accounts assigned.

On July 31 the Doe Company received a statement that the finance company had collected $26,000 of these accounts and had made an additional charge of ½% of the total accounts outstanding as of July 31—this charge to be deducted at the time of the first remittance due Doe Company from the finance company. On August 31 the Doe Company received a second statement from the finance company, together with a check for the amount due. The statement indicated that the finance company had collected an additional $18,000 and had made a further charge of ½% of the balance outstanding as of August 31.

Required (on books of Doe Company):

1. Give the entry to record the assignment of the accounts on a notification basis (July 1).
2. Give entry to record the data from the first report from the finance company (July 31).
3. Reconstruct the report submitted by the finance company on August 31; show details to explain cash remitted and the uncollected accounts still held by the finance company.
4. Give the entry to record the data in the report of August 31.
5. Explain how the items should be reported on the financial statements of Doe Company at July 31 and August 31.

(AICPA adapted)

9

Liabilities and Income Taxes

This chapter discusses liabilities of various types and accounting for income taxes. To facilitate discussion and study, Part A considers liabilities in general and Part B discusses accounting for income taxes.

PART A—MEASURING, RECORDING, AND REPORTING LIABILITIES

Liabilities are obligations of a debtor to pay assets or render services in the future that result from past transactions or events and are definite in amount, or subject to reasonable estimation, as stated or implied in oral or written contracts. The two basic problems in accounting for liabilities are identification and measurement. Since liabilities represent claims for assets or services, they are intangible.

Liabilities are classified as *(a)* short term (i.e., current) or *(b)* long term because their liquidity is important to both the debtor and the creditor. In regard to the relative timing of the cash demands of liabilities, investors and other statement users have no basis, other than these classifications on the financial statements, of assessing this important factor.

In accounting for liabilities, identification is a primary problem because certain kinds of liabilities are relatively easy to hide or overlook, such as those owed to obscure parties, product warranties, and contingencies.

Conceptually, a liability should be measured as the *present value* of all required future cash flows (or of cash flow equivalents such as services). Often the transaction that created the liability will provide an adequate basis for measurement. For example, when assets or services are acquired on credit, the asset or service is valued at cost under the cost principle, which in turn measures the amount of the liability incurred. Alternatively, this correspondence between the "price" of the asset and the valuation of the liability sometimes does not exist. To illustrate, assume a company acquired a machine for which it promised to pay $10,000 at the end of three years (with no interim interest payments). Both the valuation of the liability and the cost of the asset are measured as the present value of the required future cash flow. Assuming a 10% going rate of interest for this type of debt, measurement of the liability (and the asset) would be

$$\$10,000 \times p_{n=3; i=10\%} =$$
$$\$10,000 \times .75131 \text{ (Table 6–2)} = \$7,513.10$$

This principle is applicable to all liabilities. However, in accounting for short-term liabilities (particularly those involving open accounts payable of one to three months), the interest factor often is ignored because of immateriality and because of the provisions of *APB Opinion No. 21.*

Consistent with the measurement of liabilities at their present value, most liabilities are recorded and reported at their maturity amount because a liability with the market rate of interest plus the principal amount will always have a present value exactly the same as the maturity amount. Aside from the materiality exception noted above for some short-term liabilities, liabilities should be recorded and reported at their present value at date of acquisition and thereafter until retired. This is precisely what should be done for so-called noninterest-bearing notes (as illustrated later) and for bonds or other indebtedness issued above or below par. Bonds payable are reported net of unamortized discount or premium using the interest method. These issues are discussed in the remainder of this chapter and in Chapter 20 (bonds).

Although exchange transactions generally establish the definite amount and maturity date of a liability, there are situations where a definite liability is known to exist, or it is probable that one exists, but the exact amount and sometimes the maturity date are not known precisely. Therefore, one section of this chapter discusses estimated liabilities and loss contingencies.

CURRENT LIABILITIES

Current (i.e., short-term) liabilities are obligations reported on the balance sheet that will be paid out of assets classified on that particular balance sheet as current assets. Most current liabilities, such as accounts payable, short-term notes payable, and current maturities of long-term debt, enter the accounts as a result of completed transactions. However, this may not be true for *accrued liabilities* because of their nature; that is, at the end of the accounting period they have not yet been recorded in the accounts. For example, a company receives no recordable asset, nor is there a completed exchange transaction by the end of the period for income taxes payable. As another example, to conform to the matching principle, estimated warranties payable must be recorded for the year in which sales were made coupled with a warranty agreement that will be fulfilled in one or more later periods. Thus, it is necessary for companies to record these accrued liabilities during the end-of-the-

period adjusting process; otherwise such liabilities would not be recorded in most cases.

Current Liabilities Defined

Current liabilities for many years were defined as those obligations due within one year of balance sheet date. This definition was related to the older definition of current assets (liquidation within one year). It was recognized that these definitions were unrealistic for many companies. As a consequence, the Committee on Accounting Procedure of the AICPA defined current liabilities as follows:

> The term *current liabilities* is used principally to designate obligations whose liquidation is reasonably expected to require the use of existing resources properly classifiable as current assets, or the creation of other current liabilities.

The committee supplemented the definition of current liabilities as follows:

> As a balance-sheet category, the classification is intended to include obligations for items which have entered into the operating cycle, such as payables incurred in the acquisition of materials and supplies to be used in the production of goods or in providing services to be offered for sale; collections received in advance of the delivery of goods or performance of services; and debts which arise from operations directly related to the operating cycle, such as accruals for wages, salaries, commissions, rentals, royalties, and income and other taxes. Other liabilities whose regular and ordinary liquidation is expected to occur within a relatively short period of time, usually 12 months, are also intended for inclusion, such as short-term debts arising from the acquisition of capital assets, serial maturities of long-term obligations, amounts required to be expended within one year under sinking fund provisions, and agency obligations arising from the collection or acceptance of cash or other assets for the account of third persons.

> This concept of current liabilities would include estimated or accrued amounts which are expected to be required to cover expenditures within the year for known obligations (a) the amount of which can be determined only approximately (as in the case of provisions for accruing bonus payments) or (b) where the specific

person or persons to whom payment will be made cannot as yet be designated (as in the case of estimated costs to be incurred in connection with guaranteed servicing or repair of products already sold).[1]

The principal types of current liabilities are as follows:

1. Known liabilities of a definite amount:
   a. Accounts payable.
   b. Short-term notes payable.
   c. Cash dividends payable.
   d. Advances and funds held as short-term deposits.
   e. Accrued liabilities.
   f. Deferred credits (such as revenues collected in advance).
2. Known liabilities, amount dependent on operations:
   g. Taxes (income, sales, and social security).
   h. Bonus obligations.
   i. Accrued liabilities.
3. Known liabilities, amount estimated.
4. Loss contingencies.

Special accounting problems related to these types of current liabilities are discussed in the following sections. Normally each of the current liabilities listed above should be separately accounted for and separately reported on the balance sheet.

Accounts Payable

Accounts payable is a designation for the recurring trade obligations of the business that arise from the acquisition of merchandise, materials, supplies, and services used in the production and/or sale of goods or services. They are directly related to the regular operations of the company. Current payables not coming under this definition should be separately reported from accounts payable. Examples are income taxes payable and current payments on long-term debt.

[1] AICPA, *Accounting Research Bulletin No. 43,* "Restatement and Revision of Accounting Research Bulletins" (New York, 1961), pp. 21–22.

Notes Payable

Short-term notes payable are reported as current liabilities. They may be either trade or non-trade notes payable, and each should be separately reported. Trade notes payable are defined in the same manner as accounts payable except for the promissory note characteristic. Notes payable may be secured by collateral (pledged or mortgaged assets), or they may be unsecured. Secured notes should be reported separately, and the nature of the collateral should be reported both with respect to the notes and to the specific assets mortgaged. One approach is to disclose pledged assets in the notes to the financial statement. Another method reports the pledged assets under both the asset and liability captions similar to the following:

Investment:
    Stock in X Corporation at
       cost (pledged for $3,000
       note to Y Bank) $5,000
Current Liabilities:
    Notes payable (secured by
       stock in X Corporation) $3,000

Interest on Notes Payable

All commercial notes require the borrower to pay interest because of the unavoidable time cost of using money. Nevertheless, the commercial world uses two note designations to identify different types of interest assumptions on notes; they are

1. Interest-bearing notes—those that require payment of the principal amount (also the face amount) at maturity date plus specified interest payments. This type of note often is called *ordinary note.*
2. Noninterest-bearing notes—those that include the principal amount and the interest in the face of the note, all of which is paid at maturity date. This type of note often is called *discounted note,* which is much more descriptive.

On all notes, regardless of type, the amount of interest per period should be calculated as

$$\frac{\text{Principal}}{\text{Amount}} \times \frac{\text{Period Rate}}{\text{of Interest}} \times \text{Time} = \frac{\text{Interest}}{\text{Amount}}$$

And the *effective* rate of interest is the relationship between the interest amount and the principal amount.

Interest-Bearing (ordinary) Notes Payable. For an interest-bearing note the borrower receives cash or equivalent assets or services for the *face amount* of the note, and interest is paid at one or more subsequent dates (in addition to the face of the note which is paid at maturity). Therefore, for an interest-bearing note the principal amount (face amount) and the cost of the assets received (assuming the stated rate of interest is realistic) are the same; the interest is in addition to these amounts. On an interest-bearing note the *stated* rate of interest and the *effective* rate of interest are the same (assuming the stated rate is realistic).

To illustrate an interest-bearing note, assume X Company borrowed $10,000 cash and signed a one-year 9% interest-bearing note, dated October 1, 19A. The cash received, principal amount, face amount, and maturity amount would be $10,000 each. At maturity, the face amount of the note plus interest for one year ($900), a total of $10,900, would be paid. The borrowing transaction, accrual of interest at the end of the accounting period (December 31, 19A), and payment at maturity (September 30, 19B) would be recorded as follows:

October 1, 19A—To record an interest-bearing note:

Cash	10,000	
Note payable, short term		10,000

December 31, 19A—Adjusting entry for accrued interest:

Interest expense		
($10,000 × 9% × 3/12)	225	
Interest payable		225

September 30, 19B—Payment of face amount plus interest at maturity (assuming no reversing entry was made on January 1, 19B):

Interest payable	225	
Interest expense		
($10,000 × 9% × 9/12)	675	
Note payable, short term	10,000	
Cash		10,900

Reporting at December 31, 19A—Interest-bearing note payable:

Income statement:

Interest expense	$	225

Balance Sheet:

Current liabilities:	
Note payable, short term	10,000
Interest payable	225

Discounted (noninterest-bearing) Notes Payable (with no stated interest rate). For a discounted note, the borrower receives cash or equivalent assets or services for the face amount of the note *less* the interest amount charged. The face amount of a discounted note includes *both* the principal and interest amounts; thus, at maturity only the face amount is paid. Because of these features, neither the interest rate nor the amount of interest is explicitly stated in the note. The amount of interest should be computed on the cash (or equivalent assets or services) received since this is the principal amount of the debt. Thus, the principal amount of a discounted note is the face amount discounted (i.e., present value) at the realistic rate of interest for the obligation. To illustrate, assume $10,000 cash is borrowed and a one-year discounted note payable dated October 1, 19A, is executed at an agreed rate of interest of 9%. The face amount of the note would be

$$\$10,000 + (\$10,000 \times 9\%) = \$10,900$$

The effective rate of interest would be

Interest Paid ($10,900 − $10,000)
$$\div \text{Cash Received } (\$10,000) = 9\%$$

Entries to account for this discounted note (i.e., interest included in the face amount) would be as follows:

October 1, 19A—To record a discounted note payable:

Cash	10,000	
Discount on note payable	900	
Note payable, short term*		10,900

December 31, 19A—Adjusting entry for accrued interest:

Interest expense ($900 × 3/12)	225	
Discount on note payable		225

September 30, 19B—Payment of the face amount of the note:

Interest expense ($900 × 9/12)   675
Note payable, short term   10,900
   Discount on note payable   675
   Cash   10,900

*These entries assume the discounted note is recorded at "gross." Alternatively, notes payable could have been credited for the principal amount, $10,000. At each interest period the accrued interest payable would be credited to that account so that at maturity its balance would be $10,900. The net results over the life of the debt are the same. This approach is illustrated in Exhibit 9–2.

Reporting at December 31, 19A—Discounted note payable:

Income Statement:
   Interest expense . . . . $ 225

Balance Sheet:
   Current liabilities:
      Note payable $10,900
      Less: Unamortized discount . . .   675   10,225

Discounted Note with Interest Based on Face Amount. The interest on a discounted note sometimes is computed on the *face amount* of the note rather than on the *principal amount* (the latter was illustrated above). This basis for computing interest causes the *effective* rate of interest to be *higher* than the "quoted" rate. To illustrate interest based on the face amount of a discounted note, assume Y Company signed a $10,000 discounted note (face amount) and received cash for that amount less 10% interest on the face amount. Cash received would be $10,000 − ($10,000 × 10%) = $9,000 (which is the principal of the loan). Although the "quoted" or represented rate of interest was 10%, the effective rate was 11% (i.e., $1,000 ÷ $9,000 = 11+%). The entries to record such a discounted note would be the same as illustrated immediately above except for the dollar amounts. Interest based on the face amount of a discounted note rather than on the principal amount, although not uncommon some years past, is not common today because (a) the represented rate is different from the effective rate of interest, which tends to mislead borrowers, and (b) the truth-in-lending laws require the lender to inform the borrower of the *effective rate* of interest, as opposed to the "quoted" rate.

Dividends Payable

Cash (or property) dividends payable (i.e., dividends declared but not yet paid) should be reported as a current liability if there is an intention to pay them within the coming year or operating cycle, whichever is the longer. *Stock dividends* issuable are not reported as a current liability but as an element of stockholders' equity, as explained in Chapter 17. Cash (and property) dividends payable are reported as a liability between date of declaration and date of payment on the legal basis that declaration is an enforceable contract that the corporation has assumed by virtue of formal declaration.

Liabilities are not recognized for undeclared dividends in arrears on preferred stock nor for any other dividends not yet declared formally by the board of directors. Undeclared dividends on cumulative preferred stock often are disclosed in the notes. Scrip dividends payable (liability dividends) are reported as a current liability unless there is no intention to make payment within the near future (see Chapter 17).

Advances and Returnable Deposits

A special type of liability arises when a company receives deposits from customers and employees. Deposits may be received from customers as guarantees to cover payment of obligations that may arise in the future or to guarantee performance of a contract or service. For example, when an order is taken, a company may require an advance payment to cover losses that would be incurred should the order be canceled. Such advances are liabilities of the company receiving the order until the underlying transaction is completed; therefore, they are recorded by debiting Cash and crediting an account such as Liability—Customer Deposits.

Deposits frequently are received from customers as guarantees for noncollection or for possible damage to property left with the customer. For example, deposits taken from customers by gas, water, light, and other public utilities are liabilities of such companies to their customers. Employees may make deposits for the return of keys and other company property, for locker privileges, and for club memberships. Some of these deposits are long term; others are current. Deposits should be reported as current or long-term liabilities, depending upon the time involved between date of deposit and expected termination of the relationships. In cases where the advances or deposits are interest bearing, an adjusting entry to accrue such interest costs is required.

Accrued Liabilities

Accrued liabilities arise because accounting recognition must be given at the end of the accounting period to expenses that have been incurred but not yet paid. Accrued liabilities usually are recognized in the accounts by making adjusting entries at the end of the period. For example, property taxes usually are assessed near the end of the calendar year and are payable in the following year. The *matching principle* requires that such expenses and the related liabilities be estimated in advance, recognized in the accounts, and reported on the financial statements on an accrual basis. Determination of expense accruals may be made from an examination of the historical expense accounts and other supplementary records. In recording accrued liabilities it is especially important that appropriate account titles be used such as Wages Payable, Estimated Property Taxes Payable, and Interest Payable.

In respect to the accrual of property taxes, the Committee on Accounting Procedure of the AICPA stated:

> Generally, the most acceptable basis of providing for property taxes is monthly accrual on the taxpayer's books during the fiscal period of the taxing authority for which the taxes are levied. The books will then show, at any closing date, the appropriate accrual or prepayment.[2]

For some liabilities established on a monthly accrual basis, such as Property Taxes Payable, the amount actually paid and the amount accrued during the year sometimes will differ. Such differences should be accounted for as an adjustment at the end of the period.

Deferred Credits

A caption, "Deferred credits," positioned after liabilities and before owners' equity, sometimes is shown on published balance sheets. Usually one finds under this caption four types of items, viz:

1. Revenues collected in advance (sometimes called unearned revenue or, less descriptively, deferred revenue), such as interest, rent, and advances received for services yet to be rendered. These items require that obligations, benefits, or services be rendered in the future before the revenue is realized.
2. Credits arising through certain external transactions that are difficult to classify. Examples are premium on bonds payable, unearned deposit on royalties, and deferred income on installment sales.
3. Credits arising through certain internal transactions. Examples are deferred repairs, allowance for rearrangement costs, and equities of minority interests (on consolidated statements).
4. Credits arising from income tax allocation procedures (deferred income taxes).

Rent collected in advance creates an obligation to render future occupancy (services). Thus, revenues collected in advance are properly reported as liabilities until the services are furnished or until there is a transfer of ownership of goods, as the case may be. For example, subscriptions collected in advance on magazines represent a liability to deliver a certain number of issues to the subscriber in the future. As the issues are delivered, the liability, Subscriptions Collected in Advance, is reduced by transfers to a revenue account, such as Subscription Revenue.

Some of the items listed above (particularly types 2 and 3) are difficult to classify on the balance sheet. This difficulty underlies the wide usage of the vague balance sheet classification, "Deferred credits." Observe that this classification, reported below liabilities and above owners' equity, is not consistent with the basic accounting model Assets = Liabilities + Owners' Equity, and it fails to identify clearly for the statement user the true nature of the various items reported. Certain of these items are clearly in the nature of liabilities; others represent offsets or additions to related items. For these reasons many accountants, including the authors, consider the deferred classification on the balance sheet to be theoretically objectionable. A

---

[2] AICPA, *Accounting Research Bulletin No. 43*, "Restatement and Revision of Accounting Research Bulletins" (New York, 1961), pp. 83–84.

sound basis for classification of the various items listed above is as follows:

1. Classify as *current liabilities (a)* those short-term items that represent a future claim against current assets whether or not there is an obligation to a specific individual or entity and *(b)* those items that will represent revenue when the current obligations to deliver goods and render services are met.
2. Classify as long-term liabilities all items that are consistent with (1) above, except that they are not *current;* that is, extended periods of time are involved.
3. Classify all other items according to their characteristics as asset offsets, owners' equity, or additions to regular liabilities.

On the above basis the following classifications are suggested:

Item	Classification
Interest revenue collected in advance	Current liability
Unearned rent revenue	Current liability
Advances received for services to be rendered in the future	Current liability
Customer deposits, short term	Current liability
Magazine subscriptions collected in advance	Current liability
Deferred repairs	Current liability (represents a "claim" against current assets—may be long-term liability if related to several future periods)
Allowance for rearrangement costs	Current liability
Premium on bonds payable	Long-term liability (add to related bonds payable; see Chapter 20)
Equities of minority interests	Owners' equity (special caption separate from controlling interest; see Chapter 19)
Long-term refundable customer deposits	Long-term liability
Leasehold advances (advances on leases)	Current or long-term liability
Deferred income taxes	Current or long-term liability depending upon the element of time involved.

Funds Collected for Third Parties

Numerous state and federal laws require businesses to collect taxes from customers and employees for later remittance to certain gov-ernmental agencies. Taxes collected, but not yet remitted, represent current liabilities. To illustrate, assume there is a 5% sales tax and that sales for the period were $400,000. The indicated entries are as follows:

1. At date the tax is assessed (point of sale):

Cash and accounts receivable ...	420,000	
Sales		400,000
Sales taxes payable		20,000

2. At date of remittance to taxing authority:

Sales taxes payable	20,000	
Cash		20,000

Payroll Taxes

Take-home pay seldom is the amount of the earnings of the employee because of numerous payroll deductions, such as union dues, insurance premiums, savings plans, stock purchase plans, income taxes withheld, and "social security" taxes. Because of the high progressive tax rates and the increasing amount of payroll subject to these rates, the payroll taxes are a very significant current cost to the employee. The recent social security legislation, signed into law on December 20, 1977, substantially increased the rates and the amounts of wages subject to tax beginning in 1979. Comparative effects with the prior law are shown in Exhibit 9–1.

Federal Income Taxes Withheld. Federal income tax laws require the employer to withhold from the pay of each employee an amount representing anticipated income taxes payable by the employee. The amount withheld depends upon the number of dependents and the level of income of the employee. Employers compute the amounts withheld according to a government prescribed formula, or read them directly from withholding tax tables provided by the government. Income taxes withheld must be remitted to the Treasury through local depositaries (banks), and the amounts withheld are current liabilities of the employer until remittance.

FICA Payroll Taxes. Social security laws require that the employer deduct a tax from the pay of each employee under specified conditions. In addition to the tax paid by the employee, the employer must match the contribution of the employee and remit both taxes to the Treasury Department. The rates and amount of

EXHIBIT 9-1
Payroll Tax Rates under the Federal Insurance Contributions Act
New Law—Effective January 1, 1978

Year	Prior Law			New Law		
	Total Tax Rate	Wage Base	Maximum Tax	Total Tax Rate	Wage Base	Maximum Tax
	Employers and Employees					
1978	6.05%	$17,700	$1,071	6.05%	$17,700	$1,071
1979	6.05	18,900	1,143	6.13	22,900	1,404
1980	6.05	20,400	1,234	6.13	25,900	1,588
1981	6.30	21,900	1,380	6.65	29,700	1,975
1982	6.30	23,400	1,474	6.70	31,800	2,131
1983	6.30	24,900	1,569	6.70	33,900	2,271
1984	6.30	26,400	1,663	6.70	36,000	2,412
1985	6.30	27,900	1,758	7.05	38,100	2,686
1986	6.45	29,400	1,896	7.15	40,200	2,874
1987	6.45	31,200	2,012	7.15	42,600	3,046
	Self-Employed Individuals					
1978	8.10%	$17,700	$1,434	8.10%	$17,700	$1,434
1979	8.10	18,900	1,531	8.10	22,900	1,855
1980	8.10	20,400	1,652	8.10	25,900	2,098
1981	8.35	21,900	1,829	9.30	29,700	2,762
1982	8.35	23,400	1,954	9.35	31,800	2,973
1983	8.35	24,900	2,079	9.35	33,900	3,170
1984	8.35	26,400	2,204	9.35	36,000	3,366
1985	8.35	27,900	2,330	9.90	38,100	3,772
1986	8.50	29,400	2,499	10.00	40,200	4,020
1987	8.50	31,200	2,652	10.00	42,600	4,260

Note: The wage base through 1981 is set by statute under the new law. After 1981 the wage bases shown above are estimated under the automatic cost-of-living escalator provision (source: Arthur Young Memorandum, December 1977).

wages subject to this tax are shown in Exhibit 9-1. These payroll taxes are generally referred to as FICA taxes because the enabling legislation is the Federal Insurance Contributions Act. The purpose of the tax is to provide retirement pay and death benefits for the retiree's survivors.

FUTA Payroll Taxes. Another social security tax levied by the federal government is to finance the cost of administering the federal-state unemployment compensation program. This payroll tax is paid only by the employer (of one or more persons). These payroll taxes are usually called FUTA taxes because the enabling legislation is the Federal Unemployment Tax Act. Currently, the FUTA tax rate is 3.4% on the first $6,000 in wages paid to each employee (after December 31, 1977). The law provides that 2.7%

is payable to the state (of employment) as a participation (if the state laws qualify) and the remaining 0.7% is payable to the Federal Treasury [Code Sec. 3301 and 3306 (b)].

Accounting for withholding taxes, FICA taxes, and FUTA taxes may be illustrated simply. Assume salaries of $100,000 for the month of January and income tax withholding of $20,000.

January 31, 1979—To record salaries and *employee* payroll taxes:

Salaries	100,000	
Withholding taxes payable		20,000
FICA taxes payable—		
employees ($100,000 × 6.13%)*		6,130
Cash		73,870

* This assumes no employee exceeded the $22,900 maximum wage base.

January 31, 1979—To record *employer* payroll taxes:

Expense—payroll taxes		9,530
FICA taxes payable—		
employer ($100,000 × 6.13%) ...	6,130	
FUTA taxes payable—		
federal ($100,000 × .7%)	700	
FUTA taxes payable—state		
($100,000 × 2.7%)	2,700	

At remittance date:

Withholding taxes payable	20,000	
FICA taxes payable—employees	6,130	
FICA taxes payable—employer	6,130	
FUTA taxes payable—federal	700	
FUTA taxes payable—state	2,700	
Cash		35,660

Between the date of the payroll and the remission date, the five liabilities recorded would be reported as current liabilities.[3]

Tax and Bonus Problems

It is not unusual to find employment terms that provide for the payment of a *bonus* to an officer, branch manager, or other employee of a corporation. A bonus should be treated as an operating expense and set up as a current liability when earned and pending payment. Bonus payments generally are deductible in computing taxable income under federal tax laws. Bonus contracts relating to income are usually one of two classes, viz:

1. The bonus is computed on the income after deducting income taxes but before deducting the bonus.
2. The bonus is computed after deducting both the bonus and the income taxes.

Since the tax is not determinable before the bonus is computed or vice versa, a special computation is required, based on simultaneous equations. To illustrate a typical situation, assume Bryan Company reported income of $100,000 before deducting income taxes and before the bonus to the general manager. Assume the tax rate T is 48% and the bonus rate B is 10%. Two situations are illustrated.

[3] Observe that on a payroll of $100,000 the total taxes paid by the employees and employer combined amounted to $35,660 (36%).

Situation 1. The bonus is based on income after deducting income taxes but before deducting the bonus.

$$B = .10(\$100,000 - T) \quad (1)$$
$$T = .48(\$100,000 - B) \quad (2)$$

Substitute value of T in (2) for T in (1):

$$B = .10[\$100,000 - .48(\$100,000 - B)]$$
$$B = .10[\$100,000 - \$48,000 + .48B]$$
$$B = \$10,000 - \$4,800 + .048B$$
$$B - .048B = \$5,200$$
$$.952B = \$5,200$$
$$B = \$5,462$$

Substitute value of B in (2):

$$T = .48(\$100,000 - \$5,462)$$
$$T = \$45,378$$

Situation 2. The bonus is based on income after deducting both income taxes and the bonus.

$$B = .10(\$100,000 - B - T) \quad (1)$$
$$T = .48(\$100,000 - B) \quad (2)$$

Substitute value of T in (2) for T in (1):

$$B = .10[\$100,000 - B - .48(\$100,000 - B)]$$
$$B = .10[\$100,000 - B - \$48,000 + .48B]$$
$$B = \$10,000 - .10B - \$4,800 + .048B$$
$$B + .10B - .048B = \$5,200$$
$$1.052B = \$5,200$$
$$B = \$4,943$$

Substitute value of B in (2):

$$T = .48(\$100,000 - \$4,943)$$
$$T = \$45,627$$

Proof of Computations

	Situation 1	Situation 2
Computation of tax:		
Income before tax and bonus	$100,000	$100,000
Deduct bonus (as computed)	5,462	4,943
Taxable income	94,538	95,057
Multiply by tax rate	.48	.48
Tax	$ 45,378	$ 45,627

Computation of bonus:

Income before tax and bonus	$100,000	$100,000
Tax	45,378	45,627
	54,622	54,373
Bonus (as computed)		4,943
Income subject to bonus	54,622	49,430
Multiply by bonus rate	.10	.10
Bonus	$ 5,462	$ 4,943

The entries to record the bonus and income taxes in Situation 2 would be as follows:

1. To record bonus:

Employee compensation expense	4,943	
Bonus payable		4,943

2. To record income taxes:

Income tax expense	45,627	
Income taxes payable		45,627

3. To record payment of bonus:

Bonus payable	4,943	
Cash		4,943

LONG-TERM LIABILITIES

All liabilities not classified as current (as defined in the preceding section) should be classified as long-term liabilities; however, some financial statements carry a second noncurrent category, *other liabilities*. Bonds payable and long-term notes and mortgages are then reported under long-term liabilities, and all other long-term obligations reported under the *other liabilities* category.

Long-term liabilities are reported on the balance sheet at their present value. The present value of a liability is the sum of the discounted present values of *(a)* the cash maturity amount plus *(b)* the cash interest payments to be made, each discounted at the going market rate of interest in effect at inception for that particular type of liability. When the stated rate of interest is realistic (i.e., the going rate), the present value is equal to the par or principal amount. When the stated interest rate is not realistic, the present value may be different from the principal amount. Two situations are often encountered: (1) a note issued for cash and (2) a note issued for property, goods, or services. *APB Opinion No. 21,* "Interest on Receivables and Payables," provides the guidelines for these two situations.

Note Issued for Cash. In this situation, *Opinion No. 21* states that the note "is presumed to have a present value at issuance measured by the cash proceeds exchanged." To illustrate, assume $10,000 cash is borrowed and a note payable for that amount is executed that is due in five years and calls for annual interest at 9% in addition to the principal of $10,000. The note would be recorded at $10,000, which represents *(a)* the cash proceeds received, *(b)* the principal amount, and *(c)* the present value of the note (in this situation the 9% is viewed as a realistic rate). Entries for the first year would be as follows:

a.	Cash	10,000	
	Note payable, long term		10,000
b.	Interest expense	900	
	Cash ($10,000 × 9%)		900

The present value of this note would be computed as follows:

Maturity amount discounted:	
$10,000 × $p_{n=5;i=9\%}$ = $10,000	
× .64993 (Table 6–2) =	$ 6,499
Interest payments discounted:	
$900 × $P_{o_{n=5;i=9\%}}$ = $900	
× 3.88965 (Table 6–4) =	3,501
Present value (same as	
maturity amount)	$10,000

Note Issued for Property, Goods, or Services. In this situation, the accounting value that should be assigned to the noncash consideration received for a note payable must be carefully determined in accordance with the provisions of *APB Opinion No. 21.* In such transactions, if entered into at "arm's length," the presumption is that the interest rate and the payment terms stipulated by the parties should be accepted as realistic unless "(1) interest is not stated, or (2) the stated interest rate is unreasonable, or (3) the stated face amount of the note is materially different from the current sales price for the same or similar items or from the market value of the note at the date of the transaction." The *Opinion* also specifies that the noncash consideration received should be recorded at its market value or the market value of the note payable, whichever is the more clearly determinable. The market value of the note is its discounted

EXHIBIT 9–2
Accounting for Note Payable and Noncash Consideration

a. Computation of present value of the note payable:

Maturity amount discounted:
$10,000 \times p_{n=5;i=9\%} = \$10,000 \times .64993$ (Table 6–2) = ... $6,499.30
Interest payment discounted:
$600 \times P_{o_{n=5;i=9\%}} = \$600 \times 3.88965$ (Table 6–4) = ... 2,333.79
Net present value $8,833.09

(Discount: $10,000 − $8,833.09 = $1,166.91.)

b. Debt and interest amortization schedule (interest method):

At Year-End	Cash Interest Payments	Interest Expense	Amortization of Discount	Balance Sheet Valuation (present value)
Start				$ 8,833.09
1	$600	$8,833.09 × 9% = $794.98	$794.98 − $600 = $194.98	9,028.07
2	600	9,028.07 × 9% = 812.53	812.53 − 600 = 212.53	9,240.60
3	600	9,240.60 × 9% = 831.65	831.65 − 600 = 231.65	9,472.25
4	600	9,472.25 × 9% = 852.50	852.50 − 600 = 252.50	9,724.75
5	600	9,724.75 × 9% = 875.25	875.25 − 600 = 275.25	10,000.00*

*At maturity date.

Note: At the end of each year the balance sheet should report the amount shown in the last column above and the income statement should reflect interest expense shown in the third column.

c. Entries—The entries to account for this note (with an *effective* rate different from the *stated* rate) can be made in either of two ways with the same results.

Case A—Note Entered at "Gross"			*Case B—Note Entered at "Net"*		
Start:					
Land	8,833.09		Land	8,833.09	
Discount on note payable	1,166.91		Note payable ...		8,833.09
Note payable		10,000.00			
End of Year 1:					
Interest expense	794.98		Interest expense	794.98	
Discount on note payable		194.98	Note payable ...		194.98
Cash		600.00	Cash		600.00

d. The balance sheet presentation at the end of Year 1 would be as follows:

Case A: Long-Term Liabilities:
Note payable, due in 5 years (maturity amount).................... $10,000.00
Less: Unamortized discount ($1,166.91 − $194.98) 971.93 $9,028.07

Case B: Long-Term Liabilities:
Note payable, due in 5 years, net of discount
(maturity amount, $10,000) 9,028.07

present value based on an "appropriate" rate of interest at date of issuance.[4] The *Opinion*

[4] An appropriate rate is defined as "the prevailing rates for similar instruments of issuers with similar credit ratings" or a realistic rate considering all of the circumstances.

specifies that if the present value of the note is different from its face amount, the resulting premium or discount "should be accounted for as an element of interest over the life of the note." Amortization of the discount or premium should be based upon the "interest method" rather than the straight-line method so that the result will be "a constant rate of interest when applied to the amount outstanding at the beginning of any given period."[5]

To illustrate the issuance of notes payable for noncash considerations, assume a $10,000, five-year note payable that stipulates 6% annual interest is issued for a tract of land. The market value of the land cannot be reasonably determined; however, for this kind of transaction, the prevailing rate of interest for the issuer is 9%. Exhibit 9–2 illustrates the following for the issuer:

a. Computation of the present value of the note to be used as the valuation of the land.
b. The related debt and interest amortization schedule using the interest method of amortization.
c. Methods of recording the transactions for the first year.
d. Balance sheet presentation of the note payable.

Current Maturities of Long-Term Debt

On the balance sheet for the year preceding the maturity of a long-term debt, the amount to be paid during the upcoming current period, if payable from current assets, should be reported as a current liability. *FASB Statement No. 6*, "Classification of Short-Term Obligations Expected to be Refinanced," specifies that this classification should not be used if the payment is to be made from a sinking fund, or the cash is to be derived from other noncurrent sources. To illustrate, the current payment on a serial bond issue out of current assets would be reported as follows:

Current Liabilities:		
Current payment on bond issue ..		$100,000
Long-Term Liabilities:		
Bonds payable	$500,000	
Less: Current payment	100,000	400,000

---

[5] Other methods, such as straight-line, may be used "if the results obtained are not materially different from those that would result from the 'interest' method" (AICPA, *Accounting Principles Board Opinion No. 21* "Interest on Receivables and Payables" [New York, 1971], par. 14).

Bonds payable are discussed in depth in Chapter 20. Study of that chapter is essential for a complete understanding of liabilities.

CONTINGENCIES AND ESTIMATED LIABILITIES

Liabilities often must be estimated because (1) a known liability exists but the ultimate amount is uncertain or (2) a contingency loss exists. A contingency is defined in *FASB Statement No. 5* as "an existing condition, situation, or set of circumstances involving uncertainty as to possible gain (hereinafter a 'gain contingency') or a loss (hereinafter a 'loss contingency') to an enterprise that will ultimately be resolved when one or more future events occur or fail to occur. Resolution of the uncertainty may confirm the acquisition of an asset or the reduction of a liability or the loss or impairment of an asset or the incurrence of a liability."

FASB Statement No. 5, entitled "Accounting for Contingencies," is the basic pronouncement on contingencies and estimated liabilities and is the basis for this discussion. Therefore, this section is divided into three parts: *(a)* contingent liabilities (loss contingencies) that must be accrued and reported at estimated dollar amounts in the body of the financial statements, *(b)* contingent liabilities which are reported only in the notes to the financial statements, and *(c)* gain contingencies.

FASB Statement No. 5 delineates contingencies and specifies particular accounting treatments on the basis of whether the contingency is

a. Probable. The future event or events are likely to occur.
b. Reasonably possible. The chance of occurrence of the future event or events is more than remote but less than likely.
c. Remote. The chance of occurrence of the future event or events is slight.

The provisions of *FASB Statement No. 5* relating to contingencies may be summarized as shown at the top of the next page.

Loss Contingencies That Must Be Accrued

FASB Statement No. 5 requires that a loss contingency must be accrued as a debit to expense

Probabilistic Nature of the Contingency	Amount Can Be Reasonably Estimated	Amount Cannot Be Reasonably Estimated
	Loss Contingency	
Probable	Accrue and report in the body of the statements.	Do not accrue; report as a note in the financial statements.
Reasonably possible	Do not accrue; report as a note in the financial statements.	Do not accrue; report as a note in the financial statements.
Remote	No accrual or note required; however, a note is permitted.	No accrual or note required; however, a note is permitted.
	Gain Contingency	
Probable	No accrual except in very unusual circumstances. Note disclosure required.	Note disclosure required; exercise care to avoid misleading inferences.
Reasonably possible	Note disclosure required; exercise care to avoid misleading inferences.	Note disclosure required; exercise extreme care to avoid misleading inferences.
Remote	Disclosure not recommended.	

or loss and a credit to a liability if *both* of the following conditions are met:

a. Information received prior to the issuance of the financial statements indicates that it is *probable* that an asset has been impaired or a liability has been incurred at the date of the financial statements. Implicit in this condition is that it must be probable that one or more future events will occur confirming the fact of the loss.
b. The amount of the loss can be reasonably estimated.

This situation corresponds to the upper left cell in the above table.

The *Statement* identified a number of loss contingencies, including estimated losses on receivables (allowance for doubtful accounts); estimated warranty obligations; litigations, claims and assessments; and anticipated losses on the disposal of a segment of the business *(APB Opinion No. 30)*.

A loss contingency that meets both of the above criteria, in addition to being accrued in the accounts, must be reported *(a)* on the balance sheet as a liability and *(b)* on the income statement as an expense (or loss, as the case may be) in the period in which it occurs. Three examples will now be given of the accrual of a loss contingency.

Case A—Product Warranty. Assume Company R sold merchandise for $200,000 cash during the period. Experience has indicated that warranty and guarantee costs will approximate ½% of sales. The indicated entries are as follows:

In year of sale:

Cash	200,000	
Sales revenue		200,000
Estimated warranty expense	1,000	
Estimated warranty liability		1,000

Subsequently, during warranty period for actual expenditures:

Estimated warranty liability	987	
Cash (or other resources)		987

When warranty expense is immaterial in amount, a company would not accrue it as illustrated above; instead, they would account for it on a cash basis because, for practical reasons, the materiality concept is permitted to override the theoretical matching principle.

Case B—Liability from Premiums, Coupons, and Trading Stamps. As a promotional device, many companies offer premiums of one kind or another to customers who turn in coupons, trading stamps, labels, box tops, wrappers, and so on, received when merchandise is purchased. At the end of each accounting period, a portion of these will be outstanding (unredeemed by the customers), some of which ultimately will be turned in for redemption. These outstanding claims for premiums represent a liability that must be recognized in the period of sale of the merchandise. The estimated cost of the premiums that will be given should be recorded as an estimated expense of the period of sale and an estimated liability should be credited.

To illustrate a typical situation, assume Baker Coffee Company offered to customers a premium—a silver coffee spoon (cost to Baker 75 cents each) upon the return of 20 coupons. One coupon is placed in each can of coffee when packed. The company estimated, on the basis of experience, that only 70% of the coupons would ever be redeemed. The following additional data for two years are available:

	First Year	Second Year
Number of coffee spoons purchased @ $0.75	6,000	4,000
Number of coupons redeemed	40,000	120,000
Number of cans of coffee sold	100,000	200,000

The indicated entries are as follows:

1. To record purchases of spoons:

	First Year	Second Year
Premium inventory— silverware	4,500	3,000
Cash	4,500	3,000

2. To record estimated liability and premium expense on sales:

	First Year	Second Year
Premium expense*	2,625	5,250
Estimated premium claims payable	2,625	5,250

* Computations:
Year 1: (100,000 ÷ 20) × $0.75 × .70 = $2,625.
Year 2: (200,000 ÷ 20) × $0.75 × .70 = $5,250.

3. To record redemption of coupons:

	First Year	Second Year
Estimated premium claims payable	1,500	4,500
Premium inventory— silverware	1,500	4,500

* Computations:
Year 1: (40,000 ÷ 20) × $0.75 = $1,500.
Year 2: (120,000 ÷ 20) × $0.75 = $4,500.

Case C—Liability from Litigation. Assume Company S was sued during the last quarter of the current year as a result of an accident involving a vehicle owned and operated by the company. Plaintiff seeks $100,000 damages. In the opinion of management and company counsel, it is probable that damages will be assessed and a reasonable estimate is $50,000. The indicated entry is

Estimated loss from lawsuit pending....	50,000	
Estimated liability from lawsuit pending		50,000

Estimated losses would be classified on the income statement as extraordinary, either unusual or infrequent, or as ordinary in accordance with the provisions of *APB Opinion No. 30,* "Reporting the Results of Operations." Balance sheet classification would depend upon the expected timing of the settlement of the estimated liability. Estimated liabilities may ultimately require expenditures more or less than estimated to satisfy the actual liability. When the estimated liability turns out to be too high or too low, the difference is accounted for as a change in estimate under the provisions of *APB Opinion No. 20.* That is, there is no correction of prior years' income; the difference is accounted for *prospectively* as a deduction (or addition) in the income statement of the year of settlement and subsequent years as the case may be. Occasionally a contingency loss is of such a nature that note disclosure is needed, in addition to accrual and reporting in the body of the financial statements, to meet the requirements of the full disclosure principle. Published financial reports of companies seldom, if ever, reflect a situation where counsel said, "We may lose this suit." As an advocate, counsel does everything possible to avoid a *tacit* confession of *guilt.*

Loss Contingencies Disclosed Only in Notes

The preceding section dealt exclusively with loss contingencies that must be accrued and reported in the body of the financial statements. This section discusses loss contingencies that must be disclosed in notes to the financial statements.

FASB Statement No. 5 provides that "disclosure of the contingency (other than expense or loss accruals) shall be made when there is *at least* a reasonable possibility that a loss or an additional loss may have been incurred." Observe in the table on page 320 that this requirement appears in one cell on the "probable" line (amount cannot be reasonably estimated) and both cells of the "reasonably possible" line. *Note disclosure* must give the nature of the contingency and give an estimate of the *possible* loss, or it must state that a reasonable estimate cannot be made.

Loss contingencies that must be disclosed in notes (but not accrued or reported in the body of the financial statements) do not depend upon the kind of event but rather (as noted above) on the circumstances of probability and reasonability of dollar estimates. For example, in the case of Company S given in the preceding section, since the loss contingency was both probable and the amount reasonably estimated, accrual was required. Alternatively, if we assume that management and legal counsel conclude that the plaintiff's case is weak and that there is only a *reasonable possibility* that damages will be assessed by the court, accrual is not permitted but note disclosure is required. Finally, if we assume instead that the loss contingency is *remote,* accrual is not permitted and note disclosure is not required; however, note disclosure is permitted.

The area of litigation is complicated because of *(a)* legal complexities, *(b)* the extended time often involved, and *(c)* the fact that presettlement disclosures may prejudice the outcome of the case. In these situations, the *Statement* (par. 36) suggests that "among the factors that should be considered are . . . the opinions or views of legal counsel and other advisors, the experience of the enterprise in similar cases, the experience of other enterprises, and any decision of the enterprise's management as to how the enterprise intends to respond to the lawsuit, claim or assessment." For example, if the enterprise plans to forcefully contest the lawsuit, claim, or assessment, this is considered good evidence that in their opinion the loss contingency is not probable (no accrual is required) and may not even be reasonably possible (no accrual permitted and note disclosure not required).

Prior to the issuance of *FASB Statement No. 5,* loss contingencies were called contingent lia-

bilities. For many years disclosure of contingent liabilities was a part of generally accepted accounting principles although the specifications were vague. With respect to a category of loss contingencies that are *remote* as to probability, the *Statement* specifies that "certain loss contingencies are currently being disclosed in financial statements even though the possibility of loss may be remote. The common characteristic of these contingencies is a guarantee, normally with a right to proceed against an outside party in the event that the guarantor is called upon to satisfy the guarantee." Examples cited are guarantees of indebtedness of others and guarantees to purchase receivables. Disclosure of such loss contingencies, and others, that have the same characteristic (a guarantee) "shall be continued. The disclosure shall include the nature and amount of the guarantee."

GAIN CONTINGENCIES

A gain contingency arises when the characteristics of a contingency are present (as defined on page 319) and there may be an increase in assets or a decrease in liabilities, depending upon one or more future events.

Contingency gains are rarely accrued; however, they are accorded note disclosure, providing "misleading implications" are not given. The different treatment accorded gain contingencies, compared with loss contingencies, is due to application of the concept of conservatism. *FASB Statement No. 5* specifies the treatment of gain contingencies as follows:

a. Contingencies that might result in gains are not reflected in the accounts since to do so might be to recognize revenue prior to its realization.

b. Adequate disclosure shall be made of contingencies that might result in gains, but care shall be exercised to avoid misleading implications as to the likelihood of realization.

An example of a gain contingency would be the case where the company has sued another party for damages. Assuming that the case has been decided in favor of the company but is awaiting appeal, and in the opinion of the company counsel and management the appeal will be denied, note disclosure (but not accrual) would be appropriate. Another example would be expropriation (by a foreign government) of the assets of the company, and a concomitant probability that reimbursement will exceed book value. In these circumstances the volatile political situation there must be recognized. Therefore, note disclosure would be needed (in this situation the gain contingency may well turn out to be a loss contingency). The note disclosure should be carefully worded to avoid misleading implications about the probability of the gain and its amount. Remote gain contingencies should never be disclosed.

APPROPRIATIONS AND RESERVES OF RETAINED EARNINGS

Accrual of "reserves for general contingencies" is not permitted by *FASB Statement No. 5.* The *Statement* also provides that in those situations where *appropriations* or "reserves" of retained earnings are recorded, the debit to create them must be to Retained Earnings, not to loss or expense, and the balances in such "reserve" accounts must not be reported outside the stockholders' equity section of the balance sheet (also see Chapter 17).

PART B—ACCOUNTING FOR INCOME TAXES

Accounting for income taxes is discussed in this chapter because income taxes comprise an important liability of most corporations.[6] This liability merits special attention because accounting for income taxes is subject to specific rules, some of which are controversial. This part of the chapter does not cover all of the complexities one might encounter because that would presuppose a complete understanding of income taxes. Nevertheless, the major complexities and most of the common specific situations are discussed. The discussions are based primarily upon *APB Opinion No. 11,* "Accounting for Income Taxes." Numerous other pronouncements (*APB Opinions Nos. 23* and *24* and *FASB Statement No. 9*) deal with special areas of this topic, but they do not change the general rules specified in *Opinion No. 11.*

---

[6] Partnerships and sole proprietorships do not pay income taxes; the owners must include their shares of company income on their personal income tax returns.

APB Opinion No. 11 establishes the basic requirement that companies should match against the revenue of a period an amount of income tax expense based on the reported pretax *accounting income* of that period regardless of the amount of income taxes payable (as reflected in the income tax return for the period). Thus, *Opinion No. 11* deals exclusively with the amount of income tax *expense* that should be reported on the income statement. It does not govern computation of the amount of income taxes *payable* (to the government) because that is governed solely by the Internal Revenue Code and IRS Tax Regulations.

The complexities often encountered in accounting for income taxes arise because it is necessary to reconcile the concepts underlying financial accounting (which govern the reporting of income tax expense on the financial statements) with the provisions of the income tax laws (which govern the amount of taxes payable to the government as reflected on the income tax return). Fortunately, the two areas adopt the same general notion of income; however, enough differences exist to require special accounting and reporting guidelines.

Preliminary to the substantive discussions to follow, two terms that will be used throughout the remainder of this chapter are defined as follows:

1. Pretax accounting income (or simply accounting income)—revenues less expenses (ignoring income tax expense) reported on the income statement in conformity with generally accepted accounting principles. Income tax *expense* reported on the income statement is based on *pretax accounting income.*
2. Taxable income—revenues less expenses includable on the tax return in conformity with income tax laws and regulations. Income taxes *payable* reflected on the income tax return is based on *taxable income.*

This part of the chapter considers the following income tax topics in the order given:

1. Interperiod income tax allocation.
2. Income tax effects of prior period adjustments.

3. Tax loss carrybacks and carryforwards.
4. Intraperiod income tax allocation.
5. Disclosure of income tax allocation.

INTERPERIOD INCOME TAX ALLOCATION

Interperiod income tax allocation is defined in *APB Opinion No. 11* as "the process of apportioning income taxes among periods." This means that income tax expense reported on the income statement must be based on pretax accounting income and income taxes payable must be based on taxable income. And any difference between income tax expense and income taxes payable for the period that will reverse must be recognized as *deferred income taxes.* Thus, income tax expense results from *allocation* of income taxes to the period in which the income which caused the tax is reported. Allocation is necessary to conform to the matching principle as stated in *APB Opinion No. 11,* paragraph 12:

> Interperiod tax allocation is an integral part of the determination of income tax expense, and income tax expense should include the tax effects of revenue and expense transactions included in the determination of pretax accounting income.

Four cases are given to illustrate interperiod income tax allocation. Assume XY Corporation prepared the summarized income statements for Years 19D and 19E shown in Exhibit 9–3.

EXHIBIT 9–3

XY CORPORATION		
Pretax Income Statements		
	19D	*19E*
Revenues:		
Sales revenue	$100,000	$120,000
Rent revenue	6,000	6,000
Investment revenue	1,000	1,000
Total revenues	107,000	127,000
Expenses:		
Cost of goods sold	65,000	75,000
Depreciation expense		
(straight line)	10,000	10,000
Interest expense	2,000	2,000
Total expenses	77,000	87,000
Pretax accounting		
income	$ 30,000	$ 40,000
Assumed average income tax rate, 40%.		

Case A—Assume that all revenues and expenses shown in the two income statements for XY Corporation were properly includable on the income tax returns for the two years. Thus, for both years, *pretax accounting income* and *taxable income* were the same. The entries to record income taxes would be as follows:

19D:

Income tax expense ($30,000 ×.40)	12,000	
Income taxes payable		12,000

19E:

Income tax expense ($40,000 × .40) ...	16,000	
Income taxes payable		16,000

The income statements would report the respective amounts as expense, and the balance sheets would report the same amounts as a liability (assuming no prepayments on the tax liability). There are no *deferred income taxes* because the amounts for income tax expense and income taxes payable were the same for each period.

Case B—Assume that the rent revenue for one full year amounting to $12,000 was collected in full on July 1, 19D, for the following 12 months. Accrual accounting required XY Corporation to include six months' rent revenue on the income statement for each year. However, for income tax purposes all of the rent revenue must be included on the income tax return for the period in which collected, 19D. Therefore, for each year pretax accounting income and taxable income are different. Consequently, deferred income taxes must be recognized. Computation of income taxes and the related entries to record income taxes would be as follows:

Year 19D:	
Income tax expense (pretax accounting income, $30,000 × .40) =	$12,000
Income taxes payable [taxable income, ($30,000 + 6,000) × .40] =	14,400
Difference: Deferred income taxes (check: $6,000 × .40)	$ 2,400

Entry to record income taxes for 19D:

Income tax expense	12,000	
Deferred income taxes	2,400	
Income taxes payable		14,400

The 19D income statement would report income tax expense of $12,000, and the balance sheet for 19D would report *(a)* income taxes payable, $14,400 (assuming no prepayments), and *(b)* a current asset (a debit) for deferred income taxes, $2,400. 19E tax computations and entries would be:

Year 19E:

Income tax expense (pretax accounting income, $40,000 × .40) =	$16,000
Income taxes payable [taxable income, ($40,000 − $6,000) × .40] =	13,600
Difference: Deferred income taxes (check: $6,000 × .40)	$ 2,400

Entry to record income taxes for 19E:

Income tax expense	16,000	
Income taxes payable		13,600
Deferred income taxes		2,400

The 19E income statement would report income tax expense of $16,000, and the balance sheet for 19E would report income taxes payable of $13,600 (assuming no prepayments). Deferred income taxes would not be reported since it has a zero balance—it was debited for $2,400 in 19D and credited for the same amount in 19E. Note that at the end of 19E the deferred income tax amount of $2,400 reversed or "turned around" because at that time, for this particular transaction, the *total* (for the two years) pretax accounting income and *total* taxable income amounts were the same. In summary, the income tax expense was *allocated* to the respective periods in which the related income was reported for accounting purposes, regardless of when the income tax was actually reported on the tax return.

Case C—We will disregard the assumption in Case B and instead assume that XY Corporation uses straight-line depreciation on the income statement and double-declining balance (DDB) depreciation on the income tax return for machinery acquired January 1, 19D, that cost $50,000 and had an estimated useful life of five years and no residual value. Depreciation expense each year under each method would be as follows:

Straight-line depreciation:

$50,000 × 20% (five years) =	$10,000
Double-declining balance depreciation:	
Year D: $50,000 × 40% =	20,000
Year E: ($50,000 − $20,000) × 40% =	12,000

In this case the pretax accounting income for each year will be different from the taxable income because of the different amounts of depreciation included in the respective income amounts; as a consequence, deferred income taxes must be recognized. Computation of income taxes and the related entries to record income taxes would be as follows:

Year 19D:

Income tax expense (pretax accounting income, $30,000 × .40) =	$12,000
Income taxes payable (taxable income, $20,000[a] × .40) =	8,000
Difference: Deferred income taxes (check: $10,000[b] × .40)	$ 4,000

[a] $30,000 + $10,000 − $20,000 = $20,000.
[b] $20,000 − $10,000 = $10,000.

Entry to record income taxes for 19D:

Income tax expense	12,000	
Income taxes payable		8,000
Deferred income taxes		4,000

The income statement for 19D would report income tax expense of $12,000, and the balance sheet would report *(a)* a liability for income taxes payable of $8,000 (assuming no prepayments) and *(b)* another liability for deferred income taxes of $4,000. In this case deferred income taxes is a liability because the tax expense related to it was reported on the income statement and the tax will be paid in later periods when DDB depreciation expense becomes less per period than straight-line depreciation. Thus, the deferred taxes (a credit) will completely reverse or turn around completely by the end of the last year (fifth year) of depreciation on the machinery. 19E tax computations and entries would be:

Year 19E:

Income tax expense (pretax accounting income, $40,000 × .40) =	$16,000
Income taxes payable (taxable income, $38,000[c] × .40) =	15,200
Difference: Deferred income taxes (check: $2,000[d] × .40) = ...	$ 800

[c] $40,000 + $10,000 − $12,000 = $38,000.
[d] $12,000 − $10,000 = $2,000.

Entry to record income taxes for 19E:

Income tax expense	16,000	
Income taxes payable		15,200
Deferred income taxes		800

The income statement for 19E would report income tax expense of $16,000, and the balance sheet would report *(a)* a liability for income taxes payable of $15,200 (assuming no prepayments) and *(b)* another liability for $4,000 + $800 = $4,800 for deferred income taxes payable. During the next three years this $4,800 credit will be exactly offset by debits because straight-line depreciation expense then will be greater than DDB depreciation (i.e., the deferred taxes will completely reverse or turn around).

Timing Differences. There are two kinds of transactions that cause pretax accounting income to be different from taxable income; they are called (1) timing differences and (2) permanent differences. Cases A–C illustrated timing differences. Case D illustrates permanent difference (next column).

APB Opinion No. 11, paragraph 13, defines timing differences as "differences between the periods in which transactions affect taxable income and the periods in which they enter into the determination of pretax accounting income. Timing differences originate in one period and reverse or 'turn around' in one or more subsequent periods. Some timing differences reduce income taxes that would otherwise be payable currently; others increase income taxes that would otherwise be payable currently." Cases B (rent revenue) and C (depreciation expense) above illustrated timing differences because there was a difference between pretax accounting income and taxable income that would reverse in one or more subsequent periods. *Timing differences always give rise to deferred income taxes* (either a debit or a credit). Four types of transactions cause timing differences:

a. Revenues or gains are included in taxable income later than they are included in pretax accounting income. Examples include earlier pretax-accounting recognition of gross profits on installment sales and income on construction contracts.

b. Expenses or losses are deducted in determining taxable income later than they are de-

ducted in determining pretax accounting income. Examples include earlier pretax accounting recognition of estimated warranty expense, deferred compensation, and estimated losses on disposal of facilities and discontinued operations.

c. Revenues or gains are included in taxable income earlier than they are included in pretax accounting income. Examples are rent collected in advance and gains on the sale of property leased back (see Chapter 22.)

d. Expenses or losses are deducted in determining taxable income earlier than they are deducted in determining pretax accounting income. An example is depreciation on an accelerated basis for tax purposes but on a straight-line basis for accounting purposes.

In summary, timing differences *(a)* relate to items that will be on *both* the income statement and the income tax return, but at different times; *(b)* they always give rise to deferred income taxes; and *(c)* they will reverse over time.

Permanent Differences. *APB Opinion No. 11* defines permanent differences as differences that "arise from statutory provisions under which specified revenues are exempt from taxation and specified expenses are not allowable as deductions in determining taxable income." Examples are interest received on municipal obligations and premiums paid on officers' life insurance. Other permanent differences arise from items entering into the determination of taxable income which are not components of pretax accounting income in any period. Examples are the special deduction for certain dividends received and the excess of statutory depletion over cost depletion.

Income tax allocation is *never* applied to permanent differences because they do not give rise to income tax differences that will subsequently reverse or turn around. *For a permanent difference, there is no discrepancy between income tax expense and income taxes payable.*

To illustrate a permanent difference, we will return to Exhibit 9–3 for XY Corporation with the fourth and last case.

Case D—Assume the investment revenue of $1,000 for each year was interest received on "tax-free" municipal bonds. Disregarding Case B (rent revenue) and Case C (depreciation expense), income tax expense and income taxes payable each year would be the same amount:

Year	Computation	Income Tax Expense	Income Taxes Payable
19D ...	($30,000 − $1,000) × .40	$11,600	$11,600
19E ...	($40,000 − $1,000) × .40	15,600	15,600

Comprehensive Illustration. In an actual situation, a worksheet is used to compute interperiod tax allocation amounts and a single entry is made to record the combined effect of all tax differences. To simulate an actual situation, we will combine Cases B, C, and D for XY Corporation; present a suitable worksheet; and illustrate the presentation of the income tax effects. To restate the assumptions in each case:

Case B—On July 1, 19D, collected $12,000 rent in advance for the following 12 months. This amount is subject to income tax in the year collected (a timing difference).

Case C—On January 1, 19D, acquired machinery that cost $50,000; estimated useful life five years and no residual value. Straight-line depreciation is used for financial reporting, and DDB depreciation for tax purposes (a timing difference).

Case D—Investment revenue amounting to $1,000 each year was interest on tax-free municipal bonds (a permanent difference).

An appropriate income tax worksheet, the entry to record the combined income tax effects, and the financial statement presentations are shown in Exhibits 9–4 and 9–5.

Classification of Deferred Income Taxes. Deferred income taxes must be reported on the balance sheet *(a)* if a debit, as a current or noncurrent asset; and *(b)* if a credit, as a current or long-term liability. On this point *APB Opinion No. 11,* paragraph 57, reads:

> Deferred charges and deferred credits relating to timing differences represent the cumulative recognition given to their tax effects and as such do not represent receivables or payables in the usual sense. They should be classified in two categories—one for the net current amount and the other for the net noncurrent amount. This presentation is consistent with the customary distinction between current and noncurrent categories and also recognizes the close relationship among the various deferred tax accounts, all of which bear on the determination of income tax expense. The current portions of such deferred charges and credits should be those amounts which relate to assets and liabilities classified as current. Thus, if installment receivables are a current asset, the deferred credits representing the tax effects of uncollected installment sales should be a current item; if an estimated provision for warranties is a current liability, the deferred charge representing the tax effect of such provision should be a current item.

The key sentence relating to classification of deferred income taxes is "the current portions of such deferred charges and credits should be those amounts which relate to assets and liabilities classified as current." All other deferred income taxes and credits are reported as noncurrent. Current debits and credits are offset, and noncurrent debits and credits are offset; however, current and noncurrent debits and credits are not offset. To illustrate, the presentations shown in Exhibits 9–4 and 9–5 were classified on the following basis:

	Balance Sheet Classification	
	Current	Noncurrent
Year 19D:		
Balance in deferred income tax account, $1,600 credit allocated to:		
Debits:		
Rent revenue collected in advance, a current item ($6,000 × .40)	$2,400	
Credits:		
Depreciation of machinery, a noncurrent item ($10,000 × .40)		$4,000
Year 19E:		
Balance in deferred income tax account, $4,800 credit allocated to:		
Debits:		
None		
Credits:		
Depreciation of machinery, a noncurrent item ($10,000 + $2,000) × .40		4,800

EXHIBIT 9–4
Comprehensive Illustration—Interperiod Income Tax Allocation

XY CORPORATION
Income Tax Worksheet for the Year 19D

Tax Expense	Item	Taxes Payable
$30,000	Pretax accounting income	$30,000
(1,000)	1. Deduct investment revenue on tax-free municipal bonds (a permanent difference)	(1,000)
	2. Add rent revenue taxed in current year ($12,000 − $6,000)	6,000
	3. Deduct additional depreciation (DDB) ($10,000 − $20,000)	(10,000)
29,000	Pretax accounting income subject to tax	
	Taxable income	25,000
× .40	Income tax rate	× .40
$11,600	Income tax expense	
	Income taxes payable	$10,000
	Deferred income taxes $11,600 − $10,000 = $1,600 credit	

Entry to record combined effect of income taxes:

Income tax expense	11,600	
Income taxes payable		10,000
Deferred income taxes		1,600

Financial statements:

XY CORPORATION
Income Statement for the Year Ended December 31, 19D
(refer to Exhibit 9–3)

Revenues:		
Sales revenue	$100,000	
Rent revenue	6,000	
Investment revenue	1,000	$107,000
Expenses:		
Cost of goods sold	65,000	
Depreciation expense	10,000	
Interest expense	2,000	
Income tax expense	11,600	88,600
Net Income		$ 18,400

XY CORPORATION
Balance Sheet at December 31, 19D (partial)

Current Assets:	
*Deferred income taxes	$ 2,400
Current Liabilities:	
Income taxes payable (assuming no prepayments)	10,000
Long-Term Liabilities:	
*Deferred income taxes	4,000

* These amounts net to $1,600 (credit); see discussion on page 327.

EXHIBIT 9–5
Comprehensive Illustration—Interperiod Income Tax Allocation

XY CORPORATION
Income Tax Worksheet for the Year 19E

Tax Expense		Item	Taxes Payable
$40,000	....	Pretax accounting income	$40,000
(1,000)	....	1. Deduct investment revenue on tax-free municipal bonds (a permanent difference)	(1,000)
		2. Deduct rent revenue taxed in prior year ($6,000 − $12,000)	(6,000)
		3. Deduct additional depreciation (DDB) ($10,000 − $12,000)	(2,000)
39,000	....	Pretax accounting income subject to tax	
		Taxable income	31,000
× .40	....	Income tax rate	× .40
$15,600	....	Income tax expense	
		Income taxes payable	$12,400
		Deferred income taxes $15,600 − $12,400 = $3,200 credit	

Entry to record combined effect of income taxes:

Income tax expense	15,600	
Income taxes payable		12,400
Deferred income taxes		3,200

Financial statements:

XY CORPORATION
Income Statement for Year Ended December 31, 19E
(refer to Exhibit 9–3)

Revenues:		
Sales revenue	$120,000	
Rent revenue	6,000	
Investment revenue	1,000	$127,000
Expenses:		
Cost of goods sold	75,000	
Depreciation expense	10,000	
Interest expense...................................	2,000	
Income tax expense	15,600	102,600
Net Income		$ 24,400

XY CORPORATION
Balance Sheet at December 31, 19E (partial)

Current Liabilities:	
Income taxes payable (assuming no prepayments)	$12,400
Long-Term Liabilities:	
*Deferred income taxes	4,800

* Balance in the deferred income tax account:
$1,600 + $3,200 = $4,800; see discussion on page 327.

Changes in Tax Rates. Timing differences give rise to deferred income taxes which are computed on the basis of tax rates in effect when the timing difference occurred. Subsequently, the deferred taxes recognized reverse over the cycle of the timing difference. The reversal is based on the tax rates that were used when the deferred tax amount was initially recorded. On this point *APB Opinion No. 11,* paragraph 19, states:

The deferred taxes are determined on the basis of the tax rates in effect at the time the timing differences originate and are not adjusted for subsequent changes in tax rates or to reflect the imposition of new taxes. (Also see par. 36.)

The fundamental point is that over the cycle of the timing difference for each item, exactly the same amount should be reversed as was recognized as deferred taxes initially. When tax rates change during the timing cycle, (a) income taxes payable must be computed on the basis of the new tax rate (because that is set by law), (b) deferred taxes must be reversed at the rate used when they were initially recorded, and (c) income tax expense for the period is adjusted to accommodate the difference.

To illustrate accommodation of a change in the tax rates during the timing cycle, assume X Corporation had the following data:

	19A	19B
Pretax accounting income	$20,000	$25,000
Accelerated depreciation (used for tax purposes)	6,000	2,000
Straight-line depreciation (used for financial accounting purposes)	4,000	4,000
Average income tax rate	30%	40%

The entries to record income taxes would be as follows:

19A:

Income tax expense ($20,000 × .30)	6,000	
Income taxes payable [($20,000 + $4,000 − $6,000) × .30]		5,400
Deferred income tax—19A depreciation [($6,000 − $4,000) × .30] ..		600

19B:

Income tax expense [($25,000 ×.40) + (.40 − .30)($4,000 − $2,000)]	10,200	
Deferred income tax—19A depreciation [($4,000 − $2,000) × .30]	600	
Income taxes payable [($25,000 + $4,000 − $2,000) × .40]		10,800

In the above sequence of entries the timing difference which arose in 19A exactly reversed in 19B (at the 19A tax rate). The tax liability in each year was based on the tax rate then in effect as required by law. In 19B income tax expense was based on the 40% tax rate then in effect, *adjusted* for the reversal of the deferred

taxes. The adjustment of $200 was determined by multiplying the change in the tax rates (.40 − .30) times the difference in the two depreciation amounts for 19B ($4,000 − $2,000). It is important to note that the $200 adjustment was *added* to income tax expense because the deferred tax initially was recorded as a credit (in 19A), which means that there was an underprovision of deferred income tax in 19A. In contrast, the adjustment of tax expense for the later year would be *subtracted* when the deferred tax initially is recorded as a debit because there would turn out to be an overprovision of deferred tax (assuming the tax rate increased in the later year). If tax rates drop, these relationships reverse.

Also note in particular the care taken in this illustration to identify the deferred tax with the year during which it arose in order to be able to identify the correct tax rate to use for reversal of the deferred tax. This point emphasizes the necessity in actual practice to maintain detailed records of specific timing differences (*APB Opinion No. 11* permits certain grouping) and the tax rates in effect when they arise.

INCOME TAX EFFECTS OF PRIOR PERIOD ADJUSTMENTS

FASB Statement No. 16, "Prior Period Adjustments," limits prior period adjustments to two items: (a) correction of an error in the financial statements of a prior period and (b) adjustments for income tax benefits related to operating loss carryforwards of purchased subsidiaries.

If an error misstated reported income of a prior period and if the misstated item had an income tax effect, the prior period adjustment would also need to correct for the income tax effect of the error. In such a case, the company most likely would file an amended tax return to claim a refund or to pay additional taxes, as the case may be.

To illustrate, assume TW Corporation inadvertently understated depreciation expense in 19A by $10,000 when the income tax rate was 40%. In 19C the company discovered this error when the income tax rate was 45%. Two entries (or a single combined entry) would correct the error in 19C:

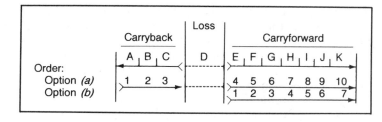

	Prior period adjustment (expense correction)	10,000	
	Accumulated depreciation		10,000
	Receivable for refund of 19A income taxes ($10,000 × 40%)	4,000	
	Prior period adjustment (tax refund on expense correction)		4,000

Note that the tax rate in effect during the year when the error was made (i.e., 40%), rather than the tax rate of the correction year (i.e., 45%) was used in the income tax entry above. The $6,000 balance in the Prior Period Adjustment account would be closed to Retained Earnings and reported on the Statement of Retained Earnings.

INCOME TAX LOSS CARRYBACKS AND CARRYFORWARDS

To permit a form of "income averaging," federal tax laws allow corporations that sustain a loss for the year to *carryback* and/or *carryforward* such losses and thereby to get a cash refund of prior taxes paid or a tax credit in future years. Under the current law, at the end of the year of loss, the company must make an irrevocable choice of either

Option (a)—Carryback (in order of year) up to three years of such losses to secure a refund

of prior taxes on income of an equivalent amount. If the loss is so large that the carryback provision does not absorb it fully, the remaining loss may become a carryforward (in order of year) until it is absorbed fully, with a limit of seven years forward. The carryforward will result in a tax credit (reduction of taxes payable) for each year forward to which it extends.

Option (b)—Carryforward (in order of years) up to seven years.

Assuming Year D is the year of loss, the tax provisions may be diagrammed as shown at the *top* of this page.

The accounting issue posed by income tax loss carrybacks and carryforwards is the extent to which in the *year of loss* any (a) carryback tax refunds and (b) potential carryforward tax credits should be accrued in the accounts. To illustrate the accounting and reporting, the situation shown at the *bottom* of this page will be used.

The choice between the two options, which must be made at the end of the year of loss, may be critical because each option may offer a different economic advantage (i.e., the amount of the tax refund and/or tax credit that will result). At the end of the year of loss, the carryback refund can be readily computed with certainty be-

Year	Actual (carryback)			Loss Year	Estimated (carryforward)						
	A	B	C	D	E	F	G	H	I	J	K
Profit (loss) —in $000s	$5	$9	$11	$(30)	$5	$5	$50	$55	$60	$75	$100
Tax Rate (%)	20	20	20		20	20	40	40	40	40	45
Tax Paid —in $000s	$1	$1.8	$2.2		$1	$1	$20	$22	$24	$30	$45

Decision:
Option (a) versus Option (b)

cause the past profits and the related tax rates are known by year. However, for the carryforward period, the profits and the related tax rates are not known at the end of the year of loss. Therefore, if Option *(b)* is to be considered, a projection must be made of them in order to make a rational choice. If future profits turn out to be sufficient to cover the loss, and if the tax rates are higher in the carryforward period than in the carryback period, a relative economic advantage rests with Option *(b)*; however, the choice is clearly speculative at the time when it must be made. Alternatively, Option *(a)* offers a certain refund rather than a speculative one except to the extent that there is a carryforward amount. In some situations certain technical adjustments may reduce some of the benefits of carrybacks and carryforwards.

Accounting for Carrybacks and Carryforwards. In a period when an operating loss follows a period of net income sufficient to offset the loss, the resultant tax *carryback* will give rise to a refund of income taxes paid in the prior period. Since the refund is virtually certain, the *tax effect* should be recorded in the accounts and reflected in the financial statement for the loss period. *APB Opinion No. 11* states the following:

> The tax effects of any realizable loss carry*backs* should be recognized in the determination of net income (loss) of the loss periods. The tax loss gives rise to a refund (or claim for refund) of past taxes, which is both measurable and currently realizable; therefore the tax effect of the loss is properly recognizable in the determination of net income (loss) for the loss period.

Carryback Option. To illustrate using the above data, assume the company selected Option *(a)*. The carryback would absorb $25,000 of the loss (i.e., $5 + $9 + $11) and result in a receivable for a tax refund of $5,000 ($1 + $1.8 + $2.2). At the end of the year of loss, the following entry would be made:

19D (year of loss):

Receivable for refund of income taxes of prior years (carryback)	5,000	
Income tax refund from loss carryback (closed to income summary)		5,000

The effect of the above accrual entry would be to *(a)* report a $5,000 receivable on the 19D balance sheet and *(b)* reduce the reported loss from $30,000 to $25,000 for 19D. Since the carryback did not fully absorb the $30,000 loss, there is a potential carryforward tax benefit relating to the $5,000 unabsorbed loss (under Option [*a*]).

When there is a carryforward, *uncertainty* necessarily attends the realization of a tax credit against future profits. One of two accounting approaches must be used for a carryforward, depending upon the degree of uncertainty involved. On this point *APB Opinion No. 11* states:

> The tax effects of loss carry*forwards* also relate to the determination of net income (loss) of the loss periods. However, a significant question generally exists as to realization of the tax effects of the carry*forwards*, since realization is dependent upon future taxable income. Accordingly, the Board has concluded that the tax benefits of loss carry*forwards* should not be recognized until they are actually realized, except in unusual circumstances when realization is *assured beyond any reasonable doubt* at the time the loss carry*forwards* arise. When the tax benefits of loss carry*forwards* are not recognized until realized in full or in part in subsequent periods, the tax benefits should be reported in the results of those periods as extraordinary items.

To illustrate, assume the above company is applying Option *(a)*. There are two situations to be considered:

Situation 1—The circumstances are unusual, and realization of the estimated future profits (and tax benefits) is *assured beyond any reasonable doubt.* In this case the loss carryforward for 19D (year of loss) should be recorded as follows:[7]

Receivable for estimated future income tax credit (loss carryforward) (carryforward year: 19E, $5,000 × .20)	1,000	
Estimated income tax credit (loss carryforward)		1,000

Because of the relatively high level of certainty, the future tax credit should be recog-

---

[7] In 19E, assuming an actual profit of $6,000:

Income tax expense ($6,000 × .20)	1,200	
Receivable for estimated future income tax credit ($5,000 × .20)		1,000
Income taxes payable		200

nized in the year of loss since that is the year in which the credit was considered "earned." This entry would increase the receivable on the 19D balance sheet and reduce the 19D reported loss by an additional $1,000 (see below). It would be reasonable to debit "prepaid expense" instead of a "receivable" since both are current assets.

Situation 2—The circumstances are such that there is significant doubt as to the ultimate realization of the tax benefit of the carryforward; that is, realization is not assured beyond any reasonable doubt (the usual situation). In this situation, the loss carryforward is *not recognized* (i.e., accrued) in the year of loss. If and when the tax credits materialize, they are recorded the year in which realization occurs as a debit to taxes payable and a credit to an extraordinary gain for the year.

Assume that the company elected Option *(a)*, the income statement and balance sheet at the end of the year of loss would reflect the following:

ward only. Since there is no carryback in this option, the accounting will depend upon the degree of certainty in the projections of future profit and income tax rates. Therefore, we will consider the two situations specified in *APB Opinion No. 11* quoted above:

1. The circumstances are unusual, such that realization of the future tax benefit is assured beyond any reasonable doubt. In this case, the above company would accrue the estimated future tax credits as follows in the year of the loss:

Receivable for estimated future
  income tax credits
  (loss carryforward) 10,000
    Estimated income tax
     credits (loss
     carryforward)   10,000

Computation:
19E	$ 5,000 × .20 = $1,000	
19F	5,000 × .20 = 1,000	
19G	20,000 × .40 = 8,000	$10,000

2. The circumstances are such that there are significant questions as to the realization of the tax benefit of the carryforward. In this

	Option (a)—Carryback Plus Carryforward	
19D Year of Loss	**Situation 1 Carryforward Reasonably Assured**	**Situation 2 Carryforward Not Reasonably Assured**
Income Statement:		
Net loss before recognition of tax effect	$30,000	$30,000
Deduct tax refund for prior years' tax due to carryback	(5,000)	(5,000)
Deduct estimated tax credit in future years due to carryforward	(1,000)	
Net loss	$24,000	$25,000
Balance Sheet:		
Current Assets:		
Receivable for tax refund and tax credits due to loss carryback and carryforward.	$ 6,000	$ 5,000

Carryforward Option. To compare the accounting for the two options, now assume the company elected Option *(b)*, that is, to carryfor-

case the loss carryforward is not recognized (i.e., accrued). The tax credits are recognized in the future when they occur as reductions in taxes payable. The related entries would be as follows under the assumptions that the projected future profits were exactly on target:

19D (year of loss)—No entry.

19E, F, and G:

	19E	19F	19G
Income tax expense	1,000	1,000	20,000
Extraordinary gain, loss carryforward* ..		1,000	1,000	8,000
Income taxes payable			12,000

* Specified in the quotation above as an extraordinary gain.

Assume that the company elected Option *(b)*; the income statement and balance sheet at the end of the year of loss would reflect the following:

cause the comparative cash flows (or cash savings) are at different times.

THE INVESTMENT TAX CREDIT

Congressional legislation entitles taxable entities, both individuals and businesses, to reduce their income taxes by up to 10% of the cost of certain long-lived assets. This tax deduction is referred to as the *investment tax credit,* and where applicable it has the economic effect of reducing the cost of the asset. Accounting for the investment tax credit is discussed and illustrated in Chapter 14.

INTRAPERIOD INCOME TAX ALLOCATION

APB Opinion No. 11 specifies two distinctly different types of income tax allocation: *(a) interperiod* income tax allocation, caused by tim-

	Option (b)—Carryforward Only	
19D Year of Loss	Situation 1 Carryforward Reasonably Assured	Situation 2 Carryforward Not Reasonably Assured
Income Statement:		
Net loss before recognition of tax effect	$30,000	$30,000
Deduct estimated tax credit in future years due to carryforward	10,000	
Net loss	$20,000	$30,000
Balance Sheet:		
Current Assets:		
Receivable for estimated tax credit due to loss carryforward......................	$10,000	

In the above example, Option *(b)* appears to be preferable because the cash saved (tax credit) amounted to $10,000 compared to a maximum of $6,000 under Option *(a)*. This resulted from the fact that the carryforward option took advantage of a 40% tax rate (as opposed to 20%). Of course, this result must be tempered with the element of uncertainty implicit in Option *(b)*. We made the unrealistic assumption that the projections were exactly on target. Additionally, in assessing the comparative advantages of the two options when the decision must be made (i.e., in the year of loss), the future projections should be discounted at a reasonable rate be-

ing differences between the income statement and the tax return (discussed above), and *(b) intraperiod* income tax allocation, which relates total income tax for the period to the various statement components that caused the tax. The discussions to follow supplement the brief discussion in Chapter 4 of intraperiod tax allocation. It is important to understand that *both* types of income tax allocation must be applied; one is not an alternative to the other.

The concept of intraperiod allocation is to report the income tax (or tax saving) associated with a particular kind of item along with that item in the financial statements. To illustrate the concept, assume the following for ABC Corporation:[8]

Pretax income before extraordinary items	$40,000
Extraordinary gain (pretax)	10,000
Total income tax expense (average tax rate 40%)	20,000

ABC Corporation would report the results of intraperiod tax allocation of the $20,000 total income tax expense as follows:

Income before income tax and before extraordinary items		$40,000
Less: Income tax expense ($40,000 × .40)		16,000
Income before extraordinary items ...		24,000
Extraordinary gain (specified)	$10,000	
Less: Applicable income tax ($10,000 × .40)	4,000	6,000
Net Income		$30,000

In this example, as in most of the examples in this textbook, average tax rates are used so that the major thrust of the particular discussion will not be obscured by the distraction of laborious income tax computations.

The specific tax rates need to be used for intraperiod income tax allocation in view of the following specification in *APB Opinion No. 11*, paragraph 52:

> The Board has concluded that tax allocation within a period should be applied to obtain an appropriate relationship between income tax expense and (a) income before extraordinary

items, (b) extraordinary items, (c) adjustments of prior periods (or of the opening balance of retained earnings), and (d) direct entries to other stockholders' equity accounts. The income tax expense attributable to income before extraordinary items is computed by determining the income tax expense related to revenue and expense transactions entering into the determination of such income, without giving effect to the tax consequences of the items excluded from the determination of income before extraordinary items. The income tax expense attributable to other items is determined by the tax consequences of transactions involving these items. If an operating loss exists before extraordinary items, the tax consequences of such loss should be associated with the loss.

Intraperiod income tax allocation involves only the reporting phase of accounting and seldom, if ever, the recording phase. Therefore, it does not give rise to entries in the accounts and does not modify the entries to record income taxes as illustrated in the prior discussion of interperiod income tax allocation.

An illustration involving five separate cases is used to show how *total income tax expense* for the period is allocated to the several components of income which caused a tax assessment (or a tax saving). Note that in each case the allocations always sum to the total tax amount.

Fact situation assumed:

1. Income tax rates: 22% on the first $25,000 of taxable income, 48% above $25,000, and 30% on capital gains. These rates, rather than the current five rates (see footnote 8), are used *only* for simplification of this illustration.

2. Pretax data from the accounts (simplified amounts used for illustrative purposes) are shown in the table at the bottom of this page.

---

[8] From 1975 through 1978 the corporate tax rates were: 20% on the first $25,000, 22% on the next $25,000, and 48% on all taxable income over $50,000. The 1978 tax law set the following rates on taxable income for 1979 and thereafter: 17% on the first $25,000, 20% on the next $25,000, 30% on the next $25,000, 40% on the next $25,000, and 46% on all income over $100,000.

	Case A	Case B	Case C	Case D	Case E
Income before extraordinary items (loss)	$30,000	$ 30,000	$(30,000)	$ 30,000	$30,000
Extraordinary gain (loss)	10,000	(40,000)	40,000	(10,000)	10,000*
Pretax income	$40,000	$(10,000)	$10,000	$ 20,000	$40,000
Total income tax expense	$12,700	$ (2,200)	$ 2,200	$ 4,400	$10,900

* Capital gain.

EXHIBIT 9–6
Intraperiod Tax Allocation

Case A:

Income before income tax and before extraordinary gain			$ 30,000
Less: Income tax expense	$25,000 × .22 =	$ 5,500	
	5,000 × .48 =	2,400	7,900
Income before extraordinary gain			22,100
Extraordinary gain (specified)		10,000	
Less: Applicable income tax *expense*	10,000 × .48 =	4,800	5,200
Net Income			$ 27,300

(Total tax allocated: $7,900 + $4,800 = $12,700 *expense*)

Case B:

Income before income tax and before extraordinary loss			$ 30,000
Less: Income tax expense	$25,000 × .22 =	$ 5,500	
	5,000 × .48 =	2,400	7,900
Income before extraordinary loss			22,100
Extraordinary loss (specified)		40,000	
Less: Applicable income tax *saving*	$25,000 × .22 = $5,500		
	5,000 × .48 = 2,400		
	10,000 × .22 = 2,200	10,100	(29,900)
Net Income (loss)			$ (7,800)

(Total tax allocated: $10,100 − $7,900 = $2,200 tax *saving*)

Case C:

Income (loss) before income tax and before extraordinary gain			$(30,000)
Less: Income tax saving	$25,000 × .22 =	$ 5,500	
	5,000 × .48 =	2,400	7,900
Income (loss) before extraordinary gain			(22,100)
Extraordinary gain (specified)		40,000	
Less: Applicable income tax *expense*	$25,000 × .22 = 5,500		
	5,000 × .48 = 2,400		
	10,000 × .22 = 2,200	10,100	29,900
Net Income			$ 7,800

(Total tax allocated: $10,100 − $7,900 = $2,200 *expense*)

Case D:

Income before income tax and before extraordinary loss			$ 30,000
Less: Income tax expense	$25,000 × .22 =	$ 5,500	
	5,000 × .48 =	2,400	7,900
Income before extraordinary loss			$ 22,100
Extraordinary loss (specified)		$10,000	
Less: Applicable income tax *saving*	$ 5,000 × .48 = $2,400		
	5,000 × .22 = 1,100	3,500	6,500
Net Income			$ 15,600

(Total tax allocated: $7,900 − $3,500 = $4,400 *expense*)

Case E:

Income before income tax and before extraordinary gain			$ 30,000
Less: Income tax expense	$25,000 × .22 =	$ 5,500	
	5,000 × .48 =	$ 2,400	7,900
Income before extraordinary gain			22,100
Extraordinary gain (specified)		10,000	
Less: Applicable income tax *expense* (capital gain)	$10,000 × .30 =	3,000	7,000
Net Income			$ 29,100

(Total tax allocated: $7,900 + $3,000 = $10,900 *expense*)

EXHIBIT 9–7
Disclosure of Income Tax Allocation

B CORPORATION
Income Statement (partial)
For the Year Ended December 31, 19B

Income from operations		$120,000
Less: Income tax expense (Note A)		48,000*
Income before extraordinary items........................		72,000
Extraordinary items:		
Loss	$30,000	
Less: Applicable tax reduction ...	12,000	18,000
Net Income		$ 54,000

* An average tax rate of 40% is assumed on all items for illustrative purposes.

B CORPORATION
Balance Sheet (partial)
At December 31, 19B

Current Liabilities:	
Income taxes payable (Note A)	$35,000
Deferred income taxes (Note B)	11,000
Long-Term Liabilities:	
Deferred income taxes (Note B)	19,000

Notes to financial statement:

Note A. Income tax payable was computed as follows:

Income tax expense on current operations	$48,000
Add decrease in current deferred tax credit	2,000
Deduct increase in noncurrent deferred tax credit	(3,000)
Income taxes payable on current operations	47,000
Deduct tax saving on extraordinary loss	12,000
Income taxes currently payable	$35,000

Note B. The current portion of deferred income taxes is related to income tax expense on the gross profit on installment sales not yet subject to tax; the net decrease for the current year was $2,000. The noncurrent portion was for the additional deduction for accelerated depreciation on the tax return over straight-line depreciation reflected on the income statement; the net increase for the year was $3,000.

Income taxes, as allocated, would be reported as shown in Exhibit 9–6 for each of the five cases. Computations are given to show how the allocated amounts were derived. Observe in all cases that, first total tax should be computed, next tax

is independently computed on income before extraordinary items, and the difference is allocated to the extraordinary items. However, detailed computations are shown in Exhibit 9–6 to indicate that the results are correct.

DISCLOSURE OF TAX ALLOCATION

Full disclosure of the components of income tax expense (including deferred income taxes) is required. In respect to the income statement, *APB Opinion No. 11* states that "the components of income tax expense should be disclosed" on the income statement; that is, in addition to *intraperiod* allocation, taxes estimated to be payable and the tax effects of timing differences should be reported. The *Opinion* states that these amounts "may be presented as separate items in the income statement or, alternatively, as combined amounts with disclosure of the components parenthetically or in a note to the financial statements." The examples presented thus far in this chapter have not been accompanied by note disclosure of related details. Note disclosures generally are needed to explain the reconciliation of the difference between the income tax expense for the period and the related additions and deductions to income taxes payable (including details of the deferred income tax accounts). In some cases the details are also presented in supplementary schedules included with the note disclosure. Exhibit 9–7 illustrates typical note disclosure. Note the reconciliation of income tax expense with income taxes payable (Note A), the recognition of *interperiod* tax allocation (Notes A and B), and the effects of *intraperiod* tax allocation (separate income tax amounts for income from operations and extraordinary items).

QUESTIONS

PART A

1. In evaluating a balance sheet, some bankers say that the liability section is one of the most important parts. What are the primary reasons for their position on this point?

2. Generally, liabilities are reported at their maturity amount. In general, when should liabilities,

prior to due date, be reported at less than their maturity amount?

3. How is the cost principle involved in accounting for current liabilities?

4. Define current liabilities.

5. Differentiate between secured and unsecured liabilities. Explain the reporting procedures for each.

6. How are cash and stock dividends declared, but not yet paid, classified on the balance sheet? Explain.

7. What are deferred revenues? What is the basis for classifying them as current liabilities?

8. Define a long-term liability.

9. When goods or services are acquired and a long-term note payable is given that either specifies (a) no interest or (b) an unrealistically low interest rate, how should the value of the note be measured?

10. Basically, what is the accounting definition of a contingency? What are the three characteristics of a contingency? Why is the concept important?

11. How does the accountant measure the likelihood of the outcome of a contingency? In general, how does this affect the accounting for and reporting of contingencies?

12. Explain why loss contingencies are accounted for and reported differently from gain contingencies.

13. Under what circumstances would you consider appropriation of retained earnings with respect to a loss contingency?

14. How would each of the following items be reported on the balance sheet? Justify doubtful items.
    a. Cash dividends payable.
    b. Bonds payable.
    c. Accommodation endorsement.
    d. Lawsuit pending.
    e. Stock dividend issuable.
    f. Estimated taxes payable.
    g. Deferred rent revenue.
    h. Unearned interest revenue.
    i. Customer deposits on containers.
    j. Current installment on serial bonds.
    k. Accounts payable.
    l. Loans from officers.
    m. Accrued wages.
    n. Deferred repairs.

PART B

15. Accounting for income taxes under interperiod income tax allocation procedures essentially is accrual accounting for income taxes; otherwise, accounting for income taxes essentially is cash basis accounting. Evaluate this statement.

16. It is common for companies to use an accelerated depreciation method for income tax purposes and straight-line depreciation for financial reporting (book) purposes. Some accountants argue that the deferred income tax liabilities of these companies will never have to be paid so long as they (a) continue this depreciation policy, (b) expand, and (c) continue to replace worn-out depreciable assets with new ones. Evaluate this argument.

17. What is the nature of a permanent difference? Do permanent differences give rise to deferred income taxes? Give three examples of items of permanent difference in accounting for income taxes.

18. What is intraperiod income tax allocation? How does it differ from interperiod income tax allocation?

19. Does the "deferred" caption in deferred income taxes mean that deferred income tax is always a long-term (noncurrent) item? Explain.

20. In respect to loss carrybacks and loss carryforwards, which can be recorded with greater certainty of realization of the benefit therefrom? How does this difference in certainty affect the accounting treatment accorded loss carrybacks and carryforwards?

EXERCISES

PART A
Exercises 9–1 to 9–11

Exercise 9–1

On September 1, 19A, B Company borrowed cash on a $4,000 note payable due in one year. Assume the going rate of interest was 9% per year on this type of note for this company. The accounting period ends December 31.

Required:

Complete the tabulation at the top of the next page (show computations and round amounts to the nearest dollar):

(Relates to Exercise 9–1)	Assuming the Note Was—		
	Interest Bearing	Noninterest Bearing (discounted)	
		(on face)	(on cash)
Assuming interest is based:			
a. Cash received	$_____	$_____	$_____
b. Cash paid at due date	$_____	$_____	$_____
c. Total interest paid (cash)	$_____	$_____	$_____
d. Interest expense in 19A	$_____	$_____	$_____
e. Interest expense in 19B	$_____	$_____	$_____
f. Amount of liability to report on balance sheet at December 31, 19A (including any accrued interest)	$_____	$_____	$_____
g. Effective rate of interest (%)	_____%	_____%	_____%

Exercise 9–2

For each of the following, indicate the balance sheet classification and preferred title; include comments on doubtful items.

a. Trade payable.
b. Deposits held from customers—trade
c. Accrued wage expense.
d. Accommodation endorsement.
e. Reserve for rearrangement costs.
f. Customer payments on orders received (goods not shipped).
g. Sales taxes collected.
h. Bonds payable, one third paid each year.
i. Advance on rent revenue.
j. Stock dividend declared.
k. Accrued property taxes (estimated).
l. Cash dividend declared but not yet paid.
m. IOU to company president.
n. Accrued interest on note payable.

Exercise 9–3

The records of the Rayburn Corporation provided the following information at December 31, 19A:

a.	Notes payable (trade), short-term (includes a $4,000 note given on the purchase of equipment that cost $20,000; the assets were mortgaged in connection with the purchase)	$30,000
b.	Bonds payable ($10,000 due each April 1)	90,000
c.	Accounts payable (including $10,000 owed to the president of the company)	50,000
d.	Accrued property taxes (estimated)	1,000
e.	Stock dividends issuable on March 1, 19B (at par value)	12,000
f.	Cash dividends, payable March 1, 19B	20,000
g.	Long-term note payable, maturity amount	15,000
h.	Discount on the note in (g) above (unamortized)	500

Required:

Assuming the fiscal year ends December 31, show how each of the above items should be reported on the balance sheet at December 31, 19A.

Exercise 9–4

Tipo Company paid salaries for the month amounting to $80,000. Of this amount, $10,000 was received by employees who had already been paid the $22,900* maximum (FICA rate 6.13%). In addition to the $10,000, another $4,000 was paid to employees who had already been paid the $6,000* maximum (FUTA rates: 2.7% state and 0.7% federal). Withholding taxes amounted to $25,000, and $1,200 was withheld for investment in company stock per an agreement with certain employees. Use the rates given in the chapter for 1979.

* These amounts refer to 1979 cut off points for wages subject to FICA and FUTA taxes.

Required:

Give entries to record the *(a)* salary payment including the deductions, *(b)* employer payroll expenses, and *(c)* remittance of the taxes.

Exercise 9–5

Tuffts Company gives the general manager a bonus equal to 20% of income after tax. The bonus is deductible for tax purposes but is not an expense for computing the bonus. Assume an average tax rate of 40%. Income prior to taxes and bonus was $80,000.

Required (round amounts to nearest dollar):

1. Compute the tax and the bonus.

2. Prove your computations.
3. Give entries to record the tax and the bonus.

Exercise 9–6

AB Company has an agreement to pay the president a bonus of 10% of income, after deducting federal income taxes and after deducting an amount equal to 6% on contributed capital (contributed capital is $300,000). Income before deductions for bonus and income taxes was $50,000. The bonus is deductible for tax purposes; assume an average income tax rate of 25%.

Required:

1. Compute the bonus, tax and net income after deducting both bonus and tax.
2. Prove the computations.
3. Give the entries to record the tax and the bonus.

Exercise 9–7

On April 1, 19A, Tuff Company purchased a heavy machine for use in operations by paying $5,000 cash and signing a $25,000 (face amount) noninterest-bearing note due in two years (on March 31, 19C). The going rate of interest for Tuff on this type of note was 10% per year. The company uses straight-line depreciation. The accounting period ends on December 31. Assume a five-year life for the machine and 10% residual value.

Required:

1. Give all entries indicated on April 1, 19A, and December 31, 19A (assume straight-line amortization of the discount). Show computations of the cost of the machine (round amounts to nearest dollar).
2. Complete a tabulation as follows (show computations):
   a. Income Statement, 19A:
      Depreciation expense .... $_____
      Interest expense .... $_____
   b. Balance Sheet, 19A:
      Operational asset—machine ...... $_____
      Accumulated depreciation .... $_____
      Current liability—interest
        payable .... $_____
      Note payable .... $_____
3. When should the interest method, rather than the straight-line method, be used to amortize the discount on the note? Compute interest expense for 19A assuming the interest method. Is the difference material?

Exercise 9–8

Small Company purchased a heavy-duty used truck (an operational asset) on April 1, 19A, for $2,000 cash plus a $6,000, two-year note payable. The principal is due on March 31, 19C, and specified 4% interest payable each March 31. Assume the going rate of interest for this type of debt for this company was 10%. The accounting period ends December 31.

Required:

1. Give the entry to record the purchase on April 1, 19A. Show computations (round to nearest dollar).
2. Complete a tabulation as follows, include computations:
   a. Amount of cash interest
      payable each March 31 .... $_____
   b. Total interest expense
      for the two-year period .... $_____
   c. Amount of interest reported
      on income statement for 19A .... $_____
   d. Amount of liability reported
      on balance sheet at December 31,
      19A (excluding accrued interest) ... $_____
   e. Depreciation expense for 19A
      assuming straight-line (use
      even months), no residual
      value, and a four-year life .... $_____

Exercise 9–9

WT Corporation sells a line of products that carry a three-year warranty against defects. Based on industry experience, the estimated warranty costs related to dollar sales are the first year after sale—1% of sales; second year after sale—3% of sales; and third year after sale—5%. Sales and actual warranty expenditures for the first three-year period were as follows:

	Cash Sales	Actual Warranty Expenditures
19A	$ 90,000	$ 900
19B	110,000	4,100
19C	130,000	9,800

Required:

1. Give entries for the three years for the (a) sales, (b) estimated warranty expense, and (c) the actual expenditures.
2. What amount should be reported as a liability on the balance sheet at the end of each year?

Exercise 9–10

Local Grocery has initiated a promotion program whereby customers are given coupons redeemable in

U.S. savings bonds. One coupon is issued for each dollar of sales. On the surrender of 750 coupons, one $25 savings bond (cost $18.75) is given. It is estimated that 20% of the coupons issued will never be presented for redemption. Sales for the first period were $400,000, and the number of coupons redeemed totaled 225,000. Sales for the second period were $440,000, and the number of coupons redeemed totaled 405,000. The savings bonds are acquired as needed.

Required:

Prepare journal entries (including closing entries) relative to the premium plan for the two periods. Show amounts that should be reported in the balance sheet and income statement for the two periods.

Exercise 9–11

X Company is preparing the annual financial statements at December 31, 19A. A customer fell on the escalator and has filed a lawsuit for $25,000 because of a claimed back injury. The lawyer employed by the company has carefully assessed all of the implications. If the suit is lost, the lawyer's opinion is that the $25,000 will be assessed by the court.

Required:

1. Assume the lawyer, the independent accountant, and management have reluctantly concluded that it is probable that the suit will be successful. Show how this contingency should be reported on the financial statements for 19A. Also, give any entries that should be made in the accounts in 19A.
2. Assume instead that the conclusion is that it is reasonably possible that the company will be liable, and it is reasonably estimated that the amount will be $25,000. In what way would your response to Requirement 1 be changed?
3. Assume that the conclusion of the legal counsel and management is that it is *remote* that there will be a contingency loss. They believe the suit is without merit. How should this contingency be reported?

PART B
Exercises 9–12 to 9–18

Exercise 9–12

Jackson Retailers, Inc., would have had identical net income before taxes on both its income tax returns and income statements for the years 19A through 19D were it not for the fact that for tax purposes opera-

tional assets that cost $120,000 were depreciated by the sum-of-the-years'-digits method, whereas for accounting purposes, the straight-line method was used. These operational assets have a four-year estimated life and zero residual value. Excess of revenue over expenses other than depreciation and income taxes for the years concerned were as follows:

	19A	19B	19C	19D
Pretax accounting income (excluding depreciation)	$60,000	$80,000	$70,000	$70,000

Assume the average income tax rate for each year was 40%.

Required:

1. Prepare a partial income statement for each year to reflect interperiod tax allocation.
2. Give journal entries at the end of each year to record income taxes.

Exercise 9–13

The pretax income statements for R Corporation for two years (summarized) were as follows:

	19A	19B
Revenues	$180,000	$200,000
Expenses	150,000	165,000
Pretax accounting income	$ 30,000	$ 35,000

For tax purposes, the following differences existed:

a. An expense of $10,000 on above income statement for 19B is not deductible for income tax purposes (it was goodwill amortization).

b. A revenue of $6,000 reported on the above income statement for 19B is taxable in 19A (it was unearned rent revenue).

c. An expense of $8,000 on the above income statement for 19A is not deductible for income tax purposes until 19B (it was estimated warranty costs).

Required:

1. Compute *(a)* income tax expense and *(b)* income taxes payable for each period. Assume an average tax rate of 40%.
2. Give the entry to record income taxes for each period.
3. Recast the above income statements to include income taxes as allocated.

Exercise 9–14

Rocky Oil Corporation, a small wildcat exploration company, earned $75,000 pretax accounting income during 19A and $125,000 during 19B. The records of the corporation showed the following additional data for the two years:

	19A	19B
Straight-line depreciation (included in pretax accounting income)	$35,000	$35,000
Accelerated depreciation (for income tax purposes)	38,000	32,000
Statutory depletion (for income tax purposes)	65,000	95,000
Cost depletion—an expense (included in pretax accounting income)	44,000	60,000

The assets subject to depreciation were five years old at the end of 19A and are expected to remain in service for an additional five years. The income tax rate is 40% for 19A and 19B.

Required:

1. Identify the item of timing differences given above. Identify the item of permanent difference.
2. Prepare the journal entries to record income taxes for the company for 19A and 19B.
3. Prepare the income statement and balance sheet presentations related to income taxes in the 19A and 19B financial statements.

Exercise 9–15

Carter Company accounts and related records revealed the following data for the first two years of operations:

	19A	19B
Pretax accounting income	$100,000	$110,000
Rent collections one year in advance	9,000	
Rent revenue allocated (included in pretax accounting income)	5,000	4,000

Carter Company had no other timing differences, no permanent differences, or other complicating income tax factors in 19A and 19B.

Required:

1. Record income taxes for the company for 19A and 19B assuming the income tax rate for each year was 30%.
2. Record the income taxes for the company for 19A and 19B assuming the income tax rate was 30% for 19A and 40% for 19B. Be prepared to explain the way you treated the impact of the change in the tax rate from 19A to 19B.

Exercise 9–16

Larson Corporation reported pretax operating income in 19A amounting to $80,000 the first year of operations. In 19B the corporation experienced a $60,000 pretax operating loss. Assume an average income tax rate of 45%.

Required:

1. Compute the income tax consequences for each year.
2. Show how the tax consequences for each year would be reflected in the income statements for each year.
3. Give appropriate entries to record income tax effect for each year.

Exercise 9–17

Ajax Corporation experienced a bad year in 19D. The company reported taxable income (loss) for 19A–19D and had average tax rates as follows:

	19A	19B	19C	19D
Taxable income (loss)	$8,000	$32,000	$20,000	$(65,000)
Income tax rate	30%	30%	35%	40%

There were no timing differences or permanent differences in 19A–19D.

Required:

1. Record income taxes for the company:
   a. For 19D under the general provisions of *APB Opinion No. 11* on tax loss carrybacks and carryforwards.
   b. For 19E assuming the company reported taxable income of $45,000 in 19E and pretax accounting income of $50,000 for 19E (a $5,000 timing difference). Assume the income tax rate for 19E was 45%.
2. Record income taxes for the company:
   a. For 19D assuming it is virtually certain that taxable income of $5,000 or more will be earned in 19E–19K.
   b. For 19E assuming the company reported taxable income of $45,000 in 19E and that pretax accounting income for 19E was the same amount (no timing differences). Assume the income tax rate for 19E was 45%.

Exercise 9–18

Wells Corporation experienced a $100,000 pretax operating loss for 19A, the first year of operations. Assume an average 40% tax rate.

Required:

1. Assume the loss resulted from an identifiable cause and that future taxable income over the next seven years is virtually certain to be sufficient to offset the loss.

   a. Give entry and a partial income statement for 19A to reflect appropriate tax allocation consequences.

   b. Assume it is now the end of 19B and that a pretax operating profit in 19B is reported amounting to $150,000. Give entry and a partial income statement for 19B to reflect appropriate tax allocation consequences.

2. Assume that at the time of the loss there was no realistic basis to conclude that profits in the next seven years would be sufficient to absorb the loss.

   a. Give entry and a partial income statement for 19A to reflect appropriate tax allocation consequences.

   b. Assume pretax operating incomes, following the year of loss, as follows: 19B, breakeven; 19C, $40,000; and 19D, $90,000. Give entry and a partial income statement for each of these three years to reflect appropriate tax allocation consequences.

PROBLEMS

PART A
Problems 9–1 to 9–11

Problem 9–1

For each of the situations below, indicate (1) correct title, (2) usual balance sheet classification, (3) the amount to report, and (4) explanation of the basis for your classification. (Suggestion: Set up four columns for your response.)

a.	Trade accounts payable (including $2,000 owed to the company president)	$30,000
b.	Trade notes payable (including $9,000 for equipment note)	29,000
c.	Long-term note payable (secured by stock in X Company)	10,000
d.	Cash dividends (not yet paid)	12,000
e.	Deposits held, from customers	4,000
f.	Prepaid rent revenue	3,000
g.	Excess of selling price over par—bonds payable	2,800
h.	Bonds (annual payment $30,000)	90,000
i.	Accrued warranty costs	1,000
j.	Deferred lease revenue	2,000
k.	Reserve for taxes	7,000
l.	Reserve for future contingencies	15,000
m.	Endorsement on note payable	2,000

Problem 9–2

DE Corporation borrowed cash on August 1, 19A, and signed a $12,000 (face amount), one-year note payable, due on July 31, 19B. The accounting period ends December 31. Assume a going rate of interest of 10% for this company for this type of borrowing.

Required (round amounts to nearest dollar):

1. How much cash should DE receive on the note assuming *(a)* an interest-bearing note and *(b)* discounted note (interest based on the cash received). What would be the effective rate of interest in each case? Show computations.
2. Give the following entries for each case:

   a. August 1, 19A, date of the loan.

   b. December 31, 19A, adjusting entry.

   c. July 31, 19B, payment of the note.

3. What liability amounts should be shown in each case on the December 31, 19A, balance sheet?

Problem 9–3

On October 1, 19A, Scott Company borrowed cash $36,000 and signed a 10%, one-year note payable, due on September 30, 19B. The accounting period ends on December 31.

Required:

1. Compute the face amount of the note assuming (show computations):

   Case A—An interest-bearing note.

   Case B—A discounted (noninterest-bearing) note, and the interest is based on the cash received.

2. Complete a tabulation as follows:

		Case A Interest Bearing	Case B Discounted
a.	Face amount of the note	$_____	$_____
b.	Total cash received	$_____	$_____
c.	Total cash paid	$_____	$_____
d.	Total interest paid	$_____	$_____
e.	Interest expense in 19A	$_____	$_____
f.	Interest expense in 19B	$_____	$_____
g.	Effective rate of interest (%)	_____%	_____%

3. Give entries indicated for each case at October 1, 19A, December 31, 19A, and September 30, 19B.
4. Show how the liability amounts should be reflected for each case on the balance sheet at December 31, 19A.

Problem 9–4

Arons Corporation was formed for the purpose of constructing buildings. The first contract involved the construction of an office building. Since the corporation was short of ready cash, an agreement was made with the supervising engineer whereby compensation would be a share of the profits. The agreement provided that the supervising engineer would receive 20% of the profits on the contract after providing for corporate income tax and after deducting the bonus.

Upon completion of the construction, the records of the corporation showed the following:

Income before tax and before payment
to the supervising engineer
(assume a 40% tax rate) $450,000
Expenses already deducted from the net
income, not allowable as deductions
in computing income taxes but
allowed as a deduction before
computing the profit to be
paid the supervising engineer 10,000

Assume the compensation to the supervising engineer is deductible for corporate income tax purposes.

Required:
1. Compute the amount of the compensation to the supervising engineer and income tax expense assuming the compensation is an expense in determining the basis for the compensation. Show proof of computations.
2. Give entries to record the compensation and tax expenses.

Problem 9–5

For the purpose of stimulating sales, Black Coffee Company places a coupon in each can of coffee sold; the coupons are redeemable in chinaware. Each premium costs the company $0.80 (the cost of printing the coupons is negligible). Ten coupons must be presented by the customers to receive one premium. The following data are available:

Month	Cans of Coffee Sold	Premiums Purchased	Coupons Redeemed
January	650,000	25,000	220,000
February	500,000	40,000	410,000
March	560,000	35,000	300,000

It is estimated that only 70% of the coupons will be presented for redemption.

Required:
Compute the amount of the premium inventory, liability for premiums outstanding, and premium ex-

pense at the end of each month and give the related entries. *Hint:* Set up parallel columns for each period.

Problem 9–6

Crunch Cereal Company gives a premium (costs $0.75 each) for "five box tops sent in plus $0.25 cash to cover premium mailing costs." Actual mailing costs average $0.15 per premium. Data covering two periods are as follows:

	Period	
	First	Second
Premiums purchased	15,000	25,000
Tops redeemed for premiums	50,000	100,000
Boxes of cereal sold at $2 per box	220,000	250,000

It is estimated that 60% of the tops distributed will never be returned.

Required:
1. Give entries for each period to record sales, premium purchases, premium expenses, redemptions, mailing costs, and closing entries. *Hint:* Set up parallel columns for each period.
2. Indicate how premiums and any related liabilities would be reported on the balance sheet at the end of each period and the amount of premium expense on the income statements for each period.

Problem 9–7

The following selected transactions were completed during the year just ended (December 31, 19A) by AB Corporation:

a. Bonds payable dated February 1 with a maturity value of $100,000 were sold at 106 on February 1. The bonds mature in ten years and bear 6% interest per annum payable on each January 30.
b. Merchandise purchased on account amounted to $400,000. Cash payments on account were $340,000, and a $3,000, one-year, 9% interest-bearing note, dated September 1, was given to one creditor. Accounts payable carried over from the preceding year were $30,000. Assume periodic inventory system.
c. Cosigned a $5,000 note payable for another party.
d. On June 1, the company borrowed cash and a $21,800, one-year, discounted (i.e., noninterest bearing) note was signed. Assume a going rate of interest of 9% and that interest is based on the cash received.
e. Payroll records showed the following (assume amounts given are correct):

Gross Wages	Employee			Employer		
	With-holding	FICA	Union Dues	FICA	FUTA State	FUTA Federal
$50,000 ...	$15,000	$3,000	$500	$3,000	$1,350	$350

Remittances were union $280; withholding taxes, $13,000; FICA, $5,800; FUTA—state, $1,200; and FUTA—federal, $340.

f. The company was sued for $50,000 damages. It appears a judgment against the company of $30,000 is probable. For problem purposes, assume this is an extraordinary item.

g. On November 1, 19A, the company rented some office space in its building to XY Company and collected six months' rent in advance, total $1,800.

h. Cash dividends declared but not paid, $14,000.

i. On December 31, accrued interest on the bonds (assume straight-line amortization).

j. Accrue interest on the notes at December 31.

Required:

1. Give the entry or entries for each of the above items.
2. Prepare a list (title and amount) of the resulting liabilities at December 31, 19A, assuming it is the end of the period. For each liability, indicate its appropriate classification on the balance sheet. *Hint:* Set up tabulations with three columns: title, amount, and classification.

Problem 9–8

Handy Appliance Company provides a product warranty for defects on two lines of items sold. Line A carries a two-year warranty for all labor and service (but not parts). The company contracts with a local service establishment to provide the requirements of the warranty. The local service establishment charges a flat fee of $50 per unit payable at date of sale.

Line B carries a three-year warranty for labor and parts on service. Handy purchases the parts needed under the warranty and has service personnel who perform the work. On the basis of experience, it is estimated that for Line B, the three-year warranty costs are 3% of dollar sales for parts and 7% for labor and overhead. Additional data available are as follows:

	Period		
	1	2	3
Sales in units, Line A	700	1,000	
Sales price per unit, Line A	$ 610	$ 660	
Sales in units, Line B	600	800	
Sales price per unit, Line B	$ 700	$ 750	
Actual warranty outlays on Line B:			
Parts	$3,000	$ 9,600	$12,000
Labor and overhead	$7,000	$22,000	$30,000

Required:

1. Give entries for period sales and expenses identified by product. *Hint:* Set up parallel columns for the three periods.
2. Complete a tabulation as follows:

	Year-End Amounts		
	Period 1	Period 2	Period 3
a. Warranty expense (on the income statement)	$_____	$_____	$_____
b. Estimated warranty liability (on the balance sheet)	$_____	$_____	$_____

Problem 9–9

On September 1, 19A, Robbins Company acquired a badly needed machine (an operational asset) by paying $5,000 cash and signing a two-year note that carried a face amount of $15,000 due at the end of the two years; the note did not specify interest. Assume the going rate of interest for this company for this type of loan was 8%. The accounting period ends December 31.

Required: (round amounts to nearest dollar):

1. Give the entry to record the purchase of the machine.
2. Complete a tabulation as follows and show computations:

	Straight-Line Method	Interest Method
a. Cash paid at maturity	$_____	$_____
b. Total interest expense	$_____	$_____
c. Interest expense on income statement for 19A	$_____	$_____
d. Amount of the liability reported on balance sheet at end of 19A	$_____	$_____
e. Depreciation expense for 19A (assume straight-line, even months, no residual value, and a useful life of four years)	$_____	$_____

3. Should the interest method be used in this situation? Explain.
4. Give the entries to record depreciation and interest expense (both methods) for 19A.
5. Show how the liability should be reflected on the balance sheet at the end of 19A for both methods.

Problem 9–10

On August 1, 19A, Massie Company purchased a large used machine for operations. Payment was made by cash $6,000 and a $30,000 (face amount), two-year, discounted note payable (due on July 31, 19C). The note did not specify interest; however, for Massie, the going rate for this type of transaction was 9%. Assume straight-line depreciation, a five-year life, and no residual value. The accounting period ends on December 31.

Required (round amounts to nearest dollar):
1. Give the entry to record the purchase of the machine.
2. Complete a tabulation as follows and show computations.

	Straight-Line Method	Interest Method
a. Face amount of the note	$_____	$_____
b. Cash paid at maturity	$_____	$_____
c. Total interest expense	$_____	$_____
d. Interest expense on income statement for 19A	$_____	$_____
e. Amount of the liability on the balance sheet at end of 19A	$_____	$_____
f. Depreciation expense for 19A	$_____	$_____

(Prepare an amortization schedule for the note that reflects the interest method.)
3. Should the interest method be used in this situation? Explain.
4. Give the entries for 19A to record depreciation and interest expense for both the interest method and the straight-line method of amortizing the discount on the note.
5. Show how the liability should be reflected on the balance sheet at the end of 19A for both methods.

Problem 9–11

Dollins Company is preparing the annual financial statements at December 31, 19A, and is concerned about application of *FASB Statement No. 5,* "Accounting for Contingencies." Four particular situations are under consideration, viz:

1. The company owns a small plant in a foreign country that has a book value of $3,000,000 and an estimated market value of $4,000,000. The foreign government has clearly indicated its intention to expropriate the plant during the coming year and to reimburse Dollins for 50% of the estimated market value.
2. An outside party has filed a claim against Dollins for $25,000 claiming that certain actions by Dollins

caused the party to lose a contract on which the estimated profit was this amount. In the opinion of the attorney hired by Dollins, the probability of the claim being successful is remote. They do not believe it will ever be brought to trial. If necessary, Dollins will defend itself in court.
3. During 19B, a third party (a potential customer) sued Dollins for $150,000 for a claimed injury that occurred on the premises owned by Dollins. No date for the trial has been set; however, the lawyer employed by Dollins has completed a thorough investigation. Because it can be proven that the third party did fall on the premises, the company lawyer believes it will not be difficult for the plaintiff to prove injury. There is evidence that it was due to negligence by the plaintiff. The attorney believes that it is not probable, but is reasonably possible, that the suit will be successful (for the plaintiff), *but* for a significantly smaller amount.
4. Dollins had a $10,000, 8%, one-year note receivable from a customer. Dollins discounted the note, with recourse, at the bank to obtain cash before its due date (due on June 1, 19B). If the maker does not pay the bank by due date, Dollins will have to pay it. The customer has an excellent credit rating (having never defaulted on a debt).

Required:
For each situation, respond to the following:

a. What accounting recognition (i.e., journal entries), if any, should be accorded each situation at the end of 19A? Explain why.
b. What should be reported on the income statement, balance sheet, and/or by footnote in each situation? Explain why.

PART B
Problems 9–12 to 9–19

Problem 9–12

Speedy Construction Company has contracts for construction of three major projects. The percentage of completion method of accounting is used for accounting purposes, while the completed contract method is used for the income tax returns. For purposes of this problem, assume there are no revenues nor expenses other than those included in the total profit figures given.

Project	Year Started	Completed	Total Profit	19A	19B	19C	19D
A	19A	19C	$ 70,000	40%	50%	10%	
B	19B	19C	90,000		20	80	
C	19B	19D	100,000		10	70	20%

Required:

1. For each year, compute *(a)* income tax expense and *(b)* income taxes payable; assume an average tax rate of 45%. (If necessary, refer to the section in Chapter 12 entitled "Inventories for Long-Term Construction Contracts.")
2. Give the entry to record income taxes for each year.
3. Complete a tabulation as follows:

	19A	19B	19C	19D
Income Statement:				
Pretax income	$_____	$_____	$_____	$_____
Income taxes	$_____	$_____	$_____	$_____
Net income	$_____	$_____	$_____	$_____
Balance Sheet:				
Income taxes payable	$_____	$_____	$_____	$_____
Deferred taxes (credit)	$_____	$_____	$_____	$_____

Problem 9–13

Parson Company financial statements for a four-year period reflected the following pretax amounts:

	19A	19B
Operating income, pretax	$100,000	$120,000
Extraordinary losses, pretax	(15,000)	(17,000)
Prior period adjustment, gain, pretax	7,000	
Timing differences included in above amounts:		
a. Revenue on income statement taxable in the following period	5,000	
b. Revenue on income statement, taxable in the preceding period		7,000
c. Expense on income statement, tax deductible in the following period	8,000	
d. Expense on income statement, tax deductible in the preceding period		6,000
e. Extraordinary loss on income statement, tax deductible in the following period	10,000	

(Relates to Problem 9–13)	19A	19B	19C	19D
Income Statement (summarized):				
Revenues *(a)*	$120,000	$130,000	$140,000	$160,000
Expenses *(b)*	(90,000)	(92,000)	(95,000)	(108,000)
Depreciation (straight line)	?	?	?	?
Pretax income	$?	$?	$?	$?
Balance Sheet (partial):				
Machine (four-year life, no residual value), at cost	$ 40,000	$ 40,000	$ 40,000	$40,000
Income taxes payable	?	?	?	?
Deferred taxes	?	?	?	?

(a) Includes $10,000 tax-free interest revenue in each of 19A and 19B.
(b) Includes $4,000 goodwill amortization in each year 19B, 19C, and 19D.

The company has an average tax rate of 40% each year and uses sum-of-the-years'-digits depreciation (no residual value) on the income tax return (for problem purposes, assume this method is acceptable for tax purposes in this situation) and straight-line depreciation for accounting purposes.

Required:

1. Complete the above income statements incorporating income taxes appropriately allocated.
2. Compute income taxes payable for each year.
3. Give the entry for each year to record income taxes. Prove the deferred tax amount for each year.
4. Explain why tax allocation provides better financial statement amounts in this situation.

Problem 9–14

Assume the following data for X Corporation are available for a two-year period:

f. Prior period gain on statement of retained earnings, taxable in the next period	4,000
Retained earnings, beginning balance 30,000	55,000

Assume an average income tax rate of 40% on all items, except extraordinary items, to which a 30% tax rate applies. Item *(d)* will require an amended tax return.

Required:

1. Compute income tax expense for each year that should be reflected on the income statement. Show operating income, extraordinary items, and prior period adjustments separately.
2. Compute income taxes payable for each year that should be reflected on the tax return. Show operating income, extraordinary items, and prior period adjustments separately.

3. Give the entry to record income taxes for each year.
4. Prepare a partial income statement and partial statement of retained earnings for each year to show how income tax expense should be reported. Include both interperiod and intraperiod allocations.

Problem 9–15

XYZ Corporation earned $80,000 pretax accounting income in 19K. During 19K the following factors complicated the accounting for 19K income taxes:

1. Gross profit on installment sales recognized in the accounts during 19K $270,000
2. Gross profit reportable for income tax purposes—based on cash collections on installment receivables during 19K that arose on installment sales made in
   19J 120,000
   19K 120,000
3. Amortization of goodwill in the accounts (not deductible for income tax purposes) 5,000
4. Ultimate disposition of remaining $60,000 of a loss carryforward recorded in 19D. The corporation reported at year-end 19J an asset (receivable) of $60,000 × .40 = $24,000, which represented the then remaining tax benefit (i.e., as yet unrealized) of the loss carry-forward which was initially recorded in 19D 24,000
5. At the end of 19J the balance sheet reported a timing difference that arose from installment sales made in 19J which were accounted for on the sales realization basis and reported for tax purposes on a cash collection basis. Deferred income tax credit from 19J 48,000
6. Income tax rate for all years 19A–19K 40%

Required:
1. Prepare the journal entry to record income taxes for 19K. Prepare an income tax worksheet similar to the illustration in the chapter to provide data for the entry.
2. Prepare partial income statements and balance sheets for 19J and 19K to report income taxes for the two years in comparative form. Assume that the ending 19J balance in income tax payable was

$28,000 and that 19J income tax expense was $30,000.

Problem 9–16

Carter Company accounts and related records revealed the following data for the first two years of operations:

	19A	19B
Pretax accounting income	$160,000	$180,000
Income tax differences:		
1. Estimated warranty expense (included in pretax account-ing income)	15,000	16,000
Cash payments on warranties arising in		
19A (deductible for tax purposes)	12,000	2,000
19B (deductible for tax purposes)		15,000
		17,000
2. Rent revenue collection one year in advance (taxable in year collected)	6,000	
Rent revenue allocated on accrual basis (included in pretax accounting income)	4,000	2,000
3. Gross profit on installment sales on sales realization basis (included in pretax accounting income)	175,000	230,000
Gross profit reportable for in-come tax purposes (on cash collection basis) on in-stallment sales made in		
19A	65,000	110,000
19B		75,000
		185,000
Income tax rates	30%	35%

Required:
1. Identify the timing differences and the permanent differences listed above in Items 1–3.
2. Using pretax accounting income as the base from which to begin, give the entries to record income taxes for 19A and 19B under each of the following assumptions:
   a. That each item was the only difference that occurred during the year. That is, give the entries for each year for each of the three items as if the other two did not occur.
   b. That all three items occurred during the year. That is, give the combined entry for each year. For this requirement you should prepare an

income tax worksheet for each year similar to the one illustrated in the chapter.

Problem 9–17

Mac Corporation acquired machinery on July 1, 19C. The list price was $35,000. Mac paid $15,000 cash and gave a note payable for the remainder with a face amount of $20,000 which included interest at 10% per year (a noninterest-bearing note). The maturity date of the note was July 1, 19E. The machinery had an estimated service life of eight years and no residual value. Mac uses straight-line depreciation for accounting purposes and double-declining balance depreciation for income tax purposes.

During 19C Mac earned $175,000 pretax accounting income. Included in this amount was a deduction of $15,000 for cost depletion of a mineral which the company mines and sells. Income tax regulations provide that taxpayers such as Mac may deduct for income tax purposes the larger of cost depletion or 6% of the gross revenue from the sale of the extracted minerals. During 19C Mac extracted 100,000 pounds of the mineral and sold 90,000 pounds at $3 per pound.

There were no other factors to complicate the company's income tax computations during 19C. The income tax rate during 19C was 20% on the first $25,000 of taxable income and 46% on the excess (for illustrative purposes only).

Required:

1. Give the journal entry to record income taxes for 19C. Mac's fiscal year ends on December 31.
2. What effect did the difference between statutory depletion and cost depletion have on income taxes for 19D (the following year)? What type of difference was involved? Explain.

Problem 9–18

Petty Corporation pretax financial statements for the first two years of operation reflected the following amounts:

	19A	19B
Revenues	$300,000	$330,000
Expenses	320,000	315,000
Pretax Income (loss)	$ (20,000)	$ 15,000

Assume an average tax rate of 40%.

Required:

1. Assume future income during the next five years is unpredictable (i.e., uncertain):
   a. Restate the above financial statements incorporating the income tax effects appropriately allocated. Show computations.
   b. Give entries to record the income tax effects for each year. Explain the basis for your entries.
2. Assume future income is reasonably certain during the next five years. Complete Requirements 1 (a) and (b) above.

Problem 9–19

Young Corporation's pretax financial statements for the first four years of operations reflected the following pretax amounts:

	19A	19B	19C	19D
Income Statement (summarized):				
Revenue	$125,000	$155,000	$180,000	$230,000
Expenses	120,000	195,000	170,000	200,000
Pretax Income (loss)	$ 5,000	$ (40,000)	$ 10,000	$ 30,000

Assume an average income tax rate of 30% during 19A and 19B and 40% in 19C and 19D, and that future incomes are uncertain at the end of each year. Also, assume that management of Young Corporation elects to carry the 19B loss back to 19A (and *then* forward) in order to "lock in" the immediate cash refund on the carryback.

Required:

1. Recast the above statement to incorporate the income tax effects appropriately allocated. Show computations.
2. Give entries to record the income tax effects for each year.

10

Inventories—General Problems

Accounting for inventories *(a)* facilitates determination of income by matching appropriate inventory costs with revenues and *(b)* provides an inventory amount for the balance sheet. Such inventory considerations as control, safeguarding, measurement, and cost allocation present problems of considerable magnitude for both accountants and management. These problems are especially critical in view of the materiality of inventories in the typical business and the fact that inventories directly affect both the income statement and the balance sheet. Such factors have caused the accounting profession to give particular attention to the problems related to inventories. This and the two following chapters present the principal accounting concepts and procedures relating to inventories.

THE NATURE OF INVENTORIES

As an accounting category, *inventories* are assets consisting of goods owned by the business at a particular time and held for future sale or for utilization in the manufacture of goods for sale. No other asset includes such an extensive variety of properties under a single heading, for practically all kinds of tangible goods and properties are found in the inventories of one business or another. Machinery and equipment are operational assets of the business using them,

but at one time they constituted part of the inventory of the manufacturer of such equipment. Even a building until finished and turned over to a buyer is an inventory item, a "contract in process," among the assets of the builder.

In many companies, inventories comprise a significant portion of current assets or even total assets. Furthermore, inventories generally represent an active asset because of their constant usage and replacement. Although many inventory items are small, they frequently have considerable value; therefore, the problem of safeguarding inventories is akin to protecting cash. The advisability of adequate stocking of items for sale, coupled with the risk of loss and cost of overstocking, creates critical management planning and control problems. Failure to control inventories and to account for inventory quantities and costs might well lead to business failure.[1]

CLASSIFICATION OF INVENTORIES

The major classifications of inventories relate to the type of business. A trading entity (i.e., wholesale or retail) acquires merchandise for

---

[1] For an introductory discussion of accounting for inventories, refer to G. A. Welsch and R. N. Anthony, *Fundamentals of Financial Accounting,* rev. ed. (Homewood, Ill.: Richard D. Irwin, Inc., 1977), chap. 7.

resale, whereas a manufacturing entity acquires raw materials and component parts, and manufactures finished products. The flow of inventory costs through these two types of entities may be diagrammed as follows (assuming a perpetual inventory system):

Trading entity:

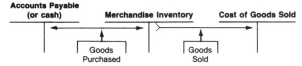

Manufacturing entity:

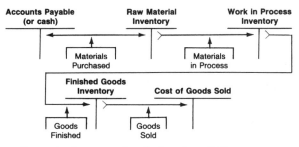

Inventories may be defined as follows:

1. Merchandise inventory—goods on hand purchased by a trading entity for resale. The physical form of the goods is not altered prior to resale.
2. Manufacturing inventory—the combined inventories of a manufacturing entity consisting of
   a. Raw materials inventory—tangible goods purchased or obtained from natural sources and on hand principally for direct use in the manufacture of goods for resale. Parts or subassemblies manufactured prior to use are sometimes classified as raw materials inventory; however, a preferable classification is *component parts inventory.*
   b. Work in process inventory—goods partly processed and requiring further processing before sale. Work (goods) in process inventory normally is valued at the sum of *direct material, direct labor,* and *allocated manufacturing overhead costs* incurred to date of the inventory.
   c. Finished goods inventory—manufactured items completed and being held for

sale. Finished goods inventory normally is valued at the sum of *direct material, direct labor,* and *allocated manufacturing overhead costs* related to their manufacture.
   d. Manufacturing supplies inventory—items on hand such as lubrication oils for the machinery, cleaning materials, and supply items which comprise an insignificant part of the finished product as, for example, the thread and glue used in binding this book.
3. Miscellaneous inventories—items such as office supplies, janitorial supplies, and shipping supplies. Inventories of this type normally are used in the near future and usually are charged to selling or general expense when used.

THE DUAL PHASE OF THE INVENTORY PROBLEM

The basic cause of many inventory accounting problems is the fact that goods sold during a fiscal period seldom correspond exactly to those produced or bought during that period. Consequently, the typical situation is one where physical inventory increases or decreases during the period. This increase or decrease in the physical quantity of inventory necessitates a corresponding *allocation of the total cost of goods available* for sale or use between *(a)* those goods that were sold or used and *(b)* those that remain on hand. This situation creates two distinct problems in inventory identification and measurement, viz:

1. Identification and measurement of the quantity of *physical goods* (items and quantities) that should be included in inventory at the end of the period.
2. Measurement of the *accounting values* assigned to the physical goods included in inventory at the end of the period.

IDENTIFICATION OF GOODS (ITEMS) THAT SHOULD BE INCLUDED IN INVENTORY

In identifying the physical quantity of goods to be included in inventory, accountants apply the general rule that all goods to which the entity has *ownership* at inventory date should be included, regardless of their location. The vendor (seller) should include in inventory, goods under contract for sale but not yet segregated and applied to the contract. Further, mere segregation does not create a "transfer of ownership"—the terms of the contract itself must be determining. Since at the close of an accounting period, a business may *(a)* hold goods which it does not own or *(b)* own goods which it does not hold, care must be exercised in identifying the goods properly includable in inventory.

Goods purchased, though not received, should be included in the inventory of the purchaser provided ownership to such goods has passed. Application of the "passage of ownership" rule generally requires the following: if, the goods are shipped *f.o.b. destination,* ownership does not pass until the purchaser receives the goods from the common carrier; if the goods are shipped *f.o.b. shipping point,* ownership passes when the seller delivers them to the common carrier.[2]

Goods *out* on consignment, those held by agents, and those located at branches should be included in inventory. On the other hand, goods *held* (but owned by someone else) for sale on commission or consignment and those received from vendors but rejected and awaiting return to vendor for credit should be excluded from inventory.[3]

In identifying items that should be included in inventory where there is a question as to whether ownership has passed, the accountant must exercise judgment in light of the particular situation. Obviously, the legal title should be acknowledged; however, a strict legal determination often is impractical. In such cases the sales agreement, policies of the parties involved, industry practices, and other available evidence of intent must be considered.

---

[2] Refer to Chapter 2, discussion of the revenue principle.

[3] Consignment is a special marketing arrangement whereby the consignor (the owner of the goods) ships merchandise to another party, known as a consignee, who is to act as a sales agent only. The consignee does not purchase the goods but assumes responsibility for their care, and upon sale remits the proceeds (less expenses and a commission). Goods out on consignment, since they are owned by the consignor until sold, should be excluded from the inventory of the consignee and included in the inventory of the consignor.

MEASUREMENT OF PHYSICAL QUANTITIES IN INVENTORY

The physical quantities in inventory may be determined by means of *(a)* a *periodic (physical) inventory system* or *(b)* a *perpetual inventory system.*

Periodic Inventory System

When a periodic system is used, an actual physical count of the goods on hand is taken at the end of each period for which financial statements are to be prepared. The goods are counted, weighed, or otherwise measured, then extended at *unit costs* to derive the inventory valuation. When a periodic inventory system is used, end-of-the-period entries are required for *(a)* transferring the beginning inventory to expense and *(b)* recording the ending inventory.

Under the periodic system, cost of goods sold (an expense) is a *residual amount* and cannot be independently verified from the records. To illustrate:

Cost of goods sold:		
Beginning inventory (carried forward from the prior period)	$ 50,000	
Merchandise purchases (accumulated in the accounts)	200,000	
Total goods available for sale	250,000	
Less: Ending inventory (determined by count)	60,000	
Cost of goods sold (a residual amount)		$190,000

The accounting entries and external financial reporting under the periodic inventory system were reviewed and illustrated in Chapters 3 and 4.

Perpetual Inventory System

When a perpetual system is used, detailed *subsidiary records,* in addition to the usual ledger accounts, are maintained for each inventory item. An *Inventory Control* account is maintained in the general ledger on a current basis. The detailed inventory record for *each* different item must provide for recording (a) receipts, (b) issues, and (c) balances on hand, usually in both quantities and dollar amounts. Thus, the physical quantity and valuation of goods that should be on hand at any time are readily available from the accounting records. Consequently, a physical inventory count is unnecessary except to check on the accuracy of the inventory records from time to time. Such checks (physical counts) are usually made at least annually or on a continuous rotation basis when large inventories are involved. When a discrepancy is found, the perpetual inventory records must be adjusted to the physical count. In such cases, the inventory account is debited or credited as necessary for correction and an inventory adjustment account such as "Inventory Shortages (loss) or Overages (gain)" is debited or credited. The inventory adjustment account is closed to Income Summary at the end of the period. The balance in the inventory shortage account usually is reported as an expense on internal financial statements, but it is combined with the cost of goods sold amount on external statements.

A perpetual inventory system also is particularly useful (a) to control and safeguard inventory and (b) to facilitate preparation of monthly statements. A perpetual inventory is generally considered to be one of the essential characteristics of a good cost accounting system. Its primary disadvantage is the recordkeeping cost.

To briefly review and compare the accounting procedures for the periodic and the perpetual inventory systems, the following simplified data are used (comparative entries are given on the following page):

	Units	Unit Amount
Merchandise inventory, beginning	500	$4.00 (cost)
Merchandise purchases during the period	1,000	4.00 (cost)
Total goods available for sale	1,500	
Merchandise sold during the period	900	6.00 (sales price)
Mechandise inventory, ending	600	

In the comparative entries illustration, two procedural differences between the two inventory systems should be noted, viz:

1. When the periodic system is used, only one entry is made to record a sale, that is, at sales price. In contrast, when the perpetual system is used, two entries are required to record a sale—one for the revenue (at sales price) and one for cost of goods sold (at cost price). Only the perpetual system provides a current accounting for the cost of goods sold amount at the date of each sale.

2. When the periodic system is used, purchases of goods during the period are debited to a purchases account to accumulate total purchases for the period. Thus, the beginning balance in the inventory account remains undisturbed throughout the period and no detailed record is maintained of the current amount of goods on hand. In contrast, under the perpetual system, purchases are debited directly to the inventory control account (and concurrently entered into the detailed inventory records), and current issues are credited to it as sales are made so that it carries a perpetual, or continuing, balance of the goods that should be on hand at each date.

A typical subsidiary inventory record (for Raw Material X) that would be maintained under the perpetual inventory system (but not under the periodic system) is shown in Exhibit 10–1.

EFFECT OF INVENTORY ERRORS

Errors in measuring inventory quantities or monetary values are common because of complicating factors such as size of the inventory, the number of different kinds of items, their physical characteristics, means of storage, unintentional oversights, and intentional errors. This section is included to demonstrate the effect of inventory errors on the financial statements.

An overstatement of the ending inventory overstates pretax income by the same amount, and an understatement of the ending inventory understates pretax income. Conversely, an overstatement of the beginning inventory understates pretax income by the same amount,

354

Comparative Entries

Periodic Inventory System			Perpetual Inventory System (assuming no shortage or overage)		
a. Merchandise purchased for resale:					
Purchases (1,000 @ $4)	4,000		Merchandise inventory	4,000	
Cash		4,000	Cash		4,000
b. Merchandise sold:					
Cash (900 @ $6)	5,400		Cash	5,400	
Sales revenue		5,400	Sales revenue		5,400
			Cost of goods sold	3,600	
			Merchandise inventory (900 @ $4)		3,600
c. Entries at end of the accounting period:					
To close purchases account:					
Income summary	4,000		None		
Purchases		4,000			
To transfer beginning inventory amount:					
Income summary	2,000		None		
Inventory (beginning)*		2,000			
To record ending inventory amount:					
Inventory (ending)*	2,400		None		
Income summary		2,400			

* These amounts may be closed to Cost of Goods Sold and then to Income Summary with the same results.

Closing entry:

Periodic			Perpetual		
None, unless above accounts are first closed to Cost of Goods Sold.			Income summary	3,600	
			Cost of goods sold		3,600

Income Statement (partial):					
Sales revenue		$5,400	Sales revenue		$5,400
Cost of goods sold:					
Beginning inventory	$2,000				
Purchases	4,000				
Goods available for sale	6,000				
Ending inventory	2,400				
Cost of goods sold		3,600	Cost of goods sold		3,600
Gross margin		$1,800	Gross margin		$1,800
Balance Sheet (partial):					
Current Assets:					
Merchandise inventory		$2,400	Merchandise inventory		$2,400

and an understatement of the beginning inventory overstates pretax income. An overstatement of purchases alone overstates cost of goods sold and understates pretax income.

Incorrect inclusion or exclusion of physical units in inventory will cause errors in the financial statements. The following errors are not uncommon:[4]

---

[4] Some of the effects of these errors will differ depending upon the inventory flow method used, that is, *Fifo, Lifo,* and so on.

EXHIBIT 10–1
Perpetual Inventory Record

						SUBSIDIARY LEDGER							Verification Dates	
						PERPETUAL INVENTORY RECORD								
Article	*Raw Material X*			Unit *lbs.*			Maximum *1,600*							
Location	*L-15*			Bin No. *32*			Reorder Level *800*							
	Ordered			Received or Completed					Issued or Sold				Balance on Hand	
Date	Order No.	Units	Order No.	Ref.	Units	Unit Cost	Total Cost	Ref.	Units	Unit Cost	Total Cost	Units	Unit Cost	Total Cost
Jan. 1												1,000	*$.40*	*$400*
10			*17*		*500*	*$.40*	*$200*					1,500	.40	600
18									*600*	*$.40*	*$240*	900	.40	360
19	*18*	*700*												

Incorrect inclusion of items that should not be in ending inventory because ownership is not present:

1. *Incorrect inclusion of items in the ending inventory, and purchase of the items on credit was recorded*—These two errors result in an overstatement of the ending inventory, purchases, and accounts payable. In this case pretax income will be correctly stated since the errors in inventory and purchases will offset; however, the assets (inventory) and liabilities (accounts payable) on the balance sheet each will be overstated by the same amount.
2. *Incorrect inclusion of items in the ending inventory, but purchase of the items was not recorded*—This error results in an overstatement of the ending inventory; hence, both pretax income and assets are overstated by the same amounts.

Incorrect exclusion of items that should be admitted to ending inventory because ownership is present:

3. *Incorrect exclusion of items from the ending inventory, but the credit purchase was correctly recorded*—This error results in an understatement of the ending inventory, hence, an understatement of both pretax income and assets by the same amount.

4. *Incorrect exclusion of items from the ending inventory, and the purchase of the items on credit was not recorded*—These two errors result in understatement of ending inventory, purchases, and accounts payable. In this case pretax income will be correctly stated since the errors in inventory and purchases will offset; however, the assets (inventory) and liabilities (accounts payable) on the balance sheet each will be understated by the same amount.

The effects of each situation are demonstrated in Exhibit 10–2.

Errors similar to those discussed above, which relate to purchases, may also arise when goods are sold. These errors not only cause the financial statements for the current period to be in error but also frequently cause future amounts to be wrong. An error in the ending inventory, if not corrected, will cause a counterbalancing error in the next period because the ending and beginning inventories have opposite effects on income.

MEASUREMENT OF THE ACCOUNTING VALUE OF INVENTORY

At date of acquisition, inventory items are recorded at cost in harmony with the *cost prin-*

EXHIBIT 10–2
Effects of Inventory Errors (pretax)

	Correct Amounts	(1) Inventory Error—Incorrectly Included $1,000 in Ending Inventory		(3) Inventory Error—Incorrectly Excluded $1,000 from Ending Inventory	
		(1) Purchases in Error (was recorded)	(2) Purchases Are Correct (was not recorded)	(3) Purchases Are Correct (was recorded)	(4) Purchases in Error (was not recorded)
Income Statement:					
Sales	$10,000	$10,000	$10,000	$10,000	$10,000
Beginning inventory	3,000	3,000	3,000	3,000	3,000
Purchases	12,000	13,000†	12,000	12,000	11,000*
Total	15,000	16,000	15,000	15,000	14,000
Ending inventory	8,000	9,000†	9,000†	7,000*	7,000*
Cost of goods sold	7,000	7,000	6,000	8,000	7,000
Gross margin	3,000	3,000	4,000†	2,000*	3,000
Expenses	1,000	1,000	1,000	1,000	1,000
Income	$ 2,000	$ 2,000	$ 3,000†	$ 1,000*	$ 2,000
Balance Sheet:					
Assets (inventory)	$ 8,000	$ 9,000†	$ 9,000†	$ 7,000*	$ 7,000*
Liabilities (payables)	12,000	13,000†	12,000	12,000	11,000*
Retained earnings	20,000	20,000	21,000†	19,000*	20,000

* Under.
† Over.

ciple; subsequently, when sold, their cost is matched with revenue in accordance with the *matching principle*. Inventory items remaining on hand at the end of an accounting period are "valued" on the basis of the cost principle except when their value decreased because of damage, obsolescence, erosion of replacement cost, and similar factors, in which case they are "valued" in accordance with the concept of *conservatism* (for example, lower-of-cost-or-market or net realizable value procedures). The discussions to follow in this and the next two chapters consider special inventory valuation problems and related procedures.

The *accounting value* of inventories represents an allocation of the total cost of goods or materials *available* between that portion used or sold (cost of goods sold) and that portion held as an asset for subsequent use or sale (inventory). The nature of the allocation is indicated in the following diagram (based on the example given on pages 353 and 354):

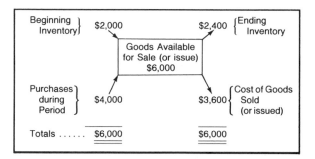

A number of procedures used for measuring the accounting value of inventories satisfy the theoretical requirements. A multiplicity of acceptable procedures suggests the wide variation in inventory characteristics and conditions depending upon the particular situations and purposes. Basically the accounting values for inventories serve two different purposes. Each purpose implies procedures that may not appear entirely appropriate for the other purpose. One purpose is to develop a monetary value for the inventory reported on the *balance sheet.* There it is appropriate to report this resource at cost or at its future utility to the business, whichever is lower. The other purpose, directed toward the *income statement,* is to measure the inventory value so there is a proper measurement of income between accounting periods in an environment where prices are usually changing. Conservatism with respect to inventory values in terms of one objective may not be conservative in terms of the other objective. In recent years the income measurement objective has predominated, as indicated by the following quotation from *Accounting Research Bulletin No. 43:*

> In accounting for the goods in the inventory at any point of time, the major objective is the matching of appropriate costs against revenues in order that there may be a proper determination of the realized income. Thus, the inventory at any given date is the balance of costs applicable to goods on hand remaining after the matching of absorbed costs with concurrent revenues. This balance is appropriately carried to future periods provided it does not exceed an amount properly chargeable against the revenues expected to be obtained from ultimate disposition of the goods carried forward.[5]

Measurement of acceptable values for (1) inventory and (2) cost of goods sold, involves two distinct problems, viz:

1. Inventory unit cost—selection of an appropriate *unit cost* for valuation of the items in inventory. The principal bases or *inventory valuation methods* are as follows:
   a. Cost basis.
   b. Departure from cost basis:
      1. Lower of cost or market (LCM).
      2. Net realizable value.
      3. Replacement cost.
      4. Selling price.
2. Inventory flow—selection of an appropriate inventory flow method, that is, selection of an appropriate *assumed flow* of inventory unit costs. The principal *inventory flow methods* (discussed in Chapter 11) are as follows:

a. Specific cost.
b. Average cost.
c. First-in, first-out.
d. Last-in, first-out.

CONTENT OF UNIT COST

The cost principle provides the theoretical foundation for measurement of unit cost for inventory and cost of goods sold, viz:

> The primary basis of accounting for inventories is cost, which has been defined generally as the price paid or consideration given to acquire an asset. As applied to inventories, cost means in principle the sum of the applicable expenditures and charges directly or indirectly incurred in bringing an article to its existing condition and location.[6]

Thus unit inventory cost is measured by the total outlay made to acquire goods and to prepare them for the market. These costs include not only the purchase price but also those incidental costs such as excise and sales taxes, duties, freight, storage, insurance on the merchandise while in transit or in storage, and all other costs incurred on the goods up to the time they are ready for use or for sale to the customer. Some incidental costs, such as freight-in, frequently can be identified directly with specific goods, while other incidental costs may require a reasonable allocation to specific goods. As a practical matter some incidental costs, although theoretically a cost of goods purchased, often are not included in inventory valuation but are reported as a separate expense; the cost of allocating may not be warranted by the slight increase in accuracy. In such cases, *consistency* in application is particularly important.

General administrative and distribution expenses and interest expense are not included in determining unit inventory costs because they are not directly related to the purchase or manufacture of goods for sale. Theoretically, a part of all such costs should be allocated to inventory; practical considerations suggest, however, that any such allocation would be too arbitrary to be meaningful. General and administrative ex-

---

[5] AICPA, *Accounting Research Bulletin No. 43, "Restatement and Revision of Accounting Research Bulletins"* (New York, 1961), Ch. 4, Statement 2.

[6] Ibid., Statement 3.

penses often are treated as *period* expenses because they more directly relate to accounting periods than to units of inventory; consequently, they are deducted on the income statement in the period in which incurred.

Freight-In (Freight on Purchases)

In conformity with the cost principle, freight and other incidental costs paid in connection with the purchase of materials for use or merchandise for resale are additions to unit cost. When such charges can be identified with specific goods, they should be charged directly to such goods. However, in some cases identification is impractical. Consequently, such costs often are recorded in a special account such as Freight-In, which is reported as an addition to cost of goods sold in the case of a trading entity and to cost of materials used in a manufacturing entity. However, this practical procedure may overstate cost of goods sold and understate inventory by the amount of such costs that should be allocated to inventory (as opposed to charging the full amount to cost of goods sold). Theoretically, freight-in should be apportioned to cost of goods sold and to the ending inventory in proportion to the relative quantities of goods included in each of the two categories.

Purchase Discounts

Cash discounts sometimes are given in respect to credit purchases to encourage early payment. Under the cost principle, the net cash equivalent paid for the specific item is cost. Payments made for the extension of credit should be accounted for as interest expense. Theoretically, all cash discounts permitted, whether taken or not, should be omitted from cost. Upon payment of invoices, any discounts not taken constitute interest expense. Since cash discounts are reductions in the cost of specific goods, they reduce both cost of purchases and inventory valuation. Therefore, credit purchases should be recorded *net of discount* to reflect the *correct cost*. Although technically incorrect, for practical reasons and because the cash discount often is immaterial, purchases sometimes are recorded at the *gross amount*. The gross approach

violates the revenue principle; clearly, no revenue should be recorded from the mere act of purchasing goods.

To illustrate each approach, assume merchandise is purchased for $1,000 on credit terms of 2/10, n/30. Assume further that three-fourths of the charge is paid within the ten-day discount period. The recording and reporting under these approaches is shown on the opposite page.

The net of discount approach correctly reflects the cost of the merchandise in conformity with the cost principle and also correctly states the amount of the liability since most companies take all discounts and pay only the net amount. Note that 2% interest saved by paying within ten days is a significantly higher rate on an annual basis. This method also correctly allocates the discount effect between inventory and cost of goods sold. It follows the cost principle because the true costs of purchases, cost of goods sold, and inventory are recorded and reported. Similarly, accounts payable is recorded and reported at the amount actually payable, appropriately excluding interest. The net approach reports *purchase discount lost* (a debit) as expense rather than reporting *purchase discount* (a credit) as a reduction in cost of goods sold or as "other" revenue.

DEPARTURES FROM THE COST PRINCIPLE IN COSTING INVENTORY

Under certain prescribed conditions, generally accepted accounting principles require exceptions to the cost principle in measuring the unit cost of inventory items. The exceptions may be classified as follows:

1. Lower of cost or market (LCM).
2. Net realizable value.
3. Replacement cost.
4. Selling price.

Lower of Cost or Market

Under the concept of conservatism, known losses, although not actually evidenced by completed transactions, are recognized in the period of occurrence. In contrast, known gains not evidenced by completed transactions are not recognized until realized. Therefore, under the lower-

Net of Discount Approach *(correct)*			Gross Amount Approach *(incorrect)*		
Recording:					
To record the purchase (perpetual inventory system):					
Merchandise inventory	980		Merchandise inventory	1,000	
Accounts payable (net) . . .		980	Accounts payable (gross)		1,000
To record payment of three-fourths of the liability within discount period:					
Accounts payable (net)	735		Accounts payable (gross)	750	
Cash		735	Cash		735
($980 × .75 = $735)			Discount on purchases		15
To record payment of one-fourth of the liability after the discount period:					
Accounts payable (net)	245		Accounts payable (gross)	250	
Interest expense*	5		Cash		250
Cash		250			
* Alternative title: Purchase discounts lost.					
To record sale of half the inventory for $1,500 for cash:					
Cash	1,500		Cash	1,500	
Sales revenue		1,500	Sales revenue		1,500
Cost of goods sold	490		Cost of goods sold	500	
Merchandise inventory		490	Merchandise inventory		500
($980 × 1/2 = $490)					
Reporting:					
Income Statement:					
Cost of goods sold		$490	Cost of goods sold ($500 less		
Interest expense		5	purchase discount, $15)		$485
Balance Sheet:					
Inventory		490	Inventory		500

of-cost-or-market "rule," the unit cost used is the lower of *(a)* original cost when purchased or *(b)* market cost (i.e., replacement cost, not selling price) at the *end of the current period.* Thus, an item purchased in June 19A for $50 which is still on hand at the end of 19A, at which time it could be purchased for $45, would be reported in the 19A ending inventory at a unit cost of $45. The $5 loss would be reported as an expense on the 19A income statement, and the $45, which becomes the cost for future accounting, would be included in cost of goods sold for the period when the item is sold.

The lower-of-cost-or-market rule was adopted on the basis of *(a)* the matching principle, in that the decline in utility of the goods on hand should be recognized as a loss in the period in which the decline in utility took place, and *(b)* the concept of balance sheet conservatism,

which directs that the asset inventory should be reported at the lower figure. It is particularly important to recognize also the implicit assumption in the lower-of-cost-or-market rule that selling prices decrease in approximate proportion to decreases in replacement cost. *Cost,* as used in this context, refers to the actual unit cost as determined in accordance with the cost principle.

Market, as used in this context by accountants and by the Treasury Department for income tax purposes, is defined as follows: "Under ordinary circumstances 'market' means the current bid price prevailing at the date of the inventory for the particular merchandise in the volume in which usually purchased by the taxpayer."

In applying the lower-of-cost-or-market (LCM) procedure, certain *exceptions* were recognized by the Committee on Accounting Procedure of the AICPA. "Judgment must always be exercised and no loss should be recognized unless the evidence indicates clearly that a loss has been sustained. There are, therefore, exceptions to such a standard." These exceptions were described as follows:

As used in the phrase *lower of cost or market* the term *market* means current replacement cost (by purchase or by reproduction, as the case may be) except that:

(1) Market should not exceed the net realizable value (i.e., estimated selling price in the ordinary course of business less reasonably predictable costs of completion and disposal); and

(2) Market should not be less than net realizable value reduced by an allowance for an approximately normal profit margin.[7]

The concepts of *net realizable value* and *net realizable value less normal profit* may be illustrated as follows for one unit of Inventory Item A:

Inventory Item A, at original cost	$ 70
Inventory Item A, at estimated current selling price in *present condition*	$100
Less: Estimated distribution expense	40
Net realizable value	60
Less: Allowance for normal profit (10% of sales price)	10
Net realizable value less normal profit	$ 50

The deduction of distribution expense (including any other expenses to ready it for sale) is necessary to prevent inclusion of the item in inventory at more than its current realizable value.

The exceptions quoted above for net realizable value and net realizable value less normal profit in effect establish a "ceiling" and a "floor" for *market* in the comparison with original *cost* in applying the procedure. Exhibit 10–3 gives several independent situations in which the LCM rule is applied. The cost and other values are those of a single unit. Observe in the illustration that "market" results from a choice of the middle amount among current replacement cost, the ceiling (net realizable value), and the floor (net realizable value less normal profit). The "market" thus derived is compared with

---
[7] *Accounting Research Bulletin No. 43*, Ch. 4, Statement 6.

EXHIBIT 10–3
Exceptions—Computation of Lower of Cost or Market

		Case			
		I	*II*	*III*	*IV*
a.	Cost (per unit)	$1.00	$1.00	$1.00	$0.45
b.	Current replacement cost (per unit)	0.55	0.65	0.45	0.40
c.	Ceiling (net realizable value—estimated sales price less predictable cost of completion and disposal)*	0.60	0.60	0.60	0.60
d.	Floor (net realizable value less a normal profit margin)*	0.51	0.51	0.52	0.52
e.	Market (selected from [b], [c], and [d] values)	0.55	0.60	0.52	0.52
f.	Inventory valuation under LCM rule (selected from [a] and [e])	0.55	0.60	0.52	0.45

* Additional data to verify ceiling and floor.

	I	*II*	*III*	*IV*
Estimated selling price (later period)	$0.85	$0.90	$0.80	$0.75
Less: Estimated to complete and sell	0.25	0.30	0.20	0.15
Net realizable value (ceiling)	$0.60	$0.60	$0.60	$0.60
Less: Estimated normal profit†	0.09	0.09	0.08	0.08
Net realizable value less profit (floor)	$0.51	$0.51	$0.52	$0.52

† 10% of sales price; rounded for instructional convenience.

cost in order to determine the appropriate inventory valuation.

The limits (ceiling and floor) are necessary to measure properly the economic utility of the items in inventory. For example, in Case II in Exhibit 10–3, current replacement cost is $0.65 and the net realizable value (ceiling) is $0.60. To carry the $0.65 forward in inventory, which is more than the net realizable value, would result in a charge against future sales greater than the economic utility of the goods and a charge of $0.35 against current income which is less than the anticipated loss of $0.40; hence, the reported profit and inventory value of each period would be incorrect. In Case III, Exhibit 10–3, the net realizable value less normal profit (floor, $0.52) is greater than current replacement cost; therefore, the floor value should be carried forward in inventory. To carry forward a market value of $0.45 would result in an understatement of the inventory, since at $0.52 a normal profit margin ($0.08) will be earned when the item is sold. Therefore, if current replacement cost as the market value ($0.45) were carried forward in this case, future profits on the inventory items would be overstated and current period profits understated.

In applying the exceptions, *Bulletin No. 43* states: "Because of the many variations of circumstances encountered in inventory pricing, Statement 6 [see the quotation on page 360] is intended as a guide rather than a literal rule. It should be applied realistically in light of the objectives expressed in this chapter and with due regard to the form, content, and composition of the inventory."[8]

ACCOUNTING PROBLEMS IN APPLYING LOWER OF COST OR MARKET

In applying the LCM procedure, two primary accounting problems arise, viz:

1. How should the procedure be applied to determine the overall inventory valuation?
2. How should the resulting inventory valuation be recorded in the accounts?

Determination of Overall Inventory Valuation

In applying the LCM procedure in determining the overall inventory valuation, three approaches are available (*ARB No. 43,* Ch. 4, Statement 7): (1) comparison of cost and market separately for each item of inventory, (2) comparison of cost and market separately for each *classification* of inventory, and (3) comparison of *total* cost with *total* market for the inventory. Exhibit 10–4 shows the application of each approach.

Generally, the LCM procedure is applied to *individual inventory items.* However, in certain circumstances, application of the procedure to classifications or totals may have greater significance for accounting purposes. For example, in applying the procedure to the raw materials inventory of a manufacturer producing only one major product and using several raw materials having common characteristics, the utility of the total stock of raw material may have more significance than the individual market prices of each raw material. Consistency in application is essential.

---

[8] The application of LCM to *Fifo* and average cost (see Chapter 11) causes their results to approximate the *Lifo* results. Furthermore, LCM cannot be applied to *Lifo* results for income tax purposes, nor would such application be reasonable for accounting purposes since *Lifo* results are usually already stated at an amount near LCM.

EXHIBIT 10–4
Applying Lower of Cost or Market

Commodity	Cost	Market	Lower of Cost or Market Applied to— Individual Items	Classification	Total
Classification A:					
Item 1	$10,000	$ 9,500	$ 9,500		
Item 2	8,000	9,000	8,000		
	18,000	18,500		$18,000	
Classification B:					
Item 3	21,000	22,000	21,000		
Item 4	32,000	29,000	29,000		
	53,000	51,000		51,000	
Total	$71,000	$69,500			$69,500
Inventory valuation			$67,500	$69,000	$69,500

A particular problem arises when several unit costs of a particular commodity must be compared with a single unit *market* price. This situation frequently occurs when first-in, first-out (discussed in Chapter 11) and similar inventory flow procedures are used. In such cases the aggregate cost for the commodity should be compared with the aggregate market, as shown in Exhibit 10–5.

With respect to departures from cost in inventory valuation, once an inventory item has been reduced to a value lower than cost, *subsequent accounting* would consider the reduced value as "cost" for that particular item. Items once reduced for inventory valuation purposes should not be subsequently restored to their original cost.

Recording Lower of Cost or Market in the Accounts

Since purchases are recorded at cost, the introduction of LCM valuation of the inventory each period poses the question of how the *difference* between cost and the LCM amount should be accounted for and reported. Since this difference arises because inventory items on hand can now be replaced for less than their original cost, it is generally called an *inventory holding loss.* The basic issue is whether the inventory holding loss should be separately accounted for and separately reported on the fi-

EXHIBIT 10–5
Lower of Cost or Market and *Fifo*

		Unit Prices				Inventory Valuation	
Commodity	Units on Hand	Actual Cost	Current Market	Aggregate Cost	Aggregate Market	Unit	Total
A	10,000	$4.00					
	10,000	3.85	$3.90	$ 78,500	$ 78,000	$3.90	$78,000
B	10,000	7.70				7.70	77,000
	10,000	8.00	7.90	157,000	158,000	8.00	80,000

nancial statements. Therefore, two distinctly different methods of recording and reporting the effects of the application of lower of cost or market are found in practice.

1. Direct inventory reduction method—The inventory holding loss is not separately recorded and reported. This is accomplished by simply recording the LCM amount for the ending inventory each period. Thus, the holding loss is merged into the ending inventory and cost of goods sold amounts.
2. Inventory allowance method—The inventory holding loss is separately recorded and reported. This is accomplished by using a contra asset account, "Allowance to Reduce Inventory to LCM." Thus, the inventory and cost of goods sold amounts are at original cost and the inventory holding loss is separately recognized.

Both methods derive the same net income and total assets; the methods differ only with respect to detail in the entries, on the income statement, and on the balance sheet.

To illustrate and compare the two methods of recording and reporting LCM, the following simplified data will be used:

		Ending Inventory (in thousands)		
	Valuation	19A	19B	19C
A.	Cost	$10	$20	$30
B.	Market (replacement cost)	11	17	28
C.	LCM (lower of A, B)	10	17	28
D.	Inventory holding loss (A − C)	-0-	3	2

Direct Inventory Reduction Method. This method is straightforward because the ending inventory LCM amount, rather than original cost, is *(a)* recorded directly in the accounts and *(b)* reported on the financial statements.

When a perpetual inventory system is used, the ending inventory accounts (i.e., the control account and the subsidiary records) must be reduced from cost to the lower market price. Exhibit 10–6 illustrates the accounting entries for both the perpetual and periodic inventory systems for each of the three years. The exhibit also illustrates reporting on the income statement and balance sheet. Observe that the holding losses in Years 19B and 19C are not separately reflected. Absent the holding losses, the inventory for 19B would have been reported at $20 instead of $17. Similarly, cost of goods sold would have been reported at $37 instead of $40 in 19B.

Inventory Allowance Method. This method uses separate entries to account for *(a)* inventory at original cost, *(b)* cost of goods sold at original cost, and *(c)* the inventory holding loss. The inventory holding loss at the end of each period is recorded as a debit to a "loss" account, usually called "Inventory Holding Loss," and is credited to "Allowance to Reduce Inventory to LCM." The separate accounting for the holding loss each period then is reflected in the financial statements. Since the latter account is a contra asset account, it is deducted from the inventory amount (at original cost) on the balance sheet. It is similar to the allowance account used to record lower of cost or market for equity securities, as explained and illustrated in Chapter 8.

EXHIBIT 10–6
Recording LCM, Direct Reduction Method

RECORDING LOWER OF COST OR MARKET—DIRECT INVENTORY REDUCTION METHOD
Inventory Holding Loss Merged with Inventory and Cost of Goods Sold
(LCM entries are in boxes for emphasis)

Year 19A:

No holding loss in 19A; account for the inventories and cost of goods sold as usual.

Year 19B: *Perpetual Inventory* *Periodic Inventory*

a. To reduce ending inventory account to LCM:

Cost of goods sold (holding loss $20 − $17) 3
    Inventory (ending) 3

b. To close beginning inventory:

Income summary (or cost of goods sold) 10
    Inventory (beginning) 10

c. To record ending inventory at LCM:

Inventory (ending at LCM direct) 17
    Income summary (or cost of goods sold) 17

Year 19C:

d. To reduce ending inventory account to LCM:

Cost of goods sold (holding loss $30 − $28) 2
    Inventory (ending) 2

e. To close beginning inventory:

Income summary (or cost of goods sold) 17
    Inventory (beginning at LCM) 17

f. To record ending inventory at LCM:

Inventory (ending at LCM direct) 28
    Income summary (or cost of goods sold) 28

REPORTING LOWER OF COST OR MARKET—DIRECT INVENTORY REDUCTION METHOD
Inventory Holding Loss Merged with Inventory and Cost of Goods Sold

	Year 19A	Year 19B	Year 19C
Balance Sheet:			
Current Assets:			
Merchandise Inventory	$10	$17*	$28*
Income Statement			
Sales revenue (assumed)	$50	$65	$81
Cost of goods sold:			
Beginning inventory (at LCM)	$ 0	$10	$17
Purchases (assumed)	40	47	61
Total available	40	57	78
Ending inventory (at LCM)	10	17	28
Cost of goods sold	30	40*	50*
Gross margin	20	25	31
Expenses (assumed)	10	13	16
Income (pretax)	$10	$12	$15

* The holding loss merged with these amounts is: 19B, $3; and 19C, $2.

EXHIBIT 10–7
Recording LCM, Allowance Method

RECORDING LOWER OF COST OR MARKET—INVENTORY ALLOWANCE METHOD
Inventory Holding Loss Accounted for Separately from Inventory and Cost of Goods Sold
(LCM entries are in boxes for emphasis)

Year 19A:

No holding loss in 19A; account for the beginning and ending inventory and cost of goods sold in the usual way.

Year 19B:

	Perpetual Inventory	Periodic Inventory
a. To reduce ending inventory account to LCM:		
Holding loss on ending inventory, LCM ($20 − $17)	3	3
Allowance to reduce inventory to LCM	3	3
b. To close beginning inventory:		
Income summary (or cost of goods sold)		10
Inventory (beginning at cost)		10
c. To record ending inventory at cost:		
Inventory (ending at cost)		20
Income summary (or cost of goods sold)		20

Year 19C:

	Perpetual Inventory	Periodic Inventory
d. To reverse 19B allowance balance (related to 19C beginning inventory):*		
Allowance to reduce inventory to LCM	3	3
Holding loss (reversal) on beginning inventory, LCM	3	3
e. To record holding loss on ending inventory:*		
Holding loss on ending inventory, LCM ($30 − $28)	2	2
Allowance to reduce inventory to LCM	2	2
f. To close beginning inventory:		
Income summary (or cost of goods sold)		20
Inventory (beginning at cost)		20
g. To record ending inventory at cost:		
Inventory (ending at cost)		30
Income summary (or cost of goods sold)		30

    * Entries d and e may be combined as one:

	Perpetual	Periodic
Allowance to reduce inventory to LCM	1	1
Holding loss on inventory, LCM ($3 − $2)	1	1

EXHIBIT 10–8

REPORTING LOWER OF COST OR MARKET—INVENTORY ALLOWANCE METHOD
Holding Losses Separately Reported for Inventory and Cost of Goods Sold

	Year 19A		Year 19B		Year 19C	
Balance Sheet:						
Current Assets:						
Merchandise inventory (at cost)	$10		$20		$30	
Less: Allowance to reduce						
inventory to LCM	0	$10	3	$17	2	$28
Income Statement:						
Sales revenue (assumed)		$50		$65		$81
Cost of goods sold:						
Beginning inventory (at cost)	$ 0		$10		$20	
Purchases (assumed)	40		47		61	
Total goods available for sale	40		57		81	
Ending inventory (at cost)	10		20		30	
Cost of goods sold (at cost)		30		37		51
Gross margin		20		28		30
Expenses (assumed)		(10)		(13)		(16)
Add: Reversal of 19B inventory						
holding loss—LCM						3
Deduct: Holding loss on reduction						
of ending inventory to LCM				(3)		(2)
Income (pretax)		$10		$12		$15

Exhibit 10–7 illustrates the accounting entries for the allowance method for both the perpetual and periodic inventory systems. The "new" entries are set out in boxes for emphasis. The related financial statement presentations for the allowance method are shown in Exhibit 10–8. Observe on both the balance sheet and the income statement that the inventory holding loss is set out separately.

To comprehend the effects of LCM on periodic income, it is important to recall the formula

$$\frac{\text{Beginning}}{\text{Inventory}} + \text{Purchases} - \frac{\text{Ending}}{\text{Inventory}} = \frac{\text{Cost of}}{\text{Goods Sold}}$$

Reduction of the ending inventory in one year (in this example 19B) *increases* total expense (and reduces income) for that year *and decreases* total expense (and increases income) for the following year, 19C. Thus, the effect of LCM (in both methods) is to shift income from one year to the following year when the goods are sold. The direct reduction method obscures this

effect (although it is there), whereas the allowance method sets it out separately. This two-year effect is demonstrated in Exhibits 10–7 and 10–8 (allowance method). Observe that in 19C there is a *reversal* of the 19B holding loss entry ($3) and a separate entry to record the 19C holding loss of $2. The net effect is a *credit* (addition) in the 19C income statement. Unfortunately, this effect sometimes *(a)* is not perceived (when one considers only the direct reduction method) or *(b)* causes a slight confusion (when considering the allowance method). Understanding this dual period effect is the key to the first entry in Exhibit 10–7 for Year 19C which was a reversal of the holding loss entry for the prior year, 19B. Accordingly, if there were a holding loss entry in the prior period, it will always be reversed in full the following period; then the holding loss for the current year should be recorded. Observe in Exhibit 10–8 that the income statement was constructed to reflect both of these effects in 19C—a credit from the reversal and a debit from the 19C holding loss (net effect, $3 − $2 = $1 credit).[9]

Comparison and Evaluation of the Two Methods. The two methods derive the same pretax income (refer to Exhibits 10–6, 10–7, and 10–8), and the same *total* asset amount is reported on the balance sheet. Thus, the central issue in evaluating the two methods hinges on whether the holding losses should be separately reported. There is not general agreement on the preferable response to this issue. Three considerations affect the evaluation:

1. Theoretical considerations—It is useful to make a distinction in accounting between "loss" and "expense" (see Chapter 4). The expense called cost of goods sold is conceptually different from the inventory holding loss because each derives from significantly different causes. On this basis, it appears sound to take the position that these two essentially different amounts should not be merged (for the same reason that a fire loss on the inventory is not merged with cost of goods sold).
2. Usefulness to the statement user—Separate reporting of inventory holding loss provides the statement user with another piece of information that could be important in certain investor (or creditor) decisions.
3. Generally accepted accounting principles—*ARB No. 43,* Chapter 4, Statement 7, paragraph 14, states: "When substantial and unusual losses result from the application of this rule [lower of cost or market] it will frequently be desirable to disclose the amount of the loss in the income statement as a charge separately identified from consumed inventory costs described as cost of goods sold." Moreover, the allowance approach, under which the holding loss is separately reported, is consistent with GAAP for invest-

ments in equity securities (*FASB Statement No. 12* requires the allowance approach).

NET REALIZABLE VALUE AND REPLACEMENT COST

Many accountants believe that inventories should be reported at either net realizable value or current replacement cost, depending upon which is the more clearly determinable, rather than at actual cost. They believe that inventories should be reported at these values whether they are *above* or below actual cost because "market value" better serves the decision maker using the financial statements.

Current generally accepted accounting principles limit the use of net realizable value or replacement cost to specific inventory items that have suffered a diminution to a value below cost because of such factors as damage, obsolescence, shop wear, repossessions, and trade-ins. Trade-ins are discussed in Chapter 13.

Inventory items subject to unusual decreases in current value (such as a fire damage) or which are difficult to value based on the transaction that gave rise to their ownership (such as repossession), should be valued at current replacement cost or net realizable value, whichever is the more clearly determinable. Current replacement cost may be determined by referral to an established "used" market for such items, from bona fide offers, or from regional surveys. Net realizable value is determined as illustrated on page 360.

To illustrate a typical situation, assume X Appliance Store has on hand a repossessed TV set that cost $300. It was sold for $500 and was repossessed when $350 was owed on it by the customer. Assumed further that similar *used* TV sets could be purchased for $290. The repossession should be recorded as follows:

```
Inventory—repossessed merchandise
    (replacement cost) .....................  290
Loss on repossession* .....................   60
    Accounts receivable ..................        350
    * In some situations this may be a gain.
```

Often replacement cost for used or damaged merchandise cannot be realistically or objectively determined. In this situation, net realizable value may be used. To illustrate, assume

[9] For reporting purposes, the net effect, rather than the two separate amounts, generally is reported. In *published* financial statements, holding losses are rarely separately reported on the income statement, although they are of considerable interest to investors and to the business press. It is not unusual to observe the allowance account on the balance sheet as a contra asset (often with nondescriptive titles).

Also, in LCM procedures the implicit assumption is that sales prices will be marked up or down to follow changes in the replacement cost, even for those goods on hand (i.e., a replacement cost pricing strategy).

the facts for X Appliance Store as above, with the added assumptions that no replacement cost is available, the used TV set can be sold for $300, and disposal (resale) costs will approximate 15% of the sales price. The repossession would be recorded as follows:

```
Inventory—repossessed merchandise
  (net realizable value)* ...................   255
Loss on repossession .....................    95
    Accounts receivable ...................          350
   * Computation of inventory value:
     Estimated sales value .....................................   $300
       Less: Estimated disposal costs (15%) ....................     45
     Net realizable value ......................................   $255
```

Assume further that the TV set is subsequently sold for $310 cash. The entry would be as follows:

```
Cash .....................................   310
  Inventory—repossessed
    merchandise .......................          255
  Selling expense (expense recovery) ......           45
  Gain on sale of repossessed
    merchandise .......................           10
```

When repossessions are a recurring feature of operations, estimates of future losses should be made and recorded in the year of sale as a debit to expense and as a credit to an allowance account similar to Allowance for Doubtful Accounts. Under this procedure, when there is a repossession, any loss determined at that subsequent date should be debited to the allowance account.

Damaged and obsolete goods should be reported at current replacement cost in their present condition or, alternatively, at net realizable value.

Inventory losses resulting from storm, fire, flood, and other unusual events should be reported separately (a) as extraordinary items or (b) as a line item listed above income before extraordinary items in conformity with the criteria set forth in *APB Opinion No. 30* "Reporting the Results of Operations" (see Chapter 4).

INVENTORIES VALUED ABOVE COST AT SELLING PRICE

Under certain unusual circumstances an inventory item may be valued at selling price. The circumstances, to conform to generally accepted accounting principles, are as follows:

It is generally recognized that income accrues only at the time of sale, and that gains may not be anticipated by reflecting assets at their current sales prices. For certain articles, however, exceptions are permissible. Inventories of [commodities for which] there is an effective government-controlled market at a fixed monetary value, are ordinarily reflected at selling prices. A similar treatment is not uncommon for inventories representing agricultural, mineral, and other products, units of which are interchangeable and have an immediate marketability at quoted prices and for which appropriate costs may be difficult to obtain. Where such inventories are stated at sales prices, they should of course be reduced by expenditures to be incurred in disposal, and the use of such basis should be fully disclosed in the financial statements.[10]

Under this method, when there is a decrease in selling price, a holding loss would be reported; conversely, when there is an increase in selling price, a holding gain would be reported. Thus, net income would include gross margin and the holding gain or loss for the period. This effect can be attained by valuing the inventory at selling price (also see Chapter 7 on CRC accounting). To illustrate, assume the following simplified data:

Year	Sales	Purchases at Cost	Ending Inventory at Selling Price	Expenses
19A	$ -0-	$1,000	$1,750	$300
19B	1,700	-0-	-0-	300

The comparative results would be the following:

	Cost Basis		Selling Price Basis	
	19A	19B	19A	19B
Income Statement:				
Revenue	$ -0-	$1,700	$750*	$1,700
Cost of goods sold	-0-	(1,000)	-0-	(1,750)
Expenses	(300)	(300)	(300)	(300)
Gain (loss)	$(300)	$ 400	$450	$ (350)
Balance Sheet:				
Inventory	$1,000	$ -0-	$1,750	$ -0-

  * $1,750 − $1,000 = $750.

[10] *Accounting Research Bulletin No. 43*, Chap. 4, par. 16.

Illustrative of several pricing methods, a published financial statement recently reported the following inventory items:

Inventories:
  At market:
    Wheat and other grains, flour and
      meal . . . . $xxxx
  At lower of cost (first-in, first-out) or
    market:
    Soybeans and other raw materials xxxx
    Supplies xxxx
  At cost (last-in, first-out):
    Soybean, linseed, sperm, and crude
      fish oil xxxx

RELATIVE SALES VALUE METHOD

The preceding sections on LCM, net realizable value, replacement cost, and valuation of inventories at selling price represented generally accepted *departures* from cost in specific circumstances. We now return to the use of historical cost in situations where two or more different kinds of inventory items are purchased for a lump sum and a separate cost for each item is required for accounting purposes. Some method of apportioning the *joint cost* must then be used. The apportionment of the lump cost logically should be related to the economic utility of each item and the quantities involved. Since the *sales value* of a particular item may be a reasonable indication of its relative utility, apportionment of the joint cost of such "basket purchases" is usually made on the basis of the *relative sales value* of the several items. Also, when joint costs are incurred subsequent to purchase, such costs frequently are allocated on the basis of relative sales value.

To illustrate, assume a packing plant purchased 1,000 bushels of orchard-run apples (ungraded) for $1,000 and that after purchase the apples were sorted into three grades at a cost of $35 with the following results: Grade A, 200 bushels; Grade B, 300 bushels; and Grade C, 500 bushels. Assume further that sorted apples were selling at the following prices: Grade A, $2; Grade B, $1.50; and Grade C, $0.60. The cost apportionment may be made as shown in Exhibit 10–9.

Assuming a perpetual inventory system, the purchase would be recorded as follows:

Raw material inventory—apples Grade A
  (200 @ $1.80) 360
Raw material inventory—apples Grade B
  (300 @ $1.35) 405
Raw material inventory—apples Grade C
  (500 @ $0.54) 270
    Cash   1,035

In cost allocations such as illustrated above, quantities lost due to shrinkage or spoilage should be assigned no cost, thereby resulting in a greater unit cost for the remaining units. In the case of real estate developments, improvements such as streets and parks may be apportioned in this manner to the cost of the salable areas.

LOSSES ON PURCHASE COMMITMENTS

Occasionally a company will contract with a supplier to purchase a specific *quantity* of ma-

EXHIBIT 10–9
Relative Sales Value Method

	Quantity (bushels)	Unit Sales Price	Total Sales Value	Multi-plier*	Apportioned Cost Total†	Apportioned Cost Per Bushel‡
A	200	$2.00	$ 400	.90	$ 360	$1.80
B	300	1.50	450	.90	405	1.35
C	500	0.60	300	.90	270	0.54
	1,000		$1,150		$1,035	

* Total cost divided by total sales value, that is, $1,035 ÷ $1,150 = .90.
† Total sales value times multiplier.
‡ Unit sales price times multiplier.
(Note: Alternatively, instead of using the multiplier, the arithmetic may be based on fractions or percents for each grade. The results would be the same.)

terials during a specified future *period* at an agreed *unit cost*. Basically, such purchase commitments (contracts) may be *(a)* subject to revision or cancellation before the end of the contract period or *(b)* not subject to revision or cancellation. Each of these situations requires different accounting and reporting procedures.

In the case of purchase contracts *subject to revision or cancellation* where a future loss is *possible* and the amount of the commitment is material, full disclosure requires a footnote. To illustrate, assume XY Company entered into a purchase contract during October 1979 that stated: "During 1980, 50,000 units of Material X will be purchased at $5 each. Upon 60 days' notice, this contract is subject to revision or cancellation by either party." A footnote similar to the following should be included in the financial statements for 1979 (no accounting entry would be made):

> Note 1. At the end of 1979 a contract for the purchase during 1980 of a maximum of $250,000 for raw materials during 1980 was in effect. The contract can be revised or canceled upon 60 days' notice by either party. At the end of 1979, the materials had a current replacement cost of $240,000.

Where purchase contracts are *not subject to revision or cancellation,* and when a loss is probable and the amount can be reasonably estimated, the loss and related liability should be recorded in the accounts and reported in the financial statements. In the above example, assume the $240,000 market price is reasonably measured and has a high probability of materializing. In *these* circumstances the loss on the purchase commitment should be recorded as follows (assuming a noncancellable contract):

```
Estimated loss on purchase
   commitment .....................  10,000
   Liability—noncancellable
     purchase commitment .........          10,000
```

The estimated loss is reported on the 1979 income statement, and the liability is reported on the balance sheet. When the goods are received in 1980, they are debited to Merchandise Inventory (or purchases) at their market value and the liability account is debited for the $10,000 estimated in 1979. To illustrate, assume the

above raw materials have a market value at date of delivery of $235,000. The purchase entry would be as follows:

```
Raw materials (or purchases) .......  235,000
Liability—noncancellable purchase
   commitment....................   10,000
Loss on purchase contract..........    5,000
   Cash ........................           250,000
```

This treatment records the loss in the period when it actually occurred. This treatment is consistent with the provisions of *ARB No. 43,* Chapter 4, Statement 10, and *FASB Statement No. 5,* "Accounting for Contingencies" (see Chapter 9).

Appendix—Replacement Cost Disclosure

Chapter 7 discusses price level effects and the replacement cost concept as applied to financial statements. The brief discussion to follow focuses on the replacement cost of *(a)* inventory and *(b)* cost of goods sold.

The Securities and Exchange Commission (SEC) issued *Accounting Series Release No. 190 (ASR No. 190),* March 23, 1976, which states:

> The new rule as adopted requires *registrants* who have *inventories* and gross property, plant and equipment which aggregates more than $100 million and which comprises more than 10% of total assets to *disclose* the estimated current replacement cost of *inventories* and productive capacity at the end of each fiscal year and the approximate amount of *cost of sales* and depreciation based on replacement cost for the two most recent full fiscal years. (Emphasis supplied.)

ASR No. 190 states the following with respect to the disclosure:

> This information may be presented *either* in a footnote to the financial statements or in a separate section of the financial statements following the notes. In either place, the information may be designated as "unaudited."
>
> These proposals were designed to enable investors to obtain more relevant information about the current economics of a business enterprise in an *inflationary economy* than that provided solely by financial statements prepared on

the basis of historical cost [and] to provide information to investors which will assist them in obtaining an understanding of the current costs of operating the business . . . [and] to provide information which will enable investors to determine the *current cost* of *inventories* and productive capacity as a measure of current economic investment in these assets. . . . (Emphasis supplied.)

Thus, the requirement includes disclosure of *(a)* the replacement cost of the ending inventory (excluding obsolete and discontinued items) and *(b)* the approximate amount of cost of goods sold as if they had been calculated by estimating the *replacement cost* of the goods sold.

SEC Staff Accounting Bulletin (SAB) No. 7, which interprets *ASR No. 190,* defines replacement cost as "the lowest amount that would have to be paid in the normal course of business to obtain a new asset of equivalent operating or productive capacity." Basically, replacement cost for the ending inventory should be estimated at its then-current market cost and cost of goods sold would be represented by the weighted average of the various current market costs incurred during the period.

Because of the wide range of situations in different industries and companies and the lack of experience in applying the replacement cost concept, numerous approaches for estimating replacement cost are being used on an experimental basis, such as

a. Market prices currently quoted by vendors.
b. Long-term contract prices.
c. Historical costs restated by applying specific price indexes (see Chapter 7).
d. Historical costs restated by applying general price indexes (see Chapter 7).
e. Estimated current cost to replace.
f. Current cost of equivalent units.
g. Updated standard costs.
h. Present value of estimated net cash flows.

ASR No. 190 does not prescribe "replacement cost" accounting. The traditional historical cost model is not disturbed. Rather, it specifies *separate disclosure* of a limited number of estimated replacement cost numbers. It is a piecemeal approach because all elements of the financial statements are not stated on a replacement cost basis in the supplements to the historical cost statements.

Exhibit 10–10 presents a typical disclosure of the replacement cost of inventories and cost of goods sold.

One of the flaws in *ASR No. 190* is that it requires the disclosure of the current replacement cost of inventory and cost of goods sold, operational assets and depreciation, but it specifically prohibits the disclosure of holding gains on inventory and operational assets. Many accountants believe that *ASR No. 190* thus allows companies to present only half the facts, and during inflation, the negative half at that. A more basic flaw is germane to replacement cost (or to any departure from historical cost). The flaw is not conceptual or theoretical because the theory is well developed. The flaw is the difficulty in operationalizing the theory. For example, it would be extremely difficult to develop, with any reasonable degree of precision, an estimate of the replacement cost of the identical productive capacity of most major operational assets (such as a plant). Factors such as technological improvements make this a very formidable task indeed. Yet, this is what *ASR No. 190* requires.

The experiment is still in the embryonic stage. Only time will tell the direction of the generally accepted accounting model of the next generation. In the meantime, many companies are busily attempting to measure current replacement costs with reasonable precision (see Chapter 7). *ASR No. 190,* which was imposed without prior experimentation, also can be criticized because it draws no distinction as to the effects of inflation on companies whose monetary liabilities significantly exceed their monetary assets and on those companies in an opposite position. The movement toward disclosure of the replacement cost of inventories will receive further emphasis if the provisions of a December, 1978 exposure draft of a proposed *FASB Financial Accounting Standards,* "Financial Reporting and Changing Prices" is adopted (see Chapter 7).

QUESTIONS

1. In general, why should the accountant and management be concerned with inventories?

EXHIBIT 10–10
Reporting Replacement Cost Information

17. Replacement cost information (unaudited)

Regulations of the Securities and Exchange Commission require that certain replacement cost data be stated in 1976 reports filed with the Commission. The corporation, believing that such information may be of interest to shareholders, is including the required data, plus additional data below.

	Millions of Dollars	
	Historical Costs	Replacement Costs
	For Year Ending 12/31/76	
Depreciation and depletion	$ 1,448	$ 2,500
Cost of sales, excluding depreciation and depletion	31,467	31,505
	At December 31, 1976	
Inventories:		
Crude, products and merchandise	3,794	6,020
Materials and supplies	440	440
Property, plant, and equipment:		
Gross investment:		
Land, leases, and easements	1,302	2,930
Incomplete construction	4,778	4,778
Producing (mineral resource)	8,340	15,420
All other	15,082	32,830
Total	29,502	55,958
Net investment:		
Land, leases, and easements	1,248	2,820
Incomplete construction	4,778	4,778
Producing (mineral resource)	4,221	7,220
All other	8,424	17,850
Total	$18,671	$32,668

The Commission has warned, and the corporation agrees, that the data set forth above should not be interpreted as showing the complete effect of inflation on net income. Among other possible effects, no consideration has been given in these data to: holding gains or losses, revised economic lives of replaced assets versus existing assets, replacement of assets with a different type, non-replacement of assets, operating cost efficiencies of replacement of existing assets, future price and cost levels, tax and other effects which might be encountered.

The replacement costs presented herein, while believed reasonable, are necessarily subjective. They do not necessarily represent amounts for which the assets could be sold, costs which will be incurred in future periods, or the manner in which actual replacement of assets will occur. Actual costs of replacement, where, when and to the extent made, may differ significantly from the amounts reported here.

The replacement cost data have been developed, for the most part, by application of appropriate indices to historical cost; no attempt has been made to reengineer or redesign worldwide facilities. Thus, for the most part, the data reflect replacement in-place, in-kind.

Replacement cost of refining and substantial amounts of other plant and equipment was determined through application of an internally developed construction cost index, available for major worldwide locations, which reflects current local labor and material markets, competition and corporation experience. Other local industry indices were applied where considered more appropriate to achieve a credible result. In the case of ocean tankers, current construction costs were used even though, for limited amounts, current market prices for purchase of existing tonnage were less. Items such as automotive equipment and office buildings were costed at current market prices.

Land, a major item in the case of the corporation, did not require updating in the Commission's requirements but has been in the foregoing data, based on appraised value or estimated current market prices. The historical cost of "mineral resource assets" on the corporation's books has been updated by use of appropriate indices; no value of the underlying oil, gas or other underground reserves is included in either the historical or replacement costs. Refining capacity in total is included in replacement cost data even though, in some areas, there is significant capacity that is currently idle.

Source: Exxon Corporation 1976 Annual Report, p. 40.

2. List and briefly explain the usual inventory classifications.

3. What general rule is applied by accountants in determining what goods should be included in inventory?

4. Assume you are in the process of adjusting and closing the books at the end of the fiscal year (for the purchaser). What treatment for inventory purposes would you accord the following goods in transit? *(a)* invoice received for $5,000, shipped f.o.b. shipping point; *(b)* invoice received for $10,000, shipped f.o.b. destination; and *(c)* invoice received for $1,000, shipped f.o.b. shipping point

and delivery refused on the last day of the period because of damaged condition.

5. Complete the following:

	Include in Inventory	
	Yes	No
a. Goods out on consignment.	___	___
b. Goods held on consignment.	___	___
c. Merchandise at our branch for sale.	___	___
d. Merchandise at conventions for display purposes.	___	___
e. Goods held by our agents for us.	___	___
f. Goods held by us for sale on commission.	___	___
g. Goods held by us but awaiting return to vendor because of damaged condition.	___	___
h. Goods returned to us from buyer, reason unknown to date.	___	___

6. Explain the principal aspects of a periodic inventory system.

7. Why is cost of goods sold often characterized as a residual amount?

8. Explain the effect of each of the following errors in the ending inventory of a trading business (ignore income taxes):
   a. Incorrectly included 100 units of Commodity A, valued at $1 per unit, in the ending inventory; the purchase was recorded.
   b. Incorrectly included 200 units of Commodity B, valued at $2 per unit, in the ending inventory; the purchase was not recorded.
   c. Incorrectly excluded 300 units of Commodity C, valued at $3 per unit, from the ending inventory; the purchase was recorded.
   d. Incorrectly excluded 400 units of Commodity D, valued at $4 per unit, from the ending inventory; the purchase was not recorded.

9. What is meant by the "accounting value" of inventory? What accounting principles predominate in measuring this value?

10. In determining *unit cost* for inventory purposes, how should the following items be treated?
   a. Freight on goods and materials purchased.
   b. Purchase returns.
   c. Purchase (cash) discounts.

11. Should purchase discounts be (a) deducted in total in the income statement for the period in which the discounts arose or (b) deducted in part in the income statement and in part from inventory in

the balance sheet? Assume that two thirds of the goods purchased were sold by year-end. Explain.

12. Cost is the primary basis for inventory valuation. List the four exceptions to cost discussed in the chapter. Under what specified conditions is each generally acceptable?

13. Why is the concept of LCM applied to inventory valuation?

14. What is the rationale underlying the use of the "ceiling" and "floor" values in determining "market" in the application of the LCM concept?

15. How should damaged or obsolete merchandise on hand at the end of the period be valued for inventory purposes?

16. What are the basic assumptions underlying the relative sales value method when used in allocating costs for inventory purposes?

17. Briefly outline the accounting and reporting of losses on purchase commitments when (a) the purchase contract is subject to revision or cancellation and (b) it is noncancellable and a loss is reasonably probable.

DECISION CASE 10–1

Ward Manufacturing Company has been in operation since 1955 and has experienced satisfactory growth since that time. L. Ward, the organizer, was an experienced and skilled machinist having operated a small custom machine shop for years. In 1955, with the financial assistance of a friend, Ward organized the company to manufacture specially designed trailers for the transportation of horses. Most of the trailers were designed to haul one horse; consequently, they were built to meet the particular desires of each customer. These trailers varied from a standard type to deluxe models in keeping with the horse-show tradition. In 1963 the company started making trailers for boats. Two standard models were developed for sale to sporting goods stores; and, in addition, trailers were made to meet the specifications of individual buyers.

The company recently experienced an unexpected demand for boat trailers which was attributed to their quality, competitive price, and design. Ward is having considerable difficulty keeping up with this demand and hesitates to add capacity, workers, and materials needed, on the basis of expectations, rather than on the basis of firm orders. As a consequence, the firm has lost some business. Customarily a 50% deposit is required on all custom-made trailers.

Ward is particularly interested in the manufacturing side of the business, and he is inclined to ignore the financial and management aspects. As a result of some income tax difficulties, Ward engaged an outside CPA to set up records and help with the financial management of the company. One employee spends part time on the present recordkeeping, which involves minimum records on cash, salaries, receivables, payables, and wages.

The company regularly stocks 23 different items of raw materials and numerous small supplies such as bolts, screws, welding materials, and paint. The company loses about two thirds of the available cash discounts on purchases through oversight. Customarily the company pays freight on the purchases. Finished goods on the lot usually consist of 8 to 15 horse trailers, 20 to 35 boat trailers, plus small quantities of eight other small items manufactured. Frequently, customers leave trailers on the lot a week or more before picking them up. Several kinds of raw material currently on hand are of such a nature that the replacement cost is less than the original cost. The company has always had difficulty with raw materials and supplies; frequently shortages hold up work on jobs for days. Often substitutions of higher cost materials are necessary due to items being out of stock. The raw materials are stored both outside and inside, and individual workers select the material as they need it on a help-yourself basis. Ward feels that the company cannot afford an inventory clerk. Items are reordered from a notebook kept on Ward's desk where individual workers are instructed to write down any items that are low or out of stock. When raw materials are received, they are moved to the storage area and placed wherever space is available. Space is a problem. No inventory records are maintained. No payments are made for raw materials unless the invoice is signed by the employee that checked in the goods. Theft is no problem for the company.

The CPA has decided to install a job order cost system so that costs will be accumulated by job for direct material, direct labor, and manufacturing overhead; and it is recognized that in view of the small size of the company, the overall system must be simple and easy to operate.

The CPA is concerned about the raw material and finished goods inventory situations in particular and has asked you to make recommendations relative to the inventory problem. The CPA has decided to employ *Fifo* and LCM. Specifically, the CPA wants your suggestions for the company relative to (1) recommendations for better inventory control, (2) determination of quantities in inventory, and (3) the appropriateness of applying LCM to the valuation of the inventory. Sound reasons are expected to support your suggestions.

Required:

Narrate your recommendations to the company giving particular attention to the raw materials and finished goods inventories. Give supporting reasons.

EXERCISES

Exercise 10–1

Listed below for Wilson Sales Company are items of inventory that are in question. The company stores a substantial portion of the merchandise in a separate warehouse and transfers damaged goods to a special inventory account. The company policy is "satisfied customers."

a.	Items counted in warehouse by inventory crew	$50,000
b.	Invoice received for goods ordered, goods shipped but not received (Wilson pays the freight)	500
c.	Items shipped today, f.o.b. destination, invoice mailed to customer	70
d.	Items currently being used for window displays	800
e.	Items on counters for sale per inventory count (not in [a])	9,000
f.	Items in shipping department, invoice not mailed to customer	140
g.	Items in receiving department, refused by Wilson because of damage (not in [a])	100
h.	Items shipped today, f.o.b. shipping point, invoice mailed to customer	400
i.	Items included in warehouse count, damaged, not returnable	200
j.	Items included in warehouse count, specifically crated and segregated for shipment to customer in 5 days per sales contract, with return privilege	300
k.	Items in receiving department, returned by customer, no communication received from customer	100
l.	Items ordered and in receiving department, invoice not received from supplier	500

Required:

Complete the following tabulation to reflect the correct inventory:

Item	Exclude or Include in Inventory	Amount	Explanation
a. Items counted in warehouse	Include	$50,000	Items on hand
b. Etc.			
Total inventory valuation		$_____	

Exercise 10-2

The records of X Company reflected the following data: sales revenue, $80,000; purchases, $58,000; net income to sales revenue, 5%; beginning inventory, $9,000; and expenses, $20,000.

Required:

1. Reconstruct the income statement. Assume a periodic inventory system.
2. Give entries at the end of the period for the inventories and the other closing entries assuming Case A—a periodic inventory system; and Case B—a perpetual inventory system.

Exercise 10-3

The records for K Company at December 31, 19A, reflected the following:

	Units	Unit Amount
Sales during the period	10,000	$13
Inventory at beginning of period	2,000	6
Merchandise purchased during the period (for cash)	18,400	6
Purchase returns during the period (cash refund)	100	6
Inventory at end of the period	?	6
Total expenses (excluding cost of goods sold), $45,000.		

Required:

In parallel columns, give entries for the above transactions, including all entries at the end of the period assuming:

Case A—Periodic inventory system.

Case B—Perpetual inventory system.

Use the following format:

Accounts	Case A	Case B

Exercise 10-4

The independent CPA for Stine Company found the following errors in the records of the company:

a. Incorrect exclusion from the ending inventory of items costing $4,000 for which the purchase was not recorded.
b. Inclusion in the ending inventory of goods costing $7,000, although a purchase was not recorded. The goods in question were being held on consignment from Conley Company.

c. Incorrect exclusion of $2,000 from the inventory count at the end of the period. The goods were in transit (f.o.b. shipping point); the invoice had been received, and the purchase was recorded.
d. Inclusion of items on the receiving dock that were being held for return to the vendor because of damage. In counting the goods in the receiving department, these items were incorrectly included. With respect to these goods, a purchase of $6,000 had been recorded.

The records (uncorrected) showed the following amounts: *(a)* purchases, $180,000; *(b)* pretax income, $20,000; *(c)* accounts payable, $30,000; and *(d)* inventory at the end of the period, $50,000.

Required:

Set up a table to reflect the uncorrected balances, changes occasioned by correction of the errors, and the corrected balances for (1) purchases, (2) pretax income, (3) accounts payable, and (4) ending inventory.

Exercise 10-5

The records of Tyler Company reflected the following:

Sales revenue		$160,000
Cost of goods sold:		
Beginning inventory	$10,000	
Purchases	85,000	
Goods available for sale	95,000	
Ending inventory	25,000	70,000
Gross margin		90,000
Expenses		60,000
Net income (pretax)		$ 30,000

The following errors were found that had not been corrected:

a. Accrued expenses not recognized, $6,000.
b. Revenues collected in advance amounting to $4,000 are included in the sales revenue amount.
c. Goods costing $10,000 were incorrectly included in the ending inventory (they were being held on consignment from Blue Company). No purchase was recorded.
d. Goods costing $3,000 were correctly included in the ending inventory; however, no purchase was recorded (assume a credit purchase).

Required:

1. Recast the income statement on a correct basis.
2. What amounts would be incorrect on the balance sheet if the errors are not corrected?

Exercise 10–6

Dawson Company uses a perpetual inventory system. The items on hand are inventoried on a rotation basis throughout the year so that all items are checked twice each year. At the end of the year, the following data relating to goods on hand are available:

Product	Per Perpetual Inventory Units	Per Perpetual Inventory Unit Cost	Per Physical Count (units)
A	200	$6	180
B	1,500	2	1,520
C	2,000	3	1,900
D	8,000	1	8,000
E	13,000	2	12,800

Required:

Determine the amount of the inventory overage or shortage and give the adjustment to the perpetual inventory records. Give the entry to record the final disposition of any discrepancy that needs to be recorded.

Exercise 10–7

On December 31, 19B, Ransom Company prepared the annual financial statements and used an ending inventory valuation of $330,000 based on a periodic inventory system. The accounts for 19B have been adjusted and closed. Subsequently, the independent auditor located several discrepancies in the 19B ending inventory. These were discussed with the company accountant who then prepared the following schedule:

a.	Merchandise in the store (at 10% above cost)	$330,000
b.	Merchandise out on consignment at sales price (including markup of 60% on selling price)	9,600
c.	Goods held on consignment from the Brown Electrical Company at sales price (sales commission, 20% of sales price included)	2,400
d.	Goods purchased, in transit (shipped f.o.b. shipping point; estimated freight, not included, $600), invoice price	5,000
e.	Goods out on approval, sales price, $1,500, cost, $1,000	1,500
	Total inventory as corrected	$348,500

Average income tax rate, 45%.

Required:

1. The auditor did not agree with the "corrected" inventory amount of $348,500. Compute the correct ending inventory amount (show computations) by modifying the "corrected" balance of $348,500.

2. List the items on the income statement and balance sheet for 19B that should be corrected for the above errors and give the amount of the error in the balance of each item affected.
3. Since the accounts have been closed for 19B, a correcting entry in January 19C is needed. Give the required correcting entry.

Exercise 10–8

Roberts Trading Company purchased merchandise on credit for $20,000; terms, 2/15, n/30. Payment for three fourths of the recorded liability was made during the discount period; the balance was paid after the discount period. The company uses a perpetual inventory system.

Required:

Give entries in parallel columns to record the purchase and payments on the liability assuming

a. Net of discount approach is used for purchase discounts.
b. Gross amount approach is used for purchase discounts.

Which approach is preferable? Why?

Exercise 10–9

Economy Trading Company purchased merchandise on credit for $40,000; terms, 2/10, n/30. Payment was made within the discount period. At the end of the fiscal period, one fourth of this merchandise was unsold. Determine (1) the cost of goods sold that would be reported on the income statement and (2) the ending inventory valuation as regards this particular lot of merchandise assuming

a. Purchases and accounts payable are recorded at gross, and purchase discounts are reported on the income statement as other income.
b. Purchases and accounts payable are recorded at gross, and purchase discounts are deducted in total from purchases on the income statement.
c. Purchases and accounts payable both are recorded at net.

Evaluate the several approaches. Which approach is preferable? Why?

Exercise 10–10

HiFi Company, a large dealer in radio and television sets, buys large quantities of a television model which costs $400. The contract reads that if 100 or more are purchased during the year, a bonus or rebate of $15 per set will be made. On December 15, the records showed that 150 sets had been purchased and that 10 remained on hand in inventory. A claim for the rebate was made to the vendor, and a check was received on January 20 after the books were closed.

Required:

1. At what valuation should the inventory be shown on December 31? Why?
2. What entry should be made relative to the rebate on December 31? Why?
3. What entry would be made on January 20? Why?

Exercise 10–11

Case A—Small Company had 1,000 units of Product A in inventory at the end of the fiscal period. The unit cost was $60; estimated distribution costs, $3 per unit; and the "normal" profit is $4 per unit. Compute the unit valuation of the inventory under each separate case listed below. Apply the LCM procedure in accordance with the "exceptions" specified by the Committee on Accounting Procedure of the AICPA.

Case	Anticipated Sales Price	Current Replacement Cost
a.	$65	$61
b.	70	62
c.	60	58
d.	58	50
e.	66	57
f.	68	61
g.	50	44
h.	59	57
i.	61	53
j.	73	59

Case B—The management of Small Company has taken the position that under the LCM procedure the two items listed below should be reported in the ending inventory at $14,600 (total). Do you agree? If not, indicate the correct inventory valuation by item. Show computations.

"Handyman" hedge clippers: 300 on hand; cost, $22 each; replacement cost, $16; estimated sales price, $30; estimated distribution cost, $9 each; and normal profit, 10% of the sales price.

"Handyman" edgers: 200 on hand; cost, $40 each; replacement cost, $36 each; estimated sales price, $90; estimated distribution cost, $28; and normal profit, 20% of sales.

Exercise 10–12

The inventories for the years 19A and 19B are shown below for Ryan Retailers, Inc.:

Inventory Date	Original Cost	Lower of Cost or Market	Difference
1/1/19A	$6,000	$6,000	$ -0-
12/31/19A	7,000	6,500	500
12/31/19B	9,000	9,000	-0-

Required:

1. Give in parallel columns the journal entries to apply the LCM procedure to the inventories for 19A and 19B, assuming the company uses the direct inventory reduction method (where the holding loss is not separately recognized) using *(a)* perpetual inventory procedures and *(b)* periodic inventory procedures.
2. Give in parallel columns the journal entries to apply the LCM procedure to the inventories for 19A and 19B, assuming the company utilizes the inventory allowance method where the holding losses in the beginning and ending inventories are separately recognized using *(a)* perpetual inventory procedures and *(b)* periodic inventory procedures.
3. What are the primary advantages and disadvantages of each method?

Exercise 10–13

Snappy Canning Company purchased 1,910 bushels of ungraded apricots at $2 per bushel. The apricots were sorted as follows: Grade One, 600 bushels; Grade Two, 400 bushels; and Grade Three, 900 bushels. Handling and sorting costs amounted to $500. The current market prices for graded apricots were Grade One, $4 per bushel; Grade Two, $3 per bushel; and Grade Three, $1 per bushel. The company utilizes a perpetual inventory system. What entry should be made to record the purchase? Show computations of total and unit costs for each grade assuming the relative sales value method of cost allocation is used.

Exercise 10–14

Community Development Corporation purchased a tract of land for development purposes. The tract was subdivided as follows: 30 lots to sell at $6,000 per lot and 80 lots to sell at $9,000 per lot. The tract cost $200,000, and an additional $25,000 was spent in general development costs. Assuming cost allocation is based on the relative sales value method, give entries for (1) purchase of the tract and payment of the development costs, (2) sale of one $6,000 lot, and (3) sale of one $9,000 lot. Assume a perpetual inventory system.

Exercise 10–15

Swift Realty Company purchased and subdivided a tract of land at a cost of $440,000. The subdivision was on the following basis:

20% used for streets, alleys, and parks.

30% divided into 100 lots to sell for $4,000 each.

40% divided into 200 lots to sell for $3,000 each.

10% divided into 50 lots to sell for $2,000 each.

Required:

1. Record the purchase of the lots. Use the relative sales value method to allocate the total cost of $440,000 to the three categories of lots. Assume a perpetual inventory system.
2. During the final month of the year, the paving was completed (included in the $440,000 cost) and sales were made. At the end of the first year, 20, $4,000 lots; 50, $3,000 lots; and 10, $2,000 lots are on hand. Compute the valuation of the inventory at year-end and record the sales and cost of goods sold amounts for each category of lots. Assume the lots are sold for cash.

Exercise 10–16

Sweet Candy Company purchased 1,000 bags of orchard-run pecans at a cost of $3,460. In addition, the company incurred $50 for transportation and grading. The pecans graded out as follows:

Grade	Quantity	Current Market Price per Bag
A	300	$7.00
B	500	6.00
C	150	5.00
Waste	50	

Required:

Assuming the relative sales value method is used to allocate joint costs, give

1. The entry for purchase assuming a perpetual inventory system (show computations).
2. Valuation of ending inventory assuming the following quantities are on hand: Grade A, 100 bags; Grade B, 80 bags; and Grade C, 20 bags.
3. Sale of 20 bags of the Grade A pecans.

Exercise 10–17

A fire damaged some of the merchandise held for sale by Thomas Appliance Company. Five television sets and six stereo sets were damaged and not covered by insurance. They will be repaired and sold as used sets. Data are as follows:

	Per Set	
	Television	Stereo
Inventory (at cost).................	$300	$200
Estimated cost to repair	40	30
Estimated cost to sell	20	20
Estimated sales price	120	90

Required:

1. Compute the appropriate inventory value for each set.
2. Give the separate entries to record the damaged goods inventory for the television and stereo sets. Assume a perpetual inventory system.
3. Give the entries to record the subsequent repair of the television sets and the stereo sets. (Credit Cash.)
4. Give the entry to record sale for cash of one television set and one stereo set. (Credit Distribution Costs.)

Exercise 10–18

Zakin Corporation, during 1979, signed a contract with Young Company to "purchase 20,000 subassemblies at $30 each during 1980."

Required:

1. On December 31, 1979, end of the annual accounting period, the financial statements are to be prepared. Under what additional contractual and economic conditions should disclosure of the contract terms be made only by means of a note in the financial statements? Prepare an appropriate note. Assume the cost is dropping and the estimated current replacement cost is $575,000.
2. What contractual and economic conditions would require accrual of a loss? Give the accrual entry.
3. Assume the subassemblies are received in 1980 when their cost was at the estimate you used in Requirement 2. The contract was paid in full. Give the required entry.

PROBLEMS

Problem 10–1

Assume you are the independent auditor for the XY Manufacturing Corporation. The ending inventory for the year ended December 31, 19A, is under consideration. The following problems related to the inventory have arisen, and the company accountant requests your advice on them:

Part A

	Units	
	Material A @ $3	Material B @ $5
Raw material unit inventory data on December 31, 19A—Items counted in warehouse (excluding the items below)	15,000	3,500
a. Purchase invoice received, items not received (f.o.b. shipping point)		300
b. Items set aside for return to vendor next period per agreement December 20, 19A; not up to guaranteed specifications, returned January 2, 19B		100
c. Items issued to factory and returned by them in damaged condition, not returnable to vendor		50
d. Items from a shipment partly damaged when received, returnable to vendor per agreement; shipped January 3, 19B		40
e. Items purchased, on receiving dock, refused because of damage	50	
f. Items purchased, on receiving dock, invoice not received	200	300
g. Items to be returned to vendor per agreement, rejected for incorrect specs	150	
h. Purchase invoice received, items not received (f.o.b. destination)	20	100

Part B

	Units	
	Product X @ $10	Product Y @ $20
Finished goods unit inventory data on December 31, 19A—Items counted in warehouse (excluding the items below)	25,000	12,000
a. Items shipped to customer on January 1, 19B, invoice mailed December 31, 19A (f.o.b. shipping point)		500
b. Items completed by factory, counted in the work in process inventory; not transported to warehouse	1,000	
c. Items on receiving dock, returned by customer because of major damage, notification from customer received		50
d. Items on trucking company dock, invoice mailed to customer, buyer pays freight	500	
e. Items in damaged condition	20	10
f. Items in shipping department, invoice not mailed to customer	80	
g. Items shipped December 31, 19A (f.o.b. destination), invoice mailed to customer January 2, 19B	100	
h. Items on consignment to Brady Distributing Company	400	800
i. Items specifically segregated and crated for shipment to XY Branch No. 10	100	100
j. Items used for display purposes	10	30
k. Items specifically segregated and crated and being held for shipment to customer January 10, 19B, per contract of sale for December 19A		500
l. Items on receiving dock, returned by customer, no notification received (not damaged)	20	

Required:

Compute the valuation of the ending inventory of raw materials and finished goods indicating specifically what items you would include and exclude. Give reasons you would present to the company relative to any doubtful items. The following format is recommended:

		Inventory Valuation				
	Inventory Include/	Material A		Material B		
Item	Exclude	Units	Amount	Units	Amount	Explanation

Problem 10–2

Darby Company's fiscal period ends December 31, 19A. The company uses a periodic inventory system. An independent CPA was engaged after the end of the year to perform an audit. Therefore, the CPA did not observe the taking of the inventory. As a result, an examination was made of the inventory records only.

The financial statements prepared by the company (uncorrected) showed the following: ending inventory, $75,000; accounts receivable, $60,000; accounts payable, $30,000; sales, $400,000; net purchases, $160,000; and pretax income, $45,000.

The following data were found during the audit:

a. Merchandise that cost $11,000 and sold on December 31, 19A, for $16,000 was included in the ending inventory. The sale was recorded. The goods were in transit; however, a clerk failed to note that the goods were shipped f.o.b. shipping point.

b. Merchandise that cost $6,000 was excluded from the ending inventory and not recorded as a sale for $7,500 on December 31, 19A. The goods had been specifically segregated. According to the terms of the contract of sale, ownership will not pass until actual delivery.

c. Merchandise that cost $15,000 was included in the ending inventory. The related purchase has not been recorded. The goods had been shipped by the vendor f.o.b. destination; and the invoice, but not the goods, was received on December 30, 19A.

d. Merchandise in transit that cost $7,000 was excluded from inventory because it was not on hand. The shipment from the vendor was f.o.b. shipping point. The purchase was recorded on December 29, 19A, when the invoice was received.

e. Merchandise in transit that cost $13,000 was excluded from inventory because it had not arrived. Although the invoice had arrived, the related purchase was not recorded by December 31, 19A. The merchandise was shipped by the vendor f.o.b. shipping point.

f. Merchandise that cost $8,000 was included in the ending inventory since it was on hand. The merchandise had been rejected because of incorrect specifications and was being held for return to the vendor. The merchandise was recorded as a purchase on December 26, 19A.

g. Merchandise that cost $18,000 was excluded from the inventory, and the related sale for $23,000 was recorded. The goods had been segregated in the warehouse for shipment; there was no contract for sale but a "tentative order by phone."

h. Merchandise that cost $10,000 was out on consignment to Goode Distributing Company and was excluded from the ending inventory. The merchandise was recorded as a sale of $25,000 when shipped to Goode on December 2, 19A.

i. Merchandise received on January 2, 19B, costing $800 was recorded on December 31, 19A. An invoice on hand showed the shipment was made f.o.b. supplier's warehouse on December 31, 19A. Since the merchandise was not on hand at December 31, 19A, it was not included in the inventory.

j. A sealed packing case containing a product costing $900 was in the Darby shipping room when the physical inventory was taken. It was included in the inventory because it was marked *"Hold for customer's shipping instructions."* Investigation revealed that the customer signed a purchase contract dated December 18, 19A, but that the case was shipped and the customer billed on January 10, 19B. A sale was recorded on December 18, 19A.

k. A special item, fabricated to order for a customer, was finished and in the shipping room on December 31, 19A. The customer had inspected it and was satisfied with it. The customer was billed in full for $1,000 on that date. The item was included in inventory because it was shipped on January 4, 19B.

l. Merchandise costing $700 was received on December 28, 19A. The goods were excluded from inventory, and a purchase was not recorded. You located the related papers in the hands of the purchasing agent; they indicated *"on consignment from Baker Company."*

m. Merchandise costing $2,000 was received on January 8, 19B, and the related purchase invoice recorded January 9. The invoice showed the shipment was made on December 29, 19A, f.o.b. *destination.* The merchandise was excluded from the inventory.

Required:

1. Prepare a schedule with one column for each of the six financial statement items (starting with the uncorrected balances), plus any other columns deemed useful. Show the specific corrections to each balance and the corrected balances. Explain the basis for your decision on all items.
2. Give the entry to correct the accounts assuming the accounts for 19A have been closed.

(AICPA adapted)

Problem 10–3

Hiam Company completed the following selected transactions during 19A for Product A:

	Units	Unit Amount
Beginning inventory	5,000	$18
Purchases	20,000	18
Purchase returns	1,000	18
Sales	18,000	40
Sales returns	100	40
Ending inventory per physical count	5,800	
Inventory shortage	?	
Expenses (excluding cost of goods sold and income taxes), $328,400.		

Required:

1. In parallel columns, give entries for the above transactions including entries at the end of the accounting period, December 31, 19A, for (assume a 40% income tax rate and cash transactions):

   Case A—A periodic inventory system.

   Case B—A perpetual inventory system.

2. Prepare a multiple-step income statement assuming a periodic inventory system and 20,000 shares of common stock outstanding.
3. What amounts, if any, would be different on the income statement assuming a perpetual inventory system is used? Explain.

Problem 10–4

Linden Company has completed the income statement and balance sheet (summarized and uncorrected shown below) at December 31, 19A. Subsequently, during the audit, the following items were discovered:

a. Expenses amounting to $3,000 were not accrued.
b. A conditional sale on credit for $9,000 was recorded on December 31, 19A. The goods, which cost $5,000, were included in the ending inventory because they had not been shipped since the cus-

tomer's address was not known and the credit had not been approved. Ownership had not passed.

c. Merchandise purchased on December 31, 19A, on credit for $6,000 was included in the ending inventory because the goods were on hand. A purchase was not recorded because the accounting department had not received the invoice from the vendor.

d. The ending inventory was overstated by $10,000 due to an addition error on the inventory sheet.

e. A sale return (on account) on December 31, 19A, was not recorded: sales amount, $15,000; cost, $8,000. The ending inventory did not include the goods returned.

	Un-corrected Amounts	Items for Correction (a) (b) (c) (d) (e)	Cor-rected Amounts
Income Statement:			
Sales revenue	$90,000		
Cost of goods sold	50,000		
Gross margin	40,000		
Expenses	30,000		
Pretax income	$10,000		
Balance Sheet:			
Accounts receivable	$32,000		
Inventory	20,000		
Remaining assets	40,000		
Accounts payable	11,000		
Remaining liabilities	6,000		
Common stock	60,000		
Retained earnings	15,000		

Required:

Set up a schedule similar to the one above; make the corrections and derive the corrected amounts. Indicate increases and decreases for each transaction. Explain any assumptions made with respect to doubtful items. Disregard income taxes.

Problem 10–5

Turner Company purchased merchandise during 19A on credit for $63,000 (includes $3,000 freight charges paid in cash); terms, 2/10, n/30. All of the purchase liability, except $10,000, was paid within the discount period; the remainder was paid within the 30-day term. At the end of the annual accounting period, December 31, 19A, 90% of the merchandise had been sold and 10% remained in inventory. The company uses a perpetual system.

Required:

1. Give entries in parallel columns for the purchase and the two payments on the liability assuming (a) purchases and accounts payable are recorded at gross and (b) purchases and accounts payable are recorded at net.

2. What amounts would be reported for the ending inventory and cost of goods sold under (a) and (b) in Requirement 1. Assume purchase discounts under the gross method are reported as a deduction from cost of goods sold. Explain why the amounts are different between the two methods.

3. Which method is preferable? Why?

Problem 10–6

The information shown below relating to the ending inventory was taken from the records of the Quick Publishing Company:

Inventory Classification	Quantity	Per Unit Cost	Per Unit Market
Newsprint:			
Stock A	200	$300	$330
B	60	250	230
Special stock (white):			
Stock H	20	70	65
I	10	60	62
Special stock (colored):			
Stock S	8	75	70
T	4	90	80
U	7	100	110

Required:

1. Determine the valuation of the above inventory at cost and at LCM assuming application by (a) individual items, (b) classifications, and (c) total inventory. The unit costs of the three categories are significantly different; however, within each category the unit costs are similar.

2. Give the entry to record the ending inventory for each approach assuming periodic inventory and
   a. Direct inventory reduction method.
   b. Allowance method.
   Which method is preferable? Why?

3. Of the three applications computed in Requirement 1, which one appears preferable in this situation? Explain.

Problem 10–7

The records of Stice Company provide the following data relating to inventories for the years 19A and 19B:

Inventory Date	Original Cost	At Lower of Cost or Market
1/ 1/19A	$ 40,000	$ 40,000
12/31/19A	50,000	46,000
12/31/19B	39,000	37,000

Other data available are as follows:

	19A	19B
Sales	$220,000	$245,000
Purchases	135,000	150,000
Administrative and selling expenses	51,000	61,000

The company values inventories on the basis of LCM and uses the periodic inventory system. For problem purposes ignore income taxes.

Required:

1. Give, in parallel columns, for 19A and 19B, the entries to apply the LCM procedure under each of the two methods: Case A—direct inventory reduction where the holding loss is not separately reported; and Case B—the allowance method. Set up a format similar to the following:

	Amounts	
	19A	19B
Case A:		
Entries		
Case B:		
Entries		

2. Prepare an income statement and show the inventory amounts for the balance sheet for each case. Follow the format illustrated in the chapter.
3. Which method is preferable? Why?

Problem 10–8

The summarized income statements for the Sharp Company are shown below as developed by the company. The inventories given below were valued at cost.

	19A	19B
Sales	$104,000	$97,000
Cost of goods sold:		
Beginning inventory	25,000	20,000
Purchases	75,000	73,000
Total	100,000	93,000
Ending inventory	20,000	15,000
Cost of goods sold	80,000	78,000
Gross margin	24,000	19,000
Less: Operating expenses	14,000	12,000
Pretax Income	$ 10,000	$ 7,000

The inventories valued at LCM would have been: at the beginning of 19A, $25,000 (the same as cost); end of 19A, $17,000; and end of 19B, $13,000.

Required:

1. Restate the 19A and 19B income statements applying the LCM rule for each of the following procedures (use a format similar to that illustrated in the text). Disregard income taxes.
   a. Direct inventory reduction method where the inventory holding loss is not reported separately.
   b. Allowance method where the inventory holding losses in both beginning and ending inventories are reported separately.
2. Which procedure is preferable? Why?

Problem 10–9

Fresh Fruit Company purchased a large quantity of mixed grapefruit for $34,300 which was graded at a cost of $900, as indicated below. Sales (at the sales prices indicated) and losses (frozen, stolen, rotten, etc.) are also listed.

Grade	Baskets Bought	Sales Price per Basket	Baskets Sold	Baskets Lost
A	3,000	$4.00	2,000	50
B	4,000	3.00	3,000	60
C	10,000	1.50	8,000	80
D	6,000	.75	4,000	
Culls	1,000	.50	900	
Loss	55			

Required:

1. Give entry for purchase assuming a perpetual inventory system. Show computations.
2. Give entries to record the sales and cost of goods sold.
3. Give entry relative to the losses assuming the losses are recorded separately from cost of goods sold.
4. Determine the valuation of the ending inventory.
5. Compute the direct contribution to pretax income for each grade of grapefruit. (Disregard operating, administrative, and selling expenses.)

Problem 10–10

On May 1, 19A, Box and Carr each invested $90,000 cash in a partnership for the purpose of purchasing and subdividing a tract of land for residential building purposes.

On June 1, they purchased 30 acres comprising the subdivision, at $5,000 per acre, paying $50,000 in cash and giving a one-year, 8% interest-bearing note (with mortgage) for the balance. Development costs amounted to $92,000.

The property was subdivided into 300 lots of equal size, 100 of which were to sell at $3,000 each and the balance at $4,000 each.

During July through December 19A the following sales were made for one-half cash and the balance on 9% interest-bearing notes, due in six months from date of sale.

	Lots
Group A (sold at $4,000 each)	30
Group B (sold at $3,000 each)	20

Cash collections on the notes receivable up to December 31, 19A, amounted to $49,000 principal plus $1,000 interest. Accrued interest recorded at December 31, 19A, amounted to $1,000.

Operating and selling expenses amounted to $95,000 by the end of December 19A. No payment was made on the note payable.

Required:

1. Journal entries for all of the above transactions. Disregard income taxes.
2. Statement of income for the period May through December of 19A.
3. Compute the inventory of unsold lots on December 31, 19A.

Problem 10–11

Broome Appliance Company completed the following selected (and summarized) transactions during 19A:

a. During the year purchased merchandise for resale, quoted at $150,000, on credit terms, 2/10, n/90; immediately paid 80% of the cash cost.
b. Paid freight charges on purchases amounting to $6,000 cash.
c. Paid 60% of the accounts payable within the discount period. The remaining amount was unpaid at year-end; however, at year-end none was beyond the discount period.
d. Returned merchandise to a vendor because of damage in shipment and received a $1,980 cash refund.
e. During the year sold merchandise for $300,000, of which 10% was on end-of-the-month credit terms.
f. Repossessed a refrigerator abandoned by a customer who left town. The sales price was $400, of which $300 was unpaid. The refrigerator cost $320. Estimates are that the used refrigerator can be sold for $250, cost of repairs will be $30, and selling costs will be $10.
g. Operating expenses paid in cash, $90,000.
h. Paid $30 to repair the repossessed refrigerator.
i. The purchases amount given in (a) included a shipment, on credit, that had a quoted gross cost of $8,000 (terms, 2/10, n/30). The liability has not been paid. The shipment was in transit, f.o.b. desti-

nation, at December 31, 19A. The invoice had been received. It was not included in the ending inventory amount.
j. The beginning inventory was $70,000 (at cost, which was the same as LCM).
k. The ending inventory (excluding the repossessed refrigerator) was $78,000 at cost; and at LCM, $73,000.

Accounting policies followed by the company are (a) annual accounting period ends December 31; (b) purchases and accounts payable are recorded net of cash discounts; (c) freight charges are allocated to the merchandise when purchased; (d) all cash discounts allowed are taken; (e) used and damaged merchandise is carried in a separate inventory account; and (f) inventories are reported at LCM, and any holding loss or gain on inventory valued at LCM is separately recognized (i.e., the allowance method).

Required:

1. Give entries for transactions (a) through (i) assuming periodic inventory system.
2. Give the end of the period entries (adjusting and closing). Assume an income tax rate of 40%.
3. Prepare a multiple-step income statement (19A). Assume 10,000 shares of common stock outstanding.
4. Show how the ending inventory should be reported on the balance sheet at December 31, 19A.

Problem 10–12

Quillen Distributing Company completed the following selected (and summarized) transactions during 19A:

a. Merchandise inventory on hand January 1, 19A: $100,000 (at cost, which was the same as LCM).
b. During the year purchased merchandise for resale at quoted price of $200,000 on credit terms, 2/10, n/30. Immediately paid 85% of the cash cost.
c. Paid freight on merchandise purchased, $9,000 cash.
d. Paid 40% of the accounts payable within the discount period. The remaining payables were unpaid at the end of 19A and were still within the discount period.
e. Merchandise that had a quoted price of $3,000 was returned to a supplier. A cash refund of $2,940 was received since the items were unsatisfactory.
f. During the year sold merchandise for $370,000, of which 10% was on credit terms, n/30.
g. A television set caught fire and was damaged internally; it was returned by the customer since it was guaranteed. The set was originally sold for

$600, of which $400 cash was refunded. The set cost the company $420. Estimates are that the set, when repaired, can be sold for $240. Estimated repair costs are $50, and selling costs are estimated to be $10.

h. Operating expenses (administrative and distribution) paid in cash, $115,000 (includes the $10 in *g*).

i. Excluded from the purchase given in *(b)* and from the ending inventory was a shipment for $7,000 (net of discount). This shipment was in transit, f.o.b. shipping point at December 31, 19A. The invoice was in hand.

j. Paid $50 cash to repair the damaged television set (see [*g*] above).

k. Sold the damaged television set for $245; selling costs allocated, $10.

l. The ending inventory (as counted) was $110,000 at cost, and $102,000 at LCM. Assume an average income tax rate of 40%.

Accounting policies followed by the company are *(a)* annual accounting period ends December 31, *(b)* purchases and accounts payable are recorded net of cash discounts, *(c)* freight charges are allocated to merchandise when purchased, *(d)* all cash discounts are taken, *(e)* used and damaged merchandise is carried in a separate inventory account, and *(f)* inventories are reported at LCM and the allowance method is used.

Required:

1. Give entries for transactions *(b)* through *(k)* assuming periodic inventory system.
2. Give the end of the period entries (adjusting and closing).
3. Prepare a multiple-step income statement (19A). Assume 10,000 shares of common stock outstanding.
4. Show how the ending inventory should be reported on the balance sheet at December 31, 19A.

11

Inventories—Flow and Matching Procedures

Chapter 10 identified two pervasive inventory problems—measurement of inventory *unit cost* and measurement of accounting values. This chapter considers the latter problem, that is, the selection of an assumed inventory cost flow such as average cost, *Fifo,* or *Lifo.* To facilitate discussion this chapter is divided into two parts: Part A—Inventory Cost Flow Methods; and Part B—Complexities in Applying *Lifo.*

PART A—INVENTORY COST FLOW METHODS

When goods are purchased or manufactured, there is an inflow of cost; when the goods are later sold or issued, there is an outflow of cost. The net difference between these cost flows is represented by the cost remaining in inventory. During an accounting period items typically are manufactured or purchased at different unit costs. Upon issue or sale of the items where more than one unit cost is involved, the accountant must select an appropriate unit cost for accounting purposes. Alternatively, the problem can be viewed as one of costing the units remaining on hand in inventory and of measuring the amount of cost of goods sold or used.

A definite policy on the assumed flow of costs for inventory and cost of goods sold (or cost of issues) is established when a particular inventory flow method is selected. Although inventory

flow methods may be consistent with the physical flow of goods in a specific case, the focus is on the flow of *costs* rather than on the flow of physical goods. In this regard, *ARB No. 43* states:

> Cost for inventory purposes may be determined under any one of several assumptions as to the flow of cost factors (such as first-in first-out, average, and last-in first-out); the major objective in selecting a method should be to choose the one which, under the circumstances, most clearly reflects periodic income.[1]

The inventory flow methods discussed in this chapter conform to the *cost principle* and do not involve departures from cost. The concept of *unit cost* discussed in Chapter 10 is applied, and the central issue is the order in which these actual unit costs are assigned to inventory and cost of goods sold. The selection of an inventory flow method reflects the manner in which the *matching principle* is applied to determine the cost of goods sold amount that is deducted from sales revenue for the period. This affects net income and income taxes (a cash outflow). Generally accepted accounting principles state that the method selected should be the one that "most clearly reflects periodic income" in each particular situation. Of course, all of the methods will

---

[1] AICPA, *Accounting Research Bulletin No. 43,* "Restatement and Revision of Accounting Research Bulletins" (New York, 1953), Statement 4.

EXHIBIT 11–1
Inventory Data

		Received			Units
			Unit	Units	on
Transactions		Units	Cost	Issued	Hand
Jan. 1	Inventory (@ $1)				200
9	Purchase ...	300	$1.10		500
10	Sale			400	100
15	Purchase ...	400	1.16		500
18	Sale			300	200
24	Purchase ...	100	1.26		300

produce the same results if costs do not change; however, this is seldom the case.

The inventory cost flow methods discussed in this chapter are as follows:

1. Specific cost identification.
2. Average cost.
3. First-in, first-out *(Fifo)* cost.
4. Last-in, first-out *(Lifo)* cost.
5. Miscellaneous cost flow methods.

For purposes of illustrating the various cost flow methods, the simplified data given in Exhibit 11–1 are used.

Using the data given in Exhibit 11–1, we can illustrate, by diagram, the problem of selecting a cost flow method for inventory and cost of goods sold purposes:

The application of some of the inventory cost flow methods will vary depending upon whether *periodic* or *perpetual* inventory procedures are used. The discussions to follow will distinguish between these procedures as they affect the application of the inventory cost flow method.

Recall that under periodic inventory procedures, the ending inventory is determined solely by a physical unit count; the unit costs (as defined in Chapter 10) are then applied by using one of the flow methods discussed in this chapter. Cost of goods sold (or used) is determined by subtracting the ending inventory cost from the total *goods available* amount. In contrast, under perpetual inventory procedures, all receipts and issues of inventory items are recorded so that an up-to-date or running inventory balance is continuously maintained directly in the records. As a consequence, the inventory records provide the amounts for inventory and cost of goods sold.

SPECIFIC COST IDENTIFICATION

When the goods involved are relatively large or expensive and small quantities are handled, it may be feasible to tag or number each item when purchased or manufactured, so that the actual unit cost can be indicated on each item by code. This procedure makes it possible to easily identify at date of sale the specific *unit cost* for each issue or sale and for each item re-

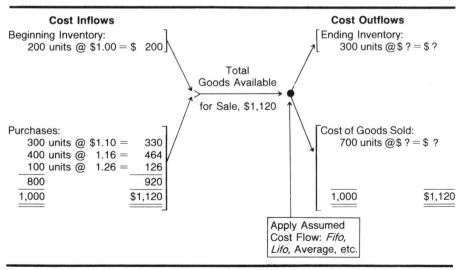

maining in inventory. The specific cost identification method relates the *cost flow* with the specific flow of physical goods, and may be applied with either periodic or perpetual inventory procedures. The specific cost method requires careful identification of each item; consequently, it is seldom used because of the practical limitation created by the detailed records that are required.

One disadvantage of the method is the possibility of profit manipulation by arbitrary selection of items at time of sale. To illustrate, assume there are three identical stereo sets available for sale that cost $400, $420, and $426. One is sold for $600. In this instance, reported cost of goods sold (and gross margin) would depend upon the particular unit selected for sale. Thus, the method often lacks objectivity in application. However, it is essential in situations where the individual units have unique characteristics which, by their relative appeal to customers, determine which unit is sold. With this kind of product, as for example, automobiles or rare gems, there is little possibility for profit manipulation.

AVERAGE COST

The average cost method is based on the concept that the best measure of inventory on the balance sheet and of cost of goods sold on the income statement is a representative unit cost for the period. The concept of average cost is applied in two ways, depending upon the inventory system: *(a)* periodic inventory system—weighted average unit cost for the period; and *(b)* perpetual inventory system—moving average unit cost.

Weighted Average Cost

Under this method, a weighted average unit cost is computed at the end of the period by using the unit purchase costs and the number of units in the beginning inventory and purchases for the period. The weighted unit cost, thus computed, is applied to *(a)* the units in the ending inventory and *(b)* the units sold (to derive cost of goods sold). Exhibit 11–2 illustrates application of the weighted average method using the

EXHIBIT 11–2
Inventory—Weighted Average Cost Illustrated

		Units	Unit Price	Total Cost
Goods available:				
Jan. 1	Inventory	200	$1.00	$ 200
9	Purchase	300	1.10	330
15	Purchase	400	1.16	464
24	Purchase	100	1.26	126
Total		1,000	1.12*	1,120
Cost of goods sold at weighted average cost:				
Jan. 10		400	1.12	448
18		300	1.12	336
		700		784
Ending inventory at weighted average cost:				
Jan. 31		300	1.12	$ 336

* Weighted average unit cost ($1,120 ÷ 1,000 = $1.12).

data given in Exhibit 11–1. Observe that the weighted average unit cost is derived by dividing the total cost for goods available for sale by the total number of units available.

The weighted average cost method is used frequently because it determines unit cost on an objective basis and is relatively easy to apply. Average cost minimizes the effect of extreme variations in purchase costs. In a rising market, weighted average cost will be lower than current cost; and in a declining market, it will be higher than current cost. The method is particularly sound because it is systematic and it is not subject to manipulation. It is appropriate for *periodic* inventory systems because *(a)* the inventory of physical units is not determined (counted) until the end of the period and *(b)* the weighted average unit cost can be determined at that time. Thus, the measurements necessary to compute ending inventory and cost of goods sold are determined at the same time, at the end of the accounting period.

Moving Average Cost

When a perpetual inventory system is used, the weighted average approach cannot be ap-

EXHIBIT 11–3
Inventory—Moving Average Cost Illustrated (perpetual inventory record)

Date	Received			Issued			Balance		
	Units	Unit Cost	Total Cost	Units	Unit Cost	Total Cost	Units	Unit Cost	Total Cost
Jan. 1							200	$1.00	$200
9	300	$1.10	$330				500	1.06*	530
10				400	$1.06	$424	100	1.06	106
15	400	1.16	464				500	1.14*	570
18				300	1.14	342	200	1.14	228
24	100	1.26	126				300	1.18*	354

* New average computed.

plied because a weighted unit cost cannot be calculated until the end of the period. To overcome this problem, a moving weighted average unit cost may be used because it provides a new unit cost *after each purchase.* Thus, when goods are sold or issued, the moving average unit cost existing at that time is used. Application of the moving average concept in a perpetual inventory system is shown in Exhibit 11–3 (based on data from Exhibit 11–1).

Note that the moving average unit cost is computed directly on the inventory card *after each purchase,* thus facilitating the current costing of issues during the period. For example, on January 9 the $1.06 moving average cost was derived by dividing the total cost ($530) by the total units (500), and so forth. The ending inventory of 300 units is costed at the latest moving average unit cost of $1.18 (total $354). Cost of goods sold is the sum of the "Issued, Total Cost" column ($766).

The moving average is objective, consistent, not subject to manipulation, and is a representative average that is more current than the weighted average. A practical problem with both methods is that the unit costs may not be even amounts. This problem can be resolved by costing the issues (cost of goods sold) in such a way that the remaining inventory unit costs are even. The averaging methods do not match the latest unit cost with sales revenue. Rather, they match the average costs of the period against revenue. Therefore, they generally provide inventory and cost of goods sold amounts between the *Lifo* and *Fifo* extremes. The amounts on the balance sheet (ending inventory) and on the income statement (cost of goods sold), however, are consistent as to valuation; and many accountants favor the use of average costs (versus *Fifo* or *Lifo*) because extreme values for inventory and cost of goods sold are avoided.

FIRST-IN, FIRST-OUT COST

The first-in, first-out method *(Fifo)* is based upon the assumption that the first goods purchased or manufactured are the first costed out upon sale or issuance. Since the costs are "flowed out" in the same order that they flowed in, goods sold (or issued) are costed at the *oldest* unit cost and the goods remaining in inventory are costed at the *newer* unit cost amounts. Application of *Fifo* requires the use of *inventory layers* for the different unit costs. The method may be used without complexity with either periodic or perpetual inventory systems.

Using the illustrative data in Exhibit 11–1 and a physical inventory count at the end of the period, *Fifo* results would be determined as follows:

Fifo **Cost—Periodic Inventory System**

	Beginning inventory (200 units @ $1)	$ 200
	Add purchases during the period (computed above)	920
	Goods available	1,120
Inventory Computation *(Fifo)*	Deduct ending inventory (300 units per physical inventory count):	
	100 units @ $1.26 (most recent purchase) $126	
	200 units @ $1.16 (next most recent purchase) 232	
	Total inventory	358
	Cost of goods sold (or issues) . .	$ 762

The same data are used in Exhibit 11–4 to illustrate the application of *Fifo* with a perpetual inventory system. Note that the maintenance of inventory layers throughout the period is necessary to assign the appropriate cost to each issue.

When the *Fifo* perpetual inventory system is used, the issues on the inventory record may be costed out either *(a)* currently throughout the period (i.e., each time there is a withdrawal) or

(b) all at the end of the period, with the same results. In Exhibit 11–4, issues from inventory on January 10 and 18 (*Fifo* basis) were costed out as they occurred (i.e., currently). If the costs had not been assigned to issues currently but instead had been assigned at the end of the period, the ending inventory would have still been valued at the same $358, comprised of the costs of obtaining the most recently acquired units (100 @ $1.26 plus 200 @ $1.16). In contrast, we shall see in the next section that under *Lifo,* different ending inventory amounts result, depending upon whether issues are costed currently or at the end of the period.

Fifo is widely used for inventory costing purposes because *(a)* it is easy to apply, *(b)* it is adaptable to either periodic or perpetual inventory procedures, *(c)* it produces an inventory amount for the balance sheet that approximates current replacement cost, *(d)* the flow of cost tends to be consistent with the usual physical flow of goods, *(e)* it is systematic and objective, and *(f)* it is not subject to manipulation. The fundamental weakness of *Fifo* is that it does not match *current cost* of goods sold with current revenues; rather the oldest unit costs are matched with the current sales revenue (also see Chapter 7). This means that when costs are rising (i.e., in a period of inflation), reported net

EXHIBIT 11–4
Inventory—*Fifo* Cost Illustrated (perpetual inventory record)

Date	Received Units	Received Unit Cost	Received Total Cost	Issued Units	Issued Unit Cost	Issued Total Cost	Balance Units	Balance Unit Cost	Balance Total Cost
Jan. 1							200	$1.00	$200
9	300	$1.10	$330				200 300	1.00 1.10	200 330
10				200 200	$1.00 1.10	$200 220	100	1.10	110
15	400	1.16	464				100 400	1.10 1.16	110 464
18				100 200	1.10 1.16	110 232	200	1.16	232
24	100	1.26	126				200 100	1.16 1.26	232⎫ 126⎭ $358

income will tend to be overstated in comparison with *Lifo* and average cost; and, conversely, when prices are falling, reported net income will tend to be understated. Some critics have said this tendency indirectly contributes to the severity of boom and bust conditions. The income tax implications can also be serious—when prices are rising, companies that use *Fifo* report more income than those using *Lifo* or average cost. Consequently, *Fifo* users pay more income taxes currently when prices are rising (other things being equal).

LAST-IN, FIRST-OUT COST

The last-in, first-out *(Lifo)* method of inventory cost flow is based on the concept that the latest unit acquisition cost should be matched with current sales revenue. Consequently, under this method the cost outflows are the inverse of the cost inflows (the opposite of *Fifo*). The units remaining in the ending inventory are costed at the oldest unit costs available; and the units in cost of goods sold, or issued, are costed at the newest unit costs available. *Lifo* application requires the use of inventory layers for the different unit costs.

Although the *Lifo* concept is simple, its application often is quite complex because of the detailed recordkeeping required, the discipline (rules) necessary to prevent inconsistent results and manipulation, and the formidable array of tax regulations that must be followed.

This section will present the *Lifo* concept assuming a *specific goods, single-product* situation.[2] Of course, such a simple situation seldom exists in actual practice; to look at it alone, without consideration of the implementation problems, would give an oversimplified view of this complex subject. Therefore, Part B presents the primary complexities encountered in *Lifo* application.

Lifo may be applied with either a periodic or perpetual inventory system. Assuming a *periodic inventory system* and a physical inventory of units at the end of the period, *Lifo* results would be determined as follows:

---

[2] This is variously called the *quantity, specific goods,* or *unit Lifo* method of applying the *Lifo* concept; see Part B for an alternate method of applying *Lifo.*

Lifo Cost—Periodic Inventory System

	Goods available (per above)	$1,120
Periodic Inventory Computation (Lifo)	Deduct ending inventory (300 units per physical inventory count):	
	200 units @ $1 (oldest costs available; from January 1 inventory) $200	
	100 units @ $1.10 (next oldest costs available; from January 9 purchase) 110	
	Total inventory	310
	Cost of goods sold (or issues)	$ 810

When *Lifo* is applied with a *perpetual inventory system,* the *issues* usually are costed on the perpetual inventory record currently throughout the period (i.e., each time there is a withdrawal), rather than at the end of the period.

With respect to *Lifo,* the timing of the costing of issues is important, since costing currently may result in a different inventory valuation and cost of goods sold amount than costing at the end of a period. The usual application of *Lifo* with a *perpetual* inventory system (i.e., costed currently during the period) is shown in Exhibit 11–5. In contrast, Exhibit 11–6 shows *Lifo* applied with a *perpetual* inventory system costed at the end of the period. This application is seldom used because it is inconsistent with the perpetual inventory concept of costing at date of issuance.

The items shown in italics in Exhibit 11–6 were entered at the *end* of the period. Note that Exhibit 11–6 (costed at end of period) provides the same inventory valuation ($310) as the *periodic* inventory computation given above. On the other hand, Exhibit 11–5 (costed currently) provides an inventory valuation of $342. The $32 difference occurs because the issues on January 10 and 18 were from different inventory layers as a result of the difference in the timing in costing issues. The difference between the *cost of issues* on the two records is also $32.

During periods of rising prices, *Lifo* costed at the end of the period will always provide a lower pretax income than will costing currently. Therefore, a company using *Lifo* for tax purposes would be motivated to cost at the end of the period. Because of this, if a perpetual *Lifo* system, costed currently, is used for internal purposes, the results are generally restated to an

EXHIBIT 11-5
Perpetual Inventory Record (*Lifo* cost illustrated—costed currently)

Date	Received			Issued or Sold			Balance		
	Units	Unit Cost	Total Cost	Units	Unit Cost	Total Cost	Units	Unit Cost	Total Cost
Jan. 1							200	$1.00	$200
9	300	$1.10	$330				200 300	1.00 1.10	200 330
10				300 100	$1.10 1.00	$330 100	100	1.00	100
15	400	1.16	464				100 400	1.00 1.16	100 464
18				300	1.16	348	100 100	1.00 1.16	100 116
24	100	1.26	126				100 100 100	1.00 1.16 1.26	100 ⎫ 116 ⎬ 126 ⎭ $342

EXHIBIT 11-6
Perpetual Inventory Record (*Lifo* cost illustrated—costed at end of period, for demonstration purposes only)

Date	Received			Issued or Sold			Balance		
	Units	Unit Cost	Total Cost	Units	Unit Cost	Total Cost	Units	Unit Cost	Total Cost
Jan. 1							200	$1.00	$200
9	300	$1.10	$330				500		
10				400* *Detail:* *100* *300*	*$1.26* *1.16*	*$126* *348*	100		
15	400	1.16	464				500		
18				300 *Detail:* *100* *200*	*1.16* *1.10*	*116* *220*	200		
24	100	1.26	126				300 *Detail:* *200* *100*	*1.00* *1.10*	*200* ⎫ *110* ⎭ $310

* Since costing of issues is delayed until the end of the period, the first issue (400 units) is costed out of the last purchase (100 units at $1.26), and so on. This is inconsistent with a perpetual inventory system.

end-of-the-period costing basis for *(a)* income tax and *(b)* external reporting purposes.

Lifo Inventory Liquidation

A serious problem occurs under *Lifo* procedures when a company fails to maintain the base year or "normal" inventory position (i.e., the *beginning* inventory of the period in which *Lifo* was first adopted by the company). This erosion of the base year inventory occurs when total usage of an inventory item exceeds acquisitions subsequent to adoption of *Lifo* (i.e., the base year). To illustrate, assume the following:

	Units	Unit Cost	Total Cost
Beginning inventory (assumed to be the base year *Lifo* inventory [Year 1])	10,000	$1.00	$10,000
Purchases	40,000	1.50	60,000
Total available for sale ...	50,000		70,000
Sales (44,000 units, costed on *Lifo* basis)	{ 40,000	1.50	60,000
	{ 4,000	1.00	4,000
	44,000		64,000
Ending inventory	6,000	1.00	$ 6,000

In the above example the company failed to maintain the base year inventory position by 4,000 units. This failure may have been due to

a. Voluntary inventory liquidation—Management may have decided to reduce normal inventory quantity for some reason, such as a decline in demand, anticipation of a decline in costs, or anticipation of an improvement in the product.[3]

b. Involuntary inventory liquidation—An inventory reduction may have been forced by uncontrollable causes, such as shortages, strikes, delayed delivery dates, or unexpected customer demands.

As a result of the liquidation of part of the base inventory, cost of goods sold includes 4,000

units costed at an old cost ($1 per unit), which is matched against current revenue, causing a distortion of reported income. Assuming the inventory liquidation is temporary, should the 4,000 units be costed out at $1 per unit or at some other cost? The problem is further complicated because the 4,000 units will be replaced in the next period at a higher cost, for example, at $1.60 per unit. Should the restoration of the base inventory position be at $1 per unit or at $1.60 per unit? One approach used, when the inventory liquidation is temporary, involves debiting Cost of Goods Sold with the estimated replacement cost, crediting Inventory at *Lifo* cost, and crediting the difference to a temporary account as follows (assuming perpetual inventory procedures):

Cost of goods sold (40,000 @ $1.50) + (4,000 @ $1.60)	66,400	
Inventory (40,000 @ $1.50) + (4,000 @ $1)		64,000
Excess of replacement cost of *Lifo* inventory temporarily liquidated (4,000 @ $0.60)		2,400

When the liquidated inventory is replaced (i.e., the base position restored at $1.60 per unit), the following entry is made:

Inventory (4,000 @ $1)	4,000	
Excess of replacement cost of *Lifo* inventory temporarily liquidated (4,000 @ $0.60)	2,400	
Accounts payable (4,000 @ $1.60) ...		6,400

If the replacement cost occurs at a price other than the estimate of $1.60 per unit, the difference represents a change in estimate. Recall that *APB Opinion No. 20,* "Accounting Changes," requires that changes in estimates be accounted for prospectively. Therefore, the difference between the actual replacement cost and the estimated replacement cost would be included in cost of goods sold for the year of replacement. Thus, if this were to occur, the last entry given above would include a debit or credit to Cost of Goods Sold (see Chapter 24).

A balance (i.e., the credit) in the Excess of Replacement Cost of *Lifo* Inventory Temporarily Liquidated should be reported as a current liability because it represents an amount which will have to be spent without a corresponding

---

[3] A major criticism of *Lifo* is that it is subject to profit manipulation. For example, year-end purchasing policy can be used (1) to reduce reported profits by heavy buying if prices have increased and (2) to overstate profits by permitting inventories to decline and "old" low prices to be charged to Cost of Goods Sold.

increase in inventory valuation. There is disagreement on the validity of this procedure. Some accountants believe it is needed to protect the integrity of the *Lifo* concept; others view it as income manipulation (i.e., a "planned" inventory liquidation). As a practical matter, erosion of the base inventory seldom occurs because the IRS usually will disallow *Lifo* for tax purposes if it does.

Recording *Lifo* in the Accounts

Few companies use *Lifo* for *internal* accounting and control purposes. Most companies using *Lifo* have changed to it from another method (such as *Fifo*) for *tax* and *external* reporting purposes. Generally, for internal purposes they prefer to continue the method used in the past. For internal purposes, and in the accounts, most companies use either *Fifo,* average, standard costs, or variable costing. At the end of the period, these results are converted to *Lifo* for income tax purposes and for *external financial reporting.* Usually this conversion is external to the accounts. However, in some cases the results of the conversion to *Lifo* are entered into the accounts as a single amount by using an inventory allowance account (Allowance to Reduce Inventory to *Lifo* Basis). Unfortunately, this account is sometimes referred to as a *"Lifo* Reserve."

In those cases where *Lifo* is used for internal purposes and entered in the accounts throughout the period, the issues are almost always costed *currently* because the management will not permit delay of interim costing of inventory and cost of goods sold until year-end because they are needed for internal financial and control reports. Current costing minimizes the *Lifo* impact on inventory and cost of goods sold, whereas costing at the end of the year maximizes its impact. Consequently, the internal results generally are *converted* to an annual *Lifo* basis to attain the maximum tax benefit (see dollar value *Lifo,* Part B of this chapter).

The Internal Revenue Code permits a company to use *Lifo* on the income tax return only if it is also used for its *external financial reports.* However, this does not require that *Lifo* must be used for internal purposes or entered into the accounts.

Comparison of *Lifo* with *Fifo*

The significant effects of *Lifo* may be emphasized by comparing it with *Fifo.* As long as unit costs remain constant, the two methods give the same results; when unit costs change materially, the two methods provide significantly different effects on assets (inventories and cash) and net income (expenses, including income taxes). Note that the comparative effects will depend upon the direction of the change in unit costs. With *rising* costs, *Fifo* matches low costs (older costs) with increased sales revenue (inflated dollars) and provides an inventory valuation approximating higher current replacement cost, whereas *Lifo* matches high costs (newer costs) with increased sales revenue and provides an inventory valuation on a low-cost (oldest cost) basis. Conversely, with *declining* costs, *Fifo* matches high costs (older costs) with decreased sales revenue and provides an inventory valuation approximating lower current replacement cost, whereas *Lifo* matches low costs (newer costs) with decreased sales revenue and provides an inventory valuation on a high-cost (older cost) basis. In summary, *Fifo* produces a more realistic ending inventory valuation because it approximates current cost. In contrast, *Lifo* matches the more recent costs with revenue and hence produces a better matching of expense with revenue.

With respect to the *cash flow* effects, when prices are rising, *Lifo* results in lower pretax income and, consequently, less income tax; therefore, because of the cash saving, cash outflow is less than when *Fifo* is used. These effects can be observed in Exhibit 11–7. The data given in that exhibit assume rising prices. Note in particular the impact of *Lifo* on income taxes, net income, and cash flow. An interesting paradox is evident in Exhibit 11–7. *Fifo* produces the higher inventory and income amounts, but *Lifo* produces more cash because it results in less income tax.

Because of a continuing worldwide inflationary trend and the pervasiveness of income taxes,

EXHIBIT 11–7
Lifo Cost Compared with *Fifo* Cost—Prices Rising

Basic Data Assumed

Beginning cash balance	$ 2,000
Beginning inventory balance, 5,000 units @	5 (base inventory)
Purchases during period, 5,000 units @	7
Sales during period, 5,000 units @	18
Expenses (excluding income taxes)	35,000
Income tax rate, 40%.	

Comparative Results

	First-In, First-Out			Last-In, First-Out			Increase (decrease) from Fifo to Lifo
	Units	@	Amount	Units	@	Amount	
Income Statement:							
Sales	5,000	$18	$90,000	5,000	$18	$90,000	$ -0-
Cost of goods sold	5,000	5	25,000	5,000	7	35,000	10,000
Gross margin			65,000			55,000	(10,000)
Expenses			35,000			35,000	-0-
Pretax income			30,000			20,000	(10,000)
Income taxes (@ 40%)			12,000			8,000	(4,000)
Net Income			$18,000			$12,000	$ (6,000)
Balance Sheet (limited to above transactions):							
Cash (assuming all transactions were cash)			$10,000			$14,000	$ 4,000
Inventory			35,000			25,000	(10,000)
Net difference (same as difference in net income)							$ (6,000)

an increasing number of companies have shifted to *Lifo*. The primary arguments generally cited for *Lifo* are (1) it provides a better matching of current costs with current revenue; (2) in periods of inflation, it results in lower income taxes, hence, less cash outflows; (3) it reflects the usual pricing policy of an enterprise—raise selling prices when replacement cost increases even though there are goods still on hand at the old lower cost; and (4) it is systematic.

The primary arguments generally cited against *Lifo* are (1) it understates assets—the inventory on the balance sheet is costed at old, out-of-date unit costs; (2) it does not correctly match replacement cost with revenue; (3) it is subject to manipulation—profits can be manipulated by changing the usual purchasing pat-

terns; (4) it is subject to involuntary inventory liquidation which often causes drastic results; (5) cost flows do not correspond to the physical flow of goods; and (6) it presents too many complexities and variations in application.

MISCELLANEOUS INVENTORY COST FLOW METHODS

Numerous methods for determining the cost of inventory, in addition to those discussed above, have been proposed. Except in a few very unusual situations, none of these has been accepted under generally accepted accounting principles for external financial reporting purposes. However, some of them are used for *internal cost accounting* purposes. As background, several miscellaneous methods are briefly discussed in this section.

Next-In, First-Out Method

Nifo refers to the concept that cost of goods sold should be costed at the unit cost anticipated for the next purchase of a like volume. The concept attempts to measure cost of goods sold as the actual cost of replacing the goods sold. It is maintained that *Lifo* fails to precisely match replacement cost with current revenues since the method employs the cost of the latest purchase *prior* to the actual sale. *Nifo* has not received general acceptance even though it is a current replacement cost concept.

Base Stock Method

The base stock (or normal stock) method is generally viewed as the predecessor of the *Lifo* method. The method assumes that there is a normal or base stock of goods that should be maintained at all times. The base stock represents a permanent commitment of resources, similar to an operational asset, that is costed at a "normal" price which is viewed as the original cost—usually the lowest cost experienced by the company. Maintenance of the base inventory at a constant amount is essential to avoid the problem of inventory profits.[4] Goods must be maintained above the minimum base stock for operational purposes. These goods are viewed as temporary increments and are recorded at cost; issues should be costed out of the increment on a *Lifo* basis, although *Fifo* or average sometimes is used for practical reasons. The base stock method is illustrated in Exhibit 11–8.

The purpose of the base stock method is similar to that of last-in, first-out, that is, the matching of current costs with current revenues. The permanency assumed with respect to the base

EXHIBIT 11–8
Base Stock Inventory Method

	Units	Unit Cost	Amount
Base stock	10,000	$0.50	$ 5,000
Extra stock	2,000	1.20	2,400
Total beginning inventory	12,000		7,400
Purchases:			
First	2,000	1.30	2,600
Second	6,000	1.40	8,400
Total available	20,000		18,400
Ending inventory (11,000 units per count):			
Base stock	10,000	0.50	5,000
Extra stock	1,000	1.20	1,200
Total	11,000		6,200
Cost of goods sold	9,000		$12,200

stock provides another avenue for justification. The method is not generally used because of the arbitrary nature of both the quantity and unit values of the assumed base stock. Essentially similar results may be obtained under *Lifo* as revealed in Exhibit 11–8. Like *Lifo*, the base stock method is subject to manipulation through selective purchasing. Erosion of the *base stock* would be treated in a manner similar to that illustrated earlier for *Lifo* liquidation. It is not permitted for income tax purposes.

Standard Cost Method

In manufacturing entities using a standard cost system, the inventories are valued, recorded, and reported for internal purposes on the basis of a standard unit cost. The standard cost approximates an ideal or expected cost, and its use prevents the inflation of inventory values because it excludes from inventory those losses and expenses due to inefficiency, waste, and abnormal conditions. Under this method the *differences* between actual cost (which includes losses due to inefficiencies, etc.) and standard cost (which excludes losses due to inefficiencies, etc.) are recorded in separate variance accounts which are written off as a current period "loss" rather than being capitalized in inventory.

---

[4] Inventory profits (sometimes called illusory profits) is an imprecise term often used to refer to the higher profits that tend to be reported during a period of rising prices as a result of the use of *Fifo* or average cost. This occurs because *Fifo* matches lower (old) inventory costs against current revenues that reflect sales prices marked up on the basis of the latest purchase costs (i.e., a *Lifo* markup strategy). *Lifo* tends to avoid such inventory profits.

Standard costing may be applied to raw materials, work in process, and finished goods inventories; and it is used more often in manufacturing situations because of its usefulness for cost control. To illustrate the use of standard costs for raw materials, assume a manufacturing company has just adopted standard cost procedures and that the beginning inventory is zero. During the current period the company makes two purchases and one issue and records them as follows:

1. To record the purchase of 10,000 units of raw material at $1.10 actual cost; standard cost has been established at $1:

```
Raw materials (10,000 units @ $1) .   10,000
Raw materials purchase price
  variance (10,000 units @ $0.10) .    1,000
  Accounts payable (10,000 units
    @ $1.10) .................               11,000
```

2. To record issuance of 8,000 units of raw material to the factory for processing:

```
Material in process  ..............   8,000
  Raw materials (8,000 units
    @ $1).....................               8,000
```

3. To record the purchase of 2,000 units of raw material at $0.95:

```
Raw materials (2,000 units @ $1) ..   2,000
Raw materials purchase price
  variance (2,000
  units @ $0.05) ............                100
  Accounts payable (2,000
    units @ $0.95) ............              1,900
```

Results for the period:

```
Purchases at actual cost:
  10,000 units @ $1.10  .........   $11,000
   2,000 units @   0.95  .........     1,900
       Total ...................             $12,900
Issues at standard cost:
  8,000 units @ $1  .............    8,000
Ending inventory at standard cost:
  4,000 units @ $1  .............    4,000   12,000
Raw materials purchase price
  variance (debit—charged
  against current income
  as a loss) ................              $    900
```

Under the procedures illustrated above for raw material, there would be no need to consider inventory flow methods such as *Lifo, Fifo,* and average, since only one cost—the standard cost—appears in the records. In addition, perpetual inventory records could be maintained in *units only,* since all issues and inventory valuations are at the same standard price. Standard cost represents a departure from the cost principle as currently interpreted. We have included only a brief discussion because for external reporting purposes, standard cost results generally are not used except in special circumstances. Therefore, for external reporting, the inventory is usually restated by applying one of the generally accepted methods discussed above. Standard costs are widely used for *internal management* planning and control. A detailed discussion of standard cost procedures is beyond the scope of this book and can be found in any complete cost accounting textbook.

Variable or Direct Cost Method

For *internal management* planning and control purposes, the concept of variable or direct costing is often used in manufacturing companies. Under this concept, fixed costs (i.e., those that tend to relate to time, such as salaries) and variable costs (i.e., those that vary with productive activities, such as direct labor) are distinctly segregated. This separation is especially useful for internal management planning and control. One important aspect of this concept is that the cost of goods manufactured is the sum of the variable costs only, that is, direct materials, direct labor, and variable manufacturing overhead. All fixed costs, including fixed manufacturing overhead, are treated as period costs and are deducted from revenues of the period rather than being capitalized and carried forward in inventory. Hence, fixed costs are not reported as part of cost of goods sold.

Valuation of inventories at only variable production costs, although highly useful for internal management purposes, is not generally acceptable for external financial reporting purposes, nor can it be used for tax purposes except in special circumstances. Consequently, for external reporting and tax purposes, companies using variable costing for internal purposes must convert the inventory and cost of goods sold to "actual" cost by using other costing methods discussed in this chapter.

SELECTION OF A COST FLOW METHOD

The use of the various inventory cost flow methods for external reporting and tax purposes is indicated in the following tabulation taken from AICPA, *Accounting Trends and Techniques, 1978* (p. 125):

Inventory Flow Methods (based on 600 companies)

	Number of Disclosures*			
	1977	1976	1975	1974†
Methods				
First-in, first-out (fifo)	392	389	376	375
Last-in, first-out (lifo)	332	331	315	303
Average cost	227	232	235	236
Standard costs	37	31	48	49
Retail method	31	26	36	35
Other	47	50	34	56
Total Disclosures	1,066	1,059	1,044	1,054

	Number of Companies			
Use of LIFO				
All inventories	10	9	11	14
50% or more of inventories ...	194	167	125	135
Less than 50% of inventories	93	84	86	67
Not determinable	35	71	93	87
Not used	268	269	285	297
Total Companies	600	600	600	600

* Some companies use more than one method.
† A period of "double-digit" inflation.

Selection of an inventory cost flow method, or a decision to change from one method to another, presents a complex problem. Although income measurement should be the primary consideration, it is difficult to realistically avoid considering income tax effects. With respect to income measurement, it is also unrealistic to ignore the problem of inventory profits. In periods of rising prices, *Lifo* tends to minimize inventory profits whereas *Fifo* tends to maximize them. The tendency to emphasize the income statement, the relatively high inflation trend, and tax effects have prompted a number of companies in recent years to switch to *Lifo*. With respect to the favorable income tax effect of *Lifo* during periods of inflation, one must recognize that the effect would be reversed in periods of deflation. Because of the complexities involved and the potential for manipulation, the Internal Revenue Code and Regulations impose a formidable array of rules governing *Lifo* for income tax purposes. On the other hand, the diverse economic impacts in the long run versus the short run and the negative impact of *Lifo* during periods of inflation on income, EPS, and certain other ratios have caused many companies to consider a switch to *Lifo* undesirable for them.

PART B—COMPLEXITIES IN APPLYING *LIFO*

Exhibits 11–5 and 11–6 illustrated different inventory and cost of goods sold amounts that may arise under *Lifo* costed currently and costed at the end of the period. The discussions and illustrations in Part A assumed *Lifo* was applied using the quantity of goods, single-item method. Although the illustrations were simplified, some of the complexities of *Lifo* application were suggested. Moreover, an array of income tax regulations further complicates the application of *Lifo* since *Lifo* must be used for the external financial statements as a condition for its use for income tax purposes.

Because of the complexities in applying *Lifo*, most companies maintain their internal accounting records on a *Fifo* or average cost basis during the year and convert those results to *Lifo* external to the accounts. Particular problems are encountered, however, by those companies which use other methods in the accounting system and convert ending inventory and cost of goods sold to a *Lifo* basis at the end of the period for income tax and external financial statement purposes.

Lifo application problems are discussed in the following order:

1. Initial adoption of *Lifo*.
2. Application of *Lifo* inventory procedures.
   a. Quantity of goods *Lifo* method.
      (1) Single-item approach.
      (2) Multiple-pools approach.
3. Dollar value *Lifo* method (for either single or multiple inventory pools).
   a. Applying the dollar value *Lifo* approach.
   b. Inventory liquidation.
   c. Technological changes in inventories.
4. Indexing.
5. *Lifo* "reserves."

INITIAL ADOPTION OF *LIFO*

Income tax regulations permit taxpayers to use *Lifo* for all or part of the total inventory of goods (i.e., for manufacturers and processors—raw materials, work in process, finished goods; for retailers and wholesalers—merchandise for sale). In the typical *Lifo* situation, the company has changed from some other method to *Lifo* for *tax* and *external* reporting purposes, although a few companies have changed in the opposite direction.

The switch to *Lifo* involves a change in accounting principle as described in *APB Opinion No. 20,* "Accounting Changes." Paragraph 20 of that *Opinion* requires that the *cumulative* effect of a change in accounting principle be shown between the captions "Income before Extraordinary Items" and "Net Income." However, paragraph 26 of that *Opinion* specifically rules out measurement of the cumulative effect when the change is *to Lifo* (but not from *Lifo*), because it is almost always impossible to reconstruct the

forma amounts for prior years. The principal example of this type of accounting change is a change in inventory pricing method from Fifo to Lifo. . . .

When there is a change to *Lifo,* the *base year* is the year in which the change is made, and the *Lifo base cost* for the beginning inventory (generally called the *base inventory*) for the base year is the ending inventory for the prior year, adjusted to cost regardless of the prior method used (Treas. Reg. §1.472-2). This means that writedowns of the prior year's ending inventory below cost (such as to lower of cost or market) must be added back. Recall that LCM is not applied to *Lifo.*

To illustrate a change to *Lifo,* assume X Company has been using *Fifo* for all purposes. The company decided to change to *Lifo* for income tax and external reporting purposes starting in 19D. *Fifo* will be continued in the internal inventory accounts.[5] The inventory data given immediately below were available for 19D:

Fifo inventory at end of 19C:

Layer 1	4,000 units @ $ 85	$ 340,000
Layer 2	6,000 units @ 110	660,000
Total	10,000 units @ 100	$1,000,000

Fifo inventory at end of 19D (per inventory records):

Purchases	30,000 units @ $112	
Sales	(28,000) units	
Ending inventory	12,000 units @ 112	$1,344,000

Lifo inventory at end of 19D:

Base inventory layer ...	10,000 units @ $100	$1,000,000	
19D *lifo* layer	2,000 units @ 112	224,000	
Total ending inventory	12,000		$1,224,000

exact composition of old inventory cost layers that the company would have reported in prior periods if it had been using *Lifo* all along. Paragraph 26 states:

> Computing the effect on retained earnings at the beginning of the period in which a change in accounting principle is made may be sometimes impossible. In those rare situations, disclosure will be limited to showing the effect of the change on the results of operations of the period of change (including per share data) and to explaining the reason for omitting accounting for the cumulative effect and disclosure of pro

External financial statements for 19D:

a. Use *Lifo* inventory amount of $1,224,000 on the income statement and balance sheet.

b. Disclosure note included with the financial statements for 19D, assuming a 40% average income tax rate:

---

[5] *FASB Interpretation No. 1,* "Accounting Changes Related to the Cost of Inventory": "In applying *APB Opinion No. 20,* preferability among accounting principles shall be determined on the basis of whether the new principle constitutes an improvement in financial reporting and not on the basis of the income tax effect alone."

At the beginning of the current year (19D) the company changed its inventory measurement basis from *Fifo* to *Lifo*. Had the *Fifo* method been continued during 19D, the ending inventory would have been $1,344,000 − $1,224,000 = $120,000 higher than reported in the attached statements. The net effect of the change to *Lifo* in 19D was to reduce net income (after income taxes) by $120,000 × (1 − .40) = $72,000 (approximately $x.xx per share). Pro forma effects of retroactive application are not realistically determinable.

The management believes that the newly adopted inventory measurement method will attain a better matching of current expenses with current revenues.

APPLICATION OF *LIFO* INVENTORY PROCEDURES

Fundamentally, there are three different *Lifo* application methods:

1. Quantity of goods *Lifo* method (discussed in Part A).
2. Dollar value *Lifo* method (discussed in Part B).
3. Retail value *Lifo* method (discussed in Chapter 12).

Quantity of Goods *Lifo* Method

This method (often called specific goods *Lifo* or unit *Lifo*) has two approaches, *(a)* the single-item approach and *(b)* the multiple-pools approach.

Single-Item Approach. The single-item approach was illustrated in Part A of this chapter. It requires that the *quantity* of each individual item or product in the ending inventory be determined either by physical inventory count or from perpetual inventory records; then unit costs are applied in *Lifo* order, in the manner shown in Exhibit 11–6, to derive the *Lifo* inventory amount. Normally, the *Lifo* inventory amount will consist of a *base Lifo inventory* amount plus subsequent incremental *Lifo* layers for each new price.

The single-item approach is used in small businesses and in situations where there are a small number of different inventory items or products. In larger and more complex situations,

the detailed recordkeeping usually is considered too burdensome, except in cases where only a few major items of inventory are on the *Lifo* basis.

Multiple-Pools Approach. The multiple-pools approach involves grouping of *substantially identical* items into *Lifo* inventory pools. Each pool is then treated as if it were a single inventory item. For the beginning inventory (the base layer when *Lifo* was adopted), all of the units in a pool are treated as though they were acquired at the same time; that is, the unit cost for the beginning inventory can be obtained by dividing the total number of units into the total inventory cost. The *ending Lifo inventory* each period, to the extent that the number of units does not exceed the beginning inventory, is obtained by multiplying the number of units remaining in inventory by the average unit cost at the start of the current period. The number of units in the ending inventory, in excess of the number at the start (an inventory increment or layer), is valued by multiplying the excess number by the average cost of purchases during the period. This is in contrast with the single-item approach in which the number of units purchased during the current year is greater than the number of units sold; the units in the ending inventory are valued by cost layers in the order of acquisition of the layers (i.e., *Lifo* order). The ending inventory then is the base layer plus the incremental layers.

To illustrate the comparative effects of the single-item approach and the multiple-pools *Lifo* approach, the following data are assumed for T Company for 19B:

	Units and Unit Cost	
Beginning Inventory:		
Product A	600 @ $ 7.00	
Product B		400 @ $14.50
Purchases:		
Product A	1,000 @ $ 7.80	
Product B		800 @ $15.00
Sales:		
Product A	900 @ $17.00	
Product B		600 @ $25.00

The single-item approach and multiple-pools approach are applied in Exhibit 11–9 using the above data. Observe that the computed ending

EXHIBIT 11–9
Lifo—Quantity of Goods Method: Single-Item and Multiple-Pools Approaches Compared

| | Lifo—Single-Item Approach | | | Lifo—Multiple-Pools Approach |
	Product A	Product B		Inventory Pool No. 1
Beginning inventory	600 @ $7.00 $ 4,200	400 @ $14.50 $ 5,800		1,000 @ $10.00* $10,000
Purchases	1,000 @ 7.80 7,800	800 @ 15.00 12,000		1,800 @ 11.00* 19,800
Total	1,600 12,000	1,200 17,800		2,800 29,800
Cost of goods sold	900 @ 7.80 7,020	600 @ 15.00 9,000		1,500 @ 11.00 16,500
Ending inventory:				
Layer 1	600 @ 7.00 4,200	400 @ 14.50 5,800		1,000 @ 10.00 10,000
Layer 2	100 @ 7.80 780	200 @ 15.00 3,000		300 @ 11.00 3,300
Total	700 $ 4,980	600 $ 8,800		1,300 $13,300

* Computations:
($4,200 + $5,800) ÷ (600 + 400) = $10.00.
($7,800 + $12,000) ÷ (1,000 + 800) = $11.00.

Lifo inventory for 19B is different by ($4,980 + $8,800) − $13,300 = $480 between the two approaches.

This simplified example demonstrates the efficiency of the multiple-pools approach. Consider the more common situation where there are several hundred different items that can be grouped into, perhaps, ten inventory pools. The saving in clerical costs could be substantial.

DOLLAR VALUE *LIFO* METHOD

Dollar value *Lifo,* in contrast to the quantity of goods method, bases the *Lifo* inventory computations on *(a)* dollars of inventory, *(b)* a specific price index for each year, and *(c)* broad inventory pools. The inventory layers are identified with the price index for the year in which the layer was added. Thus, dollar value *Lifo* is not a distinctly different inventory method; rather it is a method of estimating *Lifo* results for the ending inventory each period (and, hence, estimating cost of goods sold).

Dollar value *Lifo* is an approach for *converting* the ending inventory results derived by another method (such as *Fifo* or average) to a *Lifo* basis. Typically, a company using dollar value *Lifo* for income tax and external financial statement purposes will be using another

method (usually *Fifo* or average) in the internal inventory accounts. The problem is to take the results generated by the internal inventory records and convert them to a dollar value *Lifo* basis. Obviously, if *quantity of goods Lifo* is used in the internal inventory accounts, there is no need for dollar value *Lifo*.

The discussions and illustrations of dollar value *Lifo* will be based on the conversion of *Fifo* inventory results to dollar value *Lifo* for Tye Company for Years 19B and 19C. The *Fifo* results for each of these years are shown in Exhibit 11–10.[6]

The dollar value *Lifo* conversion method involves the following two distinct phases:

Phase A—Computation of a conversion price index for each period. The conversion index numbers are critical because, as an integral part of the conversion process, they may materially affect the results. Tax regulations and generally accepted accounting principles require that a conversion price index

---

[6] Throughout these discussions we will assume *Fifo* is used internally; however, other quantity of goods methods, based on cost, could have been asssumed. The IRS requires that the internal inventory records be maintained in such manner as to facilitate audits. Congress approved the use of unit *Lifo* in 1938 and dollar value *Lifo* in 1949.

EXHIBIT 11–10
Tye Company—Illustrative Data, *Fifo* Basis

a. Ending inventory, *Fifo* basis (per internal inventory accounts; two products will comprise the inventory pool):

	Product A			Product B			Total
	Units	Cost	Total	Units	Cost	Total	Amount
Year 19A:							
Ending inventory *(Fifo):**							
Layer 1	1,000	$1.00	$1,000	2,000	$2.00	$ 4,000	
Layer 2				500	2.20	1,100	
	1,000	$1.00	$1,000	2,500	$2.04	$ 5,100	$6,100
Year 19B:							
Purchases†	3,000	$1.20	$3,600	4,000	$2.50	$10,000	
Sales	(2,800)			(3,500)			
Ending inventory:							
Fifo	1,200	1.20	1,440	3,000	2.50	7,500	$8,940
Year 19C:							
Purchases†	3,300	1.30	4,290	4,200	2.60	10,920	
Sales	(3,200)			(4,200)			
Ending inventory:							
Fifo	1,300	1.30	1,690	3,000	2.60	7,800	$9,490

b. *Fifo* is continued in the internal inventory accounts and for internal management purposes.
c. *Lifo* was adopted at the start of 19B for (1) income tax purposes and (2) external financial statement purposes. At the end of each year the *Fifo* results will be converted to dollar value *Lifo* results.

* Beginning inventory for the year of adoption of *Lifo*.
† Totals for the year; thus, the unit purchase costs are annual averages.

be used that is *specific* to the particular inventory pool within the company as opposed to an external index or a general price index.[7] This means that an internal conversion price index for each inventory pool must be computed each period based upon the change in costs as reflected in the internal inventory and purchase records of the company. The internal conversion price index for an inventory pool must be computed on the basis of actual inventory costs (*Fifo* basis in this case) as follows:

$$\frac{\text{Ending } \textit{Fifo} \text{ Inventory for the Period Valued at } \textit{Current Year} \text{ Actual Cost}}{\text{Ending } \textit{Fifo} \text{ Inventory for the Period Valued at } \textit{Base Year} \text{ Actual Costs}} = \begin{array}{l}\text{Conversion Price} \\ \text{Index for the} \\ \text{Current Year}\end{array}$$

[7] Two exceptions to this requirement are explained in a later section, "Indexing."

Computation of the internal conversion price index is illustrated subsequently for Years 19B and 19C.

Phase B—Conversion of the Fifo *results to* Lifo *basis by using the conversion index numbers computed in Phase A.* Conversion requires that each inventory pool be costed at both *base period* dollar costs and *current period* dollar costs. When the total of the ending inventory for the current period at base year costs exceeds the dollar total of the beginning inventory for that period, at base year costs, an inventory increment or layer has been added. If the difference is less, some inventory *liquidation* has occurred. Any inventory increment, stated at base year cost, then must be converted to current year costs by using the conversion index numbers. Thus, each *Lifo* inventory layer (in dollars only) is *directly identified* with the conversion price index number that was computed for the year in which the layer was added. There is no identification with units or unit costs (as is the case with quantity of goods *Lifo*). If the inventory decreases during the year, the reduction is taken from the most recent layers (increments), that is, in *Lifo* order. Conversion computations are illustrated in Exhibits 11–11 and 11–12 for Tye Company for Years 19B and 19C.

Dollar value *Lifo* may be applied on the basis of either

a. *A single pool*—A single pool is used for the entire company when (1) the company is a manufacturer or processor and (2) overall operations constitute a "natural business unit." Thus, an automobile manufacturer may use a single pool that would encompass raw materials, component parts, work in process, and finished goods (as if it were one big inventory item).

b. *Multiple pools*—Each pool encompasses a group of inventory items that are *similar* in respect to raw materials, manufacturing, and distribution. A separate inventory pool is formed which corresponds to the "natural business" *subunits* of the company. Manufacturers may use either single pool or multiple pools; however, retailers, wholesalers, and jobbers must use multiple pools. For example, a large department store may have separate inventory pools for men's clothing, ladies' clothing, home appliances, and so on.

Because of the higher degree of aggregation and the attendant likelihood of avoiding some liquidation of the base layer, single pool generally is preferred to multiple pools where there is a choice.

Applying the Dollar Value *Lifo* Approach

There are two variations of the dollar value *Lifo* approach known as (1) double extension and (2) link chain. The link-chain variation was designed for restrictive situations where the double-extension variation is not satisfactory in coping with the computation of the index number and conversion, such as when there have been significant technological changes in the in-

ventory (discussed later). Its use for income tax purposes is strictly limited. Link chain and double extension are not alternatives for the same set of facts. Because of its limited use and because the computations are similar, the link-chain variation is not discussed and illustrated here.

The designation double extension is based upon the fact that under dollar value *Lifo,* the ending inventory each period must be double costed (i.e., at base year costs and at current year costs) in both phases of the conversion process.

The inventory data for Tye Company given in Exhibit 11–10 were used to apply the dollar value *Lifo* method for Year 19B in Exhibit 11–11 and for Year 19C in Exhibit 11–12. You should trace the data from the prior exhibit through the computation of Phase A—the internal conversion price index; and Phase B—the conversion of *Fifo* results to dollar value *Lifo* results for each year.

The computations for Phases A and B illustrated in Exhibits 11–11 and 11–12 are straightforward. Observe that in both phases the ending *Fifo* inventory is double costed: at current year cost and at base year cost. The ratio between these two amounts represents the conversion price index for the current year because it measures the change in inventory costs since the base year. The base year is centered on 1.00, and subsequent changes are measured in terms of that year. Also, observe that the two products are considered to be one inventory pool. However, the typical dollar value *Lifo* inventory pool includes numerous products. In Phase B the various inventory layers, identified by year and expressed in base year costs, are simply restated to actual costs by year of accumulation to derive the dollar value *Lifo* inventory amount.

Inventory Liquidation

Frequently there will be a full or partial *inventory liquidation* (or invasion) of one or more of the prior years' incremental layers. Inventory liquidation is taken from the most recent layers in *Lifo* order; and for each layer invaded, the conversion price index for the year that the layer was added to inventory is applied. Thus, the method requires very careful accounting for each

EXHIBIT 11–11
Conversion of *Fifo* Results to *Lifo* Basis—Year 19B (dollar value *Lifo* method)

Phase A—Computation of internal conversion price index (based on *Fifo* results provided by internal inventory records of Tye Company—per Exhibit 11–10)—19B:

	Inventory at Current Year Cost	÷	Inventory at Base Year Cost	=	Conversion Price Index
Base *Lifo* inventory (from 19A)	$6,100	÷	$6,100	=	1.00
Ending inventory:					
Product A	1,200 @ $1.20 = $1,440		1,200 @ $1.00 = $1,200		
B	3,000 @ 2.50 = 7,500		3,000 @ 2.04 = 6,120		
Totals	$8,940	÷	$7,320	=	1.221

Phase B—Conversion of *Fifo* results to dollar value *Lifo* results—19B:

	Fifo at Base Year Cost	×	Conversion Price Index	=	Lifo Results
19B ending *Fifo* inventory per above (current cost $8,940)	$ 7,320				
Base inventory layer	(6,100)	×	1.00	=	$6,100
Difference: 19B additional layer	$ 1,220	×	1.221	=	1,490
19B dollar value *Lifo* ending inventory					$7,590*

* Report this value on the 19B balance sheet and use to compute 19B cost of goods sold.

EXHIBIT 11–12
Conversion of *Fifo* Results to *Lifo* Basis—Year 19C (dollar value *Lifo* method)

Phase A—Computation of internal conversion price index (based on *Fifo* results provided by internal inventory records of Tye Company—per Exhibit 11–10)—19C:

	Inventory at Current Year Cost	÷	Inventory at Base Year Cost	=	Conversion Price Index
Ending inventory:					
Product A	1,300 @ $1.30 = $1,690		1,300 @ $1.00 = $1,300		
B	3,000 @ 2.60 = 7,800		3,000 @ 2.04 = 6,120		
Totals	$9,490	÷	$7,420	=	1.279

Phase B—Conversion of *Fifo* results to dollar value *Lifo* results—19C:

	Fifo at Base Year Cost	×	Conversion Price Index	=	Lifo Results
19C ending *Fifo* inventory per above (current cost $9,490)	$ 7,420				
Base inventory layer	(6,100)	×	1.00	=	$6,100
19B inventory layer (per above)	(1,220)	×	1.221	=	1,490
Difference: 19C additional layer	$ 100	×	1.279	=	128
19C dollar value *Lifo* ending inventory					$7,718*

* Report this value on the 19C balance sheet and use to compute 19C cost of goods sold.

layer in terms of the index applicable to that layer. Layers, once liquidated, are never added back.

To illustrate, assume Tye Company's sales of Product A (Exhibit 11–10) for 19C amounted to 3,500 units (instead of 3,200). This would cause the 19C ending inventory to be 1,000 units of Product A (instead of 1,300 units). Thus, there would be a liquidation of the inventory of the prior year for Product A by 200 units. The 19C *Fifo* inventory results would be as follows:

```
19C ending Fifo inventory:
  Product A . . . . . . . . . . . .   1,000 units @ $1.30 = $1,300
  Product B . . . . . . . . . . . .   3,000 units @  2.60 =  7,800
      Total . . . . . . . . . . . . .                        $9,100
```

The conversion computations would be as follows:

Phase A—To compute internal conversion price index for 19C:

	Inventory at Current Year Cost	÷	Inventory at Base Year Cost		Conversion Price Index
Product A . .	1,000 @ $1.30 = $1,300		1,000 @ $1.00 = $1,000		
Product B . .	3,000 @ 2.60 = 7,800		3,000 @ 2.04 = 6,120		
Total	$9,100	÷	$7,120	=	1.278

Phase B—To convert *Fifo* results to dollar value *Lifo* results for 19C:

	Fifo at Base Year Cost	×	Conversion Price Index	=	Lifo Results
19C ending inventory per above (current cost $9,100)	$7,120				
Base inventory layer	(6,100)	×	1.00	=	$6,100
19B inventory layer remaining	$1,020*	×	1.221	=	1,245
19C dollar value Lifo ending inventory					$7,345

* There was no 19C layer added and there was a partial liquidation of the 19B layer of $1,220 − $1,020 = $200 (at base year cost).

Recall that in the Tye Company example, the internal inventory accounts were maintained on a *Fifo* basis (as reflected in Exhibit 11–10). In contrast, for income tax and external financial reporting purposes, the company used dollar value *Lifo*. The *conversion* of the *Fifo* results to dollar value *Lifo* for 19B and 19C was illustrated in Exhibits 11–11 and 11–12 for Tye Company. Although the illustrative amounts are simplified, it may be useful to compare the results of *Fifo* with the results of dollar value *Lifo* as follows for Year 19C:

	Year 19C—Cost of Goods Sold Compared for—	
	Fifo—for Internal Purposes (Exhibit 11–10)	Dollar Value Lifo—for External Purposes (Exhibit 11–12)
Beginning inventory	$ 8,940	$ 7,590
Purchases	15,210	15,210
Total	24,150	22,800
Ending inventory	9,490	7,718
Cost of goods sold	$14,660	$15,082

The comparison reflects a higher cost of goods sold amount for dollar value *Lifo* than for *Fifo* as would be expected. Thus, this derives lower pretax income and lower income tax. Because of the simplified example, the difference is not large; however, our focus should be on the application of the dollar value *Lifo* conversion process. We emphasize again three important aspects of the process: (1) the computation of an *internal* price index each period, (2) application of the computed internal index to obtain the ending *Lifo* inventory amount each period, and (3) the high level of aggregation permitted by the IRS (and in the external financial reports) when dollar value *Lifo* is used. The high level of aggregation of the items in the inventory makes the method attractive; the aggregation tends to resolve the technological product change problem and maximizes the *Lifo* effect on pretax income.

We will now turn our attention to two related problems in applying dollar value *Lifo:* (1) inventory liquidation and (2) technological changes in product lines (i.e., product mix).

Technological Changes in Inventories

In the preceding discussions of dollar value *Lifo,* the point was made that it provided a better avenue for handling the effects of technological changes in inventories than did quantity of goods *Lifo*. With respect to inventories, technological changes are of two kinds: *(a)* dropping and/or adding product lines because of obsolescence, changes in demand, supply availability, competition, and so forth, and *(b)* technical improvements in product lines, such as the move from black and white to color television. Some companies experience a continuing change in the product mix.

In the quantity of goods *Lifo* method, the phasing out of an old product would cause the old *Lifo* inventory costs (usually low relative to current costs) to be moved to cost of goods sold and, when a new product is launched, to be replaced with new inventory costs which are usually much higher.

In contrast, the dollar value *Lifo* method, in large measure, retains the old *Lifo* costs when technological changes occur, because it bases the inventory calculation on dollars rather than on specific units. When an old product is dropped from the inventory pool, the base inventory amount is continued. Moreover, when a new product is added to the inventory pool, a *reconstructed* cost for it is established as the base inventory cost at *(a)* what the item would have cost at the base date (based upon base year price lists, etc.); or *(b)* if the item did not exist at that date, the first cost after the base date that can be reconstructed; or *(c)* if no prior cost can be determined, then the cost at the date that the item was first stocked for use or sale.

The effects of technological changes on *Lifo* inventory amounts for the quantity of goods *Lifo* approach compared with the dollar value *Lifo* approach may be indicated as follows:

		Lifo Inventory Unit Costs			
Product	Base Year	Year 19W	Year 19X	Year 19Y	Year 19Z
A	$1	$ 5	Discontinued		
B	2	8	$ 6	$ 6	Discontinued
C (new)		15	16	16	$17
D (new)			20	21	21

Dollar value *Lifo* would retain this in the base inventory.

Quantity of goods *Lifo* would replace base year inventory costs with these current costs.

To illustrate how dollar value *Lifo* accommodates technological changes in the *Lifo* inventory, we will adapt the Tye Company data of 19C (Exhibit 11–10). Assume that Product A was completely sold and discontinued during 19C and that Product C was added to the *Lifo* inventory pool, resulting in the following 19C ending inventory, *Fifo* basis:

19C ending inventory, *Fifo* basis:		
Product A—Discontinued		
Product B—No change in assumption	3,000 units @ $2.60 =	$ 7,800
Product C—New product*	2,000 units @ 1.10 =	2,200
Total *Fifo* inventory		$10,000

* Reconstructed base year cost $0.80 per unit.

The dollar value *Lifo* inventory valuation at the end of 19C would be computed as follows:

Phase A—To compute the internal conversion price index for 19C:

	Inventory at Current Year Cost	÷	Inventory at Base Year Cost	=	Conversion Price Index
Product B ..	3,000 @ $2.60 = $ 7,800		3,000 @ $2.04 = $6,120		
Product C ..	2,000 @ 1.10 = 2,200		2,000 @ 0.80 = 1,600		
Total	$10,000	÷	$7,720	=	1.295

Phase B—To convert the *Fifo* results to dollar value *Lifo* results for 19C:

	Fifo at Base Year Cost		Conversion Price Index		Lifo Cost
19C ending inventory (current cost $10,000)	$7,720				
Base inventory layer	(6,100)	×	1.00	=	$6,100
19B inventory layer	(1,220)	×	1.221	=	1,490
19C additional inventory layer	$ 400	×	1.295	=	518
19C dollar value *Lifo* ending inventory					$8,108

Note in the above computations that *(a)* the base layer (and other prior layers) was retained at the old costs (notwithstanding the fact that product A was dropped), and *(b)* the cost of the new product was "reconstructed" at the base year cost (not the cost in 19C when added to the pool, $1.10). These two retentions of old *Lifo* costs are not possible when the quantity of goods *Lifo* approach is used. Thus, dollar value *Lifo* maximizes the *Lifo* effect, which is considered its primary advantage.

INDEXING

In the preceding discussions and illustrations of dollar value *Lifo,* the indexes used were *internal indexes,* since they were computed from the internal inventory data of the company. No externally computed indexes were used. Recall that computation of the internal index each period required that *(a)* unit cost data and *(b)* physical quantity data for the ending inventory be available for each item in the inventory pool. In complex situations, this requirement for detailed data often poses a critical problem. As a consequence, there are two situations where the index might be derived in another way, viz:

1. Internal index derived on sampling basis— In situations where determination of detailed unit and cost data for each item in the *entire* inventory pool is impractical (because of technological changes, wide variety of items, or extreme fluctuations in the variety of items), the tax regulations state that an internal index may be computed by using a "representative portion of the inventory pool, or by use of other sound and consistent statistical methods." When this internal sampling approach is used, computation of the internal index is the same as illustrated in Exhibits 11–11 and 11–12, Phase A, except that sample data rather than total data are used.
2. External index—In situations where *neither* the entire ending inventory pool nor statistical sampling of the pool is feasible for computing an internal index, an *appropriate external price index* may be used. This is a rare situation because it is very difficult to justify in light of the IRS regulations. The selection of an external price index avoids the detailed index computations illustrated in Exhibits 11–11 and 11–12, Phase A. Therefore, only Phase B computations are necessary.

Application of the dollar value *Lifo* approach when the conversion price index is either based on a sample of the inventory or is a selected external price index is usually called *indexing.*[8]

To illustrate indexing, the following data are assumed for Doe Company for 19C:

			External Index
a.	Doe Company uses *Fifo* for internal purposes and dollar value *Lifo* with an external index for income tax and financial statement purposes.		
b.	19B ending *Lifo* inventory (from prior year):		
	Base layer—At base year cost..............	$100,000	1.00
	19B inventory layer—At base year cost........	40,000	1.05
c.	19C ending *Fifo* inventory—At current year cost..............................	176,000	1.10

Conversion of the 19C *Fifo* inventory to dollar value *Lifo* for 19C:

Phase A—Computation of conversion index for 19C—not needed.

Phase B—Conversion of *Fifo* inventory to dollar value *Lifo* using external indexes—19C:

	Fifo at Base Year Cost		Conversion Price Index		Lifo Cost
19C ending inventory (current cost) $176,000 ÷ 1.10)*	$160,000				
Base inventory layer	(100,000)	×	1.00	=	$100,000
19B inventory layer	(40,000)	×	1.05	=	42,000
19C additional inventory layer	$ 20,000	×	1.10	=	22,000
19C dollar value *Lifo* ending inventory					$164,000

* To convert current year cost to base year cost.

LIFO "RESERVES"

Companies using *Lifo* for tax and external reporting purposes and some other method, such as *Fifo,* for internal management and record-keeping purposes, sometimes employ a *Lifo* allowance account (often inappropriately called a *Lifo* "reserve" account) to reflect the difference between the two inventory amounts.

To illustrate, one company reported inventories as follows:

	19B	19A
Current Assets:		
Finished goods, work in process, and raw materials, *Lifo* basis (net of *Lifo* reserve of $3,200,000 in 19B and $2,900,000 in 19A)	$8,000,000	$6,500,000

[8] This is an assumption often used in accounting literature for *Lifo* problems. It oversimplifies dollar value *Lifo* and gives no flavor of the real life complexities encountered by all accountants. As explained above, the use of an external index is rarely permissible.

This indirectly reflects that the inventory method used for internal management purposes *(Fifo)* provided ending inventory balances of $11,200,000 in 19B and $9,400,000 in 19A. Although seldom formally entered in the accounts, the difference could be recorded in the accounts as follows, assuming *Lifo* was initially adopted in 19A:

19A (first *Lifo* year):

Cost of goods sold	2,900,000	
Allowance to reduce inventory to *Lifo* basis		2,900,000

19B:

Cost of goods sold	300,000	
Allowance to reduce inventory to *Lifo* basis ($3,200,000 − $2,900,000)		300,000

SUMMARY

The discussions in Part B explained the primary problems in *Lifo* application. Since the quantity, or specific unit, method of applying *Lifo* illustrated in Part A is not often applied for external purposes, its study alone conveys an oversimplification of the *Lifo* issue. In application, *Lifo* is comparatively complex and involves considerable clerical effort. Because of the wide range of opportunities for differences, and because it is subject to inventory manipulation, it has been accorded much attention by governmental regulatory agencies such as the SEC and the IRS. Similarly, the major accounting firms have devoted much research and study to *Lifo* because they generally view it as a conceptually sound and practical approach to the measurement of income. Also, accountants insist that the concept be applied in a conceptually sound, consistent, and realistic way in each situation. *Lifo* is generally recommended in situations where

1. Continuing price changes (inflation) can be reasonably expected.
2. Income taxes will increase or remain high.
3. Inventory quantities (volume) will not decrease materially.
4. Shortages of items stocked are not expected.
5. Long-run trends in the business can be projected with a reasonable level of confidence.

QUESTIONS

PART A

1. What are the primary purposes to be served in selecting a particular inventory cost flow method? Why is the selection particularly important?

2. Briefly explain the differences between periodic and perpetual inventory systems. Under what circumstances is each generally used?

3. Does the adoption of a perpetual inventory system eliminate the need for physical count or measurement of inventories? Explain.

4. Explain the specific identification cost method and outline the objections to it.

5. Distinguish between a weighted average and a moving average in determining unit cost. When is each generally used? Explain.

6. Explain the essential features of first-in, first-out. What are the primary advantages and disadvantages of *Fifo?* Explain the difference in the application of *Fifo* under *(a)* periodic and *(b)* perpetual inventory systems. In contrast with *Lifo*, how does *Fifo* affect cash flow?

7. Explain the essential features of last-in, first-out. What are the primary advantages and disadvantages of *Lifo?* Explain the difference in application of *Lifo* under *(a)* periodic inventory and *(b)* perpetual inventory systems.

8. Explain why *Lifo* costed currently and *Lifo* costed at the end of the period may yield different results.

9. What is meant by inventory layers? Why are they significant with respect to the *Fifo, Lifo,* and base stock methods?

10. Assuming the *Lifo* method, what is meant by inventory liquidation? Why is it a serious problem for *Lifo* but not *Fifo?*

11. How is *Lifo* usually applied *(a)* in the accounts, *(b)* on the income tax return, and *(c)* in the external financial reports.

12. Compare the balance sheet and income statement effects of *Fifo* versus *Lifo* (a) when prices are rising and (b) when prices are falling.

PART B

13. Why do IRS regulations limit reporting of the impact in a footnote for only the base year, of two

different inventory methods (where one of the methods is used for tax purposes)?

14. What is meant by the quantity of goods *Lifo* method? Identify and distinguish between the two approaches used to implement this method.

15. Explain how changes in the item or product mix of *Lifo* inventories over a period of several years will adversely affect the results of the quantity of goods approach.

16. What are the primary differences and limitations of the *Lifo* quantity of goods method versus the dollar value method?

17. Contrast the concept of a *Lifo* inventory pool as between the quantity of goods method and the dollar value method.

18. What are the basic features of the dollar value *Lifo* method?

19. What is indexing in the context of applying the dollar value *Lifo* approach? When can an external rather than an internal price index be used?

DECISION CASE 11-1

Storm Company uses *Lifo,* unit basis (costed at the end of the period), to cost the ending inventory for income tax and external reporting purposes. Near the end of 19A, the records and related estimates provided the following annual data for one item sold regularly:

	Units	Unit Cost
Beginning inventory (*Lifo* basis):		
Base inventory (normal minimum level)	10,000	$20
Increment No. 1	5,000	30
Purchases (actual)	60,000	35
* Sales (@ $50 per unit)	65,000	

* Expenses (excluding income taxes), $1,000,000.
Beginning retained earnings, $650,000.
Average income tax rate, 30%.

   * Including estimates for remainder of 19A.

On December 26, 19A, the company has an opportunity to purchase not less than 30,000 units of the above item at $33 (a special price) with ten-day credit terms. Delivery is immediate, and the offer will expire January 3, 19B. The question has been posed as to whether the purchase (and delivery) should be consummated in 19A or 19B; the management has tentatively decided to make the purchase in 19A.

Required:

1. What is your recommendation as to the purchase date? Support your recommendation with reasons and pro forma (as if) income statement and balance sheet data. Include computations. Assume 10,000 shares of common stock are outstanding.

2. Explain and illustrate why earnings per share would be changed if the purchase is made in 19A.

3. Would you suspect profit manipulation in this situation if Storm elected to make the purchase in 19A? Explain.

EXERCISES

PART A
Exercises 11–1 to 11–7

Exercise 11-1

The inventory records of the Darby Company provided the following data for one item of merchandise for sale (assume the transactions in order of the number given):

	Units	Unit Cost	Total Amount
Goods available for sale:			
Beginning inventory	500	$6.00	$ 3,000
Purchases:			
(1)	600	6.10	3,660
(3)	600	\ 6.20	3,720
(5)	400	6.30	2,520
	2,100		$12,900
Sales:			
(2)	900		
(4)	500		
(6)	300		

Required:

1. Complete the following (round unit costs to nearest cent and total amounts to nearest dollar).

	Costing Method	Valuation	
		Ending Inventory	Cost of Goods Sold
a.	Fifo	$_____	$_____
b.	Lifo (unit basis costed at end of period and assume base inventory is 400 units)	$_____	$_____
c.	Weighted average	$_____	$_____
d.	Lifo (same as [*b*] except costed currently)	$_____	$_____

2. Compute the amount of pretax income and rank the methods in order of the amount of pretax income (highest first) assuming *Fifo* pretax income is $30,000.

3. Which method is preferable in this instance? Why?

Exercise 11–2

The raw material records of the AB Manufacturing Company showed the following data relative to raw material K (assume the transactions occurred in the order given):

		Units	Unit Cost
1.	Inventory	300	$2.00
2.	Purchase	400	2.10
3.	Issue	600	
4.	Purchase	500	2.20
5.	Issue	400	
6.	Purchase	600	2.30

Required:

1. Compute the cost of issues for the period and the ending inventory assuming (round unit costs to even cents):
   a. Weighted average.
   b. Moving average.
   c. Fifo.
   d. *Lifo* (unit basis, costed at end, 300 units in base layer).
   e. *Lifo* (unit basis, costed currently, 300 units in base layer).
2. Under what general circumstances would each be preferable?

Exercise 11–3

The inventory records of Goldstein Retailers showed the following data relative to a particular unit sold regularly (assume transactions in the order given):

		Units	Unit Cost
1.	Inventory	2,000	$4.00
2.	Purchases	18,000	4.50
3.	Sales (@ $13 per unit)	7,000	
4.	Purchases	6,000	4.60
5.	Sales (@ $13.50 per unit)	16,000	
6.	Purchases	4,000	4.70

Required:

1. Complete the following tabulation (round unit costs to even cents and keep unit costs of inventory in even dollars):

	Ending Inventory	Cost of Goods Sold	Gross Margin
a. Fifo	_____	_____	_____
b. Weighted average	_____	_____	_____
c. Lifo (unit basis costed at end, 2,000 units in base layer)	_____	_____	_____
d. Lifo (unit basis costed currently, 2,000 units in base layer)	_____	_____	_____
e. Moving average (show computations)	_____	_____	_____

2. What method would be preferable? Explain the basis for your choice.

Exercise 11–4

Stanley Company uses *Lifo* (unit basis). The following data were available relative to the primary raw material for 19A:

	Units	Unit Cost
Beginning inventory (base inventory)	5,000	$3.00
Beginning inventory (excess)	1,000	3.10
Purchases	19,000	3.40
Issues	22,000	

The first purchase in period 19B was 10,000 units at $3.70 per unit.

Required:

1. Compute the ending *Lifo* inventory (costed at end of period) and the cost of issues for 19A.
2. Give the journal entries for purchases and issues; record the 19A inventory invasion in the accounts (debit purchases to Inventory and issues to Work in Process).
3. Give the journal entry for the purchase in 19B.

Exercise 11–5

Tims Company currently uses *Fifo* for internal and external reporting and tax purposes. The inventory records for 19C reflected the following for one major item sold regularly:

Beginning inventory (at cost)	10,000 units @ $ 8
Purchases during 19C	40,000 units @ 10
Sales during 19C (@ $30)	35,000 units
Expenses (excluding income taxes)	$ 40,000

Beginning cash balance	$ 20,000
Beginning retained earnings	$500,000
Income tax average rate	45%

The company is considering a change to *Lifo* (costed at the end) for all purposes. Assume the beginning inventory given above will be the *Lifo* base inventory.

Required:

1. Assuming all transactions are cash basis, compare *Lifo* and *Fifo* results by preparing for each: *(a)* an income statement and *(b)* a partial balance sheet (limited to the above transactions). Include a column for *differences* and show computation of cash balances. Assume 100,000 shares of common stock outstanding.
2. In this situation, based on the data at hand, which inventory method would you recommend? Why?
3. Under what conditions would you recommend the other method?

Exercise 11–6

Munson Company records standard costs in the accounts. The finished goods inventory records are maintained at standard. When raw material is purchased, the difference between standard cost and actual cost is recorded in a separate variance account and reported as a *loss or gain* for the period in which the goods were purchased. The records relating to one item of raw material for 19A showed the following: standard cost per unit, $8; beginning inventory, 1,000 units; purchases during the period were; No. 1—2,000 units at $8.25, No. 2—800 units at $7.90, and No. 3—1,200 units at $8; units issued to work in process (factory), 3,500; expenses paid were $31,500; total cost of goods sold was $40,000; and sales were $70,000.

Required:

1. Give journal entries for the purchases, sales, expenses, and cost of goods sold. Assume no change in the inventory balances in work in process and finished goods.
2. Prepare an income statement (disregard income taxes). Assume 5,000 shares of common stock outstanding.

Exercise 11–7

WT Manufacturing Company produces a single product in one plant that is distributed nationally. The plant is highly mechanized; therefore, fixed costs are relatively high. Full manufacturing cost and *Lifo* (unit basis and costed at the end of the period) have been used for internal and external reporting and tax purposes. Because there is only one plant and wide distribution, a large inventory of finished goods is maintained. The controller is considering a variable (direct) costing system for internal purposes. *Lifo* (unit basis) will continue to be used for income tax purposes. The following year-end amounts were determined on a *Lifo* (full historical cost) basis:

Sales (8,000 units @ $91)	$728,000
Cost of goods sold (@ $46)	368,000
Gross margin	360,000
Expenses (fixed)	160,000
Pretax income	200,000
Income taxes (@ 40%)	80,000
Net Income	$120,000
Beginning inventory, finished goods	None
Manufacturing costs (10,000 units):	
Direct material used	$ 55,000
Direct labor incurred	175,000
Factory overhead—fixed	150,000
Factory overhead—variable	80,000
Ending inventory, finished goods (2,000 units)	(92,000)
Cost of goods sold	$368,000

Required:

1. Recast the above statements for internal purposes on a direct cost basis. Use the beginning inventory as given.
2. Which basis should be used for external reporting purposes? Explain.
3. How is the total fixed expense reported for the period?

PART B
Exercises 11–8 to 11–13

Exercise 11–8

On January 1, 19B, Dawson Company changed from *Fifo* to *Lifo* for income tax and external reporting purposes. The ending inventory for 19A (*Fifo* basis) was $155,000 (this will be the base inventory amount for *Lifo*). At the end of 19B, the *Lifo* inventory amount, computed using the dollar value, double-extension approach was $160,000; had the company continued using *Fifo,* this amount would have been $184,000. The average income tax rate is 46%.

Required:

1. Compute the difference in net income for 19B attributable to the change from *Fifo* to *Lifo.* Show computations.
2. Prepare an appropriate note to the financial statements for 19B.

Exercise 11–9

XY Corporation has been using *Fifo* for all purposes for several years. Starting January 1, 19C, the company has decided to change to *Lifo* for *(a)* internal reports, *(b)* external reports to shareholders, and *(c)* income tax purposes.

Because of the limited number of items stocked and the opportunity to use *"Lifo* inventory pools" for substantially identical items, the company is considering using the quantity of goods method applied to (1) single items or (2) to multiple pools.

This problem is limited to two of the items (A and B) that are substantially identical. If pooled, they would constitute Inventory Pool No. 1. The related inventory data for a two-year period were as follows:

	Year 19C	Year 19D
Beginning inventory:		
Item A	600 units @ $10	
Item B	700 units @ 12	
Purchases during the year (at cost):		
Item A	6,000 units @ 12	7,100 units @ $13
Item B	1,200 units @ 15	800 units @ 16
Sales during the year (at sales price):		
Item A	5,800 units @ 25	7,000 units @ 28
Item B	900 units @ 32	850 units @ 34

Required:

1. Prepare a schedule to compute the *Lifo* results using the quantity of goods method, *single-item* approach. Suggested captions are given at the top of the next column.

	Item A			Item B
	Units	Unit Cost	Total Cost	(repeat)
Year 19C:				
Beginning inventory				
Purchases				
Total available				
Ending inventory				
Issues				
Year 19D:				
(repeat)				

2. Prepare a schedule to compute the *Lifo* results using the quantity of goods method, *multiple-pools* approach. Suggested captions:

	Inventory Pool No. 1		
	Total Units	Average Unit Cost	Total Cost
Year 19C:			
(Same captions as in Requirement 1)			
Year 19D:			
(Same captions as for 19C)			

Exercise 11–10

AB Corporation has been using *Fifo* since its organization for *(a)* internal management reports and control, *(b)* external reporting to shareholders, and *(c)* income tax purposes. On January 1, 19B, management decided to change from *Fifo* to *Lifo* for external reporting and income tax purposes. *Fifo* will continue in use for internal purposes.

The company has a number of *"Lifo* inventory pools"; however, this problem deals with only one of them. The company will apply the dollar value approach for converting the *Fifo* results to a *Lifo* basis and will use an internal conversion index computed each year.

The *Fifo* results for a three-year period, taken directly from the accounts and internal reports for Inventory Pool No. 1 (composed of five similar items in a "natural business unit"), showed the data at the bottom of this page.

(Relates to Problem 11–10)	Year 19A			Year 19B			Year 19C		
	Units	Unit Cost	Total	Units	Unit Cost	Total	Units	Unit Cost	Total
Sales revenue			$18,200			$24,280			$30,920
Cost of goods sold *(Fifo):*									
Beginning inventory	800	$2.50	2,000	600	$3.00	1,800	700	$3.60	2,520
Purchases	2,000	3.00	6,000	2,500	3.60	9,000	3,000	4.00	12,000
Ending inventory*	600	3.00	1,800	700	3.60	2,520	900	4.00	3,600
Cost of goods sold	2,200		6,200	2,400		8,280	2,800		10,920

* Deduction.

Required:

1. Compute the conversion price indexes needed for the dollar value *Lifo* application through 19C. Show computations and round conversion ratios to two decimal places.
2. Convert the *Fifo* results to a *Lifo* basis for 19B and 19C using the dollar value approach. Show computations.
3. Assuming $8,000 operating expenses, a 30% average tax rate, and 2,000 shares of common stock outstanding, prepare income statements for 19B and 19C with two headings for each year: *(a)* for internal reports (*Fifo* basis), and *(b)* for external reports and tax returns (*Lifo* basis). *Suggestion:* Use one set of side captions and four money columns.

Exercise 11–11

Crow Company uses *Lifo* for income tax and external reporting purposes. The *Lifo* base inventory (at end of 19A) for inventory Pool No. 1 amounted to $70,000. The periodic inventory of Pool No. 1 taken at the end of 19B, priced at 19B costs on a *Fifo* basis, amounted to $92,000. Analysis of a statistical sample of the inventory and related computations showed a price index for 19A of 100 and for 19B of 115.

Required:

1. Use the internal indexes already derived to compute the 19B ending *Lifo* inventory amount assuming the dollar value method.
2. Under what conditions is the sampling index approach appropriate?

Exercise 11–12

Ready Wholesale Grocery Company uses the *Lifo* method for income tax and external reporting purposes. The ending inventory for 19A (*Lifo* basis) amounted to $260,000 (at base cost). The physical inventory taken at the end of 19B, at 19B costs, was valued at $336,000 (*Fifo* basis). An external price index indicated a 12% increase in prices during 19B. Assume this is a rare situation in which an external price index can be used.

Required:

1. Use the external index to compute the *Lifo* inventory amount, assuming dollar value, double-extension method.
2. Under what special conditions is the external index approach appropriate for converting a *Fifo* basis inventory to the dollar value *Lifo* basis?

Exercise 11–13

At the end of the annual accounting period, the inventory records of Scott Company reflected the following:

	19A	19B
Ending inventory at *Fifo*	$350,000	$390,000
Ending inventory at *Lifo*	340,000	320,000

The company uses *Fifo* for internal purposes and *Lifo* for income tax and external reporting purposes.

Required:

1. Assume the inventory difference is recognized in the accounts. Give the appropriate journal entry for each year.
2. Show how the inventories should be shown on the 19B comparative balance sheet.

PROBLEMS

PART A
Problems 11–1 to 11–6

Problem 11–1

ST Company records showed the following transactions, in order of occurrence, relative to Raw Material Z:

		Units	Unit Cost
1.	Inventory	400	$5.00
2.	Purchase	600	5.50
3.	Issue	700	
4.	Purchase	900	5.60
5.	Issue	800	
6.	Purchase	200	5.80

Required:

Compute the cost of the issues and ending inventory in each of the following completely independent situations (round unit costs to the nearest cent for inventory; show computations):

	Units and Amount	
Assumption	Ending Inventory	Issues
a. Weighted average.		
b. Moving average.		
c. Fifo.		
d. Lifo costed currently.		
e. Lifo costed at end of period.		
f. Base stock (base stock, 100 units).		
g. Standard cost (standard cost, $4.75).		

Problem 11–2

The records of XY Trading Company showed the following transactions, in the order given, relating to the major inventory item:

		Units	Unit Cost
1.	Inventory	3,000	$7.00
2.	Purchase	5,000	7.20
3.	Sales (@ $15)	4,000	
4.	Purchase	7,000	7.50
5.	Sales (@ $15)	9,000	
6.	Purchase	8,000	7.60
7.	Sales (@ $16)	9,000	
8.	Purchase	6,000	7.90

Required:

Complete the following tabulation for each independent assumption (round unit costs to the nearest cent for computations):

		Units and Amount		
	Assumption	Ending Inventory	Cost of Goods Sold	Gross Margin
a.	Fifo.			
b.	Lifo costed at end of period (base inventory, 1,000 units).			
c.	Lifo costed currently (base inventory, 1,000 units)—support with a perpetual inventory record.			
d.	Weighted average.			
e.	Moving average—support with a perpetual inventory record.			

Problem 11–3

The records of Dawn Company showed the following data with respect to one raw material used in the manufacturing process. Assume the transactions occurred in the order given.

	Units	Unit Cost
Inventory	4,000	$7.00
Purchase No. 1	3,000	7.60
Issue No. 1	5,000	
Purchase No. 2	8,000	8.00
Issue No. 2	7,000	
Purchase No. 3	3,000	8.20

Required:

1. Compute cost of materials issued (to work in process) and the valuation of the ending inventory for each of the following independent transactions

(round unit costs to the nearest cent for inventory; show computations):
   a. *Fifo.*
   b. *Lifo,* costed at end of period (base inventory, 4,000 units).
   c. Weighted average.
   d. Moving average.
   e. Standard cost (assuming a standard unit cost of $7).

2. In parallel columns, give all entries indicated for *Fifo* assuming a count of the raw material on hand at the end showed 6,000 units:

   Case A—A perpetual inventory system.
   Case B—A periodic inventory system.

Problem 11–4

The records of Day Company showed the following data relative to one of the major items being sold. Assume the transactions occurred in the order given.

	Units	Unit Cost
Beginning inventory	7,000	$4.00
Purchase No. 1	6,000	4.20
Sale No. 1 (@ $10)	9,000	
Purchase No. 2	8,000	4.50
Sale No. 2 (@ $11)	4,000	

Required:

1. Compute cost of goods sold, valuation of the ending inventory, and gross margin under each of the following independent assumptions (round unit costs to nearest cent):

		Amount		
		Inventory	Cost of Goods Sold	Gross Margin
a.	Weighted average cost with periodic inventory system.			
b.	Fifo with perpetual inventory system.			
c.	Lifo costed at end of period (base inventory, 7,000 units).			
d.	Standard cost, assuming the standard cost is $4.			

2. Give all entries indicated by the above data assuming a perpetual inventory system:

   Case A—Fifo ([b] above).
   Case B—Standard cost ([d] above).

Problem 11–5

Davis Manufacturing Company manufactures one main product. Two raw materials are used in the manufacture of this product. The company uses standard costs in the accounts and carries the raw material, work in process, and finished goods inventories at standard. The records of the company showed the following:

	Material A	Material B
Beginning inventory (units)	8,000	5,000
Standard cost per unit	$2.00	$7.00
Purchases during the period:		
No. 1	10,000 @ $2.00	7,000 @ $7.00
No. 2	20,000 @ 1.90	8,000 @ 7.20
Issues during the period (units)	28,000	16,000
Ending inventory per physical count (units) ...	10,000	3,900

Required:

1. Give all entries indicated relative to raw materials assuming standard costs.
2. Determine the value of the ending inventory and cost issues for each raw material.
3. Accumulate the amount of the variations from standard for each raw material and explain or illustrate the reporting and accounting disposition of these amounts.

Problem 11–6 (an overview problem)

Rawlins Company maintains perpetual inventory records on a *Fifo* basis for the three main products distributed by the company. A physical inventory is taken at the end of each six months in order to check the perpetual inventory records.

The following information relating to one of the products for the year 19A was taken from the records of the company:

	Product A
Beginning inventory	9,000 units @ $8.10
Purchases and sales (in the order given):	
Purchase No. 11	5,000 units @ 8.15
Sale No. 1	10,000 units
Purchase No. 12	16,000 units @ 8.20
Sale No. 2	11,000 units
Purchase No. 13	4,000 units @ 8.30
Purchase No. 14	7,000 units @ 8.20
Sale No. 3	14,000 units
Purchase No. 15	5,000 units @ 8.10
Ending inventory (per count)	10,000
Replacement cost (per unit)	$8.00

Required:

1. Reconstruct the perpetual inventory record for Product A.
2. Give all entries indicated by the above data assuming selling price is $18 per unit and that the company employs the inventory allowance method (holding losses separately identified) in recognizing LCM.
3. Prepare the income statement for this product through gross margin.

PART B
Problems 11–7 to 11–12

Problem 11–7

Chase Company sells three main products. In the past, perpetual inventory procedures have been employed on a *Fifo* basis. The records of the company showed the following information relating to one of the products:

Beginning inventory	500 units @ $3.00
Purchases and sales (in the order given):	
Purchase No. 1	400 units @ 3.10
Purchase No. 2	600 units @ 3.15
Sale No. 1	1,000 units
Purchase No. 3	800 units @ 3.25
Sale No. 2	700 units
Sale No. 3	500 units
Purchase No. 4	700 units @ 3.30

In considering a change in inventory policy, the following summary was prepared:

	Illustration			
	(1)	*(2)*	*(3)*	*(4)*
Sales	$15,400	$15,400	$15,400	$15,400
Cost of goods sold..........	6,930	7,110	6,996	6,905
Gross margin ...	$ 8,470	$ 8,290	$ 8,404	$ 8,495

Required:

Identify the inventory flow method used for each illustration assuming only the ending inventory was affected. Show computations.

(AICPA adapted)

Problem 11–8

Fowler Company decided at the beginning of 19A to change from *Fifo* to *Lifo*. The records of the company showed the following data for 19A relative to one major inventory item distributed:

	Units	Unit Cost
Beginning inventory (*Lifo* base inventory layers averaged), January 1, 19A	10,000	$3.00
Purchases and sales (in the order given):		
1. Purchase	8,000	3.20
2. Sold (@ $8.00)	9,000	
3. Sold (@ $8.25)	5,000	
4. Purchase	7,000	3.20
5. Purchase	6,000	3.40
6. Sold (@ $8.75)	8,000	
7. Purchase	3,000	3.50

Expenses (excluding income taxes), $40,000.
Average income tax rate, 40%.

Required:

1. Prepare an income statement for 19A, unit *Lifo* basis, costed at the end of the period. Assume 10,000 shares of common stock outstanding.
2. Prepare an appropriate footnote, and any other required supporting data, for the change in 19A from *Fifo* to *Lifo*.
3. What would be disclosed in 19B relative to the change? Why?

Problem 11–9

Stanton Retailers, Incorporated, sells two main products regularly. The products are considered "substantially identical" for inventory purposes. The company used *Fifo* through 19A for all purposes. Starting in 19B, *Lifo* was adopted for external reporting and income tax purposes. The inventory pool (the two products combined) records at *Fifo* reflected the information shown at the bottom of this page.

Required:

1. Convert the ending inventory at *Fifo* to a *Lifo* basis for 19B, 19C, and 19D, assuming the dollar value method is used. Round conversion ratios to two decimal places.
2. Prepare a schedule (that includes inventory, tax, and income) to compare the results for *Fifo* and *Lifo*. For analytical purposes, assume (a) an average tax rate of 40% and (b) a pretax income amount of $300 for each year. Which method should be used? Why?
3. Prepare a suitable footnote for the financial statements for 19B assuming *Lifo* is used for external reporting and income tax purposes.

Problem 11–10

Wilson Distributing Company sells three main products regularly. The products are considered "substantially identical" for inventory purposes. The company used *Fifo* through 19A for all purposes. After 19A, *Fifo* was continued for internal management and accounting purposes; however, at the start of 19B, *Lifo* was adopted for income tax and external reporting purposes. The following data (for the three products combined) were taken from the records for the three years following the adoption of *Lifo*:

	Fifo Basis per Accounts		
	Units	Cost	Total
19A:			
Ending inventory	2,000	$3.00	$ 6,000
19B:			
Purchases	6,000	3.30	$19,800
Sales (@ $8)	5,000		
Ending inventory	3,000	3.30	9,900

(Relates to Problem 11–9)	Purchases			Issues			Balance (Fifo)		
19A:									
Ending inventory							400	1.00	400
19B:									
Purchases	700	1.20	840				400	1.00	400
							700	1.20	840
Sales (@ $3.00)				400	1.00	400			
				100	1.20	120	600	1.20	720
19C:									
Purchases	600	1.35	810				600	1.20	720
							600	1.35	810
Sales (@ $3.40)				600	1.20	720			
				200	1.35	270	400	1.35	540
19D:									
Purchases	500	1.50	750				400	1.35	540
							500	1.50	750
Sales (@ $3.75)				400	1.35	540	500	1.50	750

19C:

Purchases	10,000	3.50	$35,000
Sales (@ $9)	6,000		
Ending inventory	7,000	3.50	24,500

19D:

Purchases	3,000	4.00	$12,000
Sales (@ $9)	6,000		
Ending inventory			
Layer 1	1,000	3.50	3,500
Layer 2	3,000	4.00	12,000
Total	4,000		$15,500

Required:

1. Convert the ending inventory at *Fifo* to a *Lifo* basis for 19B, 19C, and 19D, assuming the dollar value method is used. Round conversion ratios to two decimal places.
2. Prepare a schedule (which includes inventory, tax, and income) that compares the results of the methods, *Fifo* and *Lifo*. For analytical purposes assume *(a)* an average tax rate of 40% and *(b)* a pretax income amount of $8,000 under *Fifo*. Which method should be used? Why?
3. Prepare an appropriate footnote to the financial statements for 19B assuming *Lifo* is used for external reporting and tax purposes.

Problem 11–11

Baker Company has been using *Fifo* for all internal and external reporting purposes. At the start of 19B,

it adopted *Lifo* for external financial statement and income tax purposes. The *Fifo* inventory records reported the following for one inventory pool:

	Fifo Basis
19A ending inventory	$100,000
19B ending inventory	120,000
19C ending inventory	130,000
19D ending inventory	135,000

External price index selected: 19A—1.00; 19B—1.10; 19C—1.15; and 19D—1.21

Required:

Convert the ending *Fifo* inventory amounts to a *Lifo* basis for 19B, 19C, and 19D, assuming the dollar value method, using an external price index. The external index selected is given above.

Problem 11–12

Stallings Company sells two main products that have low volume but high cost. *Fifo,* with a perpetual inventory system, is used for internal cost accounting and management purposes. On January 1, 19B, the company adopted *Lifo* for external reporting and income tax purposes; *Fifo* will continue to be used for internal purposes. The *Fifo* inventory records are shown at the bottom of this page and is continued at the top of the next page.

(Relates to Problem 11–12)

Perpetual Inventory Record

	Purchases*			Issues			Fifo Balance		
	U	UC	TC	U	UC	TC	U	UC	TC
Product X									
December 31, 19A . .							200	100	20,000
19B:									
Purchases	400	130	52,000				400	130	52,000
Sales (@ $300) . .				200	100	20,000			
				200	130	26,000	200	130	26,000
							200	130	26,000
19C:									
Purchases	500	140	70,000				500	140	70,000
Sales (@ $300) . .				200	130	26,000	500	140	70,000
							500	140	70,000
19D:									
Purchases	100	150	15,000				100	150	15,000
Sales (@ $325) . .				300	140	42,000	200	140	28,000
							100	150	15,000

Perpetual Inventory Record *(continued)*

	Purchases*			Issues			Fifo Balance		
	U	UC	TC	U	UC	TC	U	UC	TC
Product Y									
December 31, 19A ..							300	90	27,000
19B:									
Purchases	400	92	36,800				400	92	36,800
Sales (@ $275) ..				300	90	27,000	400	92	36,800
							400	92	36,800
19C:									
Purchases	100	95	9,500				100	95	9,500
Sales (@ $275) ..				400	92	36,800	100	95	9,500
							100	95	9,500
19D:									
Purchases	400	96	38,400				400	96	38,400
Sales (@ $295) ..				100	95	9,500	400	96	38,400

* U = units; UC = unit cost; and TC = total cost.

Required:

Assume the two products are "substantially identical" for inventory purposes. Convert the ending inventory at *Fifo* to a *Lifo* basis for 19B, 19C, and 19D, assuming the dollar value method is used. Round conversion ratios to two places.

Optional: If specifically assigned by your instructor, also

a. Prepare a schedule that includes inventories, income taxes, and net income that compares the *Fifo* and *Lifo* results. For analytical purposes assume an average tax rate of 40% and a pretax income amount of $30,000.

b. Prepare a suitable footnote to the financial statements for 19B assuming *Lifo* is used for external and tax purposes.

Inventories—Special Valuation Procedures

Numerous situations occur in which accountants must make estimates relating to inventories. Consequently, certain inventory estimating procedures have gained wide acceptance. They are discussed and illustrated in this chapter, which is divided into two parts as follows:

Part A–1—Estimating Procedures for Inventories
    a. Gross margin method
    b. Retail inventory method
    2—Inventories for Long-Term Construction Contracts
Part B—Dollar Value, *Lifo* Retail Method

PART A–1—ESTIMATING PROCEDURES FOR INVENTORIES

GROSS MARGIN METHOD

The gross margin[1] method represents an approach frequently used to approximate the value of an inventory independent of a physical count of the goods, and as a test check on the detailed inventory records in perpetual inventory procedures. The method is based on the assumption that the short-run *rate of gross margin* (gross margin divided by sales) will be approximately the same from one period to the next.

Computation of total goods *available* for sale is the first step in the gross margin method. This is done in the normal manner, based on data provided by the accounts. Next the estimated cost of goods sold is determined by multiplying sales revenue by an estimated gross margin rate and deducting the result from sales to derive estimated cost of goods sold. Deduction of the estimated cost of goods sold from the cost of goods available for sale gives the ending inventory at estimated cost. For example, if the rate of gross margin for a business has been uniformly 20% of sales and is estimated to continue at that rate for the current period, the ending inventory for the current year may be estimated as shown below:

Cost of goods available for sale:		
Beginning inventory		$ 50,000*
Purchases during period	$160,400*	
Freight-in	9,800*	
Total Purchases	170,200	
Less: Purchase returns and allowances	200*	
Net purchases		170,000
Cost of goods available for sale		220,000

---

[1] The method traditionally has been referred to as the gross profit method; nevertheless the descriptive modern terminology *gross margin* is used throughout these discussions. (Ref. AICPA, *Terminology Bulletin No. 2.*)

Deduct estimated cost
of goods sold:

Sales	201,000*	
Less: Sales returns	1,000*	
Net sales	200,000	
Less: Estimated gross margin ($200,000 × .20†)	40,000	
Estimated cost of goods sold		160,000
Estimated cost of ending inventory		$ 60,000

* Data directly from the records.
† Based on recent past performance.

A more comprehensive example, in which the data are rearranged to facilitate computation and study, is shown at the bottom of this page.

The gross margin method uses (1) selected *actual cost data* from the accounts and (2) a *key projection*—the expected *normal gross margin rate*.

In some problems relating to the gross margin method, a *cost* percentage (cost of goods sold divided by sales) is given rather than the gross margin percentage (gross margin divided by sales). If either percentage is known, the other is easily determinable, since the two percentages must sum to 100%. In the above example, since the rate of gross margin is 20%, the cost percentage is 80% (100% − 20%). The gross margin rate, or markup, was given as a percent of sales (20% markup on sales); however, it could have been stated as 25% of the *cost of goods sold* (markup on cost). In the latter case, a conversion of the rate on cost to a rate on sales would be desirable. Conversion of a rate on cost to a rate on sales or vice versa may be accomplished algebraically as follows:[2]

$$\text{Symbols:} \quad C = \text{Cost}$$
$$SP = \text{Selling price}$$
$$MU = \text{Markup}$$

1. The markup on cost is 25%; determine the markup (gross margin rate) on sales. Since there are two variables, two equations are needed:

(1)
$$C + .25C = SP$$
$$1.25C = SP$$
$$C = \frac{1}{1.25} SP$$
$$C = .80SP$$

(2)
$$MU = SP - C$$
$$MU = SP - .80SP$$
$$MU = .20SP$$
$$MU \text{ on sales} = MU \div SP$$
$$MU \text{ on sales} = .20SP \div SP$$
$$\underline{MU \text{ on sales} = .20}$$

2. The markup on sales is 20%; determine the markup on cost:

---

[2] A more direct computation (where markup on cost is known) giving the same results without a conversion to markup on sales could be made as follows:

Cost of goods available for sale (per above)	$220,000
Deduct estimated cost of goods sold:	
Sales reduced to estimated cost ($200,000 ÷ 1.25)	160,000
Estimated cost of ending inventory	$ 60,000

	Known Data		Computations	Sequence of Computations
Net sales		$10,000*		
Cost of goods sold:				
Beginning inventory	$ 5,000†			
Add: Purchases	8,000*			
Goods available for sale	13,000			
Less: Ending inventory	?		($13,000 − $6,000) = $7,000	3
Cost of goods sold............		?	($10,000 − $4,000) = $6,000	2
Gross margin (as a % of sales)	40%‡	?	($10,000 × .40) = $4,000	1

* From company records.
† Ending inventory from prior period.
‡ Based on recent past performance.

(1) $$SP - .20SP = C$$
$$.80SP = C$$

(2) $$MU = SP - C$$
$$MU = SP - .80SP$$
$$MU = .20SP$$
$$MU \text{ on cost} = MU \div C$$
$$MU \text{ on cost} = .20SP \div .80SP$$
$$\underline{MU \text{ on cost} = .25}$$

A more direct approach that shortcuts the algebra involves the use of fractions, as illustrated below. Note that in all cases the numerator (i.e., markup) is the same for both markup on cost and markup on sales; whereas when converting to a markup on sales, the denominator is the sum of the numerator and denominator of the cost fraction, and when converting to a markup on cost, the denominator is the difference between the numerator and the denominator of the sales fraction. Obviously the fraction or rate on sales must be smaller than the comparable fraction or markup rate on cost. Observe the relationship between the fractions on each line in the following example:

	Markup	
Problem	On Cost	On Sales
a. Markup is 25% on cost; determine the markup on sales	¼(or 25%) →	⅕(or 20%)
b. Markup is 33⅓% on sales; determine the markup on cost	½(or 50%) ←	⅓(or 33⅓%)
c. Markup is 66⅔% on cost; determine the markup on sales	⅔(or 66⅔%)→	⅖(or 40%)

The gross margin method frequently is employed in the following four different situations:

1. By auditors and others to test the reasonableness of an inventory valuation provided by some other person or determined by some other means, such as physical inventory or perpetual inventory. To illustrate, assume the bookkeeper for the company referred to above submitted to the auditor an ending inventory valuation of $85,000. The gross margin method provides an approximation of $60,000 (see page 418), which would suggest that the inventory may be overvalued.

2. To estimate the ending inventory for interim financial reports (monthly or quarterly statements, for example) prepared during the year where it is impractical to take an interim physical inventory. The method finds fairly wide application for internal reporting purposes and for external quarterly reports (see *APB Opinion No. 28,* par. 13a).

3. To estimate an inventory destroyed by a casualty such as fire or storm. Obviously, this application would be limited to those situations where the books of accounts are not destroyed, since certain basic data from the accounts are essential. Valuation of inventory lost through casualty is necessary *(a)* to estimate the market value of the loss and *(b)* to establish a basis for settlement of insurance claims related to the inventory loss. For insurance claim purposes, the results may have to be adjusted to current replacement cost because that is the basis on which such claims generally are settled.

4. To develop budget estimates of cost of goods sold, gross margin, and inventory after a sales revenue budget is developed.

The gross margin method gives an estimate based on the cost flow assumption used by the company (*Fifo, Lifo,* etc.). In applying the gross margin method, the accountant must bear in mind that the possibility of error exists because of *(a)* the assumption that the estimated gross margin rate, based on the results of past period(s), will continue in the future and *(b)* the effect of using an *average* rate. In the usual situation a company will carry a number of different lines of merchandise, each having a different markup or gross margin. Obviously, a change during the period in markup on one or more lines, or a shift in the relative quantities of each line sold, will change the average gross margin rate (markup), thereby affecting the validity of the results derived by the method.

When the gross margin method is applied in situations where significantly different markup rates are involved for different classes of merchandise, computations should be developed for each separate class if practicable. Then the estimate for total inventory can be determined by summing the estimates for the separate classes.

RETAIL INVENTORY METHOD

The retail inventory method of estimation is widely employed by retail stores, particularly department stores, which sell a wide variety of items. In such situations, perpetual inventory procedures sometimes are impractical, and taking a complete physical inventory more often than annually is uncommon. Several features of department store operation make possible utilization of the retail inventory method. Particular features are *(a)* the departments frequently are homogeneous with respect to the markup on items sold within a department and *(b)* articles purchased are immediately priced for resale and the prices are displayed. The effect of this latter feature may be observed in the tendency by retailing establishments to relate markups, analyses, budgets, estimates, markdowns, and so on, to *sales price* rather than to cost price. Whereas those in nonretailing companies tend to relate markup to cost, the retailer traditionally relates markup to selling price.

The retail inventory method is not a quantity of goods (units) method; rather it is based only on "dollar" amounts. Thus, the retail inventory method provides a special approach to measure the ending inventory on a (1) *Fifo* basis, (2) average cost basis, (3) lower-of-cost-or-market (LCM) basis, or (4) *Lifo* basis, depending on how the calculations are made.

The retail inventory method (1) uses both retail and actual cost data provided by the accounts to compute (rather than to project) the cost ratio, (2) calculates the ending inventory at retail value, and (3) converts that retail value to a cost value by using the computed cost ratio.

The retail inventory method has been actively sponsored by the National Retail Merchants Association and approved by the Internal Revenue Service; consequently, it has become an important method of inventory determination. The accounting profession has accepted the method on its own merits as fundamentally sound where properly administered. It must be realized that the retail inventory method represents an approach for *estimating* the amount of the ending inventory used in computing cost of goods sold on the income statement and for reporting on the balance sheet. If properly applied, it can be used for both financial accounting and income tax purposes. From time to time it must be supplemented with a physical inventory check.

Application of the retail inventory method requires that *internal records* be kept which will provide the following data:

1. Beginning inventory valued at both cost and retail.
2. Purchases during the period valued at both cost and retail.
3. Adjustments to the original marked retail price, such as additional markups, markup cancellations, markdowns, employee discounts, and markdown cancellations.
4. Data relating to other adjustments, such as interdepartmental transfers, returns, breakage, and damaged goods.
5. Sales revenue.

This method is similar to the gross margin method in that the inventory valuation is based on the *ratio of cost to selling price*. That is, the gross margin method uses a projection of the historical cost ratio, whereas the retail inventory method uses a computed cost ratio based upon the current cost relationship of the period. Under the retail method, records are maintained so that the ratio may be computed for the current period. The *actual* cost and retail data required for the retail method are collected on a continuing basis and, since these data are not estimates, the cost/retail ratio can be certain. However, since the computed cost ratio is an average (i.e., not specific to each kind of goods sold), the computed inventory is an estimate.

The retail method involves computation of the goods available for sale at both *cost* and *retail.* Total cost is divided by total retail to obtain the *cost ratio.* Sales are then deducted from goods available for sale (at retail); the result is the inventory at retail. Multiplication of the inventory at retail by the computed cost ratio provides the estimated ending inventory valuation at cost. Determination of the ending inventory valuation employing the retail method is illustrated as follows with simplified data:

	At Cost	At Retail
Goods available for sale:		
Beginning inventory (January 1)	$ 15,000*	$ 25,000*
Purchases during January	195,000*	275,000*
Total goods available for sale	$210,000	300,000
Cost ratio: $210,000 ÷ $300,000 = .70.		
Deduct January sales at retail		260,000*
Ending inventory (January 31):		
At retail		$ 40,000
At cost ($40,000 × .70)	$ 28,000	

* Data available from the records.

Since the retail inventory method provides an estimate of the ending inventory, a rotating physical inventory (department by department) should be taken at least annually as a check on the accuracy of the computed inventory amounts. Significant differences between the physical inventory and the retail inventory amount should be carefully analyzed because they may indicate *(a)* inventory losses due to breakage, loss, or theft; *(b)* incorrect application of the retail method; *(c)* failure of departmental managers to correctly report markdowns, additional markups, or cancellations; *(d)* errors in the records; *(e)* errors in the physical inventory; or *(f)* inventory manipulation.

The primary uses of the retail method are as follows:

1. To provide estimated inventory valuations for interim periods (usually monthly) when such physical inventories are impracticable and a perpetual inventory system is not used. The method provides inventory valuations needed for monthly statements, analyses, and purchasing policy considerations.

2. To provide a means for converting a physical inventory, priced at retail, to a cost basis. To eliminate the necessity of marking the cost (in code) on the merchandise, or referring to invoices, some retail establishments, after physically counting the stock on hand, extend the inventory sheets at retail. The retail value is then converted to cost by applying the retail inventory method without reference to individual cost prices.

3. To provide a basis for *interim* control of inventory, purchases, theft, markdowns, and additional markups when neither a traditional periodic nor perpetual inventory system is used for these interim purposes.

4. To provide a basis for external financial reports.

5. To provide data for income tax purposes.

6. To provide a test of the overall reasonableness of a physical inventory.

Markups and Markdowns

The preceding illustration assumed that there were no changes in the *original* marked sales price. The original sales price on some of the merchandise frequently is raised or lowered, particularly at the end of the selling season or when replacement costs (in present condition) are changing. The retail method requires that a careful record be kept of all adjustments to the *original* marked sales price since these adjustments must be taken into account in the computation. In order to apply this rule it is important to distinguish among the following terms:

Original sales price—the amount at which the merchandise is first marked for sale.

Markup—the original or initial amount that merchandise is marked up. Thus, it is the difference between cost and the original sales price. It may be expressed as a dollar amount or a percent of either cost or selling price. It is sometimes referred to as initial markup or markon.

Additional markup—an increase in the sales price above the original sales price. Note that the original sales price is the base from which additional markup is measured.

Additional markup cancellations—cancellation of an *additional* markup. Additional markups less additional markup cancellations usually is called net additional markup.

Markdown—a reduction in selling price below the original sales price.

Markdown cancellation—after a reduction in the original selling price (i.e., after a markdown), an increase in the selling price which does not exceed the original sales price (after the original sales price, an increase is an additional markup).

The definitions may be illustrated by assuming an item that cost $8 is originally marked to sell at $10, subsequently marked to sell at $11, then marked down to $10, and finally reduced to sell at $7:

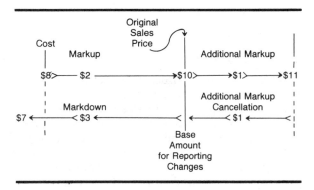

The validity of an inventory amount determined by using the retail inventory method depends largely upon the accuracy with which changes in the original selling price are reported by the merchandising personnel to the accounting department. The importance of the markup/markdown distinction, which may not seem apparent at this point, will be illustrated in the applications which follow.

APPLICATION OF THE RETAIL INVENTORY METHOD

The basic concept and computations underlying the retail inventory method were discussed and illustrated above. However, the specific ways in which the calculations are made determine the approximate valuations. The difference in calculations to derive each particular basis may be outlined as follows:

Basis Desired	Computation of Cost Ratio
1. *Fifo* cost.	Exclude beginning inventory from the computation of the cost ratio.
2. Average cost.	Include beginning inventory in the computation of the cost ratio.
3. LCM.	Exclude net markdowns from the computation of the cost ratio; include them after the cost ratio is computed.
4. *Lifo* cost.	Must use the dollar value, *Lifo* retail method (discussed in Part B).

To illustrate the first three bases above, the following data are assumed from the accounting records of KM Company at the end of the accounting period (note that units are not used):

	At Cost	At Retail
Inventory at beginning of period	$ 550	$ 900
Purchases during period	6,290	8,900
Additional markups during period		225
Additional markup cancellations during period		25
Markdowns during period		600
Markdown cancellations during period		100
Sales for the period		8,500

Retail Method, *Fifo* Cost (excluding LCM)

Recall that when *Fifo* is used, the ending inventory is costed at the latest unit costs; therefore, the costs in the beginning inventory will be included in cost of goods sold rather than in the ending inventory. If the beginning inventory is excluded from the computation of the cost ratio, the result will more nearly approximate *Fifo* results for the ending inventory. The computations for KM Company would be as follows:

Retail Method—*Fifo* Cost (not LCM)

		At Cost	At Retail
Goods available for sale:			
Beginning inventory		$ 550	$ 900
Purchases during the period		6,290	8,900
Additional markups during the period	$225		
Less: Additional markup cancellations	25		
Net additional markups			200
Deduct:			
Markdowns during the period	600		
Less: Markdown cancellations	100		
Net markdowns			(500)
Total (excluding beginning Inventory)		6,290	8,600

	At Cost	At Retail
Cost ratio: $6,290 ÷ $8,600 = .731 (based on newest costs)		
Total goods available for sale	$6,840	9,500
Deduct:		
Sales		8,500
Ending inventory:		
At retail		$1,000
At approximate *Fifo* cost ($1,000 × .731)	$ 731	

The cost ratio must express the *normal* relationship between cost and retail. For this reason the net additional markups and the net markdowns must be included as adjustments to the retail amounts because they represent changes in the marked sales prices but do not affect cost. This suggests the care that must be exercised in computing the cost ratio.

Retail Method, Average Cost (excluding LCM)

Recall that average cost is derived by dividing *total* goods available for sale in dollars of cost by total units available for sale; both totals include the beginning inventory. Therefore, if we calculate the cost ratio on the basis of totals, including the beginning inventory, the retail method derives the approximate average cost ratio. The computation for KM Company is:

Retail Method—Average Cost Basis (not LCM)

	At Cost	At Retail
Total goods available for sale including beginning inventory (from above)	$6,840	$9,500
Cost ratio: $6,840 ÷ $9,500 = .720 (based on average cost)		
Deduct:		
Sales		8,500
Ending inventory:		
At retail		$1,000
At approximate average cost ($1,000 × .72)	$ 720	

Retail Method, Lower of Cost or Market (LCM)

Lower of cost or market is a *conservative* valuation method; it derives an inventory valuation that usually is less than *Fifo* or average. By ex-

cluding net markdowns from the computation of the cost ratio, an *approximate* LCM valuation is derived. The LCM approach may be applied to either the *Fifo* or average computations illustrated above. To illustrate:

Retail Method—Average Cost Basis, LCM

		At Cost	At Retail
Goods available for sale:			
Beginning inventory		$ 550	$ 900
Purchases during period		6,290	8,900
Additional markups	$225		
Less: Additional markup cancellations	25		
Net additional markups			200
Total goods available for sale (including beginning inventory)		$6,840	10,000
Cost ratio: $6,840 ÷ $10,000 = .684.			
Deduct:			
Sales			(8,500)
Remainder			1,500
Markdowns	$600		
Less: Markdown cancellations	100		
Net markdowns			(500)
Ending inventory:			
At retail			$ 1,000
Average cost basis, LCM ($1,000 × .684)		$ 684	

Retail Method—*Fifo* Cost Basis, LCM

	At Cost	At Retail
Cost ratio (excludes the beginning inventory) $6,290 ÷ ($8,900 + $200) = .691.		
Ending inventory:		
At retail (per above)		$ 1,000
Fifo cost basis, LCM ($1,000 × .691)	$ 691	

The retail inventory LCM methods of inventory estimation, illustrated above, implicitly assume that *markdowns* usually are made because the utility of the merchandise has declined. That is, *(a)* the current purchase price of identical new goods dropped or *(b)* the goods had a lower replacement cost (i.e., the cost that would be incurred to replace the goods in their *present* condition) because of such factors as style obsolescence, shopwear, odd sizes, and excess supply. Therefore, on the basis of LCM, the net markdowns are omitted from computation of the *cost ratio,* which *lowers* the computed cost ratio (because of a larger denominator) by the effect of the net markdowns. This is assumed to approximate the LCM cost ratio. Since the net markdowns are omitted from the retail column (above the cost ratio computation), they must be reflected in the retail column (below the cost ratio) to derive the correct amount for "ending inventory at retail." This is accomplished by subtracting the net markdowns along with net sales (i.e., below the cost ratio computation). Observe in the LCM computations immediately above that the inventory amount at retail, $1,000, is the same amount shown in the earlier illustrations of retail *Fifo* (not LCM) and average (not LCM); however, each illustration produced a different *value* for the ending inventory (and LCM was the lowest).

Special Items

Several factors may complicate computation of the ending inventory when the retail inventory method is used. In resolving these issues it is essential to protect the integrity of (1) the computed "normal" cost ratio and (2) the amount of ending inventory at retail. Six complicating factors are as follows:

1. Freight-in—This expenditure adds to the *cost* of merchandise; therefore, it should be added to goods available for sale (or directly to purchases) at *cost* but not at retail.
2. Purchase returns—Since purchase returns reduce the amount of goods purchased, they should be deducted from goods available for sale at both cost and retail.
3. *Abnormal* casualty losses and missing merchandise arising from unusual and infrequent events (such as a fire or theft) should be deducted from goods available for sale at both cost and retail because they will not be sold; removal from both cost and retail avoids distortion of the normal cost ratio and the ending inventory (the damaged merchandise would be set up in a special inventory account).
4. Sales Returns and Allowances—Since this is a contra account to the Sales Revenue account, Sales Returns and Allowances should be deducted from gross sales. If the returned merchandise is placed back into inventory for resale, no change in the "At Cost" column is needed because its cost is already properly included in the purchases amount. However, if the merchandise is not returned to inven-

tory because of damage (or for other reasons), then its cost should be deducted in the "At Cost" column on the sales line after the cost ratio (because sales has been reduced and the cost also should be reduced).

5. Discounts to employees and favored customers—These discounts result from selling merchandise below the "normal" sales price and are not occasioned by market price changes (decreases). Since such discounts do not result from an assumed decrease in replacement cost, they are different from markdowns. The amount of the discounts is computed as the number of units sold at a discount multiplied by the difference between the marked selling price and the discount price. Such discounts must always be *deducted below the cost ratio,* along with sales (whether LCM or not), because they are concessions to recipients and do not reflect market price decreases. If such discounts are incorrectly deducted in deriving the cost ratio, the ratio will be overstated which will cause the ending inventory to be overstated.
6. *Normal* spoilage (including shrinkage and breakage)—This item is measured for retail inventory purposes as the number of units lost multiplied by the marked retail price. This amount must always be *deducted below the cost ratio,* along with sales (whether LCM or not), because the *expected* spoilage cost was implicitly included in the marked selling price and it does not reflect market changes. Deduction of normal spoilage in arriving at the cost ratio would overstate the cost ratio and the ending inventory at estimated cost, as well.

These six special items are illustrated below and are numbered in the same manner to facilitate study.

Special Items, Retail Inventory Method—Average Cost Basis (not LCM)

		At Cost	At Retail
Goods available for sale:			
	Beginning inventory	$ 6,050	$ 11,000
	Purchases	57,120	102,000
1.	Freight-in	1,020	
2.	Purchase returns	(560)	(1,000)
	Net additional markups		600
	Net markdowns		(4,500)

		At Cost	At Retail
3.	Casualty loss (actual loss, from beginning inventory) Computation: $6,600 × ($6,050/$11,000) = $3,630*	(3,630)	(6,600)
	Total	$60,000	$101,500
	Cost ratio: $60,000 ÷ $101,500 = .591.		
	Deduct: Gross sales $71,200		
4.	Sales returns (merchandise returned to stock) 1,200		
5.	Discounts to employees		(70,000)
6.	Normal spoilage		(200)
	Ending inventory:		(1,300)
	At retail		$ 30,000
	At average cost (not LCM) $30,000 × .591 =		$17,730
	Assuming average cost basis—LCM: Average cost, LCM ratio: $60,000 ÷ ($101,500 + $4,500) =		.566
	Ending inventory, at average cost basis—LCM $30,000 × .566 =		$16,980

* The casualty loss could have been recorded as follows per the assumed fact situation:

Cash (from insurance company)	2,000	
Casualty loss (fire damage)	1,630	
Purchases (or cost of goods sold)		3,630

The preceding discussions of the retail inventory method presumed that the merchandise included in a single set of computations is similar in that (a) the markup was essentially the same for each kind of merchandise included and (b) the relative proportion of the various kinds of merchandise in the ending inventory and in sales for the period was essentially the same. In individual departments this is generally the case; however, on a storewide basis it often is not. Consequently, the essential data should be accumulated by sales departments and the retail inventory computations then made on a *departmental basis*. The departmental inventories then are summed to derive the total inventory.

PART A–2—INVENTORIES FOR LONG-TERM CONSTRUCTION CONTRACTS

Up to this point in the chapter we have considered inventories that arise in the conventional manner; that is, inventories are either purchased from vendors or they are manufactured over a reasonably short period of time. In those discussions we considered the dual phases of the inventory accounting problem, measuring (a) cost of goods sold and (b) ending inventory.

In contrast, a very unconventional inventory measurement problem arises in the construction industry. *Construction in process inventory* is generally associated with long-term construction contracts, which are typical when such projects as buildings, bridges, ships, and dams are built. The problem is unconventional because the construction period often extends over two or more accounting periods. Since inventory valuation directly affects income measurement and reporting during the construction period, these two problems are discussed. For example, assume a 2½-year construction period. Should income be recognized as construction progresses (i.e., each period), or should income be recognized only at the end of the 2½ years?

The accounting profession and the income tax laws have recognized two distinctly different methods of accounting for long-term construction contracts. The two methods are:

1. The completed contract method—All construction costs are accumulated in an inventory account—Construction in Process—and income is recognized as earned only upon completion of the project.
2. The percentage of completion method—All construction costs *plus* all income recognized as earned during the construction period are accumulated in an inventory account—Construction in Process—and income is recognized as earned each period based upon progress of the construction (i.e., production basis—see discussion of the revenue principle in Chapter 2).

To illustrate the accounting for long-term construction contracts we will use the following data:

1. Ace Construction Company received a contract to erect a building for $1,500,000. Construction is to start February 1, 19A, and is to be completed 2½ years from that date.
2. Progress billings are to be submitted by the contractor at the end of each month based upon percentage of completion estimates developed by the independent architect as of the 15th of each month. The progress billings are payable to the contractor within ten days after the billing.

426

Long-term Construction Contracts—Illustrative Data

	Year 19A	Year 19B	Year 19C	Total
Contract price				$1,500,000
Costs incurred each year	$ 350,000	$550,000	$465,000	1,365,000
Estimated costs to complete (at year-end) ..	1,000,000	460,000	–0–	–0–
Income on construction ...				$ 135,000
Progress billings each year	300,000	575,000	625,000	$1,500,000
Collections on billings each year	270,000	555,000	675,000	1,500,000

3. Data covering the entire construction period are shown above.
4. The percentage of completion at the end of each accounting period during the construction time will be measured by the ratio of total costs incurred to date to estimated total costs to be incurred on the project (costs incurred to date plus estimated costs to complete).

COMPLETED CONTRACT METHOD

Since long-term construction contracts almost always provide for the contractor to bill the other party for progress payments (as agreed upon in the contract), such progress billings are debited to Accounts Receivable (construction contract billings) and credited to Billings on Contracts (long-term construction) as they occur. The latter account is not a revenue account; it is a contra asset (offset) to the Construction in Process account on the balance sheet. If the net difference is a debit, it is usually reported as a current asset; if a credit, as a current liability. When the contract is completed, the reported income is the difference between the accumulated credit balance in the Billings on Contracts and the Construction in Process Inventory debit balance. Under the completed contract method, during the construction period the construction in process inventory is reported on the balance sheet at the total accumulated costs to date, less the total progress billings to date, and income on construction contracts ($135,000 in the example) is reported only in the year of completion (19C in the example). The entries in the accounts of Ace Construction Company, for this

method, are illustrated in Exhibit 12–2; and the financial statement presentation for each year is shown in Exhibit 12–3.

PERCENTAGE OF COMPLETION METHOD

Under this method, accounting for a long-term construction contract is the same as the completed contract method explained above except that *income is recognized as earned each period* during the construction time. Since the *actual* income on the contract will not be known until completion, an estimate of it must be made each period. The estimated amount of income is then apportioned to each period on the basis of the percentage of the total contract completed (i.e., percentage of completion) during the period.

Percentage of completion is usually derived on the basis of either *(a)* engineering and/or architectural estimates of the work performed to date compared to the total work necessary to complete the contract or *(b)* the ratio of total costs incurred to date on the contract *to* the estimated total costs to be incurred on the contract. The estimated amount of income recognized each period is accrued by debiting Construction in Process and crediting Income on Construction (long-term contracts). The latter account is closed to Income Summary each period and is reported on the income statement.

Computation of the amount of estimated income to be recognized each year by the Ace Construction Company is illustrated in Exhibit 12–1. Observe that the estimated total income of $135,000 is apportioned each period on the basis of the ratio of costs incurred to date to total costs to be incurred. The resulting entries in the accounts of Ace Construction Company are reflected in Exhibit 12–2, and the financial statement presentation for each period is shown in Exhibit 12–3.

EXHIBIT 12–1
Apportionment of Estimated Income—
Percentage of Completion Method

	Year 19A	Year 19B	Year 19C
Contract price	$1,500,000	$1,500,000	$1,500,000*
Less costs:			
Actual cost to date (cumulative)	350,000*	900,000*	1,365,000*
Estimated cost to complete	1,000,000	460,000	
Estimated total costs	1,350,000	1,360,000	1,365,000*
Estimated total income	$ 150,000	$ 140,000	$ 135,000*
Apportionment of total income (based on ratio of costs incurred to date to estimated total construction cost):			
19A:			
($350,000/$1,350,000) × $150,000	$ 38,889		
19B:			
($900,000/$1,360,000) × $140,000		$ 92,647	
Less income recognized to date		38,889	
Income recognized in 19B		$ 53,758	
19C:			
Total income to be recognized (actual)			$ 135,000
Less income recognized to date			92,647
Income recognized in 19C			$ 42,353

* Actual.

As Exhibit 12–3 reflects, both methods derive the same results on the balance sheet during the construction period, except for the amount of the ending inventory and retained earnings. Under the percentage of completion method, the inventory prior to completion of the project is greater in amount by the accumulated pretax income recognized in the current and prior periods. Thus, for Ace Construction Company the ending inventory (i.e., costs in excess of billings) is greater by $38,889 at the end of 19A and by $38,889 + $53,758 = $92,647 at the end of 19B. Recall that the estimated income recognized as earned each year was debited to Construction in Process in the percentage of completion method.

Under either method, when there is a projected loss at any time, it must be recognized in the period in which a loss on the contract appears reasonably certain. The loss should be recognized by means of a debit to Loss on Construction Contract and a credit to Construction in Process. The credit side of the entry removes from the inventory account the amount of costs in excess of expected recovery value. Also, when an overall loss on the contract is reasonably certain, income previously recognized should be "reversed" in the period that such determination is made.

EVALUATION OF METHODS

The completed contract and percentage of completion methods of accounting for long-term construction contracts are different approaches for measuring and reporting (a) periodic income from construction and (b) the ending inventory (construction in process) during the period of construction. Exhibit 12–2 shows that the entries are identical each period under both methods except entry No. 4 (recognition of income earned on construction). Over the life of the construction period, both methods recognize the same amount of total pretax income.

Advocates of the *completed contract* method assert that it is more objective and more conservative since income is not recognized until all of the revenues and expenses for the completed job are known with certainty. It is sometimes viewed as deficient, however, because income measurement and recognition do not reflect performance each accounting period during the construction time (i.e., poor matching of expense with revenue). Although most of the work may be completed prior to the accounting period in which the construction is completed, all of the income is reported in the last period.

The *percentage of completion* method is supported on the basis that since a contract is in effect, the construction company earns revenue as it performs the work on the contract. In this view, it is unreasonable to await completion before measuring and recognizing income. It is sometimes viewed as deficient because income during the construction period is measured subjectively and recognized on the basis of (a) *estimates* of work done (percentage completion) and (b) *estimated* total construction cost. This criti-

EXHIBIT 12–2
Long-Term Construction Contracts—Journal Entries for Completed Contract and Percentage of Completion Methods Compared

	Method		
	Completed Contract		Percentage of Completion

Year 19A:

1. Costs of construction:

Construction in process	350,000*		350,000	
Cash, payables, etc		350,000		350,000

> * Under the completed contract method this may include a *reasonable allocation* of general and administrative expenses for periods prior to completion.

2. Progress billings:

Accounts receivable	300,000		300,000	
Billings on contracts		300,000		300,000

3. Collections on billings:

Cash	270,000		270,000	
Accounts receivable		270,000		270,000

4. Recognition of income:

Construction in process	(No income recognized		38,889	
Income on	until completion)			
construction†				38,889

> † Closed to Income Summary.

Year 19B:

1. Costs of construction:

Construction in process	550,000		550,000	
Cash, payables, etc.		550,000		550,000

2. Progress billings:

Accounts receivable	575,000		575,000	
Billings on contracts		575,000		575,000

3. Collections on billings:

Cash	555,000		555,000	
Accounts receivable		555,000		555,000

4. Recognition of income:

Construction in process	(No income recognized		53,758	
Income on	until completion)			
construction				53,758

Year 19C:

1. Costs of construction:

Construction in process	465,000		465,000	
Cash, payables, etc.		465,000		465,000

2. Progress billings (final billing):

Accounts receivable	625,000		625,000	
Billings on contracts		625,000		625,000

EXHIBIT 12–2 *(continued)*

	Method			
	Completed Contract		Percentage of Completion	
Year 19C (continued)				
3. Collections on billings (in full):				
Cash	675,000		675,000	
Accounts receivable		675,000		675,000
4. Recognition of income (and to close the accumulated account balances):				
Construction in process			42,353*	
Billings on contracts	1,500,000		1,500,000	
Construction in process..............		1,365,000		1,500,000
Income on construction		135,000		42,353

* Alternatively, this entry could be:

Billings on contracts	1,500,000	
Construction in process		1,457,647
Income on construction...		42,353

EXHIBIT 12–3
Long-Term Construction Contracts—Financial Statements for Completed Contract and Percentage of Completion Methods Compared

	Year 19A		Year 19B		Year 19C	
	C.C.*	P.C.*	C.C.	P.C.	C.C.	P.C.
Balance Sheet:						
Current Assets:						
Accounts receivable	$ 30,000	$ 30,000	$ 50,000	$ 50,000		
Inventory:						
Construction in process	350,000	388,889	900,000	992,647		
Less: Billings on contracts	300,000	300,000	875,000	875,000		
Costs in excess of billings†	50,000	88,889	25,000	117,647		
Income Statement:						
Income on construction	–0–	38,889	–0–	53,758	$135,000	$ 42,353

* C.C.—Completed contract method.
  P.C.—Percentage of completion method.
  † Abbreviated titles are used herein for convenience. This is usually labeled "Cost of uncompleted contracts in excess of billings."

cism notes that income may be recognized early during the construction, although in the end there may be an overall loss due to cost overruns.

The accounting profession has sanctioned the use of either method as follows:

> The committee believes that in general when estimates of costs to complete and extent of progress toward completion of long-term contracts are reasonably dependable, the percentage-of-completion method is preferable. When lack of dependable estimates or inherent hazards cause forecasts to be doubtful, the completed-contract method is preferable. Disclosure of the method followed should be made.[3]

PART B—DOLLAR VALUE, *LIFO* RETAIL METHOD

This Part discusses and illustrates another extension of the *Lifo* inventory method—the application of *Lifo* by companies that also use the retail inventory method to estimate their inventory costs. Thus, this extension is known as dollar value, *Lifo* retail. As the name implies it uses a dollar value (as opposed to a physical unit) concept of inventory valuation which is entirely consistent with the retail inventory technique discussed earlier. Finally, since it is a *Lifo* application, it employs the last-in, first-out assumption of cost flow. When *Lifo* results are desired for an inventory estimated by the conventional *Fifo* retail method, dollar value, *Lifo* retail must be used. It is acceptable for interim financial reports, external financial reports, and for income tax purposes (subject to specific constraints in the tax regulations—Treas. Reg. §1.471–8, 1.472–1).

The dollar value, *Lifo* retail method requires that *(a)* a distinction be maintained between the base year inventory and subsequent incremental layers and *(b)* the subsequent layers be costed by applying a price level index to the results derived from the retail inventory approach. That is, at the end of each period, the *Fifo* ("pure" *Fifo,* i.e., not LCM) retail inventory ap-

proach is used and the results are then converted to a *Lifo* basis using a conversion price index.

Treasury regulations specify that variety stores using the *Lifo* retail method must use an *internally computed index* as discussed and illustrated in Chapter 11, Part B. On the other hand, retailers that qualify as department stores (as defined for tax purposes) may use a published external index instead of an internally computed index when it can be shown that computation of an internal index is impractical. The published index used must be one prepared by the Bureau of Labor Statistics. In the discussions and illustrations to follow, we will assume a published index is used for conversion purposes.

APPLICATION OF THE DOLLAR VALUE, *LIFO* RETAIL METHOD

The dollar value, *Lifo* retail method, although conceptually simple, is computationally burdensome. As with the dollar value, *Lifo* method discussed and illustrated in Part B of Chapter 11, it involves the use of price level index numbers. It *also* requires use of the computed *cost ratio* of the retail inventory method in the conversion process. The dollar value, *Lifo* retail method may be outlined as follows:

a. For each period, first apply the conventional (not LCM) retail inventory method, *Fifo* cost, as illustrated on page 422. Recall that LCM cannot be used with *Lifo;* therefore, the "not LCM" method must be used. If some other retail inventory method is used, it must be recomputed on a *Fifo* (pure) basis.

b. At the end of each period the retail inventory, *Fifo* (pure) results, *at retail,* are converted to a *Lifo cost* basis by using the dollar value approach. The beginning base year inventory for the year of change to dollar value *Lifo* is the ending *Fifo* (pure) inventory carried over from the year prior to the change. At the end of each period, conversion of the *Fifo retail* results to a *Lifo cost* basis involves two distinct phases as follows:

> *Phase A*—Computation of an internal conversion index for the period similar to the illustration in Exhibit 11–11, Phase A, or selection of an external price index

[3] AICPA, *Accounting Research Bulletin No.* 45, "Long-Term Construction-Type Contracts" (New York, 1955), par. 15.

Note: If a company uses different methods for external financial reporting and income tax purposes, deferred income taxes must be recognized (see Chapter 9).

(for retail stores of the same type) for conversion purposes.

Phase B—Conversion of the ending *Fifo* (pure) inventory results, *at retail,* to a *Lifo* dollar value cost basis by using (1) the conversion price index and (2) the cost ratio for the period. Both ratios must be used for dollar value, *Lifo* computations because the conversion is from retail value to cost value. The *Fifo* retail value ([*a*] above) must be used (rather than *Fifo* cost) because the ending inventory must be identified by year, each of which has its own price index *and* cost ratio values.

Phase A will not be illustrated in this chapter because it is not applied when an external index is used (which is common in the retail industries) and because it is similar to the illustrations in Chapter 11 (except that the index is related to retail prices rather than to costs).

Phase B starts with the ending *Fifo* inventory, valued at current year retail (provided by the retail *Fifo* inventory computation for the period), which is then restated to *base year retail* by dividing it by the current year conversion price index.[4] The result is the total ending inventory for the current year at base year retail. This base year retail value then is comprised of the base layer and the additional layers (i.e., each layer at base year retail). Each such layer then is converted to dollar value *Lifo cost* by multiplying the base year retail amount by (1) the conversion index and (2) the cost ratio that relates to that particular inventory layer. The sum of the layers, as converted, provides the ending inventory at dollar value *Lifo* cost, which is reported on the balance sheet and used on the income statement to compute cost of goods sold.

Conversion computations will be illustrated using the data given in Exhibit 12–4.

---

[4] In using index numbers, there are two manipulations that must be understood:

1. A valuation at base year price, $40,000 × a current year price index, for example, 1.02 = the valuation at current year prices, $40,800; therefore, it follows that—
2. A valuation at current year prices, $40,800 ÷ a current year price index, 1.02 = the valuation at base year price, $40,000.

Required:

1. Compute the ending inventory for each period using the conventional retail inventory method, *Fifo* basis (pure) to provide the data for conversion.
2. Convert the *Fifo* retail results, computed in Requirement 1, to dollar value, *Lifo* retail.

The computations are shown separately for each year in Exhibits 12–5, 12–6, and 12–7. Each exhibit should be studied carefully.

Changing to Dollar Value *Lifo* Retail—Computation of Base Inventory

In the discussions and illustrations above for WZ Company, the base inventory (at the beginning of the base year, 19B) was given as follows: at cost, $17,400; and at retail, $30,000. These base year beginning inventory values would have been carried forward from the ending inventory of 19A assuming the company was already on *"pure" Fifo* (not LCM). However, *if the company had been on a method other than "pure" Fifo (such as average, or Fifo at LCM), the ending inventory for 19A would have to be restated to a "pure" Fifo cost basis.* The restatement usually is relatively simple.

To illustrate, assume WZ Company had been using the retail inventory method, average basis, at LCM. At the start of 19B, the company decided to change to the dollar value, *Lifo* retail method for tax and external reporting purposes. The retail method computation previously developed at the end of December 19A (at average, LCM) was as follows:

	At Cost	At Retail
Inventory, January 1, 19A	$ 5,700	$ 10,000
Purchases	78,300	138,000
Net additional markups		2,000
Total	$84,000	150,000
Cost ratio: $84,000 ÷ $150,000 = .56.		
Net markdowns		5,000
Remainder		145,000
Less: Sales		115,000
Ending inventory, December 31, 19A:		
At retail		$ 30,000
At average cost, LCM ($30,000 × .56)	$16,800	

EXHIBIT 12–4
Data from Company Inventory Records for Dollar Value, *Lifo* Retail Conversion—WZ Company

1. The company has been using the retail inventory method (*Fifo,* not LCM) for *(a)* internal reporting and control purposes, *(b)* external reporting to shareholders, and *(c)* income tax purposes. Starting on January 1, 19B, the company decided to use the dollar value, *Lifo* retail method for the latter two purposes.
2. The inventory at December 31, 19A, using the conventional retail inventory method, *Fifo* basis (not LCM) was:

Ending inventory:

At retail	$30,000
At cost ($30,000 × cost ratio .58)	17,400

3. Inventory data subsequent to change to *Lifo:* *

	19B		19C		19D	
	At Cost	*At Retail*	*At Cost*	*At Retail*	*At Cost*	*At Retail*
Purchases	$90,480	$147,000	$101,500	$172,000	$109,800	$177,000
Net additional markups		8,800		9,000		7,000
Net markdowns		5,000		6,000		4,000
Sales		140,000		162,800		197,800
4. Selected external price index (19A = 100)†		102		106		110

* A three-year period is used because a shorter time span does not adequately illustrate an application.

† When the index at the beginning of the base year is not 100, the current year index should be divided by the base index value to obtain the percentage or ratio index. To illustrate, assume the index value at the beginning of the base year is 1.05 and the index at the end of the year is 1.071. The index value to use at the end of 19B would be 1.071 ÷ 1.05 = 1.02 as above. The base year index then becomes 100.

The computation to restate the beginning base year inventory (January 1, 19B) to a *Fifo* cost basis would be as shown below. Note the exclusion of the January 1, 19A, inventory and inclusion of both markups and markdowns to determine the cost ratio.

	At Cost	At Retail
Inventory, January 1, 19A	$ 5,700	$ 10,000
Purchases	78,300	138,000
Net additional markups		2,000
Net markdowns (to avoid LCM effect)		(5,000)
Total (excluding beginning inventory)	78,300	135,000
Total (including beginning inventory)	$84,000	145,000
Cost ratio: *Fifo* cost basis: $78,300 ÷ $135,000 = .58.		
Less: Sales		115,000
Beginning base year inventory, January 1, 19B:		
At retail		$ 30,000
At cost ($30,000 × .58)	$17,400	

The two values, $30,000 and $17,400, represent the beginning base year inventory. Observe that they were given in Exhibit 12–4.

The entry to restate the January 1, 19B, inventory from average, LCM to "pure" *Fifo* cost would be as follows (for the year of change only):

Beginning inventory ($17,400 − $16,800)	600	
Inventory adjustment due to adoption of *Lifo* retail		600

The inventory adjustment account would be closed to Income Summary and reported on the income statement as an accounting change during 19B (see Chapter 24). To reemphasize, this computation is needed only at the date of the change and only if some method other than "pure" *Fifo* was used in the prior years.

Because of the increasing use, dollar value, *Lifo* retail has received considerable attention by practicing and industrial accountants. In applying the concept in actual practice and if used for tax purposes, the IRS Regulations and rulings must be carefully observed. Neither the accounting profession nor the taxing authorities have deemed it desirable to frame detailed and

EXHIBIT 12–5
Application of Dollar Value, *Lifo* Retail—WZ Company, 19B

Fact Situation for 19B:
  a. Base layer (carried over from 19A): Retail $30,000 × .58 = Cost $17,400
  b. Computation of 19B ending *Fifo* inventory (not LCM) (see Exhibit 12–4):

	At Cost	At Retail	Cost Ratio
Goods available for sale:			
Inventory, January 1, 19B	$ 17,400	$ 30,000	
Purchases	90,480	147,000	
Net additional markups		8,800	
Net markdowns		(5,000)	
Subtotal (excluding beginning inventory)	90,480 ÷	150,800 =	.60
Total goods available for sale	$107,880	180,800	
Deduct: Sales		140,000	
Ending 19B inventory: At retail		$ 40,800	
At cost, $40,800 × .60 =	$ 24,480		.60

Conversion Process for 19B:
  Phase A—Conversion price index for 19B = 1.02

      If computed: $40,800 ÷ (same amount restated to base prices) $40,000 = 1.02
      Computation of the $40,000 similar to Exhibit 11–11, Phase A)

  Phase B—Conversion of ending inventory at *Fifo* retail ($40,800) to dollar value *Lifo* cost:

	Base Year Retail	Conversion Index and Cost Ratio	Dollar Value Lifo Cost
Ending inventory at retail converted to base year retail $40,800 ÷ 1.02 =	$40,000		
Less: Base inventory layer	30,000	× 1.00 × .58 =	$17,400
19B additional inventory layer	$10,000*	× 1.02 × .60 =	6,120
Ending 19B inventory at dollar value *Lifo* cost			$23,520

  * Multiplication of this base year retail amount by the current price index restated it to current year prices (i.e., $10,000 × 1.02 = $10,200); multiplication of the result by the current year cost ratio restated this 19B layer to 19B cost (i.e., $10,200 × .60 = $6,120).

inflexible rules in this area because of the wide range of situations in which it is used. Accounting students should be familiar with the method because of its increasing use.

In summary, it is important to understand that dollar value, *Lifo* retail identifies and accounts for the *Lifo inventory layers* only in terms of the conversion price index/cost ratio combination that existed during the year when the *Lifo* layer was added to inventory. In contrast, quantity of goods *Lifo* (for both perpetual and periodic inventory systems) identifies the *Lifo* layers only with the unit purchase (acquisition) cost incurred when the items were ac-

quired. Also *Lifo* cannot be applied using the traditional retail inventory method alone; to attain *Lifo* results with the retail inventory method, the dollar value approach must be used. The dollar value, *Lifo* retail method is used primarily because of (1) potential tax savings, and (2) an overall reduction in the clerical costs associated with inventories, despite its complexities.

QUESTIONS

PART A

1. What is the basic assumption implicit in the gross margin method?

EXHIBIT 12–6
Application of Dollar Value, *Lifo* Retail—WZ Company, 19C

Fact Situation for 19C:

a. Beginning dollar value *Lifo* inventory carried over from end of 19B (from Exhibit 12–5):

	Retail at Base Cost	Conversion Index	Cost Ratio	Lifo Cost
Base inventory layer	$30,000	1.00	.58	$17,400
19B additional layer	10,000	1.02	.60	6,120
Total	$40,000			$23,520

b. Computation of 19C ending *Fifo* inventory (not LCM) (see Exhibit 12–4):

	At Cost		At Retail		Cost Ratio
Goods available for sale:					
Inventory, January 1, 19C (Exhibit 12–5)	$ 24,480		$ 40,800		
Purchases	101,500		172,000		
Net additional markups			9,000		
Net markdowns			(6,000)		
Subtotal (excluding beginning inventory)	101,500	÷	175,000	=	.58
Total goods available for sale	$125,980		215,800		
Deduct: Sales			162,800		
Ending 19C inventory: At retail			$ 53,000		
At cost, $53,000 × .58 =	$ 30,740				.58

Conversion Process for 19C:

Phase A—Conversion price index for 19C = 1.06

Phase B—Conversion of ending inventory at *Fifo* retail ($53,000) to dollar value *Lifo* cost:

	Base Year Retail	Conversion Index and Cost Ratio	Dollar Value Lifo Cost
Ending inventory at retail converted to base year retail, $53,000 ÷ 1.06 =	$50,000		
Less: Base inventory layer	(30,000)	× 1.00 × .58 =	$17,400
19B inventory layer	(10,000)	× 1.02 × .60 =	6,120
19C additional inventory layer	$10,000	× 1.06 × .58 =	6,148
Ending 19C inventory at dollar value *Lifo* cost			$29,668

EXHIBIT 12–7
Application of Dollar Value, *Lifo* Retail—WZ Company, 19D

Fact Situation for 19D:

a. Beginning dollar value *Lifo* inventory carried over from end of 19C:

	Retail at Base Cost	Conversion Index	Cost Ratio	Lifo Cost
Base inventory layer	$30,000	1.00	.58	$17,400
19B additional layer	10,000	1.02	.60	6,120
19C additional layer	10,000	1.06	.58	6,148
Total	$50,000			$29,668

b. Computation of 19D ending *Fifo* inventory (not LCM) (see Exhibit 12–4):

	At Cost		At Retail		Cost Ratio
Goods available for sale:					
Inventory, January 1, 19D (Exhibit 12–6)	$ 30,740		$ 53,000		
Purchases	109,800		177,000		
Net additional markups..............................			7,000		
Net markdowns			(4,000)		
Subtotal (excluding beginning inventory)	109,800	÷	180,000	=	.61
Total goods available for sale	$140,540		233,000		
Deduct: Sales...			197,800		
Ending 19D inventory: At retail			$ 35,200		
At cost $35,200 × .61 =	$ 21,472				.61

Conversion Process for 19D:

Phase A—Computed or selected conversion price index for 19D = 1.10

Phase B—Conversion of ending inventory at *Fifo* retail $35,200 to dollar value *Lifo* cost:

	Base Year Retail	Conversion Index and Cost Ratio	Dollar Value Lifo Cost
Ending inventory at retail converted to base year retail, $35,200 ÷ 1.10	$32,000		
Less: Base inventory layer	(30,000)	× 1.00 × .58 =	$17,400
19B inventory layer remaining	$ 2,000*	× 1.02 × .60 =	1,224
Ending 19D inventory at dollar value *Lifo* cost			$18,624

* After subtracting the base layer of $30,000, there remained only $2,000. Therefore, all of the 19C layer was liquidated and only $2,000 of the 19B layer remained (i.e., there was also liquidation of $8,000 of the 19B layer). Since only ⅕ of the 19B additional layer remained at the end of 19D (i.e., $2,000 ÷ $10,000), only ⅕ of its cost remains (i.e., ⅕ × $6,120 = $1,224). Observe that layers are liquidated in *Lifo* order and that both the conversion price index and the cost ratio are *always* identified with the layer created at those ratios. A layer once liquidated is never restored.

2. Approximate the valuation of the ending inventory assuming the following data are available:

Cost of goods available for sale $100,000
Net sales 150,000
Gross margin rate (on sales) 40%

3. Distinguish between *(a)* gross margin rate on sales, *(b)* gross margin percentage on cost of goods sold, *(c)* cost percentage, *(d)* markup on cost, and *(e)* markup on sales.

4. List the four principal uses of the gross margin method.

5. Why is it frequently desirable to apply the gross margin method by classes of merchandise?

6. Explain the basic approach of the retail method of estimating inventories. What data must be accumulated in order to apply the retail method?

7. The ending inventory estimated by the retail inventory method was $40,000. A physical inventory of the merchandise on hand extended at retail showed $35,000. Suggest possible reasons for the discrepancy.

8. What are the primary uses of the retail method of estimating inventories?

9. When are markdowns and markdown cancellations excluded in computing the cost ratio in the retail inventory method?

10. Explain the essential differences between *(a)* the completed contract method and *(b)* the percentage of completion method of accounting for long-term construction contracts.

11. Why is the ending inventory of construction in process larger in amount when the percentage of completion method is used compared with the completed contract method? How much larger will the amount be?

PART B

12. Under what circumstances is the dollar value, *Lifo* retail method used?

13. Fundamentally, what is the basic distinction between a conventional retail inventory method and the dollar value, *Lifo* retail method?

14. Explain why a conventional retail inventory method, as adapted, and the dollar value, *Lifo* retail method must be used in combination to attain *Lifo* retail results.

15. When *Lifo* retail is adopted, why must the ending inventory of the period prior to the base year usually be recomputed?

EXERCISES

PART A
Exercises 12–1 to 12–10

(Unless instructed otherwise round all markup percentages and cost ratios to two decimal places.)

Exercise 12–1

Assume the following data for Taylor Company for a particular period:

Sales $120,000
Beginning inventory 16,000
Purchases 80,000

For each of the separate situations below, estimate the ending inventory:

a. Markup is 40% on sales.
b. Markup is one fourth on cost.
c. Markup is 60% on sales.
d. Markup is 50% on cost.
e. Markup is 57% on cost.

Exercise 12–2

The books of Sutton Company provided the following information:

Inventory, January 1 .... $ 6,000
Purchases to May 10 80,000
Net sales to May 10 98,000

Before opening for business on May 11, the assets of the company were totally destroyed by fire. The insurance company adjuster found that the average rate of gross margin for the past few years had been $33\frac{1}{3}\%$.

Required:

What was the approximate value of the inventory destroyed assuming the gross margin percentage given was based on (1) sales and (2) cost of goods sold?

Exercise 12–3

You are engaged in the audit of the records of Storm Company. A physical inventory has been taken by the company under your observation, although the extensions have not been completed, to determine the valuation of the inventory. The records of the company provide the following data: sales, $300,000 (gross); return sales, $4,000 (returned to stock); purchases (gross), $155,000; beginning inventory, $50,000; freight-in, $5,000; and purchase returns and allowances, $2,000. The gross margin last period was 34% of net sales; you anticipate that it will be 35% for the year under audit. Estimate the cost of the ending inventory using the gross margin method. Show computations.

Exercise 12–4

The records of Ellis Company provided the following data for January for two products sold:

	Product A	Product B
Beginning inventory, January 1	$ 40,000	$ 60,000
Purchases during January	147,000	186,000
Freight on purchases	3,000	4,000
Sales during January	300,000	400,000

The gross margin rates on sales for the prior year were company overall, 44%; Product A, 42%; and Product B, 49%.

Required:

1. Estimate the cost of the ending inventory separately and in the aggregate.
2. Under what conditions would one of your responses to Requirement 1 be suspect?

Exercise 12–5

Dixie Retail Store uses the retail method of inventory. At the end of June, the records of the company reflected the following:

Purchases during June: at cost, $265,000; at retail, $430,000.
Sales during June: $380,000.
Inventory, June 1: at cost, $40,000; at retail, $70,000.

Estimate the ending inventory for June assuming *(a)* Fifo cost basis and *(b)* average cost basis. Show all computations.

Exercise 12–6

The records of Popular Department Store showed the following data for Department 20 for January: beginning inventory at cost, $15,000, and $26,000 at selling price; purchases at cost, $150,000, and $297,000 at selling price; gross sales, $303,000; return sales, $6,000 (returned to stock); purchase returns at cost, $4,000, and $7,000 at selling price; and freight-in, $5,960. Determine the approximate valuation of the ending inventory using the retail inventory method *(a)* at average cost and *(b)* at *Fifo*. Show all computations. Which is lower? What may have accounted for the result?

Exercise 12–7

Use the retail inventory method (LCM basis) to estimate the ending inventory *(a)* at average cost and LCM and *(b)* Fifo cost and LCM for Allan Retailers based on the following data:

	At Cost	At Retail
Beginning inventory	$ 91,000	$142,000
Purchases	330,000	561,000
Purchases returned	6,000	10,000
Freight-in	5,000	
Additional markups		12,000
Additional markup cancellations		5,000
Markdowns		9,000
Markdown cancellations		2,000
Sales		560,000
Sales returned (and restored to inventory)		4,000

How is LCM introduced into the computations? Explain the logic of this procedure. Will LCM always produce a lower inventory cost estimate under the retail method than *Fifo* or average without LCM?

Exercise 12–8

Summers Retail Store has just completed the annual physical inventory, which involved counting the goods on hand, then pricing them at selling prices. The inventory valuation derived in this manner amounted to $96,000. The records of the company provided the following data: beginning inventory, $80,000 at retail and $52,120 at cost; purchases (including freight-in and returns), $750,000 at retail and $469,920 at cost; additional markups, $20,000; additional markup cancellations, $8,000; gross sales, $703,000; return sales (restored to inventory), $9,000; and markdowns, $6,000.

Required:

1. Estimate the cost of the ending inventory assuming average cost and LCM.
2. Note any discrepancies and give possible reasons for them.

Exercise 12–9

Speedy Construction Company contracted to build a plant for $500,000. Construction started in January

19A and was completed in November 19B. Data relating to the contract are summarized below:

	19A	19B
Cost incurred during the year	$290,000	$135,000
Estimated additional costs to complete	145,000	
Billings during the year	230,000	270,000
Cash collections during the year ...	200,000	300,000

Required:

Give the journal entries for Speedy, in parallel columns, assuming *(a)* the completed contract method and *(b)* the percentage of completion method. Apportion on basis of costs incurred to date to total estimated construction cost.

Exercise 12–10

Use the data given in Exercise 12–9 to complete a tabulation as follows:

	Completed Contract Method	Percentage Completion Method*
Income Statement:		
Income:		
19A	$_____	$_____
19B	_____	_____
Balance Sheet:		
Receivables:		
19A	_____	_____
19B	_____	_____
Inventory—construction in process, net of billings:		
19A	_____	_____
19B	_____	_____

* Apportion on basis of costs incurred to date to total estimated construction cost.

PART B
Exercises 12–11 to 12–12

Exercise 12–11

Johnson Retailers uses *Fifo* retail for internal purposes and the dollar value, *Lifo* retail method to convert those results for external reporting and for income tax purposes (starting January 1, 19B).

The following data were provided by the inventory records for the year ended December 31, 19B:

	At Cost	At Retail
January 1, 19B, base inventory (carried over from 19A)	$ 6,000	$10,000

Data at end of 19B:

Sales revenue (net of returns)		80,000
Purchases (net of returns)	54,900	85,000
Net additional markups		7,000
Net markdowns		2,000
Total administrative and selling expenses	10,000	

Assume the conversion index numbers are December 31, 19A, 120; and December 31, 19B, 126. Average income tax rate, 40%.

Required:

1. Compute the *Fifo* retail inventory results that would be used for internal purposes at the end of 19B.
2. Convert the *Fifo* retail inventory results to a dollar value, *Lifo* basis for external reporting and income tax purposes.
3. Prepare an income statement using the following format:

	Year 19B	
	Fifo Basis	Lifo Basis
Sales revenue	$_____	$_____
Less expenses:		
Cost of goods sold:		
Beginning inventory	_____	_____
Purchases	_____	_____
Total	_____	_____
Ending inventory	_____	_____
Cost of goods sold	_____	_____
Administrative and selling expenses	_____	_____
Total expenses	_____	_____
Pretax income	_____	_____
Income taxes	_____	_____
Net Income	_____	_____

Exercise 12–12

Diffy's Retail Store had been using the traditional retail inventory method determined on the average cost, LCM basis, for a number of years for all purposes. On January 1, 19M, the company changed to dollar value, *Lifo* retail for external reporting and income tax purposes, but retained average cost, LCM for internal purposes.

At the end of 19L and 19M, the retail inventory computations (average, LCM) for internal purposes were as shown at the top of the next page.

(Relates to Exercise 12–12)	Year 19L		Year 19M	
	At Cost	At Retail	At Cost	At Retail
Beginning inventory, January 1	$ 17,000	$ 30,000	$ 11,200	$ 20,000
Purchases	151,000	268,000	180,000	321,789
Net additional markups		2,000		3,000
Total	$168,000	300,000	$191,200	344,789
Cost ratio ($168,000 ÷ $300,000 = .56) ..		.56		.55
Sales		(275,000)		(300,000)
Net markdowns		(5,000)		(9,000)
Inventory, December 31:				
At retail		$ 20,000		$ 35,789
At cost (average, LCM)	$ 11,200		$ 19,684	

Conversion index numbers: December 31, 19L, 150; and December 31, 19M, 168.

Required (round to nearest dollar):

1. Compute the inventory values (at cost and at retail) that should be used as the base inventory and the ending inventory for 19M for conversion purposes. Why are the above inventory values not appropriate for this purpose?
2. Convert the *Fifo* retail inventory results, computed in 1, to a dollar value, *Lifo* retail basis for the external reports and income tax use at the end of 19M.
3. Complete the following tabulation for 19M:

	Year 19M		
	Average	Fifo	Lifo
Sales revenue..............	$_____	$_____	$_____
Cost of goods sold:			
Beginning inventory	_____	_____	_____
Purchases	_____	_____	_____
Total	_____	_____	_____
Ending inventory	_____	_____	_____
Cost of goods sold ......\	_____	_____	_____
Gross margin	_____	_____	_____

PROBLEMS

PART A
Problems 12–1 to 12–12

(Unless instructed otherwise round all gross margin percentages, markup percentages, and cost ratios to two decimal places.)

Problem 12–1

The records of White Company provided the following information on August 13, 19A:

Inventory, January 1, 19A....................	$ 50,000
Purchases, January 1 to August 13	300,000
Sales, January 1 to August 13	400,000
Purchase returns and allowances	3,000
Sales returns (goods returned to stock)	1,000
Freight-in	4,000

A fire completely destroyed the inventory on August 14, 19A, except for goods marked to sell at $6,000 which had an estimated residual value of $4,000, and for goods in transit to which White Company had ownership; the purchase had been recorded. Invoices recorded on the latter show merchandise cost, $2,000, and freight-in, $100. The average rate of gross margin on sales in recent years has been 25%.

Required:

1. Compute the inventory fire loss.
2. Under what conditions would your response to Requirement 1 be suspect? Explain.

Problem 12–2

Amber Retail Company is developing a profit plan. The following planned data were developed for a three-month future period:

a. January 1 planned inventory, $90,000.
b. Planned average rate of gross margin on sales, 30%.

Complete the following profit plan:

	Profit Plan Estimates			
	January	February	March	Total
Sales planned	$160,000	$180,000	$190,000	$530,000
Cost of goods sold:				
Beginning inventory	?	?	?	?
Purchases budget	110,000	130,000	160,000	400,000
Total goods available ...	?	?	?	?
Less: Ending inventory	?	?	?	?
Cost of goods sold	?	?	?	?
Gross margin planned	?	?	?	?

Problem 12–3

Davis Retail Store burned on March 19, 19D. The following information (up to the date of the fire) was taken from the records of the company which were stored in a safe: inventory, January 1, $28,000; sales, $140,000; purchases, $90,000; sales returns (restored to stock), $3,000; purchase returns and allowances, $2,000; and freight-in, $4,000. The cost of goods sold and gross margins for the past three years were as follows:

	Cost of Goods Sold	Gross Margin
19A	$468,000	$122,000
19B	435,000	130,000
19C	472,000	127,000

Required:

1. Estimate the value of the inventory destroyed in the fire.
2. Under what conditions would your response to Requirement 1 be suspect?
3. The insurance company pays indemnity on "market value" at date of the fire. What amount would you recommend that Davis submit as an insurance claim? Explain.

Problem 12–4

Dawson Company in the past valued inventories at cost. At the end of the current period, the inventory was valued at 45% of selling price as a matter of convenience. However, the cost ratio is not 45%. The current financial statements have been prepared, and the inventory sheets inadvertently destroyed, consequently, you find it impossible to reconstruct the ending inventory at actual cost per the physical count. Fortunately, the following data are available:

Sales	$300,000
Ending inventory (at 45% of selling price)	22,500
Purchases (at cost)	182,500
Pretax income	32,000
Beginning inventory (at cost)	20,000

Required:

Prepare a corrected (and detailed) income statement. Show computations and round the cost ratio to four decimal places.

Problem 12–5

The records of Stanford Department Store provided the following data for June:

Sales (gross)	$730,000
Return sales (restored to inventory)	2,000

Additional markups	9,000
Additional markup cancellations	5,000
Markdowns	7,000
Purchases:	
At retail	749,000
At cost	419,540
Purchase returns:	
At retail	4,000
At cost	2,200
Freight on purchases	6,000
Beginning inventory:	
At cost	51,000
At retail	95,000
Employee discounts	1,000
Markdown cancellations	3,000

Required:

Estimate the valuation of the ending inventory assuming (show computations and carry cost ratios to four places and round inventory to nearest dollar):

Case A—Average cost.

Case B—Average cost, LCM.

Case C—Fifo cost.

Case D—Fifo cost, LCM.

Problem 12–6

Snowden's Department Store uses the retail inventory method. Data for the year ended January 31, 19C, for one department appear below:

Inventory, January 31, 19B:	
Cost	$ 31,850
Sales price	54,000
Purchases for the year ended	
January 31, 19C (gross):	
Cost	137,300
Sales price	245,000
Sales for year (gross)	250,000
Freight on merchandise purchased	6,000
Returns:	
Purchases:	
Cost	1,150
Sales price	2,000
Sales (merchandise restored to	
inventory)	5,000
Additional markups	4,000
Additional markup cancellations	1,000
Markdowns	12,000
Markdown cancellations	2,000
Employee discounts	500

Required:

1. Estimate the January 31, 19C, inventory valuation using the retail inventory method under each of

the following methods (carry cost ratios to three decimal places):

a. Average cost and LCM.
b. Fifo cost and LCM.
c. Average cost.
d. Fifo cost.

2. Since sales returns reenter Snowden's inventory after the customer returns the goods, why are sales returns not added back to goods available for sale at cost and at retail?

Problem 12–7

Auditors are examining the accounts of Austin Retailers, Inc. They were present when Austin's personnel physically counted the Austin inventory; however, the auditors made their own tests. The records of Austin Retailers provided the following data for the year:

	At Retail	At Cost
Inventory, January 1	$ 220,000	$145,500
Net purchases	1,573,000	973,500
Freight-in		15,000
Additional markups	16,000	
Additional markup cancellations	9,000	
Markdowns	8,000	
Employee discounts	2,000	
Sales	1,400,000	
Inventory, December 31 (per physical count valued at retail)	395,000	

Required:

1. Compute the ending inventory at average cost and LCM as an audit test of the overall reasonableness of the physical inventory count.
2. Note any discrepancies that are indicated. What factors should the auditors consider in reconciling any difference in results from the analysis?
3. What accounting treatment should be accorded the discrepancy (if any)?

Problem 12–8

Master Builders, Incorporated, contracted to construct an office building for the Carson Company for $900,000. Construction began on January 15, 19A, and was completed on December 7, 19B. Master Builders' fiscal year ends December 31. Transactions by Master Builders relating to the contract are summarized below:

	19A	19B
Cost incurred to date	$500,000	$800,000
Estimated costs to complete	320,000	
Progress billings to date	400,000	900,000
Progress collections to date	375,000	900,000

Required:

1. In parallel columns, give the entries on the contractor's books assuming (a) the completed contract method and (b) the percentage of completion method allocated on the basis of cost. Assume percentage of completion is measured by the ratio of costs incurred to date to total estimated construction costs.
2. For each method, prepare the income statement and balance sheet presentations for this contract by year.
3. What is the nature of the item "Costs in excess of billings" that appears on the balance sheet?
4. Which method would you recommend the contractor use? Why?

Problem 12–9

Mineola Construction Company contracted to build a dam for the city of Danville for $975,000. The contract provided for progress payments. Mineola Company closes the books each December 31. Work commenced under the contract on July 15, 19A, and was completed on September 30, 19C. Construction activities are summarized below by year:

19A—Construction costs incurred during the year, $180,000; estimated costs to complete, $630,000; progress billings to the city during the year, $153,000, and collections, $150,000.

19B—Construction costs incurred during the year, $450,000; estimated costs to complete, $190,000; progress billings to the city during the year, $382,500, and collections, $380,000.

19C—Construction costs incurred during the year, $195,000. Since the contract was completed, the remaining balance was billed and later collected in full per the contract.

Required:

1. Give the entries on the contractor's books assuming the percentage of completion method is used. Show computation of income apportionment on a cost basis assuming percentage of completion is measured by the ratio of costs incurred to date to total estimated construction costs.
2. Prepare income statement and balance sheet pre-

sentations for this contract by year (percentage of completion basis).

3. Prepare income statement and balance sheet presentations by year assuming completed contract method. For each amount that is different, explain the reason.

4. Which method would you recommend to this contractor? Why?

Problem 12–10

Richards Engineering Company contracted to build a bridge for the city of Temple for $750,000. The contract specified that the city would pay Richards each month the progress billings, less 10%, which was to be held as a "reserve." At the end of the construction, the final payment is to include the reserve. Each billing, less the 10% reserve, must be paid within ten days after submission of a billing to the city.

Transactions relating to the contract are summarized below:

19A—Construction costs incurred during the year, $200,000; estimated costs to complete, $400,000; progress billings, $190,000; and collections per the contract.

19B—Construction costs incurred during the year, $300,000; estimated costs to complete, $115,000; progress billings, $280,000; and collections per the contract.

19C—Construction costs incurred during the year, $110,000. The remaining billings were submitted by October 1 and final collections completed on November 30.

Required:

1. Complete a tabulation as follows:

Date	Method	Income Recognized	Receivable Ending Balance	Construction in Process Ending Balance	Contracts in Excess of Billings Ending Balance
19A	Completed contract				
	Percentage of completion*				
19B	Completed contract				
	Percentage of completion*				
19C	Completed contract				
	Percentage of completion				

* Apportion on basis of costs incurred to date compared to total estimated construction costs.

2. Explain what causes the ending balance in construction in process to be different for the two methods.

3. Which method would you recommend for this contractor? Why?

Problem 12–11

Superior Construction Company contracted to construct a building for $300,000. Construction commenced in 19A and was completed in 19C. Data relating to the contract are summarized below:

	19A	19B	19C
Costs incurred during the year	$ 80,000	$120,000	$ 40,000
Estimated costs to complete	158,000	39,000	
Billings during year	65,000	130,000	105,000
Collections during year	60,000	128,000	110,000

Required:

Complete a tabulation as follows:

Year	Method	Income Recognized	Receivable Ending Balance	Construction in Process Ending Balance	Contracts in Excess of Billings Ending Balance
19A	Completed contract				
	Percentage of completion*				
19B	Completed contract				
	Percentage of completion				
19C	Completed contract				
	Percentage of completion				

* Apportion on basis of costs incurred to date compared to total estimated construction costs.

Problem 12–12

Slow Construction Company contracted to build a large warehouse for Silver City. Construction began on October 1, 19A, and was completed at the end of the tenth working day in January 19C. Slow had estimated construction costs to be $800,000 and had submitted a bid for $900,000, which was accepted by Silver City officials. The accounting period for Slow ends December 31. The construction contract included the following provisions:

1. Contract price, $900,000; progress payments (based on costs incurred) payable within ten days of billing.

2. Completion date, December 31, 19B, with a penalty involving reduction of the contract price in the

amount of $500 per working day after that date, less the number of days Slow was unable to work because of inclement weather.

Construction activities summarized by year were as follows:

	19A	19B	19C
Costs incurred each year	$200,000	$500,000	$230,000
Estimated cost to complete	600,000	210,000	
Progress billings by year	195,000	490,000	210,000
Progress collections by year	180,000	485,000	230,000*

* Penalty reduction in contract price, 10 days @ $500 = $5,000.

Required:

1. For each year give *(a)* the journal entries and *(b)* the balance sheet and income statement reported by Slow assuming the completed contract method is used. Show computations.
2. For each year give *(a)* the entries and *(b)* the balance sheet and income statement reported by Slow assuming the percentage of completion method is used. Assume the construction income is measured and recognized on the basis of the ratio of costs incurred to date to total estimated completion costs. Show computations.

PART B
Problems 12–13 to 12–16

Problem 12–13

Sewanee Department Store keeps its internal inventory records on a *Fifo* (not LCM) basis. At interim reporting dates Sewanee accountants convert the book balances to a *Lifo* basis for reporting purposes. They use the dollar value, *Lifo* retail method for making this conversion. It is now March 31, 19E, and the fol-

lowing data that pertain to the quarter just ended are available from the accounts:

	Quarter Ended March 31, 19E	
	At Cost	At Retail
Base layer from 19C (when *Lifo* was adopted); index = 100	$ 19,750	$ 38,500
Additional *Lifo* layer added in 19D; index = 104; cost ratio .60	30,900	51,500
Beginning inventory, 19E; index = 110	49,500	90,000
Purchases (net)	231,000	400,000
Net additional markups		30,000
Net markdowns		10,000
Return sales		6,000
Sales (gross)		392,000
Price index at end of March 19E = 116.6.		

Required:

Compute the ending inventory at March 31, 19E, at dollar value, *Lifo* retail. Show all computations in order and round all cost ratios and price index ratios to three places.

Problem 12–14

Midwest Retailers has used the traditional *Fifo* retail method (cost basis) of inventory for all purposes. On January 1, 19F, the company decided to use the dollar value, *Lifo* retail method to convert the inventory to the *Lifo* basis. The results will be used for external reporting and for income tax purposes. The base inventory at the start of 19F was as follows:

	At Cost	At Retail
January 1, 19F, base inventory (carried over from December 31, 19E)	$31,000	$50,000

Data from the inventory records for 19F–19H (below):

(Relates to Problem 12–14)	19F		19G		19H	
	At Cost	At Retail	At Cost	At Retail	At Cost	At Retail
Sales (net)		$130,000		$140,000		$155,000
Purchases (net)	$100,800	153,000	$112,000	167,000	$121,600	182,000
Net markdowns		2,000		3,000		2,000
Net additional markups		9,000		11,000		10,000
Applicable price index (19E = 100)		104		107		111
Administrative and selling expenses	25,000		27,000		30,000	

Required:

1. Compute the inventory values (at cost and at retail) that should be used as the ending inventories for 19F, 19G, and 19H for conversion purposes.
2. Convert the *Fifo* inventory results for each year, computed in Requirement 1, to dollar value, *Lifo* retail for use in developing the external financial statements and the income tax return.
3. Complete the following tabulation for 19H:

	Year 19H	
	Fifo Basis	Lifo Basis
Sales revenue	$_____	$_____
Less expenses:		
Cost of goods sold:		
Beginning inventory	_____	_____
Purchases	_____	_____
Total	_____	_____
Ending inventory	_____	_____
Cost of goods sold	_____	_____
Administrative and selling		
expenses	_____	_____
Total expenses	_____	_____
Pretax income	_____	_____
Income taxes (assume a		
40% rate)	_____	_____
Net income	_____	_____
Reduction in cash outflows		
by using *Lifo*	$_____	

Problem 12–15

Goode Department Store has been using the retail inventory method (average, LCM) for a number of years. After extensive consideration the company decided to change to dollar value, *Lifo* retail for all purposes. Thus, after the change, instituted on January 1, 19W, *Fifo* retail cost basis will be computed each period, then these results will be converted to dollar value, *Lifo* retail for external reporting and income tax purposes.

The inventory records for the year 19V showed the following computations (i.e., for the year prior to the change):

	At Cost	At Retail
Inventory, January 1, 19V	$ 32,000	$ 54,000
Purchases (net)	493,400	680,000
Net additional markups		6,000
Total	$525,400	740,000

Cost ratio: $525,400 + $740,000 = .71

Sales (net)		(670,000)
Net markdowns		(10,000)
Inventory, December 31, 19V:		
At retail		$ 60,000
At average cost LCM		
($60,000 × .71)	$ 42,600	

Data for the three years 19W–19Y were as shown at the bottom of this page.

Required:

1. Compute the inventory value that should be used as the base inventory on January 1, 19W.
2. Compute the inventory values (at cost and at retail) that should be used as the ending inventories for 19W, 19X, and 19Y for conversion purposes (and for internal use).
3. In view of the change from average, LCM, the company decided to adjust the inventory account to the *Fifo* cost basis for internal purposes. Give the entry to effect this change at the start of 19W.
4. Convert the *Fifo* inventory results for each year, computed in Requirement 2, to dollar value, *Lifo* retail for use in developing the external financial statements and the income tax return.
5. Complete the tabulation for 19Y shown at the top of page 445.

(Relates to Problem 12–15)	19W		19X		19Y	
	At Cost	At Retail	At Cost	At Retail	At Cost	At Retail
Purchase (net)	$501,120	$689,000	$497,000	$711,000	$529,250	$722,000
Net additional markups		16,000		10,000		10,000
Net markdowns		9,000		11,000		7,000
Sales (net)		683,900		703,350		732,470
Applicable price index						
(19V = 200)	206		210		216	
Administrative and selling						
expenses	45,000		48,000		50,000	

	Year 19Y	
	Fifo Basis	Lifo Basis
Sales revenue	$____	$____
Less expenses:		
Cost of goods sold:		
Beginning inventory	____	____
Purchases	____	____
Total	____	____
Ending inventory	____	____
Cost of goods sold	____	____
Administrative and		
selling expenses	____	____
Total expenses	____	____
Pretax income	____	____
Income taxes (assume		
a 40% rate)	____	____
Net income	____	____
Reduction in cash		
outflows by using *Lifo*....	$____	

Problem 12–16

Sweet Department Store has used the conventional retail inventory method, average (LCM) basis for a number of years for all purposes. The company has decided to use dollar value, *Lifo* retail results for external reporting and income tax purposes. The change is to be effective January 1, 19F. Relevant data subject to the change and the next three years follow:

a. From the internal inventory records—computation of the retail inventory (average, LCM basis) for 19E:

	At Cost	At Retail
Inventory, January 1, 19E	$ 37,000	$ 60,000
Purchases, net	227,000	413,000
Net additional markups		7,000
Total	$264,000	480,000
Cost ratio: $264,000 ÷		
$480,000 = .55		
Sales, net		(416,000)
Net markdowns		(14,000)
Inventory, December 31, 19E:		

At retail		$ 50,000
At average cost LCM		
($50,000 × .55)	$ 27,500	

b. Data for 19F–19H as shown at the bottom of this page.

The company will use the retail inventory method, *Fifo* cost basis for internal purposes starting with 19F.

Required:

1. Compute the inventory value that should be used as the base inventory on January 1, 19F.
2. Compute the inventory values (at cost and retail) that should be used as the ending inventories for 19F, 19G, and 19H for conversion purposes (and for internal use).
3. In view of the change from average, LCM, the company decided to adjust the inventory account to the *Fifo* cost basis for internal purposes. Give the entry to effect this change at the start of 19F.
4. Convert the *Fifo* inventory results for each year, computed in Requirement 2, to dollar value, *Lifo* retail for use in developing the external financial statements and the income tax return.
5. Complete the following tabulation for 19H:

	For Year 19H	
	Fifo Basis	Lifo Basis
Sales revenue	$____	$____
Less expenses:		
Cost of goods sold:		
Beginning inventory	____	____
Purchases	____	____
Total	____	____
Ending inventory	____	____
Cost of goods sold	____	____
Administrative and		
selling expenses	____	____
Total expenses	____	____
Pretax income	____	____
Income taxes (assume a		
40% rate)	____	____
Net income	____	____
Reduction in cash		
outflows by using *Lifo*....	$____	

(Relates to Problem 12–16)	19F		19G		19H	
	At Cost	At Retail	At Cost	At Retail	At Cost	At Retail
Purchases (net)	$231,000	$400,000	$262,200	$450,000	$271,600	$470,000
Net additional markups		30,000		17,000		20,000
Net markdowns		10,000		7,000		5,000
Sales (net)		380,000		410,000		485,000
Applicable price index						
19E = 110	116.6		122.1		132.0	
Administrative and selling						
expenses	70,000		80,000		100,000	

13

Operational Assets: Property, Plant, and Equipment— Acquisition, Use, and Retirement

This chapter and the next two chapters focus on a broad category of assets that may be thought of as operational assets because they are used in the operations of the business and are not held for resale. Operational assets, also referred to as fixed assets, may be classified as follows for accounting purposes:

1. Tangible property, plant, and equipment— Assets in this category have five major characteristics: *(a)* actively used in operations, *(b)* not held as an investment or for resale, *(c)* relatively long lived, *(d)* have physical substance, and *(e)* provide measurable future benefits to the entity. These operational assets are variously described by the terms *property, plant, and equipment; plant assets; capital assets;* or *tangible fixed assets.* The three classes of this group of assets are
   a. Those subject to depreciation such as buildings, equipment, tools, and furniture.
   b. Those subject to depletion such as mineral deposits and timber tracts.
   c. Those not subject to depreciation or depletion such as land for plant site, farms, and ranches.
2. Intangibles—Assets in this category have no physical substance; the value is represented by grants and business rights which confer

some operating, financial, or income-producing advantages on the owner. They are amortized over their useful life in a manner that accords with the expiration of their economic value to the enterprise.

This chapter discusses property, plant, and equipment; Chapter 14 discusses depreciation and depletion; and Chapter 15 discusses intangibles.

CAPITAL EXPENDITURES (ASSET) AND REVENUE EXPENDITURES (EXPENSE)

Accounting for expenditures and obligations incident to the acquisition of property, plant, and equipment and intangible assets necessitates classification of related outlays as either *capital expenditures* (asset) or as *revenue expenditures* (expense). *Capital expenditures* relate to the acquisition of assets, the benefits of which extend over one or more accounting periods beyond the current period; hence, they are recorded in appropriate asset accounts. Capital expenditures made for assets having limited lives are subsequently allocated to the future periods benefited through depreciation, amortization, or depletion. An expenditure that is debited to an asset account or to accumulated depreciation is said to be capitalized.

Revenue expenditures relate to the acquisition of property or other benefits which do not extend beyond the current accounting period; hence, they are recorded in appropriate expense accounts for the current period.

In cases where *(a)* a capital expenditure is relatively small, or *(b)* the future benefit is insignificant, or *(c)* reasonable measurement of the future benefit is impracticable, practical considerations dictate that the outlay should be accounted for as a revenue expenditure (i.e., expensed). Many companies have adopted a realistic accounting policy in this respect such that, for example, expenditures under $500 are classed as revenue expenditures; expenditures above this amount are classified as capital expenditures only where there is clearly a significant and measurable benefit extending to a future period. Correct classification is important because an incorrect classification affects reported income for the entire life of the asset.

PRINCIPLES UNDERLYING ACCOUNTING FOR PROPERTY, PLANT, AND EQUIPMENT

The accounting for property, plant, and equipment fundamentally rests on the *cost and matching principles*. At date of acquisition, these assets are recorded in the accounts at cost. The acquisition cost is measured by the cash outlay made to acquire such assets. If a consideration other than cash is exchanged for the assets, the market value of such consideration at the time of the transaction, or the market value of the assets received, whichever is the more clearly determinable, is recorded as the cost of the assets acquired. An asset is not "acquired" until it has been placed in the position where it is to be used and is ready for productivity in the broad business sense; thus all reasonable and legitimate costs incurred in placing an asset in this status are additions to the cost of the asset.[1]

[1] Unfortunately the accounting profession uses *fair value, market value, fair market value,* and *current market value* to describe the arm's-length price of an asset used in certain transactions and valuations. We generally use *market value* in this text because it is fully descriptive of the intended meaning. The word "fair" implies that "unfair" values might be used in the accounts, and the modifier "current" is redundant because market value presumes the one prevailing at the relevant time.

Subsequent to acquisition, items of property, plant, and equipment are carried in the accounts and reported at *(a)* cost (if unlimited life) or *(b)* in the case of a limited life, at cost less accumulated depreciation, amortization, or depletion (reflecting continuing application of the matching principle.)

The following outline identifies the principal topics related to the accounting for property, plant, and equipment:

1. Acquisition cost of property, plant, and equipment when acquired
   a. For cash.
   b. On a deferred payment plan.
   c. For stock or other securities.
   d. Through exchanges.
   e. Through lump-sum purchases.
   f. Make-ready costs.
2. Departures from cost:
   a. Donated assets and discovery value.
   b. Writedowns due to impairment of use value to the company.
3. Assets constructed for own use.
4. Interest during the construction period.
5. Expenditures subsequent to the beginning of operational use:
   a. Ordinary repairs and maintenance.
   b. Extraordinary repairs.
   c. Replacements and betterments.
   d. Additions.
   e. Rearrangements of assets.
6. Retirement of operational assets.
7. Acquisition costs of specific property. (see Appendix)

The discussion to follow closely parallels the above outline.

TANGIBLE ASSETS ACQUIRED FOR CASH

If a tangible operational asset is purchased for cash, any outlay that a prudent buyer would make for the asset in an arm's-length transaction, including costs of installation and making ready to use, should be capitalized. The capitalizable costs include the invoice price (less discounts), plus incidental costs such as insurance during transit, freight, duties, ownership searching, ownership registration, installation, and breaking-in costs. All available discounts,

448

whether taken or not, should be deducted from the invoice cost. Discounts not taken should be recorded as discounts lost and treated as a current financial expense.

TANGIBLE ASSETS ACQUIRED ON DEFERRED PAYMENT PLAN

Tangible operational assets acquired on a deferred or long-term payment plan (on credit) should be recorded at the cash equivalent price, excluding all interest and financing charges. Actual and implied interest and other finance charges should be charged to financing expense and not treated as part of the asset cost (see page 457 for an exception proposed by the FASB).

If the contract of purchase does not specify interest and financing charges, such charges, nevertheless, should be deducted in determining the cost of the asset. If a current cash price for the asset is determinable, the excess charged under the deferred payment contract should be treated as interest expense and should be apportioned over the period covered by the purchase contract. If no cash price is determinable for the asset, a realistic interest charge should be

recognized in recording the purchase. Although sound in theory, these latter distinctions are not always observed in practice, since the amounts involved may not be *material.* These procedures are specified in *APB Opinion No. 21.*

To illustrate the purchase of a tangible asset on credit, assume a machine was purchased under a contract that required equal payments of $3,951 at the end of each of three years, when the going interest rate was 9% per annum. In particular, note that this hypothetical purchase

contract does not separately identify the interest. To record the asset purchased at $11,853 (i.e., $3,951 × 3) would include in the asset cost the interest expense implicit in the contract. Rather, the asset account should be debited for the *present value* of the three payments discounted at 9% as follows:

PV = Annual Payment × $P_{on=3;i=9\%}$ (Table 6–4)
= $3,951 × 2.53129 (present value of an ordinary annuity of 3 rents of 1 each at 9%).
= $10,000 (rounded)

Therefore, the indicated entries are as follows.

At date of purchase:[2]

Asset—machinery	10,000	
Installments payable—machinery contract		10,000

At payment dates (amounts rounded):

	1st Year	2d Year	3d Year
Interest expense ($10,000 × 9%, etc.)	900	625	328
Installments payable—machinery contract	3,051	3,326	3,623
Cash	3,951	3,951	3,951

A table of debt amortization and interest expense follows (see Chapters 6 and 9):

End of Period	Annual Payment (cash credit)	Interest Expense (debit)		Payment on Principal (debit)	Unpaid Principal
Start					$10,000
1	$ 3,951	$10,000 × 9% $	900	$ 3,051	6,949
2	3,951	6,949 × 9%	625	3,326	3,623
3	3,951	3,623 × 9%	328	3,623	–0–
	$11,853		$1,853	$10,000	

---

[2] Alternatively this entry could be made as follows:

Asset—machinery	10,000	
Discount on installment payable*	1,853	
Installments payable—machinery contract ($3,951 × 3)		11,853

* This amount would be shown contra to "Installments Payable—Machinery Contract" on the balance sheet, thus reporting the liability at its present value.

The payment entries would be revised accordingly; the net effect would be the same in all respects. The first payment entry would be as follows:

Interest expense	900	
Installments payable—machinery contract	3,951	
Discount on installment payable		900
Cash		3,951

TANGIBLE ASSETS ACQUIRED IN EXCHANGE FOR SECURITIES

For a number of reasons, the proper valuation of tangible operational assets received in exchange for bonds and stocks of the acquiring company frequently is difficult to determine, viz:

1. The lack of a readily determinable market value for the securities or the assets involved.
2. The absence of an arm's-length bargaining between the parties to the exchange.[3]
3. The nature of the assets involved, such as unexplored or unproven mineral deposits, manufacturing rights, patents, chemical formulas, mining claims, and the like, may make value estimates difficult.
4. The current quoted market price of the security issued may be based upon a market volume far below the volume of shares involved in the exchange (i.e., a thin market).

The cost principle holds that assets acquired should be recorded at their then current cash equivalent cost. If this amount is not determinable, the cost of assets acquired through exchange of securities should be measured as follows:

1. Determine the market value of the consideration (i.e., the securities) given. Where the securities have an established market price, it should be used as long as the market would absorb the volume of securities involved at that price.
2. If the market value of the securities in the volume exchanged cannot be determined, the market value of the assets acquired should be used. In the absence of an actual cash basis sale of the assets involved in the immediate past, an independent appraisal of them by a professionally recognized appraiser may be recorded as the cost of the assets acquired.
3. If a market value for neither the securities nor the assets received can be determined objectively, values established by the board of directors of the corporation may be used. The law generally allows the directors considerable discretion in establishing values in this situation, except in cases where fraudulent intent on the part of the directors can be shown.

When assets are acquired in exchange for securities, any actual or implied discounts or premiums on the securities should be accounted for in the normal manner. Tangible assets acquired in exchange for bonds payable should be recorded at the current cash value of the bonds, which takes into account any premium or discount on the bonds payable. If there is no currently established market price for the bonds, the cost of the asset can be computed as the *present value* of the bond principal plus the present value of the interest payments, at the going rate of interest (see Chapters 6, 9, and 20).

Operational assets acquired for a combination of cash *and* securities should be capitalized at the sum of the cash, and the market value of the securities determined in accordance with the principles discussed above. When property is financed through notes, care should be taken so that financing expenses are not charged as part of the cost of the operational asset.

TANGIBLE ASSETS ACQUIRED THROUGH EXCHANGES

Items of property, plant, and equipment (referred to in this section as "nonmonetary assets") frequently are acquired by trading in an old asset in full or as part payment. In some transactions, there is an exchange of two or more noncash assets; in other cases, an asset is acquired by exchanging another asset plus a payment or receipt of cash (often referred to as "boot"). Prior to the issuance of *APB Opinion No. 29,* "Accounting for Nonmonetary Transactions," exchanges were recorded by debiting the asset account for the item acquired at either (1) its quoted list price, or (2) the cash paid plus the book value of the old asset exchanged, or (3) its market value. These three alternatives for the same set of facts were widely used in financial accounting.

APB Opinion No. 29 specifies the accounting approach for a wide range of nonmonetary transactions, including those involving the acquisition of tangible operational assets through

---

[3] An arm's-length transaction is negotiated by unrelated parties, each acting in his or her best interest.

exchanges. The basic principle established in the *Opinion* is

> Accounting for nonmonetary transactions should be based on the fair values of the assets (or services) involved which is the same as that used in monetary transactions. This is a *fair market value concept* because realization of gain or loss on disposal of the old asset is assumed to have occurred (i.e., a purchase/sale transaction). (Emphasis supplied.)

Thus, under the *basic principle,* the cost of a tangible operational asset acquired in exchange for another nonmonetary asset is the market value of the asset surrendered to obtain it, and a gain or loss on the disposition of the old asset should be recognized in accounting for the exchange. The market value of the asset acquired should be used to measure its cost only if it is more clearly determinable than the market value of the asset surrendered. However, the *Opinion* specifies several exceptions to the basic principle and also covers exchanges where there is a cash difference (boot) paid or received in the exchange. The following discussion highlights certain provisions of the *Opinion.*

Similar versus Dissimilar Assets

The *Opinion* specifies that the accounting for exchanges of operational assets will depend upon whether the assets exchanged are *similar* or *dissimilar.* Similar *productive* assets are defined as "assets that are of the same general type, that perform the same function, or that are employed in the same line of business." All other productive assets would be classified as dissimilar. For example, the trading in of an old truck on a new truck would involve similar assets; however, the trading in of a tract of land on a new truck would involve dissimilar assets. The distinction between exchanges of similar assets and exchanges of dissimilar assets is important because the *Opinion* specifies different accounting treatments for the two types of exchanges.

Accounting Procedures for Exchanges

Both parties record exchanges of *dissimilar* assets on a *market value* basis, whether or not there is a cash difference (boot) paid or received on the theory that such exchanges represent the culmination of an earning process. Market value, when there is no cash difference, is the market value of the asset surrendered (if this is not reasonably determinable, the market value of the asset received is used). When there is a cash difference, market value is the cash paid plus the market value of the asset surrendered. If the latter is not reasonably determinable, the market value of the asset received is used.

In contrast, when *similar* assets are exchanged and no cash difference (boot) is paid or received, both parties record the exchange on a *book value* basis on the theory that such exchanges do not represent the culmination of an earning process. When a cash difference is received or paid and the assets are similar, the book value basis is altered as illustrated in (2c) below. In no case (involving either similar or dissimilar assets) is the new asset recorded at a cost in excess of its market value if the market value is known. Therefore, the accounting prescribed by the *Opinion* for the exchange of similar and dissimilar operational assets is as follows:

1. Dissimilar assets—Use the market value concept; record the asset acquired at the market value of the asset surrendered, plus or minus any cash difference, and recognize a gain or loss on disposal of the old asset because of the culmination of an earning process.

   Example: Company A has an old crane that cost $50,000; accumulated depreciation to date, $45,000 (i.e., a carrying value of $5,000). It is exchanged with Company B for a tract of land; cash boot of $12,000 was paid. The market value for the old crane is determined to be $13,000.

   To record the exchange by Company A:

Land ($13,000 + $12,000)	25,000	
Accumulated depreciation (old crane)	45,000	
Machinery (old crane)		50,000
Cash		12,000
Gain on disposal of machinery*		8,000

   * Market value recognized, $13,000 − book value, $5,000 = $8,000.

2. Similar assets—In this situation, *APB Opinion No. 29* prescribes a *book value* approach because it is assumed that nonmonetary ex-

change transactions of similar assets are not essentially the culmination of an earnings process.

The procedure for recording an exchange of similar assets depends upon whether a cash difference was also paid or received in the exchange. Accounting for the three possible situations is prescribed as follows:

a. Similar assets exchanged and *no* cash difference (boot) paid or received—In this situation, the cost of the asset acquired is recorded at the carrying (book) value of the asset surrendered.

Example: Company A exchanged an old crane that cost $50,000, accumulated depreciation to date, $45,000, for a much smaller crane having a current cash price of $8,000. No cash difference was involved in this exchange of similar assets. The exchange would be recorded as follows:

Machinery (new crane, at book value of old crane)	5,000*	
Accumulated depreciation (old crane)	45,000	
Machinery (old crane)		50,000

* Cannot exceed market value.

b. Similar assets exchanged and a cash difference (boot) is paid—In this situation, the asset acquired is recorded at the sum of the cash paid plus the book value of the old asset surrendered. As in all cases, the asset acquired cannot be recorded at more than its market value. Therefore, no gain can be recorded; however, if the market value of the asset received is less than the sum of the cash paid plus the book value of the old asset, a loss must be recorded.

Example: Company A exchanged the old crane that cost $50,000, accumulated depreciation, $45,000, for the new, smaller crane having a current cash price of $8,000, and *paid* $1,000 cash boot. The transaction would be recorded as follows:

Machinery (new crane, $1,000 + $5,000)	6,000	
Accumulated depreciation (old crane)	45,000	
Machinery (old crane)		50,000
Cash		1,000

Alternatively, had the cash difference been $4,000, the new asset would be recorded at $8,000 and a $1,000 loss would be recognized.

c. Similar assets exchanged and a cash difference (boot) is received—In this situation, *APB Opinion No. 29* specifies that a gain shall be recognized on the asset given up "to the extent that the amount of the monetary receipt exceeds a proportionate share of the recorded amount of the asset surrendered." Thus, when a cash difference is *received,* the exchange transaction is construed to involve a part sale and a part exchange of the asset surrendered. In this case, a gain on that part sold for cash may be recognized. The asset acquired is recorded as a proportionate part of the book value of the asset surrendered. Thus, this transaction is treated in part at market value and in part at book value.

Example: Company A exchanged the old crane that cost $50,000, accumulated depreciation, $45,000, for a new, smaller crane having a current cash price of $8,000, and *received* a cash difference of $2,000. The transaction would be recorded as follows:

Cash	2,000	
Machinery (new crane) [a]	4,000	
Accumulated depreciation (old crane)	45,000	
Machinery (old crane)		50,000
Gain on disposal of machinery (old crane) [b]		1,000

Computations:

[a] Cost of new crane—Book value of old crane less the proportion of book value of the old crane sold:

Book value, old crane ($50,000 − $45,000)..............................	$5,000

Proportion of book value of the old crane sold for cash:

$$\text{Book Value of old} \times \frac{\text{Cash realized on part sale}}{\text{Cash realized on part sale} + \text{MV of asset acquired on part exchange}}$$

$5,000 \times \dfrac{\$2,000}{\$2,000 + \$8,000}$	1,000
Difference—cost of asset acquired	$4,000

[b] Gain on disposal of asset surrendered—Cash received less portion sold of book value of asset surrendered:

Cash received	$2,000
Proportion of book value of old crane sold (per above)	1,000
Difference—gain on sale of old crane	$1,000

Alternatively, in case of a loss, the *Opinion* requires recognition of the full amount of such loss. To illustrate, assume in the preceding example that the accumulated depreciation was $39,000. The transaction would be recorded as follows:

Cash	2,000	
Accumulated depreciation (old crane)	39,000	
Loss on disposal of machinery (old crane)	1,000	
Machinery (new crane)	8,000	
Machinery (old crane)		50,000

Observe that the full amount of the loss is recognized because the asset acquired cannot be recorded in excess of its market value. Thus, there is no need to calculate the proportionate part of the old crane sold. A loss is reported because the book or carrying value of the asset given up (i.e., $11,000) is greater than its market value (i.e., $2,000 + $8,000), as reflected in the exchange transaction. Note that *Opinion No. 29* is written to limit recognition of gains to situations where boot is received with similar assets. This is intended to avoid manipulation of accounting values to report gains on exchanges, which was possible under procedures permitted earlier.

The *Opinion* does not recognize the list price as the cost of an operational asset in any situation unless that price is the actual cash equivalent price (market value). The list price often is merely a basis for bargaining rather than a genuine cash cost. To determine market value in exchanges of operational assets, *Opinion No. 29* states that market values should be determined by referring to "quoted market prices, independent appraisals, estimated fair values of assets or services received in exchange and other available evidence."[4]

If a business successively acquires several generations of similar assets by trading the next-to-newest asset as part payment for the newest asset, the effect of applying *Opinion No. 29* can be to cumulate past errors in accounting into the carrying value of the newest asset. Examples of such errors that can affect this carrying value include past mis-depreciation, erroneous accounting for repairs, and so forth. By requiring successive assets to be valued at the carrying value of the asset traded in plus boot paid and not recognizing gains on exchanges, effects of past errors can be perpetuated. The cycle is broken in the event of a loss on exchange of assets, in which case the new asset is recorded at market value.

LUMP-SUM PURCHASES OF ASSETS

It is not unusual for a business to acquire several dissimilar assets for a lump sum. This type of acquisition, frequently referred to as a basket, group, or lump-sum purchase, poses the problem of apportioning the lump-sum cost to the several assets acquired. The apportionment should be based upon some realistic indicator of the relative values of the several assets involved, such as appraised values, tax assessment, cost savings, or the present value of estimated future earnings.

To illustrate, assume that $90,000 was paid for property that included land, a building, and some machinery. Assume further that an independent appraisal showed appraised values of land, $30,000; building, $50,000; and machinery, $20,000. The cost apportionment and entry to record the transaction are shown below:

Asset	Appraised Value	Proportion	Apportioned Cost
Land	$ 30,000	3/10	$27,000
Building	50,000	5/10	45,000
Machinery	20,000	2/10	18,000
Total	$100,000		$90,000

Entry to record the purchase:

Land	27,000	
Building	45,000	
Machinery	18,000	
Cash		90,000

---

[4] Under generally accepted accounting principles, no asset, irrespective of its characteristics, should be recorded at acquisition at more than its then market value. This is the definition of cost under the cost principle and is in accord with that principle.

MAKE-READY COSTS

Outlays subsequent to acquisition but prior to operational use of an operational asset, made to ready the asset for use, should be capitalized as part of the cost of the asset. Prior to operational use, a secondhand asset frequently will require considerable outlays for major repairs, reconditioning, remodeling, and installation, all of which should be capitalized. Reinstallation and rearrangement costs of machinery, rearrangement of partitions, renovation of buildings, and similar outlays on operational assets purchased in a used condition should be capitalized as part of the cost. Overhead items such as insurance, taxes, supervisory salaries, and similar incidental expenditures directly related to the asset during a period of renovation also should be capitalized. Depreciation should *not* be recorded on such costs prior to the period of use.

DEPARTURES FROM COST IN ACCOUNTING FOR TANGIBLE OPERATING ASSETS

Although accounting for assets fundamentally is based upon the cost principle, there are special circumstances in which departure from the cost principle is sanctioned. These exceptions are as follows:

1. Writeup due to donation of assets to the company.
2. Writeup due to high and unexpected discovery value.
3. Writedown due to significant and permanent impairment of use value to the company.
4. Revaluations due to quasi-reorganization (see Chapter 17).
5. Capitalization of interest.

Items 1, 2, and 3 are discussed in paragraphs immediately following; item 5 is discussed following consideration of self-constructed operating assets.

Donated Assets

Assets occasionally are donated to a corporation by stockholders for various reasons, and by municipalities, or local nonprofit organizations, as an inducement to locate a plant or other facilities in the area. Frequently, such gifts are conditional upon some particular performance on the part of the corporation, such as the employment of a certain number of individuals by a given date.

Strict adherence to the cost principle would involve recording donated assets at the amount of incidental costs incurred in acceptance of the gift and in fulfilling the related agreements. Accountability for the resources of an enterprise and measurement of enterprise earning power require that every economic facility employed, regardless of origin, be recorded at acquisition date at the current cash equivalent price or some other equivalent value. *APB Opinion No. 29* states that "a nonmonetary asset received in a *nonreciprocal transfer* should be recorded at the fair market value of the asset received." In the case of a donated asset (donated assets exemplify "nonreciprocal transfers," i.e., transfers in which the donor receives nothing measurable in return), an independent and realistic appraisal of the current market value of the donated asset should be recorded, provided the donation is unconditional. Should the donor impose restrictions, however, any "negative values" arising from such conditions should be deducted from the market value of the asset in determination of the valuation to be recorded. To illustrate, assume a building, including the land on which it is located, is given by a city to XYZ Corporation as an inducement to establish a plant therein. The related transactions may be recorded as follows:[5]

1. To record the market value, per appraisal at date of donation:

Plant building	8,000	
Plant land	4,000	
Contributed capital—donated plant		12,000

2. At date of transfer and payment of transfer costs:

---

[5] Some have argued, rather illogically, that the value recorded for assets donated by nonshareholders also should be credited to a special revenue account and reported on the current income statement, while donations by shareholders should be credited to contributed capital as illustrated. Present GAAP does not permit revenue recognition for the value of donated assets.

Contributed capital—donated
plant (basis: the market
value of $12,000 already
recognized implicitly
includes this cost) 900
    Cash....................... 900

3. To record depreciation for first year assuming a ten-year life and no residual value:

Depreciation expense 800
    Accumulated depreciation—
    plant building 800

If the donation is contingent upon the fulfillment in the future of some contractual obligation on the part of the recipient, most accountants agree that the asset should be treated as a contingent asset until such time as the contingent condition has been met. In such a case, *FASB Statement No. 11,* "Accounting for Contingencies," requires that the donated asset should be disclosed in the financial statements by note only. Alternatively, when the obligation is essentially met, or upon conditional transfer of ownership, the asset may be recognized in the accounts on a contingent basis. To illustrate, assume a city donated a plant site having a market value of $25,000 to a corporation subject to a provision that ownership would transfer one year after the beginning of operations. A conditional ownership transfer agreement was executed. The transactions may be recorded as follows:

1. At date of agreement and conditional transfer:

Contingent asset—donated
plant site 25,000
    Contingent contributed capital—
    donated plant site 25,000

2. At date of transfer of actual ownership and incidental costs of $500:

Plant site...................... 25,000
Contingent contributed capital—
donated plant site 25,000
    Contingent asset—donated
    plant site 25,000
    Cash 500
    Contributed capital—donated
    plant site 24,500

Depreciable assets received by donation should be depreciated in the normal manner on the basis of the market value recorded in the accounts. A contingent asset (as recorded in entry No. 1 above), if depreciable in nature, should be depreciated on the basis of the market value from date of initial recognition.

Discovery Value

Property owned by a company may increase in value substantially as a result of the *discovery* thereon of valuable mineral or other natural resources. In such cases the original cost of the property may not provide a reasonable basis for accountability. In the case of discovery value, the accounting profession sometimes recognizes another exception to the cost principle. The market value of the property, in consideration of the valuable natural resource, should be realistically estimated, usually by appraisal, and recorded in the accounts. The resulting credit should be to Unrealized Capital Increment—Discovery Value. Depletion should be recognized on the basis of the increased value. To illustrate, assume a tract of land was purchased in 1974 for $20,000 and that in 1979 a valuable gravel deposit (that is commercially exploitable) was discovered on it. Related entries are as follows:

1. To record purchase in 1974:

Land 20,000
    Cash 20,000

2. To record discovery value (estimated total quantity exploitable, 100,000 tons; appraised at $250,000, exclusive of residual land value of $20,000) in 1979:[6]

Land—discovery value increment
(gravel deposit) 250,000
    Unrealized capital discovery value
    increment (gravel deposit) . 250,000

3. To record depletion for first year based on depletion rate of $2.50 per ton; 10,000 tons removed during first year:

Depletion expense 25,000
    Land—discovery value
    increment (gravel deposit) . 25,000

---

[6] The accounting profession has sanctioned, but not required, this procedure. Chapter 9B of *Accounting Research Bulletin No. 43* specifies that in the case of operational assets written up to appraised values, depreciation shall be based on the appraised value.

The FASB contemplated prescribing discovery value as the basis for accounting for oil and gas *reserves* when it was considering issuance of *FASB Statement No. 19.* When the final statement was issued in December 1977, however, a majority of the Board members rejected discovery value accounting for oil and gas reserves because

(a) values that were current when initially recorded quickly become out-of-date and

(b) the mixture of values of minerals measured at different dates of discovery lacks both the verifiability of historical costs and the relevance of current values. The Board believes that issues relating to the accounting measurement basis should await resolution in the conceptual framework project.[7]

At the present time it appears that relatively few natural resource companies have used discovery value.

We saw earlier that recognizing discovery values had the effect of raising depletion charges over what they would have been if the resources involved had been valued at historical cost. It should be noted that in the event an appraisal results in increasing the carrying value of a depreciable asset, depreciation expense is similarly increased. Reflecting upward appraisals in the accounts has been forbidden since the issuance of *APB Opinion No. 6* late in 1965 (which revised Chapter 9B of *ARB No. 43*). At the same time, that *Opinion* provided (for appraisals that had been recorded earlier) that income should be charged with depreciation computed on the written-up amounts.

Writedown of Operational Assets Due to Impairment of Use Value

If an operational asset suffers impairment of its operational value by a *material amount,* it should be written down or written off as the circumstances warrant. For example, a plant may become idle due to factors such as continuing decline in demand, obsolescence of its products,

or inadequate transportation facilities, so that it has little or no resale value and its decreased value, if any, can only be realized as salvage. In such cases, GAAP *requires* an immediate writedown to net realizable value and recognition of the impairment loss for the period. Normally the writedown should be accomplished through a credit to the accumulated depreciation account (in recognition of obsolescence) and a debit to a nonrecurring loss. The loss would be extraordinary only if it is *(a)* unusual and *(b)* occurs infrequently *(APB Opinion No. 30).* As a general principle operational assets should not be carried at a book value in excess of their economic value in use.

ASSETS CONSTRUCTED FOR OWN USE

Some types of companies regularly construct portions of their operational assets; utilities often extend transmission facilities and build pipelines using their own work crews and property. Other companies which would not normally build their own facilities may do so when their personnel and properties would otherwise be idle. Obviously, all labor and material costs identifiable with the construction should be charged to the new assets. Accounting treatment of *overhead* costs that may be associated with the construction is more controversial. Two problems arise: (1) What elements of overhead can be specifically identified with the new construction? (2) Should overhead be applied to self-constructed assets on the same basis as to regular production for inventory?

Identification of specific overhead costs with construction projects can become complex. Some overhead elements, such as permits and licenses, are easily associated with the construction, but others may not be so obvious. When machinery is depreciated on a machine-hours or output basis and that machinery is used on a self-construction project, it is easy to assign depreciation charges to the project. On the other hand, when the machinery is depreciated by the straight-line, sum-of-the-years'-digits, or declining balance method (especially if it would have been idle but for the self-construction), assignment of depreciation charges is likely to be more arbitrary. Other elements of overhead, such as

---

[7] *Statement of Financial Accounting Standards No. 19,* "Financial Accounting and Reporting by Oil and Gas Companies" (Stamford, Conn., December 1977), p. 71.

insurance, taxes, and utilities, may be even more difficult to assign to self-construction projects. Some believe that notwithstanding the difficulties of identifying specific overhead charges with the construction project, the only sound basis of accounting for the cost of self-constructed assets is to attempt to assign specific overhead costs to the project.

Others believe self-construction projects should bear the same proportion of overhead costs as would regular production. In their view, if overhead is assigned on the basis of labor hours and 8% of labor hours accounted for are associated with self-construction, then 8% of overhead should be charged to the self-constructed assets. This viewpoint is easier to sustain when the company's personnel and facilities are employed at or near capacity than when there are idle personnel and facilities, and one of the reasons for undertaking the self-construction was to absorb the idle capacity. Those favoring assigning overhead on the same basis to both types of production maintain that self-constructed assets should be accorded the same treatment as inventory and that unless the same procedure is followed, special favors are granted to self-constructed assets. Not assigning the same overhead to self-construction would result in an undervaluation of constructed assets and an overstatement of cost of goods sold and inventories. The counterargument is that allocation of overhead to self-constructed assets when idle capacity exists does not affect normal production, and therefore capitalization of overhead other than that occasioned by the self-construction will result in overstatement of the cost of self-constructed assets and understatement of inventory costs. In the final analysis, income would be temporarily overstated since the self-constructed assets are longer lived than inventory.

The dispute has not been resolved. The AICPA's *Accounting Research Monograph No. 1* says the central question is whether or not the overhead costs in question have "discernible future benefits." A useful criterion in answering that question is

> . . . that, in the absence of compelling evidence to the contrary, overhead costs considered to have "discernible future benefits" for the purpose of determining the cost of inventory should be presumed to have "discernible future benefits" for the purpose of determining the cost of a self-constructed depreciable asset.[8]

Under this criterion it would appear that both *normal* and *incremental* overhead costs would be charged to self-constructed assets; it should be remembered, however, that this *monograph* is not binding on accountants.

Excess Costs of Construction

Actual cost of self-constructed operational assets may differ from what their cost would have been if acquired from outsiders. When a company determines that its cost of self-constructed properties exceeds the prospective cost of acquiring similar properties of equal capacity and quality from outsiders, it should charge the excess cost to operations of the period in which the self-construction is completed. Failure to do so carries forward cost elements which have no future benefit. On the other hand, when the cost of self-constructed facilities is less than their prospective cost if acquired from outsiders, the assets should be initially valued at actual cost. Writing them up to the prospective cost and the attendant recognition of the cost saving as part of income of the current period is not permitted under generally accepted accounting principles.

INTEREST DURING THE CONSTRUCTION PERIOD

Whether assets are being self-constructed or acquired from outsiders, there is often a lengthy waiting period between the authorization and start of a project and its completion. A controversial question concerns whether to capitalize (i.e., debit the asset) interest during the construction period, or to account for it as a financing expense. Increasing amounts of an entity's borrowed or contributed capital are tied up while construction proceeds toward completion. There

---

[8] Charles W. Lambden, Dale L. Gerboth, and Thomas W. McRae, *Accounting for Depreciable Assets* (New York: AICPA, 1975), p. 57.

is general agreement that such time-related costs as taxes and insurance during construction should be charged to the asset under construction rather than being treated as current expenses. Consistent logic would support similar capitalization of interest (interest costs incurred after construction should always be expensed). However, several complications arise when attempting to capitalize interest: Unless the funds were specifically borrowed to finance the construction, it may be difficult to determine a proper amount of interest to capitalize. Where no funds were specifically borrowed for the construction, assignment of interest to the constructed assets requires imputation of an interest rate and an offsetting credit must be made to some accounts such as Interest Revenue, which has the effect of increasing income during the construction period. Capitalization of interest has been discouraged or prohibited by regulatory authorities in some instances.

Public utilities have often capitalized interest during construction. Instead of charging interest on funds borrowed to finance construction to current operations, they have capitalized it as a cost of the assets built. Utility customers are charged regulated rates set to give utility stockholders a fair rate of return on their investment, so this procedure has resulted in an equitable allocation. If the interest were charged to current operations, present customers would have to pay increased utility rates to cover the added expense and would, in effect, be financing facilities which are going to benefit future customers. By charging the interest to the constructed assets (thereby raising future depreciation charges on them), the future customers who benefit from the assets pay for the interest costs that helped make them a reality.

Capitalization of interest during construction outside the public-utility industry was not a widespread practice but became a growing one in the early 1970s. However, its spread was halted, at least temporarily, for many companies, by issuance of SEC *Accounting Series Release No. 163*. Under provisions of this release (after June 21, 1974), only electric, gas, water, and telephone utilities plus, in certain situations, those companies covered by provisions of two AICPA industry guides can capitalize interest.[9] In addition, companies that prior to June 21, 1974, had publicly disclosed an accounting policy of capitalizing interest may continue interest capitalization, but may not extend it to new types of assets. On all financial statements filed, by utilities or other companies subject to these rules, after January 1, 1975, the amount of interest capitalized must be reported. In the case of nonutility companies, the basis for capitalizing interest and the method of determining capitalized interest must be disclosed.

Interest on funds borrowed during significant time periods required to bring assets to the condition and location necessary for intended usage would be capitalized as part of the assets' historical cost if provisions of an exposure draft of a proposed FASB Statement of Financial Accounting Standards issued in December 1978, become effective. A significant time period is defined in the draft as "usually one year or longer." The standard would apply to inventories as well as to operational (fixed) assets.

Assets qualifying for interest capitalization would include those under construction for an entity's own use, those requiring a long production period prior to sale (e.g., ships or real estate projects), and inventories requiring a long maturation period (such as aging whiskey). The amount of interest to be capitalized is an allocation of interest cost incurred during the developmental period of the asset from the first expenditure on the asset and ending when the asset is substantially complete and ready for its intended use. Guidelines for the allocation generally provide that the interest rate on *recent* borrowings of the company should be associated with the qualifying assets.

To illustrate, under the draft's provisions, if $700,000 were borrowed to finance construction of an asset that cost $1,000,000, interest on the $700,000 debt and interest on other recent debt of $300,000 would be capitalized during the period required to develop the asset (but not to exceed the amount of interest cost incurred by the entity during that period). In the absence of recent debt, interest on any other currently exist-

---

[9] *Audits of Savings and Loan Associations,* an AICPA industry audit guide (1973); and *Accounting for Retail Land Sales,* an AICPA industry accounting guide (1973).

ing debt would be capitalized. The proposed Statement does not provide for imputing (capitalizing) interest cost on funds represented by owners' equity. The amount of interest capitalized cannot be amortized over the life of the debt, but must be included in the asset cost that is used to compute periodic depreciation expense over the life of the asset.

The proposed Statement requires disclosure in the financial statements or related notes of the total amount of interest cost incurred for the period and the amounts thereof that were (a) expensed and (b) capitalized.

EXPENDITURES SUBSEQUENT TO ACQUISITION

Repairs and Maintenance

After acquisition cost has been measured and recorded, numerous costs related to *utilization* of plant and equipment assets are incurred. Examples include repairs, maintenance, betterments, and replacements. What outlays should be charged to the asset account, to the accumulated depreciation account, to Retained Earnings, to expense, or to some combination of these accounts? The problem is particularly critical as a result of the difficulty in distinguishing between the several classifications of outlay, such as ordinary repairs as opposed to extraordinary repairs, because each type of outlay requires different treatment in the accounts and financial reports.

Ordinary Repairs and Maintenance. *Maintenance costs* are those costs, such as lubrication, cleaning, adjustment, and painting, which are incurred on a more or less continuous basis to keep equipment in normal usable condition. *Ordinary repairs* (as distinguished from major repairs) are outlays for parts, labor, and other related costs which are necessary to keep the equipment in normal operating condition but do not add materially to the use value of the asset, nor prolong its life appreciably. Ordinary repairs are recurring and normally involve relatively small expenditures. Examples of ordinary repairs are repairing a broken chain or electrical circuit and replacing spark plugs. Since maintenance costs and ordinary repairs are similar in many respects and are accounted for in

the same way, they usually are combined for accounting purposes.

Ordinary repair and maintenance expense may be accounted for using either of two approaches:

1. As direct expenditures—An appropriate expense account is debited for each outlay as incurred. Since use of the asset precedes repairs, it is sometimes argued that the matching principle is not adequately implemented. However, immateriality of the amount and the short time between use and repair are compensating factors.
2. Accrual procedure—In the case of a new asset, the maintenance and repair costs initially will be low, increasing in amount each year as the asset is utilized. Repair costs also follow use and tend to vary during the year. Rather than charging operating expense as the repairs are incurred, it is sometimes preferable to use the accrual procedure. The accrual procedure requires an estimate of the total cost of ordinary repairs and maintenance during *(a)* the life of the asset or *(b)* during the year, depending on the period over which apportionment is desired. The amount of estimated repairs is allocated to each interim period on the basis of time (an equal amount each month or year, as the case may be) or on the basis of production or output. Repair and Maintenance Expense is debited each period, and a liability account is credited for the estimated amount. Actual expenditures for ordinary repairs and maintenance are then debited to the allowance account when incurred. To illustrate, assume ordinary repairs and maintenance for the year have been estimated at $1,800 and that this amount is to be apportioned on a time basis (an equal amount each month). Assume that the actual repairs and maintenance costs incurred for the first month amounted to $110. The entries would be as follows:

1. To record the estimated ordinary repair and maintenance cost for the month:

Repairs and maintenance expense 150
    Estimated liability for
      repairs and maintenance 150

2. To record actual outlays for the month for ordinary repairs and maintenance:

Estimated liability for
  repairs and maintenance 110
    Cash or payables 110

The income statement would report repairs and maintenance expense of $150 for the month. The $40 credit balance in the liability account would be reported on the interim balance sheet as a current liability because it reflects a future demand on current assets. In this example, at the end of the year any balance in the liability account would be closed to the related expense account. That is, repair and maintenance expense would be adjusted to the actual cost of repairs for the period.

The accrual procedure for ordinary repairs and maintenance has been accorded general acceptability by the accounting profession. The procedure is justifiable for apportioning an expense where there is a sound basis for doing so; it is not acceptable simply as a means of equalizing profits among several periods. It is used on either an annual basis, or to cover the entire life of the asset. In the latter case, the ending balance in the liability account, each year, is reported on the balance sheet as a special liability (a claim against future assets). The accrual procedure is easiest to justify when production or other activities causing repairs are somewhat seasonal.

Extraordinary Repairs

Extraordinary or major repairs involve relatively large amounts, are not recurring in nature, and usually increase the *use value* (efficiency and use utility) or the service life of the asset beyond what it was before the repair. There are two acceptable *alternative* approaches to accounting for extraordinary repairs:

1. Increase the asset account—If the expenditure serves primarily to increase the use value (utility), the cost is debited to the related asset account.
2. Reduce the accumulated depreciation account—If the expenditure serves primarily to increase the service life of the asset (and perhaps the residual value), the cost is debited to the related accumulated depreciation account.

In either case, the revised carrying value (cost minus accumulated depreciation), taking residual value into consideration, is depreciated over the estimated remaining life. Examples of extraordinary repairs are major overhauls, major improvements in the electrical system, and strengthening the foundation of a building.

Because of the difficulty in making a realistic distinction between increase in utility and increase in useful life as a result of extraordinary repairs, and because the two methods give the same net results (with the same set of facts), both are widely used. Often the depreciation rate must be revised.

Replacements and Betterments

Replacement involves the removal of a major part or component of plant or equipment and the substitution of a new part or component of essentially the *same type and performance capabilities.* Replacement may involve specific subunits or a number of major items similar in many respects to an extraordinary repair. In fact, the line between replacements and extraordinary repairs often is difficult to draw.

In contrast, a *betterment,* or improvement, constitutes the removal of a major part or component of plant or equipment and the substitution of a different part or component having significantly *improved and superior* performance capabilities. The result of the improved substitute serves to increase the overall efficiency and tends to increase the useful life of the primary asset. The replacement of an old shingle roof with a modern fireproof tile roof, installing a more powerful engine in a shrimp boat, and replacement of an improved electrical system in a building are illustrations of betterments.

Because of the different circumstances in which replacements and betterments are made, three different approaches are used, viz:

1. Substitution—Conceptually this method assumes that there has been a disposal of the old unit and acquisition of a new unit. There-

fore, these two separate events are recorded as follows:

a. The cost of the old unit replaced is removed from the asset account, the accumulated depreciation on the old unit is removed, and a loss on disposal is recognized.

b. The new replacement unit is debited to the asset account.

To illustrate, assume the old shingle roof on Plant A, original cost $20,000, 80% depreciated, is replaced with a new fireproof tile roof that cost $60,000. The two entries (which could be combined) are as follows:

a. To remove old roof from the accounts:

Accumulated depreciation (old roof, $20,000 × 80%) ..	16,000	
Loss on disposal of plant assets	4,000	
Plant assets (old roof)		20,000

b. To record acquisition of new roof:

Plant assets (new roof)	60,000	
Cash		60,000

Theoretically, this method is sound in every respect. However, it can be applied only when the cost of the old subunit and the related accumulated depreciation are known or can be realistically estimated. The loss would not be extraordinary under the provisions of *APB Opinion No. 30.*[10]

2. Capitalize—This approach is used when the old costs and related accumulated depreciation amounts are not known, and when the primary effect is to increase efficiency (rather than to lengthen the economic life of the basic asset; a betterment). The cost of the betterment is debited to the primary asset in conformance with the cost principle. The primary asset is improved as to performance and perhaps remaining life. In this approach, the cost and accumulated depreciation on the unit replaced are not removed from the accounts because they are not realistically determinable. Often the depreciation rate must be revised.

3. Reduce accumulated depreciation—This approach is recommended when the primary effect is to lengthen the remaining life of the related asset (a replacement); however, it is used as a full-fledged alternative to capitalization in the asset account. The cost of the replacement is debited to the related accumulated depreciation account on the basis that it is a recovery of past depreciation and that the life of the primary asset is lengthened. Often the depreciation rate must be revised.

Additions

Additions are extensions, enlargements, or expansions made to an existing asset. An extra wing or room added to a building and the addition of a production unit to an existing machine are examples of additions. An addition represents a capital expenditure and should be recorded in the operational asset accounts at the full acquisition cost determined under the principles discussed above for acquisition cost of the original asset. Work done on the existing structure, such as shoring up the foundation to accommodate the addition or the cutting of an entranceway through an existing wall, should be regarded as a part of the cost of the addition and capitalized. The cost of an addition, less any estimated residual value, normally should be depreciated over its own service life or the remaining life of the original asset of which it is a part, whichever period is the shorter if it is an integral part of the older asset. If not an integral part, it should be depreciated over its own useful life.

Pollution control devices have recently been added by large numbers of entities in compliance with laws or court or administrative orders. Sometimes, either because the original assets (which are the source of the pollution) were acquired when prices were low or because of stringency of the control regulations, the antipollution devices are quite costly in relation to the original assets. The devices themselves are capitalizable as plant additions. A question arises as to the accounting disposition of fines, dam-

---

[10] Some accountants believe that this is a change in estimate (*APB Opinion No. 20,* "Accounting Changes"); therefore, the loss should not be separately recognized but should be debited to accumulated depreciation and thereby spread prospectively over the remaining life of the primary asset.

ages, or penalties which are sometimes assessed in connection with earlier pollution. Some have argued that such costs should be charged to the current period; others contend the costs should be capitalized and depreciated over future periods. The authors prefer the first of these alternatives.

Rearrangement of Assets

The cost of reinstallation, rerouting, or rearrangement of factory machinery for the purpose of securing greater efficiency in production or reduced production costs in the future should be capitalized if material in amount and if the benefits of the rearrangement definitely will extend beyond the current accounting period. Such costs should be capitalized as a deferred charge and amortized over the ensuing periods benefiting from the rearrangement. If no measurable future benefit is to be derived from such outlays, they should be expensed as incurred.

RETIREMENT OF OPERATIONAL ASSETS

Operational assets may be retired voluntarily through disposal by sale, trade, or abandonment—or involuntarily lost as a result of casualty such as fire or storm. Irrespective of the cause of retirement, if the asset is subject to depreciation, it should be depreciated to the date of such retirement. Likewise, taxes, insurance premium costs, and similar costs should be accrued up to the date of retirement. At the date of retirement the cost of the asset and its related accumulated depreciation should be removed from the accounts. To illustrate, assume a truck costing $32,000 on February 1, 1976, is sold on July 1, 1980, for $6,500. Straight-line depreciation has been recorded on the basis of an estimated service life of five years and an estimated residual value of $2,000. The company closes its books on December 31 of each year. The entries at date of sale would be as follows:

1. Depreciation expense   3,000
    Accumulated depreciation—
       equipment   3,000
    To record 6 months' depreciation for 1980 at $500 per month computed as follows:
    Amount to be depreciated ($32,000 − $2,000) $30,000
    Service life—5 years or 60 months.
    Depreciation, $30,000 × 6/60 ························· $3,000

2. Cash   6,500
    Accumulated depreciation—
      equipment*   26,500
        Delivery equipment   32,000
        Gain on sale of equipment*   1,000
    To record retirement of old truck by sale.

* Sales price			$6,500
Less book value of asset sold:			
Original cost		$32,000	
Accumulated depreciation:			
1976—11 months	$5,500		
1977—12 months	6,000		
1978—12 months	6,000		
1979—12 months	6,000		
1980— 6 months	3,000	26,500	5,500
Gain on sale			$1,000

The accounting entries for an exchange were discussed and illustrated earlier in the chapter. If an operational asset is abandoned or disposed of because it has no value, the cost and accumulated depreciation amounts should be removed from the accounts and any loss on abandonment, including costs of disposal, recognized.

Outlays made to restore and repair uninsured assets damaged through fire, storm, or other casualty should be recorded as losses and closed to the Income Summary account. Outlays made to improve properties beyond their approximate operating condition prior to the casualty should be apportioned between losses and the asset.[11] Damaged assets not restored should be reduced to a carrying value consistent with the decrease in going-concern utility. Accounting for *insured* casualty losses is discussed in Chapter 15.

Appendix—Acquisition Costs of Specific Property

In determining the acquisition cost of an operational asset, the general principles discussed heretofore are applicable; however, certain items of property give rise to special problems in applying the general principles. These special problems are considered below.

Land

The acquisition cost of land should be recorded in an account captioned Land or Real

---

[11] In instances where the casualty loss is both (a) unusual and (b) occurs infrequently, as defined in *APB Opinion No. 30,* it must be reported as an extraordinary item.

Estate. Some of the specific elements of land cost include the following:

1. Original contract price.
2. Brokers' commissions.
3. Legal fees for examining and recording ownership.
4. Cost of ownership guarantee insurance policies.
5. Cost of real estate surveys.
6. Cost of an option when it is exercised.
7. Cost of razing an old building (net of any salvage).
8. Cost of cancelling an unexpired lease.
9. Payment by the purchaser of accrued or unpaid taxes on the land to date of purchase.

On the other hand, the cost of land does not include fees for surveying, ownership searches, geological options, legal and other expert services on land *not* purchased; nor does it include expenditures in connection with disposal of refuse, costs of easements or rights-of-way which are limited as to time, assessments for repairs to roads and sidewalks, or repairs to other improvements.

Land improvements, such as paving, fencing, and lighting, should be set up in separate asset accounts and depreciated. Unlike the land itself, these items have finite lives. Some costs incurred to improve the usefulness of land confer such lasting or permanent benefits that they can be legitimately debited to the Land account. Examples include costs associated with draining, clearing, landscaping, landfilling, grading, and installing of sewers.

Companies sometimes acquire rights to use land for long periods. These include leases and easements (i.e., rights to use the land for facilities such as tracks, building sites, and parking lots).

Lease accounting is discussed in Chapter 22. Where amounts are paid over a specific period, it is necessary to amortize any advanced down payment (in excess of the periodic rents) over the term of the contract. Periodic rentals are charged to current income.

A special problem arises concerning the treatment of taxes and carrying charges in respect to real estate held for investment or for future use. From a conservative point of view, such charges should be recorded as current expenses. However, accounting theory tends to hold the view that since the asset is not producing revenue against which the charges may be offset, the carrying charges should be capitalized, particularly when the market value of the property is increasing. If the real estate is producing revenue through rent, for example, or is declining in value, there are sound reasons for treating the carrying costs as a current expense. Such charges may be either capitalized or expensed for income tax purposes.

Buildings

Specific cost elements of buildings include the following:

1. Original contract price or cost of construction.
2. Expenses incurred in remodeling, reconditioning, or altering a purchased building to make it suitable for the purpose for which it was acquired.
3. Cost of excavation or grading or filling of land for the specific building.
4. Expenses incurred for the preparation of plans, specifications, blueprints, and so on.
5. Cost of building permits.
6. Payment by the purchaser of unpaid or accrued taxes on the building to date of purchase.
7. Architects' and engineers' fees for design and supervision.
8. Other costs such as temporary buildings used during the construction period.
9. Unanticipated expenditures such as rock blasting, piling, or relocation of the channel of an underground stream.

The cost of a building should include neither extraordinary costs incidental to the erection of the building, such as those due to a strike, flood, fire, or other casualty, nor the cost of abandoned construction.

Removable building equipment may have a shorter life than the building and may be subject to replacement without impairment of the integrity of the building, in which case it should be separately recorded as building equipment and separately depreciated. Razing costs of a building that has been used by an entity should be identified with the retirement of the old building.

Machinery, Furniture, Fixtures, and Equipment

Specific cost elements of machinery, furniture, fixtures, and equipment include the following:

1. Original contract or invoice cost.
2. Freight-in, import duties, handling and storage costs.
3. Specific in-transit insurance charges.
4. Sales, use, and other taxes imposed on the acquisition.
5. Costs of preparation of foundations, protective apparatus, and other costs in connection with making a proper situs for the asset.
6. Installation charges, including company overhead on the same basis as it is charged to inventory.
7. Charges for testing and preparation for use.
8. Costs of reconditioning used items when purchased.

Since machine and hand tools are relatively low in cost per unit, are frequently lost or broken, and thus have a short service life, they normally are not accorded the same treatment as other tangible operational assets; rather they are accounted for in one of three ways, viz:

1. Capitalized at date of purchase, periodically inventoried, and the asset account adjusted to their inventory value in present condition, thereby charging the losses due to wear and tear, breakage, theft, and disappearance to current expense.
2. Capitalized as an asset at a conservative valuation for the ordinary or normal stock; all subsequent tool purchases are then charged to current expense.
3. Expensed as acquired (see Chapter 14).

Patterns and Dies

Patterns and dies are used in the fabrication of many manufactured items such as automobile bodies and firearms. Patterns and dies used for regular production over a period of time should be recorded in an operational asset account, Patterns and Dies, and depreciated over their estimated service lives. Patterns and dies that are purchased or constructed for a particular job or order should be charged directly to the cost of that job.

Returnable Containers

Products are frequently sold in reusable containers that have a relatively high value. Gas cylinders, oil drums, and steel tanks generally can be returned by the purchaser for value. In some cases the purchaser is charged a deposit for the container and will receive a credit or refund when it is returned. In such cases, until returned, the containers should be carried in the vendor's accounts as an operational asset and depreciated over their estimated useful lives. Containers not returned within a reasonable time are accounted for as being retired by sale; the deposit becomes the sales price. In contrast, some companies do not bill the customer for the container, although the customer is expected to hold the container available for pickup. In such cases, the vendor may account for the containers as operating supplies rather than as operational assets and measure any loss by an inventory procedure similar to the procedure described above for tools.

Leasehold Improvements

Improvements on *leased* property, such as buildings, walks, landscaping, and certain types of permanent equipment (generally referred to as fixtures), unless specifically exempted in the lease agreement, revert to the owner of the property upon termination of the lease. Improvements on leased property of this nature are referred to as *leasehold improvements*. The cost of such improvements should be capitalized by the lessee in a tangible operational asset account entitled Leasehold Improvements (considered by some to be an intangible asset). The cost of the leasehold improvements should be depreciated over the term of the lease or the service life of the improvement, whichever is shorter. Renewal provisions in the lease agreement normally are disregarded in depreciating leasehold improvements.

QUESTIONS

1. Operational assets used in day-to-day business operations can be classified as tangible or intangible; distinguish between the two, giving examples. Under what balance sheet caption are tangible operational assets reported? Give at least one synonym for whatever title you specify.

2. Distinguish between capital and revenue expenditures. What accounting implications are involved?

3. Relate the *cost principle* to the acquisition of operational assets. Relate the *matching principle* to operational asset accounting.

4. How is asset acquisition cost determined when the consideration given is securities?

5. In determining the cost of an operational asset, how should the following items be treated: *(a)* invoice price, *(b)* freight, *(c)* discounts, *(d)* title verification costs, *(e)* installation costs, *(f)* breaking-in costs, *(g)* cost of major overhaul before operational use, and *(h)* interest on debt incurred to purchase the asset?

6. A machine is purchased on the following terms: cash, $10,000, plus ten semiannual payments of $3,000 each. How should the acquisition cost of the machine be recorded? Explain.

7. Basically, how are assets recorded when they are acquired by trading in an old asset?

8. When several assets are bought for a single lump-sum consideration, a cost apportionment procedure is usually employed. Explain the procedure. Why is apportionment necessary?

9. Should donated assets be reflected in the accounts? If so, how should they be recorded and at what value?

10. What is discovery value? If discovery value is reflected in the accounts, what is the effect on subsequent expense charges?

11. Some businesses self-construct plant assets. What costs should be capitalized? In connection with self-construction of assets, explain what to do with *(a)* general company overhead and *(b)* any excess costs incurred.

12. Capitalization of interest during the period operational assets were under construction has been a widespread practice in one industry. Identify the industry; explain why interest capitalization was practiced.

13. Distinguish between maintenance, ordinary repairs, and extraordinary repairs.

14. Explain the accounting for *(a)* extraordinary repairs, *(b)* replacements, and *(c)* betterments.

15. The XY Corporation added a new wing at a cost of $50,000, plus $1,000 spent in making passageways through the walls of an old structure to the existing plant. The plant was 10 years old and was being depreciated by an equal amount each year over a 30-year life. Over what period should the new wing be depreciated?

16. What are leasehold improvements? How should they be accounted for?

17. Outline the accounting steps related to the disposition of an operational asset assuming it is not traded in on another asset.

DECISION CASE 13–1

One of your clients, a savings bank with several local branches, recently acquired ownership to a lot and building located in a historical part of the city. The building was in a dilapidated condition, unsuitable for human habitation. The bank thought at the time that it was acquiring a site for a new branch. Although a firm of architects recommended demolition, the city council, in whose discretion such activity rests, refused consent to demolish the building in view of its historical and architectural value.

In order to comply with safety requirements and to make the building suitable for use as a branch location, the bank spent $125,000 restoring and altering the old building. It had paid $25,000 for the building and lot and had contemplated spending $80,000 on a new building after demolishing the old structure. Somewhat similar old buildings in less run-down condition could have been bought in the same area for about the same $25,000 price. It is possible, even likely, that some of these which were not so old could have been demolished without governmental intervention, and the bank could have carried out its original plan.

Now that the restoration has been completed and the bank is making final plans to open its newest branch in the restored building, the bank has been informed by the State Historical Commission that the building qualifies for and will receive a plaque designating it as a historical site. This designation will be of some value in attracting traffic to the site, will probably result in the building being pointed out when tours of the city visit the area, and so on. Under present laws, receipt of the designation may well mean that the bank can never demolish the structure and is obligated to preserve it even if the property is later vacated.

Required:

1. Discuss the pros and cons of capitalizing the entire $125,000 spent on restoration of the building.
2. How should the $25,000 original expenditure be treated? What would have been the cost of the land if the bank had been able to carry out its original plans?
3. Sooner or later, your client is likely to seek advice as to proper accounting for subsequent costs—repairs, depreciation, possible improvements, and so on. What advice would you give?

DECISION CASE 13–2

A corporation which does not have a subsidiary ledger for plant recorded the construction of a new factory building by the following entry:

Factory building .... $xx
    Cash .... $xx

After reviewing contracts and cost data, the corporation's public accountant recommended that the company use the following classifications in future accounting for the building:

Building foundation .... $xx
Framing and sheathing xx
Outside finish xx
Roof xx
Interior finish xx
Partitions xx
Acoustical ceiling xx
Electric wiring xx
Electric fixtures xx
Furnace xx
Boiler xx
Plumbing system xx

What might be the advantages (or disadvantages) of following the recommendation? Discuss fully from the standpoint of the effect of the recommendation on maintenance, depreciation, and retirement.

(AICPA adapted)

DECISION CASE 13–3

The invoice price of a machine is $10,000. Various other costs relating to the acquisition and installation of the machine amount to $2,000 and include such things as transportation, electrical wiring, special

base, and so forth. The machine has an estimated life of ten years and no residual value.

The owner of the business suggests that the incidental costs of $2,000 be charged to expense immediately for three reasons: (1) if the machine should be sold, these costs cannot be recovered in the sales price; (2) the inclusion of the $2,000 in the machinery account will not necessarily result in a closer approximation of the market price of this asset over the years because of the possibility of changing price levels; and (3) charging the $2,000 to expense immediately will reduce federal income taxes.

Required:

Discuss each of the points raised by the owner of the business.

(AICPA adapted)

DECISION CASE 13–4

The annual reports for 1976 of some leading corporations included the excerpts cited below. You are to comment specifically on them as indicated.

From PepsiCo, Inc. (Part A):

"Valuation of returnable bottles and cases is based on periodic physical inventories of those in-plant and on estimates of those in-trade. In-plant and estimated in-trade breakage is charged to cost of sales. Returnable bottles and cases are adjusted to deposit value within one year of acquisition."

1. Why is it necessary to make estimates as to cases and bottles categorized as "in-trade"?
2. Is the company's policy likely to result in a misvaluation of bottles and cases?

From Owens-Illinois, Inc. (Part B):

". . . the estimated cost of the next periodic rebuild of a glass melting furnace is accrued during the furnace's current operating life and carried in the reserve for rebuilding furnaces. No tax deduction is allowed for this provision. When the furnace is rebuilt, the actual cost is charged against the reserve and is deducted as an expense for tax purposes."

1. Where would you report "reserve for rebuilding furnaces" on a classified balance sheet? Give reasons for your answer.
2. Assuming inflation persists, what is the likely effect of the company's policies on current earnings? On the carrying value of future furnaces?

From American Broadcasting Companies, Inc. (Part C):

"In 1975 operating expenses include a charge of $10,378,000 for the writedown to estimated realizable value of the park facilities of the Wildlife Preserve at Largo, Maryland. The Company has been unsuccessful in selling the facilities as a park and an additional writedown of $3,500,000 to estimated land value was made in 1976. The remaining balance is classified as other assets in the accompanying balance sheets."

1. Do you agree with the company's classification? Give reasons for your answer.
2. Should the charges aggregating almost $14 million have been made to operating expenses? Under what circumstances should the writedowns have been set out separately or given other treatment?

EXERCISES

Exercise 13–1

When examining the accounts of a new corporate client, you encounter the following items at year end:

	Identity	Description or Added Data	Valuation Data
a.	Franchise	Just acquired as perpetual franchise.	Cost, $90,000
b.	Land	Purchased last year for future plant site.	Cost, $260,000
c.	Building	Purchased 12 years ago for warehouse. (Being depreciated over 45-year life by straight-line method; no residual value.)	Cost, $450,000
d.	Patent	Purchased three years ago. (Half of useful life has elapsed and is reflected by amortization recorded.)	Cost, $78,000
e.	Fixtures	Purchased at start of current year (straight line, 20-year life, no residual value)	Cost, $30,000
f.	Returnable containers	Bought three years ago. (Being depreciated on basis of ten-year life by straight-line method; 20% are expected not to be returned.)	Cost, $30,000
g.	Goodwill	Arose when business acquired a division in 1971 which has since been merged in as integral part of client corporation.	Remaining unamortized balance, $64,000
h.	Land	Bought for speculative purposes last year.	Cost, $65,000
i.	Hand tools	Bought at various times.	Remaining balance is value at date of examination, $8,000

Required:

Indicate the balance sheet classification and amount for each of the foregoing items.

Exercise 13–2

What is the proper cost to use for recording the land in each of the following independent cases? Give reasons in support of your answer.

Case A—Issued 14,000 shares (par value per share of $1) par value capital stock with a "market value" of $1.50 per share (based upon a recent sale of ten shares) for the land. The land was recently appraised at $17,000 by competent appraisers.

Case B—Rejected an offer two years ago by the vendor to sell the land for $7,500 cash. Issued 1,000 shares of capital stock for the land (market value of the stock based on several recent large transactions, $7.20 with normal weekly stock trading volume).

Case C—At the middle of the current year gave a check for $5,000 for the land and assumed the liability for unpaid taxes: taxes in arrears last year, $200; assessed for current year, $100.

Case D—Issued 1,000 shares of capital stock for the land. The par value of the stock was $50 per share; the market value (stock sells daily with an average daily volume of 5,000 shares) was $63 per share at time of purchase of land. Vendor offered to sell the land for $62,000 cash. Competent appraisers valued the land at $64,000.

Exercise 13–3

a. Delivery equipment was purchased having a list price of $8,000; terms were 2/10, n/30. Payment was made within the discount period.
b. Delivery equipment was purchased having a list price of $5,000; terms were 2/10, n/30. Payment was made after the discount period.
c. Delivery equipment listed at $10,000 was purchased and invoiced at 2/10, n/30. In order to take advantage of the discount, the company borrowed $8,000 of the purchase price by issuance of a 60-day, 9% note which was paid with interest at maturity.

Required:

Give entries in each separate situation for costs, borrowing, and any expenses involved.

Exercise 13–4

Farmer Company purchased a machine, having an estimated ten-year useful life, on a time payment plan. The list price of the machine was $32,500. Terms were $4,000 cash down payment plus three equal annual payments of $10,000 each to include interest on the unpaid balance at 9% per annum.

Required (round to nearest dollar):
a. Give entry to record the purchase.
b. Give entry for depreciation at the end of one year

assuming straight-line depreciation and no residual value.

c. Give entry to record the last $10,000 payment.

Exercise 13–5

For each of the following numbered items, indicate, by using one of the five lettered choices listed below, which accounting treatment is correct. Explain questionable items and assumptions you make. Each cost, identified as a numbered item, was incurred by a corporation incident to acquisition of a new machine.

Lettered Choices:

a. Increases or decreases Machinery account.
b. Debit an expense account for current period.
c. Debit Prepaid Expense or Deferred Charge and amortize separately from machinery.
d. Debit Plant, Property, and Equipment account (other than machinery).
e. An accounting treatment other than the four choices above. Explain.

Items Affecting Cost:

1. Invoice price of the machinery, before discount.
2. Cash discount for prompt payment of foregoing invoice, not taken.
3. Cost of moving machinery into place.
4. Cost of removing old machine which this machinery replaced.
5. Sales tax based on purchase price of new machinery.
6. Special electrical wiring required to connect new machine.
7. Enlargement of electrical system of plant to accommodate new machine and provide for some expected future needs.
8. Service contract paid in full covering first two years' operation of the machine.
9. Cost of materials used while testing new machine.
10. Payment to technicians who assisted with break-in of new machine.
11. Cost of training three of our employees who will operate machine.
12. Charge to machine which was offest by credit to "Miscellaneous Revenue" amounting to anticipated first years' savings from use of new machine.
13. Insurance premium paid covering first year of protection of new machine against hazards to which it will be exposed.
14. Repair charges incurred during first year of operations.
15. Cost of installing sound insulation so new machine will not disturb those who work near it.

Exercise 13–6

Smith Company purchased a tract of land on which were located a warehouse and an office building. The cash purchase price was $154,000 plus $800 fees in connection with the purchase. The following data were collected concerning the property:

	Tax Assessment	Vendor's Book Value	Original Cost
Land	$10,000	$10,000	$10,000
Warehouse	20,000	15,000	30,000
Office building	30,000	25,000	60,000

Required:

Journalize the purchase; show computations.

Exercise 13–7

Cohen Company bought a machine on a time payment plan. The cash purchase price was $20,561. Terms were $4,000 cash down payment plus four equal annual payments of $5,000 which includes interest on the unpaid balance at 8% per annum.

Required:

1. Give entry to record the purchase. Show computations (round to nearest dollar).
2. Give entry to record depreciation at the end of the first full year assuming straight-line depreciation, an eight-year life, and no residual value.
3. Prepare a table to reflect the accounting entries for each of the four installment payments. Round amounts in table to nearest dollar.

Exercise 13–8

Charmaine Company manufactured a new machine for its own use. The ledger account below reflects related charges and credits made during the year to the Machinery account.

Machinery (new)

Debit		Credit	
Cost of dismantling old machine replaced	1,200	Cash proceeds from sale of old machine	300
Labor charges	22,000		
Raw materials used	24,000		
Installation charges	3,000		
Materials spoiled	800		
Profit on construction	5,000		
Spare parts	4,500		
Auxiliary tools	3,000		

Your investigation revealed the following additional facts:

1. The old machine that was removed had originally cost $30,000; accumulated depreciation was $29,600.
2. The manufacturing overhead account balance is $200,000; you determine that 96% of this relates to ordinary manufacture and the rest to the self-construction.
3. Cash discounts average 2% on all raw material purchases; the entire amount of discounts taken was recorded as Purchase Discounts.
4. The installation charges represent a payment to outsiders for technical assistance during the break-in period of the machine.
5. Materials spoiled represent the cost of materials used during the testing and break-in period.
6. Profit on construction was credited to an account with that title. Charmaine Company estimates it saved at least $5,000 by self-constructing the machinery instead of purchasing it.
7. The charge for spare parts represents the cost of parts purchased and set aside to cover breakdowns and maintenance during the first two years of normal use of the machinery.
8. Auxiliary tools are items used in conjunction with the machine which have an estimated useful life of five years. The machine is expected to last from 10 to 12 years.

Required:

Prepare journal entries to correct the machinery account and other accounts of Charmaine Company. Insofar as possible, key your entries to the numbers identifying data above.

Exercise 13–9

Select the best answer for each of the following. Briefly justify your choice for each item.

1. If the present value of a note issued in exchange for a plant asset is less than its face amount, the difference should be
   a. Included in the cost of the asset.
   b. Amortized as interest expense over the life of the note.
   c. Amortized as interest expense over the life of the asset.
   d. Included in interest expense in the year of issuance.
2. When a closely held corporation issues preferred stock for land, the land should be recorded at the
   a. Total par value of the stock issued.
   b. Total book value of the stock issued.
   c. Appraised value of the land.
   d. Total liquidating value of the stock issued.
3. The debit for a sales tax levied and paid on the purchase of machinery preferably would be to
   a. The Machinery account.
   b. A separate Deferred Charge account.
   c. Miscellaneous Tax Expense (which includes all taxes other than those on income).
   d. Accumulated Depreciation—Machinery.
4. The Wise Corporation purchased a new machine on October 31, 19A. A $250 down payment was made, and three monthly installments of $800 each are to be made beginning on November 30, 19A. The cash price would have been $2,500. Wise paid no installation charges under the monthly payment plan, but a $50 installation charge would have been incurred with a cash purchase. The amount to be capitalized as the cost of the machine during 19A would be
   a. $2,700.
   b. $2,650.
   c. $2,550.
   d. $1,850.
   e. None of the above.
5. If a corporation purchased a lot and building and subsequently demolished the building and now uses the property as a parking lot, the accounting treatment of the cost of the building at acquisition would depend on
   a. The significance of the cost allocated to the building in relation to the combined cost of the lot and building.
   b. The length of time for which the building was held prior to its demolition.
   c. The contemplated future use of the parking lot.
   d. The intention of management for the property when the building was acquired.
6. Property, plant, and equipment may properly include
   a. Cash paid on machinery purchased but not yet received.
   b. Idle equipment awaiting sale.
   c. Property held for investment purposes.
   d. Land held for possible future plant site.
   e. None of the above.

(AICPA adapted)

Exercise 13–10

Parkins Company has some old equipment that cost $57,500; accumulated depreciation is $36,000. This equipment was traded in on a new machine that had a list price of $70,000; however, the new machine could be purchased without a trade-in for $68,000 cash. The difference is to be paid as cash boot.

Required:

Give the entry to record the acquisition of the new machine under each of the following independent cases:

Case A—The new machine was purchased for cash with no trade-in.

Case B—The equipment and the machine are dissimilar. The old machine is traded in, and $45,000 cash boot is paid.

Case C—Same as Case B except that the equipment and the machine are similar.

Exercise 13–11

Frank Company operates two separate plants. In Plant A, the accounting policy is to consider all ordinary (minor) repairs as revenue expenditures when incurred. In contrast, in Plant B, the accounting policy is to use the accrual procedure that charges repairs equally each period. Selected data for 19A are as follows:

	Plant A	Plant B
Estimated repair costs budgeted for the year	3,000	$3,600
Actual repair costs incurred and paid:		
First quarter	150	400
Second quarter	1,400	700
Third quarter	900	2,100
Fourth quarter	550	500

Required:

1. Give the entries in parallel columns for each plant for each of the four quarters.
2. Would you recommend any changes in the accounting policies? Explain and justify your response.

Exercise 13–12

In this exercise all items of property concerned are operational assets, not inventory, unless specified to the contrary. "List prices" are not necessarily market values.

Required:

Give journal entries where specified to record the following transactions:

1. Land carried on the books of P Company at $10,000 is exchanged for a computer carried on the books of Q Corporation at $20,000 (cost, $25,000; accumulated depreciation, $5,000). Market value of both assets is $25,000. Journalize on books of both P and Q.
2. Land carried on the books of P Company at $15,000 is exchanged for land carried on the books of Q Corporation at $13,000. Market value of each tract is $20,000. Journalize on Q's books.
3. A truck which cost P Company $6,000, on which $5,000 depreciation has been accumulated, has a market value of $1,400. It is traded to a dealer along with cash boot of $5,600 for a new truck which has a $7,400 list price. Journalize on P's books.
4. A truck which cost P Company $6,000, on which $5,000 depreciation has been accumulated, is traded to a dealer along with $6,300 cash boot. The new truck would have cost $7,000 if only cash had been paid; its list price is $7,500. Journalize on P's books.
5. Fixtures which cost P Company $15,000, on which $9,000 depreciation is recorded, and for which the market value is $8,000, are traded to Q Corporation along with $500 cash boot. In exchange, P received fixtures from Q carried on Q's books at cost of $13,000 less $6,000 accumulated depreciation. Journalize on books of both P and Q; if necessary, round amounts to the nearest dollar.

Exercise 13–13

Select the best choice for each of the following. Briefly justify your choice for each item.

1. The Maddox Corporation acquired land, buildings, and equipment from a bankrupt company at a lump-sum price of $90,000. At the time of acquisition, Maddox paid $6,000 to have the assets appraised. The appraisal disclosed the following values:

Land	$60,000
Building	40,000
Equipment	20,000

What cost should be assigned to the land, buildings, and equipment, respectively?
   a. $30,000, $30,000, and $30,000.
   b. $32,000, $32,000, and $32,000.
   c. $45,000, $30,000, and $15,000.
   d. $48,000, $32,000, and $16,000.

2. An improvement made to a machine increased its market value and its production capacity by 25% without extending the machine's useful life. The cost of the improvement should be
   a. Expensed.
   b. Debited to accumulated depreciation.

c. Capitalized in the machine account.

d. Allocated between accumulated depreciation and the machine account.

3. The debit for a sales tax properly levied and paid on the purchase of machinery preferably would be a charge to

a. The machinery account.

b. A separate deferred charge account.

c. Miscellaneous tax expense (which includes all taxes other than those on income).

d. Accumulated Depreciation—Machinery.

4. Hardy, Inc., purchased certain plant assets under a deferred payment contract. The agreement was to pay $10,000 per year for five years. The plant assets should be valued at

a. $50,000.

b. $50,000 plus a "going" interest charge.

c. Present value of a $10,000 annuity for five years at the "going" interest rate.

d. Present value of a $10,000 annuity for five years discounted at the bank prime interest rate.

5. When a closely held corporation issues preferred stock for land, the land should be recorded at the

a. Total par value of the stock issued.

b. Total book value of the stock issued.

c. Appraised value of the land.

d. Total liquidating value of the stock issued.

Items 6, 7, and 8 are based on the following information:

Two independent companies, Beam and Wall, are in the home building business. Each owns a tract of land, being held for development, but each company would prefer to build on the other's land. Accordingly, they agree to exchange their land.

An appraiser was hired, and from his report and the companies' records, the following information was obtained:

	Beam Company's Land	Wall Company's Land
Cost and book value	$ 80,000	$50,000
Market value based upon appraisal	100,000	90,000

The exchange of land was made, and based on the difference in appraised values, Wall paid $10,000 cash to Beam.

6. For financial reporting purposes, Beam would recognize a pretax gain on this exchange in the amount of

a. $0.

b. $2,000.

c. $10,000.

d. $20,000.

7. For financial reporting purposes, Wall would recognize a pretax gain on this exchange in the amount of

a. $0.

b. $10,000.

c. $30,000.

d. $40,000.

8. After the exchange, Beam would record its newly acquired land on its books at

a. $70,000.

b. $72,000.

c. $80,000.

d. $92,000.

(AICPA adapted)

Exercise 13–14

Select the best choice for each of the following. Briefly justify your choice for each item.

1. Kelly Company exchanged inventory items that cost $8,000 and normally sold for $12,000 for a new delivery truck with a list price of $13,000. The delivery truck should be recorded on Kelly's books at

a. $8,000.

b. $8,667.

c. $12,000.

d. $13,000.

2. Good Deal Company received $20,000 in cash and a used computer with a market value of $180,000 from Harvest Corporation for Good Deal's existing computer having a market value of $200,000 and an undepreciated cost of $160,000 recorded on its books. How much gain should Good Deal recognize on this exchange, and at what amount should the acquired computer be recorded, respectively?

a. Zero and $140,000.

b. $4,000 and $144,000.

c. $20,000 and $160,000.

d. $40,000 and $180,000.

3. The Ackley Company exchanged 100 shares of Burke Company common stock, which Ackley was holding as an investment, for a piece of equipment from the Flynn Company. The Burke Company common stock, which had been purchased by Ackley for $30 per share, had a quoted market price of $34 per share at the date of exchange. The piece of equipment had a recorded amount on Flynn's books of $3,100. What journal entry should Ackley have made to record this exchange?

	Debit	Credit
a. Equipment	3,000	
Investment in Burke Company common stock		3,000

b. Equipment 3,100
    Investment in Burke Com-
       pany common stock   3,000
       Gain   100

c. Equipment 3,100
    Other expense   300
    Investment in Burke Com-
       pany common stock   3,400

d. Equipment 3,400
    Investment in Burke Com-
       pany common stock   3,000
       Gain   400

4. Blacker Company exchanged a business machine for a new machine. The old machine had an original cost of $3,500, an undepreciated cost of $1,600, and a market value of $2,000 when exchanged. In addition, Blacker paid $2,200 cash for the new machine. The list price of the new machine was $4,300. At what amount should the new machine be recorded for financial accounting purposes?
  a. $3,500.
  b. $3,800.
  c. $4,200.
  d. $4,300.

5. Brauch Theatre Corporation recently purchased the Bergstrom Theatre and the land on which it is located. Brauch plans to raze the building immediately and to build a new modern theater on the site. The cost of the Bergstrom Theatre should be
  a. Written off as an extraordinary loss in the year the theater is razed.
  b. Capitalized as part of the cost of the land.
  c. Depreciated over the period from the date of acquisition to the date that the theater is to be razed.
  d. Capitalized as part of the cost of the new theater.

6. Property, plant, and equipment are conventionally presented in the balance sheet at
  a. Replacement cost less accumulated depreciation.
  b. Historical cost less residual value.
  c. Original cost adjusted for general price level changes.
  d. Acquisition cost less depreciated portion thereof.

7. In those rare instances where appraisal increments in the value of plant and equipment have been recorded, depreciation on the appraisal increments should be
  a. Ignored because the increments have not been paid for and should not be matched with revenue.
  b. Charged to retained earnings.
  c. Charged to expense.

d. Charged to an appropriation of retained earnings.

(AICPA adapted)

Exercise 13–15

The plant building of Lindy Company is old (estimated remaining useful life, ten years) and demands continuous maintenance and repairs. The company's books show that the building cost $200,000, and that accumulated depreciation was $150,000 at the beginning of the current year. During the current year the following expenditures relating to the plant building were made:

a. Continuing, frequent, and low
   cost repairs $14,000
b. Complete overhaul of the plumbing
   system (old costs not known) 8,500
c. Added a new storage shed attached to
   the building, estimated useful
   life of eight years 24,000
d. Removed the original roof, original cost,
   $16,000, and replaced it with a new
   modern roof that was guaranteed 30,000
e. Unusual, infrequent, and costly repairs 4,000

Required:

Give the journal entry to record each of the above items. Explain the basis for your treatment of each item.

PROBLEMS

Problem 13–1

An examination of the property, plant, and equipment accounts of Stanley Company disclosed the following transactions:

a. Bought a delivery truck for which the list price was $4,500; paid cash $1,500 and gave a one-year, noninterest-bearing (discounted) note payable for the balance. The current interest rate for this type of note was 9%. Round to nearest dollar.

b. Contracted for a building at a price of $400,000. Settlement was effected with the contractor by transferring $400,000 face value of 20-year, 8% company bonds payable, at which time financial consultants advised that the bonds would sell at 94.

c. Purchased a new machine having a list price of $20,000. Failed to take a 1% cash discount available upon full payment of the invoice within ten days. Shipping costs paid by the vendor amounted to $100. Installation costs amounted to $250, including $100 which represented 10% of the monthly salary of the factory superintendent (installation period, two days). A wall was torn out and replaced (moved two feet) at a cost of $500 to make room for the machine.

d. Purchased an automatic counter to be attached to a machine in use. The counter cost $630. The estimated useful life of the counter was seven years, whereas the estimated life of the machine was ten years.

e. During the first month of operations the machine (see [c] above) became inoperative due to a defect in manufacture. The vendor repaired the machine at no cost; however, the specially trained operator was idle during the two weeks the machine was inoperative. The operator was paid the regular wages ($540) during the period, although the only work performed was to observe the repair by the factory representative.

f. After one year of use, exchanged the electric motor on a machine for a heavier motor at an exchange cash cost of $400. The new motor had a list price of $1,250. The parts list indicated a list price for the original motor of $900 (estimated life, 10 years).

Required:

1. Prepare entries to record each of the above transactions. Explain and justify your decision on questionable items.
2. Record depreciation at the end of the year in which the foregoing transactions took place. Assume that all of the transactions affecting depreciation, except *(b)* and *(f)*, occurred early enough in the year to warrant recording a full year's depreciation and that *(b)* occurred at a time that would warrant depreciation for one-half year. Stanley Company uses straight-line depreciation. None of the assets is expected to have a residual value except the delivery truck (for which the residual value is $400). Estimated useful lives: truck, 6 years; machinery, 10 years; and building, 40 years. Make three separate entries—one for the truck, one for the building, and one for the machinery and related items. Transaction *(f)* took place in the year following the year for which you are to record depreciation.

Problem 13–2

Hulburd Haulers contracted to buy three Master Loaders, agreeing to make five equal annual payments of $6,800 each at the end of each of the next five years. Master Loaders have a list price of $9,050 each, which also is the cash price, and an estimated service life of nine years and residual value of $350.

Required (round to nearest dollar):

1. Determine the approximate interest rate implicit in the contract and then record the purchase of the loaders in accordance with GAAP.
2. Assuming Hulburd Haulers' fiscal year coincides with the payment dates, record the first payment and reflect depreciation at the end of the first year.
3. Give similar entries at the end of the fifth year.

Problem 13–3

Clark Corporation bought equipment on July 1, 19A, for which its entries throughout the 1½ years of ownership were as below:

July 1, 19A:

Equipment	25,000	
Installment note payable		25,000

December 31, 19A:

Depreciation expense (½ year)	1,250	
Accumulated depreciation		1,250

July 1, 19B:

Installment note payable	5,000	
Cash		5,000

December 31, 19B:

Depreciation expense.................	2,500	
Accumulated depreciation		2,500

As can be inferred from the foregoing, the equipment is being depreciated on a straight-line basis with an assumed ten-year life and zero residual value. The $25,000 installment note is payable in five equal annual installments which includes interest. Assume 8% is a reasonable interest rate on debts with the risk characteristics of this installment note.

Required (round amounts to nearest dollar):

1. Prepare a table to reflect the entries for the note.
2. Give the journal entry or entries to correct Clark Corporation's books as of December 31, 19B, on the basis that the books are still open as of that date.

Problem 13–4

GH Corporation acquired a new machine by trading in an old machine and paying $35,000 cash. The old machine originally cost $40,000 and had accumulated depreciation at the date of exchange of $30,000. The market value of the old machine at date of exchange was $7,500. GH Corporation is considering recording this transaction by one of the two following methods:

	Method 1		Method 2	
Machinery (new)	42,500		45,000	
Accumulated depreciation (old)	30,000		30,000	
Loss on disposal of machinery	2,500			
Cash		35,000		35,000
Machinery (old) ...		40,000		40,000

Required:

1. Identify and discuss the reasons for recording the above transaction using Method 1.
2. Identify and discuss the reasons for recording the above transaction using Method 2.
3. Suppose the market value of the used machine traded in was $18,000 at the time of the exchange, how would the exchange be recorded in accordance with generally accepted accounting principles? (Assume the same amount of cash boot as above, $35,000.)

(AICPA adapted)

Problem 13–5

The city of Delford entered into an agreement with Kitt Manufacturing Company whereby the city would donate to Kitt Company a tract of land near the city on which was located a vacant building suitable for manufacturing operations. The agreement provided that ownership would transfer to the company at the end of five years (from January 1, 19A) if a plant was put in operation for not less than three years and that the company would employ 300 or more employees. Kitt Company entered into the agreement on January 1, 19A, and started operations on November 1, 19A, on a reduced scale; by the end of 19B the plant was in full production and 325 persons were on the payroll.

Just prior to signing the agreement the city had hired a competent appraiser to appraise the property with the following results: plant site, $20,000; and building, $780,000. The appraiser estimated the remaining useful life for the building at 20 years. Kitt Company spent $3,500 in connection with the transfer of ownership of the site and $490,000 on renovating the building.

Required:

1. Give entries to record the donation, incidental costs, renovating costs, depreciation for 19A and 19B (if any), and to record the transfer of ownership. Disregard residual values.
2. Give entries assuming that Kitt Company did not complete the agreement and abandoned the plant in January 19C.

Problem 13–6

XYZ Company utilized its own facilities to construct a small addition to its office building. Construction began on March 1 and was completed on June 30 of the same year. Prior to the decision to construct the asset with its own facilities, the company accepted bids from outside contracts; the lowest bid was $240,000. Detailed costs accumulated during the construction period are summarized as follows:

Materials used (including $120,000 for normal production)	$180,000
Direct labor (including $300,000 for normal production)	450,000
General supplies used on construction	8,000
Rent paid on construction machinery	3,000
Insurance premiums on construction	1,700
Supervisory salary on construction	5,000
Total general administrative overhead for the year	115,000
Total factory overhead for the year:	
Fixed ($10,000 due to construction)	100,000
Variable	60,000
Direct labor hours (including 100,000 hours for normal production)	150,000

The company allocates factory overhead to normal production on the basis of direct labor hours.

Required:

Compute the amounts that might be capitalized

a. Assuming the plant capacity to be 150,000 direct labor hours and that the construction displaced production for sale to the extent indicated.
b. Assuming the plant capacity to be 200,000 direct labor hours and that idle capacity was utilized for the construction.

Hint: Use overhead rates for factory overhead.

Problem 13–7

Prepare journal entries to record the following transactions related to the acquisition of operational assets. Justify your position on doubtful items.

a. Purchased a tract of land for $20,000; assumed taxes already assessed amounting to $180. Paid title fees, $50, and attorney fees of $300 in connection with the purchase. Payments were in cash.
b. Purchased property which included land and buildings for $78,900 cash. The purchase price included an offset of $300 for unpaid taxes. Purchaser borrowed $30,000 at 7% interest (principal and interest due one year from date) from the bank to help make the cash payment. The property was

appraised for taxes as follows: land, $22,000; and building, $44,000.

c. Prior to use of the property purchased in *(b)* above, the following expenditures were made:

Repair and renovation of building	$7,000
Installation of 220-volt electrical wiring	4,000
Removal of separate shed of no use (sold scrap lumber for $50)	300
Construction of a new driveway	1,000
Repair of existing driveways	600
Deposits with utilities for connections	50
Painting the company name on two sides of the building	400
Installation of wire fence around property	2,500

d. The land purchased in *(a)* above was leveled and two retaining walls were built to stop erosion that had created two rather large gulleys across the property. Total cash cost of the work was $4,500. The property is being held as a future plant site.

e. Purchased a used machine at a cash cost of $12,500. Subsequent to purchase the following expenditures were made:

General overhaul prior to use	$1,500
Installation of machine	500
Cost of moving the machine	150
Cost of removing two small machines to make way for the larger machine purchased	100
Cost of reinforcing the floor prior to installation	140
Testing costs prior to operation	60
Cost of tool kit (new) essential to adjustment of machine for various types of work	170

Problem 13–8

This problem deals with the effects of accounting errors on financial statements of a manufacturing company whose fiscal year is the calendar year. The company has a 6-month inventory turnover; most of its depreciable assets are depreciated over an eight-year life by the straight-line method, with zero estimated residual value. If an error makes a statement element too high, a "+" should be used; if it causes the element to be too low, a "−"; if the error has no effect or is completely counterbalanced, a "0." There are, however, in the exhibit at the top of page 475, certain mistakes in reflecting the effects of the errors. You are to indicate for each line the number of mistakes and to identify which items are wrong and why. Answer each question independently of the others.

Hint: Remember that depreciation of factory machinery is an element of factory overhead (see the tabulation at the top of page 475).

Problem 13–9

Two *dissimilar* operational assets were exchanged when the accounts of the two companies involved reflected the following:

Account	Company A (designate as Asset A)	Company B (designate as Asset B)
Operational asset	$5,000	$8,000
Accumulated depreciation	3,000	5,300

The market value of Asset A was realistically determined to be $2,600; no realistic estimate of market value could be made for Asset B.

Required:

1. Give the exchange entry for each company assuming no cash difference was involved.
2. Give the exchange entry for both companies assuming a cash difference of $100 was paid by Company A to Company B.

Problem 13–10

Part 1

Company X had an old machine that originally cost $10,000 and has accumulated depreciation to date of $7,500. The old machine was exchanged for a new *similar* machine that had a cash price of $4,500. Two independent cases are assumed:

Case A—There was a direct exchange (no cash difference was paid or received).

Case B—Company X exchanged the old machine for the new machine and paid a cash difference of $2,100.

Part 2

Company Y had an old machine that originally cost $12,000 and has accumulated depreciation to date of $8,000. The old machine was exchanged for a new *similar* machine that had a firm cash price of $3,600. Two independent cases are assumed:

Case C—There was a direct exchange (no cash difference was paid or received).

Case D—Company Y exchanged the old machine for the new machine and received a cash difference of $500.

	Statement for 19A			Statements for 19B		
(Relates to Problem 13–8) Transactions	Net Operational Assets (book value)	Selling or General Expense	Cost of Goods Sold	Total Assets on Balance Sheet	Net Income	Owners' Equity
1. Repairs which kept office fixtures in normal operating condition were made June 30, 19A, and charged to Office Fixtures.	+	+	0	+	0	+
2. The company completed self-construction of an annex to the Office Building on April 1, 19A, and failed to charge any overhead to the project.	0	0	+	0	+	0
3. Replacement of a major component of Factory Machinery early in 19A was charged to Factory Overhead. The component cost twice as much as the one replaced (the latter was 60% depreciated).	–	0	+	–	+	–
4. Cost of rearranging Factory Machinery late in 19A was not recorded at all that year. When the invoice was received early in 19B, payment was charged to Factory Overhead.	–	0	–	0	–	–
5. Deposits paid to electric utilities early in 19A for added meters installed in the factory were charged to Factory Machinery.	+	0	+	–	–	–
6. Early in 19A the company paid legal fees of $1,500 in connection with title search for a site bought for employee parking. The fee was charged to Legal Fees (a general expense).	–	0	0	–	0	–
7. In midyear 19A the company paid $2,000 for engineering services related to testing new factory machinery. Factor Overhead was charged.	–	0	+	–	0	+

Required (round amounts to nearest dollar):

1. Give the entries to record the exchange of similar assets in Cases A, B, C, and D.
2. Give the entries for each case assuming the assets were dissimilar.

Problem 13–11

Two *similar* operational assets were exchanged when the accounts of the two companies involved reflected the following:

Account	Company A (designate as Asset A)	Company B (designate as Asset B)
Operational asset	$5,000	$8,000
Accumulated depreciation	3,000	5,300

The market value of Asset A was realistically determined to be $2,400; no realistic estimate could be made for Asset B.

Required (round amounts to nearest dollar):

1. Give the exchange entry for each company assuming no cash difference is involved.

2. Give the exchange entry for each company assuming a cash difference of $500 was paid by Company A to Company B.

Problem 13–12

Argo Company, a manufacturer, operates three plants in different locations. This problem focuses on Plant No. 1. The plant asset records reflected the following at the beginning of the current year, January 1, 19A:

Plant building (residual value, $20,000;
    estimated useful life, 30 years) $120,000
Accumulated depreciation 80,000
Machinery (residual value, $35,000;
    estimated useful life, 15 years) 200,000
Accumulated depreciation 115,500

During the current year ending December 31, 19A, the following transactions (summarized) relating to the above accounts were completed:

a. Expenditures for nonrecurring, relatively large repairs that tend to increase the economic utility but not the economic life of the assets:
    Plant building $34,000
    Machinery 21,000
b. Replacement of the original electrical wiring system of the plant building (original cost, $21,000) 42,000
c. Additions:
    Plant building—added a small wing to the plant building to accommodate new equipment acquired. The wing has a useful life of 15 years and no residual value 45,000
    Machinery—added special protection devices to ten machines. These devices are attached to the machines and will have to be replaced every five years (no residual value) 2,000
d. Outlays for maintenance parts, labor, etc., to keep the assets in normal working condition:

Quarter	Plant Building	Machinery
1	$1,700	$ 2,000
2	1,500	6,000
3	1,800	1,000
4	2,000	10,000

Required:

1. Give appropriate entries to record transactions (a) through (c). Explain the basis underlying your decisions.
2. Give appropriate entries by quarter, in parallel columns, for transaction (d) assuming the accounting policy is (1) to record all ordinary repairs incurred as revenue expenditures as outlays are made and (2) to use the accrual procedure. The annual budgeted amounts for maintenance and repair expense were plant building, $7,200; and machinery, $17,000.
3. Which method used in Requirement 2 do you prefer? Explain.

Problem 13–13

The books of Cooper Manufacturing Company had never been audited prior to 1976. In auditing the books for the year ended December 31, 1979, the auditor found the following account for the plant:

Plant and Equipment

1976:		1976:	
Plant purchased	90,000	Sale of scrap	300
Repairs	5,300	Depreciation (6%)	6,000
Legal	600	1977:	
Title fees	50	Depreciation (6%)	8,040
Insurance	3,000	1978:	
Taxes	1,200	Cash proceeds	
1977:		from old	
Addition to plant	15,000	machine	1,150
Writeup	20,000	Depreciation (6%)	8,160
Interest expense	1,500	1979:	
Repairs	500	Depreciation (6.4%)	8,520
Machinery for new			
addition	2,000		
1978:			
New machine	3,000		
Installation	600		
1979:			
Machinery			
overhaul	1,350		
Replaced roof	900		
Fence	3,400		

(Balance, $116,230)

Additional data relating to plant and equipment developed during the audit follow:

a. The plant was purchased during January 1976. At that time the tax assessment listed the plant as follows: plant site at $10,000, the building at $20,000, and the machinery therein at $30,000. The estimated life of the plant and machinery was 20 years.
b. During the first six months of 1976 the company expended the amounts listed in the account for the year in getting the plant ready for operation; operations began July 1. The repairs pertain to both the building and machinery. No breakdown was available. The legal fees were incurred in connection with the plant purchase and applied to

all components of it. The $3,000 insurance premium represented a one-year policy on the plant and equipment, dated January 1, 1976 ($1,000 of the premium applied to the machinery). The property tax rate for the year was 2%. The scrap was accumulated during the "repair period."

c. In 1977 a plant addition was completed costing $15,000, at which time the company was paying 10% on some borrowed funds. The addition was under construction for four months. During the year $1,500 was spent for ordinary repairs, of which one third was capitalized. Machinery costing $2,000 was purchased. The asset account was written up by $20,000 to bring it in line with the bank's security allowance on loans (Contributed Capital was credited).

d. During 1978 a new machine was purchased (July 1) for $3,000 plus installation costs of $600; an old machine costing an estimated $2,100 was sold for $1,150. The old machine was acquired when the plant was acquired.

e. During 1979 several items of equipment were completely reconditioned at a cost of $1,350. Minor repairs were charged to expense during the year. The roof was replaced on one wing of the plant. A fence was constructed around the plant to keep unauthorized personnel out; it is estimated that the fence will have 10 years of remaining life.

Required:

1. Set up a worksheet to compute the correct balances for the following accounts (suggested columnar captions): Land, Buildings, Machinery, Land Improvements, and Accumulated Depreciation (assume 6% straight-line depreciation on ending balances except for Land Improvements. Disregard residual value and round amounts to nearest dollar). Suggested line captions: list each item by year. Justify any assumptions that you make.
2. Give one compound entry to correct the accounts assuming the books have already been closed for 1979.

Problem 13–14*

Ellford Corporation received a $400,000 low bid from a reputable manufacturer for the construction of special production equipment needed by Ellford in an expansion program. Because the company's own

plant was not operating at capacity, Ellford decided to construct the equipment itself and the company accountant recorded the following production costs related to the construction:

Services of consulting engineer	$ 10,000
Work subcontracted	20,000
Materials	200,000
Plant labor normally assigned to production	65,000
Plant labor normally assigned to maintenance*	100,000
Total	$395,000

* Included in manufacturing overhead.

Management prefers to record the cost of the equipment under the incremental cost method. Approximately 40% of the corporation activities are devoted to government supply contracts, which are all based in some way on cost. The contracts require that any self-constructed equipment be allocated its full share of all costs related to the construction.

The following information is also available:

a. The above production labor was for partial fabrication of the equipment in the plant. Skilled personnel were required and were assigned from other projects. The maintenance labor would have been idle time of nonproduction plant employees who would have been retained on the payroll whether or not their services were utilized.
b. Payroll taxes and employee fringe benefits are approximately 30% of labor cost and are included in manufacturing overhead cost. Total manufacturing overhead for the year was $5,630,000.
c. Manufacturing overhead is approximately 50% variable and is applied on the basis of production labor cost. Production labor cost for the corporation's normal products totaled $6,810,000.
d. General and administrative expenses include $22,500 of executive salary cost and $10,500 of postage, telephone, supplies, and miscellaneous expenses identifiable with this equipment construction.

Required:

1. Prepare a schedule computing the amount which should be reported as the full cost of the constructed equipment to meet the requirements of the government contracts. Any supporting computations should be in good form.
2. Prepare a schedule computing the incremental cost of the constructed equipment.
3. What is the greatest amount that should be capitalized as the cost of the equipment? Why?

(AICPA adapted)

---

* This problem is an appropriate assignment where class members are reasonably well grounded in cost accounting. It is perhaps inadvisable to assign the problem where the cost accounting foundation is marginal.

Problem 13–15

Valley Manufacturing Company was incorporated on January 2, 19A, but was unable to begin manufacturing activities until July 1, 19A, because new factory facilities were not completed until that date.

The Land and Building account at December 31, 19A, was as follows:

Date	Item	Amount
19A:		
Jan. 31	Land and building	$ 98,000
Feb. 28	Cost of removal of building	1,500
May 1	Partial payment of new construction	35,000
May 1	Legal fees paid	2,000
June 1	Second payment on new construction	30,000
June 1	Insurance premium	1,800
June 1	Special tax assessment	2,500
June 30	General expenses	12,000
July 1	Final payment on new construction	35,000
Dec. 31	Asset writeup	12,500
		230,300
Dec. 31	Depreciation—19A at 1%	2,300
	Account balance	$228,000

The following additional information is to be considered:

a. To acquire land and building the company paid $48,000 cash and 500 shares of its 5% cumulative preferred stock, par value $100 per share.

b. Cost of removal of old buildings amounted to $1,500 with the demolition company retaining all materials of the building.

c. Legal fees covered the following:

Cost of organization	$ 500
Examination of title covering purchase of land	1,000
Legal work in connection with construction work	500
	$2,000

d. Insurance premium covered premiums for three-year term beginning May 1, 19A.

e. The special tax assessment covered street improvements.

f. General expenses covered the following for the period from January 2, 19A, to June 30, 19A:

President's salary	$ 6,000
Plant superintendent covering supervision on new building	5,000
Office salaries	1,000
	$12,000

g. Because of a general increase in construction costs after entering into the building contract, the board of directors increased the value of the building $12,500, believing such increase was justified to reflect current market at the time the building was completed. Retained Earnings was credited for this amount.

h. Estimated life of building—50 years. Writeoff for 19A—1% of asset value (1% of $230,300 = $2,300).

Required:

1. Prepare entries to reflect correct land, building, and accumulated depreciation accounts at December 31, 19A.
2. Show the proper presentation of land, building, and accumulated depreciation on the balance sheet at December 31, 19A.

(AICPA adapted)

Problem 13–16

Equipment which cost $12,800 on January 1, 19A, was sold for $4,000 on June 30, 19F. It had been depreciated over a ten-year life by the straight-line method on the assumption its residual value would be $800.

A warehouse that cost $110,000, residual value $5,000, was being depreciated over 35 years by the straight-line method. When the structure was 20 years old, an additional wing was constructed at a cost of $36,000. The estimated life of the wing considered separately was 25 years, and its residual value is $1,000. The accounting period ends December 31.

Required:

1. Give entries (and show computations) to record
   a. The sale of the equipment. Include current depreciation in the sale entry.
   b. The addition; cash was paid.
   c. Depreciation for the warehouse and its addition after the latter has been in use for one year.
2. Show how the building and attached wing would be reported on a balance sheet prepared immediately after entry *(c)*.

Problem 13–17

At December 31, 19A, certain amounts included in the operating assets section of Townsend Company's balance sheet had the following balances:

Land	$100,000
Buildings	800,000
Leasehold improvements	500,000
Machinery and equipment	700,000

During 19B the following transactions occurred:
1. Land site No. 621 was acquired for $1,000,000. Additionally, to acquire the land Townsend paid a $60,000 commission to a realtor. Costs of $15,000 were incurred to clear the land. During the course of the clearing, timber and gravel were recovered and sold for $5,000.
2. A second tract of land (No. 622) with a building was acquired early in 19B for $300,000. The realtor's records indicated the land cost $200,000 and the building cost $100,000. The realtor was paid an $18,000 commission by Townsend. Shortly after the acquisition, the building was demolished at a cost of $30,000. A new building was constructed for $150,000, plus the following costs:

Excavation fees	$11,000
Architectural design fees	8,000
Building permit fee	1,000
Imputed interest on funds used during construction	6,000

The new building was completed and occupied September 30, 19B.
3. A third tract of land (site No. 623) was acquired for $600,000 and put on the market for resale.
4. Extensive work was done to a building occupied by Townsend under a lease agreement that expires December 31, 19L. Total cost of the work consisted of the following:

Paintings of ceilings	$10,000 (estimated useful life is 1 year)
Electrical work	35,000 (estimated useful life is 10 years)
Connection of extension to current working area	80,000 (estimated useful life is 30 years)

The lessor paid half of the costs incurred in connection with the extension to the current working area.
5. During December 19B, costs of $65,000 were incurred to improve leased office space. The related lease will terminate on December 31, 19D, and will not be renewed.
6. A new group of machines was bought under a royalty agreement which provides for payments of royalties based on units of production for the machines. Invoice price of the machines was $75,000, freight costs were $2,000, unloading charges were $1,500, and royalty payments for 19B were $13,000.

Required:

1. Prepare a detailed analysis of the changes in each of the following balance sheet accounts for 19B:

> Land
> Buildings
> Leasehold improvements
> Machinery and equipment

Disregard related accumulated depreciation accounts. Use the following format:

	12/31/19A Balances	19B Additions	19B Reductions	12/31/19B Balances
Land:				
Buildings:				
Leasehold improvements:				
Machinery and equipment:				
Other accounts:				

2. Indicate where on a classified balance sheet, items not fitting the four categories specified above would be reported as of December 31, 19B.

(AICPA adapted)

14

Property, Plant, and Equipment—Depreciation and Depletion

At the outset of the preceding chapter we delineated the primary characteristics of operational assets. The attribute common to all operational assets is that they are acquired and utilized because of their revenue generating *potentials,* rather than for resale purposes. They can be viewed by the enterprise as comprising a store of economic service values that will expire as they are utilized in the revenue generating process. Therefore, as their economic service values are used in generating revenue, a portion of their total cost periodically must be matched with (allocated against) revenues generated during the period in order to fulfill the requirements of historical cost income measurement. The process of periodically allocating a portion of the total cost of property, plant, and equipment against the revenue generated must be applied to most operational assets (land is an exception). This entails application of allocation procedures to three distinct classes of assets; the accounting terminology commonly utilized in this respect is the following:

1. Depreciation—The accounting process of allocating against periodic revenue the cost expiration of *tangible* property, plant, and equipment.
2. Depletion—The accounting process of allocating against periodic revenue the cost expiration of an asset represented by a *natural resource,* such as mineral deposits, gravel deposits, and timber stands.
3. Amortization—The accounting process of allocating against periodic revenue the cost expiration of *intangible assets* represented by *special rights* or benefits, such as prepaid insurance, patents, copyrights, and leaseholds. Sometimes "amortized" is used as a general term to include all types of periodic apportionments.

This chapter discusses depreciation and depletion. Chapter 15 considers the amortization of intangibles.

The three categories of cost apportionments just described are similar in application; the only difference is that each focuses on a different class of assets. Conceptually, they represent the process of cost allocation as opposed to asset valuation. They constitute an application of the *matching principle.*

The cost of property, plant, and equipment may be compared with a prepaid expense; the cost is prepaid (in advance of utilization of the asset), and hence, is recorded as an asset. As the economic service life of the asset expires with the passage of time or through use, the cost thereof must be systematically allocated to operations as a current expense. Operational assets contribute long-term *future* benefits to the enterprise, whereas prepaid expenses normally are used up within one operating cycle after acquisition. *Accounting Terminology Bulletin No. 1*, paragraph 56, defines depreciation as follows:

> *Depreciation accounting* is a system of accounting which aims to distribute the cost or other basic value of tangible capital assets, less salvage value (if any), over the estimated useful life of the unit (which may be a group of assets) in a systematic and rational manner. It is a process of allocation, not of valuation. *Depreciation for the year* is the portion of the total charge under such a system that is allocated to the year.

In accounting for operational assets, the underlying principles are *(a)* at acquisition, the assets are recorded at cost on the basis of the *cost principle; (b)* subsequent to acquisition, those assets that have a determinable limited life are reported at the cost recognized at acquisition less the accumulated allocations of such costs (depreciation, depletion and amortization), and *(c)* periodic allocations of cost are recognized as current expense in conformance with the *matching principle.*

DEPRECIATION

Now let's turn our attention specifically to depreciation as defined above. In order to understand fully the nature of depreciation accounting, it is necessary to examine its effects on *(a)* the income statement, *(b)* retained earnings and dividends, *(c)* cash flow, *(d)* balance sheet, and *(e)* statement of changes in financial position.

Depreciation is recognized on the income statement as selling, administrative, or manufacturing expenses, depending upon the nature and use of the assets involved. The periodic depreciation charge may affect the income statement in two ways. One way is a direct charge to expense. For instance, depreciation on company automobiles used by salespersons would be classified as selling expenses. On the other hand, depreciation on machinery used in the factory would be reported as a part of the cost of inventory; and when the inventory is sold, the cost of the inventory (including an element of depreciation) is debited to cost of goods sold. But, that portion of depreciation charge remaining in the valuation of goods on hand at the end

of the period is reported as an *asset* (inventory) and deferred until the goods are sold. It follows that income of a given period is reduced by depreciation initially charged to inventory only to the extent that such goods are sold during that period.

Depreciation and Dividends

Since depreciation expense reduces reported pretax income, the amount of retained earnings is likewise reduced. This effect reduces the reported amount of retained earnings available for dividends; consequently, over the life of the operational asset an amount equivalent to the cost of the tangible operational asset (less any residual value) is "held back" from retained earnings and dividend availability. Thus one of the results of depreciation accounting is to prevent the impairment of capital through dividends based upon overstated earnings. Failure to recognize depreciation causes overstatement of income with an attendant possible dissipation of capital through liquidating dividends. As we pointed out in Chapter 7, it is possible for capital to be dissipated in this manner as a result of recording depreciation on the historical cost basis in accordance with GAAP—when prices are rising and no adjustments are made to pricing and dividend policies. The following paragraph explores this same notion in the context of depreciation and cash flow.

Depreciation and Cash Flow

Depreciation accounting attempts to measure an expense and to charge it against income. Where revenue is sufficient, depreciation, like other expenses, is recovered. It should be apparent, however, that the mere booking of depreciation can have no effect upon the amount of assets coming into the business through sales of product. But if a business can sell its product for enough to cover all operating costs including depreciation, the assets received from customers (cash and receivables) will exceed total expense outlays by at least the amount of the depreciation. Since dividends normally are declared out of net income, net assets equal to the amount of the depreciation expense will be retained in the business which operates at a profit or merely at breakeven.[1]

In view of the above discussion it is important to realize that although the depreciation provision will result in holding back assets from dividends equivalent to the provision, it does not specifically provide or "hold back" cash. The relationship of depreciation and cash flow is simply that although most costs and expenses require cash when incurred, the depreciation charge is a noncash reduction of net income; the cash was disbursed when the operational asset was acquired. Therefore, the *cash generated by net income is greater* than reported net income by the amount of noncash expenses (less noncash revenues) reported on the income statement. The fact that depreciation has been recognized does not mean that cash (or even other assets) necessarily will be available to replace the assets when their service lives expire. The assets retained as a result of deducting depreciation from income are not automatically segregated into a fund for replacements. On the contrary, the retained funds will probably find uses in paying off liabilities and in purchasing new and different types of assets which can also be used to generate cash. Therefore, while such funds are not automatically segregated for asset replacement, the revenue generating process of most companies is intended to produce the cash for replacement of old assets.

Depreciation Is an Estimate

The importance of depreciation varies with the nature of the business and the degree of mechanization or automation involved. Significantly, reported net income is no more accurate than the estimate of the periodic depreciation figure. Since periodic depreciation expense, as well as certain other expenses, are estimates, reported net income reflects such estimates. In view of these considerations, any attempt to compute and report the depreciation provision to even pennies, for example, implies a degree of accuracy that does not exist. With respect to accounting, rounding of the periodic depreciation charge should be consistent with the probable margin of error involved in the estimate.

CAUSES OF DEPRECIATION

The causes of depreciation may be classified as follows:

Physical Factors	*Functional Factors*
1. Wear and tear from operation.	1. Inadequacy.
2. Action of time and other elements.	2. Obsolescence, including supersession.
3. Deterioration and decay.	

Significantly, a *change in market value* is not recognized as one of the causes of depreciation under generally accepted accounting principles.[2] The three physical factors, as they affect the service life of a tangible operational asset, are self-explanatory. The two functional factors are less obvious. Inadequacy is brought about by expansion of a business, as the operational asset becomes unequal to the increased service required, even though it may still be in good condition and quite capable of the service originally expected of it.

Obsolescence may arise from inadequacy, supersession, and other causes such as the outmoding of the product being produced or the service being rendered. Supersession occurs when new assets can render improved service. In such cases it may be desirable to discard the old asset.

Depreciation accounting takes into account all predictable factors that tend to limit the economic usefulness of an operational asset to the enterprise. The periodic apportionment of cost through depreciation must be based upon both the physical and functional causes of depreciation. Generally those factors that operate more

---

[1] Different methods of depreciation have different effects on cash flow, which is reflected on the statement of changes in financial position. For example, accelerated depreciation in the early years will give a higher depreciation expense amount than will straight line; consequently, income taxes would be lower. This would result in a saving of cash paid for income taxes during the early periods. See Chapter 6 for discussion of the present value aspects of the time value of money and Chapter 23 for discussion of cash flows.

[2] Depreciation is not caused by changes in the market value of an operational asset; however, when the carrying value is significantly above the use value to the entity, in terms of market value (such as an idle plant), the asset must be written down to reflect the impairment of value (this is not depreciation expense). See Chapter 13.

or less continuously are given recognition in depreciation accounting, whereas sudden and unexpected factors such as storms, floods, sudden change in demand, and radical outmoding of the asset must be accorded special treatment. One of these special treatments, for example, might result in the immediate removal of an asset from the accounts and the recording of a related loss.

The useful life of an operational asset generally is influenced directly by the repair and maintenance policies of the firm. Low standards of maintenance and repair may reduce costs temporarily; however, the useful life of the asset will be shortened, thereby increasing the periodic depreciation expense. Although some have contended that depreciation should include both amortization of the original cost and current repair costs, accountants have viewed ordinary repairs and depreciation (as previously defined) as separate expenses.

In the case of facilities temporarily idle or being held for possible future use, depreciation should continue since the physical and functional causes, which tend to reduce the ultimate economic usefulness of the asset to the firm, continue. Operational assets that will not be returned to service should be reduced to their estimated net realizable value in anticipation of disposal. Special accounts normally should be established in accounting for idle facilities.

FACTORS IN DETERMINING DEPRECIATION EXPENSE

The periodic depreciation expense should represent the allocation of the original cost (less the estimated residual value) of the asset to operations in proportion to the economic benefit received per period from the asset. The factors which must be considered in calculating the periodic depreciation expense are as follows:

1. Actual cost (as defined in the preceding chapter).
2. Estimated residual (scrap or salvage) value.
3. Estimated service life.

Computation of depreciation is based on one "actual" and two "estimated" factors. The residual value is the estimated amount which may be recovered through sale, trade-in allowance, or by other means when the asset is finally retired from service. In estimating the residual value, allowance must be made for the costs of dismantling and disposing of the retired asset. For example, assume it is estimated that upon retirement the asset can be sold for $2,500 and that the costs of dismantling and selling are estimated at $500. In this case the residual value would be $2,000. In practice, recovery value and dismantling and selling costs are frequently disregarded entirely—a procedure which is acceptable when the recovery and disposal amounts may offset (in which case residual value is zero), when the amounts involved are immaterial, or when the estimates involve a wide margin of error.

In estimating the service life of an asset for accounting purposes it is important to realize that service life implies (a) use of the asset by the owner, (b) use of the asset for the purpose for which acquired, and (c) a specific repair and maintenance policy over the life of the asset. Allocation of depreciation charges should be representative of the expiration of the "economic service potentials" of the asset to the enterprise. Thus, the service life should be determined on a basis which is integrally linked with the expiration of such values. For example, service life may be measured in terms of (a) definite time periods such as months or years, (b) units of output, or (c) hours of operating time. Selection of the appropriate measure of service life should depend upon the nature of the asset involved and the primary causes of its depreciation.

RECORDING DEPRECIATION

The periodic depreciation amount is recorded as a debit to an expense account or a cost of manufacturing account (factory overhead) and a credit to a contra asset account entitled Accumulated Depreciation. Rather than a direct credit to the related asset account, this special contra account traditionally has been credited to maintain a separation of the original cost and the amount of that cost expired through depreciation. The contra account should not be labeled "reserve" for depreciation, since depreciation provides no such "reserve."

The periodic depreciation charges and accumulated depreciation are recorded for each individual asset or group of assets in subsidiary records which detail the various depreciable assets.

METHODS OF DEPRECIATION

Methods of depreciation focus on computation of the amount of depreciation expense that should be recorded each period. A number of methods have been developed, each of which provides a somewhat different pattern of depreciation charges over the life of the tangible asset. The methods may be classified as follows:

a. Based on time:
   1. Straight line.
b. Based on output:
   2. Service hours.
   3. Units of output.
c. Reducing depreciation charge:
   4. Sum-of-the-years' digits.
   5. Fixed-percentage-on-declining-base.
   6. Double-declining balance.
d. Based on investment and interest concepts:
   7. Annuity.
   8. Sinking fund.

To illustrate these methods the following symbols and simplified amounts are used:

Item	Symbol	Illustrative
Acquisition cost	C	$ 100
Residual value	R	10
Estimated service life	n	
Years		3
Service hours		6,000
Productive output in units		9,000
Depreciation rate (per year, per service hour, or per unit of productive output)	r	
Dollar amount of depreciation per period	D	

Straight-Line Method

The straight-line method has been used widely because of its simplicity. This method relates depreciation directly to the passage of time rather than to specific use. It is called straight line because it results in an equal charge for depreciation in each of the periods of the service life of the asset; thus, when graphed against time, the periodic depreciation charge, the accumulated depreciation, and the undepreciated asset cost are all indicated by straight lines. The use of the formula for computing the periodic depreciation charge (annual in this case) is illustrated below.

$$D = \frac{C - R}{n}$$

or

$$D = \frac{\$100 - \$10}{3} = \$30 \text{ per Period}$$

Depreciation frequently is expressed as a *rate*. For the illustrative figures, the periodic (annual) rate *(r)* may be expressed as either *(a)* 33⅓% on net depreciable value (i.e., $30 ÷ $90 = 33⅓%)[3] or *(b)* 30% on cost (i.e., $30 ÷ $100 = 30%); the percent on cost generally is used.

Exhibit 14–1 illustrates application of straight-line depreciation over the life of the illustrative asset and the accounting entries involved.

The straight-line method is simple, easy to understand, and is widely used. It meets the cri-

EXHIBIT 14–1

Depreciation Table and Entries, Straight-Line Method (life, three years)

Year	Depreciation Expense (debit)	Accumulated Depreciation (credit)	Balance Accumulated Depreciation	Undepreciated Asset Balance (book value)
0				$100
1	$30	$30	$30	70
2	30	30	60	40
3	30	30	90	10 (residual value)
	$90	$90		

---

[3] In this case, to compute the periodic charge, the "net to be depreciated" is multiplied by the rate.

terion of being "systematic and rational" (*ARB No. 44*, revised, par. 2). It is theoretically acceptable when the following conditions prevail:

1. The decline in economic service potential of the asset is approximately the same each period.
2. The decline in economic service potential of the asset is related to the passage of time rather than to use.
3. Use of the asset is consistent from period to period.
4. Repairs and maintenance are essentially the same each period.

Straight-line depreciation is deficient in that *(a)* depreciation is considered a function of time rather than a function of use, which often is not the case; *(b)* it may not satisfactorily match expense with revenue; and *(c)* it causes a distortion, relative to a pure rate of return concept, in certain rate of return computations.

The latter effect occurs because depreciation expense remains constant each period (and affects the rate of return numerator, net income, in this way), whereas the asset (and total assets, the denominator) is reduced each year. The net result is that the periodic rate of return on the asset mistakenly appears to increase over time.

Service Hours Method

The service hours method is based upon the assumption that the decrease in service life is conditioned primarily by the actual running time of the asset rather than by the mere passage of time. Rather than an equal periodic charge for depreciation, this method results in a periodic charge which correlates with the amount of time the asset is operated. If a machine is operated twice as much in the current period as in the prior period, the depreciation charge for the current period will be twice as much as that of the last period. In utilizing this method the service life of the asset must be estimated in terms of total probable service or working hours prior to retirement; then a rate per service hour is computed.

Assuming a 6,000-hour estimated useful life, the formula for the depreciation rate would be as follows:

$$r = \frac{C - R}{n}$$

or

$$r = \frac{\$100 - \$10}{6,000} = \$0.015 \text{ per Service Hour}$$

Assuming 3,000 actual hours of running time the first year, depreciation expense would be as follows:

$$D = r \times \text{Service Hours Current Period}$$

or

$$D = \$0.015 \times 3,000 = \$45$$

Exhibit 14–2 illustrates application of the service hours method over the life of the illustrative asset.

The service hours method accords with the GAAP criterion of "rational and systematic" and produces a logical matching of expense and revenue if the asset loses service potential on the basis of running time. Under this method the amount of cost allocated would tend to vary with the productive output of the asset. However, to the extent that there was running time without productive output, this relationship would not hold. Where obsolescence is not a primary factor and where the economic service potentials of the asset to the company are used up primarily by running time, the service hours method would seem appropriate. Also wide variations in use from period to period would suggest application of the service hours method. For many

EXHIBIT 14–2
Depreciation Table and Entries, Service Hours Method (life, 6,000 hours)

Year	Service Hours Worked*	Depreciation Expense (debit)		Accumulated Depreciation (credit)	Balance Accumulated Depreciation	Undepreciated Asset Balance (book value)
0						$100
1	3,000	(3,000 × $0.015)	$45	$45	$45	55
2	2,000	(2,000 × $0.015)	30	30	75	25
3	1,000	(1,000 × $0.015)	15	15	90	10 (residual value)
	6,000		$90	$90		

* It is assumed that the asset was actually used in this manner and that the original estimate of useful life was confirmed.

assets, such as buildings, furniture, and typewriters, it would be impracticable, if not impossible, to apply the service hours method. In contrast, it would be appropriate for some assets, like delivery equipment.

Productive Output Method

Under this method the service life of the asset is estimated in terms of the number of *units* of output. A proportionate part of the total cost to be depreciated (cost less residual value) is charged to each unit of output as a cost of production; consequently, depreciation charges fluctuate periodically with changes in the volume of production or output. Each unit of output is charged with a constant amount of depreciation, in contrast to the straight-line method where each unit of output will be charged with a different amount of depreciation if output varies from period to period.

The cost to be depreciated over the life of the asset is divided by the estimated service life in units to derive a depreciation rate per unit of output; multiplication of this rate times the output for the period gives the periodic depreciation charge. Thus computation of the rate, assuming an estimated productive life of 9,000 units of output, would be as follows:

$$r = \frac{C - R}{n}$$

or

$$r = \frac{\$100 - \$10}{9,000} = \$0.01 \text{ per Unit of Output}$$

Assuming 4,000 units of actual output during the first year, the depreciation charge would be as follows:

$$D = r \times \text{Units of Output Current Period}$$

or

$$D = \$0.01 \times 4,000 = \$40$$

Exhibit 14–3 illustrates an application of the productive output method over the life of the asset.

The productive output method and the service hours method both reflect the fact that some assets, such as trucks and machinery, usually

EXHIBIT 14–3
Depreciation Table and Entries, Productive Output Method (life, 9,000 units)

Year	Units of Output*	Depreciation Expense (debit)		Accumulated Depreciation (credit)	Balance Accumulated Depreciation	Undepreciated Asset Balance (book value)
0						$100
1	4,000	(4,000 × $0.01)	$40	$40	$40	60
2	3,000	(3,000 × $0.01)	30	30	70	30
3	2,000	(2,000 × $0.01)	20	20	90	10 (residual value)
	9,000		$90	$90		

* It is assumed that the asset was actually used in this manner and that the original estimate of useful life was confirmed.

depreciate in direct proportion to usage. These methods more closely relate the benefit derived from the use of the asset to the depreciation cost allocated than do other methods. The productive output method is particularly appropriate where obsolescence is not a major factor, where actual output can be realistically measured, and where the service life in units of output can be reasonably estimated.

The differences between the periodic depreciation in the service hours method and the productive output method in the illustrative problem are due to a change in the efficiency of operations—the asset was used more efficiently in some periods than in others. This observation would lead to the conclusion that in situations where either method could be applied, the productive output method generally would be preferable.

It is important to recognize the effect of the different methods on *total cost of products* and on *unit product cost* when the depreciation is on assets used in manufacturing. The straight-line method reports depreciation as *fixed cost in total* but *variable cost per unit* of output. In contrast, the service hours method and the productive output method report depreciation as *variable in total* but *fixed per unit of output*. To illustrate, assume an asset costing $600 (no residual value) with an estimated life of five years or 500 units of output. Assume further that output was Year 1–90; Year 2–100; Year 3–110; Year 4–120; and Year 5–80. The comparative depreciation charges and unit cost figures for the straight-line and output methods are compared below:

Year	Units of Output	Output Depreciation		Straight-Line Depreciation	
		Amount	Unit Cost	Amount	Unit Cost
1.........	90	$108	$1.20	$120	$1.33
2.........	100	120	1.20	120	1.20
3.........	110	132	1.20	120	1.09
4.........	120	144	1.20	120	1.00
5.........	80	96	1.20	120	1.50
	500	$600		$600	

These distinctions are particularly important in cost analyses for managerial pricing, control, and decision-making considerations. These relative effects should be considered in selecting a method of depreciation.

Accelerated (reducing charge) Methods

The accelerated methods are designed to allocate the cost to be depreciated in such a manner that periodic depreciation charges are higher in the early years and lower in the later years of the life of the operational asset. The accelerated methods are based upon the assumption that new assets are more efficient than old assets; therefore, the economic service potentials rendered by the asset are greater during the early life of the asset. If the cost of these greater values being consumed through utilization of the asset is to be matched with the resulting revenue, some form of accelerated depreciation (sometimes referred to as reducing charge depreciation) is theoretically desirable. The accelerated methods are also defended on the grounds that the annual depreciation charge should decrease as repair expenses on the asset increase, thus resulting in a more equitable (smoother) charge to the operating periods for the use of the operational asset.

Numerous procedures have been proposed for computing accelerated depreciation expense; however, the principal methods currently being used are the following:

1. Sum-of-the-years' digits.
2. Fixed percentage on declining base.
3. Double-declining balance.

Sum-of-the-Years'-Digits Method

This method (abbreviated as SYD) applies a decreasing fraction each succeeding period to the cost to be depreciated. The fractions are determined by using as the denominator the sum-of-the-years' digits for the life of the asset. The numerator, which changes each period, is the years' digits in reverse order. For example, the asset in the illustration, having an estimated service life of three years, would be depreciated as follows:

Denominator:
  Sum-of-the-years' digits; $1 + 2 + 3 = 6$.

Numerators:
  Digits in reverse order; 3, 2, and 1.

Fractions:
  First period, $\frac{3}{6}$.
  Second period, $\frac{2}{6}$.
  Third period, $\frac{1}{6}$.

Exhibit 14–4 illustrates an application of the method for the illustrative asset.

Note that the reducing fraction is multiplied by the cost to be depreciated (cost less residual value) in each period. When the life of the asset is relatively long, the denominator (sum of the

EXHIBIT 14–4
Depreciation Table and Entries, Sum-of-the-Years'-Digits Method (life, three years)

Year	Depreciation Expense (debit)		Accumulated Depreciation (credit)	Balance Accumulated Depreciation	Undepreciated Asset Balance (book value)
0.........					$100
1.........	($\frac{3}{6}$ × $90)	$45	$45	$45	55
2.........	($\frac{2}{6}$ × $90)	30	30	75	25
3.........	($\frac{1}{6}$ × $90)	15	15	90	10 (residual value)
		$90	$90		

EXHIBIT 14–5

Depreciation Table and Entries, Fixed-Percentage-on-Declining-Base Method (life, three years)

Year	Depreciation Expense (debit)		Accumulated Depreciation (credit)	Balance Accumulated Depreciation	Undepreciated Asset Balance (book value)
0					$100.00
1	(53.6% × $100)	$53.60*	$53.60	$53.60	46.40
2	(53.6% × $46.40)	24.87	24.87	78.47	21.53
3	(53.6% × $21.53)	11.53	11.53	90.00	10.00 (residual value)
		$90.00	$90.00		

* Carried to nearest cent to demonstrate that the correct residual value remains.

digits) can be readily computed by using the following formula. Computation of SYD for an asset with a 25-year life is illustrated.

$$SYD = n\left(\frac{n+1}{2}\right)$$

or

$$SYD = 25\left(\frac{25+1}{2}\right) = 325$$

Fixed-Percentage-on-Declining-Base Method

To apply this method the book value of the asset (undepreciated asset balance) is multiplied by a constant percentage rate. Since a constant rate is applied to a *declining base,* each subsequent periodic depreciation charge will be less. The rate must be computed taking into account the cost, estimated life, and residual value; consequently, the rate will automatically provide for the residual value at the end of the service life of the asset. The depreciation rate (the fixed percentage) and its application are illustrated below:

$$r = 1 - \sqrt[n]{\frac{R}{C}}$$

or

$$r = 1 - \sqrt[3]{\frac{\$10}{\$100}} = .536, \text{ or } 53.6\%$$

Calculation of $\sqrt[n]{\frac{R}{C}}$ can be done by use of logarithms or some hand calculators.

Observe in Exhibit 14–5 that the book value at the end of the service life is precisely the estimated residual value. It should be pointed out that where the asset has no residual value, the formula given above for calculation of the depreciation percentage or rate cannot be used unless a nominal residual value of, say, $1, is assumed. As a matter of practical application, it is usually desirable to round the rate to an even percentage.

Double-Declining Balance Method

Reducing charge depreciation is acceptable for federal income tax purposes, except the regulations provide that the amount of depreciation must not be more than double the amount that would result under the straight-line method *when the residual value is ignored.*[4] This provision gave rise to the double-declining balance method. Under this method the fixed percentage used is simply double the straight-line rate; residual value is ignored. Each year this rate is multiplied by the declining book value. Based on the data given at the outset of the discussion of depreciation methods, the rate would be 67%

[4] For income tax purposes there are numerous restrictions on the double-declining balance method. Double the straight-line rate may be used only on certain types of new property acquired within a certain range of dates. Used property, certain types of new property, and property acquired before 1954 may be depreciated at 150% of the straight-line rate. Although residual value is ignored in the depreciation computations, an asset may not be depreciated below a reasonable residual value.

EXHIBIT 14–6
Depreciation Table and Entries, Double-Declining Balance Method (life, three years)

Year	Annual Rate	Depreciation Expense (debit)	Accumulated Depreciation (credit)	Balance Accumulated Depreciation	Undepreciated Asset Balance (book value)
0.....					$100
1.....	67%	67% × $100 = $67	$67	$67	33
2.....	67%	67% × $ 33 = 22	22	89	11
3.....	67%	1*	1*	90	10 (residual value)

* Rounding amount needed for total depreciation of $90 and residual vaue of $10.

(i.e., 33⅓% × 2). The depreciation would be as shown in Exhibit 14–6.

The accelerated methods discussed above can be classed as rational and systematic. They are not difficult to apply. For all practical purposes the sum-of-the-years'-digits and double-declining balance methods are the only accelerated methods used. The important criterion to apply is whether they properly match periodic depreciation expense with periodic revenue.

With respect to acceptability of the accelerated approach, the Committee on Accounting Procedure of the AICPA stated in *Accounting Research Bulletin No. 44* that

> The declining-balance method is one of those which meets the requirements of being "systematic and rational." In those cases where the expected productivity or revenue-earning power of the asset is relatively greater during the earlier years of its life, or where maintenance charges tend to increase during the later years, the declining-balance method may well provide the most satisfactory allocation of cost. The conclusions of this bulletin also apply to other methods, including the "sum-of-the-years'-digits" method, which produce substantially similar results.

DEPRECIATION BASED ON INVESTMENT CONCEPTS

The preceding paragraphs discussed depreciation approaches that provided (1) a *constant* depreciation expense charge per period, (2) a *decreasing* depreciation charge per period, or (3) a *varying* depreciation charge per period (out-

put methods). The *compound interest methods* represent a distinctly different approach since they provide an *increasing periodic* expense effect. The other approaches to depreciation have been criticized because among other things, they ignore the investment characteristics of the ownership of property, plant, and equipment. Depreciation based on investment concepts views such an investment in property, plant, and equipment, and the return on that investment, in the same manner as if an annuity investment were made. Implicit is the concept that the subsequent periodic returns received over the life of the asset comprise both principal and interest. Therefore, the total depreciation expense amount each period would embody two elements: (1) the recovery of principal would be credited to accumulated depreciation and (2) the remainder would be credited to an account for *imputed interest revenue.* The effect of this entry each period, since, in the total depreciation expense amount each period, the principal amount increases each period and the interest amount decreases, is an increasing reduction in net income because of depreciation. The two methods—annuity and sinking fund—give the same net effect on income; they are illustrated in the Appendix to this chapter.

FRACTIONAL YEAR DEPRECIATION

Implicit in the preceding illustrations has been the assumption that the asset year and the company's fiscal year coincide; however, assets seldom are purchased on the first day of a fiscal period and are seldom retired at the end of the fiscal year. Therefore, depreciation often must be computed for fractional parts of the year. An accounting policy generally is established so that consistent amounts of depreciation are recorded for fractional parts of the year. Most companies do not count days because depreciation is an estimate and such precision would be irrelevant. Policies widely used are as follows:

1. Compute depreciation on the basis of even months.
2. Depreciate from the first of the month all assets *acquired* on or before the 15th of the month; if *acquired* after the 15th, do not depreciate for the partial month. Assets *disposed of* on or before the 15th of the month are not depreciated for the partial month; if *disposed of* after the 15th, record a full month's depreciation.
3. To determine the monthly depreciation amount, divide the annual amount by 12 regardless of the method of depreciation used.
4. For methods other than straight-line depreciation, when the asset year and the fiscal year do not coincide, compute partial depreciation on the basis of the months for each of the partial years of the asset life and sum the results.

To illustrate implementation of the fourth policy, assume the asset used in the preceding illustration was acquired on May 5, Year 1, and was retired on April 25, Year 4. The fiscal year ends on December 31. Using sum-of-the-years'-digits depreciation, as given in Exhibit 14–4, the computations and results would be as follows:

Year	Annual Depre-ciation (Exhibit 14–4)	Months	Computation	Depre-ciation Expense
1	$45	8	($45 × $\frac{8}{12}$)	$30
2	30	12	($45 × $\frac{4}{12}$) + ($30 × $\frac{8}{12}$)	35
3	15	12	($30 × $\frac{4}{12}$) + ($15 × $\frac{8}{12}$)	20
4		4	($15 × $\frac{4}{12}$)	5
	$90	36		$90

Other viable alternatives include (1) depreciation computed on the balance in the asset account at the beginning of the year; (2) depreciation computed on the balance in the asset account at the end of the year; (3) depreciation computed only on assets acquired during the first half of the year, and no depreciation on assets disposed of during the first half of the year; and (4) depreciation computed on a semiannual basis.

SPECIAL DEPRECIATION SYSTEMS

Unique features of certain kinds of depreciable assets have caused adaptations of the depreciation methods discussed above. The most common adaptations, generally referred to as "systems," are discussed in this section under the following captions:

1. Inventory (or appraisal) system.
2. Retirement and replacement systems.
3. Group and composite life systems.

Inventory (or appraisal) System

Under this system, purchases of depreciable assets are debited to an appropriate asset account in the usual manner, and depreciation is credited to the same account. The amount recorded as depreciation for the period is determined by estimating the "value" of the asset on hand in its present condition; the asset account then is reduced to this amount, and depreciation expense is charged. Residual recovery serves to reduce depreciation expense for the period. The value of the asset on hand is determined by inventory procedures and an estimate of its *acquisition cost* taking into account its present condition. As implied by its name, the inventory system is almost identical to the procedures used to take a physical count of inventory for sale.

To illustrate, assume the Hand Tools account showed a balance of $680; an inventory of the tools on hand at the end of the period, valued at *acquisition cost* and adjusted for present condition, indicated a value of $560. The broken and obsolete tools were sold for $10. The entry to record the periodic depreciation is as follows:

Cash	10	
Depreciation expense—hand tools		
($120 − $10)	110	
Hand tools ($680 − $560)		120

The inventory system is appropriate for situations where the asset account represents numerous asset items of a small unit cost, such as hand tools, machine tools, patterns and dies, and dishes, flatware, and so forth, in a restaurant.

In particular, care must be exercised to exclude changes in value due to changes in the price level or other market fluctuations; otherwise the depreciation charge will include noncost elements such as unrealized (holding) market gains and losses. A conventional matching of depreciation expense and periodic revenues requires that the items be valued at original cost adjusted for present condition.

Retirement and Replacement Systems

The retirement and replacement systems of depreciation frequently are used by public utilities because of the peculiar problems of accounting for certain assets such as poles and other line items. They are also used in accounting for low-cost items such as hand tools. Under retirement and replacement systems, no periodic entry is made for depreciation in the normal manner; instead depreciation is recognized at the *time of replacement* of the asset. The basic distinction between the methods is that under the *retirement* system, the cost of the *old* asset (less its residual value) is charged to depreciation expense when it is replaced, whereas under the *replacement* system the cost of the *new* asset (less residual value of the *old* asset) is charged to depreciation expense when it replaces the old asset. To illustrate both systems, assume the Hi-Power Utility Company replaced ten utility poles at a cost of $100 each. The old poles replaced originally cost $50 each and have a residual value of $10 each.

Retirement system:

1. To record the retirement of the old poles:

Depreciation expense [10 × ($50 − $10)]	400	
Salvage inventory (residual value, old poles) (10 × $10)	100	
Transmission line (cost of old poles) (10 × $50)		500

2. To record installation of the new asset:

Transmission line (cost of new poles)	1,000	
Cash or Pole inventory (cost of new poles)		1,000

Replacement system:

Depreciation expense [10 × ($100 − $10)]	900	
Salvage inventory (residual value, old poles) (10 × $10)	100	
Cash or Pole inventory (cost of new poles)		1,000

From this example it should be clear that the retirement system represents a *Fifo* approach, whereas the replacement system represents a *Lifo* system in allocating the asset cost to depreciation. The retirement system provides depreciation charges based on older costs and reports the operational asset at newer costs, whereas the replacement system provides depreciation charges based on newer costs and reports the operational asset at the older cost. Neither system adequately matches expense with revenue, inasmuch as depreciation is recognized only when assets are being replaced. Once the company has reached a relatively stable level of growth and replacement, however, the resulting periodic depreciation charges may approximate the amounts that would be computed under one of the usual methods such as straight line. The systems have been used by utility companies because of the practical difficulty in depreciating large numbers of relatively low-cost items such as poles, cross-members, brackets, and conduits at many locations. In such situations the distinction between ordinary repairs and capitalizable replacements is difficult to establish and apply on a practical basis. Although lacking in theoretical justification, the retirement system has some appeal from a practical standpoint, especially where retirement system depreciation closely approximates depreciation expense under one of the usual methods such as straight line.

Group and Composite Life Systems

The discussions up to this point have assumed that each item of property will be depreciated as a separate unit. In actual practice, many companies group certain operational assets for depreciation purposes. For example, all of the one-ton trucks may be grouped, or an entire operating assembly, such as a refinery, may be depreciated as a single unit. In such cases an average depreciation rate is applied to the group or assembly. Where an average rate of depreciation is applied to a number of *homogeneous* assets having similar characteristics and service lives, such as the trucks mentioned above, the procedure is referred to as *group depreciation.* Where an average rate of depreciation is applied to a number of *heterogeneous* assets having dissimilar characteristics and service lives, such as the refinery mentioned above, the procedure is referred to as *composite depreciation.* Many accountants view composite depreciation as a special variation of group depreciation. It is difficult to clearly distinguish between them. From the accounting standpoint there is no difference in mechanical application of the average rate nor in the resulting journal entries as between the two systems.[5]

Under the group system, all of the assets in the group are recorded in one asset account, and one accumulated depreciation account is established for the entire group; consequently, it would be incorrect to consider that any item in the group has a "book value" because the book value appearing in the account applies to the entire group and not to individual items. Subsequent acquisitions of items belonging to the group are similarly debited to the group asset account at cost. Depreciation is computed by multiplying an *average depreciation rate* times the balance in the group asset account regardless of the age of the individual assets represented therein. The rate may be computed and applied to cost or cost less residual value, as desired. The depreciation entry is made by debiting Depreciation Expense and crediting Accumulated Depreciation for the periodic amount of depreciation thus computed.

Upon retirement of a unit which is a part of the group, the group asset account is credited for the *original cost* of the item and the Accumulated Depreciation account is debited for the *same amount less any residual recovery.* The

system, therefore, does not recognize "losses or gains" on retirement of single assets in the group.[6]

To illustrate the group system, assume the Lawman Wholesale Corporation purchased ten fork lift trucks for warehousing purposes, each costing $4,800. Each truck has an estimated residual value of $800 at the end of the estimated service life of five years. The company depreciates the trucks on a group basis. Assuming depreciation is recognized on the *ending* balance in the asset account, typical entries under the group system are indicated below:

1. To record the initial purchase of ten trucks at $4,800 each:

Trucks 48,000
   Cash 48,000

2. To record group depreciation at the end of the first year:

Depreciation expense
($48,000 × 16⅔%) 8,000
   Accumulated depreciation 8,000

Computation:
Cost.................... $48,000
Estimated residual value 8,000
To be depreciated over
  5 years $40,000
Depreciation per year
  ($40,000 ÷ 5) .... $ 8,000
Depreciation rate on asset
  balance ($8,000 ÷ $48,000) .. 16⅔%

3. To record retirement of one truck at the end of the second year due to wreck; amount received from insurance, $3,000:

Cash 3,000
Accumulated depreciation (cost
less residual recovery) 1,800
   Trucks 4,800

4. To record purchase of two additional trucks at $5,000 each:

Trucks 10,000
   Cash 10,000

5. To record the retirement of a truck that has been used for 5½ years, and then sold to a salvage yard for $300, original cost, $4,800:

Cash 300
Accumulated depreciation 4,500
   Trucks 4,800

[5] For a full discussion of depreciation of multiple asset accounts (group and composite), see Joseph D. Coughlan and William K. Strand, *Depreciation: Accounting, Taxes and Business Decisions* (New York: The Ronald Press Co., 1969), chap. 5. Group depreciation can utilize the straight-line or double-declining balance formulas but cannot be based on sum-of-the-years' digits or output formulas.

[6] Ibid.

In applying the group system it may be necessary to approximate the "book value" of a specific unit that is a part of the group. For example, when a unit is transferred from one group account to another group account, as might be done when the asset is moved from one organizational division of the company to another, it is desirable that the original acquisition cost and accumulated depreciation to date be transferred in the accounts. In such cases the accumulated depreciation under the group system may be approximated as follows:

$$\frac{\text{Present Age}}{\text{Service Life}} \times \left(\frac{\text{Acquisition}}{\text{Cost}} - \frac{\text{Residual}}{\text{Value}} \right)$$

To illustrate, assume a truck is being transferred from Division A to Division B; the truck originally cost $4,800 and has been in operation two years. Its estimated service life is five years, and the estimated residual value, $800. The truck has been depreciated on a group basis; the *average* group rate being used is 16⅔%. The entry to record the transfer might be as follows:

```
Truck—Division B .................... 4,800
Accumulated depreciation—machin-
   ery—Division A* .................... 1,600
      Truck—Division A ................     4,800
      Accumulated depreciation—
         machinery—Division B* ..........     1,600
   * Computation:
      ($4,800 − $800) × ⅖ = $1,600.
```

Under the *composite system* the units making up the operating unit or assembly may have a fairly wide range of service lives. Because of this condition, composite life depreciation is subject to theoretical objections. In establishing the average rate under composite depreciation, a *composite rate* (which is a weighted average) may be computed. Composite life is the average life of the various units which make up an operating unit or assembly, and the composite rate is the ratio of the periodic depreciation to the acquisition cost of all components of the operating unit, as illustrated in Exhibit 14–7.

If there are no changes in the asset account, the assembly will be depreciated to the residual value (at the end of the 11th year in the above example).

The group and composite methods are easier to apply than the unit methods and would there-

EXHIBIT 14–7
Life Calculation under Composite Depreciation— Operating Assembly XY

Component Item	Original Cost	Residual Value	Amount to Be Depreciated	Estimated Service Life (years)	Annual Depreciation
A	$50,000	$5,000	$45,000	15	$3,000
B	20,000	4,000	16,000	10	1,600
C	7,000	600	6,400	8	800
D	3,000	-0-	3,000	3	1,000
	$80,000	$9,600	$70,400		$6,400*

```
* Composite life: $70,400 ÷        Depreciation first period:
  $6,400 = 11 years.                Depreciation expense
Composite depreciation rate:         ($80,000 × 8%) .. 6,400
  $6,400 ÷ $80,000 = 8%               Accumulated de-
  on cost                               preciation ....      6,400
```

fore result in reductions in recordkeeping costs for many entities. For entities using computers, this factor may be insignificant. Group and composite systems recognize that depreciation estimates are based on averages and that gains or losses on disposition of single assets are of minor significance.

The chief disadvantage of the group and composite methods is that it is possible for them to conceal faulty estimates for long periods and through their failure to recognize gains or losses, not correct for changes in asset usage or for other errors. Unit methods are simple, and they facilitate computation of gains or losses on retirements of particular assets. In case portions of the assets should become idle, depreciation on those could be more readily isolated under unit methods.

DEPRECIATION POLICY

With the possible exception of inventories, no single area of accounting offers as much potential variety of practice or choice as does depreciation accounting. About the only "constant" is the starting point, which usually is historical cost; there are not many variables in the calculation of cost, though such matters as capitalizing or not capitalizing interest during construction, determining market values in nonmonetary exchanges, and treatment of overhead on self-construction afford examples of how identical assets acquired at the same time can begin with different costs. During the life of an asset there are often many judgmental decisions on whether a related expenditure is to be capitalized or expensed. As to capitalized balances (original cost plus postacquisition expenditures), we have presented different patterns and formulas which can be adopted for depreciation expense. It is necessary to estimate in advance such uncertain elements as life in years, productive output, hours of use, and rate of return. It is also usually necessary to estimate residual value; sometimes it is necessary to anticipate cost of dismantling or of restoration incident to retirement of a plant asset. There is small wonder, then, that great variability attends depreciation accounting.

For larger companies, it is easier to report their depreciation practices than to assess whether these practices conform to theoretical ideals. To judge whether a particular company's depreciation policies are sound requires an intimate knowledge of maintenance policies, particulars about obsolescence, plans for replacement, and financial considerations, among other things.

Accounting Trends and Techniques, 1978, the AICPA annual survey of practices of 600 selected industrial corporations, indicates that in 1977 annual reports, the straight-line method is used more than the other methods, accounting for 73% of the total usage. Accelerated depreciation methods account for over 21% of the total, while unit of production methods account for over 5%.[7] Details from the 1978 survey covering the four most recent years are set out in Exhibit 14–8. The same study indicates that approximately 79% of the companies had material differences between depreciation reported on published financial statements and depreciation reported for income tax purposes: this requires income tax allocation. For the most part, accelerated methods were used for tax purposes while straight line was used for financial reporting.

---

[7] The depreciation practices of small companies for financial reporting purposes are known only on a piecemeal basis. Those public accountants who have large numbers of small clients and those banks which receive large numbers of reports from small customers can tell what *their* clients' practices are, but overall data on small businesses at large are not available.

EXHIBIT 14–8
Depreciation Methods*

	Number of Companies			
	1977	1976	1975	1974
Straight line	559	567	567	563
Declining balance	67	66	80	71
Sum-of-the-years' digits	34	37	46	45
Accelerated method— not specified	60	71	73	74
Unit of production	40	41	38	35
Sinking fund	1	1	1	1

* AICPA, *Accounting Trends and Techniques, 1978* (New York, 1978), p. 270. The columns sum to more than 600 because some companies use different depreciation methods for different classes of depreciable assets.

DEPRECIATION DISCLOSURES

Because of the significant effects of the depreciation methods used, on both financial position and the results of operations, the APB in *Opinion No. 12* reaffirmed an earlier ARB that the following disclosures should be made in the financial statements or accompanying notes:

a. Depreciation expense for the period.
b. Balances of major classes of depreciable assets, by nature or function, at the balance sheet date.
c. Accumulated depreciation, either by major classes of depreciable assets or in total, at the balance sheet date.
d. A general description of the methods used in computing depreciation on major classes of depreciable assets.

This was augmented in *APB Opinion No. 22,* "Disclosure of Accounting Policies" (April 1972), where depreciation methods and amortization policies were cited as examples of required disclosures.

CHANGES AND CORRECTION OF DEPRECIATION

Occasionally a business will change the method of depreciation used, change estimates of service life or residual value, or locate prior errors. *APB Opinion No. 20,* "Accounting Changes" (July 1971), carefully specifies how each of these three different situations should be accounted for and reported. The provisions of the *Opinion,* as they relate to depreciation, may be summarized as follows:

1. Changes in accounting principle—A change from one generally accepted method to another generally accepted method (such as from SYD to straight line). Changes of this type require an adjustment for the differences in accumulated depreciation to date between the old and new methods. This difference is recorded as a "depreciation adjustment" which is reported on the income statement for the period of change between the captions "Income before Extraordinary Items" and "Net Income."

   To illustrate, assume XY Corporation has a machine that cost $150,000, having an estimated life of five years and no residual value. After the end of Year 2, the company decided to change from SYD to straight-line depreciation. Computation of the adjustment, the change entry, and reporting on the income statement are illustrated below:

   a. Computation of adjustment:

Year	Prior Method—SYD		New Method—Straight Line	Difference to Date
	SYD	Amount		
1	5/15	$50,000	$30,000	$20,000
2	4/15	40,000	30,000	10,000
Total		$90,000	$60,000	$30,000

   b. Change entry at start of Year 3:

   ```
   Accumulated depreciation .....  30,000
       Depreciation adjustment,
       change in accounting
       method ...............                 30,000
   ```

   c. Reporting on the current income statement:

   ```
   Income before extraordinary items ....  $60,000
       Extraordinary items (detailed) .......  (10,000)
       Adjustment due to accounting
       change (depreciation) ..........   30,000*
   Net income .......................  $80,000
   ```
   * Net of income tax; also an appropriate note.

   This treatment is theoretically sound since it *(a)* does not permit the adjustment

to be reflected as an operating item, *(b)* documents the item, *(c)* does not permit it to "bypass" the income statement, and *(d)* establishes better values for future financial reports.

2. Change in estimate—A change in the estimated useful life and/or the residual value. Changes of this type are made *prospectively.* This means that the undepreciated balance is apportioned to the new remaining life taking into account the new estimated life and/or new residual value.

   To illustrate, assume XY Corporation has another machine that cost $160,000, with an estimated useful life of five years, no residual value, and uses straight-line depreciation. At the start of the fourth year, it is decided that an eight-year estimated life would be more realistic with no change in the residual value. Computation of annual depreciation for the remaining life of five years and the depreciation entry for the fourth year follows:

   a. Computation of depreciation expense:

   ```
   Undepreciated balance (book value):
           $160,000 × ⅖ = $64,000.
   Annual depreciation, straight line:
           $64,000 ÷ 5 years = $12,800.
   ```

   b. Regular adjusting entry for depreciation expense end of fourth year (there is no special accounting change entry):

   ```
   Depreciation expense ........  12,800
       Accumulated
       depreciation ...........           12,800
   ```

3. Accounting error—Errors in depreciation recorded in prior years should be corrected when found. A correcting entry is required to record a *prior period adjustment* (reported on the statement of retained earnings) for the net effect of the error up to the beginning of the year during which the error is corrected. To illustrate, assume that a machine that cost $10,000, estimated service life of five years, no residual value, was incorrectly debited to expense when acquired. The error was discovered during the third year after acquisition. The correcting entry

and the depreciation entry for the third year follow:

a. Correcting entry:

Machine	10,000	
Accumulated depreciation ($10,000 × ⅖)		4,000
Prior period adjustment— error correction		6,000

b. Adjusting entry for depreciation expense, end of third year:

Depreciation expense ($10,000 ÷ 5)	2,000	
Accumulated depreciation ..		2,000

Accounting changes, as prescribed in *APB Opinion No. 20*, are discussed more comprehensively in Chapter 24.

THE INVESTMENT TAX CREDIT

From time to time Congress has included in the income tax laws provisions designed to encourage certain kinds of investments. The *investment tax credit* which relates to investment in productive facilities is such a provision. Details concerning this credit have changed over the years.[8] The most recent changes provide that taxpayers who acquire qualified property receive a 10% investment credit. Within certain

---

[8] The first investment tax credit was provided by the Revenue Act of 1962. Its provisions were revised by the 1964 Act, suspended in 1966, and restored in 1967. After yet another suspension, the credit was again restored. The Revenue Act of 1978 sets the credit "permanently" at 10% of the cost of qualifying property. It provides for limits on the amount of investment credit usable in a single year. Generally, the first $25,000 of investment credit can be used without limit to offset what would otherwise be the first $25,000 of income tax liability. For 1979 the upper limit on the excess of tax liability over the initial $25,000 which can be offset by the investment tax credit is 60%; by 1982 the limit will rise to 90%. Thus, if a taxpayer in 1982 initially determines tax liability at $125,000, up to $115,000 of investment tax credit can be used as an offset against the liability. This is computed as below:

		Investment Credit
Initial tax liability........................	$125,000	
Deduct first $25,000 (unlimited part)	25,000	$ 25,000
Remainder to which limit applies...........................	100,000	
1982 limit percent	×90%	
Additional investment credit (limited)		90,000
Total investment credit usable in 1982		$115,000

limits, the effect is to reduce by the amount of the investment credit the amount of taxes that would otherwise have to be paid. To illustrate the essential nature of the investment credit, assume data pertaining to X Corporation for 1979 as follows:

a.	Equipment bought early in 1979 that qualified for the investment credit (ten-year life, zero residual value)	$200,000
b.	Straight-line depreciation on equipment for 1979	20,000
c.	Income subject to tax for 1979 (after deducting $20,000 depreciation on equipment)	60,000
d.	Income tax before investment credit	24,000*

* Assuming a 40% rate for illustrative purposes.

The effect of the investment credit would be:

Income taxes for 1979 before investment credit....................................	$24,000
Less investment credit (10% of $200,000)	20,000
Amount of tax to be paid	$ 4,000

In the above example the significant reduction in income taxes, as a result of the investment credit, obviously would be viewed with considerable interest by taxpayers and surely would influence some of their investment decisions. With respect to proper accounting, the question is posed as to how the $20,000 tax credit should be recorded and reported on the income statement (the balance sheet aspect of accounting for the tax credit is straightforward; reduce current period income tax payable). Fundamentally, two distinctly different accounting approaches have been vigorously debated by the accounting profession. In these discussions the nature of the investment credit has been viewed as follows:

a. Current period reduction in income tax expense, that is, the *flow-through method*— The proponents of this view argue that since the investment credit was made available by the Revenue Act, it is in substance a selective reduction in taxes related to the taxable income of the year in which the credit arises. They note that various tax consequences as well as the investment credit affect a wide range of managerial decisions.

They argue that the investment credit, as a reduction in income tax expense, should increase income by the full amount of the tax credit in the year in which the tax credit arises.

b. Cost reduction or *deferral method*—Proponents of this position argue that it is the *use,* not the *purchase,* of the asset that gives rise to the benefits to be received from the investment credit. Support for this argument rests on the fact that if the property which gave rise to the credit is not retained, part or all of the credit will be lost. It can also be noted that shorter lived property receives a smaller credit. The original tax provision, although later revised, required that the credit be treated for tax purposes as a reduction of asset cost.

The effects of these two diverse positions may now be emphasized by comparing the accounting entries that would result from the illustrative data given above. Entries in 1979 would be as shown at the bottom of this page.

The tabulation of 1979 entries reveals that when the investment credit is treated as a reduction in income taxes, its effects "flow through" the income statement in the year during which the asset was placed in service. In contrast, under the deferral method, with a ten-year asset only one tenth of the benefit is recognized as a reduction in income tax expense in any one year of service life of the asset. *The credit balance in the Deferred Investment Credit account is a contra account on the balance sheet to the related asset account;* however, *APB Opinion No. 2,* paragraph 14, somewhat illogically, also permits it to be reported as a "deferred credit."

Either the flow-through method or the deferral method may be followed at the present time under generally accepted accounting principles as specified in *APB Opinion Nos. 2* and *4.* This not altogether ideal state of affairs is the result of some early indecision on the part of the Accounting Principles Board. To the Board's credit, however, it should be pointed out that it moved to correct the situation in 1971 by issuing an exposure draft of an *Opinion* which would have allowed only the deferral method. The Board lost the battle in the political arena when business executives pressured Congress to insert a provision in the Revenue Act of 1971 which legally permitted choice of either method of accounting for the investment credit. Whichever method is adopted must be used consistently and disclosed.

DEPLETION

Nature of Depletion

Depletion in the accounting sense represents allocation of the cost of a natural resource (wasting asset) against revenue as it is exploited. Ex-

Investment Credit Treated as a Reduction in Income Tax (flow-through method)		Investment Credit Treated as a Cost Reduction (deferral method)	
a. To record purchase of equipment early in 1979 for $200,000:			
Equipment 200,000		Equipment 200,000	
Cash	200,000	Cash	200,000
b. To record income taxes for 1979:			
Income tax expense 4,000		Income tax expense 24,000	
Income tax payable	4,000	Income tax payable	4,000
		Deferred investment credit . . .	20,000
		Deferred investment credit 2,000	
		Income tax expense (¹⁄₁₀ of $20,000)	2,000
c. Depreciation on equipment for 1979 (ten-year life):			
Depreciation expense 20,000		Depreciation expense 20,000	
Accumulated depreciation	20,000	Accumulated depreciation	20,000

amples of such resources are ore, oil, coal, timber, and gravel. In accounting for such assets, the original cost is recorded in harmony with the *cost principle* and subsequently amortized over the total production available. Allocation between periods, consistent with the *matching principle,* usually is accomplished by dividing the cost of the asset (less any residual value) by the estimated number of units that can be withdrawn economically; the *unit depletion rate* thus computed is multiplied by the actual units withdrawn during the period to determine the depletion charge for the period. As with other tangible assets, three factors are involved: (1) cost, including all development costs that can be related to the resource; (2) estimated residual value of the property upon exhaustion of the natural resource; and (3) the estimated production over the life of the resource. To illustrate, assume that it is estimated by competent reserve geologists that a given mineral lease has a potential production of two million units, and that the total cost of the lease, including development costs, is $160,000 with no residual value. The depletion rate per unit of mineral produced and its application would be computed as follows:

Depletion rate:
$160,000 ÷ 2,000,000 = $0.08 per unit

Production for period:
10,000 units

Depletion charge for period:
10,000 × $0.08 = $800

This method generally is used for financial and cost accounting purposes. For federal income tax purposes, other depletion methods may be employed in accordance with the Internal Revenue Code. For example, the Code permits the taxpayer to elect *statutory* or *percentage depletion* rather than cost depletion illustrated above. Under statutory depletion a stated percentage of gross income may be taken as the depletion deduction on the tax return. The percentage varies from 5% on some deposits to 22% on others. Some of the more common depletion percentages follow:

Sulphur and uranium; and, if from deposits in the United States, asbestos, lead, zinc, nickel, and certain others 22%

Oil and gas*	22%
Gold, silver, copper, iron ore, and oil shale (from U.S. deposits)	15
Coal and sodium chloride	10
Clay and shale used for certain purposes	7½
Other clay	5
Certain other minerals and metallic ores	14

* For many years the percentage rate on oil and gas was 27½%; in 1969 it was reduced to 22%. Recently it was eliminated for larger oil producers but still has some applicability on a greatly reduced scale.

Under the Code the sum of the statutory depletion charges allowed may (and in practice frequently does) exceed the original cost of the resource. The use of cost depletion for financial reporting purposes and statutory depletion for income tax purposes gives rise to a *permanent tax difference,* as discussed in Chapter 9.

Original acquisition costs, development costs, and tangible property costs associated with a natural resource should be set up in separate accounts. If any of the resulting facilities are likely to have a shorter life than the natural resource, their acquisition cost should be amortized over the shorter period. When buildings and similar improvements are constructed in connection with the exploitation of the specific resource, their lives may be limited by the duration of the resource. In such cases costs should be amortized on the same basis as the other costs related to the resource.

In view of the difficulties in estimating underground deposits of minerals, the evaluation of additional information derived through further developmental work and the additional costs incident thereto, the depletion rate must be changed from time to time. The new rate is determined by dividing the unamortized cost plus any additional development costs by the *remaining* estimated reserves. Past depletion charges are not revised.

Dividends sometimes are paid by companies exploiting natural resources equivalent to accumulated net income plus the accumulated depletion charge. State laws generally permit such dividends. This practice is common where there are no plans to replace the natural resource in kind and operations are to cease upon exhaustion of the deposit. In such cases, the stockholders should be informed of the portion of each dividend that represents a return of capital (i.e., the depletion charge). To illustrate, assume the Tex Oil Company accounts showed the following (summarized):

Assets	$1,000,000
Accumulated depreciation	(200,000)
Accumulated depletion	(100,000)
	$ 700,000
Liabilities	$ 150,000
Capital stock	500,000
Retained earnings	50,000
	$ 700,000

The board of directors could declare a dividend of $150,000 which would be recorded as follows:

Retained earnings	50,000	
Return of capital to stockholders	100,000	
Cash		150,000

The return of capital to stockholders would be reported as a deduction in the owners' equity section of the balance sheet.

Appendix—Annuity and Sinking Fund Methods of Depreciation

The annuity and sinking fund methods of depreciation are based on the same concepts that underlie an annuity investment. In this situation an investment is made and subsequently returns are received, usually each period. Each periodic return includes two separate elements: *(a)* a return of principal and *(b)* investment revenue. Over time, the periodic return of principal is larger (this represents depreciation) and the periodic interest element is smaller as the asset diminishes in value with use. The annuity and sinking fund methods yield the same overall effect on the income statement and balance sheet; their differences relate to the *reporting* of depreciation expense and imputed interest revenue on the income statement.

To illustrate the annuity and sinking fund methods of depreciation, assume the following simplified data:

Investment in plant item at cost at beginning of Year 1	$100
Residual or scrap value estimated at end of Year 3	$ 10
Estimated useful life of the plant item	3 years
Average cost of capital	10%
Present value of 1 for 3 periods at 10% (from Table 6–2)	.75131
Present value of ordinary annuity of 3 rents at 10% (from Table 6–4)	2.48685

ANNUITY METHOD OF DEPRECIATION

To apply this method the annual depreciation charge is computed on an annuity basis. The amount of the annual return on the investment is assumed to represent depreciation expense; accumulated depreciation is credited for the portion that represents return of principal, and the difference is credited to *imputed* interest revenue.

To illustrate, the periodic charge to depreciation expense would be computed as follows:

$$\text{Depreciation Expense} = \frac{C - (R \times p)}{P_o}$$

$$= \frac{\$100 - (\$10 \times .75131)}{2.48685}$$

$$= \$37.19$$

where C refers to cost, R refers to residual value, p refers to the present value of 1, and P_o refers to the present value of an ordinary annuity.

With this value we can construct a depreciation table reflecting the entries for depreciation and the periodic carrying value of the asset from acquisition to retirement. The table would be as follows:

Depreciation Table and Journal Entries—Annuity Method

Year	(a) Depreciation Expense Dr.	(b) Accumulated Depreciation Cr.	(c) Interest Revenue Cr.	(d) Unamortized Asset Balance
0	—	—	—	$100.00
1	$ 37.19	$27.19	$ 10.00	72.81
2	37.19	29.91	7.28	42.90
3	37.19	32.90	4.29	10.00
	$111.57	$90.00	$21.57	

(a) Constant amount from formula as computed above.
(b) *(a)* minus *(c)*.
(c) Previous unamortized asset balance times .10.
(d) Previous balance minus current *(b)*.

Observe that the above table is identical with an annuity amortization table (Chapter 6) except for the column captions. Also observe the following characteristics of the annuity method, as revealed by the entries in the above table, viz:

1. Depreciation Expense is debited each period for a *constant* amount, and total depreciation expense exceeds the cost to be depreciated ($90 in the example) because it *includes* the imputed interest.
2. Accumulated Depreciation is credited for an *increasing* amount each period, and in total it is the same as the amount to be depreciated.
3. Interest Revenue (this is imputed interest) is credited for a *decreasing* amount each period to reflect the constant rate of return on a declining investment.
4. Because of the net effect of Depreciation Expense and Interest Revenue, there is an *increasing net expense* effect on the income statement. It is the same as the credit to accumulated depreciation each period.
5. The carrying value of the asset decreases each period by a continuously increasing amount.

SINKING FUND METHOD OF DEPRECIATION

The sinking fund method is similar to the annuity method. The chief difference is that under the sinking fund method interest is not separately recorded and reported (and is not added to Depreciation Expense), while under the annuity method imputed interest is accorded separate recognition (and is added to Depreciation Expense). It should be pointed out that while a sinking fund to replace the asset being depreciated might be maintained, most companies would prefer to invest in other productive assets and that formal sinking funds (asset replacement funds) are quite rare. The journal entries, assuming depreciation only and no actual sinking fund, for the two methods are as follows:

Annuity and Sinking Fund Depreciation Methods Compared

	Annuity Method		Sinking Fund Method	
Year 1:				
Depreciation expense	37.19		27.19	
Accumulated depreciation		27.19		27.19
Interest revenue		10.00		
Year 2:				
Depreciation expense	37.19		29.91	
Accumulated depreciation		29.91		29.91
Interest revenue		7.28		
Year 3:				
Depreciation expense	37.19		32.90	
Accumulated depreciation		32.90		32.90
Interest revenue		4.29		

Observe in the illustration that the sum of the three annual amounts *credited to accumulated* depreciation under both methods is $90 (enough to replace the asset if its replacement cost does not rise and if the $10 estimated residual value is realized). Also observe that if a series of three payments of $27.19 (i.e., $90 ÷ 3.31) were made to a sinking fund earning 10%, $90 would accumulate at the end of three years. To summarize, the above entries reveal that the only difference between the two methods is the treatment of *imputed* interest: Both credit the same periodic amounts to accumulated depreciation; both produce the same periodic income; however, the annuity method produces a *higher* periodic depreciation expense, which is reduced by the credit to imputed interest.

The compound interest methods have been criticized on the grounds that they are not "rational" since an increasing charge for depreciation over the life of the asset is inconsistent with the fact that ownership costs based on value tend to decrease in later years. Also a part of the depreciation charge under the *annuity method* is for imputed or theoretical interest; the offsetting credit for this element is made to Interest Revenue and therefore affects the income or loss of the period in which the depreciation is recorded.

For a combination of reasons the compound interest methods have been used relatively little in practice. Many entities, for reasons already cited, prefer to adopt depreciation methods which result in a somewhat opposite pattern of depreciation charges (i.e., more depreciation in earlier years and less depreciation in later years).

The limited extent to which the methods have been used seems to be confined largely to public utilities. There is some theoretical justification for their use by regulated businesses where a precalculated rate of return on investment is virtually assured by the rate-setting process and revenues and rates are set on the basis of a regulated rate of return on invested capital. Generally, it can be said that they do not conform to current GAAP.

QUESTIONS

1. Distinguish between amortization, depletion, and depreciation.

2. Explain the effects of depreciation on (a) the income statement and (b) the balance sheet.

3. Explain the relationship of depreciation to (a) cash flow and (b) assets.

4. What is the relationship of depreciation to replacement of the assets being depreciated?

5. What are the primary causes of depreciation? What effect do changes in the market value of the asset being depreciated have on the depreciation estimates?

6. List and briefly explain the three factors which must be considered in allocating the cost of an operational asset.

7. What is meant by accelerated methods of depreciation? Under what circumstances would these methods generally be appropriate?

8. What accounting policy problems arise when the entity's fiscal year and the asset year do not coincide? Consider the case of a company that closes its books on June 30 but has bought a depreciable asset on January 1.

9. Briefly explain the inventory system of depreciation. Under what circumstances is such a system appropriate?

10. Compare the retirement and replacement depreciation systems.

11. How are composite life depreciation and group depreciation similar?

12. There are three categories in respect to change and correction of depreciation. Briefly explain each and outline the accounting involved as specified in *APB Opinion No. 20*.

13. What is the investment credit? What are the accepted ways of accounting for it?

14. Define depletion. How is depletion generally computed for financial and cost accounting purposes?

15. What depreciation methods are based on compound interest principles? How are the methods similar? Dissimilar?

16. As between the sum-of-the-years' digits and double-declining balance depreciation methods, which method will always produce the larger amount of depreciation in the first year of use of an asset?

DECISION CASE 14–1

a. A new client has certain fully depreciated tangible operational assets which are still used in the business.
   (1) Discuss the possible reasons why this could happen.
   (2) Comment on the significance of the continued use of these fully depreciated assets.
b. In the past these fully depreciated assets and their accumulated depreciation have been merged with other operational assets and related depreciation on the balance sheet. Discuss the propriety of this accounting treatment, including a discussion of other possible treatments and the circumstances in which they would be appropriate.

(AICPA adapted)

DECISION CASE 14–2

Kwik-Bild Corporation sells and erects shell houses. These are frame structures that are completely finished on the outside but are unfinished on the inside except for flooring, partition studding, and ceiling joists. Shell houses are sold chiefly to customers who are handy with tools and who have time to do the interior wiring, plumbing, wall completion, finishing, and other work necessary to make the shell houses livable dwellings.

Kwik-Bild buys shell houses from a manufacturer in unassembled packages consisting of all lumber, roofing, doors, windows, and similar materials necessary to complete a shell house. Upon commencing operations in a new area, Kwik-Bild buys or leases land as a site for its local warehouse, field office, and display houses. Sample display houses are erected at a total cost of from $13,000 to $17,000, including the cost of the unassembled packages. The chief element of cost of the display houses is the unassembled packages, since erection is a short-term, low-cost operation. Old sample models are torn down or altered into new models every three to seven years. Sample display houses have little salvage value because dismantling and moving costs amount to nearly as much as the salvage value of an unassembled package.

Required:

a. A choice must be made between (1) expensing the costs of sample display houses in the period in which the expenditure is made and (2) spreading the costs over more than one period. Discuss the relative merits of each method.

b. Would it be preferable to depreciate the cost of display houses on the basis of (1) the passage of time or (2) the number of shell houses sold? Explain.

(AICPA adapted)

EXERCISES

Exercise 14–1

To demonstrate the mechanical computations involved in several methods of depreciation, the following simplified situation is presented:

Acquisition cost	$ 8,600
Residual value	$ 600
Estimated service life:	
Years	4
Service hours	10,000
Productive output	32,000

Required:

Compute the annual depreciation under each of the following situations (show computations and round to the nearest dollar):

1. Straight-line depreciation; compute the depreciation charge and rate for each year.
2. Service hours method; compute the depreciation rate and charge for the first year assuming 2,200 service hours of actual operation.
3. Productive output method of depreciation; compute the depreciation rate and charge for the first year assuming 3,800 units of output. Is all of the depreciation amount (computed in your answer) expensed during the current period?
4. Sum-of-the-years' digits method; compute the depreciation charge for each year.
5. Double-declining balance method; compute the depreciation charge for each year.

Exercise 14–2

Equipment which cost Dean Company $15,000 will be depreciated on the assumption it will last eight years and have a $1,000 residual value. Several possible methods of depreciation are under consideration.

Required:

1. Prepare a schedule which shows annual depreciation expense, accumulated depreciation, and book values for the *first two* years assuming (show computations and round to nearest dollar):
   a. Fixed-percentage-on-declining-base method. The eighth root of .06667 is .71283.
   b. Productive output method. Estimated output is a total of 84,000 units, of which 9,000 will be produced the first year; 12,000 for each of the next two years; 15,000 the fourth year; 10,000 the fifth, sixth, and seventh years; and 6,000 the final year.
   c. Sum-of-the-years' digits method.
2. What criteria would you consider in selecting a method?

Exercise 14–3

Marsalles Company acquired a depreciable asset at a cost of $9,600 which is estimated to have a useful life of four years and residual value of $800.

Required:

1. Prepare a depreciation table for the entire life of the asset reflecting use of the following methods (show computations and round to nearest dollar):
   a. Straight-line method.
   b. Sum-of-the-years' digits method.
   c. Double-declining balance method.
2. What criteria should be considered in selecting a method?

Exercise 14–4

Nancy Company bought a machine for $10,000 which has an estimated service life of four years and a residual value of $750.

Required:

1. Prepare a depreciation table covering the life of the asset reflecting use of the following methods (show computations and round to nearest dollar):
   a. Sum-of-the-years'-digits method.
   b. Productive output method. Total output is estimated at 36,000 units. Assume actual output for the four years was sequentially: 11,000; 8,000; 7,000; and 10,000 units. Round the rate to four decimal places.
   c. Double-declining balance method.
2. Assume same facts as in Requirement 1 (a) except that in the fourth year, after ten months, the machine was sold for $950 cash. Journalize the depreciation and the sale.

Exercise 14–5

Ben Company bought equipment on January 1, 19A, for $22,000 for which the expected life is ten years and residual value is $2,000. Under three acceptable depreciation methods, the annual depreciation expense and cumulative balance of accumulated depreciation at the end of 19A and 19B are shown below:

	Method A		Method B		Method C	
	(Relates to Exercise 14–5)					
Year	Annual Expense	Accumulated Amount	Annual Expense	Accumulated Amount	Annual Expense	Accumulated Amount
19A	$4,400	$4,400	$2,000	$2,000	$3,636	$3,636
19B	3,520	7,920	2,000	4,000	3,272	6,908

Required:

1. Identify the depreciation method used in each instance.
2. Project continued use of the same method through years 19C and 19D and determine the annual depreciation expense and accumulated depreciation amount for each year under each method.

Exercise 14–6

City Utility Company purchased 500 poles at $120 per pole, the debit being to the Inventory—Poles P-113 account. Subsequent to the purchase, 100 of the new poles were used to replace an equal number of old poles (Poles M-101) which were carried in the tangible operational asset account, Poles—Austin Line. The old poles originally cost $30 each and had an estimated residual value of $10 per pole.

Required:

1. Give all indicated entries (a) assuming the retirement system is employed and (b) assuming the replacement system is used.
2. Compare the effect on the periodic depreciation expense and the asset accounts as between the two systems.

Exercise 14–7

Metz Company owned a power plant which consisted of the following, all acquired on January 1, 19A:

	Cost	Estimated Residual Value	Estimated Life (years)
Building	$600,000	None	15
Machinery, etc.	180,000	$18,000	10
Other equipment	150,000	10,000	5

Required (carry decimals to two places):

1. Compute the total straight-line depreciation for 19D on all items combined.
2. Compute the composite depreciation rate on the plant.
3. Determine the composite life of the plant.

Exercise 14–8

Bobbin Company owned the following machines, all acquired at the same time:

Machine	Cost	Estimated Residual Value	Estimated Life (years)
A	$12,000	None	5
B	20,000	$2,400	8
C	30,000	2,000	10
D	38,000	2,000	12

Required:

1. Calculate total depreciation if machines are depreciated on a unit basis by the straight-line method.
2. Determine the composite depreciation rate if the machines are depreciated as a group.
3. Determine the composite life of the machines.
4. If the machines are depreciated as a group, what

depreciation methods can be used? What methods cannot? Give reasons for your answers.

Exercise 14–9

The Low Company depreciates its spot welders on a straight-line group basis. Transactions relative to spot welders in Plant A were as follows:

a. January 2, 19A: Bought six spot welders for an aggregate price of $16,500, paying cash.
b. December 31, 19A: On the assumption the residual value of the group would total 10% of original cost and have a useful life of five years, recorded depreciation at year-end.
c. Recorded depreciation at year-end, December 31, 19B.
d. January 2, 19C: One unit which performed unsatisfactorily was sold for $1,250 cash.
e. Two additional spot welders were bought January 10, 19C, at the same unit price as the original elements of the group and added to the group.
f. Recorded depreciation at December 31, 19C, for full year for all units in group.
g. Transferred one of the original spot welders to Plant C on January 2, 19D.

Required:

Give entries for each transaction; show computations; closing entries are not required.

Exercise 14–10

Zeno Company's records show the following property acquisitions and retirements during the first two years of operations:

Year	Cost of Property Acquired	Estimated Useful Life (years)	Sales or Retirements Year of Acquisition	Amount
19A	$50,000	10	—	—
19B	20,000	10	19A	$7,000

Property is depreciated for one-half year in the year of acquisition. Retired property is to be depreciated for the full year in its year of retirement. Assume zero residual values.

Required:

Determine depreciation expense for 19A and for 19B and the balances of the Property and related Accumulated Depreciation accounts at the end of each year under the following depreciation methods (show computations and round to the nearest dollar):

a. Straight-line method.
b. Sum-of-the-years' digits method.

(AICPA adapted)

Exercise 14–11

White Company owned ten warehouses of a similar type except for varying size. The group system is applied to the ten warehouses, the rate being 8% per year on cost. At the end of the tenth year the asset account Warehouses showed a balance of $5,300,000 (residual value $300,000), and the Accumulated Depreciation account showed a balance of $2,400,000. Shortly after the end of the tenth year, Warehouse No. 8, costing $600,000, was retired and demolished. Materials salvaged from the demolition were sold for $40,000, and $15,000 was spent on demolition.

Required:

Give entries to record (a) depreciation for the 10th year, (b) retirement of the warehouse, and (c) depreciation for the 11th year.

Exercise 14–12

Baum Corporation purchased a machine (which qualified for the 10% investment tax credit) on January 1, 19A, at a cost of $75,000, having an estimated useful life of 12 years and no residual value. The company uses straight-line depreciation and has an average tax rate of 35%. Income (after deducting depreciation expense, but before income tax expense) was 19A, $42,000; and 19B, $50,000.

Required:

Give the entries for income taxes and depreciation at December 31, 19A, and December 31, 19B, end of the fiscal period, assuming the

a. Flow-through method.
b. Deferral method.

Exercise 14–13

XT Company's investment in a gravel quarry amounted to $4,000,000, of which $400,000 could be ascribed to land value after the gravel has been removed. Geologists who were engaged to estimate the removable gravel reported originally that six million cubic yards (units) could be extracted. In the first year 900,000 units were extracted and 820,000 units were sold. In the second year 800,000 units were extracted and sales were 850,000 units.

At the start of the third year management of XT Company had the quarry examined again, at which time it was determined the remaining removable gravel was 2.5 million units. Production and sales for the third year amounted to 300,000 units. In the fourth year production was 750,000 units while sales amounted to 600,000 units.

Required:

1. Calculate depletion expense to be reported on XT's income statement for each of the four years. Show supporting computations.
2. Show how the gravel inventory (*Fifo* basis) and the gravel deposit would be reported on XT's balance sheet at the end of the fourth year. Assume an accumulated depletion account is used.

Exercise 14–14

Saegert Minerals, Inc., paid $1,700,000 for property with removable ore estimated at 2,000,000 tons. The property has an estimated value of $100,000 after the ore has been extracted. Before any ore could be removed it was necessary to incur $400,000 of developmental costs. In the first year, 200,000 tons were removed and 175,000 tons of ore were sold; in the second year, 300,000 tons were removed and 325,000 tons were sold. In the course of the second year's production, discoveries were made which indicated that if an added $300,000 is spent on developmental costs during the third year, future removable ore will total 2,700,000 tons. After incurring these added costs, production for the third year amounts to 540,000 tons, and sales, 531,000 tons.

Required:

1. Calculate depletion expense to be reported on Saegert's income statement for each of the three years. Show supporting computations and round unit costs to three decimal places.
2. Show how the resource and the inventory would be reported on Seagert's balance sheet at the end of the third year (*Fifo* basis). Assume an accumulated depletion account is used.
3. Give the journal entry to record depletion expense at the end of the three years.

Exercise 14–15

There are both similarities and differences to be found in the accounting treatments of depreciation and depletion.

Required:

1. Describe cost depletion and statutory depletion. Under what conditions, if any, is percentage depletion permitted?

2. List *(a)* the similarities and *(b)* the differences in accounting treatments of depreciation and cost depletion.
3. Operational assets donated to corporations are placed on the books, and their depreciation or depletion is recorded. Discuss the accounting justification for recording on the books *(a)* operational assets received as a gift and *(b)* their depreciation or depletion.

(AICPA adapted)

Exercise 14–16

Select the best choice for each of the following. Briefly justify your selection of each item.

1. Upon purchase of certain depreciable assets utilized in its production process, a company expects to be able to replace these assets by adopting a policy of never declaring dividends in amounts larger than net income (after deducting depreciation). If a net income is earned each year, recording depreciation will coincidentally result in sufficient assets being retained within the enterprise which, if in liquid form, could be used to replace those fully depreciated assets if
   a. Prices remain reasonably constant during the life of the property.
   b. Prices rise throughout the life of the property.
   c. The retirement depreciation method is used.
   d. Obsolescence was an unexpected factor in bringing about retirement of the assets replaced.
2. In 19x1 Anton Company purchased a tract of land as a possible future plant site. In January 19x9 valuable sulphur deposits were discovered on adjoining property and Anton Company immediately began explorations on its property. In December 19x9, after incurring $100,000 exploration costs, which were accumulated in an asset account, the company discovered sulphur deposits appraised at $1,000,000 more than the value of the land. To record the discovery value the company should debit:
   a. $100,000 to an expense account.
   b. $100,000 to an asset account.
   c. $1,000,000 to an asset account and $100,000 to an expense account.
   d. $1,000,000 to an asset account.
3. The Exploitation Company acquired a tract of land containing an extractable natural resource. Exploitation Company is required by its purchase contract to restore the land to a condition suitable for recreational use after it extracts the natural resource. Geological surveys estimate the recoverable natural resource will be 3,000,000 tons, and

that the land will have a value of $600,000 after restoration. Relevant cost information follows:

Land	$6,000,000
Restoration	900,000
Geological surveys	300,000

If Exploitation Company maintains no inventories of extracted material, what should be the charge to depletion expense per ton of material extracted?
a. $1.80.
b. $1.90.
c. $2.00.
d. $2.20.

4. As generally used in accounting, what is depreciation?
 a. It is a process of asset valuation for balance sheet purposes.
 b. It applies only to long-lived intangible assets.
 c. It is used to indicate a decline in market value of a long-lived asset.
 d. It is an accounting process which allocates long-lived asset cost to accounting periods.

5. Property, plant, and equipment should be reported as valued at cost less accumulated depreciation on a balance sheet dated December 31, 19x9, unless
 a. Some obsolescence is known to have occurred.
 b. An appraisal made during 19x9 disclosed a higher value.
 c. The amount of insurance carried on the property is well in excess of its book value.
 d. Some of the property still on hand was written down in 19x5 pursuant to a quasi-reorganization.

6. Which of the following statements is the assumption on which straight-line depreciation is based?
 a. The operating efficiency of the asset decreases in later years.
 b. Service value declines as a function of time rather than use.
 c. Service value declines as a function of obsolescence rather than time.
 d. Physical wear and tear are more important than economic obsolescence.

(AICPA adapted)

Exercise 14–17

Select the best choice for each of the following. Briefly justify your selection of each item.

1. Which of the following reasons provides the best theoretical support for accelerated depreciation?
 a. Assets are more efficient in early years and initially generate more revenue.
 b. Expenses should be allocated in a manner that "smooths" earnings.
 c. Repairs and maintenance costs will probably increase in later periods, so depreciation should decline.
 d. Accelerated depreciation provides easier replacement because of the time value of money.

2. A principal objection to the straight-line method of depreciation is that it
 a. Provides for the declining productivity of an aging asset.
 b. Ignores variations in the rate of asset use.
 c. Tends to result in a constant rate of return on a diminishing investment base.
 d. Gives smaller periodic writeoffs than decreasing charge methods.

3. Lay Corporation, which has a calendar year accounting period, purchased a new machine for $10,000 on April 1, 19x1. At that time Lay expected to use the machine for nine years and then sell it for $1,000. The machine was sold for $5,000 on September 30, 19x7. Assuming straight-line depreciation, no depreciation in year of acquisition, and a full year of depreciation in the year of retirement, the gain to be recognized at the time of the sale would be
 a. $1,000.
 b. $500.
 c. $445.
 d. $0.
 e. None of the above.

4. A graph is set up with "depreciation expense" on the vertical axis and "time" on the horizontal axis. Assuming linear relationships, how would the graphs for straight-line and sum-of-the-years' digits depreciation, respectively, be drawn?
 a. Vertically and sloping down to the right.
 b. Vertically and sloping up to the right.
 c. Horizontally and sloping down to the right.
 d. Horizontally and sloping up to the right.

5. On July 1, 19x1, Gusto Corporation purchased equipment at a cost of $22,000. The equipment has an estimated residual value of $3,000 and is being depreciated over an estimated life of eight years under the double-declining balance method of depreciation. For the six months ended December 31, 19x1, Gusto recorded one-half year's depreciation. What should be the charge for depreciation (rounded to the nearest dollar) of this equipment for the year ended December 31, 19x2?
 a. $4,158.
 b. $4,750.
 c. $4,813.
 d. $5,500.

6. The depreciation method that does not result in decreasing charges is
   a. Double-declining balance.
   b. Fixed-percentage-on-book value.
   c. Sinking fund.
   d. Sum-of-the-years' digits.
7. Use of the annuity method of calculating depreciation over an asset's life results in
   a. Constant charges to depreciation expense.
   b. Decreasing charges to depreciation expense.
   c. Increasing credits to interest revenue.
   d. Constant credits to interest revenue.
8. Odell Corporation quarries limestone at two locations, crushes it, and sells it to be used in road building. The Internal Revenue Code provides for 5% depletion on such limestone. Quarry No. 1 is leased, the company paying a royalty of $0.01 per ton of limestone quarried. Quarry No. 2 is owned, the company having paid $100,000 for the site; the company estimates that the property can be sold for $30,000 after production ceases. Other data follow:

	Quarry No. 1	Quarry No. 2
Estimated total reserves, tons	30,000,000	100,000,000
Tons quarried through December 31, 19x1	2,000,000	40,000,000
Tons quarried, 19x2	800,000	1,380,000
Sales, 19x2	$600,000	$1,000,000

19x2 depletion of Quarry No. 1 for financial reporting purposes is
   a. $3,000.
   b. $8,000.
   c. $30,000.
   d. $29,600.
   e. None of the above.
9. Assume the same facts as in item 8. 19x2 depletion of Quarry No. 2 for financial reporting purposes is
   a. $0.
   b. $1,380.
   c. $966.
   d. $50,000.
   e. None of the above.
10. Assume the same facts as in item 8, except that a new engineering study performed early in 19x2 indicated that as of January 1, 19x2, 75,000,000 tons of limestone were available in Quarry No. 2. 19x2 depletion of Quarry No. 2 for financial reporting purposes is
   a. $772.80.
   b. $840.
   c. $0.

   d. $50,000.
   e. None of the above.

   (AICPA adapted)

Exercise 14–18

Management of the company where you are employed as chief accountant is contemplating applying the "fixed-percentage-on-declining-base" depreciation method to some newly acquired properties. You have been asked to develop schedules which will show annual depreciation expense and carrying values of assets at the end of each year if the contemplated method is adopted. (Round amounts to nearest dollar.)

Case 1

Machinery which will cost $10,000 and have a residual value of $500 with an estimated life of five years. The fifth root of .05 is .54928. Round the annual depreciation rate to three decimal places.

Case 2

Fixtures which will cost $6,000 and have a residual value of $1,500 with an estimated life of four years. The fourth root of .25 is .7071. Round the annual depreciation rate to four decimal places.

Exercise 14–19 (based on Appendix)

Equipment costing $50,000 and an estimated life of five years with a residual value of $8,000 is to be depreciated by compound-interest methods.

Required (round to nearest dollar):

Using a 7% rate prepare a depreciation table covering the entire life of the asset assuming

1. Annuity method.
2. Sinking fund method (round latter to nearest dollar).

PROBLEMS

Problem 14–1

Depreciation continues to be one of the most controversial, difficult, and important problem areas in accounting.

Required:

1. a. Explain the conventional accounting concept of depreciation accounting.
   b. Discuss its conceptual merit with respect to (i) the value of the asset, (ii) the charge(s) to

expense, and *(iii)* the discretion of management in selecting the method.

2. *a.* Explain the factors that should be considered when applying the conventional concept of depreciation to the determination of how the value of a newly acquired computer system should be assigned to expense for financial reporting purposes. (Ignore income tax considerations.)

 b. What depreciation methods might be used for the computer system?

(AICPA adapted)

Problem 14–2

Sands Company purchased a special machine at a cost of $91,000. It was estimated that the machine would have a net resale value at the end of its useful life for the company of $7,000. Statistics relating to the machine over its service life were as follows:

Estimated service life:
Years	5
Output, units	6,000

Actual operations:

Year	Units of Output
1	1,400
2	1,300
3	1,000
4	1,100
5	1,200

Required:

Prepare a depreciation table for each assumption below indicating entries for the asset over the useful life under the following methods: *(a)* straight line, *(b)* output, *(c)* sum-of-the-years' digits, *(d)* fixed percentage of 40% on declining base, and *(e)* double-declining balance. Show computations and round to nearest dollar.

Problem 14–3

Royal Company purchased a piece of special factory equipment on January 1, 19A, costing $63,750. In view of pending technological developments it is estimated that the machine will have a resale value upon disposal in four years of $15,500 and that disposal cost will be $1,750.

Data relating to the equipment follow:

Estimated service life:
Years	4
Service hours	20,000

Actual operations:

Calendar Year	Service Hours
19A	5,500
19B	5,000
19C	4,800
19D	4,600

Required (round to nearest dollar and show computations):

1. Prepare a depreciation table for the service hours method assuming the books are closed each December 31.
2. Compute depreciation expense for the first and second years assuming *(a)* straight line, *(b)* sum-of-the-years' digits, *(c)* fixed percent on declining base (30% rate), and *(d)* double-declining balance.

Problem 14–4

Machinery which cost Keene Corporation $10,000 is expected to last ten years and have a $500 residual value. Several depreciation methods in common use were applied to these data. The results in terms of annual charges covering Year 2 and Year 3 are set out below:

Year	Method A	Method B	Method C	Method D
1	?	?	?	?
2	$1,924	$1,600	$1,555	$950
3	1,424	1,280	1,382	950

Required (round to nearest dollar):

1. What is the book value of the asset at the end of Year 3 for each of the four methods used to compute Year 2 and Year 3 depreciation given in the table above? *Hint:* The tenth root of .05 is .74.
2. In connection with Methods C and D, suppose that after the completion of Year 3, it is determined the total remaining life of the machinery is five instead of seven years. Determine the annual charge and the balance of Accumulated Depreciation at the end of Year 4 and Year 5.

Problem 14–5

Equipment which cost $50,000 and has a five-year estimated life and residual value of $8,000 will depreciate various amounts in its second full year under various depreciation methods and formulas.

Second-year depreciation under the methods listed (but not in the same order) amounted to (1) $11,200; (2) $10,638; (3) $8,400; (4) $10,000; and (5) $10,803. The depreciation methods used were *(a)* annuity, *(b)* fixed percent on declining base, *(c)* productive output, *(d)* straight line, and *(e)* sum-of-the-years' digits.

In connection with the annuity method, a 7% interest rate was used. For the fixed percent on declining base, a 30.7% rate was used. The productive output method assumed 672,000 units could be produced; in the first two years actual output was 200,000 units and 160,000 units, respectively.

Required:

Alongside the letters identifying the five methods, write the number associated with the amounts of second-year depreciation. Support each answer with calculations.

Problem 14–6

Fresh Company bought a new machine for $30,000. It is expected to have a six-year useful life and a residual value of $6,000 at the end of that time. You have been requested to draw up schedules which will show annual depreciation for the machine each year under each of several different depreciation methods and assumptions as to how the machine will be used throughout its productive life (round to the nearest dollar).

The independent methods for which you are to supply depreciation data are as follows:

a. Use of sum-of-the-years'-digits depreciation with no revision in life estimate or residual value.
b. Use of units of production depreciation on the assumption the machinery can produce 96,000 units, and production throughout the six years of use will occur as follows: Year 1, 18,000 units; Year 2, 17,000; Year 3, 17,000; Year 4, 16,000; Year 5, 13,000; and Year 6, 15,000.
c. Use of units of production depreciation with the same starting assumption as in *(b)* and the same production in the first three years. In the fourth year, however, the total production estimate over the entire service life of the machine was revised to 107,000 units, and production for Years 4, 5, and 6 was, respectively, 24,000 units; 14,000 units; and 17,000 units.
d. Use of the fixed-percent-on-declining-base method. The sixth root of .2 is .765.
e. Use of the straight-line method. After using the method four years, at the start of the fifth year the residual value is revised downward to an estimated $3,000.
f. Use of the sinking fund method. An 8% interest rate should be assumed.

Problem 14–7

Management of a company which has just acquired an operational asset at a cost of $50,000 that is to be depreciated over five years to a residual value of $8,000 has asked you to develop alternate depreciation schedules based on various depreciation methods and assumptions as to usage.

a. Show depreciation under the productive output method if scheduled production using the asset will be Year 1, 200,000 units; Year 2, 160,000 units; Year 3, 140,000 units; Year 4, 100,000 units; and Year 5, 72,000 units.
b. Instead, the productive output method will be used as in *(a)* and through the first two years the total expectation and planned production are the same. However, at the start of Year 3 the total production estimate over the service life of the asset is revised to 750,000 units, and scheduled production in Years 3, 4, and 5 will be 200,000 units; 90,000 units; and 100,000 units, respectively.
c. The sum-of-the-years'-digits method will be used.
d. The annuity method will be used in conjunction with a 7% annual interest rate.
e. The fixed-percent-on-declining-base method will be used. The fifth root of .16 is .693.
f. The straight-line method will be used. After recording depreciation three years in accordance with the original assumptions, the residual value is changed to $10,000.

Required:

Prepare depreciation schedules which show depreciation expense for each year together with accumulated depreciation and book value for each situation and method described above.

Problem 14–8

Operational assets being depreciated on a composite basis by a manufacturer are set out in the schedule below:

Component	Cost	Estimated Residual Value	Estimated Life (years)
A........	$44,700	$2,700	10
B........	14,000	0	7
C........	38,000	8,000	15
D........	6,200	200	5
E........	12,000	2,000	5

Required:

1. Calculate the composite life and annual composite depreciation rate for the group of assets listed above. Record depreciation after one full year of use. Round the depreciation rate to three decimal places.
2. During the second year it became necessary to replace component B, which was sold for $8,000. The

replacement component cost $16,000 and has an estimated residual value of $2,600 at the end of its estimated six-year useful life. Record the retirement and substitution, which was a cash acquisition.

3. Record depreciation at the end of the second full year.

Problem 14–9

As of December 31, 19F, the Machinery account on the books of Black Corporation was as below:

Machinery

1/1/A	Purchase	$50,000	12/31/A	Depreciation	$5,000
7/1/B	Purchase	10,000	9/ 1/B	Machinery sold	2,000
11/1/C	Purchase	36,000	12/31/C	Depreciation	6,300
			12/31/D	Depreciation	7,800
			7/ 1/E	Machinery sold	1,000
			12/31/E	Depreciation	7,800
			12/31/F	Depreciation	9,300

Additional data:

Machinery sold September 1, 19B, cost $3,600 on January 1, 19A; machinery sold July 1, 19E, cost $2,500 on January 1, 19A. Machinery costing $2,000, which was purchased on July 1, 19B, was destroyed on July 1, 19F, and was a total loss. Assume the debits in the machinery account are correct.

Required:

1. Prepare a depreciation schedule showing *correct annual depreciation* and *account balances.* Assume ten-year life on all items, straight-line depreciation, and no residual value. Suggested captions: Date acquired, Machinery (debit-credit*), Correct Depreciation by Year (six columns), and Accumulated Depreciation (debit-credit*).
2. Prepare journal entry or entries to correct the books on December 31, 19F, assuming the books are not closed for 19F.

Problem 14–10

The accounts for Trucks and Accumulated Depreciation on the books of Dacy Hardware Store are as shown below:

Trucks

1/1/19A	Trucks No. 1 and 2	7,200	1/1/19C	Truck No. 1 scrapped	3,600
1/1/19C	Truck No. 3	3,780	1/1/19D	Truck No. 2 scrapped	3,600
1/1/19D	Truck No. 4	3,840			
7/1/19D	New tires, Truck 3	600			

Accumulated Depreciation

1/1/19C	Truck No. 1 scrapped ($1,500 received as salvage)	2,400	12/31/19A	Depreciation	2,400
			12/31/19B	Depreciation	2,400
1/1/19D	Truck No. 2 scrapped ($300 received as salvage)	3,300	12/31/19C	Depreciation	2,460
			12/31/19D	Depreciation	2,460
			12/31/19E	Depreciation	1,905

Required:

1. Prepare a depreciation schedule showing correct account balances and depreciation by year, assuming the estimated lives of Trucks No. 3 and No. 4 were changed from three to four years (other trucks have estimated service lives of three years and no estimated residual value) on January 1, 19E. Suggested captions: Date acquired, Truck No., Trucks (debit-credit*), Correct Depreciation by Year (five columns), and Accumulated Depreciation (debit-credit*).
2. Prepare journal entry or entries to correct the books as of December 31, 19E, assuming they were not yet closed for 19E. The schedule prepared for Requirement 1 should provide the data needed.

Problem 14–11

Hotstrike Minerals Company bought mineral-bearing land for $135,000 which engineers say will yield 200,000 pounds of economically removable ore; the land will have a value of $30,000 after the ore is removed.

To work the property, the company built structures and sheds on the site which cost $30,000; these will last 12 years, and because their use is confined to mining and it would be expensive to dismantle and move them, they will have no residual value. Machinery which cost $30,000 was installed at the mine, and added cost for installation was $6,000. This machinery should last 15 years; like the structures, usefulness of the machinery is confined to these mining operations. Dismantling and removal costs when the property has been fully worked will approximately equal the value of the machinery at that time; therefore, Hotstrike does not plan to use the structures or the machinery after the minerals have been removed.

In the first year, Hotstrike removed only 10,000 pounds of ore; however, production was doubled in the second year. It is expected that all of the removable ore will be extracted within eight years from the start of operations.

Required:

1. Prepare a schedule showing unit and total depletion and depreciation and book value for the first and second year of operation.
2. On the assumption that in the first year 90% of production was sold, and in the second year, the inventory carried over from the first year plus 90% of the second year's production was sold, give entries to record accumulated depreciation and depletion. To show the effect of these costs, make the offsetting debits to cost of goods sold and inventory. Use "accumulated" accounts.

Problem 14–12

Thompson Corporation, a manufacturer of steel products, began operations on October 1, 19A. The accounting department of Thompson has started the operational asset and depreciation schedule presented on the next page. You have been asked to assist in completing this schedule. In addition to ascertaining that the data already on the schedule are correct, you have obtained the following information from the company's records and personnel:

a. Depreciation is computed from the first of the month of acquisition to the first of the month of disposition.
b. Land A and Building A were acquired from a predecessor corporation. Thompson paid $812,500 for the land and building together. At the time of acquisition, the land had an appraised value of $72,000 and the building had an appraised value of $828,000.
c. Land B was acquired on October 2, 19A, in exchange for 3,000 newly issued shares of Thompson's common stock. At the date of acquisition, the stock had a par value of $5 per share and a market value of $25 per share. During October 19A, Thompson paid $10,400 to demolish an existing building on this land so it could construct a new building.
d. Construction of Building B on the newly acquired land began on October 1, 19B. By September 30, 19C, Thompson had paid $210,000 of the estimated total construction costs of $300,000. Estimated completion and occupancy date is July 19D.
e. Certain equipment was donated to the corporation by a local university. An independent appraisal of the equipment when donated placed the market value at $16,000 and the residual value at $2,000.
f. Machinery A's total cost of $110,000 includes installation expense of $550 and normal repairs and maintenance of $11,000. Residual value is estimated at $5,500. Machinery A was sold on February 1, 19C.
g. On October 1, 19B, Machinery B was acquired with a down payment of $4,000 and the remaining payments to be made in ten annual installments of $4,000 each beginning October 1, 19C. The prevailing interest rate was 8% on debts with similar risk characteristics to this debt. The following data were abstracted from present value tables:

Present Value of 1 at 8%

10 rents	.463
11 rents	.429
15 rents	.315

Present Value of Ordinary Annuity of 1 at 8%

10 rents	6.710
11 rents	7.139
15 rents	8.559

Required:

Number your answer sheet from 1 to 14. For each numbered item on schedule at the top of page 512, supply the correct amount next to the corresponding number on your answer sheet. Round each answer to the nearest dollar. *Do not recopy the schedule.* Show supporting computations in good form.

(AICPA adapted)

Problem 14–13

LM Manufacturing Company utilizes a number of small machine tools in their operations. Although there are numerous variations in the tools, they cost approximately the same and have similar useful lives. The company carries a Machine Tools account in the records; the account showed a balance of $1,600 (200 tools) at the end of 19A. Acquisitions, retirements, and other data for a period of two years are given below:

	19B	19C
Acquisitions	100 @ $7.50	120 @ $7.75
Retirements:		
Number	150	80
Salvage proceeds	$40	$20
Inventory	150 @ $5.20	190 @ $5.40

Required:

1. Give entries for each of the two years assuming (round to even dollars and show computations):
   a. The inventory system is used.
   b. The retirement system is used.
   c. The replacement system is used.
2. Prepare a tabulation covering the two years to

(Relates to Problem 14–12)

THOMPSON CORPORATION
Operational Asset and Depreciation Schedule
For Fiscal Years Ended September 30, 19B, and September 30, 19C

Assets	Acquisition Date	Cost	Residual	Depreciation Method	Estimated Life in Years	Depreciation Expense Year Ended September 30, 19B	19C
Land A	October 1, 19A	$ (1)	N/A	N/A	N/A	N/A	N/A
Building A	October 1, 19A	(2)	$47,500	Straight line	(3)	$14,000	$ (4)
Land B	October 2, 19A	(5)	N/A	N/A	N/A	N/A	N/A
Building B	Under construction	210,000 to date	—	Straight line	Thirty	—	(6)
Donated equipment	October 2, 19A	(7)	2,000	150% declining balance	Ten	(8)	(9)
Machinery A	October 2, 19A	(10)	5,500	Sum-of-the-years' digits	Ten	(11)	(12)
Machinery B	October 1, 19B	(13)	—	Straight line	Fifteen	—	(14)

N/A—Not applicable.

present the annual depreciation charge and the balance in the Machine Tools account under each system.

Problem 14–14

Sandra Company utilizes a large number of identical small tools in operations. On January 1, 19A, the first year of operations, 1,000 of these tools were purchased at a cost of $4 each. On December 31, 19A, 200 of the tools were sold or scrapped for $40, the estimated residual value being $40 ($0.20 each). During the year the 200 were replaced at a cost of $4.20 each. On December 31, 19B, 300 of the tools were sold or scrapped for $75, having an estimated residual value of $0.25 each and replaced at a cost of $4.50 each. On December 31, 19C, 140 of the tools were sold or scrapped for $35 (residual value $0.25 each) each being replaced at a cost of $3.60.

Required:

1. Give entries to record all indicated transactions, assuming the company employed the *(a)* retirement system and *(b)* the replacement system.
2. Compare the results under the two systems by showing periodic depreciation for each year and the balance in the Tools account at each December 31, 19A–19D.

Problem 14–15 (reviews Chapters 9 and 14)

Rocky Gravel Company mines and processes rock and gravel. It started in business on January 1, 19A,

when it purchased the assets of another company. You have examined its financial statements at December 31, 19A, and have been requested to assist in planning and projecting operations for 19B. The company also wants to know the maximum amount by which notes payable to officers can be reduced at December 31, 19B.

The adjusted trial balance on December 31, 19A, was as follows:

Cash	$ 17,000	
Accounts receivable	24,000	
Mining properties	60,000	
Accumulated depletion		$ 3,000
Equipment	150,000	
Accumulated depreciation		10,000
Organization cost	5,000	
Accumulated amortization		1,000
Accounts payable		12,000
Federal income taxes payable.....		22,000
Notes payable to officers		40,000
Capital stock		100,000
Contributed capital in excess of par		34,000
Sales		300,000
Production costs (including depreciation and depletion)	184,000	
Administrative expense (including amortization and interest) ...	60,000	
Federal income tax expense	22,000	
	$522,000	$522,000

You are able to develop the following information:

1. The total yards of material sold is expected to increase 10% in 19B, and the average sales price

per cubic yard will be increased from $1.50 to $1.60.

2. The estimated recoverable reserves of rock and gravel were 4,000,000 cubic yards when the properties were purchased.

3. Production costs include direct labor of $110,000 of which $10,000 was attributed to inefficiencies in the early stages of operation. The union contract calls for 5% increases in hourly rates effective January 1, 19B. Production costs, other than depreciation, depletion, and direct labor, will increase 4% in 19B.

4. Administrative expense, other than amortization and interest, will increase $8,000 in 19B.

5. The company has contracted for additional movable equipment costing $60,000 to be in production on July 1, 19B. This equipment will result in a direct labor hour savings of 8% as compared with the last half of 19A. The new equipment will have a life of 20 years. All depreciation is computed on the straight-line method. The old equipment will continue in use.

6. The new equipment will be financed by a 20% down payment and a 10% three-year chattel mortgage. Interest and principal payments are due semiannually on June 30 and December 31, beginning December 31, 19B. The notes payable to officers are demand notes dated January 1, 19A, on which 9% interest is provided for and was paid on December 31, 19A.

7. Accounts receivable will increase in proportion to sales. No bad debts are anticipated. Accounts payable will remain substantially the same.

8. Percentage depletion allowable on rock and gravel is to be computed at 5% of gross income and is limited to 50% of taxable income before depletion.

9. It is customary in the rock and gravel business not to place any value on stock-piles of processed material which are awaiting sale.

10. Assume an income tax rate of 40%.

11. The company has decided to maintain a minimum cash balance of $20,000.

12. The client understands that the ethical considerations involved in preparing the following statements will be taken care of by your letter accompanying the statements. (Do not prepare the letter.)

Required:

1. Prepare a statement showing the net income projection for 19B. Note: Round all amounts to the nearest $100. If the amount to be rounded is exactly $50, round to the next highest $100.

2. Prepare a statement which will show cash flow

projection for 19B and will indicate the amount that notes payable to officers can be reduced at December 31, 19B.

(AICPA adapted)

Problem 14–16 (reviews Chapter 13 and 14)

For each of the following situations, *(a)* select the best response from those given and *(b)* explain the basis for your choice, showing computations where appropriate.

The following data pertain to questions 1 and 2 only. On July 1, 19A, Miller Mining, a calendar year corporation, purchased the rights to a copper mine. Of the total purchase price, $2,800,000 was allocable to the copper. Estimated reserves were 800,000 tons of copper. Miller expects to extract and sell 10,000 tons of copper each month. Production began immediately. The selling price is $25 per ton. Miller uses percentage depletion (15%) for tax purposes. To aid production, Miller also purchased some new equipment on July 1, 19A. The equipment cost $76,000 and had an estimated useful life of eight years. However, after all the copper is removed from this mine, the equipment will be of no use to Miller and will be sold for an estimated $4,000. Use straight-line depreciation.

1. If sales and production conform to expectations, what is Miller's depletion expense on this mine for financial accounting purposes for the calendar year 19A?
   a. $105,000.
   b. $210,000.
   c. $225,000.
   d. $420,000.

2. If sales and production conform to expectations, what is Miller's depreciation expense on the new equipment for financial accounting purposes for the calendar year 19A?
   a. $4,500.
   b. $5,400.
   c. $9,000.
   d. $10,800.

3. Willard, Inc., purchased some equipment on January 2, 19A, for $24,000 (no residual value). Willard used straight-line depreciation based on a ten-year estimated life. During 19D, Willard decided that this equipment would be used only three more years and then replaced with a technologically superior model. What entry, if any, should Willard make as of January 1, 19D, to reflect this change?
   a. No entry.
   b. Debit an extraordinary item for $4,800, and credit accumulated depreciation for $4,800.

c. Debit a prior period adjustment for $4,800, and credit accumulated depreciation for $4,800.

d. Debit depreciation expense for $4,800, and credit accumulated depreciation for $4,800.

4. Gorch Company sold an item of plant equipment. Gorch received a noninterest-bearing note to be paid $1,000 per year for ten years. The "going" rate of interest for this transaction is 8%. What discount should Gorch reflect on this transaction?

a. Zero.
b. $3,290.
c. $4,630.
d. $6,710.

5. Blacker Company exchanged a business car for a new car. The old car had an original cost of $7,500, an undepreciated cost of $1,600, and a market value of $2,000 when exchanged. In addition, Blacker paid $6,200 cash for the new car. The list price of the new car was $8,300. At what amount should the new car be recorded for financial accounting purposes?

a. $7,500.
b. $7,800.
c. $8,200.
d. $8,300.

Items 6 and 7 are based on the following information: On January 2, 19A, Kirk Manufacturing Company acquired some equipment from Quarter Corporation. The sale contract requires Kirk to make 12 annual payments of $10,800 at the end of each year. The first payment was made on December 31, 19A, and no deposit was required. The equipment has an estimated useful life of 20 years with no anticipated residual value. The prevailing interest rate for Kirk in similar financing arrangements is 8%.

6. At what amount should Kirk have capitalized this equipment?

a. $77,100.

b. $81,390.
c. $103,720.
d. $106,040.

7. If the equipment was capitalized at $80,000 and all other facts remain as originally stated, how much interest expense should Kirk have recorded in 19A?

a. Zero.
b. $6,500.
c. $7,200.
d. $9,600.

(AICPA adapted)

Problem 14–17 (based on Appendix)

Equipment costing $100,000 has an estimated five-year life and $20,000 residual value.

Required (round to nearest dollar):

Using a 10% annual earnings rate on the equipment, prepare a depreciation table covering the entire life of the equipment assuming:

1. Annuity method.
2. Sinking fund method.

Problem 14–18 (based on Appendix)

Machinery with an estimated life of ten years and a residual value of 15% was acquired for $10,000. If the company can earn 7% annually on the machinery, what depreciation entries would be made at the end of each of the first two years assuming (a) the annuity method and (b) the sinking fund method. Derive the formula for annual depreciation under the annuity method. *Hint:* The formula is a rearrangement of the basic present value equation expressing the theoretical cost of an asset.

15

Intangible Assets

Intangible assets are those properties, *without physical substance,* which are useful to an entity because of the special *rights* their ownership confers. The accounting classification of assets reports some intangibles as *(a)* current assets, such as cash, receivables, short-term investments, and prepaid insurance; *(b)* funds and investments, such as bond sinking funds, and investments in stocks and bonds; *(c)* other assets, such as noncurrent claims to cash; *(d)* operational or fixed assets, such as patents, franchises, and goodwill; and *(e)* deferred charges (i.e., long-term expense prepayments).

Since a number of different kinds of intangibles have been discussed in prior chapters, this chapter focuses on three different kinds of intangible assets, viz: (1) intangible operational assets, (2) deferred charges, and (3) cash surrender value of insurance and expense prepayments. Each will be considered separately.

The long-term intangibles used in operating a business are generally classified for accounting purposes as *intangible* assets; other titles used are intangible operational assets, intangible fixed assets, or simply, intangibles. This classification includes intangible long-lived assets such as patents, copyrights, franchises, trademarks, trade names, secret processes, and goodwill. The primary characteristics of these in-

tangible assets are *(a)* they have no physical substance, *(b)* their ownership confers some exclusive rights, *(c)* they provide future benefits to operations, and *(d)* they are relatively long-lived. For example, a company that owns a patent used in making one of its products has a valuable intangible asset.[1]

Intangible assets may be further classified on the basis of

1. Identifiability—Most intangibles have separate identities and can be sold individually; examples include patents, copyrights, and trademarks. Other intangibles are inseparable from the entity itself and cannot be realized without selling the enterprise; the principal example is goodwill.
2. Manner of acquisition—acquired from external sources by purchase (such as a franchise) or internally developed (such as a trademark).
3. Expected period of benefit—limited by law or contract such as the 17-year legal life of a patent or the 10-year contract term of a franchise, or having indeterminate life, such as goodwill.

---

[1] A patent held for speculative rather than for operational purposes would be classified as "Investments and Funds."

ACCOUNTING FOR INTANGIBLE ASSETS

Accounting for intangible assets involves essentially the same accounting principles and procedures as for tangible property, plant, and equipment (discussed in Chapters 13 and 14), that is,

1. At acquisition—measuring and recording acquisition cost.
2. During period of use—measuring, recording, and reporting expiration of the service potential over the period of benefit. This process of recording allocation of the acquisition cost of intangibles is usually referred to as *amortization.*
3. At disposition—recording and reporting disposal at date of sale, exchange, or end of the economic useful life.

Accounting and reporting for intangible assets acquired after October 1970 is prescribed by *APB Opinion No. 17,* "Intangible Assets." Accounting for intangible assets acquired on or before October 31, 1970, may be accounted for in accordance with *APB Opinion No. 17* or *ARB No. 43,* chapter 5 (otherwise this *ARB* was superseded by the *Opinion*).

Prior to *APB Opinion No. 17,* intangible assets were accounted for on the basis of *life expectancy.* Intangible assets having limited lives were identified as *Type A;* they were amortized over their estimated period of future use. Intangible assets having indeterminate lives were identified as *Type B* and were not amortized until a realistic determination of useful life could be made. Often this determination was never made; hence, the cost of many Type B intangibles were never amortized. *Opinion No. 17,* among other things, stopped this practice (for assets acquired after October 1970) by providing that

> . . . the value of intangible assets at any one date eventually disappears and . . . the recorded costs of intangible assets should be amortized by systematic charges to income over the periods estimated to be benefited. . . . The cost of each type of intangible should be amortized on the basis of the estimated life of that specific asset. . . . The period of amortization should not, however, exceed 40 years.

MEASURING AND RECORDING INTANGIBLE ASSETS AT ACQUISITION

Intangible assets should be recorded at acquisition at their current cash equivalent cost in conformity with the cost principle. When an intangible asset is acquired for some consideration other than cash, cost is determined by either the market value of the consideration given or by the market value of the right acquired, whichever is the more clearly determinable. For example, if a patent is acquired by the issuance of capital stock, the cost of the patent may be determined as the market value of the shares of stock issued; or if the shares issued do not have an established market value consistent with the volume issued for the patent, then evidence of the market value of the patent should be sought as the measurement of cost in the transaction.[2]

Classification of the Cost of Intangible Assets

With intangibles, as in the case of property, plant, and equipment, costs must be carefully classified in the accounts to facilitate subsequent accounting. Proper accounting for cost requires that where two or more intangible assets are acquired at a single lump-sum purchase price, an allocation of the joint cost should be made to determine the cost basis of each intangible involved. Allocation of the cost of intangibles acquired in a "basket purchase" may be made by using the methods described for tangible assets, such as the relative sales value method (see Chapter 13).

AMORTIZATION OF THE COST OF INTANGIBLE ASSETS

The cost of intangible assets should be *amortized* by systematic debits to expense over

---

[2] Unfortunately the accounting profession uses *fair value, market value, fair market value,* and *current market value* to describe the arm's-length price of an asset used in certain transactions and valuations. We generally use *market value* in this text because it is fully descriptive of the intended meaning. The word "fair" implies that "unfair" values might be used in the accounts, and the modifier "current" is redundant because market value presumes the one prevailing at the relevant time.

the estimated periods of useful life, just as the cost of tangible assets having a limited period of usefulness is depreciated. Capricious and arbitrary determination of the amount to be amortized as expense from period to period distorts income and violates the *matching principle.* Neither is it desirable from the standpoint of income determination to accelerate the amortization process and write off the cost of intangibles substantially before the end of their usefulness. Intangible assets often are (because of precedent) amortized by a direct credit to the asset account rather than to an allowance (contra) account and a debit to expense.

In estimating the future useful life of an intangible asset the following factors should be considered:[3]

a. Legal, regulatory, or contractual provisions may limit the maximum useful life.

b. Provisions for renewal or extension may alter a specified limit on useful life.

c. Effects of obsolescence, demand, and other economic factors may reduce useful life.

d. Useful life may parallel the service life expectancies of individuals or groups of employees.

e. Expected actions of competitors and others may restrict present competitive advantages.

f. An apparently unlimited useful life may in fact be indefinite, and benefits cannot be reasonably projected.

g. An intangible asset may be a composite of many individual factors with varying effective useful lives.

The method of amortization should be systematic and should reflect over time the decline in economic service value of the intangible. Thus, any of the depreciation methods discussed in Chapter 14 may be appropriate. Perhaps reflecting precedent rather than economic realities, *APB Opinion No. 17* states that "the straight-line method of amortization—equal annual amounts—should be applied unless a company demonstrates that another systematic method is more appropriate." The *Opinion* also

states that changes in amortization rates should be *prospective;* that is, the remaining unamortized cost should be amortized over the remaining life, but not to exceed 40 years after acquisition. Intangibles very rarely have a residual value.

DISPOSAL OF INTANGIBLE ASSETS

When an intangible asset is sold, exchanged, or otherwise disposed of, the unamortized cost (or cost and accumulated amortization if separately recorded) must be removed from the accounts and a gain or loss on disposal recorded.

Because analysts often viewed intangibles as of questionable asset value and because of over-conservatism, accounting practice in the past tended to encourage their arbitrary writedown to a nominal amount, either by lump sum in one period or over an unrealistically short estimated life. Contemporary accounting principles and practice do not permit this arbitrary practice, because it misstates income and financial position. On this point, *APB Opinion No. 17* states that intangible assets "should not be written off in the period of acquisition" and "analysis of all factors should result in a reasonable estimate of the useful life. . . ."

On the other hand, in common with all assets, during the period of use, an estimate of value and future benefits of an intangible asset may indicate that the unamortized cost exceeds the economic utility (i.e., use value) to the enterprise. In such situations the unamortized cost should be written down to reflect the evident *impairment* of value. The revised value should be amortized over the estimated remaining useful life, not to exceed 40 years from date of acquisition (see *APB Opinion No. 17,* par. 31). When there is a writedown because of impairment of value, disclosure is required in notes to the financial statements.

IDENTIFIABLE INTANGIBLE ASSETS

Identifiable intangible assets are so designated because they can be specifically and separately identified from the enterprise itself. Thus, they can be sold separately. Examples are patents, copyrights, franchises, and trademarks

---

[3] AICPA, *APB Opinion No. 17,* "Intangible Assets" (New York, 1970), par. 27.

(but not goodwill). They may be *(a)* acquired by purchase or *(b)* developed internally. In either instance, they are recorded initially at cost, in conformance with the cost principle, and the cost is expensed in the same period or amortized as economic service value declines in conformance with the matching principle.

Because of the wide variety of intangible assets, the procedures tend to vary somewhat in applying the foregoing principles and guidelines. In the next few paragraphs, we will discuss the specifically identifiable intangible assets commonly encountered in business.

Patents

A patent is an exclusive right recognized by law and registered with the U.S. Patent Office; a patent enables the holder to use, manufacture, sell, and control the patent without interference or infringement by others. In reality the registration of the patent with the Patent Office is no guarantee of protection. Therefore, the patent is not conclusive until it has been successfully defended in court. For this reason there is general agreement that the cost of *successful* court tests should be capitalized as part of the cost of the patent.

The cost of a patent acquired by purchase is determined according to the *cost principle;* that is, cost of a purchased patent is the market value of the consideration given or of the asset received, whichever is more clearly determinable. Internally developed patents resulting from the company's own research and development activities must be accounted for as specified by *FASB Statement No. 2* as discussed under the heading "Research and Development Costs." Succinctly, this means that laboratory costs leading to the development of the patent must be expensed as incurred. The only costs of an internally developed patent that can be capitalized are legal fees and other costs associated with registration of the patent such as models and drawings required for the registration.

Patents have a legal life of 17 years. The useful life of most patents is shorter because technological progress, substitute products, and other improvements cause the product or process covered by the patents to lose their competitive advantage before 17 years elapse. Patent costs should be amortized over the useful life or legal life, whichever is shorter.

Copyrights

A copyright is a form of protection given by law to the authors of literary, musical, artistic, and similar works. Owners of copyrights are granted certain exclusive rights such as *(a)* to print, reprint, and copy the work; *(b)* to sell or distribute copies; and *(c)* to perform and record the work.

A new copyright law became effective in January 1978. Under its provisions, copyrighted works already protected by law retain the then-existing copyright term of 28 years, renewable under some conditions for an additional period of protection of 47 years. For works created after January 1978, the new law provides a term lasting for the author's life plus an added 50 years. Copyrights can be transferred, and most business entities owning copyrights have received them by transfer. Under the new law, authors or certain heirs can terminate transfers of copyrights after 35 years under certain conditions.

As a practical matter, few copyrights have economic value for nearly so long a period as their legal lives or the terms for which transfers are effective. Costs of copyrights should be amortized over the period the copyrighted items are expected to produce revenue. In no case is it permissible to amortize a copyright acquired after October 1970 over a period exceeding 40 years.

Franchises

A common type of franchise is a grant by a governmental unit for use of public properties or to furnish public-utility type services. Costs of obtaining a franchise should be recorded in a Franchise account and should be amortized over the term of the franchise or 40 years, whichever is shorter.

Another common type of franchise involves the granting of a right by one entity to another entity to use a specific designation (such as Kentucky Fried Chicken) subject to certain obligations agreed to by the contracting parties. Again, accounting for the franchise by the franchisee (i.e., the purchaser) involves initial capitalization of the cost of the asset (the right under franchise) and its subsequent amortization over the shorter of useful life or 40 years.

Trademarks

Trademarks can be registered with the federal patent office to help prove ownership. Thus, names, symbols, or other devices providing distinctive identity for a product are afforded a degree of legal protection. Amounts paid or incurred directly for the acquisition, protection, expansion, registration, or defense of a trademark or trade name should be capitalized. Such capitalized balances should be amortized over the useful life of the trademark or 40 years, whichever is shorter.

UNIDENTIFIABLE INTANGIBLE ASSETS

Unidentifiable intangible assets are so designated because they result from a number of concurrent economic factors and cannot be separately identified from the enterprise. Examples are goodwill and going value. Unidentifiable intangible assets can be *(a)* purchased externally through the acquisition of a going business (not purchased singly) or *(b)* developed internally by excellent business practices, providing superior goods and services, promotion, and so on, all of which build long-range customer appeal.

In contrast to identifiable intangible assets, unidentifiable intangible assets are recorded and reported *only when acquired by purchase.* In this situation, the cost of unidentifiable intangible assets usually can be realistically measured. *APB Opinion No. 17* states:

> The cost of unidentifiable intangible assets is measured by the difference between the cost of the group of assets or enterprise acquired and the sum of the assigned costs of individual tangible and identifiable intangible assets acquired less liabilities assumed.

To illustrate the *purchase* of unidentifiable intangible assets (collectively often called goodwill), assume X Company purchased Y Company with the following results:

Purchase price		$900,000
Assets acquired from Y Company (at market value):		
Tangible assets	$890,000	
Identifiable intangibles:		
Patent	14,000	
Franchise	16,000	
Total.	920,000	
Less: Liabilities of Y Company assumed.	120,000	
Net identifiable market values acquired		800,000
Difference—unidentifiable intangible assets (i.e., goodwill). . .		$100,000

In contrast, unidentifiable intangible assets *developed internally* by the company are not capitalized under generally accepted accounting principles. *APB Opinion No. 17* states that continuing costs (as opposed to the purchase cost) of developing, maintaining, or restoring unidentifiable intangible assets "inherent in a continuing business and related to the enterprise as a whole—such as goodwill—should be deducted from income when incurred."

Goodwill

Goodwill represents the potential of a business to earn "above-normal" profits. It arises as a result of such factors as customer acceptance, efficient operations, reputation for dependability, location, and the like. Goodwill should be recorded only when a business is purchased and the price paid exceeds the market value of all tangible and identifiable intangible assets acquired minus any liabilities assumed. The cost of goodwill should represent a valuation placed on the *above-normal earning capacity* of the business. Conceptually, goodwill is the *present value* of the expected future excess (i.e., above-normal) earnings.

In the normal process of building up a business over time, an element of goodwill is developed. This "internally developed goodwill," in contrast to purchased goodwill, is not properly reflected in the accounts for two basic reasons: (1) there has been no direct and identifiable disbursement for it, as was the case for other assets such as fixtures and purchased assets; and (2) to the extent that expenses (such as promotion costs) have been incurred that may have indirectly contributed to goodwill, they have been reflected in past income statements as expenses and any attempt to separate them out would be arbitrary.[4]

Amortization of Goodwill. Accounting for purchased goodwill is controversial. One view is that it should not be amortized but should be reported as an intangible asset until there is definite evidence of its demise (such as failure to earn excess profits). Another view is that it should be deducted in full from capital at date of acquisition. Still another view is that it should be amortized over a realistic period during which the above-normal or superior earnings contemplated in the purchase decision are being realized.[5]

Some argue that there should be no amortization of goodwill so long as profits are above normal. The logical extension of this argument would be *(a)* to write it off directly to capital or *(b)* to amortize goodwill only when "excess" profits fail to materialize.

The argument in favor of amortization is that purchased goodwill, like any other operational asset, was acquired to generate earnings and,

like other assets, its cost should be amortized against those earnings. Thus, the conclusion of traditional accounting thought is that goodwill should be amortized when the superior earnings are being realized. The argument continues that the purchase decision contemplated a specific amount of goodwill which had already been developed at the date of purchase. The purchaser envisioned a particularly profitable period in the future for which a price would be paid, the price for this "excess" profitability is the cost of the *original goodwill purchased.* The cost of acquired goodwill should then be amortized over the expected period of excess earnings contemplated in the purchase decision.

These arguments were resolved, as far as current practice is concerned, by *APB Opinion No. 17.* It requires that goodwill be amortized by systematic charges each period, using the straight-line method, "unless a company demonstrates that another systematic method is more appropriate." The amortization period must be the estimated useful life, but not more than 40 years from date of purchase.

Amortization of goodwill is not permitted for income tax purposes—it causes a permanent tax difference (discussed in Chapter 9); therefore, allocation of income taxes is inappropriate.

Estimating Goodwill. In negotiations relating to the purchase or sale of a business, the accountant may be requested to assist in valuing goodwill. Computations based upon an analysis of asset values and income potential frequently are useful in such negotiations, since goodwill relates to the excess earning capacity of the business. *However, in such circumstances goodwill is the result of bargaining between the purchaser and seller.* In such analyses it must be emphasized that *future earning potentials* rather than past earnings are significant. However, past earnings, properly adjusted, may provide a sound basis for estimating future potentials. In estimating future earnings, the earnings history of the firm should be studied. As a basis for estimating future earnings, the following steps may be suggested:

1. Select for study a series of past years' earnings which appear to be most representative

---

[4] A business that is established and operating but with only average profits is more valuable than a collection of similar assets and liabilities about to be launched as a business. This difference, the "more valuable" aspect, is the essence of *going value* (sometimes called *going concern value*). Thus, going value is akin to goodwill but different from it. Goodwill relates to above-average profitability; going value does not. Goodwill is fairly commonly recorded and reported on financial statements. Going value is seldom found on books or statements. In acquisition transactions where goodwill is properly recognized, a portion of the payment may actually represent a payment for going value, but separation of the two is almost never attempted. Any going value in such a case is usually subsumed under goodwill.

[5] It is sometimes alleged that goodwill can be negative. Cases cited are where the book value of assets purchased exceeds the overall purchase price paid for an entity, or alternatively where the sum of the market values of individual assets exceeds the overall purchase price. In the opinion of the authors, such an excess is not negative goodwill. Book value has no inherent relationship to market value. Market values of assets sold individually may not be the same as what can be realized if the assets are sold as a package, but an informed seller is unlikely to dispose of a group of assets for less than could be realized by selling them individually. There are situations where the cost of a business may be less than book value or less than the sum of the market values of specific assets; however, this does not give rise to *negative goodwill. APB Opinion No. 16* requires revaluation of the tangible and intangible assets acquired in a purchase transaction so that no negative goodwill is recognized.

of usual operations and indicative of future expectations. The period of years should be long enough to reveal the pattern of earnings fluctuations experienced by the company and short enough to use the data most relevant to the prediction.

2. Adjust these past earnings for all
   a. Unusual and/or nonrecurring gains and losses.
   b. Earnings effects of accounting changes, estimates, and methods.
   c. Changes which are expected to occur in expenses and revenues in the future.
3. Analyze the trend and uniformity of past earnings. Even though past earnings have been above normal, any observed downward trend in the immediate past may indicate the disappearance of above-normal earning capacity. Such a downward trend may negate any basis for goodwill value.
4. On the basis of the above analysis, project the future earnings and assets. Econometric methods are available for this estimation process.

Within the above framework, several approaches to *estimating* the value of goodwill are discussed below. To illustrate, assume that on January 1, 1979, it is desired to estimate the goodwill for Company X and that the data in Exhibit 15–1 are available.

Assume after careful analysis of the data in Part A of Exhibit 15–1, appraisal of the assets, and other pertinent factors, that the projections in Part B were derived.

We will illustrate four unsophisticated methods and one conceptually sound approach to the estimation of goodwill.

Capitalization of Earnings. The expected earnings may be capitalized at a "normal" rate of return for the industry in order to estimate the total net asset value. The difference between this value (total asset value implied) and the average net assets expected (exclusive of goodwill) may be used as a rough approximation of goodwill. To illustrate, assuming an estimated "normal" rate of return of 12%, goodwill for Company X may be computed as follows:

Estimated future average annual earnings	$20,000	
Normal rate of return for the industry	12%	
Total net asset value implied ($20,000 ÷ 12%)		$166,667
Average net assets expected (exclusive of goodwill)		100,000
Estimated goodwill		$ 66,667
Total net asset valuation including goodwill ($100,000 + $66,667)		$166,667

Capitalization of Excess Earnings. The preceding method is deficient in that it does not recognize *excess* earnings as a special factor. Capitalization of excess earnings requires the projection of a special rate to be applied to such earnings. The special capitalization rate should represent the planned annual rate of recovery of investment in the intangible as a result of excess earnings. The special rate should be higher than the normal rate because of the greater risk of not earning above the "normal" rate. The greater the risk, the higher the rate should be.

To illustrate the computation for Company X, assume an estimated normal rate on assets of 12% and a capitalization rate of 15% for the excess earnings.

EXHIBIT 15–1
Estimation of Goodwill

A. Historical Data

Year	Earnings (adjusted for nonrecurring and/or unusual items)	Book Values		
		Total Assets	Liabilities	Owners' Equity
1974	$18,000	$162,000	$ 82,000	$ 80,000
1975	17,000	172,000	90,000	82,000
1976	19,000	190,000	105,000	85,000
1977	19,000	187,000	90,000	97,000
1978	21,000	200,000	98,000	102,000
Total	$94,000	$911,000	$465,000	$446,000
Five-year average	$18,800	$182,200	$ 93,000	$ 89,200

B. Projections

Estimated future average annual earnings expected	$ 20,000
Estimated average net asset value (i.e., net assets exclusive of goodwill)	100,000

Estimated future average annual earnings	$20,000	
Return on average net assets expected (exclusive of goodwill) at the normal rate ($100,000 × 12%)	12,000	
Excess earnings expected	$ 8,000	
Goodwill: Excess earnings capitalized at 15% ($8,000 ÷ 15%)		$ 53,333
Total net asset valuation including goodwill ($100,000 + $53,333)		$153,333

Years' Purchase of Average Excess Earnings.
The goodwill may be estimated more directly by multiplying the estimated excess earnings by the number of years over which the investor expects to recover the investment in goodwill from the above-normal earnings of the business. To illustrate, assume the expected period of recovery is six years:

Excess earnings (computed above)	$ 8,000
Expected period of recovery	6 years
Estimated goodwill	$ 48,000
Total net asset valuation including goodwill ($100,000 + $48,000)	$148,000

This last method implicitly assumes an amortization period of six years for goodwill.

Years' Purchase of Average Earnings. A modification of the above method ignores excess earnings and focuses instead on average annual earnings. It is conceptually deficient because it does not use *excess* earnings to estimate goodwill; recall that goodwill is the asset representation of the cost of purchasing *excess* earning potential.

Estimated future average annual earnings	$ 20,000
Purchase of four years' earnings (multiply by 4)	× 4
Estimated goodwill	$ 80,000
Total net asset valuation including goodwill ($100,000 + $80,000)	$180,000

Under this method some goodwill could be estimated even though below-normal earnings were

expected. For example, if average annual earnings expected were $7,000, an estimated goodwill of $28,000 would result despite the fact that annual earnings were *below* the average earnings for the preceding five-year period (see Exhibit 15–1).

Present Value Estimation of Goodwill

A conceptually sound approach to estimating (and amortizing) goodwill is to determine the *present value of the future excess earnings purchased.* To illustrate, assume for the above example that the negotiations implied the purchase of estimated future excess earnings for ten years in addition to the identifiable net assets and that the expected earnings rate on goodwill was 15%. Computation of the implied goodwill would be as follows:

Excess earnings (computed above)	$ 8,000
Present value of excess earnings: $8,000 × $P_{o_{n=10, i=15\%}}$ $8,000 × 5.01877 (Table 6–4)	$ 40,150
Estimated average value of net assets excluding goodwill	100,000
Total net asset valuation including goodwill	$140,150

The purchase at $140,150 would be recorded as follows:

Identifiable assets (detailed)	100,000	
Goodwill	40,150	
Cash (or other considerations)		140,150

The goodwill would then be amortized over ten years as in Exhibit 15–2.

Straight-line amortization over the ten-year period could be used; however, the present value approach shown in Exhibit 15–2 is in harmony with the nature of goodwill, since the present value amortization implicitly recognizes a constant rate of return per period on the investment in goodwill. As the goodwill loses value over time, the return per period (dollar amount) correspondingly decreases (column [b] of Exhibit 15–2). Thus, the recovery of the principal amount of investment in goodwill (column [c]) increases over time, and this results in a greater periodic amortization of goodwill in the later years. This expense configuration may be espe-

EXHIBIT 15-2
Goodwill Amortized on Present Value (or interest) Method

Year	(a) Annual Excess Earnings	(b) (15%) Return on Goodwill Investment	(c) Goodwill Amortization Expense (dr.) Goodwill (cr.)	(d) Goodwill Carrying Value
Start				$40,150
1	$8,000	$6,023	$1,977	38,173
2	8,000	5,726	2,274	35,899
3	8,000	5,385	2,615	33,284
4	8,000	4,993	3,007	30,277
5	8,000	4,542	3,458	26,819
6	8,000	4,023	3,977	22,842
7	8,000	3,426	4,574	18,268
8	8,000	2,740	5,260	13,008
9	8,000	1,951	6,049	6,959
10	8,000	1,041	6,959	—

(a) Projected annual excess earnings.
(b) 15% of previous goodwill balance ($40,150 × .15 = $6,023, etc.).
(c) Column (a) − (b).
(d) Previous balance minus column (c).

cially appropriate in many cases since the purchased goodwill, as part of the price of acquiring a going business, may diminish less per year in the early years (after an ownership change) and more in the later years.

DEFERRED CHARGES

Deferred charges are intangibles and are closely related to intangible assets as defined in the preceding section of this chapter. Whereas intangible assets derive value based on *rights*, deferred charges derive asset value in a different way because long-term prepayments of expenses contribute to the production of future revenues. Also, deferred charges are akin to prepaid expenses (a short-term intangible reported as a current asset). Examples of deferred charges are bond and capital stock issue costs, organization costs, machinery rearrangement costs, long-term prepaid insurance premiums, and prepaid leasehold costs.

A special item, debit balances, arising from interperiod income tax allocation, is reported under the classification of deferred charges.

Deferred charges are amortized over the future periods during which they will contribute to the generation of future revenues. The 40-year rule specified in *APB Opinion No. 17* does not apply to deferred charges; however, they seldom, if ever, have lives that long.

In the next few paragraphs we will discuss the deferred charges usually encountered in accounting.

Organization Costs

Expenditures are incurred as an integral part of organization and promotion of a corporation. Costs such as legal fees, state incorporation fees, stock certificate costs, stamp taxes, underwriting costs, and office expenses incident to organizing are capitalized as *organization costs* on the basis that such costs benefit the operations of future years. To expense the total amount in the first year of operation would result in an incorrect matching of expense and revenue. Since the life of a corporation generally is indefinite, the length of the period which will receive the benefits of this cost is usually indeterminate. For this reason, and because the recognition of organization costs as a business asset depends entirely upon intangible values presumably attached to the corporate form of organization for the particular business, organization expenses generally are amortized over an arbitrarily selected short period. This practice is encouraged by the tax rules, which permit the corporation to amortize most organization costs ratably over such period as the company desires as long as that period is not less than five years.

There is a troublesome amortization problem in accounting for *stock issue costs;* that is, the costs of printing stock certificates, attorney fees related directly to the issue of stock, commissions paid for sale, and accountants' fees (such as the cost of filing with the SEC). Three approaches to accounting for stock issue costs are found in practice:

1. *Debit such costs to the asset account Organization Costs and amortize under the "40-year" rule.* Although this is a fairly common practice, many accountants feel that it is conceptually deficient because (a) the cost relationship to future revenues is tenuous, (b) costs should be amortized over the indefinite life of the corporation, and (c) this treatment is applied only at date of organization.

2. *Offset such costs against the sales price of the stock.* Under this practice they would be included in the determination of stock discount or premium. In this alternative such costs would not be separately recognized and amortized against future revenues. It poses a troublesome problem when the net amount received by the corporation is less than the total amount paid by the stockholders so that a discount is created. This approach appears to be the most widely used primarily because *(a)* frequently the issue costs are not separable from the issue transaction, *(b)* the costs often are not material in amount, *(c)* amortization problems are avoided, and *(d)* it is equally appropriate for all issues of stock.

3. *Debit such costs to a deferred charge and amortize them in a manner similar to organization expense.* This approach is similar in concept, advantages, and disadvantages to Method 1 above except for the balance sheet classification. As a practical matter, under this method the costs generally are amortized over a short period.

Leaseholds

When a business leases property from its owner under an operating lease and makes prepayments which cover the term of the lease (such as a "lease bonus" payment to secure the lease), the prepayment is properly charged to an asset account commonly called Leasehold. The balance is amortized over the period benefited (which is usually the lease term), and the periodic amortization is usually accorded the same accounting treatment as periodic rental payments under the lease. Leasehold improvements such as costly modifications of the leased property are sometimes charged to the Leasehold account and are sometimes set up in a separate Leasehold Improvements account. Leasehold Improvements should be amortized over the term of the lease or the life of the improvements, whichever is shorter. Accounting for leaseholds is illustrated in Chapter 22.

Research and Development Costs

Research and development costs, commonly called R&D, are among the most important expenditures made by modern industrial companies. The tabulation in Exhibit 15–3 indicates the significance of R&D.

At one time, unamortized R&D costs were a significant balance sheet asset and were properly reported as a deferred charge. Accounting practice for R&D costs was, however, quite varied; some companies charged R&D costs to expense in the period they were incurred; others deferred varying portions of their R&D expenditures as assets, and practice as to amortization of the deferred portion was far from uniform. This variety of practice as to accounting for such

EXHIBIT 15–3
Significance of R&D

	Millions		R&D Costs as % of Sales	R&D Costs as % of Profits	R&D Costs per Employee
	Sales of Industry	R&D Expense			
Industry					
Aerospace	$ 25,589	$ 884.5	3.5	131.3	$1,668
Automotive	116,799	2,941.7	2.5	57.8	1,501
Chemicals	56,221	1,438.8	2.6	39.7	1,720
Food and beverages	59,888	301.9	.5	12.4	337
Office equipment and computers	36,839	1,978.1	5.4	55.8	2,347
All industries	867,174	16,224.7	1.9	33.9	1,149

Source: *Business Week,* June 27, 1977, pp. 62–84.

an important expenditure received the attention of the FASB and resulted in the issuance of *FASB Statement No. 2,* "Accounting for Research and Development Costs," in 1974. This *Statement* specifies accounting practices for R&D costs.

Among other things, *Statement No. 2* provided that

1. All R&D costs covered by the *Statement* shall be charged to expense when incurred. Stated another way, R&D expenditures (except for item 3 below) must not be capitalized.
2. Financial statements must disclose *total* R&D costs charged to expense in each period for which an income statement is presented.
3. Item 1 above does not apply to R&D costs where work is done for others under contract. Also, exceptions were made for certain government-regulated entities. In other words, in these areas, R&D costs can be charged to an asset account when incurred.
4. The *Statement* became effective for fiscal years beginning on or after January 1, 1975. Those entities that had capitalized R&D costs on their books at that date were required to write them off by means of a prior period adjustment.

As specified by the FASB in *Statement No. 2,* R&D costs encompass those costs of materials, equipment and facilities, personnel, intangibles purchased from others, contract services, and allocated indirect costs specifically related to R&D and not having alternative future uses. These would include the following

a. Laboratory research aimed at discovery of new knowledge.
b. Searching for applications of new research findings or other knowledge.
c. Conceptual formulation and design of possible product or process alternatives.
d. Testing in search for or evaluation of product or process alternatives.
e. Modification of the formulation or design of a product or process.
f. Design, construction, and testing of preproduction prototypes and models.

g. Design of tools, jigs, molds, and dies involving new technology.
h. Design, construction, and operation of a pilot plant that is not of a scale economically feasible to the enterprise for commercial production.
i. Engineering activity required to advance the design of a product to the point that it meets specific functional and economic requirements and is ready for manufacture.

It can be argued that *Statement No. 2* represents a practical solution to what had been a serious problem. Study had indicated it was difficult to establish criteria for deferment of R&D costs and, as noted above, there was considerable diversity of practice in accounting for R&D. One of the chief aims of standard-setting bodies such as the FASB is to reduce diversity of accounting practice.

Critics of *Statement No. 2* argue that while direct charge-off of R&D costs might yield about the same periodic expense as capitalization and amortization of R&D, the balance sheet consequences are hard to defend. In essence, the standard requires companies to report that none of their R&D expenditures has future benefit since no intangible or deferred charge related to R&D can appear on the balance sheet.[6] Successful companies operating in areas such as those for which R&D amounts were cited at the start of this discussion actually have almost priceless assets as a result of their R&D efforts, but no amount related to R&D costs appears on their balance sheets. Regardless of which side of the argument has more appeal to you, the standard has had strong support as reflected in accounting practice and has eliminated a major area of diversity.

As noted in the earlier discussion of patents, companies can no longer apportion a part of their R&D expenditures to the cost of an internally developed patent. Patent costs can include cost of *securing* the patent but not expenditures

---

[6] A company owning a laboratory facility in which R&D activities are conducted and which has alternative future uses (in R&D projects or otherwise) should account for the facility as an operational asset. Depreciation and other costs related to such facilities should be accounted for as R&D expenses.

which led to the development of what is being patented.

ACCOUNTING FOR EXPLORATION COSTS

Oil and gas producing companies have, for many years, used either of two accounting methods to account for costs incurred in searching for and developing oil and gas reserves. Many smaller companies used the *full cost* method under which they capitalized the costs associated with both producing wells and those which were unsuccessful (dry holes). The full cost method was based largely on the theoretical argument that the cost of drilling dry holes is as much a part of exploration activities as is the cost of drilling producing wells. Stated differently, "You have to drill dry holes to find oil and gas." In this view, such dry hole costs should be capitalized and amortized over the future because such dry hole costs were incurred to benefit the operations of future periods.

Most larger oil companies used the *successful efforts* method under which they capitalized only the costs of searching for and developing producing wells; they charged to expense the costs associated with dry holes (as soon as they were sure of the outcome) on the theory that dry hole costs produce no oil and provide no benefit for future periods.

In February 1978, the FASB attempted to eliminate this dichotomy when it issued *FASB Statement No. 19,* "Financial Accounting and Reporting by Oil and Gas Producing Companies." This *Statement* rejected the full cost method and required all oil and gas producing companies to use the successful efforts method. In articulating its position, the FASB asserted that similar activities should be accounted for similarly and that they found no basis for allowing different methods of accounting for the same type of event to produce different asset values and income amounts.

Accounting requirements of *FASB Statement No. 19* include the following:

1. Oil and gas companies are required to use a version of the "successful efforts" method of accounting for costs incurred in searching for and developing oil and gas reserves. In essence, this means that only the costs of *successful* wells can be capitalized and subsequently amortized. Costs of *unsuccessful* exploratory wells (dry holes) must be charged off to expense as soon as a determination is made they are unsuccessful. See also Item 6 below. Full costing (a procedure which would capitalize costs of both successful and unsuccessful wells with subsequent amortization of the capitalized costs) is prohibited.

2. Mineral interests in properties are recorded as assets when acquired.

3. All exploration costs except the costs of drilling exploratory wells are recorded as expense when incurred.

4. The costs of drilling exploratory wells are accumulated in a temporary inventory account, "Construction in Process," when incurred. Later, if a well is unsuccessful, the accumulated costs are transferred to expense. On the other hand, if proved reserves result from the well, the costs are reclassified as an amortizable asset.

5. In the case of offshore wells or those in remote areas, if producible quantities of reserves are found but classification of those reserves as "proved" depends on whether additional exploratory wells confirm sufficient additional reserves to justify major expenditures (such as additional offshore drilling platforms or a gathering system), the cost of drilling the wells can be deferred as "Construction in Process" if the added exploratory drilling is definitely planned or is under way.

6. After recoverable reserves have been confirmed, the costs of drilling *developmental* wells are capitalized as amortizable assets. Even costs of dry holes drilled to develop proved reserves can be capitalized.

7. Capitalized acquisition, exploration, and development costs are related to proved reserves.

Unfortunately, in a move which many perceived as a severe setback to the private sector's efforts to determine accounting principles, in August 1978 the SEC determined that "traditional accounting methods—successful efforts and full cost—failed to provide sufficient useful information on the financial position and operating results of oil and gas producers." It went on to say that requiring either method as a uniform basis of accounting and reporting would be unwarranted.

The Commission indicated that it would undertake a major effort to develop "Reserve Recognition Accounting" (RRA) which ultimately may evolve as a form of exit value accounting (see Part B of Chapter 7). The SEC plans to develop RRA sufficiently so that by 1981 RRA will replace the two traditional methods. Meanwhile, it will continue to accept financial statements prepared under the successful efforts method as prescribed in *Statement No. 19* or the full cost method under rules it will promulgate. In light of these developments *FASB Statement No. 25,* "Suspension of Certain Accounting Requirements for Oil and Gas Producing Companies," was issued in February 1979. It suspended the effective data of applying *FASB Statement No. 19* related to the successful efforts method. Oil and gas producing companies *not* subject to SEC reporting requirements can use either the successful efforts or full costing methods. As RRA is developed, other companies must move to it as directed by the SEC.

DEVELOPMENT STAGE COMPANIES

The subject of accounting for companies in the development stage is closely akin to deferred charges because such companies in the past deferred a wide range of costs. This was done because, during the development stage, they incur high start-up costs and generally have little or no revenues against which they can be matched.

Because of the lack of guidelines and the wide variety of practices, the FASB issued *Statement of Financial Accounting Standards No. 7,* "Accounting and Reporting by Development Stage Companies" (June 1975).

The *Statement* defines development stage companies essentially as follows:

> An enterprise shall be considered to be in the development stage if it is devoting substantially all of its efforts to establishing a new business and either of the following conditions exists: (a)

planned principal operations have not commenced or (b) planned principal operations have commenced but there has been no significant revenue therefrom. A development stage enterprise will typically be devoting most of its efforts to activities such as financial planning; raising capital; exploring for natural resources; developing natural resources; research and development; establishing sources of supply; acquiring property, plant, or other operating assets, such as mineral rights; recruiting and training personnel; developing markets; and starting up production.

Prior to the issuance of *Statement No. 7,* the accounting practices of development stage companies included the following, which many accountants felt did not accord with generally accepted accounting principles: (a) deferral of various types of costs without regard to their future benefits and recoverability; (b) issuance of special types of statements, including statements of assets and unrecovered preoperating costs; and (c) other related practices which were outside the mainstream of generally accepted accounting principles.

To correct these abuses, *Statement No. 7* requires development stage companies to present financial statements prepared on the same basis as other businesses; special reporting formats are unacceptable. Capitalization and deferral of costs are subject to the same assessment of future benefit and recoverability applicable to established businesses. Thus, the Statement specifies that a development stage company is required to prepare basic statements and provide additional disclosure as follows:

a. A balance sheet, including any cumulative net losses reported with a descriptive caption such as "deficit accumulated during the development stage" in the owners' equity section.

b. An income statement, showing amounts of revenue and expenses for each period covered by the income statement and, in addition, cumulative amounts from the enterprise's inception.

c. A statement of changes in financial position, showing the sources and uses of financial resources for each period for which an income statement is presented and, in addition, cumulative amounts from the enterprise's inception.

d. A statement of stockholders' equity, showing from the enterprise's inception for each stock issuance:
1. Date and number of shares issued for cash or other consideration.
2. Dollar amounts (per share or other equity unit) assigned to consideration received for securities.
3. Where there is noncash consideration, its nature and the basis of determining amounts.[7]

The *Statement* also required that the financial statements be *specifically identified* as those of a development stage enterprise and include a description of the nature of the development stage in which the enterprise is engaged.

INSURANCE

Practically all businesses carry one or more kinds of insurance. Insurance requires prepayment of the premium, at which time an asset having intangible characteristics is created. Depending on the type of insurance and time covered, the prepaid premium may be *(a)* a current asset (i.e., short-term prepayments), *(b)* a long-term investment (i.e., cash surrender value of life insurance policies), or *(c)* a deferred charge (i.e., long-term prepayments).

Although there are many different kinds of insurance, the usual kinds carried by businesses include *(a)* liability insurance, *(b)* casualty insurance, and *(c)* life insurance on key executives. The remainder of the chapter discusses and illustrates the accounting for various aspects of intangibles related to insurance.

Liability Insurance

Liability insurance involves a contract whereby the insurance company, in consideration for a stated premium, is contractually obligated for certain liabilities to third parties that arise from specified events such as damages

---

[7] Adapted from FASB *Statement of Financial Accounting Standards No. 7,* "Accounting and Reporting by Development Stage Enterprises" (Stamford, Conn., June 1975), par. 11.

sought by a customer for injuries in an accident on company premises. The premium typically is paid in advance for periods of one to five years. Prepaid premiums represent an intangible asset. To illustrate, assume that on January 1, 19A, Company B paid a $2,500 five-year premium for a liability insurance policy. The accounting and reporting for 19A would be as follows:

Entries:

January 1, 19A—insurance premium paid:

Prepaid insurance	2,500	
Cash		2,500

December 31, 19A—adjusting entry:

Insurance expense	500	
Prepaid insurance		500

Reporting at December 31, 19A:

Income Statement:	
Insurance expense	500
Balance Sheet:	
Current Assets:	
Prepaid insurance	500
Deferred Charges:	
Prepaid insurance, long term	1,500

Casualty Insurance

Casualty insurance involves a contract whereby the insurance company in consideration for a premium payment assumes an obligation under certain circumstances to reimburse the policyholder an amount not exceeding the *market value* (at date of loss) of the property lost due to storm, fire, and so forth, as specified in the policy. The indemnity in no case exceeds the amount stipulated in the contract, that is, the *face* of the policy.

The great diversity in the forms of policies and the legal status of their provisions in the past caused most states to adopt a standard policy. The companies are allowed a certain degree of flexibility in varying the terms of the standard policy by attaching "riders" or endorsements (standardized paragraphs).

The premium, a charge per $100 of insurance carried, usually is computed on a standard basis, depending upon the nature of the asset insured. For example, in the case of insurance on a building, the premium is adjusted for such things as type of construction, kind of roof, types of flues, occupancy by owner or tenant, space rented for commercial use in the building, and location.

When a policy is canceled at the request of the insurance company, the insured is entitled to a refund of a pro rata portion of the premium, which covers the unexpired policy term. If the cancellation is requested by the insured, the premium to be returned is computed by reference to a short-rate table which refunds less than the pro rata portion of the premium. For example, one state's schedule provides that the insured who pays 2½ times the annual rate for a three-year policy may recover 60% of the premium if the insured cancels the policy at the end of one year.

Coinsurance

To encourage adequate insurance coverage related to the current market value of the insured property, many policies carry a *coinsurance clause* which provides that if the property is insured for less than a stated percentage (often 80%) of its market value at the time of a loss, the insured is a *coinsurer* with the insurance company. As a coinsurer the insured must stand a share of losses. The share of a loss, when there is a coinsurance clause, is determined by application of the policy provision that the insurance company will pay the *lowest* of the three following amounts:

1. Face of the policy.
2. Market value of the loss.
3. Coinsurance indemnity (determined by formula).

To illustrate the effect of a coinsurance clause, assume the following for Company C:

1. Policy on casualties—face, $7,000; coinsurance clause, 80%.
2. Casualty—fire, market value of the loss at date of fire (there was a partial loss of the property), $5,680.
3. Market value of the property immediately prior to the fire, $10,000.

Computation of the coinsurance indemnity (by formula):

$$\frac{\text{Face of Policy}}{.80 \times \text{Market Value of Property at Date of Casualty}} \times \begin{array}{c}\text{Market}\\ \text{Value of the}\\ \text{Loss}\end{array}$$

$$= \text{Coinsurance Indemnity}$$

$$\frac{\$7,000}{.80 \times \$10,000} \times \$5,680 = \$4,970$$

Thus, the insurance company would reimburse the insured for $4,970 because it is lower than either the face of the policy ($7,000) or the amount of the loss ($5,680). In this case, the insured had to absorb ⅛ of the loss because only ⅞ of the "required" insurance was carried.

Application of this rule is further illustrated by the cases shown in Exhibit 15–4 (assuming in each case that the policy contains an 80% coinsurance clause).

EXHIBIT 15–4
Indemnity under Coinsurance (80%)

	Case 1 (when formula is lowest)	Case 2 (when loss is lowest)	Case 3 (when policy is lowest)
Market value of property at date of loss	$10,000	$10,000	$10,000
Face of policy carried by insured	7,000	8,800	6,000
Market value of loss	5,680	6,000	10,000
Maximum indemnity (formula)	4,970*	6,600†	7,500‡
Actual indemnity payable	4,970	6,000	6,000

* Computed above.   † $\frac{\$8,800}{.80 \times \$10,000} \times \$6,000 = \$6,600$ ‡ $\frac{\$6,000}{.80 \times \$10,000} \times \$10,000 = \$7,500$

Blanket Policy

When a company takes out a fire insurance policy covering several items of property (frequently called a blanket policy), the policy usually includes an "average" clause, which provides that the protection will pertain to each item of property in such proportion as each property bears to the entire value (market value at time of loss) of the property insured. For example, assume that a blanket policy for $9,000, containing the 80% coinsurance clause, insured two buildings—A having a market value at the date of the fire of $10,000 and B of $5,000. The face of the policy would be allocated as $6,000 on A and $3,000 on B. If a fire loss of $2,000 occurred in B, the maximum indemnity would be as follows:

$$\frac{\$3,000}{.80 \times \$5,000} \times \$2,000 = \$1,500$$

Since $1,500 is less than either the loss ($2,000) or the effective policy ($3,000), the actual indemnity would be $1,500, the maximum set by the formula.

Indemnity under Several Policies

Where more than one insurance policy covers the same property and all policies have the same or no coinsurance clause, the total insurance is computed as though all the insurance was issued in a single policy. The indemnity thus computed is then allocated among the different policies in proportion to the face of each policy. To illustrate, assume that property having a market

EXHIBIT 15–5
Indemnity under Four Policies with No Coinsurance Clause

Policy	Insurance Carried (face)	Computation	Indemnity (amount collectible)
1	$10,000	10/80 × $60,000	$ 7,500
2	25,000	25/80 × $60,000	18,750
3	40,000	40/80 × $60,000	30,000
4	5,000	5/80 × $60,000	3,750
	$80,000		$60,000

EXHIBIT 15–6
Indemnity under Four Policies with Common Coinsurance Clause

Policy	Coinsurance	Face of Policy	Loss Proration*	Formula†	Indemnity (lowest)
1	90%	$10,000	$ 7,500	$ 6,667	$ 6,667
2	90	25,000	18,750	16,667	16,667
3	90	40,000	30,000	26,667	26,667
4	90	5,000	3,750	3,333	3,333
		$80,000	$60,000		$53,334

* $10,000/$80,000 × $60,000 = $7,500, etc.

† $\dfrac{\$10,000}{.90\,(\$100,000)} \times \$60,000 = \$6,667$, etc.

value of $100,000 is insured under the respective policies shown in Exhibits 15–5, 15–6, and 15–7 (first two columns), and a fire loss of $60,000 was incurred. If the policies do not contain coinsurance clauses, the actual indemnity would be as shown in Exhibit 15–5.

If the policies all contained 90% coinsurance clauses, the actual indemnity would be as shown in Exhibit 15–6.

If property is insured by several policies having *different* coinsurance clauses, each coinsurance requirement must be taken into account. To illustrate, assume the above example except that the coinsurance clauses are as indicated in Exhibit 15–7. With property worth

EXHIBIT 15–7
Indemnity under Four Policies with Variable Coinsurance Clauses

Policy	Coinsurance	Face of Policy	Loss Proration*	Formula†	Indemnity (lowest)
1	None	$10,000	$ 7,500	Not applicable	$ 7,500
2	75%	25,000	18,750	$20,000	18,750
3	80	40,000	30,000	30,000	30,000
4	90	5,000	3,750	3,333	3,333
		$80,000	$60,000		$59,583

* Computed as in Exhibit 15–6.

† $\dfrac{\$25,000}{.75\,(\$100,000)} \times \$60,000 = \$20,000$

$\dfrac{\$40,000}{.80\,(\$100,000)} \times \$60,000 = \$30,000$

$\dfrac{\$5,000}{.90\,(\$100,000)} \times \$60,000 = \$3,333$

$100,000 and total coverage of $80,000, policies 1, 2, and 3 met the coinsurance requirements of zero, $75,000, and $80,000. Only policy 4 failed to meet the requirement ($90,000).

Accounting for a Casualty Loss

When there is a casualty loss, prepaid insurance must be adjusted accordingly. To illustrate the nature of the adjustment we will utilize a *fire loss*. When a fire has occurred, an orderly accounting procedure is essential for *separately reporting the loss* and for proper matching of operating expense and the loss against revenue. In accounting for a fire loss, certain procedures should be followed, viz:

1. Determine to what extent the accounting records have been damaged or destroyed. Take steps to supplement damaged records, or to reconstruct them if they have been destroyed.
2. Adjust the books to the date of the fire for all operating items affected by the fire. Make all necessary adjusting entries for depreciation, amortization, accrued and prepaid expense, and revenue items affected by the fire.
3. Determine the *book value* of all assets destroyed by the fire.
4. Open a Casualty Loss account in the general ledger and transfer to it the book value of all assets destroyed. Charge the Casualty Loss account with any *unexpired* insurance premium on that portion of the policy which is paid by the insurance company as a result of the casualty, and with any expenses incurred in connection with the fire and the settlement.
5. Determine the amounts recoverable under the policies in force. Credit the Casualty Loss account for these amounts plus any proceeds received from the sale of damaged assets whose cost has been charged to Casualty Loss.[8]
6. Close the balance of the Casualty Loss account to Income Summary. It is advisable

---

[8] Proceeds from sale of damaged assets may, instead, go to the insurance company under terms of the settlement.

to close the books as of the date of the fire when the fire is of major proportions.

In determining the book value of assets destroyed, cognizance must be taken not only of the estimated depreciation recorded for past periods but also of the depreciation to be recorded for the elapsed portion of the present period to date of loss. The portion of the insurance premium to be charged to the Casualty Loss account is the unexpired portion at the date of the fire if the full amount of the policy is paid. If only a portion of the policy is paid, then the amount of the payment is endorsed on the policy and the remainder continues in force. In this case, that proportion of the unexpired premium which the endorsement bears to the face of the policy is taken out of Prepaid Insurance and charged to Casualty Loss. If the policy is continued, the remainder is left in the Prepaid Insurance account; if canceled, this remainder is a cash refund.

If a perpetual inventory system is used, and if the records are not destroyed, the amount of the merchandise on hand at the time of the fire can be determined from the records. In the absence of such records, the amount of the inventory may be estimated by the "gross margin" method as described in Chapter 12.

Accounting for Casualty Loss Illustrated. Assume the Fire Alarm Company suffered a fire loss on July 1 of the current year; the relevant values were as follows:

a. Market values at date of the fire (July 1):	
Inventory (same as cost), 100% loss	$ 3,000
Furniture and equipment, 100% loss	1,000
Building—total market value	26,250
Building—amount of loss at market value, ⅔ loss	17,500
b. Insurance coverage:	
Inventory—none.	
Furniture and equipment, insured—face of policy, $2,400 (no coinsurance clause). Unexpired insurance on January 1 of current year (30 months unexpired)	50
Building, insured—face of policy, $16,800 (includes an 80% coinsurance clause). Unexpired insurance on January 1 of current year (24 months unexpired)	320

c. Account balances January 1 of current
   year:

Prepaid insurance ($50 + $320)	370
Inventory (at cost)	1,500
Furniture and equipment (at cost)	2,400
Accumulated depreciation, furniture and equipment (depreciation rate, 25% per year on cost)	1,200
Building (at cost)	30,000
Accumulated depreciation, building (depreciation rate, 3⅓% per year on cost)	10,000

The entries to adjust the books to the date of the fire, to record the fire loss, and to record the settlement with the insurance company follow with explanations and computations:

1. Entries to adjust the books to the date of the fire for operating items affected:

Casualty loss (goods destroyed) . . .	3,000	
Merchandise inventory (inventory destroyed)		3,000

To record inventory of unsold merchandise destroyed by fire. (Note: Merchandise Inventory is closed to Income Summary at regular closing. This amount offsets the charges to regular income from the beginning inventory and purchases, part of which was burned. An alternative treatment would be to credit the beginning inventory and purchases to the extent of the loss and to debit the Casualty Loss account).

Depreciation expense on furniture and equipment	300	
Accumulated depreciation on furniture and equipment		300

To record depreciation, at a rate of 25% per year from January 1 to July 1 ($2,400 × 25% × 6/12).

Depreciation expense on building . .	500	
Accumulated depreciation on building		500

To record depreciation, from January 1 to July 1 ($30,000 × 3⅓% × 6/12 = $500).

Insurance expense	90	
Prepaid insurance		90

To record the expired insurance premium from January 1 to July 1, as follows:

Furniture and equipment ($50 × 6/30)	10
Building ($320 × 6/24) . . .	80

2. Entries to close the book value of assets destroyed:

Casualty loss	900	
Accumulated depreciation on furniture and equipment	1,500	
Furniture and equipment		2,400

To close the accumulated depreciation and the asset accounts into the Casualty Loss account.

Casualty loss	13,000	
Accumulated depreciation on building	7,000	
Building		20,000

To close two thirds of the accumulated depreciation and of the asset accounts into the Casualty Loss account ($10,000 + $500) × ⅔ = $7,000.

3. Entry to record the settlement with the insurance company:

Cash ($14,000 + $1,000)	15,000	
Casualty loss		15,000

To record the receipt of indemnity proceeds from the insurance company, computed as follows: furniture and equipment $1,000 (full settlement); building, per formula [$16,800 ÷ ($26,250 × 80%)] × $17,500 = $14,000 (which is less than face of policy or market value of the loss). No insurance on inventory loss.

4. To adjust the balance in Prepaid Insurance:

If Policies Continued

Casualty loss	217	
Prepaid insurance		217

If Policies Not Continued

Casualty loss	217	
Cash	63	
Prepaid insurance		280

Analysis of prepaid insurance:

	Furniture and Fixtures	Building	Total
Unexpired January 1	$50	$320	$370
Amortized to July 1	10	80	90
Unexpired July 1	40	240	280
Amount related to indemnity:			
$1,000/$2,400 × $40 =	17		17
$14,000/$16,800 × $240 =		200	200
Unexpired after fire loss (or cash refund)	$23	$ 40	$ 63

The Casualty Loss account is closed to Income Summary. For the insured assets above the Casualty Loss account reflected a credit balance (i.e., a gain) since the indemnity was based on market values at the date of the casualty whereas the book value of the assets destroyed was less than the market value (i.e., the replacement cost).

Life Insurance

Life insurance companies sell insurance policies that call for a stipulated payment (indemnity) in case of death of the insured, receiving in return compensation in the form of premiums. In an *ordinary life* policy, the premiums are paid until the death of the insured at which time the stipulated benefit is paid to the beneficiary. During the period the policy is in force, it has both a cash surrender value and a loan value. In a *limited payment* policy, the premiums are paid for a stated number of periods or until the death of the insured (if prior to the end of the stipulated period) and the benefit is paid at death or after a stipulated date as an endowment. As with the ordinary life policy, there is a cash surrender value and a loan value. In *term insurance,* the premium payments are made for a stated number of periods or until death (if prior to the end of the stipulated period); the benefit is paid only if death occurs within the stated number of periods. In term insurance, there is no cash surrender or loan value and the policy must be renewed at the end of the stipulated period; otherwise it lapses. At renewal, a new premium scale is effective based on the advanced age. Because there are no complexities in accounting for term insurance, the discussion to follow will be limited to ordinary life policies.

The law and insurance companies have long recognized that a company has an insurable interest in certain of its *executives.* Thus, it is common for companies to insure the lives of certain key executives; the proceeds are payable to the company to compensate for the loss incurred in replacing a deceased executive.

In accounting for a life insurance policy of this type, premiums paid (cash paid less any dividends earned on the policy) and the related asset (intangible) must be recorded and reported.

Cash Surrender and Loan Value. The cash surrender value of a policy is the sum payable upon the cancellation of the policy at the request of the insured. The loan value of a policy is the amount the insurance company will loan on a policy maintained in force. The cash surrender value is computed as of the end of the year; the loan value is computed as of the beginning of the year (thus, it is less by interest for one year). Each policy carries a table that indicates the cash surrender value and the loan value for specific policy years. Since the policy could be canceled and a portion of the premiums which have been paid may be returned in the form of the cash surrender value, not all of the premiums paid constitute an expense but only the excess of the total premiums paid over the cash surrender value.[9]

The portion of premiums paid equal to the cash surrender value is an asset and should be shown as such on the balance sheet under the caption "Investments and Funds."

To illustrate one sequence of entries, assume the following data taken from an insurance policy having an indemnity of $25,000:

Year	Premium (beginning of year)	Cash Surrender Value (end of year)
1	$720	–0–
2	720	–0–
3	720	$210
4	720	290
5	(Etc., as specified in the policy)	

---

[9] The diagram below illustrates that in the early years of an ordinary life policy, substantially all of each periodic premium is for insurance protection. Cash surrender value customarily starts accumulating in the third year or later. As more time passes, an increasing portion of each premium payment adds to the cash surrender value. This is a general pattern; individual policies differ widely with respect to accumulation of cash values.

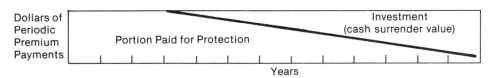

Indicated entries:

Year 1:

Life insurance expense 650
Cash surrender value of life insurance 70*
    Cash 720

   * $210 ÷ 3 years = $70. Recognition of this addition to cash surrender value anticipates that the policy will be kept in force at least through the third policy year when the cash surrender value actually arises. An alternative (and more conservative) treatment would recognize the $210 in the third year and reduce insurance expense for that year by the same amount.

Year 2:
Same as year 1

Year 3:
Same as year 1

Year 4:

Life insurance expense 720
    Cash 720

At year-end:

Cash surrender value of life insurance
  ($290 − $210) 80
    Life insurance expense (current) 80

A balance in the account, Cash Surrender Value of Life Insurance, is reported on the balance sheet under the caption, "Funds and Investments." Each year thereafter the Cash Surrender Value of Life Insurance account would be debited for the increase in the cash surrender value as shown by the table in the policy. The above example was simplified by assuming the policy year and the accounting year coincided. If they do not coincide, as in the normal case, an adjusting entry at the end of each accounting period would be required for the prepaid amount of insurance expense.

The following entry would be made when the face of the policy is paid at the death of the president, assuming the cash surrender value of the policy at date of death was $3,500 and that three months' premium is to be refunded in accordance with the insurance policy whereby premiums paid beyond date of death are refunded.

Cash [$25,000 + (³⁄₁₂ × $720)] 25,180
  Life insurance expense
    (³⁄₁₂ × $720) 180
  Cash surrender value of life
    insurance 3,500
  Gain on settlement of life
    insurance indemnity 21,500

The gain normally would be extraordinary.

REPORTING INTANGIBLES

Noncurrent assets properly classified as intangibles are variously reported under the balance sheet captions (or similar captions): "Intangibles," "Deferred charges," and "Other assets." Although reasonably precise definitions have been provided in this chapter, in the practical world of accounting there are no comparable authoritative distinctions among the three captions. Therefore, considerable variation among companies can be observed in the balance sheet reporting of noncurrent intangibles. Often each intangible is descriptively titled in the statement with additional note disclosure to provide relevant details.

QUESTIONS

1. What distinguishes intangible assets from the remaining assets traditionally reported outside the current asset category? How are intangible assets reported on the balance sheet?

2. What outlays are properly considered part of the cost of an intangible asset?

3. Cite the factors that should determine whether or not an intangible asset is amortized and, if so, over what span of time.

4. What is an identifiable intangible asset? Give some examples of such assets.

5. What is the nature of a franchise? Of a trademark?

6. Explain the conceptual nature of goodwill and the basis on which goodwill is amortized.

7. What is the proper role of the accountant in valuation of goodwill?

8. Briefly describe going value. How can it be distinguished from goodwill?

9. Define a deferred charge. Is it an intangible?

10. How are deferred charges distinguished from prepaid expenses? Give examples of each.

11. What items are properly chargeable to organization costs? Should organization costs be amortized? Explain.

12. What are the basic provisions of the *FASB Statement* on accounting for research and development costs?

13. What kinds of costs are oil and gas companies permitted to capitalize under provisions of *FASB Statement No. 19?* Succinctly describe "full costing" and indicate whether or not it is permitted under provisions of the *Statement.*

14. What is a development stage company? Are development stage companies subject to the same or different accounting rules than other companies? Explain briefly.

15. Some casualty policies have coinsurance clauses. What is the purpose of such a clause? How does its presence in a policy affect the indemnity which the insured can collect if the insured property is totally destroyed?

16. When a casualty occurs for which insurance is in force, certain accounting steps should be taken. What are these accounting measures?

17. What is the relationship between cash surrender value and loan value of a life insurance policy? Which one affects accounting entries? How?

18. For what reasons do some companies insure the lives of executives and name the companies as beneficiaries?

DECISION CASE 15–1

The National Broadcasting Company (NBC) was reported to have incurred costs of $750,000 in the development of its "N" logo shown at intervals in its TV broadcasts. Shortly after the N was announced and first used by NBC, it was discovered that an educational TV network in Nebraska had already been using a similar logo. To obtain exclusive rights to its already costly N, NBC agreed, in an out-of-court settlement, to pay $55,000 cash to the Nebraska network and to furnish it with various new and used color TV equipment without cost. The equipment to be transferred was conservatively valued at $500,000. A spokesman for the Nebraska network said the equipment to be provided by NBC would have cost $750,000 if bought new and that for the two years preceding the settlement, efforts to get a $750,000 appropriation from the Nebraska legislature to buy such equipment had been unsuccessful. Terms of the settlement provided that $2,500 of the cash settlement was to be paid to William Korbus. He had designed the Nebraska network's N at a cost of $100. Delivery of the equipment to the Nebraska network was to begin approximately three months after the announced settlement and was to occur over a four-month interval. (Source: *The Wall Street Journal,* March 8, 1976.)

Required:

1. How should NBC account for its original costs of $750,000 related to the logo? How should it account for the settlement with the Nebraska network and Korbus?
2. Assuming that accounting principles for not-for-profit organizations such as the Nebraska network were similar to those for a commercial network, how should the Nebraska network account for the settlement?
3. What are the accounting implications of the fact that two different networks could spend such different sums for items that were almost identical?

DECISION CASE 15–2

Exxon Corporation and two partners, Mobil Oil and Champlin Petroleum Company, paid cash bonuses of $632 million for rights to drill for oil and gas on six different offshore tracts in the Gulf of Mexico near Florida.

Required:

1. Between the date of the bonus payment and the time drilling begins, how should the $632 million expenditure be accounted for? What about other costs?
2. After spending an added $15 million to drill seven wells on the acreage, the venturers unfortunately found no oil or gas in commercial quantities and announced there were no plans for additional drilling on the tracts. Assuming the rights to drill do not expire for another ten years, what accounting is indicated?

DECISION CASE 15–3

The time lapse between the date a new product is conceived and the date it is available for sale to customers is often lengthy. The following listing of commonplace products and the number of years it took to make them marketable realities is indicative.

Antibiotics	30
Automatic transmission	16
Cellophane	12
Dry soup mixes	19
Fluorescent lights	33
Frozen foods	15
Instant coffee	22
Instant rice	18
Nylon	12
Photography	56
Radio	24
Television	63
Zippers	30

On the other hand, instant cameras and filter cigarettes made it to the stores in two years, and long-playing records took only three.

In the light of the foregoing, if you were a member of a standards-setting body such as the FASB, what would be your basic position as to proper accounting for R&D costs? Cite the considerations that cause you to reach your basic conclusions.

DECISION CASE 15–4

Under provisions of *FASB Statement No. 2*, R&D costs must be expensed in the period in which they are incurred except for costs of R&D activities conducted for others under contract and indirect costs that are specifically reimbursable under terms of a contract.

How should these exception-type costs be accounted for and reported? Support whatever conclusions you reach.

EXERCISES

Exercise 15–1

The data below pertain to two separate intangible assets:

	Asset X	Asset Y
Cost	$8,400	$9,800
Estimated economic life	Indefinite	14 years

Required (assume straight-line amortization):

1. Give annual entry for amortization, if any, for each asset. (Assume both were acquired after 1970.)
2. Assume Asset Y has been in use for eight full years and it is determined at the start of the ninth year that its remaining life will be four years. Give the appropriate amortization entry for Asset Y at the end of its ninth year.

Exercise 15–2

Check the best answer in each of the following and indicate the basis for your choice.

1. On January 15, 19A, a corporation was granted a patent on a product. On January 2, 19J, to protect its patent, the corporation purchased a patent on a competing product that originally was issued on January 10, 19F. Because of its unique plant, the corporation does not feel the competing patent can be used in producing a product. The cost of the competing patent should be

   a. Amortized over a maximum period of 17 years.
   b. Amortized over a maximum period of 13 years.
   c. Amortized over a maximum period of 8 years.
   d. Expensed in 19J.

2. Goodwill should be written off
   a. As soon as possible against retained earnings.
   b. As soon as possible as an extraordinary item.
   c. By systematic charges against retained earnings over the period benefited, but not more than 40 years.
   d. By systematic charges to expense over the period benefited, but not more than 40 years.

3. A large publicly held company has developed and registered a trademark during 19A. How should the cost of developing and registering the trademark be accounted for?
   a. Charged to an asset account that should not be amortized.
   b. Expensed as incurred.
   c. Amortized over 25 years if in accordance with management's evaluation.
   d. Amortized over its useful life or 17 years, whichever is shorter.

4. A deferred charge should be
   a. Expensed as incurred.
   b. Capitalized and not amortized until it clearly has no value.
   c. Capitalized and amortized over the estimated period benefited.
   d. Capitalized and amortized over the estimated period benefited but not exceeding 40 years.

5. Research and development costs incurred after 1975 should be
   a. Capitalized on a selective basis and not amortized.
   b. Capitalized, then amortized over 40 years.
   c. Expensed in the year in which they are incurred.
   d. Charged directly to retained earnings.

6. Goodwill is most closely akin to
   a. Going value.
   b. Franchises.
   c. Trademarks.
   d. Copyrights.

                     (Items 1–3, 6, AICPA adapted)

Exercise 15–3

In 1978 Rocher Electronics Company signed a long-term contract which it accounts for under the code name "Starfare." The purpose of the Starfare project is to develop advanced radar gear for a government agency.

To facilitate its work, Rocher purchased a five-year-old patent from Jupiter Technologies, Ltd. It expects to apply the technology covered by this patent over the estimated three-year life of the Starfare project to it and subsequently to apply it to other company work and/or projects for a total of eight years. Rocher's fiscal year is the calendar year.

In February 1979, after the books were adjusted and closed for 1978, your examination of debits to the Starfare project account reveals the following:

Date		Item	Debit
1978:			
July	1	Cost of patent bought from Jupiter Technologies	$ 40,000
	15	Legal fees related to acquisition of Jupiter patent	2,000
Jan. to		Direct labor applicable to Starfare project	40,000
Dec.		Direct materials applicable to Starfare project	23,800
Dec.	31	Amortization of R&D costs applicable to Starfare	2,500
	31	Income earned on Starfare project	8,824
		Total debits in 1978	$117,124
1979:			
Jan.	3	Legal fees incurred in successful defense of Jupiter patent	$ 15,000

Further investigation reveals the following:

1. There were no credits to the Starfare project account. The $117,124 balance was reported as Inventory—Research in Progress on the December 31 balance sheet.
2. Rocher Company has accumulated all R&D costs in a deferred charge account which it amortizes at year-end. Actual R&D applicable to Starfare for 1978 was $8,500.
3. The Starfare project contract provides that Rocher is entitled to
   a. Apply overhead at 40% of direct labor costs to the project; overhead does not include R&D charges or patent amortization. Analysis reveals that in 1978, 90% of overhead was allocated to cost of goods sold and 10% to inventory.
   b. Accrue income at 8% of its costs subject to subsequent audit and approval by government auditors.
   c. Bill the government agency which let the contract for 96% of its accumulated costs (including accrued profits) at three-month intervals. (No billing was made until December 31, 1978, at which time Rocher debited $114,359 to a Due from U.S. Government account and credited Progress Billings.)

Required:

Give journal entries as of February 1979 to correct Rocher's accounts. Round amounts to nearest dollar.

Exercise 15–4

For the past five years, the total assets of Majestic Store have averaged $700,000 while average liabilities

amounted to $150,000. Cumulative total earnings for the five-year period have been $280,000. Included in the latter figure are extraordinary gains of $45,000 and nonrecurring losses of $30,000. An 8% return on investment is considered normal for the industry. In calculating goodwill where a transfer of the business to new interests is contemplated, the parties agree that excess earnings should be capitalized at 20%.

Required:

In light of the foregoing, calculate the implied goodwill using the second approach illustrated in the chapter. Show computations.

Exercise 15–5

A small mining operation which is available for purchase can be expected to produce for the next three years; it will be exhausted at that time and have a zero residual value due to restoration cost obligations. Best estimates place its net receipts at $40,000 for the first year; thereafter, there will be an annual $10,000 drop in net receipts.

Required:

Using an assumed 9% return rate and assuming net receipts occur at year-end, calculate the goodwill implicit in an offer of $85,000 for the business. Round calculations to nearest dollar.

Exercise 15–6

The following projections were developed as a basis for estimating goodwill:

Average annual expected earnings	$10,000
Average future value of net assets (excluding goodwill)	66,000

Required:

Estimate goodwill under each independent approach below:

a. Goodwill equal to the difference between (1) earnings capitalized at 12½% (normal rate for industry) and (2) expected average assets.
b. Goodwill equal to excess earnings capitalized at 20%; normal rate for industry, 10%.
c. Goodwill equal to six years of excess earnings; normal earnings rate for industry, 10%.
d. Goodwill based on present value of excess earnings as computed in *(b)* at an 15% expected earnings rate for five years. Prepare an amortization table to be used as a basis for amortizing the good-

will on a present value basis. Round amounts to nearest dollar.

Exercise 15–7

New Corporation is negotiating with the Old Company with a view to purchasing the entire assets and liabilities of the latter. You have been asked to help evaluate the "goodwill on the basis of the latest concepts." Accordingly, you decide to utilize the present value approach. The following data have been assembled on Old Company:

	Market Value	Book Value
Total identifiable assets (exclusive of goodwill)	$8,000,000	$5,000,000
Liabilities	3,000,000	3,000,000
Average annual earnings expected (next five years) ..	520,000	

Required (round to nearest dollar):
1. Compute goodwill assuming a 9% expected earnings rate.
2. Assume the deal is consummated; New's offer, as accepted, was cash equal to the market value of the net identifiable assets plus the goodwill computed in Requirement 1. Give entry on New's books to record the transaction.
3. Prepare an amortization table that is conceptually consistent with your computations in Requirement 1.

Exercise 15–8

Jackson Company is contemplating the acquisition of Jones Company. Jackson estimates that Jones can earn $15,000 per year over the indefinite future. Jackson also believes that an appropriate normal earnings rate for Jones is 9% on (Jackson's estimate of) the market value of Jones's average owners' equity (over the indefinite future) of $120,000. Finally, Jackson customarily requires a 12% return on excess earnings of companies it purchases to compensate for the greater risk associated with excess earnings.

Required (round amounts to nearest dollar):
1. Compute the purchase price (including goodwill) which Jackson Company should be willing to pay for the investment in Jones Company, assuming Jackson uses the theoretically best method of valuing goodwill and is willing to pay for ten years of excess earnings.
2. Compute the annual amount of goodwill amortization assuming Jackson Company amortizes goodwill using the straight-line method.

Exercise 15–9

Company Y suffered a fire loss on July 1. Between January 1 and July 1 the company had made sales of $60,000 and inventory purchases of $44,000. January 1 beginning inventory was $6,400. The costs of both beginning inventory and purchases were evenly divided between inventory items that had different markup percentages. Company Y made half its sales at a 50% markup on cost and the other half at a markup that represented 25% of the sales price.

The fire destroyed 60% of Company Y's July 1 inventory (stated in dollars rather than units), but fortunately the inventory was insured for market value (i.e., replacement cost) of $10,000, with an 80% coinsurance clause. Company Y determines that the replacement cost of its inventory at July 1 exceeds its cost by 5%. Prepaid insurance is not a consideration in this exercise.

Required:
1. Compute the cost of Company Y inventory destroyed by the fire.
2. Compute the amount of the insurance recovery on the fire loss.
3. Prepare journal entries to record the fire loss and insurance recovery. Company Y uses a perpetual inventory system.

Exercise 15–10

Select the best answer in each of the following and indicate the basis for your choice (show computations if appropriate).

1. Inger Company bought a patent in January 19A for $6,800. For the first four years, it was amortized on the assumption that the total useful life would be eight years. At the start of the fifth year, it was determined six years would be the probable total life. Amortization at the end of the fifth year should be
   a. $1,133.
   b. $1,700.
   c. $850.
   d. None of the foregoing.
2. XY Company has a lease on a site which does not expire for 25 years. With the land owner's permission, XY erected a building on the site which will last 50 years. XY should recognize expense in connection with the building's cost—
   a. One fortieth each year.
   b. One twenty-fifth each year.
   c. In totality as soon as it is completed.
   d. One fiftieth each year.

3. Where there is an 80% coinsurance clause, the market value of the insured property is $30,000 and the amount of loss and of the face of the policy are, respectively, $15,000 and $12,000; indemnity collectible would be
   a. $7,500.
   b. $12,000.
   c. $15,000.
   d. $30,000.

4. Where the policy has an 80% coinsurance clause, if the market value of the property is $10,000, the amount of loss is $8,500, and insurance carried is $7,000, the indemnity collectible would be
   a. $10,000.
   b. $8,500.
   c. $8,000.
   d. $7,000.
   e. None of the foregoing.

5. Suppose the facts are as in 4 above except that the amount of the loss is $7,000; then the indemnity collectible would be
   a. $10,000.
   b. $8,000.
   c. $7,000.
   d. $6,000.
   e. None of the foregoing.

6. Which of the following is not properly reported as a deferred charge?
   a. Bond issue costs.
   b. Discount on bonds payable.
   c. Organization costs.
   d. Deferred income taxes.

7. Prepaid expenses and deferred charges are alike in that they are both
   a. Reported as current assets on a classified balance sheet.
   b. Destined to be charged to expense in some subsequent period in harmony with the matching principle.
   c. Reported as other assets.
   d. Applicable to the fiscal period immediately following the balance sheet on which they appear.

Exercise 15–11

Select the best answer in each of the following. Briefly justify your choices.

1. Why are certain costs of doing business capitalized when incurred and then depreciated or amortized over subsequent accounting cycles?
   a. To reduce the federal income tax liability.
   b. To aid management in the decision-making process.

   c. To match the costs of production with revenues as earned.
   d. To adhere to the accounting concept of conservatism.

2. In January 1975 the Idea Company purchased a patent for a new consumer product for $170,000. At the time of purchase the patent was valid for 17 years. Due to the competitive nature of the product, the patent was estimated to have a useful life of ten years. During 1979 the product was removed from the market under governmental order because of a potential health hazard present in the product.
   What amount should Idea charge to expense during 1979, assuming amortization is recorded at the end of each year?
   a. $10,000.
   b. $17,000.
   c. $102,000.
   d. $130,000.

3. In accordance with GAAP, which of the following methods of amortization is normally recommended for intangible assets?
   a. Sum-of-the-years' digits.
   b. Straight line.
   c. Units of production.
   d. Double-declining balance.

4. On December 31 of the current year (last day of the corporation's fiscal year), M Corporation sold for $15,000 a patent for which M had paid $50,000 and which had a book value of $6,000 at the time. The terms of sale were as follows:

   $5,000 down payment.
   $5,000 payable on December 31 of each of the next two years.

   The sale agreement made no mention of interest, however, 10% would be a reasonable rate for this type of transaction. What should be the amount of the notes receivable net of any unamortized discount on December 31 of the year of sale (rounded to the nearest dollar)?
   a. $8,678.
   b. $9,091.
   c. $10,000.
   d. $11,000.

5. If a company constructs a laboratory building to be used as a research and development facility, the cost of the building is matched against earnings as
   a. Research and development expense in the period(s) of construction.
   b. Depreciation deducted as part of research and development costs.

c. Depreciation or immediate writeoff depending on company policy.

d. An expense at such time as productive research and development has been obtained from the facility.

(AICPA adapted)

Exercise 15–12

By means of a check mark in the appropriate column, indicate how each of the following expenditures should be accounted for at the time it is incurred. If the amount should be split, check more than a single column. Assume that each expenditure occurred late in the current fiscal year of the entity making payment. Give reasons for each answer.

Exercise 15–13

Select the best answer in each of the following. Briefly justify each selection.

1. Patents and copyrights have definite legal lives and should be amortized over
   a. Their legal lives.
   b. Their useful lives.
   c. Their legal or useful life, whichever is shorter.
   d. A period not to exceed 40 years.
2. X Company incurred $50,000 of costs in R&D activities. These costs need not be expensed if
   a. They give promise of a successful outcome.
   b. The projects are completed and have culminated in a profitable patent for X.
   c. X is doing contract research for another com-

(Relates to Exercise 15–12) Transactions	Debit to Retained Earnings	Debit to Current Expenses	Capitalize as an Intangible	None of the Foregoing
1. As a result of an out-of-court settlement, X Company paid $14 million to another corporation because it had infringed on the payee's patent. Most of the agreed payment relates to sales made by X in prior years; the remainder to current sales.				
2. X incurred legal costs of $750,000 in connection with the litigation described in No. 1.				
3. Acting on recommendations of High Technology, Inc., Y spends $60,000 rearranging its machinery. Benefits are expected to last six years.				
4. Y paid High Technology $90,000 for R&D work the latter has done under contract for Y. The results are expected to increase Y's profits over the next seven years.				
5. D Corporation incurs legal costs of $500,000 successfully defending one of its patents in an infringement suit. The patent runs six more years.				
6. Assume D's suit in No. 5 had turned out adversely and that D was forced to write off its patent carried at $80,000. How should the writeoff be treated?				
7. Jay Company paid Zippy Corporation $50,000 for the exclusive right to repair auto transmissions in the City of Erehwon, using the Zippy name and logo in signs, ads, and the like. The franchise runs for as long as Jay is in business but cannot be transferred.				
8. P Company spent $400,000 developing a new manufacturing process on which it will apply for a patent.				
9. P incurs $50,000 legal and registration costs related to securing a patent on the process described in No. 8.				
10. In 1979 Uno Company paid an author $40,000 for the copyright to the author's novel and for rights to produce a movie based on it. The copyright was issued in 1978, and the author is elderly.				

pany, and the costs relate to the contract which is still in progress.

  d. The projects were begun before the issuance of *FASB Statement No. 2*.

3. Organization costs

  a. Are not covered by *APB Opinion No. 17* and need not be amortized.

  b. Must be amortized over a period not to exceed 40 years.

  c. Should be reported as a contra item under "Owners' Equity."

  d. Should be expensed as soon as they are incurred.

4. Some intangibles are characterized as specifically identifiable, while others lack the property of specific identifiability. An example of the latter is

  a. A trademark.

  b. A perpetual franchise.

  c. A franchise for a limited term.

  d. Goodwill.

5. The legal life of a patent is

  a. 28 years.

  b. 17 years.

  c. The life of the holder of the patent (if a natural person).

  d. 40 years.

6. A copyright granted to a composer in 1979 has a legal life of

  a. 17 years.

  b. 28 years.

  c. The life of the composer plus 50 years.

  d. 40 years.

7. Which of the following is not properly classified as an intangible asset?

  a. A copyright acquired by transfer.

  b. Goodwill.

  c. A patent acquired as an outgrowth of the owner's R&D activities.

  d. Losses incurred by a development stage company.

8. P Corporation acquired A Company in 1968 and B Company in 1979. In both instances the acquired companies were dissolved and their assets and operations merged with other assets and activities of P. In both instances P paid more than book value for its acquisitions and most of the difference was attributable to goodwill. In accounting for the goodwill

  a. P must amortize the goodwill of each company over a similar time period.

  b. P need not amortize the goodwill of either company.

  c. P need not amortize the goodwill associated with A but must amortize the goodwill associated with B.

  d. P need not amortize the goodwill associated with B but must amortize the goodwill associated with A.

Exercise 15–14

Assuming that all policies contain an 80% coinsurance clause, show what the insurance company would pay under each of the following cases:

	Case A	Case B	Case C
Market value of property	$30,000	$18,000	$12,000
Amount of loss	28,800	3,600	3,840
Face of policy	27,000	15,000	9,000

Exercise 15–15

On January 1, a store had $120 unexpired premiums on an 80% coinsurance fire policy, which ran one year, for $15,000 on its merchandise. On January 1, the inventory was $20,000. January purchases were $44,000, and January sales were $60,000. A fire on February 1 destroyed the entire stock on hand. The insurance policy was canceled upon payment of the indemnity, and any unexpired (i.e., unearned) premium after the fire was refunded.

Required:

Give journal entries to record the estimated inventory and the fire loss assuming a 30% gross margin rate on sales.

Exercise 15–16

ABC Company sustained a fire loss on February 28. The following data were available (fiscal year ends December 31):

  a. Sixty percent of the inventory burned; cost and market value of loss were both $1,800 (assume periodic inventory procedures).

  b. Furniture and fixtures: depreciation $20 per month; market value of the item burned, $3,600 (original cost, $3,000; accumulated depreciation to January 1, $480).

  c. Insurance premium $60 per year paid on last January 1 for one year; payment of the indemnity canceled the policy and the unexpired (i.e., prepaid) premium after the fire was refunded in cash. No insurance expense has been recorded for January or February.

  d. Settled with insurance company; face of policy, $5,000, 90% coinsurance clause; market value of property insured, $7,500. Close Causalty Loss account.

Required:

Give indicated journal entries.

Exercise 15–17

Assuming that each policy contains an 80% coinsurance clause, indicate what each insurance company would pay under the following cases:

	Case A	Case B	Case C
Market value of property	$25,000	$15,000	$10,000
Amount of loss	24,000	3,000	3,200
Face of policies:			
Written by X Company ...	10,000	7,500	4,000
Written by Y Company ...	12,500	5,000	3,500

Exercise 15–18

A company carried casualty insurance on an asset with four different insurance companies. Determine the liability of each insurance company under policies for the amounts indicated and with the coinsurance clauses shown. At the date of the fire the insured property had a current market value of $120,000 and the market value of the loss was $12,960.

Company	Coinsurance Clause	Face of Policy
A	100%	$30,000
B	70	30,000
C	90	20,000
D	None	10,000

Exercise 15–19

On January 1, Wilkins Company purchased a $100,000 ordinary life insurance policy on its president. The following data relate to the first five years:

Year	Annual Advance Premium	Cash Surrender Value (year-end) Increase	Cash Surrender Value (year-end) Cumulative
1	$3,000	-0-	-0-
2	3,000	-0-	-0-
3	3,000	$3,150	$3,150
4	3,000	1,080	4,230
5	3,000	1,125	5,355
6	Etc.	Etc.	Etc.

Required:

1. Give all entries indicated up to death of the president on July 2 of the fifth year.
2. Give entry to record insurance settlement upon death of the president. The premium unexpired was refunded. Assume the policy year and accounting year coincide.

PROBLEMS

Problem 15–1

Case A—One of your corporate clients bought all of the assets of another company whose operations were compatible with those of the client and continued to operate the business of the acquired entity as a separate division. The purchase price paid included an excess consideration for such items as customers' lists, going concern value, and goodwill, aside from what was paid for identifiable tangibles and intangibles. Under terms of the original contract, if the division (i.e., the acquired unit) proves sufficiently profitable, an added payment will become due. This added payment is almost certain to materialize and will approximately equal what was already paid for customer lists, going concern value, and goodwill. These intangibles have been amortized since acquisition over a more or less arbitrary eight-year total life. The client has inquired whether the added payment, which is clearly related, can be amortized over 12 years from the date the payment is to be made. If this were to be done, vestiges of the balance related to the new payment would remain on the books as much as seven years after the last of the first payment had been fully amortized.

Case B—Another corporate client is in a regulated industry and has franchise rights granted by a federal commission. The rights are worth considerably more than the cost of obtaining them; they can be transferred with the permission of the commission (which usually is not difficult to obtain). The rights do not lapse as long as the client is a going concern, although they could be revoked. Revocation of such rights has rarely occurred. The client's management contends there is no need to amortize the franchise rights over 40 years, much less a shorter period. Indeed, some of the managers feel they should be written up in value.

Required:

Draft memoranda setting forth your recommendations concerning the above situations. Support whatever positions you take.

Problem 15–2

The Tiger Corporation, a retail farm implements dealer, has increased its annual sales volume to a level three times greater than the annual sales of a dealer purchased eight years ago in order to begin operations.

The board of directors of Tiger Corporation recently received an offer to negotiate the sale of Tiger

Corporation to a larger competitor. As a result, the majority of the board wants to increase the stated value of goodwill on the balance sheet to reflect the larger sales volume developed through intensive promotion and the current market prices of the company's products. However, a few of the company's board members would prefer to eliminate goodwill altogether from the balance sheet in order to prevent "possible misinterpretations." Goodwill was properly recorded when the business was acquired eight years ago.

Required:

1. *a.* Discuss the meaning of the term "goodwill." Do not discuss goodwill arising from consolidated statements or the conditions under which goodwill is recorded.
   b. List the techniques used to calculate the tentative value of goodwill in negotiations to purchase a going concern.
2. Why are the book and market values of the goodwill of Tiger Corporation different?
3. Discuss the propriety of
   a. Increasing the stated value of goodwill prior to the negotiations.
   b. Eliminating goodwill completely from the balance sheet prior to negotiations.

(AICPA adapted)

Problem 15–3

Transactions during the first year of the newly organized Stephanie Corporation included the following:

Jan. 2 Paid $4,000 attorney's fees for assistance in securing the corporate charter, drafting bylaws, and advising on operating in other states (which the company intends).

31 Paid $700 for television commercials advertising the grand opening. In addition, during the grand opening the company gave premiums taken from inventory to customers and visitors which cost $8,000.

Feb. 1 Paid invoice received from financial institution which underwrote and sold the company's $400,000 par value stock at a 10% premium. Per agreement, the underwriter charged 1% of the gross proceeds from the stock sale.

Mar. 1 Paid $18,000 to a franchisor for the right to open in the company premises a "Tastee Food" lunch counter. The initial franchise runs ten years from March 1 and can be renewed upon payment of a second amount negotiated on the basis of sales under the initial franchise.

May 1 Acquired for $10,200 a newly issued patent to be held to produce royalty income.

July 1 Paid consultants $6,000 for services in securing a trademark enabling the company to market under the now-protected name "Stephanie Styling."

Oct. 1 Obtained a license from the city to conduct operations in a newly opened department. The license, which cost $600, runs for one year from date and is renewable.

Nov. 1 Acquired another business and paid (among other amounts) $6,000 for its goodwill. The payment represents an amount based on purchase of five years' expected above-normal profits.

Dec. 31 Amortized those assets subject to amortization over their indicated lives. Where no life is specified, amortized over the longest term possible. Amortization is on a monthly basis; in other words, acquisition of an intangible in July would call for a half year's amortization.

Required:

1. Journalize the foregoing transactions.
2. Present the "Intangibles Assets" section of Stephanie's balance sheet in good form as of December 31.

Problem 15–4

On June 30, 19A, your client, Vandiver Corporation, was granted two patents covering plastic cartons that it has been producing and marketing profitably for the past three years. One patent covers the manufacturing process, and the other covers the related products.

Vandiver executives tell you that these patents represent the most significant breakthrough in the industry in the past 30 years. The products have been marketed under the registered trademarks Safetainer, Duratainer, and Sealrite. Licenses under the patents have already been granted by your client to other manufacturers in the United States and abroad and are producing substantial royalties.

On July 1, Vandiver commenced patent infringement actions against several companies whose names you recognize as those of substantial and prominent competitors. Vandiver's management is optimistic that these suits will result in a permanent injunction against the manufacture and sale of the infringing products and collection of damages for loss of profits caused by the alleged infringement.

The financial vice president has suggested that the patents be recorded at the discounted value of expected net royalty receipts.

Required:

1. What is an intangible asset? Explain.
2. *a.* What is the meaning of "discounted value of expected net receipts"? Explain.

b. How would such a value be calculated for net royalty receipts?

3. What basis of valuation for Vandiver's patents would be generally accepted in accounting? Give supporting reasons for this basis.

(AICPA adapted)

Problem 15–5

After considerable analysis the following projections were derived as a basis for estimating the potential value of goodwill in anticipation of negotiations for the sale of the business:

Average annual earnings projected............ $ 44,000
Average market value of net assets expected .. 350,000
"Normal" rate of return for the industry, 10%.
Rate of return expected on excess profits, 12½%.
Expected recovery period for excess earnings, five years.
Years' purchase of average annual earnings, three.

Estimate the value of goodwill under five different approaches (including a present value determination at 15%). Round amounts to the nearest dollar.

Problem 15–6

Your new client, PQR Company, is being audited for the first time. In the course of your examination, you encounter in the ledger an account titled "Intangibles" which is presented below:

Intangibles

6/30/19A	Goodwill	5,000	12/31/19B	Amortization	480
12/31/19A	R&D	10,700	12/31/19C	Amortization	1,200
4/1/19B	Goodwill	11,400			
6/30/19B	Patent	9,600			
12/31/19B	R&D	13,900			
6/1/19C	Goodwill	16,500			
7/1/19C	Bond discount	4,800			
12/31/19C	R&D	17,100			

By tracing entries to the journal and other supporting documents, you ascertain the following facts:

a. The June 30, 19A, entry was made when, somewhat surprisingly, the first six months' operations were profitable; a loss had been anticipated. At the direction of the company president, and with the approval of the board of directors, an entry was made debiting Intangibles and crediting Retained Earnings for $5,000.

b. All debit entries dated December 31 pertaining to R&D arise from the fact that the company has continuously engaged in an extensive research

and development program to keep its products competitive and to develop new products. The charges represent half of the costs of the R&D program for each year and were transferred at year-end from the R&D expense account.

c. The April 1, 19B, entry was made after an extensive advertising campaign had seemingly proved particularly successful. Sales rose 8% after the campaign and never dropped again to less than a 4% increase over their former level. The charge represents the cost of the campaign.

d. The $9,600 charge on June 30, 19B, represents the purchase price of a patent bought because the company feared if it fell into other hands, it would damage the company's products competitively.

e. The June 1, 19C, charge was made after PQR acquired a division of another profitable company. The price represented an excess payment of $16,500 over the market values of identifiable assets acquired and was based on an expectation of continued high profitability. This cost of goodwill should properly be carried in an Investment in Affiliate account (covered in Chapter 19).

f. The July 1, 19C, charge for $4,800 represents discount on a ten-year $100,000 bond issue marketed by the company on that date. (Since the amount is relatively immaterial, use of straight-line amortization need not be changed.)

g. The credits to the Intangibles account represent an attempt by the company bookkeeper to amortize the year-end balances 10% each year (subject to the policy described below). When you question the bookkeeper and company officials, you learn the company's policy is to amortize those intangibles it regards as having limited lives over ten years. For this purpose, acquisitions and retirements are accounted for in terms of the most proximate quarter in which they entered or were removed from the books. All items are regarded as amortizable except R&D and Goodwill, You concur with the judgment as to the ten-year life of those intangibles properly subject to amortization.

Required:

Make journal entries to correct PQR's books as of December 31, 19C, on the assumption the books have been adjusted but not closed for the year as of that date. (Although years such as 19A and 19B have not been specifically identified as particular calendar years, for purposes of your solution, assume all events of the problem have occurred recently and that the current pronouncements of authoritative bodies reflected in the text apply to the various items.)

It is suggested that you key your entries to the letter, identifying the items in the problem. Explain each correcting entry. For the most part, compound entries should be avoided unless elements of the entry are closely related.

Problem 15–7

Sorenson Manufacturing Corporation was incorporated on January 3, 1977. The corporation's financial statements for its first year's operations were not examined by a CPA. You have been engaged to examine the financial statements for the year ended December 31, 1978, and your examination is substantially completed. The corporation's trial balance appears below.

SORENSON MANUFACTURING CORPORATION
Trial Balance
December 31, 1978

	Debit	Credit
Cash	$ 11,000	
Accounts receivable	68,500	
Allowance for doubtful accounts		$ 500
Inventories	38,500	
Machinery	75,000	
Equipment	29,000	
Accumulated depreciation		10,000
Patents	85,000	
Prepaid expenses	10,500	
Organization costs	29,000	
Goodwill	24,000	
Licensing agreement No. 1	50,000	
Licensing agreement No. 2	49,000	
Accounts payable		147,500
Unearned revenue		12,500
Capital stock		300,000
Retained earnings, January 1, 1978	27,000	
Sales		668,500
Cost of goods sold	454,000	
Selling and general expenses	173,000	
Interest expense	3,500	
Extraordinary losses	12,000	
Totals	$1,139,000	$1,139,000

The following information relates to accounts that may yet require adjustment:

1. Patents for Sorenson's manufacturing process were acquired January 2, 1978, at a cost of $68,000. An additional $17,000 was spent in December 1978, to improve machinery covered by the patents and charged to the Patents account. Depreciation on operational assets has been properly recorded for 1978 in accordance with Sorenson's practice, which provides a full year's depreciation for property on hand June 30 and no depreciation otherwise. Sorenson uses the straight-line method for all depreciation and amortization.

2. On January 3, 1977, Sorenson purchased licensing agreement No. 1, which was believed to have an unlimited useful life. The balance in the Licensing Agreement No. 1 account includes its purchase price of $48,000 and expenses of $2,000 related to the acquisition. On January 1, 1978, Sorenson bought licensing agreement No. 2, which has a life expectancy of ten years. The balance in the Licensing Agreement No. 2 account includes its $48,000 purchase price and $2,000 in acquisition expenses, but it has been reduced by a credit of $1,000 for the advance collection of 1979 revenue from the agreement.

   In late December 1977 an explosion caused a permanent 60% reduction in the expected revenue producing value of licensing agreement No. 1, and in January 1979 a flood caused additional damage that rendered the agreement worthless.

3. The balance in the Goodwill account includes (a) $8,000 paid December 30, 1977, for an advertising program it is estimated will assist in increasing Sorenson's sales over a period of four years following the disbursement and (b) legal expenses of $16,000 incurred for Sorenson's incorporation on January 3, 1977.

4. The balance in the Organization Costs account properly includes costs incurred during the organization period. Sorenson has exercised its option to amortize Organization Costs over a five-year period beginning January 1977 for federal income tax purposes and wishes to amortize these costs for accounting purposes in the same manner. No amortization has yet been recorded.

5. No amortization has yet been recorded for 1978.

Required:

Prepare journal entries as of December 31, 1978, as required by the information given. Note: Prior to the explosion, Licensing Agreement No. 1 should have been amortized in accordance with provisions of *APB Opinion No. 17.*

(AICPA adapted)

Problem 15–8

The XYZ Corporation is a small manufacturing company producing a highly flammable cleaning fluid. On May 31, 1979, the company had a fire which completely destoyed the processing building and the in-process inventory; some of the equipment was saved.

The cost of the operational assets destroyed and their related accumulated depreciation at May 31, 1979, were as follows:

	Cost	Accumulated Depreciation
Building	$40,000	$24,667
Machinery and equipment	15,000	4,375

At present prices the cost to replace the destroyed property would be building, $80,000; and machinery and equipment, $37,500. At the time of the fire it was determined that the destroyed building was 62.5% depreciated and the destroyed machinery and equipment was 33.3% depreciated. The insurable (i.e., market) value of all the building and machinery and equipment was determined to be $75,000, but insurance premiums were structured in such a way as to only provide indemnification equal to the market value (i.e., current replacement cost) of the *undepreciated portion* of the building and the machinery and equipment.

After the fire a physical inventory was taken. The raw materials were valued at $30,000, the finished goods at $60,000, and supplies at $5,000.

The inventories on January 1, 1979, consisted of

Raw materials	$ 15,000
Work in process	50,000
Finished goods	70,000
Supplies	2,000
Total	$137,000

A review of the accounts showed that the sales and gross margin for the last five years were as follows:

	Sales	Gross Margin
1974	$300,000	$ 86,200
1975	320,000	102,400
1976	330,000	108,900
1977	250,000	62,500
1978	280,000	84,000

The sales for the first five months of 1979 were $150,000. Raw material purchases were $50,000. Freight on purchases was $5,000. Direct labor for the five months was $40,000; for the past five years manufacturing overhead was 50% of direct labor.

Insurance on the property and inventory was carried with three companies. Each policy included an 80% coinsurance clause. The amount of insurance carried with the various companies was as follows:

	Building, Machinery, and Equipment	Inventories
Company A	$30,000	$38,000
Company B	20,000	35,000
Company C	15,000	35,000

The cost of cleaning up the debris was $7,000. The value of the scrap salvaged from the fire was $600.

Required:

1. Compute the value of inventory lost.
2. Compute the expected recovery from each insurance company.

(AICPA adapted)

Problem 15–9

Smith Mercantile Company operates retail branches in various cities. Branches in four cities are served out of Warehouse No. 16, which sustained fire damage on April 10.

Between January 1 and April 10 recorded shipments from Warehouse No. 16 to its four stores were as below:

Branch	Shipments
W	$80,500
X	92,000
Y	69,000
Z	23,000

Shipments to branches are marked up 15% above cost, and sales prices are reflected in the foregoing amounts. The January 1 inventory at Warehouse No. 16 was $48,100; purchases between January 1 and April 10 totaled $224,600; freight-in was $2,300; and purchase returns were $9,200.

To arrive at the April 10 inventory for insurance settlement purposes it was agreed to deduct 10% for goods shopworn and damaged prior to the fire.

A compromise agreement between the insurance adjuster and Smith Company management set the amount of inventory lost in the fire at $21,480.

Required:

1. Estimate the amount of inventory in the warehouse at April 10.
2. Determine the indemnity claim if the warehouse contents were insured by a single $20,000 policy having an 80% coinsurance clause. Calculate to nearest dollar.

Problem 15–10

The records of Company X showed at date of fire (all merchandise destroyed): sales, $240,000; beginning inventory, $15,000; purchases, $205,000; insurance (one-year policy for $12,000 with 80% coinsurance clause) premium, $200; salespersons' salaries, $15,000; and general expense, $13,000. The fire occurred six months after the premium was paid; payment of the indemnity canceled the insurance policy. It was agreed that the gross margin percentage based on sales was 16⅔%.

Required:

1. Compute the indemnity to be received from the insurance company
2. Give entries relating to the fire loss.
3. Prepare a classified income statement for the period ending on a date immediately following the fire. Ignore income taxes.

Problem 15–11

Estimate the amount (to the nearest dollar) of insurance collectible on each of the following assets assuming the policies include an 80% coinsurance clause:

Asset	Market Value	Loss Suffered	Insurance Carried
Buildings	$80,000	$42,000	$65,000
Furniture	20,000	18,000	15,000
Delivery equipment ...	9,000	4,000	5,000
Merchandise	?	60%	10,000

To find the value of the merchandise destroyed, the following facts are submitted from which to select the significant data:

The gross margin averages 30% of sales.
The market value (i.e. the replacement cost) of the inventory is the same as its cost.

Purchases for the period	$65,000
Beginning inventory	19,400
Return purchases	2,000
Salespersons' commissions and advertising	8,000
Interest revenue	200
Postage and stationery	1,000
Sales	84,000
Credit department expense	700
Sales returns	2,000

Problem 15–12

Dawn Company operates in a leased building; it adjusts and closes books each December 31. On April 30 a fire seriously damaged its inventory and fixtures. Inventory was totally destroyed; fixtures were half destroyed. Different insurance policies cover the assets, but both have a common feature under which they are canceled for future or remaining coverage to whatever extent a portion of the total potential indemnity is collected by the insured.

The company uses a periodic inventory system, and the accounting records were saved; these reveal that in the past three years gross margin has averaged 38% of sales price. The January 1 inventory was $73,280. Between January 1 and April 30 purchases and sales were respectively $116,320 and $206,500. Inventory was insured by a $65,000 policy with no coinsurance clause. The latest premium payment covering a one-year period from September 1 of last year amounted to $720.

When the books were closed last December 31, the fixtures were 2½ years old. Accounts related to the fixtures and their insurance policy are set forth below.

Fixtures		Accumulated Depreciation	
Balance 20,000		Year 1	900
		Year 2	1,800
		Year 3	1,800

Prepaid Insurance	
Policy A 42	
Policy B 480	

Policy A expired February 28 of the current year. Policy B was immediately put in force to replace it and covers a two-year period. It is for $10,000 maximum coverage, provides for indemnity on the basis of market value of any loss, and has an 80% coinsurance clause. It is determined that the market value of the fixtures when the fire occurred was $15,000 and that the damage amounted to a loss of half their market value.

Required (round amounts to nearest dollar):

1. Adjust the books to April 30 and reflect the inventory as of that date.
2. Open a Casualty Loss account; set up the indemnities collectible as a receivable due from the Insurance Company.
3. Transfer the net balance in Casualty Loss to Income Summary.

Problem 15–13

On April 1, 19A, Clara Company insured the life of its president, T. Lee, for $75,000, naming itself as beneficiary. Annual premiums paid each April 1 are $3,600. As a result of the third premium payment and at the end of the third policy year, the policy has a cash surrender value of $1,800. One year later this will increase to $2,430. Allocate the 3rd year cash surrender value equally to each of the first three years.

Clara Company adjusts and closes its books on December 31 and charges premium payments to Prepaid Insurance. All premiums are paid when due. Lee died

April 3, 19D. No refund of unexpired premiums as of date of death is provided for in the policy.

Required:

Make all entries related to the policy through April 3, 19D, including adjusting and closing entries at the end of each year the policy is in force.

Problem 15–14

One of your corporate clients is somewhat "insurance minded" and maintains in force, several life insurance policies which have a cash surrender value feature on which the corporation is beneficiary. Several questions have arisen concerning the accounting presentation or treatment of these policies and their cash surrender value aspects.

a. One policy is on the life of the company president (who is not a stockholder). A substantially high proportion of what could be borrowed against this policy has been borrowed; the loan amounts to 88% of the cash surrender value at balance sheet date. One reason for borrowing this way is that the interest rate is about half the rate at which other loans could be obtained. You are asked for advice as to how to report the loan on the company's balance sheet and whether the fact that there may be a current liability against the policy changes the classification of cash surrender value.

b. Most of the stock of the corporation is held by a few large stockholders. To retain control within a limited group, your client has bought policies on the lives of these principal stockholders which will provide for repurchase of their stock in the event of a stockholder's death. The cash surrender value of these policies has been reported on the balance sheet. You are asked whether further disclosure is necessary.

c. Looking to the future and possible repayment of the loan on the policy mentioned, especially if interest rates should fall, a hypothetical question is posed. Assuming the loan is repaid, would it be mandatory to report cash surrender value on this policy since the insurance is carried to cover the loss it is anticipated would be sustained as the result of the death of a key official?

d. For a time, another officer of the corporation (who also is not a stockholder) personally "owned" and paid premiums on a substantial life insurance policy on which his wife was beneficiary. For business reasons, your client bought the policy from him at a price equal to his past premium payments ($80,000). The corporation became beneficiary of the policy and beneficial owner of its cash surren-

der value ($45,000); the latter amount was recorded in the accounts as an asset. The $35,000 difference is being amortized over the life expectancy of the insured as disclosed in a mortality table. You are asked for your concurrence or disagreement with this accounting treatment.

Required:

Draft a reply responding to the above questions. Give reasons to support whatever positions you take.

Problem 15–15

Select the best answer in each of the following. Briefly justify your choice.

1. H Company incurred R&D costs in 1978 as follows:

Materials used in R&D projects	$ 400,000
Equipment acquired that will have alternate future uses in future R&D projects	2,000,000
Depreciation for 1978 on above equipment	500,000
Personnel costs of persons involved in R&D projects	1,000,000
Consulting fees paid to outsiders for R&D projects	100,000
Indirect costs reasonably allocable to R&D projects	200,000
	$4,200,000

The amount of R&D costs charged to H's 1978 income statement should be

a. $1,500,000.
b. $1,700,000.
c. $2,200,000.
d. $3,500,000.

2. P Company is planning to invest $40,000 in a royalty-producing copyright. P's expected rate of return from the three-year project is 10%. The present value of $1 at 10% for one year is .909, for two years it is .826, and for three years it is .751. The cash flow, net of income taxes, will be $15,000 for the first year (present value, $13,635) and $18,000 for the second year (present value, $14,868). Assuming the rate of return is exactly 10%, what would be the cash flow, net of income taxes, for the third year?

a. $8,634.
b. $11,000.
c. $11,497.
d. $15,309.

3. Which of the following cost items would be matched with current revenues on a basis other than association of cause and effect?

a. Goodwill.
b. Sales commissions.
c. Cost of goods sold.
d. Purchases on account.

4. If four separate carriers have written fire insurance policies totaling $60,000 on a single property with a market value at $100,000, what fraction of a loss of $20,000 would be collectible from a carrier whose $30,000 policy contains a 90% coinsurance clause?
   a. 60/90.
   b. 30/90.
   c. 30/60.
   d. 20/100.

5. Four separate carriers have written fire insurance policies totaling $160,000 on a single property valued at $200,000. The fraction of a partial loss of $40,000 that will be collectible from a carrier whose $60,000 policy contains a 90% coinsurance clause would be
   a. 9/10.
   b. 4/5.
   c. 2/3.

d. 1/5.
e. None of the above.

6. How should research and development costs be accounted for according to a Financial Accounting Standards Board Statement?
   a. Must be capitalized when incurred and then amortized over their estimated useful lives.
   b. Must be expensed in the period incurred unless contractually reimbursable.
   c. May be either capitalized or expensed when incurred, depending upon the facts of the situation.
   d. Must be expensed in the period incurred unless it can be clearly demonstrated that the expenditure will have significant future benefits.

7. Cash surrender value of life insurance policies on corporate executives should be shown in the balance sheet as
   a. Cash.
   b. Short-term investment.
   c. Prepaid expense.
   d. Long-term investment.

(AICPA adapted)

16

Corporations—Formation and Contributed Capital

The corporate form of business organization has become a dominant one in the United States. This particular form gained widespread use primarily as a result of the legal foundations upon which it is built. A corporation is, in the eyes of the law, an entity separate and apart from the owners. Limited liability of corporate owners, provision for succession of ownership, facility for capital accumulation, separation of management from ownership, and the legal right to act in the same capacity as an individual in the transaction of authorized business are five important factors contributing to the growth of the corporate form of business. In view of the unique features of the corporate form and its extensive use, accountants have considerable concern with respect to the special accounting problems encountered. This chapter and the next two consider these special accounting problems.

Unique problems are encountered in accounting for a corporation in respect to the *owners' equity.* In other respects the accounting treatment of transactions is largely unaffected by the form of business organization. At the outset it is well to realize that there is not complete agreement in the accounting profession on a number of the issues related to accounting for owners' equity. In a sole proprietorship, owners' equity usually is represented by a single equity account; and in a partnership, by separate equity accounts for each partner. In contrast, accounting

for a corporation generally requires a number of owners' equity accounts.

In accounting for corporate owners' equities, accountants adhere to the concept of *source of capital* primarily to comply with legal requirements which are stated in the laws of the various states in terms of the sources of capital. In order to apply this concept, owners' equity accounts are established so that the *sources* of the capital used in the enterprise are clearly segregated. In accounting by *source,* aside from the funds supplied by creditors (liabilities), the primary sources of corporate capital are *(a)* contributions by the owners and *(b)* earnings retained in the business. The term "capital" has long been used to refer to the resources provided by owners, that is, the shareholders. It includes contributions by owners plus retained earnings. In recent years it has been more often called shareholders' or stockholders' equity. The accountant should be familiar with the four following classes of equities and capital:

1. *Total equity (enterprise capital)*—Total equity represents the total interests of all creditors and owners of a particular corporation in the properties of that business; it is the sum of the creditors' equity and the owners' equity.

2. *Owners' equity (proprietary equity)*—Owners' equity represents the total equity at a

given time of the legal owners of the enterprise; it is the total of contributed capital and all subsequent accretions in the form of additional contributions and retained earnings.

3. *Contributed capital*—Contributed capital is the investment made by the owners; in a corporation it is the total amount paid in by all parties other than creditors, plus retained earnings that have been capitalized. It does not include appropriated or unappropriated retained earnings.

4. *Legal or stated capital*—Legal capital is that portion of corporate capital that is required by statute to be retained in the business for the protection of creditors.

CLASSIFICATIONS OF CORPORATIONS

The laws of each state, rather than federal laws, provide for the formation and operation of corporations. Although state laws relating to corporations vary in many respects, there is much similarity in basic provisions. The statutes of all states provide for the existence of a separate entity and for the basic capital structure (capital stock).[1] Corporations are brought into legal existence by submitting an application (articles of incorporation) for a charter to the secretary of state. If approved, a charter is issued by the state which specifies the detailed conditions under which the corporation may operate, such as what business activities are permitted, types of capital stock to be issued, and the method of electing officers. The charter is supplemented with bylaws which are adopted by the stockholders.

Corporations may be classified as follows:

By ownership:

1. Public corporations, when they relate to governmental units or business operations owned by governmental units.

2. Private corporations, when they are privately owned. Such corporations may be nonstock (nonprofit organizations such as colleges and churches) or stock (usually organized for profit making).

By state of incorporation and operation:

3. Domestic corporations, when operating in the state in which incorporated.

4. Foreign corporations, when operating in states other than the one in which incorporated.

By availability of ownership interests:

5. Open, or publicly held, corporations, when the stock is available for purchase. The shares of open corporations often are "listed" by one of the stock exchanges.

6. Closed, or closely held, corporations, when the stock is not available for purchase and is generally held by few shareholders.

NATURE OF CAPITAL STOCK

Shares of capital stock, represented by stock certificates, evidence ownership in a corporation. Shares may be transferred freely by shareholders unless there is an enforceable agreement not to do so. Ownership of shares entitles the holder to certain basic rights. These rights are as follows:

1. The right to participate in the *management* of the corporation through participating and voting in stockholder meetings.

2. The right to participate in the *profits* of the corporation through dividends declared by the board of directors.

3. The right to share in the distribution of *assets* of the corporation at liquidation or through liquidating dividends.

4. The right to purchase shares of stock on a *pro rata basis* in the corporation when such shares represent additional capital stock issues. This pre-emptive right is designed to protect the proportional interests of each shareholder in the ownership. Some publicly held companies have withdrawn this pre-emptive right.

These rights are shared equitably and proportionately by all stockholders unless the charter

---

[1] The formation and operation (particularly with respect to shareholders' equity) is subject to the laws of the various states. These laws vary significantly in many respects. Some years ago the American Bar Association (specifically its Committee on Corporate Laws) developed a recommendation called the Model Business Corporation Act. Unfortunately, the act uses some obsolete terminology. Over the years the various states have tended to adopt many (but not all) of the recommendations in the *Model Act*. Nevertheless, wide differences in state statutes continue to prevail.

or bylaws (and stock certificates) specifically provide otherwise. In the case of one class of stock, all holders enjoy equal rights; in the case of two or more classes of stock, the holders of one class of stock may have rights that have been withheld from the others.

In order to comprehend clearly the nature of capital stock, and to account for it correctly, the accountant must understand the following terms:

1. Authorized capital stock—the number of shares of stock that can be issued legally as specified in the charter.
2. Issued capital stock—the number of shares of authorized capital stock that have been issued to date.
3. Unissued capital stock—the number of shares of authorized capital stock that have *never* been issued.
4. Outstanding capital stock—the number of shares of capital stock that have been issued and are being held by shareholders at a given date.
5. Treasury stock—those shares once issued and later reacquired by the corporation, that is, the difference between issued shares and outstanding shares.
6. Subscribed stock—unissued shares of stock set aside to meet subscription contracts. Subscribed stock often is not issued until the subscription price is paid in full.

In accounting for stockholders' equity, descriptive (and some nondescriptive) terms have evolved. Although in practice there is some variation in terminology, the following terminology appears to represent current trends:[2]

1. Contributed capital (sometimes referred to as paid-in capital):
   a. Capital stock:
      (1) Preferred stock.
      (2) Common stock.
   b. Other contributed capital or additional paid-in capital (an obsolete term, capital surplus, is sometimes used):

   (1) From owners:
      Contributed capital in excess of par or stated value (sometimes called premium on capital stock) and contributed capital from treasury stock and stock retirement transactions.
   (2) From outsiders:
      Donation of assets.
2. Retained earnings (an obsolete term, earned surplus, is sometimes used).
   a. Prior period adjustments (see Chapter 4).
   b. Appropriated (frequently referred to as reserves).
   c. Unappropriated.
3. Unrealized capital increment or decrement.

Exhibit 16–1 presents a typical stockholders' equity section of a balance sheet. Observe in the exhibit the reporting of owners' equity by *source*.

CLASSES OF CAPITAL STOCK

Corporations tend to use several different types of capital stock which give the respective shareholders specific privileges, restrictions, and responsibilities. Some of these restrictions may result from provisions of state statutes, the charter, or the bylaws of the corporation, and

EXHIBIT 16–1
Stockholders' Equity Section of a Typical Balance Sheet

Stockholders' Equity		
Contributed Capital:		
Capital stock:		
Preferred stock, 6%, par $10, cumulative and nonparticipating, 20,000 shares authorized, 15,000 issued and outstanding	$150,000	
Preferred stock subscribed, 100 shares	1,000	
Total preferred stock	151,000	
Common stock, nopar value, 10,000 shares authorized; 8,000 shares issued and outstanding, stated value $5	40,000	$191,000
Other Contributed Capital:		
In excess of par value, preferred stock	12,000	
In excess of stated value, common stock	3,000	
Donation of plant site	5,000	20,000
Total Contributed Capital		211,000
Retained Earnings:		
Appropriated:		
Reserve for bond sinking fund	50,000	
Unappropriated	70,000	
Total Retained Earnings		120,000
Unrealized increment, discovery value of natural resource		50,000
Unrealized loss on long-term investments in equity securities		(6,000)
Total Stockholders' Equity		$375,000

[2] In AICPA *Accounting Terminology Bulletin No. 1,* "Review and Resumé," the Committee on Terminology recommended: "The use of the term *surplus* (whether standing alone or in such combination as *capital surplus, paid-in surplus, earned surplus, appraisal surplus,* etc.) [should] be discontinued."

are made operative by contract between the corporation and the shareholders. The two primary classifications of capital stock are *(a)* par value and nopar value stock and *(b)* common and preferred stock.

Par Value Stock

The laws of each state (and the Model Act) provide for the issuance of par value stock, that is, shares of stock with a designated dollar "value" per share as provided for in the articles of incorporation and as printed on the face of the stock certificates. Par value stock may be either common or preferred. In the early history of corporations in the United States, only par value stock was authorized. Since the owners of a corporation under earlier laws were not liable to creditors (beyond the assets of the corporation), later statutes provided for a par value to afford some measure of protection to creditors. In this respect the courts tended to hold that shareholders who had paid *less* than par value for their stock could be assessed for an amount equal to the discount to satisfy creditors' claims. Par value stock sold initially at less than par is said to have been issued at a discount, whereas par value stock sold above par is said to have been issued at a premium. Today, the issuance of par value stock at a discount is illegal in most states (and by the Model Act). Fundamentally, par value has no particular relationship to market value. However, par value has significance in most states in that (1) it represents the minimum amount that must be paid in at initial sale of the stock; (2) in the case of insolvency, if the par value of all outstanding shares was fully paid in (or an equivalent amount of retained earnings was capitalized as in a stock dividend), the shareholders cannot be held additionally liable; and (3) it establishes the minimum amount of owners' equity the law requires to be maintained.

In order to avoid a real or implied discount, most new corporations, and those distributing new issues, use a very low par value, such as $1, and offer the stock at a higher price, such as $10, $20, or even $100 per share.[3]

---

[3] Despite laws that forbid selling par value capital stock at a discount, it sometimes happens de facto when promoters, and others, receive shares of stock in exchange for noncash assets or services which are overvalued.

Nopar Stock

True nopar stock does not carry a designated or assigned value per share—nor is such provided for in the articles of incorporation. However, the laws of some states (and the Model Act) authorize the issuance of nopar stock with a *stated* or *assigned* value. The stated or assigned value is established by the corporate directors or the bylaws of the corporation.

The use of an assigned or stated value serves to place the nopar stock on practically the same basis as par value stock for accounting purposes. Both common and preferred stock may be represented by nopar shares. Nopar stock was first permitted by statute in New York in 1912; since that date the authorization of stock without par value has become so generally accepted that today practically all states permit its issuance. The chief advantages *claimed* for this type of stock are as follows:

1. It avoids a contingent liability of stockholders to creditors for stock discount.
2. It places the investor on guard to determine the true value of the stock rather than blindly to assume it to bear some relationship to the par value.
3. It facilitates the accounting for capital in that the total amount paid in generally is credited to the capital stock account.
4. It does away with the dubious expediency, sometimes encountered in par value stock, of overvaluing assets received for stock in order to report such stock fully paid.
5. In some jurisdictions there is less tax on nopar shares.

The claimed disadvantages of nopar stock are (1) excessive franchise and other taxes levied by some jurisdictions, (2) the frequent recording of a large amount of "additional" contributed capital, and (3) the tendency to exercise less care in the valuation of noncash assets received in exchange for the nopar shares.

Legal Capital

The distinction between par and nopar capital stock may be more fully appreciated by a consideration of legal capital. The total owners' equity in a corporation is represented by capital contributed by owners, capital contributed by outsiders, retained earnings, and unrealized capital increments and decrements. *Legal capital* is defined by the laws of each state somewhat differently. Recall that the stockholders in a corporation have limited liability; that is, they cannot be held legally liable for the debts of the corporation (except to the extent that legal capital is impaired). In order to afford some measure of protection to creditors, state laws designate some minimum investment in the corporation as legal capital. This legal capital usually cannot be returned to the owners through dividends or by purchase of their shares by the corporation unless creditor claims are adequately protected.

When par value stock is issued, most states specify that the par value of all issued (and not formally retired) shares constitutes legal capital. In the case of nopar stock the legal capital generally is regarded as the stated or assigned value per share. In the case of true nopar stock most states require that the full proceeds from the sale of nopar stock be treated as legal capital. In case the legal capital is impaired through dividend payments or purchase of the corporation's own shares (treasury stock), the courts generally have held that creditors may obtain payment from the shareholders for claims to the extent of such impairment.

The concept of legal capital is important in accounting for corporate ownership equities. The capital accounts should be maintained so that sources are known, thereby providing appropriate data for determination of legal capital in conformance with the statutes of the particular state in which incorporated. Since state statutes define legal capital, and there is considerable variation in statutes among states, careful accounting for corporate capital is essential. For example, some states exclude capital stock subscribed (and unissued) from legal capital.

The amount of legal capital should be entered in the capital stock account, and amounts received in excess of legal capital should be recorded in other appropriately designated capital accounts.

Common Stock

Common stock represents the basic issue of shares and normally carries all of the basic rights listed in a preceding paragraph. When there is only one class of stock, all of the shares are common stock.

Preferred Stock

Preferred stock is so designated because it confers certain preferences or privileges over the common stock. The preferences or privileges may relate to the following:

1. Dividends.
   a. Cumulative or noncumulative.
   b. Fully participating, partially participating, or nonparticipating.
2. Assets.
3. Redemption.
4. Convertibility.

Since the right to vote is a basic right, preferred shareholders have full voting rights unless specifically prohibited in the charter. Likewise, all the other basic rights of stock ownership apply to preferred stock unless specifically withheld in the charter.[4]

Preferred stock is usually par value stock, in which case the dividend preference is expressed as a percentage. For example, 6% preferred stock would carry a dividend preference of 6% of the *par value* of each share. In the case of nopar preferred stock a dividend preference necessarily is expressed as a specific dollar *amount* per share. Occasionally a corporation may issue two or more classes of preferred stock each having different preferences.

To identify specifically the preferences relating to preferred stock, corporations must indicate on the stock certificate the exact nature of the preferences, that is, whether the stock is cumulative, participating, callable, or convertible.[5]

Cumulative Preferences on Preferred Stock

Noncumulative preferred stock provides that dividends not declared (i.e., dividends "passed" or in arrears) for any prior year or series of prior years are lost permanently as far as the pre-

---

[4] Frequently preferred stock is specified as nonvoting.

[5] In some cases the distinction between common and preferred stock represents restrictive or negative features. For example, noncumulative, nonparticipating, and nonvoting are negative features.

ferred shareholders are concerned. As a result the noncumulative restriction generally is viewed as an undesirable feature by potential investors.

Cumulative preferred stock provides that dividends in arrears for any prior year or series of prior years accumulate and must be paid in full to the preferred shareholders when dividends are declared, before the common stockholders may receive a dividend. If only a part of the preference is met for any one year, then the balance of the cumulative preference remains in arrears. Cumulative preferred stock does not carry the right, in liquidation of the corporation, to dividends in arrears if there are no retained earnings. However, express provisions may be made in the charter and stock specifications concerning dividends in arrears in such situations. At common law, where the charter is silent as to the cumulative feature, preferred stock is considered to be cumulative.

APB Opinion No. 9, "Reporting the Results of Operations," par. 35, states: "When cumulative preferred dividends are in arrears, the per share and aggregate amounts thereof should be disclosed."

Participating Preferences on Preferred Stock

Preferred stock is *fully participating* when the preferred shareholders are entitled to dividends (in addition to the basic preference rate) on a pro rata basis (based on par or stated value) with the holders of common stock. In this case the preference relates to a prior claim to dividends up to a stated percent of par (the basic preference rate), after which both classes of stock share ratably in dividends in excess of the basic preference.

Preferred stock is *nonparticipating* when the dividends on such stock for any one year are limited in the charter to a specified preference rate (plus any cumulative preferences). *Partially participating* preferred stock provides that the shareholders thereof participate above the preferential rate with the common stockholders, but only up to an additional rate which is specified in the charter and on the stock certificate. For example, a corporation may issue 6% preferred stock, with participation up to a total of 8%, in which case participation privileges

with the common shareholders would be limited to an additional 2%.

In the absence of an expressed stipulation, most courts have taken the view that preferred stock has no right to participate with the common stock, unless this preference is stated expressly in the preferred stock specifications in the charter.

Since accountants are called upon to advise management with respect to dividend declarations, it is important that computation of dividends be clearly understood. To illustrate dividend computations, assume the following:

Preferred stock, 5% ($100 par value per share— 1,000 shares outstanding)	$100,000
Common stock ($50 par value per share— 4,000 shares outstanding)	200,000

Dividend Computations

	Preferred	Common
Illustration No. 1: Preferred stock is cumulative, nonparticipating; dividends two years in arrears; dividends declared, $28,000.		
Step 1—Preferred in arrears	$10,000	
Step 2—Preferred, current (5% × $100,000)	5,000	
Step 3—Common (balance)		$13,000
	$15,000	$13,000
Illustration No. 2: Preferred stock is cumulative, fully participating; dividends two years in arrears; dividends declared, $28,000.		
Step 1—Preferred in arrears	$10,000	
Step 2—Preferred, current (5%)	5,000	
Step 3—Common, current (to match preferred 5%)		$10,000
Step 4—Balance (ratably with par)	1,000	2,000
	$16,000	$12,000
Illustration No. 3: Preferred stock is noncumulative, partially participating up to an additional 2%; dividends declared, $28,000.		
Step 1—Preferred, current (5%)	$ 5,000	
Step 2—Common, current (to match preferred 5%)		$10,000
Step 3—Preferred, partial participation, additional 2%	2,000	
Step 4—Common (balance)		11,000
	$ 7,000	$21,000
Illustration No. 4: Preferred stock is noncumulative; partially participating up to an additional 2%; dividends declared, $16,000.		
Step 1—Preferred, current (5%)	$ 5,000	
Step 2—Common, current (to match preferred 5%)		$10,000
Step 3—Preferred, partial participation	333*	
Step 3—Common		667
	$ 5,333	$10,667

* Cannot exceed, $100,000 × 2% = $2,000.

In Illustrations 2, 3, and 4, the "Common, current (to match preferred 5%)" does not mean that the common stock also is 5%; no such provision attaches to the common. Rather in computing participation preferences, the common must be given a "match" equal to the preferred rate; otherwise the common would suffer another disadvantage. The percent rate on the preferred gives it a preference only when dividends are inadequate to accord each class of stock proportionately equal treatment. The allocation of dividends among the various classes of stock may be affected by state laws.

If the common stock is *nopar* and the preferred stock has participating privileges, a specified dollar amount per common share must be established at the outset for the participation matching computations. To illustrate, assume the following fact situation:

Preferred stock, 5%, par $100, cumulative and fully participating; 1,000 shares outstanding.
Common stock, nopar, 10,000 shares outstanding; participation matching amount, $1 per share.
Total dividends to be paid in 19C, $43,000; no dividends were declared or paid in 19A or 19B.

Dividend Computations

	Preferred	Common
Preferred, in arrears (1,000 shares × $100 × 5% × 2 years)	$10,000	
Preferred, current (1,000 shares × $100 × 5%)	5,000	
Common, to match (10,000 shares × $1)		$10,000
Participation:*		
Preferred	6,000	
Common		12,000
Total	$21,000	$22,000

* Computations:

$$\frac{(1,000 \text{ shares} \times \$100 \times 5\% = \$5,000)}{\$15,000} \times \$18,000\dagger = \$ 6,000$$

$$\frac{(10,000 \text{ shares} \times \$1 = \$10,000)}{\$15,000} \times \$18,000 = \frac{12,000}{\$18,000}$$

$\dagger$ $43,000 - $10,000 - $5,000 - $10,000 = $18,000.

Asset Preference

Preferred stock that is *preferred as to assets* (i.e., a liquidation preference) provides that the holders, in case of corporate dissolution, have a priority up to par value or other stated amount per share over common shareholders. Once the priority for the preferred is satisfied, the remainder of the assets is distributed to the common shareholders. *APB Opinion No. 10*, "Omnibus Opinion," par. 10, requires that "the liquidation preference of the preferred stock be disclosed in the equity section of the balance sheet in the aggregate, either parenthetically or 'in short' rather than on a per share basis or by disclosure in notes."

Redemption Preference

Preferred stock having a *redemption* privilege (redeemable stock) provides that the shareholder, at his or her option, may, under the conditions specified, turn in the shares owned to the corporation at a specified price per share.

Redeemable preferred stock, with mandatory redemption dates and amounts, and a cumulative dividend preference, is very much like debt. Consequently, some accountants believe that such preferred stock should be reported as a liability and that the related dividends should be accounted for as interest expense.

Convertibility Privilege

Preferred stock may carry a provision of *convertibility* (convertible stock), which means that at the option of the holder, the preferred shares owned may be exchanged (converted to) for other securities such as common stock. Conversion privileges frequently turn out to be particularly valuable and hence are favored by investors.

Callable Preferred Stock

Preferred stock may be *callable;* that is, the corporation may, at its option, call the stock (purchase it) for cancellation under specified conditions of time and price. *APB Opinion No. 10*, paragraph 11, states that there should be disclosure "on the face of the balance sheet or in notes pertaining thereto: the aggregate or per share amounts at which preferred shares may be called or are subject to redemption through sinking fund operations or otherwise."

ACCOUNTING FOR ISSUANCE OF PAR VALUE STOCK

In accounting for stockholders' equity, recall that *source* is particularly important; accordingly, if a corporation has more than one class of stock, separate accounts must be maintained for each class. In case there is only one class of stock, an account "Capital Stock" is usually employed. In cases where there are two or more classes of stock, titles such as "Common Stock," "Preferred Stock, 5%," and "Common Stock, Nopar" are appropriate. The complete sequence of transactions related to issuance of stock is *(a)* authorization of shares, *(b)* subscriptions, *(c)* collections on subscriptions, and *(d)* issuance of the shares.

Authorization

The authorization in the charter to issue a specified number of shares may be recorded *(a)* by notation or *(b)* by a formal journal entry, viz:

a. Notation:

> Common Stock—Par Value $100 per Share
> (authorized 5,000 shares)

b. Journal entry:

Unissued common stock	500,000	
Common stock, par $100		
(5,000 shares)		500,000

To record authorization of 5,000 shares of common stock, par value $100 per share.

Observe that these two accounts are offsetting. The notation approach is more common. For this reason, the discussions below assume the notation approach.

Stock Issued for Cash

In most situations capital stock is sold and issued for cash rather than on a subscription basis (i.e., installment basis). Using the above example and assuming the sale of 1,000 shares at $102 per share, the issue entry would be as follows:

Notation method:

Cash	102,000	
Common stock, par $100		
(1,000 shares)		100,000
Contributed capital in excess		
of par, common stock		2,000

The capital stock account is credited for the par value of the stock times the number of shares issued, and the excess over par is credited to a descriptively named contributed capital account to record *source* in detail.

ACCOUNTING FOR NOPAR CAPITAL STOCK

Because the statutes in many states permit two types of nopar stock—*true* nopar stock and *stated value* nopar stock—there is some variation in accounting. Nopar stock with a stated value is accounted for as discussed above for par value stock since the stated value places the nopar stock on practically the same basis as par value stock. Amounts received in excess of stated value should be credited to an account with a descriptive title such as Contributed Capital in Excess of Stated Value, Nopar Common Stock.

In the case of *true* nopar stock, no entry can be made for the authorization; instead, notation may be made in the journal and in the ledger account heading such as

> Common Stock—Nopar Value
> (authorized 10,000 shares)

With respect to nopar stock, most states require that the total number of shares authorized, in addition to the customary imprint of the number of shares represented by the individual stock certificate, be shown on the face of each such certificate. It is important to note that entries to record true nopar stock should indicate the *number of shares* as well as the dollar amounts. In the case of true nopar stock, the accounting treatment should follow the applicable legal requirements. If the statutes provide that all proceeds represent legal capital, then the capital stock account should be credited for the full amount received. If the statutes establish a minimum amount per share, then at least this amount should be credited to the capital stock account. In the absence of legal requirements, the total amount received should be credited to the nopar capital stock account.

SUBSCRIPTIONS

Prospective stockholders may sign a contract to purchase a specified number of shares with payment to be made at one or more specified dates in the future. Such a contract is known as a *stock subscription.* Since a legal contract is involved, accounting recognition must be given to this transaction. The purchase price is debited to Stock Subscriptions Receivable; Capital Stock Subscribed is credited for the par, stated, or assigned amount per share; and the difference is credited to Contributed Capital in Excess of Par (or stated value).

To illustrate, assume 100 shares of preferred stock, par $10, are subscribed for at $12; the entry would be as follows:

```
Stock subscriptions receivable—
   preferred stock ..................  1,200
   Preferred stock subscribed,
      par $10 (100 shares) ............        1,000
   Contributed capital in excess
      of par, preferred stock ...........          200
```

Observe that the premium is recorded when the subscription is recorded rather than later when the cash is collected. The Capital Stock Subscribed account recognizes the corporation's obligation to issue the 100 shares upon fulfillment of the terms of the agreement by the subscribers. This account is reported on the balance sheet in a manner similar to the related capital stock account (see Exhibit 16–1). Subscriptions receivable is classified as a current asset if the corporation expects current collection (if noncurrent, it is a long-term asset). Alternatively, if there are *no plans for collection,* subscriptions receivable cannot be considered a realizable asset and, therefore, should be offset against capital stock subscribed in the owners' equity section of the balance sheet. In some cases subscription contracts call for installment payments. In such cases separate "call" accounts may be set up for each installment. If there are a number of subscriptions, it is usually desirable to maintain a *subscribers' ledger* as a subsidiary record to the subscriptions receivable account in a manner similar to that maintained for regular accounts receivable.

Collections on stock subscriptions may be in cash, property, or services. The appropriate account is debited, and subscriptions receivable is credited. If a service or property is received, the *amount* recorded would be based on the market value of the property or services.

Stock certificates usually are not issued until the subscription price is paid in full.[6] Therefore, the last collection often requires two entries. To illustrate, assume the last collection on the above subscription (for $1,200) was $400; the entries would be as follows:

To record collection:

```
Cash .............................    400
   Stock subscriptions receivable—
      preferred stock ..................        400
```

To record issuance of the stock:

```
Preferred stock subscribed ..............  1,000
   Preferred stock, par $10
      (100 shares) ....................        1,000
```

Accounting for *nopar stock* and stock subscriptions are illustrated in Exhibit 16–2.

To issue the stock, a *stock certificate* is prepared for each shareholder which specifies the number of shares represented. An entry to reflect the number of shares held by each shareholder is made in the *stockholder ledger,* which is a subsidiary ledger to the capital stock account.

When a subscriber *defaults* after fulfilling a part of the subscription contract, certain complexities arise. In case of default, the corporation simply may decide to (1) return to the subscriber all payments made or (2) issue shares equivalent to the number paid for in full, rather than the total number contracted. These two options obviously involve no disadvantage to the subscriber, although the corporation may incur a later economic loss if the stock prices drop. The laws of most states cover the contingency where the corporation does not elect either of these alternatives. Such laws vary considerably; two contrasting provisions follow:

a. The subscribed stock is *forfeited,* and all payments made by the defaulting subscriber are lost to the subscriber; hence, the amount

---

[6] Whether some of the shares are issued or not, the subscriber is accorded all the privileges of a stockholder unless the subscription contract specifies otherwise.

EXHIBIT 16–2
Entries for Nopar Stock

	Stated Value Stock		True Nopar Value Stock	
1. To record authorization of nopar stock:				
Notation—10,000 shares of nopar common stock authorized.	Stated value, $5*		No stated value	
2. To record sale of 5,000 shares @ $6:				
Cash	30,000		30,000	
Common stock, nopar, stated value $5		25,000		
Common stock, nopar				30,000
Contributed capital in excess of stated value, nopar common stock		5,000		
3. To record subscription of 5,000 shares @ $6; 20% collected in cash:				
Cash	6,000		6,000	
Stock subscriptions receivable—nopar common stock	24,000		24,000	
Nopar common stock subscribed (5,000 shares)		25,000		30,000
Contributed capital in excess of stated value, nopar common stock		5,000		
4. To record collection of subscription and issuance of stock:				
Cash	24,000		24,000	
Stock subscriptions receivable—nopar common stock		24,000		24,000
Nopar common stock subscribed	25,000		30,000	
Common stock, nopar, stated value $5 (5,000 shares)		25,000		
Common stock, nopar (5,000 shares)				30,000

* Note: This could take the form of a journal entry as illustrated above for par value stock.

paid in is credited to the contributed capital to the corporation. Further, the corporation is free to sell the shares again. Provisions of this type favor the corporation.

b. The stock is forfeited, and the corporation must resell the stock under a *lien,* whereby the original subscriber must be reimbursed for the amount that the *net receipts* for the stock (i.e., the total cash collected from both the first and second sales, less the costs incurred by the corporation in making the second sale) exceed the *original subscription price.* The refund to the defaulting subscriber cannot exceed the amount paid to the date of default less resale costs.

To illustrate Provision *(b),* assume the subscriber in the illustration on page 558 (subscription for 100 shares of preferred stock, par $10, at $12 per share) defaulted after paying $400 cash. The stock is resold later, and cash collected.

To record the default:

Preferred stock subscribed (100 shares)	1,000	
Contributed capital in excess of par, preferred stock	200	
Subscriptions receivable		800
Payable to subscriber (pending resale)		400

To record resale for cash (Case A, $11; Case B, $15; both net of $50 resale cost):

| | Resale Price (net of $50 resale costs) | |
	Case A—$11	Case B—$15
Cash	1,100	1,500
Payable to subscriber	400	400
Preferred stock, par $10 (100 shares)		
Preferred stock, par $10 (100 shares)	1,000	1,000
Contributed capital in excess of par, preferred stock	200	550
Cash (to subscriber)	300*	350†

* The subscriber had to absorb the $50 drop in the net sales price (i.e., $1,200 − $1,150 = $50) and the resale cost of $50.

† The subscriber cannot receive more than the amount paid on the original subscription, less any resale costs (i.e., $400 − $50 = $350 in this example).

ACCOUNTING FOR STOCK PREMIUM AND DISCOUNT

In the preceding discussions, amounts received in excess of par value were credited to an appropriately designated stock "premium" account. Similarly, amounts received less than par are debited to an appropriately titled stock "discount" account. Stock premium constitutes an increase in total corporate capital, whereas stock discount serves to reduce total corporate capital. In view of the advent of nopar stock and the passage of laws in most states forbidding the sale of stock at a discount and the potential legal entanglements, accountants seldom encounter the problem of stock discount.

Contributed capital in excess of par value is classified as contributed or paid-in capital and should remain in the accounts until retirement of the stock. Upon retirement of the stock the related premium should be removed from the accounts. Some states allow such contributed capital to be charged (i.e., "used") for stock dividends; a few allow charges to such accounts for cash dividends as well. When state laws allow these charges, the shareholders receiving the dividends should be informed that they represent a return of original investment (i.e., a liquidating dividend) rather than a distribution of earnings.

Separate premium and discount accounts should be established for each class of stock as needed. Premium and discount should not be offset against each other. Discount can be eliminated by additional collections (stock assessments) from shareholders, capitalization of retained earnings, or through retirement of the related stock. Discount is reported on the balance sheet (a) as a negative item directly under the particular class of stock to which it relates or (b) as a negative item under the "Other Contributed" capital.

Accounting for stock issue costs was discussed in Chapter 15.

SPECIAL SALES OF STOCK

A corporation may sell (issue) each class of stock separately as assumed in the preceding discussions or it may sell two or more classes of securities for one lump sum. Further, a corporation may issue stock for services or property rather than for cash. Each of these situations presents special accounting problems.

In the situation where two or more classes of securities are sold (issued) for a single lump sum, the proceeds must be allocated among the several classes of securities on some logical basis. Two methods available for such situations are (a) the proportional method, where the lump sum received is allocated proportionally among the classes of stock on the basis of relative market value of each security and (b) the incremental method, where the market value of one security is used as a basis for that security and the remainder of the lump sum is allocated to the other class of security. Selection of an appropriate method should depend upon the information available. To illustrate several situations, assume 100 shares of common stock (par value $100 per share) and 50 shares of preferred stock (par value $80 per share) are sold for a lump sum of $15,000.

Assumption 1: The common stock is selling at $104 and the preferred stock at $101—apportionment on basis of relative market values (proportional method):

Cash	15,000	
Common stock, par $100 (100 shares).............................		10,000
Preferred stock, par $80 (50 shares)		4,000
Contributed capital in excess of par, common stock		100
Contributed capital in excess of par, preferred stock		900

Computations (rounded):

Common:
$$\frac{(100 \times \$104)}{(\$10,400 + \$5,050)} \times \$15,000 = \$10,100 : \$10,100 - \$10,000 = \$100$$

Preferred:
$$\frac{(50 \times \$101)}{(\$10,400 + \$5,050)} \times \$15,000 = \underline{\$4,900} : \$4,900 - \$4,000 = \$900$$
$$\underline{\underline{\$15,000}}$$

Assumption 2: The common stock is selling at $104; no market has been established for the preferred stock—apportionment on basis of market value of one class of shares (incremental method):

Cash		15,000
Common stock, par $100 (100 shares)	10,000	
Preferred stock, par $80 (50 shares)	4,000	
Contributed capital in excess of par,		
common stock ($4 per share)	400	
Contributed capital in excess of par,		
preferred stock ($1,000 − $400)	600	

Assumption 3: No market value is determinable for either class of stock. In this case an arbitrary allocation is the only alternative. In the absence of any other logical basis, a *temporary* allocation may be made on the basis of relative par values. Should a market value be established for one of the securities in the relatively near future, a correcting entry based on such value would be appropriate. The entry to record the arbitrary allocation—on the basis of relative par values—would be as follows:

Cash		15,000
Common stock, par $100 (100 shares)	10,000	
Preferred stock, par $80 (50 shares)	4,000	
Contributed capital in excess of par,		
common stock	714	
Contributed capital in excess of par,		
preferred stock	286	

Computations:

Common:
$$\frac{\$10,000}{\$14,000} \times \$15,000 = \$10,714: \$10,714 - \$10,000 = \underline{\underline{\$714}}$$

Preferred:
$$\frac{\$4,000}{\$14,000} \times \$15,000 = \underline{\frac{4,286}{\$15,000}}: \$4,286 - \$4,000 = \underline{\underline{\$286}}$$

Noncash Sale of Stock

When a corporation issues stock as payment for assets or services, the question of stock valuation for accounting purposes arises. The values to apply in this situation, in determination of the proceeds, are as follows, in order of preference:[7]

1. Current market value of the stock issued or the current market value of the assets or services received, whichever is the more clearly determinable.

2. Appraised value of the assets or services received.

3. Valuation of the assets or services established by the board of directors.

The exchange of noncash assets for stock has given rise to many abuses over the years through improper valuation of the assets received. Overvalued assets create an overstatement of corporate capital—a condition frequently referred to as *watered stock.* On the other hand, undervaluation of assets creates an understatement of corporate capital giving rise to what is frequently referred to as *secret reserves.* Secret reserves also may be created by depreciating or amortizing assets over a period substantially less than their useful lives.

UNREALIZED CAPITAL INCREMENT

Unrealized capital *increment,* as a category of stockholders' equity, is not widely used in practice. It arises when assets are written up from cost; thus, it violates the cost principle. Because of adherence to the cost principle and the concept of conservatism, assets rarely are written up from cost to market value. An example of such writeups involves *discovery value* of natural resources. Other examples are to be found in financial companies. Typically, in insurance and mutual fund companies, the investment portfolio is adjusted to market value periodically because it is current GAAP in these industries to account for their investments at market value. An upward adjustment of the asset account requires an offsetting credit to either revenue or unrealized capital increment (see Chapters 13 and 19).

There are a number of unsettled issues such as *(a)* measurement of market value, *(b)* classification of the credit, and *(c)* adequate disclosure. As the profession moves toward "value accounting," these issues will necessarily come into sharper focus and demand definitive solutions.

The writeup of operational (fixed) assets to appraisal (market) value was discussed briefly in Chapter 13 with respect to discovery value of natural resources. However, except in very limited situations, current GAAP does not permit the writeup of assets to market value. Recall

---

[7] *APB Opinion No. 29,* "Accounting for Nonmonetary Transactions," par. 4, specifically states that it does not apply to the "c. Acquisition of nonmonetary assets or services on issuance of the capital stock of an enterprise, . . ." Preference 1 is consistent with the spirit of the *Opinion.*

from Chapter 13 that the writeup for discovery value created a credit "Unrealized capital increment—discovery value" which is not reported in the current income statement (as a gain or revenue) but rather as a positive increment in stockholders' equity.

UNREALIZED CAPITAL DECREMENT

Unrealized capital *decrement* (i.e., a debit balance) is a contra, or negative, amount in stockholders' equity. It arises when assets are written down under special circumstances. The *debit* from the writedown may be reflected in the financial statements in either of two ways, viz:

1. Reported currently as a deduction in the income statement—The application of the lower-of-cost-or-market (LCM) approach to *(a)* short-term investments and *(b)* inventories gives rise to a debit which is reported as a deduction (a loss) in the current income statement (see Chapters 8 and 10). Another example is the writedown of an operational asset due to a "diminution of going value," such as the writedown of an idle plant (see Chapter 13). Still another example is the recognition of a loss due to the discontinuance of a segment of a business at a loss. These kinds of writedowns are reported on the income statement as ordinary or extraordinary losses, depending on the circumstances.
2. Reported as a deduction, or contra amount, in stockholders' equity on the balance sheet—*FASB Statement No. 12,* "Accounting for Certain Marketable Securities," (December 1975) requires the recording of an "Unrealize loss on long-term investments in equity securities." This unrealized capital decrement on long-term investments must be reported as a contra item in stockholders' equity as discussed in Chapter 19, Part A.

ASSESSMENTS ON SHAREHOLDERS

Some states permit the issuance of *assessable stock,* providing the charter includes such a provision. Also in some states, under certain conditions, the board of directors may assess the stockholders a certain amount per share, although the stock held is not identified as assessable stock. A stock assessment involves the collection of cash from the stockholders in proportion to the shares held without the issuance of additional stock. Stock assessments may be used when a corporation is in dire need of cash, facing probable bankruptcy, or when the stock originally was issued at a discount. If the stock was issued originally at a discount, the assessment (up to the amount of the discount) is credited to the discount account. If no stock discount is carried in the accounts, the credit is to a contributed capital account with an appropriate title such as Contributed Capital, Stock Assessments.

INCORPORATION OF A GOING BUSINESS

The owner, or owners, of a sole proprietorship or partnership may decide to incorporate, or a corporation may acquire another business in exchange for shares of stock.[8] Certain accounting problems arise in such situations, particularly with respect to the values to be placed on the assets received for shares of stock.

In accounting for assets in the situation where an unincorporated business is selling its assets, the cost principle requires that the assets be recorded by the buyer at their market value as of the date of the exchange. The market value of the stock issued for the assets should be used as the value of the assets acquired; if this is not reasonably determinable, then the assets should be valued by other means—usually by appraisal. In some situations neither of these values can be reasonably determined; in such cases the parties involved must be relied upon to establish a realistic estimate of market value. It is not unusual, in the case of a going business, for the parties to agree to an exchange value in excess of the total market value of the identifiable net assets acquired because of the recognition of *goodwill.* In cases where goodwill is paid for, it should be recorded as an intangible asset at its purchased price.

In some situations the only change is in the form of organization; that is, the ownership and management continue unchanged, as where a

---

[8] See Chapter 19 on business combinations.

partnership is simply incorporated. Here a strong case can be made for carrying forward the book values with no recognition of goodwill.

The entries to record the exchange of a going business for shares of stock will depend upon whether the original books of the acquired business will be continued or whether new books will be opened for the corporation and any adjustments made to market values.

If the *original books* are retained, two basic steps are required in cases where the *cost principle* applies, in which case *market values* are recorded as follows:

1. Entries must be made to revalue the assets (and any other items agreed upon) in accordance with the cost principle.
2. Entries must be made to close out the old owners' equity accounts and to replace them with corporate capital accounts.

If *new books* are to be started, the old books must be closed and new books for the corporation opened. Entries should be made on the *old books* to

1. Revalue the assets (and any other items agreed upon) in accordance with the cost principle.
2. Record the transfer of the assets.
3. Record receipt of the stock and its distribution.

Entries must be made on the *new books* to

1. Record the stock authorization.
2. Record the receipt of the assets.
3. Record issuance of the stock.

To illustrate each situation, assume the books for the AB Partnership showed the following:

Cash	$ 2,000
Accounts receivable	10,000
Allowance for doubtful accounts	(1,000)
Inventory	21,000
Operational assets	40,000
Accumulated depreciation	(15,000)
	$57,000
Accounts payable	$ 5,000
Notes payable	2,000
A, capital	30,000
B, capital	20,000
	$57,000

The XYZ Corporation is formed with 20,000 shares of common stock authorized (par value $5 per share); 12,000 of the shares are issued in exchange for the assets, except the cash; the liabilities are assumed by the corporation. It was agreed that the inventory should be written down to $16,000 and that the accumulated depreciation should be $14,000. The book value of the remaining assets essentially represented market value at the time of transfer to XYZ Corporation. The 12,000 shares and the $2,000 cash are to be divided between A and B according to their capital balances after the above adjustments. The partners had divided profits and losses equally. The remaining 8,000 shares were sold to the public at $5.10 per share.

Assumption 1: The old books are to be retained.

1. To record the adjustments:

Accumulated depreciation	1,000	
Adjustment account	4,000	
Inventory		5,000

2. To record goodwill:[9]

Goodwill*	17,200	
Adjustment account		17,200

* Computation:		
Value of shares exchanged (12,000 at $5.10)		$61,200
Value of net assets (after adjustment and excluding cash)		44,000†
Goodwill		$17,200

† $30,000 + $20,000 − $2,000 − $4,000 = $44,000.

3. To close Adjustment account to partners' capital accounts and to divide the gain equally.

Adjustment account	13,200	
A, capital		6,600
B, capital		6,600

4. Notation: Capital stock authorized, 20,000 shares, par $5 per share.

5. To record distribution of $2,000 cash and issuance of 12,000 shares of stock to the partners for the other assets (net):

A, capital ($30,000 + $6,600)	36,600	
B, capital ($20,000 + $6,600)	26,600	
Cash		2,000
Common stock, par $5 (12,000 shares)		60,000
Contributed capital in excess of par, common stock		1,200

---

[9] See Chapter 15 for discussion of amortization of goodwill.

EXHIBIT 16–3
Incorporation of a Partnership

Entries on New Books (Corporation)			*Entries on Old Books (Partnership)*		
1. To record authorization of capital stock:					
Notation: Common stock, par $5; authorized 20,000 shares.					
2. To record adjustments agreed upon:					
			Accumulated depreciation	1,000	
			Adjustment account	4,000	
			Inventory		5,000
3. To record goodwill (as computed in Assumption 1):					
			Goodwill	17,200	
			Adjustment account		17,200
4. To close Adjustment account to capital accounts:					
			Adjustment account	13,200	
			A, capital		6,600
			B, capital		6,600
5. To record transfer of assets and liabilities as adjusted:					
Accounts receivable	10,000		Allowance for doubtful accounts	1,000	
Inventory	16,000		Accumulated depreciation	14,000	
Operational assets	40,000		Accounts payable	5,000	
Goodwill	17,200		Notes payable	2,000	
Allowance for doubtful accounts		1,000	* Receivable from XY Corporation	61,200	
Accumulated depreciation		14,000	Accounts receivable		10,000
Accounts payable		5,000	Inventory		16,000
Notes payable		2,000	Operational assets		40,000
*Payable to AB partnership		61,200	Goodwill		17,200
6. To record transfer of stock:					
*Payable to AB Partnership	61,200		Stock in XY Corporation	61,200	
Common stock		60,000	*Receivable from XY Corporation		61,200
Contributed capital in excess of par, common stock		1,200			
7. Distribution of stock and cash:					
			A, capital	36,600	
			B, capital	26,600	
			Stock in XY Corporation		61,200
			Cash		2,000
8. To record sale of 8,000 shares at $5.10 per share:					
Cash	40,800				
Common stock		40,000			
Contributed capital in excess of par, common stock		800			

* These are clearance accounts that can be avoided by combining Entries 5 and 6.

6. To record sale of 8,000 shares at $5.10 per share:

Cash	40,800	
Common stock, par $5 (8,000 shares) .		40,000
Contributed capital in excess of par, common stock		800

Assumption 2: New books are opened and the old books closed. See Exhibit 16–3.

QUESTIONS

1. Explain the meaning of each of the following: total equity, contributed capital, owners' equity, and legal capital.

2. Define public, private, domestic, foreign, open, and closed corporations.

3. What are the four basic rights of shareholders?

How may one or more of these rights be withheld from the shareholder?

4. Explain each of the following: authorized capital stock, issued capital stock, unissued capital stock, outstanding capital stock, subscribed stock, and treasury stock

5. In accounting for corporate capital, why is *source* particularly important?

6. Distinguish between par and nopar stock.

7. Distinguish between common and preferred stock.

8. Explain the difference between cumulative and noncumulative preferred stock.

9. Explain the difference between nonparticipating, partially participating, and fully participating preferred stock.

10. Under what circumstances should stock subscriptions receivable be reported *(a)* as a current asset, *(b)* as a noncurrent asset, and *(c)* as a deduction in the stockholders' equity section of the balance sheet?

11. What is a liquidating dividend? Why is it important that a liquidating dividend be identified separately?

12. Explain and illustrate "secret reserves" and "watered stock."

13. How should premium and discount on capital stock be accounted for and reported?

14. How are assets valued when shares of stock are given in payment thereof.

15. What is the difference between unrealized capital increment and unrealized capital decrement?

16. What is a stock assessment?

DECISION CASE 16–1

C. Banfield, an engineer, developed a special device to be installed in backyard swimming pools that would set off an alarm should anything fall into the water. Over a two-year period Banfield's spare time was spent developing and testing the device. After receiving a patent, three of Banfield's friends, including a lawyer, considered plans to market the device. Accordingly, a charter was obtained which authorized 25,000 shares of $10 par value stock. Each of the four organizers contributed $1,000, and each received in return 100 shares of stock. They also agreed that each would re-

ceive 500 additional shares. The remaining shares were to be held as unissued stock. Each organizer made a proposal as to how the additional 500 shares would be paid for. These individual proposals were made independently; then the group considered them as a package. The four proposals were as follows:

Banfield: The patent would be turned over to the corporation as payment for the 500 shares.

Lawyer: One hundred shares to be received for legal fees already rendered during organization, 100 shares to be received as advance payment for legal retainer fees for the next three years, and the balance to be paid for in cash at par.

Friend No. 2: A small building, suitable for operations, would be given to the corporation for the 500 shares of stock. It was estimated that $750 would be needed for renovation. The owner estimates that the market value of the building is $25,000 and there is an $18,000 loan on it to be assumed by the corporation.

Friend No. 3: To pay $1,000 cash on the stock and to give an interest-bearing note for $4,000 (subscriptions receivable) to be paid out of dividends over the next five years.

Required:

You have been engaged as an independent CPA to advise the group. Specifically, you have been asked the following questions:

1. How would the above proposals be recorded in the accounts? Evaluate the valuation basis for each.
2. What are your recommendations for an agreement that would be equitable to each organizer? Explain the basis for such recommendations.

EXERCISES

Exercise 16–1

Burns Corporation received a charter authorizing 100,000 shares of $10 par value stock. During the first year, 40,000 shares were sold at $15 per share. One hundred additional shares were issued in payment for legal fees. At the end of the first year, reported net income was $20,000. Dividends of $8,000 were paid on the last day of the year. Liabilities at the year-end amounted to $10,000.

Required:

Complete the following tabulation (show calculations):

	Item	Amount	Assumptions
a.	Total equities	$	
b.	Owners' equity	$	
c.	Contributed capital	$	
d.	Legal capital	$	
e.	Issued capital stock	$	
f.	Outstanding capital stock	$	
g.	Unissued capital stock	$	
h.	Treasury stock	$	

Exercise 16–2

Georgia Corporation's charter authorized 60,000 shares of nopar common stock and 20,000 shares of 6%, cumulative and nonparticipating preferred stock, par value $10 per share. Stock issued to date: 40,000 shares of common sold at $200,000 and 10,000 shares of preferred stock sold at $18 per share. In addition, subscriptions for 2,000 shares of preferred have been taken, and 30% of the purchase price of $18 has been collected. The stock will be issued upon collection in full. The Retained Earnings balance is $70,000. At year-end there was a $6,000 unrealized loss on long-term investments in equity securities.

Required:

Prepare the stockholders' equity section of the balance sheet in good form.

Exercise 16–3

Prepare, in good form, the stockholders' equity section of the balance sheet for Idaho Manufacturing Company.

Retained earnings	$ 60,000
Premium on common stock	40,000
Preferred stock subscribed (2,000 shares)	20,000
Preferred stock, 6%, par $10, authorized 25,000 shares	140,000 (issued)
Common stock, par $20, authorized 50,000 shares	200,000 (issued)
Stock subscriptions receivable, preferred	4,000
Donation of plant site	10,000
Premium on preferred stock	30,000
Unrealized loss on long-term investment in equity securities	5,000

Exercise 16–4

The following data were provided by the accounts of Baker Corporation at December 31, 19C:

Subscriptions receivable (noncurrent)	$ 5,000
Retained earnings, January 1, 19C	150,000
Capital stock, par ?, authorized 100,000 shares	600,000
Future site for office donated (to Baker)	15,000
Capital stock subscribed, 1,000 shares (to be issued upon collection in full)	10,000
Premium on capital stock	300,000
Subscriptions receivable, capital stock (due in three months)	2,000
Bonds payable	100,000
Net income for 19C (not included in retained earnings)	120,000
Dividends declared and paid during 19C	40,000

Required:

1. Respond to the following (state any assumptions made):

a.	Total retained earnings at end of 19C is		$_____
b.	Retained earnings on January 1, 19C, was		$_____
c.	The number of shares outstanding is	shares	_____
d.	Legal capital is		$_____
e.	Total stockholders' equity is .		$_____
f.	Number of shares issued is .	shares	_____
g.	The average selling price per share was		$_____
h.	The number of shares sold was	shares	_____
i.	The par value per share is ..		$_____

2. Prepare the stockholders' equity section of the balance sheet at December 31, 19C. Use good form, complete with respect to details.

Exercise 16–5

Miller Corporation has the following stock outstanding:

Common, $50 par value—6,000 shares.

Preferred, 6%, $100 par value—1,000 shares.

Required:

Compute the amount of dividends payable in total and per share on the common and preferred for each separate case:

Case A—Preferred is noncumulative and nonparticipating; dividends declared, $18,000.

Case B—Preferred is cumulative and nonparticipating; three years in arrears; dividends declared, $40,000.

Case C—Preferred is noncumulative and fully participating; dividends declared, $24,000.

Case D—Preferred is noncumulative and fully participating; dividends declared, $40,000.

Case E—Preferred is cumulative and participating up to an additional 3%; three years in arrears; dividends declared, $60,000.

Case F—Preferred is cumulative and fully participating; three years in arrears; dividends declared, $50,000.

Exercise 16–6

Foster Corporation reported net income during four successive years as follows: $1,000; $2,000; $1,000; and $20,000.

The capital stock consisted of $70,000 common (par $20 per share) and $30,000 of 5% preferred (par $10 per share).

Required:

If net income in full were declared and paid as dividends each year, determine the amount to be paid on each class of stock for each of the four years assuming:

Case A—Preferred is noncumulative and nonparticipating.

Case B—Preferred is cumulative and nonparticipating.

Case C—Preferred is noncumulative and fully participating.

Case D—Preferred is cumulative and fully participating.

Exercise 16–7

Fisher Corporation received a charter authorizing the issuance of 200,000 shares of common stock. Give the journal entries in parallel columns for the following transactions during the first year assuming Case A—par value of $5 per share; and Case B—true nopar stock.

a. To record authorization (memorandum).
b. Sold 100,000 shares at $7; collected in full and issued the shares.
c. Received subscriptions for 10,000 shares at $7 per share; collected 60% of the subscription price. The stock will not be issued until collection is in full.
d. Issued 200 shares to an attorney in payment for legal fees.
e. Issued 8,000 shares and paid cash $100,000 in payment for a building.
f. Collected balance on subscriptions receivable in (c).

State and justify any assumptions you made. Assume a short time span.

Exercise 16–8

Henke Manufacturing Company's charter authorized the issuance of 400,000 shares of nopar common stock. Give journal entries for the following transactions assuming Case A—the board of directors set a stated value of $1 per share; and Case B—the stock is true nopar. Set up two columns so that Case A is to the left and Case B is to the right. Explain and justify any assumptions you make. Assume a short time span.

a. Authorization recognized (memorandum).
b. Sold 100,000 shares at $5 and collected in full; the shares were issued.
c. Received subscriptions for 10,000 shares at $5 per share; collected 40% of the subscription price. The shares will be issued upon collection in full.
d. Issued 500 shares for legal services.
e. Issued 2,000 shares and paid $15,000 cash for some used machinery.
f. Collected balance of subscriptions in (c).

Exercise 16–9

Morley Corporation charter authorized 100,000 shares of $10 par value stock. A. B. Cook subscribed for 500 shares at $25 per share, paying $2,500 down, the balance to be paid $1,000 per month. The stock will not be issued until collection in full. After paying for three months, Cook defaulted. Subsequently, the corporation sold the stock for $30 per share.

Required:

1. Give all entries relative to the 500 shares originally subscribed for by Cook assuming Morley refunded all collections made to date of default.
2. Give the entry for the default assuming shares equivalent to the collections were issued to Cook (at $25 per share). Also give the entry for the sale of the remaining shares at $30.

Exercise 16–10

The charter for Weir Manufacturing Company authorized 100,000 shares of common stock ($10 par value) and 10,000 shares of preferred stock ($50 par value). The company issued 500 shares of common and 200 shares of preferred stock for used machinery.

Required:

For each separate situation, give the entry to record the purchase of the machinery assuming Case A—the common stock currently is selling at $80 and the preferred at $60; Case B—the common stock has been selling at $80, and there have been no recent sales of the preferred stock; and Case C—there is no current market price for either class of stock (however, the machinery has been appraised at $48,000).

State and justify any assumptions made.

Exercise 16–11

The charter of DM Corporation authorized 10,000 shares of common stock, par $20, and 10,000 shares of preferred stock, par $10. The following transactions were completed. Assume each is completely independent.

a. Sold 200 shares of common and 100 shares of preferred for a lump sum amounting to $6,076. The common had been selling during the current week at $25, and the preferred at $12.

b. Issued 90 shares of preferred stock for some used equipment. The equipment had been appraised at $1,200; the book value shown by the seller was $600.

c. A 10% assessment on par was voted on both the common and preferred when 6,000 shares of common and 4,000 shares of preferred were outstanding. The assessment was collected in full.

d. Sold 300 shares of common and 200 shares of preferred to one person for a total cash price of $10,000. The common recently had been selling at $26; there were no recent sales of the preferred.

Required:

Give the journal entries for each transaction. State and justify any assumptions you made.

Exercise 16–12

Garcia Corporation was incorporated with 500 shares of capital stock, par $100; 400 of the shares were issued for the equity in the Doe and Roe Partnership. The remaining 100 shares were sold at $102. The balances in the accounts of the partnership were as follows:

Cash	$ 1,000
Notes receivable	8,000
Accounts receivable	17,000
Inventory	6,000
Operational assets	15,000
	$47,000

Accounts payable	$10,000
Allowance for doubtful accounts	1,000
Accumulated depreciation	2,000
Doe, capital	20,000
Roe, capital	14,000
	$47,000

The following adjustments were to be made prior to the exchange: decrease inventory to $4,000 and increase accumulated depreciation to $6,000. The partners shared profits equally.

Required:

Give entries to record the changes to the corporate form assuming the old books are to be continued (compute goodwill assuming the market value of the stock issued was $102 per share).

PROBLEMS

Problem 16–1

Using appropriate data from the information given below, prepare, in good form, the stockholders' equity section of a balance sheet for Oliphant Corporation.

Stock subscriptions receivable, preferred stock	$ 8,000
Reserve for bond sinking fund	60,000
Unrealized capital increment per appraisal of natural resources (discovery value)	45,000
Preferred stock, 6%, authorized 1,000 shares, par $100 per share, cumulative and fully participating	70,000
Bonds payable, 7%	125,000
Common stock, nopar, 5,000 shares authorized and outstanding	260,000
Donation of future plant site (to Oliphant)	6,000
Premium on preferred stock	14,000
Discount on bonds payable	1,000
Retained earnings, unappropriated	50,000
Preferred stock subscribed (to be issued upon collection in full)	10,000
Unrealized loss on long-term investments in equity securities	5,000

Problem 16–2

Summers Corporation was granted a charter authorizing 10,000 shares of 6% preferred stock, par value $10 per share, and 50,000 shares of common stock, nopar value. No stated or assigned value was identified with the common stock. During the first year, the following transactions occurred:

a. 20,000 shares of common stock were sold for cash at $10 per share.

b. 1,000 shares of preferred stock sold for cash at $25 per share.

c. Subscriptions were received for 1,000 shares of preferred stock at $25 per share; 50% was received as a down payment, and the balance was payable in two equal installments. The shares will be issued upon collection in full.

d. 5,000 shares of common stock, 500 shares of preferred stock, and $15,500 cash were given as payment for a small plant that the company needed. This plant originally cost $40,000 and had a depreciated value on the books of the selling company of $20,000. Assume the prior market price per share did not change.

e. The first installment on the preferred subscriptions was collected.

Required:

1. Give journal entries to record the above transactions. State and justify any assumptions you made.
2. Prepare the stockholders' equity section of the balance sheet at year-end. Retained earnings at the end of the year amounted to $47,000. There was an $11,000 balance in the account; "Unrealized Loss on Long-Term Investments in Equity Securities."

Problem 16–3

Mehos Corporation's charter authorized 500,000 shares of $5 par value stock. John Doe subscribed for 10,000 shares at $20 per share and paid a 40% cash downpayment. The remaining 60% was payable in three equal semiannual amounts. After paying the first semiannual amount, Doe defaulted. The stock is issuable at date of full payment.

Required

1. Give the entries to record (a) the subscription and (b) collection of the first semiannual amount.
2. Assumption A—Give the entries to record (a) the default by Doe and the issuance to Doe of shares equivalent to the cash paid by Doe, and (b) sale of the remaining subscribed shares to another party for cash at $22 per share (the cost of reselling was $0.10 per share).
3. Assumption B—Give the entries to record (a) the default by Doe and (b) resale under lien of all of the subscribed shares to another party for cash at $22 per share (the cost of reselling was $0.10 per share) including any cash refunded to Doe.

Problem 16–4

The charter for Dawson Corporation, to conduct a manufacturing business, authorized common stock, 100,000 shares, nopar value, and 6% preferred stock

10,000 shares, cumulative and nonparticipating with par value per share of $10. During the early part of the first year, the following transactions occurred:

a. Each of the six incorporators subscribed to 1,000 shares of the common at $15 per share and 500 shares of the preferred at $12 per share. Half of the subscription price was paid, and half of the subscribed shares issued.
b. Another individual purchased 500 shares of common and 100 shares of preferred stock paying $9,135 cash.
c. One of the incorporators purchased a used machine for $40,000 and immediately transferred it to the corporation for 2,000 shares of common stock, 200 shares of preferred stock, and a one-year, 9% interest-bearing note for $8,000.
d. The investors paid the subscriptions, and the remaining stock was issued.

Required:

1. Give all entries indicated for the Dawson Corporation.
2. Prepare the stockholders' equity section of the balance sheet. Assume retained earnings of $25,000 at year-end.

Problem 16–5

Stinson Corporation received a charter that authorized 100,000 shares of common stock. During the first year, the following transactions affecting stockholders' equity were completed:

a. Immediately after incorporation sold 60,000 shares at $25 per share for cash.
b. Near year-end received a subscription for 1,000 shares at $25 per share, collected 60% in cash, balance due in two equal installments within one year. The stock will be issued upon collection in full.
c. Near year-end issued 500 shares for a used machine that would be used in operations. The machine had cost $20,000 new and was carried by the seller at a book value of $11,000. It was appraised at $13,000 six months previously by a reputable independent appraiser.
d. Collected half of the unpaid subscriptions in (b).

Required:

1. Give entries for each of the above transactions assuming: Case A—the stock has a par value of $10 per share; Case B—the stock is true nopar value; and Case C—the stock is nopar (however, it is assigned a stated value of $5 per share). Set up paral-

lel amount columns for each case. State and justify any assumptions you make.

2. Prepare the stockholders' equity section of the balance sheet at the end of the first year for each case. Assume a balance in Retained Earnings of $124,000 at year-end.

Problem 16–6

The charter for Douglas Corporation authorized 500,000 shares of common stock. During the first year of operations, the following transactions affected stockholders' equity:

a. Immediately after incorporation sold 400,000 shares of capital stock at $10 per share; collected cash.

b. Immediately after incorporation received a subscription for 10,000 shares of capital stock from one individual at $10 per share. Collected 40% of the subscription, and the balance is due at the end of one year. The shares will be issued upon collection in full.

c. Near year-end exchanged 6,000 shares of capital stock for a plant site. The site was carried on the books of the seller at $25,000, and it had been appraised within the past month at $65,000.

d. Collected $12,000 on the subscription in (b).

Required:

1. Give entries for the above transactions assuming:

   Case A—Par value stock; $2 par value per share.

   Case B—True nopar value stock.

   Case C—Nopar value stock with a stated value of $1 per share.

   Set up parallel amount columns for each case. State and justify any assumptions you make.

2. Prepare the stockholders' equity section of the balance sheet at the end of the first year for each case. Assume a $119,000 ending balance in the Unappropriated Retained Earnings account, a reserve for bond sinking fund of $10,000, and unrealized loss on long-term equity investments of $13,000.

Problem 16–7

The charter of Ford Corporation authorized the issuance of 20,000 shares of 6% cumulative, nonparticipating preferred stock, par $10 per share, and 100,000 shares of common stock, nopar value. During the first year of operations, the following transactions affecting stockholders' equity were completed:

a. The promoters sold 9,000 shares of the preferred stock at $25 cash; the stock was issued.

b. Subscriptions were received for an additional 1,000 shares of preferred stock at $25 per share; 20% was collected, the balance is to be paid in four equal installments; the stock will be issued upon collection in full.

c. Each of the three promoters was issued 1,000 shares of common stock (only the common stock carried voting privileges) at $20 per share, each paid one fifth in cash, the remainder was considered to be reimbursement for promotional activities; the shares were issued. Debit Organization Expense.

d. An individual purchased 100 shares of preferred and 100 shares of common stock and paid a single sum of $4,400. The stock was issued. Assume a current market price of $25 for the preferred stock and that no current market value for the common was firmly established.

e. Collected cash from the promoters ([b] above) for the first installment.

f. Issued 5,000 shares of common stock for a used plant. The plant had been appraised during the past month at $110,000 and was carried by the seller at a book value of $60,000.

Required:

1. Prepare journal entries to record the foregoing transactions. State and justify any assumptions you make.

2. Prepare the stockholders' equity section of the balance sheet assuming retained earnings at year-end of $131,000 and unrealized loss on long-term investment in equity securities of $20,000.

Problem 16–8

The stockholders' equity section of the balance sheet for the Austin Metals Corporation at the end of its first fiscal year was reported as follows:

Stockholders' Equity

Contributed capital:		
Capital stock:		
Preferred, 6%, cumulative, nonparticipating, $100 par value, redeemable at $125 per share, authorized 5,000 shares, issued and outstanding 4,185	$ 418,500	
Preferred stock subscribed, 465 shares	46,500	$ 465,000
Common stock, stated value $8 per share, authorized 1,500,000 shares, issued and outstanding 954,000 shares	7,632,000	
Common stock subscribed, 106,000 shares ...	848,000	8,480,000
Other contributed capital:		
Excess of par, preferred stock	15,000	
Excess of stated value, common stock	21,200	36,200
Retained earnings		110,000
Total Stockholders' Equity		$9,091,200

Required:

Prepare journal entries during the first year as indicated by the above report. Use the memorandum approach to record the authorization and assume that all stock was purchased through subscriptions under terms of 60% cash downpayment and 40% payable six months later. Also assume that of the 40%, all but 10% of the subscribers had paid in full by year-end. Shares are not issued until collection in full from the subscriber.

Problem 16–9

Watson Corporation reported net income during five successive years as follows: $20,000; $30,000; $9,000; $5,000; and $60,000. The capital stock consisted of $300,000, $20 par value common, and $200,000, $10 par value 6% preferred.

Required:

For each separate case, prepare a tabulation showing the amount (and computations) each class of stock would receive in dividends (1) if the entire net income were distributed each year and (2) if 60% of each year's earnings were distributed that year.

Case A—Preferred stock is noncumulative and nonparticipating.

Case B—Preferred stock is cumulative and nonparticipating.

Case C—Preferred stock is cumulative and fully participating.

Problem 16–10

The charter for Stone Corporation authorized 5,000 shares of 6% preferred stock, par value $20 per share, and 8,000 shares of common stock, par value $50 per share. All of the authorized shares have been issued. In a five-year period, annual dividends paid were $4,000; $40,000; $32,000; $5,000; and $41,000, respectively.

Required:

Prepare a tabulation (including computations) of the amount of dividends that would be paid to each class of stock for each year under the following separate case:

Case A—Preferred stock is noncumulative and nonparticipating.

Case B—Preferred stock is cumulative and nonparticipating.

Case C—Preferred stock is noncumulative and fully participating.

Case D—Preferred stock is cumulative and fully participating.

Case E—Preferred stock is cumulative and partially participating up to an additional 2%; assume the dividend for year five was $42,000 instead of $41,000.

Problem 16–11

Ace Corporation was authorized 5,000 shares of capital stock, par $50 per share. The shares were issued as follows:

a. 4,000 shares sold for cash at $102 per share.
b. 1,000 shares for the owners' equity of the RT Partnership, which reported the following balance sheet at "appraised market value."

Accounts receivable (net)	$ 13,000
Inventory	20,000
Operational assets (net)	67,000
	$100,000

Notes payable	$ 20,000
R, capital	40,000
T, capital	40,000
	$100,000

Required:

1. Give the required entries on the books of RT Partnership to reflect the recognition of goodwill (based on $102 per share) and to close out the partnership books. Assume the partners shared profits equally.
2. Give all entries required on the books of Ace Corporation from organization through acquisition of RT Partnership.
3. Prepare an unclassified balance sheet for Ace Corporation immediately after recording the acquisition of RT Partnership.

Problem 16–12

National Corporation was organized to take over the partnership of Brown and Smith. The charter authorized 10,000 shares of capital stock, par value $100 per share. The balance sheet as of June 30, 19X, for Brown and Smith was as follows (at book value):

BROWN & SMITH PARTNERSHIP
Assets

Cash	$ 10,000
Accounts receivable	13,000
Allowance for doubtful accounts	(1,000)
Prepaid expenses	1,000
Buildings	90,000

Accumulated depreciation	(20,000)
Equipment	60,000
Accumulated depreciation	(30,000)
Land	10,000
	$133,000

Liabilities and Owners' Equity

Accounts payable	$ 29,000
Accrued expenses payable	4,000
Brown, capital	60,000
Smith, capital	40,000
	$133,000

The partnership profits and losses were divided 70% to Brown and 30% to Smith. Incorporators were Brown, Smith, Franks, Box, and Cane. The latter three purchased 2,000 shares each at $102. According to the agreement, 1,500 shares will be issued to Brown and Smith in the ratio of their capital balances at the end in payment for the business (including the liabilities).

Prior to dissolution, the $10,000 cash on hand will be distributed to Brown and Smith based on their capital ratios prior to adjustment. The following adjustments, based on appraised market values prior to the exchange, were agreed upon:

Allowance for doubtful accounts increased to $3,000.

Accumulated depreciation, buildings decreased to $7,000.

Land revalued to $20,000.

Goodwill recognition based on the "appraised market values" and $102 per share for the capital stock.

Required:

1. Prepare entries for National Corporation assuming the old partnership books are to be continued and used by the corporation. The partnership will go out of existence.
2. Prepare an unclassified balance sheet immediately after the above entries.

17

Corporations—Retained Earnings and Changes in Stockholders' Equity after Formation

In Chapter 16 the three major categories of corporate capital were identified as contributed capital, retained earnings, and unrealized capital. Contributed capital was discussed there; this chapter focuses on *retained earnings* and dividends in Part A and contraction and expansion of corporate capital after formation in Part B.

PART A—RETAINED EARNINGS AND DIVIDENDS

Retained earnings represent accumulated net income, gains and losses, and prior period adjustments of a corporation to date reduced by dividend distributions to shareholders and amounts transferred to permanent capital accounts as a result of stock dividends. Net income and net loss come from regular operations, nonrecurring or unusual transactions, and extraordinary items. If the accumulated losses and distributions of retained earnings exceed the accumulated gains, a *deficit* in retained earnings exists and must be reported.

Some variation in terminology with respect to retained earnings can be noted in practice. The term *earned surplus* once was commonly used to denote what was defined above as retained earnings. More descriptive terminology is preferable because the statement users are provided with a clearer description of the nature

of each account. Also, the older term is quite inappropriate because there is no "surplus." On this point the AICPA Committee on Terminology recommended that:

> The use of the term *surplus* (whether standing alone or in such combinations as *capital surplus, paid-in surplus, earned surplus, appraisal surplus,* etc.) be discontinued. . . .
>
> The term *earned surplus* be replaced by terms which will indicate source, such as *retained income, retained earnings, accumulated earnings* or *earnings retained for use in the business.*[1]

In accounting for stockholders' equity, a careful distinction is maintained between contributed capital (comprised of the capital stock and other contributed capital accounts) and retained earnings.

In accounting for *total* retained earnings, often more than one account is involved. Total retained earnings at a given date may be comprised of two categories of accounts. The Retained Earnings account (if not designated otherwise) represents the *unappropriated* portion of retained earnings, that is, retained earnings not set aside or appropriated for specific reasons. The second category is often called

---

[1] AICPA, *Accounting Terminology Bulletin No. 1,* "Review and Résumé" (New York, 1961), par. 69.

appropriated retained earnings, and the accounts comprising it are given special designations such as Retained Earnings Appropriated for Bond Sinking Fund (or Reserve for Bond Sinking Fund). This category is discussed in a subsequent section. The *usual* debits and credits to the Retained Earnings account are as follows:

Retained Earnings

Debits	Credits
Net losses (including extraordinary losses)	Net income (including extraordinary gains)
Prior period adjustments	Prior period adjustments
Cash dividends	
Stock dividends	

Observe that no *credits* are included that occur as a result of the sale, issuance, purchase (of treasury stock), or exchange of capital stock. These credits are accounted for as elements of contributed capital. In certain circumstances, *debits* to Retained Earnings may occur as a result of treasury stock and stock retirement transactions, as discussed in Chapter 18. Such debits represent de facto cash dividends.

DIVIDENDS

Dividends consist of distributions to the corporation's stockholders in proportion to the number of shares of each class of stock held. Such distributions generally take place at regular intervals, and on occasion, extraordinary dividends may be distributed. The term *dividends* used alone usually refers to cash dividends. When dividends in a form other than cash are distributed, they should be labeled according to what is distributed. The following types of dividends are encountered with some frequency:

1. Cash dividends.
2. Property dividends.
3. Liability or scrip dividends.
4. Liquidating dividends.
5. Stock dividends.

Distributions to stockholders may involve

1. The distribution of corporate assets and a decrease in *total* corporate capital, as in the case of cash, property, or liquidating dividends.
2. The creation of a liability and a decrease in *total* corporate capital, as in the case of liability dividends or a cash dividend declared but not yet paid.
3. No change in assets, liabilities, or *total* corporate capital, but only a change in the internal categories of corporate capital, as in the case of a stock dividend.

The question always arises on the "use" of retained earnings for dividends. Obviously, dividends are not *paid* with retained earnings but are paid with cash or some other asset (except in the case of a stock dividend). More specifically, dividends generally reduce *both* retained earnings and assets. Cash or property dividends cannot be paid without this dual effect. As noted above, assets other than cash, and even liabilities, may be involved in dividend distributions. Similarly, other elements of corporate capital may be affected rather than retained earnings. The laws of all states allow retained earnings to be used as a basis for dividends, although some states place restrictions even here, such as a provision that dividends in any one year may not exceed the earnings for the preceding year. Some states permit debits to certain contributed capital accounts, such as contributed capital in excess of par, as a basis for cash dividends, providing creditor interests are not jeopardized.[2] Generally, statutes are more liberal with respect to stock dividends since no assets are distributable. The statutes of the particular state are controlling; however, in the absence of any statement or information to the contrary, one should assume a debit to Retained Earnings when dividend distributions are recorded.

Four dates are important in accounting for dividends: (1) date of declaration, (2) date of record, (3) ex-dividend date, and (4) date of payment. Prior to payment, dividends must be formally *declared* by the board of directors of the corporation. Stockholders normally cannot force

---

[2] A liquidating dividend may be involved; see subsequent section on liquidating dividends.

a dividend declaration; the courts have consistently held that dividend declaration is a matter of prudent management to be decided upon by the duly elected board of directors. Of course, the board must meet all statutory, charter, and bylaw requirements, act in good faith, and protect the interests of all parties involved. In deciding whether to declare a dividend (and of what type), the board of directors should consider the financial impact on the company, the adequacy of cash and retained earnings, expectations for the future, and corporate growth and expansion needs.

On the *date of declaration* the board formally announces the dividend declaration. In the case of a cash or property dividend, the declaration is recorded on this date by debiting Retained Earnings and crediting Dividends Payable. In the absence of fraud or illegality,[3] the courts have held that formal announcement of the declaration of a cash, property, or liability dividend constitutes an enforceable contract (i.e., an irrevocable declaration) between the corporation and the shareholders. In view of the irrevocability of this action, such dividends are recorded on declaration date. In the case of *stock dividends,* no assets are involved, directly or indirectly, as far as the corporation is concerned; therefore, the courts generally have held that a stock dividend declaration is revocable. Consequently, no entry is made on declaration date in the case of a stock dividend.[4]

The *date of record* is selected by the board and is stated in the announcement of the declaration. The date of record is the date on which the list of stockholders of record is prepared. Individuals holding stock at this date, as shown in the corporate stockholders' record, receive the dividend, regardless of sales or purchases of stock after this date. No dividend entry is made in the accounts on this date.

Technically, the *ex-dividend date* is the day after the date of record. To provide time for stock transfer of listed stocks, the stock exchanges advance the effective ex-dividend date by three or four days. Thus, one who holds the stock on the day prior to the stipulated ex-dividend date receives the *dividend.* Between the declaration date and the ex-dividend date, the *market price* of the stock includes the dividend. On the ex-dividend date, the price of the stock drops because the recipient of the dividend already has been set. Thus, dividend revenue is earned on the declaration date and not on the date of record, the ex-dividend date, or the date of payment.

The *date of payment* also is determined by the board of directors, and generally is stated in the announcement of the declaration. At the date of payment, in the case of cash or property dividends, the liability recorded at date of declaration is debited and the appropriate asset account is credited. A stock dividend distribution usually is recorded only on this date, as illustrated in a subsequent section.

Dividends on par value stock may be stated as a certain percent of the par value, but dividends on nopar stock must be stated as a dollar amount per share.

Cash Dividends

Cash dividends constitute the usual form of distributions to stockholders. The declaration must meet the preferences of the preferred stockholders and then may extend to the common stockholders (see discussion and illustration of dividend computations in Chapter 16). In declaring a cash dividend the board of directors should be careful that the cash position for the coming months is not jeopardized and the Retained Earnings balance is sufficient. The cash problem may be met, in part, by careful selection of the *payment* date.

To illustrate a cash dividend, assume the following announcement is made: The Board of Directors of Bass Company, at their meeting on January 20, 19A, declared a dividend of $0.50 per share, payable March 20, 19A, to shareholders of record as of March 1, 19A. Assume further

---

[3] Questions of legality should be referred to an attorney.

[4] A few accountants prefer to make an entry at this date. See subsequent section on stock dividends. Also, in the case of cash dividends, if the declaration date and payment date are in the same accounting period, there would be no compelling reason to make an entry in the accounts on the declaration date.

that 10,000 shares of nopar capital stock are outstanding.

At date of declaration (January 20, 19A):[5]

| Retained earnings (10,000 shares × $0.50) | 5,000 | |
| Cash dividends payable | | 5,000 |

At date of record (March 1, 19A):

No entry. The corporate stockholders' record is "closed," and the list of dividend recipients is prepared.

At date of payment (March 20, 19A):

| Cash dividends payable | 5,000 | |
| Cash | | 5,000 |

Cash Dividends Payable is reported on the balance sheet as a current liability because the duration of the dividend liability usually is short term.

Property Dividends

Corporations occasionally pay dividends in assets other than cash. Such dividends are known as property dividends. The property may be securities of other companies held by the corporation, real estate, merchandise, or any other asset designated by the board of directors. Property received by the stockholder as a dividend is subject to income tax at its market value. The market value at the declaration date is used because, as in the case of a cash dividend, it is the date when the dividend is recorded. This is the date that the corporation gives up (by implicit contract) all alternative uses of the assets to be distributed. Subsequent market price changes (upward or downward) accrue to the shareholder (recipient of the asset).

A property dividend should be recorded at the current market value of the assets transferred. On this point *APB Opinion No. 29* (May 1973), "Accounting for Nonmonetary Transactions," states:

> A transfer of a nonmonetary asset to a stockholder or to another entity in a nonreciprocal

transfer should be recorded at the fair value of the asset transferred, and a gain or loss should be recognized on disposition of the asset.

Most property dividends are paid with the securities of other companies. Among other advantages, this avoids the problem of indivisibility of units as would be the case with most assets other than cash.

To illustrate a sequence of entries for a property dividend, assume AB Corporation has an investment in 100 shares of XY Corporation that cost $10,000. AB Corporation declared a property dividend, using the XY shares, when the quoted price was $150 per share. The dividend transactions would be recorded as follows:

At declaration date:

Investment in stock of XY Corporation [100 shares × ($150 − $100)]	5,000	
Gain on disposal of investment		5,000
Retained earnings (100 shares × $150)	15,000	
Property dividends payable		15,000

At issue date:

| Property dividends payable | 15,000 | |
| Investment in stock of XY Corporation | | 15,000 |

Liability Dividends

Strictly speaking, any dividend involving the distribution of assets is a liability dividend *between* the declaration date and the date of payment. Nevertheless, liability or *scrip* dividends refer to instances where the board of directors declares a dividend and issues promissory notes, bonds, or scrip to the stockholders. In essence, this means that a comparatively long time will lapse between the declaration and payment dates. In most cases scrip dividends are declared when a corporation has sufficient retained earnings to serve as a basis for dividends but is short of cash. The stockholder may hold the scrip until due date and collect the dividend or possibly may discount it to obtain immediate cash. When bonds or notes are involved, the due date and rate of interest are specified. Scrip often is interest bearing and is usually payable at a specified future date. The immediate effect of a scrip or liability dividend is a debit to Retained Earnings

---

[5] Sometimes a temporary account, Dividends Paid, is debited at this date and subsequently closed to Retained Earnings. Note that in this procedure the word "paid" is used loosely because the cash obviously is not paid on declaration date.

and a credit to a liability account such as Scrip Dividends Payable or Notes Payable to Stockholders. Upon payment, Cash is credited and the liability account debited. Since interest paid on a liability dividend is not a part of the dividend, the interest payments should be debited to Interest Expense rather than directly to Retained Earnings as a part of the dividend.

Liquidating Dividends

Distributions that constitute a *return of contributed capital* rather than earnings are known as liquidating dividends, and owners' equity accounts other than Retained Earnings are debited. Liquidating dividends may be either intentional or unintentional. *Intentional* liquidating dividends occur when the board of directors knowingly declares dividends which will, in effect, represent a return of investment to the shareholders, as in the case when a corporation is reducing permanent capital.

Mining companies may pay dividends on the basis of earnings computed prior to deduction of depletion. In such cases there is an intentional liquidating dividend equal to the amount of depletion. Stockholders should be informed of the portion of any dividend that represents a return of capital. Such dividends usually are not taxable to the shareholder as income but serve to reduce the cost basis of the stock investment.

In accounting for liquidating dividends, Contributed Capital rather than Retained Earnings should be debited, since a portion of stockholder investment is returned. Rather than debiting the capital stock accounts, as would be done if shares were being retired, other contributed capital accounts such as the "in excess of par" accounts may be debited. In some cases it may be desirable to set up a special account, Capital Repayment, which would be treated as a deduction (contra account) in the stockholders' equity section of the balance sheet.

Unintentional liquidating dividends may occur when income, and hence retained earnings, is overstated because of errors or inappropriate accounting. For example, the omission or understatement of depreciation, amortization, or depletion charges would cause retained earnings to be overstated. In such cases, if reported retained earnings (prior to correction) were used in full as a basis for dividends, part of the resulting dividend would represent a liquidating dividend.

Stock Dividends

A stock dividend is a distribution of *additional shares of stock* of the corporation (not a transfer of assets to the shareholders), in proportion to their prior stock holdings. A stock dividend does not change the assets, liabilities, or total stockholders' equity of the issuing corporation. Rather, it only causes the transfer of an amount from Retained Earnings to the permanent capital accounts (i.e., capital stock and contributed capital in excess of par). Therefore, it only causes a change in the "internal content" of stockholders' equity.[6]

A stock dividend may be from treasury stock or unissued stock, and common or preferred shares may be issued. When the stock dividend is of the same class as that held by the recipients, it is called an *ordinary* stock dividend. Alternatively, when a different class of stock is issued, it is called a *special* stock dividend (e.g., preferred shares issued to the common shareholders). It was noted in a preceding section that state laws vary as to the availability of various classes of stockholders' equity for stock dividends. Some states permit the use of certain *contributed* capital, such as contributed capital in excess of par and even unrealized capital. All states permit retained earnings to be used as a basis for stock dividends.

In the absence of information to the contrary, it should be assumed that the debit is to Retained Earnings. The credit always is to the respective contributed capital accounts for the particular shares issued.

There are several reasons for a stock dividend. The principal reasons are as follows:

1. To permanently retain profits in the business by *capitalizing* a portion of the retained earnings. The effect of a stock dividend, through a debit to Retained Earnings and

---

[6] In the unusual situation where Contributed Capital rather than Retained Earnings is debited for a stock dividend, this effect would not result.

offsetting credits to permanent capital accounts, is to raise the contributed (and legal) capital and thereby "shelter" the new legal capital from use to declare cash dividends.

2. To continue dividends without distributing assets needed for expansion and working capital. This action may be motivated by a desire to pacify stockholders, since many of them may be willing to accept a stock dividend representing accumulated earnings almost as readily as a cash dividend because the additional shares received can be sold for cash. Ordinary stock dividends are not subject to income tax; they serve instead to reduce the investment cost per share to the investor.

3. To increase the number of shares outstanding, which reduces the market price per share. Thus, a stock dividend *may* cause increased trading of the shares in the market with a consequent increase in total share market values.

It is especially important that the exact nature of a stock dividend be understood and that it be clearly differentiated from a *stock split.* A *stock dividend* does not require the distribution of assets or the creation of a liability. It does not change *total* corporate capital. Rather, a stock dividend is no more than an interequity transaction. Normally, the only effect on the issuing corporation's balance sheet is a transfer of part of the retained earnings to contributed capital and an increase in the number of shares outstanding. A stock dividend does not affect the par value per share. Thus, a stock dividend does not affect the assets, liabilities, or total capital but only the internal content of stockholders' equity.

In contrast, a *stock split* increases the number of shares and at the same time it involves a *pro rata reduction in the par value per share.* A stock split is accomplished by replacing the old shares with a greater number of new shares which have a smaller par value per share; total par value outstanding remains the same after a stock split. A stock split does not cause a transfer of retained earnings to contributed capital; thus, neither contributed capital nor retained earnings is changed. In the case of a stock split,

the number of shares, but not the dollar amount of *contributed capital,* is changed. In contrast, in a stock dividend, the dollar amount of contributed capital is changed.

To illustrate the different effects of a stock dividend and a stock split, assume X Corporation is authorized to issue 40,000 shares of common stock, par $100, of which 10,000 shares were sold initially at par, and there is a current balance of $1,600,000 in retained earnings. The effects of a 100% stock dividend and a two-for-one stock split may be summarized as follows:

X Corporation

	Prior to Change	After Stock Dividend	After Stock Split
Stock outstanding:			
10,000 shares, par $100	$1,000,000		
20,000 shares, par $100		$2,000,000	
20,000 shares, par $50			$1,000,000
Retained earnings	1,600,000	600,000	1,600,000
Total capital	$2,600,000	$2,600,000	$2,600,000

Since a stock dividend requires capitalization of retained earnings, the question arises as to the amount of retained earnings that should be capitalized (transferred to contributed capital) for the additional shares issued. The *statutory minimum* in most states is par or stated value.[7] In the case of preferred stock it may be either par value or the liquidating value. However, the amount transferred from retained earnings to contributed capital should not necessarily be limited to the statutory minimum. Generally accepted accounting principles reflect a definite position on this issue. Two distinct situations affecting the amount to be capitalized are recognized as follows:

Situation 1—A small stock dividend: When the proportion of the additional shares issued is *small* in relation to the total shares *previously outstanding,* the *current market value* of the additional shares should be capitalized. The Committee on Accounting Procedure of the AICPA stated:

> . . . many recipients of stock dividends look upon them as distributions of corporate earnings and usually in an amount equivalent to the fair

---

[7] In the case of *true* nopar stock, it appears that the amount capitalized is almost always the current market value.

value of the additional shares received. Furthermore, it is to be presumed that such views of recipients are materially strengthened in those instances, which are by far the most numerous, where the issuances are so small in comparison with the shares previously outstanding that they do not have any apparent effect upon the share market price and, consequently, the market value of the shares previously held remains substantially unchanged. The committee therefore believes that where these circumstances exist the corporation should in the public interest account for the transaction by transferring from [retained earnings] to the category of permanent capitalization . . . an amount equal to the fair value of the additional shares issued [i.e., the market value immediately after issuance].[8]

Use of *market value immediately after issuance* is further buttressed by the fact that the market price per share, in the case of a small stock dividend, usually does not drop proportionately to the increased number of shares outstanding after the dividend. Thus, if this is the case, the shareholders receive a real value increase in their holdings.

Situation 2—A large stock dividend: When the proportion of the additional shares issued is *large* in relation to the total shares previously outstanding, no less than the legal minimum (generally par value) should be capitalized, as the Committee stated:

> Where the number of additional shares issued as a stock dividend is so great that it has, or may reasonably be expected to have, the effect of materially reducing the share market value, the committee believes that the implications and possible constructions discussed in the preceding paragraph are not likely to exist. . . . Consequently, the committee considers that under such circumstances there is no need to capitalize earned surplus [retained earnings], other than to the extent occasioned by legal requirements.[9]

The dividing line between the two situations described above (a small versus a large stock dividend) is very difficult to draw. The significant distinction is the behavior of the per share stock price rather than the exact proportion be-

tween the new and old shares. The market price per share will depend upon a number of factors, such as the economic characteristics of the company, and the general condition of the economy. However, stock dividends sometimes serve as "signals" about the economic characteristics of companies using stock dividends. It seems clear that the Committee on Accounting Procedures believed good "signals" (i.e., those "signals" which keep stock prices from adjusting down proportionately for the number of new shares issued) are more coincidental with *small* stock dividends than with *large* stock dividends. In considering this problem the Committee further stated: "It would appear that there would be few instances involving the issuance of additional shares of less than, say, 20% or 25% of the number previously outstanding where the effect would not be such as to call for the procedure" for a small stock dividend outlined above as *Situation 1.*

To summarize, no less than the minimum amount per share (the legal amount required) should be capitalized, and a higher amount per share (market value) should be capitalized for a "small" stock dividend. Some corporate managements elect to capitalize the *average* contributed capital per share on the old shares if it is not less than the minimum.

The above discussions are particularly applicable to *ordinary* stock dividends. In the case of special stock dividends, such as a stock dividend in preferred stock issued to common shareholders, theoretical considerations would suggest that market value be capitalized.

To illustrate several situations involving stock dividends, assume the following for Z Corporation:

Z Corporation:

Preferred stock, par value $20, 10,000 shares authorized, 5,000 shares outstanding	$100,000
Common stock, par value $10, 20,000 shares authorized, 10,000 shares outstanding	100,000
Contributed capital in excess of par, preferred stock	10,000
Contributed capital in excess of par, common stock	15,000
Retained earnings	150,000
Total Stockholders' Equity	$375,000

Market price per share immediately before issuance:

Preferred	$25
Common	12

Situation 1—A small stock dividend: A 10% common stock dividend (i.e., one additional

[8] AICPA, *Accounting Research Bulletin No. 43,* "Restatement and Revision of Accounting Research Bulletins" (New York, 1961), Ch. 7, Sec. B, par. 10.

[9] Ibid., par. 11.

share is issued for each ten shares held) is declared on the common stock. The market price remains $12 per share.

At issue date:[10]

Retained earnings (1,000 shares at market, $12)	12,000	
Common stock, par $10 (1,000 shares)		10,000
Contributed capital in excess of par, common stock		2,000

Situation 2—A large stock dividend: A 50% common stock dividend (i.e., one additional share for each two shares held) is declared. The market value per share drops immediately to $7.50.

At issue date:

Retained earnings (5,000 shares at par, $10)	50,000	
Common stock, par $10 (5,000 shares)		50,000

Situation 3—A large stock dividend: A 50% common stock dividend is declared. The market value drops to $7.50 per share. Management decides to capitalize on the basis of the average paid in.

At issue date:

Retained earnings (5,000 shares at $11.50*)	57,500	
Common stock, par $10 (5,000 shares)		50,000
Contributed capital in excess of par, common stock		7,500

* Computation: ($100,000 + $15,000) ÷ 10,000 shares = $11.50.

Situation 4—A small stock dividend: A 20% common stock dividend (i.e., one additional

---

[10] A few accountants prefer to make an entry on declaration date and another entry on issue date by using a temporary contributed capital account entitled Stock Dividend Distributable. The two entries would be as follows:

Declaration date:

Retained earnings	12,000	
Stock dividends distributable (an element of stockholders' equity)		10,000
Contributed capital in excess of par, common stock		2,000

Issuance date:

Stock dividends distributable	10,000	
Common stock		10,000

share for each five shares held) is issued to *both common and preferred shareholders.* The market price per share does not change appreciably after issuance from $12.

At issue date:

Retained earnings (3,000 shares* at $12)	36,000	
Common stock, par $10 (3,000 shares)		30,000
Contributed capital in excess of par, common stock		6,000

* Computation: (10,000 + 5,000) × .20 = 3,000 shares.

To conclude the discussion of stock dividends, we reemphasize that an important aspect of such dividends is that a part of the retained earnings often is transferred to *permanent* capital (i.e., capitalized). This transfer reflects that the company has "grown through earnings" by permanently removing such earnings from dividend availability. For many of the large corporations a significant amount of total owners' equity reported as contributed capital came from this source. Thus, the amount of accumulated retained earnings reported on many balance sheets is far short of the actual total accumulated earnings (less cash dividends paid) over the life of the corporation. Theoretically, the amount of accumulated retained earnings that has been capitalized over the life of the corporation should be reported as a separate element of permanent contributed capital. Although separate reporting of accumulated capitalized earnings is not required, it would appear to be a particularly useful amount for many statement users.

DIVIDENDS IN ARREARS ON PREFERRED STOCK

Dividends in arrears on *cumulative* preferred stock, prior to declaration of such dividends, do not constitute a liability to the corporation. However, full disclosure requires that cumulative dividends in arrears be reported. A note to the financial statements may be used to indicate the number of years and amounts of dividends in arrears. An alternative method is to report the amount of dividends in arrears as an appropriation of retained earnings. For example, retained earnings of $30,000 may be reported as follows:[11]

Retained earnings:
Unappropriated	$20,000	
Appropriated for preferred dividends in arrears	10,000	$30,000

FRACTIONAL SHARE RIGHTS

Stock rights are agreements issued to shareholders that entitle them to acquire a particular class of stock in the future from the corporation under specified conditions (at a specified cost or at no cost per share). Stock rights are evidenced by the issuance of a certificate called a *stock warrant* which represents one or more stock rights. A stock right may call for one share of stock, or for less than one share, in which case it is called a fractional share right.

Fractional share rights often must be issued with a stock dividend (such as when the stock dividend is *not* on a one-for-one basis). Soon after issuance, stock rights generally are freely traded on the market (see Chapter 18). To illustrate the accounting for fractional share rights related to a stock dividend, assume Z Corporation (page 579) declared a 20% stock dividend whereby each common shareholder is to receive one share of common stock, par $10, for each five shares currently held (i.e., a stock dividend of 2,000 common shares). The market value of the shares was $12 per share. Assume further that 1,730 shares of common stock and 1,350 fractional share rights were issued to various common shareholders calling for the remaining 270 stock dividend shares (i.e., 270 shares × 5 = 1,350 fractional share rights). These fractional share rights were issued to shareholders that held numbers of shares not divisible by five (e.g., a holder of nine shares would receive one additional share plus four fractional share warrants). Each *fractional share* right calls for one fifth of a share of common stock; thus, to obtain a common share, five such rights must be pre-

sented. Z Corporation would record the issuance of the stock dividend (assumed to be a small stock dividend) and the rights as follows:

Retained earnings (2,000 shares at market, $12)	24,000	
Common stock, par $10 (1,730 shares × $10)		17,300
Common stock rights outstanding (1,350 rights for 270 shares of par $10)		2,700
Contributed capital in excess of par, common stock (2,000 shares × $2)		4,000

The shareholders receiving the fractional share rights may sell their rights, buy rights, and/or turn them in for shares of common stock (or through oversight let them lapse since they will have an expiration date). Five cases are given below to illustrate typical situations.

Case A—All of the rights are turned in to Z Corporation, and the common shares are issued.

Common stock rights outstanding (1,350 rights)	2,700	
Common stock, par $10 (270 shares)		2,700

Case B—Only 90% of the rights are turned in, and the remainder lapse.

Common stock rights outstanding (1,350 rights × $2)	2,700	
Common stock, par $10 (243 shares)		2,430
Contributed capital, lapse of stock rights (135 rights × $2)* .		270

* A credit to Contributed Capital leaves the full amount capitalized ($24,000). Some accountants prefer to credit Retained Earnings because the effect would be to capitalize $23,730 only.

Case C— Assume the fractional share rights specified that *(a)* five such rights could be turned in for one share of stock at no cost or *(b)* each right could be turned in for $2.40 cash. Cash was disbursed for 350 rights, and the remaining 1,000 rights were turned in for the requisite number of shares.

Common stock rights outstanding (1,350 rights)	2,700	
Contributed capital in excess of par, 350 × ($2.40 − $2.00)	140	
Common stock, par $10 (1,000 rights ÷ 5 = 200 shares)		2,000
Cash (350 rights × $2.40)		840

---

[11] *APB Opinion No. 10* states that "the liquidation preference of the stock be disclosed in the equity section of the balance sheet in the aggregate, either parenthetically or 'in short' rather than on a per share basis or by disclosure in notes"; and *APB Opinion No. 9*, par. 35, specifies that amounts in arrearage on cumulative preferred stock should be disclosed.

Case D—Assume that Z Corporation did not issue fractional share warrants. Instead it paid $2.40 cash for each fractional share (in lieu of the rights). The *issuance* of the stock dividend would be recorded as follows:

Retained earnings (2,000 shares at market, $12)	24,000	
Common stock, par $10 (1,730 shares)		17,300
Contributed capital in excess of par, common stock [1,730 shares × ($12 − $10)]		3,460
Cash (1,350 fractional shares × $2.40)		3,240

If a balance sheet for Z Corporation is prepared between the date of issuance of the stock rights and their receipt later, the outstanding rights would be reported as follows (refer to the data on page 579 and the issuance entry on page 581).

Z CORPORATION

Stockholders' Equity

Contributed Capital:			
Capital Stock:			
Preferred stock, $20 par value, 10,000 shares authorized, 5,000 shares outstanding		$100,000	
Common stock, $10 par value, 20,000 shares authorized, 11,730 shares outstanding	$117,300		
Common stock rights outstanding (for 270 shares)	2,700	120,000	
Total Capital Stock		220,000	
Other Contributed Capital:			
Contributed capital in excess of par, preferred stock	10,000		
Contributed capital in excess of par, common stock	19,000	29,000	
Total Contributed Capital		249,000	
Retained Earnings:			
Unappropriated		126,000	
Total Stockholders' Equity		$375,000	

Observe that stock rights outstanding are reported next to the related stock account. This reports the obligation to issue the requisite number of shares.

DIVIDENDS AND TREASURY STOCK

Dividends are not paid on treasury stock. However, treasury stock occasionally is used to pay a stock dividend. If treasury stock is used for this purpose, it should be recorded as having been distributed at its current market value (also see discussion of treasury stock in Chapter 18).

To illustrate a stock dividend from treasury stock, assume a corporation issued 6,000 shares of $20 par value common stock at $22 per share of which 5,000 shares are currently outstanding and 1,000 shares are held as treasury stock acquired (and recorded) at $21 per share. The board of directors declared a stock dividend whereby one share of treasury stock would be transferred for each five shares of stock held. The current market value per share remained essentially unchanged after the stock dividend at $23 per share. The indicated entry assuming a small stock dividend is as follows:

Retained earnings (1,000 shares at market of $23)	23,000	
Treasury stock (1,000 shares at cost of $21)		21,000
Contributed capital, treasury stock transactions		2,000

LEGALITY OF DIVIDENDS

The availability of retained earnings and certain elements of contributed capital as a basis for dividends was mentioned in the first section of this chapter. To attempt to identify precisely what elements of corporate capital are available as a basis for cash, property, and stock dividends, respectively, would require a minute and detailed study of the laws of each state. Such a study is beyond the scope of this text; further, questions of law rather than accounting are involved. There are at least two provisions which appear uniform—namely, that dividends may not be paid from *legal capital* (usually represented by the capital *stock* accounts) and that unappropriated retained earnings are available for dividends.[12] Aside from these two provisions, there are numerous variations, depending upon the respective state statutes, such as the following:

1. All contributed capital, other than legal capital, is available for dividends.
2. Specified items of contributed capital, other than legal capital, are available for dividends.
3. Contributed capital, other than legal capital,

---

[12] Some states permit the payment of dividends from current earnings even though the corporation has an accumulated deficit in Retained Earnings.

is available for dividends on preferred stock but not on common stock.

4. Unrealized capital is not available for dividends.
5. Unrealized capital is available for stock dividends only.
6. Debits in the contributed capital accounts and a deficit in Retained Earnings must be restored before payment of any dividends.
7. Dividends from retained earnings must not reduce the Retained Earnings balance below the cost of treasury stock held.

The accountant has a responsibility in circumstances where the propriety and legality of dividends are at issue to *(a)* insure that such matters are referred to an attorney and *(b)* ascertain that the financial statements fully disclose all known and material facts concerning such dividends.

APPROPRIATIONS OF RETAINED EARNINGS

From time to time *appropriations* of retained earnings may be made as a result of management action, by contract, or by law. Appropriations of retained earnings constitute a *restriction* on a specified portion of accumulated earnings for specific purposes. Such specific appropriations nevertheless represent a part of *total* retained earnings. Thus, retained earnings is comprised of two subcategories: (1) appropriated retained earnings and (2) unappropriated retained earnings.

Retained earnings are appropriated to protect the cash position of the corporation by reducing the amount of cash dividends that otherwise might be paid during the period covered by the appropriation. Restrictions arise in the following situations:

1. To fulfill a *legal requirement,* as in the case of a restriction on retained earnings equivalent to the cost of treasury stock held as required by the law of the specific state.
2. To fulfill a *contractual agreement,* as in the case of a bond issue where the bond indenture carries a stipulation providing for a restriction on retained earnings.
3. To record a discretionary action by the board

of directors to restrict a portion of retained earnings as an aspect of *financial planning.*
4. To record a discretionary action by the board of directors to restrict a portion of retained earnings in anticipation of *possible future losses.*

Item 1 in the above list will be discussed in Chapter 18; the remaining items will be discussed below. Preliminary to the discussions to follow, observe that appropriations of retained earnings have no direct effect upon assets. An appropriation is a "clerical" identification and does not set aside specific assets such as cash; this would occur only if cash is set aside in a separate fund, such as a Bond Sinking Fund (somewhat similar to a savings account).

Appropriations of retained earnings may be accounted for and reported using either of two approaches, viz:

1. Make no entries in the accounts. Report the appropriations or restrictions either parenthetically on the balance sheet (or statement of retained earnings) or by notes to the statements.
2. Make entries in the accounts and report the appropriations as appropriated retained earnings in the balance sheet.

In recent years the first approach has been used by an increasing number of companies. Sometimes it is desirable to supplement the reporting under the second approach with note disclosure. Both approaches will be discussed.

When the need for an appropriation ceases or management decides to remove the appropriation, it is no longer reported; and prior entries recording the restriction (if the second approach is used) are reversed so that the appropriated amount is returned to unappropriated retained earnings.

When the second approach is used, the restriction is entered in the accounts as a debit to the Retained Earnings account (i.e., unappropriated retained earnings) and as a credit to a descriptively designated appropriated account.[13]

---

[13] Recall the discussion of *reserves* in Chapter 5. The term reserve should be limited in usage to appropriations of retained earnings, AICPA, *Accounting Terminology Bulletin No. 1,* "Review and Resumé" (New York, 1961), pars. 57–64.

Under this approach the basic principle is that an appropriation account is *never* debited for a loss, or for any other reason, except to return the balance to the original source, that is, to the Retained Earnings account. Even in the case of a stock dividend (which usually requires a debit to Retained Earnings) or when a new appropriation is established as the consequence of closing another such account, balances of any appropriated retained earnings account should be returned first to the regular Retained Earnings account, and the new restriction should be recorded in the normal manner. On this point *FASB Statement No. 5* states the following:

> Some enterprises have classified a portion of retained earnings as "appropriated" for loss contingencies. In some cases, the appropriation has been shown outside the stockholders' equity section of the balance sheet. Appropriation of retained earnings is not prohibited by this Statement provided that it is shown within the stockholders' equity section of the balance sheet and is clearly identified as an appropriation of retained earnings. Costs or losses should not be charged to an appropriation of retained earnings, and no part of the appropriation shall be transferred to income.[14]

Appropriation Related to a Contractual Agreement

To offer more security to purchasers of a bond issue, the bond indenture may include various provisions favorable to the bondholders (see Chapter 20). One such provision, generally referred to as a bond sinking or redemption *fund,* calls for the periodic deposit of a specified amount of cash in a fund, held by a trustee, to be used to retire the bonds at maturity. A second provision, when used, calls for the periodic *appropriation* of a specific amount of retained earnings. The amount to be appropriated may or may not be the same as the cash contributed to the fund.

To illustrate, assume a $1 million bond issue was sold at par, with the provisions that *(a)* $100,000 per year for ten years shall be deposited

in a special fund and *(b)* an equal amount shall be designated as an appropriation of retained earnings. Assuming the appropriation is recorded in the accounts (the second approach discussed above), the entries would be as follows:

1. At date of issuance of bonds:

Cash	1,000,000	
Bonds payable		1,000,000

2. At end of each of the ten years:[15]

Bond redemption fund (or Bond sinking fund)	100,000	
Cash		100,000
Retained earnings	100,000	
Retained earnings appropriated for bond redemption fund (or Reserve for bond sinking fund)		100,000

3. At date of maturity:

Bonds payable	1,000,000	
Bond redemption fund		1,000,000
Retained earnings appropriated for bond redemption fund	1,000,000	
Retained earnings		1,000,000

Since the original proceeds of the bond issue may have been used to acquire operational assets, upon payment of the bonds management may desire to reappropriate the $1,000,000 or, to "capitalize" it through a stock dividend. To illustrate each situation:

1. Assume the board of directors voted that $1,000,000 be reappropriated in view of investment in plant:

Retained earnings	1,000,000	
Retained earnings appropriated for investment in plant		1,000,000

2. Assume the board of directors declared and issued a $1,000,000 stock dividend (to be capitalized at par value, $10 per share):

---

[14] FASB, *Statement of Financial Accounting Standards No. 5,* "Accounting for Contingencies" (March 1975), par. 15.

[15] Interest revenue on the fund balance is disregarded in this example. Interest earned on the fund normally is recorded as a credit to interest revenue and a debit to the sinking fund. This serves to reduce the amount of cash that must be transferred to the sinking fund each year.

Retained earnings	1,000,000
Capital stock, par $10	
(100,000 shares)......	1,000,000

Similar contractual appropriations may relate to agreements such as the retirement of preferred stock and payment of various obligations.

If the appropriation is not recorded in the accounts (approach 1), a footnote often is used to report the restriction. However, in any event, the entries relating to the *fund* (but not to the appropriation) would be necessary.

Appropriations as an Aspect of Financial Planning

Many corporations began with a small initial capital investment and have grown large by retaining a large portion of the earnings in the business. In such circumstances it may be desirable to capitalize a portion of accumulated earnings by issuing stock dividends. Alternatively the board of directors, at least temporarily, may set aside a portion of accumulated earnings in one or more appropriation accounts such as the following:

Retained Earnings Appropriated for Investment in Plant (as illustrated above)

Retained Earnings Appropriated for Working Capital

Retained Earnings Invested in Operational Assets

Appropriation for Possible Future Losses

In anticipation of possible future losses, the board of directors sometimes will direct that a portion of retained earnings be appropriated and specifically identified with titles such as the following:

Retained Earnings Appropriated for Contingencies

Retained Earnings Appropriated for Possible Storm Damage

Retained Earnings Appropriated for Possible Future Inventory Cost Declines

Retained Earnings Appropriated for Possible Loss in Pending Lawsuit

Retained Earnings Appropriated for Self-Insurance

As stated earlier, even though the anticipated contingency does materialize, any actual loss arising therefrom should be recorded as an ordinary, unusual or infrequent, or extraordinary item, as would be done when there is no related appropriation account; such losses are not properly charged to the appropriation account.

An appropriation for possible future inventory cost decline is not the same account discussed in Chapter 10 which related to the valuation of inventory at lower of cost or market (Allowance to Reduce Inventory to Lower of Cost or Market). That account was related to a cost decline that had *already* materialized, whereas the appropriation account relates to a possible cost decline in the future, that is, one that has not yet materialized and may not ever materialize but the possibility does exist.

The use of this type of appropriation is subject to specific constraints given in *FASB Statement No. 5,* "Accounting for Contingencies" (see quotation on page 584). This *FASB Statement* is discussed in detail in Chapter 9.

REPORTING RETAINED EARNINGS

The statement of retained earnings was discussed in Chapter 4, and illustrative examples were given. For a number of years there has been considerable diversity of views as to what should be reported on the income statement versus the statement of retained earnings. The issue has focused primarily on how *(a)* extraordinary items and *(b)* prior period adjustments should be reported. Recall that *APB Opinion No. 9* (December 1966) specifies that extraordinary items must be reported on the income statement and that prior period adjustments must be reported on the statement of retained earnings.

In June 1977 the FASB issued *Statement No. 16,* "Prior Period Adjustments," which amended the older definition of prior period adjustments (specified in *APB Opinion No. 9*). *FASB Statement No. 16* states the following with respect to annual financial statements (as distinguished from interim statements of less than one year):[16]

---

[16] *FASB Statement No. 16* amends certain paragraphs in *APB Opinion No. 9;* the remaining parts of the latter continue in effect.

Par. 11. Items of profit and loss related to the following shall be accounted for and reported as prior period adjustments and excluded from the determination of net income for the current period:

a) Correction of an error in the financial statements of a prior period and

b) Adjustments that result from realization of income tax benefits of preacquisition operating loss carryforwards of purchased subsidiaries.

Par. 16. Those items that are reported as prior period adjustments shall, in single period statements, be reflected as adjustments of the opening balance of retained earnings.

Clearly, the effect of *FASB Statement No. 16* is to narrow the definition of prior period adjustments to the extent that, for all practical purposes, the income statement comes very close to expressing the all-inclusive concept (see Chapter 4). Correction of errors is discussed in detail in Chapter 24, and the second category of prior period adjustments specified above—preacquisition operating loss carryforwards—is deferred to texts that concentrate on mergers and consolidations.[17]

APB Opinion No. 9, par. 26, specifies a full disclosure requirement for prior period adjustments as follows:

When financial statements for a single period only are presented, this disclosure should indicate the effects of such restatement on the balance of retained earnings at the beginning of the period. When financial statements for more than one period are presented, which is ordinarily the preferable procedure, the disclosure should include the effects for each of the periods included in the statements. Such disclosure should include the amounts of income tax applicable to the prior period adjustments.

Under generally accepted accounting principles, as specified in these and other pronouncements, the statement of retained earnings should report the following:

---

[17] See, for example, C. H. Griffin, T. H. Williams, and K. D. Larson, *Advanced Accounting,* 3d ed. (Homewood, Ill.: Richard D. Irwin, Inc., 1977).

1. Beginning balance.
2. Prior period adjustments (supplemented by an appropriate note).
3. Net income or loss for the period.
4. Dividends.
5. Appropriations of retained earnings.
6. Adjustments made pursuant to a quasi-reorganization.
7. Ending balance.

To illustrate the reporting of retained earnings, the following data from the records of Model Stores, Incorporated, are used:

For Year Ended December 31, 1979

Sales		$520,000
Cost of goods sold		300,000
Expenses		120,000
Income taxes on ordinary income		52,000
Extraordinary gain		7,000
Income taxes on extraordinary item		3,000
Balance in retained earnings, January 1, 1979:		
Unappropriated	$158,000	
Appropriation for plant expansion	60,000	
Appropriation for bond sinking fund	40,000	258,000
Prior period adjustment, correction of accounting error from 1978 (deduction net of $7,000 income tax saving)		19,000
Dividends for 1979		30,000
Appropriation of retained earnings for bond sinking fund for 1979		10,000

The income statement and statement of retained earnings for Model Stores are shown in Exhibit 17–1.

When the statement of retained earnings is not complex, it is sometimes included with the income statement in a combined income and retained earnings statement. In complex situations, full disclosure may necessitate the use of notes to the statement of retained earnings.

APB Opinion No. 12 ("Omnibus Opinion," 1967) also has had an impact on the reporting of retained earnings; paragraph 10 of the *Opinion* states:

When both financial position and results of operations are presented, disclosure of changes in

EXHIBIT 17–1
Income Statement and Statement of Retained Earnings Illustrated

MODEL STORES, INCORPORATED
Income Statement
For the Year Ended December 31, 1979

Sales		$520,000
Less: Cost of goods sold		300,000
Gross margin		220,000
Less: Expenses	$120,000	
Income taxes	52,000	172,000
Income before extraordinary items		48,000
Extraordinary items:		
Gain (designated, net of applicable income tax, $3,000)		4,000
Net Income		$ 52,000
Earnings per share (not illustrated).		

MODEL STORES, INCORPORATED
Statement of Retained Earnings
For the Year Ended December 31, 1979

Unappropriated Retained Earnings:			
Unappropriated balance, January 1, 1979		$158,000	
Adjustments applicable to prior periods:			
Correction of accounting error from 1978 (net of $7,000 income tax saving)		(19,000)	
Corrected beginning balance		139,000	
Add: Net Income for 1979		52,000	
		191,000	
Deductions and appropriations during 1979:			
Dividends for 1979	$30,000		
Appropriation for bond sinking fund	10,000	40,000	
Unappropriated balance, December 31, 1979			$151,000
Appropriated Retained Earnings:			
For plant expansion		60,000	
For bond sinking fund:			
Balance, January 1, 1979	40,000		
Addition during 1979	10,000	50,000	
Appropriated balance, December 31, 1979			110,000
Total Appropriated and Unappropriated, Balance December 31, 1979			$261,000

the separate accounts comprising stockholders' equity (in addition to retained earnings) and of the changes in the number of shares of equity securities during at least the most recent annual fiscal period and any subsequent interim period presented is required to make the financial statements sufficiently informative. Disclosure of such changes may take the form of separate statements or may be made in the basic financial statements or notes thereto.

Consequently, in recent years there has been widespread use of comprehensive supplemen-

tary statements of all changes in owners' equity similar to that illustrated in Chapter 5, Exhibit 5–3.

PART B—CONTRACTION AND EXPANSION OF CORPORATE CAPITAL AFTER FORMATION

Once the corporate charter is granted and the bylaws are approved, provisions governing corporate capital (i.e., stockholders' equity) are established; however, this does not mean that such provisions may not be changed. Aside from the sale of unissued shares already authorized (or distribution of stock dividends), a corporation may obtain authorization for additional classes of stock, expansion of the number of shares of currently authorized stock, or change of the par or stated values. Or it may contract and expand corporate capital by purchasing and selling its own shares in the marketplace. Callable and redeemable shares may be acquired and retired and convertible shares may be exchanged. The corporation may undergo a corporate reorganization involving a significant change in the entire capital structure; or it may combine with other entities. These changes are controlled in various manners: by state laws, by charter and bylaw provisions, or by the shareholders themselves. Upon approval of the shareholders, the bylaws may be changed and even a new or amended charter obtained. In the long term the primary source of expansion of stockholders' equity is income not distributed as cash or property dividends. Retained earnings frequently is capitalized by means of a stock dividend (see Part A) or through other kinds of capital changes.

In accounting for and reporting changes in corporate capital, other than as a result of earning income (or loss), five basic principles have general applicability, viz:

1. Sources of stockholders' equity should be separately recorded and reported.
2. Information must be accumulated and reported to meet the requirements of the accounting profession and the prevailing laws.
3. A corporation cannot recognize, as income or as increases in retained earnings, gains that result from capital stock transactions

between itself and its owners; accounting recognition of net asset *increases* resulting from transactions relating to the corporation's own stock are recorded as changes in contributed capital rather than as gains. Net asset decreases, however, can be debited to retained earnings.

4. Increases in authorized shares, authorized legal capital, changes in par or stated values, or exchanges of its own equity shares (such as its own preferred shares for its own common shares) do not create income, losses, or credits to retained earnings. Debits to retained earnings from such capital transactions are viewed as similar to dividends.

5. Certain payments (of assets) by a corporation for its own shares above the contributed capital per share may be considered to be a form of cash (or property) dividends which would decrease retained earnings.

TREASURY STOCK

Expansion and contraction of contributed capital after formation frequently arise from treasury stock transactions. The statutes of most states permit a corporation to purchase its own stock subject to certain limitations. *Treasury stock* is a corporation's own stock (preferred or common) that *(a)* has been issued, *(b)* is subsequently reacquired by the issuing corporation, and *(c)* after acquisition has not been resold or formally retired. Thus, treasury stock does not reduce the number of *issued* shares but does reduce the number of *outstanding* shares. Treasury shares may be subsequently resold and then are again classified as outstanding shares. The courts generally have held that discount liability does not apply to treasury stock resold (see Chapter 16), assuming the second purchaser did not have knowledge of any prior discount liability.

The purchase of treasury stock contracts both assets and stockholders' equity, whereas a sale of treasury stock expands both assets and stockholders' equity. Treasury shares may be obtained by purchase, by settlement of an obligation, or through donation. Treasury stock does not carry voting, dividend, or liquidation privileges. Although the acquisition of treasury stock involves the disbursement of assets, basically treasury stock is not an asset since a corporation cannot own itself.[18] In this respect, treasury stock is generally viewed as similar to unissued stock, which is not an asset.

Treasury stock may be acquired for the following reasons: (1) the corporation has ready cash, and the stock is considered to be unrealistically underpriced; (2) to use for employee stock options, bonus plans, and direct sale to employees (when there are no unissued shares); (3) to use in exchange for other securities or assets; (4) to use for a stock dividend; (5) to increase earnings per share; (6) to buy out one or more particular stockholders; and (7) to support the market price of the stock.

RECORDING AND REPORTING TREASURY STOCK TRANSACTIONS

There are several prevailing views as to the approach that should be used in accounting for, and reporting, treasury stock. These views may be grouped broadly under two methods, viz:

1. Cost method (one-transaction concept).
2. Par value method (dual-transaction concept).

Both of these methods are generally accepted; however, they yield different results for certain individual items within the stockholders' equity section of the balance sheet. Assuming a common set of facts, the *total* amount of stockholders' equity is the same under both methods.

---

[18] *ARB No. 43*, chap. 1, par. 4, states: "While it is perhaps in some circumstances permissible to show stock of a corporation held in its own treasury as an asset, if adequately disclosed, the dividends on stock so held should not be treated as a credit to the income account of the company." Despite the fact that this statement is inconsistent (in that income recognition is not permitted on something that would be called an asset), this source has been used by a few to argue for classifying treasury stock as an asset. A typical case is where there is a future obligation under an employee stock incentive plan that will require the future issuance of corporation stock acquired by repurchase. This practice has serious theoretical flaws because the obligation is to issue corporation stock in the future (an owners' equity item similar to subscribed stock) and is not in the nature of a true liability (coupled with a dubious asset composed of the corporation's own capital stock).

Cost Method

This method sometimes is referred to as the one-transaction concept because the *purchase and subsequent sale* of the treasury stock is viewed as one extended transaction. At acquisition, the *cost* of the treasury stock is debited to a "holding" account called Treasury Stock. At date of subsequent resale, the Treasury Stock account is credited for *cost;* and any difference between selling price and cost is recorded as a change in one or more stockholders' equity accounts as illustrated below.

Separate treasury stock accounts should be established for each class of stock. When treasury shares are acquired at different costs, specific shares should be identified; otherwise a *Fifo* or average cost per share must be used to determine the credit to the Treasury Stock account (at cost) at resale date.

Under the cost method the balance in the Treasury Stock account at the end of the accounting period is viewed as an *unallocated reduction* of the total amount of stockholders' equity (see page 590).

The following entries illustrate accounting for treasury stock assuming the *cost method* is used:

Recording Treasury Stock—Cost Method for Par Value Stock

1. To record the initial sale and issuance of 10,000 shares of common stock, par $25, at $26 per share:

Cash (10,000 shares @ $26)	260,000	
Common stock, par $25 (10,000 shares)		250,000
Contributed capital in excess of par, common stock		10,000

2. To record the acquisition of 2,000 shares of treasury common stock at $28 per share:

Treasury stock, common stock (2,000 shares @ $28)	56,000	
Cash		56,000

Note: Observe that the acquisition entry will never reflect a "debit or credit difference" under the cost method because the cash price paid is always the amount debited to the treasury stock account.

3. To record sale of 500 shares of the treasury stock at $30 per share (above cost and above par):

Cash (500 shares @ $30)	15,000	
Treasury stock, common stock (500 shares @ cost, $28)		14,000
Contributed capital from treasury stock transactions, common stock ...		1,000

(Had this sale been at cost [$28 per share], no entry would have been made to the Contributed Capital Account.)

4. To record the sale of another 500 shares of the treasury stock at $19 per share (below cost and below par):

Cash (500 shares @ $19)	9,500	
Contributed capital from treasury stock transactions, common stock*	1,000	
Retained earnings	3,500	
Treasury stock, common stock (500 shares @ cost, $28)		14,000

* Debit limited to the current balance in this account (see Entry 3); any remainder is allocated to Retained Earnings.

Under the cost method, when treasury stock is resold at a price in excess of its cost, the full amount of the "gain" (the credit difference) should be recorded as contributed capital from treasury stock transactions, as in Transaction 3 above, and not credited to Income, Gain, or Retained Earnings.

Alternatively, when treasury stock is sold at less than cost, the debit difference should be allocated first to whatever balance there is in the account for Contributed Capital from *Treasury Stock Transactions* (for the same class of stock); and any remainder should be debited to Retained Earnings. The portion debited to Retained Earnings represents a "distribution" of retained earnings to certain shareholders.[19] For

---

[19] This is consistent with *APB Opinion No. 6*, par. 12, which states: " 'Gains' on sales of treasury stock not previously accounted for as constructively retired should be credited to capital surplus [i.e., Contributed Capital from Treasury Stock Transactions]; 'losses' may be charged to capital surplus to the extent that previous net 'gains' from sales or retirements of the same class of stock are included therein, otherwise to retained earnings." This rule does not extend to contributed capital in excess of par or stated value.

example, in Transaction 4 above, had there been no balance in the account for contributed capital from treasury stock transactions (for common stock), the entire $4,500 would have been debited to the Retained Earnings account; alternatively, had the balance in the account for contributed capital from treasury stock transactions (for common stock) been $4,500 or more, there would have been no debit to the Retained Earnings account.

When the cost method is used, treasury stock (at cost) is reported as an *unallocated reduction* of stockholders' equity. Assuming Transactions 1 through 4 above, and a beginning balance in Retained Earnings of $40,000, the balance sheet would reflect the following:

Stockholders' Equity
(cost method for treasury stock)

Contributed Capital:	
Common stock, par $25, authorized 50,000 shares, issued 10,000 shares, of which 1,000 are held as treasury stock	$250,000
Contributed capital in excess of par, common stock	10,000
Total Contributed Capital	260,000
Retained earnings ($40,000 − $3,500)	36,500
Total Contributed Capital and Retained Earnings	296,500
Less: Treasury stock, 1,000 shares at cost, $28	28,000
Total Stockholders' Equity	$268,500

The cost method is frequently used because of its simplicity. It may avoid the necessity of developing specific data concerning the original premiums, discounts, and so on, relating to the specific stock involved. Therefore, it can be defended on practical grounds. However, theoretical justification is lacking because the *sources* of the various components of capital are not maintained.

Par Value Method

This method is sometimes referred to as the dual-transaction concept because it views the purchase and sale of treasury stock as two completely independent and unrelated transactions. Thus, the two objectives of the par value method are as follows:

1. At date of acquisition of treasury stock—to make a final accounting with the retiring stockholder and to adjust the capital accounts on a "stock retirement" basis.

2. At date of resale of treasury stock—to record the reissuance essentially in the same manner as for the sale and issuance of unissued stock.

To accomplish these two purposes, the treasury stock account is carried at the par or stated value per share; hence, the designation par value method. The accounting at each transaction date is as follows:

1. Date of acquisition—The final accounting with the retiring stockholder is recorded as a credit to Cash for the price paid and a debit to the treasury stock account for the par value (in the case of par value stock), stated value (in the case of nopar stock with a stated value), or average amount credited to the capital stock account (in the case of true nopar stock). In the case of a *debit difference* between the price paid and the amount recorded in the treasury stock account, a step allocation, subject to account balances, is made as follows: First, remove from the account for contributed capital in excess of par, or stated value, or average paid in, the *proportionate part* which agrees with the number of treasury shares acquired (as would be done if the shares were retired, which reflects the nature of the par value method); second, debit the account for contributed capital from treasury stock transactions (to the extent needed, but not in excess of any balance from the same class of stock); and third, allocate any remainder to the Retained Earnings account. In addition, *APB Opinion No. 6*, paragraph 12a, states: "Alternatively the excess may be charged entirely to retained earnings in recognition of the fact that a corporation can always capitalize or allocate retained earnings for such purposes."

In the case of a *credit difference*, there must be a debit to the account for contributed capital in excess of par (if there is such an account balance) for the proportionate part; then the sum of the proportionate part *plus* the credit difference must be credited to contributed capital from treasury stock transactions.

2. *Date of resale*—The entry for resale of treasury stock is essentially the same as the entry for original sale: Cash is debited and Treasury Stock is credited for par value, stated value, or average paid in (the case of true nopar stock); i.e., the same cost per share that was recorded at acquisition date. A *credit difference* between sales price and the amount credited to the Treasury Stock account is credited in full to the account for contributed capital from treasury stock transactions. A *debit difference* is allocated first to contributed capital from treasury stock transactions (to the extent that there is a balance), and any remainder is debited to Retained Earnings.

Recording Treasury Stock—Par Value Method for Par Value Stock

The preceding example is used to illustrate the accounting for treasury stock assuming the *par value method* is used.

1. To record the initial sale and issuance of 10,000 shares of common stock, par $25, at $26 per share:

Cash (10,000 shares @ $26)	260,000	
Common stock, par $25 (10,000 shares)		250,000
Contributed capital in excess of par, common stock (@ $1)		10,000

2. To record acquisition of 2,000 shares of treasury common stock at $28 per share (a debit difference):

Treasury stock, common stock (2,000 shares @ par, $25)	50,000	
Contributed capital in excess of par, common stock (@ $1)	2,000	
Contributed capital from treasury stock transactions, common stock	–0–*	
Retained earnings	4,000	
Cash (2,000 shares @ $28)		56,000

* No available balance to absorb a debit.

Alternatively, had the 2,000 shares been acquired for $46,000 cash, the debits to the treasury stock and contributed capital accounts would be as above; a credit to Contributed Capital from Treasury Stock Transactions, Common Stock for $6,000 would be necessary.

3. To record the sale of 500 shares of treasury stock at $30 per share (above cost and above par; a credit difference):

Cash (500 shares @ $30)	15,000	
Treasury stock, common stock (500 shares @ par, $25)		12,500
Contributed capital from treasury stock transactions, common stock ...		2,500

(Had this sale been at cost [$28 per share], a credit of $1,500 would have been made to Contributed Capital from Treasury Stock Transactions, Common Stock).

4. To record the sale of another 500 shares of treasury stock at $19 per share (below cost and below par; a debit difference):

Cash (500 shares @ $19)	9,500	
Contributed capital from treasury stock transactions, common stock*	2,500	
Retained earnings	500	
Treasury stock, common stock (500 shares @ par, $25)		12,500

* Debit limited to the current balance in this account.

The above entries conform with the concept of the par value method, and the integrity of each source is maintained to the fullest extent possible. Observe that at date of acquisition, the treasury stock was recorded essentially as if it were a recall of the shares and each resale was recorded essentially as if it were an original sale. Thus, the method is conceptually superior to the cost method, although somewhat more complex in application.

When the par value method is used, treasury stock is reported on the balance sheet as a direct deduction, at par or stated value, or average paid in (in the case of true nopar stock), from the class of stock to which it relates (i.e., as a contra amount). Stockholders' equity, assuming Transactions 1 through 4 above and a beginning balance in Retained Earnings of $40,000, would be reported as follows:

Stockholders' Equity
(par value method for treasury stock)

Contributed Capital:
Common stock, par $25, authorized 50,000 shares, issued 10,000 shares	$250,000
Less: Treasury stock, 1,000 shares at par, $25	25,000
Total Common Stock Outstanding, 9,000 Shares	225,000
Contributed capital in excess of par, common stock ($10,000 − $2,000)	8,000
Contributed capital from treasury stock transactions, common stock	–0–
Total Contributed Capital	233,000
Retained earnings ($40,000 − $4,000 − $500)	35,500
Total Stockholders' Equity	$268,500

Observe that the *total* amount of stockholders' equity reported under the cost method (page 590) and the par value method is the same ($268,500); the basic difference between the two methods is reflected only in the detailed accounts that comprise stockholders' equity.

In overall perspective, the cost method is somewhat more simple whereas the par value method is theoretically consistent with the concept of reporting capital by sources. Because of its simplicity the cost method appears to be used more; however, the laws of some states appear to specify the method to be used, and in other states the two methods are alternatives (as they are under GAAP).

ACCOUNTING FOR NOPAR TREASURY STOCK

Nopar stock having a *stated* or *assigned* value per share is accounted for in the same manner as illustrated above for par value stock under each of the two methods. The stated or assigned value per share is treated as if it were par.

In the case of *true nopar stock,* the cost method almost always is used because it can be applied exactly the same as for par value stock (as discussed above). When the par value method is used with true nopar stock, the *average amount per share* reflected in the nopar capital stock account (i.e., the average amount paid in) usually is used as the "basic value" in the place of par or stated value. Other than the fact that with true nopar stock there is no account for Contributed Capital in Excess of Par (or stated value), the accounting for true nopar stock under the par value method would be as illustrated above.

TREASURY STOCK RECEIVED BY DONATION

Shareholders sometimes donate shares of a corporation's stock back to the corporation. Such donations may *(a)* be to raise needed working capital through resale of donated stock or *(b)* constitute return of the stock in recognition of an overvaluation of assets originally given in exchange for the stock. Stock received by donation is classified as treasury stock unless it is formally retired. Neither total assets nor *total equity* is changed by the donation of treasury stock. Three methods have been employed in recording the receipt of donated treasury stock, viz:

1. Cost method—When the donated stock is received, debit the treasury stock account for the current market value of the stock and credit Contributed Capital, Donated Treasury Stock for the same amount. Upon subsequent sale, any "gains" or "losses" (i.e., net asset increases or decreases) would be accounted for as illustrated above for the cost method.

2. Par value method—When the donated stock is received, debit the treasury stock account for the par or stated value (or in the case of true nopar stock, average paid in) and credit an appropriately designated donated capital account. Subsequent sales would be recorded as illustrated above for the par value method.

3. Memo method—When donated stock is received, a memorandum entry is made on the basis that there was no cost. Subsequent sales amounts would be credited to contributed capital for the full sales price. This method is seldom used.

RETIREMENT OF TREASURY STOCK

A corporation may decide to formally retire treasury shares and have them revert to unissued status. When treasury stock is retired in this manner, all capital account balances *related to the treasury shares* (including contributed capital from treasury *stock transac-*

tions) are reduced on a *proportional basis,* and any net debit difference is debited to Retained Earnings. A net credit difference is credited to Contributed Capital from Stock Retirement.

To illustrate, we will continue the preceding example assuming par value stock. Recall that the capital balances, after the illustrative entries, reflected the following (refer to the balance sheet examples on pages 590 and 592):

	Cost Method	Par Value Method
Common stock, par $25, 10,000 shares issued	$250,000	$250,000
Contributed capital in excess of par, common stock	10,000	8,000
Treasury stock (1,000 shares):		
At cost	(28,000)	
At par value		(25,000)
Retained earnings	36,500	35,500
Total Stockholders' Equity	$268,500	$268,500

The entry to record retirement of all of the 1,000 shares of treasury stock would be as follows:

	Cost Method	Par Value Method
Common stock, par $25 (1,000 shares)	25,000	25,000
Contributed capital in excess of par, common stock [($10,000 ÷ 10,000 shares) × 1,000 shares]	1,000	
Retained earnings	2,000	
Treasury stock:		
At cost	28,000	
At par		25,000

Had there been a balance in Contributed Capital from Treasury Stock Transactions, Common Stock, it would have been closed out and the difference, if a debit, recorded in Retained Earnings and, if a credit, to Contributed Capital from Retirement of Common Stock. In the highly unlikely event that fewer than all of the treasury shares are retired, the various debits and credits would be proportionately less.

RESTRICTION OF RETAINED EARNINGS FOR TREASURY STOCK

In Chapter 16 legal capital was discussed and the point was made that state laws frequently were originally designed to protect creditor interests through the maintenance of legal capital and restriction of cash and property dividends. When treasury stock is purchased, assets of the corporation are disbursed to the owners of the shares purchased. Should a corporation have a completely free hand in this matter, it is not difficult to perceive how creditor interests (or the interests of another class of shareholders) may be jeopardized through the distribution of corporate assets via treasury stock purchases, even though legal capital may be "reported intact." To prevent this situation, many states have laws limiting the amount of treasury stock that may be held at any one time to some amount such as the total retained earnings. This provision has the effect of *(a)* requiring restriction of retained earnings equivalent to the cost of treasury stock held and *(b)* reducing the amount of retained earnings that may be used for dividends until the treasury shares are resold.[20] To illustrate, assume a corporation reported the following stockholders' equity:

Capital stock, par $25, 10,000 shares authorized and issued	$250,000
Contributed capital in excess of par	10,000
Retained earnings	38,000

Assuming a statutory limitation that the cost of treasury stock held cannot exceed the balance of Retained Earnings, the corporation could purchase treasury stock costing $38,000; if it did, no dividends could be declared. Should the corporation purchase treasury stock with a cost of $30,000, dividends up to $8,000 could be declared. The restriction on retained earnings would be removed *(a)* by sale of the treasury shares or *(b)* by formal retirement of the shares. The restriction on retained earnings is reported either

---

[20] In some states the restriction applies to retained earnings; on the other hand, some states permit the purchase of treasury stock equivalent in cost to other capital items such as contributed capital in excess of par. Throughout these discussions we will assume that the cost of treasury stock held cannot exceed the balance of Retained Earnings.

as a separate item on the balance sheet or as a note.

RETIREMENT OF CALLABLE AND REDEEMABLE STOCK

Corporations frequently issue *callable* preferred stock which provides that the corporation, *at its option* after a certain date, can call in the shares at a specified price for retirement. In contrast, *redeemable* stock provides that *at the option of the stockholder,* and under certain conditions, the shares tendered will be retired at a specified price per share. Redemption signifies both acquisition and retirement of the stock. The call or redemption price is at or above par and is usually above the original issue price.[21] Shares called, or redeemed, are not classified as treasury stock.

When callable or redeemable stock is acquired and immediately retired, all capital balances relating to the specific shares are removed from the accounts; any "loss" is debited to Retained Earnings as a form of dividends, and any "gain" is credited to a contributed capital account appropriately designated. If the stock is cumulative preferred and there are dividends in arrears, such dividends are debited to Retained Earnings when paid.

To illustrate several typical situations, assume a corporation had 2,500 shares of callable preferred stock (par value $100) outstanding, $250,000; contributed capital in excess of par, preferred stock, $10,000; and retained earnings, $45,000. Now assume the corporation called and retired 1,000 shares of the preferred stock. Three different assumptions as to the *call and retirement* are illustrated below:

Assumption 1: The preferred stock is callable at the original issue price of $104 per share.

Preferred stock (1,000 shares at par, $100)	100,000	
Contributed capital in excess of par, preferred stock ($4 per share)	4,000	
Cash (1,000 shares @ $104)		104,000

---

[21] *APB Opinion No. 10,* par 10, recommends that "any liquidation preference of the stock be disclosed in the equity section of the balance sheet in the aggregate, either parenthetically or 'in short' rather than on a per share basis or by disclosure in notes." Amounts of arrearages on cumulative preferred dividends also should be disclosed.

Assumption 2: The preferred stock is callable at $110 per share—$6 per share above the original issue price of $104.

Preferred stock (1,000 shares at par, $100)	100,000	
Contributed capital in excess of par, preferred stock ($4 per share)	4,000	
Retained earnings	6,000	
Cash (1,000 shares @ $110)		110,000

Assumption 3: The preferred stock is 5% cumulative; three years' dividends are in arrears. The stock is callable at 101 plus the dividends in arrears.

Retained earnings ($100,000 × 5% × 3 years)	15,000	
Cash		15,000

Note: Dividends on the remaining preferred shares are not considered in this entry; cumulative dividends on them also would be paid and recorded at this time.

Preferred stock (1,000 shares at par, $100)	100,000	
Contributed capital in excess of par, preferred stock ($4 per share)	4,000	
Contributed capital from retirement of preferred stock		3,000
Cash (1,000 shares @ $101)		101,000

If true nopar stock is retired, the average price per share originally credited to the stock account is removed and the "loss" or "gain" is accounted for as illustrated above. If nopar stock with a stated or assigned value is retired, the procedures illustrated above for par value stock are followed.

CONVERTIBLE STOCK

Corporations sometimes issue *convertible* preferred stock which gives the shareholder an option, within a specified time period, to exchange convertible shares currently held for other classes of capital stock (or bonds) at a specified rate. The converted shares usually are retired when received by the corporation. Conversion privileges require the issuing corporation to set aside a sufficient number of shares to fulfill the conversion rights until they are exercised, or expire.

At date of conversion, all account balances related to the converted shares are removed and the new shares issued are recorded at their par or stated value; any difference, if a credit, is recorded in an appropriately designated contributed capital account; if a debit, Retained Earnings is reduced. To illustrate three typical situations, assume the following data:

Preferred stock, par $2, shares outstanding, 100,000 ...	$200,000
Contributed capital in excess of par, preferred stock	20,000
Common stock, par $1, shares authorized, 500,000;	
shares outstanding, 150,000	150,000
Contributed capital in excess of par, common stock	50,000

Situation 1: The conversion privilege specifies the issuance of one share of common stock for each share of preferred stock turned in for conversion. Shareholders turn in 10,000 shares of preferred stock for conversion.

Preferred stock (10,000 shares at par, $2)	20,000	
Contributed capital in excess of par, pre-		
ferred stock ($0.20 per share)	2,000	
Common stock (10,000 shares at		
par, $1)		10,000
Contributed capital from conversion		
of preferred stock		12,000

Situation 2: The conversion privilege specifies the issuance of two shares of common stock for each share of preferred stock converted. Shareholders turn in 10,000 shares of preferred stock for conversion.

Preferred stock (10,000 shares at par, $2)	20,000	
Contributed capital in excess of par, pre-		
ferred stock ($0.20 per share)	2,000	
Common stock (20,000 shares at par, $1) ..		20,000
Contributed capital from conversion of		
preferred stock		2,000

Situation 3: The conversion privilege specifies the issuance of three shares of common stock for each share of preferred stock converted. Shareholders turn in 10,000 shares of preferred stock for conversion.

Preferred stock (10,000 shares at par, $2)	20,000	
Contributed capital in excess of par, pre-		
ferred stock ($0.20 per share)	2,000	
Retained earnings	8,000	
Common stock (30,000 shares at		
par, $1)		30,000

Conversion of bonds for capital stock is discussed in Chapter 20.

CHANGING PAR VALUE

A corporation, if it conforms with the applicable state laws, may amend the charter and by-laws to change the par value of one or more classes of authorized stock. Par value stock may be called in and replaced with nopar stock or stock of a different par value; conversely, nopar stock may be replaced with par value stock.[22]

The entries to record changes in par value follow the principles enunciated on pages 587–88 and illustrated in the preceding paragraphs. In particular, all capital account balances pertaining to the old stock are removed from the accounts and the new stock issued is recorded. If an additional credit is needed, an appropriately designated contributed capital account is credited; if an additional debit is needed, Retained Earnings is debited. The entries are similar to those illustrated above for recording the conversion of convertible stock.

QUASI-REORGANIZATIONS

When a corporation has sustained heavy losses over an extended period of time so that there is a significant *deficit* in Retained Earnings and an unrealistic carrying value for assets, a quasi-reorganization may be desirable from the prudent management and accounting points of view.

A quasi-reorganization refers to a procedure whereby a corporation may, without *formal* court proceedings of dissolution, establish a new basis for accounting for assets and stockholders' equity. In effect, a quasi-reorganization is an accounting reorganization in which a "fresh start" is effected in the accounts with respect to certain assets, liabilities, legal capital, and retained earnings.

The Committee on Accounting Procedure of the AICPA recognized the procedure, provided it is properly safeguarded.[23] The Securities and Exchange Commission also recognized it and listed certain safeguards or conditions with respect to a quasi-reorganization. These conditions are summarized below:

1. Retained earnings after the quasi-reorganization must be zero.

---

[22] In a stock split the par value is reduced and the number of shares outstanding is increased proportionally; therefore, the balance in the capital stock account is unchanged. Only a memorandum entry in the original stock account is needed to reflect the new par value per share and the number of shares outstanding after the split.

[23] *Accounting Research Bulletin No. 43,* Chapter 7, Sec. A.

2. Upon completion of the quasi-reorganization no deficit shall remain in any corporate capital account.

3. The effects of the whole procedure shall be made known to all stockholders entitled to vote and appropriate approval in advance obtained from them.

4. A fair and conservative balance sheet shall be presented as of the date of the reorganization and the readjustment of values should be reasonably complete, in order to obviate as far as possible future readjustments of like nature.[24]

Characteristics of a quasi-reorganization are *(a)* the recorded values relating to appropriately selected assets are restated; *(b)* the capital accounts are restated, and the Retained Earnings account is restated to a zero balance; *(c)* the Retained Earnings account is "dated" for a period of time (three to ten years) following the reorganization (illustrated below); *(d)* full disclosure of the procedure and the effects thereof are reported on the financial statements; and *(e)* the corporate entity is unchanged.[25]

To illustrate the accounting for a quasi-reorganization, assume the following simplified balance sheet at January 1, 19A:

Current assets	$ 200,000
Operational assets	1,300,000
	$1,500,000
Liabilities	$ 300,000
Capital stock	1,500,000
Contributed capital in excess of par	100,000
Retained earnings	(400,000)
	$1,500,000

Assume it is determined that the inventories are overvalued by $50,000 and that the operational asset carrying value should be reduced by $350,000.

Under these conditions the company could consider two alternatives. First, the corporation may be dissolved, pay creditors, and form a new corporation. The new corporation would receive the assets, pay off the creditors, and report $800,000 as the new stockholders' equity.

Alternatively, the corporation may undergo a quasi-reorganization (without dissolution) which would be less cumbersome and less expensive than legal reorganization. By complying with the conditions set forth above, including creditors and stockholder approval, the quasi-reorganization may be effected without paying off the creditors at this time. The entries needed are reflected in Exhibit 17–2. That exhibit also shows the restated balance sheet amounts immediately after the quasi-reorganization. The quasi-reorganization restatements of specific account balances are reflected in retained earnings, which is then restated to a zero balance and legal capital is reduced accordingly.

In general, a quasi-reorganization is justified when *(a)* a large deficit from operations exists, *(b)* it is approved by the stockholders, *(c)* the cost basis of accounting for operational assets becomes unrealistic in terms of going-concern values,[26] *(d)* a break in continuity of the historical cost basis is clearly needed so that realistic financial reporting is possible, *(e)* the Retained Earnings balance is totally inadequate to absorb an obvious decrease in going-concern asset values, and *(f)* a "fresh start," in the accounting sense, appears to be desirable or advantageous to all parties properly concerned with the corporation. A quasi-reorganization, by approval of the creditors and shareholders, is supervised by a court to assume adequate protection of the interests of both parties. Since legal capital, as measured in the accounts, is reduced in a quasi-reorganization, all concerned parties seek equity through the court supervision to avoid future misunderstanding and litigation.

---

[24] Securities and Exchange Commission, *Accounting Series Release No. 25.*

[25] For a detailed treatment of quasi-reorganization, see James S. Schindler, *Quasi-Reorganization* (Michigan Business Studies, vol. XIII, no. 5) (Ann Arbor: Bureau of Business Research, University of Michigan, 1958).

[26] The AICPA *Technical Aids* (CCH, Sec. 4220.01) state: "Thus, the official statements of the SEC and the APB can be interpreted as indicating that a quasi-reorganization, if otherwise appropriate, could result in a write-up as well as a write-down of assets." *APB Opinion No. 6,* par. 17, states: "The Board is of the opinion that property, plant and equipment should not be written up by an entity to reflect appraisal, market or current values which are above cost. This statement is not intended to change the accounting practice followed in connection with quasi-reorganizations or reorganizations."

Also, restructure of debt that sometimes occurs in a quasi-reorganization does not come under the provisions of *APB Opinion No. 26* or *FASB Statement No. 15* (see Chapter 20, Part C).

EXHIBIT 17–2
Entries to Record Quasi-Reorganization (January 1, 19A)

Accounts	Balances before Quasi-Reorganization	Entries to Record Quasi-Reorganization		Balances after Quasi-Reorganization
Current assets	$ 200,000		*(a)* $ 50,000	$ 150,000
Operational assets	1,300,000		*(b)* 350,000	950,000
Total Assets	$1,500,000			$1,100,000
Liabilities	$ 300,000			$ 300,000
Capital stock.....................	1,500,000	*(d)* $700,000		800,000
Contributed capital in				
excess of par	100,000	*(c)* 100,000		–0–
Retained earnings	(400,000)	*(a)* 50,000 *(c)* 100,000		(Note 1)
		(b) 350,000 *(d)* 700,000		
Total Liabilities and				
Stockholders' Equity	$1,500,000			$1,100,000

Note 1 (on balance sheet). Retained earnings represents accumulations since January 1, 19A, at which time a $400,000 deficit was eliminated as a result of a quasi-reorganization.

Explanation of entries:
  (a) To write down a current asset (inventory) by $50,000.
  (b) To write down an operational asset by $350,000.
  (c) To write off contributed capital in excess of par as a partial offset to the deficit in retained earnings, $100,000.
  (d) To change retained earnings to a zero balance and to restate legal capital by the same amount (i.e., $400,000 + $50,000 + $350,000 − $100,000 = $700,000). This leaves legal capital at $800,000, the amount necessary to reconcile the basic accounting model after quasi-reorganization. Legal capital can be restated by (1) reducing par value per share (requires a charter change) or (2) reducing the shares outstanding (no charter change required).

QUESTIONS

PART A

1. What are the principal sources and dispositions of retained earnings?

2. Differentiate between total retained earnings and the balance of the Retained Earnings account.

3. What is the position of the accounting profession on use of the word *surplus?* What is the basis for this position?

4. What are the four important dates relative to dividends? Explain the significance of each.

5. Distinguish between cash dividends, property dividends, and liability dividends.

6. What is a liquidating dividend? What are the responsibilities of the accountant with respect to such dividends?

7. Explain the difference between intentional and unintentional liquidating dividends.

8. Basically what is the difference between a cash or property dividend and a stock dividend?

9. Distinguish between a stock dividend and a stock split.

10. What are the reasons for appropriations of retained earnings?

11. Explain the distinction between *(a)* a bond sinking fund and *(b)* an appropriation of retained earnings for bond sinking fund.

12. What items are properly reported on the statement of retained earnings?

13. Is the following statement correct? "Retained earnings was reduced by $10,000 appropriated for plant expansion." Explain.

PART B

14. Define treasury stock.

15. Explain the basic difference in theory between the one-transaction concept and the dual-transaction concept in accounting for treasury stock.

16. In comparing the recording of treasury stock at cost with recording at par, "total capital is unaffected; however, subdivisions thereof are affected." Explain this statement.

17. Why have many states limited purchases of treasury stock to the amount reported as retained earnings? How may the restriction on retained earnings be removed?

18. In recording treasury stock transactions why are "gains" recorded in a contributed capital account whereas "losses" may involve a debit to Retained Earnings?

19. How is treasury stock reported on the balance sheet (a) under the cost method and (b) under the par value method?

20. How is the restriction on retained earnings, equal to the cost of treasury stock held, reported on the balance sheet?

21. How is stock donated back to the corporation recorded?

22. What is a quasi-reorganization? Under what conditions is it acceptable?

DECISION CASE 17–1

Bland Plastics, Incorporated, was started in 1972 to manufacture a wide range of plastic products from three basic components. The company was originally owned by 23 shareholders; however, five years after formation, the capital structure was expanded considerably, at which time preferred stock was issued for the first time. At the present time there are more than 250 holders of preferred and common stock. The preferred is nonvoting, cumulative, nonparticipating, 6% stock. The company has experienced a substantial growth in business over the years. This growth was due to two principal factors: (a) the dynamic management and (b) geographic location. The firm served a rapidly expanding area with relatively few regionally situated competitors.

The last audited balance sheet showed the following (summarized):

Balance Sheet
December 31, 1979

Cash	$ 11,000
Other current assets	76,000
Investment in K Company stock (at cost)	30,000
Plant and equipment (net)	310,000
Intangible assets	15,000
Other assets	8,000
	$450,000
Current liabilities	$ 38,000
Long-term notes	60,000
Preferred stock, par value $100* (500 shares)	50,000
Common stock, $15 par value (10,000 shares)*	150,000
Premium on preferred stock	2,000
Retained earnings	25,000
Profits invested in plant	125,000
	$450,000

* Authorized shares—preferred, 2,000; common, 20,000.

The board of directors have not declared a dividend since organization; instead, the profits are used to expand the company. This decision was based on the facts that the original capital was small and there was a decision to limit the number of shareholders. At the present time the common stock is held by slightly fewer than 50 individuals. Each of these individuals also owns preferred shares; their total holdings approximate 46% of the outstanding preferred. The preferred was issued at the time of the expansion of capital.

The board of directors have been planning to declare a dividend during the early part of 1980, payable June 30. However, the cash position as shown by the balance sheet has raised serious doubts as to the advisability of a dividend in 1980. The president has explained that most of the cash was temporarily tied up in inventory and plant.

The company has a chief accountant but no controller. The board relies on an outside CPA for advice concerning financial management. The CPA was asked to advise about the contemplated dividend declaration. Four of the seven members of the board felt very strongly that some kind of dividend must be declared and paid and that all shareholders "should get something."

Required:

You have been asked to analyze the situation and make whatever dividend proposals that appear to be worthy of consideration by the board. Present figures to support your recommendations in a form suitable for consideration by the board in reaching a decision. Provide the basis for your proposals and indicate any preferences that you may have.

DECISION CASE 17–2

Unknown Corporation purchased equipment with a cash price of $144,000 in 1979 for $90,000 cash and a promise to deliver an indeterminate number of shares of its $5 par common stock, with a market value of $15,000 on January 1 of each year for the next four years. Hence, $60,000 in "market value" of shares will be required to discharge the $54,000 balance due on the equipment.

The corporation then acquired 5,000 shares of its own stock (which became treasury shares) in the expectation that the market value of the stock would increase substantially before the delivery dates.

Required:

1. Discuss the propriety of recording the equipment at

a. $90,000 (the cash payment).

b. $144,000 (the cash price of the equipment).

c. $150,000 (the $90,000 cash payment + the $60,000 market value of treasury stock that must be transferred to the vendor in order to settle the obligation according to the terms of the agreement). Assume an ordinary annuity.

2. Discuss the arguments *for* treating the balance due as

a. A liability.

b. Treasury stock subscribed.

3. Assuming that legal requirements do not affect the decision, discuss the arguments *for* treating the corporation's treasury shares as

a. An asset awaiting ultimate disposition.

b. A capital element awaiting ultimate disposition.

(AICPA adapted)

EXERCISES

PART A
Exercises 17–1 to 17–10

Exercise 17–1

Campbell Corporation's books on January 1 showed the following balances (summarized):

Cash	$ 20,000
Other current assets	25,000
Operational assets (net)	250,000
Other assets	55,000
	$350,000

Current liabilities	$ 30,000
Long-term liabilities	60,000
Capital stock, 2,000 shares	200,000
Contributed capital in excess of par	10,000
Retained earnings	50,000
	$350,000

The board of directors is considering a cash dividend, and you have been requested to provide certain assistance as the independent CPA. The following matters have been referred to you:

1. What is the maximum amount of cash dividends that can be paid at January 1? Explain.

2. Approximately what amount of dividends would you recommend based upon the data from the accounts? Explain.

3. What entries would be made assuming a $15,000 cash dividend is declared with the following dates specified: *(a)* declaration date, *(b)* date of record, and *(c)* date of payment.

4. Assuming a balance sheet is prepared between declaration date and payment date, how would the dividend declaration be reported?

Exercise 17–2

On June 1, 1979, Tims Manufacturing Corporation had outstanding 10,000 shares of capital stock, par value $10 per share. The shares were held by ten stockholders, each having an equal number of shares. The Retained Earnings account showed a credit balance of $60,000, although the company was short of cash. The company owned 20,000 shares of stock in AB Company that had been purchased for $20,000. The current market value is $1.25 per share. On June 1, 1979, the board of directors of Tims Corporation declared a dividend of $3 per share "to be paid with AB stock within 30 days after declaration date and scrip to be issued for the difference. The scrip will be payable at the end of 12 months from declaration date and will earn 6% interest per annum." The accounting period ends December 31.

Required:

1. Give all entries related to dividends through date of payment of the scrip.

2. Report all items related to the dividend declaration as they should be reported on *(a)* the balance sheet and *(b)* the income statement at the end of 1979, including any notes needed for full disclosure (i.e., write the notes as they should appear in the statements).

Exercise 17–3

The records of MB Corporation showed the following at the end of 19C:

Preferred stock, 6% cumulative, non-participating, par $20	$200,000
Common stock, nopar value, (50,000 shares issued)	240,000
Contributed capital in excess of par, preferred stock	30,000
Retained earnings	125,000
Investment in stock of X Corporation (500 shares at cost)	10,000

The preferred stock has dividends in arrears for 19A and 19B. On January 15, 19C, the board of directors passed the following resolution: "The 19C dividend shall be 6% on the preferred stock and $0.90 per share on the common stock; the dividends including those in arrears are to be paid on March 1, 19C, by issuing a property dividend using the requisite amount of X Corporation stock." On January 15, 19C, the stock of

X Corporation was selling at $60 per share and at $62 on March 1, 19C.

Required:

1. Compute the amount of the dividends to be paid to each class of shareholders, including the number of shares of X Corporation stock required and the amount of cash. Assume that divisibility of the shares of X Corporation poses no problem.
2. Give journal entries to record all aspects of the dividend declaration and the subsequent payment.

Exercise 17–4

On December 1, 1979, the board of directors of GT Mining Company declared a maximum dividend permitted by the state law. There were 100 stockholders, each holding 200 shares of stock with a par value of $5 per share. The laws of the state provide that "dividends may be paid equal to all accumulated profits prior to depletion charges." Retained Earnings showed a balance of $30,000; depletion for the year amounted to $20,000 (accumulated depletion was $80,000). The dividend was payable 60 days after declaration date.

Required:

1. Give all entries related to the dividend through the payment date.
2. What special notification, if any, should be given the shareholders?
3. What items related to the dividend declaration would be reported on a balance sheet dated December 31, 1979, assuming net income for 1979 of $15,000 (included in the $30,000 balance of retained earnings given above)? Write any note that may be needed to fully disclose the dividend.

Exercise 17–5

The records of Caster Corporation showed the following balances on November 1, 19A:

Capital stock, par $10	$275,000
Contributed capital in excess of par	82,500
Retained earnings	195,000

On November 5, 19A, the board of directors declared a stock dividend of one additional share for each five shares outstanding; issue date, January 10, 19B. The market value of the stock immediately after the declaration was $18 per share.

Required:

1. Give entries in parallel columns for the stock dividend assuming, for problem purposes, *(a)* market value is capitalized, *(b)* par value is capitalized,

and *(c)* average paid in is capitalized. Assume the company records the dividend on declaration and credits an account titled, Stock Dividends Distributable (not a liability).
2. Explain when each value should be used.
3. What should be reported on the balance sheet at December 31, 19A, assuming no intervening transactions?

Exercise 17–6

The accounts of Henke Corporation provide the following data at December 31, 19C:

Capital stock, par $5, authorized shares 100,000; issued and outstanding 20,000 shares	$100,000
Contributed capital in excess of par	60,000
Retained earnings	120,000

On May 1, 19D, the board of directors of Henke Corporation declared a 50% stock dividend (i.e., for each two shares outstanding one additional share is to be issued) to be issued on June 1, 19D. The stock dividend is to be capitalized at the average of contributed capital per share at December 31, 19C.

On June 1, 19D, all of the required shares were issued for the stock dividend except for those required by 1,200 fractional share rights issued.

On December 1, 19D, the company honored 1,000 of the fractional share rights by issuing the requisite number of shares. The remaining fractional share rights were still outstanding at the end of 19D.

Required:

1. Give the required entries by Henke Corporation at each of the following dates:
   a. May 1, 19D.
   b. June 1, 19D.
   c. December 1, 19D.
2. Prepare the stockholders' equity section of the balance sheet at December 31, 19D, assuming net income for 19D was $30,000.
3. Assume instead that the fractional share rights specified that *(a)* two such rights could be turned in for one share of stock without cost or *(b)* each right could be turned in for $2.50 cash. As a result, 900 rights were turned in for shares, 200 rights for cash, and the remainder lapsed. Give the entry to record the ultimate disposition of all the fractional share rights.

Exercise 17–7

Corporation S made the following entry to record the ultimate disposition of all fractional share warrants issued in connection with a "small" stock dividend:

Fractional share rights outstanding	3,000	
Common stock, par $10		2,000
Additional contributed capital		500
Cash		500

Required:

1. What dispositions were made of the total of the fractional share rights, as evidenced by the above entry?
2. On what date would Corporation S have known the number of fractional share rights it would have to issue as a part of the stock dividend distribution?
3. How would the above entry be altered if the stock dividend had been "large" instead of "small"?
4. How may the dollar amount of the debit to the Fractional Rights Outstanding account exceed the amount credited to the Common Stock account?

Exercise 17–8

Bryan Manufacturing Company's books carried an account entitled "Reserve for Profits Invested in Fixed Assets, $450,000" and another account entitled "Reserve for General Contingencies, $80,000." Capital stock outstanding, par value $20, amount to $400,000.

The company also had bonds outstanding of $200,000. The following accounts also were carried: Bond Sinking Fund, $90,000; and Bond Sinking Fund Reserve, $90,000.

The board of directors voted a 10% stock dividend and directed that the market value of the stock, $150 per share, be capitalized using as a basis "the general reserves" to the extent possible.

Required:

Give entries for the following using preferable titles:

a. To originally establish the reserves related to fixed assets and general contingencies.
b. To record the issuance of the stock dividend.
c. To originally establish the bond sinking fund.
d. To originally establish the reserve for bond sinking fund.
e. To record payment of the bonds assuming the bond sinking fund and the reserve each have a $160,000 balance at retirement date.

Exercise 17–9

Using the simplified data below for the year ended December 31, 19X, construct (1) a single-step income statement and (2) a statement of retained earnings. Assume all amounts are material and annual data.

Current items:		
a. Sales revenue		$400,000
b. Cost of goods sold		160,000
c. Expenses		120,000
d. Extraordinary loss (pretax)		20,000
e. Prior period adjustment—correction of error in recording income taxes of a prior year (a debit)		2,400
f. Appropriation to reserve for bond sinking fund		10,000
g. Dividends paid		40,000
Balances—beginning of period:		
h. Retained earnings		130,000
i. Reserve for bond sinking fund		60,000

Income taxes—assume a 40% average rate.

Exercise 17–10

Using the simplified data below, construct comparative statements of (1) income (single step) and (2) retained earnings for 19A and 19B. Assume all amounts are material, annual data, and an average tax rate of 40% on all items.

	19A	19B
Current items:		
a. Sales	$110,000	$120,000
b. Cost of goods sold	45,000	50,000
c. Expenses	25,000	29,000
d. Extraordinary gain	3,000	
e. Extraordinary loss		6,000
f. Dividends declared and paid	12,000	10,000
g. Appropriation for profits invested in operational assets	40,000	
h. Prior period adjustment—correction of accounting error made in prior period; no tax effect (a credit)		2,000
Beginning balances:		
Unappropriated retained earnings	$130,000	?
Appropriation for profits invested in operational assets	-0-	?

PART B
Exercises 17–11 to 17–20

Exercise 17–11

Young Corporation issued 5,000 shares of $20 par value common stock outstanding, originally sold at $50 per share. On January 15, Young purchased 20 shares of its own stock at $55 per share. On March 1, twelve of the treasury shares were sold at $58. The balance in Retained Earnings was $25,000 prior to these transactions.

Required:

1. Give all entries indicated in parallel columns assuming for treasury stock *(a)* the cost method and *(b)* the par value method.
2. What would be the resulting balances in the stockholders' equity accounts for each method?

Exercise 17–12

Thomas Corporation had the following stock outstanding:

Common stock, nopar, 20,000 shares
  (sold at $15) $300,000
Preferred stock, par $10, 5,000 shares
  (sold at $25) 50,000

The following treasury stock transactions were completed:

a. Purchased 50 shares of the common stock at $17 per share.
b. Purchased 20 shares of the preferred stock at $27.
c. Sold 30 shares of the common stock at $14.
d. Sold 10 shares of the preferred stock at $30.

Required:

1. Give entries for all of the above stock transactions assuming the par value method is used.
2. Give resulting balances in the stockholders' equity accounts; assume a beginning balance in Retained Earnings of $20,000.

Exercise 17–13

Johnson Corporation had outstanding 10,000 shares of preferred stock, par value $10 and 10,000 shares of nopar common stock sold initially for $20 per share. Contributed capital in excess of par on the preferred stock amounted to $40,000; the Retained Earnings balance is $30,000. The corporation purchased 200 shares of preferred at $22 per share and 300 shares of common stock at $25 per share. Subsequently, 100 shares of the common treasury stock were sold for $20 per share.

Required:

1. Give entries to record the treasury stock transactions assuming the cost method is used.

2. Prepare the resulting stockholders' equity section of the balance sheet.

Exercise 17–14

At January 1, 19A, the records of Sobel Corporation showed the following:

Capital stock, par $10, 50,000 shares
  outstanding $500,000
Contributed capital in excess of par 250,000
Retained earnings 150,000

During the year, the following transactions affecting stockholders' equity were recorded:

a. Purchased 500 shares of treasury stock at $20 per share.
b. Purchased 500 shares of treasury stock at $22 per share.
c. Sold 600 shares of treasury stock at $25.
d. Net income for 19A was $40,000.

The state law places a restriction on retained earnings equal to the cost of treasury stock held.

Required:

1. Give entries for the initial issuance and for each of the above transactions, in parallel columns, assuming *(a)* the cost method and *(b)* the par value method. Assume *Fifo* flow for treasury stock. Set up an account for the appropriation of retained earnings.
2. Give the resulting balances in the capital accounts. Include any required disclosure related to the treasury stock.

Exercise 17–15

During Year 19B, Masters Corporation had several changes in stockholders' equity. The comparative balance sheets for 19A and 19B reflected the following amounts in stockholders' equity:

	Balances December 31	
	19A	*19B*
Capital stock, par $10, issued	$600,000*	$700,000†
Contributed capital in excess of par	180,000	230,000
Contributed capital, sale of treasury stock		1,000
Retained earnings	120,000	150,000
Treasury stock	18,000	1,700

* Includes 1,000 shares of treasury stock.
† Includes 100 shares of treasury stock (the 1,000 shares were sold and 100 shares were bought).

Required:

1. What method was used to account for treasury stock? Explain the basis for your conclusion.
2. Give the required entry for each transaction that affected stockholders' equity during 19B. Explain how you determined the amounts used in each entry.

Exercise 17–16

The records for Day Corporation at December 31, 19A, showed the following, assuming the cost method was used for treasury stock:

Assets	$127,000
Liabilities	20,000
Stockholders' equity:	
Capital stock, par $10, 7,000 shares	70,000
Treasury stock, 1,000 shares (at cost)	17,000
Contributed capital in excess of par	14,000
Retained earnings	40,000

Required:

Prepare balance sheets for the corporation with special emphasis on the stockholders' equity section if the state law places a restriction on retained earnings equal to the cost of treasury stock held and if the corporation sets up a special appropriated account for this requirement. Also assume the following:

1. The cost method is used.
2. The par value method is used. *Hint:* Certain of the above account balances must be modified.

Exercise 17–17

AB Corporation had 30,000 shares of $10 par value capital stock authorized, of which 20,000 shares were issued three years ago at $15 per share. During the current year, the corporation received 500 shares of the capital stock as a bequest from a deceased shareholder; in addition (at approximately the same date), 1,000 shares were purchased at $14 per share. State law places a restriction on retained earnings equal to the cost of treasury stock held. At the end of the year, a cash dividend of $0.50 per share was paid; prior to the dividend, retained earnings amounted to $40,000.

Required:

1. Prepare entries to record all of the transactions assuming the cost method for recording treasury stock is used. Record the donated stock at its market value.
2. Prepare the stockholders' equity section of the bal-ance sheet at year-end and include all required disclosures related to the treasury stock.

Exercise 17–18

The records for XY Corporation reflected the following data on stockholders' equity:

a. Preferred stock, par $50, issued 2,000 shares.
b. Preferred treasury stock, 200 shares (cost $54 per share).
c. Premium on preferred stock at original issue, $2 per share.
d. Common stock, par $100, issued 3,000 shares.
e. Common treasury stock, 300 shares (cost $98 per share).
f. Premium on common stock at original issue was $3 per share.
g. Retained earnings, unappropriated, $110,000.
h. Retained earnings appropriated for cost of treasury stock held, $40,200. The state law places a restriction on retained earnings equal to the cost of treasury stock held.

The shareholders voted to retire all of the treasury stock forthwith and to purchase and retire another 400 shares of common stock that could be purchased immediately at $108 per share.

Required:

Give entries in parallel columns for the following transactions, assuming the (1) cost method and (2) par value method:

a. Purchase of the 400 shares of outstanding common stock and their retirement.
b. To retire all of the treasury shares. Give separate entries for the preferred and common.

Exercise 17–19

The records of Henke Corporation reflected the following:

Preferred stock, 1,000 shares outstanding, par $100	$100,000
Common stock, 1,000 shares outstanding, par $50	50,000
Contributed capital in excess of par, preferred stock	5,000
Contributed capital in excess of par, common stock	2,000
Retained earnings	50,000

The preferred stock is convertible into common stock. Give entry, or entries, required in each of the following cases:

Case A—The preferred shares are converted to common stock on a par-for-par basis; that is, two shares of common are issued for each share of preferred.

Case B—The preferred shares are converted to common share for share.

Case C—The preferred shares are converted to common stock on a one-for-three basis; that is, three shares of common are issued for each share of preferred.

Case D—The preferred shares are converted, on a share-for-share basis, for a new class of stock known as Common Class B, nopar.

Case E—The preferred shares are converted to common stock on a one-for-five basis (i.e., five shares of common are issued for each share of preferred) plus a cash payment by the holders of the preferred in the amount of $35 per share of common received.

Exercise 17–20

AB Company had experienced a net loss for a number of years. Recently a new president was hired. The board of directors agreed to a quasi-reorganization and to restate certain items in the accounts as outlined by the new president, subject to stockholder approval. Prior to the restatement, the balance sheet reported the following (summarized at June 30, 19A):

Cash	$ 5,000
Receivables	16,000
Inventories	210,000
Operational assets (net)	560,000
Other assets	44,000
	$835,000

Current liabilities	$ 50,000
Long-term liabilities	85,000
Capital stock (8,000 shares)	800,000
Contributed capital in excess of par	40,000
Retained earnings	(150,000)
Reserve for contingencies	10,000
	$835,000

The stockholders approved the quasi-reorganization effective July 1, 19A, which carried the following provisions:

a. The inventories to be reduced to a LCM value of $140,000.
b. Receivables of $3,000 to be written off as worthless.
c. The operational assets to be reduced to a net carrying value of $400,000.
d. The capital structure to be adjusted so that the deficit will be eliminated and the capital reduced (including a reduction in shares outstanding if needed) by the net adjustment made to assets.

Required:
1. Give entries to record the quasi-reorganization as approved by the stockholders.
2. Prepare an unclassified balance sheet after the quasi-reorganization, including an explanatory note to fully disclose the effect of the quasi-reorganization.

PROBLEMS

PART A
Problems 17–1 to 17–9

Problem 17–1

The balance sheet at December 31, 19A, for Ward Manufacturing Company is shown below in summary:

Cash	$ 28,000
Receivables	36,000
Inventory	110,000
Investments—4,000 shares of Taylor stock at cost	6,000
Operational assets (net)	80,000
Other assets	10,000
	$270,000

Current liabilities	$ 26,000
Bonds payable	50,000
Preferred stock	20,000
Common stock, nopar (5,000 shares)	100,000
Contributed capital in excess of par, preferred	5,000
Retained earnings	69,000
	$270,000

The preferred stock is 6%, $100 par value, and cumulative. Dividends are three years in arrears (excluding the current year, 19B).

The investment in stock of Taylor Company has been held for a number of years; that stock is now selling for $5 per share.

On November 1, 19B, the board of directors of Ward declared dividends as follows:

a. Preferred stock, all dividends in arrears plus current year dividend; payment to be made by transferring the requisite number of shares of Taylor stock at $5 per share.
b. Common stock, $4 per share for the current year, payment to be made by transferring the remainder of the Taylor stock and issuing a scrip dividend for the balance. The scrip will earn 8% annual

interest and will be paid at the end of six months from date of declaration.

Required:

1. Compute the amount of dividends payable to each class of shareholder and indicate the amount of the scrip dividend.
2. Give entries to record the transfer of the Taylor stock and the issuance of the scrip dividend (assume declaration and payment dates are the same). Make separate entries for the common and preferred stock.
3. Give the adjusting entry at December 31, 19B, for the interest on the scrip dividend.
4. Give the entry to record payment of the scrip dividend and interest on April 30, 19C.
5. Prepare the stockholders' equity section of the balance sheet as of December 31, 19B. Assume reported net income of $30,000 for 19B (including the interest on the scrip dividend and gain on disposal of Taylor stock).

Problem 17–2

On November 5, 19A, the board of directors of Sharp Corporation declared *(a)* a stock dividend whereby each holder of common stock is to receive one share of common for each five shares held and *(b)* a cash dividend on the preferred stock for the one year in arrears and for the current year. The board of directors directed that the average originally paid in per share of common will be capitalized for the stock dividend. Assume the declaration and issue (or payment) dates are the same. At November 1, 19A, the records of the corporation showed:

Stockholders' Equity

Preferred stock, 6%, $10 par value, authorized 20,000 shares, issued 10,000 shares . . .	$100,000
Common stock, nopar, stated value $5, authorized 50,000, issued 30,000 shares	150,000
Contributed capital in excess of par, preferred	20,000
Contributed capital in excess of stated value, common	30,000
Retained earnings	160,000

Upon issuance of the stock dividend, 5,000 fractional share warrants were distributed to stockholders. On December 30, 19A, 4,500 fractional share rights were exercised. The remaining rights are outstanding to date.

Required:

1. Give entries to record *(a)* issuance of the stock dividend, *(b)* payment of the cash dividend, and *(c)* exercise of the rights.

2. Prepare the stockholders' equity section of the balance sheet after giving effect to the entries in Requirement 1 above, assuming net income for 19A was $18,000.
3. Give the entry assuming the remaining rights lapsed on October 30, 19B.

Problem 17–3

On December 31, 19A, the accounts for Butts Corporation showed the following balances:

Stockholders' Equity

Preferred stock, 6%, par value $25, authorized 10,000 shares, outstanding 8,000 shares	$200,000
Common stock, nopar, stated value $10, authorized 20,000 shares, outstanding 12,000 shares	120,000
Contributed capital in excess of par, preferred	15,000
Contributed capital in excess of stated value, common	30,000
Retained earnings	175,000

During 19B the following sequential transactions were recorded relating to the capital accounts:

a. Apr. 1   A stock dividend was issued whereby (1) each holder of ten preferred shares received one share of common stock and (2) each holder of six shares of common stock received one share of common. The market price of the common stock was $15 per share immediately after issuance of the stock dividend. In issuing the stock dividend, 2,700 shares of common stock and 1,000 fractional share rights were issued.

b. Nov. 1   All of the rights were redeemed except 100 which remained outstanding.

c. Dec. 15   A 6% cash dividend on the preferred shares and a $0.50 per share dividend on the common shares were declared and paid.

d. Dec. 31   Reported net income was $60,395.

Required:

1. Prepare journal entries for each of the above transactions during 19B.
2. Prepare the stockholders' equity section of the balance sheet at December 31, 19B.
3. Now assume that Butts had paid cash to the shareholders in lieu of issuing fractional share warrants. The cash distribution was based on the market value of $15 per share. Give the entry on April 1, 19B, to record the dividend transaction. What would be the total stockholders' equity of Butts Corporation on December 31, 19B, in this situation if all other factors remain as they were given above?

Problem 17–4

The records for Miller Corporation showed the following balances at the end of 19A:

Current assets	$ 165,000
Operational assets	960,000
Other assets	300,000
Investment in X Corporation stock (5,000 shares at cost)	5,000
	$1,430,000

Current liabilities	$ 60,000
Long-term liabilities	100,000
Preferred stock, par $10	300,000
Common stock, no par, 100,000 shares outstanding	800,000
Contributed capital in excess of par, preferred	12,000
Retained earnings	158,000
	$1,430,000

To date 3,000 shares of the preferred stock (6%, $100 par value, cumulative, nonparticipating) have been issued. Authorized shares were common, 200,000; and ·preferred, 3,000. No dividends were declared or paid for 19A. During the subsequent two years the following transactions affected stockholders' equity:

Year 19B:

a. Feb. 1 Declared and immediately issued one share of X Corporation stock for each share of preferred stock as a property dividend. The current market value of X stock was $3.50 per share. In addition, a cash dividend was paid to complete payment of the dividends in arrears.

b. Oct. 1 Declared and immediately issued scrip dividends amounting to 6% on the preferred and $0.80 per share on the common stock. Interest on the scrip is 7% per year.

c. Dec. 31 Reported net income was $150,000 including any effects of the above transactions.

Year 19C:

d. Sept. 30 Paid the scrip dividends including 7% per annum interest for 12 months.

e. Nov. 1 Declared and issued a stock dividend, payable in common stock to holders of both preferred and common stock. The preferred holders to receive "value" equivalent to 6%, and the common holders to receive one share for each five shares held. The "value" and the amount capitalized per share as a debit to Retained Earnings to be the market value. The current price per share on the common stock is $1.50.

    Issued the stock dividend in full to the preferred. Fractional share rights for 500 shares (i.e., 2,500 rights) were issued to common stockholders.

f. Dec. 1 The fractional share rights specified that five such rights could be turned in for one share of common stock. On this basis, 2,000 of the outstanding fractional share rights were turned in. The remaining 500 rights are outstanding.

g. Dec. 31 Reported net income was $86,000, including any effects of the above transactions.

Required:

1. Prepare journal entries for each of the foregoing transactions (round amounts to nearest dollar).
2. Prepare the stockholders' equity section of the balance sheet at December 31, 19C, after giving recognition to the foregoing transactions.

Problem 17–5

Super Manufacturing Company was organized with an authorization for 50,000 shares of $10 par value stock. During the first five years of operations, the following transactions affected stockholders' equity. Assume they occurred in the order given.

Year 19A:

a. Received subscriptions for 20,000 shares of stock at $15 per share; 50% was collected from each subscriber as a down payment; the stock is not issued until fully paid.

b. Balance was collected on all shares except 1,500.

c. Reported net income was $5,000.

Year 19B:

d. The balance was collected on 1,400 of the subscribed shares. Subscriptions for the other 100 shares were defaulted. The subscriber was refunded the amount paid in less 20% of the purchase price per agreement. Issued the 1,400 shares.

e. Reported net income was $7,000.

Year 19C:

f. Declared and paid a cash dividend amounting to $0.50 per share on the shares outstanding.

g. Reported net income was $18,000.

Year 19D:

h. Sold 5,000 shares of stock at $18; collected cash and issued stock.

i. Reported net income, $20,000.

Year 19E:

j. Declared a 10% stock dividend on the shares outstanding. The board of directors voted that the "average paid in to date per share" be capitalized (exclude the default recovery). Immediately issued the stock dividend and fractional share rights for 200 of the shares.

k. Rights for 190 shares received and stock issued; the balance lapsed.

l. Declared and paid a $0.50 per share dividend—half payable in cash, balance in scrip payable in six months with interest at 7% per annum.

m. Accrued two months' interest on the scrip dividends.

n. Reported net income $18,000 (includes the interest on the scrip).

Required (round amounts to nearest dollar):

1. Prepare entries for each of the foregoing transactions.
2. Prepare the stockholders' equity section of the balance sheet at the end of 19E, after giving effect to the foregoing entries.

Problem 17–6

The following annual data were taken from the records of Rawlins Corporation at December 31, 19X (assume all amounts are material, the items in parentheses are credit balances):

Current items:

a.	Sales	$(402,000)
b.	Cost of goods sold	230,000
c.	Expenses	85,000
d.	Extraordinary loss	20,000
e.	Stock dividend issued	50,000
f.	Cash dividend declared and paid	19,000
g.	Correction of accounting error involving income taxes from prior period	8,000
h.	Current appropriation to reserve for bond sinking fund	10,000
i.	Current appropriation to reserve for plant expansion	40,000

Income taxes:

Assume an average tax rate of 40% on all items except any prior period adjustments.

Balances, January 1, 19X:

j.	Unappropriated retained earnings	(120,000)
k.	Reserve for bond sinking fund	(50,000)
l.	Reserve for plant expansion	(60,000)

Required:

1. Prepare a single-step income statement for the year ended December 31, 19X.
2. Prepare a statement of retained earnings for the year ended December 31, 19X.

Problem 17–7

Cooper Corporation records provided the following annual data at December 31, 19A, and 19B (assume all amounts are material):

			19A	19B
Current items:				
a.	Sales		$240,000	$260,000
b.	Cost of goods sold		134,000	143,000
c.	Expenses		71,000	77,000
d.	Extraordinary loss		7,000	2,000
e.	Cash dividend declared and paid		20,000	
f.	Stock dividend issued			30,000
g.	Appropriation to reserve for bond sinking fund		10,000	10,000
h.	Increase in bond sinking fund		10,000	10,000
i.	Prior period adjustment—error correction (debit)		6,000	
j.	Income taxes—assume an average rate of 46% on all items including extraordinary items and prior period adjustments.			
Balances, January 1, 19X:				
k.	Reserve for bond sinking fund		70,000	?
l.	Unappropriated retained earnings		160,000	?
m.	Reserve for plant expansion		100,000	?
n.	Bond sinking fund		70,000	?
o.	Bonds payable		100,000	?

Required:

1. Prepare a single-step comparative income statement for Years 19A and 19B.
2. Prepare a comparative statement of retained earnings.

Problem 17–8

Random Corporation records provided the following unclassified data at December 31, 19X.

a. Appropriation during the year of retained earnings for reserve for bond sinking fund, $15,000; the prior balance was $65,000.

b. Balance in Retained Earnings, Unappropriated account per books at end of prior year, $100,000.

c. Cash dividends declared on preferred stock December 31 of the year just ended, payable the following January 15 amounting to $10,000.

d. Declared and issued a small stock dividend on common stock July 1, 19X; par $20,000; and market value, $30,000.

e. Preferred stock sold during 19X: 200 shares, par $100; and market, $130.

f. Income statement data for 19X: sales, $350,000; cost of goods sold, $160,000; and expenses, $80,000.

g. Correction of accounting error from a prior period (a debit), $8,000.

Income taxes—assume an average rate of 45% on all items including extraordinary items and the correction (item [g]).

Required:

1. Prepare a single-step income statement.
2. Prepare a statement of retained earnings.

Problem 17–9

Baker Corporation is undergoing an audit. The books show an account entitled Surplus which is reproduced below covering a five-year period, January 1, 1975, to December 31, 1979.

Credits

1975–78	Net income carried to surplus	$	800,000
1975	By debit to goodwill—authorized by management		50,000
12/31/76	Contributed capital in excess of par		6,000
1/ 1/77	Correction of prior accounting error		2,000
1/ 1/77	Donation to company—operational asset		5,000
3/31/77	Refund of prior years' income taxes		9,000
7/ 1/78	Reduction in capital stock from par value, $100, to par value, $50, with no change in the number of shares outstanding (10,000); approved by shareholders		500,000
12/31/79	Net income, 1979		170,000
			$1,542,000

Debits

1975–79	Cash dividends paid	$	600,000
12/31/75	To reserve for bond sinking fund (required annually)		20,000
12/31/77	Reserve for bond sinking fund ...		20,000
12/31/78	Reserve for bond sinking fund ...		20,000
9/ 1/79	Fifty percent stock dividend		250,000
		$	910,000

Required:

1. The above account is to be closed and replaced with appropriate accounts. Complete a worksheet analysis of the above account to reflect the correct account balances and the corrections needed. It is suggested that the worksheet carry the following columns: *(a)* surplus account per books; *(b)* net income, 1979; *(c)* corrected unappropriated retained earnings, 12/31/79; and *(d)* columns for debits and credits to any other specific accounts needed.
2. Give the appropriate entry or entries to close this account and to set up appropriate accounts in its place.

(AICPA adapted)

PROBLEMS

PART B
Problems 17–10 to 17–17

Problem 17–10

Stopke Corporation reported the following summarized data prior to the transactions given below:

Assets	$660,000
Less: Liabilities	100,000
	$560,000

Stockholders' Equity:	
Preferred stock, $10 par	$300,000
Common stock, $5 par	150,000
Contributed capital in excess of par, preferred stock	30,000
Retained earnings	80,000
	$560,000

The state law places a restriction on retained earnings equal to the cost of treasury stock held, and Stopke sets up an appropriation of retained earnings to meet this requirement.

The following transactions affecting stockholders' equity were recorded:

a. Purchased preferred treasury stock, 500 shares at $15.
b. Purchased common treasury stock, 1,000 shares at $20.
c. Sold preferred treasury stock, 100 shares at $17.
d. Sold common treasury stock, 400 shares at $18.

Required:

1. Give entries in parallel columns for the treasury stock transactions *(a)* through *(d),* assuming (1) the cost method and (2) the par value method is used.
2. Prepare the resulting balance sheet (unclassified) for each method.

Problem 17–11

For each question given below, select the best answer from among those given. Explain the basis for your choice.

1. Company G originally issued 100,000 shares of its $20 par common stock at $40 per share. Over its first ten years of operations the company earned $75,000 and declared no dividends. In the 11th year of operations, Company G purchased 500 shares of its own stock (as treasury stock) at a cost of $65 per share. One year later, Company G formally retired the treasury stock. If Company G uses the

cost method of accounting for treasury stock, it should record the retirement of the treasury stock as follows:

A. Common stock 30,000
        Treasury stock   20,000
        Contributed capital from
        treasury stock trans-
        actions   10,000

B. Common stock 30,000
        Contributed capital from trea-
        sury stock transactions   2,500
        Treasury stock   32,500

C. Common stock 20,000
        Contributed capital in excess
        of par, common stock 12,500
        Treasury stock   32,500

D. Common stock 10,000
        Retained earnings 22,500
        Treasury stock   32,500

E. If E is selected, give the correct entry.

2. Which of the following statements is true in respect to the differences and similarities between the cost and par value methods of accounting for treasury stock?

A. Company A paid $26,000 cash for treasury stock that the company had originally issued for $15,000 (which was $10,000 above par). If Company A uses the par value method of accounting for treasury stock, it will report more contributed capital and less retained earnings than under the cost method at any time the company currently holds treasury stock.

B. The cost method results in a larger total owners' equity than the par value method.

C. Under the par value method, the balances in the contributed capital accounts are more realistically reported than under the cost method.

D. The balance in Retained Earnings is the same under the two methods for a given set of facts; however, the total contributed capital is different under the two methods.

E. All of the above statements are true.

3. When preferred stock is purchased and retired by the issuing corporation for less than its original issue price, proper accounting for the retirement

A. Increases the amount of dividends available to common shareholders.

B. Increases the contributed capital.

C. Increases reported income for the period.

D. Increases the treasury stock held by the corporation.

E. None of the above.

4. The spread between the cost of treasury stock and a subsequent higher selling price of the treasury stock should be credited to
A. Contributed capital.
B. Capital stock.
C. Retained earnings.
D. "Other" income.

5. Hillside Corporation has 80,000 shares of $50 par value common stock authorized, issued and outstanding. The 80,000 shares were issued at $55 each. Retained earnings of the company are $160,000. If 1,000 shares of Hillside common stock were reacquired at $62 and the par value method of accounting for treasury stock were used, the balance in the common stock account would decrease by
A. $62,000.
B. $55,000.
C. $50,000.
D. None of the above.

Problem 17–12

California Corporation had authorized and outstanding 5,000 shares of capital stock, par value $50 per share. The stockholders approved the exchange of two new shares for each share of the old stock.

Required:

Prepare entries to record the change under each of the following separate cases (assume a sufficient balance in retained earnings):

Case A—The old stock originally was sold at a premium of $2 per share, and the new stock was $25 par value.

Case B—The old stock was sold at a premium of $3 per share, and the new stock was nopar value stock with no stated or assigned value.

Case C—The old stock was sold at a premium of $1 per share, and the new stock was nopar value stock with no stated or assigned value.

Case D—The old stock was sold at par, and the new stock was nopar value stock with no stated or assigned value.

Case E—The old stock was sold at a premium of $4 per share, and the new stock was nopar value stock with a stated value of $20 per share.

Case F—The old stock was sold at a premium of $5 per share, and the new stock was nopar value stock with a stated value of $30 per share.

Case G—The old stock was sold at par, and the new stock was nopar value stock with a stated value of $27.50 per share.

Problem 17–13

At the end of 19B the comparative balance sheets for X Corporation reported the following stockholders' equity amounts:

	Balances December 31	
	19A	19B
Preferred stock, par $10, shares authorized 20,000	$150,000	$200,000
Common stock, nopar, share authorized 100,000, issued near the end of 19A, 30,000; 19B, 31,000	210,000	218,000
Contributed capital in excess of par, preferred stock	74,000	154,000
Contributed capital, sale of preferred treasury stock		1,600
Treasury stock, preferred stock	2,000	1,000
Treasury stock, common stock	2,100	3,500*
Retained earnings appropriated for treasury stock:		
Preferred (at cost)	5,124	2,462
Common (at cost)	1,950	3,550
Retained earnings unappropriated† .	40,000	65,962

* Increased for 200 shares.
† No dividends were declared during 19B.

Required

1. At the end of 19A, what had been the average selling price per share (by the corporation) of the *(a)* preferred and *(b)* common shares?
2. What method is being used to account for treasury stock? Explain.
3. Complete the following tabulation for the treasury stock held at December 31, 19A (show computations):

	Number of Treasury Shares Held	Average Cost per Share
Preferred	_____	_____
Common	_____	_____

4. How many shares were outstanding at December 31, 19A, for *(a)* preferred and *(b)* common?
5. What was the total amount of shareholders' equity at December 31, 19A?
6. Give the required entry for each transaction that affected stockholders' equity during 19B.

Problem 17–14

The following account balances were shown on the books of XY Corporation at December 31:

Noncumulative preferred stock, par $100, 5%, 2,000 shares	$200,000
Common stock, par $50, 5,000 shares	250,000
Retained earnings (deficit)	(45,000)

At a stockholders' meeting (including holders of preferred shares) the following actions related to the quasi-reorganization were decided upon:

a. That an amendment to the charter be obtained authorizing a total issue of 5,000 shares of cumulative, 6% preferred, par $100 per share, and 40,000 shares of nopar common stock.
b. That all outstanding stock be returned in exchange for new stock as follows:
   (1) For each share of old preferred, one share of new preferred. Purchased for cash at par 20 shares of old preferred stock from a dissatisfied stockholder and the remainder exchanged.
   (2) For each share of old common, two shares of new common; the credit to the nopar stock account shall be at an amount which creates a credit balance in contributed capital from conversion sufficient to exactly provide for the deficit in retained earnings. All of the old shares were exchanged.
c. That the past operating deficit be written off against the credit created by the conversion of the common stock.

During the ensuing year the following transactions were effected:

d. Sold 200 shares of the new preferred stock at $105 per share.
e. The company issued 1,200 shares of nopar common in payment for a patent tentatively valued by the seller at $20,000. (The current market value of a share was $15).
f. The company sold 50 shares of nopar common at $19 per share, receiving cash. Also issued 100, $1,000 bonds at 102; one share of common stock, as a bonus, was given with each bond.
g. At the end of the year the board of directors met and was informed that the net income before deductions for bonuses to officers was $100,000. The directors took the following actions:
   (1) Ordered that 500 shares of nopar common stock (from authorized but unissued shares) be issued to officers as a bonus. The market price of a nopar common share on this date was $16.
   (2) Declared and paid dividends (for one year) on the preferred stock outstanding.

Required:

1. Prepare journal entries to record the above transactions.
2. Prepare the stockholders' equity section of the balance sheet after giving effect to the above transactions.

Problem 17–15

You have just commenced your audit of Shaky Company for the year ended December 31, 19B. The president advises you that the company is insolvent and must declare bankruptcy unless a large loan can be obtained immediately. At the start of 19C, a lender who is willing to advance $450,000 to the company has been located, but will only make the loan subject to the following conditions:

1. A $450,000, 8% mortgage note payable annually over 15 years on the land and buildings will be given as security on a new loan (cash to be received $450,000).
2. A new issue of 500 shares of $100 par value, 5%, noncumulative, nonparticipating preferred stock will replace 500 outstanding shares of $100 par value, 7%, cumulative, participating preferred stock. Preferred stockholders will give up all claims to $21,000 of dividends in arrears. The company has never formally declared the dividends.
3. A new issue of 600 shares of $50 par value, class A common stock will replace 600 outstanding shares of $100 par value, class A common stock.
4. A new issue of 650 shares of $40 par value, class B common stock will replace 650 outstanding shares of $100 par value, class B common stock.
5. A $600,000, 6% mortgage payable on the company's land and buildings held by a major stockholder will be canceled along with four months' accrued interest already recorded. The mortgage will be replaced by 5,000 shares of $100 par value, 6%, cumulative if earned, nonparticipating preferred stock.
6. On May 1, 19A, the company's trade creditors had accepted $360,000 in notes payable on demand at 6% interest in settlement of all past-due accounts (recorded in 19A). No payment has been made to date on the accrued interest (recorded for 19A and 19B) or principal. The company will offer to settle these liabilities at $0.75 per $1 owed or to replace the notes payable on demand with new notes payable for full indebtedness over five years at 6% interest. It is estimated that $200,000 of the demand notes and the accrued interest thereon will be exchanged for the longer term notes and that the balance will accept the offer of a reduced cash settlement.

The president of the Shaky Company requests that you determine the effect of the foregoing on the company and furnishes the following data, which you believe are correct (prior to the above conditions):

Bank overdraft	$ 15,000
Other current assets	410,000
Operational assets (net)	840,000
Trade accounts payable	235,000
Other current liabilities	85,000
Contributed capital in excess of par value	125,000
Retained earnings, deficit	345,000

Required:

1. Prepare pro forma (as if) journal entries that you would suggest to give effect to the foregoing as of January 1, 19C. Entries should be keyed to numbered information in order.
2. Prepare a pro forma (as if) balance sheet for the Shaky Company at January 1, 19C, as if the recapitalization had been consummated. *Hint:* Leave a zero balance in Retained Earnings.

(AICPA adapted)

Problem 17–16

During the last five years, Hanson Corporation has experienced severe losses. A new president has been tentatively employed who is confident the company can be saved from bankruptcy (and dissolution). Working with an independent CPA, the new president has proposed a quasi-reorganization with the constraints that *(a)* the capital structure must be changed to eliminate the deficit in retained earnings and *(b)* it must be approved by the stockholders and creditors. The board approved the proposal and submitted it to a vote of the stockholders and creditors.

Prior to reorganization, the balance sheet (summarized) reflected the following:

Cash	$ 20,000
Accounts receivable	94,000
Allowance for doubtful accounts	(4,000)
Inventory	150,000
Operational assets	800,000
Accumulated depreciation	(300,000)
Deferred charges	40,000
	$800,000
Current liabilities	$150,000
Long-term liabilities	240,000
Common stock, par $50	500,000
Preferred stock, par $100	100,000
Contributed capital in excess of par on preferred stock	30,000
Retained earnings, deficit	(220,000)
	$800,000

The reorganization proposal, as approved by the stockholders and creditors, provided the following:

a. To adequately provide for probable losses on accounts receivable, increase the allowance by $6,000.

b. Write down the inventory to $100,000 because of obsolete and damaged goods.

c. Reduce the book value of the operational assets to $400,000 by increasing accumulated depreciation.

d. By agreement of the creditors, reduce all liabilities by 5%.

e. Reduce the par value of the preferred shares to $60.

f. Close out the contributed capital in excess of par on the preferred stock.

g. Call in the old common stock and issue a new common stock, nopar. Set up a new nopar common stock account with the balance needed to reduce retained earnings to zero.

Required:

1. Give a separate entry for each of the above changes.
2. Prepare an unclassified balance sheet immediately after the quasi-reorganization.

Problem 17–17

Weston Corporation, a medium-sized manufacturer, has experienced losses for the past five years.

Although operations for the year ended resulted in a loss, several important changes resulted in a profitable fourth quarter; as a result, future operations of the company are expected to be profitable.

The treasurer suggested a quasi-reorganization to *(a)* eliminate the accumulated deficit of $423,620 in retained earnings, *(b)* write up the $493,100 cost of operating land and buildings to their market value, and *(c)* set up an asset of $203,337 representing the estimated future tax benefit of the losses accumulated to date.

Required:

1. What are the characteristics of a quasi-reorganization? That is, of what does it consist?
2. List the conditions under which a quasi-reorganization generally would be justified.
3. Discuss the propriety of the treasurer's proposals to
   a. Eliminate the deficit of $423,620.
   b. Write up the value of the operating land and buildings of $493,100 to their market value.
   c. Set up an asset of $203,337 representing the future tax benefit of the losses accumulated to date.

(AICPA adapted)

18

Stock Rights and Options and Earnings per Share

This chapter concludes the discussion of corporate capital by focusing, in Part A, on stock rights and employee stock compensation plans and, in Part B, on earnings per share.

PART A—STOCK RIGHTS AND EMPLOYEE STOCK COMPENSATION PLANS

STOCK RIGHTS

Corporations often issue *stock rights* that provide for the future acquisition, without cost or by purchase, of capital stock under specified conditions. Thus, a stock right is an option to acquire specified capital stock in the corporation under prescribed conditions and within a stated future time period. When rights are issued to current stockholders (as in the case of fractional share rights as part of a stock dividend), there is one right issued per share owned; however, it may take more than one right to acquire an additional share of stock.

As evidence of the ownership of stock rights, a certificate commonly known as a *stock warrant* is issued by the corporation which conveys to the holder one or more stock rights. A warrant specifies *(a)* the option price per share of the specified stock (there may be no price), *(b)* the number of rights required to obtain a share of the stock, *(c)* the number of rights represented by the warrant, *(d)* the expiration date of the rights, and *(e)* instructions for exercising the rights. When more than one right is required to obtain one share of stock in the future, such rights represent fractional shares and they are often referred to as *fractional share* rights.[1]

Stock rights usually have value and, as a consequence, are bought and sold in the capital markets. Three dates are important with respect to the valuation of stock rights: (1) date of announcement, (2) date of issuance of the rights, and (3) date of expiration. Between the date of announcement and the date of issuance of the rights, the stock to which they relate will sell *rights on;* that is, the price of the stock will be incremented by the value of the rights because the stock and the rights are not separable during that period of time. After the rights are issued and until the rights expire, the shares and rights sell separately; consequently, the shares sell *ex rights* during this period of time and the rights have a separate price.

Situations in which stock rights often are issued include the following:

---

[1] Stock rights sometimes are referred to as stock warrants.

1. To represent fractional shares when a stock dividend is declared and issued (discussed and illustrated in Chapter 17).
2. To enhance the marketability of other securities issued by the corporation, such as giving common stock rights with convertible bonds payable (discussed and illustrated in Chapter 20).
3. To give existing shareholders the first opportunity to buy additional shares when the corporation decides to raise additional equity capital by selling *unissued* (old) shares to its current shareholders.
4. To provide evidence of the right of stockholders to buy additional shares of *new* stock issues in proportion to their current holdings.
5. As compensation to outsiders (such as underwriters, promoters, and professionals) for services rendered to the corporation.
6. As additional compensation to officers and other employees of the corporation; these are often referred to as *stock options.*

The issuance of stock rights poses accounting problems for both the recipient and the issuing corporation. Accounting for stock rights received by an investor is discussed in Chapter 19.

In respect to the *issuing corporation,* at least a memorandum entry must be made at date of issuance of stock rights because the balance sheet, or notes to the statements, must disclose the number of stock rights outstanding by class of stock. However, accounting entries usually are made in the accounts for most of the situations listed above. Since Situations 1 and 2 are discussed in other chapters, this Part will focus on the remaining four.

Situations 3 and 4—The issuance of stock rights related to the sale and issuance of additional shares (or new stock issues) to current shareholders may be illustrated as follows:

	Amount
Balances prior to decision to issue rights:	
Common stock, par $10 authorized 100,000 shares, outstanding 30,000 shares	$300,000
Contributed capital in excess of par, common stock	150,000
Retained earnings	70,000

Decision:
To increase the outstanding shares by 50 percent (i.e., issue 15,000 additional shares).
Issue price to current shareholders—$30 per share plus two stock rights.
Announcement date: January 1, 1979.
Issue date for rights: March 1, 1979.
Expiration date for rights: September 1, 1979.
Market prices:
Rights—between announcement and issue dates, average $1 per right.
Stock—At announcement date, $30 per share.
—At expiration date, $34 per share.

The indicated entries by X Corporation are as follows:

January 1, 1979—date of announcement: None.

March 1, 1979—date of issuance: Memorandum only, viz:

Issued 30,000 stock rights to current shareholders for 15,000 shares of stock to be sold. Each share will be sold for $30 cash plus the receipt of two stock rights. After September 1, 1979, all outstanding rights will expire and the remaining shares will be sold on the market at the then current market price.

July 1, 1979—date of exercise by one shareholder holding 1,000 rights:

Cash (1,000 rights ÷ 2 = 500 shares) × $30	15,000	
Common stock, par $10 (500 shares)		5,000
Contributed capital in excess of par, common stock		10,000
(Remaining rights outstanding, 29,000 for 14,500 shares of common stock.)		

Situation 5—It is not unusual for a corporation to be short of cash during the early part of its life and, as a consequence, to issue its own shares for professional services rendered. In some instances, stock rights rather than shares are issued. To illustrate, assume that at the end of year one, 500 stock rights were issued to an attorney for legal services when the rights were selling at $2 each. The rights specify that for each five rights tendered, one share of common stock, par $20, will be issued for $40 cash at any time up to the end of the fifth year of the life

of the corporation. The indicated entries would be as follows:

Year 1—Date of issuance:

Expense—legal services (500 rights @ $2)*	1,000	
Stock rights outstanding (500 rights for 100 shares of common stock) ..		1,000

* Observe that these are valued at their current market price.

Year 5—The 500 rights are tendered for 100 shares:

Cash (100 shares @ $40)	4,000	
Stock rights outstanding (500 rights)	1,000	
Common stock, par $20 (100 shares)		2,000
Contributed capital in excess of par ..		3,000

During the period the stock rights are outstanding, the item "Stock rights outstanding (for 100 shares), $1,000" should be reported under stockholders' equity along with the capital stock account to which it relates.

ACCOUNTING FOR STOCK OPTIONS ISSUED TO EMPLOYEES

Corporations often establish plans whereby shares of stock in the company are issued to employees. The purposes of stock option plans are quite varied, ranging from a desire to encourage ownership in the company by the employees, to raising equity capital, to providing additional compensation to one or more employees.

Often *stock rights* are given because it has been decided to issue shares of stock to the employees or a particular group of employees (such as top executives) at some *future date* as a form of compensation (situation 6 on page 614). In this situation the stock rights generally are specified as *nontransferable;* the shares received through exercise of the rights are *transferable.*

Plans for the issuance of stock to employees are designated with a variety of terms, none of which has been accorded standard usage. Typical terms used are stock purchase plans, stock option plans, stock bonus plans, stock award plans, stock thrift plans, and stock savings plans. It is important that the accountant carefully examines the specifications of a plan in order to determine the rights and obligations of the issuing corporation (sometimes called the grantor) and of the recipient of the shares (sometimes called the grantee) in order to determine the appropriate accounting, reporting, and disclosures.[2]

Fundamentally, there are two basic characteristics of stock option plans that significantly affect the accounting and reporting. These characteristics differentiate as to the *additional cost to the company,* viz:

1. Noncompensatory plans—These plans specify the issuance of company stock to employees at *(a)* no additional cost to the company and *(b)* no additional compensation to the employee. Examples are stock purchase plans whereby employees, at their option, can purchase shares of company stock directly from the company (often by payroll deductions) at approximate market price and thereby save certain marketing commissions and related costs.

2. Compensatory plans—These plans may specify the issuance of company stock to employees at a set price per share to be paid by the employee; however, that price must be less than the current market price of the stock to involve additional compensation. In some cases, the employee receives the stock under specified conditions at no cost. Typically, in compensatory plans the issuance of stock to employees *(a)* causes the company to incur an additional cost and *(b)* provides additional compensation (income) to those receiving the stock options.

Stock option plans often pose important income tax implications for the company and the affected employees because as a general rule the tax laws permit a tax deduction for the corporation when the employee is subject to income taxes on the options or shares received. In this regard, a plan is said to be a *qualified plan* if there is no income tax to the recipient initially (the shares, when sold by the employee, qualify as a long-term capital gain). If such is not the case, there is no tax benefit to the company and

---

[2] Stock option plans are so varied and so continually evolving that it would be useless to *(a)* speculate on which will be the most "popular," *(b)* attempt to discuss a wide variety of such plans, and *(c)* single out specific examples for extended elaboration. Instead, the discussions to follow focus directly on the underlying fundamentals upon which the accounting for most plans can be based.

the options are taxed as income to the employee, in which case the plan is said to be a *nonqualified plan.*

Fundamentally, the accounting, reporting, and disclosure requirements for all plans whereby stock is, or will be, issued to employees is determined by whether the plan is *compensatory* or *noncompensatory.* Within these two broad categories, certain accounting differences exist.

The accounting, reporting, and disclosure requirements, with respect to plans for the issuance of stock to employees, must be in conformity with *Accounting Research Bulletin (ARB) No. 43,* chapter 13B, as amended and supplemented by *APB Opinion No. 25,* "Accounting for Stock Issued to Employees" (October 1972). The discussions to follow are based on these two pronouncements.

Theoretical Considerations

Historically, and continuing to date, there has been considerable controversy over the appropriate accounting for *compensatory plans.* The controversy centers upon the timing of the recognition and measurement of compensation expense to the granting company. There is a theoretical answer, upon which most informed accountants tend to agree, and a practical answer (provided by *ARB No. 43* and *APB Opinion No. 25*) designed to cope with the real-world complexities caused by the wide variations in plans and *practical measurement problems.* The basic issues can best be pinpointed by illustration. For this purpose, assume the following continuing situation:

1. AB Corporation—executive stock option plan:
   Options approved for *each* of the ten designated top executives.
   a. Five thousand shares of common stock, par $5.
   b. Nontransferable, exercisable three years after grant and prior to expiration date (five years from date of grant and requiring continuing employment).
   c. Option price, $20 per share.
2. On January 1, 1979, Executive Z was granted an option for 5,000 shares:

a. For services performed 1979 through 1983 (approximately equal each year).
b. At January 1, 1979, the quoted market price was $30 per share.
c. The option was exercised by Executive Z in December 1983 when the quoted market price per share was $40 (a relatively steady increase since 1979).

The fundamental question for the accountant is to determine the appropriate accounting, reporting, and disclosure procedures for the plan during the period 1979 through 1983. To do this, the following questions must be answered:

1. Is the plan compensatory?
   a. If no, there are no unique accounting problems (discussed below).
   b. If yes, then
2. At what date should the compensation be measured?
3. What is the total amount of the compensation?
4. To what accounting periods should the compensation cost, as measured, be assigned as expense?
5. What entries should be made in the accounts?
6. How should the effects be reported and disclosed on the financial statements?

The *theoretical* responses to these questions are not complicated; they may be summarized as follows:

1. The issuance of options to employees that involve *(a)* additional cost to the company and *(b)* additional compensation to the employee constitutes a compensatory plan; all other plans are noncompensatory.
2. The compensation cost should be measured when the corporation foregoes the principal alternative use (sale) of the shares. This is usually identified as the date on which the option is granted to a specific individual; that is, the *date of grant.*
3. The total amount of the compensation cost should be measured as the *market value* of the *stock rights* (not the shares themselves) at the date of the grant to the specific individual.

4. The total amount of compensation cost, thus measured, should be assigned as *expense* of the accounting periods in which the services are rendered. This serves to match the compensation expense with the related revenues in conformity with the matching principle.

Practical Considerations

The accounting profession, despite continued efforts, has not been able to promulgate accounting rules for stock options which attain theoretical positions satisfactory to many accountants. The primary problem is one of *measurement.* Let's review the practical guidelines provided by *ARB No. 43* and *APB Opinion No. 25.* We will consider each of the questions listed above separately.

Is the Plan Compensatory? Because the decision on this point fundamentally affects the accounting procedures to be followed, and because the precise lines of distinction are not obvious in many plans, *APB Opinion No. 25,* paragraph 7, carefully defines a *noncompensatory* plan as follows:

> . . . at least four characteristics are essential in a noncompensatory plan: (a) substantially all full-time employees meeting limited employment qualifications may participate (employees owning a specified percent of the outstanding stock and executives may be excluded), (b) stock is offered to eligible employees equally or based on a uniform percentage of salary or wages (the plan may limit the number of shares of stock that an employee may purchase through the plan), (c) the time permitted for exercise of an option or purchase right is limited to a reasonable period, and (d) the discount from the market price of the stock is no greater than would be reasonable in an offer of stock to stockholders or others.

All other plans are classified as *compensatory.*

Accounting for Noncompensatory Plans

Since noncompensatory plans involve no additional expense to the company and no additional compensation to the employees, there are no unique accounting problems involved. To illustrate, assume Company Y has a stock pur-chase plan whereby employees may acquire stock from the company either by direct purchase or through payroll deductions. The option price of the stock is 5% below the quoted market price. Assuming payroll deductions, typical entries would be (data assumed as given in the entries):

1. To record the monthly payroll and related deductions:

Salary and wage expense	90,000	
Income taxes withheld		18,000
Payroll taxes withheld		
(FICA, FUTA, etc.)		6,000
Union dues payable		440
Liability—employee stock		
purchase plan*		7,600
Cash (or salary and wages		
payable)		57,960

    * Per payroll deductions authorized by employees.

2. To record issuance of shares to employees (market price, $20):

Liability—employee stock pur-		
chase plan	7,600	
Capital stock, par $15,		
(400 shares*)		6,000
Contributed capital in ex-		
cess of par		1,600

    * $7,600 ÷ ($20 × .95) = 400 shares.

Accounting for Compensatory Plans

Since accounting for compensatory plans involves measurement of the amount of compensation expense to the company (in addition to regular salary) and its recognition in appropriate periods, the accounting complexities are significantly increased. To discuss these complexities, we will proceed to the remaining questions posed above and, for illustrative purposes, return to the data given on page 616 for AB Corporation.

When Should the Compensation Cost Be Measured? In a compensatory plan, the amount of additional compensation theoretically should be measured on the date of grant (see page 616). However, because of real-world measurement problems, *APB Opinion No. 25* specifies that compensation should be measured at a *measurement date* defined in paragraph 10 of the *Opinion* as follows:

The *measurement date* for determining compensation cost in stock option, purchase, and award plans is the first date on which are known both (1) the number of shares that an individual employee is entitled to receive and (2) the option or purchase price, if any.

Thus, depending on the specific circumstances, the *measurement date* may be either

a. The date the option is granted to the individual employee. This *date of grant* is the usual case because both the number of shares and the purchase price generally are set at that date.

b. A date subsequent to the date of grant; that is, the earliest subsequent date when both the number of shares and the purchase price are known. This situation occurs, for example, when either the number of shares or their purchase price is contingent upon future earnings of the company or upon future market prices of the stock. Use of this later date, rather than the date of grant, is a concession to the measurement problem—additional compensation expense must be measured when both the purchase price and the number of shares to which the employee is entitled are known.

In respect to AB Corporation (page 616), the measurement date is the date of grant because in this case both the *(a)* number of shares (5,000) and *(b)* purchase, or option, price ($20) are known at that date.

What Is the Total Amount of Compensation Cost? Theoretically, the total amount of the compensation cost is the current market value of the *rights* (not the stock) at the date of grant. However, because of practical measurement problems, *APB Opinion No. 25* states that compensation for

> . . . services that a corporation receives as consideration for stock issued through employee stock option, purchase, and award plans should be measured by the quoted market price of the stock at the measurement date less the amount, if any, that the employee is required to pay.

The difference between the quoted market price of the stock at measurement date and the option price is used as a surrogate for the *market value* of the rights. The valuation of stock options has received considerable attention in finance, primarily due to increased trading in options on the Chicago Board Options Exchange. Option valuation is complex because the option price depends on (a) the time to maturity of the option, (b) the risk-free interest rate, and (c) the variance rate on the stock price—in addition to the stock price and the option price of the stock. GAAP uses the last two factors, stock price and option price in *approximating* the value of an option. *APB Opinion No. 25* states that "if a quoted market price is unavailable, the best estimate of the market value of the stock should be used to measure compensation."

In respect to the plan outlined above for AB Corporation (page 616), total additional compensation, which is measurable in this instance on the date of grant, January 1, 1979, is $30 − $20 = $10 per share, or $50,000 for Executive Z. This situation is illustrated on page 619 (Case A).

When the measurement date is at a date subsequent to the date of grant, the number of shares, the option price, and market price generally must be *estimated* for the measurement of the compensation because *accruals* of *estimated* annual compensation expense must be recorded for each period between the date of grant and the measurement date (when these dates are different). Total *actual* compensation cost then is measured and recorded as a deferred expense on the measurement date. Annual compensation expense is recorded for the remaining periods prior to expiration or exercise date. This situation is illustrated on pages 620–22 (Case B).

If the grantee exercises the option prior to the end of the expiration date, the amount of total compensation not assigned to specific periods usually is assigned to the period in which exercise occurs.

To What Accounting Periods Should the Measured Compensation Cost Be Assigned as Expense? The total amount of additional compensation cost theoretically should be assigned to the periods in which the services are rendered so that compensation expense is matched with the related revenues. This generally requires accrual, and/or deferral, of the compensation expense. The theoretical response essentially is specified in *APB Opinion No. 25* as follows:

> 12. *Accruing Compensation Cost.* Compensation cost in stock option, purchase, and award plans should be recognized as an expense of one or more periods in which an employee performs services and also as part or all of the consideration received for stock issued to the employee through a plan. The grant or award may specify the period or periods during which the employee performs services, or the period or periods may be inferred from the terms or from the past pattern of grants or awards [ARB No. 43, chapter 13B, paragraph 14; APB Opinion No. 12, *Omnibus Opinion-1967,* paragraph 6].
>
> 13. An employee may perform services in several periods before an employer corporation issues stock to him for those services. The employer corporation should *accrue* compensation expense in each period in which the services are performed. If the measurement date is later than the date of grant or award, an employer corporation should record the compensation expense *each period from date of grant or award to date of measurement based on the quoted market price of the stock at the end of each period.*
>
> 14. If stock is issued in a plan before some or all of the services are performed, part of the consideration recorded for the stock issued is unearned compensation and should be shown as a *separate reduction of stockholders' equity.* The unearned compensation should be accounted for as expense of the period or periods in which the employee performs service.
>
> 15. Accruing compensation expense may require estimates, and adjustment of those estimates in later periods may be necessary [APB Opinion No. 20, *Accounting Changes,* paragraphs 31 to 33]. For example, if a stock option is not exercised (or awarded stock is returned to the corporation) because an employee fails to fulfill an obligation, the estimate of compensation expense recorded in previous periods should be adjusted by decreasing compensation expense in the period of forfeiture. (Emphasis supplied.)

Thus, the *Opinion* specifies precise guidelines for accrual and deferral of total additional compensation cost when the measurement date is *(a)* at the date of grant or *(b)* at a date subsequent to the date of grant. Observe that the phrase in italics in paragraph 13 is significant because it does not permit allocation of any of the compensation cost to periods prior to the date of *grant.*

With respect to AB Corporation, the total compensation cost of $50,000 should be assigned as expense equally to each year of the five-year period 1979–83 because Executive Z will work full-time for the company during that period, which is the period "covered" by the option grant.

ILLUSTRATIVE ENTRIES FOR COMPENSATORY STOCK OPTION PLANS

Illustrative entries will be given for *compensatory* stock option plans for the two basic situations, viz:[3]

Case A—The date of grant and the measurement date are identical.

Case B—The date of grant and the measurement date are different.

For illustrative purposes the data given on page 616 for AB Corporation will be used.

Case A—Compensatory plan; date of grant and measurement date are identical.

For convenience the fact situation for AB Corporation is summarized as follows:

a. January 1, 1979—Stock option granted to each of the ten top executives. For illustrative purposes we will use the option granted to Executive Z for 5,000 shares of common stock (par $5) at an option price of $20 per share.

b. Consideration—Additional compensation for services 1979 through 1983 (five years); approximately equal services each year.

c. Market price per share of stock on January 1, 1979, $30 (date of grant).

d. December 1983—Executive Z exercised the option when the quoted price of the stock

---

[3] Currently, very few compensatory plans are initiated because of recent changes in the tax laws, the 1976–79 period of depressed stock prices, and the complex accounting requirements. However, common stock options may again become common. For those instructors who prefer, the remainder of this Part of the chapter may be omitted without affecting the continuity of the chapter.

was $40 per share (a relatively steady increase since 1979).

Analysis: In the preceding discussions we have established (in accordance with *ARB No. 43* and *APB Opinion No. 25*) that

1. The AB Corporation plan is compensatory—There is additional compensation cost to the company and additional compensation to Executive Z because of the spread between the market price of the stock ($30) and the option price ($20) at the date of grant (i.e., the measurement date in this instance).
2. The date of grant and the measurement date are identical, January 1, 1979, because on that date both the number of shares (5,000) and the stock option price ($20) are known.
3. The total additional compensation cost is 5,000 shares × ($30 − $20) = $50,000.
4. The additional compensation cost to the company of $50,000 should be allocated as expense equally (because the services to be rendered by Executive Z will be approximately equal each year) to each of the five years (1979–83).

Based on the above analysis, the employer, AB Corporation, should make the following entries with respect to participation by Executive Z in the stock option plan:

a. January 1, 1979—date of grant; to record total deferred compensation cost and the stock options outstanding:

Deferred compensation cost	50,000	
Executive stock options outstanding (for 5,000 shares of common stock)		50,000

($30 − $20) × 5,000 shares = $50,000.

b. December 31, 1979, through 1983—to record the annual apportionment of compensation cost to compensation expense (for each of the five years):

Executive compensation expense	10,000	
Deferred compensation cost		10,000

$50,000 ÷ 5 years = $10,000 per year.

c. December 31, 1983—exercise date, to record the stock rights tendered by Executive Z and issuance of the 5,000 shares:

Cash (5,000 shares @ $20 option price)	100,000	
Executive stock options outstanding (for 5,000 shares)	50,000	
Common stock, par $5 (5,000 shares)		25,000
Contributed capital in excess of par, common stock		125,000

Compensation expense ($10,000) is reported on the income statement each year as a normal operating expense. Stock options outstanding and deferred compensation cost would be reported on the balance sheet December 31, 1979, as follows:

Stockholders' Equity

Contributed Capital:		
Common stock, par $5, authorized 500,000 shares, issued and outstanding 200,000 shares (assumed) ...		$1,000,000
Executive stock options outstanding (for 5,000 shares of common stock)	$50,000	
Less: Unamortized deferred compensation cost	40,000	10,000
Other contributed capital (etc.)	(not illustrated)	

Note that Deferred Compensation Cost is a *contra account* to stockholders' equity, rather than a deferred charge, as might be implied by the account title.

Case B—Compensatory plan; date of grant and measurement date are different.

When either the number of shares to be issued or the option price is not known at the date of grant, the measurement difficulties become more complex.[4] To accommodate this uncertainty, estimates of the unknown variables must be made until the measurement date arrives. Re-

---

[4] In some cases the option price but not the number of shares is known; in other cases the reverse is true; and in still other cases neither is known at the date of grant because they are contingent upon future events as specified in the stock option plan. Each of these situations would require the use of estimates of the unknown variables prior to the measurement date.

call that the measurement date is the first date on which *both* the number of shares to be issued and the option price are known.

To illustrate this situation, the data for AB Corporation (page 616) are *adapted* as follows:

Provisions of the option plan:

January 1, 1979—A stock option for 5,000 shares is granted to Executive Z, exercisable after three years from this date and within five years from this date.

Option price—To be established on December 31, 1981, by reducing the basic option price of $20 by the percentage increase in total profits for 1979 through 1981 (a three-year period).

Additional compensation will be for services to be rendered from January 1, 1979, to December 31, 1983, assuming approximately equal services each year.

Market price per share on January 1, 1979, $20 (date of grant).

Exercise of option—Executive Z exercised the option during December 1983 when the quoted price of the shares was $40 each.

Estimates made on December 31, 1979 (to simplify, assume they are not revised in 1980):

a. Percentage increase in profits for 1979 through December 31, 1981: 15%.
b. Resulting estimated option price: $20 × (1 − .15) = $17 per share.
c. Market price estimated for December 31, 1981: $28 per share.

Actual amounts on December 31, 1981:

a. Percentage increase in actual profits for 1979 through December 31, 1981: 10%.
b. Resulting actual option price: $20 × (1−.10) = $18 per share.
c. Market price quoted on December 31, 1981: $27.20 per share.

The grantor, AB Corporation, should make the entries given below over the life of the option agreement with Executive Z (end of accounting period December 31):

a. January 1, 1979—date of grant:

No entry—measurement and recording of compensation cost are based on estimates until the measurement date, December 31, 1981.

b. December 31, 1979 and 1980—end of period; to record accrual of *estimated* annual compensation expense:

	1979	1980
Compensation expense	11,000	11,000
Executive stock options outstanding	11,000	11,000

Computation of estimated compensation expense:
Total estimated compensation cost ($28 − $17) × 5,000 shares = $55,000.
Allocation to periods: $55,000 ÷ 5 years = $11,000.

c. December 31, 1981—measurement date; to record the stock options and the remaining compensation cost (i.e., revision of the estimated amounts recorded in 1979 and 1980):

Deferred compensation cost ($46,000 − $22,000)	24,000	
Executive stock options outstanding		24,000

Computation of total compensation cost:
($27.20 − $18) × 5,000 shares = $46,000.

d. December 31, 1981, 1982, and 1983—end of period; to record the annual compensation expense for each of the remaining three years:

Compensation expense	8,000	
Deferred compensation cost		8,000

$24,000 ÷ 3 years = $8,000.

e. December, 1983—exercise date; to record the stock rights tendered by Executive Z and the issuance of the 5,000 shares:

Cash ($18 × 5,000 shares)	90,000	
Executive stock options outstanding (for 5,000 shares)	46,000	
Common stock, par $5 (5,000 shares)		25,000
Contributed capital in excess of par		111,000

The stock option effects would be reported on the financial statements for two representative years as follows:

	1980	1981
Income statement:		
Expenses:		
Compensation expense	$ 11,000	$ 8,000
Balance Sheet:		
Contributed Capital:		
Common stock, par $5, authorized 500,000 shares; issued and outstanding 200,000 shares (assumed)	$1,000,000	$1,000,000
Executive stock options outstanding (for 5,000 shares); see note X	22,000*	$46,000
Less: Unamortized deferred compensation cost	16,000†	30,000
Other contributed capital, etc.		

* $11,000 × 2 years = $22,000.
† $24,000 − $8,000 = $16,000.

Note X must disclose the following information about the stock option plan, as required by *ARB No. 43*, Chapter 13B paragraph 15:

    a. The status of the option plan at the end of the period.

    b. The number of shares under option.

    c. The option price.

    d. The number of shares to which options were exercisable.

    e. The number of shares exercised during the period and the option price thereof.

A chart is shown in Exhibit 18–1 which summarizes the decisions and sequence of entries for

1. Noncompensatory plans.
2. Compensatory plans:
    a. Measurement date on date of grant.
    b. Measurement date subsequent to date of grant.

Occasionally employee stock options outstanding lapse because of

a. Failure of an employee to fulfill the option obligations due to severance, disability, or death. Such situations should be accounted for as a change in accounting estimate in conformity with *APB Opinion No. 20* (refer to the quotation on page 619, of paragraph 15, *APB Opinion No. 25*). The *credit* balance, relating to the particular lapsed option carried in the stock options outstanding account, and any directly related *debit* balance carried in the deferred compensation cost account, should be removed and the "net credit difference" should be accounted for as a reduction of *compensation expense* (re-

lated to the remaining options outstanding) for the current and any future relevant periods.

b. Failure to exercise when the option price of the stock is higher than the quoted market price of the stock by expiration date of the options (i.e., it would not be rational to exercise the options). In this situation, there is no future compensation expense related to options because they have already been "earned"; therefore, many accountants would record the "net credit difference" for the options as a credit to Contributed Capital from Stock Options. In this scenario, the recipients of the options received the market value from the corporation and effectively contributed that "value" back to the corporation by letting the options lapse. Other accountants believe *APB Opinion No. 20,* mentioned above, also applies to this situation and that the "net credit difference" should serve to reduce *normal* compensation expense for the current and any relevant future periods.

PART B—EARNINGS PER SHARE (EPS)

The concept of earnings per share (EPS) was discussed briefly in Chapter 4. Earnings per share applies *only* to common stock. For many years earnings per share amounts were computed and reported in various ways on an optional basis. *APB Opinion No. 9,* "Reporting the Results of Operations" (December 1966), recommended, but did not require, that earnings per share be disclosed in the income statement. *APB Opinion No. 15,* "Earnings per Share," was issued in May 1969; it changed the recommendation to a requirement. This complex and long *Opinion* was soon supplemented with a 186-page Interpretation.[5] The discussions and illustrations to follow focus on *APB Opinion No. 15.*

FASB Statement No. 21, "Suspension of the Reporting of Earnings per Share and Segment Information by Nonpublic Enterprises" (April 1978), suspended the EPS requirement for enter-

---

[5] J. T. Ball, *Computing Earnings per Share—Unofficial Accounting Interpretations of APB Opinion No. 15* (New York: AICPA, 1970).

EXHIBIT 18–1
Stock Issued to Employees—Summarized

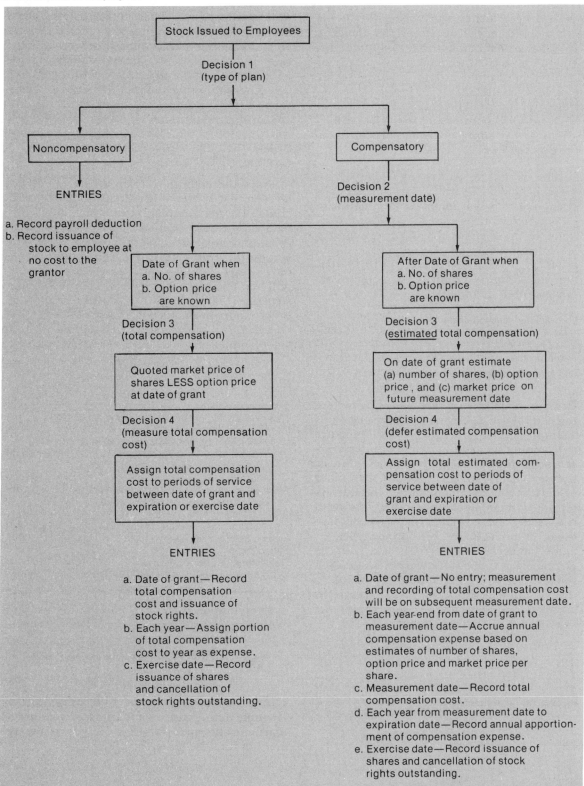

prises (a) whose debt or equity securities do not trade in a public market on a foreign or domestic stock exchange, nor in the over-the-counter market (including securities quoted only locally or regionally), or (b) that are not required to file statements with the SEC.

APB Opinion No. 15 identifies *two* different types of capital structures and prescribes different earnings per share presentations for each; they are as follows:

1. Simple capital structures—the case where the stockholders' equity "either consists only of common stock or includes no *potentially dilutive* convertible securities, options, warrants, or other rights that upon conversion or exercise could in the aggregate dilute earnings per common share." In this situation the *Opinion* prescribes a "single EPS presentation" as follows:

Earnings per common share:
Income before extraordinary items	$1.50
Extraordinary loss	(.11)*
Net Income	$1.39

* Not required but usually presented.

2. Complex capital structure—the case where the capital arrangement does not qualify as a simple capital structure because there are outstanding securities or rights that are *potentially dilutive* to common stock; that is, they may cause an increase in the number of outstanding common shares. In addition to the common stock outstanding, the dilutive securities and rights that may increase the outstanding shares of common stock include *convertible* preferred stock, *convertible* bonds payable, stock warrants, stock options, rights, and other similar securities. In this situation *APB Opinion No. 15* prescribes a "dual EPS presentation" that recognizes the dilutive effects as follows:

	Primary Earnings per Share	Fully Diluted Earnings per Share
Income before extraordinary items......................	$1.40	$1.25
Extraordinary loss	(.10)	(.08)
Net Income	$1.30	$1.17

Basically, earnings per share is computed by dividing the *average* number of common shares outstanding into net income. However, both the numerator and the denominator must be adjusted for certain items because of the complexities inherent in many capital structures. Therefore, *APB Opinion No. 15* is quite specific concerning these items.

COMPUTING EPS WITH A SIMPLE CAPITAL STRUCTURE

From the definition given at the left it can be seen that a *simple capital structure* may include (1) only common stock (including fully paid subscribed common stock) or (2) common stock and *nonconvertible* preferred stock. The several illustrations given in Chapter 4 involved only simple capital structures. At this point we will add one more example of a simple capital structure; that is, the situation where in addition to the common shares outstanding there is *nonconvertible* preferred stock. We will also reconsider computation of the average number of shares of common stock outstanding.

Assume the following data for MW Corporation:

Common stock, par $10, authorized 200,000 shares:	
Outstanding at beginning of year, 90,000 shares	$900,000
Issued during the year, on May 1, 6,000 shares	60,000
Preferred stock, par $20, 6% *nonconvertible,* cumulative, authorized 5,000 shares, outstanding at end of the year, 2,500 shares	50,000
Income before extraordinary items	144,000
Extraordinary loss (net of income tax)	(10,000)
Net income	134,000
Assume an average income tax rate of 45%.	

Computation of the EPS amount for a simple capital structure may be generalized as follows:

$$EPS = \frac{Income - \begin{array}{c}Dividend\ Claim\ of\\Nonconvertible\ Preferred\ Stock\end{array}}{\begin{array}{c}Average\ Number\ of\ Common\\Shares\ Outstanding\end{array}}$$

To compute the "simple EPS presentation" amounts in this case, two preliminary computations must be made—one with respect to the numerator and the other for the denominator.

EXHIBIT 18–2
Computation of Weighted Average Number of Shares Outstanding—MW Corporation

Dates	Shares	Time Outstanding	Weighted Shares
January 1, shares outstanding	90,000		
January 1—April 30	90,000	×4	360,000
May 1, sold additional shares	+6,000		
May 1—December 31	96,000	×8	768,000
December 31, shares outstanding	96,000		
Total share—months		12	1,128,000

Average number of shares outstanding, 1,128,000 ÷ 12 = 94,000

1. Nonconvertible preferred stock dividend claim—Since earnings per share relates only to common stock, the dividend claims of any outstanding nonconvertible preferred stock must be recognized in the computation of earnings per common share. That portion of the income for the period that is subject to the period's dividend claim of the nonconvertible preferred stock must be subtracted in the numerator. Two situations are possible:

   a. If the nonconvertible preferred stock is *noncumulative,* the subtraction of one year's dividend claim is made only if preferred dividends have been *declared* for the current year, because if those dividends are "passed," they are lost to the noncumulative preferred shareholders.
   b. If the nonconvertible preferred stock is *cumulative* (the usual case), subtraction of the current year's dividend must be made whether preferred dividends have been *declared or not* for the current year, because dividends "passed" are not lost by the cumulative preferred shareholders. An addition to the loss is made in the case of a loss.

   The nonconvertible preferred stock of MW Corporation is cumulative; therefore, the preferred stock dividend claim for the current year is

$$\begin{array}{c} \$50,000 \\ \text{(par value)} \end{array} \times \begin{array}{c} 6\% \text{ (dividend} \\ \text{preference rate)} \end{array} = \$3,000$$

2. Weighted average number of shares outstanding—In both simple and complex capital structures the denominator must be the weighted average number of common shares outstanding (adjusted in some situations as explained later). The shares outstanding must be weighted by the fraction of the period they were *outstanding* during the period.

Using the data for MW Corporation given on page 624 and the computations given in Exhibit 18–2 (average number of shares outstanding), the single EPS presentation required for a simple capital structure would be as shown in Exhibit 18–3.

The weighted average number of shares of common stock outstanding for MW Corporation would be computed as shown in Exhibit 18–2.

Observe in computing the average that the additional shares were included only for the months outstanding; similarly, reacquired (i.e., treasury) shares would be included only for the part of the year they were outstanding.

EXHIBIT 18–3
Earnings per Share for Simple Capital Structure

Earnings per common share outstanding:
Income before extraordinary items
($144,000 − $3,000) ÷ 94,000 shares = $1.50
Extraordinary loss
($ 10,000   ) ÷ 94,000 shares = (.11)
Net Income
($134,000 − $3,000) ÷ 94,000 shares = $1.39

When *stock dividends, stock splits,* or reverse stock splits occur during the period, *Opinion No. 15* par. 48, states that computation of the average number of shares of common stock outstanding (for EPS) purposes ". . . should give retroactive recognition to an appropriate change in capital structure for all periods presented." The Unofficial Accounting Interpretations of APB Opinion No. 15 (AICPA, By J. T. Ball), p. 115, states that "stock dividends and stock splits are retroactive adjustments rather than transactions to be weighted by the number of days a stock dividend or stock split was outstanding." This means that the computed average must be based on the assumption that the stock-dividend and stock-split shares were outstanding for the entire period. To accomplish this effect, all *actual shares outstanding prior* to the issuance of any stock dividends and/or splits (the actual shares outstanding *subsequent* to issuance of any stock

Illustrative Data

CASE A—A stock dividend:

Share data for 19X:	Shares
January 1, shares outstanding	10,000
April 1, sold new shares	1,000
Balance	11,000
June 1, stock dividend (100%)	11,000
Balance	22,000
September 1, sold new shares	2,000
December 31, shares outstanding	24,000

CASE B—A stock dividend and stock split share data for 19X (adapted from J. T. Ball, *Computing Earnings Per Share,* AICPA, Unofficial Accounting Interpretations of APB Opinion No. 15, page 114):

January 1, shares outstanding	100,000
February 25, stock dividend (5%)	5,000
March 21, treasury stock purchased	(525)
Balance	104,475
October 9, sold new shares	10,000
Balance	114,475
November 21, stock split (2-for-1)	114,475
December 31, shares outstanding	228,950

Computations

CASE A—Computation of Average Shares Outstanding (including a stock dividend):

Dates	Actual Shares	Retroactive Adjustment	Year-End Equivalent Shares Outstanding	Months Outstanding	Weighted Shares
Jan. 1–Apr. 1	10,000	× 2	= 20,000	× 3	= 60,000
Apr. 1–June 1	11,000	× 2	= 22,000	× 2	= 44,000
June 1–Sept. 1	22,000		= 22,000	× 3	= 66,000
Sept. 1–Dec. 31	24,000		= 24,000	× 4	= 96,000
Total weighted shares				12	266,000

Weighted average number of shares outstanding: 266,000 ÷ 12 = 22,167

CASE B—Computation of Average Shares Outstanding (including a stock dividend and a stock split):

Dates	Actual Shares	Retroactive Adjustment Stock Dividend	Stock Split	Year-End Equivalent Shares Outstanding	Days Outstanding	Weighted Shares
Jan. 1–March 20	100,000	× 1.05	× 2.00	= 210,000	× 79	= 16,590,000
Mar. 21–Oct. 8	104,475		× 2.00	= 208,950	× 202	= 42,207,900
Oct. 9–Dec. 31	228,950			= 228,950	× 84	= 19,231,800
Total weighted shares					365	78,029,700

Weighted average number of shares outstanding: 78,029,700 ÷ 365 = 213,780 dividends and/or splits already include their effects) must be *restated to year-end equivalent shares outstanding* (i.e., weighted shares).

Two cases are presented here to illustrate computation of the average number of shares outstanding during the year (for EPS) when there are stock dividends and stock splits. The computations for both are shown on page 626.

COMPUTING EPS WITH A COMPLEX CAPITAL STRUCTURE

Corporations with capital structures that do not meet the definition of a simple capital structure should present two sets of EPS data with equal prominence on the income statement. *APB Opinion No. 15* describes these as follows:

1. Primary earnings per share: The first presentation is based on the outstanding common shares and those securities that are in substance equivalent to common shares and have a dilutive effect.[6]
2. Fully diluted earnings per share: The second is a pro forma presentation which reflects the dilution of earnings per share that would have occurred if *all* contingent issuances of common stock that would individually reduce earnings per share had taken place at the beginning of the period (or time of issuance of the convertible security, etc., if later).

Primary Earnings per Share. Primary EPS is based on the weighted average of the common shares outstanding (as discussed above) *plus all common stock equivalents. APB Opinion No. 15* defines a common stock equivalent (CSE) as "a security which is not, in form, a common stock but which usually contains provisions to enable its holder to become a common stockholder and which, because of its terms and the circumstances under which it was issued, is in sub-

stance equivalent to a common stock." The value of a common stock equivalent derives in large part from the related common stock. Neither conversion nor anticipated conversion is necessary for a security to be considered as a common stock equivalent. The two most common types of common stock equivalents are *convertible securities* and *stock rights.* The determination of whether a convertible security or a stock right is a CSE (but not the determination of the number of CSE's) should be made "only at time of issuance and should not be changed thereafter so long as the security remains outstanding."

To determine when a security is a common stock equivalent and to compute the *number of equivalent shares* for EPS purposes, separate consideration must be given to:

a. Stock options, stock rights, stock warrants and other stock purchase contracts, subscribed common stock, if not fully paid, and
b. Securities convertible to common shares such as convertible preferred stock and convertible bonds payable.

These two distinctly different categories must be separately considered because they have different characteristics. As a consequence, their *dilutive* effects on the computation of earnings per share are quite different.[7]

These two different sources of common stock equivalents will be discussed and illustrated next. For illustrative purposes, the data given for MW Corporation are adapted and assume the following additional data *at date of issuance:*

Additional data for MW Corporation (see page 624 for basic data)

1.	Stock rights outstanding for common shares	2,000 shares
	Option or exercise price per share	$ 20
	Average market price per share for the period of issuance	$ 25
2.	Convertible securities:	
	A. Convertible bonds payable, Series A, $100,000, 4%,	

---

[6] Any reduction of EPS from dilutive securities of *less* than 3% in the aggregate *need not* be considered as dilution in the computation and presentation of EPS discussed throughout the *Opinion.* This *optional* test is based on materiality and is applied in practice on the net income line for EPS. There are two independent tests: (1) the difference between EPS ignoring all dilutive securities and primary EPS, and (2) the difference between EPS ignoring all dilutive securities and fully diluted EPS. Example: EPS ignoring all dilutive securities, $1.00 and primary EPS, $.98; the difference is less than 3%; may report *either* $.98 or $1.00 as primary EPS. Fully diluted EPS, $.97, difference 3%; *must* report fully diluted EPS of $.97.

---

[7] Dilution (dilutive) is defined in the *Opinion* as *"[a]* reduction in earnings per share resulting from the assumption that convertible securities have been converted or that options and warrants have been exercised or other shares have been issued upon the fulfillment of certain conditions." The opposite, called *antidilution,* occurs if their inclusion would have the effect of increasing the earnings per share amount. Antidilutive common stock equivalents are not included in the computations (see page 632).

each $1,000 bond convertible to 60 shares of common stock.
Bond issue price [a] 101
Bank prime interest rate at date of issuance [b] 7½%

B. Convertible bonds payable, Series B, $500,000, 6%, each $1,000 bond convertible to 50 shares of common stock.
Bond issue price [a] 98
Bank prime interest rate at date of issuance [b] 7½%

[a] "Due to the high conversion ratio (60 shares), Series A sold at a premium; in contrast Series B sold at a discount, despite the higher interest rate (6% versus 4%), due to the lower conversion ratio (50 shares). Assume straight-line amortization.
[b] Although the bonds were sold at different dates, the same bank prime rate is used for instructional convenience.

Equity contracts—Options, rights, warrants, and other stock purchase contracts that call for common shares when exercised, increase the common shares outstanding. Therefore, they comprise one category of common stock equivalents. A particular characteristic of these contracts is that when exercised there usually is a cash inflow to the corporation because the acquirer must pay the specified option price if there is one. If conversion is assumed, this would increase the number of shares outstanding; therefore, to compute the common stock equivalents, an assumption also must be made regarding the "as if" use of the resulting cash inflow. Since the cash inflow cannot be added to the numerator, *APB Opinion No. 15* specifies that the *treasury stock method* must be used.

The treasury stock method computes common stock equivalents as the number of common shares that would be issued upon exercise of the rights or options (at the option price), *less* the number of shares that could be bought back as treasury stock (at the *average* market price of the stock).[8] Computation of common stock equivalents, using the treasury stock method, is illustrated for MW Corporation in Exhibit 18–4.

[8] *Average* market price of the stock is *always* used to compute the number of common stock equivalents for purposes of computing primary EPS. In contrast, for computing fully diluted EPS *only,* the *ending* market price per share of stock is substituted for the average market price per share if the ending market price is *higher.* Thus, when the ending market price is higher, fully diluted EPS is reduced below primary EPS because of use of the treasury stock method.

EXHIBIT 18–4
Stock Rights—Treasury Stock Method to Compute CSE—MW Corporation

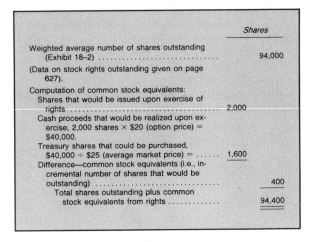

	Shares
Weighted average number of shares outstanding (Exhibit 18–2)	94,000
(Data on stock rights outstanding given on page 627).	
Computation of common stock equivalents:	
Shares that would be issued upon exercise of rights	2,000
Cash proceeds that would be realized upon exercise, 2,000 shares × $20 (option price) = $40,000.	
Treasury shares that could be purchased, $40,000 ÷ $25 (average market price) = ...	1,600
Difference—common stock equivalents (i.e., incremental number of shares that would be outstanding)	400
Total shares outstanding plus common stock equivalents from rights	94,400

In Exhibit 18–4 the stock rights were *dilutive* because they increased the number of "as if" shares outstanding by 400 and there was no dollar offset added to the numerator. In contrast, if the average market price is below the option price, the above computation would reduce the shares outstanding, in which case the effect would be *antidilutive.* For all practical purposes, the *Opinion* limits use of the treasury stock method to those situations where it is dilutive.[9] The options would not be exercised if the option price exceeded the market price.

The *Opinion* specifies a *variation* of the treasury stock method when the "number of shares of common stock obtainable upon exercise of outstanding options and warrants in the aggregate exceeds 20% of the number of common shares outstanding at the end of the period for which the computation is being made. . . ." In these situations, exercise of all options and warrants should be assumed; however, the cash inflow assumed would be applied in two steps:

1. First apply the funds to repurchase common shares at the average market price, but not

[9] *APB Opinion No. 15* (par. 36) recommends that assumption of exercise not be reflected in EPS data until the market price of the common stock has been in excess of the exercise or option price for substantially all of three consecutive months ending with the last month of the period to which EPS data relate. Also refer to paragraphs 37 and 38 of the *Opinion.*

to exceed 20% of the outstanding shares, and then

2. Apply the balance of the funds to *(a)* reduce any short-term or long-term borrowings and *(b)* any remaining funds to investments in U.S. government securities or commercial paper. In these situations the "as if" interest reduction, net of income taxes, must be considered as an increase in income (i.e., added to the numerator in the EPS computation).[10]

In Exhibit 18–4 the 2,000 additional shares that would be issued upon exercise of the rights is not in excess of 20% of the number of shares outstanding at the end of the period (i.e., 96,000 × 20% = 19,200 shares).

Convertible securities typically encompass *convertible preferred stock* and *convertible bonds payable* that generally contain provisions whereby the holder, under specified conditions, can convert them to common shares. Thus, they may constitute common stock equivalents when issued. The *Opinion* states that "convertible securities should be considered common stock equivalents if the cash yield to the holder at time of issuance is significantly below what would be a comparable rate for a similar security of the issuer without the conversion option." To il-

lustrate, assume a corporation can sell a new issue of nonconvertible bonds at a 6% annual interest rate; however, it has been advised that the same bonds, if convertible to common stock, probably would be marketable at a 4% annual interest rate. The 2% difference in interest rates (yield) provides a measure of the value of the conversion privilege. Of course, in an actual situation both rates seldom, if ever, would be known. However, in this example, the *convertible* bonds probably would qualify as common stock equivalents.

To determine whether a *convertible security* in a given situation should be considered as a common stock equivalent, *APB Opinion No. 15* applies an "if converted" concept; it states that "a convertible security should be considered as a common stock equivalent at the time of issuance if, based on its market price, it has a cash yield of less than 66⅔% of the then current bank prime interest rate."[11] The "cash yield" is the ratio of cash interest to be paid each year divided by the cash received at date of issuance. This *prime rate test* must be used to determine whether a convertible security represents common stock equivalents as illustrated at the bottom of this page (based on the additional data given for MW Corporation on pages 627–28).

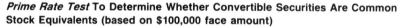

***Prime Rate Test* To Determine Whether Convertible Securities Are Common Stock Equivalents (based on $100,000 face amount)**

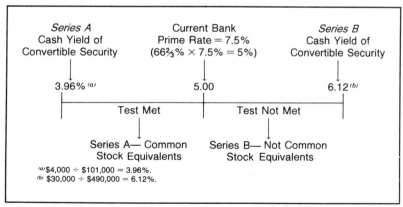

---

[11] If no market price of the convertible security is available, this test should be based on the "fair" value of the security. If there is a scheduled change in the interest rate or dividend rate during the first five years after issuance, the lowest scheduled rate should be used (par. 33).

This is an arbitrary test; nevertheless, it is a pragmatic solution to the very difficult problem of defining a CSE. The *Opinion* states: "The Board believes that the current bank prime rate in general use for short-term loans represents a practical, simple and readily available basis on which to establish the criteria for determining a common stock equivalent. . . ."[12] From a realistic point of view, a security bought to yield less than two thirds of the bank prime rate probably was acquired for potential appreciation and not for current yield; therefore, its conversion feature was an important element in the total consideration paid for it. Consequently, a test such as this one is necessary for defining common stock equivalents for convertible securities.

The prime rate test was devised to determine whether a *convertible security* is more in the nature of an equity security than a debt security. The prime rate test assumes that when the cash yield to the holder (from the security held) is *less* than a comparable rate (without the conversion privilege), measured as two thirds of the current prime interest rate, the convertible security is more in the nature of an equity security, particularly since conversion in the future may be likely. Therefore, *when the prime rate test is met, the convertible security represents common stock equivalents.*

If the prime rate test is met, the *number* of common stock equivalents related to the convertible securities is computed using an "if converted" approach. This approach assumes the following:

a. That the convertible securities are converted to common shares at the *beginning* of the period (or at time of issuance, if later), and
b. That, in view of the "as if" reduction in debt (convertible bonds), there would be a reduction in interest expense. Since income was reduced by interest expense on the debt (net of tax) this assumption requires that the interest, net of income tax, be added back to income (i.e., added to the numerator in the EPS computation). In the case of convertible preferred stock, if the prime rate test is passed, the CSE shares would be added to the denominator; the dividends would not be added to income in the numerator because dividends are not deducted in computing income.

Computation of Primary Earnings per Share

When there is a complex capital structure, primary *and* fully diluted EPS amounts are computed for (1) income before extraordinary items, (2) extraordinary items, and (3) net income. The computation of each amount may be summarized as follows:[13]

Primary Earnings per Share*

	Numerator	Denominator
1.	Income before extraordinary items:	
	Income before extraordinary items minus claims of *nonconvertible* preferred stock and minus dividend claims of convertible preferred stock that is not CSE, and plus interest (net of tax) on convertible debt classified as common stock equivalents.	Weighted average number of shares outstanding plus all common stock equivalents.
2.	Extraordinary items:	
	Extraordinary gain or loss (net of tax).	Same as above.
3.	Net income:	
	Same as (1) plus or minus extraordinary items.	Same as above.

* Excluding all antidilutive securities.

Particularly observe that the numerator and denominator must be consistent.

Computation of primary EPS, including the adjustments to the numerator and denominator, is shown in Exhibits 18–5 and 18–6.

Fully Diluted Earnings per Share. Recall that when there is a complex capital structure, *APB*

---

[12] The current bank prime interest rate is the rate banks locally are charging on short-term loans to borrowers with the best credit risk. Note that the cash yield is based on pretax yield because the prime rate is pretax. For determining whether convertible preferred stock qualifies as a CSE the yield rate on convertible preferred stock is the specified dividend rate.

[13] This summary does not specify all the numerous exceptions and certain detailed computations because they would serve to confuse the broader issues. It is not feasible to cover all of the complexities, and memorization of them would be fruitless. As stated earlier our objective is to focus on the broad issues. APB *Opinion No. 15,* recommends, but does not require the presentation of the EPS amount on extraordinary items.

EXHIBIT 18–5
Common Stock Equivalents for Primary EPS, including convertible debt securities (MW Corporation)

	Shares
Weighted average number of shares outstanding (Exhibit 18–2)	94,000
Common stock equivalents from *stock rights* (Exhibit 18–4)	400

Convertible debt securities, if-converted method:
  (Data on convertible securities given on pages 627 and 628.)
  Prime rate tests:
    Series A, convertible bonds payable, $100,000, 4%:

$$\frac{\text{Cash Yield (interest) per Year}}{\text{Market Price at Issuance}} = \frac{\$100,000 \times 4\%}{\$100,000 \times 1.01} = \frac{\$4,000}{\$101,000} = 3.96\%$$

Two thirds of bank prime interest rate: $7.5\% \times \frac{2}{3}$ = 5.00%

Computation of the number of common stock equivalents—Since the yield rate (3.96%) is less than two thirds of the bank prime rate (5.00%), the Series A convertible bonds are common stock equivalents computed as ($100,000 ÷ $1,000) × 60 shares = ... **6,000**

Series B, convertible bonds payable, $500,000, 6%:

$$\frac{\text{Cash Yield (interest) per Year}}{\text{Market Price at Issuance}} = \frac{\$500,000 \times 6\%}{\$500,000 \times .98} = \frac{\$30,000}{\$490,000} = 6.12\%$$

Two thirds of bank prime interest rate: $7.5\% \times \frac{2}{3}$ = 5.00%

Computation of the number of common stock equivalents—Since the yield rate (6.12%) is higher than two thirds of the bank prime rate (5.00%), the Series B convertible bonds are *not* common stock equivalents. (Note: We will see below that they *are* included in fully diluted EPS.)

| Total shares of common stock outstanding plus all common stock equivalents (used for primary EPS computation see Exhibit 18–6) .... | **100,400** |

Opinion No. 15 requires a dual EPS presentation—primary earnings per share and fully diluted earnings per share (refer to pages 624 and 627). Fully diluted earnings per share reflects the maximum possible dilution; therefore, the number of shares in the denominator of the EPS computation includes *(a)* the average number of common shares outstanding *plus (b)* all common stock equivalents (i.e., those used in computing primary EPS) *plus (c)* all other contingent issuances of common stock that would reduce earnings per share. If *(c)* is zero, primary and fully diluted EPS would be the same.[14]

Computation of fully diluted earnings per share may be summarized as follows:

[14] If primary and fully diluted EPS are the same, only primary needs to be reported; however, a note should disclose this fact.

Fully Diluted Earnings per Share*

Numerator	Denominator
1. Income before extraordinary items:	
Income before extraordinary items minus claims of *nonconvertible* preferred stock, plus interest expense (net of tax) on all convertible debt.	Weighted average number of shares outstanding plus all common stock equivalents plus all *other common shares that would be issued on convertible securities.*
2. Extraordinary items:	
Extraordinary gain or loss (net of tax).	Same as above.
3. Net income:	
Same as (1) plus or minus extraordinary items.	Same as above.

* Excluding all antidilutive securities.

For MW Corporation, computation of fully diluted earnings per share also would require inclusion of all the shares that would be issued

EXHIBIT 18–6
Computation of Primary Earnings per Share (MW Corporation)

	Shares
Number of shares (i.e., the denominator):	
Average number of common shares outstanding (Exhibit 18–2)	94,000
Add common stock equivalents (Exhibit 18–5)	6,400
Total number of shares for primary EPS computation	100,400
Income (i.e., the numerator):	
Income before extraordinary items (page 624)	$144,000
Less: Preferred stock, *nonconvertible,* dividend preference (page 624)	(3,000)
	141,000
Add: Interest expense (net of income tax effect on convertible bonds that are CSE, Series A [($100,000 × 4%) − $50 premium amortization] × (1.00 − .45)*	2,173
Income before extraordinary items, adjusted	143,173
Extraordinary loss	(10,000)
Net Income, Adjusted	$133,173
Primary earnings per share amounts:	
Income before extraordinary items ($143,173 ÷ 100,400 shares) = $1.43	
Extraordinary loss ($ 10,000 ÷ 100,400 shares) = (.10)	
Net income ($133,173 ÷ 100,400 shares) = $1.33†	

* Premium amortization assumed, straight line, over 20 years (pages 627 and 628; $1,000 ÷ 20 years = $50). Income tax rate 45% (page 624).

† The dilutive effect of common stock equivalents was $1.39 − $1.33 = $0.06 (i.e., $.06 ÷ $1.39 = 4.3% dilution from $1.39 in Exhibit 18–3, which ignored the effect of common stock equivalents). Since the 4.3% difference is material (i.e., 3% or more), primary EPS must be reported as $1.33.

for the Series B bonds (recall that they did not qualify as CSE, thus were not used in computing *Primary* EPS) and an addback to income for the assumed net-of-tax interest deduction (if including the bonds on an as-if converted basis would decrease fully-diluted EPS below primary EPS). Computations for these two items are reflected in Exhibit 18–7.

Antidilution

A reduction in earnings per share amounts resulting from common stock equivalents or convertible securities that do not represent common stock equivalents is known as *dilution,* and the stock purchase contracts and convertible securities that cause this effect are called *dilutive securities.*

Antidilution, caused by *antidilutive* stock purchase contracts and convertible securities, has the opposite effect. Antidilution causes an increase in earnings per share amounts above the amounts that would otherwise be reported. To attain the maximum dilutive effect on EPS (because of conservatism), all *antidilutive* securities are excluded in computing *both* primary and fully diluted earnings per share amounts. To repeat, antidilution may arise from either stock purchase contracts (options, warrants, rights, etc.) or convertible securities (convertible debt or preferred stock).

Antidilutive effects can be illustrated as follows:

Stock rights, options, and other stock purchase contracts: Was the option or exercise price *above* the average market price of the optioned stock? If yes, the common stock equiv-

EXHIBIT 18–7
Computation of Fully Diluted Earnings per Share (MW Corporation)

		Shares
Number of shares (i.e., the denominator):		
Average number of common shares outstanding (Exhibit 18–2)		94,000
Add common stock equivalents:		
From stock rights (Exhibit 18–4)	400	
From convertible debt (Exhibit 18–5)	6,000	6,400
Contingent issuances of common stock from convertible securities that are not common stock equivalents:		
Series B, bonds payable ($500,000 ÷ $1,000) × 50		25,000
Total number of shares for fully diluted EPS Computation		125,400
Income (i.e., the numerator):		
Income before extraordinary items (page 624)		$144,000
Less: Preferred stock dividend preference (page 624)		(3,000)
		141,000
Add: Interest expense (net of income tax effect) on convertible securities:		
Series A bonds payable (Exhibit 18–6)		2,173
Series B Bonds payable:[($500,000 × 6%) + ($500 discount amortization)] × (1.00 − .45)*		16,775
Income before extraordinary items, adjusted		159,948
Extraordinary loss		(10,000)
Net Income, Adjusted		$149,948
Fully diluted earnings per share amounts:		
Income before extraordinary items ($159,948 ÷ 125,400 shares) = $1.28		
Extraordinary loss ($ 10,000 ÷ 125,400 shares) = (.08)		
Net income ($149,948 ÷ 125,400 shares) = $1.20†		

* Assumed 20-year, straight-line, amortization of bond discount and a 45% income tax rate (see note at bottom of Exhibit 18–6).
† Optional materiality test: ($1.39 − $1.20) ÷ $1.39 = 13.7%; material, report $1.20.

alents would be antidilutive and would not be included in any EPS calculations.

Illustration for MW Corporation:
a. Dilutive—option price *below* market price:
As illustrated above—option price, $20; market price, $25.
Computation: 2,000 shares − ($40,000 ÷ $25) = +400, positive common stock equivalents (see Exhibit 18–4). Clearly, this amount added to the denominator, with no compensating effect in the numerator would *decrease* the EPS amounts below what they would be without the rights and options. Thus, they are *dilutive.*

b. Antidilutive—option price *above* market price:
Assumption—option price, $20; market price, $18.
Computation: 2,000 shares − ($40,000 ÷ $18) = −222, negative common stock equivalents. This negative amount would decrease the denominator, which would serve to *increase* the EPS amounts above what they would be without the rights and options. Thus, they are *antidilutive* and would not be included in any EPS computations.

Furthermore, if the option price exceeded the market price, it is unlikely that the options would be exercised. This is an example of the logic underlying the antidilutive provisions in *APB Opinion No. 15.*[15]

Reporting Earnings per Share

APB Opinion No. 15, as amended by *FASB Statement No. 21,* requires that earnings per share data be "shown on the face of the income statement," for all periods presented by "publicly held" corporations. In addition, the following should be disclosed (paraphrased from *APB Opinion No. 15,* pars. 19–21):

a. A description, in summary form, sufficient to explain the pertinent rights and privileges of the various securities outstanding.
b. A schedule or note relating to the earnings per share data to explain the bases upon which both primary and fully diluted earnings per share are calculated.
c. All assumptions and any resulting adjustments used in deriving the earnings per share data.
d. The number of shares issued upon conversion, exercise or satisfaction of required conditions, and so forth, during at least the most recent annual fiscal period and any subsequent interim period presented.

e. Computations and/or reconciliations as needed to provide a clear understanding of the manner in which the earnings per share amounts were obtained.

An illustration of income statement presentation for the example used in the preceding discussions (MW Corporation) is shown in Exhibit 18–8.

EXHIBIT 18–8
Reporting Earnings per Share—Complex Capital Structures

MW Corporation
Income Statement (partial)
For the Year Ended December 31, 19X

Income before extraordinary items		$144,000
Extraordinary loss (net of income taxes of $8,182)		10,000
Net Income		$134,000

Earnings per share (Note X):

	Primary	Fully Diluted
Income before extraordinary items	$1.43	$1.28
Extraordinary loss (net of tax)	(.10)	(.08)
Net Income	$1.33	$1.20

Notes to the financial statements:

Note X. Earnings per share amounts were computed in accordance with the provisions of *APB Opinion No. 15.* Primary earnings per share includes all common stock equivalents based on stock rights and options outstanding (using the treasury stock method) plus those based on convertible securities (using the "if-converted" method). Fully diluted earnings per share includes all additional contingent common shares that would be issued for all convertible securities; thus, it represents maximum dilution.

The outstanding stock rights and Series A convertible bonds payable were determined to be common stock equivalents, and the Series B convertible bonds, although not common stock equivalents, were included in the computation of fully diluted amounts. The income amounts were adjusted for the interest (net of income taxes) effects of these securities.

The pertinent rights and privileges of the stock rights and the convertible securities are explained in the notes related to those items (refer to the balance sheet).

No shares were issued during the past two years for exercise of stock rights or conversion of convertible securities.

A chart is shown in Exhibit 18–9 which summarizes the primary decisions, their sequence, and the computation process for earnings per share in both simple and complex capital structures.

---

[15] Footnote 8 to *APB Opinion No. 15* states: "The presence of a common stock equivalent or other dilutive securities together with income from continuing operations and extraordinary items may result in diluting one of the per share amounts which are required to be disclosed on the face of the income statement—i.e., income from continuing operations, income before extraordinary items, and before the cumulative effect of accounting changes, if any, and net income—while increasing another. In such a case, the common stock equivalent or other dilutive securities should be recognized for all computations even though they have an antidilutive effect on one of the per share amounts."

EXHIBIT 18-9
Computing Earnings per Share—Summarized

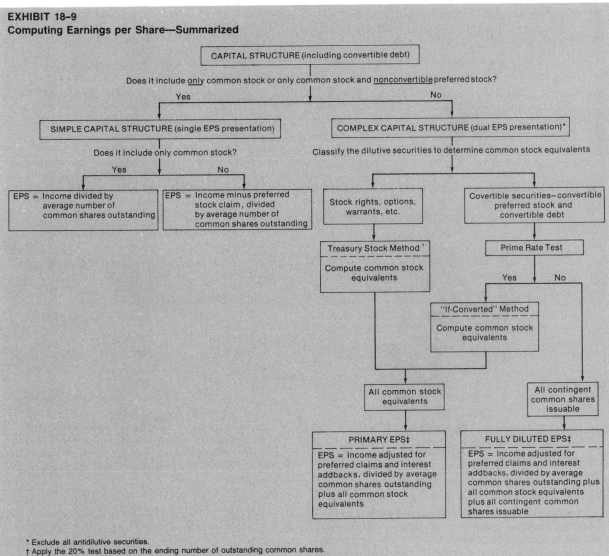

* Exclude all antidilutive securities.
† Apply the 20% test based on the ending number of outstanding common shares.
‡ Apply the 3% materiality test.

QUESTIONS

PART A

1. What are stock rights?

2. In what situations are stock rights frequently issued?

3. Distinguish between a compensatory and a noncompensatory stock option plan.

4. What is meant by the measurement date? Why is it sometimes later than the date of grant?

5. What is the amount of total compensation in a stock option plan?

6. Why are estimates necessary when the measurement date is later than the date of grant of a stock option that is compensatory?

PART B

7. What is the difference in earnings per share computations and reporting as between a simple capital structure and a complex capital structure?

8. What is a common stock equivalent? How do common stock equivalents affect earnings per share computations?

9. What is the 3% materiality rule in EPS computations and how is it used?

10. Contrast primary earnings per share and fully diluted earnings per share.

11. What is the treasury stock method?

12. What is the prime interest rate test and when is it used?

13. What is the difference between a dilutive security and an antidilutive security? Why is the distinction important in earnings per share considerations?

14. A company split its common stock two for one on June 30 of its fiscal year ended December 31. Before the split, there were 4,000 shares of common stock outstanding. How many shares of common stock should be used in computing EPS? How many shares of common stock should be used in computing a comparative EPS amount for the preceding year?

EXERCISES

PART A
Exercises 18–1 to 18–3

Exercise 18–1

This exercise focuses on stock rights by presenting two separate cases.

Case A—AB Corporation has outstanding 50,000 shares of common stock, par $1. The company has decided to sell an additional 25,000 shares of unissued common stock at $12 per share and to give the current stockholders first chance to buy shares proportionally equivalent to the number now held. To facilitate this plan each shareholder was issued one right for each share currently held. Two rights must be submitted to acquire one additional share for $12. Rights not exercised lapse on April 2, 19A.

Required:

Give any entry or memorandum that should be made in the accounts of AB Corporation on each of the following dates:

January 15, 19A, the date of the announcement that the rights will be issued on March 1, 19A.

March 1, 19A, issuance of all the rights. At this date the stock of AB Corporation was quoted on the market at $12.50 per share.

March 30, 19A, exercise by current shareholders of 98% of the rights issued.

April 2, 19A, the remaining rights outstanding lapsed because of the deadline.

Case B—CD Corporation had outstanding 60,000 shares of common stock, par $5. A one-for-three stock dividend (i.e., for each three shares outstanding one additional share was issued) was declared and issued. Because of fractional shares, 1,500 stock rights were issued (one stock right calls for $\frac{1}{3}$ share of stock).

Required:

1. Give the entry to record the stock dividend assuming $8 per share is debited to Retained Earnings.
2. Give the entry assuming 1,485 of the rights are exercised.
3. Give the entry assuming the remaining rights outstanding are allowed to lapse.

Exercise 18–2

SW Corporation has a stock purchase plan with the following provisions:

Each full-time employee, with a minimum of one year's service, may acquire common stock, par $5, in the company through payroll deductions at 4% below the market price on the date selected by the employee for stock purchase, up until the day before the second year of service begins.

Employee Jones signed a payroll deduction form on January 1, 1979, for $40 per month. At that date, the market price of the stock was $27. Assume a monthly salary of $1,000 and other payroll deductions in the aggregate of 20%. At the end of 1979, Jones requested that stock be purchased equal to the amount accumulated to his credit. At that date, the market price of the stock was $25.

Required:

1. Is this a compensatory plan? Explain.
2. What is the total additional compensation to Jones? Explain.
3. How many shares is Jones entitled to? Show computations.
4. Give entries to record (a) the monthly payroll and (b) issuance of the shares assuming unissued shares are used.

Exercise 18–3

BC Corporation is authorized to issue 300,000 shares of common stock, par $1; to date 140,000 shares have been issued. The corporation initiated a stock bonus plan during 1979 for designated managers. Each manager will receive stock options to purchase 1,000 shares of common stock, if still employed by the company, any time after two years from date of grant, January 1, 1979. The rights are nontransferable and expire after December 31, 1983. The option price is $15 per share; the market price on date of grant was $20. The services will be rendered approximately equally over the five-year period ending December 31, 1983.

Required:

1. Is this a noncompensatory plan? Explain.
2. What is the measurement date? Explain.
3. What is the amount of total compensation for each manager?
4. Over what period should this compensation expense be assigned? How much should be assigned to 1979? to 1980? Explain.
5. What entry should be made on the date of grant (for one manager)?
6. What entry should be made on December 31, 1979?
7. Give the entry to record the exercise of the option by one manager on December 31, 1983, when the market price of the common stock was $35 per share.

PART B
Exercises 18–4 to 18–9

Exercise 18–4

The records for WT Corporation, at year-end, reflected the following:

Common stock, nopar, authorized shares 500,000:	
Outstanding at beginning of year:	
100,000 shares	$175,000
Sold and issued during the year, September 1,	
3,000 shares	8,000
Preferred stock, 6%, par $10, nonconvertible,	
cumulative, authorized 20,000 shares:	
Outstanding during the year, 6,000 shares	60,000
Contributed capital in excess of par,	
preferred stock	3,000
Retained earnings	150,000
Bonds payable, 6½%, nonconvertible	100,000
Income before extraordinary items	90,000
Extraordinary loss (net of tax)	(20,000)
Net income	70,000

Required:

1. Is this a simple or complex capital structure? Explain.
2. What kind of EPS presentation is *required?* Explain.
3. Compute the required EPS amounts (show computations).
4. Compute the required EPS amounts assuming the preferred stock is noncumulative and the current year's dividend has not been declared and that the current year's dividend was passed.

Exercise 18–5

At the end of 19A the records of Jones Corporation reflected the following:

Common stock, par $5, authorized	
500,000 shares:	
Outstanding January 1, 19A, 200,000	
shares	$1,000,000
Sold and issued April 1, 19A, 1,000	
shares	5,000
Issued 10% stock dividend, November 30,	
19A, 20,100 shares	100,500
Preferred stock, 6%, par $10, noncon-	
vertible, noncumulative, authorized	
50,000 shares, outstanding during	
the year, 20,000 shares	200,000
Contributed capital in excess of par,	
common stock	150,000
Contributed capital in excess of par,	
preferred stock	100,000
Retained earnings (the effect given to	
current preferred dividends declared	
during 19A)	640,000
Bonds payable, 6½%, nonconvertible	500,000
Income before extraordinary items	182,000
Extraordinary gain (net of tax)	18,000
Net income	200,000
Average income tax rate, 45%.	

Required:

1. Is this a simple or complex capital structure? Explain.
2. What kind of EPS presentation is required? Explain.
3. Compute the required EPS amounts (show computations).
4. Compute the required EPS amounts assuming the preferred is cumulative.

Exercise 18–6

At the end of 19A the records of Midas Corporation showed the following:

Common stock, nopar, authorized 200,000
shares:
Outstanding January 1, 19A 52,000
shares $624,000
Purchased treasury shares April 1, 19A,
2,000 shares (at cost) .... (50,000)
Issued a 100% stock dividend on
December 1, 19A, on the outstanding
shares (50,000 additional shares)
Preferred stock, par $10:
Class A, 6%, nonconvertible, noncumula-
tive, outstanding 10,000 shares 100,000
Class B, 5%, nonconvertible, cumulative,
outstanding 20,000 shares 200,000
Contributed capital in excess of par,
preferred stock 80,000
Retained earnings (no dividends were
declared in 19A) 420,000
Bonds payable, 7%, nonconvertible 150,000
Income before extraordinary items 180,500
Extraordinary loss (net of tax) 40,000
Net income 140,500
Average income tax rate, 40%.

Required:

1. Is this a simple or complex capital structure? Explain.
2. What kind of EPS presentation is required? Explain. Disregard the materiality test.
3. Compute the required EPS amounts (show computations).

Exercise 18-7

At the end of 19A the records of Sterling Corporation reflected the following:

Common stock, nopar, authorized 100,000
shares; issued and outstanding throughout
the year, 50,000 shares $600,000
Stock rights outstanding (for 10,000 shares of
common stock at $15 per share) 150,000
Preferred stock, 6%, par $10, nonconvertible,
cumulative, authorized 25,000 shares; is-
sued and outstanding throughout the year,
10,000 shares 100,000
Contributed capital in excess of par, preferred
stock 30,000
Retained earnings (no dividends declared dur-
ing the year) 290,000
Bonds payable, 9½%, nonconvertible 90,000
Income before extraordinary items 85,000
Extraordinary loss (net of tax) 15,000
Net income 70,000
Average income tax rate, 40%.
Average market price of the common stock
during 19A, $25 per share.
Bank prime interest rate at date of issuance
of bonds, 8%.

Required:

1. Is this a simple or complex capital structure? Explain.
2. What kinds of EPS presentation is required? Explain.
3. Compute the required EPS amounts (show computations and assume all amounts are material).

Exercise 18-8

At the end of 19A the records of Collins Corporation
reflected the following:

Common stock, nopar, authorized 200,000
shares; issued and outstanding throughout
the period to December 1, 19A, 60,000
shares. A stock split issued, December 1,
19A, which doubled the outstanding
shares. $750,000
Preferred stock, 5%, par $10, nonconvertible,
cumulative, nonparticipating, shares authorized, issued, and outstanding during the year,
10,000 100,000
Contributed capital in excess of par, preferred
stock 20,000
Retained earnings (no dividends declared during the year) 440,000
Bonds payable, 5%, each $1,000 bond is con-
vertible to 75 shares of the common stock
(bonds initially sold at 101.5) 200,000
Income before extraordinary items 86,000
Extraordinary loss .... (14,000)
Net income 72,000
Premium amortization on bonds payable for
19A, $60.
Average income tax rate, 40%.
Average market price of the common stock
during 19A, $9.
Bank prime interest rate (at date of issuance
of bonds), 8%.

Required:

1. Is this a simple or complex capital structure? Explain.
2. What kind of EPS presentation is required? Explain.
3. Compute the required EPS amounts (show computations, rounded to three decimal places, and assume all amounts are material).

Exercise 18-9

At the end of 19A the records of Fisher Corporation
reflected the following:

Common stock, nopar, authorized 500,000
shares; issued and outstanding throughout
the period, 100,000 shares $850,000

Stock dividend issued, December 31, 19A, 50,000 shares (not included in the 100,000 shares above)	425,000
Retained earnings (includes effect of dividends on all shares)	480,000
Bonds payable, 4½%, each $1,000 bond is convertible to 80 shares of the common stock (bonds initially sold at 99)	60,000
Bonds payable, 6½%, each $1,000 bond is convertible to 90 shares of the common stock (bonds initially sold at 97)	300,000
Income before extraordinary items	125,000
Extraordinary gain	12,000
Net income	137,000

Discount amortization for 19A: 4½% bonds, $20; 6½% bonds, $600.

Average income tax rate, 40%.

Average market price of the common stock during 19A, $13.

Bank prime interest rate at date of issuance: 4½% bonds, 6⅞%; 6½% bonds, 8%.

Required:

1. Is this a simple or complex capital structure? Explain.
2. What kind of EPS presentation is required? Explain. Disregard the materiality test.
3. Compute the required EPS amounts (show computations, rounded to three decimal places, and assume all amounts are material).

PROBLEMS

PART A
Problems 18–1 to 18–5

Problem 18–1

Dawson Corporation is authorized to issue 100,000 shares of common stock, par $25, of which 60,000 are outstanding. During 1979, the company initiated a stock bonus plan for certain executives. The plan provides for each qualified executive to receive an option for 1,000 shares of the common stock. Subject to continued employment, the option is exercisable at any time after three years and prior to expiration, which is five years from the date of grant. The option is nontransferable, and the specified option price is $60 per share. The option is considered to be additional compensation, prorated equally, for the year of the grant and the following four years. On January 1, 1979, J. Doe, the company president, was granted an option under the plan when the market price of the stock was $68. Assume Doe exercised the grant during the latter part of 1983 when the market price of the stock was $90 per share.

Required:

1. Is this a compensatory plan? Explain.
2. What is the measurement date? Explain.
3. What is the amount of the total compensation?
4. Over what period should this compensation be assigned as expense? How much should be assigned to 1979? to 1980? Explain.
5. Give appropriate entries on the following dates (if none, explain why):
   a. Date of grant.
   b. Measurement date.
   c. End of each year, starting on December 31, 1979.
   d. Exercise date.
6. Illustrate how the option would affect the income statements and balance sheets at the end of 1979 and 1980.

Problem 18–2

Samuels Corporation has a stock option plan for the top managers that includes the following provisions:

a. Each manager that qualifies will receive an option to acquire 10,000 shares of Samuels common stock, par $1, at an option price of $10 per share.
b. The option is nontransferable and, if not exercised, expires after five years from date of grant.
c. The option cannot be exercised prior to the end of two years from date of grant and requires continued employment in the company.
d. The stock option is for additional compensation for the year of the grant and the following four years; approximately equal each year.

An option was granted to the president on January 1, 1979, at which time the common stock was selling at $17 per share. Assume the option is exercised on December 31, 1983, when the stock is quoted at $35 per share.

At January 1, 1979, common stock, par $1 (authorized 200,000 shares), 90,000 were outstanding.

Required:

1. Is this a compensatory plan? Explain.
2. What is the measurement date? Explain.
3. Compute the total compensation expense
4. Over what period of time should this total compensation be assigned as expense? Explain.
5. Give appropriate entries for the following dates (if none, explain why):
   a. Date of grant.
   b. Measurement date.

c. End of each year, starting on December 31, 1979.

d. Exercise date.

6. Illustrate how the option would affect the income statements and balance sheets at the end of 1979 and 1980.

Problem 18–3

Henley Corporation has 100,000 shares of common stock, par $20, authorized, of which 40,000 shares are outstanding. The company has a stock option plan that provides the following:

a. Each qualified manager shall receive on January 1, a computed number of shares of common stock at a computed option price per share. The computation of each amount shall be made three years after the option is granted and will be related to the increase in net income over the three-year period. The plan provides additional compensation for qualified managers for services to be performed approximately equally during the years 1979–83.

b. The options are nontransferable and must be exercised not earlier than three years and not later than five years from date of grant. Affiliation with the company is required to the exercise date.

On January 1, 1979, an option was granted to A. B. Cox, the controller. At that date, the common stock was quoted on the market at $50 per share. Assume Cox exercised the option near the end of 1983.

	Estimates Made on December 31, 1979, of What the Amount Would Be on December 31, 1981*	Actual Amount on December 31, 1981
Number of shares optioned	500	510
Option price	$60	$62
Market price per share (a relatively steady increase each year)	$75	$78

  * Estimate at 12/31/80 same as estimate at 12/31/79.

Required:

1. Is this a compensatory plan? Explain.
2. When is the measurement date? Explain.
3. Over what period should total compensation expense for Cox be assigned?
4. Give appropriate entries (related to Cox) for the following dates (if none, explain why):
   a. Date of grant.
   b. End of 1979 and 1980.
   c. Measurement date.
   d. End of 1981, 1982, and 1983.
   e. Exercise date.

5. Show how the option would affect the income statements and balance sheets for 1980 and 1981

Problem 18–4

Davidson Corporation is authorized to issue 200,000 shares of common stock, par $10; to date 75,000 shares have been issued. On January 1, 1979, the corporation initiated a stock option plan for the three top managers. The plan provides that each manager will receive an option to purchase, no later than December 31, 1983, 2,000 shares of the common stock at a base option price of $48, adjusted for changes in earnings per share, and providing continued employment. The option price is to be established on December 31, 1981, and will be based on changes in earnings per share. EPS for 1978 was $2. The option price will be established at the end of 1981 as follows:

> The option price per share will be the base option price of $48 adjusted proportionately upward or downward in inverse relationship to changes in EPS from December 31, 1978, through 1981.

The options are nontransferable and expire on December 31, 1983. The stock was quoted at $45 per share on the market on January 1, 1979. On December 31, 1979, the management has made what they consider to be realistic estimates that earnings per share would increase steadily to $3.20 at December 31, 1981, and that the stock would increase steadily to $46 per share on that date. These estimates were not revised in 1980. EPS on December 31, 1981, actually turned out to be $3, and the actual market price was $50.

The president received the options with the option price unknown at January 1, 1979. Assume the president exercised the option, the last day possible, on December 31, 1983.

Required:

1. Is this a compensatory plan? Explain.
2. What is the measurement date? Explain.
3. Over what period should total compensation expense for the president be assigned?
4. Give appropriate entries (related to the president) on the following dates (if none, explain why):
   a. Date of grant.
   b. End of 1979 and 1980.
   c. Measurement date.
   d. End of 1981, 1982, and 1983.
   e. Exercise date.
5. Show how the option would affect the income statements and balance sheets for 1980 and 1981.

Problem 18–5

On January 1, 19A, the board of directors of Ebeneezer Corporation approved two stock purchase plans with respect to its common stock, par $10. The specifications of each plan were as follows:

Plan	Employees Eligible	Discount from Market Price	Date on Which the Number of Shares and Option Price Determined	Exercise Period
No. 1 ...	Executives	20%—Minimum option price of $28.	December 31, 19B	On January 2 and June 2 of 19E
No. 2 ...	All hourly employees	4%	January 2 of each year 19A–E	January 2 of each year 19A–E

Under Plan No. 1 employees will earn the options evenly over 19A–D. Plan No. 1 options expire on June 3, 19E.

During the years 19A–E, Ebeneezer Corporation completed the following transactions relating to the two plans (the accounting fiscal year ends December 31):

January 2, 19A:
   Plan No. 1—Granted an option for 1,000 shares to each of five executives.
   Plan No. 2—Granted an option for 50 shares to each of the 90 employees.
   Quoted price of the stock, $30 per share.

December 31, 19A:
   Quoted price of the stock, $35 per share.
   Estimated market price expected to be $37 per share on December 31, 19B.

December 31, 19B:
   Quoted market price, $40 per share.

January 2, 19C:
   Plan No. 2—Issued 4,500 shares based on the quoted market price of $40 per share.

January 2, 19E:
   Plan No. 1—Issued 1,500 shares.
   Quoted market price of the stock, $44 per share.

June 2, 19E:
   Plan No. 1—Issued 3,400 shares.
   Quoted market price of the stock, $45 per share.

June 3, 19E:
   All outstanding options lapse.

Required:

1. Is each plan compensatory or noncompensatory? Explain. When is the measurement date?
2. Give the required journal entries to record all transactions listed for
   a. Plan No. 1.
   b. Plan No. 2.

PROBLEMS

PART B
Problems 18–6 to 18–9

Problem 18–6

Beamer Corporation is developing the EPS presentation at December 31, 19A. The records of the company provide the following information:

Liabilities

Convertible bonds payable, 7% (each $1,000 bond is convertible to 20 shares of common stock)	$200,000

Stockholders' Equity

Common stock, nopar, authorized 100,000 shares:	
Outstanding January 1, 19A, 59,000 shares	236,000
Sold and issued 10,000 shares on April 1, 19A	40,000
Common stock rights outstanding (for 4,000 shares of common stock)	16,000
Preferred stock, 6%, par $10, nonconvertible, cumulative, authorized 20,000 shares, outstanding during 19A, 5,000 shares	50,000
Contributed capital in excess of par, preferred stock	10,000
Retained earnings	380,000
Income before extraordinary items	150,000
Extraordinary loss (net of tax)	(20,000)
Net income	130,000

Additional data:

a. Stock rights—option price, $4 per share; average market price of the common stock over 19A, $6 (also during last quarter).
b. Convertible bonds—issue price, 115; prime interest rate at date of issuance was 8%; premium amortization during 19A, $1,500.
c. Average income tax rate of 45%.

Required:

1. Is this a simple, or a complex, capital structure? Explain.
2. What kind of EPS presentation is required? Explain.
3. Prepare the required EPS presentation for 19A. Show all computations.
4. Were there any antidilutive securities? How was this determined?
5. How should antidilutive securities be treated in the computations of EPS? Why?

Problem 18–7

The records of Indus Corporation reflected the following data at the end of 19A:

Liabilities

Bonds payable, 6½%, convertible (each $1,000 bond is convertible to 30 shares of common stock)	$150,000

Stockholders' Equity

Common stock, par $2, authorized 300,000 shares:	
Outstanding January 1, 19A, 150,000 shares	300,000
Sold and issued on October 1, 19A, 20,000 shares	40,000
Common stock warrants outstanding (for 6,000 shares)	12,000
Preferred stock, 6%, par $5, nonconvertible, cumulative, authorized 100,000 shares, outstanding during 19A, 20,000 shares	100,000
Contributed capital in excess of par, common stock	340,000
Contributed capital in excess of par, preferred stock	60,000
Retained earnings	310,000
Income before extraordinary items	170,000
Extraordinary loss (net of tax)	(20,000)
Net income	150,000

Additional data:

a. Stock warrants—option price, $3 per share; average market price of common stock during 19A, $3.60 per share (also during last quarter).
b. Convertible bonds—issue price, 125; prime interest rate at date of issuance of the bonds was 8½%; premium amortization during 19A, $2,250.
c. Average income tax rate of 40%.

Required

1. Is this a simple, or a complex, capital structure? Explain.
2. What kind of EPS presentation is required? Explain.
3. Prepare the required EPS presentation for 19A. Show all computations. Disregard materiality test.
4. Were there any antidilutive securities? How was this determined?
5. How should antidilutive securities be treated in EPS computations? Why?

Problem 18–8

At the end of 19A, the records of AB Corporation showed the following:

Common stock, nopar, authorized 500,000 shares:	
Outstanding January 1, 19A, 200,000 shares	$1,800,000
Treasury shares acquired June 1, 19A, 1,000 shares (at cost)	(12,000)
Stock dividend issued, November 1, 19A, 19,900 shares (10%)	199,000
Stock rights outstanding for 20,000 shares of common stock at $15 per share.	
Preferred stock, 5%, par $20, cumulative, nonconvertible, authorized, issued, and outstanding throughout the year, 10,000 shares.	200,000
Contributed capital in excess of par, preferred stock	30,000
Retained earnings (after deducting current year dividends)	760,000
Bonds payable, Series A, 5%, each $1,000 bond is convertible to 20 shares of common stock (bonds issued at 101)	50,000
Bonds payable, Series B, 6½%, each $1,000 bond is convertible to 57 shares of common stock (bonds issued at 96)	400,000
Income before extraordinary loss	192,000
Extraordinary loss (net of tax)	(20,000)
Net income	172,000

Average income tax rate for 19A, 40%.
Average market price of the common stock during the last quarter of 19A, $20 per share.
Bank prime interest rate at date of issuance of: 5% bonds, 7½%; 6½% bonds, 8%.
Amortization for 19A: 5% bonds—premium, $40; 6½% bonds—discount, $800.

Required:

1. Is this a simple or complex capital structure? Explain.
2. What kind of EPS presentation is required? Explain.

Problem 18–9

The Ronson Automatic balance sheet at December 31, 19D, reported the following:

Long-term notes payable, 10%, due in 19G	$ 50,000
Bonds payable, 7%, each $1,000 of face value is convertible into 90 shares of common stock; bonds mature in 19M	800,000
Preferred stock, 5%, nonconvertible, cumulative, par value $100	300,000
Common stock, par value $5	700,000
Common stock rights outstanding entitling holders to acquire 40,000 shares of common stock at $9 per share	200,000
Net loss for 19D	125,000

Additional data:

1. During 19D, 1,000 shares of preferred stock were issued at par on September 1. Dividends are paid semiannually, or. May 31 and November 30. Declaration precedes payment by three weeks. On newly issued shares dividends are prorated from issue date.
2. Bank prime rate of interest was 7¾% when the convertible bonds were issued at 102. Premium amortization for 19D was $900.
3. Average market price of common stock during 19D was $15 (also during last quarter).
4. Income tax rate of Ronson is 40%.
5. Ronson earned taxable income of $400,000 during 19A–C.

Required:

Present the EPS data on the 19D income statement of Ronson Automatic in good form, along with supporting computations.

Long-Term Investments in Equity Securities

A company may invest in another company by acquiring either *(a)* debt securities (i.e., notes, mortgages, and bonds) or *(b)* equity securities (i.e., common and preferred stock). The investments may be acquired with the intention of holding them on a short-term or long-term basis. Short-term investments were discussed in Chapter 8.

Investments are classified as current assets when they meet the dual test of (1) ready *marketability* and (2) a clear *intention* by management to convert them to cash during the upcoming year or normal operating cycle, whichever is the longer. All investments that do not meet both of these criteria are classified as noncurrent assets on the balance sheet under the caption "Investments and Funds" (see Chapter 5). Investments classified under this category are referred to as long-term investments. They include debt and equity securities and other assets, such as land held for investment purposes. They may or may not meet the test of ready marketability; however, the intention of management must be to retain them beyond the time span for current assets.

The purpose of this chapter is to discuss the measuring, accounting, and reporting of long-term investments in *equity securities*. To accomplish this purpose, the chapter is divided into three parts: Part A—Cost, Equity, and Market Value Methods; Part B—Consolidated Statements, and Part C—Special Problems in Accounting for Stock Investments.[1] There is a general discussion at the start of the chapter. Long-term investments in *debt* securities are discussed in Chapter 20.

RECORDING LONG-TERM INVESTMENTS AT DATE OF ACQUISITION

At date of acquisition of a long-term investment, an appropriately designated investment account is debited for the full cost of the investment (i.e., market value), in accordance with the cost principle. Full cost includes the basic cost of the security plus brokerage fees, excise taxes, and any other transfer costs incurred by the purchaser. Stocks may be purchased for cash, on margin, or on a subscription basis. When stock is acquired on margin, only part of the purchase price is paid initially and the balance is borrowed. The stock should be recorded at its full cost, and the liability to the lender should be

---

[1] Subdivision of the chapter provides flexibility should consideration of consolidated statements be deferred to a more advanced course. However, consolidated statements are discussed briefly in this chapter because some accounting majors do not take an advanced course in consolidations and mergers.

recognized. A stock subscription to buy the stock of another corporation creates an asset represented by the stock investment and a liability for the amount to be paid. Interest paid on a subscription contract, or on funds borrowed to purchase the investment, should be recorded as interest expense and not capitalized as part of the cost of the investment.

When noncash considerations (property or services) are given for long-term investments, the cost assigned to the securities should be (1) the market value of the consideration given or (2) the market value of the securities received, whichever is the more reasonably determinable.[2] Inability to determine either value in an exchange of unlisted or closely held securities for property for which no established market value exists may require the use of appraisals or estimates.

Securities frequently are purchased between regular interest or dividend dates. Under generally accepted accounting principles, interest is accrued on debt securities but dividends are not accrued. In the case of a purchase of cumulative preferred stock on which the issuing corporation has been regularly paying dividends, the correct treatment is debatable. The authors would not accrue dividends (even in this case) because dividends legally do not accrue.[3]

To illustrate, assume that on October 1, 19A, X Corporation purchased 500 shares of the common stock of Y Corporation, par $5, at $20 per share. Dividends are paid regularly around July 1 of each year; the last dividend was $0.50 per share. The investment would be recorded as follows:

| Long-term investment, Y Corporation common stock (500 shares) | 10,000 | |
| Cash | | 10,000 |

(Note: No dividends are accrued.)

Alternatively, assume that on October 1, 19A, X Corporation purchased a $10,000, 6% bond (interest payable each July 1) of Y Corporation for $10,000 plus accrued interest. The acquisition of this long-term investment in *debt securities* would be recorded as follows:

Long-term investment, Y Corporation bond (at cost)	10,000	
Investment revenue ($10,000 \times .06 \times \frac{3}{12}$)	150	
Cash		10,150

(Note: Interest accrued to date of purchase is discussed in detail in Chapter 20.)

Special Cost Problems

A purchase of two or more classes of securities for a single lump sum (sometimes called a lump-sum or basket purchase) necessitates allocation of the total cost to each class of securities based upon their relative market values. For example, if a block of Security A purchased alone would cost $1,000 and a block of Security B purchased separately would cost $2,000, one third of the total lump-sum cost would be allocated to A and two thirds to B whether the combined cost was $3,000 or some other amount. In case one class of securities has a known market value and the other does not, the known market value is used for that class and the remainder of the lump-sum price is allocated to the other. If neither has a known market value, it is better to defer any apportionment until evidence of at least one market value is established.

Securities sometimes are acquired in exchange for other securities. The securities acquired should be recorded at the market value of those given up or their own market value at the time of the exchange, whichever is more clearly determinable. To illustrate an exchange of securities, assume that each holder of a share of $100 par value preferred stock in AB Corporation becomes entitled to receive in exchange five shares of nopar common stock of the company. An investor who had paid $6,000 for 50 shares of preferred stock makes the exchange. At the time of the exchange, the nopar common shares

---

[2] Unfortunately the accounting profession uses *fair value, market value, fair market value,* and *current market value* to describe the arm's-length price of an asset used in certain transactions and valuations. We generally use *market value* in this text because it is fully descriptive of the intended meaning. The word "fair" implies that "unfair" values might be used in the accounts, and the modifier "current" is redundant because market value presumes the one prevailing at the relevant time.

[3] Theoretically, dividends should be recognized when stock is purchased between the declaration date and record date (ex-dividend date). The price of a listed stock (especially preferred) tends to rise as the regular dividend date approaches and to decline by approximately the amount of the dividend as soon as the stock goes "ex dividends". Prices of stocks are subject to many variables which may obscure these price movements, even though they are present.

were selling at $27. The exchange would be recorded as follows:[4]

```
Investment in nopar common stock of
  AB Corporation ($27 × 250 shares).....  6,750
    Investment in preferred stock of AB
      Corporation......................          6,000
    Gain on exchange of stock
      investment ......................            750
```

In accounting for investments, generally, it is necessary to maintain an identification of each security acquired, which can be done by using the stock or bond certificate number. In effect, this requires the maintenance of inventory records with respect to securities in order that they may be properly "costed out" upon disposition. For example, if 10 shares of X Corporation stock are purchased at $150 per share and later an additional 30 shares are purchased at $200 per share, the subsequent sale of 5 shares at $180 per share would pose a cost identification problem. If the five shares can be identified by certificate number as a part of the first purchase, a gain of $30 per share should be recognized. Alternatively, if they are identified with the second purchase, a loss of $20 per share should be recognized. If an averaging procedure were applied, the result would be a loss of $7.50 per share computed as follows:

```
First purchase ............ 10 shares @ $150 =   $1,500
Second purchase.......... 30 shares @   200 =    6,000
      Total ..............  40                   $7,500

Average cost per share $7,500 ÷ 40 shares   = $187.50
Sales price per share.....................   =  180.00
      Loss per share .....................      $  7.50
```

Identification of shares sold ordinarily is not difficult. However, where blocks of shares have been transferred through an estate, or where the issuing corporation has exchanged substitute securities for those originally purchased, an identification problem can arise. Federal tax laws require use of "first-in, first-out" where specific identification cannot be made. Use of either *Fifo*

or an *average cost* procedure is acceptable from the standpoint of accounting theory; however, most companies use the same approach for tax and accounting purposes to avoid having to record deferred income taxes.

ACCOUNTING AND REPORTING FOR STOCK INVESTMENTS SUBSEQUENT TO ACQUISITION

In accounting for long-term investments in stock subsequent to acquisition date, *(a)* careful distinction is observed between voting common stock and nonvoting stock, such as nonvoting preferred stock and *(b)* the proportion of voting shares owned to the total shares outstanding (i.e., the level of ownership of the voting shares).[5]

Fundamentally, there are three different methods of accounting for and reporting stock investments, viz: (1) cost method, (2) equity method, and (3) market value method. Each of these methods is used under certain specified conditions. In addition, when one company owns a controlling interest in the voting stock of another company, the controlling company usually must prepare *consolidated financial statements* (discussed in Part B of this chapter).

The distinction between *voting common stock* and nonvoting stock is important because the former permits the owner to exercise some influence or control through voting on the operating and financial policies of the other company. The degree of influence or control depends upon the *proportion of outstanding voting shares owned* as an investment (usually the common stock) to the total of such shares outstanding. Therefore, in accounting for and reporting long-term investments in the voting capital stock of another company, *APB Opinion No.*

---

[4] A more extended discussion of the exchange of securities is presented in Chapter 20; there an alternate treatment whereby no gain or loss is recognized also is presented. The authors are of the opinion that the treatment illustrated here is preferable.

[5] Level of ownership refers to the proportion of shares owned to the total shares outstanding. To illustrate, assume Company X purchased 20,000 shares of common stock of Company Y when there were 100,000 total shares outstanding. The level of ownership by Company X in Company Y would be $20,000 ÷ 100,000 = 20\%$. Ownership of exactly 50% of the voting shares may fit the "significant influence" category or the controlling interest category, depending on other factors.

18, "Equity Method for Investments in Common Stock" (March 1971), defined two important concepts, "significant influence" and "control," essentially as follows:

1. Significant influence—This is the ability of the investor company to affect, in an important degree, the operating and financing policies of another company through ownership of a sufficient number of shares of its voting stock. Ability to exercise significant influence also may be indicated in several other ways, such as representation on the board of directors, participation in policy-making processes, material intercompany transactions, interchange of managerial personnel, or technological dependency. In order to achieve a reasonable degree of uniformity, the APB provided an operational rule that an investment of *20% or more of the outstanding voting stock* should lead to the presumption that in the absence of evidence to the contrary, an investor has the ability to exercise *significant influence* over the other company.

2. Controlling interest—A controlling interest exists when the investing company owns enough of the voting stock of the other company to effectively control its operating and financing policies. Ownership of *over 50%* of the outstanding voting stock usually would assure *control;* however, there are situations where this may not be the case (discussed in Part B). On the other hand, circumstances sometimes exist where ownership of less than 50% may create a controlling interest. Factors such as number of shares outstanding, number of shareholders, and the extent of shareholder participation in voting bear on the point at which a controlling interest is attained. Operationally, the presumption is that a controlling interest is represented by over 50% of the voting stock.

The issuance of *APB Opinion No. 18* had a significant impact on the accounting for long-term investments in capital stock. In accordance with certain prior pronouncements and *Opinion No. 18,* accounting for long-term investments in stock may be outlined as follows:

Accounting for Long-Term Equity Investments

Investment Characteristics	Level of Ownership	Reporting Method
A. No significant influence or control:		
1. Nonvoting stock owned.	All levels	Cost
2. Voting stock owned.	Less than 20%	Cost
B. Significant influence but not control:		
3. Voting stock owned.	20% through 50%	Equity
C. Controlling interest:		
4. Voting stock owned, but for special reasons not appropriate to consolidate.	Over 50%	Equity
5. Voting stock owned, appropriate to consolidate.	Over 50%	Consolidated statement basis

Part A of this chapter discusses and illustrates categories 1 through 4 above and the market value method. Part B discusses the accounting and reporting where there is a controlling interest and when *consolidated statements* are required—category 5.

PART A—COST, EQUITY, AND MARKET VALUE METHODS

COST METHOD

Under the cost method, a long-term investment in *equity securities* is recorded in the accounts at cost. Subsequently, it is reflected in the accounts and reported on the balance sheet at lower of cost or market (LCM). On this point, *FASB Statement No. 12* (December 31, 1975) states:

> The carrying value of a marketable equity securities portfolio shall be the lower of its aggregate cost or market value, determined at the balance sheet date. The amount by which aggregate cost of the portfolio exceeds market value shall be accounted for as the valuation allowance.

Marketable equity securities owned by an entity shall, in the case of a classified balance sheet, be grouped into separate portfolios according to the current or noncurrent classification of the securities for the purpose of comparing aggregate cost and market value to determine carrying amount. In the case of an unclassified balance sheet, marketable equity securities shall for the purposes of this Statement be considered as noncurrent assets.

Equity securities, as used in *Statement No. 12,* encompasses all capital stock (including warrants, rights, and stock options) except preferred stock that by its terms either must be redeemed by the issuing enterprise or is redeemable at the option of the investor. Treasury stock (see Chapter 17) and convertible bonds are excluded (see Chapter 20).

To apply the LCM concept, *Statement No. 12* defines *cost* after acquisition as the original cost of the equity security, except a *new cost basis* is established after acquisition in these situations:

a. When a marketable equity security is transferred between current and noncurrent classification if its market value is below cost.
b. When an individual marketable security (rather than the portfolio) has been written down to a market value below cost to reflect a permanent, as opposed to a temporary, decline in market value.

These two situations are discussed later.

Statement No. 12 makes a careful distinction between realized and unrealized gains and losses on marketable equity securities. A *realized* gain or loss represents the difference between the net proceeds received and the investment cost of an equity security at date of sale. In contrast, an *unrealized* gain or loss on a marketable equity security represents the difference between the aggregate market value and aggregate cost of the long-term investment portfolio on a given date. Realized gains and losses on a marketable equity security are recognized only when securities are sold (or written down because of a permanent decline), whereas unrealized gains and losses are recognized only at the end of the accounting period when the adjusting entry is made to apply the LCM concept to the *portfolio.*

In the adjusting entry, an allowance account (a contra asset account) is used to record the difference between aggregate (portfolio) cost and aggregate (portfolio) market, and an unrealized loss (or loss recovery) account is used for the other side of the entry. On the balance sheet, the allowance account balance is subtracted from the cost of the portfolio and the accumulated unrealized loss amount is reported under the owners' equity caption as unrealized capital. In contrast, recall from Chapter 8 that for short-term equity securities classified as *current assets, both* the realized and unrealized gains and losses are reported on the current income statement. Under no circumstances can the cumulative unrealized gains recorded exceed the cumulative unrealized losses on the long-term portfolio of equity securities.

Under the cost method, cash dividends received are recorded as investment revenue. Cash dividends should be recorded as a receivable on declaration date; however, if declaration and payment dates are during the same period, the same effect is attained by a single entry on the payment date as follows:

Cash (amount assumed)	7,500	
Investment revenue		7,500

Occasionally, an investor receives a dividend that is entirely, or in part, a *liquidating dividend* (see Chapter 17). Dividends received in excess of earnings accumulated since the acquisition date of the investment are considered liquidating dividends. In such instances, the investor should reduce the investment account for the amount of the liquidating dividend. Dividends received in noncash assets should be recorded at the market value of the assets received.

To illustrate application of the cost method for long-term investments in equity securities, the following series of transactions and entries for X Corporation are presented:

January 5, 19A—Purchased the following equity securities as a long-term investment (less than 20% of the outstanding shares in each case):

Y Corporation, common stock (par $5), 5,000 shares at $12.

Z Corporation, preferred stock (par $10, nonredeemable), 4,000 shares at $20.

Long-term investment in equity
securities 140,000
   Cash [(5,000 × $12) +
   (4,000 × $20)] 140,000

December 31, 19A—Adjusting entry to LCM. Market value: Y stock, $10; and Z stock, $21.

Unrealized loss on long-term
investment in equity se-
curities 6,000
   Allowance to reduce long-
   term investment in
   equity securities to market 6,000

Computation:

Security	Shares	Cost	Market	Unrealized Gain (Loss)
Y	5,000	@ $12 = $ 60,000	@ $10 = $ 50,000	$(10,000)
Z	4,000	@ 20 = 80,000	@ 21 = 84,000	4,000
Total ...		$140,000	$134,000	$ (6,000)*

*Note that the *unrealized* loss of $6,000 is the difference between aggregate (portfolio) *market* and aggregate (portfolio) *original cost.*

August 10, 19B—Unexpectedly sold 1,000 shares of the Z Corporation stock at $24.

Cash (1,000 × $24) 24,000
   Long-term investment in
   equity securities
   (1,000 × $20) 20,000
   Realized gain on sale of long-
   term investments* 4,000

* Closed to Income Summary. Note that the *realized* gain is the difference between *selling price* and *original cost.*

December 31, 19B—Adjusting entry to LCM. Market value: Y stock, $10.50; and Z stock, $22.00.

Allowance to reduce long-term investment in equity securities to
market 4,500
   Unrealized loss on long-term
   investment in equity securities 4,500

Computation:

Security	Shares	Cost	Market	Unrealized Gain (Loss)
Y	5,000	@ $12 = $ 60,000	@ $10.50 = $ 52,500	$(7,500)
Z	3,000	@ 20 = 60,000	@ 22.00 = 66,000	6,000
Total ...		$120,000	$118,500	$(1,500)

Balance in allowance account (before
December 31, 19B, adjustment) $6,000
Balance needed in allowance account 1,500
   Adjustment needed (debit) $4,500*

* Note that this amount is in fact a recovery of a previously recorded unrealized loss. Thus, the unrealized loss account is credited (i.e., reduced) for the loss recovery. The unrealized loss account is reported on the balance sheet.

The financial statements for X Corporation would reflect the following:

	19A	19B
Income Statement:		
Realized gain on long-		
term investment		$ 4,000
Balance Sheet:		
Funds and Investments:		
Investment in equity		
securities, at cost	$140,000	120,000
Less: Allowance to		
reduce equity in-		
vestment to market ..	6,000	1,500
Investment portfolio		
at LCM	$134,000	$118,500
Stockholders' Equity:		
Unrealized capital:		
Unrealized loss on		
investment in		
equity securities	(6,000)	(1,500)

In the case of a *permanent decline* (as opposed to a temporary decline) in the value of a long-term marketable equity security, the *individual* security (not the entire portfolio) must be written down to market. This reduced valuation thereafter is considered to be *cost;* that is, the amount of the writedown is accounted for as a *realized* loss and is reported on the current income statement.

To illustrate, refer to the above example. Assume Y Corporation stock was selling at $5 per share at the end of 19B and that the drop in value was clearly not temporary. This situation would be recorded as follows:

December 31, 19B—To record permanent decline in value of Y Corporation common stock (5,000 shares).

Realized loss, permanent decline in
valuation of equity security 35,000
   Long-term investment in equity
   securities [5,000 × ($12 − $5)] ... 35,000

Then, the unrealized loss and the allowance accounts would be adjusted to the end-of-period balances for LCM in the manner illustrated above. Observe in this particular case, the balances in the two accounts would be adjusted to zero because the market value of the *remainder* of the portfolio (i.e., the Z stock) exceeds cost.

In the case of a change in *classification* between short term (current) and long term (noncurrent) of an individual security, the security must be transferred at the LCM value at date of transfer. This value then becomes *cost* for subsequent periods. If market is below cost, the difference must be accounted for as a realized loss and reported on the current income statement.

To illustrate, refer to the earlier example. Assume Y Corporation stock was selected during 19B for sale during 19C and, therefore, was reclassified as a short-term investment at the end of 19B when the market value was $10.50 (cost was $12). This change in classification would be recorded as follows:

December 31, 19B—To record reclassification of Y Corporation stock (5,000 shares):

Short-term investment in equity securities (at market, $10.50)	52,500	
Realized loss on marketable equity securities*	7,500	
Long-term investment in equity securities (at cost, $12.00)		60,000

* Closed to Income Summary.

As explained above, the unrealized loss and the allowance accounts would be adjusted at the end of the period for the LCM effect.

The cost method is relatively simple and limits the recognition of revenue to cash or property dividends since the investor is presumed to have no ability to significantly influence or control the other company. Disclosure requirements are given in Chapter 8.

EQUITY METHOD

The equity method is conceptually different from the cost method. It is based on the presumption that the investor owns a sufficient number of the outstanding voting shares of another company (usually called the investee company) to exercise significant influence (although not control) over the operating and financial policies of the other company. An important element is influence over the *dividend policy* of the investee. This presumption radically changes the basis for recognition of *investment revenue* from that used in the cost method.

APB Opinion No. 18 states that investors should use the equity method in accounting for investments in common stock of unconsolidated subsidiaries (foreign as well as domestic) and also for investments in common stock where the "investment in voting stock gives it the ability to exercise significant influence over operating and financial policies of an investee even though the investor holds 50% or less of the voting stock." The *Opinion* also states that "an invest-

ment (direct or indirect) of 20% or more of the voting stock of an investee should lead to a presumption that in the absence of evidence to the contrary an investor has the ability to exercise significant influence over an investee."[6] *Opinion No. 18* sets forth procedures for applying the equity method. Among them are the following:

  a. Intercompany profits and losses should be eliminated until realized by the investor or investee as if a subsidiary, corporate joint venture or investee company were consolidated.

  b. A difference between the cost of an investment and the amount of underlying equity in net assets of an investee should be accounted for as if the investee were a consolidated subsidiary.

  c. The investment(s) in common stock should be shown in the balance sheet of an investor as a single amount, and the investor's share of earnings or losses of an investee(s) should ordinarily be shown in the income statement as a single amount except for the extraordinary items as specified in (d) below.

  d. The investor's share of extraordinary items and its share of prior-period adjustments reported in the financial statements of the investee in accordance with *APB Opinions Nos. 9* and *30* [and *FASB Statement No. 16*] should be classified in a similar manner unless they are immaterial in the income statement of the investor.

  e. A transaction of an investee of a capital nature that affects the investor's share of stockholders' equity of the investee should be accounted for as if the investee were a consolidated subsidiary.

  f. Sales of stock of an investee by an investor should be accounted for as gains or losses equal to the difference at the time of sale between selling price and carrying amount of the stock sold.

Thus, under the equity method the *cost* of the investment at acquisition date is recorded as a

---

[6] The equity method gives the same net results on the financial statements as would consolidation procedures discussed in Part B; as a consequence it is frequently referred to as "one-line consolidation". Recognition and amortization of goodwill as well as the elimination of intercompany transactions must be accounted for. Explanations and illustrations of the equity method often assume that the stock was purchased at its book value. This "book-value assumption" seldom if ever occurs; therefore, it imparts misleading knowledge of the concept and essence of the equity method.

debit to the *investment account.* Subsequently, each period the investment account is *(a)* increased for the investor's proportionate share (i.e., the percent of outstanding voting shares acquired) of the earnings (or decreased for losses) reported by the investee company and *(b)* decreased by all dividends received from the investee. Entries are then made to adjust the periodic reported income recognized *(a)* to eliminate any intercompany gains and losses ([*a*] above) and *(b)* for any differences in expenses (such as depreciation) arising when such expenses were reported by the investee and were based on the investee's carrying values that are different from market values at acquisition date. These latter entries are necessary because the investor must account for such expenses on the basis of the market value (i.e., investor's cost) of the related assets at acquisition date of the shares. Also if the investee's income statement reports extraordinary gains or losses, they likewise must be separately accounted for by the investor. Subsequent to acquisition, each period the investor:

1. Records the proportionate share of the investee's reported income by debiting the Investment account and crediting the Investment Revenue account. In case of a loss, the Investment account is credited and Investment Loss is debited. If the investee reports extraordinary items, they must be separately recorded in this entry. Thus, the investor's investment account increases and decreases with the gains and losses of the investee company. When the investee earns income, the investor is presumed to *earn* a proportionate part of that income, with a consequent increase in asset value (and vice versa for losses).
2. Records dividends received as a debit to the Cash account and a credit to the Investment account. In effect, dividends paid by the investee company to the investor are viewed as a conversion of part of the Investment account balance to Cash.
3. Records the proportionate share of additional expense if the investor's cost (i.e., market value on date of acquisition) was in excess of the investee's book value at that date.

Examples of additional expenses that must be recorded are as follows:

a. Depreciation expense. Assume Investor Company acquired 20% of the outstanding voting shares (hence a 20% interest in the net assets) of Investee Company. Assume further that at date of acquisition, depreciable assets owned by Investee Company were carried at $500,000, but the market value (cost to the investor) was $700,000 (a difference of $200,000). Assuming straight-line depreciation, a ten-year remaining life, and no residual value, Investor Company would have to recognize additional depreciation of $4,000 [i.e., ($200,000 × .20) ÷ 10 years]. Otherwise, the investment revenue recognized by the Investor Company and the investment account will be overstated. The additional depreciation amount is debited to the Investment Revenue account and credited to the Investment account since the depreciation reduces the revenue amount the Investor Company earns on the acquisition cost of the equipment. It would not be appropriate for Investor Company to record depreciation by debiting Depreciation Expense and crediting Accumulated Depreciation, because Investor Company reports the market value of depreciable assets of Investee Company as an implicit part of the cost in the investment account rather than in a separate operational asset account. A similar example would be the amortization of patents (or other intangibles) owned by Investee Company.

b. In a similar manner, assets held by the Investee Company at date of acquisition, such as inventory and short-term investments, may necessitate recognition of additional expense. For example, if the Investee's carrying value for inventory or short-term investments, is less than the market value (cost to the Investor), additional expense would have to be recognized as a credit to the Investment account and a debit to the Investment Revenue account. When this occurs, the entry is usually made in the year following acquisition because as current assets their disposal normally will be within that period. Likewise, when a long-term asset is disposed of subsequent to acquisition date of the investment, any gain or loss reported by the Investee Company must be adjusted for any "accounting differences" between the carrying value of the Investee and the market value recognized by the Investor. It is important to recall that all such adjustments to the investment account and the revenue account must be related to the proportionate ownership.

4. Records amortization each year of any purchased *goodwill* resulting from the acquisition transaction. As explained in Chapter 15, goodwill is measured as the excess of the cost of the investment to the investor over the *market value* of the identifiable net assets of the investee. Identifiable assets exclude goodwill because it is not physically identifiable or separately recorded in the accounts of the investee company in any form. For example, if goodwill purchased is computed to be $56,000 at acquisition date and if a forty-year amortization period is used, additional expense of $1,400 (i.e., $56,000 ÷ 40) would be recognized each year by the investor as a debit to Investment Revenue and a credit to the investment account. Good-

will is amortized against Investment Revenue because it reduces the amount the investor earns on the investment; it is credited to the investment account because it is included as an implicit element of acquisition cost that was recorded in that account.

5. Eliminates intercompany gains and losses (discussed in Part B).

6. Records gain or loss on the sale of all or a part of the investment equal to the difference between the sales price and the then carrying value of the investment (as reflected in the investment account).

To illustrate application of the equity method, assume that on January 1, 19A, Investor Company purchased 1,800 shares (representing 20%) of the outstanding voting common stock of Investee Company for $300,000 cash. Assume on date of acquisition the values given at the bottom of this page relating to Investee Company were assembled by Investor Company.

The *equity method* must be applied in this situation because Investor Company owns 20% of the outstanding stock of Investee Company as a long-term investment. The purchase of this investment would be recorded by Investor Company as follows:

a. January 1, 19A, date of acquisition—Purchase of 1,800 shares of Investee Company

	Data on Investee Company	
	Book Values Reported by Investee Company	Market Values Used by Investor Company
Assets not subject to depreciation:		
Inventory (*Fifo* basis)	$ 400,000	$ 405,000
Land	150,000	165,000
Total	550,000	570,000
Assets subject to depreciation (net of accumulated depreciation; remaining life, ten years)	500,000	700,000
Total Assets	$1,050,000	$1,270,000
Liabilities	$ 50,000	
Common stock (9,000 shares, par $100) $900,000		
Retained earnings 100,000	1,000,000	
Total Liabilities and Shareholders' Equity	$1,050,000	

stock (20% ownership) as a long-term investment:

```
Investment, Investee Company
   common stock (1,800 shares) .  300,000
      Cash . . . . . . . . . . . . . . . . . . . .        300,000
```

Assume further that at the end of the fiscal year, December 31, 19A, Investee Company reported the following:

```
1.  Income before extraordinary items  . . . .  $ 80,000
    Extraordinary gain (net of tax)  . . . . . . . .   30,000
    Net income  . . . . . . . . . . . . . . . . . . . . . .  $110,000
2.  Total cash dividends
    declared and paid during 19A  . . . . . . . .  $ 50,000
```

To apply the equity method, the first step is to compute the *goodwill purchased* and to identify the assets of the investee that have a market value different from their book value at acquisition date, viz:[7]

Computation of Goodwill and Related Asset Values

```
Purchase price for 20% interest
   of Investee Company . . . . . . . . . . . . . .          $300,000
Market value of identifiable
   net assets purchased:
   Total market value of assets
      of Investee Company . . . . . . . . . . . . .  $1,270,000
   Less total liabilities
      of Investee Company . . . . . . . . . . . . .      50,000
         Total identifiable net assets
            of Investee Company . . . . . . . . . .   1,220,000
   Proportionate part purchased
      by Investor Company . . . . . . . . . . . . .        × .20
   Market value of identifiable
      net assets purchased . . . . . . . . . . . . .                244,000
Goodwill purchased (20%) . . . . . . . . . . . .          $ 56,000
```

Proportionate part of each asset adjusted to market value:

	Investor's Cost (Market Value)		Investee's Book Value	Proportionate Part of Excess of Cost (Market) over Book Value
Inventory	$405,000	−	$400,000	(× 20%) = $ 1,000
Land	165,000	−	150,000	(× 20%) = 3,000
Depreciable assets	700,000	−	500,000	(× 20%) = 40,000*
Goodwill (per above) . . .	56,000	−	–0–	= 56,000†

```
* Additional annual depreciation: $40,000 ÷ 10 years = $4,000.
† Annual amortization of goodwill: $56,000 ÷ 40 years = $1,400.
```

---

[7] Recall the discussion of goodwill in Chapter 15. Purchased goodwill is the difference between the purchase price of all, or a proportionate part of, a business and the market value of the same proportion of the net assets of that business. Under generally accepted accounting principles, goodwill is recorded only when purchased. *APB Opinion No. 17* requires that all intangibles, including goodwill, be amortized over a reasonable period not exceeding 40 years.

The entries, *subsequent to acquisition date,* to reflect the effects in the accounts of Investor Company at the end of 19A would be as follows:

b. December 31, 19A—To recognize revenue and an increase in the investment account, based on the proportionate share of income reported by Investee Company:

```
Investment, Investee Company
   common stock
   ($110,000 × .20) . . . . . . . . . . . . . .  22,000
      Investment revenue (ordi-
         nary) ($80,000 × .20) . . . . . . .        16,000
      Extraordinary gain (appropri-
         ately identified) ($30,000
         × .20) . . . . . . . . . . . . . . . . . . . .          6,000
```

c. December 31, 19A—To record cash dividend received on Investee Company shares:

```
Cash ($50,000 × .20) . . . . . . . . . . . . .  10,000
      Investment, Investee Company
         common stock  . . . . . . . . . . .        10,000
```

d. December 31, 19A—To record depreciation on the $40,000 *increase* in depreciable assets implicit in the purchase (see tabulation at left):

```
Investment revenue (ordinary)
   ($40,000 ÷ 10 years) . . . . . . . . . . .  4,000
      Investment, Investee Company
         common stock  . . . . . . . . . . .         4,000
```

e. December 31, 19A—To record periodic amortization of the $56,000 goodwill purchased (as computed at left). Assume straight-line amortization over 40 years (maximum permitted by *APB Opinion No. 17*):

```
Investment revenue (ordinary)
   ($56,000 ÷ 40 years) . . . . . . . . . . .  1,400
      Investment, Investee Company
         common stock  . . . . . . . . . . .         1,400
```

f. December 31, 19A—To record additional cost of goods sold associated with excess of market value over book value of inventory of Investee Company (see above), assuming the goods were sold during 19A:

```
Investment revenue (ordinary)
   [($405,000 − $400,000) × .20] . .  1,000
      Investment, Investee Company
         common stock  . . . . . . . . . . .         1,000
```

No entry is required for the land because *(a)* it is not being sold and *(b)* it involves no depreciation or amortization.

The investment account and the two revenue accounts in the above illustration would be as follows:

**Investment, Investee Company Common Stock
(1,800 shares; 20%)**

a.	Acquisition (cost)	300,000	*c.*	Dividends received	10,000
b.	Proportionate share of net income of investee	22,000	*d.*	Additional depreciation	4,000
			e.	Amortization of goodwill	1,400
			f.	Inventory cost	1,000

(Ending debit balance, $305,600)

Investment Revenue (ordinary)

d.	Depreciation	4,000	*b.*	Reported income	16,000
e.	Amortization of goodwill	1,400			
f.	Inventory	1,000			
	To income summary	9,600			

Extraordinary Gain (appropriately identified)

To income summary	6,000	*b.*	Reported gain	6,000

The ending balance in the investment account represents the adjusted 20% ownership interest of Investor Company in the net assets of Investee Company. The $305,600 ending balance is reported on the balance sheet of Investor Company. The two revenue accounts represent the proportionate share of the income (as adjusted) of Investee Company that is recognized in the accounts of Investor Company.

For the investor, the equity method has significant conceptual and measurement differences from the cost method because each is based upon different concepts of (1) investment valuation and (2) revenue recognition. The conceptual difference is that the equity method effectively treats the Investor and Investee companies as one entity for investment valuation and income recognition purposes. In contrast, the cost method is used for investments in which this close relationship between the Investor and Investee does not exist. To illustrate the differences:

	Amount	Difference
Investment valuation:		
Cost method (remains at original cost)	$300,000	
Equity method (adjusted to proportionate share of net assets)	305,600	$5,600
Revenue recognition:		
Cost method (limited to dividends received):		
Investment revenue	$ 10,000	
Equity method (proportionate share of net income, adjusted):		
Investment revenue $9,600		
Extraordinary gain 6,000	15,600	$5,600

The two differences ($5,600) are the same because under the equity method the investment account is adjusted from the cost basis by the investor's share of the income of the investee, less dividends received. Similarly, investment revenue is different, as between the cost and equity methods by the investor's proportionate share of the income of the investee, less dividends received from the investee.

MARKET VALUE METHOD

The market value method of accounting for long-term investments is fundamentally different from the other methods. The market value method is based upon the concept of *current market value accounting;* that is, the investment is revalued at each balance sheet date to the then current market price of the securities held. Thus, *investment valuation* is at current market value and *investment revenue* for the period is comprised of dividends received plus or minus the change in the market value of the securities held during the period.

Many accountants believe that all marketable securities, whether short term or long term, should be accounted for using the market value method because market value data *(a)* report the economic consequences of holding the investment, *(b)* are more useful to decision makers than cost or equity data in projecting future cash flows, and *(c)* are objectively determinable for many stocks.

At the present time, the market value method is not in accordance with generally accepted accounting principles except in a few special circumstances.[8] Its use in special circumstances

---

[8] AICPA, *APB Opinion No. 18,* "The Equity Method of Accounting for Investments in Common Stock" (New York, March 1971), par 9. Also see Chapter 8.

is permitted under the modifying principle—industry peculiarities (see Chapter 2). The market value method is widely used today by insurance companies, pension funds, and mutual funds in accounting for their investment portfolios. The method is applied in those situations only to securities which are readily marketable; other methods are used for "nonmarketable" securities. The market value method may be outlined as follows:

1. At date of acquisition, investments are recorded at cost in accordance with the cost principle.
2. Subsequent to acquisition, the investment account periodically is adjusted to the then current market value of the securities held. The adjusted amount then becomes the "carrying value" for subsequent accounting.
3. Revenue recognized each period includes
   a. All cash or property dividends received during the period.
   b. The increase (or decrease) in the market value of the portfolio during the period. This is often referred to as the *market* or *holding gain* or *loss.*
4. At disposition of the investment, the difference between carrying value and sales price is recognized as a gain or loss.

To illustrate the market value method, assume Mutual Fund A purchased 3,000 shares (10%) of the outstanding common stock of Company B for $50 per share. The events and related journal entries for Mutual Fund A for a three-year period are given below for the *market value method:*

a. Year 1—purchased 3,000 shares of common stock of Company B at $50 per share.

Investment in Company B common stock (3,000 shares × $50)	150,000	
Cash		150,000

b. End of Year 1—Company B reported net income, $20,000.

No entry on books of Mutual Fund A.

c. End of Year 1—market price per share on Company B common stock, $55.

Investment in Company B common stock	15,000	
Investment revenue (holding gain on stock investment)		15,000
($55 − $50) × 3,000 shares = $15,000.		

d. End of Year 2—Company B reported net income, $22,000.

No entry on books of Mutual Fund A.

e. End of Year 2—Company B paid a cash dividend of $0.80 per share.

Cash (3,000 shares × $0.80)	2,400	
Investment revenue (dividends)		2,400

f. End of Year 2—market price of Company B common stock, $55.

No entry on books of Mutual Fund A, since market price is unchanged.

g. Year 3—sold 1,000 shares of the Company B stock at $54 per share.

Cash	54,000	
Loss on sale of investment in equity securities	1,000	
Investment in Company B common stock (1,000 shares × $55)		55,000

The market value method poses several critical problems in application; among them are the following:

1. Determination of market value—For instance, in a "thin market," a large block of stock may be overvalued if the price per share prevailing at a given time is simply multiplied by the number of shares held. Additionally, many accountants seriously question the appropriateness of using a price per share on a given day (such as last day of the period). To counter this alleged problem, arguments have been made for use of some form of average price per share.

2. Reporting the market gain or loss—Many take the position that the market gain or loss (such as the $15,000 gain recognized at the end of Year 1) should be viewed as an unrealized increment (or decrement) and reported separately as an element of owners' equity. In this view, only realized gain or loss would be reported on the income statement as "realized" upon disposal of the investment. In contrast, others believe that market gains and losses should

be reported on the income statement in the period in which they occur. In the illustration immediately above, this position was assumed. In contrast, if the market changes are accounted for as *unrealized,* the above entries would be changed as follows:

Entry *(c):* End of Year 1—market price per share on Company B common stock, $55.

Investment in Company B common stock	15,000	
Unrealized market gain on investments (stockholders' equity) [3,000 shares × ($55 − $50)] . . .		15,000

Entry *(g):* Year 3—sold 1,000 shares of Company B common stock at $54 per share.

Cash (1,000 shares × $54)	54,000	
Unrealized market gain on investments ($15,000 ÷ 3)	5,000	
Investment in Company B common stock (1,000 × $55)		55,000
Gain on sale of stock investment		4,000

Numerous arguments have been advanced in respect to the valuation of marketable securities at market value. The principal arguments cited against this are *(a)* it violates the cost principle and places on the balance sheet values that may not be objectively determined and may be temporary; *(b)* it introduces another variance between book and tax amounts; *(c)* it violates the traditional realization principle since revenue is recognized on market changes rather than on sale; and *(d)* because of the volatility of some stock prices, it introduces a possible "yo-yo" effect on net income. In contrast, the proponents disagree with the first two points and argue that *(a)* valuation at market value is more relevant information for decision making than costs which might have been incurred in the distant past; *(b)* it avoids "managed" earnings through the sale of selected investments acquired at a low original cost and a high current market value; *(c)* it avoids the LCM inconsistency; and *(d)* stock yield including both dividends and holding gains and losses should be reported on the income statement each period since that best reflects the current economic situation of the investment.

PART B—CONSOLIDATED STATEMENTS

The purpose of Part B is to present the fundamental concepts underlying consolidated financial statements. The numerous complexities involved are deferred to advanced texts that devote considerable attention to the topic.

CONCEPT OF A CONTROLLING INTEREST

When an investor company owns over 50% of the outstanding voting stock of another company, in the absence of overriding constraints, a controlling interest is deemed to exist. The investor company is called the *parent* company, and the other company is known as a *subsidiary.* In a parent-subsidiary relationship, both corporations continue as separate legal entities; consequently, they are separate accounting entities (refer to separate entity assumption, Chapter 2). As separate entities, they have separate accounting systems and separate financial statements. Because of the ownership relationship, the *parent company* (but not the subsidiary) is required to prepare *consolidated financial statements* which view the parent and the subsidiary (or subsidiaries) as a single economic entity. To prepare consolidated financial statements, the *separate* financial statements of the parent and the subsidiary are combined each period by the parent company into one overall set of financial statements as if they were one single entity. The income statement, balance sheet, and statement of changes in financial position are consolidated in this manner.

Consolidated financial statements are not always prepared when over 50% of the stock of another corporation is owned because certain constraints may preclude the exercise of a controlling interest. To qualify for consolidation as a single economic entity, two basic elements must be present (*ARB No. 51,* pars. 2 and 3):

1. Control of voting rights—This is presumed to exist when over 50% of the outstanding *voting* stock of another entity is owned by the investor. Nonvoting stock is excluded because it does not provide an avenue for control by vote. However, control may not exist even though over 50% of the voting stock is

owned, as in the case of a foreign subsidiary where restrictions are imposed by the foreign country such that effective control cannot be exercised by the parent company. In such situations, the subsidiary would not qualify for consolidation. These are commonly called *unconsolidated subsidiaries* and must be accounted for under the equity method (see Part A of this Chapter).

2. Most meaningful financial presentation—This means that the statement user must be given financial statements that best present the operating circumstances. In some situations this may result in "unconsolidated subsidiaries" because they are in different lines of business which are sufficiently incompatible that meaningful consolidation is not possible. For example, separate statements may be required for a bank or an insurance company where the parent is engaged primarily in manufacturing.

Although each affiliate (parent and subsidiaries) keeps separate books and prepares separate financial statements, these individualized statements do not present a comprehensive report of the *economic unit* as a whole. Since the entire economic unit is effectively under one management (and one group of stockholders), a financial report for that unit is essential to meet the needs of owners, creditors, and management. When a subsidiary is less than 100% owned, there is a group of minority shareholders (minority interest) to be recognized in the consolidated financial statements.

ACQUIRING A CONTROLLING INTEREST

There are often a number of economic, legal, and operational advantages to a parent-subsidiary relationship. A company may acquire a controlling interest in the voting stock of another company in two basic ways, viz:

1. Pooling of interests—The voting stock of an existing corporation is acquired by the parent by exchanging shares of its own capital stock for the acquired shares of the subsidiary. In this situation, the parent disburses

no cash or other assets and incurs no liabilities for the acquisition.

2. Purchase—The voting stock of an existing corporation is acquired by the parent by paying cash, transferring noncash assets, or incurring debt. In this situation, the parent disburses a significant amount of resources.

ACCOUNTING AND REPORTING PROBLEMS

Generally accepted accounting principles require that each subsidiary prepare its own financial statements in the usual manner. However, the parent company is required to prepare *consolidated* financial statements which include all subsidiaries, except those designated *unconsolidated* subsidiaries as described above. In consolidated financial statements, there is an item by item combination (aggregation) of the parent and subsidiary statements. For example, the amount of cash shown on a consolidated statement would be the sum of the amounts of cash shown on the separate statements of the parent and the subsidiaries.

The emphasis in accounting for a controlling interest is on the consolidated financial statements. Either the cost or equity method may be used by the parent company in its accounts; however, the resulting consolidated financial statements must be the same regardless of the accounting method used in the accounts.[9] There-

---

[9] In the case of a controlling interest, the investment account may be carried on either the cost or equity basis. The cost basis is often used because the parent company does not desire to formally enter into its accounts the income, dividend offset, additional depreciation, amortization of goodwill, and so on, required by the equity method. Also, the accounting periods may be different, and changes in percentage of ownership complicate the formal approach. Not infrequently, a company, when it moves from the equity approach range (i.e., 20%–50%) to a controlling interest range (over 50%), will adjust the accounts from the equity basis to the cost basis for these reasons. Since consolidation is a *reporting* approach, as opposed to an accounts approach, a worksheet is used; and the accounts of the parent are unaffected by the consolidation procedures. Under either method, the consolidation procedures are adapted on the worksheet so that the consolidated results are precisely the same whether the cost or equity method is used in the accounts. The cost method is used in the discussions in this chapter primarily for instructional convenience. When a parent company prepares unconsolidated statements for special purposes, all subsidiary and other stock investments that qualify must be reported on the equity basis.

fore, this part of the chapter will focus on the *preparation* of consolidated financial statements.

In preparing consolidated financial statements, the method of acquisition—pooling of interests versus purchase—has a significant impact both on the parent company and the consolidated statements.

Consolidated financial statements are prepared by means of a worksheet, and there is no need to make separate consolidation entries in the accounts. In practically all situations, a special worksheet approach is essential. The essential steps in preparation of the worksheet can be summarized as follows:[10]

1. The assets and liabilities of the subsidiary are substituted for the investment account reflected on the books of the parent. This is accomplished by "eliminating" the owners' equity accounts of the subsidiary against the investment account of the parent.
2. Elimination of intercompany receivables and payables.
3. Elimination of intercompany revenues, expenses, gains, and losses.
4. Elimination of other intercompany items.
5. Adjustments on the worksheet are made to reflect certain acquisition effects that differ from the book values, such as goodwill purchased by the parent as part of the cost of the investment in the subsidiary.
6. The remaining revenues and expenses of the parent and subsidiary are combined to derive a consolidated income statement.
7. The assets and liabilities of the parent and subsidiary are combined to derive a consolidated balance sheet.
8. The resource inflows and outflows of the parent and subsidiary are combined to derive a consolidated statement of changes in financial position.

Consolidated financial statements are commonly prepared *(a)* at the date of acquisition of

---

[10] It is important to realize that these steps refer to worksheet entries and to the resultant financial statements and not to the books of accounts of the respective entities which are continued as the records of separate legal entities.

a controlling interest (balance sheet only) and *(b)* for each accounting period subsequent to acquisition (income statement, balance sheet, and statement of changes in financial position). Consolidation results are significantly influenced by the way the stock of the subsidiary was acquired, that is, by pooling of interests or by purchase.

COMBINATION BY POOLING OF INTERESTS

The acquisition of a controlling interest by the parent company in the stock of the subsidiary company by an exchange of shares of stock often occurs because the combination can be effected without the disbursement of cash or other resources by the parent company. The exchange of shares is viewed as the *uniting of ownership interests* and not as a purchase/sale transaction between two companies and their shareholders. As a consequence, the recorded assets, liabilities, revenues, expenses, and so forth, for both entities are combined for consolidated statement purposes at their *recorded* book values. The incomes of the parent and its subsidiaries are combined and restated as consolidated income. Since a purchase/sale transaction is not presumed for the exchange of shares, market values of the assets of the subsidiary are not considered in consolidation.

APB Opinion No. 16, "Business Combinations," specifies "the combining of existing voting common stock interests by the exchange of stock is the essence of a business combination accounted for by the pooling of interests method." However, the *Opinion* specifies 12 conditions that must be met in order for the pooling of interests method to be appropriate; and if they are met, the pooling of interests method *must be used.* All combinations not meeting all 12 specifications *must* use the purchase method. Not all stock exchanges will meet the criteria for pooling of interests.

The general characteristics of the pooling of interests method of preparing consolidated statements may be summarized as follows:

1. The assets and liabilities of the combining companies are reported at the previously es-

tablished *book values* of each company. Although adjustments may be made to reflect consistent applications of accounting principles, the current market values of the assets of the subsidiary at the time of the combination are not used as a substitute for the book values at that date.

2. No goodwill results from the combination.
3. The Retained Earnings balances of the combining companies are added to determine the Retained Earnings balance of the combined companies at date of acquisition.
4. After combination, financial statements which pertain to precombination periods must be restated on the combined basis "as if" the companies were combined throughout those periods.

As stated above, at date of acquisition a consolidated balance sheet usually is prepared by the parent company; at the end of each subsequent period, a consolidated income statement, balance sheet, and a statement of changes in financial position are prepared.

Consolidated Balance Sheet Immediately after Acquisition, Pooling of Interests Basis. Assume that Company P (parent) acquired 90% of the outstanding voting stock of Company S (subsidiary); therefore, minority shareholders own the remaining 10%. Immediately prior to the exchange, their respective balance sheets reflected the following:

Amounts Immediately Prior to Acquisition—Company P and Company S

	Company P Book Value	Company S Book Value	Company S Market Value
Cash	$610,000	$ 20,000	$ 20,000
Accounts receivable (net)	10,000*	40,000	40,000
Inventories	20,000	30,000	25,000
Plant and equipment (net)	200,000	110,000	151,000
Patents (net)	20,000	10,000	14,000
	$860,000	$210,000	$250,000
Current liabilities	$ 10,000	$ 20,000*	
Long-term liabilities	50,000	40,000	
Common stock (par $100)	600,000	100,000	
Retained earnings	200,000	50,000	
	$860,000	$210,000	

* At date of acquisition, Company S owed Company P $5,000 accounts payable. For liabilities, carrying and market value are assumed to be the same.

Company P issued 900 shares of its $100 par common stock to the shareholders of Company S for 900 shares of the outstanding $100 par common stock of Company S. This is an exchange of shares (a continuity of the previously existing ownership), and we will assume that it meets the 12 conditions (specified in *APB Opinion No. 16*) for pooling of interests (one of the criteria requires at least 90% ownership). Company S will continue as a separate legal entity and as a 90% subsidiary of Company P. The exchange would not affect the books of Company S; however, Company P would make the following entry at date of acquisition:[11]

At date of acquisition:

Investment in Company S common
  stock (90% ownership) 90,000
    Common stock (900 shares at
      $100 par) 90,000

Now, assume that Company P prepares a consolidated balance sheet *immediately after* the acquisition; the worksheet used, on a pooling of interests basis, is shown in Exhibit 19–1.

The worksheet is started by entering the two separate balance sheets, using *book values* for each company immediately *after* the acquisition entry. Note that two account balances on the Company *P* balance sheet (i.e., the investment and parent common stock accounts) were changed to reflect the above acquisition entry. The worksheet is designed to provide an orderly procedure for combining the two separate balance sheets into a consolidated statement (the last column). The pair of columns for *eliminations* is used to prevent double counting of *reciprocal items* (i.e., items that are strictly

---

[11] Since this entry, under the pooling of interests concept, is not viewed as a purchase/sale transaction, it is generally recorded at par value of the stock issued or the proportionate share acquired of the subsidiary's contributed capital. Some accountants prefer to use average contributed capital per share. This is an unsettled issue; however, in any case, the elimination entry is adapted to attain the pooling of interests result. Par value equal to the proportionate share of the subsidiary's contributed capital is used in this discussion because of its instructional convenience. Consideration of the broader issue is beyond the scope of this chapter (refer to *Advanced Accounting* of this series). The exchange ratio is largely conditioned by the economic worth of the two entities involved.

EXHIBIT 19-1
Consolidation Worksheet to Develop Balance Sheet

COMPANY P AND ITS SUBSIDIARY, COMPANY S (90% INTEREST)
Pooling of Interests Basis
Immediately after Acquisition

Account	Balance Sheet per Books		Eliminations		Consolidated Balance Sheet
	Company P	Company S	Debit	Credit	
Cash	610,000	20,000			630,000
Accounts receivable	10,000	40,000		(b) 5,000	45,000
Inventories	20,000	30,000			50,000
Investment in Company S	90,000*			(a) 90,000	
Plant and equipment (net)	200,000	110,000			310,000
Patents	20,000	10,000			30,000
	950,000	210,000			1,065,000
Current liabilities	10,000	20,000	(b) 5,000		25,000
Long-term liabilities	50,000	40,000			90,000
Common stock (par $100):					
Parent	690,000*				690,000
Subsidiary		100,000	(a) 90,000		10,000M
Retained earnings:					
Parent	200,000				200,000
Subsidiary		50,000			45,000 5,000M
	950,000	210,000			1,065,000

M—minority shareholders' 10% interest in Company S.
* Includes effects of acquisition entry.
Eliminations:
  (a) To eliminate the investment account balance against the stockholders' equity (90%) of the subsidiary.
  (b) To eliminate the intercompany debt of $5,000.

between the two companies). In this instance, there are two such items that must be eliminated, viz:

a. The investment account balance reflected on the balance sheet of Company P ($90,000) must be eliminated because in its place the various assets and liabilities of Company S will be added to those of the parent. Similarly, 90% of the common stock reported by Company S must be offset because it is owned now by the parent. Thus, entry *(a)* on the worksheet offsets the investment account balance on the balance sheet of the parent against the stock account reflected on the balance sheet of the subsidiary.

b. Intercompany debt—Included in current lia-

bilities of Company S is $5,000 accounts payable owed to Company P; therefore, accounts receivable on the balance sheet of Company P also includes this amount. When the two balance sheets are combined, this intercompany debt must be eliminated, since it is not a payable or receivable involving the combined entity and outsiders. Entry *(b)* on the worksheet effects this elimination.

After the elimination entries for all intercompany items are reflected on the worksheet, the two balance sheets are aggregated horizontally line by line. The 10% interest of the *minority shareholders* of Company S represented by their proportionate share of the stockholders' equity is set out separately (denoted as M). The last column provides all the data needed to prepare a formal consolidated balance sheet. Note that the *book values* of Company S are added to the *book values* of Company P; the market values given in the data above do not affect a combination by pooling of interests.

COMBINATION BY PURCHASE

The acquisition of a controlling interest by purchase occurs when the combination does not meet all of the 12 conditions for a pooling of interests. Typically, an acquisition by purchase occurs when the parent company acquires a controlling interest in the subsidiary company by purchasing the voting stock with cash or other resources. This situation is viewed as a purchase/sale transaction, and the *market values* related to the *subsidiary* must be introduced into the consolidation procedures in accordance with the cost principle. *APB Opinion No. 16* states: "Accounting for a business combination by the purchase method follows the principles normally applicable under historical cost accounting to recording acquisitions of assets and issuances of stock and to accounting for assets and liabilities after acquisition." This means that the parent company must debit the investment account for the market value of the shares of the subsidiary acquired, on the presumption that the parent paid market value for the investment. The significant implication of this requirement is that in preparing consolidated statements, the assets of the *subsidiary* (including any purchased goodwill) must be valued at their *market value at date of acquisition* before being aggregated with the *book values* of the assets of the parent company. Recall that in a pooling of interests, book values rather than market values of the subsidiary are used in consolidation.

Although there are numerous additional complexities in application of the purchase method, the general characteristics may be outlined as follows:

1. The assets and liabilities of the subsidiary are reported by the parent company at their date of acquisition cost in conformity with the cost principle. Cost is the price paid for the stock of the subsidiary (cash equivalent cost) and is the *market value* at that date.

2. Individual assets of the subsidiary are reported at their individual market values as of the date of acquisition. These include all identifiable tangible and intangible assets (receivables, inventory, land, equipment, patents, etc.). Liabilities of the subsidiary usually are reported at their book values.

3. The difference between the total purchase cost and the market value of the *identifiable* assets acquired (less the liabilities assumed) is reported as "goodwill from acquisition." Goodwill from acquisition is subsequently amortized as an expense on the parent's income statements.

4. At date of combination, the Retained Earnings balance of the combined entity is defined as the Retained Earnings balance of the parent company; that is, the Retained Earnings balance of the subsidiary is eliminated (not carried forward).

5. After the combination, financial statements which pertain to precombination periods must depict the historical data of the parent company only.

Consolidated Balance Sheet Immediately after Acquisition, Purchase Basis. To illustrate preparation of a consolidated balance sheet on a *purchase basis* immediately after acquisition, we will again use the data given for Company P and Company S on page 659. Assume Company P purchased, in the open market, 90% of the 1,000 shares of outstanding stock of Company S for $211,000 cash. Company S will not make an entry to recognize this sale of stock by its stockholders because it did not engage in the transaction; however, Company P will record the purchase, at cost, as follows:

At date of acquisition:

Investment in Company S common stock, (90% ownership)	211,000	
Cash		211,000

Assume that Company P prepares a consolidated balance sheet *immediately after* acquisition and the purchase method must be used. The first step is to determine the amount of *goodwill purchased* in consideration of the market values and to identify the assets of the subsidiary that have a market value different from their book value as follows:

Computation of Goodwill and Related Asset Values*

Purchase price for 90% interest in Company S		$211,000
Market value of identifiable *net* assets purchased:		
Total market value of identifiable assets of company S (page 659)	$250,000	
Less total liabilities of Company S	60,000	
Total identifiable *net* assets of Company S	190,000	
Proportional part purchased by Company P	×.90	
Market value of identifiable *net* assets purchased		171,000
Goodwill purchased		$ 40,000

Proportionate part of each asset adjusted to market value:

	Parent's Cost (Market Value)		Subsidiary's Book Value	Proportionate Part of Excess of Cost (Market) over Book Value
Inventory	$ 25,000	—	$ 30,000	(×.90) = $ (4,500)
Plant and equipment	151,000	—	110,000	(×.90) = 36,900
Patents	14,000	—	10,000	(×.90) = 3,600
Goodwill (per above)	40,000		-0-	40,000
Total (see worksheet entry [a])				$76,000

* If total purchase cost is less than the summed market values of individual assets less liabilities, the difference is applied to reduce the valuations of the identifiable tangible and intangible assets. That is, negative goodwill is not recognized.

The worksheet shown in Exhibit 19–2 is started by entering the two balance sheets, using amounts immediately after the acquisition entry. Observe that two accounts (i.e., Cash and Investments) on Company P balance sheets have been changed to reflect the acquisition entry. Also, the middle pair of columns are headed "Eliminations and Adjustments" because (a) the eliminating entries must be made and (b) the assets of Company S must be *adjusted* from book value by the proportionate part of the market value. The above computation of goodwill and

related asset amounts indicates that inventories must be reduced by $4,500; plant and equipment increased by $36,900; patents increased by $3,600; and goodwill recorded in the amount of $40,000 to reflect the proportionate part of the excess of market value over book value of each of these items acquired by Company P. The net offset for these amounts is recorded in the Investment account as an elimination because that account was debited at acquisition for the market value of the total net assets acquired (90%). Elimination entries also must be made for (a) the proportionate part of the stockholders' equity of the subsidiary owned by the parent and (b) the intercompany debt. All of these adjustments and eliminations are reflected on the worksheet in Exhibit 19–2. Each entry is explained immediately below the worksheet.

The worksheet is completed by extending each item horizontally, taking into consideration the eliminations and adjustments. The last column provides all of the data needed to prepare a formal consolidated balance sheet on the purchase basis.

In summary, a comparison of Exhibit 19–1 with Exhibit 19–2 reflects the following underlying conceptual difference: in pooling of interests the book values of the subsidiary are added to the book values of the parent, whereas in a purchase the market values of the subsidiary at acquisition are added to the book values of the parent. In the illustrations of consolidation to follow, this basic difference will be maintained in the combined statements for subsequent periods.

PREPARING CONSOLIDATED STATEMENTS SUBSEQUENT TO ACQUISITION

At the end of each accounting period subsequent to acquisition of a controlling interest in another company, the parent company will prepare a consolidated balance sheet, consolidated income statement, and consolidated statement of changes in financial position. The worksheet illustrated above can be expanded to develop a consolidated balance sheet and income statement. A separate worksheet usually

EXHIBIT 19–2
Consolidation Worksheet to Develop Balance Sheet

COMPANY P AND ITS SUBSIDIARY, COMPANY S (90% OWNERSHIP)
Purchase Basis
Immediately after Acquisition

Account	Balance Sheet per Books		Eliminations and Adjustments		Consolidated Balance Sheet
	Company P	Company S	Debit	Credit	
Cash	399,000*	20,000			419,000
Accounts receivable	10,000	40,000		(c) 5,000	45,000
Inventories	20,000	30,000		(a) 4,500	45,500
Investment in Company S	211,000*			(a) 76,000	
				(b) 135,000	
Plant and equipment (net)	200,000	110,000	(a) 36,900		346,900
Patents	20,000	10,000	(a) 3,600		33,600
Goodwill			(a) 40,000		40,000
	860,000	210,000			930,000
Current liabilities	10,000	20,000	(c) 5,000		25,000
Long-term liabilities	50,000	40,000			90,000
Common stock:					
Company P	600,000				600,000
Company S		100,000	(b) 90,000		10,000M
Retained earnings:					
Company P	200,000				200,000
Company S		50,000	(b) 45,000		5,000M
	860,000	210,000			930,000

M—minority shareholders' 10% interest in Company S.
* Includes effects of the acquisition entry ($610,000 − $211,000 = $399,000).
Eliminations and adjustments:
(a) To record the adjustment of assets to market value and to eliminate the net effect from the investment account (per goodwill computation above).
(b) To eliminate the proportionate part of the stockholders' equity of the subsidiary (90%) and to eliminate an equal amount from the investment account (which is now zero).
  (Note: Entries [a] and [b] may be combined.)
(c) To eliminate the intercompany payable/receivable of $5,000.

is needed to develop a consolidated statement of changes in financial position.

In this section, an expanded worksheet to develop a consolidated balance sheet and income statement subsequent to acquisition will be illustrated assuming (a) pooling of interests and (b) purchase. The same data will be used for both illustrations. The section will conclude with an illustration of the formal consolidated statements on a purchase basis.

Consolidated Statements Subsequent to Acquisition, Pooling of Interests Basis. To illustrate the preparation of a consolidated balance sheet and income statement one year after acquisition, the illustration of Companies P and S given on page 659 will be continued (also refer to Exhibits 19–1 and 19–2). Assume it is one year later, December 31, 19A, and that the *separate* financial statements for Companies P and S reflect the following:

Amounts at End of 19A—Pooling of Interests Basis

	At December 31, 19A	
	Company P	Company S
Income Statement:		
Sales revenue	$520,000	$105,000 (a)
Cost of goods sold	300,000 (a)	53,000
Depreciation	20,000	4,000
Patent amortization	2,000	1,000
Other expenses	138,000	35,000
Total expenses	460,000	93,000
Net Income	$ 60,000	$ 12,000
Balance Sheet:		
Cash	$639,000	$ 24,000
Accounts receivable (net)	15,000 (b)	45,000
Inventories	30,000	29,000
Investment in Company S		
(pooling basis)	90,000 (c)	
Plant and equipment (net)	180,000	106,000
Patents (net)	18,000	9,000
Total assets	$972,000	$213,000
Current liabilities	$ 12,000	$ 21,000 (b)
Long-term liabilities	40,000	30,000
Common stock (par $100)....	690,000	100,000
Retained earnings	230,000 (d)	62,000
Total equities	$972,000	$213,000

(a) Includes intercompany sales of $7,000; transferred at cost.
(b) Includes intercompany debt of $3,000.
(c) Carried forward at amount recorded at date of acquisition.
(d) During 19A, Company P declared and paid a $30,000 cash dividend.

The expanded consolidation worksheet is shown in Exhibit 19–3 for the pooling of interests basis. Note that it is the same type as the worksheet shown in Exhibit 19–1 (consolidated balance sheet at acquisition) with the income statement added. The reported amounts from the separate statements are entered directly on the worksheet. For worksheet convenience, and to facilitate understanding, common stock, retained earnings at date of acquisition, and income since acquisition are set out separately. The worksheet involves only one item not previously discussed—the $7,000 intercompany sales. During the year, Company S transferred to Company P goods with a cost of $7,000. Company S recorded this as a sale, and Company P recorded it as a purchase (cost of goods sold). This is an intercompany item that must be eliminated to prevent double counting of sales and cost of goods sold; when Company P sold the goods to outsiders, a sale was recorded at that time.[12] The eliminations are explained at the bottom of the worksheet. Since the consolidated statements are prepared on a pooling of interests basis, the *book values* of the two companies are aggregated item by item. Note that consolidated income is the sum of the net income amounts reported by the companies separately; the same is true with respect to consolidated retained earnings.

Consolidated Statements Subsequent to Acquisition, Purchase Basis. To illustrate the preparation of a consolidated balance sheet and income statement one year after acquisition, the financial statements for Companies P and S given on on this page at the left will be used. Since that information assumes pooling of interests, the following adaptations are necessary to reflect the *purchase* basis:

Company P balance sheet:

a. Reduce the cash balance to $428,000 (i.e., $639,000 − $211,000) because of the cash paid at acquisition date for the stock of Company S (see entry on page 661).
b. Increase Investment in Company S to $211,000 to reflect the cost recorded at acquisition date.
c. Decrease Common stock, Company P to $600,000 because no such shares were issued to acquire the shares of Company P.
d. Assume the following estimated remaining lives from acquisition date for Company S:
Plant and equipment, 10 years.
Patents, 10 years.
Goodwill, 40 years.

The goodwill and related asset values computed at date of acquisition (page 662) are used, *without change,* for consolidation purposes in subsequent years. Recall the following amounts: goodwill, $40,000; inventory decrease, $4,500; plant and equipment increase, $36,900; and patents, increase $3,600.

---

[12] The elimination of intercompany sales of $7,000 assumed the goods were transferred at cost. If (a) the transfer price included an element of profit for the selling entity and (b) the goods were still held by the purchasing entity, the profit residue (unrealized intercompany inventory profit) would be eliminated by debiting Sales for the sales price, crediting Cost of Goods Sold for the cost price, and crediting Ending Inventory for the seller's markup.

EXHIBIT 19–3
Worksheet to Develop Consolidated Income Statement and Balance Sheet

COMPANY P AND ITS SUBSIDIARY, COMPANY S (90% OWNERSHIP)
At December 31, 19A
Pooling of Interests Basis

Items	Reported Amounts		Eliminations		Consolidated Statements
	Company P	Company S	Debit	Credit	
Income Statement:					
Sales revenue	520,000	105,000	(c) 7,000		618,000
Cost of goods sold	300,000	53,000		(c) 7,000	346,000
Depreciation	20,000	4,000			24,000
Patent amortization	2,000	1,000			3,000
Other expenses	138,000	35,000			173,000
	460,000	93,000			546,000
Income (to balance sheet)	60,000	12,000			72,000
Apportioned for consolidation:					
Minority interest					
(10% × $12,000)					1,200M
Parent interest					70,800
Balance Sheet:					
Cash	639,000	24,000			663,000
Accounts receivable (net)	15,000	45,000		(b) 3,000	57,000
Inventories	30,000	29,000			59,000
Investment in Company S	90,000*			(a) 90,000	–0–
Plant and equipment (net)	180,000	106,000			286,000
Patents	18,000	9,000			27,000
	972,000	213,000			1,092,000
Current liabilities	12,000	21,000	(b) 3,000		30,000
Long-term liabilities	40,000	30,000			70,000
Common stock:					
Company P	690,000*				690,000
Company S		100,000	(a) 90,000		10,000M
Retained earnings (at acquisition):					
Company P ($200,000 − $30,000)	170,000				170,000
Company S		50,000			5,000M
					45,000
Income (from income statement)	60,000	12,000			1,200M
					70,800
	972,000	213,000			1,092,000

M—minority shareholders' interest of 10% in Company S.
* Includes effects of the acquisition entry (page 659).
Eliminations:
   (a) To eliminate investment account balance against stockholders' equity (90% ownership) of the subsidiary.
   (b) To eliminate intercompany debt of $3,000.
   (c) To eliminate intercompany sales of $7,000 (at cost).

The expanded consolidation worksheet is shown in Exhibit 19–4 on the purchase basis. Note that it follows the format shown in Exhibit 19–2 (consolidated balance sheet at date of acquisition) with the addition of the income state-

ment. Recall on the worksheet (Exhibit 19–2) there were *(a)* adjustments of the assets of Company S to market value, including goodwill; *(b)* elimination of subsidiary owners' equity; and *(c)* elimination of intercompany debt. Exhibit 19–4

EXHIBIT 19–4
Worksheet to Develop Consolidated Income Statement and Balance Sheet

COMPANY P AND ITS SUBSIDIARY, COMPANY S (90% OWNERSHIP)
At December 31, 19A
Purchase Basis

Items	Reported Amounts		Adjustments and Eliminations		Consolidated Statements
	Company P	Company S	Debit	Credit	
Income Statement:					
Sales revenue	520,000	105,000	(e) 7,000		618,000
Cost of goods sold	300,000	53,000		(e) 7,000	346,000
Depreciation	20,000	4,000	(d) 3,690		27,690
Patent amortization	2,000	1,000	(d) 360		3,360
Goodwill amortization			(d) 1,000		1,000
Other expenses	138,000	35,000			173,000
	460,000	93,000			551,050
Income (to balance sheet)	60,000	12,000			66,950
Apportioned for consolidation:					
Minority interest					
(10% × $12,000)					1,200M
Parent interest					65,750
Balance Sheet:					
Cash	428,000*	24,000			452,000
Accounts receivable (net)	15,000	45,000		(c) 3,000	57,000
Inventories	30,000	29,000		(a) 4,500†	54,500
Investment in Company S	211,000*			(a) 76,000	
				(b) 135,000	–0–
Plant and equipment (net)	180,000	106,000	(a) 36,900	(d) 3,690	319,210
Patents	18,000	9,000	(a) 3,600	(d) 360	30,240
Goodwill			(a) 40,000	(d) 1,000	39,000
	882,000	213,000			951,950
Current liabilities	12,000	21,000	(c) 3,000		30,000
Long-term liabilities	40,000	30,000			70,000
Common stock:					
Company P	600,000				600,000
Company S		100,000	(b) 90,000		10,000M
Retained earnings (at acquisition):					
Company P ($200,000 − $30,000)	170,000				170,000
Company S		50,000	(b) 45,000		5,000M
Income (from income statement)	60,000	12,000			1,200M
					65,750
	882,000	213,000			951,950

M—minority interest share in Company S (10%).
* Includes effects of acquisition entry.
† *Lifo* assumed. When this cost flows out of inventory this credit would be to cost of goods sold, subsequently it would be credited to Company P retained earnings.
Adjustments and eliminations:
   (a) To adjust the assets of Company S to market and to eliminate the net effect from the investment account (per goodwill computations page 662).
   (b) To eliminate the proportionate part of stockholders' equity (90%) and to eliminate an equal amount from the investment account (which is now zero).
   (c) To eliminate the intercompany debt, $3,000.
   (d) To recognize additional market value expenses: depreciation, $36,900 ÷ 10 years = $3,690; patent amortization, $3,600 ÷ 10 years = $360; and goodwill amortization, $40,000 ÷ 40 years = $1,000.
   (e) To eliminate intercompany sales, $7,000 (at cost).

includes one additional concept not previously discussed; that is, the writeup of Company S assets, including goodwill, necessitates *adjustments* for *additional* depreciation, patent amortization, and amortization of goodwill for the period (adjustment [d]). The eliminations and adjustments are explained below the worksheet.

The consolidated income statement and balance sheet (purchase basis) for Company P is shown in Exhibit 19–5. Note the manner of presenting the minority interest and the more descriptive caption for goodwill, "Cost of investment in excess of market value of identifiable net assets of subsidiary."

Alternatively, the minority interest reported in Exhibit 19–5 often is reported along the following lines:

Stockholders' Equity		
Common stock, par $100, 6,000 shares outstanding		$600,000
Retained earnings		235,750
Total interest of parent company		835,750
Interest of minority stockholders in subsidiary:		
Common stock	$ 10,000	
Retained earnings	6,200	16,200
Total stockholders' interest including interest of minority stockholders		$851,950

Most *published* corporate financial statements are consolidated statements involving one or more subsidiaries. Full disclosure on consolidated statements normally requires extensive use of notes to the statements, as illustrated in the Appendixes to Chapters 4 and 5.

In summary, we can compare the results of pooling of interests with purchase as reflected in the common situation as illustrated in Exhibits 19–3 and 19–4, viz:

	Basis		Difference— Pooling over Purchase
	Pooling	Purchase	
Net income:			
Parent interest	$ 70,800	$ 65,750	$ 5,050
Minority interest	1,200	1,200	-0-
Cash	663,000	452,000	211,000
Plant and equipment (net)	286,000	319,210	(33,210)
Goodwill	-0-	39,000	(39,000)
Liabilities	100,000	100,000	-0-
Capital stock, Company P	690,000	600,000	90,000
Retained earnings:			
Parent interest	285,800	235,750	50,050
Minority interest	6,200	6,200	-0-

EXHIBIT 19–5

COMPANY P AND SUBSIDIARY, COMPANY S
Consolidated Income Statement (purchase basis)
For the Year Ended December 31, 19A

Sales		$618,000
Expenses:		
Cost of goods sold	$346,000	
Depreciation	27,690	
Patent amortization	3,360	
Goodwill amortization	1,000	
Other expenses	173,000	551,050
Consolidated net income including minority interest		66,950
Minority interest in net income of subsidiary (10%)		1,200
Consolidated net income		$ 65,750

Consolidated Balance Sheet (purchase basis)
At December 31, 19A

Assets

Cash		$452,000
Accounts receivable (net)		57,000
Inventories		54,500
Plant and equipment (net)		319,210
Patents		30,240
Cost of investment in excess of market value of identifiable net assets of subsidiary		39,000
Total Assets		$951,950

Liabilities

Current liabilities	$ 30,000	
Long-term liabilities	70,000	$100,000

Interest of Minority Stockholders in Subsidiary

Common stock	10,000	
Retained earnings	6,200	16,200

Stockholders' Equity

Common stock par $100, 6,000 shares outstanding	600,000	
Retained earnings ($170,000 + $65,750)	235,750	835,750
Total Liabilities and Stockholders' Equity		$951,950

Net income is lower (by $5,050) under the purchase basis because that approach requires adjustment of the subsidiary's assets to market value and that goodwill be recognized, each of which must be allocated on an annual basis to *expense* ($3,690 + $360 + $1,000 = $5,050). Cash and capital stock are lower under the purchase basis because, at acquisition, cash rather than capital stock is used to acquire the controlling interest. Purchase basis requires recognition of market values (for subsidiary assets) and purchased goodwill which caused the goodwill of $39,000 to be reported under the purchase basis. Retained earnings is higher under pooling of interests because it is the sum of the parent and subsidiary amounts, whereas when the purchase method is used, retained earnings of the subsidiary at acquisition is eliminated. The minority interest in net income and retained earnings is the same under both methods.

Principally because of (a) the effect on cash and (b) the accounting effects on net income and retained earnings, companies prefer pooling of interests. Also, because the pooling of interests method retains the book value basis of accounting for subsidiary assets, pooling provides the parent company with the opportunity to later report gains on the sale of subsidiary assets with market values in excess of cost. This is not possible under the purchase method because the assets of the subsidiary are recorded at market value when they are acquired by the parent. Pooling transactions were fairly common during the mid-1960s, prior to the issuance of *APB Opinion No. 16*. On the other hand, the stockholders of the acquired company often prefer to receive cash rather than stock of the parent company. In respect to the accounting aspects and the opportunity to manipulate reported earnings, the APB in *Opinion No. 16* placed severe restrictions on use of the pooling of interests approach. Also, in conformity with the full disclosure concept, *Opinion No. 16*, paragraphs 64 and 95, specifies a number of items that must be explained in the notes to the consolidated financial statements; these vary somewhat between pooling of interests and purchase.

PART C—SOME SPECIAL PROBLEMS IN ACCOUNTING FOR STOCK INVESTMENTS

Several special problems relating to the acquisition, holding, and sale of stock investments are discussed in the remaining paragraphs.

Stock Dividends Received on Investment Shares

To conserve cash and yet make a distribution to shareholders, a corporation may issue a stock dividend. When a stock dividend is issued, the distributing corporation debits Retained Earnings and credits the appropriate capital stock accounts (see Chapter 17). The effect of a stock dividend as far as the issuing corporation is concerned is to "capitalize" a part of retained earnings; significantly, a stock dividend does not decrease the assets of the issuing corporation.

From the *investor's* point of view, the nature of a stock dividend is suggested by the effect on the issuing corporation. The investor does not receive assets or revenue from the corporation; neither does the investor own more of the issuing corporation. The investor does have more shares to represent the same prior proportional ownership. Thus, the receipt of a stock dividend in the same class of shares as already owned results, from the standpoint of the investor's records, in more shares but no increase in the cost (carrying value) of the holdings.

The investor should make no entry for revenue nor change the investment account other than to record a memorandum entry for the number of shares received. In case of a sale of any of the shares, a new cost per share is computed by adding the new shares to the old and dividing this sum into the carrying value. To illustrate, assume X purchased 100 shares of stock at $90 and subsequently received a 50% dividend payable in identical stock, and later sold 20 shares at $85. A schedule showing the gain or loss on the sale and the balance remaining in the investment account (cost method) follows:[13]

	Shares	Cost per Share	Total Cost	Sales Proceeds	Gain (Loss)
Purchase	100	$90	$9,000		
Stock dividend	50		0		
Total	150	60 [a]	9,000		
Sold	20	60	1,200	$1,700 [b]	$500
Ending balance	130	60	$7,800		

[a] $9,000 ÷ 150 shares = $60.
[b] $85 × 20 shares = $1,700.

If the stock dividend is of a different class of stock than that on which the dividend was

---

[13] Under the Internal Revenue Code stock dividends are exempt from taxation except (a) where the shareholder can elect to take cash rather than stock for the dividend and (b) when stock dividends satisfy dividend preference requirements.

declared, such as preferred stock received as a dividend on common stock, three methods of accounting for the dividend have been suggested:

1. Record the new stock in terms of shares only, and when it is sold recognize the total sales price as a gain.
2. Record the new stock at an amount determined by apportioning the carrying value of the old stock between the new stock and the old stock on the basis of the relative market values of the different classes of stock *after* issuance of the dividend.
3. Do not change the carrying value of the old stock but record the new stock on the books at its market value upon receipt with an offsetting credit to dividend revenue. This method is predicated on the assumption that stock of a different class received as a dividend is no different from a property dividend.

Of these three methods the first is the most conservative, but the second is the most consistent with generally accepted accounting principles, while the third appears to be seldom used. To illustrate the second method, assume an investor purchased 50 shares of X Company common stock for $7,500. When the market value of the common stock was $10,000 the investor received a stock dividend of 20 shares of X preferred stock with a market value of $2,500. Using the relative sales value method, the cost may be apportioned as follows:

$$\text{Apportioned Cost to Common} = \$7,500 \times \frac{\$10,000}{\$12,500} = \$6,000$$

$$\text{Apportioned Cost to Preferred} = \$7,500 \times \frac{\$2,500}{\$12,500} = \underline{1,500}$$
$$\$7,500$$

Indicated entry:

Investment in preferred stock of
X Company 1,500
    Investment in common stock of
    X Company 1,500

Stock Split of Investment Shares

A stock split is effected when a corporation issues new or additional shares without "capital-

izing" (debiting) retained earnings or otherwise adding to the dollar amount of *legal capital*. In a stock split the number of shares outstanding is increased, accompanied by a proportionate decrease in the par or stated value per share of stock (refer to Chapters 16 and 17). Although a stock split is basically different from a stock dividend from the point of view of the issuer, the two are virtually identical from the point of view of the investor. In both cases the investor has more shares than before the split or dividend, but with the same total cost as before.[14] For instance, a two-for-one stock split means that the holder of shares at the date of the split will receive two shares in place of each old share held; concurrently, the par or stated value per share of the stock is halved. This merely means that the investor has twice as many shares after the split to represent the same total cost as before the split. To the investor, the accounting for a stock split is the same as for a stock dividend of the same class as already owned; that is, a memorandum entry is made to record the number of new shares received and the revised cost per share.

Convertible Securities

An enterprise may invest in preferred stock or bonds that are convertible into common stock under specified conditions. An accounting measurement problem arises at the time of conversion since the cost or book value of the convertible securities generally is different from the market value of the common stock received at the time of conversion. Two alternative views are held on this point:

1. At date of conversion record the book value of the convertible security given up as the cost of the new security received; thus no gain or loss on conversion would be recognized. This position is supported by the argument that the original transaction established the value of both securities, the original as well as the potential, because the investor purchased the convertible security with full knowledge of the conversion option.

---

[14] In a reverse split, such as a two-for-three split, the number of outstanding shares is reduced rather than increased. Reverse stock splits are rare.

In this view, prearranged conversion does not constitute a distinct exchange transaction.

2. At date of conversion record the new security received at its market value and recognize a gain or loss on conversion. This position is supported by the argument that a distinct and separate exchange transaction has occurred at conversion. In this view the very fact of conversion points to a shift in value in favor of the new security.

The former view tends to prevail in practice, although the latter accords more closely with economic reality. Also see Chapter 20 for the accounting treatment of convertible bonds payable.

Stock Rights on Investment Shares

The privilege accorded stockholders (investors) of purchasing additional shares of stock from the issuing corporation at a specific price and by a specified future date commonly is known as a *stock right*. The term *stock right* is usually interpreted to mean one right for *each share of old stock*. For example, a holder of two shares of stock who receives the rights to subscribe for one new share is said to own two stock rights rather than one; that is, there is one right per old share regardless of the "new" share arrangement. Rights have value when the holder can buy additional shares through *exercise* of the rights at a lower price per share than on the open market without rights. As the spread between the privileged price and the market price changes subsequent to issuance of the rights, the value of the rights will change.

When the intention to issue stock rights is declared, the stock will start selling in the market "rights on"; that is, the market price of the share sold "rights on" includes the value of a share and the value of a right. After the rights are issued, the shares will sell in the market "ex rights". After issuance, rights usually have a separate market from that of the related stock and thus will be separately quoted at a specific market price. After rights are received, the investor has shares of stock and stock rights, both arising out of the single original cost.

To determine the gain or loss on the sale of either the stock or the rights, it is necessary to apportion the total cost of the investment between the stock and the rights. This usually is done by the use of the relative sales value method; that is, the total cost of the old shares is divided between the old stock and the rights in proportion to their relative market values at the time that the rights are issued.

Illustrative Problem

To illustrate accounting for stock rights, assume an investor purchased 500 shares of stock in the XY Corporation at $93 per share and later received 500 stock rights entitling the investor to subscribe to 100 additional shares at $100 per share. Upon the issuance of the rights, each share of stock on which the rights were issued had a market value of $120 (ex rights), and the rights had a market value of $4 each when issued.

Case A—Assume that instead of subscribing for the additional shares, the investor later sold the rights at $4.50 each. The investor's entries are:

1. To record acquisition of stock investment:

Investment—stock of XY Corporation (500 shares × $93)	46,500	
Cash		46,500

2. To record receipt of 500 rights on XY Corporation stock investment:

Investment—stock rights of XY Corporation*	1,500	
Investment—stock of XY Corporation		1,500

* Allocation of investment cost to stock rights on basis of relative market values:

Shares: $\frac{\$120}{\$124} \times \$46,500 = \$45,000$ (i.e., $90 per share)

Rights: $\frac{\$4}{\$124} \times \$46,500 = \underline{1,500}$ (i.e., $3 per right)

Total cost . . . . . . $\underline{\underline{\$46,500}}$

3. To record sale of the 500 stock rights of XY Corporation:

Cash (500 rights × $4.50)	2,250	
Investment—stock rights of XY Corporation (500 rights @ $3)		1,500
Gain on sale of stock rights . . .		750

Case B—Assume the investor exercised the rights to subscribe to the additional shares and later sold one of the *new* shares for $140. The investor's entries are:

1. To record acquisition of stock investment—Same as entry 1 above.
2. To record receipt of stock rights—Same as entry 2 above.
3. To record exercise of the 500 rights and receipt of 100 new shares of stock of XY Corporation:

```
Investment—stock of XY Corpora-
  tion [100 shares × $115
  (i.e., $100 cash + 5
  rights @ $3)]  .................11,500
    Investment—stock rights of XY
      Corporation (500 rights @ $3) .    1,500
    Cash (100 shares @ $100) ......   10,000
```

4. To record sale of one of the new shares for $140 cash:

```
Cash (1 share @ $140) .............    140
  Investment—stock of XY Corpo-
    ration (1 share @ $115) .......    115
  Gain on sale of stock invest-
    ment ......................     25
```

In the unlikely event the rights are not sold or exercised, they will lapse. In this situation, theoretically a loss equivalent to the allocated cost of the rights should be recognized. However, as a practical matter, the allocation entry (entry 2 above) usually is simply reversed.

SPECIAL-PURPOSE FUNDS

Companies often set aside cash, and sometimes other assets, in special funds to be used in the future for a specific purpose. Funds may be set aside by contract, as in the case of a bond sinking fund; by law as in the case of rent deposits; or voluntarily, as in the case of a plant expansion fund. Special-purpose funds may be either a current asset, as in the case of short-term savings accounts, or a noncurrent asset, when they are not directly related to current operations. The latter are classified under the caption "Investments and Funds" (see Chapter 5). Typical long-term funds are as follows:

1. Funds set aside to retire a specific long-term liability, such as bonds payable, mortgages payable, long-term notes payable (see Chapters 6 and 9).
2. Funds set aside to retire preferred stock.
3. Funds set aside to purchase major assets, such as land, buildings, and plant (see Chapters 6 and 14).

Typically, special-purpose funds are deposited with an independent *trustee,* such as a financial institution. In this situation, arrangements often are agreed upon whereby a specific rate of interest will be earned each period on the balance in the fund. Usually, the return earned on the fund each period is added to the fund balance. Depending upon the agreement, a fund increases *(a)* on a compound interest basis at an agreed rate or *(b)* by the actual amount earned on the fund.

A special-purpose fund may be created *(a)* by making a single contribution at the start (use a FV of 1) or *(b)* by making equal periodic contributions (an annuity). The concepts of present and future value, fund accumulation tables, and related accounting entries were comprehensively discussed and illustrated in Chapter 6. Liability funds were discussed in Chapter 9, and future asset acquisition funds in Chapter 14.

QUESTIONS

PART A

1. Distinguish between debt and equity securities; also between short-term and long-term investments.

2. What accounting principle is applied in recording the acquisition of an investment? Explain its application in cash and noncash acquisitions.

3. Explain why interest revenue is accrued on investments but dividend revenue is not accrued.

4. Under the cost method, no distinction is made between voting and nonvoting stock, but the distinction is important with respect to the equity and consolidation methods. Explain why.

5. Explain when the cost method of accounting for equity investments is applicable.

6. Explain how the LCM concept is applied to long-term investments in equity securities. How is "cost" determined when an investment is reclassified from short-term to long-term or vice versa?

7. Explain the basic features of the equity method of accounting for long-term investments. When is it applicable? To what other method is it most closely related? Explain.

8. Assume Company R acquired, as a long-term investment, 30% of the outstanding voting common stock of Company S at a cash cost of $100,000. At date of acquisition, the balance sheet of Company S showed total shareholders' equity of $250,000. The market value of the assets of Company S was $20,000 greater than their book value at date of acquisition. Compute goodwill purchased. What accounting method should be used? Explain why.

9. Assume the same facts as given in Question 8, with the additional data that the net assets have a remaining estimated life of 10 years and goodwill will be amortized over 20 years (assume no residual values and straight-line depreciation). How much additional depreciation and amortization expense should be reflected by the investor, Company R, each year in accounting for this long-term investment? Give the entries to record additional depreciation and amortization of goodwill.

10. The equity method of accounting for a long-term investment usually will reflect a larger amount of investment revenue than would the cost method in the same circumstances. Explain why.

11. Explain the basic features of the market value method of accounting for investments. Is it a generally accepted method? Explain.

12. How would the market value method of accounting for investments, in contrast to the cost method, tend to prevent "managed" earnings?

PART B

13. Outline the characteristics of an acquisition transaction of a long-term investment that would be accounted for as a (a) pooling of interests and (b) purchase.

14. Contrast the primary effects on the balance sheet and income statement of a pooling of interest versus a purchase. Why are the effects different?

15. Explain why market values are used in the purchase method but not in the pooling of interest method.

16. Explain why goodwill is recognized in a purchase but not in a pooling of interests.

17. What are intercompany items? Why must they be eliminated in preparing consolidated financial statements?

18. What is meant by minority interest in consolidated statements? How is this interest reported on (a) the income statement and (b) the balance sheet?

19. Explain the basic reasons why many companies, other things being equal, would prefer the pooling of interests method over the purchase method of accounting for parent/subsidiary relationships.

PART C

20. Fundamentally, the investor accounts for a stock dividend and a stock split in the same way. Briefly, explain the accounting that should be followed by the investor in these situations.

21. What is a convertible security? Assume an investor has a convertible security with a book value of $200,000 which is turned in to the issuer for conversion. The investor receives, in conformance with the conversion, common stock with a current market value of $225,000. Explain how the investor should account for the conversion of this long-term investment.

22. What is a stock right (or warrant)? If stock rights have a market value, how would the investor account for the receipt of stock rights?

DECISION CASE 19–1

May Corporation is currently negotiating a combination with Nott Corporation, a successful enterprise that would complement the operations of May. An important factor in the negotiations has been the potential effects of the merger on May's financial statements. Accordingly, May management has requested that pro forma (i.e., as if) financial statements be prepared under two assumptions.

The balance sheets for the two corporations for the year just ended (prior to combination) are shown in the following table:

	May Corporation	Nott Corporation Book Value	Nott Corporation Appraised Value
Balance Sheet:			
Cash	$ 485,000	$ 15,000	$ 15,000
Receivables (net)	30,000	65,000	50,000
Inventories	85,000	70,000	70,000
Land	50,000		
Plant	600,000	100,000	230,000
Patents	10,000	30,000	40,000
	$1,260,000	$ 280,000	
Current liabilities	$ 40,000	$ 15,000	
Long-term liabilities	110,000	25,000	
Common stock (par $100)	1,000,000	200,000	
Retained earnings	110,000	40,000	
	$1,260,000	$ 280,000	

Income Statement:		
Sales......................	$6,000,000	$1,000,000
Costs and expenses (ex-		
cluding depreciation and		
amortization)	5,754,000	967,000
Depreciation	65,000	10,000
Amortization of patents	1,000	3,000
Income	180,000	20,000

At year-end Nott Corporation owed a $10,000 current liability to May Corporation. For case purposes, assume that all depreciable assets and intangible assets have a remaining useful life of ten years from date of combination.

Required:

1. Assume that May will purchase all of the outstanding stock of Nott for a cash consideration of $460,000.
   a. Give the pro forma entry for the investment.
   b. Prepare a pro forma balance sheet on a purchase basis (or if you prefer, present a pro forma consolidation worksheet).
2. Assume instead that May will acquire all of the outstanding shares of Nott by exchanging stock on a share-for-share basis.
   a. Give the pro forma entry for the exchange.
   b. Prepare a pro forma balance sheet (or worksheet) on a pooling of interests basis.
3. Identify the amounts on the two pro forma consolidated balance sheets that will be different between (1) and (2) above and explain the reasons for each. Identify and explain the amounts that would be different on the income statements for the next period as between (1) and (2).

EXERCISES

PART A
Exercises 19–1 to 19–8

Exercise 19–1

During 19A Franklin Company purchased shares in two corporations, as indicated below, with the intention of holding them as long-term investments. Purchases were in the following order:

a. Purchased 100 shares of the 10,000 shares outstanding of common stock of M Corporation at $31 per share plus a 5% brokerage fee and a transfer cost of $45.
b. Purchased 200 shares of preferred stock (nonvoting) of N Corporation at $78 per share plus a 3% brokerage fee and transfer costs of $42.
c. Purchased 20 shares of common stock of M Corporation at $35 per share plus a 5% brokerage fee and transfer costs of $5.
d. Received $4 per share cash dividend on the N Corporation stock (from earnings since acquisition).

Required:

1. Give the indicated entries in the accounts of Franklin Company for transactions *(a), (b), (c),* and *(d).* Assume the cost method is appropriate and that these are the only long-term equity investments held.
2. The market values of the shares held at the end of 19A were: M stock, $34; and N stock, $75. Give the appropriate adjusting entry for Franklin Company; show computations and assume the decline is temporary.
3. The market values of the shares held at the end of 19B were: M stock, $36; and N stock, $77. Give the appropriate adjusting entry with computations. Assume the decline is temporary.
4. Show how the income statement and balance sheet for Franklin Company would reflect the long-term investments for 19A and 19B.

Exercise 19–2

Adams Company purchased common stock (par value $50) of the Baker Corporation as a long-term investment. Transactions related to this investment were as follows and in the order given.

a. Purchased 500 shares of the common stock at $90 per share (designated as Lot No. 1).
b. Purchased 2,000 shares of the common stock at $95 per share (designated as Lot No. 2).
c. At the end of the first year, Baker Corporation reported net income of $52,000.
d. Baker Corporation paid a cash dividend on the common stock of $2 per share.
e. After reporting net income of $5,000 for the second year, Baker Corporation issued a stock dividend whereby each stockholder received one additional share for each two shares owned. At the time of the stock dividend the stock was selling at $85.
f. Baker Corporation revised its charter to provide for a stock split. The par value was reduced to $25. The "old" common stock was turned in, and the holders received in exchange two shares of the new stock for each old share owned.

Required:

Give the entries for each transaction as they should be made in the accounts of Adams Company. Show computations. Assume the cost method and less than 20% ownership throughout. (Also, refer to Part C of this chapter.)

Exercise 19–3

On January 1, 19A, Smith Company purchased 300 of the 1,000 outstanding shares of common stock of

Rankin Corporation for $23,200. At that date, the balance sheet of Rankin showed the following book values:

Assets not subject to depreciation	$40,000
Assets subject to depreciation (net)	26,000*
Liabilities	6,000
Common stock (par $50)	50,000
Retained earnings	10,000

* Market value, $30,000; the assets have a ten-year remaining life (straight-line depreciation).

Required:

1. Assuming the equity method is appropriate, give the entry by Smith to record the acquisition at a cost of $23,200. Assume a long-term investment.
2. Show the computation of goodwill purchased at acquisition.
3. Assume at December 31, 19A (end of the accounting period), Rankin Corporation reported a net income of $12,000. Assume goodwill amortization over a ten-year period. Give all entries indicated on the records of Smith Company.
4. In February 19B, Rankin Corporation paid a $2 cash dividend. Give the necessary entry.

Exercise 19–4

On January 1, 19A, Kyle Corporation purchased 2,000 of the 8,000 outstanding shares of common stock of Low Corporation for $20,000 cash. At that date, Low's balance sheet reflected the following book values:

Assets not subject to depreciation	$25,000
Assets subject to depreciation (net)	30,000*
Liabilities	5,000
Common stock (par $5)	40,000
Retained earnings	10,000

* Market value, $38,000; estimated remaining life of ten years (straight-line depreciation).

Required:

1. Assuming the equity method is appropriate, show the computation of goodwill purchased at acquisition.
2. At the end of 19A, Low reported income before extraordinary items, $19,000, extraordinary loss, $2,000, and net income, $17,000. In December 19A, Low Corporation paid a $1 per share cash dividend. Reconstruct the following accounts (use T-account format) for Kyle Corporation: Cash, Investment in Low Corporation Stock, Investment Revenue—Ordinary, and Investment Revenue—Extraordinary. Assume the equity method is appropriate and straight-line amortization of goodwill is over ten years. Date and identify all amounts entered in the accounts.

Exercise 19–5

On January 3, 19A, Bloomington Company purchased 2,000 shares of the 10,000 outstanding shares of common stock of Kokomo Corporation for $14,600 cash. At that date, the balance sheet of Kokomo reflected total shareholders' equity of $60,000. In addition, the market value of the assets, subject to depreciation, was $3,000 in excess of their book value reported on the Kokomo balance sheet. Assume a ten-year remaining life (straight-line depreciation) and amortization of goodwill over ten years.

Required:

Set up captions as follows and enter the indicated information (show computations):

Information— Bloomington Accounts	Assuming Cost Method Appropriate	Assuming Equity Method Appropriate
a. Entry at date of acquisition.		
b. Goodwill purchased—computation only.		
c. Entry on December 31, 19A, to record $15,000 net income reported by Kokomo.		
d. Entry on December 31, 19A, for additional depreciation expense.		
e. Entry on December 31, 19A, for amortization of goodwill.		
f. Entry on December 31, 19A, to recognize decrease in market value of Kokomo stock, quoted market price, $7 per share. Assume this is the only long-term equity security held.		
g. Entry on March 3, 19B, for a cash dividend of $1 per share paid by Kokomo.		

Exercise 19–6

On January 10, 19A, Company X purchased as a long-term investment 12% of the 10,000 shares of the outstanding common stock of Company Y (par value $40 per share) at $50 per share. During 19A, 19B, and 19C the following additional data were available:

	19A	19B
Reported net income by Company Y at year-end	$30,000	$35,000

Cash dividends by Company Y at
  year-end $10,000 $15,000
Quoted market price per share of
  Company Y stock at year-end   57   55

On January 2, 19C, Company X sold 100 shares of the Company Y shares at $56 per share.

Required:

1. Assuming the market value method is used, give all entries indicated in the accounts of Company X assuming market changes are reported on the income statement.
2. Prepare a tabulation to show the investment revenue of Company X and the balance in the investment account at year-end 19A, 19B, and 19C. Assume no cash dividends were paid by Company Y during 19C and that the quoted market price of Company Y common stock was $56 per share at December 31, 19C.

Exercise 19–7

On January 1, 19A, Company R purchased, as a long-term investment, 6% of the 50,000 (par $10) shares of the outstanding common stock of Company S at $11 per share. During the years 19A, 19B, and 19C, the following additional data were available:

	Company S
End of 19A:	
Reported net income	$30,000
Cash dividends paid	20,000
Market value per share	15
End of 19B:	
Reported net income	25,000
Cash dividends paid	15,000
Market value per share	14

January 10, 19C:
  Company R sold 200 shares of the
  Company S stock at $17.50 per share.

Required:

1. Assuming the market value method is used, give all entries related to the investment for Company R assuming
    a. Market changes are reported on the income statement.
    b. Market changes are reported on the balance sheet as a separate element of owners' equity.
2. In parallel columns for each assumption, show at the end of 19A, 19B, and on January 10, 19C (after sale of the 200 shares) the following:
    a. Balance of the investment account.
    b. Balance in the unrealized owners equity each year-end.
    c. Revenue from the investment for each period.

For this requirement assume there were no additional investment transactions during 19C and the market value of Company S stock was $17.50 per share on December 31, 19C.

Exercise 19–8

During January 19A, Company A purchased 20% of the 5,000 shares of outstanding common stock of Company B at $20 per share. At that date, the following data were available:

	Company B	
	At Book Value	Market Value per Appraisal
Assets not subject to depreciation	$ 60,000	$63,000*
Assets subject to depreciation (ten-year remaining life)	40,000	45,000
	$100,000	
Liabilities	$ 20,000	20,000
Common stock (par value $10)	50,000	
Retained earnings	30,000	
	$100,000	

* Difference due to inventory *(Fifo)*.

At the end of 19A, Company B reported net income of $15,000 and paid cash dividends of $5,000. At the end of 19A, Company B common stock was quoted on the market at $22 per share.

In January 19B, Company A sold 100 shares of the Company B common stock at $23 per share.

Required:

In parallel columns prepare entries for the accounts of Company A from the date of the purchase of the long-term investment through date of sale of the 100 shares assuming: Case A—the cost method is used; Case B—the equity method is used; and Case C—the market value method is used (market value changes are reported as revenue on the income statement). Assume goodwill is amortized over a 20-year period and the Company B stock is the only long-term equity investment held. Use straight-line depreciation and amortization.

PART B
Exercises 19–9 to 19–14

Exercise 19–9

On January 1, 19A, Company P acquired all of the outstanding shares of Company S common stock by exchanging, on a share-for-share basis, 4,000 shares of its own stock. The balance sheets reflected the following summarized data immediately before acquisition:

	Company P	Company S
Assets not subject to depreciation	$180,000	$40,000*
Assets subject to depreciation (ten-year remaining life)	120,000	25,000
	$300,000	$65,000
Liabilities	$ 20,000*	$ 5,000
Common stock (par $10)	200,000	40,000
Retained earnings	80,000	20,000
	$300,000	$65,000

* Includes a $4,000 debt owed by Company P to Company S.

Required:

1. Give entry in the accounts of Company P for the acquisition of this long-term investment on a pooling of interests basis.
2. Prepare a consolidation worksheet immediately after acquisition. Assume the pooling of interests method.

Exercise 19–10

Refer to the balance sheets immediately before acquisition for Companies P and S as given in Exercise 19–9.

Assume the same requirements and facts except that Company P exchanged, on a share-for-share basis, 3,600 shares of its own stock for a 90% interest in Company S.

Exercise 19–11

In January 19A, Company P purchased, for $149,000 cash, all of the 10,000 outstanding voting shares of the common stock of Company S. Immediately before acquisition the following additional summarized data were available:

		Company S	
	Company P Book Value	Book Value	Market Value (appraised)
Assets not subject to depreciation	$410,000	$ 80,000*	$ 85,000†
Assets subject to depreciation	200,000	60,000	67,000‡
Total	$610,000	$140,000	$152,000
Liabilities	$ 40,000*	$ 10,000	
Common stock (par $10)	500,000	100,000	
Retained earnings	70,000	30,000	
Total	$610,000	$140,000	

* Includes a $12,000 debt owed by Company P to Company S.
† Market value excess over cost is all on short-term investments.
‡ Estimated remaining life, ten years (straight-line depreciation).

Required:

1. Give entry in the accounts of Company P to record acquisition of this long-term investment assuming the purchase method.
2. Compute the amount of goodwill purchased.
3. Prepare a consolidation worksheet immediately after acquisition using the purchase method.
4. How much additional expense (assume a 20-year amortization period for goodwill) will be reflected on the consolidated income statement each year after the acquisition?

Exercise 19–12

Refer to the balance sheets immediately before acquisition for Companies P and S given in Exercise 19–11. Assume the same facts except that Company P purchased 60% of the outstanding shares of Company S for $96,200 cash.

Required:

1. Give entry in the accounts of Company P to record acquisition of this long-term investment assuming the purchase method.
2. Compute the amount of goodwill purchased.
3. Prepare a consolidated worksheet immediately after acquisition using the purchase method.
4. How much additional depreciation expense and goodwill amortization (assume a 20-year amortization period) will be reflected on the consolidated income statement each year after the acquisition?

Exercise 19–13

On January 1, 19A, Par Company purchased an 80% interest in Sub Company for $116,400. At acquisition, the goodwill purchased was computed as follows:

Purchase price for 80% interest in Sub Company		$116,400
Market value of identifiable assets	$153,000*	
Less liabilities	20,000	
Market value of identifiable net assets	133,000	
Proportion purchased	×.80	
Market value of identifiable net assets purchased		106,400
Goodwill purchased		$ 10,000

* Includes $5,000 excess over book value of operational assets.

At the end of 19A, the financial statements reflected the following (summarized):

	Reported at End of Year 19A	
	Par Company	Sub Company
Income Statement:		
Sales......................	$360,000	$ 80,000
Interest revenue		400
	360,000	80,400
Cost of goods sold	150,000	42,000
Other operating expenses	109,600	26,300
Interest expense...............	400	100
	260,000	68,400
Net Income	$100,000	$ 12,000
Balance Sheet:		
Current assets	$172,000	$ 80,000
Investment in Sub Company	116,400	
Operational assets (net)	400,000	90,000
	$688,400	$170,000
Current liabilities	$ 50,000	$ 30,000
Common stock	500,000	100,000
Retained earnings	138,400	40,000*
	$688,400	$170,000

* At acquisition, the balance was $28,000.

Intercompany items at year-end were as follows:

a. Par Company sold Sub Company goods (at cost) during the year amounting to $5,000.
b. Par Company paid Sub Company $400 interest during the year.
c. Par Company owed Sub Company $3,000 at the end of the year.

Required:

Prepare a worksheet to develop a consolidated income statement and balance sheet at the end of 19A assuming the purchase method. Assume straight-line depreciation is used, the operational assets have a 10-year remaining life, and goodwill will be amortized over 20 years.

Exercise 19–14

On January 1, 19A, X Company purchased 80% of the outstanding common stock of Y Company at a cost of $137,200. At acquisition, the goodwill purchased was computed as follows:

Purchase price for 80% interest in Y Company	$137,200
Market value of identifiable assets.............................	$191,500*
Less liabilities	25,000
Market value of identifiable net assets	166,500
Proportion purchased	×.80

Market value of identifiable net assets purchased		133,200
Goodwill		$ 4,000

* Includes excess over book value of inventory, $1,250; and operational assets, $6,250.

After one year of operations, each company prepared a balance sheet and income statement as follows (summarized):

	Reported at End of Year 19A	
	X Company	Y Company
Income Statement:		
Sales	$340,000	$ 90,000
Cost of goods sold	190,000	46,000
Depreciation	32,000	15,000
Other operating expenses ..	72,000	17,000
Interest expense..........	2,000	1,000
	296,000	79,000
Net Income	$ 44,000	$ 11,000
Balance Sheet:		
Current assets	$170,800	$ 40,000
Investment in Y Company ..	137,200	
Operational assets (net)	330,000	160,000
	$638,000	$200,000
Liabilities	$138,000	$ 30,000
Common stock	400,000	150,000
Retained earnings	100,000	20,000*
	$638,000	$200,000

* Balance at date of acquisition, $9,000.

Additional data:

a. Sales of X Company to Y Company during the year were $15,000 (at cost).
b. Depreciation on operational assets—assume a ten-year remaining life and straight-line method.
c. Amortization of any goodwill—assume a 20-year amortization period.

Required:

Prepare a worksheet to develop a consolidated income statement and balance sheet at the end of 19A assuming the purchase method.

PART C
Exercises 19–15 to 19–18

Exercise 19–15

Brown Company purchased, for a lump sum of $104,070, the three different stocks listed on the next page.

Company and Stock	Number of Shares
X Corporation, common stock, par $10	200
Y Corporation, preferred stock, par $100	400
Z Corporation, common stock, nopar	500

In addition, Brown paid transfer fees and other costs related to the acquisition amounting to $790. At the time of purchase, the stocks were quoted on the local market at the following prices per share: X common, $70; Y preferred, $120; and Z common, $90.

Required:

Give entry to record the purchase of these long-term investments and payment of the transfer fees. Show computations. Record each stock in a separate account.

Exercise 19–16

Each of the following situations is completely independent; however, both relate to the receipt of a stock dividend by an investor.

Case A—Corporation K had 20,000 shares of $50 par value stock outstanding at which time the board of directors voted to issue a 25% stock dividend (i.e., one additional share for each four [4] shares owned).

Required:

Company L owns 2,000 shares of the Corporation K stock (a long-term investment) acquired at a cost of $65 per share. After receiving the stock dividend, Company L sold 200 shares of the additional stock for $70 per share. Give the entries for Company L to record (1) acquisition of the 2,000 shares, (2) receipt of the stock dividend, and (3) sale of the 200 shares. Assume the cost method.

Cash B—During the course of an audit, you find accounts as follows:

Investments—Stock in A Company ($100 par per share)
Debits

Jan. 1	Cost of 100 shares	$17,500
Feb. 1	50 shares received as a stock dividend (at par $100)	5,000

Credits

July 1	25 shares of dividend stock sold at $125	3,125

Income Summary
Credits

Feb. 1	Stock dividend on A Company stock . . .	$ 5,000
Aug. 1	Cash dividend on A Company stock	3,000

Required:

Assuming the cost method, restate these accounts on a correct basis. Give reasons for each change.

Exercise 19–17

Box Corporation issued one stock right for each share of common stock owned by investors. The rights provided that for each six rights held, a share of preferred stock could be purchased for $100 cash (par of the preferred was $80 per share). When the rights were issued, they had a market value of $7 each and the common stock was selling at $142 per share (ex rights). Roy Company owned 300 shares of Box common stock, acquired as a long-term investment at a cost of $22,350. Assume the cost method.

Required:

1. How many rights did Roy Company receive?
2. Determine the cost of the stock rights to Roy Company and give any entry that should be made upon receipt of the rights.
3. Assume Roy Company exercised the rights. Determine the cost of the new stock and give the entry to record the exercise of the rights.
4. Assume instead that Roy Company sold its rights for $7.40 each. Give entry to record the sale.

Exercise 19–18

Give entries in the accounts of XY Corporation under the cost method for the following transactions which occurred over a period of time and in the chronological order shown:

a. XY Corporation purchased 100 shares of Bell Corporation common stock at $99 per share as a long-term investment.
b. Bell Corporation issued a 10% stock dividend in additional common shares.
c. Bell Corporation issued rights to present common stockholders entitling each holder of five old shares to buy one additional share of new common stock at 95. At the time, the rights sold for $4 per right and the shares outstanding sold for $116 each (ex rights). Make an allocation to the rights.
d. XY Corporation exercised its rights and bought new shares.
e. XY Corporation sold 120 shares of Bell stock for $12,000, failing to identify the specific shares disposed of. (Use *Fifo* procedures.)

PROBLEMS

PART A
Problems 19–1 to 19–5

Problem 19–1

On January 1, 19A, Freeze Company purchased 4,000 shares of the 20,000 shares outstanding of common stock (par $10) of Gray Corporation for $64,000 cash and 3,000 shares of the 100,000 shares outstanding of common stock (nopar) of Hobbs Corporation for $21,000 cash as a long-term investment. These are the only long-term equity investments held. The accounting periods for the companies end on December 31. Subsequent information was as follows:

	Gray	Hobbs
December 31, 19A:		
Income reported for 19A	$40,000	$20,000
Cash dividend per share paid at		
the end of 19A	1.50	None
Market price per share of stock	12	8
October 20, 19B:		
Sold 1,000 shares of the Hobbs stock at $10 per share.		
December 31, 19B:		
Income reported for 19B	50,000	26,000
Cash dividends per share paid at		
the end of 19B	1.00	.50
Market price per share of stock	14	11
Reclassified Hobbs stock as a current asset (short-term investment).		

Required:

1. Assuming the cost method, give all entries indicated for Freeze Company for 19A and 19B.
2. Show how the long-term investments in equity securities and the related investment revenue would be reported on the financial statements of Freeze Company at the end of each year.

Problem 19–2

On January 1, 19B, Abel Company purchased 3,000 of the 15,000 outstanding shares of common stock of Briggs Corporation for $80,000 cash as a long-term investment (the only long-term equity investment held). At that date, the balance sheet of Briggs Corporation showed the following book values (summarized):

Assets not subject to depreciation	$140,000 *(a)*
Assets subject to depreciation (net)	100,000 *(b)*
Liabilities	40,000
Common stock (par $10)	150,000
Retained earnings	50,000

(a) Market value, $150,000; difference relates to short-term investments.
(b) Market value, $140,000, estimated remaining life, ten years. Assume straight-line depreciation and amortization of goodwill over 20 years.

Additional subsequent data on Briggs Corporation:

	19B	19C
Income before extraordinary items	$25,000	$26,000
Extraordinary item—gain		5,000
Cash dividends paid	10,000	12,000
Market value per share	25	26

Required:

1. Set up captions as follows and enter the indicated information (show computations):

Information (Abel's accounts)	Assuming Cost Method Is Appropriate	Assuming Equity Method Is Appropriate
a. Entry at date of acquisition.		
b. Amount of goodwill purchased.		
c. Entries at December 31, 19B.		
(1) Investment revenue and dividends.		
(2) Additional depreciation expense.		
(3) Amortization of goodwill.		
(4) Additional expense associated with the short-term investments (held by Briggs) for which market value (i.e., purchase price to Abel) exceeded book value.		
(5) Recognition of change in market value of Briggs stock.		
d. Entries at December 31, 19C.		
(1) Investment revenue and dividends.		
(2) Additional depreciation expense.		
(3) Amortization of goodwill.		
(4) Recognition of change in market value of Briggs stock.		

2. Reconstruct the investment account for each assumption; also include the "allowance" and "unrealized capital" accounts.
3. Explain why the investment account balance is different between the cost and equity methods.

Problem 19–3

During January 19A, Riley Company purchased 1,000 shares of the 10,000 shares of the outstanding common stock (par $20) of Swanson Corporation for $36,000 cash as a long-term investment (the only long-term equity investment held). During 19A, 19B, and 19C, the following additional data were available:

	19A	19B
Net income reported by Swanson at year-end	$15,000	$20,000
Cash dividends paid by Swanson at year-end	10,000	12,000
Market price per share	40	37

On January 2, 19C, Riley sold 100 shares of the Swanson stock at $38 per share.

Required:

(Suggestion—Set up a three-column tabulation for Requirements 1–3.)

1. Give all entries indicated in the accounts of Riley Company assuming the cost method is used.
2. Give all entries indicated in the accounts of Riley Company assuming the market value method is

used and that market value changes are reported on the income statement.

3. Give all entries indicated in the accounts of Riley Company assuming the market value is used and that market value changes are reported as unrealized capital on the balance sheet.

4. Explain why the investment account balance is different between Requirements 1 and 2.

Problem 19–4

In January 19A, Bricker Company purchased 10% of the 100,000 outstanding common shares of Core Company at $6 per share as a long-term investment (the only long-term equity investment held). During the years 19A and 19B, the following additional data were available:

	Core Company
End 19A:	
Reported net income	$30,000
Cash dividends paid	15,000
Market value per share	9
End 19B:	
Reported net income	(4,000) loss
Cash dividends paid	10,000
Market value per share	7

Required:

(Suggestion: Set up a three-column tabulation for Requirements 1–3.)

1. Give all entries indicated in the accounts of Bricker Company assuming the cost method is used.

2. Give all entries indicated assuming that the market value method is used and that market value changes are reported on the income statement.

3. Give all entries indicated assuming that the market value method is used and that market value changes are reported as unrealized capital on the balance sheet.

4. Prepare a tabulation to reflect at each year-end, for each of the above requirements the following: *(a)* the balance in the investment account at each year-end, *(b)* the balance in any unrealized capital accounts, and *(c)* investment revenue for Bricker Company.

5. Give entry assuming 1,000 shares of Core Company were sold by Bricker early in 19C at $8 per share.

Problem 19–5

During January 19A, Company P purchased 20% of the 30,000 outstanding common shares of Company S at $16 per share as a long-term investment (the only long-term equity investment held). At date of acquisi-

tion of the shares, the following data in respect to Company S had been assembled by Company P:

	Company S	
	At Book Value	At Market Value
Assets not subject to depreciation	$250,000	$260,000*
Assets subject to depreciation (ten-year remaining life; straight line)	200,000	220,000
	$450,000	
Liabilities	$ 50,000	
Common stock (par $10)	300,000	
Retained earnings	100,000	
	$450,000	

* Difference due to inventory *(Fifo)*.

Selected data available at year-end:

	19A	19B
Reported net income, Company S:		
Income before extraordinary items	$20,000	$(10,000) loss
Extraordinary gain	10,000	
Cash dividends paid:		
Company S	8,000	5,000
Quoted market price per share, Company S	21	15

Required:

1. In parallel columns, prepare all entries for Company P in respect to the investment assuming *(a)* the cost method is appropriate, *(b)* the equity method is appropriate (amortize any goodwill over 20 years using the straight-line method), and *(c)* the market value method is used and market value changes are reported on the income statement.

2. Prepare a tabulation for each assumption in Requirement 1 to reflect *(a)* the balance in the investment account at each year-end, *(b)* investment revenue for each period, and *(c)* the allowance account.

PART B
Problems 19–6 to 19–10

Problem 19–6

In January 19A, Company P acquired, as a long-term investment, 9,000 of the 10,000 outstanding common stock shares of Company S (par $20) by issuing 18,000 shares of its own common stock (par $10). Immediately prior to acquisition, the balance sheets reflected the following (summarized):

	Company P Book Value	Company S Book Value	Company S Market Value
Cash	$290,000	$ 70,000	$ 70,000
Receivables (net)	63,000†	36,000	33,000
Inventories	237,000	170,000	160,000
Operational assets (net)	260,000	100,000	150,000*
Patents (net)		14,000	10,000*
Total	$850,000	$390,000	$423,000
Current liabilities	$ 60,000	$ 10,000†	
Long-term liabilities	150,000	140,000	
Common stock	514,000	200,000	
Retained earnings	126,000	40,000	
Total	$850,000	$390,000	

* Estimated useful life: operational assets, ten years; patent, five years. Assume purchased goodwill recognized will be amortized over 20 years.
† Includes a $4,000 debt owed by Company S to Company P.

Required:

1. Assume the acquisition meets all of the criteria for the pooling of interests method.
   a. Give the entry to record the stock exchange in the accounts of Company P at date of acquisition.
   b. Prepare a consolidation worksheet for the balance sheet immediately after acquisition.
2. Assume the same facts as above except that instead of the exchange of shares, Company P paid $286,700 cash for the 9,000 shares of Company S. Also assume the acquisition qualifies as a purchase.
   a. Give the entry to record the acquisition in the accounts of Company P.
   b. Compute the amount of goodwill purchased (show computations).
   c. Prepare a consolidation worksheet for the balance sheet immediately after acquisition.
3. To compare the two methods, pooling of interests versus purchase, complete the tabulation as follows:

Item (consolidated)	Consolidated Amounts the Same or Different?	Explanation of Reasons
1. Current assets.		
2. Investment account balances.		
3. Liabilities.		
4. Common stock balance.		
5. Retained earnings balance.		
6. Minority interest amount.		
7. Future net income.		

Problem 19–7

On January 1, 19A, P Company acquired 90% of the common stock of S Company by issuing 13,500 shares of its own common stock to the shareholders of S Company for an equal number of S Company shares. After one year of operations, each company prepared an income statement and balance sheet as follows (summarized):

	Reported at End of Year 19A	
	P Company	S Company
Income Statement:		
Sales	$620,000	$140,000
Interest revenue	700	
	620,700	140,000
Cost of goods sold	370,000	75,000
Depreciation expense	40,000	15,000
Other operating expenses	132,700	36,300
Interest expense	1,000	700
	543,700	127,000
Net Income	$ 77,000	$ 13,000
Balance Sheet:		
Current assets	$335,000	$101,000
Investment in S Company	135,000	
Operational assets (net—remaining life, ten years)	330,000	149,000
	$800,000	$250,000
Liabilities	$ 80,000	$ 40,000
Common stock (par $10)	600,000	150,000
Retained earnings	120,000	60,000*
	$800,000	$250,000

* Balance at acquisition date, $47,000.

Intercompany items and adjustments for 19A:

a. S Company sold $17,000 worth of goods (at cost) to P Company during the year.
b. S Company paid P Company $700 interest during the year.
c. At the end of 19A, S Company owed P Company $20,000.

Required:

1. Prepare a worksheet for 19A to develop a consolidated income statement and balance sheet. Use the pooling of interests basis. Assume straight-line depreciation.
2. Prepare a consolidated income statement and balance sheet clearly identifying the minority interest.

682

Problem 19–8

Refer to the balance sheets for Companies P and S given in Problem 19–7. Assume the same facts except that Company P purchased 13,500 shares (90%) of the common stock of Company S at a cash cost of $226,000. At date of acquisition, the depreciable operational assets, at market value, were $43,000 above book value.

The purchase method changes the trial balance for Company P given in Problem 19–7 as follows (new balances):

Current assets	$109,000
Investment account (at cost)	226,000
Common stock (par $10)	465,000

Required:

1. Compute the purchased goodwill at date of acquisition. Show computations.
2. Prepare a worksheet for 19A to develop a consolidated balance sheet and income statement. Use the purchase basis. Use straight-line depreciation and amortize goodwill over 20 years.

Problem 19–9

On January 1, 19A, Company A purchased for cash, in the open market, 80% of the outstanding common stock of Company B at a cost of $188,000. At date of acquisition, based upon an appraisal of Company B assets for consolidation purposes, the depreciable operational assets had a market value of $10,000 above their book value (because of their unique features) and the current assets had a market value of $7,500 less than their book value.

After one year of operations, each company prepared an income statement and balance sheet as follows (summarized):

	Reported at End of Year 19A	
	Company A	Company B
Income Statement:		
Sales	$630,000	$180,000
Interest revenue	1,000	
	631,000	180,000
Cost of goods sold	370,000	98,000
Depreciation expense	37,000	16,000
Other operating expenses	140,000	45,000
Interest expense	4,000	1,000
	551,000	160,000
Net Income	$ 80,000	$ 20,000

Balance Sheet:		
Current assets	$372,000	$110,000
Investment in Company B (at cost)	188,000	
Operational assets (net)	360,000	160,000
Total	$920,000	$270,000
Current liabilities	$ 70,000	$ 30,000
Common stock (par $10)	760,000	200,000
Retained earnings	90,000	40,000*
Total	$920,000	$270,000

* Balance at date of acquisition, $20,000.

Data relating to 19A eliminations and adjustments:

a. During the year, Company A sold merchandise to Company B for $35,000 (at cost).
b. During 19A, Company B paid Company A $1,000 interest on loans.
c. At the end of 19A, Company B owed Company A $20,000.
d. The depreciable assets of Company B have an estimated remaining life of ten years (no residual value, straight-line depreciation).
e. Goodwill is to be amortized over a 20-year life.

Required:

1. Compute the goodwill purchased at date of acquisition; show computations.
2. Prepare a worksheet to develop a consolidated income statement and balance sheet on the purchase basis.

Problem 19–10

Refer to the balance sheets for Companies A and B given in Problem 19–9. Assume the same facts except that Company A acquired the 90% interest in Company B by exchanging 18,000 shares of its own common stock for an equal number of shares in Company B.

The pooling of interests method changes the trial balance given for Company A in Problem 19–9 as follows:

Current assets	$560,000
Investment account	180,000
Common stock (par $10)	940,000

Required:

1. Prepare a worksheet for 19A to develop a consolidated income statement and balance sheet. Use the pooling of interest basis.
2. Prepare a consolidated income statement and balance sheet clearly identifying the minority interest.

Problem 19–11

Foster Corporation completed the following transactions, in the order given, relative to the portfolio of stocks held as long-term investments:

a. Purchased 200 shares of common stock (par value $50) of M Corporation at $70 per share plus a brokerage commission of 4% and transfer costs of $20.

b. Purchased, for a lump sum of $96,000, the following stocks of N Corporation:

Stocks	Number of Shares	Market Price at Date of Purchase
Class A, common, par value $100 ...	200	$ 50
Preferred, par value $50	300	100
Class B, nopar common stock (stated value $100)	400	150

c. Purchased 300 shares common stock of M Corporation at $80 per share plus a brokerage commission of 4% and transfer costs of $60.

d. Received a stock dividend on the M Corporation stock; for each share held, an additional share was received.

e. Sold 100 shares of M Corporation stock at $45 per share (from Lot 1).

f. Received a two-for-one stock split on the Class A common stock of the N Corporation (the number of shares doubled).

g. Received cash dividends as follows:
M Corporation common stock—$5 per share.
N, Class A, common stock—$3 per share.
N preferred—6%.
N, Class B, nopar common stock—$1.50 per share.

Required:

1. Give entries for Foster Corporation for the above transactions assuming the cost method is appropriate. Show calculations and assume *Fifo* order when shares are sold.

2. Prepare an inventory of the long-term investment portfolio; include number of shares and balance sheet valuations after giving effect to the above transactions.

20

Accounting for Bonds as Long-Term Liabilities and Investments

The preceding chapter discussed long-term investments in equity securities (i.e., capital stock), and Chapter 9 discussed short-term and long-term liabilities. Because of their unique characteristics, discussion of bonds was deferred to this chapter. This chapter analyzes bonds from the viewpoints of (a) the issuer (i.e., the borrower) and (b) the investor (i.e., the lender). This dual approach is logical because the accounting and reporting concepts and procedures for the issuer and the investor are essentially the same; that is, there is "accounting symmetry" between the debtor and creditor. Bonds represent a long-term liability for the issuer and usually a long-term investment for the investor.[1]

Certain recent pronouncements of the FASB have considered the accounting for various changes in debt arrangements prior to maturity date. These issues also are discussed in this chapter. The chapter is divided into three parts and includes an Appendix: Part A—Accounting for Bonds Compared: The Issuer and the Investor; Part B—Special Problems in Accounting for

Bonds; Part C—Changes in Obligations Prior to Maturity Date; and the Appendix—Serial Bonds.

NATURE OF BONDS

Bonds, evidenced by outstanding bond certificates, are contractual representations that a debt is owed by one party, the issuer, to one or more other parties, the investors. A bond certificate indicates the principal amount, specified interest dates (usually semiannual), the stated rate of interest based upon the principal amount, and any other special agreements. Thus, a bond may be defined as a formal (i.e., written) promise to pay a specified principal at a designated date in the future and, in addition, periodic interest on the principal at a specified rate per period.

Bonds are used to borrow a large amount from the investment community, including individuals, by dividing the total long-term debt into a number of small units, usually in denominations of $10,000 and $1,000 (sometimes $100). The total amount to be borrowed, evidenced by the bond certificates, is usually referred to as a *bond issue*. A bond issue requires the preparation of a *bond indenture,* which is the basic contract between the borrower and the investors who acquire the bonds. The bond indenture usually includes provision for an outside *independent trustee* who is given the authority to protect the rights

---

[1] Bonds are sometimes held as short-term investments, in which case they are accounted for in the manner discussed in Chapter 8. They are recorded at cost and subsequently are carried at lower of cost or market (LCM). Any premium or discount generally is not amortized in view of the short holding period. In contrast, this chapter focuses on long-term investments in bonds.

of both the investors and the issuer. A bond indenture specifies the following information which is particularly important in accounting and reporting (1) the liability of the issuer and (2) the investment of the investor:

1. Maturity date.
2. Interest payments—dates and stated rate of interest.
3. Denominations of principal.
4. Call and/or conversion provisions.
5. Security (i.e., whether supported by pledged assets or not).
6. The trustee.
7. Repayment plans, such as a bond sinking fund.
8. Special provisions such as restrictions on retained earnings of the issuer and the maintenance of certain minimum ratios (such as the ratio of debt to owners' equity).

CLASSIFICATION OF BONDS

Bonds are classified in various ways as follows:

1. Character of the issuing corporation—The borrower may be a private corporation issuing *industrial* bonds or a public entity issuing *municipal* or other *government* bonds.

2. Character of the security—Secured bonds are supported by a lien, or mortgage, on specific assets, whereas unsecured bonds have no such support. Unsecured bonds are frequently called *debenture bonds. Guaranty security bonds* are those which in case of default will be paid as to principal and interest by a third party, the guarantor. For example, a parent corporation may guarantee payment of bonds issued by one or more of its subsidiary companies. *Lien security bonds* are secured by a lien on particular kinds of property, such as securities (collateral trust bonds), rolling stock (car trust and equipment bonds), or on realty (real estate bonds).

3. Purpose of issue—*Purchase money bonds* are issued in full or part payment for property. *Refunding bonds* are issued to retire existing obligations and may have the same security as the retired debt. *Consolidated bonds* replace several prior issues with a single issue and consolidate the securities for the retired issues.

4. Payment of interest—*Income bonds* differ from *ordinary* bonds in that the payment of interest each period on income bonds depends on the earning of income by the issuer. *Participating bonds* have a specified minimum stated rate of interest plus a stated participation in the income of the issuer; they may have a specified limited participation or an unlimited participation.

Registered bonds are recorded in the name of the investor, and the periodic interest payments are sent only to that person; therefore, a sale or transfer by the investor must be reported to the issuer, trustee, or other party designated for this purpose. In contrast, *coupon bonds* have a coupon attached for each periodic interest payment. At each coupon due date, the holder of the bond simply detaches the appropriate coupon, signs it, and cashes it as if it were a check. Sale of a coupon bond does not require registration of title transfer.

5. Maturity of principal—Bonds maturing at a specified date are called *straight* (or ordinary) *bonds;* that is, the entire bond issue matures at a single date. Bonds maturing at a series of stated installment dates, say one fifth each year, are called *serial bonds* (see the Appendix to this chapter). *Callable bonds* give the *issuer* the option to retire them at a stated price before the obligatory maturity date. *Redeemable bonds* give the *investor* the option to turn them in for a stated redemption price prior to maturity. *Convertible bonds* give the *investor* the option to turn them in and to receive, in exchange, other specified securities of the borrower (usually common stock).

FINANCIAL MARKET CONDITIONS

In going to the money market, a borrower needing a large sum of money must make the fundamental decision whether to employ debt or capital stock, or a combination. This decision depends on a number of factors, some peculiar to the company and some based on the vagaries of the money market. Long-term debt has the advantage to the issuer that interest payments are deductible as an expense for income tax purposes; thus, a 45% tax bracket reduces the net interest rate (i.e., after tax) on an 8% loan to

[.08 × (1 − .45)] = 4.4%. In contrast, dividends paid on capital stock are not deductible for tax purposes.

The periodic interest payments on bonds are fixed legal obligations that must be paid in cash each interest period. In contrast, dividends on capital stock are discretionary with the board of directors and are paid only when there are sufficient retained earnings and cash. Debt has a fixed maturity date, whereas most capital stock does not.

In considering an investment decision the investor should weigh the *guaranteed* fixed interest rate and the bond maturity specifications against the *potential* for dividends. Thus, bonds generally are less risky as investments than stock. Consequently, investors demand a higher rate of return on stock investments than on bond investments. Both interest revenue (except for tax-free municipal bonds) and dividend revenue (there are certain limited exceptions) are subject to income tax to the investor.

Bonds may be marketed initially by the borrower in several ways. Typically, an entire bond issue is sold to investment bankers who *underwrite* the bond issue at a specified price and then market the bonds at a higher price to individual investors, thus realizing underwriter's compensation. Alternatively, the investment banker may agree to act as a selling agent for the borrower for an agreed commission; the selling price less the costs of selling is remitted to the issuer. Occasionally, the issuer may sell the bonds privately to financial institutions and individual investors.

Often, when there is no underwriter, the issuer may choose not to sell the entire bond issue if the bonds do not have sufficient appeal in the market. In these situations, unissued bonds should be disclosed in the financial statements, either parenthetically or by note.

PART A—ACCOUNTING FOR BONDS COMPARED: THE ISSUER AND THE INVESTOR

ILLUSTRATIVE DATA FOR BONDS

For illustration of bonds in Part A, a common set of facts will be used. Typically, bonds specify a long term from date of issuance to date of maturity (i.e., 10, 20, or more years), fractional in-

terest rates, and semiannual interest payments. However, to simplify and shorten the illustrations at the outset, we will use a five-year term, even interest rates, and annual rather than semiannual interest. These simplifications will not affect the basic concepts and accounting procedures.[2] The common set of facts used in this section are as follows:

Issuer (i.e., the borrower)	X Corporation
Investor (i.e., the lender)	Y Corporation

Terms of the bond indenture:

a.	Maturity amount of the bonds.	$100,000 (in $10,000 and $1,000 denominations).
b.	Date of the bonds.	January 1, 19A.
c.	Maturity date.	December 31, 19E (term, five years).
d.	Stated interest rate.	7% per year.
e.	Interest payments (cash).	Annually each December 31 (amount, $100,000 × .07 = $7,000).
f.	Date sold.	January 1, 19A (unless otherwise stated).
g.	Price or effective interest rate.	As specified in the examples to follow.

End of the accounting period—December 31 for both companies (unless otherwise specified).

To facilitate study, analysis, and problem solving, it is often helpful to prepare a *time scale* for the bond issue (or investment) that details important data such as issue date, interest dates, maturity date, period outstanding, and interest rates. A time scale for the above bond issue would appear as follows:

Time Scale (amount, $100,000; stated interest, 7%)

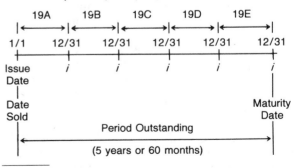

---

[2] After the introductory illustrations, semiannual interest payments are assumed in the chapter.

BOND INTEREST AND PRICES

Because bonds have fixed maturity amounts, definite maturity dates, and specified interest payments, they tend to fluctuate less in price than stocks. The market price of bonds fluctuates inversely with changes in the market interest rate. When the market interest rate rises, the market price of outstanding bonds falls; when the market interest rate falls, the market price of bonds rises. Although the market price of bonds tends to move with the interest market, the price also is influenced by changes in the issuer's financial standing and the approach of maturity (at which time the market value and maturity amount normally will coincide).

The bond indenture and the face of each bond certificate always specify a *stated*[3] interest rate which is applied to the principal amount of the bond to determine the amount of *cash interest* that will be paid each period. For example, each bond certificate of X Corporation (see data above) will specify a stated rate of 7% per year. Thus, each of the $10,000 bonds will always pay $700 cash interest each annual interest period (December 31), and a $1,000 denomination bond will always pay $70 cash, regardless of its issue or market price. In the case of semiannual interest payments, the bonds of X Corporation would pay 3.5% stated interest each six months (refer to Chapter 6 for discussion of interest calculations).

In contrast to the stated rate of interest, the *yield* or *effective* rate is the true rate of interest paid by the issuer and earned by the investor after taking into account the issue (or purchase) price of the bond.[4] Because the money market may establish a rate of interest on the bonds different from the stated rate, bonds may sell at more or less than their face or par amount.

A bond sold at *par* will incur interest expense for the issuer at the stated rate of interest and will earn interest revenue for the investor at the same rate of interest. Only in this situation will the stated and the yield rates of interest be the same. A bond sold at a *discount* (less than par) will incur interest expense for the issuer at a

yield rate higher than the stated rate, and it will earn for the investor the higher effective rate. Conversely, a bond sold at a *premium* (more than par) will incur interest expense for the issuer at a yield rate which is lower than the stated rate and likewise will earn interest revenue for the investor at the lower yield rate.[5]

Investment firms often quote bonds on a yield basis. A 7% bond quoted at 7–50 can be bought at a price that will yield 7.5% on the price of the bond each year from date of sale to maturity date. Thus, a $1,000 bond with a stated rate of 7%, payable 3.5% semiannually, sold on a 7.50% basis (yield rate) five years before maturity would have a price of $979.47 (see Exhibit 20–1, Table B). The $20.53 discount is an adjustment of the stated interest rate to the higher yield rate. Bonds may be quoted in relation to their par or maturity amount. For example, a $1,000 bond quoted at 100 is selling for $1,000 (i.e., at par); if quoted at 97, it is selling at $970 (i.e., at a discount of $30); and if quoted at 103, it is selling at $1,030 (i.e., at a premium of $30).

Determination of Bond Prices

The price of a bond is the *present value* of all of its expected net future cash inflows discounted at the market (as opposed to the stated) rate of interest. Thus, the present value of a bond is the sum of two present value amounts: *(a)* the present value of its maturity amount plus *(b)* the present value of the series of future interest payments. Computation of the price of a bond (its present value) is shown below because it is an especially important aspect of this chapter.

The *bond price* may be computed by either of two ways, each of which use tables that incorporate the same present value determinations, viz:

1. Based on the yield rate, compute the present value of *(a)* the future cash principal (i.e., the face amount) plus *(b)* the present value of the future *cash* interest payments.

    To illustrate, assume the $100,000, 7% (annual interest payments), five-year bonds were sold by X Corporation to Y Corporation at a yield rate of 8% (see page 686 and 688).

---

[3] The stated rate also is referred to as the contract, nominal, or coupon rate of interest. The principal also often is referred to as the face, maturity, or par amount.

[4] The yield rate is also called the effective, true, or market rate.

[5] This discussion assumes that the issuer sells the bonds directly to the investors with no bond issue costs. Bond issue costs will be discussed in a later section.

Computation of the bond price:
Present value of the future principal:
$100,000 × $p_{n=5;i=8\%}$ (Table 6–2) =
$100,000 × .68058 .... = $68,058
Present value of future annual
interest payments:
$7,000 × $P_{o_{n=5;i=8\%}}$ (Table 6–4) =
$7,000 × 3.99271 .... = 27,949
Bond price at 8% yield rate $96,007

Since the yield rate (8%) was higher than the stated rate (7%), the bond issue was sold at a *discount* of $100,000 − $96,007 = $3,993.

To illustrate a premium, assume instead that the bonds were sold at a yield rate of 6%.

Computation of the bond price:
$100,000 × $p_{n=5;i=6\%}$ (Table 6–2) =
$100,000 × .74726 .... = $ 74,726
$7,000 × $P_{o_{n=5;i=6\%}}$ (Table 6–4) =
$7,000 × 4.21236 .... = 29,486
Bond price at 6% yield rate $104,212

Amount of premium: $104,212 − $100,000 = $4,212.

2. Refer to a *bond table* that gives bond prices for various stated rates, yield rates, and time to maturity. Exhibit 20–1 shows excerpts from three typical bond tables. The bond prices computed above can be verified by referring to Exhibit 20–1, Table A.

It is important to note that a bond sold (or purchased) at par has a present value *identical* to the par or maturity amount. In contrast, a bond sold (or purchased) at a discount has a present value *lower* than par or maturity amount (by the amount of the discount); a bond sold (or purchased) at a premium has a present value *higher* than par or maturity amount (by the amount of the premium).

An understanding of the computation of bond prices and the related accounting is especially important because it develops a sound knowledge of the application of present value concepts. In the "real world" *(a)* bonds are priced via present value computations and *(b)* the virtual *certainty* of the future cash flows (principal and interest payments) removes much of the

EXHIBIT 20–1
Excerpts from Three Typical Bond Tables

Table A—Face of Bond, $100,000; Stated Interest, 7% Payable Annually

Yield	3 Years	4 Years	5 Years
		Time to Maturity	
6.00	102,673.01	103,465.11	104,212.37
6.50	101,324.24	101,712.90	102,077.84
7.00	100,000.00	100,000.00	100,000.00
7.50	98,699.74	98,325.33	97,977.05
8.00	97,422.90	96,687.88	96,007.29

Table B—Face of Bond, $100,000; Stated Interest, 7% Payable Semiannually

Yield	3 Years	3½ Years	4 Years	4½ Years	5 Years
			Time to Maturity		
6.00	102,708.60	103,115.14	103,509.84	103,893.05	104,265.10
6.50	101,343.14	101,543.00	101,736.56	101,924.03	102,105.60
7.00	100,000.00	100,000.00	100,000.00	100,000.00	100,000.00
7.50	98,678.73	98,485.52	98,299.30	98,119.80	97,946.81
8.00	97,378.93	96,998.97	96,633.63	96,282.33	95,944.56

Table C—Face of Bond, $100,000; Stated Interest, 8% Payable Semiannually

Yield	2 Years	2½ Years	3 Years	3½ Years	4 Years
			Time to Maturity		
6.00	103,717.09	104,579.71	105,417.20	106,230.28	107,019.69
6.50	102,771.24	103,410.40	104,029.44	104,629.00	105,209.69
7.00	101,836.54	102,257.53	102,664.27	103,057.28	103,436.98
7.50	100,912.85	101,120.82	101,321.27	101,514.47	101,700.70
8.00	100,000.00	100,000.00	100,000.00	100,000.00	100,000.00
8.50	99,097.85	98,894.82	98,700.07	98,513.25	98,334.06
9.00	98,206.23	97,805.01	97,421.06	97,053.65	96,702.05

Yield	4½ Years	5 Years	6 Years	10 Years	15 Years
6.00	107,786.11	108,530.20	109,954.01	114,877.48	119,600.45
6.50	105,772.09	106,316.80	107,355.31	110,904.51	114,236.44
7.00	103,803.85	104,158.30	104,831.67	107,106.20	109,196.02
7.50	101,880.19	102,053.20	102,380.68	103,474.05	104,457.31
8.00	100,000.00	100,000.00	100,000.00	100,000.00	100,000.00
8.50	98,162.16	97,997.28	97,687.40	96,676.41	95,805.25
9.00	96,365.60	96,043.64	95,440.71	93,496.04	91,855.55

guesswork from the application. Therefore, bond valuation is a clear-cut, "real-world" application of abstract present value concepts.

ACCOUNTING FOR AND REPORTING BONDS (ISSUER AND INVESTOR)

In accounting for bonds the *issuer* records the cash amount received for a bond as the value of the liability (i.e., the maturity amount minus

Issuer's Books—X Corporation		Investor's Books—Y Corporation	

Case A—The bond issue was sold (and purchased) at par, $100,000 on January 1, 19A:

Cash	100,000	Bond investment (at cost)	100,000
Bonds payable	100,000	Cash	100,000

Case B—The bond issue was sold (and purchased) at a discount, $96,007:*

Cash	96,007	Bond investment	100,000
Discount on bonds		Discount on bond	
payable	3,993	investment	3,993
Bonds payable	100,000	Cash	96,007

Case C—The bond issue was sold (and purchased) at a premium, $104,212:*

Cash	104,212	Bond investment	100,000
Premium on bonds		Premium on bond	
payable	4,212	investment	4,212
Bonds payable	100,000	Cash	104,212

 * Some accountants do not record the discount and premium in separate contra accounts. Under this approach, the entries would be as follows:

Case B—

Borrower		*Investor*	
Cash	96,007	Bond investment	96,007
Bonds payable	96,007	Cash	96,007

Case C—

Cash	104,212	Bond investment	104,212
Bonds payable	104,212	Cash	104,212

The latter approach records the liability and the investment at the net amount that would be reported on the balance sheet. It also simplifies the amortization of premium and discount since the periodic amortization entries are made directly to the liability and investment accounts so that at maturity date, they both reflect the maturity amount. Either approach derives precisely the same results on the periodic financial statements. Also the issuer and investor may use different recording methods.

any discount or plus any premium). Similarly, the *investor* records the cash amount paid for a bond as the cost (present value) of the bond investment.

The data on page 686 for X and Y Corporations and the computation of bond prices on page 688 are used to illustrate the entries to record the issuance of bonds (see entries at the top of this page) which assumes the entire issue, $100,000, was sold by X Corporation to Y Corporation on January 1, 19A (date of the bonds).

Amortization of Discount and Premium

Bond discount and premium affect the *reported* amounts of interest expense for the issuer and interest revenue for the investor. For example, the interest effects in each of the three cases given above can be summarized as follows:

	Case A (sold at par)	Case B (sold at discount)	Case C (sold at premium)
Price of the bonds (cash)	$100,000	$ 96,007	$104,212
Payment of principal at maturity (cash)	(100,000)	(100,000)	(100,000)
Payment of periodic interest ($7,000 × 5)	(35,000)	(35,000)	(35,000)
Difference—total interest expense	$ 35,000	$ 38,993	$ 30,788
Average interest expense per period (÷ 5)	$ 7,000	$ 7,799	$ 6,158

When sold at par, the total interest expense of $35,000 reflects both a stated and yield rate of 7%. In contrast, the total interest in Case B is greater than $35,000 by the amount of the discount ($3,993), since the bond price reflects a yield rate of 8%; in Case C, the total interest is less than $35,000 by the amount of the premium ($4,212), since the bond price reflects a yield rate of 6%. Thus, we see that bond discount and premium affect *(a)* balance sheet investment or liability amounts and *(b)* interest revenue or expense amounts on the income statement. To record and report these effects in accordance with the matching principle, bond discount and premium must be *amortized* as interest over the *period the bond is outstanding, that is, the period from date of sale to maturity date.* The two amortization methods used are (1) the *straight-line* method and (2) the *interest* method.

Straight-Line Amortization. Under this method, an *equal dollar amount* of the discount or premium is amortized each period over the period the bonds are outstanding. To illustrate for Cases B and C above, the amortization each period for the five-year life of the bonds would be recorded as shown at the bottom of this page.

The straight-line method of amortization, as illustrated, produces a constant dollar *amount* of interest each period rather than a constant *rate* of interest each period. It can be used under generally accepted accounting principles *only* when the results obtained are not materially different from the interest method results (refer to modifying principle, materiality, Chapter 2, page 35). This has been the case since the issuance of *APB Opinion No. 21* (August 1971), which reads:

> . . . the difference between the present value and the face amount should be treated as discount or premium and amortized as interest expense or income over the life of the note in such

a way as to result in a constant rate of interest when applied to the amount outstanding at the beginning of any given period. This is the "interest" method. . . . However, other methods of amortization may be used if the results obtained are not materially different from those which would result from the "interest" method.

Straight-line amortization is simple, although not theoretically sound.

Interest Method of Amortization. The interest method is sometimes called present value amortization. As explained in the preceding paragraph, it is required by *APB Opinion No. 21* (unless the results of another approach are not materially different). The interest method is based upon the concept of an annuity (see Chapter 6) because *(a)* the constant dollar amount of cash interest each period is viewed as a "rent" and *(b)* periodic interest expense (i.e., the effective interest amount) is computed by applying a *constant rate* to the periodic book value or carrying amount of the bonds. The constant rate is the yield rate of interest as illustrated in Exhibits 20-2 (8%) and 20-3 (6%). Because Exhibit 20-2 is based on a *discount,* the effective interest amount (item *[b]*) *increases* each period since the carrying value in item *(e)* is increasing. In contrast, since Exhibit 20-3 is based on a *premium,* the effective interest amount (item *[b]*) *decreases* each period because the carrying value in item *(e)* is decreasing.

When the interest method is used, it is con-

Issuer's Books—X Corporation			Investor's Books—Y Corporation		

December 31, annual interest and amortization (each year for five years):

Case B—bonds sold at a discount (straight-line amortization):

Interest expense	7,799		Cash	7,000	
Discount on bonds			Discount on bond investment	799	
payable		799*	Interest revenue		7,799
Cash		7,000†			

Note: To simpify, it is assumed that the investor receives the cash on the same date that the issuer disburses the cash.

Case C—bonds sold at a premium (straight-line amortization):

Interest expense	6,158		Cash	7,000	
Premium on bonds payable	842‡		Premium on bond in-		
Cash		7,000	vestment		842
			Interest revenue		6,158

* Amortization: $3,993 ÷ 5 yrs. = $799.
† Cash: $100,000 × .07 = $7,000.
‡ Amortization: $4,212 ÷ 5 yrs. = $842.

EXHIBIT 20–2
Bond Interest and Discount Amortization, Interest Method—Annual Interest Payments (face amount—$100,000)

Date	Cash Interest (7% annual)	Effective Interest (8% annual)	Discount Amortization	Balance Unamortized Discount	Carrying Value of Bonds
1/1/19A starting date				3,993	96,007
12/31/19A	7,000 (a)	7,681 (b)	681 (c)	3,312 (d)	96,688 (e)
12/31/19B	7,000	7,735	735	2,577	97,423
12/31/19C	7,000	7,794	794	1,783	98,217
12/31/19D	7,000	7,857	857	926	99,074
12/31/19E	7,000	7,926	926	-0-	100,000

(a) $100,000 × .07 = $7,000 (based on stated rate).
(b) $96,007 × .08 = $7,681 (based on yield rate of interest).
(c) $7,681 − $7,000 = $681.
(d) $3,993 − $681 = $3,312.
(e) $96,007 + $681 = $96,688 (or $100,000 − $3,312 = $96,688).

EXHIBIT 20–3
Bond Interest and Premium Amortization, Interest Method—Annual Interest Payments (face amount—$100,000)

Date	Cash Interest (7% annual)	Effective Interest (6% annual)	Premium Amortization	Balance Unamortized Premium	Carrying Value of Bonds
1/1/19A starting date				4,212	104,212
12/31/19A	7,000 (a)	6,253 (b)	747 (c)	3,465 (d)	103,465 (e)
12/31/19B	7,000	6,208	792	2,673	102,673
12/31/19C	7,000	6,160	840	1,833	101,833
12/31/19D	7,000	6,110	890	943	100,943
12/31/19E	7,000	6,057	943	-0-	100,000

(a) $100,000 × .07 = $7,000 (based on stated rate).
(b) $104,212 × .06 = $6,253 (based on yield rate of interest).
(c) $7,000 − $6,253 = $747.
(d) $4,212 − $747 = $3,465.
(e) $104,212 − $747 = $103,465 (or $100,000 + $3,465 = $103,465).

venient to prepare an *amortization schedule* such as those illustrated in Exhibits 20–2 and 20–3. The entries for both the issuer and the investor, for the periodic interest and amortization of premium or discount, can be taken directly from the schedule. To illustrate, the entries at the end of the first year would be as shown at the top of page 692.

REPORTING BONDS ON THE FINANCIAL STATEMENTS

The unamortized bond discount (or premium) on the bond liability or investment should be reported *(a)* as a direct deduction from (or addition to) the basic account balance or *(b)* indirectly when the maturity value is reported parenthetically.

Reporting by the Issuer

Bonds payable should be reported at their carrying value under the balance sheet caption "Long-Term Liabilities" (except for bonds to be paid during the next current period). The issuer should deduct unamortized bond discount (a debit balance) from the face amount of the related bonds payable, whereas unamortized bond premium (a credit balance) should be added to the face amount of the bonds. *APB Opinion No.*

Issuer's Books—X Corporation			Investor's Books—Y Corporation		

December 31, 19A, annual interest and amortization:*

Case B—Bonds sold at a discount (interest method amortization):

Interest expense	7,681		Cash	7,000	
Discount on bonds payable		681	Discount on bond investment	681	
Cash		7,000	Interest revenue		7,681

Computations: Exhibit 20–2.

Case C—Bonds sold at a premium (interest method amortization):

Interest expense	6,253		Cash	7,000	
Premium on bonds payable	747		Premium on bond investment		747
Cash		7,000	Interest revenue		6,253

Computations: Exhibit 20–3.

* If separate accounts are not used to record discount or premium, the amortization entry would be made directly to the respective liability or investment accounts. See footnote* to the tabulation of entries on page 689.

21 specifically states that bond discount or premium "should not be classified as a deferred charge or deferred credit." To assure full disclosure, the *Opinion* also states that the face of a note (or bond) payable and the yield rate of interest should be disclosed in the financial statements or in the notes to the statements.[6] To illustrate, the long-term liability for bonds payable should be reported essentially as follows (refer to Exhibit 20–2):

X CORPORATION—ISSUER
Balance Sheet (partial)
At December 31, 19A

Long-Term Liabilities:		
Bonds payable, maturity amount (due December 31, 19E, 7% interest, payable annually)		$100,000
Less unamortized discount (based on 8% effective interest)		3,312
Bonds payable less unamortized discount		$96,688

Reporting by the Investor

Long-term investments in bonds should be reported under the balance sheet caption, "Investments and Funds." The amount reported as the

carrying value should be the face amount of the bonds, plus or minus any unamortized premium or discount. In addition, the current market value, if determinable and materially different from the carrying value, and the yield rate of interest used for amortization purposes, should be reported to assure full disclosure. For example, the long-term investment analyzed in Exhibit 20–2 usually is reported essentially as follows:

Y CORPORATION—INVESTOR
Balance Sheet (partial)
At December 31, 19A

Investments and Funds:	
Investment in 7% bonds of X Corporation (amortized cost based on 8% effective interest, due December 31, 19E)	$96,688

The maturity amount ($100,000), the unamortized discount ($3,312), and the difference ($96,688) could be shown separately in a manner similar to that illustrated earlier for the issuer.

ACCOUNTING FOR SEMIANNUAL INTEREST PAYMENTS

Most bonds specify interest as an annual rate but require semiannual interest payments. In this situation, the semiannual rate used is half the annual rate and the number of interest periods is double the number of years to maturity (see Chapter 6).

To illustrate the accounting process when in-

[6] *APB Opinion No. 21,* "Interest on Receivables and Payables" (New York, August 1971), Appendix, par. 20. Also, the provisions of *FASB Statement No. 12* do not apply to long-term investments in debt securities and the LCM concept is not applied to them.

EXHIBIT 20–4

Bond Interest and Discount Amortization, Interest Method—Semiannual Interest Payments (face amount—$100,000)

Date	Cash Interest (3½% semi-annual)	Yield Interest (4% semi-annual)	Discount Amortization	Balance Unamortized Discount	Carrying Value of Bonds
1/1/19A starting date				4,056	95,944
6/30/19A	3,500 (a)	3,838 (b)	338 (c)	3,718 (d)	96,282 (e)
12/31/19A	3,500	3,851	351	3,367	96,633
6/30/19B	3,500	3,865	365	3,002	96,998
12/31/19B	3,500	3,880	380	2,622	97,378
6/30/19C	3,500	3,895	395	2,227	97,773
12/31/19C	3,500	3,911	411	1,816	98,184
6/30/19D	3,500	3,927	427	1,389	98,611
12/31/19D	3,500	3,944	444	945	99,055
6/30/19E	3,500	3,962	462	483	99,517
12/31/19E	3,500	3,983	483	-0-	100,000

(a) $100,000 × .035 = $3,500 (based on stated interest rate).
(b) $95,944 × .04 = $3,838 (based on yield rate).
(c) $3,838 − $3,500 = $338.
(d) $4,056 − $338 = $3,718.
(e) $95,944 + $338 = $96,282 (or $100,000 − $3,718 = $96,282).

terest is paid semiannually, assume the bonds issued on January 1, 19A, by X Corporation specified semiannual interest payments on June 30 and December 31. The stated semiannual interest rate would be 3.5%, and the number of semiannual *interest periods* would be 10; if sold at an annual yield rate of 8%, the semiannual *effective rate* would be 4%. The price of this bond issue on January 1, 19A, would be computed as follows:

Present value of future principal:
$100,000 × $p_{n=10;i=4\%}$ (Table 6–2) =
  $100,000 × .67556 .... = $67,556
Present value of future semiannual interest payments:
$3,500 × $P_{o_{n=10;i=4\%}}$ (Table 6–4) =
  $3,500 × 8.11090 .... = 28,388
Bond price (semiannual interest
  payments assumed) $95,944

The bond amortization table for this situation is presented in Exhibit 20–4. The entries for the issuer and the investor for this example are the same as previously illustrated except that *(a)* an interest entry (including amortization for six months) must be made at each semiannual in-

terest date and *(b)* the amounts of cash, interest, and discount amortization will be as reflected in Exhibit 20–4.

PART B—SPECIAL PROBLEMS IN ACCOUNTING FOR BONDS

In Part A, certain complexities were excluded to compare the fundamentals of accounting for and reporting bonds for the issuer and the investor. Some complexities that often occur in accounting for and reporting bonds are discussed in this part of the chapter.

For illustrative purposes, a different fact situation will be used that specifies semiannual interest payments. However, early maturity and even interest rates again will be used to shorten the illustrations. The fact situation is as follows:

Issuer: Cox Corporation
Investor: Day Corporation

Terms of the bond indenture:

a.	Maturity amount of the bonds.	$200,000 ($10,000 and $1,000 denominations).
b.	Date of the bonds.	January 1, 19A.
c.	Maturity date.	December 31, 19C (3 years).

d. Stated interest rate.   8%, payable 4% semiannually.

e. Interest payments (cash). $8,000 each June 30 and December 31.

f. Date sold.   As specified in each example to follow.

g. Yield interest rate and bond price.   7% (3½ % semiannually); price, $205,329 (Exhibit 20–1: 102,664.27 × 2 = $205,329)

h. Amortization schedule (interest method), assuming sale and issuance on January 1, 19A:

Date	Cash Interest (4% semi-annual)	Yield Interest (3½% semi-annual)	Premium Amorti-zation	Balance Unamor-tized Pre-mium	Carrying Value of Bonds
1/1/19A starting date				5,329	205,329
6/30/19A	8,000 (a)	7,187 (b)	813 (c)	4,516 (d)	204,516 (e)
12/31/19A	8,000	7,158	842	3,674	203,674
6/30/19B	8,000	7,129	871	2,803	202,803
12/31/19B	8,000	7,098	902	1,901	201,901
6/30/19C	8,000	7,067	933	968	200,968
12/31/19C	8,000	7,032	968	-0-	200,000

(a) $200,000 × .04 = $8,000 (based on stated rate).
(b) $205,329 × .035 = $7,187 (based on yield rate).
(c) $8,000 − $7,187 = $813.
(d) $5,329 − $813 = $4,516.
(e) $200,000 + $4,516 = $204,516 (or $205,329 − $813 = $204,516).

BONDS SOLD AND PURCHASED BETWEEN INTEREST DATES

Bonds are rarely traded on interest dates. This situation necessitates recognition in the accounts of accrued interest from the *last interest date* to the date of the transaction. The amount of cash is increased by the amount of the accrued interest for the same period. Accrued interest arises because of a particular characteristic of bonds. That is, the *full amount* of the periodic *stated* interest on a bond will be paid in cash on each interest date after sale, regardless of its sale date. Therefore, when a bond is purchased between interest dates, the amount paid for the bond by the investor will be *(a)* the price of the bond plus *(b)* any accrued interest from the last interest date. Otherwise, the seller would have no way of collecting the interest earned since the last interest date.

Bonds Sold between Interest Dates at Par

To illustrate when bonds are sold at par between interest dates, assume Cox Corporation sold $100,000 of the 8% bonds, dated January 1, 19A, to Day Corporation on November 1, 19A, at par plus the four months' accrued interest. This situation can be diagrammed on a time scale as follows:

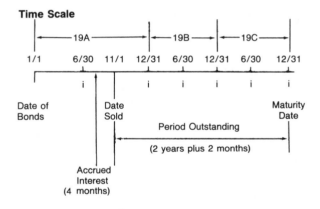

Time Scale

	Cox Corporation—Issuer		Day Corporation—Investor	
November 1, 19A—To record sale and purchase of the bonds (including four months' accrued interest):				
Cash 102,667			Investment in bonds 100,000	
Bonds payable		100,000	Interest revenue* 2,667	
Interest expense*		2,667	Cash	102,667
December 31, 19A—To record payment of stated semiannual interest:				
Interest expense 4,000			Cash 4,000	
Cash ($100,000 × .04)		4,000	Interest revenue	4,000

* If the purchase/sale transaction date is in one accounting period and the next interest date is in the following accounting period most accountants use interest payable and interest receivable, respectively, in these latter two entries. Both approaches derive the same ultimate net effect.

The amount of cash flowing from the investor to the issuer can be computed as follows:

Sale price of the bond issue on 11/1/19A (at par)	$100,000
Add: Accrued interest since last interest date (June 30 to November 1—$100,000 × .04 × ⁴⁄₆)	2,667
Total cash paid on date of sale/purchase transaction	$102,667

The issuer and the investor would make the entries in 19A shown at the bottom of page 694.

After posting both entries, the respective interest expense and interest revenue accounts will stand at $1,333 (i.e., $4,000 − $2,667), which represents interest for the two months outstanding ($100,000 × .04 × ²⁄₆ = $1,333). Similarly, bond transactions between *individual investors* when not on an interest date require recognition of accrued interest by both parties.

Bonds Sold between Interest Dates at a Discount or Premium

When a bond is traded between interest dates at a *discount,* or *premium,* the accounting illustrated immediately above is followed except that the discount or premium must be recorded and then amortized over the *period outstanding,* that is, *the period from the date of sale (not the date of the bond) to the maturity date.*

To illustrate, assume Cox Corporation sold $100,000 of the 8% bond issue, reflected on the time scale on page 694, at a 7% yield rate on November 1, 19A. Recall that the bonds were dated January 1, 19A, and mature on December 31, 19C; thus they are sold two years plus two months before maturity. The bond price on November 1, 19A, to yield 7%, and the cash flow would be computed as follows:

Bond price computed ($100,000, 8% semiannually, sold to yield 7%, two years plus two months before maturity date; see Exhibit 20–1 Table C):	
Bond price if sold on prior interest date, June 30, 19A (2½ yrs.)	$102,258
Bond price if sold on next interest date, December 31, 19A (2 yrs.)	101,837
Difference	$ 421

Interpolation for bond price on November 1, 19A:	
$101,837 + ($421 × ²⁄₆) =	
$101,837 + $140	= $101,977
Total cash flow at date of sale (November 1, 19A):	
$101,977 + accrued interest ($100,000 × .04 × ⁴⁄₆) = ...	$104,644

Note: Straight-line interpolation was used for simplicity. In practice, bond prices between interest dates usually are computed on a daily discounting basis using the number of days between the date of sale and the maturity date.

The issuer and investor would record the transaction as follows:

Issuer:

November 1, 19A—to record sale/purchase of bond issue:

Cash	104,644	
Interest expense		2,667
Premium on bonds payable		1,977
Bonds payable		100,000

Investor:

Bond investment	100,000	
Interest revenue	2,667	
Premium on bond investment	1,977	
Cash		104,644

The premium ($1,977) must be amortized over the total period outstanding (26 months). Assume straight-line amortization can be used because the results would not be materially different from interest method results. On the next interest date, the cash interest for the full six months and amortization of premium for the two months since date of sale would be recorded as shown at the top of page 696.[7]

After these two entries are posted to the accounts, the respective interest expense and revenue accounts will reflect net interest amounts (of $3,848 − $2,667 = $1,181) for two months, the period outstanding since the date of sale.

Alternatively, amortization based on the *interest method* would be as reflected in Exhibit 20–5. When the transaction is between interest dates, as in this illustration (two months before

---

[7] These entries assume amortization on interest dates; amortization often is delayed until the end of the accounting period. These entries also assume discount and premium are not recorded in the bond accounts. If the approach shown in footnote* to the tabulation of entries on page 689 is followed, the amount amortized would be recorded directly in the liability and investment accounts, respectively.

	Issuer		Investor	

December 31, 19A—to record semiannual interest payment and amortization of bond premium using straight-line amortization:

Issuer			Investor	
Interest expense	3,848		Cash	4,000	
Premium on bonds payable	152		Premium on bond investment		152
Cash ($100,000 × .04)		4,000	Interest revenue		3,848

Amortization: $1,977 ÷ 26 (total months outstanding) = $76 per month.
$76 × 2 (months outstanding this period) = $152.

the next interest date), the amortization amount at the first interest date after acquisition must be uniquely determined. It is computed as the difference between the sales price at transaction date (November 1, 19A, in the example) and the sales price at the next interest date (i.e., December 31, 19A). This computation is shown in Exhibit 20–5. Entries to reflect the semiannual interest and premium amortization also are reflected in that exhibit. This is an important example because typically bonds are bought and sold between interest dates, at a discount or premium, and the interest method should be used.

ACCOUNTING WHEN INTEREST PERIODS AND FISCAL PERIODS DO NOT COINCIDE

Typically, the interest date on bonds (and other debt securities) does not coincide with the end of the accounting period. In this situation, an issuer must *accrue* interest on a bond from the last interest date to the end of the accounting period. Similarly, an investor must accrue interest revenue on a bond investment.

In respect to bonds with a discount or premium, the discount or premium must be amortized for the period between the last amortiza-

EXHIBIT 20–5
Bond Interest and Premium Amortization between Interest Dates, Interest Method (semiannual interest payments)

Date	Cash Interest (4% semiannual)	Effective Interest (3½% semiannual)	Premium Amortization	Balance Unamortized Premium	Carrying Value of Bonds
11/1/19A starting date				1,977	101,977 (a)
12/31/19A	4,000 (b)	3,860 (b)	140 (c)	1,837	101,837
6/30/19B	4,000	3,564 (d)	436 (e)	1,401 (f)	101,401 (f)
12/31/19B	4,000	3,549	451	950	100,950
6/30/19C	4,000	3,533	467	483	100,483
12/31/19C	4,000	3,517	483	-0-	100,000

Computations:
(a) Per bond price computation on page 695.
(b) $100,000 × 4% = $4,000, and $4,000 − $140 = $3,860.
(c) Amortization to December 31, 19A:

Bond price on date of sale, November 1, 19A	$101,977
Bond price on *next* interest date, December 31, 19A (per above)	101,837
Amortization for 2 months	$ 140

Sequential computations:
(d) $101,837 × 3.5% = $3,564, etc.
(e) $4,000 − $3,564 = $436, etc.
(f) $1,837 − $436 = $1,401; $101,837 − $436 = $101,401, etc.

tion date and the year-end date; otherwise, interest for the period is misstated.

To illustrate, assume (for this example only) that the accounting periods for Cox Corporation and Day Corporation end on March 31 and that the bonds were sold on January 1, 19A as assumed on pages 693 and 694. At the end of the accounting period, the following adjusting entries would be made:[8]

March 31, 19A—Adjusting entry for accrued interest and premium amortization for the three months, January–March 19A, (computations based on data from the amortization schedule shown on page 694):

Issuer—Cox Corporation:

Interest expense ($7,187 × 3⁄6)	3,594	
Premium on bonds payable ($813 × 3⁄6) . . .	406	
Interest payable ($200,000 × .04 × 3⁄6)		4,000

(Note: Assuming the straight-line method, the amortization would be $5,329 × 3⁄36 = $444).

Investor—Day Corporation:

Interest receivable	4,000	
Premium on bond investment		406
Interest revenue		3,594

BOND ISSUE COSTS

Typically a number of costs are incurred in preparing and selling a bond issue. Bond issue costs include legal, accounting, other professional fees, commissions, engraving, printing, registration, and promotion costs. Generally accepted accounting principles classify these expenditures collectively as a *deferred charge* rather than as an element of bond discount or premium.[9] Bond issue costs should be accounted for separately from bond premium and bond discount. Bond issue costs should be amortized over the period the bonds will be outstanding (between the sale date and the maturity date) because it is assumed that related future revenue benefits will flow from the proceeds of the financing. Theoretically, bond issue costs should

be amortized using the interest method; however, the straight-line method generally is used because of immateriality.

To illustrate accounting for bond issue costs, assume Cox Corporation sold the $200,000 bonds for $205,329 (see pages 693 and 694) on January 1, 19A (also date of the bonds). Bond issue costs were $1,500.

a. January 1, 19A—to record sale:

Cash ($205,329 − $1,500)	203,829	
Bond issue costs deferred	1,500	
Premium on bonds payable		5,329
Bonds payable		200,000

b. June 30, 19A—To record amortization on bond issue costs using straight-line basis:

Interest expense (or bond issue expense)	250	
Bond issue costs deferred ($1,500 ÷ 6)		250

NONCONVERTIBLE BONDS WITH DETACHABLE STOCK WARRANTS

Debt securities, usually bonds, sometimes are issued with *stock warrants* attached. A stock warrant gives the holder an option to purchase from the issuer, within a stated time period, a specified number of shares of common stock at a specified price per share. Detachable stock warrants are often "attached" to bonds to enhance the marketability of the bonds. Bonds with detachable stock warrants usually carry a lower interest rate and tend to sell for a higher price than ordinary bonds.

Detachable stock warrants can be separated from the bonds and traded on the market; that is, they are *equity* instruments that are *separable* from the debt instrument. Because of this separability, *APB Opinion No. 14,* "Accounting for Convertible Debt and Debt Issued with Stock Purchase Warrants," states that "the portion of the proceeds of debt securities issued with detachable stock purchase warrants which is allocable to the warrants should be accounted for as paid-in capital. The allocation should be based on the relative [market] values of the two securities at time of issuance." When the market value of one security (i.e., the bond or the detach-

---

[8] These entries assume amortization on interest dates; amortization often is delayed until the end of the accounting period.

[9] *APB Opinion No. 21,* "Interest on Receivables and Payables," par. 16.

able stock warrant) cannot be determined, the market value of the other should be subtracted from the total consideration to determine the value of the other security.

In contrast with detachable stock warrants, if stock warrants are *not* detachable, there will be no separate market for them. In this case, *APB Opinion No. 14* stipulates that the full amount of the proceeds be recognized in the bond accounts and that the stock warrants *not* be recorded as owners' equity (i.e., as stock warrants outstanding).

To illustrate accounting for nonconvertible bonds with detachable stock warrants, assume AB Corporation issued $100,000, 5%, ten-year, *nonconvertible bonds with detachable stock warrants.* Each $1,000 bond carried ten detachable warrants; each warrant was for one share of common stock, par $10, at the specified option price of $15 per share. The bonds, including the warrants, sold at $105,000 and shortly after issuance, the warrants were quoted on the market for $4 each. Since no market value could be determined for the bonds under these conditions, the bond issuance would be recorded as follows:

Issuer:

Cash	105,000	
Bonds payable, 5% (with detachable stock warrants)		100,000
Premium on bonds payable		1,000
Detachable stock warrants outstanding (1,000 warrants @ $4)		4,000

Investor:

Bond investment	100,000	
Premium on bond investment	1,000	
Investment—detachable stock warrants (1,000 warrants @ $4)	4,000	
Cash		105,000

Subsequently, tender of the 1,000 detachable stock warrants for shares of stock would be recorded as follows:

Issuer:

Cash (1,000 × $15)	15,000	
Detachable stock warrants outstanding	4,000	
Common stock, 1,000 shares, par $10		10,000
Contributed capital in excess of par, common stock		9,000

Investor:

Investment in common stock, 1,000 shares	19,000	
Investment—detachable stock warrants		4,000
Cash (1,000 × $15)		15,000

Because of the contractual option price, the market value of the stock, at the date the warrants are tendered, is not recognized.

CONVERTIBLE BONDS

A convertible bond is a debt security which may be converted under specified conditions (usually must be on an interest date) to capital stock (usually common stock) of the issuer, at the option of the *investor*. Typically, convertible bonds also are *callable* (usually on an interest date) at a specified redemption or call price at the option of the *issuer* and are subordinated to nonconvertible debt. Subordinated means a lower class; that is, the convertible debt ranks below nonconvertible debt as a claim against assets. In case of insolvency, the nonconvertible debt would be paid first. Generally, convertible bonds can be sold at an interest rate lower than for nonconvertible bonds because investors impute a value to the conversion privilege. Convertible bonds also have a conversion ratio and/or a conversion price specified in the bond indenture. The *conversion ratio* is the number of shares of common stock the holder of a convertible bond will receive when it is tendered for conversion. In contrast, the *conversion price* is the face amount of the convertible bond divided by the number of shares of common stock (per bond) to be received upon conversion.

To illustrate, assume AB Corporation issued $1,000 convertible bonds, each of which could be converted, at the option of the holder at any interest date after the second year from issuance, for ten shares of AB Corporation common stock. The conversion ratio for each bond would be 10 (shares of stock) to 1 (bond). Or, stated differently, the conversion price would be $1,000 ÷ 10 shares = $100.

Convertible bonds offer certain advantages to both the issuer and the investor. The primary advantages to the issuer are *(a)* a lower rate of interest and *(b)* a means of securing equity (stockholder) financing in the long run (after conversion, this is the net effect since the debt is not paid in cash). The call option can be used by the issuer to force conversion when the aggregate price of the stock to be issued on conversion is greater than the call price of the bonds; in this case, only an uninformed investor would take cash in lieu of the stock.

The primary advantages of convertible bonds to the investor are *(a)* an option to receive either the face of the bond at maturity or to convert to common stock of the issuer, *(b)* a guaranteed rate of interest to conversion date or maturity, and *(c)* the opportunity to realize the benefits of appreciation in the price of the common stock of the issuer.

Accounting for the Issuance of Convertible Bonds

Since convertible bonds specify a lower rate of interest than would nonconvertible debt for the same company, and since they can be converted to common stock, there is the basic question upon issuance as to what portion of the sales price should relate to *debt* and what portion should be allocated to stockholders' equity. The problem is similar to that illustrated on page 698 for detachable stock warrants. Because of the inseparability of the debt and the conversion option, *APB Opinion No. 14* specifies that the issuance should be recorded as debt and that "no portion of the proceeds from the issuance should be accounted for as attributable to the conversion feature."

To illustrate, assume AB Corporation sold $100,000, 5%, *convertible* bonds for $106,000. The conversion feature specified that at the option of the *investor,* each $1,000 bond was convertible to ten shares of AB Corporation common stock, par $75, on any interest date after the end of the second year from date of issuance. The issuer and investor would record the transaction as follows:

Issuer:

Cash	106,000	
Premium on bonds payable		6,000
Bonds payable, 5%, convertible		100,000

Investor:

Bond investment (AB Corporation, convertible bonds)	100,000	
Premium on bond investment	6,000	
Cash		106,000

Accounting for Conversion

When convertible bonds are tendered by the *investor* for conversion, the issuer and investor must *(a)* bring all related amounts to a current status as of the date of the conversion (interest accruals and discount or premium amortization) and *(b)* remove the resulting carrying values from the accounts. When conversion is on an interest date, all related account balances are current.

Recording the conversion transaction poses a question as to the correct valuation to record for the new security issued. Two methods are available: (1) record the new security issued at the amount of the carrying value of the old security converted or (2) record the new security issued at either its current market value or the current market value of the old security converted, whichever is the more clearly determinable. To illustrate, assume all of the AB Corporation bonds (above) are tendered for conversion on an interest date when the unamortized premium amounted to $3,000 and the common stock had a current market price of $110 per share. The entries under each method would be as follows:

Issuer—AB Corporation:

	Book Value Method	Market Value Method
Bonds payable, 5%, convertible	100,000	100,000
Premium on bonds payable	3,000	3,000
Loss on conversion of convertible bonds		7,000
Common stock (1,000 shares @ $75)	75,000	75,000
Contributed capital in excess of par*	28,000	35,000

* $103,000 − $75,000 = $28,000; 1,000 shares × ($110 − $75) = $35,000.

Investor:

Investment in stock, AB Corporation	103,000	110,000
Bond investment, AB Corporation	100,000	100,000
Premium on bond investment	3,000	3,000
Gain on conversion of bond investment		7,000

The book value method is used almost exclusively. Although it appears deficient conceptually for the *measurement of the new security,* it is widely accepted because *(a)* it does not recognize a gain or loss on the issuance of equity securities; *(b)* it recognizes the conversion as the completion of a prior transaction (the issuance of the convertible debt); and *(c)* conversion does not represent the culmination of a completed earning process.[10]

Convertible bonds that are reacquired by exercise of a call provision (i.e., at the option of the issuer), rather than by conversion by the investor, are accounted for under the provisions of *APB Opinion No. 26,* "Early Extinguishment of Debt," and *FASB Statement No. 4,* "Reporting Gains and Losses from Early Extinguishment of Debt," as discussed in Part C of this chapter.

PART C—CHANGES IN OBLIGATIONS PRIOR TO MATURITY

In recent years there has been a significant increase in situations in which debtors (borrowers) have been unable to meet specific debt obligations because of financial difficulties. Also, for a number of reasons there have been an increasing number of early extinguishments of debt including bond refunding transactions. This part of the chapter discusses three topics that focus on changes in debt obligations prior to maturity date; they are as follows:

Topic	Basic Reference
1. Early extinguishment of debt.	*APB Opinion No. 26,* "Early Extinguishment of Debt."
	FASB Statement No. 4, "Reporting Gains and Losses from Extinguishment of Debt."
2. Classification of short-term obligations expected to be refinanced.	*FASB Statement No. 6,* "Classification of Short-Term Obligations Expected to Be Refinanced."
3. Troubled debt restructuring.	*FASB Statement No. 15,* "Accounting by Debtors and Creditors for Troubled Debt Restructurings."

---

[10] *APB Opinion No. 29,* "Accounting for Nonmonetary Transactions" (New York, May 1973), does not apply to transactions involving only the company's own securities.

EARLY EXTINGUISHMENT OF DEBT

APB Opinion No. 26 defines early extinguishment as "the reacquisition of any form of debt security or instrument before its scheduled maturity *except through conversion by the holder,* regardless of whether the debt is viewed as terminated or is held as so-called 'treasury bonds.' All open-market or mandatory reacquisitions of debt securities to meet sinking fund requirements are early extinguishments" (emphasis supplied). Thus, early extinguishment of debt may be *(a)* by exercise of a call privilege by the issuer or *(b)* by purchase in the open market.

Call Provisions. Bonds and certain other debt instruments frequently carry a *call provision* stating that, at the option of the issuer, the debt may be called for payment prior to maturity. Call time limits and call reacquisition price are specified in the bond indenture and are printed on each bond certificate. Early extinguishment by call is normally required to be on an interest date, in which case the amortization of any discount or premium and bond issue costs will be up to date and there will be no accrued interest.

Purchase in the Open Market. The issuer may purchase debt securities in the open market (for extinguishment) by paying the current market price. Such open-market purchases may or may not be on an interest date. If not on an interest date, the amortization of any discount, premium, bond issue costs, and accrued interest must be recorded from the last interest date to the date of purchase.

APB Opinion No. 26, "Early Extinguishment of Debt" (October 1972), specifies the appropriate accounting for early extinguishment of debt. The *Opinion* is based upon the fundamental concept that "all extinguishments of debt before scheduled maturities are fundamentally alike. The accounting for such transactions should be the same regardless of the means used to achieve the extinguishment." Therefore, the accounting and reporting should be essentially the same when debt is extinguished by

1. Paying cash.
2. Transferring assets other than cash.
3. Transferring equity securities by the debtor.
4. Refunding old debt by issuing new debt.

FASB Statement No. 4 "Reporting Gains and Losses from Early Extinguishment of Debt" (March 1975), specifies that "gains and losses from extinguishment of debt that are included in the determination of net income shall be aggregated and, if material, classified as an extraordinary item, net of related income tax effect. That conclusion shall apply whether an extinguishment is early or at a scheduled maturity date or later."[11]

Three typical illustrations of early extinguishment of debt will be given:

Case A—Exercise of call provision. On January 1, 19A, Corporation A issued ten-year, $100,000, 6% (payable semiannually on June 30 and December 31), callable bonds. The bonds can be called by the issuer at 101 at any time after December 31, 19C. At issuance date the bonds sold for $107,794 based on a 5% yield rate.

On July 1, 19D, Corporation A called in all of the bonds and retired them. For simplicity, assume the company used the straight-line method of amortizing bond premium.

The indicated entries at issuance and recall are as follows:

January 1, 19A—Issuance:

Cash	107,794	
Bonds payable, 6%, callable at 101		100,000
Premium on bonds payable		7,794

July 1, 19D—Recall at 101:

Bonds payable, 6%, callable at 101	100,000	
Premium on bonds payable (unamortized, $7,794 × 13/20)	5,066	
Cash		101,000
Extraordinary gain, early extinguishment of debt		4,066

Case B—Purchase in the open market. On January 1, 19A, Corporation B issued ten-year, $100,000, 5% (payable semiannually on June 30 and December 31) bonds. At issuance date the bonds sold for $92,562.

[11] *FASB Statement No. 15,* "Accounting for Debtors and Creditors for Troubled Debt Restructurings," June 1977, amended *FASB Statement No. 4* to exclude from its provisions all transactions that qualify as troubled debt restructuring (discussed later).

On January 1, 19D, Corporation B purchased all of the bonds in the open market at $99,000. For simplicity, assume the company used straight-line amortization of bond discount.

The indicated entries at issuance and reacquisition are as follows:

January 1, 19A—Issuance:

Cash	92,562	
Discount on bonds payable	7,438	
Bonds payable, 5%		100,000

January 1, 19D—Reacquisition:

Bonds payable, 5%	100,000	
Extraordinary loss, early extinguishment of debt	4,207	
Discount on bonds payable (unamortized, $7,438 × 14/20)		5,207
Cash		99,000

Refunding Bonds Payable. Early extinguishment of an outstanding issue of old bonds by the issuance of new bonds is called *refunding.* The refunding decision may involve one of the following transactions:

1. Direct exchange of the new bonds for the old bonds held by the current bondholders. In this case the old bondholders become the new bondholders.
2. Issuance of new bonds to obtain cash to purchase the old bonds in the bond market. In this case there is a new group of bondholders that replaces the old group.
3. Issuance of new bonds to obtain cash to *call* the old (callable) bonds.

APB Opinion No. 26 specifies that the accounting for all three transactions shall be essentially the same regardless of the means used to achieve the extinguishment. Refunding is viewed as a continuing transaction rather than as a series of separate transactions. Case C is presented below with three different assumptions as to the refunding decision (recall that Case A was exercise of the call and Case B was purchase of the old bonds in the open market). As in previous examples, we ignore bond issue costs to avoid excessive detail which may obscure the main points.

Case C—Refunding bonds payable. On January 1, 19A, Corporation C issued ten-year, $100,000, 5% (payable semiannually on June 30 and December 31) bonds that are callable after 19C at 101. The bonds were initially sold at par.

Refunding issue—On January 1, 19E (i.e., after 4 years), due to significant increases in the "going" market rate of interest, the 5% bonds were quoted on the market at $860 for a $1,000 bond; this quotation reflected the current market rate of 8% (with a slight rounding for instructional convenience).

To refund the old issue on this date, Corporation C issued a new series of 8% (stated interest rate payable semiannually on June 30 and December 31), six-year bonds. Since both the stated and market rates were 8%, the new bonds sold at par.

Assumption 1:

Direct exchange of bonds—On January 1, 19E, new 8% bonds were issued to the holders of the old bonds per an agreement with the bondholders. The agreement stipulated that for each $1,000, 5% bond turned in, a $900, 8% bond would be issued. This exchange rate was favorable to the bondholders because the *present value* of the old bonds at the current 8% "going" rate of interest was as follows:

Principal: $1,000 \times p_{n=12;i=4\%}$ (Table 6–2)
  $1,000 \times .62460$ .... = $625
Interest: ($1,000 \times 2\frac{1}{2}\%) \times P_{o_{n=12;i=4\%}}$ (Table 6–4)
  25×9.38507. .... = 235

  Total present value (theoretical
    market price) $860*

---

* Rounded for instructional convenience.

Receipt of a bond worth more than $860 would provide an incentive for exchange by the bondholders, and any value below that amount would provide a disincentive.

The exchange under the specified conditions, would be recorded as follows:

Bonds payable, 5% 100,000
  Bonds payable, 8% 90,000
  Extraordinary gain, early ex-
    tinguishment of debt 10,000

In this refunding decision, new bonds worth $90,000 were issued to extinguish the old bonds which had a market value of $86,000. Thus, the company incurred an *economic loss* of $4,000, although they reported an *accounting gain* of $10,000. The accounting gain of $10,000 represents the accumulated reduction of $14,000 in

the market value of the old bonds since issuance (i.e., $100,000 − $86,000), less the $4,000 exesss of market value of new bonds given to the bondholders, over the market value of the old bonds (i.e., $90,000 − $86,000).

Assumption 2:

Issuance of new bonds to obtain cash to purchase the old bonds—On January 1, 19E, new 8% bonds were sold to obtain cash for acquisition of the old bonds on the market at the quoted price of $860 per $1,000 bond. The new bonds issued amounted to $86,000 (face), 8% semiannual interest, six years to maturity. The entries to record this early extinguishment of debt by refunding would be:

1. To issue the new bonds:
   Cash 86,000
     Bonds payable, 8% 86,000
2. To retire the old bonds:
   Bonds payable, 5% 100,000
     Cash 86,000
     Extraordinary gain, early ex-
       tinguishment of debt 14,000

The issuing company would report a $14,000 *accounting gain,* although the company actually would incur an *economic* loss (pretax) equal to the bond issue costs (had there been such costs on the new issue). If there had been no bond issue costs, the *economic* gain (or loss) would be exactly zero because the present value of *each* bond issue at the market interest rate of 8% at date of refunding was $86,000, viz:

	Old 5% Bonds	New 8% Bonds
PV of principal (face amount):		
Old: $100,000 × $p_{n=12;i=4\%}$ (.62460)	$62,500	
New: $86,000 × $p_{n=12;i=4\%}$ (.62460)		$53,700
PV of interest payments:		
Old: $2,500 × $P_{o_{n=12;i=4\%}}$ (9.38507)	23,500	
New: $3,440 × $P_{o_{n=12;i=4\%}}$ (9.38507)		32,300
Total present value (theoretical market)	$86,000	$86,000

Assumption 3:

Issuance of new bonds to exercise the call privilege—In Assumptions 1 and 2 above, extraordinary *accounting gains* were reported from refunding bonds payable even though the company either incurred an *economic loss* (in Assumption 1) or fared a little worse, in terms of the present value of cash flows, than break even (in Assumption 2). Assumption 3 illustrates a situation in which the company earns an *economic gain* from refunding. That is, in Assumption 3 it is advantageous for Corporation C to refund and paradoxically, in this situation, the company reports an *accounting loss*. To illustrate this, the fact situation is changed slightly. Retain the basic data of Case C except as follows: Assume the current market rate of interest is 4%, rather than 8% as in Assumptions 1 and 2. In this case, the *theoretical* price of the outstanding 5% bonds *would be* $105,300. However, because Corporation C can call the bonds at 101, the actual bond price will not rise above $101,000 (because investors would be aware of the call privilege at 101). Under these conditions Corporation C can issue new 4% bonds with a face value of $101,000, at par, to obtain the cash needed to retire the old 5% bonds. Thus, the company will earn an *economic gain* of $4,300 (i.e., $105,300 − $101,000) on refunding. However, the accounting entries for the refunding would record an *accounting loss,* as follows:

1. Sale of new bonds:
   Cash 101,000
      Bonds payable, 4% 101,000
2. To retire the old bonds:
   Bonds payable, 5% 100,000
   Extraordinary loss, early extinguishment of debt 1,000
      Cash ($100,000 × 1.01) 101,000

In Assumption 3, as well as in Assumptions 1 and 2, the difference between the *accounting* results and the *economic* results of refunding are due to the fact that under historical cost accounting, changes in the market value of outstanding bonds payable are *not* recognized as changes occur in market value. Instead, market value changes are recognized only when a completed transaction occurs. Of course, this situation is germane to the historical cost model; however, the paradoxical nature of the results are depicted more clearly in the case of bond refunding than in some other types of transactions. In summary, the general model for determining whether to extinguish debt early (such as refunding bonds payable) can be stated as follows:

> Refund if (and only if) the *present value* of the old debt extinguished is *greater* than the sum of the present value of the new debt, plus any cash or other assets given up to extinguish the old issue, subject to the following discussion of income tax effects.

Assessing the Income Tax Effects. To focus on the basic concepts, the above illustrations omitted the income tax effects of the refunding. Now we will add the tax effects to *Assumption 2* by assuming a present and future income tax rate of 40%, that the $14,000 accounting gain is subject to tax, and that the interest paid on each bond issue is subject to tax.[12]

Economic Analysis of Refunding, Aftertax

		Advantage (Disadvantage) of Refunding
Pretax:		
Present value of old bonds (per above)	$86,000	
Present value of new bonds (per above)	86,000	$ -0-
Income tax effects:		
Tax on accounting gain ($14,000 × 40%)		(5,600)
Interest expense on old bonds, present value (per above)	23,500	
Interest expense on new bonds, present value (per above)	32,300	
Additional interest with new bonds	8,800	
Expected tax rate	×.40	
Tax savings on interest in favor of new bonds		3,520
Differential present value— economic gain (loss) from refunding		$(2,080)*

* This amount would be affected by any bond issue costs.

[12] Gains and losses on refunding are subject to income taxes (Code Section 108). There are some technical tax considerations beyond the scope of this discussion. For example, the availability of a large tax loss carryforward may have a major economic impact (favorable) on the issuer's decision to refund.

For Assumption 2 a large refunding gain will be reported on the income statement, although there was an economic loss; the amounts were as follows:

	Pretax	Aftertax
Income statement—accounting gain (loss)	$14,000	$8,400*
Economic gain (loss)		(2,080)

* $14,000 × (1 − .40) = $8,400.

In summary, the decision on early extinguishment of debt should be based on an expected present value analysis (i.e., an economic analysis) of the respective future cash flows, although the accounting must be based on the historical amounts (carrying value) of the debt extinguished.

Because of the significance of early extinguishment of debt, *FASB Statement No. 4* requires, in addition to classification of the accounting gain or loss as *extraordinary,* disclosure in the notes to the financial statements of the following:

a. A description of the extinguishment transactions, including the sources of any funds used to extinguish debt if it is practicable to identify the sources.
b. The income tax effect in the period of extinguishment.
c. The per share amount of the aggregate gain or loss net of related income tax effect.

Classification of Short-Term Obligations Expected to Be Refinanced

Occasionally, a short-term obligation (i.e., a current liability) is expected to be refinanced on a long-term basis which would not require the use of current assets during the ensuing fiscal year (or operating cycle, if longer). Examples are construction loans and currently maturing portions of long-term debt that will be refunded. Prior to the issuance of *FASB Statement No. 6* (May 1975), such obligations were variously reported as *(a)* current liabilities, *(b)* long-term liabilities, and *(c)* special noncurrent liabilities (such as "other" liabilities).

To attain uniformity in reporting, *Statement No. 6* reaffirmed the definition of current liabilities (see Chapter 5) and stated that a short-term obligation shall be *excluded* from current liabilities *only* if the following conditions are met:

> The enterprise's intent to refinance the short-term obligation is supported by an ability to consummate the refinancing demonstrated in either of the following ways: (a) After the date of an enterprise's balance sheet but before that balance sheet is issued, a long-term obligation or equity securities have been issued for the purpose of refinancing the short-term obligation on a long-term basis; or (b) Before the balance sheet is issued, the enterprise has entered into a financing agreement that clearly permits the enterprise to refinance the short-term obligation on a long-term basis on terms that are readily determinable. . . .

Thus, liabilities that meet these conditions must be reported as long-term liabilities and the disclosure in notes to the statements must include "a general description of the financing agreement and the terms of any new obligation incurred or expected to be incurred or equity securities issued or expected to be issued as a result of a refinancing."[13]

TROUBLED DEBT RESTRUCTURING

When interest rates rise and economic conditions become depressed, debtors sometimes experience severe financial strains and even bankruptcy. Foreclosures, repossessions, reorganizations, and a relaxing of contractual interest and principal payments on existing debt often occur. Generally, creditors are inclined to agree to restructure current debt in order to make it possible for the debtor to continue in business rather than moving into bankruptcy. Because of an increasing number of troubled debt restructurings, the FASB issued *Statement No. 15* (June 1977), which specifies precise accounting and reporting guidelines for both the debtor (borrower) and the creditor (lender). This section discusses and illustrates the accounting for troubled debt restructuring.

Troubled debt restructuring is defined as a

---

[13] FASB, *Statement No. 6,* "Classification of Short-Term Obligations Expected to be Refinanced" (Stamford, Conn., May 1975).

situation "when the creditor for economic or legal reasons related to the debtor's financial difficulties grants a *concession* to the debtor that it would not otherwise consider. That concession stems from an agreement between the creditor and the debtor or is imposed by law or a court."[14] The provisions of *FASB Statement No. 15* apply to restructurings consummated under reorganization, arrangement, or other provisions of the Federal Bankruptcy Act, repossession and foreclosure (par. 20).

Troubled debt restructurings may occur before, at, or after the stated maturity of the debt. The date of *consummation* is the date of the restructuring (i.e., the date for accounting recognition).[15] Fundamentally, there are two types of restructuring arrangements:

1. Transfer of assets or equity interests from the debtor to the creditor to satisfy a debt fully or partially.
2. Modification of terms of the debt with respect to *(a)* interest payments and/or *(b)* face amount. This type may involve amounts only, timing only, or both. There are two important subsets to this type:
    a. The restructured total of future cash payments (face plus interest) is equal to, or greater than, the prerestructure carrying (book) value of the debt. In this situation, no entry is made on date of restructure.
    b. The restructured total of future cash payments (face plus interest) is less than the prerestructure carrying (book) value of the debt. In this situation, an entry to recognize a *gain* (by the debtor) and a *loss* (by the creditor) must be made on date of restructure.

Each of these restructuring arrangements is discussed and illustrated in the paragraphs to follow. In those illustrations observe that there

is "accounting symmetry" between the debtor and creditor except for the *classification* of certain gains and losses (*FASB Statement No. 15*, par. 173).

The basic principle in *FASB Statement No. 15* for troubled debt restructuring is that the restructuring *gain to the debtor* and the restructuring *loss to the creditor* are based upon the *carrying value* of the obligation immediately prior to restructuring (i.e., prerestructure or consummation date) related to the *total cash flows* (or cash equivalents) required after restructuring. Thus, if the prerestructure carrying value of the obligation is less than the total future cash flows no restructure gain (debtor) or restructure loss (creditor) is recognized. Alternatively, if the prerestructure carrying value of the obligation is greater than the total future cash flows, the difference is recognized *at date of restructure* as a gain by the debtor and as a loss by the creditor.

To illustrate troubled debt restructuring, the simplified data in Exhibit 20–6 are assumed.

EXHIBIT 20–6
Illustrative Data

Debtor Company		Creditor Company	
Note payable to be restructured:		Note receivable to be restructured:	
Maturity 5 years (10% stated interest rate, annual payments) ..	$ 1,000	Maturity 5 years (10% stated interest rate, annual receipts) ..	$1,000
Accrued interest payable...............	50	Accrued interest receivable	50
Asset X (at date of restructuring):			
Carrying (book) value	500		
Current market value	700		
Common stock, par $1	50,000		
Market price per share, $1.50.			

In the discussions to follow, six cases will be used to illustrate some typical restructuring arrangements:

Transfer of assets or equity interests to settle debt:
  Case A—Transfer of assets from debtor to creditor.
  Case B—Transfer of equity interests from debtor to creditor.

Modification of terms of debt payment (restructured total future cash to be paid by debtor is equal to or greater than the prerestructured carrying value of the debt):

---

[14] A debt restructuring is not necessarily a troubled debt restructuring for purposes of the *Statement,* even if the debtor is experiencing some financial difficulties. Instead, the critical issue in a *troubled* debt restructuring is the granting of *concessions* to the debtor.

[15] *FASB Statement No. 15* amends AICPA, *APB Opinion No. 26,* "Early Extinguishment of Debt" (New York, October 1972), to the extent needed to exclude from that *Opinion's* scope early extinguishment of debt through troubled debt restructurings.

Case C—Defer all interest payments until maturity date (timing change).

Case D—Reduce the face amount (at maturity) of the debt.

Case E—A multiple change; defer all interest payments until maturity and reduce the face amount of the debt.

Modification of terms of debt payment (restructured total future cash to be paid by debtor is less than the prerestructured carrying value of the debt):

Case F—Reduce the amount of the annual interest and reduce the face amount of the debt.

Assume all cases meet the definition of a troubled debt restructure.

Transfer of Assets and Equity Interests

The basic concept underlying the transfer of assets and equity interests by the debtor to the creditor in troubled debt restructuring is that the items transferred should be recorded by both parties at current market value (i.e., cash equivalent value) at the time of restructuring, and the carrying value of the debt should be removed from the records.[16]

Transfer of Assets. For the *debtor* this situation requires recognition of two different "gains or losses": (1) the difference between the carrying (book) value of the asset and its market value must be recorded as a gain or loss on *disposal,* and (2) the excess of the carrying (book) value of the debt settled over the market value of the assets transferred must be recorded as a gain by the debtor (there would never be a loss) on *restructuring. Statement No. 15* specifies that the gain or loss on *disposal* shall be classified as ordinary, unusual or infrequent, or extraordinary in accordance with the provisions of *APB Opinion No. 30.* In contrast, the gain on *restructuring* recognized by the debtor must be reported as an *extraordinary item* net of related income tax effect (par. 21, *FASB Statement No. 15*). The related accounting entries are shown below for Case A based on the data given in Exhibit 20–6.

---

[16] Market value of assets is measured by their market price if an active market for them exists. If no active market exists for the assets transferred but exists for similar assets, the selling prices in that market may be helpful in estimating the market value of the assets transferred. If no market price is available, a forecast of expected cash flows may aid in estimating the market value of assets transferred, provided the expected cash flows are discounted at a rate commensurate with the risk involved.

For the *creditor,* at date of restructuring, recognition must be given in the accounts of the loss on receivable restructuring (there would never be a gain), which is the excess of the carrying (book) value of the receivable settled over the current market value of the assets (or other considerations) received. This loss is classified as ordinary, unusual or infrequent, or extraordinary in accordance with the provisions of *APB Opinion No. 30.* The related accounting entries are shown below for Case A. Subsequent to the restructure date the creditor must account for the asset on the same basis as if it were purchased for cash at the market value recorded.

Case A—Transfer of assets to settle the debt in full.

Assume the debtor transferred Asset X to the creditor to settle the note payable and all related obligations.

Entries at Date of Restructure

Debtor

*Asset X ($700 − $500)	200	
Gain on disposal of asset†		200
To recognize gain on disposal of nondepreciable asset.		
Note payable	1,000	
Interest payable	50	
Asset X		700
Extraordinary gain on debt restructure .		350
To record settlement of debt by transfer of asset. (Note: If this were a depreciable asset the accumulated depreciation account also would be debited in this entry.)		

Creditor

Asset X	700	
Loss on receivable restructure†	350	
Note receivable		1,000
Interest receivable		50
To record asset received in settlement of receivable.		

* If the asset transferred is a receivable from a third party, *FASB Statement No. 15* states that recognition must be given to estimated uncollectible accounts included in the receivables.

† *FASB Statement No. 15,* par. 14, states: "A difference between the fair value and the carrying amount of assets transferred to a creditor to settle a payable is a gain or loss on transfer of assets. The debtor shall include that gain or loss in measuring net income for the period of transfer, reported as provided in *APB Opinion No. 30,* "Reporting the Results of Operations" (June 1973). (Note: The term "fair value" was used in the *Opinion* to mean market value.)

Transfer of Equity Interest. When an equity interest (i.e., stock of the debtor) is issued, both parties must record it at the market value at date of restructure. For the *debtor,* this requires that the stock issued be recorded in the normal manner with the difference between par or stated value and the market value of the stock recorded as contributed capital in excess of par, as reflected in Case B. Any excess of the prerestructure carrying value of the debt over the market value of the stock issued must be recorded as an *extraordinary gain.*

For the *creditor,* the stock received must be recorded as an investment in addition to a loss (ordinary) on receivable restructure equal to any excess of the carrying (book) value of the debt settled over the *market value* of the stock received as reflected in Case B.

Case B—Transfer of an equity interest to settle the debt in full.

Assume the debtor transferred 600 shares of its common stock to the creditor to settle the note payable and all related obligations.

Entries at Date of Restructure

Debtor

Note payable	1,000	
Interest payable	50	
Common stock, par $1		
(600 shares)		600
Contributed capital in excess of par		300
Extraordinary gain on debt		
restructure		150

To record settlement of debt by transfer of stock.

  * 600 shares × ($1.50 − $1.00) = $300.

Creditor

Investment in common stock,		
Debtor Company		
(600 shares)	900	
Loss on receivable restructure*	150	
Note receivable		1,000
Interest receivable		50

  * Classify according to provisions of *APB Opinion No. 30* as ordinary, unusual or infrequent, or extraordinary.

Modification of Terms of Debt

Modification of terms of debt in a troubled debt situation may involve one or more of the following changes: *(a)* reduction in the interest rate, *(b)* extension of the payment date for interest, *(c)* reduction of the face amount, *(d)* extension of the payment date of the face amount, and *(e)* reduction in any accrued interest (i.e., interest accrued before the restructure date). In these modifications of terms no assets or equity interests are transferred from the debtor to the creditor on the restructure date.

The basic concept in accounting for modification of terms of troubled debt is that the effects must be treated *prospectively.* On this point *FASB Statement No. 15* specifies that the debtor in a troubled debt restructuring "shall account for the effects of the restructuring prospectively from the time of restructuring, and shall not change the carrying amount of the payable at the time of restructuring unless the (prerestructure) carrying amount exceeds the total future cash payments specified by the new terms." Also, "a debtor shall not recognize a gain on a restructured payable involving indeterminate future cash payments as long as the maximum total future cash payments may exceed the carrying amount of the payable." Clearly, this means that neither the creditor nor the debtor will make an entry at date of restructuring *except* when the prerestructure carrying amount of the debt is *more* than the total future cash payments required.

Subsequent to restructure date, both the creditor and the debtor must recognize periodic interest which is specified in *FASB Statement No. 15* as follows: "computed in a way that a constant effective interest rate is applied to the carrying amount of the payable at the beginning of each period between restructuring and maturity [in substance the "interest" method prescribed in paragraph 15 of *APB Opinion No. 21*]. The new effective interest rate shall be the discount rate that equates the present value of the future cash payments specified by the new terms (excluding amounts contingently payable) with the carrying amount of the payable."[17] This means that a *new effective rate of interest* must be computed as of the date of restructure and used throughout the remaining *restructured* life of the debt. In some situations the new effective rate can be computed directly using appropriately selected values from present and future

---

[17] Carrying amount of a payable for the creditor includes face amount, plus or minus unamortized premium or discount, and for the debtor, these amounts plus unamortized issue costs.

value tables (like those given in Chapter 6). In other instances the effective rate usually must be determined by the trial-and-error (iteration) method. Cases C through F illustrate computation of the new effective interest rate and the *prospective* accounting for both the debtor and the creditor. Case F illustrates a situation in which the prestructured carrying amount of the debt *exceeds* the total future cash payments required (in contrast to the other situations, this one does require an entry on the restructure date).

Case C—Modification of Terms—Defer all interest payments to maturity date (end of year 5).

Assume the only modification is to defer collection of the five $100 interest payments so that there will be a single $500 collection of interest at the end of the fifth year in addition to the $1,000 face amount. Assume the $50 accrued interest is paid prior to restructure. Since the change in timing of the interest affects the interest rate, a new prospective interest rate must be computed as follows (refer to Chapter 6):

Set the carrying value of the debt equal to the present value of the restructured cash flows and solve for the new interest rate. In this case,

$$\$1,000 = \$1,500 \times p_{n=5;i=?}$$

Rearranging for use of Table 6–2:

$$\$1,000 \div \$1,500 = p_{n=5;i=?} = .66667$$

The value of .66667 for five periods implies an interest rate of approximately 8.5% (read from Table 6–2).

The formula may be rearranged for computation by calculator as follows:

$$\$1,500 = \$1,000 \, (1 + i)^5$$
$$1.5 = (1 + i)^5$$
$$(1.5)^{.2} = 1 + i$$
$$1.0845 = 1 + i$$
$$i = 8.5\%$$

Required Entries

Debtor

At restructure date: No entry is made since the prerestructured carrying amount of the debt, $1,000, does not exceed the restructured total future cash payments, $1,500. No cash is paid on restructure date.

At each interest date subsequent to restructure:*

	Year 1	Year 2	Year 3	Year 4	Year 5
Interest expense	85	92	100	108	115
Note payable		85	92	100	108	115

At maturity date   (by this date the above interest entries would have increased the balance in the note payable account to $1,500):

Note payable	1,500	
Cash		1,500

Creditor

At restructure date: No entry is made (same reason as given for debtor).

At each interest date subsequent to restructure:*

	Year 1	Year 2	Year 3	Year 4	Year 5
Note receivable	85	92	100	108	115
Interest revenue		85	92	100	108	115

At maturity date:

Cash	1,500	
Note receivable		1,500

* Computations:

	Interest Expense	Increase Principal	Liability Balance
Start			$1,000
Year 1.........	$1,000 × 8.5% = $ 85	$ 85	1,085
2.........	1,085 × 8.5% = 92	92	1,177
3.........	1,177 × 8.5% = 100	100	1,277
4.........	1,277 × 8.5% = 108	108	1,385
5.........	1,385 × 8.5% = 115†	115	1,500
	$500	$500	

† Rounding error $2.

A variation of this modification of terms would involve simply reducing the amount of the periodic interest amount, say from $100 to $60 (i.e., a reduction in the interest rate from 10% to 6% for the remainder of the debt term). In this instance, no entry would be made on restructure date. On each interest date the usual interest entry (debit Interest Expense and credit Cash) would be recorded for $60 (instead of $100), and at maturity the $1,000 face amount would be paid.

Case D—Modification of Terms—Reduce the face amount of the debt.

Assume the only modification is to reduce the face amount of the note from $1,000 to $800, and the interest payments are not changed. Assume the $50 accrued interest is paid prior to restructure.

Since the reduction of the face amount changes the rate of interest, the new effective rate must be computed. We must find the interest rate that equates the present value of the net future cash flows with the prerestructure carrying amount of $1,000. In this case we set the sum of *(a)* the present value of the new face amount ($800) plus *(b)* the present value of the five $100 interest payments equal to the carrying amount of the debt, and solve for the new interest rate. In this case,

$$\$1,000 = (\$800 \times p_{n=5; i=?}) + (\$100 \times P_{o_{n}=5; i=?})$$

In this situation the only way to solve for "i" is by trial and error; there are no mathematical algorithms to express the solution for "i" (even computers iterate through different "i" values to find the one which equates the right-hand side of the equation to the amount on the left). Thus, we must refer to a "p" table (Table 6–2) and a "P" table (Table 6–4). The trial-and-error computations below show the rate to be 6.5%, viz:

	Present Value at—		
	6%	6.5%	7%
Principal:			
$800 × "$p$" table for $n=5$			
(6.0 = .74726)	$ 598		
(6.5 = .72988)		$ 584	
(7.0 = .71299)			$570
Interest:			
$100 × "$P$" table for $n=5$			
(6.0 = 4.21236)	421		
(6.5 = 4.15568)		416	
(7.0 = 4.10020)			410
Total present value	$1,019	$1,000	$980

When the rate falls between two table values, straight-line interpolation usually will produce results that are reasonably accurate.

Required Entries

Debtor

At date of restructure: None since the carrying amount of the debt ($1,000) does not exceed the future cash payments ($1,300). No cash is paid at restructure.

At each interest date:*

	Year 1	Year 2	Year 3	Year 4	Year 5
Interest					
expense	65	63	60	58	54
Note payable	35	37	40	42	46
Cash	100	100	100	100	100

At maturity date (by maturity date the interest entries would have decreased the balance in the note payable account to $800):

Note payable	800	
Cash		800

Creditor

At date of restructure: None

At each interest date:*

	Year 1	Year 2	Year 3	Year 4	Year 5
Cash	100	100	100	100	100
Interest revenue	65	63	60	58	54
Note receivable	35	37	40	42	46

At maturity date:

Cash	800	
Note receivable		800

* Computations:

	Cash Payment	Interest Expense	Reduction of Principal	Liability Balance
Start				$1,000
Year 1	$100	$1,000 × 6.5% = $ 65	$35	965
2	100	965 × 6.5% = 63	37	928
3	100	928 × 6.5% = 60	40	888
4	100	888 × 6.5% = 58	42	846
5	100	846 × 6.5% = 54†	46	800
		$300	$200	

† $1 rounding error.

Case E—Modification of Terms—Defer interest payments and reduce face amount.

Assume two modifications: (1) defer the five annual interest payments of $100 each to maturity date (as in Case C), in addition to the face amount and (2) reduce the face amount from $1,000 to $800 (as in Case D). Assume the $50 accrued interest is paid before restructure.

Since both of these modifications affect the interest rate, the new effective rate may be computed as follows (refer to Chapter 6 and see Cases C and D for the setup of the interest computations):

Computation by use of Table 6–2:

$1,000 ÷ $1,300 = .76923, the value for $p_{n=5;\ i=?}$

Reference to Table 6–2 indicates the new effective rate to be approximately 5.4% (interpolated).

The formula may be rearranged for computation by calculator:

$$\$1,300 = \$1,000\,(1+i)^5$$
$$1.3 = (1+i)^5$$
$$(1.3)^{.2} = 1+i$$
$$i = 5.4\%$$

In this case the accounting entries for both the debtor and creditor are essentially the same as for Case C except for the amounts. They may be summarized as follows:

At restructure date: No entry is made by either the debtor or creditor because the prerestructured carrying amount of the debt, $1,000, does not exceed the restructured total future cash payments, $1,300.

At each interest date subsequent to restructure: Each party records interest based on the new effective rate of 5.4%. Computation of periodic interest would be as follows:

Computations:

	Interest Expense	Increase Principal	Liability Balance
Start			$1,000
Year 1	$1,000 × 5.4% = $ 54	$ 54	1,054
2	1,054 × 5.4% = 57	57	1,111
3	1,111 × 5.4% = 60	60	1,171
4	1,171 × 5.4% = 63	63	1,234
5	1,234 × 5.4% = 66†	66	1,300
	$300	$300	

† Rounding error $1.

At maturity date: Each party records settlement of the maturity amount, which will have been increased through the interest entries to $1,300.

Modification When Carrying Amount Exceeds Cash Payments

Recall that modifications of the terms of a troubled debt are accounted for *prospectively.* However, when the prerestructure carrying amount of the debt *exceeds* the total restructured future cash payments (principal plus all future interest), on the restructure date "the *debtor* shall reduce the carrying amount to an amount equal to the total future cash payments specified by the new terms and shall recognize a gain on restructuring of payables equal to the amount of the reduction." This gain must be classified as *extraordinary.* "Thereafter, all cash payments under the terms of the payable shall be accounted for as reductions of the carrying amount of the payable, and no interest expense shall be recognized on the payable for any period between the restructuring and maturity of the payable."[18]

The *creditor* must apply the same concepts as the debtor in accounting for the receivable restructuring. However, the loss recorded must be classified as ordinary, unusual or infrequent, or extraordinary in accordance with the provisions of *APB Opinion No. 30.* In this situation, although the effective rate of interest is changed, it need not be computed to make the required accounting entries because the interest actually collected is applied to reduce the balance in the debt account and no interest revenue or expense is recorded after restructure date. Case F illustrates this "exception" to the general approach.

---

[18] *FASB Statement No. 15,* par. 17.

Case F—Modification of Terms (reduce annual interest and reduce face amount of the debt)—Restructured total cash receipts less than the prerestructured carrying value of the debt.

Assume there are two modifications of terms: (1) reduce annual interest collected at the end of each year from $100 to $60 per period and (2) reduce the face amount at the end of the 5 years from $1,000 to $600. Assume the accrued interest of $50 is paid prior to restructure.

Analysis: Since the restructured total cash payments ($600 + $300 = $900) is less than the prerestructured carrying value of $1,000, an entry must be made at restructure date (to recognize the gain or loss on restructuring), and all cash collections are recorded in the note account. This means that no interest revenue or expense is recorded after restructure date.

Required Entries

Debtor

At date of restructure: Adjust the note account to the total cash payments.

Note payable ($1,000 − $900)	100	
Extraordinary gain on debt restructure		100

At each interest date, Years 1–5 (all payments applied to carrying value):

Note payable	60	
Cash		60

At maturity date (the five entries on interest dates will have reduced the balance in the note account from $1,000 to $600):

Note payable	600	
Cash		600

Creditor

At date of restructure: Adjust the note account to the total cash collections.

Loss on receivable restructure	100	
Note receivable		100

At each interest date, Years 1–5:

Cash	60	
Note receivable		60

At maturity date:

Cash	600	
Note receivable		600

DISCLOSURE REQUIREMENTS

FASB Statement No. 15 prescribes detailed disclosure requirements for both the debtor and creditor.

In substance, disclosure by the *debtor* must include (a) a description of the major changes for each restructuring; (b) the aggregate gain on restructuring and the related income tax effect; (c) aggregate loss or gain on transfers of assets; (d) the per share amount of the aggregate gain on restructuring of payables, net of related income tax effect; and (e) information on any related contingent payments.

Disclosure by the *creditor* must include, for outstanding receivables that have been restructured, by major category: (a) the aggregate recorded investment, (b) gross interest revenue that would have been recorded without restructure, (c) the amount of interest revenue on those receivables that was included in net income for the period, and (d) the amount of commitments to lend additional funds to debtors whose terms have been modified in troubled debt restructurings.

Appendix—Serial Bonds

CHARACTERISTICS OF SERIAL BONDS

An issue of bonds with provision for repayment of principal in a series of *installments* is called a serial bond issue. Serial bonds are well adapted for use by school districts and other taxing authorities which borrow money upon agreement that a special tax will be levied to pay off the obligation. As the taxes are collected, the cash can be used to pay off parts of the indebtedness.

DETERMINING SELLING PRICE OF SERIAL BONDS

The selling price of serial bonds may be derived by computing the selling price for each series separately in the same way that a straight bond issue is valued, and then totaling the prices of the several series. For example, assume that serial bonds carrying 7% interest payable 3½%

semiannually are sold to yield 5% per annum with the following maturity dates: $10,000 at end of 12 months, $20,000 at end of 18 months, and $30,000 at end of 24 months. The selling price of each of the three series, as well as that of the whole issue, may be (a) derived from a bond table (similar to Exhibit 20–1) or (b) computed as follows (see pages 687–88).[19]

	Bond Price	Premium
Series No. 1 (due in 12 months— 2 interest periods):		
Principal: $10,000 × .951814*	$ 9,518.14	
Interest payments:		
$350 × 1.9274242†	674.60	
	10,192.74	$ 192.74
Series No. 2 (due in 18 months— 3 interest periods):		
Principal: $20,000 × .928599	18,571.99	
Interest payments:		
$700 × 2.85602	1,999.21	
	20,571.20	571.20
Series No. 3 (due in 24 months— 4 interest periods):		
Principal: $30,000 × .90595	27,178.52	
Interest payments:		
$1,050 × 3.761974	3,950.07	
	31,128.59	1,128.59
Total price of all series	$61,892.53	
Total premium on all series		$1,892.53

* Table 6–2—$p_{n=2;i=2\,1/2\%}$.
† Table 6–4—$P_{o_{n=2;i=2\,1/2\%}}$.

AMORTIZATION OF PREMIUM AND DISCOUNT ON SERIAL BONDS

Amortization of premium or discount on serial bonds is identical with that on ordinary bonds; however, the computations involve more arithmetic. When the results are *not* materially different from the interest method, the straight-line method may be used; otherwise, the interest method must be used. In both methods, the amount of periodic amortization must be related to the amount of bonds *outstanding* during the period. Therefore, the amount of periodic amortization of premium or discount will decrease as each serial is paid off at its maturity date.

Straight-line amortization of the $1,892.53 premium from the above example is computed

---

[19] Although not realistic, a short time span is used to simplify the computations.

EXHIBIT 20–7
Amortization of Premium on Serial Bonds—Straight Line

Serial No.	Total Premium to Be Amortized	Amortization of Premium—Straight Line			
		At End of 6 Months	At End of 12 Months	At End of 18 Months	At End of 24 Months
1	$ 192.74	$ 96.37	$ 96.37		
2	571.20	190.40	190.40	$190.40	
3	1,128.59	282.15	282.15	282.15	$282.14
	$1,892.53	$568.92	$568.92	$472.55	$282.14

for each period in Exhibit 20–7. Observe that the premium on each serial is apportioned to the number of periods the serial is outstanding.[20]

The entries for the foregoing example are given below, with the added assumption that $5,000 par of the Serial No. 3 bonds, which were to mature at the end of 24 months, were purchased for $5,100 and retired (early extinguishment) at the end of 12 months.

1. To record sale of the bonds:

Cash......................	61,892.53	
Premium on bonds payable		1,892.53
Bonds payable		60,000.00

2. To record payment of interest and straight-line amortization of premium at the end of six months:

Interest expense	1,531.08	
Premium on bonds payable (Exhibit 20–7)	568.92	
Cash ($60,000 × 3½%)		2,100.00

[20] Occasionally problems are given that do not provide a basis for determining the amount of premium or discount applicable to each series. In this situation, an approximation, known as dollar-periods or "bonds outstanding" allocation is used. It is appropriate only for the straight-line method. To illustrate, the $1,892.53 total premium could be allocated as follows:

Serial	Par	Periods Outstanding (semiannual)	Dollar Periods	Allocation Fraction	Allocation to Serials
1	$10,000	2	$ 20,000	20/200 × $1,892.53 =	$ 189.25
2	20,000	3	60,000	60/200 × $1,892.53 =	567.76
3	30,000	4	120,000	120/200 × $1,892.53 =	1,135.52
			$200,000		$1,892.53

The amounts in the last column are then allocated to each period on a straight-line basis, as illustrated in Exhibit 20–7.

3. To record payment of interest and amortization of premium at end of 12 months:

Interest expense	1,531.08	
Premium on bonds payable ..	568.92	
Cash		2,100.00

4. To record payment of Serial No. 1 bonds at the end of 12 months:

Bonds payable (Serial No. 1)	10,000.00	
Cash		10,000.00

5. To record retirement of $5,000 of Serial No. 3 bonds at end of 12 months for $5,100 cash:

Bonds payable	5,000.00	
Bond premium	94.05*	
Loss on bonds retired	5.95	
Cash		5,100.00

* ($5,000/$30,000) × ($282.15 + $282.14) = $94.05.

6. To pay interest, amortize premium, and pay off Serial No. 2 bonds at end of 18 months:

Interest expense	1,149.47	
Bond premium [$190.40 + (⅚ × $282.15)]	425.53	
Cash		1,575.00
Bonds payable	20,000.00	
Cash		20,000.00

7. To pay interest, amortize premium, and pay off Serial No. 3 bonds at end of 24 months:

Interest expense	639.88	
Bond premium (⅚ × $282.14)	235.12	
Cash		875.00
Bonds payable	25,000.00	
Cash		25,000.00

Interest method amortization requires knowledge of the yield rate of interest and the selling price. When serial bonds are involved,

EXHIBIT 20–8
Serial Bond Entries Tabulated—Interest Method Amortization

Date	Cash Cr.	Interest Expense Dr.	Bond Premium Dr.	Bonds Payable Dr.	Carrying Value
At issue	—	—	—	—	61,892.53
End 6 months	2,100.00	1,547.31*	552.69	—	61,339.84
End 12 months	2,100.00	1,533.50	566.50	—	60,773.34
End 12 months	10,000.00	—	—	10,000.00	50,773.34
End 18 months	1,750.00	1,269.33	480.67	—	50,292.67
End 18 months	20,000.00	—	—	20,000.00	30,292.67
End 24 months	1,050.00	757.33	292.67	—	30,000.00
End 24 months	30,000.00	—	—	30,000.00	—
	67,000.00	5,107.47	1,892.53	60,000.00	

* $61,892.53 × .025 = $1,547.31.

an amortization table should be prepared in the same manner as the amortization table for ordinary (nonserial) bonds except that the maturity values of each installment must be deducted from the "carrying value" amounts when the installments are paid. An amortization table showing present value amortization of the premium and payment of the three serial installments on the serial bond issue illustrated in the preceding section is given in Exhibit 20–8. In the example, recall that the sales price was $61,892.53 and the yield rate was 2½% semian-

nually. In Exhibit 20–8, observe that the computations are identical to those previously illustrated for nonserial bonds (Exhibit 20–3), except for the payments on principal as each serial matures.

When the interest method is used and some portion of a serial is retired before maturity, the carrying value at the date of early extinguishment must be reduced by the present value of the portion retired. To illustrate, assume $5,000 par of Serial No. 3 bonds are purchased for retirement at the end of 12 months (i.e., two inter-

EXHIBIT 20–9
Serial Bond Entries Tabulated—Interest Method Amortization (effect of early extinguishment)

Date	Cash Cr.	Interest Expense Dr.	Bond Premium Dr.	Bonds Payable Dr.	Extraordinary Loss on Retirement Dr.	Carrying Value
Balance end 12 months	—	—	—	—	—	50,773.34*
End 12 months . .	5,100.00	—	96.37	5,000.00	3.63	45,676.97†
End 18 months . .	1,575.00	1,141.92	433.08	—	—	45,243.89
End 18 months . .	20,000.00	—	—	20,000.00	—	25,243.89
End 24 months . .	875.00	631.11	243.89	—	—	25,000.00
End 24 months . .	25,000.00	—	—	25,000.00	—	—

* From Exhibit 20–8, line 4.
† $50,773.34 − $96.37 − $5,000 = $45,676.97.

est periods before maturity date); the reduction in carrying value would be as follows:

Principal: $5,000 × .951814 (i.e., $P_{n=2;i=.025\%}$
Table 6–2)   = $4,759.07
Interest payments: $175 × 1.927424 (i.e.,
$P_{o_{n=2;i=.025\%}}$Table 6–4)   =   337.30
Present value retired (including premium
retired, $96.37) $5,096.37

The retirement, using the present value computed above, is reflected in Exhibit 20–9, which is a continuation of Exhibit 20–8, starting with line 4. Observe that the first line of Exhibit 20–9 reflects the entry for early extinguishment. The loss, if material in amount, would be reported as an extraordinary item in conformance with *FASB Statement No. 4*, "Reporting Gains and Losses from Early Extinguishment of Debt" (see page 700).

The straight-line method appears to be used much less than in prior years in view of the APB and FASB pronouncements and the ease with which the interest method calculations can be made using computers.

QUESTIONS

PART A

1. What are the primary characteristics of a bond? What distinguishes it from capital stock?

2. Contrast each of the following classes of bonds: (a) industrial versus governmental, (b) secured versus unsecured, (c) ordinary versus income, (d) ordinary versus serial, (e) callable versus convertible, and (f) registered versus coupon.

3. What are the principal advantages and disadvantages of bonds versus common stock for (a) the issuer and (b) the investor?

4. Explain the stated and yield (effective) rates of interest on a bond. Describe their relationship to the market price of a bond.

5. Distinguish between the face (or par) amount and the price of a bond. When are they the same? When different? Explain.

6. Explain the significance of bond discount and bond premium to (a) the issuer and (b) the investor.

7. Assume a $1,000, 6% (payable semiannually), ten-year bond is sold at an effective rate of 8%. Explain two ways for determining the sale price of this bond.

8. Explain why and how bond discount and bond premium affect (a) the balance sheet and (b) the income statement of the investor.

9. Conceptually, what is the basic difference between the straight-line and interest methods of amortizing bond discount and premium?

10. Under generally accepted accounting principles, when is it appropriate to use (a) straight-line and (b) interest method amortization for bond discount or premium?

PART B

11. When the end of the accounting period of the investor is not on a bond interest date, adjusting entries must be made for (a) accrued interest and (b) discount or premium amortization. Explain in general terms what the amount of each represents.

12. When bonds are sold (or purchased) between interest dates, accrued interest must be recognized. Explain why.

13. What are convertible bonds? What are the primary reasons for their use?

14. Why is the accounting different for convertible bonds with detachable stock warrants and those without detachable stock warrants?

PART C

15. What is meant by early extinguishment of debt? How should any resultant gain or loss be reported?

16. What is meant by refunding? When would it generally be advantageous to the issuer?

17. What is meant by troubled debt restructuring? What are some of the typical restructuring arrangements?

DECISION CASE 20–1

Allied Bananas is a major seller of food products with annual sales of more than $1.5 billion. Average net income for the most recent five years has been only $6.5 million. This is an annual profit margin of around .4 percent, which is very low. Thus, A. B. Crown, president of the company, desperately needs to enhance the investment attractiveness of Allied common shares, which are currently selling at $9.50 on the stock exchange.

Allied has outstanding $125 million of 5⅜% convertible bonds payable with 21 years to maturity. The bonds were issued at par nine years ago. Each $1,000 bond is convertible, at the discretion of the bondholder, into 37.5 shares of common stock. The current market rate of interest on bonds with the term to maturity and risk characteristics of Allied bonds is 10%. Thus, the current market value of Allied bonds payable is $75 million.

Recently the Accounting Principles Board issued an *Opinion* which requires companies that pay off or refund their outstanding bonds payable before scheduled maturity dates to report any gain or loss from early extinguishment of debt on the income statement of the year during which the early extinguishment occurs. The president of Allied discerns that this rule may make it possible to increase the reported net income of Allied by refunding the 5⅜% bonds payable. Of course, Allied will have to make the refunding offer sufficiently attractive to its present bondholders to induce them to exchange their 5⅜% bonds for new, higher interest bonds.

After consulting with the Allied financial staff and underwriters, Crown decided to offer the holders of the old bonds $75 million of new 9% bonds to mature in 24 years, plus $12.5 million in cash. In addition, Allied will incur $1 million of issue costs on the new bonds. For simplicity, assume that interest on both bond issues is paid annually.

Required:

1. Prepare the journal entry which Allied would currently make under GAAP to record the refunding. Assume refunding immediately after recording a regular cash interest payment (round amounts to the nearest $50,000). Note: At the time this case actually occurred, in 1973, the FASB had not issued its *Statement No. 4* (1975), which requires the gain or loss on early extinguishment of debt to be labeled as extraordinary. It seems reasonable to conjecture that this was one of a number of such cases that prompted the FASB to issue *Statement No. 4.*
2. Compute Allied's economic gain or loss, measured in terms of the present value of future cash flows, as a result of the refunding. Ignore income taxes.
3. Why is there such a large difference between the gains or losses computed in Requirements 1 and 2 above?

EXERCISES

PART A
Exercises 20-1 to 20-6

Exercise 20-1

BA Corporation issued $600,000, 8% (payable 4% semiannually), ten-year bonds payable. The bonds were dated January 1, 19A; interest dates are June 30 and December 31.

Assume four different cases with respect to the sale of the bonds:

Case A—Sold on January 1, 19A, at par.
Case B—Sold on January 1, 19A, at 102.
Case C—Sold on January 1, 19A, at 98.
Case D—Sold on March 1, 19A, at par.

Required:

1. For each case, what amount of cash interest will be paid on the first interest date, June 30, 19A?
2. In what cases are the stated rate of interest not 4% each semiannual period?
3. In what cases will the yield rate of interest be (a) the same, (b) higher, or (c) lower than the stated rate?
4. After sale of the bonds, in what cases will the carrying or book value of the bonds (as reported on the balance sheet) be (a) the same, (b) higher, or (c) lower than the maturity or face amount?
5. After the sale of the bonds, in Cases A, B, and C, which case will report interest expense (as reported on the income statement) (a) the same, (b) higher, or (c) lower than the amount of cash interest paid each period?

Exercise 20-2

A $10,000 bond, 8% (payable 4% semiannually), ten-year (remaining period outstanding), was sold by A to B, on an interest date, at an effective rate of 10%. The bond price was computed as follows: $3,769 + $4,985 = $8,754.

Required:

Explain in detail, using values for "i" and "n" how each of the two dollar amounts was computed. Explain why the computation correctly derives the bond price.

Exercise 20-3

Compute the bond price for each of the following situations (show computations and round to nearest dollar):

a. A ten-year $1,000 bond; annual interest at 7% (payable 3½% semiannually) purchased to yield 6% interest.

b. An eight-year, $1,000 bond; annual interest at 6% (payable annually) purchased to yield 7% interest.

c. A ten-year, $1,000 bond; annual interest at 6% (payable semiannually) purchased to yield 8% interest.

d. An eight-year, $1,000 bond; annual interest at 6% (payable annually) purchased to yield 6% interest.

Exercise 20–4

S Corporation issued to T Corporation a $30,000, 8% (payable 4% semiannually on June 30 and December 31), ten-year bond dated and sold on January 1, 19A. Assumptions: Case A—sold at par; Case B—sold at 103; and Case C—sold at 97.

Required:

In parallel columns for the issuer and the investor (as a long-term investment), give the appropriate journal entries for each case on (1) January 1, 19A, and (2) June 30, 19A. Assume the difference between amortization amounts is not material; therefore, use straight-line amortization.

Exercise 20–5

M Corporation sold to N Corporation a $10,000, 9% (payable 4½% semiannually on June 30 and December 31), ten-year bond, dated and sold on January 1, 19A. The bond was sold at an 8% yield rate (4% semiannually). Round to nearest dollar.

Required:

1. Compute the price of the bond.
2. In parallel columns for the issuer and the investor (as a long-term investment), give the appropriate journal entries on (a) January 1, 19A, and (b) June 30, 19A. Assume the difference between the amortization amounts is material; therefore, use the interest method.

Exercise 20–6

X Corporation issued Y Corporation a $10,000 bond, 8% interest (payable semiannually on June 30 and December 31). The bond was sold on January 1, 19A, matures December 31, 19B, and the yield rate was 7%. Table values for $n = 4$ and $i = 3½$%: Present value of 1, .871442, and present value of annuity of 1, 3.673079.

Required (round to nearest dollar):

1. Determine the selling price of the bond by reference to Exhibit 20–1. Prove your answer by computing the present value of each of the future cash flows. Show computations.
2. Prepare a bond amortization schedule using the interest method.
3. In parallel columns give entries for the issuer and the investor (a long-term investment) for the following, assuming the interest method of amortization: (a) sale of the bonds, (b) first interest payment, and (c) all entries on the maturity date, December 31, 19B.
4. Show how the bonds should be reported on the balance sheets of the issuer and the investor at December 31, 19A.

PART B
Exercises 20–7 to 20–12

Exercise 20–7

On September 1, 19A, Day Company sold Eden Company $30,000, five-year, 9% (payable 4½% semiannually) bonds for $32,320 plus accrued interest. The bonds were dated July 1, 19A, and interest is payable each June 30 and December 31. The accounting period for each company ends on December 31.

Required:

In parallel columns, give entries on the books of the borrower and investor (as a long-term investment) for the following dates: September 1, 19A; December 31, 19A; January 1, 19B; and June 30, 19B. Assume the difference between the amortization amounts is not material; therefore, use straight-line amortization.

Exercise 20–8

XY Corporation sold $150,000, three-year, 8% (payable 4% semiannually) bonds payable for $156,400 plus accrued interest. Interest is payable each February 28 and August 31. The bonds were dated March 1, 19A, and were sold on July 1, 19A. The accounting period ends on December 31.

Required:

1. How much accrued interest should be recognized at date of sale?
2. How long is the amortization period?
3. Give entries for XY Corporation through February 19B (including reversing entries). Use straight-line amortization.

4. Would the above amounts also be recorded by the investor? Explain.

Exercise 20–9

B Corporation sold C Corporation (as a long-term investment) $50,000, four-year, 8% bonds on September 1, 19A. Interest is payable (4% semiannually) on August 31 and February 28. The bonds mature on August 31, 19E, and were sold to yield 7% interest. The accounting period for both companies ends on December 31. Present value amounts for 8 periods at 3½% per semiannual period: PV of 1, .75941; PV of annuity of 1, 6.87396.

Required:
1. Compute the price of the bond (show computations and round to nearest dollar).
2. In parallel columns, give all entries required through February 19B (including reversing entries) in the accounts of the borrower and the investor. Assume the difference between the amortization amounts is not material; therefore, use straight-line amortization.

Exercise 20–10

Goodson Company sold Hobson Company $30,000, four-year, 8% bonds dated June 1, 19A. Interest is payable 4% semiannually on May 31 and November 30. The bonds were sold on March 1, 19B, for $29,171 plus accrued interest. The accounting period ends December 31 for both companies. The yield interest rate was 9%.

Required (round to nearest dollar):
1. Verify the bond price by using values from Exhibit 20–1. Use straight-line interpolation.
2. Prepare a bond amortization table starting on March 1, 19B, and continuing to maturity, May 31, 19E. Use the interest method.
3. In parallel columns, give entries for the issuer and the investor (as a long-term investment) for the following dates: March 1, 19B, and May 31, 19B. Use interest-method amortization.

Exercise 20–11

Yates Corporation issued $150,000, 6%, ten-year bonds with detachable stock warrants. Each $1,000 bond carried 20 detachable warrants, each of which was for one share of Yates common stock, par $20, with a specified option price of $60. The bonds sold at 102 including the warrants (no bond price exwar-

rants was available), and, shortly after date of issuance, the detachable stock warrants were selling at $4 each.

The entire issue was acquired by Zinn Company as a long-term investment.

Required:
1. Give entries for the issuer and the investor at date of acquisition of the bonds.
2. Give entry for the investor assuming subsequent sale of all the warrants to another investor at $5.50 each.
3. Give entries for the issuer and investor assuming subsequent tender of all of the warrants by the investor for exercise at the specified option price. At this date the stock was selling at $75 per share.

Exercise 20–12

Walters Corporation issued $40,000, 5%, ten-year convertible bonds. Each $1,000 bond was convertible to ten shares of common stock (par $50) of Walters Corporation at any interest date after three years from issuance. The bonds were sold at 105 to Young Corporation as a long-term investment.

Required:
1. Give entry for the issuer and investor at the date of issuance.
2. Give entries for the issuer and investor assuming that the conversion privilege is subsequently exercised by Young Corporation immediately after the end of the third year. Assume 30% of any premium or discount has been amortized and that, at date of conversion, the common stock was selling at $125 per share.

PART C
Exercises 20–13 to 20–19

Exercise 20–13

On January 1, 1969, Company T issued $100,000 face value bonds payable with a stated interest rate of 5%, payable annually each December 31. The bonds mature in 25 years and have a call price of 103, exercisable by Company T after the fifth year. The bonds originally sold at par.

On January 1 of the 11th year the company contemplated calling the bonds at 103. At that time the bonds were quoted on the market at a price to yield 8%.

Required:
1. Give the issuance entry required on January 1, 1969.

2. Give the entry for extinguishment of the bonds by calling them on January 1 of the 11th year.
3. Was exercise of the call economically favorable for the issuer? Disregard income taxes and show computations.

Exercise 20-14

On January 1, 19A, Company W issued $200,000 face value bonds payable with a stated rate of interest of 5%, payable annually each December 31. The bonds mature in 25 years and are callable after the 5th year at 101. The bonds originally sold on January 1, 19A, at par.

On January 1 of the 11th year, the bonds (a) could be called at 101 or (b) acquired in the open market for $148,643 (a yield rate of 8%).

Required:

1. Give the issuance entry on January 1, 19A.
2. Give the entry on January 1 of the 11th year for early extinguishment assuming (a) the call privilege is exercised and (b) the bonds are acquired in the open market.
3. Was the early extinguishment economically favorable to the issuer (a) if the call privilege is exercised and (b) if the bonds are acquired in the open market? Disregard income taxes and show computations.

Exercise 20-15

Company X owed Super Bank a $50,000, one-year, 10% (payable on December 31) note payable dated January 1, 19A. During 19A, X Company experienced unusual difficulties and was unable to pay the note and interest. On January 1, 19B, the bank agreed to settle the debt and interest (for 19A) for $2,000 cash plus some land that had a current market value of $30,000. At December 31, 19A, the records of Company X reflected the acquisition cost of the land to be $20,000.

Required:

Give all entries required on January 1, 19B, to record this debt restructure (a) for Company X and (b) for Super Bank.

Exercise 20-16

Dawson Company owed Quick Finance Company a $100,000, 10% (payable annually each December 31) note payable dated January 1, 19A. At December 31, 19C, Dawson was experiencing serious financial problems and could not pay the principal and interest (for 19C). Since this was the maturity date for the note, an agreement was reached whereby Quick would settle the debt and interest in full for $12,000 cash plus a tract of land (Dawson's acquisition cost was $7,000) plus 1,000 shares of Dawson common stock (par $10 per share) that had a current market price of $35 per share. The current market value of the land on January 2, 19D, was $20,000. The agreement was accepted by both parties and settlement was effected on January 2, 19D.

Required:

Give all entries required to record the debt restructure for (a) Dawson Company and (b) Quick Finance Company. Show details and computations.

Exercise 20-17

Company V owed Company W a $20,000, 10% (annual interest payable each December 31), four-year note payable dated January 1, 19A. Company V was unable to pay the accrued interest at December 31, 19B, due to extreme financial difficulties. As a consequence, neither company had recorded accrued interest at the end of 19B. On January 2, 19C, an agreement was reached that the interest for 19B would not be paid; instead, the interest charge for the remainder of the term of the note would be reduced to $1,218 in total, payable on December 31, 19D (maturity date).

Required:

1. Compute the new effective rate of interest. Show computations.
2. Give all entries required on date of restructure (January 2, 19C) for each company.
3. Give all entries required on December 31, 19C, and 19D, for each company.

Exercise 20-18

Company F owed Bank G a $50,000, 10% (payable each December 31), four-year note payable dated January 1, 19A. At the end of 19B Company F experienced great difficulty in making the annual interest payment. Due to expected continuing difficulties the company may default on the note (as well as other obligations). On January 2, 19C, the two parties agreed to restructure the debt by (a) reducing the remaining annual interest payments to $2,240 each and (b) to reduce the principal amount (maturity amount) to $48,000.

Required:

1. Compute the new effective rate of interest. Show computations.

2. Give all entries required on date of restructure (January 2, 19C) for each company. If no entry is required, explain the reason.
3. Give all entries required at December 31, 19C, and 19D, for each company.

Exercise 20–19

Company D owed Bank E a $60,000, 10% (payable each December 31), four-year note payable dated January 1, 19A. Company D has experienced severe financial difficulties and is likely to default on the note and interest during 19C unless some concessions are made. Consequently, on January 2, 19C, the parties agreed to restructure the debt as follows: (a) interest payments each year to be reduced to $1,000 per year for 19C and 19D, and (b) reduce the principal amount to $30,000.

Required:

1. Does this restructure change the effective interest rate? Explain. Is the new effective rate of interest needed for accounting purposes in this situation? Explain.
2. Give all entries required for each party on the date of restructure, January 2, 19C.
3. Give all entries required for each party on December 31, 19C, and 19D.

PROBLEMS

PART A
Problems 20–1 to 20–3

Problem 20–1

Cox Corporation sold Dow Corporation (as a long-term investment) a $20,000, 7%, ten-year bond. The bond was dated January 1, 19A, and interest is payable annually each December 31. Assume the accounting periods end December 31. Assume three different cases in respect to the sale of the bond:

Case A—sold on January 1, 19A, at 7% yield.

Case B—sold on January 1, 19A, at 6% yield.

Case C—sold on January 1, 19A, at 8% yield.

Required:

1. For each case, compute the amount of interest that will be paid (i.e., cash) on the first interest date, December 31, 19A.
2. Identify which cases sold at (a) par, (b) a discount, and (c) a premium.

3. For each case, indicate (a) the stated interest rate and (b) the yield rate of interest.
4. Identify those cases where the amount of cash paid and received for the bond was (a) the same as par, (b) greater than par, and (c) less than par.
5. Subsequent to the transaction, in which cases will the respective balance sheets report the bonds at (a) par, (b) more than par, and (c) less than par?
6. Subsequent to the transaction, what cases will report interest expense and interest revenue (on the respective income statements) at more or less than the periodic amount of interest paid in cash?
7. Identify those cases where the maturity value of the bond liability (or bond investment) will be (a) the same as, (b) higher, or (c) lower than the book value.
8. Can straight-line amortization be used in each case? Explain.
9. What is the effect of periodic amortization of bond premium and discount on (a) interest expense (as reported on the income statement) and (b) bond carrying value (as reported on the balance sheet).

Problem 20–2

DE Corporation sold CB Corporation $200,000, 8% (payable 4% semiannually on June 30 and December 31), three-year bonds. The bonds were dated and sold on January 1, 19A, at a yield rate of 9%. The accounting period for each company ends on December 31. Present value amounts for six periods at 4½% per semiannual period: PV of 1, .767896; and PV of annuity of 1, 5.157872.

Required:

1. Compute the price of the bonds (round to nearest dollar).
2. Prepare an amortization table for the life of the bonds (round to nearest dollar).
3. Prepare in parallel columns, entries for the issuer and the investor (as a long-term investment) through December 31, 19A.
4. Show how the issuer and the investor would report the bonds on their respective balance sheets at December 31, 19A.
5. What would be reported on the income statement for each party for the year ended December 31, 19A?

Problem 20–3

Park Corporation sold to King Company, $40,000, 7% (payable 3½% semiannually on June 30 and December 31), four-year bonds dated January 1, 19A. The bonds were sold on January 1, 19A, at a yield rate of 6%.

Required (round to nearest dollar):

1. Compute the price of the bonds.
2. Prepare an amortization table over the life of the bonds assuming the interest method of amortization.
3. In parallel columns for the issuer and investor (as a long-term investment) give all journal entries from issuance through December 31, 19A. Assume the accounting period for Park ends on December 31 and for King, on November 30.
4. Show how the issuer and the investor should report the bonds on their respective balance sheets on December 31, 19A, and November 30, 19A, respectively.
5. What would be reported on the income statement for each party for the year ended December 31, 19A, and November 30, 19A, respectively?

PART B
Problems 20–4 to 20–9

Problem 20–4

Jackson Corporation sold King Corporation $50,000 bonds on June 1, 19A, for $51,320 plus accrued interest. The bond indenture provided the following information:

Maturity amount	$50,000
Date of bonds	April 1, 19A
Maturity date	March 31, 19C (2 years)
Stated interest rate . .	6½%, payable 3¼% semiannually
Interest payments	March 31 and September 30

Required:

1. In parallel columns, give entries for the issuer and investor (as a long-term investment) from date of sale to maturity. Assume the difference between the amortization amounts is not material; therefore, use straight-line amortization. Also assume the accounting periods end December 31.
2. Show how the bonds would be reported on the balance sheet of each company at December 31, 19A.
3. What would be reported on the income statement for each party for the year ended December 31, 19A?

Problem 20–5

B Corporation issued bonds, face amount $100,000, three-year, 8% (payable 4% semiannually on June 30 and December 31). The bonds were dated January 1,

19A, and were sold on November 1, 19A, to yield 9% interest. The bonds mature on December 31, 19C. The bonds were purchased as a long-term investment by I Corporation. Refer to Exhibit 20–1 for appropriate table values.

Required (round to nearest dollar):

1. Construct a time scale that depicts the important dates for this bond issue.
2. Determine *(a)* the price of the bond issue on the date of sale and *(b)* the total cash paid by I Corporation.
3. In parallel columns, give the entries at November 1, 19A, for the issuer and the investor.
4. Prepare a bond amortization table from date of sale to maturity date using the interest method.
5. In parallel columns, give the entries for interest and amortization at the interest date, December 31, 19A.
6. Determine and verify the balance in the interest accounts of the two parties to the transaction immediately after Requirement 5.
7. Assume the accounting period for each party ends on February 28. In parallel columns, give the adjusting entries for each party on February 28, 19B. Assume the interest method of amortization.
8. Compute the amount of amortization per month for each party assuming straight-line amortization is appropriate (i.e., the difference between the amortization amounts is not material).

Problem 20–6

Bliss Corporation issued $200,000, 8% (payable each February 28 and August 31), four-year bonds. The bonds were dated March 1, 19A, and mature on February 28, 19E. They were sold on August 1, 19A, to yield 8½% interest. The bonds were purchased by Ivy Corporation as a long-term investment. The accounting period for each company ends on December 31. Refer to Exhibit 20–1 for appropriate table values.

Required (round to nearest dollar):

1. Diagram a time scale depicting the important dates for this bond issue.
2. Determine *(a)* the price of the bond issue on the date of sale and *(b)* the total cash paid by Ivy Corporation.
3. Prepare an amortization table from date of sale to maturity using the interest method of amortization.
4. In parallel columns, give entries for the borrower and the investor from date of sale through February 28, 19B. Base amortization on Requirement 3.

5. Compute the amount of amortization per month for each party assuming the straight-line method is appropriate (i.e., the difference between the amortization amounts is not material).

Problem 20–7

Myers Corporation issued $500,000, 6%, nonconvertible bonds with detachable stock warrants. Each $1,000 bond carried 20 detachable stock warrants, each of which called for one share of Myers common stock, par $50, at a specified option price of $60 per share. The bonds sold at 106, and the warrants were immediately quoted at $1 each on the market.

Nabors Company purchased the entire issue as a long-term investment.

Required:

1. Give the following entries for Myers Corporation (the borrower):
   a. To record the issuance of the bonds.
   b. To record the subsequent exercise by investor of the 10,000 stock warrants.
2. Give the following entries for Nabors Company (the investor):
   a. Acquisition of the bonds (including the warrants).
   b. Subsequent sale to another investor of half of the stock warrants at $1.50 each.
   c. Subsequent exercise of the remaining half of the stock warrants (by tendering them to Myers Corporation.) The market value of the stock was $62 per share.

Problem 20–8

On January 1, 19A, Brown Corporation issued $50,000, 5%, five-year convertible bonds with the provision that the holder of each $1,000 bond could tender it for conversion to 15 shares of Brown common stock, par $50, at any time after 19B. The company estimated that nonconvertible bonds would have to carry an interest rate of 7½% to sell at par. The bonds were sold for $54,000. On July 1, 19C, the stock was selling at $75 per share. Assume straight-line amortization.

Required:

1. Give entries for Brown at
   a. Date of issuance—January 1, 19A.
   b. Date of conversion—July 1, 19C, assuming all bonds were turned in for conversion.
2. Assume Cooper Corporation acquired all of the bonds. Give entries by Cooper at
   a. Date of acquisition.
   b. Date of conversion.

Problem 20–9

Assume the same situation given in Problem 20–8 except that instead of being convertible, each $1,000 bond had 15 detachable stock warrants. Each warrant was for one share of common stock at a specified price of $60 per share. Immediately upon issuance of the bonds on January 1, 19A, the warrants sold on the market at $2.

Required:

1. Give entry by Brown Corporation at date of issuance, January 1, 19A.
2. Give entries for Cooper Corporation at date of acquisition (as a long-term investment) on January 1, 19A.
3. Explain the basis for the values recognized in Requirements 1 and 2.
4. Assume 100 of the detachable stock warrants are tendered on July 1, 19C. At that date the stock was selling at $70 per share. Give entry for (a) Brown Corporation and (b) Cooper Corporation.

PART C
Problems 20–10 to 20–14

Problem 20–10

On July 1, 19A, Anderson Corporation issued $500,000, 5% (payable each June 30 and December 31), ten-year bonds payable. The bonds were callable at the option of the issuer at 102 at any time after the third year. The bonds were issued at 97, and issue costs of $1,400 were paid. Assume straight-line amortization of discount and bond issue costs. Assume an average income tax rate of 40%.

Due to an increase in interest rates, these bonds were selling in the market at the end of June 19D at a yield rate of 8%. Since the company had available cash, $100,000 (face amount) of the bonds were purchased in the market on July 1, 19D, for $84,156. The accounting periods end December 31.

Required:

1. Give entry by Anderson Corporation to record issuance of the bonds on July 1, 19A.
2. Give entry to record retirement of the bonds ($100,000) on July 1, 19D. How should the gain or loss be reported on the 19D financial statements?
3. Was the early extinguishment favorable to Anderson? Consider both pretax and aftertax results. Assume bond interest and any loss or gain are subject to income tax.

Problem 20–11

Capps Corporation issued $200,000, 4½% (payable each December 31), ten-year bonds on January 1, 19A. The issuer could call them at any time after 19D at 104. The bonds sold on January 1, 19A, at 98. Straight-line amortization is used.

Due to a large increase in interest rates, the bonds were being sold in the market at the end of 19E at 86 (i.e., at a yield rate of 8%). In view of this situation, Capps decided to issue a new series of bonds (a refunding issue) in the amount of $150,000 (8% payable annually, five-year term) on January 1, 19F; the new issue was sold at par. Capps has cash on hand sufficient for the remaining cost of retirement of the old bonds. Assume an income tax rate of 40%.

Required:

1. Give entry to record issuance of the bonds on January 1, 19A.
2. Assume the refunding issue is sold at par; give the required entry for Capps.
3. Assume all of the old bonds are purchased in the open market at 86 on January 2, 19F. Give the required entry for Capps. How should the gain or loss be reported on the financial statements?
4. Was the refunding transaction favorable to Capps Corporation? Consider both pretax and aftertax results. Assume any loss or gain on refunding and bond interest are subject to income tax.

Problem 20–12

On January 1, 1973, Conners Corporation issued $100,000, 9% (4½% payable each June 30 and December 31), ten-year bonds payable (convertible and callable) at a 10% yield rate of interest. Each $1,000 bond is convertible, at the option of the holder, into Conners common stock (par $10) as follows: first five years— 25 shares for each bond tendered; second five years— 20 shares for each bond. The bonds can be called, at the option of Conners, after the fifth year at 101.

On July 1, 1979, the market interest rate on comparable bonds is 8%, and the common stock is quoted on the market at $52 per share.

Required (round to nearest dollar):

1. Record issuance of bonds on January 1, 1973. Show computation of the bond issue price.
2. Give entry to record payment of bond interest and the amortization of bond premium or discount on June 30, 1973. Assume interest method amortization.
3. Prepare the journal entries at July 1, 1979, to record

each of the following separate assumptions (use straight-line amortization):

Assumption A—All of the bondholders turned in their bonds for conversion to common stock. Use the market value method to record the conversion.

Assumption B—Conners called all of the bonds at the stipulated call price.

Assumption C—Conners refunded all of the outstanding 9% bonds by purchasing them in the open market at the current yield rate of interest. Cash for the refunding was obtained by issuing new 8% bonds (interest payable semiannually) at par; cash proceeds were $103,000 (face amount of bonds sold).

4. Which of the three above alternative means of retiring the old 9% bonds payable was most likely to occur? Why?

Problem 20–13

On January 1, 19A, Corporation B issued $100,000, 7% (payable annually on December 31), ten-year bonds payable to yield 8% interest. After paying interest for 19A and 19B, the corporation encountered severe financial difficulties which made it apparent that the bondholders would have to make some accommodations as to debt terms. Therefore, a debt restructure was effected on January 1, 19C, that provided *(a)* the remaining term to maturity would be 20 years from January 1, 19C, and *(b)* interest would be reduced so that the same amount of total dollar interest would be paid over the new term to maturity (20 years) as would have been paid over the old term to the old maturity date (8 years). Assume straight-line amortization of bond premium or discount.

Required (round to nearest dollar):

1. Give entry to record issuance of the bonds payable on January 1, 19A. Show computations of the original bond issuance price.
2. Compute the carrying value of the bonds on January 1, 19C.
3. Compute the new effective rate of interest (round to the nearest percent; then use straight-line interpolation to compute approximate interest rate to two decimal places).
4. Give all entries for both the issuer and the investor on the date of restructure, January 1, 19C. If no entry is required, explain why. Use the approximate interpolated interest rate computed in Requirement 3 and then round to the nearest dollar.
5. Give all entries for both the issuer and the investor on two interest dates, December 31, 19C, and 19D.

Problem 20–14

On January 1, 19F, DEF Corporation owed a $65,000 note payable that required the payment of 10% interest on each December 31; the note was due on June 30, 19F. Because of continuing serious financial difficulties, DEF informed the creditor that default (and discontinuance of the business) was highly probable unless some concessions on terms could be negotiated. Therefore, on January 5, 19F, the creditor agreed to the following restructure of the debt:

a. DEF will transfer immediately $15,000 of its accounts receivable to the creditor in settlement of $17,000 of the debt. The accounts of DEF reflected $1,000 in the allowance for doubtful accounts that related to these receivables; thus, the current net realizable value of the receivables was reasonably stated at $14,000.

b. DEF will transfer immediately its long-term investment in 800 shares of common stock (par $10) of ROE Corporation in settlement of $38,000 of the debt. DEF accounts reflected a carrying value of $30,000 for the ROE stock, and its current market value was $32,000.

c. DEF will pay in cash the remainder of the principal $10,000 (i.e., $65,000 − $17,000 − $38,000 = $10,000) at the end of five years from January 1, 19F (date of restructure). That is, the maturity date is December 31, 19J.

d. DEF will pay $5,000 total interest over the five-year period from January 1, 19F (i.e., $1,000 interest per year).

Required:

1. Give the required journal entries for the debtor and the creditor on date of restructure, January 1, 19F. Explain how you made the decision as to *(a)* whether entries are required and *(b)* the basis for the "values" you used. How would other values produce a biased measure of restructure gain or loss?

2. Give the required entries for the debtor and the creditor on the next interest date, December 31, 19F, and on the maturity date, December 31, 19J.

APPENDIX
Problems 20–15 to 20–16

Problem 20–15

A serial issue of $700,000 of bonds dated April 1, 19A, was sold on that date for $707,600. The interest rate is 8%, payable 4% semiannually on March 31 and September 30. Scheduled maturities are as follows:

Serial	Date Due	Amount
B	March 31, 19B	$100,000
C	March 31, 19C	200,000
D	March 31, 19D	200,000
E	March 31, 19E	200,000

Required:

1. Prepare an amortization table; use straight-line and dollar-period allocation.
2. Give all entries relating to the bonds including reversing entries through March 31, 19B. The company adjusts and closes its books each December 31. Use straight-line amortization.

Problem 20–16

On January 1, 1979, ABC Corporation sold serial bonds (dated January 1, 1979) due as follows: Series A, $10,000, December 31, 1983; Series B, $15,000, December 31, 1984; and Series C, $25,000, December 31, 1985. The bonds carried a 3% coupon (stated) interest rate per semiannual period (each June 30 and December 31) and were sold to yield 4% interest per semiannual period.

Required (round to nearest dollar):

1. Compute the selling price of the bond issue.
2. Prepare an amortization schedule for the life of the bond issue assuming the interest method is used.
3. Give entry to record retirement of half of Series C at 99½ on June 30, 1985. Assume the accounting period ends December 31.

Accounting for Pension Costs

Pension plans sponsored by private employers have become pervasive and increasingly important, and the assets controlled by pension plans now account for a staggering dollar amount. Between 1950 and 1975 the number of persons covered by private pension and deferred profit sharing plans rose from fewer than 10 million to more than 30 million. Total assets of private, noninsured pension plans amounted to more than $160 billion in 1976 (up from $33 billion in 1960).[1]

PENSION PLAN FUNDAMENTALS

The primary purpose of pension plans is to provide retirement income to employees. Companies with many employees often establish *defined benefit* plans which state the amount of benefits or the method of determining the benefits to be received by employees after retirement. In plans for hourly paid employees, the benefit is ordinarily a specified amount per month, based on years of credited service. In plans for salaried employees, benefits usually are related to their compensation (e.g., a percent of the highest five years' earnings). Other types of plans do not provide specific benefits; rather,

they specify that the retired employees will receive whatever benefits can be paid from the pension fund accumulation and its earnings. In this latter type of plan, the amount of the benefits is uncertain; it is the employer's contribution that is specified or defined.

Most pension plans are formally established through a "retirement plan" that meets Internal Revenue Code qualifications so that

1. Contributions paid by the employer are deductible for income tax purposes.
2. Earnings of the pension fund are not subject to income tax.
3. Employer contributions in behalf of employees are not taxable to employees when the contributions are made.
4. Retirement benefits are taxable to retirees, but in most instances retirees are in lower income tax brackets than when they were employed and earning the pension benefits.

Accounting treatments presented in this chapter are largely based on *APB Opinion No. 8,* "Accounting for the Cost of Pension Plans," and Interpretations of that *Opinion.*

The FASB has had the topic of pension accounting (along with other aspects of employee benefits) under consideration for some time, but at the publication date of this book, no definitive pronouncement which materially affected ac-

---

[1] *The U.S. Fact Book* (New York: Grosset & Dunlap, 1978), p. 332.

counting for pension plans had yet been issued.

Federal legislation, entitled The Employee Retirement Income Security Act of 1974 (ERISA, and also known as the Pension Reform Act of 1974), has had substantial impact on the *administration* of pension plans. Also, some phases of accounting for pension plans have been affected. For example, prior to ERISA, employers with *defined benefit plans* had the option of funding or not funding *past service cost*[2] connected with their plans. Although under some plans the past service cost was funded rapidly (in periods only slightly in excess of ten years), there were many others which did not fund past service cost at all. Under ERISA, for plans which existed on January 1, 1974, funding of past service cost must be accomplished in 40 years or less. Past service cost which arises after January 1, 1974, must be funded in 30 years or less. Similarly, prior to ERISA, employers had the option of funding or not funding *normal* (current) *pension cost* and *vesting* cost. The act requires that these continuing pension costs (as opposed to past service cost, which is a one-time cost) also be funded.

Vesting refers to an employee's right to receive a present or future pension benefit even though that person does not remain an employee of the company until retirement. Vesting occurs at the latest when the employee retires, but may occur prior to that date. For example, a benefit may vest after a specified number of years of service or at a specified age.[3]

Actuarial factors are the probabilistic data used to determine current pension cost. Actuarial determinations and estimates are an integral part of pension plans since pension costs are inherently future oriented. Pension related events with uncertain outcomes which pension actuaries must estimate include retirement age, mortality (the life expectancies of employees both before and after retirement), employee turnover, interest rates, gains and losses of pension plan investments, administrative requirements, future salary levels, pension benefits, and vesting provisions.

The above discussion referred to two different kinds of pension costs, viz:

1. *Normal pension cost*—A pension plan may be initiated when the company is organized, in which case persons upon initial employment would qualify for the pension plan. Subsequent to inception of the plan, only *normal pension cost* would be incurred (each year) by the company.

2. *Past service cost*—A pension plan may be initiated some years after the company was organized. In this case *present* employees, as well as new employees subsequently hired, would qualify for the plan. *Past service cost* is the pension cost associated with employee service performed for the company prior to the inception of the pension plan. Past service cost is explained more fully below. *Normal* pension cost would be incurred (each year) by the company for both groups of employees. In addition, all employees working for the enterprise at the date of inception of the pension plan generally are given past service credits under the plan for prior years' employment with the company. Thus, in such situations the company must bear a one-time pension cost (in addition to the normal pension cost incurred on a year-to-year basis) to provide for the "catch-up" for prior employees. This cost is referred to as *past service pension cost,* or more simply, as past service cost.

A SIMPLIFIED PENSION PLAN EXAMPLE

Most pension plans provide for equal periodic payments to each qualified employee after retirement. To illustrate some basic concepts, assume that an employer desires to provide a $10,000 annual pension paid at the end of each year for an employee who is expected to live ten years after retirement—long enough to re-

---

[2] In the past, some employers did not fund their past service cost but simply funded the accrued interest on such costs.

[3] The 1974 act imposed stringent safeguards in behalf of employees' vesting rights. An employee now must be at least 25% vested in accrued benefits derived from employer contributions after five years of covered service. By the time an employee has 15 years of covered service, the vesting must have risen (according to a table in the law) to 100%. Under another provision an employee with five years of covered service must be at least 50% vested in the accrued benefit from employer contributions when the sum of the employee's age and years of covered service totals 45.

EXHIBIT 21–1
Disbursement of Pension Fund

End of Year	Interest Revenue	Payments to Employee	Reduction of Fund Balance	Fund Principal on Deposit
Start . . .				$70,236
1	$4,917 [a]	$10,000	$5,083 [b]	65,153 [c]
2	4,561	10,000	5,439	59,714
3	4,180	10,000	5,820	53,894
4	3,773	10,000	6,227	47,667
5	3,337	10,000	6,663	41,004
6	2,870	10,000	7,130	33,874
7	2,371	10,000	7,629	26,245
8	1,837	10,000	8,163	18,082
9	1,266	10,000	8,734	9,348
10	652 [d]	10,000	9,348	

[a] $70,236 × .07 = $4,917.
[b] $10,000 − $4,917 = $5,083.
[c] $70,236 − $5,083 = $65,153.
[d] Rounded $2.

ceive $100,000. Assuming pension fund assets can be invested to earn 7%, one way for the *employer* to provide for the pension payments to the employee would be to set aside or accumulate $70,236 as a pension plan fund by the time the employee retires.[4] Exhibit 21–1 illustrates how the $70,236 would be disbursed to the employee after retirement.

Pensions are sometimes funded by the employer by making a single payment (such as the $70,236 needed here) to the plan administrator; however, single-payment funding is rare. More commonly, periodic payments into a pension fund are made during the term of employment until the date of retirement.[5]

Assume this hypothetical pension plan was adopted at or before the time the employee was hired, and that the employee had to work 12 years before qualifying for the $10,000 annual

pension payments subsequent to retirement. If the employer paid $3,926 to a pension fund at the *end* of each of the 12 years of employment, the requisite $70,236 would be accumulated. In this instance the $70,236 is the *future value* of an ordinary annuity of 12 annual amounts at 7% per year (refer to Chapter 6). The annual payment is determined by dividing $70,236 by the future value of an ordinary annuity of 12 annual payments of $1 each at 7% [i.e., $70,236 ÷ 17.88845 (Table 6–3) = $3,926]. In this instance the $3,926 annual payments would be referred to as the *normal pension cost* of the plan because the plan was not started before the employee was hired, therefore, there was no past service cost to cover.

Past Service Cost Illustrated. If the plan illustrated above had been adopted two years *after* the employee was hired, and if the *employer* decided to recognize employee service rendered *prior* to inception of the plan, the employee would have worked 10 years, instead of 12, to qualify for the same benefits. In this instance, the employer has assumed a "catch-up" obligation (for the two years of employee service); and if the full $70,236 is to be funded by the employee's retirement date, ten years hence, the amount of each annual contribution to the pension fund must be increased to $5,084 [i.e., $70,236 ÷ $F_{o_{n=10;i=7\%}}$; $70,236 ÷ 13.81645 (Table 6–3) = $5,084]. The resulting past service cost must be measured at date of inception of the pension plan.

The procedure for computing the amount of *past service cost* requires recognition that if the pension plan had been in effect when the person commenced employment, the employer would have paid annual amounts to the pension fund for the periods between the *actual* employment date and the later date on which the pension plan was *actually* started. The amount that the pension fund would have accumulated between the two dates equals past service cost. To illustrate, in the example above the employer would have paid two annual amounts of $3,926 each into the pension fund prior to the actual date of inception of the plan. Since this was not done, there is a past service cost. For those two years, the fund would have accumulated $8,127 [i.e., $3,926 × $F_{o_{n=2;i=7\%}}$; $3,926 × 2.07 (Table 6–3) =

---

[4] The $70,236 is computed as the present value of ten equal amounts of $10,000 each, at 7% per year, or $10,000 × 7.02358 (Table 6–4) = $70,236.

[5] Funding the entire pension cost when employees retire is known as *terminal funding*. Accounting recognition of pension *costs* on a one-time basis is not permitted. Periodic pension payments can remain uniform (until a plan is modified and/or evaluated), can be higher in earlier years, or can rise in later years. Their direction and pattern depend largely on the actuarial cost method used. Exhibit 21–2 shows representative annual cost patterns under five actuarial cost methods.

$8,127], which equals the *past service cost* at date of inception of the pension plan.

It is the function of the actuary, not the accountant, to measure past service cost. The actuary will determine past service cost and recommend how to fund it. The important conceptual point in accounting for past service cost is this: When a company does not immediately *fund* past service liability at the inception of the plan (and immediate funding is rare), the past service cost, although clearly related to past periods, is not charged to Retained Earnings nor to expense of the current period. Instead, it is recognized as expense over a period of *future* years, as specified in *APB Opinion No. 8* (discussed below).

It is easy to forecast with confidence how much must be paid periodically into a pension fund to attain a given future amount if the *assumed* interest rate (7% in the above example) is actually earned throughout the period of fund contributions and also throughout the later period the employees receive pension payments. In actual practice, however, earnings rates change from time to time and may fluctuate above or below the rate initially assumed. Another variable that affects the forecast of required fund accumulation is the level of pension benefits. When they increase, as frequently happens, pension costs will increase and "catch-up" funding payments will be necessary. Such cumulative "catch-up" costs are called *prior service cost* (as opposed to past service cost). In other words, after a pension plan is modified and/or after an *actuarial valuation,*[6] *prior service cost* can arise. Prior service cost includes any related past service cost that remains. Prior service cost, like the past service cost, is allocated over current and future periods.

APB OPINION NO. 8 AND PENSION ACCOUNTING

Issuance of *APB Opinion No. 8,* "Accounting for the Cost of Pension Plans," in 1966, marked

---

[6] An actuarial valuation is a formal estimate of the present value of benefits to be paid under a pension plan and a calculation of the amounts of employer contributions or accounting charges for pension cost. Pension plans are reviewed at intervals (sometimes annually) with the result that new valuations result in modifications of prior service cost and of current (normal) cost.

the first successful effort by the accounting profession to standardize pension plan accounting. Prior to the *Opinion,* accounting for pension costs varied considerably among companies. The *Opinion* recognized that there are different valid perceptions of the computation of pension costs; thus, while it specified certain standards, it did not aim for total uniformity. Two companies having almost identical pension plans, adopted at the same time, can be in compliance with the *Opinion* and yet have different patterns of reported pension expense.

The principal items mandated by the *Opinion* are as follows:

1. Pension costs (including related administrative expense) should be accounted for on the accrual basis.
2. Annual pension costs recorded should be based on an accounting method that uses an acceptable *actuarial cost method* and results in a pension cost that falls between a determinable maximum and minimum. Actuarial cost methods are discussed in the next section, and maximum and minimum limits are discussed on page 734.
3. Past service costs and prior service costs should be recognized over current and future periods; they do not constitute corrections of prior period earnings.
4. Accounting for pension costs is independent of the funding of pension costs. However, funding of a plan may affect the amount of the periodic pension expenses.
5. Certain disclosures in the body of financial statements and in the notes are required (see page 735).

ACTUARIAL COST METHODS

Actuarial cost methods were developed primarily as funding techniques in that they provide the specific amounts for periodic funding payments. Since determination of the funding requirements explicitly requires estimation of the underlying pension costs, the actuarial cost methods are also useful in determining *pension costs for accounting purposes.* Although the various actuarial cost methods are alike in that they use present value concepts and rely on actuarial assumptions, they differ significantly in their approaches and can produce different results for the same situation.

We noted above that in accordance with *APB Opinion No. 8,* the *accounting method* utilized in accounting for pension plans must use an acceptable *actuarial cost method.* The *Opinion* categorizes actuarial methods broadly as follows:

(1) Accrued Benefit Cost Method (Unit Credit Method)—under the unit credit method, future service benefits . . . are funded as they accrue—that is, each employee works out the service period involved. The past service cost . . . is the present value at the plan's inception date of the units of future benefit credited to employees for service prior to inception of the plan. Thus, the annual contribution (and cost) comprises primarily *(a)* the normal cost and *(b)* the past service cost.

(2) Projected Benefit Cost Methods—There are four methods in this group; *entry age normal, individual level premium, aggregate,* and *attained age normal* methods. The amount assigned (for funding) to the current year usually represents a constant amount that will provide for the estimated projected retirement benefits over the service lives of either the individual employees or the employee group, depending on the method selected. Pension cost projected under these methods tends to be stable or to decline year by year, depending on the method selected.

Although the APB, in *Opinion No. 8,* listed these methods as acceptable, it recognized that other methods may be acceptable if they conform to the guidelines established in the *Opinion.* It is important to understand that the above methods are applied by the actuary that determines the funding amounts each year for the company. *They provide both the amounts needed by the accountant to record pension costs and the amounts for funding requirements as illustrated later.*

The annual cost patterns for typical pension plans under the five actuarial cost methods mentioned above were graphically depicted in a

Journal of Accountancy article by William A. Dreher[7] and are shown in Exhibit 21–2. In each diagram it is assumed that the annual contributions depicted on the vertical axis will accumulate, at the end of 30 years, to a pension fund equal to the actuarial liability at that date.

ILLUSTRATION OF RECORDING PENSION COSTS AND FUNDING

The essential steps leading to development of periodic accounting entries for pension costs are as follows:

1. Determination of *past service cost* (if it exists) by the actuary. This involves an estimate derived by applying an actuarial method to factors including the expected level of future benefits, expected rates of employee mortality and turnover, and estimated net earnings of the pension fund.[8] Based on the actuary's evaluation of these factors, the actuary determines the *present value* of the cost of "credits" extended to employees for their services prior to inception of the pension plan.

2. Development of an *amortization schedule* (using an appropriate interest rate), which is used to allocate the past service cost to the current and future periods (if past service cost exists).

3. Determination of the *normal (current) pension cost* for the period. This involves estimation of the future costs of pension benefits earned as a result of services rendered by employees during the current period.

4. Development of a *funding schedule,* which specifies the periodic contributions required to fund both current and past service costs. (This schedule and the one from Step 2 may be combined into a single schedule, as shown in Exhibit 21–3.)

5. Development of the *accounting entries* for

---

[7] William A. Dreher, "Alternatives Available under *APB Opinion No. 8:* An Actuary's View," *Journal of Accountancy* (September 1967), p. 41.

[8] Net earnings will be determined by interest and dividend rates, changes in the value of pension fund investments, and administrative costs.

EXHIBIT 21-2
Annual Cost Patterns for a Typical Pension Plan under Acceptable Actuarial Cost Methods

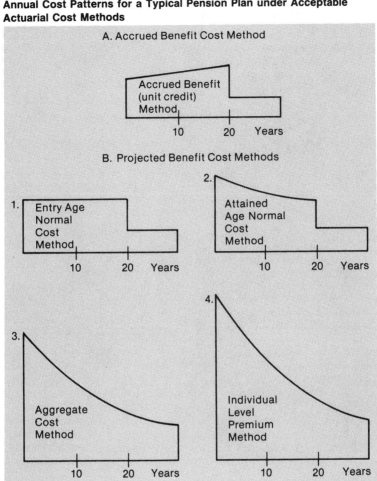

the period. These are based on *(a)* normal pension cost of the period, *(b)* past service cost of the period (i.e., amortization of total past service cost—to use the parlance of *APB Opinion No. 8*), and *(c)* funding.

The illustrative amortization and funding schedules and entries which follow are based on the following assumptions: The employer adopted a pension plan in January 1979, at which time the actuarial consultant estimated that the past service cost was $350,000 and that the normal pension cost would be $40,000 per year. Management decided to amortize and fund the past service cost over 15 years, with funding based on an expected 4% net earning rate. Past service cost will be amortized over *Case A,* 15 years (same as the funding period); *Case B,* 13 years; and *Case C,* 17 years. Under provisions of ERISA, *funding* can extend for as long as 40 years, and under income tax provisions 12 years is the minimum practical funding period. Choice of the term over which *past service cost* is *amortized* is discretionary, within a practical minimum of approximately 10 years and a maximum of 40 years (due to ERISA considerations).

EXHIBIT 21-3

Schedule of Past Service Pension Cost and Related Funding (Case B—amortization period 13 years; funding period 15 years)

	Amortization of Past Service Cost—13 Years			Funding 15 Years	Balance Sheet— Liability	
	(a) 13-Year Amortization Factor	(b) Addition for Interest	(c) Past Service Pension Expense (Dr.)	(d) Cash (Cr.)	(e) Credit Debit*	(f) Account Balance
Year						
1979	$ 35,050	—	$ 35,050	$ 31,479	$ 3,571	$ 3,571
1980	35,050	$ 143	35,193	31,479	3,714	7,285
1981	35,050	291	35,341	31,479	3,862	11,147
1982	35,050	446	35,496	31,479	4,017	15,164
1983	35,050	607	35,657	31,479	4,178	19,342
1984	35,050	774	35,824	31,479	4,345	23,687
1985	35,050	947	35,997	31,479	4,518	28,205
1986	35,050	1,128	36,178	31,479	4,699	32,904
1987	35,050	1,316	36,366	31,479	4,887	37,791
1988	35,050	1,512	36,562	31,479	5,083	42,874
1989	35,050	1,715	36,765	31,479	5,286	48,160
1990	35,050	1,926	36,976	31,479	5,497	53,657
1991	35,050	2,146	37,196	31,479	5,717	59,374
1992	—	2,375	2,375	31,479	29,104*	30,270
1993	—	1,209	1,209	31,479	30,270*	—
	$455,650	$16,535	$472,185	$472,185	-0-	-0-

(a) Periodic amortization = $350,000 ÷ 9.98565 (Table 6-4, $n = 13$; $i = 4\%$)
= $35,050 to column (a).
(b) 4% of preceding balance of column (f).
(c) Column (a) + (b).
(d) Periodic funding = $350,000 ÷ 11.11839 (Table 6-4, $n = 15$; $i = 4\%$)
= $31,479 to column (d).
(e) Column (c) − (d).
(f) Preceding balance in (f), plus or minus column (e).

Case A—To amortize and fund a *past service* cost of $350,000 over 15 years, assuming a 4% interest rate, an employer would have to record pension expense of $31,479 at the end of each year. This amount is calculated by dividing the past service cost by the present value of an ordinary annuity of $n = 15$; $i = 4\%$ (Table 6-4), that is, $350,000 ÷ 11.11839 = $31,479.

When the number of funding and amortization periods coincide, the amount calculated ($31,479 in the preceding paragraph) is recorded as expense, and is also added to the funding payment required for normal cost (this current service cost was assumed to be $40,000 for illustrative purposes) to determine the total cash funding payment. The 1979 entry would be as follows:

December 31, 1979:

Pension expense (normal pension cost)	40,000	
Pension expense (amortization of past service cost)	31,479	
Cash (paid to pension fund trustee)		71,479

The two debits in the above entry may be combined as a single debit to Pension Expense. If normal cost remains constant each year and the pension plan is not changed or revalued in an actuarial valuation, similar entries will be made through the end of 1993, that is, for a total of 15 years. After that date only *normal* pension cost must be funded and recorded each year.

Case B—When the number of funding and amortization periods differ, it is helpful to prepare a schedule to provide the data needed for the accounting entries. The schedule for this purpose, shown in Exhibit 21–3, assumes the $350,000 of *past service cost* is to be funded over 15 years and amortized over 13 years.

Note the following about the schedule:

1. It relates only to past service cost (not normal pension cost).
2. The periodic amortization of past service cost is increased by the interest on the cumulative amount by which amortization differs from funding. In terms of columns, the interest in column [b] is added to the amortization in column [a]. Interest is computed on the amount by which the cumulative amount in column [a] exceeds the cumulative amount in column [d]. A liability is recorded at the end of each of the first 13 years because expense, including interest on the liability (recorded over 13 years), exceeds the cash payment (for funding over 15 years). Interest accrues on this liability, and the interest becomes a part of pension expense. This is an exception to the general rule that interest is separately reported in financial statements.
3. The periodic past service funding payments cease at the end of Year 15 (1993).
4. Payments to the fund are constant each year.
5. The amortization of past service cost terminates at the end of the 13th year (1991).
6. A liability is recorded and reported on the balance sheet, for each year except the last one, because the funding is *slower* than the amortization (i.e., the expense recognition).

The schedule is started by first computing the 13-year amortization factor (column [a]) and, second, the 15-year periodic funding (column [d]). The remaining columns are completed as shown below the schedule.

Entries at the *end* of 1979, 1991 and 1992, based on Exhibit 21–3, assuming that normal cost remains at $40,000 per year, are as follows:

	1979 Year End	1991 Year End
Pension expense (normal pension cost)	40,000	40,000
Pension expense (past service cost)	35,050	37,196
Liability—pension cost in excess of funding	3,571	5,717
Cash (paid to pension fund trustee)	71,479	71,479

In the entry at the end of 1992 the *liability* account is *debited* as below:

Pension expense (normal pension cost)	40,000	
Pension expense (past service cost)	2,375	
Liability—pension cost in excess of funding	29,104	
Cash (paid to pension fund trustee)		71,479

Case C—Recall in this case that amortization of past service cost is over 17 years and funding is over 15 years. Because funding is *faster* than amortization of cost, a *deferred charge* is recorded, and reported on the balance sheet, for all years except the last one.

Entries based on Exhibit 21–4 at the *end* of 1979, 1990, and 1994, assuming normal pension cost remains at $40,000 per year, are as follows:

	1979 Year-End	1990 Year-End
Pension expense (normal pension cost)	40,000	40,000
Pension expense (past service cost)	28,769	27,307
Deferred charge—funding in excess of pension costs	2,710	4,172
Cash (paid to pension fund trustee)	71,479	71,479

In the entry at the end of 1994 the *deferred charge* account is *credited* as below:

Pension expense (normal pension cost)	40,000	
Pension expense (past service cost)	26,599	
Deferred charge—funding in excess of pension costs		26,599
Cash (paid to pension fund trustee)		40,000

It is important to observe that *APB Opinion No. 8* does not require immediate recognition of the full amount of the liability assumed for *past* service cost ($350,000 in the above examples). Rather, only the liability or deferred charge, caused by the *interest* difference when funding and amortization are over different lengths of time, is usually recorded. However, paragraph 20 of the Interpretation of the *Opinion* specifies: ". . . determine, at the end of each year, the amount of the legal liability not yet covered by the pension fund and balance sheet accruals. A liability and deferred charge equal to this amount would then be recorded and classified with any other pension-cost accruals and deferred charges appearing in the balance sheet."

EXHIBIT 21-4

Schedule of Past Service Cost and Related Funding (Case C—amortization period 17 years; funding period 15 years)

Year	Amortization of Past Service Cost—17 Years			Funding 15 Years	Balance Sheet— Deferred Charge	
	(a) 17-Year Amortization Factor	(b) Reduction for Interest	(c) Past Service Pension Expense (Dr.)	(d) Cash (Cr.)	(e) Debit Credit*	(f) Account Balance
1979	$ 28,769	—	$ 28,769	$ 31,479	$ 2,710	$ 2,710
1980	28,769	$ 108	28,661	31,479	2,818	5,528
1981	28,769	221	28,548	31,479	2,931	8,459
1982	28,769	338	28,431	31,479	3,048	11,507
1983	28,769	460	28,309	31,479	3,170	14,677
1984	28,769	587	28,182	31,479	3,297	17,974
1985	28,769	719	28,050	31,479	3,429	21,403
1986	28,769	856	27,913	31,479	3,566	24,969
1987	28,769	999	27,770	31,479	3,709	28,678
1988	28,769	1,147	27,622	31,479	3,857	32,535
1989	28,769	1,301	27,468	31,479	4,011	36,546
1990	28,769	1,462	27,307	31,479	4,172	40,718
1991	28,769	1,629	27,140	31,479	4,339	45,057
1992	28,769	1,802	26,967	31,479	4,512	49,569
1993	28,769	1,983	26,786	31,479	4,693	54,262
1994	28,769	2,170	26,599	—	26,599*	27,663
1995	28,769	1,106	27,663	—	27,663*	—
	$489,073	$16,888	$472,185	$472,185	–0–	–0–

(a) Periodic amortization: $350,000 ÷ 12.16567 (Table 6–4, n = 17; i = 4%) = $28,769.
(b) 4% of preceding balance of column (f).
(c) Column (a) – (b).
(d) Periodic funding = $350,000 ÷ 11.11839 (Table 6–4, n = 15; i = 4%)
       = $31,479.
(e) Column (d) – (c).
(f) Preceding balance + or – column (e).

ACTUARIAL GAINS AND LOSSES

APB Opinion No. 8 defines actuarial gains and losses as "the effects on actuarially calculated pension cost of (a) deviations, between actual prior experience and the actuarial assumptions used or (b) changes in actuarial assumptions as to future events."

Actuarial assumptions used in estimating pension funding and expenses are based on *estimates of future events.* As time passes, the actual events usually do not coincide with the prior estimates. As actual conditions change, assumptions about the future events must be revised. Thus, from time to time, it is necessary to reflect actual experience and to revise as-sumptions to be used in the future. These revisions cause *actuarial gains or losses,* which must be reflected in the accounting entries.

Paragraphs 30–33 of *APB Opinion No. 8* specify the accounting procedures for actuarial gains and losses. Actuarial gains and losses should be allocated to the current and future periods (in a manner similar to changes in accounting estimates). Two approaches commonly used are as follows:

1. Straight-line allocation (sometimes called spreading)—Ten to twenty years was suggested as reasonable.
2. Moving average allocation—A five-year moving average usually is used.

Exhibits 21–5 and 21–6 were adapted from interpretations of *APB Opinion No. 8.* Exhibit 21–5 illustrates how a ten-year straight-line allocation of actuarial gains and losses would be used as an adjustment of the *normal cost* of pension expense. Exhibit 21–6 illustrates the allocation on the basis of a five-year moving average.

The method of allocation does not affect the entries (except for the amounts) needed each year to record the allocation of actuarial gains and losses. The amount allocated to the year, if a loss (i.e., a debit), is recorded as an increase in *normal* pension expense; if it is a gain (i.e., a credit), it is recorded as a decrease in normal pension expense for the period. To illustrate, refer to Exhibit 21–6. In Year 1, there was a $5,000 actuarial gain and the moving average, computed for allocation purposes, was $2,200. Assuming the employer company has already *(a)* recorded pension expense of $50,000 for the year, *(b)* paid the predetermined funding amount to the trustee, and *(c)* received cash for the full amount of the actuarial gain for the year, the actuarial gain would be recorded as follows:

```
Cash .................................  5,000
    Pension expense (normal) ..........         2,200
    Deferred actuarial gain on
        pension fund ..................         2,800
```

The company would report the above data as follows:

```
Income Statement:
    Pension expense ($50,000 − $2,200) ........ $47,800

Balance Sheet:
    Liabilities:
        Deferred actuarial gain on
            pension fund .........................  2,800
```

Certain actuarial gains and losses call for exceptional treatment. The following use different procedures than those of the preceding paragraph in that they are recognized immediately. Actuarial gains and losses *(a)* arising from a *single occurrence* not directly related to the operation of the pension plan and *(b)* not in the normal course of the employer's business, are accorded immediate recognition. An example of such an occurrence is a plant closing, in which case the actuarial gain or loss should be treated

EXHIBIT 21–5
Allocation of Actuarial Gains and Losses
(ten-year straight-line basis)

	Actuarial Gains and Losses		
Year	Actual Gain (Loss)	Applied to Reduce (Increase) Pension Expense	Gain (Loss) Deferred to Future Years
1	$ 5,000	$ 500 *(a)*	$ 4,500 *(b)*
2	2,000	700 *(c)*	5,800 *(d)*
3	6,000	1,300	10,500
4	(1,000)	1,200	8,300
5	7,000	1,900	13,400
6	3,000	2,200	14,200
7	(8,000)	1,400	4,800
8	1,000	1,500	4,300
9	10,000	2,500	11,800
10	1,000	2,600	10,200

(a) $5,000 × 10% = $500.
(b) $5,000 − $500 = $4,500.
(c) ($5,000 + $2,000) ÷ 10 = $700.
(d) ($5,000 + $2,000) − ($500 + $700) = $5,800.

EXHIBIT 21–6
Allocation of Actuarial Gains and Losses
(five-year moving average)

	Actuarial Gains and Losses			
Year	Actual Gain (Loss)	5-Year Total	Applied to Reduce (Increase) Pension Expense	Gain (Loss) Deferred to Future Years
4	$ 1,000			
3	4,000	See Note		
2	(2,000)			
1	3,000			
1	5,000	$11,000 *(a)*	$2,200 *(b)*	$ 2,800 *(c)*
2	2,000	12,000 *(d)*	2,400 *(e)*	2,400 *(f)*
3	6,000	14,000	2,800	5,600
4	(1,000)	15,000	3,000	1,600
5	7,000	19,000	3,800	4,800
6	3,000	17,000	3,400	4,400
7	(8,000)	7,000	1,400	(5,000)
8	1,000	2,000	400	(4,400)
9	10,000	13,000	2,600	3,000
10	1,000	7,000	1,400	2,600

Note: Before Year 1, the gains and losses were recognized in the year of determination; they are used here, however, to develop a starting point in the averaging computation.
(a) $1,000 + $4,000 − $2,000 + $3,000 + $5,000 = $11,000 (five-year total).
(b) $11,000 ÷ 5 years = $2,200.
(c) $5,000 − $2,200 = $2,800.
(d) $4,000 − $2,000 + $3,000 + $5,000 + $2,000 = $12,000 (total for latest five years).
(e) $12,000 ÷ 5 years = $2,400.
(f) $2,800 + $2,000 − $2,400 = $2,400.

EXHIBIT 21–7
Minimum and Maximum Limits for Annual Pension Expense

Element of Annual Amount of Pension Expense	Minimum Annual Expense	Maximum Annual Expense
1. Normal cost.	Recognize full amount.	Recognize full amount.
2. Past service cost.	Recognize only interest on unfunded portion.	Recognize 10% until fully amortized.
3. Prior service cost (resulting from amendments of pension plan).	Recognize only interest on unfunded portion.	Recognize 10% until fully amortized.
4. Vested benefits.	Recognize actuarially computed value of vested benefits in excess of the sum of (1) pension fund and (2) any balance sheet pension accruals minus (3) any balance sheet prepayments or deferred charges at year-end.*	Not applicable since already in above amounts.
5. Interest equivalents on the difference between pension expense and amounts actually funded.	Include (or deduct) in certain limited cases in connection with vested benefits.†	Include (or deduct).

* *APB Opinion No. 8*, par. 17.
† *APB Opinion No. 8*, pars. 17, 42, and 43.

as an adjustment of the net gain or loss from that occurrence, and not as an adjustment of pension expense for the year. Another example is a merger or acquisition accounted for as a *purchase,* in which case the actuarial gain or loss should be treated as an adjustment of the purchase price of the subsidiary.

Accounting for *unrealized* (i.e., market value changes) increases or decreases in the value of pension fund investments is particularly troublesome. *APB Opinion No. 8* specifies that such changes should be accounted for as actuarial gains or losses, but states that undue weight should not be given to short-term fluctuations in the market prices of securities held in the pension fund, and that in the case of *debt* securities, it would ordinarily not be advisable to recognize changes in their market value if they are to be held to maturity.

MAXIMUM AND MINIMUM LIMITS ON ANNUAL PENSION COST

APB Opinion No. 8 recognizes that when different actuarial cost methods are applied to the

same set of facts, different accounting results may be obtained. While the *Opinion* was deliberately flexible to accommodate different funding practices, concomitantly it set maximum and minimum limits for the amounts recorded as *annual pension expense.* Computation of the maximum and minimum limits for the annual pension expense is summarized in Exhibit 21–7 and shown in Exhibit 21–8.

The maximum and minimum amounts are always the same *(a)* when the past service cost is fully amortized or *(b)* when either the "individual level premium" or the "aggregate" method is used. The maximum and minimum amounts are the same in these situations because these methods do not separately compute and identify past service cost or other prior service costs. Although actuaries compute the maximum and minimum limits, accountants are expected to have a keen understanding of them and their application.

Application of the maximum and minimum limits, based on Exhibits 21–3 and 21–4, is illustrated in Exhibit 21–8 for 1980. The added assumptions are (1) normal cost, $40,000 (funded

EXHIBIT 21–8
Maximum and Minimum Limits

	Based on Exhibit	
Component of Limitation	21–3	21–4
Minimum provision:		
1. Normal cost..	$40,000	$40,000
2. Interest on unfunded past service cost [a]	13,301	13,301
3. Interest on unfunded prior service cost [b] (due to plan amendments)	2,000	2,000
4. Additional provision for vested benefits	-0-	-0-
Total minimum provision for 1980	$55,301	$55,301
Maximum provision:		
1. Normal cost..	$40,000	$40,000
2. Ten percent of past service cost	35,000	35,000
3. Ten percent of prior service cost (due to plan amendments)	5,000	5,000
4. Interest on difference between accruals and funding (Exhibits 21–3 and 21–4)	143	(108)
Total maximum provision for 1980	$80,143	$79,892

[a] .04 [($350,000 × 1.04*) − $31,479] = $13,301
* This is for the interest buildup in 1980. For more detail, see Accounting Interpretations of *APB Opinion No. 8*, pars. 9–10.
[b] .04 × $50,000 = $2,000

in 1980), (2) prior service cost from amendment of the pension plan, $50,000, (recognized at the start of 1980 but not funded that year), and (3) vested benefits are significantly less than the pension fund.

Note that the $50,000 prior service cost, due to plan amendments, would have been included in Exhibits 21–3 and 21–4 had it been assumed there. The results would have been the same as items 2 plus 3 above, that is, .04[($350,000 × 1.04) − $31,479 + $50,000] = $15,301.

Pension expense computed for 1980 in either Exhibit 21–3 ($35,193 + $40,000 = $75,193) or 21–4 ($28,661 + $40,000 = $68,661) would be reported in the 1980 income statement (including normal pension expense) because the amount in each situation is between the computed maximum and minimum limits.

The computed pension expense will be below, between, or above the minimum-maximum limits depending on the relationships among three variables: *(a)* the funding period, *(b)* the amortization period, and *(c)* the interest rate. Not infrequently, the computed pension expense is out-

side the limits. When the computed pension expense is greater than the maximum limit, the excess should be recorded as a deferred charge. Alternatively, any amount less than the minimum should be recorded as a liability. Such differences would be amortized in subsequent years.

PENSION PLAN DISCLOSURES

Pension expense is the principal account arising from the existence of a pension plan insofar as most employers are concerned. If pension expense is not reported separately in the income statement, *APB Opinion No. 8* requires that the amount of pension expense be reported in notes to the statements. Also, when the rates of amortization and of funding past service cost differ, a deferred charge or a liability balance results. Until one of these is amortized fully at the end of the amortization or funding period (whichever is longer), it must be reported on the balance sheet (see Exhibits 21–3 and 21–4).

Under some circumstances other account balances related to pension plans may arise. When employees have vested pension rights, any excess of the actuarial present value of such rights over the amounts funded or accrued should be reported as a liability. Normally such an unfunded pension amount should be reported as a long-term liability. The debit, when such a liability is recognized, would be treated as a deferred charge and reported under the title Deferred Pension Cost or some similar caption.

In addition to disclosure of the amount of the annual pension expense, notes to the financial statements also should contain the following:

1. A brief statement that a pension plan exists, identifying or describing the employee groups covered.
2. A statement of the company's accounting and funding policies.
3. A recital of the nature and effect of significant matters affecting comparability for all periods for which statements are presented. This includes changes in accounting methods (actuarial cost method, amortization of past or prior service cost, treatment of actuarial gains and losses, etc.), changes in actuarial assumptions or other circumstances, and any plan adoptions or amendments.

The 1978 edition of *Accounting Trends and Techniques* reveals that for 534 companies the current year expense for pension and retirement plans was reported as follows:

Elements of Current Year Expense	Percent Reporting the Item
Normal cost and amortization of prior service cost	88
Normal cost and interest on unfunded prior service cost	1
Normal cost—no reference to prior service cost	6
Normal cost—no unfunded prior service cost	5
	100

EFFECTS OF ERISA

Although the 1974 ERISA legislation affected the *administration* of pension plans and aimed at making employee benefits under plans more secure, it had relatively little impact on financial accounting. A larger volume of reports containing more detailed information is now required of plan administrators, but these do not significantly affect accounting procedures or the basic financial accounting statements.

After the passage of ERISA, the FASB issued *Interpretation No. 3* (dated December 1974) and placed the subject of employee benefit accounting on its agenda. No new *FASB Statements* have been issued on the subject yet. Some of the highlights of the Interpretation include the following:

1. ERISA does not change minimum or maximum limits for the annual provision for pension expense.
2. Compliance with the participation, vesting, or funding requirements of ERISA may result in a change in the *amount* of periodic pension cost to be charged to expense for financial reporting purposes, even though no change in accounting methods is made.
3. The FASB does not believe ERISA creates an additional legal obligation for unfunded pension cost that warrants accounting recognition as a liability except in two circumstances:
   a. An entity with a plan subject to the Act's provisions must fund a minimum annual amount unless a waiver is obtained. If no waiver is obtained, the amount currently required to be funded shall be recognized as a liability by a debit to Pension Expense or to a deferred charge or both as appropriate under *APB Opinion No. 8*.
   b. If a plan is terminated, the Act imposes a liability on the employer. When there is convincing evidence a plan will be terminated and "the liability on termination will exceed fund assets and related prior accruals [i.e., expense minus funding], the excess liability shall be accrued. If the amount of the liability cannot be reasonably determined, disclosure of the circumstances shall be made in the notes to the financial statements, and an estimate of the possible range of the liability."

DISCLOSURE OF UNFUNDED PENSION LIABILITIES

Many analysts are concerned that under current GAAP, companies are not required to disclose amounts of *unfunded* past or prior service costs. A recent survey of the 100 largest U.S. corporations (on the basis of sales) revealed that *unfunded* past or prior service costs amounted to almost 91% of their three-year average pretax profits. Put another way, the average company in the survey could barely cover its past or prior service cost obligation with one year's pretax profit. On the average, *unfunded* vested benefits amounted to more than 7% of owners' equity of these companies. Fiscal years of the companies ended on various dates, but for their most recent fiscal years (ended in 1977 or 1978) *pension and retirement expense* averaged 7.7% of their $11,767 million labor expense. While such a proportion of pension and retirement expense might seem manageable, for some companies in the survey, pension and retirement costs exceeded 10% of their labor expense. More alarming is the fact that for several *profitable* companies, *unfunded* past or prior service costs, which currently do not have to be disclosed, exceeded 1,000% of their three-year average *pretax* profits. In other words, it would take ten or more years at their current profit levels just to fund past or prior service cost out of *pretax* profits. While more than 25% of the companies surveyed had no significant unfunded vested benefits, for two companies the amount of such unfunded benefits exceeded their owners' equity.[9]

This chapter only introduces accounting for pension costs, but it serves to indicate that pension accounting is complex and that a wholly satisfactory solution to some of its problems has not yet been attained. Resolution of the complexities is not easy. The FASB is working on pension accounting problems in cooperation with the actuarial profession. Pension accounting and reporting requirements seem certain to change within the next few years.

---

[9] "Unfunded Pension Liabilities: A Continuing Burden," *Business Week,* August 14, 1978, pp. 60–64. A three-year average was used to smooth out the effects of a single year's results (which could deviate significantly from normal results).

QUESTIONS

1. What are some of the uncertainties with which actuaries must deal when they estimate the cost of future benefits under a pension plan?

2. What is vesting?

3. How does past service cost arise? What is the relationship of past service cost to prior service cost?

4. What is an actuarial cost method? Do the acceptable actuarial cost methods produce similar or dissimilar expense patterns over the term of a pension plan? Explain.

5. What is normal pension cost? How is normal pension cost accounted for?

6. If accounting charges for past service cost exceeds funding payments for a period, what kind of account arises, and how should it be reported in the financial statements? Suppose the reverse is true; that is, payments exceed charges, what then?

7. What guidelines as to the *minimum* and *maximum* annual pension expense are set out in *APB Opinion No. 8?*

8. What are actuarial gains and losses? How should they be treated?

9. What are the financial statement disclosure provisions of *APB Opinion No. 8?*

10. What are the main provisions of *FASB Interpretation No. 3?*

11. What does the acronym ERISA stand for? Thus far, has financial accounting been greatly affected by it?

12. The Pasther Company has a contributory pension plan for all of its employees. In 19A, a total of $100,000 was withheld from employees' salaries and deposited into a pension fund administered by an outside trustee. In addition, Pasther deposited $200,000 of its own money into the fund in 19A. Based on the report of Pasther's outside actuaries which was received in December 19A, the 19A actuarial cost of the pension plan was $320,000. As a result of this report, Pasther deposited $20,000 of its own money into the fund on January 12, 19B. How much should be reported as pension expense in Pasther's 19A income statement?

    a. $200,000.
    b. $220,000.

c. $300,000.

d. $320,000.

Briefly support your answer choice.

(AICPA adapted)

DECISION CASE 21–1

The corporation where you are employed as controller has not had a pension plan but its directors are seriously considering adopting one. You have been called in to explain several matters to the board of directors from an accounting standpoint and to comment on them.

Item 1:

A substantial number of the employees have worked for the corporation for many years. From an accounting and financial standpoint what would happen if the company does not adopt a pension plan now but does adopt one at a future date?

Item 2:

The directors are concerned about recognition of the company's liability for past service cost. One of them, who has some familiarity with accounting, asked "If we book the liability for past service cost, what account or accounts will we debit?" Respond in terms of generally accepted accounting principles. Consider also what the company might do if it were not required to conform to GAAP.

Item 3:

What are the effects in the accounts of a fast amortization of past service cost (compared with the rate of funding)? What are the arguments favoring slow amortization of past service cost (compared with the rate of funding)?

EXERCISES

Exercise 21–1

Expected annual pension benefits to be received by a group of Fry Company's employees due to retire in eight years and to be paid one year to four years after retirement are as follows:

End of Year 1	$30,000
End of Year 2	25,000
End of Year 3	13,000
End of Year 4	8,000
Thereafter	0
Total pension payments	$76,000

Funds deposited with the pension fund trustee are expected to earn 7% per annum. The contract states

that a sum sufficient to fund all of the prospective payments must be on deposit by the date the employees plan to retire, assuming the first pension payment is made one year after retirement date.

Required (round amounts to nearest dollar):

1. *(a)* Compute the amount that must be on deposit as of the employee's retirement date. *(b)* Prove the correctness of your calculation by preparing a schedule which reflects earnings and the payout over the four-year period.

2. Using the funding amount computed in Requirement 1, determine the equal annual contributions to the pension fund trustee which will fully fund the pension payout requirements. Assume the accumulation is to occur over the next eight years, that is, the last eight years the employees are on the payroll, and that the last deposit is made on retirement date.

3. Suppose (instead of as in Requirement 2 above) that the pension plan was adopted six years before the employees would retire and that they were to be given credit for the two years of employment preceding adoption of the plan. Determine *(a)* the amount of past service cost as of the date of inception of the plan and *(b)* how much must be contributed in equal annual payments over the six-year period in order to fully fund the pension arrangement.

Exercise 21–2

Plans are being made to fund the prospective pension benefits of a group of employees of Benton Company due to retire in nine years and to be paid amounts from one to five years after retirement as below:

End of Year 1	$ 70,000
End of Year 2	50,000
End of Year 3	30,000
End of Year 4	15,000
End of Year 5	5,000
Thereafter	0
Total pension payments	$170,000

Funds deposited with the pension fund trustee will earn 6% per annum. The pension plan contract calls for deposit of an amount sufficient to fund all of the expected payments from the fund by the date the employees retire.

Required (round amounts to nearest dollar and disregard maximum-minimum limits):

1. *(a)* Compute the amount required by the trustee as of the employees' retirement date and *(b)* prepare a table reflecting the 6% earnings on un-

used funds and pension payments by the trustee, to retirees scheduled over the five-year period.

2. Compute the amount of each of nine equal annual payments which will fully fund the pensions. The payments will be made the last nine years of employment, and the last payment will coincide with the retirement date of the employees.

3. Assume (instead of as in Requirement 2 above) that the pension plan was adopted seven years before the employees' retirement date and that they will be credited for benefit purposes with the two years of employment preceding adoption of the plan. Compute (a) the amount of past service cost as of the date of inception of the plan and (b) the amount which must be contributed in equal annual payments at year-end over the seven-year period in order to fully fund the plan.

Exercise 21-3

O'Brien Company initiated a pension plan on a funded basis several years after the company began operations. Its consulting actuary determined that at inception of the plan the past service cost amounted to $338,721.

Required (disregard maximum-minimum limits):

1. Using a 7% interest table, prepare a schedule that reflects amortization of the past service cost over a four-year period and funding over a three-year period. Round to nearest dollar.

2. Give journal entries relating to the pension plan covering its first two years of operation based upon funding in accordance with the table developed for Requirement 1 and on the assumptions that the plan year and the fiscal year coincided and normal costs for the first two years were $50,000 for Year 1 and $53,000 for Year 2.

Exercise 21-4

The independent actuary engaged by Jack Company determined that should it adopt the type of pension plan contemplated, its unfunded past service cost would amount to $331,213.

Required (disregard maximum-minimum limits):

1. Prepare a schedule that reflects amortization of the past service cost over a four-year period and funding over a six-year period based on 8% annual interest rates. Round to nearest dollar.

2. Assume the actuary determined the normal pension cost to be $120,000 for Year 1 and $132,000 for Year 2. Record pension expense for both years.

3. Indicate what would be reported on Jack Company's income statement and balance sheet for each of the two years. If note disclosures are required, write the note.

Exercise 21-5

Richards Company initiated a funded pension plan and gave employees credit for past service. The actuary estimated the past service cost at inception of the plan at $50,000.

Required (round amounts to nearest dollar and disregard maximum-minimum limits):

1. Using a 5% annual rate, calculate the periodic amortization factor and periodic funding payments assuming

   Case A—Funding and amortization are over three years.

   Case B—Funding is over four years; amortization is over three.

   Case C—Funding is over two years; amortization is over three.

2. Prepare an amortization and funding schedule for the past service cost for Case C.

3. Give entries for four years for Case C. Normal costs for the years are, respectively, $12,000, $14,000, $18,000, and $22,000.

4. Indicate what would be reflected on the income statement and the balance sheet under Case C for the four years. If note disclosures are required, write the note.

Exercise 21-6

Select the best answer in each of the following. Briefly justify each selection.

1. When a company adopts a pension plan for accounting purposes, past service cost should be
   a. Treated as a prior period adjustment because no future periods are benefited.
   b. Amortized in accordance with procedures used for income tax purposes.
   c. Amortized under accrual accounting to current and future periods benefited.
   d. Treated as an expense of the period during which the funding occurs.

2. The Thoughtful Corporation adopted an employee pension plan on January 1, 19A, for all of its eligible employees. Thoughtful has agreed to make annual payments to a designated trustee at the end of each year. Data relating to the plan follow:

Normal cost $100,000
Past service cost on
  January 1, 19A (unfunded) 500,000
Funds held by trustee are expected
  to earn a 5% return.

In accordance with *APB Opinion No. 8,* what is the maximum pension expense that Thoughtful can record for 19A?

a. $105,000.
b. $125,000.
c. $150,000.
d. $175,000.

3. When pension expense is presented in a statement of income, past and current service costs
   a. Must be shown separately in computing income before extraordinary items.
   b. Must be separated so that past service cost can be treated as a prior period adjustment.
   c. Must be separated so that past service cost can be treated as an extraordinary item.
   d. May be either combined or shown separately in computing income before extraordinary items.

4. The terminal funding method and pay-as-you-go method of accounting for pension plans are not generally accepted accounting methods because
   a. They do not require the funding of past service cost.
   b. They are not actuarially sound.
   c. They do not recognize pension costs prior to the retirement of employees.
   d. They are not acceptable methods for federal income tax purposes.

5. What is the difference between the terms past service cost and prior service cost?
   a. Past service cost refers to cost applicable to periods prior to a particular date of actuarial valuation, and prior service cost refers to costs applicable to employee service prior to inception of a pension plan.
   b. Past service cost refers to costs applicable to employee service prior to inception of a pension plan, and prior service cost refers to costs applicable to periods prior to a particular date of actuarial valuation.
   c. Past service cost refers to costs applicable to a pension plan for an employee who enters the plan after inception of the plan in order to bring the employee's benefits into line with the other participants in the plan, and prior service cost refers to changes in prior period pension cost that are caused by a change in actuarial valuation.
   d. There is no difference between the two terms, and they may be used interchangeably.

(AICPA adapted)

Exercise 21–7

Set forth below is an amortization table of a company which adopted a pension plan at a time when its past service cost amounted to $1,000,000. This past service cost is being funded in a lesser number of years than it is being amortized.

(Relates to Exercise 21–7)

(a)	(b)	(c)	(d)	(e)	(f)	(g)
1	$123,290.94	—	$123,290.94	$148,527.83	$ 25,236.89	$ 25,236.89
2	123,290.94	$1,009.48	122,281.46	148,527.83	26,246.37	51,483.26
3	123,290.94	2,059.33	121,231.61	148,527.83	27,296.22	78,779.48
4	123,290.94	3,151.18	120,139.76	148,527.83	28,388.07	107,167.55
5	123,290.94	4,286.70	119,004.24	148,527.83	29,523.59	136,691.14
6	123,290.94	5,467.65	117,823.29	148,527.83	30,704.54	167,395.68
7	123,290.94	6,695.83	116,595.11	148,527.83	31,932.72	199,328.40
8	123,290.94	7,973.14	115,317.80	148,527.83	33,210.03	232,538.43
9	123,290.94	9,301.54	113,989.40	—	113,989.40*	118,549.03
10	123,290.94	4,741.91*	118,549.03	—	118,549.03*	—

* Reflects rounding.

Required (disregard maximum-minimum limits):

1. What interest rate was assumed in making the amortization and funding calculations? Show how you arrived at your results.
2. Supply appropriate titles for columns *(a)* through *(g)* of the table.
3. If the normal costs in Years 1, 2, and 3 were, respectively, $90,000, $100,000, and $110,000, what were *(a)* total disbursements for pensions for these three years and *(b)* total pension expense for these three years?
4. What balance sheet amounts would be shown by this company in respect to its pension plan at the end of Years 7, 8, and 9, and what is the nature of the account under which the amounts would be reported?

Exercise 21–8

Select the best answer in each of the following and explain the basis for your choice.

1. The amount of cost, on an accrual basis, that should be assigned each period to the pension plan for current services is known as
   a. Past service cost.
   b. Prior service cost.
   c. Normal cost.
   d. Vesting cost.
2. In accounting for a pension plan, any difference between the pension cost charged to expense and payments into the fund should be reported as
   a. An offset to the liability for past service cost.
   b. Accrued or prepaid pension cost.
   c. An operating expense in this period.
   d. An accrued actuarial liability.
3. When accounting for pension cost, a company
   a. Allocates total pension costs systematically and rationally.
   b. Records fluctuating gains and losses on pension fund investments as they occur.
   c. Gives immediate recognition to all pension costs for which legal liability exists.
   d. Establishes a positive relationship between contributions to the fund and the recorded provision.
4. Benefits under a pension plan that are not contingent upon an employee's continuing service are
   a. Granted under a plan of defined contribution.
   b. Based upon terminal funding.
   c. Actuarially unsound.
   d. Vested.
5. The account "Deferred Pension Expense" would arise when
   a. The rate of funding and amortization are the same.
   b. Funding is accomplished in a shorter period than amortization of past service cost.
   c. Amortization of past service cost and funding are ignored.
   d. Amortization of past service cost is over a shorter period than funding.
   (2, 3, and 4, AICPA adapted)

Exercise 21–9

The following tabulation was prepared for a company which had $70,000 past service cost and decided 4% was an appropriate interest rate to use. Funding payments for past service cost are made at the end of each year.

Required (disregard maximum-minimum limits):

1. Indicate how the value marked † was calculated.
2. Indicate how the value marked ‡ was calculated.
3. Show how the amounts in columns *(b), (c), (e),* and *(f)* were computed.

(Relates to Exercise 21–9)
Schedule of Past Service Pension Cost and Related Funding (amortization period 10 years; funding period 12 years)

Year	Amortization of Past Service Cost—10 Years			Funding—12 Years	Balance Sheet—Liability	
	(a) 10-Year Amortization Factor	(b) Addition for Interest	(c) Past Service Pension Expense (debit)	(d) Cash (credit)	(e) Credit Debit*	(f) Account Balance
1976	$8,630.37†		$ 8,630.37	$ 7,458.65‡	$1,171.72	$ 1,171.72
1977	8,630.37	$ 46.87	8,677.24	7,458.65	1,218.59	2,390.31
1978	8,630.37	95.61	8,725.98	7,458.65	1,267.33	3,657.64
1979	8,630.37	146.31	8,776.68	7,458.65	1,318.03	4,975.67
1980	8,630.37	199.03	8,829.40	7,458.65	1,370.75	6,346.42
1981	8,630.37	253.86	8,884.23	7,458.65	1,425.58	7,772.00
1982	8,630.37	310.88	8,941.25	7,458.65	1,482.60	9,254.60
1983	8,630.37	370.18	9,000.55	7,458.65	1,541.90	10,796.50
1984	8,630.37	431.86	9,062.23	7,458.65	1,603.58	12,400.08
1985	8,630.37	496.00	9,126.37	7,458.65	1,667.72	14,067.80
1986	–0–	562.71	562.71	7,458.65	6,895.94*	7,171.86
1987	–0–	286.79	286.79	7,458.65	7,171.86*	–0–
			$89,503.80	$89,503.80		

4. Give the company's entry to record pension expense at the end of 1985 if in addition to the amount paid to the sinking fund trustee for past service cost, $10,000 was paid for 1985 normal pension cost.
5. Give entry to record pension expense at the end of 1986, if in addition to the amount paid for past service cost, $9,000 was paid for 1986 normal cost.

Exercise 21–10

Indicate the best answer in each of the following and briefly explain the basis of your choices.

1. The terms "accrued benefit," "entry-age normal," "attained age normal," "aggregate cost," and "individual level premium"
   a. Are synonymous in meaning.
   b. Relate to vesting.
   c. Identify actuarial cost methods.
   d. Are unacceptable for use in modern pension accounting.
2. Following the guides set by the Accounting Principles Board, the minimum charge to expense permitted in accounting for pension plan expense is
   a. Normal cost.
   b. Normal cost, plus a prescribed percentage of prior (or past) service cost.
   c. Normal cost, plus interest on unfunded prior (or past) service cost, plus a prescribed percentage of any increase in prior service costs arising from amendments to the plan.
   d. Normal cost, plus interest on unfunded prior (or past) service cost, plus a possible provision for vested benefits.
3. A pension fund actuarial gain or loss that is caused by a plant closing should
   a. Be recognized immediately as a gain or loss.
   b. Be spread over the current year and future years.
   c. Be charged or credited to the current pension expense.
   d. Be recognized as a prior period adjustment.
4. Which of the following actuarial cost methods is not an acceptable method for determining pension cost?
   a. Unit credit.
   b. Individual level premium.
   c. Terminal funding.
   d. Entry age normal.
5. In March 19A, Rocka Company adopted a pension plan for its eligible employees. Unfunded past service cost was determined to be $7,000,000, and this amount will be paid in ten annual installments of $1,000,000 to an outside funding agency administering the plan.

Additional information:

Past service cost will be amortized over 20 years.	
Normal cost for 19A (remitted to funding agency in 19A).	$560,000
Amortization of past service cost for 19A.	650,000

What is the deferred pension cost for 19A?
   a. $350,000.
   b. $440,000.
   c. $500,000.
   d. $560,000.
6. Which of the following disclosures of pension plan information is not required by *APB Opinion No. 8* to be included in the financial statements?
   a. The estimated pension expense for the period.
   b. The amount paid from the pension fund to retirees during the period.
   c. A statement of the company's accounting and funding policies for the pension plan.
   d. The nature and effect of significant pension plan matters affecting comparability for all periods presented.

(All except No. 1 AICPA adapted)

Exercise 21–11

Fischer Company has its pension plan actuarially evaluated annually with the result that it evaluates the actuarial gains or losses on an annual basis. The history of its actuarial gains and losses appears below.

Year	Gain (Loss)	Year	Gain (Loss)
19A	$6,000	19G	$(4,000)
19B	3,000	19H	6,000
19C	7,000	19I	3,000
19D	4,000	19J	4,000
19E	(2,000)	19K	2,000
19F	5,000	19L	3,000

Required:

1. Prepare a schedule showing for each year the amount that would be applied to reduce Fischer Company's normal pension expense if the actuarial losses and gains are amortized on a ten-year straight-line basis. Your schedule should also show the cumulative balance of the unamortized actuarial gain or loss carried forward to future years.
2. Assume instead that before 19E the actuarial gains or losses were recognized in the year of determination and that starting with 19E they are to be applied to normal cost on the basis of using a five-year moving average. Although the actuarial gains of the first four years have already been reflected as an adjustment of normal pension cost of those years, they are to be used merely to develop a starting point in the averaging computation. As above,

prepare a schedule which shows (starting with 19E) the annual adjustment of normal pension expense and the cumulative amount deferred to future years.

Exercise 21–12

1. Unfunded past service cost of Petrox Company was $400,000 at January 1, 19A, and unfunded prior service cost (in addition to any past service cost), due to plan amendments, was $100,000. Normal cost for the year amounted to $55,000 which was fully funded. No benefits vested during the year. The past and prior service costs (due to amendment of the plan) will be amortized over 25 years from January 1, 19A. Calculate the minimum and maximum pension cost limits for the company for 19A assuming a 5% interest rate. Round to nearest dollar.

2. Unfunded prior service cost (including past service cost) of Keene Company on January 1, 19A, amounted to $550,000. This amount will be amortized over 15 years from January 1, 19A. Normal cost for the year was $70,000. Payment to the pension fund at year-end amounted to $110,000. No benefits vested during the year. Calculate the minimum and maximum pension cost limits for the company for 19A (assuming a 6% return on pension fund assets). Round to nearest dollar.

Exercise 21–13

An actuary computed a present value of the past service cost of $700,000 for Louis Company. Assume normal pension cost of $90,000 each year. Round all required computations to nearest dollar.

1. Assume the past service cost is both fully funded and amortized over 13 years by an annual amount of $70,101 each year-end. What interest rate is being used? What amount of total annual pension expense should be recognized until something changes either the normal cost or past or prior service cost? Consider the limits on pension expense specified in *APB Opinion No. 8.*

2. Assume the past service cost is amortized as in Requirement 1 above, and funding is over 12 years. What would be the annual funding payments? Assuming no other change through the second year, what is the annual pension expense for the first and second years?

PROBLEMS

Problem 21–1

Pension benefits of $150,000 per year are to be paid to a group of employees who are scheduled to retire in 15 years. It is expected the benefits will be paid for eight years, then cease. The first benefit payment is to occur one year after retirement. Money on deposit to fund the pensions is expected to earn 6% per year.

Required (round amounts to nearest dollar):

1. Calculate *(a)* the amount that would have to be deposited in a single lump sum on the date the employees retire and *(b)* instead, the amount of each annual payment required to a pension fund trustee if 15 funding payments are to be made, the last of which is on the retirement date.

2. Assume the same level of benefits based on 15 years' service but the plan was not adopted until five years later. Thus, ten equal annual payments, the last of which is on the employees' retirement date, are to be paid to the pension fund trustee. Calculate the amount of each annual funding payment under this modification.

3. Assume that pension payments are to be made at the start of each year for eight years; in other words the first payment is to occur on the date the employees retire.

   a. Calculate the amount of each equal annual payment to the pension fund if there are 15 payments and the last payment to the sinking fund trustee is on the same date as the first payment to the pensioners.

   b. Prove the accuracy of your results with a table reflecting the trustee's payouts and interest revenue over the eight-year period.

Problem 21–2

The actuary for XYZ Company determined that the past service cost under the pension plan about to be adopted will be $70,000 and that pension fund investments can be expected to earn 4%. Management accepts the actuary's recommendations and has decided to fund the past service cost over a eight-year period but to amortize it over a ten-year period.

Required (disregard maximum-minimum limits):

1. Prepare a schedule of past service pension costs and related funding if the first payment and first amortization are to be made at the end of 19A. The plan was adopted early in January 19A. Round to nearest dollar.

2. Based on amounts derived in the schedule, give the entries at the end of 19D to record the 19D funding payment on the past service cost amount plus $8,000 paid for normal pension costs for 19D.

3. Based on amounts derived in the schedule, give the entries at the end of 19I to record the funding

payment on the past service cost amount plus $9,000 paid for normal pension cost for 19I.

Problem 21–3

After having been in business a number of years without a pension plan, Dawe Corporation adopted a funded noncontributory pension plan. For simplicity, the number of periods will be limited and the first year of the pension plan will be designated as 19A. Past service cost as of January 1, 19A, amounted to $60,000. Normal pension costs for 19A were $9,000; in the four succeeding years they were $9,500, $10,000, $10,400, and $10,900

Required (round amounts to nearest dollar and disregard maximum-minium limits):

1. Using an 8% interest rate and assuming year-end funding, prepare schedules of amortization and funding for each of the following sets of assumptions as to years over which amortization and funding of past service is to occur:

	Periods	
	Amortization	Funding
Case A	4	4
Case B	3	4
Case C	4	3
Case D	4	1

2. For each case, give the entries related to pension expense and cash payments for 19A, 19D, and 19E (round all computations to nearest dollar). Use present value.
3. For each case, indicate amounts that would be reported on the income statement and balance sheet for 19A, 19D, and 19E concerning the pension plan.

Problem 21–4

Miller Company initiated a funded, noncontributory pension plan effective January 1, 19A. This was several years after the company began operations. There was a past service cost of $30,000. Because the company had excess cash, it decided to fund the past service cost fully as of year-end 19A, and to amortize the past service cost over four years. In connection with the latter, the pension fund trustee estimated that the pension fund investments will earn 7% over the foreseeable future. The funding payments will be made to the pension fund trustee.

Required (disregard maximum-minium limits and round amounts to nearest dollar):

1. Prepare a schedule of amortization and funding of the past service cost. Round all amounts to the nearest dollar.
2. Assuming that normal pension costs are 19A, $9,000; 19B, $9,400; 19C, $10,000; and 19D, $10,500, give the entries related to pension expense and cash payments for each year.
3. Suppose the first eligible employee retired late in 19C and was paid first benefits amounting to $500 late that year. Give any entries indicated for Miller. Explain.
4. Indicate amounts that would be reported on the income statement and balance sheet for 19A, 19B, 19C, and 19D.

Problem 21–5

Set forth below is an amortization and funding schedule for a company whose past service cost was

(Relates to Problem 21–5)
Schedule of Amortization of Past Service Cost and Related Funding
Amortization of Past Service Pension Cost— 10 Years

Year	10-Year Amortizaton Factor	Addition for 6% Interest	Past Service Pension Expense	12-Year Funding	Balance Sheet—Liability	
					Credit Debit*	Account Balance
1 ...	$135,867.96	—	$135,867.96	$119,277.03	$ 16,590.93	$ 16,590.93
2 ...	135,867.96	$ 995.46	136,863.42	119,277.03	17,586.39	34,177.32
3 ...	135,867.96	2,050.64	137,918.60	119,277.03	18,641.57	52,818.89
4 ...	135,867.96	3,169.13	139,037.09	119,277.03	19,760.06	72,578.95
5 ...	135,867.96	4,354.74	140,222.70	119,277.03	20,945.67	93,524.62
6 ...	135,867.96	5,611.48	141,479.44	119,277.03	22,202.41	115,727.03
7 ...	135,867.96	6,943.62	142,811.58	119,277.03	23,534.55	139,261.58
8 ...	135,867.96	8,355.69	144,223.65	119,277.03	24,946.62	164,208.20
9 ...	135,867.96	9,852.49	145,720.45	119,277.03	26,443.42	190,651.62
10 ...	135,867.96	11,439.10	147,307.06	119,277.03	28,030.03	218,681.65
11 ...	—	13,120.90	13,120.90	119,277.03	106,156.13*	112,525.52
12 ...	—	6,751.51	6,751.51	119,277.03	112,525.52*	—

determined to be $1,000,000 when its pension plan was adopted. If the company were to amortize this amount of past service cost over a 10-year period and to fund it over a 12-year period, and if the expected earnings rate on pension fund investments were 6%, the schedule presented below would apply.

Required (round amounts to nearest dollar):

1. If the company's normal pension cost for Years 1 and 2, respectively, amounted to $140,000 and $148,000, and management had decided initially to postpone funding of the past service cost, what is the *minimum* pension expense the company could report under provisions of *APB Opinion No. 8?* Show computations. (Assume there are no vesting requirements.)
2. If the company instead decided to implement the funding and amortization as reflected on the schedule, what is the *maximum* pension expense the company could report for Years 1 and 2 if normal pension costs are the same as given in Requirement 1?
3. Again assume the normal pension costs for the first two years are the same as given in Requirement 1. In this instance management decided to amortize the $1,000,000 past service cost over ten years but to fund it over eight years and to use a 5% annual rate in connection with past service cost. Calculate the ten-year amortization factor and the eight-year funding factor; prepare a partial schedule (through the first two years) and indicate the *maximum* allowed pension expense for Years 1 and 2 under provisions of *APB Opinion No. 8.* Round to nearest dollar.

Problem 21–6

Part A

Pension plans have developed in an environment characterized by a complex interaction of social concepts, legal considerations, actuarial techniques, income tax laws, and accounting practices. *APB Opinion No. 8* delineates acceptable accounting practices for the cost of pension plans.

Required:

1. The following terms are relevant to accounting for the cost of pension plans. Define or explain briefly each of the following:
   a. Normal cost.
   b. Past service cost.
   c. Prior service cost.
   d. Funded plan.
   e. Vested benefits.
   f. Actuarial gains and losses.
   g. Interest.
2. Identify the disclosures required in financial statements regarding a company's pension plan.

Part B

Liberty, Inc., a calendar-year corporation, adopted a company pension plan at the beginning of 1979. This plan is to be funded and noncontributory. Liberty used an appropriate actuarial cost method to determine its normal annual pension expense for 1979 and 1980 as $15,000 and $16,000, respectively, which as paid in the same year.

Liberty's actuarially determined past service cost was funded on December 31, 1979, at an amount properly computed as $106,000. This past service cost is to be amortized at the maximum amount permitted by generally accepted accounting principles. The interest factor assumed by the actuary is 6%.

Required:

Prepare entries to record the funding of past service cost on December 31, 1979, and the pension expenses for the years 1979 and 1980. Under each journal entry give the reasoning to support your entry. Round to the nearest dollar.

(AICPA adapted)

Problem 21–7

Hays Corporation has been in business for approximately 25 years. Recently management made a decision to institute a funded, noncontributory pension plan. An independent trustee has been selected to receive and disburse the pension funds in accordance with the plan. To shorten this problem the amounts are relatively small and the number of periods limited. Assume that the program started on January 1, 1979, and that estimates through 1983 made by the actuary were as follows:

1. Past service cost at the beginning of 1979, $60,000.
2. Normal pension costs are 1979, $8,000; 1980, $8,400; 1981, $9,000; 1982, $9,500; and 1983, $10,200.
3. Interest rate, 5%.

In respect to amortization of past service costs and their funding, there are four separate cases:

	Periods	
Case	Amortization	Funding
A	4	4
B	3	4
C	4	3
D	4	1

Required (for each case, show computations and round amounts to nearest dollar; disregard maximum-minimum limits):

1. Prepare a schedule of amortization and funding (assume funding at year-end).
2. Give the entries for years 1979, 1982, and 1983.
3. Give the balances to be reported on financial statements for 1979, 1982, and 1983.

Problem 21–8

An actuary determined that the past service cost of Carson Company was $67,100 and recommended that an 8% interest rate be used in its funding and amortization calculations.

Required (round all amounts to the nearest dollar; payments are at year-end):

Prepare a schedule to reflect past service pension costs for the company over the terms indicated.

1. Management of Carson Company has determined that the past service cost is to be funded over a 10-year period and to be amortized over 12 years.
2. Instead, assume the decision is to amortize the past service cost over eight years but (as above) to fund it over ten years.
3. In conjunction with the table prepared for Requirement 1, assume that in addition to the year-end payment for past service cost funding, the company also pays $9,000 normal costs at the end of each year (10 and 11). Give journal entries to reflect pension expense and the payments at the end of the 10th and 11th years.

Problem 21–9

Dotty Company was organized in 1967. The decision was made to initiate a funded, noncontributory pension plan starting January 1, 1979. The First Security Bank will be the independent funding agency. The actuary determined the past service cost at date of inception of the plan (as of January 1, 1979) to be $30,000 and the normal pension cost for the year 1979 to be $9,000. Since the company had excess cash, it decided to completely fund the past pension cost at the end of 1979. Past pension cost will be amortized over four years; a 6% rate of interest can be earned on pension fund investments.

Required (round amounts to nearest dollar and disregard maximum-minimum limits):

1. Prepare a schedule of funding and amortization of past service costs.

2. Give all entries indicated for 1979.
3. Give entries for 1980–84 assuming the following normal pension costs: 1980, $10,000; 1981, $11,000; 1982, $13,000; 1983, $14,000; and 1984, $15,000.
4. Assume a long-time employee retired during 1984 and was paid a first monthly pension benefit of $300. Give any entries indicated. Explain.
5. What would be reported on the income statement and balance sheet for each period 1979–84 inclusive?

Problem 21–10

Bohls Distributing Company began operations a number of years ago. Recently its management decided to add pensions as a fringe benefit for the employees. The actuary employed determined that as of the year the pension plan was to begin, past service costs amounted to $800,000. A decision was made to amortize these costs over eight years and to fund them over six years. Star Trust Company will serve as the independent trustee of the noncontributory pension trust; a 7% interest rate can be earned on pension fund investments.

Required (disregard maximum-minimum limits):

1. Prepare a schedule of amortization and funding for the past service cost. Round all calculations to the nearest dollar.
2. Give journal entries for Years 1, 3, 6, and 7 if normal pension costs paid for these years are, respectively, $76,000, $78,000, $95,000, and $104,000, and other payments are in accordance with the schedule developed in Requirement 1.
3. Give any necessary entry to record payments in Year 6 to long-time employee Carol who retired in that year and who drew pension benefits that year amounting to $1,800. Explain.
4. What would be reflected on the income statement and balance sheet of Bohls Distributing Company for Years 1, 3, 6, and 7 in respect to its pension plan?

Problem 21–11

C & L Printers, Inc., was organized more than a decade ago. Four years ago the company established a formal pension plan to provide retirement benefits for all employees. The plan is noncontributory and funded through an independent trustee, X Bank, which pays all pension benefits as they become due. Past service cost of $110,000 is being amortized over 15 years and funded over 10 years. C & L also funds an amount equal to current normal cost net of actuarial gains and losses. There have been no plan amendments since inception. Portions of the independent actuary's report covering the latest year appear below.

I. Current year's funding and
   pension cost:
   Normal cost (before adjustment for
   actuarial gains) computed
   under the entry age normal
   method $34,150
   Actuarial gains:
     Investment gains (losses):
       Excess of expected dividend
       revenue over actual dividend
       revenue . . . .   (350)
       Gain on sale of investments   4,050
     Gains in actuarial assumptions for:
       Mortality   3,400
       Employee turnover   5,050
     Reduction in pension cost from
       closing of plant   8,000
                                          Net actuarial gains   20,150
   Normal cost (funded currently) . . . . $ 14,000   14,000
   Past service costs:
     Funding   14,245
     Amortization   10,597
                       Total funded . . . . $ 28,245
                       Total pension expense
                       for financial state-
                       ment purposes $24,597

II. Fund assets:
    Cash . . . . $ 4,200
    Dividends receivable   1,525
    Investment in common stocks,
    at cost (market value,
    $177,800)   162,750
                       Total fund assets $168,475

Required:

1. Comment on (a) treatment of actuarial gains and losses and (b) computation of pension expense for financial statement purposes on the basis of requirements for accounting for pension plan costs.
2. What interest rate is being used in connection with the past service cost amortization and funding? Support your findings.

(AICPA adapted)

Problem 21–12

A partial schedule reflecting amortization and funding of past service cost appears below. Amounts are rounded to the nearest dollar.

Year	(a)	(b)	(c)	(d)	(e)	(f)
1	$17,686	—	$17,686	$20,000	$2,314	$ 2,314
2	17,686	$162	17,524	20,000	2,476	4,790
3	17,686	335	17,351	20,000	2,649	7,439
4	17,686	521	17,165	20,000	2,835	10,274

Required (round amounts to nearest dollar and disregard maximum-minimum limits):

1. What interest rate is being used?
2. Based on the funding amounts in column (d), which are to continue through the end of the tenth year, what amount of past service cost is being funded? (Answer to the nearest dollar.)
3. What is the length of the amortization period? Show computations.
4. Assign appropriate captions to columns (a) through (f) and complete the schedule for the funding and amortization. (A slight rounding error is expected.)
5. Record pension expense and the pension funding payments for the 10th and 11th years if, in addition to the year-end funding, payment of $15,000 is made for normal pension cost for each of these years.

Problem 21–13

Pension payments of $150,000 are to be paid to retired employees at the start of each year based on past service credits already earned by employees. The payments are expected to continue seven years beyond the initial payment. An interest rate of 6% is considered appropriate.

Required (round amounts to nearest dollar):

1. Calculate the present value of the past service benefits.
2. Assuming a fund equal to the amount calculated in Requirement 1 is held by the pension fund trustee at the time the pension payments to the retirees are to begin, show in tabular form how the payments will deplete the fund over the term of the payments.
3. Describe how the present value of the past service benefits would be calculated if the first payments of $150,000 were paid immediately and later payments were made at one-year intervals thereafter, the second payment was $120,000 the third payment was $95,000.

22

Accounting for Leases

Standards of financial accounting and reporting for leases have been evolving since 1949 when *Accounting Research Bulletin No. 38* was issued. The latest of the accounting profession's major efforts to set standards for lease accounting is *FASB Statement No. 13*, "Accounting for Leases" (November 1976), as amended and interpreted.

LEASE ACCOUNTING TERMINOLOGY

Paragraph 1 of *Statement No. 13* defines a *lease* "as an agreement conveying the right to use property, plant, or equipment (land and/or depreciable assets) usually for a stated period of time." The *Statement* applies to agreements that "although not nominally identified as leases, meet the above definition."

At a minimum, a lease contract involves two parties, a lessor and a lessee. The *lessor* owns the leased property and receives periodic rents in exchange for allowing its use. The *lessee* is the tenant, the one who has the contractual right to use the lessor's property. Some lease contracts such as *leveraged leases* (described in this chapter's Appendix) involve several other parties.

The *inception of a lease* is specified in paragraph 6, *FASB Statement No. 23*, "Inception of the Lease" (August 1978), as "the date of the lease agreement or commitment, if earlier. For purposes of the definition, a commitment shall be in writing, signed by the parties, and shall set forth the principal provisions of the transaction. If any of the principal provisions are yet to be negotiated, such a preliminary agreement or commitment does not qualify for purposes of this definition." See also the discussion in footnote 5 of this chapter. *Fair value of leased property*[1] is the "price for which the property could be sold in an arm's-length transaction between unrelated parties."

A *bargain purchase option* is defined as a provision allowing the lessee the option to purchase the leased property for a price which, at the inception of the lease, is sufficiently lower than the expected market value of the property at the date the option becomes exercisable that exercise of the option seems reasonably assured.

A *bargain renewal option* allows the lessee to renew the lease for a rental which, at the inception of the lease, appears to be sufficiently lower than the expected fair rental at the date the option becomes exercisable, that at the inception of the lease exercise of the renewal option appears reasonably assured. Other terms used in the chapter will be defined or explained when first used.

---

[1] Since *Statement No. 13* uses this terminology, it is used in this chapter. In the context of our earlier discussion and footnotes, fair value means *market value*.

Initial direct costs almost always are incurred by lessors in connection with leases. *FASB Statement No. 13* defines these costs as *incremental* direct costs incurred "in negotiating and consummating leasing transactions (e.g., commissions and legal fees)." *Statement No. 13* prescribes that lessors capitalize such costs and allocate them over the lease term in proportion to the recognition of rental revenue unless immediate expensing of the costs would not produce results materially different from those under the prescribed treatment. Where the results would not be materially different, immediate expensing by the lessor is allowed.

FASB Statement No. 17, "Accounting for Leases—Initial Direct Costs," effective after January 1, 1978, expanded the definition of *initial direct costs* without changing the accounting for them. Under the new, broader definition, initial direct costs include costs of credit investigations and costs of preparing and processing documents for new leases acquired. In addition, allocable commissions and portions of salaries related to *completion* of leasing agreements are now included, but payments for time spent negotiating leases that are *not consummated* are excluded. Also specifically excluded are such indirect costs as supervisory and administrative expense, and rent and facilities costs.

Leases are classified for recording and reporting purposes in paragraph 6 of *FASB Statement No. 13* as follows:

Standpoint of Lessee:

1. Capital lease—Broadly defined as a lease that transfers most of the risks and rewards of ownership from lessor to lessee or includes a "bargain purchase" option.
2. Operating leases—all other leases.

Standpoint of Lessor:

1. Capital leases—defined as above, but for which the FASB used the following subclassifications and terminology:
   a. Sales type leases.
   b. Direct financing leases.
   c. Leveraged leases.
2. Operating leases—all other leases.

The above classifications will be discussed in the paragraphs to follow. At this point it is important to understand that the *accounting* and *reporting* by the lessee and the lessor are generally symmetrical for a lease properly classified by *both* parties as an operating lease. This is also true for the lessee and lessor for a lease properly classified by both parties as a capital lease. This "accounting symmetry" for recording and reporting by the lessee and lessor will be illustrated in some of the examples to follow. Note, however, that there are leases which may be classified by one party as an operating lease and by the other party as a capital lease.

ACCOUNTING FOR OPERATING LEASES

From the lessee's standpoint, leases are classified as *operating* or *capital* leases. An operating lease is a simple rental agreement which does not meet the criteria (discussed below) for classification as a capital lease. An example of an operating lease situation is presented in Exhibit 22–1, in which Lessor A owns an office building and a small part of the space therein is rented to Lessee B for an annual rental of $1,200, payable in advance each January 1. The fiscal years of both parties end October 31.

Rent Paid in Advance on Operating Leases. An operating lease becomes slightly more complex when in addition to the periodic rent there is a payment made in advance (a down payment). In this situation, the additional payment is credited to Unearned Rent Revenue by the *lessor* and debited to an asset account called Leasehold (sometimes called Prepaid Rent Expense) by the *lessee*. Each party must amortize the prepayment over the life of the lease on a systematic and rational basis. Two amortization methods commonly used are as follows:

1. Straight-line method—A constant *dollar amount* of the prepayment is allocated to each period covered by the lease.
2. Interest (present value) method—A constant *rate* of allocation is utilized per period, as determined by application of the annuity concept to the prepayment. This method uses the present value concept (Table 6–4).

Recording by both parties for this type of situation, including both methods of amortization

EXHIBIT 22–1
Simple Operating Lease Situation—Accounting by Lessor and Lessee

Lessor A's Entries			Lessee B's Entries		
January 1, 19A:					
To record annual rentals:					
Cash	1,200		Rent expense	1,200	
Rent revenue		1,200	Cash		1,200
October 10, 19A:					
To record payment of property taxes by lessor:					
Expense	60		No entry.		
Cash		60			
October 13, 19A:					
To report payment of monthly telephone bill incurred by lessee:					
No entry.			Expense	15	
			Cash		15
October 31, 19A (end of accounting year):					
To record adjusting entry (two months' rent unearned by lessor and prepaid by lessee):					
Rent revenue	200		Prepaid rent expense	200	
Unearned rent revenue		200	Rent expense		200

of the prepayment, is presented in Exhibit 22–2. This example is similar to Exhibit 22–1, with the additional assumptions of *(a)* a three-year lease agreement, *(b)* an advance rental of $3,000 (in addition to the $1,200 annual rentals), *(c)* the fiscal years for both parties ending on December 31, and *(d)* an annual interest rate of 6%.

Observe in Exhibit 22–2 that when the straight-line method is used (Case A), $1,000 per year is amortized by each party. In contrast, when the interest method is used (Case B), *(a)* the amount amortized increases each year and *(b)* a decreasing annual interest amount is recognized on the declining unamortized balance. This produces a constant amount of rent each period ($1,122). For example, in Case B for 19A, each party recognized interest of $180. In Case B, interest was recognized by each party to reflect the time value of money because the initial prepayment was for services (usage of the property) that were used during later periods. Bargaining between lessor and lessee considered

this interest factor in setting the amount of the advance payment.

Paragraph 15 of *FASB Statement No. 13* states: "Normally, rental on an operating lease shall be charged to expense over the lease term as it becomes payable. If rental payments are not made on a straight-line basis, rental expense nevertheless shall be recognized on a straight-line basis unless another systematic and rational basis is more representative of the time pattern in which use benefit is derived from the leased property, in which case that basis shall be used." In the case of an advance payment at the outset of an operating lease (as illustrated in Exhibit 22–2), the *interest method* is theoretically preferable, nevertheless, the straight-line method frequently is used because *(a)* it is less complex, *(b)* the amortization amounts produced by the two methods often are not materially different, and *(c)* many interpret the above quotation from *Statement No. 13* to specify straight line for most situations.

EXHIBIT 22-2
Operating Lease with Amortization of Advance Rental—Accounting by Lessor and Lessee

Lessor A's Entries		*Lessee B's Entries*	

January 1, 19A:

To record advance rental:

| Cash .... | 3,000 | Leasehold (prepaid rent expense) ... | 3,000 | |
| Unearned rent revenue ...... | | 3,000 | Cash .... | | 3,000 |

To record annual rental:

| Cash .... | 1,200 | Rent expense .... | 1,200 | |
| Rent revenue .... | | 1,200 | Cash .... | | 1,200 |

December 31, 19A (end of the accounting period):

To record amortization of advance rental (for 12 months):

CASE A—Straight-line method:

Unearned rent revenue	1,000	Rent expense	1,000	
Rent revenue		1,000	Leasehold		1,000
Computation: $3,000 × 12/36 = $1,000.				

CASE B—Interest method (see computations below):

Unearned rent revenue	942	Rent expense	1,122	
Interest expense	180	Interest revenue		180
Rent revenue		1,122	Leasehold		942

December 31, 19A:

Closing entry (Case B):

Rent revenue ($1,200 + $1,122) .	2,322	Income summary	2,142	
Interest expense		180	Interest revenue		180
Income summary		2,142	Rent expense		2,322

Computations: Schedule of Amortization of Advance Rental Payment—Interest Method (see note)

Period	Periodic Rent	Interest (6%)	Amortization of Prepayment	Unamortized Balance
1/ 1/19A				$3,000
12/31/19A	$1,122 [a]	$180 [b]	$ 942 [c]	2,058 [d]
12/31/19B	1,122	123	999	1,059
12/31/19C	1,122	63	1,059	-0-

Note: An *ordinary annuity* is assumed, that is, that the advance payment represents the present value of three equal year-end amounts of $1,122 each. Alternatively, an *annuity due* could have been assumed, that is, that the three payments would be at the *beginning* of each period.

[a] Implied periodic rent = $3,000 ÷ Present value of ordinary annuity (3 rents, 6%).
        = $3,000 ÷ 2.67301 (Table 6–4).
        = $1,122.
[b] $3,000 × 6% = $180.
[c] $1,122 − $180 = $942.
[d] $3,000 − $942 = $2,058.

CAPITALIZATION OF LEASES

Until *FASB Statement No. 13* became effective, a preponderance of lessees accounted for leases using the operating lease procedures described above. Many accounting theorists contended that this was improper. In their view, a noncancelable long-term lease creates an asset for the *lessee*—a right to use the leased property. They contended that this right should be recognized by the lessee by capitalizing the lease rentals at their present value. Further, the reasoning went, signing a long-term lease creates a liability equal to the present value of the future rents, which also should be recognized by the lessee. Under this theory, the "right to use leased property" should be *amortized* like other *intangible assets,* and the lease rental payments should be accounted for in the same manner as periodic payments on a long-term liability, that is, as a combination of interest and reduction of debt.

Proponents of lease capitalization also pointed out that recognition of an asset and a liability on lessees' financial statements would make their statements more comparable with those of entities which purchased their operating properties instead of leasing them and which financed much of the purchase price with long-term debt. They argued that a company which leased operating properties under long-term leases and a company that owned similar properties financed by long-term debt were in essentially the same economic position. Both companies were committed to a series of regular payments over a long term; lessees paid "rents," while owners paid interest and either paid to a debt retirement fund or serially retired their indebtedness. Both had exclusive right to use similar assets over most or all of the useful lives of the assets. For many long-term lease contracts, both were committed to paying for repairs and maintenance, taxes and insurance, and similar *executory costs* associated with assets over their useful lives. If lessees could avoid recognition of assets and liabilities while owners could not, their financial statements would not be comparable even though they were in similar economic positions and, to some extent, were in analogous legal positions.

Opposition to the capitalization of lease rentals centered mainly around reluctance of lessees, and those who extended them credit, to recognize a liability. They pointed out that various other long-term executory contracts[2] are not recognized under GAAP, and that leases should not be singled out for different treatment. For many lessees, a switch from operating lease accounting to lease capitalization would reduce earnings for periods shortly after the change, but would not change aggregate long-term earnings. It was also noted that sudden recognition of large, previously unrecorded long-term lease liabilities would cause many lessees to be in technical default on some of their debt covenants. In other words, when lessees incurred other generally recognized debt, they often agreed concurrently to limit their indebtedness to a certain amount or to maintain a certain ratio of assets to debt; sudden recognition of amounts not previously regarded as debt could cause the lessees to be in violation of these debt agreements. In consideration of these arguments, when the FASB decided to mandate the capitalization of certain leases in *Statement No. 13,* the requirement to capitalize was not required for all existing leases.

The FASB specified that capitalization of those leases which met its criteria for capitalization was immediately mandatory only for those qualifying lease agreements entered into or revised on or after January 1, 1977.[3] Certain disclosures as to lease commitments already in effect at December 31, 1976, were required. Retroactive application to leases negotiated before 1977 was not required until calendar or fiscal years beginning after December 30, 1980. When *Statement No. 13* becomes fully effective, retroactive restatement of financial statements for years before 1981 will be required.

---

[2] Employment contracts whereby employers agree to pay certain salaries for future services, purchase commitments (which do not involve probable losses), and pensions are but a few of the types of executory contracts for which an asset and corresponding liability are not recognized under generally accepted accounting principles.

[3] Leasing transactions or revisions of agreements consummated on or after January 1, 1977, pursuant to terms of a commitment made prior to that date and renewal options exercised under agreements existing or committed prior to that date were declared exceptions to the immediate capitalization requirement.

CRITERIA FOR CAPITAL LEASES

We have explained that *operating* leases must be accounted for as executory contracts; that is, no capitalization of rent payments yet to be made is permitted. To the lessee, the only assets arising from an operating lease would relate to prepayments of rent or to leasehold improvements. Since some lease contracts may justify capitalization while others do not, and since many lessees would prefer not to capitalize with the concomitant recognition of liabilities, it was not surprising that the FASB specified rather detailed capitalization criteria in *FASB Statement No. 13.*

Criteria for Capital Leases for Lessees

As the outline on page 749 indicates, from the standpoint of the *lessee,* leases must be classed as *operating* leases (which do not permit capitalization) or as *capital* leases (which require recognition of an asset and the related long-term liability). For *lessees,* a *capital lease* is one which meets *any one* of the following four criteria:

1. The lease transfers ownership of the property to the lessee by the end of the lease term.
2. The lease contains a bargain purchase option (see pages 748 and 757).
3. The lease term is equal to 75% or more of the estimated economic life of the property.[4]
4. The present value of the minimum lease payments at the inception of the lease is at least 90% of the market value of the leased property at that time.[5]

Criteria for Capital Type Leases by Lessors

In order to qualify as a capital type lease from the standpoint of the *lessor,* the lease must meet *any one* of the four criteria set out in the left column on these pages (for capital leases by lessees) and *both* of the following additional criteria:

1. Collectibility of the lease payments is reasonably assured.
2. No important uncertainties surround the amount of unreimbursable costs yet to be incurred by the lessor under the lease.[6]

Because of the two additional criteria that the *lessor* must meet for a capital type lease, not all leases that qualify as capital leases to the lessee would necessarily qualify as capital type leases to the lessor. That is, a capital lease to the lessee could be an operating lease to the lessor. However, all leases classified by the lessor as capital type leases would qualify as capital leases to the lessee.

The general category of capital type leases for the *lessor* is further subclassified for *accounting* and *reporting* purposes as

a. Sales type leases—At inception the lease includes a "manufacturer's or dealer's profit (or loss)."

---

[4] Determination of the *lease term* is sometimes a complex matter. For most leases the fixed noncancelable period the lease is in effect and over which the lessee is obligated to make payments is the lease term. However, the lease term can be extended to cover also the period in which a bargain renewal option is in effect, periods for which failure to renew would subject the lessee to substantial penalties, and for other reasons which are detailed in paragraph 5, *FASB Statement No. 13.*

[5] Criteria 3 and 4 do not apply if the start of the lease term falls within the last 25% of the total estimated economic life of the property. In connection with criterion 4 (when applied by lessors), that portion of payments representing executory costs, such as insurance, maintenance, and taxes (including any profit thereon by the lessor) is excluded from consideration. Any investment tax credit retained by the lessor and expected to be realized by the lessor is also excluded.

FASB Statement No. 23, "Inception of the Lease" (August 1978), amends criterion 4 insofar as it applies to leased property whose value changes between the date of the lease agreement and the date the property is placed in service by the lessee. The amendment provides that the market value of the leased property be determined at the agreement date, not at the time that construction is completed or the property is acquired by the lessor. *Statement No. 23* also generally prohibits the recording of increases in estimated residual value that may occur between the agreement date and the beginning of the lease term when the agreement date is a date before the lease term starts.

FASB Interpretation No. 24, "Leases Involving Only Part of a Building" (generally effective December 1, 1978), concerns that part of *Statement No. 13* which says "when the leased property is part of a larger whole, its cost (or carrying amount) and fair value may not be objectively determinable. . . ." The *Interpretation* recognizes that reasonable estimates of the leased property's market value might be objectively determined, even if no sales of similar property are available for comparison, by referring to an independent appraisal or to estimated replacement cost information.

[6] Important uncertainties might include commitments by the lessor to guarantee performance of the leased property in a manner more extensive than the typical product warranty or to effectively protect the lessee from obsolescence of the leased property. However, the necessity of estimating executory costs such as insurance, maintenance, and taxes to be paid by the lessor does not by itself constitute an important uncertainty as referred to herein.

b. Direct financing lease—At inception the lease does not include a "manufacturer's or dealer's profit (or loss)."

SALES TYPE LEASES (LESSOR)

When manufacturers or dealers use leasing as a means of marketing their products, the lessors recognize gross profit or loss (i.e., gross margin or its negative equivalent) at the inception of the lease. Prior to discussing sales type leases, a simplified example will be presented to indicate their primary characteristics.

Assume that Lessor Company has in *inventory* a computer recorded at a cost of $70,000; the regular selling price is $100,000. Instead of selling the computer to Lessee Corporation, the two parties agree that Lessee will lease it for the next four years, paying eight semiannual rents of $15,000 (total consideration, including interest, $120,000). At the end of the lease term Lessee Corporation will take formal title to the computer upon payment of $100. *Lessor Company,* which uses a perpetual inventory system, would record this transaction as follows at date of inception of the *sales type lease:*

Lease receivables		
(8 × $15,000)	120,000	
Cost of goods sold	70,000	
Inventory (asset on		
sales type lease)		70,000
Sales revenue		100,000
Unearned interest revenue		
($120,000 − $100,000)		20,000

Alternatively, the entry may be made without using cost of goods sold as follows:

Lease receivables	120,000	
Machine (on sales type		
lease)		70,000
Dealer's profit		
($100,000 − $70,000)		30,000
Unearned interest revenue		
($120,000 − $100,000)		20,000

This is called a sales type lease because, as the above entry indicates, the lessor realized a gross profit at the inception of the lease. It can be seen from this entry that a dealer's (gross) profit of $30,000 (i.e., $100,000 − $70,000) was recognized, and it will be reflected in Income Summary at the end of the accounting period. On the other hand, only a small part of the unearned interest revenue will have been earned by year-end (even if the above entry occurred early in Lessor's fiscal year). The interest relates to the entire time there is a balance in Lease Receivables, and the interest will be earned over the four-year collection period.

DIRECT FINANCING LEASES (LESSOR)

Leases which meet the criteria for classification as capital type leases, but which do not give rise to a gross profit or loss to the *lessor* at the inception of the lease, are called direct financing leases. As the name implies, direct financing leases are financing arrangements by lessors who normally lease only (and do not sell). For the lessor, leasing property under a direct financing lease can be likened to the purchase of an annuity. The leased property is exchanged for a series of regular future rents which assure the lessor both a predetermined rate of return on the unrecovered investment in the asset leased and a return of cost. Also, the lease usually frees the *lessor* from assuming the risks of property ownership because the *lessee* assumes responsibility for such executory costs as maintenance, taxes, and insurance (paying for these items or reimbursing the lessor for them). To illustrate, assume a lessor's investment (i.e., cost) in Machinery is $235,000, which is the current market value of the machinery, and the lessor contracts with a lessee to lease the machine for four years with an initial rent of $35,000 due at the inception of the lease and seven additional $35,000 payments at six-month intervals. The lessor's entry, at *date of inception* of the *direct financing lease* would be as follows:

Cash	35,000	
Lease receivables (7 × $35,000)	245,000	
Machinery (asset		
on financing lease)		235,000
Unearned interest revenue		45,000

In this situation, no gross profit or loss is recognized by the lessor because the lessor's cost is the same as the market value of the leased asset. Thus, in the fiscal period in which the lease was signed, the lessor would earn interest revenue on the lease receivable over the period between the inception date of the lease and the end of the fiscal period.

Leveraged leases, another category of capital leases, are discussed in the Appendix to this chapter. Attention is now turned to accounting for leases other than operating leases.

LESSEE ACCOUNTING UNDER CAPITAL LEASES

The lessee must record a capital lease, at date of inception, by debiting Leased Property and crediting Lease Liability for the *present value* of all future rents required. Thus, the lessee's basic approach to lease valuation, expressed as a formula, is as follows:

$$\begin{matrix} \text{Valuation of} \\ \text{Leased Asset} \\ \text{and Related} \\ \text{Liability} \end{matrix} = \begin{matrix} \text{Periodic} \\ \text{Lease Rent} \end{matrix} \times \begin{matrix} \text{Present Value of an} \\ \text{Annuity of } n \text{ Rents at } i \\ \text{Rate of Interest} \end{matrix}$$

Determination of a reasonable rate of interest (i.e., the discount rate) is very important because it significantly affects the valuation of the leased asset and the related lease liability at inception date. The higher the rate, the lower will be the amount capitalized for the asset and the amount recorded for the liability, and vice versa.

FASB Statement No. 13 provides guidance for the *lessee* in the selection of a reasonable interest rate for present value computations. Paragraph 7 states that a lessee "shall compute the present value of lease payments using [as a discount rate] his *incremental borrowing rate* unless it is practicable for the lessee to learn the *implicit rate* computed by the lessor." If both rates are known, the lessor's implicit rate must be used if it is lower than the lessee's incremental borrowing rate.[7] Paragraph 5 of *Statement No. 13* specifies that the lessee's incremental borrowing rate is the rate that at the inception of the lease, the lessee would have incurred to borrow funds necessary to buy the leased property over a term similar to the length of the lease. Paragraph 10 sets a constraint on the lease value thus computed by the lessee; that is, if the present value of the lease payments exceeds the market value

of the leased property at the inception of the lease, the amount recorded as the asset and liability must be the market value.

The above specification in *Statement No. 13* that requires the lessee to use the lower of the lessee's incremental borrowing rate or the lessor's implicit rate (if known to the lessee) was soon abused because "leases that would otherwise be classified as capital leases are being classified as operating leases by lessees merely because of the differential between the lessee's incremental borrowing rate and the lessor's computed interest rate implicit in the lease." This was possible because the higher incremental borrowing rate often was used, which caused the computed present value of the minimum lease payments to be low, thus failing to meet the "90 percent recovery criterion for capital leases" given on page 753. To close this loophole, in November 1978, the FASB issued an exposure draft of an amendment of *FASB Statement No. 13*. The exposure draft, entitled "Lessee's Use of the Interest Rate Implicit in the Lease," states:

> A lessee shall compute the present value of the minimum lease payments using his incremental borrowing rate . . . , unless (i) it is practicable for the lessee to ascertain the implicit rate computed by the lessor or, if unable to ascertain that rate and the lease is not otherwise classified as a capital lease, to make a *reasonable estimate* of the interest rate implicit in the lease and (ii) the implicit rate is less than the lessee's incremental borrowing rate. If both of those conditions are met, the lessee shall use the implicit rate. (Emphasis supplied.)

The *reasonable estimate* required in the above quotation can be made by the lessee, using data otherwise available to the lessee plus an estimate by the lessee of the *residual value* of the leased property at the termination of the lease term.

To illustrate accounting by the lessee, assume that on June 30, 19A, a lessee signed a lease that met one or more of the criteria for a capital lease, and that the lessee's incremental borrowing rate of 10% per year coincided with the lessor's implicit rate. The lease calls for six semiannual payments of $20,000 at the *end* of each six-month period of the three-year lease term. Due to high obsolescence, the property will have no residual value at the end of the lease

---

[7] The lessor's implicit rate is the discount rate applied to compute the minimum lease payments (which includes any residual value guaranteed by the lessee) plus any *unguaranteed* residual value. This means that the lessor includes total estimated residual value. The lessor's implicit rate is discussed in the subsequent section on accounting by the lessor (see page 759).

EXHIBIT 22–3
Capital Lease—Lessee's Amortization Schedule (ordinary annuity basis)

Date	(a) Semiannual Lease Payments	(b) Semiannual Interest at 5%	(c) Reduction of Lease Liability	(d) Lease Liability Balance
6/30/19A .... Initial value				$101,514
12/31/19A	$ 20,000	$ 5,076	$ 14,924	86,590
6/30/19B	20,000	4,330	15,670	70,920
12/31/19B	20,000	3,546	16,454	54,466
6/30/19C	20,000	2,723	17,277	37,189
12/31/19C	20,000	1,859	18,141	19,048
6/30/19D	20,000	952	19,048	–0–
	$120,000	$18,486	$101,514	

Amounts in column *(b)* are 5% of the preceding balance in column *(d)*.
Column *(c)* = column *(a)* − *(b)*.
Amounts in column *(d)* are preceding balance minus amount in *(c)*.

term. The lessee computes the "value" of an asset, the service potential of which is acquired under a capital lease, as follows:

$$\begin{matrix} \text{Present Value} \\ \text{of Leased} \\ \text{Asset} \\ \text{(and Related} \\ \text{Liability)} \end{matrix} = \text{Periodic Rent} \times P_{o_{n=6;i=5\%}}$$

$$= \$20,000 \times 5.07569 \text{ (Table 6–4)}$$

$$= \$101,514$$

Exhibit 22–3 is a lease amortization table based on this set of facts.

Paragraph 11 of *FASB Statement No. 13* provides that the lessee shall amortize asset balances arising under capitalized leases ($101,514 in this example) in a manner consistent with the lessee's normal depreciation policy, and that the period of amortization must be the *lease term* rather than the life of the leased property.[8] Assume that the lessee uses straight-line depre-

ciation and has a fiscal year ending December 31. The lessee's entries through December 31, 19B, related to this lease would be as follows:

Lessee's Entries—Capital Lease (ordinary annuity basis)

June 30, 19A (inception of the lease):

Leased property under capital lease	101,514	
Liability under capital lease		101,514

To capitalize lease calling for six $20,000 semiannual payments at 10% per year.

December 31, 19A (end of accounting period):

Interest expense (see Exhibit 22–3)	5,076	
Liability under capital lease	14,924	
Cash		20,000

To record first semiannual rental payment.

Depreciation expense ($101,514 × ⅙)	16,919	
Leased property under capital lease		16,919

To record first six months' depreciation of leased property; straight line assumed.

Income summary	21,995	
Interest expense		5,076
Depreciation expense		16,919

To close expense accounts related to leased property.

June 30, 19B (second rental payment):

Interest expense ($86,590 × 5%)	4,330	
Liability under capital lease	15,670	
Cash		20,000

To record second semiannual rental payment.

---

[8] However, if a lease transfers ownership of the property to the lessee at the end of the lease term or contains a bargain purchase option, capitalized balances must be amortized in a manner consistent with the lessee's normal depreciation policy for owned assets; that is, the amounts capitalized (less estimated residual value at the end of the useful life) in such situations should be amortized over the estimated useful life of the *lessed asset* rather than over the lease term.

December 31, 19B (end of accounting period):

Interest expense ($70,920 × 5%)	3,546	
Liability under capital lease	16,454	
Cash		20,000
To record third semiannual rental payment.		
Depreciation expense ($101,514 × ⅔₆)	33,838	
Leased property under capital lease		33,838
To record full year's depreciation.		
Income summary	41,714	
Interest expense		7,876
Depreciation expense		33,838
To close expense accounts related to leased property.		

The account titles used in the above entries can vary. For example, if machinery were leased, the account debited at inception date could be called Machinery under Capital Lease. Also, instead of using an Accumulated Depreciation (or Amortization) account, credits in the depreciation entries could be made directly to the asset account (which parallels the procedures outlined in *FASB Statement No. 13*). The "depreciation" is more in the nature of amortization of an intangible (i.e., a right to use the leased property). Thus, the debit could be to "Expense— Amortization of Leased Property Rights," instead of Depreciation Expense.

If payments under the lease in this illustration had been at the *start* of each period (which

EXHIBIT 22–4
Capital Lease—Lessee's Amortization Schedule (annuity due basis)

Date	(a) Semi-annual Lease Payments	(b) Semi-annual Interest at 5%	(c) Reduc-tion of Lease Liability	(d) Lease Liability Balance
6/30/19A	Initial value			$106,590
6/30/19A	$ 20,000	–0– (a)	$ 20,000	86,590
12/31/19A	20,000	$ 4,330	15,670	70,920
6/30/19B	20,000	3,546	16,454	54,466
12/31/19B	20,000	2,723	17,277	37,189
6/30/19C	20,000	1,859	18,141	19,048
12/31/19C	20,000	952	19,048	–0–
	$120,000	$13,410	$106,590	

(a) There is no interest at the outset because the date of the first rental payment coincides with the inception of the lease; since no time has elapsed, there can be no interest. Other calculations in this table are as in Exhibit 22–3.

is the usual situation), the situation would involve an *annuity due,* and the valuation of the lease at inception would be calculated by multiplying the $20,000 rental payment by the present value of an *annuity due* at 5% for six periods [i.e., $20,000 × (4.32948 + 1) = $106,590]. The annuity due amortization table would be as shown in Exhibit 22–4.

The *pattern of entries* in this modification of the example would be the same as was illustrated on page 756, in connection with Exhibit 22–3, except that the amounts of interest and depreciation each period would differ. The total amount of expense for the three years would be the same as in the earlier example but would be recorded differently as between interest and depreciation. A comparison of the two situations would show:

	Ordinary Annuity Exhibit 22–3 (payments at end)	Annuity Due Exhibit 22–4 (payments at start)
Total depreciation (amount capitalized)	$101,514	$106,590
Total interest (per column [b] Exhibits 22–3 and 22–4)	18,486	13,410
Total expense for the three years	$120,000	$120,000

BARGAIN PURCHASE OPTIONS

Recall from the discussion of bargain purchase options (BPO) on page 748 that a BPO permits the lessee to purchase the leased property during the lease term for a future price which, at *inception of the lease,* is sufficiently lower than the *expected future value* of the property at the date the option becomes exercisable that exercise of the option appears to be reasonably assured. The effect of adding a BPO to a lease contract is to add the *present value of the option price* to the present value of the lease payments under the lease up to the date on which exercise of the option appears to be reasonably assured.

To illustrate a BPO, assume, related to the annuity due example in Exhibit 22–4, that there was a BPO permitting the *lessee* to buy the leased property three years after the inception of the

EXHIBIT 22–5
Capital Lease—Lessee's Amortization Schedule (annuity due basis; includes the six rental payments and the bargain purchase payment)

Date	Payments	Semi-annual Interest at 5%	Reduc-tion of Lease Liability	Lease Liability Balance
6/30/19A	Initial value			$128,977
6/30/19A	$ 20,000	—	$ 20,000	108,977
12/31/19A	20,000	$ 5,449	14,551	94,426
6/30/19B	20,000	4,721	15,279	79,147
12/31/19B	20,000	3,957	16,043	63,104
6/30/19C	20,000	3,155	16,845	46,259
12/31/19C	20,000	2,313	17,687	28,572
6/30/19D (BPO)	30,000	1,428	28,572	–0–
	$150,000	$21,023	$128,977	

lease (i.e., from June 30, 19A) by paying $30,000, which is significantly less than the $40,000 expected market value of the leased asset on the expected exercise date, June 30, 19D. Also, assume the useful life of the property is *five* years (instead of three). The rental payment terms are as in Exhibit 22–4; that is, six semiannual rental payments of $20,000 payable at the start of each six-month period (an annuity due situation). The interest or discount rate is unchanged (10% per year). To determine the asset valuation and the related liability to be recognized by the lessee, it is necessary to add the present value of the $30,000 BPO price to the present value of the six $20,000 rental payments as follows:

Present value of six semiannual rental payments at start of each period Exhibit 22–4	$106,590
Present value of BPO price six periods after start of lease: $30,000 × Present Value of 1 at 5% for six periods; $30,000 × .74622 (Table 6–2)	22,387
Total amount to capitalize as value of the leased asset (including the BPO valuation) ...	$128,977

Exhibit 22–5 reflects the lease amortization during the lease term and the BPO payment at June 30, 19D.

Lessee entries (except for closing entries) based on Exhibit 22–5 for 19A and 19D are as follows:

Lessee's Entries—Capital Lease and Bargain Purchase Option (annuity due basis)

June 30, 19A (inception of lease):

Leased property under capital lease	128,977	
Liability under capital lease		128,977

To capitalize lease calling for six semiannual advance payments of $20,000 and a bargain purchase payment of $30,000 at termination.

Liability under capital lease	20,000	
Cash		20,000

To record initial rental payment under lease.

December 31, 19A (end of accounting period):

Interest expense (5% × $108,977) .	5,449	
Liability under capital lease	14,551	
Cash		20,000

To record second rental payment under lease (see Exhibit 22–5).

Depreciation expense ($128,977 × $\frac{1}{10}$)	12,898	
Leased property under capital lease		12,898

To record first six months' depreciation of asset with five-year life; straight-line method assumed.

June 30, 19D:

Interest expense	1,428	
Liability under capital lease	28,572	
Cash		30,000

To record exercise of bargain purchase option at termination of lease and the related interest.

December 31, 19D (end of accounting period):

Depreciation expense ($128,977 × $\frac{1}{5}$)	25,795	
Leased property under capital lease		25,795

To record one year's depreciation.

Alternatively, assume that at June 30, 19D, the lessee let the bargain purchase option lapse. It would be necessary to recognize usual expenses for the first half of the year and all remaining balances related to the lease contract would be removed from the accounts and a loss recognized. The June 30, 19D, entry, assuming lapse of the bargain purchase option on that date, would be as follows:

Interest expense (5% × $28,572)	1,428	
Depreciation expense ($\frac{1}{10}$ × $128,977)	12,898	

Liability under capital lease (from
  Exhibit 22–5) 28,572
Loss on lapse of bargain purchase
  option* 21,591
    Leased property under capital
    lease ($128,977 × 5/10) 64,489
To write off remaining balances related to the leased property and to
recognize regular depreciation and
interest for six months.

* Computation of the loss:		
Cash disbursed from 6/30/19A through		
12/31/19C............................		$120,000
Expenses recognized through 6/30/19D:		
Interest (Exhibit 22–5, second column)	$21,023	
Depreciation ($128,977 × 6/10)	77,386	
Total expenses recognized		98,409
Excess of payments over amount		
charged off (i.e., the loss)		$ 21,591

Recall that depreciation of $12,898 had not
been recorded for the six months ended June
30, 19D. Therefore, although at that date 60%
of the asset life had expired, only 50% of the
original amount capitalized had been reduced
by earlier depreciation. Therefore, it is necessary in the writeoff entry to record depreciation
for the six months ended June 30, 19D, in addition to interest expense for this same period. The
balances in the liability and leased property accounts also are cleared by the entry.[9]

**Accruals When Fiscal and Lease Dates Do Not
Agree.** Before discussing lessor accounting for
capitalized leases, recall that in all of the preceding examples the end of the lessee's fiscal
year coincided with a rental payment date. This
would not be the usual situation. Accrual of interest and depreciation expense to the end of
the fiscal year would be necessary to properly
match expense with revenue. The adjustments
necessary when the two dates do not coincide
are illustrated in the context of the lessee's entries for Exhibit 22–5. If the lessee's fiscal year
ended on March 31 (instead of December 31),
the amount of the depreciation adjustment at
March 31, 19B, would have been $19,347 (i.e.,
$128,977 × 9/60 = $19,347) and accrued interest
would be recognized by the lessee as follows:

[9] *FASB Interpretation No. 26* (effective December 1, 1978)
provides that the purchase by the *lessee* of property under a
capital lease and the related lease termination are accounted
for as a single transaction. Any difference between the purchase price and the carrying amount of the lease obligation
is recorded by the lessee as an adjustment of the carrying
amount of the asset.

Interest expense (3/6 × $4,721)   2,361
  Interest payable 2,361
    To adjust for three months' accrued
    interest.

This interest entry could be reversed in the usual
manner on April 1, 19B.

LESSOR ACCOUNTING UNDER CAPITAL LEASES

Lessor accounting under capital type leases
is somewhat different for direct financing leases
than for sales type leases. Each of these different
situations will be discussed in the paragraphs
to follow.

Lessor Accounting under Direct Financing Leases

A capital lease to the lessee is also a capital
lease to the lessor if the lease also meets the
two additional criteria given on page 753. Even
in this situation, it is possible for the same lease
to be recorded at different values (at date of inception) in the records of the two parties. The
lessor's basic approach is to set the periodic
rents at a level sufficiently high to yield a target
rate of return on the investment in the property.
This target rate was briefly referred to in the
discussion of lessee accounting as the *lessor's
implicit rate* (see page 755).

Expressed as a formula, the *lessor's* basic approach is as follows:

$$\text{Periodic Rent} = \frac{\begin{array}{c}\text{Investment}\\ \text{in Leased Property}\end{array}}{\begin{array}{c}\text{Present Value of an Annuity}\\ \text{of } n \text{ Rents at Lessor's}\\ \text{Implicit Rate, } i\end{array}}$$

Recall that the *lessee's* basic approach to valuation by the *lessee* (page 755) was as follows:

$$\begin{array}{c}\text{Valuation}\\ \text{of Leased}\\ \text{Asset}\end{array} = \begin{array}{c}\text{Periodic}\\ \text{Rent}\end{array} \times \begin{array}{c}\text{Present Value of an}\\ \text{Annuity of } n \text{ Rents at}\\ \text{Incremental}\\ \text{Borrowing Rate, } i\end{array}$$

Observe that the second equation is a rearrangement of the first equation, and that the two
interest rates may be different.[10]

[10] If a lessee knows the lessor's implicit rate and it is lower
than the lessee's incremental borrowing rate, the lessee must
use the lessor's rate. In such a case the present values recognized by both the lessor and the lessee may be the same.

Lessor's Implicit Rate. *FASB Statement No. 13* defines the lessor's implicit interest (discount) rate as follows:

> *Interest rate implicit in the lease.* The discount rate that, when applied to (i) the minimum lease payments (as defined in paragraph 5(j)), excluding that portion of the payments representing executory costs to be paid by the lessor, together with any profit thereon, and (ii) the unguaranteed residual value (as defined in paragraph 5(i)) accruing to the benefit of the lessor, causes the aggregate present value at the beginning of the lease term to be equal to the fair value of the leased property (as defined in paragraph 5(c)) to the lessor at the inception of the lease, minus any investment tax credit retained by the lessor and expected to be realized by him.

The above quotation defines the lessor's implicit rate as that rate which will equate the cost (i.e., market value) of the leased asset at inception date to the present value of:

1. The minimum lease payments (defined to include any residual value guaranteed by the lessee, but to exclude any executory costs paid by the lessor) *plus*
2. Any unguaranteed residual value (in effect, this, plus the guaranteed residual value discounted in 1, includes the total residual value). The market value of the leased property must be reduced by any *investment tax credit* (ITC) expected to be realized by the lessor.

To illustrate this complex definition, assume the following data are provided by the lessor:

a.	Cost of the leased asset (i.e., market value at inception of the lease)	$40,000
b.	Estimated residual value at lease termination date (none guaranteed by lessee)	6,000
c.	Investment tax credit on cost, expected to be realized by lessor	10%
d.	Lease rentals, ten annual payments at each year-end	?
e.	Lessor's implicit interest rate	?

Requirement 1:

Compute the lessor's implicit rate assuming the annual lease rental is $6,878.

This requires iteration (trial and error) as follows (ordinary annuity situation):

$$\text{Cost} - \text{ITC} = \left\{ \begin{array}{l} \text{Rent} \times \\ P_{o_{n=10;i=?}} \end{array} \right\} + \left\{ \begin{array}{l} \text{Residual Value} \times \\ p_{n=10;i=?} \end{array} \right\}$$

First trial, at 14%:

$40,000 - $4,000 = ($6,878 \times 5.21612^*)$
$\qquad\qquad + ($6,000 \times .26974^*)$
$36,000 < $35,876 + $1,618$
$36,000 < $37,494$ (14% is too low)

Second trial, at 16%:

$36,000 > ($6,878 \times 4.83323^*)$
$\qquad\qquad + ($6,000 \times .22668^*)$
$36,000 > $34,603$ (16% is too high)

* Not shown in Tables 6–2 and 6–4; computed in the same way as the table values.

Third trial, at 15%:

$36,000 \approx ($6,878 \times 5.01877)$
$\qquad\qquad + ($6,000 \times .24718)$
$36,000 \approx $36,000$ (very close to 15%)

Requirement 2:

Compute the annual lease rental assuming the lessor's implicit rate is 15%.

Cost of leased asset	$40,000
Less: Investment tax credit ($40,000 × .10)	4,000
Net cost to lessor	36,000
Present value of estimated residual value:	
$6,000 × $p_{n=10;i=15\%}$ (.24718, Table 6–2)	1,483
Net investment to be recovered	$34,517
Periodic rents = ($34,517 ÷ $P_{o_{n=10;i=15\%}}$ (5.01877, from Table 6–4)	$ 6,878

Although lessors and lessees may have different lease valuations for the same lease because they used different interest rates, the illustration to follow will use the same interest rate because it better illustrates the desired accounting symmetry between the lessee and lessor. If the lessee and lessor used the same interest discount rate (which would happen if the lessor's implicit rate was lower than the lessee's incremental borrowing rate and also the lessee knew, or could reasonably estimate, the lessor's rate), then they would begin with the same present value. Thus, if a lessor has an investment of $101,514 in an asset to be leased under a direct financing lease, for three years with rents of $20,000 at the end of each semiannual period, and the lessor's tar-

EXHIBIT 22–6
Direct Financing Lease—Lessor's Amortization Schedule (ordinary annuity basis)

Date	(a) Semiannual Lease Receipts	(b) Semiannual Interest at 5%	(c) Recovery of Investment	(d) Investment Balance
6/30/19A	Initial value			$101,514
12/31/19A	$ 20,000	$ 5,076	$ 14,924	86,590
6/30/19B	20,000	4,330	15,670	70,920
12/31/19B	20,000	3,546	16,454	54,466
6/30/19C	20,000	2,723	17,277	37,189
12/31/19C	20,000	1,859	18,141	19,048
6/30/19D	20,000	952	19,048	–0–
	$120,000	$18,486	$101,514	

Amounts in column (b) are 5% of preceding balance in column (d).
Column (c) = column (a) − (b).
Amounts in column (d) are preceding balance minus amount in column (c).

get rate of return is 5% per semiannual interest period, the lessor's amortization schedule would be similar to the lessee's amortization schedule which was shown in Exhibit 22–3. In this example, the lessor calculated the periodic rent as follows:

$$\text{Periodic Rents} = \left(\frac{\$101,514 \div P_{o_{n=6;i=5\%}}}{(5.07569, \text{Table } 6\text{–}4)}\right) = \$20,000$$

Exhibit 22–6 reflects the lessor's amortization schedule based on this situation.

If the lessor's fiscal year ends December 31, the entries for 19A would be as follows:

Lessor's Entries—Direct Financing Lease (ordinary annuity basis)

June 30, 19A (inception of lease):

Lease receivable	120,000	
Asset (on financing lease)		101,514
Unearned interest revenue		18,486

December 31, 19A (end of accounting period):

Cash	20,000	
Lease receivable		20,000

To record collection of first rent under lease.

Unearned interest revenue	5,076	
Interest revenue		5,076

To adjust unearned revenue for portion earned during year.

Interest revenue	5,076	
Income summary		5,076

To close revenue account associated with the direct financing lease.

Comparison of Exhibit 22–6 and the *lessor's* entries immediately above with Exhibit 22–3 and the *lessee's* entries on page 756 will reveal symmetry between them.

LESSOR ACCOUNTING UNDER SALES TYPE LEASES

Sales type leases were briefly defined and discussed on pages 753 and 754. Recall that the distinction between direct financing leases and sales type leases applies only to the *lessor*, and that the basic distinction between them is on "manufacturer's or dealer's profit (or loss)."

FASB Statement No. 13 defines sales type leases as "leases that give rise to manufacturer's or dealer's profit (or loss) to the lessor (i.e., the fair value of the leased property at the inception of the lease is greater or less than its cost or carrying amount, if different)"—and meet the specified criteria for a capital type lease otherwise. Sales type leases normally will arise when manufacturers or dealers use leasing as a way to market their products (in addition to regular sales outlets). The *Statement* also explains that a lessor need not be a manufacturer or dealer to realize a "profit or loss" at inception of the lease if the market value of the leased asset is greater (or less) than the cost or the carrying amount of the leased asset.

For a sales type lease, two distinctly different "profits" are recognized over the term of the lease:

1. Manufacturer's or dealer's profit (more precisely, gross margin or gross profit), recognized in full at date of inception of the lease is

$$\text{Normal Sales Price (market value)} - \text{Cost or Carrying Amount}$$

2. Unearned interest revenue, allocated to interest revenue over the lease term is

$$\begin{array}{c}\text{Gross Lease Receivable} \\ \text{(principal + interest} \\ \text{before any} \\ \text{cash collection)}\end{array} - \begin{array}{c}\text{Normal Sales} \\ \text{Price (market value} \\ \text{of leased asset)}\end{array}$$

FASB Statement No. 13 provides precise definitions of the above terms for the lessor as follows:

A. Cost of the leased asset—the original cost to the manufacturer or dealer (including initial direct costs) restated for any adjustments since acquisition (i.e., carrying value at inception date).
B. Minimum lease receipts required over the lease term—minimum lease receipts required under the lease plus any residual value *guaranteed* by the lessee, but excluding any executory costs paid by the lessee.
C. *Present value* of the minimum lease payments (as defined in B).
D. Manufacturer's or dealer's profit (or loss) = C (equivalent to normal sales price) − A (cost).
E. Unearned interest revenue = B (equivalent to gross receivable) − C (above).

To illustrate accounting for a sales type lease, refer to Exhibit 22–6 (a direct financing lease was assumed). We will convert this to a sales type lease by assuming that *(a)* the lessor was

a manufacturer or dealer, *(b)* there was a manufacturer's or dealer's profit, and *(c)* that the leased asset was reflected in the lessor's inventory accounts at a cost (or carrying value) of $85,000 and that the regular sales price was $101,514. Assuming no other changes in the fact situation, this sales type lease would be accounted for by the lessor as follows:

Lessor's Entries—Sales Type Lease (ordinary annuity basis)
June 30, 19A (inception of the lease):

Lease receivable ($20,000 × 6)	120,000	
Cost of goods sold (as given)	85,000	
Inventory (asset on sales type lease)		85,000
Sales revenue (regular sales price as given)		101,514
Unearned interest revenue ($120,000 − $101,514)		18,486

Note. Comparison of the above entry with its direct financing counterpart on page 761 reveals the basic difference between the two types of leases. In the above entry the "profit" (more precisely gross margin) recognized is $16,514 (i.e., $101,514 − $85,000).

December 31, 19A (end of accounting period):

Cash	20,000	
Lease receivable		20,000

To record collection of the first rent under the lease.

Unearned interest revenue	5,076	
Interest revenue (per Exhibit 22–6)		5,076

To adjust unearned interest revenue for portion earned during the year.

Interest revenue	5,076	
Sales revenue	101,514	
Cost of goods sold		85,000
Income summary ($5,076 + $16,514)		21,590

To close the nominal accounts associated with the sales type lease.

To illustrate accounting for lessor's receipt of reimbursement by the lessee for executory costs, such as taxes and insurance, assume that the December 31, 19A, rent collection illustrated above included an additional $1,000 to cover such costs, which had already been incurred and debited to Executory Expense on Leased Property. The collection entry would be as follows:

```
Cash ...........................   21,000
  Lease receivable................          20,000
  Executory expense on leased
    property ....................            1,000
```

Residual Value and Investment Tax Credit. If the lessor has good reason to believe the leased property will be returned by the end of the term of a capital lease, the *net investment* to be recovered through rentals would be the original investment (cost) less the amount of any investment tax credit expected to be realized by the lessor and less the present value of the expected residual value to be recovered at the termination of the lease. To illustrate, assume lessor purchased a machine for lease at a cost of $10,000. It qualified for the 10% investment tax credit and had an estimated residual value of $2,000 at the termination of the lease. This direct financing lease called for three annual year-end rentals and the lessor's implicit rate was 10%. The amount of the periodic rentals would be computed as follows (ordinary annuity basis; refer to page 760):

```
Cost of leased asset .......................   $10,000
Less: Investment tax credit ($10,000 × .10) .....    1,000
  Net cost to lessor.......................     9,000
Present value of residual value: $2,000 ×
  p_{n=3;i=10%} (.75131 from Table 6–2) ...........    1,503
  Net investment to be recovered ..........   $ 7,497
Rents = $7,497 ÷ Po_{n=3;i=10%}
  (2.48685 from Table 6–4) .................   $ 3,015
```

The lease amortization table for the lessor (which illustrates the effects of the residual value of the leased asset and the investment tax credit) would be as shown below for a direct financing lease:

The related entries for the *lessor* would be as follows:

a. To acquire the machine for lease:

```
Machine .......................   10,000
  Cash .......................          10,000
```

b. To record the investment tax credit at acquisition ($10,000 × .10):

```
Income taxes payable ...........    1,000
  Machine ....................           1,000
```

c. To record lease at inception date:

```
Lease receivable ($3,015 × 3) .....    9,045
  Machine* ...................           7,000
  Unrealized interest
    revenue ..................            2,045
```
* This leaves the estimated residual value in the asset account. There is no dealer's profit; hence, it is a direct financing lease.

d. To record the first lease payment:

```
Cash .........................    3,015
Unrealized interest revenue
  (per amortization schedule) .....     900
    Lease receivable ...........          3,015
    Interest revenue ...........            900
```

If the market value of the leased asset is less than $2,000 at termination of the lease, a loss is recognized at that time for the difference. If the market value exceeds $2,000, no gain would be recognized and the asset would be reflected in the accounts of the lessor at $2,000.

TERMINATION OF LEASE AGREEMENTS

A capital lease agreement may terminate due to *(a)* a change of provisions in the lease, *(b)* renewal or extension of the lease, or *(c)* expiration of the lease term. *FASB Statement No. 13* specifies the accounting for termination by

Date	Annual Rent	Interest at 10%	Recovery of Investment	Original Investment
Start Year 1	Initial value			$9,000*
End Year 1	$3,015	$ 900	$2,115	6,885
End Year 2	3,015	689	2,326	4,559
End Year 3	3,015	456	2,559	2,000(RV)
	$9,045	$2,045	$7,000	$2,000

* Present value of lease payments ($7,497) plus present value of the residual value ($1,503) = $9,000.
RV = residual value.

the lessee and lessor as follows:

By lessee: "A termination of a capital lease shall be accounted for by removing the asset and obligation, with gain or loss recognized for the difference," (par. 14c).

By lessor: "A termination of the lease shall be accounted for by removing the net investment from the accounts, recording the leased asset at the lower of its original cost, present fair value, or present carrying amount,* and the

* At the termination of the lease, the carrying amount would be the lessor's estimated residual value, which is the remaining balance in the asset account for the leased asset (i.e., cost minus any investment credit realized).

net adjustment shall be charged to income of the period" (par. 17, f,iii).

SALE AND LEASEBACK

When the owner of property, appropriate for leasing, sells it and immediately leases it back from the buyer, the transaction is identified as a *sale and leaseback* and becomes subject to the provisions of paragraphs 32–34 of *FASB Statement No. 13.* Like other leases, sale and leaseback transactions enable a lessee to use costly properties with a minimum investment because the buyer-lessor's resources are tied up in the leased property and yet the lessee has use of the property. Because the rent payments are usually

Sale and Leaseback Illustrated

	Lessee (former owner A)			Lessor (new owner B)		
1. Sale transaction: [a]						
Cash	400,000			Building	400,000	
Building		400,000		Cash		400,000
2. Lease transaction (at inception date): [b]						
a. If an operating lease:						
No entry				No entry		
b. If a direct financing (capital) lease:						
Leased property on capital lease	400,000			Lease receivable	651,000	
Lease liability, Capital lease		400,000		Building (net)		400,000
				Unearned interest revenue		251,000

[a] If the *seller-lessee* has a gain or loss on the sale, it must be *deferred* and amortized (1) if an *operating lease,* over the lease term, and (2) if a *direct financing (capital) lease,* in proportion to amortization of the leased asset.* *FASB Statement No. 13,* paragraph 33, specifies one exception in case of a loss on sale: if at time of sale, the market value (not the net cash proceeds from sale) of the asset is *less* than its then carrying value, a diminution in value has already occurred, and the difference (diminution loss) is recognized immediately. Any other gain or loss (between sales price, net of selling cost, and the revised carrying value) must be deferred and amortized as specified in the basic rule given below.†

[b] The lessee and lessor must account for either an operating or capital lease, depending on whether the respective criteria for each are met. Thus, the lease transaction and subsequent related entries must conform to the discussions and illustrations in prior sections of this chapter.

* When the leased asset is land only, straight-line amortization over the lease term is prescribed.

† Deferral of recognition of gain or loss generally is required for sale and leaseback transactions. However, immediate recognition is required for certain other specified situations. For example, *FASB Statement No. 22* deals with revisions of lease agreements resulting from refundings of tax-exempt debt. Gains or losses from such revisions must be recognized *when they occur* rather than over the remaining term of the lease. An example would be the refunding of tax-exempt debt issued to finance construction of a hospital which is subject to a lease that serves as security for the tax-exempt debt. In the refunding, the perceived economic advantages are passed through to the lessee by modifying the terms of the lease.

fully deductible for income tax purposes by the *lessee* and because the lessor can usually *(a)* get an investment tax credit on the asset, *(b)* depreciate it by an accelerated method, and *(c)* also deduct interest (if a loan is associated with the purchase of the property), both the lessor and lessee derive significant income tax advantages from the transaction.

The general characteristics of a sale and leaseback can be illustrated with a simple situation. Assume owner A has a new building, suitable for use by retailers, that was acquired (i.e., either purchased or built) at a cost of $400,000. Owner A sold the building to new owner B for cash, at cost. At the same time, a ten-year lease agreement was signed by new owner B (now the lessor) to rent the building back to former owner A (now the lessee) for a $65,100 ten-year annual rental payable at each year-end and an approximate implicit rate of 10%. The *two* transactions would be recorded as shown at the bottom of page 764.

FINANCIAL STATEMENT DISCLOSURE

FASB Statement No. 13 requires disclosure of many details concerning leasing arrangements in the financial statements or their accompanying notes. For *lessees* the requirements are as follows:

1. For capital leases—disclosure, as of the date of each balance sheet presented, of—
   a. The gross amount of assets recorded under capital leases presented by major classes according to nature or function. This information may be combined with the comparable information for owned assets.
   b. Future minimum lease payments in the aggregate and for each of the five succeeding fiscal years, with separate deductions from the total for executory costs (including any profit thereon) included in the minimum lease payments and for the amount of the imputed interest necessary to reduce the net minimum lease payments to present value.
   c. The total of minimum sublease rentals to be received in the future under noncancelable subleases.

d. Total contingent rentals (rentals on which the amounts are dependent on some factor other than the passage of time) actually incurred for each period for which an income statement is presented.

2. For operating leases having initial or remaining noncancelable lease terms in excess of one year—disclosure, as of the date of the *latest* balance sheet presented, of—
   a. Future minimum rental payments required in the aggregate and for each of the five succeeding fiscal years.
   b. The total of minimum rentals to be received in the future under noncancelable subleases.

3. For all operating leases, disclose rental expense for each period for which an income statement is presented, with separate amounts for minimum rentals, contingent rentals, and sublease rentals.

4. Provide a general description of the lessee's leasing arrangements including, but not limited to, the following:
   a. The basis on which contingent rental payments are determined.
   b. The existence and terms of renewal or purchase options and escalation clauses.
   c. Restrictions imposed by lease agreements, such as those concerning dividends, additional debt, and further leasing.

For *lessors* (in other than leveraged leasing situations), when leasing a significant part of business activities in terms of revenues, net income or assets, the disclosure requirements are as follows:

1. For sales type and direct financing leases disclose—
   a. The components of the net investment in sales type and direct financing leases as of the date of each balance sheet presented:
      (1) Future minimum lease payments to be received, with separate deductions for *(i)* amounts representing executory costs, including any profit thereon, included in the minimum lease payments and *(ii)* the accumulated allowance for uncollectible

minimum lease payments receivable.

(2) The unguaranteed residual values accruing to the benefit of the lessor.

(3) Unearned interest revenue.

b. Future minimum lease payments to be received for each of the five succeeding fiscal years as of the date of the latest balance sheet presented.

c. The amount of unearned revenue included in income to offset initial direct costs charged against income for each period for which an income statement is presented (for direct financing leases only).

d. Total contingent rentals included in income for each period for which an income statement is presented.

2. For operating leases—disclosure, as of the date of the latest balance sheet presented, of—

a. The cost and carrying amount, if different, of property on lease or held for leasing by major classes of property according to nature or function, and the amount of accumulated depreciation in total.

b. Minimum future rentals on noncancelable leases in the aggregate and for each of the five succeeding fiscal years.

c. Total contingent rentals included in income for each period for which an income statement is presented.

3. Provide a general description of the lessor's leasing arrangements.

Classification of Lease Receivables. When a lessor has *lease receivables* which extend beyond one year (assuming the operating cycle of the business is one year or less), a problem of reporting a portion of the balances due as *current* and another portion as *noncurrent* arises. This problem will be discussed in the context of Exhibit 22–6, page 761. The lessor's lease receivables, as well as the lessee's payables, should be reported on the balance sheet, net of interest relating to them or, in other words, at their present values.

For a balance sheet prepared at December 31, 19A, the lessor would classify the next two upcoming lease receivables of $20,000 each collectible by December 31, 19B, as *current assets*

and three receivables of $20,000 each due after that date as *noncurrent assets.* However, these amounts must be reduced by the *unearned interest* included therein. Although at the time the June 30, 19B, receivable will be collected the lessor can properly recognize $4,330 of previously unearned interest revenue as earned, the receivable due at that time does not have a present value of $15,670 (i.e., $20,000 − $4,330 = $15,670). Rather, its present value at the 5% per period interest rate being used is $19,048 (i.e., $20,000 × .95238 [from Table 6–2], present value of 1 at 5% for one period). Similarly, the receivable due on December 31, 19B, has a present value at December 31, 19A, of $18,141 (which can be read from Exhibit 22–6 on the second line from the bottom). If this seems confusing, perhaps it will help to recall that the interest earned relates to the *unrecovered investment* (shown in column [d]), not to the receivables. The other three uncollected payments of $20,000 each will not be collected until after more than one year from the December 31, 19A, balance sheet date; therefore, they are subject to larger discounts because of the time value of money. Thus, a partial balance sheet at December 31, 19A, would show the following:

Current Assets:		
Lease receivables ($20,000 + $20,000)	$40,000	
Less unearned interest ($952 + $1,859)	2,811	$37,189
Noncurrent Assets:		
Lease receivables ($20,000 + $20,000 + $20,000)	60,000	
Less unearned interest ($2,723 + $3,546 + $4,330)	10,599	49,401
Total assets		$86,590

Appendix—Leveraged Leases

Fundamental Characteristics

A *leveraged lease* is a complex form of a financing lease which involves one or more parties in addition to a lessor and lessee. Debt is a key element of a leveraged lease arrangement; the lender (loan participant) is an added party. Instead of providing 100% of the cost of *depre-*

ciable property to be leased, the lessor usually provides from 20% to 40% and the lender furnishes the remaining needed funds with a nonrecourse loan. Nonrecourse in this context means that the lender cannot take assets other than the leased property in the event the lessor fails to pay the amount owed to the lender.

A lessor having taxable income from other sources is in a position to profit from leveraged leasing because, for *tax* purposes, the lessor can deduct depreciation expense on the leased property from taxable income and use the investment tax credit to further reduce income taxes—even though the lease would otherwise qualify as a capital lease for *financial accounting* purposes. Although the lessor may put up only 20% of the cost of depreciable property to be leased, 100% of the investment tax credit and depreciation can be used by the lessor to reduce income taxes.

The lender's loan is secured by a first lien on the leased property, by assignment of the lease, and assignment of the lease rentals. This means that the lender has first priority on the leased property and the lease receivables under the lease agreement in the event the leveraged lessor fails to pay the lender the amount owed on the debt incurred to purchase the leased property. Creditworthiness of the lessee is important. Title to the leased property is vested in an *owner trustee* who issues trust certificates evidencing each participant's equity interest. An *indenture trustee* holds the security interest in the leased property for the benefit of the lender and receives rental payments from the lessee which are then distributed to the lender and to the lessor through the owner trustee. The relationships among the various parties are diagrammed in Exhibit 22–7.

Because the contractual arrangements are complex and costly, it is seldom feasible to apply leveraged leasing to properties costing less than $1,000,000. It would cost as much to arrange a leveraged lease on a $50,000 asset as on a $1,000,000 one, and since the "front end" costs are large, rentals from the less costly asset would not justify the "front end" expenses. Typically, lessors depreciate property under leveraged leases by an accelerated method to delay payment of income taxes. Lessees often pay smaller rents under leveraged leases because lessors are able to leverage their tax benefits in so many ways.

Cash Flows under Leveraged Leases

In a typical leveraged lease the *lessor* experiences a net cash inflow during the early years of the lease, a net cash outflow in the later years, and a terminal receipt of cash if the property has a residual value and is sold after the lease terminates. Early reportable and tax-deductible expenses are relatively large because interest on the unpaid debt is high in the early years and because of accelerated depreciation. This combination which causes tax losses in the early years of the lease creates, in effect, a cash inflow because of the reduction of tax that would otherwise be paid on income *from other sources.* Taking full benefit of the investment tax credit in the first year has a similar effect; cash that would otherwise be paid as income tax on income from other sources is conserved. In the later years a reverse effect is experienced: lower interest and depreciation amounts cause taxable income to rise and tax payments to increase. However, due to the time value of money, the early cash inflows create a distinct advantage in favor of leveraged leasing.

To illustrate a leveraged lease, Exhibit 22–8 is used, based on the assumptions that the lessor acquired an asset for $1,000,000 on which a down payment of $200,000 was paid, leaving $800,000 to be paid in equal annual installments over the next seven years. If the interest rate agreed to between the lessor and the lender was 9% and seven equal annual payments are to be made at the *end* of each year, annual payments of $158,952 will fully pay the debt and related interest.[11] The payments are reflected in col-

---

[11] Debt payment amounts were calculated by dividing $800,000 by the present value of an ordinary annuity of 7 rents of 1 at 9%. Refer to Table 6–4: $800,000 ÷ 5.03295 = $158,952. Columns *(c)* and *(d)* in Exhibit 22–8 were based on these values; for example, the first two years' data are as follows:

Year	Payment	Interest	Reduction of Principal	Unamortized Principal
1a				$800,000
1b	$158,952	$800,000 × 9% = $72,000	$86,952	713,048
2	158,952	$713,048 × 9% = $64,174	94,778	618,270

Etc.

EXHIBIT 22–7
Leveraged Lease Transaction Participants

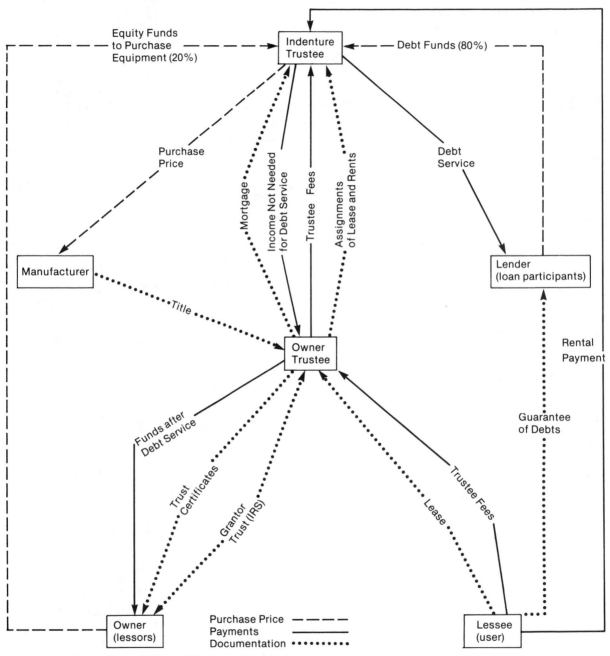

Source: R. J. Ryan, Jr., "Leveraged Leasing," *Management Accounting,* April 1977, p. 46.

EXHIBIT 22–8
Schedule of Cash Flows—Leveraged Lease

Year	(a) Annual Rentals	(b) Annual Depreciation	(c) Interest at 9%	(d) Reduce Principal	(e) Total Expense (b)+(c)	(f) Taxable Income (loss) (a)−(e)	(g) Tax Saving (expense) 50% of (f)	(h) Annual Cash Flow (a)+(g) −([c]+[d])	(i) Cumulative Cash Flow
1a								$(100,000)	$(100,000)
1b	$ 205,400	$280,000	$ 72,000	$ 86,952	$ 352,000	$(146,600)	$ 73,300	119,748	19,748
2	205,400	201,600	64,174	94,778	265,774	(60,374)	30,187	76,635	96,383
3	205,400	145,152	55,644	103,308	200,796	4,604	(2,302)	44,146	140,529
4	205,400	104,509	46,347	112,605	150,856	54,544	(27,272)	19,176	159,705
5	205,400	75,247	36,212	122,740	111,459	93,941	(46,971)	(523)	159,182
6	205,400	54,178	25,166	133,786	79,344	126,056	(63,028)	(16,580)	142,602
7	205,400	39,314*	13,121	145,831	52,435	152,965	(76,482)	(30,034)	112,568
Residual								100,000	100,000
Totals	$1,437,800	$900,000	$312,664	$800,000	$1,212,664	$225,136	$(112,568)	$212,568	$212,568

Proof of Cash Flows and Proof of Income

Proof of Cash Flows		Proof of Income	
Cash inflows:		Revenue:	
Rents (7 × $205,400)	$1,437,800	Rents	$1,437,800
Investment credit	100,000	Expenses:	
Residual value	100,000	Depreciation	900,000
Total inflows	$1,637,800	Interest	312,664
Cash outflows:		Total expenses	1,212,664
Down payment	$ 200,000	Income before taxes	225,136
Payments (7 × $158,952)	1,112,664	Taxes	(112,568)
Income taxes	112,568	Income	112,568
Total outflows	1,425,232	Add: Investment tax credit	100,000
Cumulative flow	$ 212,568	Net Income	$ 212,568

* Adjusted depreciation to sum to $900,000.

umns *(c)* and *(d)* of Exhibit 22–8. The first year's interest is \$72,000 (i.e., 9% × \$800,000), and the remainder of the payment, \$86,952 (i.e., \$158,952 − \$72,000 = \$86,952), reduces the principal.

Assume the lessor depreciates the \$1,000,000 cost of the asset down to \$100,000 using the fixed-percentage-on-declining-base method and a 28% annual rate. The asset is assumed to have a residual value of \$100,000 at the end of the seven-year lease term. Thus, depreciation for the first year at 28% amounts to \$280,000 (first amount in column [*b*]) and the second year it is \$201,600 (i.e., [\$1,000,000 − \$280,000] × 28% = \$201,600). Annual depreciation is reflected in column *(b)*. The lessor leases the asset for seven annual *year-end* rents of \$205,400 reported in column *(a)*. The lessor's expenses are added and the total is reflected in column *(e)*. Subtraction of column *(e)* from the rents in column *(a)* yields taxable income in column *(f)*. The income or loss in column *(f)* is combined with the lessor's other income (not shown) and taxed at 50%. Thus, when the result in column *(f)* is a loss, insofar as the leveraged lease is concerned, the lessor experiences a tax saving of 50% of the amount of the loss because losses on the leveraged lease activities reduce income that would otherwise be taxable at 50%. Whenever the result in column *(f)* reflects income before tax, the lessor must pay 50% of that amount as income tax. The lessor's annual cash flow is shown in column *(h)*. Many elements of the cash flow are fixed; the debt payments cause a periodic outflow of \$158,952 and the rents cause a periodic inflow of \$205,400. Were it not for income tax savings (treated as an inflow) or income tax expense (treated as an outflow), the net inflow each year would be \$46,448 (i.e., \$205,400 − \$158,952 = \$46,448). Two other inflows and outflows warrant brief attention. Recall that the lessor's down payment is \$200,000; this would cause an outflow, before regular operations begin, of that amount were it not for the fact that the investor receives a 10% investment credit of \$100,000 (i.e., \$1,000,000 × 10% = \$100,000). The difference between the \$200,000 down payment and the \$100,000 investment credit is reflected as a \$100,000 net outflow on line 1*a*. Line 1*b* reflects regular first-year leasing activities. One other special inflow needs to be mentioned.

Recall that the asset has a residual value of \$100,000 after seven years. It is assumed that this amount is realized by cash sale of the asset at book value after the seventh year and that inflow is reflected after the seventh year on the line captioned "Residual."

From above note that the net cash inflow each year would be \$46,448 were it not for income taxes. For the first year's operations reported on line 1*b*, we see that the result is a tax saving of \$73,300; this, added to the regular net inflow (i.e., \$205,400 − \$158,952), gives the \$119,748 reflected in line 1*b* in column *(h)*. When this amount is combined with \$100,000 outflow on line 1*a*, we arrive at the cumulative net cash inflow of \$19,478 shown in column *(i)* on line 1*b*.

A proof of cash flows and of income appears in the bottom portion of Exhibit 22–8.

The most revealing aspect of Exhibit 22–8 is column *(h)* which shows the timing of the cash flows, because this is the distinguishing characteristic of leveraged leases. Observe in particular that the flows are positive in Years 1–4 and negative during Years 5–7. As indicated above, the time value of money helps make leveraged leases advantageous to the lessor.

This example has shown that the lessor would be \$212,568 "better off" at the conclusion of the seven-year lease term. However, under the specifications of *FASB Statement No. 13,* annual income of the lessor from a leveraged lease is measured in such a way that annual income would differ from the net of column *(f)* minus column *(g)*, that is, aftertax income. *Statement No. 13* requires leveraged lessors to recognize lease revenue in years when the lessor's net investment[12] in leased property is positive, but no loss for years when the net investment is negative.

The FASB income formula is quite complex, and the results for any particular leveraged lease can only be obtained by calculation of a

---

[12] Net investment of a leveraged lessor in leased property is defined in *FASB Statement No. 13* as (1) rentals receivable under the leveraged lease, plus (2) any receivable for investment tax credit to be realized, plus (3) any residual value of the leased property, minus (4) lessor's nonrecourse debt on borrowing to acquire the leased property, minus (5) unearned lease revenue, minus (6) any investment tax credit deferred for recognition in future periods.

yield rate for the lessor for that particular lease. This determination is difficult without a computer because of the large number of iterative attempts that would ordinarily be necessary to derive the yield rate.

The details of the FASB approach can be learned by careful study of Appendix E of *FASB Statement No. 13.* Computer programs for the calculation of the yield rate for a leveraged lease have been published in professional journals and are available from some of the larger computer manufacturers. More detailed coverage of this topic is beyond the scope of an intermediate accounting text.

QUESTIONS

1. Match the numbered items listed immediately below with the lettered items that follow.

   1. Lessor; 2. Leveraged lease; 3. Operating lease; 4. Lessee.
   a. Contract in which lessor finances property leased with relatively large amount of debt.
   b. Lender in a lease contract transaction.
   c. Tenant in a lease contract transaction.
   d. Type of lease which requires capitalization.
   e. Type of lease which does not require capitalization.
   f. Property owner in a lease contract transaction.

   Questions 2 and 3 below are based on the following information: Briefly explain your choices.

   The Marne Company purchased a machine on January 1, 19A, for $900,000 for the express purpose of leasing it. The machine is expected to have a five-year life, no residual value, and be depreciated on a straight-line basis. On March 1, 19A, Marne leased the machine to the Dal Company for $300,000 a year for a four-year period ending February 28, 19E. Marne incurred total maintenance and other related costs under the provisions of the lease of $15,000 relating to the year ended December 31, 19A. Dal paid $300,000 to Marne on March 1, 19A.

2. Under the operating method, what should be the income before income taxes derived by Marne from this lease for the year ended December 31, 19A?
   a. $55,000.
   b. $70,000.
   c. $85,000.
   d. $100,000.

3. What should be the amount of rent expense incurred by Dal from this lease for the year ended December 31, 19A?
   a. $70,000.
   b. $120,000.
   c. $250,000.
   d. $300,000.

   (2 and 3 AICPA adapted)

4. Give highlights of the generally accepted accounting methods for operating leases.
5. Often advance rental payments are received under operating lease contracts that extend well beyond a single fiscal year. Outline possible accounting procedures to be followed in respect to such prepayments.
6. What is meant by *capitalization* of leases?
7. What are executory costs?
8. From a lease standpoint, leases are classified as capital or operating leases. By what criteria can a capital lease be identified?
9. From a lessor standpoint, a lease that is a capital lease to a lessee is likely to be one of two types. Identify the types and distinguish between them.
10. How does a lessee determine what interest rate is appropriate for capitalization of a lease?
11. What distinguishes leveraged leases from other leases? What pattern of cash flows can normally be expected in a leveraged lease?

DECISION CASE 22–1

The corporation where you are employed as controller is contemplating leasing (as a lessee) a greater proportion of its operational assets than in the past. As assets become fully depreciated and/or are retired, many of them would be replaced by leased assets. You have been asked by the board of directors to advise about certain specific financial accounting issues.

Item 1:

Having learned that interest must be recognized in connection with lease obligations and that within modest limits there may be some discretion as to interest rates chosen, some board members want to use the lowest possible rate while others want to use the highest rate. Specifically, you are asked what would be the difference insofar as the financial statements are concerned between the two alternatives.

Item 2:

If some of the lease contracts contemplated could be drawn so as to avoid the lease capitalization requirements of *FASB Statement No. 13,* what would be the effect on the financial statements of using such lease contracts?

Item 3:

Although the company is not heavily in debt, one director is concerned about becoming a lessee under a capital lease because we "do not want all that debt on the balance sheet." Can you offer any comments that might assuage these anxieties?

DECISION CASE 22-2

Pertinent provisions of *FASB Statement No. 13* concerning the interest rate to be used in capitalizing leases are cited below:

"A lessor shall compute the present value of the minimum lease payments using the *interest rate implicit in the lease.* . . . A lessee shall compute the present value of the minimum lease payments using his incremental borrowing rate . . . unless *(i)* it is practicable for him to learn [or estimate] the implicit rate computed by the lessor, and (ii) the implicit rate computed by the lessor is less than the lessee's incremental borrowing rate. If both of these conditions are met, the lessee shall use the implicit rate."

Interest rate implicit in the lease is defined as the discount rate which, when applied to the minimum lease payments (excluding executory costs) and to the unguaranteed residual value of the property to the lessor, causes the present value at the start of the lease term to equal the [market] value of the property to the lessor at the inception of the lease.*

APB Opinion No. 21, which deals with the imputation of interest to receivables and payables, indicates that the choice of an interest rate "may be affected by the credit standing of the issuer, restrictive covenants, the collateral, payment and other terms pertaining to the debt, and, if appropriate, the tax consequences to the buyer and seller."

Required:

Evaluate the foregoing criteria in light of the following assertions:

1. The assumption that a lease has an implicit interest rate, in many cases, represents circular reasoning in that the market value of the leased asset itself (i.e., the benchmark value used in determining the implicit rate) is determined by market forces. The value of the property stems from the rentals it will command rather than the rentals stemming from the value of the property.

2. Asking a lessor what interest rate is inherent in a lease transaction would be similar to asking a farmer what rate is implicit in the price the farmer can expect *now* for next fall's corn crop. There are varying degrees of risk in any operation having a distant future; the higher the farmer's future risks are thought to be, the higher the farmer will set his or her rate and, likewise, on the lessor.

3. One determinant of the implicit interest rate in a lease is the residual value of the property to be leased. This is a subjective judgment which, depending on the property, can be substantially in error. Lessors will not disclose what this guess is.

EXERCISES

Exercise 22-1

Hampton Company signed an operating lease contract effective for ten years from January 1, 19A. Hampton is to pay $60,000 at the start of the lease plus $6,000 per month rentals throughout the lease term. Prior to occupancy, Hampton spent $20,000 renovating the property to be leased and also built an addition to the leased property with the lessor's consent at a cost of $150,000. The estimated life of the addition is 15 years, and its residual value is zero. The lease contract does not contain a renewal option.

Required:

Give all entries on Hampton's books to reflect the preoccupancy outlays, leasehold, and rental payments for 19A and entries at the end of 19A assuming Hampton's fiscal year is the calendar year. Straight-line amortization is to be used.

Exercise 22-2

In lieu of paying six $7,000 rentals at six-month intervals with each payment due in advance, a lessor and lessee agree upon a single lump-sum advance payment of $37,306 which covers the entire lease period. This reflects recognition of interest at an annual rate of 10% over the lease term.

Required:

1. Show how the lump-sum amount was calculated, and prepare an amortization table on an annuity due basis covering the three-year lease term.
2. Give the entry by the lessee to record the initial payment under this operating lease and entries at end of the first year assuming the lease year and the lessee's fiscal year coincide.

---

* There are some qualifications to this abstracted definition, but they are not important for present purposes. Italics supplied in the first quotation.

Exercise 22–3

Margo Company paid $5,000 on January 1, 19A, to Dexter Properties as a lease bonus to secure a three-year lease on premises it will occupy starting from that date. Additionally, $6,000 per annum paid on each December 31 throughout the term of the lease will be paid as rent. There is no specific renewal agreement. Margo adjusts and closes its books each December 31. Dexter will maintain the property, pay taxes, and other ownership costs.

Required (round to the nearest dollar):

1. What type of lease contract is involved?
2. What are Margo's alternatives as to treatment of the $5,000? Develop an interest method amortization table using a 9% rate.
3. What is Margo's total occupancy cost for 19B under each alternative given in your response to Requirement 2?
4. What lease-related items should Margo's financial statements reflect as of December 31, 19A, if the amortization table developed in Requirement 2 is used?

Exercise 22–4

Alpha Leasing Company agreed with Koz Corporation to provide the latter with equipment under lease for a four-year period. The equipment cost Alpha $18,500 and will have no residual value when the lease term ends. Alpha expects to collect all rentals from Koz and has no material unreimbursable cost uncertainties. The market value of the equipment was $18,500 at the inception of the lease. The four equal annual rents (amount to be determined by the student) are to be paid in advance starting January 1, 19A, at which time the equipment was delivered. Koz has agreed to pay taxes, maintenance, and insurance throughout the lease term as well as any other "ownership" costs. Alpha expects a 9% return. Koz's incremental borrowing rate is 10%, but management of Koz Corporation is aware of Alpha's rate of return. The fiscal year of both companies ends December 31.

Required:

1. What kind of lease is this to Koz? To Alpha? What interest rate should Koz use?
2. Prepare an amortization table reflecting the interest and principal elements of Koz's payments over the four-year term of the lease. Give all journal entries relating to the lease for Koz Corporation for 19A including year-end adjusting and closing entries.
3. Give all journal entries for Alpha Leasing Company relating to the lease for 19A including year-end adjusting and closing entries.

Exercise 22–5

Choose the best answer in each of the following. Briefly justify each choice.

1. On the first day of its fiscal year, Lessor, Inc., leased certain property at an annual rental of $100,000 receivable at the beginning of each year for ten years. The first payment was received immediately. The leased property which is new had cost $650,000 and has an estimated useful life of 13 years and no residual value. Lessor's borrowing rate is 8%. The present value of an annuity due of 1 payable at the beginning of the period at 8% for ten years is 7.24689. Lessor had no other costs associated with this lease. Lessor should have accounted for this lease as a sale but it mistakenly treated the lease as an operating lease. What was the effect on net earnings during the first year of the lease by having treated this lease as an operating lease rather than as a sale?
   a. No effect.
   b. Understated.
   c. Overstated.
   d. The effect depends on the method selected for income tax purposes.
2. Your client constructed an office building at a cost of $500,000. He sold this building to Jones at a material gain and then leased it back from Jones for a stipulated annual rental. How should this gain be treated?
   a. Recognized in full as an ordinary item in the year of the transaction.
   b. Recognized in full as an extraordinary item in the year of the transaction.
   c. Amortized, net of tax, as an adjustment of the rental cost, an ordinary item, over the life of the lease.
   d. Amortized as an ordinary item over the life of the lease, but with the tax effect recognized in full in the year of the transaction.
3. The appropriate valuation of leased assets under an operating lease on the statement of financial position of a lessee is as follows:
   a. Zero.
   b. The absolute sum of the lease payments.
   c. The sum of the present values of the lease payments discounted at an apppropriate rate.
   d. The market value of the asset at the date of the inception of the lease.
4. What are the three types of period costs that a lessee experiences with capital leases?

a. Lease expense, interest expense, amortization expense.

b. Interest expense, amortization expense, executory costs.

c. Amortization expense, executory costs, lease expense.

d. Executory costs, interest expense, lease expense.

5. When measuring the present value of future rentals to be capitalized in connection with a lease, identifiable payments to cover taxes, insurance and maintenance should be as follows:

a. Included with the future rentals to be capitalized.

b. Excluded from future rentals to be capitalized.

c. Capitalized, but at a different rate and recorded in a different account than future rentals.

d. Capitalized, but at a different rate and period from the rate and period used for the future rental payments.

6. Generally accepted accounting principles require that certain lease agreements be accounted for as purchases. The theoretical basis for this treatment is that a lease of this type:

a. Effectively conveys all of the benefits and risks incident to the ownership of property.

b. Is an example of form over substance.

c. Provides the use of the leased asset to the lessee for a limited period of time.

d. Must be recorded in accordance with the concept of cause and effect.

(AICPA adapted)

Exercise 22–6

XY Company (as a lessee) leased a computer under a capital lease for a period of three years, contracting to pay $9,600 rent in advance at the start of the lease term and five like amounts of rent semiannually thereafter. The lease was negotiated July 1, 19A, at which time the first payment was made. XY's fiscal year is the calendar year. Straight-line depreciation is to be reflected. Assume an annual effective interest rate of 6.5%.

An incomplete amortization schedule related to the lease follows:

	Cash	Interest	Reduction	Balance
7/1/19A Initial balance				$53,250
7/1/19A First payment	$9,600	—	$9,600	43,650
1/1/19B Second payment	9,600	$1,419	8,181	35,469
7/1/19B Third payment	9,600	1,153	8,447	27,022

Required:

1. Prepare appropriate headings and complete the above amortization schedule through the final payment.

2. Prepare the entry XY Company should make at the inception of the lease.

3. On the assumptions that XY's fiscal year ends December 31 and that straight-line depreciation is used, prepare adjusting and closing entries at December 31, 19A.

4. Indicate what would be reflected on XY's December 31, 19A, balance sheet in respect to the lease. Assume XY's operating cycle is less than one year. Include also in your answer any disclosures appropriate to notes accompanying XY's financial statements.

5. If XY has the right to buy the computer on the day of the last lease payment for $5,000, this "bargain purchase option" should, in effect, be discounted on July 1, 19A, for five periods at .0325 ($5,000 × .85222 = $4,261), which adds $4,261 to the initial valuation. Thus, the amortization schedule becomes the following:

	Cash	Interest	Reduction	Balance
7/1/19A Initial balance				$57,511
7/1/19A First payment	$9,600		$9,600	47,911
1/1/19B Second payment	9,600	$1,557	8,043	39,868
7/1/19C Fifth payment	9,600	747	8,853	14,137

a. Show what would appear for the last line of the amortization schedule.

b. Record the sixth payment and exercise of the "bargain purchase option."

c. Assume instead that the computer is not purchased and that the lease is canceled by mutual agreement when the fifth payment became due. The balance of the liability prior to the fifth payment was $22,990, and the computer had been depreciated on the assumption of a seven-year life with zero residual value at the end of seven years.

Exercise 22–7

Lessee A and Lessor Z contract for the lease of a machine for six rentals of $6,000 each paid at the inception of the lease and at the start of each of five quarters thereafter. They also agree that at the time of the sixth payment, for an added $6,930 payment, A can buy the property. The interest rate is 2.5% per quarter. The present value of an annuity due of six rents at 2.5% is 5.64583 and the present value of 1 at 2.5% for five periods is .88385.

Required (round to nearest dollar):

1. Calculate the value of the lease and prepare an amortization schedule for the lessee covering the six-quarter term of the lease. Assume $6,930 is a bargain price.

2. Give the lessee's entries at the inception of the lease and at the time of the sixth payment if the lessee exercises the purchase option.

Exercise 22–8

Milholland Company uses leases as a means of selling its products. The company contracted with M. Jones Corporation to lease the latter a product to be used by Jones as an operational asset. The market value of the asset at the inception of the lease is $40,000; it cost Milholland $33,000 and is carried in its inventory at that value. Payments of $7,384 are to be made by Jones at the end of each of the six quarters following inception of the lease. Milholland's implicit interest rate is 3% per quarter.

Required (round to the nearest dollar):

1. Prepare an amortization schedule for use by Milholland covering the six-quarter term of the lease.
2. Give Milholland's journal entries at the inception of the lease and upon receipt of the first payment. Assume the first receipt coincides with the end of Milholland's fiscal year. Record its closing entries insofar as the lease transactions are concerned.

Exercise 22–9 (based on Appendix)

Loring Lessors, Inc., leased a machine to Davis Company for a five-year period beginning January 1, 19A. Loring acquired the machine at a cost of $250,000, paying $50,000 cash, and borrowing the remainder at 8% per annum. The loan agreement provides for four equal annual payments starting on December 31, 19A.

Davis agreed to pay five equal annual year-end rents of $64,273. Loring will realize a 10% investment credit the first year and will depreciate the machine (which has no residual value) by the straight-line method over its five-year life. Loring has extensive income from other sources and pays income tax at a 45% rate; any losses on a single phase of its operations result in a 45% income tax saving.

Required (round amounts to the nearest dollar):

1. Prepare a loan amortization schedule.
2. Prepare a cash flow analysis similar to Exhibit 22–8.

PROBLEMS

Problem 22–1

Select the best answer in each of the following. Briefly justify your choices.

1. On June 30, 19A, Gulch Corporation sold equipment to an unaffiliated company for $550,000. The equipment had a book value of $500,000 and a remaining useful life of ten years. That same day, Gulch leased back the equipment at $1,500 per month for five years with no option to renew the lease or repurchase the equipment. Gulch's equipment rent expense for this equipment for the year ended December 31, 19A, should be
   a. $4,000.
   b. $5,000.
   c. $9,000.
   d. $11,000.
2. What is the cost basis of an asset acquired by a lease which is in substance a purchase?
   a. The net realizable value of the asset determined at the date of the lease agreement plus the sum of the future minimum lease payments under the lease.
   b. The sum of the future minimum lease payments under the lease.
   c. The present value of the amount of future minimum lease payments under the lease (exclusive of executory costs and any profit thereon) discounted at an appropriate rate.
   d. The present value of the market price of the asset discounted at an appropriate rate as an amount to be received at the end of the lease.
3. While only certain leases are currently accounted for as a sale or purchase there is theoretical justification for considering all leases to be sales or purchases. The principal reason that supports this idea is that
   a. All leases are generally for the economic life of the property and the residual value of the property at the end of the lease is minimal.
   b. At the end of the lease the property usually can be purchased by the lessee.
   c. A lease reflects the purchase or sale of a quantifiable right to the use of property.
   d. During the life of the lease the lessee can effectively treat the property as if it were owned by the lessee.
4. What journal entry should Lessor have made on January 2, 19A, if the lease were to have been accounted for as an operating lease?

a.	Cash 10,000	
	Unearned rental	
	revenue	10,000
b.	Receivable 35,000	
	Cash 10,000	
	Equipment inventory	45,000
c.	Receivable 48,680	
	Cash 10,000	

Cost of goods sold	45,000	
Sales		58,680
Equipment inventory		45,000

d. Receivable	70,000	
Cash	10,000	
Cost of goods sold	45,000	
Sales		80,000
Equipment inventory		45,000

5. Beth Company leased equipment to Wolf, Inc., on April 1, 19A. The lease was appropriately recorded as a sale for accounting purposes by Beth. The lease is for an eight-year period expiring March 31, 19I. The first equal annual payment of $500,000 was made on April 1, 19A. Beth had purchased the equipment on January 1, 19A, for $2,800,000. The equipment has an estimated useful life of eight years with no residual value expected. Beth uses straight-line depreciation and takes a full year's depreciation in the year of purchase. The cash selling price of the equipment is $2,934,000. Assuming an interest rate of 10%, what amount of interest revenue should Beth record in 19A as a result of the lease?
   a. $0.
   b. $182,550.
   c. $243,400.
   d. $280,000.

6. On January 1, 19A, The Anson Company leased a machine to Scovil Company. The lease was for a ten-year period, which approximated the useful life of the machine. Anson purchased the machine for $80,000 and expects to earn a 10% return on its investment, based upon an annual rental of $11,836 payable in advance each January 1.

   Assuming that the lease was a direct financing lease, what should be the interest entry on Anson's books on December 31, 19A?

a. Cash	3,836	
Interest revenue		3,836
b. Unearned interest revenue	6,816	
Interest revenue		6,816
c. Cash	8,000	
Interest revenue		8,000
d. Cash	11,836	
Interest revenue		8,000
Equipment		3,836

Questions 7 and 8 are based on the following information:

On January 1, 19A, the Green Company entered into a noncancelable lease agreement with the Blatt Company for a machine which was carried on the accounting records of Green at $2,000,000. Total payments under the lease agreement which expires on December 31, 19J, aggregate $3,550,800 of which $2,400,000 represents the cost of the machine to Blatt. Payments of $355,080 are due each January 1. The first payment was made on January 1, 19A, when the lease agreement was finalized. The interest rate of 10% which was stipulated in the lease agreement is considered fair and adequate compensation to Green for the use of its funds. The "interest" method of amortization is being used. Blatt expects the machine to have a ten-year life, no residual value, and be depreciated on a straight-line basis. The lease agreement should be accounted for as a lease equivalent to a sale by Green and as a capital lease which is in substance a purchase by Blatt.

7. What should be the income before income taxes derived by Green from the lease for the year ended December 31, 19A?
   a. $204,492.
   b. $355,080.
   c. $604,492.
   d. $755,080.

8. Ignoring income taxes, what should be the expenses incurred by Blatt from this lease for the year ended December 31, 19A?
   a. $204,492.
   b. $355,080.
   c. $444,492.
   d. $595,080.

(AICPA adapted)

Problem 22–2

On January 1, 19A, Company A rented an office to Company B for an annual rental of $1,200 due each January 1. In addition, an advance payment of $5,000 was required. The lease was for a three-year period. The advance amount represented three annual rentals that would have been payable each January 1; thus, the $5,000 was somewhat less than the sum of the three annual payments that would have been made in addition to the normal rent of $1,200. This is an operating lease as to both parties.

Required (round to the nearest dollar):

1. Give all entries, including closing entries, for both the lessor and lessee assuming (a) both parties' fiscal years end December 31 and (b) a 9% interest rate is appropriate for amortization purposes. Utilize interest method amortization and present the two sets of entries in parallel columns. Show all computations.
2. Show amounts that would be reported on the income statement and balance sheet for each year for both the lessor and lessee.

Problem 22–3

In lieu of making an initial rental payment of $10,000 at the inception of an operating lease to be followed by four additional $10,000 rent payments spaced at one-year intervals, the lessee and lessor agree that the lessee can make a single initial payment of $41,699 at the start of the five-year lease term. This amount was calculated on the basis of an agreed 10% annual interest rate.

Required (round all amounts to the nearest dollar):

1. Show how the lump-sum initial payment amount was calculated.
2. Prepare an amortization schedule for the lessor covering the entire lease term. Show the lessor's entries to reflect receipt of the initial rental and adjusting entries at the end of the first, second, and last years if the lease year and fiscal year of the lessor coincide. Entries are to be based on the amortization schedule.
3. On the assumption the lessee amortizes the prepayment on a straight-line basis, give the lessee's entries to record the initial payment and year-end adjustments if the lease year and lessee fiscal year coincide.
4. Has the lessor or lessee adopted a more realistic approach to recognition of the periodic effects of the lease? Explain.

Problem 22–4

Shelton Leasing Company leased a new machine to Condon Contractors that cost $18,000. The lease is a direct financing lease to Shelton and a capital lease to Condon, who agreed to pay all executory costs and assume other risks and costs of ownership. Shelton sets the rents at an amount which will yield an annual return of 7%, and the lessee, being aware of this rate, also uses it to record the lease and calculate interest expense. The property is expected to have no residual value at the end of the four-year lease term. Both lessor and lessee have fiscal years ending December 31.

Required (round all amounts to the nearest dollar):

1. If the annual rents are payable at the end of each year, complete the following: *(a)* lessor computation of periodic rental payments and *(b)* an amortization schedule for the lessor reflecting interest and recovery of investment throughout the four-year lease term.
2. Assume instead that the annual rentals are payable at the start of the lease and annually there-

after. Complete the same items as for Requirement 1.
3. Condon depreciates all assets by the straight-line method. Give entries under Requirement 1 for both lessor and lessee relating to the lease for 19A. This includes adjusting and closing entries.
4. Indicate the asset and liability under Requirement 1 amounts that would be reported on the classified December 31, 19A, balance sheets of the lessor and lessee.

Problem 22–5

A lessor and lessee began negotiations which would have provided that the lessee would pay six annual $8,000 rents for the use of property with the first payment to be at the beginning of the lease term. However, after agreeing that money was worth 7% at the time, the parties finally agreed that the lessee would instead pay $40,801.60 at the outset and that this single advance payment would be in lieu of all other rents for the six-year lease term. Assume a direct financing lease.

Required:

1. Show how the lump-sum amount was calculated and prepare an amortization schedule covering the entire term of the lease.
2. Give journal entries for both the lessor and lessee, based on the amortization schedule, which reflect the initial payment and adjusting entries (assuming the lease year and fiscal years of the parties coincide) at the end of Years 1, 2, and 6.
3. Instead of using present value methods as in Requirement 2, assume that the lessor and lessee amortize the $40,801.60 by the straight-line method. Give entries for both parties to record amortization at the end of the year if the lease year and fiscal years of the parties coincide.

Problem 22–6

Whatley Company uses leases as a means of selling its products. It contracted with Miller Corporation to lease machinery which had a market value of $110,000 and which cost Whatley $85,000 (its carrying value in inventory). A downpayment of $22,961 is to be paid at the inception of the lease, and annually thereafter at the start of each of the next five years similar payments are to be made. Whatley's implicit interest rate is 10%. Miller's incremental borrowing rate is 12%, and the lessor's implicit rate is unknown to Miller and cannot be reasonably estimated.

Required (round to the nearest dollar):

1. Prepare amortization schedules for use by Whatley and by Miller covering the six-year lease term.
2. Give the lessor's and lessee's entries at the inception of the contract. On the assumption that both the lessor and lessee adjust and close books at the end of the year (one day before the second payment is due) and that the lessee uses straight-line depreciation and assumes zero residual value of the asset after six years, give adjusting and closing entries for both parties.

Problem 22–7

Given the following data about a noncancelable lease:

Leased asset is new at inception of lease term.

Lease term	5 years
Interest rate implicit in the lease	10%
Lessee's incremental borrowing rate	12%
Amount of each lease payment	$2,000
Lessor's cost of asset	$7,582

Lessee has no way of knowing interest rate implicit in the lease.

Fair value of leased asset at inception of lease term	$7,582

Each lease payment occurs at the end of each period, i.e., an ordinary annuity.

Unreimbursable cost uncertainties of lessor . .	None
Credit standing of lessee	Excellent
Ignore executory cost	
Depreciation method, if appropriate	Straight line
Estimated residual value of leased asset after five years	Zero

Required (round to the nearest dollar):

1. What type of lease is this to the lessee? To the lessor? Explain.
2. Make entries in parallel columns for lessee and lessor to record:
   a. The inception of the lease on January 1, 19A.
   b. All entries needed at year-end, December 31, 19A, for both parties to record lease payment (receipt), interest, depreciation, and so forth, including closing entries.

Problem 22–8

Lessor and Lessee agreed to a noncancelable lease which specified the following:

a. Lessor's cost of the asset leased, $25,000. The asset was new at the inception of the lease term.

b. Lease term, four years starting January 1, 19C.
c. Estimated useful life of the leased asset, six years.
d. On January 1, 19C, estimated that the residual value of the leased asset one day after the end of the term of the lease will be zero.
e. Depreciation method for the leased asset, straight-line.
f. Lessee's incremental borrowing rate on January 1, 19C, 12%.
g. Bank prime rate of interest on January 1, 19C, 8%.
h. Purchase option price of leased asset exercisable one day after the lease term, $7,000.
i. Title to the leased asset retained by the lessor unless the purchase option is exercised.
j. Market value of leased asset on January 1, 19C, $30,000.
k. Lessor's unreimbursable cost uncertainties, none.
l. Four annual lease rentals due on January 1 of each year during the lease term, with the first payment due at inception of the lease term, $8,495.

Required (round to the nearest dollar):
Part A:

1. What was the lessor's implicit interest rate in this lease? Assume the lessee knew all of the facts given above.
2. What type of lease was this to the lessee? To the lessor? Explain.
3. In parallel columns for the lessee and lessor, record the
   a. Inception of the lease on January 1, 19C, if appropriate.
   b. Adjusting and closing entries on December 31, 19C.

Part B:

Modify the above data as follows, assuming all other data items are unchanged:
   a. The annual rental is $7,492.
   b. Purchase option price of leased asset exercisable one day after the lease term, $5,000.
   c. Lessor's implicit rate and lessee's incremental borrowing rate on January 1, 19C, were as computed for the lessor in Part A, Requirement 1.
   d. Residual value of leased asset at end of lease term $7,000, and at end of its useful life of six years, $1,000.

4. Compute the lessee's capitalizable cost of the leased asset. Is this an operating lease or a capital lease to the lessee? Explain why.
5. What type of lease was this to the lessor? Explain.
6. In parallel columns for the lessee and lessor, record the inception of the lease on January 1, 19C,

(if appropriate) and the adjusting and closing entries on December 31, 19C.

Problem 22-9

On December 31, 19A, a lessor acquired a machine (for leasing purposes) for $120,000 cash and realized a 10% investment credit (i.e., a reduction of 19A income taxes payable of 10% on cost). The machine was leased on January 1, 19B, for five years under a direct financing lease which required annual payments of $27,180 at the end of each year. At the end of the lease term the machine will revert to the lessor, at which time the estimated residual value will be $8,000 (none of which is guaranteed by the lessee). The lessor's implicit rate of return was 10% on the net investment (after taking into consideration the investment tax credit and the residual value).

Required (round amounts to the nearest dollar):

1. Prepare a lease amortization schedule for the lessor.
2. Give the following entries for the lessor:
   a. To record acquisition of the machine on December 31, 19A.
   b. To record the investment tax credit on December 31, 19A.
   c. To record the inception of the lease on January 1, 19B.
   d. To record collection of the first rental and recognition of interest revenue on December 31, 19B (end of the fiscal period).
   e. To record, at termination of the lease on December 31, 19F, the last rent, interest revenue, and return of the asset assuming the estimate of residual value remained correct.
3. How would the lessor's entries differ at the end of the lease term assuming the market value of the returned machine was $6,000 (instead of the $8,000 estimated residual value)?
4. Show how the lessor computed the annual rental of $27,180.

Problem 22-10

Schoedsack Company purchased a machine (for leasing purposes) on December 31, 19A, for $300,000 cash on which it received a 10% investment credit (i.e., a reduction in its 19A income taxes payable equal to 10% of the cost). By prior agreement the machine was delivered to Cooper Corporation (lessee) under a direct financing lease whereby Cooper paid the first lease rental of $73,516 on December 31, 19A, and agreed to pay three more such annual rentals at each

year-end. At the end of the four-year lease term the machine will revert to the lessor, at which time it is expected to have a residual value of $20,000 (none of which was guaranteed by the lessee). The lessor's implicit interest rate was 10% on the net investment (after considering the investment tax credit and the residual value).

Required (round amounts to the nearest dollar):

1. Prepare a lease amortization schedule for the lessor.
2. Give the following entries for the lessor:
   a. To record purchase of the machine on December 31, 19A.
   b. To record the investment tax credit on December 31, 19A.
   c. To record inception of the lease on December 31, 19A.
   d. To record collection of the first rent on December 31, 19A.
   e. To record collection of the second rent on December 31, 19B. This is the end of the fiscal period; recognize rent revenue.
   f. To record interest earned on December 31, 19E.
   g. To record return of the machine by the lessee at the termination of the lease term on December 31, 19E. At this date assume the machine has an actual market value of $17,500 (instead of the $20,000 estimated residual value).
3. How would the lessor's entries differ at the end of the lease term assuming the actual market value of the machine was $23,000 (instead of the estimated residual value of $20,000)?
4. Show how the lessor computed the annual rental of $73,516.

Problem 22-11

Rentit Company entered into a lease with Needit Company on January 1, 19D. The following data relate to the leased asset and the lease agreement:

a. Asset leased—large construction crane.
b. Cost to Rentit, $121,632.
c. Estimated useful life, ten years.
d. Estimated residual value at end of useful life, $4,000.
e. Rentit's normal sales price, $146,913.
f. Lease provisions:
   (1) Noncancelable; the asset will revert to Rentit at the end of the lease term.
   (2) Estimated residual value at end of lease term, $10,000 (none guaranteed by lessee).
   (3) Title does not transfer to the lessee by the end of the lease term.

(4) No bargain purchase option is included.
(5) Lease term, seven years starting January 1, 19D.
(6) Lease payment on each year-end, starting December 31, 19D, $31,200.

Rentit's implicit rate of return, 12% (assume lessee knows this rate).

g. Needit's incremental borrowing rate, 15% (assumed to evidence a good credit rating for problem purposes).

h. Needit has a good credit rating.

i. Rentit has no material cost uncertainties.

Required (show computations and round to the nearest dollar):

1. What kind of lease was this to Needit Company? Give the basis for your response.
2. What kind of lease was this to Rentit Company? Give the basis for your response.
3. For Rentit Company give the entries to record *(a)* the lease at inception date and *(b)* the first rental.
4. For Needit Company give the entries to record *(a)* the lease at inception date and *(b)* the first rental.

Problem 22–12 (based on Appendix)

A lessor arranges financing of property to be leased to a lessee under a leveraged lease contract. The property cost $1,000,000 and is expected to have an eight-year life and zero residual value. It will be depreciated by the lessor by the sum-of-the-years'-digits method. The 10% investment credit will be realized by the lessor in the first year. The lessor has other income as well as from this lease; all income is taxed at a rate of 45% and any losses result in a similar 45% tax saving. The parties agree on eight annual payments of $180,674 each for the use of the property.

The lessor pays $300,000 toward purchase price of the property and borrows the remaining $700,000 at an annual interest rate of 8%. Eight annual payments of $121,810 will amortize the debt and interest.

Required (round all amounts to nearest dollar):

Prepare a schedule similar to Exhibit 22–8 covering the entire lease term. Present proof reconciling cash flow to net income as in that exhibit.

The Statement of Changes in Financial Position

Throughout the preceding chapters, references have been made to the statement of changes in financial position. Since the issuance of *APB Opinion No. 19,* "Reporting Changes in Financial Position" (March 1971), this statement has been one of the three *basic* financial statements (along with the income statement and balance sheet). The APB made it mandatory in the following terms:

> The Board concludes that information concerning the financing and investing activities of a business enterprise and the changes in its financial position for a period is essential for financial statement users, particularly owners and creditors, in making economic decisions. When financial statements purporting to present both financial position (balance sheet) and results of operations (statement of income and retained earnings) are issued, a statement summarizing changes in financial position should also be presented as a basic financial statement for each period for which an income statement is presented. These conclusions apply to all profit-oriented business entities, whether or not the reporting entity normally classifies its assets and liabilities as current and noncurrent.

Opinion No. 19 is particularly noteworthy in that it *(a)* made the statement mandatory, *(b)* required that it be developed on an *all-resources* basis, and *(c)* strongly recommended the title,

statement of changes in financial position. This title is now used almost exclusively. The significance of the statement, as prescribed by *Opinion No. 19,* is that it requires the reporting of comprehensive information on the financing and investing activities of the business. The *financing activities* result in inflows of resources, and the *investing activities* result in outflows of resources.

The words "changes in financial position" are descriptive of the report because the inflows and outflows of resources cause the changes in the asset, liability, and owners' equity accounts during the period. The statement focuses on reporting these changes.

The balance sheet reports financial position at a *specific point in time;* consequently, it is not a change statement. In contrast, the income statement is a change statement; it reports the change in retained earnings *during* a specified period due to operations. The details on the income statement report the specific factors that underlie net income. Similarly, the statement of retained earnings (or statement of stockholders' equity) is a change statement; it reports all of the changes in retained earnings (or the changes in all stockholders' equity accounts) *during* the specified period. Observe, that neither of these change statements reports the *causes* of the changes in assets and liabilities.

The statement of changes in financial position has the objective of filling this gap by reporting the other changes *during* the specified period. To do this, it reports changes in asset, liability, and owners' equity accounts measured in terms of *funds flow.*

This chapter discusses and illustrates development of the statement of changes in financial position in conformity with *APB Opinion No. 19.*

BASIC CHARACTERISTICS OF THE STATEMENT OF CHANGES IN FINANCIAL POSITION

The statement of changes in financial position (abbreviated SCFP) measures the changes in assets, liabilities, and owners' equity during a specified period in terms of the inflows and outflows of funds. The key concept is that assets, liabilities, and owners' equity increase and decrease during a period only because funds are generated and used. For example, the disposition of an asset or incurrence of a liability generates an inflow of funds, and the acquisition of an asset or the payment of a liability causes an outflow or use of funds. In this context the word *funds* is used broadly to mean cash, cash plus near-cash assets, or working capital.

The SCFP, as prescribed in *APB Opinion No. 19,* must be based on an *all-resources concept,* viz: ". . . the statement summarizing changes in financial position should be based on a broad concept embracing all changes in financial position," and "each reporting entity should disclose all important aspects of its financial and investing activities regardless of whether cash or other elements of working capital are directly affected." This means that the statement also must include all direct exchanges of nonfund items, that is, those transactions that involve neither the direct inflow or outflow of funds. For example, if a business acquires a machine (an asset acquisition) and pays for it in full by issuing its own capital stock to the vendor, there has been no inflow or outflow of funds. Nevertheless, under *Opinion No. 19,* transactions of this type must be reported as (a) an inflow of funds (from the issuance of the stock) and (b) an outflow of

funds (due to acquisition of the asset).[1] This means that the statement must report the following:

1. The inflows of all funds during the period and an identification of these inflows with specific changes in assets, liabilities, and owners' equity.
2. The outflows of all funds during the period and an identification of these outflows with specific changes in assets, liabilities, and owners' equity.
3. The net increase or decrease in funds during the period.

In the preceding paragraphs, the terms "funds" and "resources" have been used interchangeably. The inflows and outflows reported on the SCFP are measured in dollars of "funds." For measurement purposes, we must be precise in defining "funds." This general term is used throughout financial and accounting literature with diverse meanings.[2] Because of this diversity, and the need for precise measurement, *APB Opinion No. 19* stated:

> The Statement may be in balanced form or in a form expressing the changes in financial position in terms of *cash,* or *cash and [short-term] investments combined,* of *all quick assets,* or of *working capital.* (Emphasis supplied.)

Basically, this means that the inflows and outflows of funds may be measured in terms of *either*

1. Cash (or cash plus short-term investments; often called the near-cash basis), or
2. Working capital (i.e., current assets minus current liabilities).

In elaborating upon these two bases for measurement, the *Opinion* states:

---

[1] Prior to *APB Opinion No. 19,* these types of transactions were not reported on the old "funds flow statements." This was a significant improvement in meeting the requirements of the full disclosure principle.

[2] Funds is a particularly troublesome term because of the wide diversity of use. It is sometimes viewed as cash only, cash plus near-cash items (such as short-term investments), working capital (i.e., current assets minus current liabilities), assets set aside for a specific purpose (such as a bond sinking fund), and it has yet another special meaning in governmental accounting.

a. If the format shows the flow of cash, changes in other elements of working capital (e.g., in receivables, inventories, and payables) constitute sources and uses of cash and should accordingly be disclosed in appropriate detail in the body of the statement.

b. If the format shows the flow of working capital and two-year comparative balance sheets are presented, the changes in each element of working capital for the current period (but not for earlier periods) can be computed by the user of the statements. Nevertheless, the Board believes that the objectives of the Statement usually require that the net change in working capital be analyzed in appropriate detail in a tabulation accompanying the Statement, and accordingly this detail should be furnished.

Because of these specifications, the SCFP typically has the following general formats:

Funds Measured as Cash, or Cash plus Short-Term Investments

1. Sources of cash, or cash plus short-term investments (inflows).
2. Uses of cash, or cash plus short-term investments (outflows).
3. Net increase or decrease in cash, or cash plus short-term investments.

Funds Measured as Working Capital

Part A*—Sources and Uses of Working Capital:
  1. Sources of working capital (inflows).
  2. Uses of working capital (outflows).
  3. Net increase or decrease in working capital.

Part B*—Changes in Working Capital Accounts:
  4. Net Change in current asset accounts.
  5. Net change in current liability accounts.
  6. Net increase or decrease in working capital.

* The designations "Part A and Part B" are not specifically reflected on the statement; they are used here to facilitate explanation.

The *Opinion* permits the use of either approach. However, the specific basis used must be clearly disclosed, for example, "Cash Provided from Operations" or "Working Capital Provided from Operations."[3]

---

[3] Since cash flows are generally viewed as more critical than working capital flows, and the latter often are larger in amount, there continue to be instances where an entity, by vague terminology, has not clearly disclosed whether the statement reflects working capital or cash. The *Opinion* recognizes this problem by stating: "Terms referring to 'cash' should not be used to describe amounts provided from operations unless all non-cash items have been appropriately adjusted."

To establish a clear-cut delineation between the two approaches to measuring "funds" and to facilitate discussion, this chapter separately discusses changes in financial position on a working capital basis and changes in financial position on a cash (or cash plus short-term investments) basis.

Illustration of Cash Flows versus Working Capital Flows

The SCFP reports significant differences in results when the flow of funds is measured on a cash flow basis rather than on a working capital basis. The distinction between the cash and working capital bases is important in understanding the analyses and discussions in this chapter.

Exhibits 23–1 and 23–2 present analyses of a series of situations to illustrate the distinction between the cash and working capital bases. The resulting SCFP is summarized in Exhibit 23–3. These exhibits should be studied carefully.

In Exhibit 23–1, observe that more cash than working capital was generated in only one of the first three transactions. In item *(d)*, note that total sales caused an increase in working capital, whereas only cash sales caused an increase in cash. Expenses, whether paid or accrued as a current liability, caused a decrease in working capital, whereas only cash expenses caused a decrease in cash. *Depreciation expense does not affect either working capital or cash flow.*

In transactions *(a)*, *(b)*, and *(c)*, the differences between working capital flows and cash flows resulted from the short-term (current) receivables and payables. In contrast, long-term receivables and payables affect cash flows and working capital flows by the same amounts.

In transaction *(b)* of Exhibit 23–1 the $2,000 gain on sale of plant assets did not generate cash or working capital; rather, cash was increased by the amount of the sales price collected during the period and working capital was increased by the amount of the sales price collected in cash *plus* the short-term receivable recorded. Other similar situations will be discussed in detail later.

EXHIBIT 23–1
Inflows of Cash and Working Capital Compared

Transaction			Cash Generated	Working Capital Generated
a. Sold and issued 1,000 shares of common stock during the period, resulting in the following entry:				
Cash	3,000		$ 3,000	$ 3,000
Special receivable (current)	4,000			4,000
Special receivable (noncurrent)	5,000			
Common stock (par $10)		10,000		
Contributed capital in excess of par		2,000		
Total generated			3,000	7,000

Observe that working capital was generated by the amount of current assets received and not by the selling price, the par value of the stock, or the noncurrent receivable.

b. Sold a plant asset during the period, resulting in the following entry:				
Cash	4,000		4,000	4,000
Notes receivable, short term	5,000			5,000
Mortgage receivable, long term	14,000			
Accumulated depreciation	10,000			
Plant asset		31,000		
Gain on sale of plant asset		2,000		
Total generated			4,000	9,000

Observe that working capital generated was the sum of cash and current receivables recognized and not the amount of the sales price, the gain recognized on the sale, or the noncurrent receivable.

c. Borrowed from the bank, resulting in the following entry:				
Cash	30,000		30,000	+30,000
Notes payable, short term		20,000		−20,000
Notes payable, long term		10,000		
Total generated			30,000	10,000

Observe that although there was an inflow of cash of $30,000, working capital increased by only $10,000. This was because the increase in current liabilities for the short-term debt "offset" $20,000 of the inflow. Thus, working capital was increased by the amount of the increase in long-term debt.

d. Net income for the period was as follows:				
Sales: Cash	$40,000		+40,000	+40,000
On account	10,000	$50,000		+10,000
Cost of goods sold:				
Goods purchased for cash	18,000		−18,000	−18,000
Goods purchased on account......	7,000			− 7,000
Reduction in inventory	3,000	28,000		− 3,000
Gross margin		22,000		
Expenses:				
Paid in cash	10,000		−10,000	−10,000
Accrued (liability)	2,000			− 2,000
Depreciation	4,000	16,000		
Income from operations		6,000		
Gain on sale of plant asset		2,000		
Net Income		$ 8,000		
Total generated from continuing operations*			12,000	10,000
Total generated for the period (all transactions)			$49,000	$36,000

* The results of this analysis are *(a)* net income of $8,000 on accrual basis converted to a working capital basis is $10,000 and *(b)* net income of $8,000 on accrual basis converted to a cash basis is $12,000.

EXHIBIT 23–2
Outflows of Cash and Working Capital Compared

Transaction		Cash Applied	Working Capital Applied
a. Purchased a plant asset during the period resulting in the following entry:			
Plant asset	30,000		
Cash	3,000	$ 3,000	$ 3,000
Note payable, short term	7,000		7,000
Mortgage payable, long term	20,000		
Total applied		3,000	10,000

Observe that working capital applied was the sum of the cash paid plus the current liability recognized, not the purchase price or the long-term debt incurred.

Transaction		Cash Applied	Working Capital Applied
b. Cash dividends resulted in the following entry:			
Retained earnings	12,000		
Cash	8,000	8,000	8,000
Dividends payable (current)	4,000		4,000
Total applied		8,000	12,000
c. Payments on debts during the period resulted in the following entry:			
Accounts payable	15,000		−15,000
Notes payable, long term	25,000		
Cash	40,000	40,000	+40,000
Total applied		40,000	25,000

Observe that although $40,000 cash (and working capital) was disbursed, the decrease in working capital was only $25,000. This was because the $15,000 paid on a working capital debt constituted an "offset." Thus, the working capital applied was equivalent to the decrease in long-term debt only.

Transaction		Cash Applied	Working Capital Applied
d. Treasury stock purchased during the period resulted in the following entry:			
Treasury stock (at cost)	8,000		
Cash	5,000	5,000	5,000
Special payable, short term	3,000		3,000
Total applied		5,000	8,000
Total applied for the period (all transactions)		$56,000	$55,000

EXHIBIT 23–3

Statement of Changes in Financial Position (summarized)*
For the Year Ended December 31, 19X

	Cash Basis	Working Capital Basis		Cash Basis	Working Capital Basis
Resources generated (inflows):			**Resources applied (outflows):**		
From continuing operations	$12,000	$ 10,000	Purchase of plant asset	3,000	10,000
Issuance of common stock	3,000	7,000	Dividends	8,000	12,000
Sale of plant asset	4,000	9,000	Debt retirement	40,000	25,000
Borrowing	30,000	10,000	Acquisition of treasury stock	5,000	8,000
Total resources generated	49,000	36,000	Total resources applied	56,000	55,000
			Net increase (decrease) in resources during period:		
			Cash	$(7,000)	
			Working capital		$(19,000)

* This summarized statement omits some details required for full disclosure. It is summarized in this manner for instructional purposes; detailed statements will be presented subsequently.

Criteria for the Statement of Changes in Financial Position

In view of the wide diversity in the old funds statements, *APB Opinion No. 19* specifies certain criteria for developing a SCFP. These criteria may be summarized as follows:

1. The statement should be presented as a basic financial statement for each period in which a balance sheet and an income statement are prepared.

2. The statement applies to all profit-oriented business entities whether or not there is a classification of assets and liabilities between current and noncurrent.

3. The statement should be based on a broad concept embracing all changes in financial position (not limited to working capital or cash). The statement should disclose all important changes in financial position for the period.

4. The statement should begin with the income or loss before extraordinary items, if any, and add back (or deduct) items recognized in determining income (or loss) which did not use (or provide) working capital or cash during the period.[4]

5. The items to be added back (or deleted) in 4 above should be clearly presented to avoid the interpretation that they provided funds (e.g., "Add—Expenses not requiring outlay of working capital in the current period").

6. The effects of extraordinary items should be reported separately from the effects of normal operating items.

7. The effects of all financing and investing activities, including those which have no direct effect on working capital or cash, should be *individually* disclosed.

8. If the format shows the flow of working capital and two-year comparative balance sheets are presented, the detailed changes in working capital accounts nevertheless must be presented.

9. Working capital or cash provided from (or used in) operations should be appropriately described.

10. If the format shows the flow of cash, detailed changes in other working capital accounts should be disclosed in the body of the statement.

11. Terms referring to cash should not be used unless all noncash items have been appropriately adjusted (i.e., unless the cash basis is used).

12. There should be flexibility in form, content, and terminology in the statement; flexibility should be used to develop the presentation that is most informative in the circumstances.

13. It is strongly recommended that isolated statistics of working capital and cash, especially on a per share basis, *not* be presented.

Next we discuss and illustrate the development of the statement of changes in financial position on the *working capital* basis in Part A and on the *cash* basis in Part B.

PART A—STATEMENT OF CHANGES IN FINANCIAL POSITION, WORKING CAPITAL BASIS

Working capital is composed of positive *current* items (cash, short-term investments, receivables, inventories, prepaid expenses, etc.) and negative *current* items (accounts payable, short-term notes payable, accrued liabilities, etc.); the dollar amount of the difference between the two categories of current items represents a "liquid pool" of net working resources. In a transaction which produces a net increase in working capital, it is said that working capital has been generated, or provided; where there is a net decrease in working capital, it is said that working capital has been applied or used. Thus, transactions that involve debits and credits *only* to working capital accounts, such as the payment of a current liability, the collection of a current receivable, or the purchase of inven-

---

[4] An alternative procedure preferred by many accountants, which gives the same result, starts with revenues that generated working capital or cash during the period and deducts therefrom operating expenses that required the outflow of working capital or cash. This approach has the advantage of not suggesting that "adjustments" to net income, such as depreciation, generated working capital, or cash.

tory for cash, neither generate nor use working capital; they merely rearrange the internal *content* of working capital. In contrast, certain transactions that involve debits or credits to *one or more noncurrent* accounts *and also one or more current* accounts, such as the purchase of a *noncurrent asset* with cash or the payment of a *noncurrent debt* will cause *both* the *content* and the *amount* of working capital to change. This distinction is fundamental in the analysis required to develop a SCFP.

A SCFP, working capital basis, necessitates considerable analysis, except in simple situations because the accounts often do not directly provide the required data. Recall from the discussions above that the inflows and outflows of working capital are the result of changes in assets, liabilities, and owners' equity. Thus, the key to developing the SCFP on a working capital basis is an analysis of the *causes* of changes in the current asset and current liability accounts. Such an analysis entails a complementary analysis of the *noncurrent* asset and liability accounts, as well as of the owners' equity accounts. Stated differently, we do not gain additional understanding of the *causes* of changes in working capital by analyzing working capital; we can thereby observe the changes, but an explanation of the causes of the changes in working capital requires an analysis of the nonworking capital (i.e., the noncurrent) accounts.

On page 783 the SCFP, working capital basis, was outlined and two distinct parts were identified: Part A—sources and uses of working capital; and Part B—changes in working capital accounts. A statement for the Adamson Company detailed in this way is shown in Exhibit 23–5. This statement was developed from the comparative balance sheets and other data given in Exhibit 23–4.

The SCFP for Adamson Company (Exhibit 23–5) has four main captions, viz: (1) working capital generated (sources of working capital), (2) working capital applied (uses of working capital), (3) financing and investing activities not directly affecting working capital, and (4) a detailed report of changes in the internal content of working capital (i.e., Part B of the statement).

EXHIBIT 23–4

ADAMSON COMPANY
Summarized Data for the Year Ended December 31, 19E

	Dec. 31, 19E	Dec. 31, 19D
1. Balance Sheet:		
Cash	$ 45,000	$ 30,000
Accounts receivable (net)	38,000	40,000
Inventory	67,000	60,000
Investments, long term	162,000	200,000
Land	128,000	100,000
Building (net)	98,000	
Total assets	$538,000	$430,000
Accounts payable	$ 36,000	$ 40,000
Notes payable, short term (nontrade)	24,000	30,000
Bonds payable	35,000	50,000
Mortgage note payable	100,000	
Common stock	295,000	270,000
Retained earnings	48,000	40,000
Total equities	$538,000	$430,000
2. Income Statement:		
Sales	$100,000	
Cost of goods sold	51,000	
Expenses (including depreciation, interest, and taxes)	16,000	
Total expenses	67,000	
Net Income	$ 33,000	

3. Summary of transactions for 19E:
   a. Net income, $33,000.
   b. Credit purchases, $58,000.
   c. Increase in inventory, $7,000.
   d. All sales were on credit, $100,000.
   e. Cash expenses, $14,000.
   f. Collection on accounts receivable, $102,000.
   g. Paid on accounts payable, $62,000.
   h. Sold bonds payable for cash at par value, $10,000.
   i. Purchased land with cash $28,000.
   j. Declared and paid cash dividend, $25,000.
   k. Paid nontrade short-term notes payable, $6,000.
   l. Sold long-term investment for cash, $38,000 (at book value).
   m. Retired $25,000 bonds payable by issuing common stock. The bonds retired were equivalent to the market value of the $25,000 stock issued.
   n. A new building was completed on the land in January 19E at a cost of $100,000; gave an interest-bearing mortgage for the full amount. The building had an estimated life of 50 years and no residual value; straight-line depreciation.
   o. Depreciation expense, building, $2,000.

APPROACHES TO PREPARATION OF THE STATEMENT OF CHANGES IN FINANCIAL POSITION, WORKING CAPITAL BASIS

There are two basic approaches to preparation of the SCFP: (1) the T-account approach and (2) the worksheet approach. The objective in both approaches is to identify all changes during the period in the balances of all noncurrent balance sheet accounts (i.e., to reconcile beginning and ending account balances). Only by isolating the working capital effects of *all transactions* affecting all *noncurrent balance sheet accounts* can the accountant be certain of having explained *(a)* all the working capital changes, as well as *(b)* all the financing and investing activities not directly affecting working capital of the period.

The T-account approach to preparation of the SCFP is preferred by some for instructional purposes; it works reasonably well for simple situations, such as the Adamson Company. For more complex situations, however, the worksheet approach is recommended because it assimilates all relevant data (including the statement format) on one worksheet page. The T-account approach is illustrated for the preparation of the 19E SCFP of the Adamson Company, and the worksheet approach is illustrated for the more complex situation presented later in the chapter.

Fundamentals of the T-Account Approach

The T-account approach encompasses four steps, as follows:

1. From the beginning and ending balance sheets, compute the change in total working capital during the period. The SCFP explains what caused this change and identifies the financing and investing activities that did not directly affect working capital during the period.
2. Draft the basic format of the statement, using the categories outlined on page 783.
3. In order to identify all sources and uses of working capital and the other financing and investing activities (needed for Step 4), reproduce the original journal entries made to record the various transactions that affected the noncurrent balance sheet accounts. Then analyze the entries for working capital effects and other financing and investing activities. Enter the results of this analysis into appropriate T-accounts for each *noncurrent* account. Do not be satisfied until changes in *all* noncurrent balance sheet account balances of the period have been accounted for. The sources and uses of working capital are summarized below in T-accounts.

4. Based on the data entered in the T-accounts in Step 3, complete the SCFP (i.e., the amounts) by inserting into the basic format (Step 2) the sources and uses of working capital and the financing and investing activities that did not directly affect working capital.

Now we implement these steps using the Adamson Company data:

Step 1—Compute the change in working capital for 19E; it increased by $30,000, as would be shown in Part B of the SCFP in Exhibit 23–5.

Step 2—Set up the basic format of the SCFP as given on page 783 with added details as shown in Part A of the SCFP in Exhibit 23–5.

Step 3—Set up T-accounts for each noncurrent balance sheet account with the beginning balances (i.e., 12/31/19D) as follows:

Long-Term Investments

Beg.	200,000	

Land

Beg.	100,000	

Building (net)

Bonds Payable

	Beg.	50,000

Mortgage Note Payable

Common Stock

	Beg.	270,000

Retained Earnings

	Beg.	40,000

Next summarize the *original* related journal entries and post them to the related *noncurrent* T-accounts so that the data needed for Step 4 (i.e., completion of the SCFP) are all assembled in one place. The journal entries to record transactions (item 3 in Exhibit 23–4) which affected these noncurrent accounts during 19E are presented below. *Working capital accounts are italicized* for emphasis (the letters to the left are keyed to Exhibit 23–5).

a. To close net income to Retained Earnings:

| Income summary | 33,000 | |
| Retained earnings | | 33,000 |

h. To record sale of bonds payable at par:

| *Cash* | 10,000 | |
| Bonds payable | | 10,000 |

i. To record purchase of land with cash:

| Land | 28,000 | |
| *Cash* | | 28,000 |

j. To record cash dividend declared and paid:

| Retained earnings | 25,000 | |
| *Cash* | | 25,000 |

l. To record sale of long-term investments at book value:

| *Cash* | 38,000 | |
| Long-term investments | | 38,000 |

m. To record retirement of bonds payable by issuing common stock:

| Bonds payable | 25,000 | |
| Common stock | | 25,000 |

n. To record purchase of building by giving mortgage note payable:

| Building | 100,000 | |
| Mortgage note payable | | 100,000 |

o. To record depreciation on building:

| Depreciation expense | 2,000 | |
| Building (net) | | 2,000 |

Explanation of the Analysis. Transactions *b, c, d, e, f, g,* and *k* (see Exhibit 23–4) did *not* affect any of the noncurrent accounts and, therefore, need no special attention in the preparation of the SCFP. In contrast, transactions *a, h, i, j, l, m, n,* and *o* did affect the noncurrent accounts. Therefore, each should be analyzed for *(a)* work-

ing capital effects and *(b)* evidence of financing and investing activities not directly affecting working capital. The working capital analysis involves examination of the entries for effects on working capital. These effects were indicated by the italics in each of the above entries. For example, in entry *h,* Cash, a working capital account, was debited for $10,000 and Bonds Payable, a noncurrent account, was credited for the same amount. This transaction generated working capital in the amount of the Cash debit, $10,000.

Similar analysis was used for transactions *a, i, j,* and *l.* In this respect, transaction *a* is an anomaly because no working capital account was involved in closing net income into Retained Earnings. Remember, however, that net income is the difference between (1) all revenues and gains less (2) all expenses and losses of the period. Since revenues usually generate cash or accounts receivable, and since expenses require cash or accounts payable (all working capital accounts), it is assumed in the preparation of the SCFP that all revenues and gains and all expenses and losses affect working capital. This is why the SCFP starts with income, as directed by criterion 4 on page 786.

Nevertheless, certain expenses, as well as some revenues, do not affect working capital of the period. For example, in transaction *o* Depreciation Expense is debited. Depreciation, like all other expenses, reduces income, but the credit side of the entry is a noncurrent account, which has no effect on working capital. Starting the SCFP with income or loss reflects the assumption that all expenses reduced working capital. Because depreciation expense is one expense that does not accord with this assumption, it is necessary to add depreciation expense back into income. In the Adamson Company example, the sum of net income and depreciation expense is working capital generated by *continuing operations,* as shown in Part A of the SCFP in Exhibit 23–5. For similar reasons, certain other expenses, such as amortization of bond discount, amortization of patents, amortization of goodwill, and income tax expense for which the taxes payable are deferred to future periods under interperiod income tax allocation procedures, are also added back to net income to derive working capital generated by operations. On the other

EXHIBIT 23–5

ADAMSON COMPANY
Statement of Changes in Financial Position, Working Capital Basis
For the Year Ended December 31, 19E

Part A—Sources and Uses of Working Capital

Working capital generated:
From operations:
a. Net income $33,000
    Add expenses not affecting working capital in
      the current period:
o. Depreciation 2,000
        Total working capital generated by
            continuing operations .... $ 35,000
Other sources of working capital:
l. Long-term investments sold at book value 38,000
h. Bonds sold 10,000
        Total working capital generated 83,000

Working capital applied:
i. Land purchased $28,000
j. Cash dividends declared and paid 25,000
        Total working capital applied 53,000
    Net increase in working capital
      during the period .... $ 30,000

Financing and investing activities not directly affect-
  ing working capital:*
m. Bonds retired by issuing common stock 25,000
n. Building acquired in exchange for long-
    term mortgage payable 100,000
        Total $125,000

Must Agree

Part B—Changes in Working Capital Accounts

	Balances December 31		Working Capital Increase (Decrease)
	19E	19D	
Current Assets:			
Cash	$ 45,000	$ 30,000	$ 15,000
Accounts receivable (net)	38,000	40,000	(2,000)
Inventory	67,000	60,000	7,000
Total Current Assets	150,000	130,000	
Current Liabilities:			
Accounts payable	$ 36,000	$ 40,000	4,000
Notes payable—short term			
(nontrade)	24,000	30,000	6,000
Total Current Liabilities	60,000	70,000	
Working Capital	$ 90,000	$ 60,000	$30,000

* Each of these items often is reported as both a source and application. Either approach is permissible under *APB Opinion No. 19.*

hand, revenues for which the seller received a long-term receivable, amortization of bond premium, and deferred income tax expense (from interperiod tax allocation) are deducted from net income to derive working capital generated by continuing operations. To accommodate this latter category of *deductions,* the caption under net income in Exhibit 23–5 would be modified to read: "Add or deduct operating items of expense or revenue not affecting working capital in the current period." For each such item, the determination that it should be so treated would be made on the basis of an analysis of the journal entry (to record the item) for its effect on *(a)* net income and *(b)* working capital. In all cases, except for extraordinary gains and losses (which are accorded special treatment), items affecting net income, but not affecting working capital, should be reported in this section of the SCFP, immediately under net income.

In transactions *m* and *n* there were *concurrent* financing and investing activities that did not directly affect working capital because each one involved a *direct exchange.* This can be determined from the fact that no working capital account was debited or credited in either entry. Nevertheless, because such transactions encompass both financing and investing activities of the enterprise, they must be reported on the SCFP. For example, in transaction *m* the issuance of common stock was a financing activity and the retirement of bonds payable was an investing activity, although working capital neither increased nor decreased. One way to report such concurrent financing and investing activities is in a separate section of the SCFP captioned "Financing and investing activities not directly affecting working capital," as shown in the last caption of the SCFP, Part A, in Exhibit 23–5. Another way to report such transactions is shown in Exhibit 23–9, where they are reported as "Financial resources *generated* not directly affecting working capital," and concurrently on the same statement as "Financial resources applied not directly affecting working capital." In Exhibit 23–9, the net effect of the two listings on working capital is zero because they are added to working capital in the "generated" section and deducted from working capital in the "applied" section. The latter reporting procedure is more consistent with the thrust of

the *APB Opinion No. 19;* however, either approach is acceptable.

Now that all of the types of transactions reported on the SCFP have been discussed, we return to the reconciliation of the beginning and ending account balances for the noncurrent balance sheet accounts (the beginning account balances were shown in the T-accounts on page 788). The T-accounts presented in Exhibit 23–6 reflect (1) the beginning balances, along with (2) the *postings* of the above journal entries for transactions *a, h, i, j, l, m, n,* and *o,* which affected the noncurrent accounts (keyed by identifying letters), and (3) ending balances which agree with the ending balances on the December 31, 19E, balance sheet given in Exhibit 23–4. The sources and uses of working capital are summarized below the T-accounts by entering therein the offsetting debit or credit for each entry, *a, h, i, j, l, m, n,* and *o.*

The T-account analysis in Exhibit 23–6 completes the reconciliation of the beginning and ending balances in the noncurrent accounts and provides the necessary assurance that all working capital effects and all financing and investing activities not directly affecting working capital have been identified.

Step 4—The only remaining step in the preparation of the SCFP is to transfer the balances from the T-accounts (as completed above) directly to the appropriate captions on the SCFP. The leftmost column of Exhibit 23–5 gives the identifying letters of the transactions. Observe that each amount that was *posted* from the original entries (page 789), in turn was *transferred,* from the completed T-accounts, directly to Part A of the SCFP. Part B of the statement was taken directly from the comparative balance sheets given in Exhibit 23–4, as required by *APB Opinion No. 19.*

As previously stated, the T-account approach works well for simple situations. This approach can serve as an effective introduction to preparation of the SCFP because the concepts involved in its implementation are identical to the concepts underlying the worksheet approach discussed next (i.e., reconciliation of the beginning and ending balances of all *noncurrent* balance sheet accounts).

EXHIBIT 23–6
T-Account Analysis to Develop Statement of Changes in Financial Position (working capital basis), Adamson Company

Long-Term Investments				Land			
Beg.	200,000			Beg.	100,000		
		l.	38,000	*i.*	28,000		
End.	162,000			End.	128,000		

Building (net)				Bonds Payable			
n.	100,000	*o.*	2,000			Beg.	50,000
End.	98,000			*m.*	25,000		
						h.	10,000
						End.	35,000

Mortgage Note Payable				Common Stock			
		n.	100,000			Beg.	270,000
		End.	100,000			*m.*	25,000
						End.	295,000

Retained Earnings			
		Beg.	40,000
j.	25,000		
		a.	33,000
		End.	48,000

Sources of Working Capital				Uses of Working Capital		
a.	Income	33,000		*i.*	Land	28,000
h.	Bonds payable	10,000		*j.*	Dividends	25,000
l.	Long-term investments	38,000		*m.*	Bonds payable	25,000*
m.	Common stock	25,000*		*n.*	Building	100,000*
n.	Mortgage note payable	100,000*				
o.	Depreciation	2,000†				

* A direct exchange.
† Actually an adjustment to income, rather than a literal "source."

FUNDAMENTALS OF THE WORKSHEET APPROACH

In simple situations, such as in the case of Adamson Company, it is possible to develop the SCFP by *inspection* of the data, or in a more rational way by using the basic T-account approach previously illustrated. However, for more complex and typical situations, one would find the use of a worksheet more convenient if not essential. A worksheet has the virtue of as-similating all of the data in a systematic manner on one page. Another important attribute is that the formal SCFP, Part A, can be copied directly from the lower portion of the worksheet.[5] Ex-

[5] For examination and problem-solving purposes by students, a worksheet generally should suffice without the added onerous burden of copying a formal SCFP. Part B of the SCFP, working capital basis, is purely clerical since it is copied directly from the comparative balance sheets (current assets and current liabilities). For this reason it is wholly redundant; however, it is required by *APB Opinion No. 19.*

hibit 23–8 presents a worksheet that has been designed for analysis of the *nonworking capital accounts* and for sorting the data needed for each major classification on the SCFP. This worksheet provides for the same type of analysis presented above for the T-account approach. Each line in the upper portion of the worksheet can be viewed as a T-account. The worksheet entries are keyed to the list of transactions given in Exhibit 23–7.

Observe that this worksheet is based on the premise that the *causes* of the changes in working capital and nonworking capital financing and investing activities can be found only in an analysis of the *nonworking capital accounts*. In contrast, an analysis of *only* the working capital accounts will divulge only changes in the *content* of working capital. The worksheet deals not with the content of working capital but rather with the *causes* of the change in working capital.

The worksheet is set up with four amount columns and six major side captions. The first column (beginning balance) and last column (ending balance) are taken from the two consecutive balance sheets. The two interim columns (debit and credit) are provided for "reconciling through analysis" the beginning and ending balances for each account listed. The six side captions may be explained as follows:

1. Working capital—This is the working capital at the beginning and ending dates; it is entered on the worksheet *only* for balancing purposes.
2. Nonworking capital accounts—These are the *noncurrent* balance sheet accounts that must be analyzed in detail. They are grouped by debit and credit balances for convenience in analysis. The amounts were taken directly from the two consecutive balance sheets given in Exhibit 23–7. Sufficient lines should be provided for accounts that generally have high activity during the period (see retained earnings in Exhibit 23–8).
3. Working capital generated—This section, paralleling the SCFP, provides for listing the various sources of working capital (inflow). The amounts under this section are reflected on the worksheet as debits.
4. Nonworking capital financing activities—

This section parallels the SCFP and reflects each direct exchange (not directly affecting working capital) as a *debit* (see No. 6 below).
5. Working capital applied—This section, paralleling the SCFP, provides for listing uses (outflows), and the amounts are reflected on the worksheet as credits.
6. Nonworking capital investing activities—This section parallels the SCFP and reflects each direct exchange (not directly affecting working capital) as a *credit* (see No. 4 above). The dual effect of direct exchanges occurs because such exchanges represent simultaneous financing and investing activities.

Completion of the worksheet involves an analysis of each transaction that affected a *nonworking capital account* in a manner similar to that illustrated in the T-account approach (transactions that affect working capital *only* are not entered on the worksheet). Each such transaction is entered on the worksheet in the debit-credit format used when originally recorded in the accounts. All debits and credits to working capital accounts (such accounts are not on the worksheet) are reflected under the analysis of interim entries on the worksheet (second and third amount columns). Transactions that did not directly affect working capital result in debits or credits under the fourth and sixth *side* captions (financing and investing activities not affecting working capital). The following is a step-by-step approach used in completing the worksheet (Exhibit 23–8) for F. P. Corporation:

Step 1: Set up the four amount columns and the six major side captions.

Step 2: Enter the original data from the beginning and ending balance sheets for each nonworking capital (i.e., noncurrent) account from Exhibit 23–7.

Step 3: Analyze each listed account; enter on the worksheet under "analysis of interim entries" only those transactions that affected one or more *nonworking capital accounts* so that all differences between the beginning and ending balances are fully accounted for. The analysis is explained in the next section (the entries are keyed to the transactions listed in Exhibit 23–7).

The illustration for F. P. Corporation presents a situation where the data are more complex than for the Adamson Company and the analysis more involved than those shown in the previous example. This illustration includes the following:

Exhibit 23–7—Basic data for illustration.

Exhibit 23–8—Worksheet to develop SCFP, working capital basis.

Exhibit 23–9—SCFP, working capital basis.

The analysis of transactions and the related entries on the worksheet (Exhibit 23–8) are explained below; the discussions and entries are keyed to the basic data given in Exhibit 23–7. Only those transactions that represent situations different from those explained earlier for Adamson Company are discussed in detail.

	Original Entry	Worksheet Entry
a. Net income for the period:		
Income summary	44,000	
Working capital generated, net income		44,000
Retained earnings	44,000	44,000

Analysis: Net income for the period (1) generated working capital, and (2) affected a noncurrent account (Retained Earnings). The worksheet entry repeats the original entry except for the debit; on the worksheet this debit reflects the generation of working capital from net income, *unadjusted* for nonworking capital charges and credits.

Items *(b)* through *(d)* are not entered on the worksheet because they do not affect a *noncurrent* account and, therefore, do not change the *amount* of working capital.

e. Depreciation expense:		
Expenses, depreciation	7,900	
Working capital generated, adjustment of net income		7,900
Accumulated depreciation	7,900	7,900

f. Prepaid expenses increased $2,000—Not entered on worksheet because there was no effect on a *noncurrent* account (and no change in the amount of working capital).

g. Cash dividend declared:		
Retained earnings	15,000	15,000
Dividends payable	15,000	
Working capital applied		15,000

EXHIBIT 23–7

F. P. CORPORATION
Basic Data for Illustration

Comparative Balance Sheet Data:

	Amounts Reported at—	
	12/31/19A	12/31/19B
Debits		
Cash	$ 30,000	$ 84,000
Investment, short term (X Company stock)	10,000	8,000
Accounts receivable (net)	50,000	80,000
Inventory	20,000	30,000
Prepaid expenses		2,000
Land	60,000	25,000
Machinery	80,000	90,000
Accumulated depreciation	(20,000)	(27,900)
Other assets	29,000	39,000
Discount on bonds payable	1,000	900
Total debits	$260,000	$331,000
Credits		
Accounts payable	$ 40,000	$ 55,000
Dividends payable		15,000
Bonds payable	70,000	55,000
Common stock, nopar	100,000	131,000
Preferred stock, nopar	20,000	30,000
Retained earnings	30,000	45,000
Total credits	$260,000	$331,000

Income Statement Data:	12/31/19B
Sales (all on credit)	$180,000
Cost of goods sold	90,000
Expenses	55,000
Depreciation	7,900
Amortization of discount on bonds payable	100
Total expenses	153,000
Income before extraordinary items	27,000
Extraordinary items:	
Gain on special sale of land	18,000
Loss on bond retirement	(1,000)
Net Income	$ 44,000

Additional data; summary of selected transactions for the year:

a. Net income (per above), $44,000.
b. Purchases (on account), $100,000.
c. Inventory increase, $10,000.
d. Expenses (including income taxes), $55,000.
e. Depreciation, $7,900.
f. Prepaid expenses increased during the year, $2,000.
g. Cash dividend declared, $15,000.
h. Common stock dividend issued; retained earnings debited for $10,000.
i. Issued bonds payable for cash, $5,000.
j. Sold land for $53,000 cash; book value, $35,000; for illustrative purposes, the gain is assumed to be an extraordinary item.
k. Purchased machinery for cash, $10,000.
l. Purchased short-term investments for cash, $2,000.
m. Paid dividend on preferred stock with short-term investments, $4,000.
n. Retired $20,000 bonds payable by issuing common stock; the common stock had a market value of $21,000 (assumed to be extraordinary for illustrative purposes).
o. Collected cash on accounts receivables, $150,000.
p. Paid cash on accounts payable, $85,000.
q. Acquired other assets by issuing preferred stock, $10,000.
r. Amortization of discount on bonds payable, $100.

EXHIBIT 23–8

F. P. CORPORATION
Worksheet to Develop Statement of Changes in Financial Position, Working Capital Basis
For the Year Ended December 31, 19B

Item	Balance Dec. 31, 19A	Analysis of Interim Entries Debit	Analysis of Interim Entries Credit	Balance Dec. 31, 19B
Debits				
1. **Working capital**	70,000	(s) 64,000		134,000
2. **Nonworking capital accounts:**				
Land	60,000		(j) 35,000	25,000
Machinery	80,000	(k) 10,000		90,000
Other assets	29,000	(q–1) 10,000		39,000
Discount on bonds payable	1,000		(r) 100	900
Total debits	240,000			288,900
Credits				
Accumulated depreciation	20,000		(e) 7,900	27,900
Bonds payable	70,000	(n–2) 20,000	(i) 5,000	55,000
Common stock	100,000		(h) 10,000	131,000
			(n–1) 21,000	
Preferred stock	20,000		(q–2) 10,000	30,000
Retained earnings	30,000	(g) 15,000	(a) 44,000	45,000
		(h) 10,000		
		(m) 4,000		
Total credits	240,000	133,000	133,000	288,900
3. **Working capital generated:**				
Net income		(a) 44,000		
Adjustments to working capital basis:				
To remove gain on land			(j) 18,000	
To remove loss on bonds		(n–2) 1,000		
Depreciation expense		(e) 7,900		
Amortization of bond discount		(r) 100		
Extraordinary items:				
Land sold		(j) 53,000		
Other sources of working capital:				
Bonds payable sold		(i) 5,000		
4. ***Nonworking capital financing activities:**				
Common stock issued to retire bonds		(n–1) 21,000		
Preferred stock issued for other assets		(q–2) 10,000		
5. **Working capital applied:**				
Cash dividends declared			(g) 15,000	
Machinery purchased			(k) 10,000	
Dividends on preferred stock, paid with short-term investments			(m) 4,000	
6. ***Nonworking capital investing activities:**				
Bonds payable retired by issuing common stock			(n–2) 21,000	
Other assets acquired by issuing preferred stock			(q–1) 10,000	
Increase in working capital for the period			(s) 64,000	
Total		142,000	142,000	

Note. The following entries were not entered on the worksheet since they caused no change in working capital: *(b), (c), (f), (l), (o),* and *(p); (d)* was subsumed in net income.

* On this worksheet these two captions are illustrative of a variation in format; these two captions may be combined. For example, they are often combined as one item on the SCFP (see Exhibit 23–5).

	Original Entry	Worksheet Entry
h. Common stock dividend issued:		
Retained earnings	10,000	10,000
Common stock	10,000	10,000

Analysis: This transaction (1) did not affect working capital and (2) did not represent a financing or investing activity, although two noncurrent accounts were affected. It merely represents a transfer from one owners' equity account to another, and is generally considered not to be a financing or investing activity under the provisions of *APB Opinion No. 19*. The worksheet entry, identical to the original entry, must be made merely to complete reconciliation of the beginning and ending balances of the two accounts.

	Original Entry	Worksheet Entry
i. Bonds payable issued:		
Cash	5,000	
Working capital generated, other sources		5,000
Bonds payable	5,000	5,000
j. Sold land for cash at a gain:		
Cash	53,000	
Working capital generated, extraordinary item		53,000
Land	35,000	35,000
Gain on sale of land (assumed to be an extraordinary item)	18,000	
Working capital generated, net income (adjustment)		18,000

Analysis: This transaction generated working capital by the amount of cash received ($53,000), rather than by the amount of the gain ($18,000). Since *net* income included the extraordinary gain, and since *APB Opinion No. 19* specifically requires the SCFP to begin with *income before extraordinary items,* the extraordinary gain must be *removed from the net income amount* through an adjustment (credit on the worksheet). This has the effect of restoring net income to the amount desired—income before extraordinary items. Note the subcaption "Adjustments to working capital basis," which includes all items to convert net income (accrual basis) to "working capital generated by income before extraordinary items." This transaction should be traced through the worksheet and then to the SCFP (Exhibit 23–9).

	Original Entry	Worksheet Entry
k. Purchased machinery for cash:		
Machinery	10,000	10,000
Cash	10,000	
Working capital applied		10,000

l. Purchased short-term investments for cash; no entry on worksheet because there was no effect on noncurrent accounts and the total amount of working capital was not changed.

	Original Entry	Worksheet Entry
m. Paid dividends with short-term investments (X Company stock):		
Retained earnings	4,000	4,000
Investments, short term	4,000	
Working capital applied		4,000

Analysis: This transaction used (decreased) working capital (short-term investments) and affected a nonworking capital account.

	Original Entry	Worksheet Entry
n. Retired bonds payable by issuing common stock:		
Bonds payable	20,000	20,000 (n–2)
Extraordinary loss on bond retirement	1,000	1,000 (n–2)
Common stock	21,000	21,000 (n–1)
Financing and investing activities not directly affecting working capital		21,000 (n–1) / 21,000 (n–2)

Analysis: This transaction was a *direct exchange* that affected two nonworking capital accounts but did not directly affect working capital; it is an "in and out" item that must be reported on the SCFP (see page 791). Since common stock with a market value of $21,000 was issued to retire bonds payable with a carrying value of $20,000, a $1,000 loss on retirement was recognized (as required by *APB Opinion No. 29*) which is classified as an extraordinary item (as required by *FASB Statement No. 4*).[6] The $1,000 extraordinary loss is entered in the above entry as an *addition* to net income for the same reason that the gain on the sale of the land was de-

---

[6] *APB Opinion No. 29,* "Accounting for Nonmonetary Transactions" (May 1973), specifies with certain exceptions that direct exchanges shall be recorded to recognize current market value. *FASB Statement of Financial Accounting Standards No. 4* "Reporting Gains and Losses from Early Extinguishment of Debt," (March 1975), specifies that loss or gain on early extinguishment of debt shall be reported as an extraordinary item net of tax. The above amounts are assumed to be net of tax.

EXHIBIT 23–9

F. P. CORPORATION
Statement of Changes in Financial Position, Working Capital Basis
For the Year Ended December 31, 19B

Financial resources generated:

Working capital generated:		
Income before extraordinary items ($44,000 − $18,000 + $1,000)	$27,000	
Add: (Deduct) items to convert to working capital basis:		
Depreciation expense	7,900	
Amortization of bond discount	100	
Working capital generated by continuing operations exclusive of extraordinary items		$ 35,000
Extraordinary items:		
Land sold		53,000
Other sources of working capital:		
Bonds payable issued		5,000
Total working capital generated		93,000

**Financial resources generated not directly affecting
working capital:**

Common stock issued to retire bonds payable	21,000	
Preferred stock issued to acquire other assets	10,000	
Total		31,000
Total financial resources generated		$124,000

Financial resources applied:

Working capital applied:		
Cash dividends declared	$15,000	
Machinery purchased	10,000	
Dividends paid on preferred stock with short-term investments	4,000	
Total working capital applied		$ 29,000

**Financial resources applied not directly affecting
working capital:**

Bonds payable retired by issuing common stock	21,000	
Other assets acquired by issuing preferred stock	10,000	
Total		31,000
Increase in working capital during the period		64,000 ←
Total financial resources applied		$124,000

Changes in working capital accounts:

	Account Balances		Working Capital Increase	Must
	12/31/19B	12/31/19A	(Decrease)	Agree
Current Assets:				
Cash	$ 84,000	$ 30,000	$54,000	
Investments, short term	8,000	10,000	(2,000)	
Accounts receivable (net)	80,000	50,000	30,000	
Inventory	30,000	20,000	10,000	
Prepaid expenses	2,000		2,000	
Total Current Assets	204,000	110,000		
Current Liabilities:				
Accounts payable	55,000	40,000	(15,000)	
Dividends payable	15,000		(15,000)	
Total Current Liabilities	70,000	40,000		
Working Capital	$134,000	$ 70,000	$64,000 ←	

ducted (i.e., to convert net income to the amount "income before extraordinary gains and losses"). In accordance with *APB Opinion No. 19,* the funds implicit in the exchange amounted to $21,000, the market value involved in the transaction. This amount is reported on the SCFP as financing and investing activities, as shown in Exhibits 23–5 and 23–9.

o. & p. Neither *o,* collection of cash on receivables, nor *p,* payment of cash on accounts payable, is entered on the worksheet because there were no effects on noncurrent accounts (and no change in total working capital).

q. Acquired other assets by issuing preferred stock:

Other assets	10,000		10,000 (q–1)	
Preferred stock		10,000		10,000 (q–2)
Financing and investing activities not directly affecting working capital			10,000 (q–2)	10,000 (q–1)

Analysis: This transaction is a direct exchange that did not directly affect working capital; it affected two nonworking capital accounts. It is an "in and out" item that represents concurrent financing and investing activities; hence, it must be recognized on the worksheet (see prior discussion of direct exchanges on page 791).

r. Amortization of discount on bonds payable:

Expenses, interest, for amortization of bond discount	100	
Working capital generated, net income (adjustment)		100
Discount on bonds payable	100	100

Analysis: This transaction did not affect working capital; it affected a nonworking capital account—Discount on Bonds Payable—and reported net income (through interest expense). Since it was deducted from net income but did not affect working capital, it must be *added back to net income as a nonworking capital charge.* This item is similar in effect to depreciation expense previously discussed (see page 789).

s. Entry *(s)* does not represent a transaction; it is an optional entry that may be made simply to balance the worksheet. After this entry is made, two internal checks for accuracy and completeness can be made, viz:

1. Check each line on the worksheet horizontally to ascertain that the interim entries clear out all differences between the beginning and ending balances.

2. Total the debit and credit columns under "Analysis of Interim Entries" at two levels on the worksheet as illustrated; the worksheet debits and credits in these columns must balance at each of these two levels.

STATEMENT FORMAT

APB Opinion No. 19 states: "Provided that these guides are met, the statement may take whatever form gives the most useful portrayal of the financing and investing activities and the changes in financial position of the reporting entity." In light of this statement there is a range of variation in the formats used in practice. It appears that variations of form and terminology can meet the criteria specified in *Opinion No. 19* (see list of criteria on page 786).

In Exhibits 23–5 and 23–9 and at the end of Chapters 4, 5, and 25, various statement formats are illustrated. A SCFP that maximizes explanation and disclosure is presented in Exhibit 23–9 for F. P. Corporation.

PART B—STATEMENT OF CHANGES IN FINANCIAL POSITION, CASH BASIS (OR CASH PLUS SHORT-TERM INVESTMENTS)

The critical problems of cash planning and cash control underlie the need by internal management for meaningful statements of cash inflows and outflows. Also investors need relevant information about the ability of the enterprise to generate cash inflows, the cash requirements, and the related noncash financing and investing activities. Although a SCFP prepared on a working capital basis, as discussed in the first part of this chapter, may serve useful purposes, similar statements prepared on a *cash flow basis* are more relevant both for internal management and investors. The cash flow basis is less subject to manipulation through accounting changes and classifications. Cash is more widely understood than working capital. Statement users may not understand all of the ramifications of the residual known as working capital. Also, working capital problems tend to be reflected first in a weak cash position. The working capital basis is much less objective than the cash basis because of the alternative methods and/or estimates inherent in valuing accounts receivable, inventories, prepaid expenses, current liabilities, and the imprecision in classifying items as current and noncurrent.

In view of the advantages of cash-based statements, one may ask why working capital based statements have tended to dominate in published financial statements. The answer probably lies in the facts that working capital statements *(a)* developed first in external reports, *(b)* divulge less about the critical financing strengths and weaknesses of the enterprise, *(c)* have been given more attention in textbooks on financial accounting, and *(d)* represent precedent (which is difficult to change). In *Opinion No. 19* the APB specified that the SCFP could be presented either on a working capital or cash basis. Unfortunately the APB did not specifically require the cash flow approach.[7] The difference in reporting on a cash basis versus a working capital basis can be observed by comparing the illustrations in Parts A and B in this chapter, since identical data (for Adamson Company and F. P. Corporation) are used in both parts.

Changing from the working capital basis to the cash basis is not difficult since it simply requires the additional analysis of the *noncash* working capital items. Thus, a few more transactions must be analyzed and reported. In the SCFP, cash basis, a separate schedule of the changes in working capital accounts (Part B of the statement illustrated in Exhibit 23–5) is *not required* because the cash flow analysis automatically incorporates these data in the basic report.[8]

The SCFP on a cash basis can be developed by measuring funds as *(a)* cash only or *(b)* cash plus short-term investments. The total of cash plus short-term investments is generally used because both are liquid assets. Cash only is illustrated for the Adamson Company, and cash plus short-term investments for the F. P. Corporation.

In Exhibits 23–1 and 23–2, a series of transactions were analyzed to compare cash flow and working capital effects. The resulting SCFP (summarized) for each basis was presented in Exhibit 23–3. You should return to those illustrations and the related discussions for restudy at this point. Observe that cash generated *from net income* was $12,000. Alternatively, this amount could have been derived by starting with reported net income and adding and deducting as appropriate the noncash items, as was done in Exhibits 23–5 and 23–9 to derive cash generated by operations. In effect, this would convert accrual basis net income as reported on the income statement, to a cash flow basis. Using the data in Item *d* of Exhibit 23–1, the cash basis computation is as follows:

Net income reported (accrual basis)	$ 8,000
Add (deduct) noncash items affecting the income statement:	
Trade receivables increase	(10,000)
Trade payables increase	7,000
Inventory decrease	3,000
Depreciation expense	4,000
Accrued expense increase	2,000
Gain on sale of plant asset	(2,000)
Cash generated from continuing operations	$12,000

In Exhibit 23–3, you can observe the fundamental distinctions between cash and working capital effects of transactions. With these distinctions in mind, we can proceed directly to the development of the SCFP on a cash basis and a cash plus short-term investments basis in more complex situations.

PREPARATION OF THE STATEMENT OF CHANGES IN FINANCIAL POSITION, CASH BASIS

Development of a SCFP, cash basis, requires use of the same techniques discussed and illustrated in Part A of the chapter for working capital. The difference is that instead of focusing on the change in working capital of the period,

---

[7] There are a few situations in which the cash basis statement is required, such as in the land development industry and for companies that do not classify assets and liabilities as current (primarily financial institutions). *FASB Statement of Financial Accounting Concepts No. 1* (November 1978) has recently taken a strong stand for cash flow reports on the ground that users are concerned about cash flows.

[8] It is sometimes suggested that a simple summary of the Cash account, or a conversion of the income statement to a cash basis, adequately reports cash flows for the period. Both of these approaches would be inadequate and apt to be misleading. In contrast, a SCFP, cash basis, focuses on the changes in assets, liabilities, and owners' equity, on an all-resources basis, measured in terms of cash. Conceptually, it is the same as the working capital basis except that funds are measured as cash rather than as working capital.

the analysis is of the *causes* of the change in *cash* during the period. This simply means that *all* of the *noncash* balance sheet accounts (rather than just the nonworking capital balance sheet accounts) must be analyzed. Either the T-account or the worksheet approach may be used. In practice, the worksheet approach is almost always used.

The Worksheet Approach

Since the general format of the SCFP is the same under either the working capital or cash basis, the same worksheet format can be used for both. Thus, the worksheet used to prepare the cash basis SCFP parallels the worksheet format shown in Exhibit 23–8 and reflects some changes in terminology (essentially from the words *working capital to cash*). In the first example, we use the data for Adamson Company given in Exhibit 23–4. The cash basis worksheet for these data is shown in Exhibit 23–10. In preparing the worksheet the summarized transactions are analyzed and entered in debit-credit format under the pair of columns headed "Analysis of Interim Entries." Observe that similar to the working capital basis, the original entries are repeated with adaptation and entry at the bottom of the worksheet for the original debits and credits to Cash. The worksheet reflects the following major side captions:

Cash—Entered on the worksheet simply as a balancing feature.

Noncash accounts—All of the *noncash* accounts from the beginning and ending balance sheets are entered on the worksheet for analysis and reconciliation of the beginning and ending balances. Analysis of the transactions affecting the noncash accounts identifies the sources and applications of cash. As with the working capital approach, we can identify the noncash financing and investing activities that did not directly affect cash.

Cash generated (or sources)—This major caption is subdivided for net income, adjustments to convert accrual-basis income to cash-basis income, extraordinary items, and other sources of cash.

Noncash financing activities.

Cash applied (or used)—This major caption is for cash applied for nonoperating items.

Noncash investing activities.

Net increase (decrease) in cash for the period.

To develop the worksheet (and the related statement) on a working capital basis, *net income* and other amounts were converted from an accrual basis to a working capital basis (i.e., working capital generated by operations exclusive of extraordinary items). This concept is carried over to the cash basis worksheet (and the related statement); that is, net income on an accrual basis must be converted to a *cash basis* (i.e., cash generated by operations exclusive of extraordinary items). Therefore, in Exhibits 23–10 and 23–11, observe that there are "adjustments to convert to cash basis." The adjustments under this caption convert net income (accrual basis) to income *before* extraordinary items, cash basis.[9]

Exhibit 23–10 presents the worksheet, cash basis, for Adamson Company. Detailed explanation of its development follows below.

To develop the worksheet for Adamson Company (Exhibit 23–10), the first amount column (Balance December 31, 19D) and the last amount column (Balance December 31, 19E) were copied directly from the two balance sheets given in Exhibit 23–4. The interim entries reflected on the worksheet for *all* transactions affecting cash (and the direct noncash exchanges) are entered in the pair of columns headed "Analysis of Interim Entries." Each debit and credit to *Cash* is entered in the lower portion of the worksheet and classified as cash generated (inflow) or cash

---

[9] General practice is to start with net income and add (or deduct) the "adjustment" items to derive the cash or working capital generated from operations. Alternatively, some accountants prefer to use a revenue-expense approach rather than a net income approach. This approach gives precisely the same cash or working capital generated by operations. On this point *APB Opinion No. 19* states: "An acceptable alternative procedure, which gives the same result, is to begin with total revenue that provided working capital or cash during the period and deduct operating costs and expenses that required the outlay of working capital or cash during the period. This total should be appropriately described, e.g., 'Working capital provided from [used in] operations for the period, exclusive of extraordinary items.' This total should be immediately followed by working capital or cash provided or used by income or loss from extraordinary items, if any; extraordinary income or loss should be similarly adjusted for items recognized that did not provide or use working capital or cash during the period."

applied (use). When the worksheet is completed, the lower portion reflects the statement of changes in financial position, cash basis. Each entry on the worksheet is briefly analyzed below (keyed by letters with the basic data given in Exhibit 23–4):

	Original Entry	Worksheet Entry
a. Net income, $33,000:		
Income summary	33,000	
Cash generated, net income		33,000
Retained earnings	33,000	33,000

Analysis: This entry on the worksheet reflects net income as a source of cash; it will be adjusted in subsequent entries for *all* items necessary to convert net income (accrual basis) to income *before* extraordinary items, *cash basis.*

b. & g. Purchases of merchandise on credit $58,000 and payment on accounts payable $62,000, which caused Accounts Payable to decrease by $4,000:

	Original Entry	Worksheet Entry
Accounts payable	4,000	4,000
Cash	4,000	
Cash generated, net income (adjustment) .		4,000

Analysis: The *net* effect of the two entries to Accounts Payable was recorded for convenience (two separate entries could have been used on the worksheet). This entry on the worksheet reconciles the beginning and ending balances in Accounts Payable and adjusts net income for the decrease in cash which resulted from the $4,000 decrease in Accounts Payable. In effect, the company paid $4,000 more cash than was implicitly included as cash outflow in cost of goods sold.

c. Inventory increase, $7,000:

	Original Entry	Worksheet Entry
Inventory	7,000	7,000
Cost of goods sold	7,000	
Cash generated, net income (adjustment) .		7,000

Analysis: The Inventory increase required cash and/or accounts payable. However, the entries in *b* and *g* above isolated the effect of purchases and cash payments on accounts payable; thus, the only other element of cost of goods sold is the increase in inventory during the period. Since the full effect of the period's inventory transactions in accounts payable was accounted for in entries *b* and *g* above, the inventory increase must not have been financed with accounts payable. By deduction then, the $7,000 inventory increase must have required an outflow of cash. Therefore, the credit side of the worksheet entry is to adjust net income to a cash basis for this item.

	Original Entry	Worksheet Entry
d. & f. Sales on credit $100,000 and collections on accounts receivable $102,000, which caused accounts receivable to decrease $2,000:		
Cash	2,000	
Cash generated, net income (adjustment)		2,000
Accounts receivable ...	2,000	2,000

Analysis: The *net* effect of these two entries on Accounts Receivable was recorded (as one entry) for convenience (two separate entries could have been used on the worksheet). This entry on the worksheet reconciles the beginning and ending balances in Accounts Receivable and adjusts net income for the cash effect of the decrease in Accounts Receivable.

h. Sold and issued bonds payable at par $10,000 for cash:

	Original Entry	Worksheet Entry
Cash	10,000	
Cash from other sources ...		10,000
Bonds payable	10,000	10,000

Analysis: The sale of bonds was a direct source of cash as reflected in the worksheet entry.

i. Purchased land, $28,000 cash:

	Original Entry	Worksheet Entry
Land	28,000	28,000
Cash	28,000	
Cash applied, land purchased		28,000

Analysis: To reflect use of cash to purchase an asset.

j. Paid cash dividend, $25,000:

	Original Entry	Worksheet Entry
Retained earnings	25,000	25,000
Cash	25,000	
Cash applied, dividends		25,000

Analysis: To reflect use of cash for dividends.

k. Paid short-term note (nontrade), $6,000:

	Original Entry	Worksheet Entry
Note payable, short term (nontrade)	6,000	6,000
Cash	6,000	
Cash applied, nontrade note paid		6,000

Analysis: To reflect use of cash to pay a liability.

l. Sold long-term investment (at cost), $38,000:

	Original Entry	Worksheet Entry
Cash	38,000	
Cash from other sources ...		38,000
Investment, long term	38,000	38,000

EXHIBIT 23–10

ADAMSON COMPANY
Worksheet to Develop Statement of Changes in Financial Position, Cash Basis
For the Year Ended December 31, 19E

Item	Balance Dec. 31, 19D	Analysis of Interim Entries Debit		Analysis of Interim Entries Credit		Balance Dec. 31, 19E
Debits						
1. **Cash**	30,000	*(p)*	15,000			45,000
2. **Noncash accounts:**						
Accounts receivable (net)	40,000			*(d & f)*	2,000	38,000
Inventory	60,000	*(c)*	7,000			67,000
Investments, long term	200,000			*(l)*	38,000	162,000
Land	100,000	*(i)*	28,000			128,000
Building (net)		*(n–1)*	100,000	*(o)*	2,000	98,000
Total debits	430,000					538,000
Credits						
Accounts payable	40,000	*(b & g)*	4,000			36,000
Notes payable, short term (nontrade)	30,000	*(k)*	6,000			24,000
Bonds payable	50,000	*(m–1)*	25,000	*(h)*	10,000	35,000
Mortgage note payable				*(n–2)*	100,000	100,000
Common stock, no par	270,000			*(m–2)*	25,000	295,000
Retained earnings	40,000	*(j)*	25,000	*(a)*	33,000	48,000
Total credits...................	430,000		210,000		210,000	538,000
3. **Cash generated:**						
Net income		*(a)*	33,000			
Adjustments to derive cash basis:						
Inventory increase				*(c)*	7,000	
Accounts payable decrease				*(b & g)*	4,000	
Accounts receivable decrease		*(d & f)*	2,000			
Depreciation expense		*(o)*	2,000			
Cash from other sources:						
Long-term investments sold		*(l)*	38,000			
Bonds payable sold		*(h)*	10,000			
4. **Noncash financing activities:**						
Common stock issued to retire bonds payable		*(m–2)*	25,000			
Mortgage note payable issued for building		*(n–2)*	100,000			
5. **Cash applied:**						
Land purchased				*(i)*	28,000	
Dividends declared and paid				*(j)*	25,000	
Notes paid, short term (nontrade)				*(k)*	6,000	
6. **Noncash investing activities:**						
Bonds payable retired by issuing common stock				*(m–1)*	25,000	
Building acquired, gave long-term mortgage				*(n–1)*	100,000	
Net increase in cash for the period				*(p)*	15,000	
			210,000		210,000	

Based on data provided in Exhibit 23–4.

EXHIBIT 23–11

ADAMSON COMPANY
Statement of Changes in Financial Position, Cash Basis
For the Year Ended December 31, 19E

Cash generated:

Income before extraordinary items	$33,000	
Add (deduct) items to convert to cash basis:		
Inventory increase	(7,000)	
Trade payables decrease	(4,000)	
Trade receivables decrease	2,000	
Depreciation expense	2,000	
Total cash generated by continuing operations		$ 26,000
Other sources of cash:		
Long-term investment sold	38,000	
Bonds payable sold	10,000	48,000
Total cash generated		74,000

Cash applied:

Land purchased	$28,000	
Dividends paid	25,000	
Notes—short term (nontrade) paid	6,000	
Total cash applied		59,000
Increase in cash for the period		$ 15,000

**Financing and investing activities
not directly affecting cash:***

Bonds payable retired by issuing common stock	$ 25,000
Building acquired, gave long-term mortgage note payable	100,000
Total	$125,000

* Each of these items often is shown as both a source and an application.

Analysis: To reflect a source of cash (other than from sales revenue). There was no gain or loss because the disposal of the investment was at cost. Had there been a gain or loss, an "adjustment" of net income for the amount of the gain or loss would be necessary (see Exhibit 23–12) to adjust net income to income before extraordinary items.

m. Retired $25,000 bonds payable by issuing common stock of an equivalent value:

	Original Entry	Worksheet Entry
Bonds payable	25,000	25,000 (*m*–1)
Common stock	25,000	25,000 (*m*–2)
Financing activities		25,000 (*m*–2)
Investing activities		25,000 (*m*–1)

Analysis: This transaction is a *direct exchange;* therefore, (1) it did not directly affect cash and (2) it affected only noncash accounts, yet it constituted concurrent financing and investing activities. To report on an all-resources basis it must be included as both a source and use of cash. This is accomplished with two entries on the worksheet: *m*–1 reflects the use of cash (an investing activity—retirement of the debt), and *m*–2 reflects the source of cash (a financing activity—issuance of the common stock).

n. Purchased new building; gave a long-term mortgage for the purchase price, $100,000:

Building	100,000	100,000 (*n*–1)
Mortgage note payable		100,000 (*n*–2)
Financing activities		100,000 (*n*–2)
Investing activities		100,000 (*n*–1)

Analysis: This transaction is a *direct exchange* similar to entry *(m)* above, and is analyzed and recorded on the worksheet in a similar manner. *(Continued on p. 805)*

EXHIBIT 23–12

F. P. CORPORATION
Worksheet to Develop a Statement of Changes in Financial Position, Cash Plus Short-term Investments Basis
For the Year Ended December 31, 19B

Item	Balance Dec. 31, 19A	Analysis of Interim Entries — Debit	Analysis of Interim Entries — Credit	Balance Dec. 31, 19B
Debits				
1. **Cash plus short-term investments**	40,000	(s) 52,000		92,000
2. **Noncash accounts:**				
Accounts receivable (net)	50,000	(a & o) 30,000		80,000
Inventory	20,000	(c) 10,000		30,000
Prepaid expenses		(f) 2,000		2,000
Land	60,000		(j) 35,000	25,000
Machinery	80,000	(k) 10,000		90,000
Other assets	29,000	(q–1) 10,000		39,000
Discount on bonds payable	1,000		(r) 100	900
Total debits	280,000			358,900
Credits				
Accumulated depreciation	20,000		(e) 7,900	27,900
Accounts payable	40,000		(b & p) 15,000	55,000
Dividends payable			(g–2) 15,000	15,000
Bonds payable	70,000	(n–2) 20,000	(i) 5,000	55,000
Common stock	100,000		(h) 10,000	131,000
			(n–1) 21,000	
Preferred stock	20,000		(q–2) 10,000	30,000
Retained earnings	30,000	(g–1) 15,000	(a) 44,000	45,000
		(h) 10,000		
		(m) 4,000		
Total credits	280,000	163,000	163,000	358,900
3. **Financial resources generated:**				
Net income		(a) 44,000		
Adjustments to cash basis:				
To remove gain on land			(j) 18,000	
To remove loss on bonds		(n–2) 1,000		
Depreciation expense		(e) 7,900		
Amortization of bond discount......		(r) 100		
Inventory increase			(c) 10,000	
Prepaid expenses increase			(f) 2,000	
Accounts receivable increase			(a & o) 30,000	
Accounts payable increase		(b & p) 15,000		
Extraordinary items generating cash:				
Land sold		(j) 53,000		
Cash from other sources:				
Bonds payable sold		(i) 5,000		
4. **Noncash financing activities:**				
Liability for dividends declared		(g–2) 15,000		
Common stock issued to retire bonds ...		(n–1) 21,000		
Preferred stock issued for other assets .		(q–2) 10,000		
5. **Financial resources applied:**				
Cash applied for nonoperating items:				
Machinery purchased			(k) 10,000	
Dividends on preferred stock paid				
with short-term investments			(m) 4,000	
6. **Noncash investing activities:**				
Dividends declared but not paid			(g–1) 15,000	
Bonds retired by issuing common				
stock			(n–2) 21,000	
Other assets acquired by issuing				
preferred stock			(q–1) 10,000	
Increase in cash during the period			(s) 52,000	
		172,000	172,000	

Based on data provided in Exhibit 23–7.

EXHIBIT 23–13

F. P. CORPORATION
Statement of Changes in Financial Position,
Cash Plus Short-Term Investments Basis
For the Year Ended December 31, 19B

Financial resources generated:
Cash generated:
  Net income before extraordinary items $27,000
  Add (deduct) items to convert to cash basis:
    Depreciation expense 7,900
    Amortization of discount on bonds payable 100
    Inventory increase .... (10,000)
    Prepaid expenses increase .... (2,000)
    Trade accounts receivable increase .... (30,000)
    Trade accounts payable increase 15,000

Total cash generated by continuing operations exclusive of extraordinary items .		$ 8,000
Extraordinary items generating cash:		
Land sold		53,000
Total cash generated by operations		61,000
Other sources of cash:		
Bonds issued		5,000
Total cash generated		66,000
Financial resources generated not directly affecting cash:		
Liability for dividends declared but not paid	15,000	
Common stock issued to retire bonds payable	21,000	
Preferred stock issued for other assets	10,000	
Total		46,000
Total financial resources generated		$112,000

Financial resources applied:

Cash applied:		
Machinery purchased	10,000	
Dividends on preferred stock paid with short-term investments	4,000	
Total		14,000
Financial resources applied not directly affecting cash:		
Cash dividends declared but not paid	15,000	
Bonds payable retired by issuing common stock	21,000	
Other assets acquired by issuing preferred stock	10,000	
Total		46,000
Increase in cash and short-term investments during the period		52,000
Total financial resources applied		$112,000

Based on analysis given in Exhibit 23–12.

---

o. Depreciation expense for the period, $2,000:

	Original Entry	Worksheet Entry
Expenses, depreciation	2,000	
Cash generated, net		
income (adjustment)		2,000
Accumulated		
depreciation	2,000	2,000

Analysis: This was not a transaction; rather it was an accounting entry that recognized the expense resulting from the use of operational

assets. A noncurrent account Accumulated Depreciation, was credited, and income was reduced. Because it is a *noncash* expense, the amount must be added back to Net Income to adjust it to a cash basis. The worksheet entry attains this affect.

p. This entry is made on the worksheet merely for balancing purposes. After this entry is made, the two internal checks for accuracy, in the Analysis of Interim Entries columns, can be made as reflected in Exhibit 23–10.

The above entries identify on the worksheet all of the cash inflows, cash outflows, and the noncash financing and investing activities for the period in the manner needed for the SCFP, cash basis.

The completed worksheet in Exhibit 23–10 provides all of the details needed to prepare the SCFP on a cash basis in conformity with the criteria of *APB Opinion No. 19.* Observe on the cash basis statement, in contrast to the working capital basis statement, that it is not necessary to include a section comparable to "Changes in Working Capital Accounts." As was discussed in respect to the working capital basis, the SCFP on a cash basis may be prepared under flexible guidelines. The cash basis statement is illustrated in Exhibit 23–11.

COMPREHENSIVE ILLUSTRATION, CASH PLUS SHORT-TERM INVESTMENTS

The data for F. P. Corporation provided in Exhibit 23–7 are used to illustrate some of the complexities omitted from the previous illustration. The cash equivalent (i.e., cash plus short-term investments) basis worksheet is reflected in Exhibit 23–12 and the resulting SCFP, cash equivalent basis, is shown in Exhibit 23–13. You are urged to follow each transaction through the worksheet, remembering the principles and concepts previously discussed. In this respect it should be helpful to compare this worksheet and statement with those for the F. P. Corporation on a working capital basis as reflected in Exhibits 23–8 and 23–9.

A comparison of the SCFP, cash basis, for Adamson Company with that for F. P. Corporation, as well as those presented at the end of Chapters 4, 5, and 25, will reflect the flexibility in format and terminology permitted by *APB Opinion No. 19.* No single format can universally be declared to be the best because of the differing characteristics of each situation. However, reasonable uniformity as to terminology and format will better serve the users of financial statements.

QUESTIONS

1. Briefly explain the objectives and significance of the SCFP.

2. Distinguish between an investing activity and a financing activity.

3. Explain the all-resources concept as applied to the SCFP.

4. Explain the basic measurement distinction between the cash basis and the working capital basis for the SCFP.

5. Why is it necessary to analyze the changes in the noncurrent accounts, rather than the changes in the current accounts, in developing the SCFP, working capital basis?

6. The income statement for X Company reported a net income of $10,000. The statement also showed a deduction for depreciation of $5,000 and an increase in accounts receivable of $8,000. Give the (a) cash and (b) working capital generated by operations and explain why each is different from net income.

7. The income statement for Y Company reported a net loss of $7,000. The statement also showed a deduction for depreciation of $6,000 and amortization of patents of $3,000. In addition, the statement showed amortization of premium on bonds payable of $1,000. Compute the working capital generated by operations and explain why it is different from the net loss.

8. There are two "parts" to the SCFP, working capital basis, and only one part to the cash basis statement. Explain.

9. Give an example of working capital generated involving (a) noncurrent assets, (b) noncurrent liabilities, (c) capital stock, and (d) retained earnings.

10. Give an example of working capital applied involving (a) noncurrent assets, (b) noncurrent liabilities, (c) capital stock, and (d) retained earnings.

11. Assume the sale of an operational asset that cost $50,000, half depreciated, for $5,000 cash plus a $15,000, one-year, interest-bearing note. How much cash was generated? How much working capital was generated? Explain why an adjustment to the net income for the loss or gain on this transaction is necessary to determine the amount of cash or working capital generated from operations.

12. Explain why net income is adjusted for the depreciation amount but not for the estimated bad debt

amount in determining working capital generated. How do the two expenses affect cash flow?

13. Why is the cash basis often more relevant than the working capital basis for evaluating the financing and investing activities of an enterprise?

DECISION CASE 23-1

The following statement was prepared by the controller of the Clovis Company. The controller indicated that this statement was prepared under the "all financial resources" concept of funds, which is the broadest concept of funds and includes all financing and investing activities.

CLOVIS COMPANY
Statement of Source and Application of Funds
December 31, 19B

Funds were provided by:
Contribution of plant site by the city of Camden (Note 1)	$115,000
Net income after extraordinary items per income statement (Note 2)	75,000
Issuance of note payable—due 19F	60,000
Depreciation and amortization	50,000
Deferred income taxes relating to accelerated depreciation	10,000
Sale of equipment—book value (Note 3).....	5,000
Total funds provided	$315,000

Funds were applied to:
Acquisition of future plant site (Note 1)	$250,000
Increase in working capital	30,000
Cash dividends declared but not paid	20,000
Acquisition of equipment	15,000
Total funds applied.................	$315,000

Notes to Financial Statement

1. The city of Camden donated a plant site to Clovis Company valued by the board of directors at $115,000. The company purchased adjoining property for $135,000.
2. Research and development expenditures of $25,000 incurred in 19B were expensed.
3. Equipment with a book value of $5,000 was sold for $8,000. The gain was included as an extraordinary item on the income statement.

Required:

1. Why is it considered desirable to present a statement similar to the above in the financial reports?
2. Define and discuss the relative merits of the following three concepts used in funds flow analysis in terms of their measurement accuracy and freedom from manipulation (window dressing) in one accounting period:
   a. Cash concept of funds.
   b. Cash plus short-term investments concept of funds.
   c. Working capital concept of funds.
3. In view of *APB Opinion No. 19,* identify and discuss the weaknesses in presentation and disclosure in the above statement for Clovis Company. Your discussion should explain why you consider them to be weaknesses and what you consider the proper treatment of the items to be. Comment on the accounting treatment Clovis accorded research and development costs, depreciation and amortization, deferred income taxes, extraordinary items, the acquisition of future plant site, and the adequacy of the note disclosures. Do not prepare a revised statement.

(AICPA adapted)

EXERCISES

PART A
Exercises 23-1 to 23-3

Exercise 23-1

The balance sheets for TS Company showed the following information:

	December 31	
	19A	*19B*
Cash	$ 4,000	$17,000
Accounts receivable (net)	5,000	9,000
Inventory	10,000	12,000
Investment, long term	2,000	
Operational assets	30,000	47,000
Total debits	$51,000	$85,000
Accumulated depreciation	$ 5,000	$ 7,000
Accounts payable	3,000	5,000
Notes payable, short term (nontrade)	4,000	3,000
Notes payable, long term	10,000	18,000
Common stock	25,000	40,000
Retained earnings	4,000	12,000
Total credits	$51,000	$85,000

Additional data concerning changes in the noncurrent accounts:

a. Net income for the year 19B, $26,000.
b. Depreciation on operational assets for the year, $2,000.

808

c. Sold the long-term investment at cost.
d. Paid dividends of $7,000.
e. Purchased operational assets costing $5,000; paid cash.
f. Purchased operational assets and gave a $12,000 long-term note payable.
g. Paid a $4,000 long-term note payable by issuing common stock.
h. Issued a stock dividend; $11,000 debited to Retained Earnings and credited to Capital Stock.

Required:

1. Prepare a SCFP, working capital basis, for 19B without the benefit of a worksheet.
2. Prepare a SCFP, cash basis, for 19B without the benefit of a worksheet.

Exercise 23–2

The worksheet at the bottom of this page has been set up; you are to complete it in every respect on a working capital basis.

Additional data for 19B:

a. Net income, $23,000 (after tax).
b. Cash payment to retire bonds payable—at par value, $20,000.
c. Amortization of patent, $300.
d. Purchased long-term investment, $10,000.
e. Purchased operational asset, paid cash, $7,000.
f. Purchased short-term investment, $3,000.
g. Depreciation expense, $8,000.
h. Paid cash dividend, $4,000.
i. Sold unissued stock, 500 shares at $19 per share.

(Relates to Exercise 23–2)

DOLLEY CORPORATION
Worksheet, Statement of Changes in Financial Position, Working Capital Basis
For the Year Ended December 31, 19B

Item	Balances Dec. 31, 19A	Analysis Debit	Analysis Credit	Balances Dec. 31, 19B
Debits				
Working capital	30,000			29,800
Nonworking capital accounts:				
Investments, long-term				10,000
Operational assets (net)	60,000			59,000
Patent (net)	3,000			2,700
Other assets	7,000			7,000
	100,000			108,500
Credits				
Bonds payable	40,000			20,000
Capital stock, par $10	35,000			40,000
Contributed capital in excess of par				4,500
Retained earnings	25,000			44,000
	100,000			108,500
Sources of working capital:				
Uses of working capital:				
Change in working capital accounts:				

Exercise 23-3

The records of K Company reflected the following data:

Balance Sheet Data

	December 31	
	19A	19B
Cash	$ 34,000	$ 33,500
Accounts receivable (net)	12,000	17,000
Inventory	16,000	14,000
Long-term investments	6,000	
Operational assets	80,000	98,000
Treasury stock		11,500
Total debits	$148,000	$174,000
Accumulated depreciation	$ 48,000	$ 39,000
Accounts payable.................	19,000	12,000
Bonds payable	10,000	30,000
Common stock, nopar	50,000	65,000
Retained earnings	21,000	28,000
Total credits	$148,000	$174,000

Additional data for the period January 1, 19B, through December 31, 19B:

a. Sales on account, $70,000.
b. Purchases on account, $40,000.
c. Depreciation, $5,000.
d. Expenses paid in cash, $18,000.
e. Decrease in inventory, $2,000.
f. Sold operational assets for $6,000 cash; cost, $21,000, and two-thirds depreciated (the loss or gain is not an extraordinary item).
g. Purchased operational assets for cash, $9,000.
h. Purchased operational assets; exchanged unissued bonds payable of $30,000 in payment.
i. Sold the long-term investments for $9,000 cash (assume this is an extraordinary item).
j. Purchased treasury stock for cash, $11,500.
k. Retired bonds payable by issuing common stock, $10,000.
l. Collections on accounts receivable, $65,000.
m. Payments on accounts payable, $47,000.
n. Sold unissued common stock for cash, $5,000.

Required:

Prepare a worksheet to develop a SCFP, working capital basis, for 19B.

PART B
Exercises 23-4 to 23-7

Exercise 23-4

On January 1, 19A, AC Corporation was organized. During the year ended December 31, 19A, the corporation completed the following transactions:

a. Sold 2,000 shares of common stock, par $10, for $20 per share, collected cash.
b. Borrowed $10,000 on a one-year, 9%, interest-bearing note; the note was dated June 1.
c. On December 31, 19A, purchased machinery that cost $25,000; paid $5,000 cash and signed two notes: (1) a 60-day, 8%, interest-bearing note, face $15,000; and (2) a 1-year, 7%, interest-bearing note, face $5,000.
d. Purchased merchandise for resale at a cost of $40,000 (debited purchases); paid $30,000 cash, balance credited to Accounts Payable.
e. Declared a cash dividend of $6,000; paid $2,000 in December 19A, the balance will be paid March 1, 19B.
f. Income statement:

Sales:		
Cash	$55,000	
On credit	20,000	$75,000
Cost of goods sold:		
Purchases *(d)* above	40,000	
Less: ending inventory	10,000	(30,000)
Expenses (including income taxes):		
Paid in cash	10,000	
Accrued (unpaid)	17,000	
Depreciation	2,000	(29,000)
Net Income		$16,000

Required:

1. Set up a tabulation to derive the fund flows for each item on a *(a)* cash basis and *(b)* working capital basis. Use parallel columns.
2. Prepare a summarized SCFP (cash basis compared with working capital basis for the year ended December 31, 19A, similar to Exhibit 23-3).

Exercise 23-5

Use the data given below to compute *(a)* total cash generated by *operations* and *(b)* total working capital generated by *operations*.

Transaction	Cash Basis	Working Capital Basis
Net income reported (accrual basis)*	$50,000	$50,000
Depreciation expense, $6,000	_____	
Increase in wages payable, $1,000	_____	_____
Increase in trade accounts receivable, $1,800	_____	_____
Decrease in merchandise inventory, $2,300	_____	_____
Amortization of patent, $200	_____	_____

Transaction	Cash Basis	Working Capital Basis
Decrease in long-term liabilities, $10,000	____	____
Sale of capital stock for cash, $25,000	____	____
Amortization of bond discount, $300	____	____
Total cash generated by operations	____	
Total working capital generated by operations		____

* Revenues, $190,000; expenses, $140,000.

Additional data:

a. Net income (after tax), $28,000.
b. Acquisition of operational asset, $30,000; issued 1,000 shares of capital stock in full payment.
c. Depreciation expense, $6,000.
d. Increase in merchandise inventory, $7,000.
e. Decrease in accounts payable, $2,000.
f. Amortization of bond premium, $300.
g. Purchased long-term investment, $10,000.
h. Increase in income taxes payable, $1,500.
i. Decrease in wages payable $1,000.
j. Declared and paid cash dividend, $10,000.
k. Sold operational assets for $5,000 that cost $18,000; accumulated depreciation, $16,000 (not an extraordinary item).
l. Sold 500 shares of capital stock at $11 per share.

Exercise 23–6

The SCFP worksheet at the bottom of this page has been set up; you are to complete it in every respect on a cash basis assuming cash is construed broadly to include short-term investments.

Exercise 23–7

Use the data given in Exercise 23–3 to prepare a worksheet to develop a SCFP, cash basis.

(Relates to Exercise 23–6)

Item	Balances Dec. 31, 19A	Analysis Debit	Analysis Credit	Balances Dec. 31, 19B
Debits				
Cash plus short-term investments	19,500			32,200
Accounts receivable (net)	34,000			34,000
Merchandise inventory	78,000			85,000
Investments, long term				10,000
Operational assets	168,500			180,500
	300,000			341,700
Credits				
Accumulated depreciation	44,000			34,000
Accounts payable	21,000			19,000
Wages payable	1,500			500
Income taxes payable	2,000			3,500
Bonds payable	100,000			100,000
Premium on bonds payable	4,000			3,700
Capital stock, nopar	120,000			155,500
Retained earnings	7,500			25,500
	300,000			341,700
Sources of cash:				
Uses of cash:				

PROBLEMS

PART A
Problems 23-1 to 23-3

Problem 23-1

The SCFP worksheet at the bottom of this page has been set up; you are to complete it in every respect on a working capital basis:

Additional data for 19B:

a. Revenues, $400,000—expenses (including all gains, losses, and income taxes), $375,000 = net income, $25,000.
b. Depreciation expense, $14,000.
c. Cash dividends declared and paid, $30,000.
d. Increase in income taxes payable, $4,400.
e. Amortization of patent, $200.
f. Purchased operational asset, cost $9,000; payment by issuing 600 shares of stock.
g. Decrease in wages payable, $500.
h. Payment to retire bonds payable at par, $50,000.
i. Sold the long-term investments for $40,000 after tax (assume this is an extraordinary item).

j. Decrease in accounts receivable (net), $7,500.
k. Decrease in prepaid insurance, $1,200.
l. Decrease in merchandise inventory, $38,400.
m. Increase in accounts payable, $3,000.
n. Amortization of bond premium, $3,300.
o. Error in recording prior years' income taxes; paid during 19B (a prior period adjustment), $6,600.
p. Purchased land, $28,400, paid cash.

Problem 23-2

The balance sheets of Murray Company provided the information shown below.

Debits	December 31 19A	19B
Cash	$ 4,000	$ 11,000
Accounts receivable (net)	9,000	12,000
Inventory	8,000	5,000
Long-term investments	2,000	
Plant	30,000	30,000
Equipment	20,000	22,000
Land	10,000	40,000
Patents	8,000	7,000
	$91,000	$127,000

(Relates to Problem 23-1)

Item	Balances Dec. 31, 19A	Analysis Debit	Analysis Credit	Balances Dec. 31, 19B
Debits				
Cash plus short-term investments	40,000			44,900
Accounts receivable (net)	60,000			52,500
Merchandise inventory	180,000			141,600
Prepaid insurance	2,400			1,200
Investments, long term	30,000			
Land	10,000			38,400
Operational assets	250,000			259,000
Patent (net)	1,600			1,400
	574,000			539,000
Credits				
Accumulated depreciation	65,000			79,000
Accounts payable	50,000			53,000
Wages payable	2,000			1,500
Income taxes payable	9,000			13,400
Bonds payable	100,000			50,000
Premium on bonds payable	5,000			1,700
Capital stock, par $10	300,000			306,000
Contributed capital in excess of par	15,000			18,000
Retained earnings	28,000			16,400
	574,000			539,000
Sources of working capital:				
Uses of working capital:				

	December 31	
Credits	19A	19B
Accumulated depreciation—plant	$ 7,000	$ 10,000
Accumulated depreciation—equipment	10,000	8,000
Accounts payable	8,000	2,000
Wages payable	1,000	
Notes payable, long term	10,000	19,000
Common stock, par $10	50,000	75,000
Retained earnings	5,000	13,000
	$91,000	$127,000

Additional data:

a. Net income for the year, $12,000.
b. Depreciation on plant for the year, $3,000.
c. Depreciation on equipment for the year, $2,000.
d. Amortization of patents for the year, $1,000.
e. Sales on account, $67,000.
f. Purchases on account, $35,000.
g. Expenses paid in cash (including any prior years accrued wages), $15,000.
h. At the end of the year sold equipment costing $8,000 (50% depreciated) for $3,000 cash, net of tax (this was not an extraordinary item).
i. Purchased land costing $10,000; paid $2,000 cash, gave long-term note for the balance.
j. Paid $4,000 on long-term notes.
k. Sold $10,000 capital stock at par.
l. Purchased equipment costing $10,000; paid half in cash, balance due in three years (interest-bearing note).
m. Issued 1,500 shares common stock (at par) for land that cost $20,000, balance in cash.
n. Collections on accounts receivable, $64,000.
o. Payment on accounts payable, $41,000.
p. Sold the long-term investments for $8,000 cash, net of tax (assume this was an extraordinary item).
q. Paid dividends, $4,000.

Required:

1. Prepare a worksheet (or use the T-account approach) to develop a SCFP, working capital basis, for 19B. Key your entries.
2. If you used the T-account approach, prepare a SCFP (unless directed otherwise by your instructor).

Problem 23–3

The records of Mills Trading Company provided the following summaries and data:

1. Income statement for the month of April 19A:

Sales			$ 80,000
Less: Purchases	$ 40,000		
Increase in inventory	(5,000)	35,000	
		45,000	
Expenses:			
Depreciation	$ 5,000		
Bad debts	1,000		
Insurance	1,000		
Interest	2,000		
Salaries and wages	12,000		
Other expenses (including income taxes)	16,000		
Loss on sale of operational assets	2,000		
Total expenses		39,000	
Net Income		$ 6,000	

2. Balance sheets (unclassified):

	March 31, 19A	April 30, 19A
Cash	$ 15,000	$ 31,000
Accounts receivable	30,000	28,500
Allowance for doubtful accounts	1,500*	2,000*
Inventory	10,000	15,000
Prepaid insurance	2,400	1,400
Operational assets	80,000	81,000
Accumulated depreciation	20,000*	16,000*
Land	40,100	81,100
Total	$156,000	$220,000
Accounts payable	$ 10,000	$ 11,000
Wages payable	2,000	1,000
Interest payable		1,000
Notes payable, long term	20,000	46,000
Common stock, nopar	100,000	136,000
Retained earnings	24,000	25,000
Total	$156,000	$220,000

* Deductions.

3. Cash account:

Debits

Balance	$15,000
Sales	20,000
Operational assets	4,000
Sales	15,000
Notes payable	20,000
Sales	15,000
Accounts receivable	31,000
Common stock	5,000

Credits

Purchases	$10,000
Salaries and wages	5,000
Accounts payable	4,000
Salaries and wages	2,000
Purchases	5,000
Expenses	6,000

Dividends	5,000
Purchases	5,000
Expenses	10,000
Accounts payable	6,000
Land	20,000
Accounts payable	9,000
Wages	6,000
Interest	1,000

4. Retained Earnings account showed a debit for dividends.
5. Wrote off $500 accounts receivable as uncollectible.
6. Acquired land for common stock issued.
7. Acquired operational assets costing $16,000; gave three-year, interest-bearing note.
8. Paid a $10,000 long-term note by issuing common stock to the creditor.

Required:

1. Prepare a worksheet (or use the T-account approach) to develop a SCFP, working capital basis.
2. If you used the T-account approach, prepare a SCFP (unless directed otherwise by your instructor).

PART B
Problems 23–4 to 23–6

Problem 23–4

Use the data given in Problem 23–1.

Required:

1. Prepare a worksheet to develop a SCFP, cash (including short-term investments) basis.
2. Unless directed otherwise by your instructor, prepare a SCFP, cash (including short-term investments) basis.

Problem 23–5

Use the data given in Problem 23–2.

Required:

1. Prepare a worksheet to develop a SCFP, cash basis.
2. Unless directed otherwise by your instructor, prepare a SCFP, cash basis.

Problem 23–6

Use the data given in Problem 23–3.

Required:

1. Prepare a worksheet to develop a SCFP, cash basis.
2. Unless directed otherwise by your instructor, prepare a SCFP, cash basis.

Problem 23–7

(A review that also emphasizes Chapters 9 and 19.)
The year-end financial statements of Acres Company are presented below:

(Relates to Problem 23–7)

Balance Sheets
December 31, 19B, and 19C

	19B		19C	
Cash		$ 8,000		$ 9,000
Accounts receivable	$19,000		$16,000	
Less: Allowance for doubtful accounts	1,000	18,000	1,000	15,000
Inventories at lower of cost or market		45,000		44,000
Long-term investment, Jones, Inc., at equity				15,000
Long-term investment, Campbell Company:				
Common stock, at cost	14,000		12,000	
Less: Allowance to reduce to market	2,000	12,000	–0–	12,000
Property, plant, and equipment	60,000		74,000	
Less: Accumulated depreciation	18,000	42,000	19,000	55,000
Total Assets		$125,000		$150,000
Accounts payable		$ 6,000		$ 11,300
Income taxes payable		2,000		4,000
Deferred income taxes payable, current		2,000		3,000
Current maturity on serial bonds payable		1,000		1,000
Deferred income taxes payable, long term				1,000
Serial bonds payable, 5%, maturing in $1,000				
annual serials beginning January 1, 19A		22,000		21,000
Premium on serial bonds payable		1,100		1,000
Notes payable, long term				4,000

	19B	19C
Common stock, par $10	45,000	50,000
Contributed capital in excess of par	3,900	5,000
Retained earnings.......................................	44,000	48,700
Unrealized loss on long-term investments	(2,000)	
Total Equities	$125,000	$150,000

Income Statement
Year Ended December 31, 19C

Sales revenue		$100,000
Cost of goods sold		65,000
Gross margin		35,000
Operating expenses:		
Depreciation..	$4,000	
Interest	1,000	
Income taxes:		
Current payable	8,000	
Deferred, current	3,000	
Deferred, long term	1,000	17,000
Operating income		18,000
Investment revenue (Jones, Inc.)..		2,700
Income before extraordinary items		20,700
Extraordinary gains and losses (assumed extraordinary for problem purposes only):		
Realized gain on sale of investments (net of tax)	3,000	
Loss on sale of machinery (net of tax)	1,000	2,000
Net Income		$ 22,700

Additional information:

1. During 19C part of the long-term investment in the common stock of Campbell Company was sold for $5,000. The acquisition cost of these shares was $2,000.
2. During 19C machinery was sold for $1,000 cash; the cost of this machinery was $5,000; accumulated depreciation to date of disposal was $3,000.
3. During 19C Acres Company purchased machinery. The total cost was paid in cash except for $4,000 which was financed by a long-term note payable.
4. Dividends declared and paid during 19C amounted to $18,000.
5. During 19C Acres Company issued common stock with a par value of $5,000.
6. As a matter of accounting policy, due to the immateriality of the amounts involved, Acres Company amortizes the premium on the serial bonds payable each year on a straight-line basis (an equal amount each year). For problem purposes only, assume this practice accords with GAAP.
7. Acres' investment in Jones, Inc., is 30% of the outstanding voting common stock of Jones, Inc. The investment was made on January 1, 19C, with a cash outlay of $12,900. On that date Jones, Inc., balance sheet and related data were as follows:

	Book Value	Market Value
Cash	$15,000	$15,000
Receivables (net)	22,000	22,000
Inventories (Fifo)...............	20,000	23,000
Operational assets (net)	28,000	28,000
	$85,000	$88,000
Liabilities.....................	$45,000	$45,000
Common stock, nopar	30,000	
Retained earnings.............	10,000	
	$85,000	

During 19C, Jones, Inc., earned net income of $12,000 and paid cash dividends of $2,000. All long-term assets of Jones, Inc., have a ten-year estimated useful life and no residual value.

Required:

Prepare a SCFP for the company on the working capital basis for 19C. You need not prepare the bottom portion of the statement for "Changes in Working Capital Accounts." Also, you may use the T-account approach, the worksheet approach, or any other approach to develop the data for the SCFP (unless directed otherwise by your instructor).

Accounting Changes, Error Correction, and Incomplete Records

Accountants sometimes encounter situations in which changes in accounting methods and estimates and error corrections must be made. Incomplete records, particularly prevalent in very small businesses, constitute a similar problem area for the accountant. In recognition of these distinct problems, this chapter is divided into two parts: Part A discusses the categories of accounting changes and error correction. Part B discusses the preparation of financial statements from incomplete records. There are no new accounting principles and concepts introduced in this chapter; rather, the chapter deals exclusively with guidelines and techniques designed for orderly resolution of the two problems mentioned above.

PART A—ACCOUNTING CHANGES AND ERROR CORRECTION

Current practices and procedures for accommodating accounting changes and errors evolved gradually, and no authoritative body such as the APB dealt with them comprehensively prior to *APB Opinion No. 20,* "Accounting Changes" (August 1971). As a consequence there existed a range of accounting approaches for recording and reporting accounting changes and error correction. Prior to *Opinion No. 20* it was not unusual for changes in accounting, depending on how they were recorded and reported,

to result in a particular amount of revenue or expense over time *(a)* "passing through" the income statement twice (or even three times in a few cases) or *(b)* completely missing the income statement. Accounting changes were widely used for "doctoring" net income or loss. *APB Opinion No. 20* significantly narrowed the alternatives available by specifying the accounting for *recording* and *reporting* accounting changes.

Because of the diversity of accounting changes and errors, *Opinion No. 20,* as a basis for specifying the accounting and reporting requirements, provides the following classifications:

A. Accounting Changes
   1. Change in accounting principle. This is the situation when an enterprise adopts a generally accepted accounting principle or procedure that is different from the one previously used. An example would be a change from straight-line to double-declining balance depreciation.
   2. Change in accounting estimate. As more current and improved data are obtained in respect to accounting determinations based on estimates, a prior estimate may be changed. An example would be the following: Based on new information it is decided that the economic life of Asset

X is 12 years, rather than the 10-year life currently being utilized.

3. Change in reporting entity. Because of changes from the prior period, such as including or excluding certain financial statements of subsidiaries in consolidated statements, the reporting entity is different.

B. Error Correction

Accounting errors may be made and detected in the same period, in which case the correction simply involves correcting the entry that was omitted or recorded incorrectly in the accounts. Alternatively, accounting errors sometimes are found in one period that were made in a prior period. In this latter case, correction of the error is somewhat more complex. Accounting errors may result from the use of inappropriate accounting principles (or procedures), application of *insupportable* estimates, mathematical mistakes, entries to wrong accounts, or failure to properly analyze the economic effects when recording a transaction. An example would be debiting expense for the cost of an operational asset when acquired. The cost, instead, should be capitalized and depreciated over the useful life of the asset.

METHODS FOR RECORDING AND REPORTING ACCOUNTING CHANGES AND ERROR CORRECTIONS

APB Opinion No. 20 recognizes three fundamental ways in which accounting changes and error corrections can be recorded in the accounts and reported on the financial statements. They are as follows:

1. Currently—The cumulative effect of the accounting change is determined. The "adjustment" for this amount is *recorded* in the accounts as a special item (similar to an extraordinary item), and is *reported* in the same manner on the current financial statements.
2. Prospectively—The cumulative effect of the accounting change is *not* determined. No "adjustment" is recognized or reported; rather, the effect of the change is spread over the current and future periods.

3. Retroactively—The account balances in error are corrected and the cumulative effect of the error on Retained Earnings is determined. The correction for this amount is *recorded* in the accounts as a prior period adjustment (which is closed directly to Retained Earnings) and is *reported* as an adjustment to the beginning balance of Retained Earnings.

Because of the dissimilar characteristics of the three accounting changes and error correction listed above, the *Opinion* specifies each of these fundamental approaches. Basically, the *Opinion* prescribes the following (with certain exceptions explained later):

Type of Change	Basic Method
1. Change in accounting principle	Currently
2. Change in accounting estimate	Prospectively
3. Change in accounting entity	Retroactively
4. Error correction	Retroactively

With these fundamentals in mind we can now proceed to a detailed discussion of each of the accounting changes and error correction. In the discussions to follow we will focus on (1) the *recording* in the accounts and (2) *reporting* on the *comparative* financial statements affected.

CHANGE IN ACCOUNTING PRINCIPLE

A change in accounting principle occurs when a company adopts a generally accepted accounting principle different from a previously used one that *also* was generally accepted at the time adopted. The *Opinion* states that the term accounting principle includes "not only accounting principles and practices but also the methods of applying them." It excludes the adoption of a principle occasioned by events occurring for the first time or that were previously immaterial in their effect. Examples of a change in accounting principle are as follows:

1. A change from straight-line to some other acceptable method of depreciation, or vice versa.

2. A change in inventory cost flow, such as from *Fifo* to weighted average.
3. A change in accounting for long-term construction contracts from completed contract basis to percentage of completion.
4. A change from expensing certain costs to capitalizing the costs and depreciating them, or vice versa.
5. A change in the method of accounting for the investment tax credit.

The *Opinion* states that *most* changes in accounting principle should be recognized by including the cumulative effect (often called a "catch-up" adjustment) "in net income of the period of the change," but that a *few* specific changes in accounting principles "should be reported by restating the financial statements of prior periods" (i.e., retroactively) when presented for comparative purposes. The latter quotation specifies an exception to the basic rule; examples are (1) a change from *Lifo* inventory to another method (see Chapter 11 and Decision Case 24–1), (2) a change in the method of accounting for long-term construction contracts (see Chapter 12), and (3) a change to or from "full cost" to another method in the extractive industries (see Chapter 15). These exceptions were deemed advisable to prevent income manipulation.

The cumulative effect of the change is computed for all prior periods to the beginning of the period in which the change is made, since the financial statements for the period of change must reflect the newly adopted principle. The amount of the cumulative effect should be shown separately *between* "Income before extraordinary items" and "Net Income." The *Opinion* states that it is "not an extraordinary item but should be shown in a manner similar to an extraordinary item." Per share amounts should be shown for the cumulative adjustment reported.

The *Opinion* also requires that income before extraordinary items and net income be shown on a *pro forma* basis on the "face of the income statements for all periods presented as if the newly adopted accounting principle had been applied during all periods affected." This re-

quirement is specified to satisfy the full disclosure principle; it is illustrated below.[1]

To illustrate *a change in accounting principle,* assume Company M has been depreciating a machine for two years which cost $200,000, on a straight-line basis over ten years and no residual value. Starting in the third year the decision was made to adopt double-declining balance depreciation.[2]

The recording and reporting would be as follows:

a. To compute the cumulative effect to beginning of year of change:

Depreciation based on new method—double-declining balance:		
Year 1—$200,000 × 20%	$40,000	
Year 2—($200,000 − $40,000) × 20%	32,000	
Amount that should be reflected in accumulated depreciation		$72,000
Depreciation recorded to date—straight-line method:		
Years 1 and 2—$200,000 × $\frac{1}{10}$ × 2		40,000
Cumulative effect of change (catch-up adjustment, increase in accumulated depreciation balance required)		$32,000

b. *Recording*—To record the catch-up adjustment in Year 3:

Adjustment due to change in accounting principle (depreciation)	32,000	
Accumulated depreciation		32,000

Note. If we assume an IRS-approved amended tax return is submitted and a 40% income tax refund amounting to $32,000 × .40 = $12,800 (less any interest and penalty assessed) is received, the related entry would be a debit to Cash (or special receivable) and a credit to the above adjustment account.

---

[1] *Pro forma* is defined in *Webster's Dictionary* as "for the sake of or as a matter of form." Pro forma statements are "as if" statements; the "as if" assumptions should be clearly stated.

[2] This illustration disregards the tax effects; depending upon the circumstances, deferred taxes should be taken into account and the catch-up adjustment should be shown net of any tax effect. See Chapter 9.

c. *Reporting*—Comparative income statement presentation (ignoring income taxes) at the end of Year 3:

	Year 2	Year 3
Income before depreciation ...	$120,000	$135,600
Depreciation expense (SL)	20,000	
(DDB) — ($200,000 — $40,000— $32,000) × 20% = $25,600 (Note 3)		25,600
Income before extraordinary items	100,000	110,000
Extraordinary gain (loss)	(6,000)	10,000
Adjustment due to accounting change (Note 3)		(32,000)
Net Income	$ 94,000	$ 88,000
Earnings per share (100,000 shares outstanding):		
Income before extraordinary items and changes ..	$1.00	$1.10
Extraordinary gain (loss)	(0.06)	0.10
Change in accounting principle	—	(0.32)
Net income	$0.94	$0.88
Pro forma net income, assuming retroactive application of accounting change*	$ 82,000	$120,000
Pro forma EPS assuming retroactive application of accounting change:†		
Income before extraordinary items	$.88	$1.10
Net Income	.82	1.20

Note 3: Accounting change—During Year 3 the company changed from the straight-line method to the double-declining balance method of depreciation for machinery. The change was made because management believes that the latter method provides a more realistic matching of depreciation expense with revenue. The effect of the change in depreciation method was to increase depreciation expense of Year 3 by $5,600 over the amount of depreciation expense if the straight-line method had been retained. Also, Year 3 income was further reduced by the $32,000 resulting adjustment reported on the income statement.

In accordance with *APB Opinion No. 20*, Year 2 results (depreciation expense, $20,000, and net income, $94,000) are reported on the basis of straight-line depreciation, which was in effect during that year. However, the pro forma presentation below net income provides income data for Years 2 and 3, both reflecting double-declining balance depreciation amounts in comparative form.

	Year 2	Year 3
* Computations:		
Income before extraordinary items, as reported	$100,000	$110,000
Add back straight-line depreciation	20,000	
Deduct double-declining depreciation	(32,000)	(already deducted)
Income before extraordinary items.......	88,000	110,000
Extraordinary gain (loss)	(6,000)	10,000
Net Income	$ 82,000	$120,000

† The pro forma share amounts represent what "would have been" had the new method been used from the beginning. *APB Opinion No. 15* recommends, but does not require, earnings per share amounts for the extraordinary items.

Opinion No. 20 states that a change to another principle can be made only if the enterprise justifies the change "on the basis that it is preferable." The *Opinion* did not specify the criteria for determining when another principle is "preferable."

CHANGE IN ACCOUNTING ESTIMATE

Accounting necessarily requires the use of estimates because future developments and events cannot be known with certainty. For example, the periodic depreciation charge is the result of one known (cost) and two estimates (residual value and useful life). Estimates result from judgments which are based on specific assumptions and projections concerning future events. As the anticipated event or events come closer, it is generally possible to improve on the accuracy of the estimates. As a consequence, the accountant is frequently faced with the problem of what to do about improved estimates. For example, during the first few years' life of a company, the estimated loss rate due to uncollectible accounts necessarily may have a relatively wide range of error because of the lack of historical experience on collections; as time passes the estimated rate is refined as a result of additional information. Thus, changes in accounting estimates are a *natural consequence* of the accounting process. A change in an accounting estimate is viewed as being basically different from a change in accounting principle or an accounting error. Examples of changes in accounting estimates are as follows:

1. Change in the estimated residual value or useful life of an asset subject to depreciation, amortization, or depletion.
2. Change in the estimated loss rate on receivables.
3. Change in the expected recovery of a deferred charge.
4. Change in the estimated realized revenue collected in advance.
5. Change in the expected warranty cost on goods sold under guarantee.

When a change in an estimate has been decided upon, the accountant is faced with the dual problem of *(a)* how to record the effect of the change of estimate in the accounts and *(b)* how to report the change on the comparative financial statements. The accountant presumes that a change in an accounting estimate will be made only when there are sound reasons for doing so, as opposed to intent to manipulate reported income.[3]

Since estimates are necessary in accounting, and since changes in accounting estimates are bound to occur with some frequency, it appears reasonable to account for such changes *prospectively.* This means that the *new* estimate is incorporated in revenue and expense determinations of the current and future periods based on the existing balance in the related accounts. On this point *APB Opinion No. 20* states:

> The Board concludes that the effect of a change in accounting estimate should be accounted for in (a) the period of change if the change affects that period only, or (b) the period of change and future periods if the change affects both.

Since there is no change (or catch-up) adjustment to be made, the only additional disclosure required by the *Opinion* is "The effect on income before extraordinary items, net income and related per share amounts of the current period should be disclosed."

In some situations a change in accounting principle and a change in estimate for the same item are made concurrently. When the effects of each can be separated, two changes should be reflected. However, when the two are indistinguishable, the one that is clearly dominant should be used; if neither is clearly dominant, a change in estimate should be assumed.

To illustrate a *change* in *estimate,* assume an asset that cost $120,000 (no residual value) is being depreciated over a 10-year life. On the basis of new information available after 4 years' use, a 12-year life appears more realistic. The change in the depreciation estimate, starting in the fifth year, would be recognized as follows:

a. To compute annual depreciation for the current and subsequent years (no catch-up adjustment to be made):

Original cost of the asset	$120,000
Accumulated depreciation to date of change in estimate ($120,000 × 4/10)	48,000
Undepreciated balance at beginning of year of change in estimate	$ 72,000
Annual depreciation after change $72,000 ÷ (12 − 4 years)	$9,000

b. Recording—no catch-up adjustment.

To record depreciation for Year 5:

Depreciation expense	9,000	
Accumulated depreciation		9,000

c. Reporting—income statement for year of change, Year 5:

Depreciation expense	$9,000

CHANGE IN REPORTING ENTITY

Changes in reporting entity are to be effected and reported through retroactive restatement; that is, they "should be reported by restating the financial statements of all prior periods presented in order to show financial information for the new reporting entity for all periods." *APB Opinion No. 20,* par. 12, also defines this type of accounting change as follows:

> One special type of accounting change in accounting principle results in financial statements which, in effect, are those of a different reporting entity. This type is limited mainly to (a) presenting consolidated or combined statements in place of statements of individual companies, (b) changing specific subsidiaries comprising the group of companies for which consolidated statements are presented, and (c) changing the companies included in combined financial statements. A different group of companies comprise the reporting entity after each change.

This type of change is discussed in detail in another book in this series.[4]

---

[3] The definition of a change in estimate assumes that the original estimate and the new estimate both represent realistic and good faith determinations based upon the information available at the time the respective estimates are made. A change in estimate not meeting these criteria must be classified as an "accounting error," as defined and discussed in the next section of this chapter.

[4] C. H. Griffin, T. H. Williams, and K. L. Larson, *Advanced Accounting* (Homewood, Ill., Richard D. Irwin, Inc.), 1977.

CORRECTION OF ERRORS

Accounting errors are of two basic types: (1) those that occur and are discovered in the same accounting period and (2) those that occur in one accounting period and are discovered in a later accounting period. When an accounting error is discovered, it should be corrected immediately. The former type of error is not difficult to deal with since the accounts have not been closed and the financial statements have not been issued. This type of error can be readily corrected either *(a)* by reversing the incorrect entry and then entering the correct entry or *(b)* by making a single correcting entry designed to directly correct the account balances. *APB Opinion No. 20* deals with the second type of error; those discovered in a subsequent period.

An accounting error is specifically defined as the *misapplication* of facts existing at the time an event or transaction is recorded. The following are examples of accounting errors, as distinguished from changes in accounting principles or changes in estimates:

a. Use of an inappropriate or unacceptable accounting principle. Thus a change from an unacceptable accounting principle to a generally accepted one would require the correction of an error (not a change in accounting principle).

b. Use of an unrealistic accounting estimate, that is, the misapplication in the accounts of known information at the date of the decision in respect to the estimate. Thus, the adoption of an unrealistic depreciation rate, when discovered later, would require the correction of an error (not a change in accounting estimate).

c. Misstatement of an accounting value, such as for inventory, operational assets, liabilities, or owners' equity.

d. Failure to recognize accruals or deferrals.

e. Incorrect classification of an expenditure as between expense and asset.

f. Incorrect or unrealistic allocations of accounting values, such as, in the allocation of overhead costs during the construction of operational assets for self use.

g. Failure to record a completed transaction.

Errors discovered in the current period that were made in a prior period require that all of the cumulative effects of the error be computed up to the beginning of the current period and a correcting entry to Retained Earnings be made on a retroactive basis. The correcting entry should be made in order to correct the current beginning balance of Retained Earnings and all other accounts affected by the error. The effect of the error correction should be recorded in an account Prior Period Adjustment—Correction of Accounting Error. This account is closed directly to Retained Earnings and serves to correct the beginning balance of that account.

The prior period adjustment, in accordance with *APB Opinion No. 9* (par. 18), and *FASB Statement No. 16,* is reported on the statement of retained earnings as a retroactive adjustment of the beginning balance. As to disclosure, *Opinion No. 20* states: "The nature of an error in previously issued financial statements and the effect of its correction on income before extraordinary items, net income, and the related per share amounts should be disclosed in the period in which the error was discovered and corrected. Financial statements of subsequent periods need not repeat the disclosures."

Below we discuss and illustrate the recording (i.e., the journal entry) and the reporting (in the financial statements) of prior period adjustments under two assumptions:

Assumption 1—Only single-period financial statements for 1979 are presented. In this situation the recording and reporting are parallel.

Assumption 2—Comparative financial statements that include 1979 and 1978 are presented. In this situation the recording and reporting are *not* parallel.

The following data from the accounts of Reagan Company are used:

	1979	1978
Sales revenue	$480,000	$450,000
Cost of goods sold	(310,000)	(300,000)
Depreciation expense	(25,000)	(20,000)
Other expenses	(65,000)	(55,000)
Income tax (at 40%)	(32,000)	(30,000)
Net income	$ 48,000	$ 45,000

Balance in retained earnings,		
January 1	165,000	135,000
Dividends declared and paid		
for the year	17,000	15,000

Assume that during 1978 the company failed to record depreciation of $5,000 on machinery (i.e., depreciation expense in 1978 should have been $25,000). The error was detected and corrected during 1979 (before the books were closed for 1979).

Assumption 1—Only single-period statements for 1979 are presented.

Recording: The 1979 journal entry to correct the account balances affected by the error in recording depreciation for 1978 would be as follows:

Retained earnings, prior period		
adjustment	3,000	
Income tax payable	2,000	
Accumulated depreciation,		
machinery		5,000

Reporting:

REAGAN COMPANY
Income Statement
For the Year Ended December 31, 1979

Sales revenue		$480,000
Cost of goods sold	$310,000	
Depreciation expense	25,000	
Other expenses	65,000	
Income tax expense (at 40%).............	32,000	432,000
Net Income.............................		$ 48,000

REAGAN COMPANY
Statement of Retained Earnings
For the Year Ended December 31, 1979

Beginning balance, as previously reported ...		$165,000
Less: Prior period adjustment from error		
in depreciation for 1978	$ 5,000	
Less: Income tax effect (tax		
reduction)	2,000	3,000
Beginning balance, as adjusted		162,000
Add net income for the year		48,000
Deduct dividends for the year		(17,000)
Balance, December 31, 1979		$193,000

The $5,000 understatement of 1978 depreciation expense caused the December 31, 1978, balance in the Retained Earnings account to be overstated by $3,000 (i.e., the aftertax effect of the error). The entry to *record* the prior period adjustment given above corrects all account balances affected by the error. The correction is *reported* in the statement of retained earnings

for 1979, the period in which the correcting entry was made. When single-period financial statements are presented, the erroneous 1978 financial statements are *not* retroactively restated on a correct basis.

Assumption 2—Comparative statements that include 1979 and 1978 are presented.

Recording: The 1979 journal entry to correct the account balances affected by the error made in 1978 would be the *same* as given above for the single-period statement case, viz:

Retained earnings, prior period		
adjustment	3,000	
Income tax payable	2,000	
Accumulated depreciation,		
machinery		5,000

Reporting: First, we present the 1978–77 comparative statements as they were presented (in error) at December 31, 1978. The 1978 part of these statements should be contrasted with the 1978 part of the 1979–78 comparative statements, which will be shown below on a "restated" basis to reflect the reporting of the prior period adjustment (i.e., for the 1978 error discovered in 1979).

REAGAN COMPANY
Income Statements
For Years Ended December 31, 1978, and 1977

		1978	1977
Sales revenue		$450,000	
Cost of goods sold	$300,000		Assume 1977
Depreciation expense	20,000		data are
Other expenses	55,000		presented
Income tax expense			here.
(at 40%)	30,000	405,000	
Net Income		$ 45,000	

REAGAN COMPANY
Statement of Retained Earnings
For Years Ended December 31, 1978, and 1977

	1978	1977
Beginning balance, from		
prior year	$135,000	Assume 1977
Add net income for the		data are
year	45,000	presented
Deduct dividends for		here.
the year	(15,000)	
Ending balance	$165,000	$135,000

In the two statements immediately above, the following amounts are misstated because of the error in depreciation in 1978: depreciation expense, income tax expense, net income, and the 1978 ending balance in Retained Earnings. The

1979–78 comparative statements below, "restated" on a correct basis, indicate the manner of reporting the prior period adjustment (correction) in comparative statements.

REAGAN COMPANY
Income Statements
For the Years Ended December 31, 1979, and 1978, Restated

	1979		1978 Restated	
Sales revenue		$480,000		$450,000
Cost of goods sold	$310,000		$300,000	
Depreciation expense (see Note 3)	25,000		25,000	
Other expenses	65,000		55,000	
Income tax expense (at 40%)	32,000	432,000	28,000	408,000
Net Income (see Note 3)		$ 48,000		$ 42,000

REAGAN COMPANY
Statement of Retained Earnings
For the Years Ended December 31, 1979, and 1978, Restated

	1979	1978 Restated
Beginning balance (restated for 1979— see Note 3)	$162,000	$135,000
Add net income for the year (restated for 1978—see Note 3)	48,000	42,000
Deduct dividends for the year	(17,000)	(15,000)
Ending balance (restated for 1978— see Note 3)	$193,000	$162,000

Note 3. Prior period adjustment—During 1979 the company discovered that depreciation expense for 1978 had been understated by $5,000 (aftertax effect on net income was $3,000). Accordingly, the 1978 statements, as reported above, have been restated on a correct basis.

Depreciation expense of $25,000 for 1978 on the income statement reflects the prior period adjustment for the correction of the error. Also, the parenthetical notations in the statement of retained earnings draw attention to elements of retained earnings which were restated as a consequence of the error correction. Note that although the *recording* of the error correction was in 1979, the *reporting* was in the 1978 portion of the comparative statements.

Now suppose the error that was detected and corrected in 1979 had occurred in 1977 (or earlier). In this instance the 1979 journal entry to *record* the prior period adjustment (error correction) would be as given above for *both* single-period and comparative statement assumptions. Likewise, single-period statements for 1979 would *report* the prior period adjustment on the 1979 statement of retained earnings—exactly as shown above for Assumption 1.

Under Assumption 2, the comparative statements for 1979–78 would be different from those

reported above. The error occurred in 1977, but the 1977 statements are not presented along with 1979–78 statements. Therefore, the only feasible way to report the prior period adjustment pertaining to 1977 (or earlier) is as an adjustment to beginning retained earnings for *1978* in the same manner as shown for Assumption 1 above for 1979.

In a supplementary summary of income statements covering, for example, five or ten years ending with 1979, the 1977 statements would be restated on a correct basis, regardless of whether single-period or two-year comparative statements were presented for the current year financial statements.

Often the issuance of a new *FASB Statement* requires application of *APB Opinion No. 20;* such statements frequently specify exactly how the change should be accounted for. One example is *FASB Statement No. 2,* which required companies with preexisting asset balances for deferred research and development costs to write the asset off by a direct debit to Retained Earnings.

ANALYTICAL PROCEDURES FOR CORRECTING ERRORS

The accountant needs to use efficient analytical procedures for dealing with accounting changes, whether they relate to principles, estimates, or errors. Changes and correcting entries must be determined, and notes prepared to augment the statement disclosure. This section presents some analytical techniques that are useful for these purposes as well as for problem-solving purposes for students, CPA candidates, and others.

Errors may be classified according to which financial statements are affected. Some may affect only the balance sheet. For example, a credit to Retained Earnings that should have been to Contributed Capital would affect only the balance sheet. Correction would involve a transfer from one *real* account to another *real* account. In this case, balance sheets for future periods would be in error until correction of the respective account balances. Other changes affect only the income statement. For example, a credit to the Sales account instead of Interest Revenue would affect only the income statement. Correction of this error would involve a transfer from one *nominal* account to another *nominal* account. In this case, financial reports of future periods would be unaffected whether or not the error is corrected (since nominal accounts are closed).

A third, and more common type of error affects both the balance sheet and the current income statement. This type may be further classified on the basis of the effect on the current and future financial statements as follows:

1. *Counterbalancing errors.* This kind of error results from failure to allocate properly an expense or revenue item between two consecutive accounting periods. There is no *pretax* effect upon the balance sheet at the end of the second period, since the total revenue and total expense to that date are correct; no error would be left in Retained Earnings or other balance sheet accounts, since the error effect is exactly counterbalanced by an opposite effect the next period. Examples of counterbalancing errors are as follows:

   a. Errors in adjusting for prepaid expenses, accrued expenses, unearned revenues, or accrued revenues (revenues earned but not yet collected). Such errors cause an incorrect income statement in the period in which the error was made, with an equal misstatement in the opposite direction on the income statement for the following period. To illustrate, assume accrued wages were not recognized in 19A. The effect of this error is as follows:

19A Income statement	—Wage expense understated
	—Income overstated
19A Balance sheet	—Current liabilities understated
	—Retained earnings overstated
19B Income statement	—Wage expense overstated (because Wage Expense was debited when wages were paid)
	—Income understated
19B Balance sheet	—No misstatements

   b. Errors in the merchandise inventory. Errors of this type are counterbalancing because the ending inventory of the current period is the beginning inventory of the next period and the beginning and ending inventories have opposite effects on income of the two periods. To illustrate, assume the ending inventory for 19A is understated. The effect of this error is as follows:

19A Income statement	—Ending inventory understated
	—Cost of goods sold overstated
	—Income understated
19A Balance sheet	—Assets (inventory) understated
	—Retained earnings understated
19B Income statement	—Beginning inventory understated
	—Cost of goods sold understated
	—Income overstated
19B Balance sheet	—No misstatements

2. *Noncounterbalancing errors.* This kind of error continues to affect account balances until corrected; hence, one or more balance sheet accounts continue to be reported in error. Examples of noncounterbalancing errors are as follows:

   a. Over- or understatement of the depreciation charge; the accumulated depreciation and retained earnings balances are in error until corrected or until the asset is disposed of or fully depreciated. The income statements are in error for the periods in which incorrect amounts of depreciation expense are recorded.

   b. Recognition of a capital expenditure as an expense, or vice versa, results in incorrect asset balances, expense amounts, and retained earnings until corrected or until the asset is disposed of or fully depreciated.

Preparing Correcting Entries for Errors

Correcting entries will vary depending on (a) whether the error is counterbalancing (i.e., self-correcting) and (b) the lapsed time since the error was made. To illustrate, the following situations involving both counterbalancing and non-counterbalancing errors are analyzed and corrected (in the assumed absence of any income tax effects) at two different points in time. Recall that when an error made in a prior period is corrected, the cumulative misstatement of prior years' net income is reflected in the period of correction as a *prior period adjustment.* Since prior period adjustments are closed to Retained Earnings, this serves to correct the beginning balance of that account.

Situation 1—Error in merchandise inventory. Assume that the ending inventory for 19A was understated by $1,000.

Case A—The error was found at the end of 19B (before books were closed for 19B).

Analysis: Income for 19A was understated by $1,000; hence, retained earnings at the start of 19B is understated by this amount. Beginning inventory for 19B is understated by $1,000.

Correcting entry at the end of 19B:

Inventory, beginning	1,000	
Prior period adjustment (retained earnings)		1,000

Case B—The error was found during 19C.

Analysis: Counterbalanced; income for 19A was understated by $1,000, and income for 19B was overstated by the same amount. Therefore, Retained Earnings and all other balance sheet accounts are correct at the end of 19B. No correcting entry is needed in 19C. Restate 19A and 19B financial statements to a correct basis for all subsequent reporting purposes.

Situation 2—Error in both purchases and inventory. Assume that a $2,000 credit purchase in 19A was not recorded until 19B, when cash was paid, and the goods were not included in the 19A ending inventory.

Case A—The two errors were discovered in 19B (before books were closed for 19B).

Analysis: In 19A both purchases and ending inventory were understated by the same amounts; therefore, since they have opposite effects on income, that amount for 19A was correct. However, on the 19A year-end balance

sheet both inventory and payables were understated by $2,000. In 19B both inventory (beginning) and purchases are in error.

Correcting entry in 19B:

Inventory, beginning	2,000	
Purchases		2,000

Case B—The two errors were discovered in 19C.

Analysis: Both errors counterbalanced in 19B; therefore, no correcting entry is needed in 19C. Restate 19A and 19B financial statements to a correct basis for all subsequent reporting purposes.

Situation 3—Error in prepaid expense. Assume that a five-year fire insurance policy was acquired on January 1, 19A. The five-year premium of $500 was paid and charged in full to insurance expense in 19A.

Case A—The error was discovered at the end of 19B (before books were closed for 19B).

Analysis: In 19A, insurance expense was overstated and income understated by $400. Also in 19A prepaid insurance and retained earnings were understated by $400. No insurance expense for 19B has been recorded since the full $500 was expensed in 19A.

Correcting entry at the end of 19B:

Prepaid insurance	400	
Prior period adjustment (retained earnings)		400
(An adjusting entry for $100 expired insurance must also be made for 19B.)		

Case B—The error was discovered in 19C.

Correcting entry in 19C:

Prepaid insurance	300	
Prior period adjustment (retained earnings)		300
(An adjusting entry for $100 expired insurance also must be made for 19C.)		

Situation 4—Error in accrued expense. Assume accrued property taxes for $100 for 19A were not recorded. They were paid early in 19B and were recorded as expense when paid.

Case A—The error was found at the end of 19B (before books were closed for 19B).

Analysis: In 19A, tax expense was understated and income overstated. Also liabilities were understated and retained earnings overstated by $100. Tax expense for 19B is overstated by $100 because of the payment entry in 19B.

Correcting entry at end of 19B:

Prior period adjustment
   (retained earnings)   100
      Tax expense   100

Case B—The error was found during 19C.

Analysis: The error counterbalanced in 19B because 19A income was overstated and 19B income understated by the same amount. No correcting entry is needed for 19C. Restate 19A and 19B financial statements to a correct basis for all subsequent reporting purposes.

Situation 5—Error in revenue earned but not yet collected. Assume interest receivable of $75 at the end of 19A was not recorded. The interest was collected in 19B and recorded as revenue when collected.

Case A—The error was found at the end of 19B (before books were closed).

Analysis: In 19A, interest revenue and income were understated. On the balance sheet receivables and retained earnings were understated. In 19B interest revenue is overstated because of the collection entry in 19B.

Correcting entry at end of 19B:

Interest revenue   75
   Prior period adjustment
      (retained earnings)   75

Case B—The error was discovered during 19C.

Analysis: The error counterbalanced in 19B because 19A income was understated and 19B income was overstated by the same amount. No correcting entry is needed in 19C. Restate 19A and 19B financial statements to a correct basis for all subsequent reporting purposes.

Situation 6—Expense capitalized. Assume that on January 1, 19A, $500 was expended for ordinary repairs; the $500 was debited to the Machinery account, which was being depreciated 10% per year.

Case A—The error was discovered at the end of 19B (before books were adjusted for 19B).

Analysis: For 19A, repair expense was understated, depreciation expense overstated, and income overstated by the difference. On the balance sheet, assets were overstated and retained earnings overstated by $500 × .90 = $450.

Correcting entry at end of 19B:

Accumulated depreciation
   (for 19A)   50
Prior period adjustment
   (retained earnings)   450
      Machinery   500

Case B—The error was discovered during 19C (before the adjustment for depreciation expense was made for 19C).

Correcting entry during 19C:

Accumulated depreciation
   (for 19A and 19B)   100
Prior period adjustment
   (retained earnings)   400
      Machinery   500

These illustrations should be sufficient to indicate the care that must be taken in analyzing and correcting errors. Fundamental to the analysis are the following: (1) a clear understanding of how the *incorrect entry* was made, (2) a determination of what the *correct entry* should have been, and (3) development of a *correcting entry* to bring *(a)* into conformity with *(b)* by taking into account all effects of the error between the date of the error and the date of the correction.

Worksheet Techniques for Correcting Errors

Usually errors can be analyzed and appropriate accounting developed without a worksheet. However, when errors are numerous and complicated a worksheet approach often is helpful. An efficient worksheet usually can be designed to meet the needs of the particular situation. Of necessity, the worksheet will be unique to the situation; therefore, the accountant should develop an ability to design efficient worksheets for specific problems as they arise.[5] In the re-

---

[5] A reasonable skill in worksheet design often is quite helpful in tackling problems on the CPA examination.

mainder of this part, two different worksheets which are often used will be presented.

Worksheet to Correct Net Income and Provide Correcting Entries

A type of problem sometimes encountered involves correction of a number of errors in pretax income. Usually the situation requires (a) determination of correct income for a series of periods and (b) preparation of a correcting entry (or entries) at the time the errors are discovered.

To illustrate, assume the following data have been developed for Company A:

	Amounts Incorrectly Reported at Year-End		
	19A	19B	19C
Reported pretax income, uncorrected for the errors listed below	$5,000	$7,000	$6,000
a. Prepaid expense not recognized at year-end (i.e., the amount was incorrectly expensed when the cash was paid earlier; example, unexpired insurance)	100	300	400
b. Revenue collected in advance at year-end (i.e., the revenue was incorrectly recognized as earned when the cash was collected earlier; example, unearned rent revenue)	300	500	100
c. Accrued expense not recognized at year-end (i.e., the expense was incurred by year-end but was not recognized until paid next period; example, accrued wages payable)	600	800	500
d. Accrued (earned) revenue not recognized at year-end (i.e., the revenue had been earned by year-end but was uncollected; the revenue was incorrectly recognized as earned in the next period when collected; example, rent revenue receivable) ..	500	400	600
e. Depreciation expense understated (i.e., depreciation not recorded at year-end)	200	200	200

Required:

1. Determine correct pretax income for each year.
2. Give the correcting entries needed, assuming:

   Case A—the errors were discovered at the end of 19C (before the adjusting and closing entries were made for 19C).

   Case B—the errors were discovered during 19D (before the 19D adjusting and closing entries were made).

Solution for Requirement 1—Exhibit 24–1 is designed to meet this requirement. The worksheet begins with the uncorrected amounts and provides for correction of income for *each year.* To explain the mechanics of the worksheet, observe prepaid expenses. Since prepaid expenses of $100 were not recognized in 19A, expenses were overstated and income was understated for that year by $100. In the following year the $100 opposite effect occurred because of this item. Therefore, to correct, income for 19A is increased and income for 19B is decreased on the worksheet by $100. At the end of 19C the $400 prepaid expense has not counterbalanced; that amount should be reflected as a debit balance in prepaid expenses (to be reported on the 19C balance sheet). The remaining analyses on the worksheet follow this pattern. You should carefully study each item on the worksheet.

Solution for Requirement 2—The required correcting entry must be related to a specific date (i.e., when the error was discovered) because the catch-up adjustment, which is recorded as a *prior period adjustment,* must be made to correct the balance in the Retained Earnings account as of the beginning date of the period during which the error is detected and corrected. For this requirement, the discovery date in each case is assumed to be different; hence, the correcting entries in each case are different.

Case A—Assume that the errors were discovered at the end of 19C prior to the 19C closing process.

In this case, at year-end two separate entries are given for each item. The first is the *correcting entry* needed to correct retained earnings for the prior period (catch-up) adjustment, and the

EXHIBIT 24–1
Worksheet to Correct Income
At End of Year 19C

			Income	
Item		19A	19B	19C
Reported income		5,000	7,000	6,000
Corrections:				
a. Prepaid expense	19A	+100	−100	
not recognized	19B		+300	−300
as asset	19C			+400
b. Unearned revenue	19A	−300	+300	
not recognized	19B		−500	+500
as liability	19C			−100
c. Accrued expense	19A	−600	+600	
not recognized	19B		−800	+800
at all	19C			−500
d. Accrued revenue	19A	+500	−500	
not recognized	19B		+400	−400
at all	19C			+600
e. Depreciation	19A	−200		
understated	19B		−200	
	19C			−200
Correct income		4,500	6,500	6,800

second entry is the normal end-of-the-period *adjusting entry* for the item. Although the two entries may be combined, because they are related and are at a common date, it is important to understand that they are quite different—one *corrects,* the other *adjusts.* Based on the data given on page 826, or as analyzed in Exhibit 24–1, the correcting and adjusting entries at the end of 19C would be as follows for Case A:

a. *Prepaid expense* not recorded as prepaid (hence, was reflected as 19B expense):

Correcting entry:

Expense (for 19C)	300	
Prior period adjustment (closed to retained earnings)		300

Correction needed because the 19B prepaid amount was incorrectly left in 19B expense, thus, it was incorrectly excluded from 19C expense. The 19A error has already self-corrected.

Adjusting entry (at end of 19C):

Prepaid expense.	400	
Expense (for 19C)		400

b. *Revenue collected in advance* (unearned rent revenue) not recorded as unearned as of the end of 19B and

hence, earned in 19C (instead was reflected as 19B revenue):

Correcting entry:

Prior period adjustment	500	
Rent revenue (for 19C)		500

Correction needed because the 19B unearned amount was incorrectly left in 19B revenue, thus, it was incorrectly excluded from 19C revenue. The 19A error has already self-corrected.

Adjusting entry (at end of 19C):

Revenue (for 19C)	100	
Unearned revenue		100

c. *Accrued expense* not recorded as accrued (nor reflected as expense):

Correcting entry:

Prior period adjustment	800	
Expense (for 19C)		800

Correction needed because the 19B accrued amount was incorrectly not expensed in 19B; thus, it was incorrectly included in 19C expense (when paid). The 19A error has already self-corrected.

Adjusting entry (at end of 19C):

Expense	500	
Accrued expense payable		500

d. Accrued revenue (revenue earned but not yet collected) was not recorded when earned (hence, not reflected as revenue):

Correcting entry:

Revenue (for 19C)	400	
Prior period adjustment		400

Correction needed because the 19B amount earned was incorrectly not recorded in 19B; thus, it was incorrectly included in 19C revenue (when collected). The 19A error has already self-corrected.

Adjusting entry (at end of 19C):

Revenue receivable	600	
Revenue (for 19C)		600

e. *Annual depreciation* not recorded (either as expense or as accumulated):

Correcting entry:

Prior period adjustment	400	
Accumulated depreciation		
(for 2 years, 19A and 19B)		400

Correction needed because depreciation was not recorded in 19A or 19B and this is *not* a self-correcting type of error.

Adjusting entry (at end of 19C):

Depreciation expense (for 19C only)	200	
Accumulated depreciation		200

Each of the above entries ([*a*]–[*e*]) could be combined into one entry for convenience. For example, the correcting and adjusting entries for item *(e)* immediately above could be combined as follows:

Depreciation expense (for 19C only)	200	
Prior period adjustment (to correct		
for 19A and 19B)	400	
Accumulated depreciation (for 19A,		
19B, and 19C)		600

Case B—Assume that the errors made in 19A, 19B, and 19C were discovered during 19D (prior to the adjusting and closing entries for 19D).

In this case, the date of discovery of the errors is not at year-end; therefore, only a correcting entry is required for each item. Based on the data given on page 826, and as analyzed in Exhibit 24–1, the *correcting entries* needed would reflect the errors caused by the omission of adjusting entries. Observe that the errors made in 19A and 19B for items *(a)* through *(d)* would have

self-corrected; however, the error in depreciation for the full three years would have to be corrected (it is not self-correcting). The correcting entries in 19D would be as follows for Case B:

a.

Prepaid expense	400	
Prior period adjustment (for		
19C error)		400

b.

Prior period adjustment (for 19C error) . . .	100	
Unearned revenue		100

c.

Prior period adjustment (for 19C error) . . .	500	
Accrued expense payable		500

d.

Revenue receivable	600	
Prior period adjustment		
(for 19C error)		600

e.

Prior period adjustment		
(for 19A, 19B, and 19C errors)	600	
Accumulated depreciation		600

Worksheets to Recast Financial Statements

Another group of problems commonly requires recasting of a correct income statement, balance sheet, and statement of retained earnings. To demonstrate a worksheet designed to solve problems of this type, the following illustrative problem is presented. To simplify, income tax effects are disregarded.

ILLUSTRATIVE PROBLEM

1. Uncorrected and unadjusted trial balance at December 31, 19B—As shown in the first two amount columns of Exhibit 24–2.
2. Additional data:
   a. Merchandise inventory December 31, 19A, overstated $4,000 (periodic inventory).
   b. Prepaid advertising of $2,000 at December 31, 19B, not recorded.
   c. Prepaid insurance of $2,000 at December 31, 19B, not recognized because the entire premium, paid on June 1, 19B, was debited to general expense.
   d. Accrued sales salaries of $1,000 at December 31, 19A, not recorded.
   e. Accrued utilities expense of $1,000 at December 31, 19B, not recorded (classify as general expense).
   f. No provision was made for doubtful accounts. The following estimates have

EXHIBIT 24-2
Worksheet to Correct Financial Statements—December 31, 19B

Account	Uncorrected Trial Balance Debit	Credit	Entries Debit	Credit	Income Summary Debit	Credit	Retained Earnings Debit	Credit	Balance Sheet Debit	Credit
Cash	9,000			(h) 1,000					8,000	
Receivables	20,000								20,000	
Allowance for doubtful accounts				(f) 4,000						4,000
Inventory, beginning(a)	30,000			(a) 4,000	26,000					
Equipment	60,000								60,000	
Accumulated depreciation				(g) 20,000						20,000
Accounts payable		5,000								5,000
Capital stock, par $10, 7,500 shares outstanding		76,000	(i) 1,000							75,000
Retained earnings, beginning		25,000		(k) 8,000				33,000		
Prior period adjustments:										
Inventory correction			(a) 4,000				4,000			
Salaries correction			(d) 1,000				1,000			
Bad debt correction			(f) 1,000				1,000			
Depreciation correction			(g) 15,000				15,000			
Sales		130,000				130,000				
Purchases	90,000				90,000					
Selling expenses	17,000			(b) 2,000 (d) 1,000	14,000					
General expenses	10,000		(e) 1,000 (f) 3,000 (g) 5,000 (h) 1,000	(c) 2,000	18,000					
	236,000	236,000								
Prepaid advertising			(b) 2,000						2,000	
Prepaid insurance			(c) 2,000						2,000	
Utilities payable				(e) 1,000						1,000
Dividends paid 19B(b)			(k) 8,000				8,000			
Inventory, ending(a)						32,000			32,000	
Contributed capital in excess of par				(i) 1,000						1,000
Net income					14,000			14,000		
Retained earnings balance							18,000			18,000
			44,000	44,000	162,000	162,000	47,000	47,000	124,000	124,000

Notes:

(a) Other entries could be made for the beginning and ending inventories with the same results.

(b) Entry (k) is not necessary; here it is made simply to provide all of the detailed amounts affecting Retained earnings.

been made: 19A, $1,000; and 19B, $3,000 (classify as general expense).

g. No provision was made for depreciation. The following amounts have been computed: prior to 19B, $15,000; and 19B, $5,000 (classify as general expense).

h. Cash shortage, $1,000 at end of 19B (classify as a general espense).

i. Correction for premium on capital stock, originally credited to the capital stock account (7,500 shares, par $10 per share).

j. The inventory was $32,000 at the end of 19B.

k. Dividends paid and properly recorded in 19B, $8,000. (Note: Transactions occurring during the current year and affecting retained earnings, if desired, may be entered on the worksheet so that the worksheet will reflect the beginning balance and the detail concerning all changes in retained earnings.)

Required:

Complete a worksheet to provide corrected amounts for the 19C income statement, statement of retained earnings, and balance sheet. Key all entries on the worksheet to the data given.

Exhibit 24–2 shows an efficient worksheet that meets the "solution" needs for this situation. Observe that it is similar to the worksheets illustrated in Chapter 3. The entries include both (a) current adjusting entries and (b) correcting entries. You should follow each item through the worksheet. Corrected financial statements can be prepared from the worksheet.

This type of worksheet is especially important throughout accounting because (1) it can be adapted to many different problem situations and (2) its built-in debit/credit feature assures a degree of accuracy and completeness not otherwise attainable.

PART B—STATEMENTS FROM SINGLE-ENTRY AND OTHER INCOMPLETE RECORDS

Most businesses maintain a reasonably complete record of all transactions directly affecting them. Usually complete records are best accomplished through a systematic model based on (a) the double-entry concept and (b) the accounting model. However, many small businesses, especially sole proprietorships, maintain only a single-entry system that records the "bare essentials."

Single-entry recordkeeping includes all those records, whether kept systematically or not, deemed necessary by the proprietor but which do not record the *dual effect* of each transaction on both assets and equities as expressed in the accounting model. In some cases only records of cash, accounts receivable, accounts payable, and taxes paid may be maintained. No record may be kept, except perhaps in memorandum form, of operational assets, inventories, expenses, revenues, and other elements usually considered essential in an accounting system. However, the incomplete data, plus other information that often can be assembled, generally can be analyzed sufficiently to provide a reasonably accurate income statement and balance sheet.

Preparation of Balance Sheet from Single-Entry Records

Since single-entry records usually provide little information about assets (other than cash and accounts receivable), preparation of the balance sheet in such situations involves identification and measurement of various assets and liabilities. The cost of the operational assets must be determined or estimated from such data as are available. Canceled checks, receipts, bills of sale, deeds, papers transferring title to real estate, and other similar records provide much of the needed data. Once the cost of each operational asset is determined, depreciation can be computed. The amount of merchandise, supplies, and other inventories on hand may be obtained by actual count. If original cost cannot be determined, merchandise and supplies can be recorded at current replacement cost.

Similarly, notes payable and other liabilities (except accounts payable for which there is generally an invoice from the seller) must be obtained from memoranda, correspondence, and even by consultation with creditors.

EXHIBIT 24–3

A. A. BROWN COMPANY
Balance Sheet
At December 31, 19A

Assets

Current Assets:
Cash		$2,345
Accounts receivable		90
Notes receivable, trade		50
Merchandise inventory		1,550
Total Current Assets		4,035

Property and Equipment:
Office and store equipment	$500	
Less: Accumulated depreciation	25	475
Total Assets		$4,510

Liabilities

Current Liabilities:
Accounts payable	$ 240
Long-term Liabilities	None
Total Liabilities	240

Owner's Equity

A. A. Brown, proprietorship ($4,510 − $240)	4,270
Total Liabilities and Owner's Equity	$4,510

EXHIBIT 24–4

A. A. BROWN COMPANY
Computation of Net Loss
For the Year Ended December 31, 19A

Owner's equity, January 1, 19A	$4,500
Owner's equity, December 31, 19A	4,270
Net loss for period	$ 230

customers as owing a total of $90; Brown was positive that the bills were outstanding. You called the customers for verification.

g. Accounts payable, $240—The "unpaid invoices" file contained two invoices that totaled to this amount; Brown assured you that they had not been paid.

A balance sheet prepared from the above data is shown in Exhibit 24–3. Owner's equity was determined by subtracting total liabilities from total assets.

To illustrate preparation of a balance sheet from single-entry records, assume the following data have been gathered for the sole proprietorship, A. A. Brown Company, for 19A:

a. Cash on hand and on deposit, $2,345—from count of cash and bank statement.

b. Merchandise inventory, $1,550—Count made by Brown, costed at current replacement cost since purchase invoices were not available.

c. Store and office equipment acquired on January 1, 19A, $500—from invoice found in the files.

d. Brown agreed that a depreciation rate of 5% per annum, with no material amount of residual value, was reasonable.

e. Note receivable, dated December 31, 19A, $50—This note, signed by a customer for goods purchased, was in the files.

f. Accounts receivable, $90—Brown maintained a "Charge Book" which listed four

Computation of Income

The computation of income where single-entry records are kept may be based on an analysis of the changes in owner's equity for the period. For example, if it is determined that the only change in owner's equity for Brown Company resulted from a gain or loss from operations, the summary income statement in Exhibit 24–4 may be prepared (proprietorship, January 1, 19A, taken from balance sheet for prior period, or reconstructed).

If there had been additional investments or withdrawals during the period, these would have to be considered in the computation of income or loss. The following equation indicates the procedure for determining income when there have been investments or withdrawals during the period:

Income = Ending Owner's Equity
− Beginning Owner's Equity
+ Withdrawals
− Additional Investments

The two examples of the single-entry income statement computations shown in Exhibit 24–5

EXHIBIT 24–5
Income Determination—Single Entry

	Computation Where There Was—	
	An Income	A Loss
Owner's equity, end of period	$8,000	$5,500
Owner's equity, beginning of period	7,100	6,300
Change increase (decrease)	900	(800)
Add: Withdrawals during period	1,200	1,000
	2,100	200
Deduct: Additional investments during period	500	400
Income for period	$1,600	
Loss for period		$ (200)

J. R. Mercer Company

	19A	
	January 1	December 31
Accounts and trade notes receivable (no doubtful accounts)	$35,000	$48,000
Inventory (per physical count)	6,900	8,700
Building and equipment (appraised at estimated cost less depreciation)	17,000	17,400
Prepaid expenses (per memoranda)	100	110
Accounts payable (per files)	8,100	9,200
Notes payable (for equipment per files)		500
Cash on hand (per cash register)	60	110
Liability for accrued expenses (per memoranda)	120	150
Salaries paid		7,000

indicate the procedure when there have been investments and withdrawals during the period.

PREPARATION OF A DETAILED INCOME STATEMENT FROM INCOMPLETE DATA

Income or loss for the period can be computed as shown in the preceding section. However, knowing only the amount of income or loss does not identify the components of income for management, nor does it meet the needs of other interested parties. For example, banks and other credit grantors usually request a statement setting out the details of operations. The Internal Revenue Service requires a detailed statement of revenues and expenses for income tax purposes.

An itemized income statement in the conventional form may be prepared from single-entry records and supplemental data without converting the records to double-entry form. By analyzing the cash receipts and disbursements, much of the needed detail may be obtained. The preparation of an income statement from single-entry data may be illustrated as follows:

The following information was obtained from the single-entry records of J. R. Mercer Company. Balance sheets as of January 1 and December 31 and an income statement for 19A are to be prepared:

An analysis of the bank statements indicated deposits and disbursements as follows:

Bank overdraft, January 1, 19A	$ 2,800
Deposits during year:	
Collections on account	42,000
Additional capital contributions by owner	10,000
Checks drawn during year for:	
Purchases	26,000
Expenses	6,000
Salaries of employees	7,000
Withdrawals by owner	3,000
Purchase of equipment	340

Balance Sheet Preparation

In preparing the balance sheets, cash in the bank on December 31, 19A, must be computed. There was an overdraft on January 1, 19A. Total deposits of $52,000 less the January 1 overdraft of $2,800 and total checks drawn of $42,340 indicate a December 31, 19A, balance of $6,860. The balance sheets are shown in Exhibit 24–6.

Computation of Net Income

Using the method described above, net income may be computed by analysis of the change in proprietorship as follows:

Owner's equity, December 31, 19A	$71,330
Owner's equity, January 1, 19A	48,040
Increase in owner's equity	23,290
Add withdrawals during year	3,000
	26,290
Deduct additional investments during year	10,000
Net income, 19A	$16,290

EXHIBIT 24–6

J. R. MERCER COMPANY
Balance Sheets

	19A	
	January 1	December 31
Assets		
Cash in bank	$ —	$ 6,860
Cash in register	60	110
Accounts and notes receivable	35,000	48,000
Inventory	6,900	8,700
Prepaid expenses	100	110
Buildings and equipment	17,000	17,400
	$59,060	$81,180
Liabilities		
Notes payable	$ —	$ 500
Bank overdraft	2,800	—
Accounts payable	8,100	9,200
Accrued expenses payable	120	150
	11,020	9,850
Owner's Equity (difference)		
J. R. Mercer, proprietorship	$48,040	$71,330

Analysis of Revenue and Expenses. To prepare a detailed income statement, each item of revenue and expense to be included thereon must be determined. Such a determination may be made by summarizing all the transactions in debit and credit form, which in effect would involve conversion to double-entry procedures. This approach is subsequently illustrated (in worksheet form) in this chapter. Alternatively, the desired figures may be derived directly by analyzing the respective items or in T-account form as illustrated at the bottom of this page.

Computation of Sales. Cash and credit sales combined for J. R. Mercer Company may be determined by analyzing cash receipts and changes in accounts receivable and trade notes receivable as follows (refer to the problem data given on page 832):

Schedule 1

Accounts and trade notes receivable, December 31, 19A	$48,000
Cash collected from customers and deposited	42,000
Increase in cash on hand ($110 — $60)	50
	90,050
Less: Accounts and trade notes receivable, January 1, 19A	35,000
Sales for the period, 19A	$55,050

Alternatively, to determine the sales for the period, you may prefer simply to reconstruct the T-accounts for the *accounts receivable* and *sales* accounts as shown at the bottom of this page. Some people find the T-account approach preferable to the schedule in that the problem of whether to add or subtract a given amount is easily resolved by making the normal debit-

Accounts Receivable

Beg. bal. (Jan. 1)	35,000	Cash collections (deposited)	42,000
a. Sales (amount necessary to complete account)	55,050	Cash collections (on hand)	50
		End. balance (Dec. 31)	48,000
	90,050		90,050
Balance carried forward	48,000		

Sales

	a. From reconstructed accounts receivable	55,050

credit entries; also, there is a built-in self-check. The items are simply entered in the account in the normal manner and the missing amount (sales in the above case) is the balancing (plug) figure. Note that the *ending* balance is always entered on the "opposite side" for balancing purposes in reconstructing the account, as is done in the normal year-end closing of accounts with balances to be carried forward.

Note that the increase of cash on hand is assumed to represent collections from customers. If there had been data relative to cash discounts on sales, returned sales, or accounts written off as uncollectible, both the sales discounts and the bad debts written off should be added to the total in Schedule 1. In such cases if the T-account analysis is used, it would appear advisable to reconstruct the following accounts: Accounts Receivable, Allowance for Doubtful Accounts, Bad Debt Expense, Sales Discounts, Sales Returns, and Sales.

Computation of Purchases

The amount of purchases may be determined by the analysis of cash disbursements and changes in both accounts payable and trade notes payable as follows (refer to the problem data given on page 832 for J. R. Mercer Company):

Schedule 2	
Accounts and trade notes payable, December 31, 19A	$ 9,200
Payments to creditors	26,000
	35,200
Less: Accounts and trade notes payable, January 1, 19A	8,100
Purchases for the period, 19A	$27,100

It should be noted that cash discounts may have been taken. If this is the case, such discounts should be added into the schedule (or included in the T-account analysis) to derive gross purchases.

Computation of Depreciation

The building and equipment were valued at appraised cost less depreciation. The decrease in the net book value of the asset, taking into account additions and dispositions of equipment during the period, is the amount of depreciation for the period as computed below:

Schedule 3	
Net balance of buildings and equipment, January 1, 19A	$17,000
Purchases of equipment during 19A:	
By issue of note payable	500
By cash payment	340
Balance before depreciation	17,840
Less: Net balance on December 31, 19A (after current depreciation)	17,400
Depreciation for the period, 19A	$ 440

Computation of Expenses

The expenses paid in cash by J. R. Mercer Company, determined from an analysis of cash disbursements, must be adjusted for prepaid and accrued items at the beginning and at the end of the period as follows:

Schedule 4		
Expenses paid in cash during 19A		$6,000
Add: Expenses accrued on December 31, 19A		150
Prepaid expenses on January 1, 19A		100
		6,250
Deduct: Accrued expenses, January 1, 19A	$120	
Prepaid expenses, December 31, 19A	110	230
Expenses for the period, 19A		$6,020

Again, you may find it easier to analyze the more involved situations, such as this one, by reconstructing the related accounts in the following manner:

Prepaid Expenses

Beginning balance (Jan. 1)	100		a. Reversing entry to expense	100
c. Adjusting entry to record ending balance (Dec. 31)	110			

Liability for Accrued Expenses

b. Reversing entry to expense	120		Beginning balance (Jan. 1)	120
			d. Adjusting entry to record ending balance (Dec. 31)	150

Expenses

Paid in cash during 19A (includes beginning accrued expense)	6,000	b.	Reversing entry from accrued	120
a. Reversing entry for prepaid	100	c.	Adjusting entry for prepaid	110
d. Ending balance accrued	150			

(Expenses for 19A—account balance, $6,020.)

Note again that the beginning balances are entered, then the "normal" accounting entries are made in the accounts. The information does not reveal any adjustments to salary expense; therefore, that expense is $7,000 as given.

Preparation of the Income Statement

All information needed to prepare the income statement has now been determined. That statement would appear as shown in Exhibit 24–7.

WORKSHEETS FOR PROBLEMS FROM SINGLE-ENTRY AND OTHER INCOMPLETE RECORDS

The preceding example, although simplified, suggests the need for a worksheet approach to reduce clerical work and minimize the possibility of errors and omissions. A worksheet provides several internal checks on accuracy and recognizes each group of transactions in terms of their debit and credit effects. In order to provide a "track record," such worksheets should be accompanied by explanations and computations of the analyses involved.

The following illustrative problem is presented to demonstrate the use of a worksheet to solve problems involving extensive incomplete data.

J. C. Main has been in business two years and has not maintained double-entry records. A financial statement was prepared by an accountant at the end of last year, 19A. This balance sheet (balances at January 1, 19B) and one developed at the end of the current year (dated December 31, 19B) are presented in Exhibit 24–8. They were developed by "inventorying" all assets and liabilities.

EXHIBIT 24–7

J. R. MERCER COMPANY
Income Statement
For Year Ended December 31, 19A

Sales (Schedule 1)		$55,050
Cost of goods sold:		
Inventory, January 1, 19A (given)	$ 6,900	
Purchases (Schedule 2)	27,100	
Goods available for sale	34,000	
Less: Inventory, December 31, 19A (given)	8,700	
Cost of goods sold		25,300
Gross margin on sales		29,750
Less: Expenses:		
Depreciation (Schedule 3)	440	
Expenses (Schedule 4)	6,020	
Salaries (given)	7,000	13,460
Net Income		$16,290

The following additional information for 19B was developed:

a. Main kept no record of cash receipts and disbursements, but an analysis of canceled checks provided the following summary of payments: accounts payable, $71,000; expenses, $20,700; and purchase of equipment, $3,700. No checks appeared to be outstanding.

b. Main stated that $100 cash was withdrawn

EXHIBIT 24–8

J. C. MAIN COMPANY
Balance Sheets

	19B	
	January 1	December 31
Cash	$ 10,000	$ 22,000
Notes receivable	5,000	3,000
Accounts receivable	61,000	68,000
Inventories	25,000	27,000
Prepaid expenses	500	200
Furniture and equipment (net)	10,600	12,400
	$112,100	$132,600
Bank loan	$ —	$ 5,000
Accounts payable	30,000	36,000
Accrued expenses payable	800	650
J. C. Main, proprietorship	81,300	90,950
	$112,100	$132,600

regularly each week from the cash register for personal use. No record was made of these personal withdrawals.

c. The $5,000 bank loan was for one year, the note was dated July 1, 19B, and 6% interest was taken out of the face amount (cash proceeds, $4,700).

d. Main stated that equipment listed in the January 1 balance sheet at $900 was sold for $620 cash.

e. The bank reported that it had credited Main with $4,000 during the year for customers' notes that Main left for collection.

f. One $400 note on hand December 31, 19B, was past due and appeared worthless. Therefore, this note was not included in the $3,000 notes receivable listed in the December 31, 19B, balance sheet. Assume no allowance for doubtful accounts; bad debts are written off directly to expense because of immateriality.

Main needs a detailed income statement for the current year, 19B.

Solution: A seven-column or five-column interim worksheet may be adapted for this problem. A five-column worksheet is shown in Exhibit 24–9. Note that a five-column worksheet is achieved by placing "debits over credits" (since this eliminates two more columns). Columns are set up for beginning balances, interim entries (debit and credit), income statement, and ending balances.

The beginning and ending balances, taken from the two balance sheets, are entered directly on the worksheet as illustrated, with sufficient line spacing for the anticipated entries. Next the interim entries for all transactions are reconstructed (as explained below) to account for all changes in each account during the period. Last, all items not listed in the column "ending balances" are carried as debits or credits to the column headed "Income Statement." At this point in the solution the *net income* (or loss) is the difference between the debits and credits in the Income Statement column. Particular attention should be called to the fact that considerable data needed for reconstruction of the entries may not be available (as in this case); therefore, care must be exercised in the sequence of developing the entries. Note that all of the data available are used first (entries [a] through [f]), then subsequent entries are developed by computing the "missing data" as illustrated in entry (g) and following. Problems such as this one are frequently referred to as missing data problems.

Explanation of Entries on the Worksheet:

a. To record cash payments shown by analysis of canceled checks.

b. To record Main's cash withdrawals of $100 per week for 52 weeks.

c. To record bank loan of $5,000 less $300 interest of which $150 was prepaid as of December 31, 19B.

d. To record sale of equipment, cost less depreciation, $900, for $620 cash.

e. To record $4,000 notes receivable collected by bank.

f. To record writeoff of bad note, $400.

g. To record notes from customers, computed as follows (data taken directly from worksheet):

Notes collected	$4,000
Note written off	400
Notes on hand, December 31, 19B	3,000
	7,400
Less: Notes on hand, January 1, 19B	5,000
Notes receivable (received on accounts)	$2,400

h. Cash collected from customers (observe that it does not matter whether the collection was at time of sale or on account) is computed as follows from data shown in the Cash account on the worksheet:

Cash paid out ($95,400 + $5,200)	$100,600
Cash balance, December 31, 19B	22,000
	122,600
Cash collected from all sources other than from customers:	
($4,700 + $620 + $4,000)	9,320
	113,280
Less: Cash balance, January 1, 19B	10,000
Cash collected from customers	$103,280

i. Sales are computed by finding the only "missing entry" in *accounts receivable,*

EXHIBIT 24–9

J. C. MAIN COMPANY
Worksheet for Year Ended December 31, 19B

Account	Beginning Balances January 1, 19B	Interim Entries Debit		Interim Entries Credit		Income Statement	Ending Balances December 31, 19B
Debit accounts:							
Cash	10,000	(c)	4,700	(a)	95,400		22,000
		(d)	620	(b)	5,200		
		(e)	4,000				
		(h)	103,280				
Notes receivable	5,000	(g)	2,400	(e)	4,000		3,000
				(f)	400		
Accounts receivable	61,000	(i)	112,680	(g)	2,400		68,000
				(h)	103,280		
Inventories	25,000	(j)	27,000	(j)	25,000		27,000
Prepaid expenses	500	(c)	150	(k)	500		200
		(k)	50				
Furniture and equipment (net)	10,600	(a)	3,700	(d)	900		12,400
				(l)	1,000		
Expenses		(a)	20,700	(k)	50	21,000	
		(k)	500	(n)	800		
		(n)	650				
Interest expense		(c)	150			150	
Loss on sale of equipment		(d)	280			280	
Loss on worthless note		(f)	400			400	
Depreciation		(l)	1,000			1,000	
Purchases		(m)	77,000			77,000	
Net income		(o)	14,850			14,850	
	112,100					114,680	132,600
Credit accounts:							
Bank loan				(c)	5,000		5,000
Accounts payable	30,000	(a)	71,000	(m)	77,000		36,000
Accrued expenses payable	800	(n)	800	(n)	650		650
J. C. Main, proprietorship	81,300	(b)	5,200	(o)	14,850		90,950
Sales				(i)	112,680	112,680	
Income summary (inventory change)		(j)	25,000	(j)	27,000	2,000	
	112,100		476,110		476,110	114,680	132,600

which entry is for sales on account. (Balance in notes receivable has already been reconciled on the worksheet.)

Notes received on account (item *g*)	$ 2,400
Cash collected from customers (item *h*) . .	103,280
Final balance of accounts receivable	68,000
Total credits and balance	173,680
Less: January 1 balance	61,000
Total debits for the year (sales)	$112,680

j. To close the January 1 inventory and to record the December 31 inventory (to income summary).

k. To close the January 1 balance of prepaid expenses and to increase the prepaid expense balance as of December 31 to $200 as given.

l. To set up the depreciation expense for the period. All entries have been made in the Furniture and Equipment account on the

EXHIBIT 24–10

J. C. MAIN COMPANY Income Statement For Year Ended December 31, 19B		
Revenues:		
Sales		$112,680
Cost of goods sold:		
Beginning inventory, January 1, 19B	$ 25,000	
Purchases	77,000	
Total goods available for sale	102,000	
Less: Ending inventory, December 31, 19B	27,000	75,000
Gross margin on sales		37,680
Less: Expenses:		
Expenses	21,000	
Depreciation	1,000	
Loss on worthless note	400	22,400
Operating income		15,280
Less: Other expenses and losses:		
Interest expense	150	
Loss on sale of equipment	280	430
Net Income		$ 14,850

worksheet except the 19B depreciation credit. Depreciation is computed as follows:

Furniture and equipment, January 1, 19B	$10,600
Equipment purchased	3,700
	14,300
Less: Equipment sold	900
	13,400
Less: Balance of furniture and equipment, December 31, 19B	12,400
Depreciation for the period	$ 1,000

m. Purchases are computed by finding the missing entry in accounts payable on the worksheet as follows:

Payments on accounts payable	$ 71,000
Balance of accounts payable, December 31, 19B	36,000
	107,000
Less: Accounts payable, January 1, 19B	30,000
Purchases for the period	$ 77,000

n. To close the January 1 balance of accrued expenses payable and to record accrued expenses payable as of December 31.

o. To close net income to proprietorship. The net income may be computed by analyzing the changes in capital from January 1 to December 31, 19B, as illustrated previously or by extending the balances in the nominal accounts to the column "Income Statement" and then computing the difference between the debits and credits. Obviously, one computation would serve as a check on the other.

The resulting income statement, taken directly from the worksheet, is shown in Exhibit 24–10.

LIMITATIONS OF SINGLE-ENTRY RECORDKEEPING

Single-entry recordkeeping is employed by a large number of particularly small businesses, by nonprofit organizations, by persons acting in a fiduciary capacity as administrators or executors of estates, and by many individuals relative to their personal affairs. Even some regular systems of recordkeeping recommended for retail outlets by trade associations and by manufacturers are maintained on a single-entry basis. For example, one such system is used by a large number of small retail druggists. Single-entry records are used in the interest of simplicity, and generally are less expensive to maintain than double-entry system, since they do not require the services of a trained person. In fact, more often than not, single-entry records are maintained by the proprietor or someone closely associated with the activities being recorded.

Single-entry recordkeeping is generally inadequate except where operations are especially simple and the volume of activity is small. Some of the more important disadvantages of single-entry systems are as follows:

1. Data may not be available to the management for effectively planning and controlling the business.
2. Lack of systematic and precise recordkeeping may lead to inefficient administration and reduced control over the affairs of the business.
3. Do not provide a check against clerical errors, as does a double-entry system. This is one of the most serious of the defects of single-entry records.

4. Seldom makes provision for recording all transactions. Many internal transactions (i.e., those normally reflected through adjusting entries), in particular, are not recorded.
5. Since no accounts are provided for many of the items appearing in both the balance sheet and income statement, omission of important data is always a possibility.
6. In the absence of detailed records of all assets, lax administration of those assets may occur.
7. Theft and other losses are less likely to be detected.

QUESTIONS

1. Briefly distinguish between the following: *(a)* change in principle, *(b)* change in estimate, *(c)* change in reporting entry, and *(d)* accounting error.
2. What are the three basic alternatives for reflecting the effects of accounting changes and error corrections?
3. Complete the following matrix:

	Method of Reflecting the Effect *		
	(1)_____	(2)_____	(3)_____
a. Change in estimate	___	___	___
b. Change in principle	___	___	___
c. Correction of error	___	___	___

* Identify these three captions; then enter appropriate check on each line.

4. What are pro forma statements? Why are they used in respect to some accounting changes?
5. What is the difference between a counterbalancing and a noncounterbalancing error? Basically, why is the distinction significant in the analysis of errors?
6. Complete the matrix at the bottom of this page by entering a plus to indicate overstatement and a minus to indicate understatement.
7. Give two examples of each of the following types of errors:
   a. Affects income statement only.
   b. Affects balance sheet only.
   c. Affects both income statement and balance sheet.
8. Briefly explain the differences between a double-entry and a single-entry system.
9. What are the primary shortcomings of a single-entry system? What are the advantages?

DECISION CASE 24–1

This decision case is adapted from an actual situation. It focuses on the change from *Lifo* to the *Fifo* method of accounting for inventory. This particular kind of accounting change has received considerable interest because when prices are rising it causes a *credit* (often very large in amount) to be recorded, which if reported on the income statement significantly increases *reported* net income. The case is presented in three parts, each of which has its own requirement.

		Effect of Error on—			
(Relates to Question 6)		Net Income	Assets	Liabilities	Owners' Equity
a.	Ending inventory for 19A understated:				
	19A financial statements	___	___	___	___
	19B financial statements	___	___	___	___
b.	Ending inventory for 19B overstated:				
	19B financial statements	___	___	___	___
	19C financial statements	___	___	___	___
c.	Failed to record depreciation in 19A:				
	19A financial statements	—	___	___	___
	19B financial statements	—	___	___	___
d.	Failed to record a liability resulting from revenue collected in advance at end of 19A; instead, credited revenue erroneously:				
	19A financial statements	___	___	___	___
	19B financial statements	___	___	___	___

Part A

Effective January 1, 19C, Kowalski Corporation changed its inventory method from *Lifo* to *Fifo*. In its 19C annual report (Kowalski's fiscal year ends December 31) the company disclosed that the change decreased the net loss for 19C by $20 million relative to the net loss that would have been reported if the change had not been made. The 19C net loss, including the $20 million effect from the accounting change, was $7.6 million. The change also increased 19C year-end inventories by $150 million over the *Lifo* inventory amount at December 31, 19C.

The following tabulation gives the relevant amounts (in millions of dollars):

Year	Purchases	Fifo Ending Inventory	Lifo Ending Inventory
19A	$5,802	$1,372	$1,240
19B	6,040	1,445	1,335
19C	6,199	1,541	1,391

Required:

Present the inventory and cost of goods sold as they should be reported on the comparative balance sheet and income statements for 19B–19C. Show the computation of the cost of goods sold amounts.

Part B

The accounting entry made by Kowalski on December 31, 19C, to record the accounting change from *Lifo* to *Fifo* was (in millions of dollars) as follows:

Recording:

Inventory	150.0	
Income taxes payable		76.5*
Gain on inventory change from *Lifo* to		
Fifo (closed to income		
summary)—19C		20.0
Prior period adjustment, inventory		
change (closed to retained		
earnings)—19C		53.5

* Assume this tax amount is correct; it is the net effect of numerous tax items. This case does not focus on income taxes.

Required:

Briefly explain the reason for the debit or credit to each account shown in the above entry to record the accounting change.

Part C

Long-term notes and debenture bonds payable of Kowalski Corporation require the company to maintain a current ratio of 1.4 to 1 as a condition for retaining the stated interest rate on the debt. Specifically, for every .01 or fraction thereof by which the current ratio of Kowalski falls below 1.4 to 1, the interest rate on Kowalski's outstanding debt automatically increases by ½% (i.e., .005). Total long-term debt at December 31, 19C, was $791 million. The debt matures, on average, in 15 years.

The Internal Revenue Code requires companies to use *Lifo* for financial reporting purposes as a condition for being allowed to use *Lifo* for income tax purposes. Therefore, when Kowalski changed to *Fifo* for accounting purposes, it also had to change to *Fifo* for income tax purposes. The change caused a $76.5 million increase in income taxes currently payable.

The following table gives relevant accounts (in millions of dollars):

	Current Assets		Current Liabilities	
Year-End	Fifo Basis	Lifo Basis	Fifo Basis	Lifo Basis
19C	$2,168	$2,017	$1,548	$1,471.5

Required:

1. Based on the above description of this case situation, why does it appear that Kowalski made the accounting change?
2. In terms of cash flows (i.e., the present value of future cash flows, where appropriate) evaluate whether Kowlaski made the correct choice by changing inventory methods. Company accountants conservatively estimate that the annual increase in income taxes due to the change will be $2 million over each of the next ten years. An appropriate discount rate for all present value computations is 10%. Round current ratios to two decimal places.

EXERCISES

PART A
Exercises 24–1 to 24–7

Exercise 24–1

Lyle Corporation has been depreciating equipment over a ten-year life using the sum-of-the-years'-digits method. The equipment cost $68,000 (estimated residual value of $13,000). On the basis of an engineering study of its economic potential to the company, completed during the fifth year (19E), management decided to change to straight-line depreciation, effective as of the beginning of the fifth year (19E), with no change in the estimated useful life or the residual value. The annual financial statements are prepared on a comparative basis (two years presented). Net incomes (no extraordinary items) prior to giving effect to this change (i.e., on the old basis) were 19D, $48,000; and 19E, $51,000. Shares of stock outstanding, 100,000. Disregard income tax considerations.

Required:

1. Identify the type of accounting change involved and analyze the effects of the change.
2. Prepare entry, or entries, to appropriately reflect the change in the accounts in 19E (fifth year), the year of the change.
3. Illustrate how the change should be reflected on the 19E financial statement, which includes 19D results for comparative purposes.

Exercise 24–2

Lyle Corporation has been depreciating equipment over a ten-year life on a straight-line basis. The equipment cost $24,000 and has an estimated residual value of $6,000. On the basis of experience since acquisition (four years prior to 19E), management has decided to depreciate it over a total life of 14 years instead of 10, and with no change in the estimated residual value. The change is to be effective on January 1, 19E. The annual financial statements are prepared on a comparative basis (two years presented). Net incomes (no extraordinary items) prior to giving effect to the change (i.e., on the old basis) were 19D, $48,000; and 19E, $51,000. Shares of stock outstanding, 100,000. Disregard income tax considerations.

Required:

1. Identify the type of accounting change involved and analyze the effects of the change.
2. Prepare entry, or entries, to appropriately reflect the change in the accounts for 19E (fifth year), the year of the change.
3. Illustrate how the change should be reflected on the 19E financial statements, which include 19D results for comparative purposes.

Exercise 24–3

AB Corporation has never had an audit prior to 19D, the current year. Prior to the arrival of the auditor the company accountant had prepared a comparative set of financial statements with 19C and 19D shown thereon for comparative purposes. The books for 19D have not been closed. During the audit it was discovered that an invoice dated January 19A for $9,000 (paid in cash at that time) was debited to operating expenses, although it was for the purchase of equipment. The equipment has an estimated useful life of ten years and no estimated residual value.

Reported incomes reflected on the comparative financial statement prepared by the company auditor (prior to discovery of the error) were 19C, $30,000; and 19D, $33,000. Shares of stock outstanding, 100,000. Disregard income tax considerations.

Required:

1. Identify the type of item involved and analyze the effects of the change.
2. Prepare the entry, or entries, to appropriately reflect the change in the accounts for 19D, the year of the change.
3. Illustrate how the change should be reflected on the 19D financial statements, which include 19C results for comparative purposes.

Exercise 24–4

Give journal entries to correct the accounts, and the subsequent adjusting entry, for each of the errors listed below assuming (1) the errors were discovered on December 31, 19B, before the books were adjusted and closed; and (2) the errors were discovered in January 19C (after the books for 19B were adjusted and closed). Assume each item is material. Disregard income tax considerations.

a. Merchandise costing $6,000 was received on December 28, 19A, and was included in the ending inventory of 19A, but the credit purchase was not recorded in the purchases journal until January 3, 19B.

b. An entry was made on December 30, 19B, for writeoff of organization expense as follows (assume only one year's amortization was justified for 19B; amortization per year, $1,000):

General expense	5,000	
Deferred organization expense		5,000

c. Discount of $3,300 on a long-term bond investment purchased on May 1, 19A, was written off to Retained Earnings on that date. These bonds mature on July 1, 19J. Use straight-line amortization.

d. Machinery costing $900 was purchased and charged to repair expense on June 30, 19A. The depreciation rate on machinery is 10% per year.

Exercise 24–5

You are auditing the accounts of Zero Merchandising Corporation for the year ended December 31, 19B. You discover that the adjustments made on the previous audit for the year 19A were not entered in the accounts; therefore, the accounts are not in agreement with the audited amounts as of December 31, 19A. The following adjustments were included in the 19A audit report:

a. Invoices for merchandise purchased in December 19A, not entered on the books until January 19B and not included in the December 31, 19A, inventory, $6,000.

b. Invoices for merchandise received in December 19A were not recorded in the accounts until January 19B; the goods were included in the 19A ending inventory, $9,000.

c. Provision for doubtful accounts for 19A understated by $1,000.

d. Selling expense for 19A not recorded in the accounts until paid in January 19B, $2,500.

e. Accrued wages at December 31, 19A, not recorded at that date, $2,000.

f. Unexpired insurance at December 31, 19A, understated by $300.

g. Taxes for year ended December 31, 19A, not entered in the accounts until January 19B, $1,200.

h. Depreciation not recorded prior to January 19A, $3,000; for year ended December 31, 19A, $1,500.

Required:

Assume you have the uncorrected and unadjusted trial balance dated December 31, 19B. Give the journal entry for each of the above items that should be made to the trial balance before using it for further audit purposes. Disregard income tax implications.

Exercise 24–6

XY Sales Company has made several accounting changes with a view to improving the matching of expenses with revenue. Assume it is at the end of 19H, and that the accounting period ends on December 31. The books have not been adjusted or closed at the end of 19H. Among the changes were the following:

a. Machinery that cost $25,000 (estimated useful life ten years, residual value $3,000) has been depreciated using the sum-of-the-years'-digits method. Early in the eighth year (19H), it was decided to change to straight-line depreciation (with no change in residual value or estimated life).

b. A patent that cost $8,500 is being depreciated over the legal life of 17 years. Early in the 6th year since its acquisition (19H), it was decided that the economic benefits would not last longer than 13 years from date of acquisition.

c. During 19F and 19G, all ordinary repair expenditures were debited to the Machinery account. The repair expenditures were made in January of each year; the capitalized amounts were $7,000 and $11,000 during the two years, respectively. The machinery was being depreciated 12% per year on cost. It is now 19H, and the error has just been discovered.

Required:

1. For each of the above situations, identify the type of accounting change or error that was involved, and briefly explain how it should be accounted for.

2. Give the appropriate entry to reflect the change and the 19H adjusting entry in each instance. Show computations and disregard income tax considerations. If no entry is required in a particular instance, explain why.

Exercise 24–7

RB Company failed to recognize accruals and prepayments since organization three years previously. The net income, accruals, and prepayments at year-end are given below:

	Amounts Incorrectly Reported at Year-End		
	19A	19B	19C
Reported income (pretax)	$4,000	$1,000*	$5,000
Items not recognized at year-end (i.e., no adjusting entry was made for these items):			
a. Prepaid expense†	200	280	109
b. Accrued expense	250	225	247
c. Revenue collected in advance‡	325	360	293
d. Revenue earned but not yet collected	275	230	196

* Net loss.
† Insurance premiums debited to insurance expense when paid.
‡ Revenue credited when cash collected.

Required:

1. Compute the correct income for each year (disregard income tax effects).

2. Give entry to correct each item assuming the errors were discovered at year-end 19C (books were not closed).

3. Give entry to correct each item assuming the errors were discovered during 19D, after the 19C books

were closed, but prior to the 19D adjusting and closing entries.

PART B
Exercises 24–8 to 24–13

Exercise 24–8

During the year ended December 31, 19A, M. Lane, a retail merchant who had started a business January 2, 19A, paid trade creditors $49,062 in cash and had an ending inventory per count (*Fifo* basis) of $9,563. Balances available on December 31, 19A, were the following: accounts payable, $16,125; expenses, $2,450; capital (representing total investment in cash January 2, 19A), $45,000; accounts receivable, $13,188; and sales, $50,000. There were no withdrawals. All sales and purchases were on credit.

Required:

1. Develop a worksheet and complete it to provide information for a corrected income statement and balance sheet. *Hint:* Set up four columns for the following: interim entries debit, interim entries credit, income statement, and balance sheet.
2. Prepare a statement of cash inflows and outflows for the year ended December 31, 19A.

Exercise 24–9

On January 1, 19A, A. B. Cline invested $5,000 cash in a television repair shop. Memoranda revealed that $50 per week was withdrawn for living expenses. Cline's personal automobile, having a market value of $2,500 at that time, was invested in the business for use as a service car. The shop then paid $500 for body changes on the car to make it suitable for their needs; this amount was capitalized. On January 1, 19A, F. Frye also invested as a partner. Frye invested equipment valued at $3,000 and $1,000 cash. It was agreed that the partners would share profits equally after January 1, 19A. Frye withdrew $800 cash during the year.

On December 31, 19A, the following assets and liabilities were determined from memoranda and other records: cash, $4,810; equipment (less depreciation), $4,600; receivables, $1,200; car (net of depreciation), $2,250; notes payable, $1,000.

Required:

Prepare a balance sheet showing capital balances for each partner and a separate computation of net income.

Exercise 24–10

Compute the four account balances needed for the 19B income statement from the following data (each item is independent):

a. Wages: amount paid during 19B, $15,000; accrued on December 31, 19A, $1,000; and accrued on December 31, 19B, $2,000.

b. Rent revenue: amount collected during 19B, $8,000; unearned (collected in advance), $500 on December 31, 19A, and $300 on December 31, 19B; earned but not collected, $200 on December 31, 19A, and $600 on December 31, 19B.

c. Total sales: Cash account, balance, December 31, 19A, $26,000; balance, December 31, 19B, $33,000; and total disbursements for 19B, $39,000. All cash receipts were from customers. Accounts receivable: balance, December 31, 19A, $40,160; and balance, December 31, 19B, $59,000. Accounts written off during 19B as uncollectible, $960.

d. Purchases (before discounts): accounts payable balance on December 31, 19A, $28,320, and on December 31, 19B, $33,000; payments made on accounts during 19B, $46,000; cash discounts taken, $820.

Exercise 24–11

Give the journal entry to account for the missing amount in each of the following situations:

a. Prepaid Insurance: starting balance, $1,400; ending balance, $1,900; amount expired, $1,200.

b. Allowance for Doubtful Accounts: starting balance, $5,000; ending balance, $6,000; bad debts written off, $2,700.

c. Bond Sinking Fund: starting balance, $90,000; ending balance, $102,000; current contribution to sinking fund, $20,000; interest on the sinking fund, $10,000.

d. Premium on Bonds Payable: starting balance, $6,000; ending balance, $4,500; no change in bonds payable.

e. Capital Stock: starting balance, $200,000; ending balance, $250,000; stock sold at par during the year, $30,000.

f. Retained Earnings: starting balance, $34,000 (credit); appropriation to reserve for bond sinking fund, $10,000; charge for stock dividend, $20,000; net income, $42,000; ending balance, $36,000 (credit).

g. Accounts Receivable: starting balance, $25,000;

collections on accounts, $27,000; bad accounts written off, $1,200; sales returns on account, $900; notes received on accounts, $3,000; ending balance, $25,900.

h. Accounts Payable: starting balance, $17,300; cash paid on accounts, $30,200; cash discounts taken, $600; ending balance, $15,500.

Exercise 24–12

For each account indicate the amount that should be reported on the income statement. Show computations.

	Beginning of Period	End of Period
a. Interest revenue collected		
in advance (unearned)	$ 50	$ 75
Uncollected interest revenue (earned)	65	20
Interest collected during period, $200.		
Interest revenue should be reported as $_____.		
b. Accrued wages payable	$ 1,000	$ 1,800
Prepaid wages	400	200
Wages paid during period, $12,000.		
Wages expense should be reported as $_____.		
c. Accounts receivable	$10,000	$14,000
Notes receivable (trade)	2,000	1,000

Cash sales	$120,000
Collections on accounts	40,000
Return sales (on account)	2,000
Collection on trade notes	5,000
Accounts written off as bad	500
Discounts given (on account)	600
Gross sales should be reported as $_____.	

	Beginning	End of
d. Accounts payable	$ 5,000	$ 7,000
Notes payable (trade)	10,000	6,000

Payments on accounts	$ 40,000
Cash purchases	100,000
Discounts taken on credit purchases	1,000
Purchase returns (on account)	1,500
Payments on trade notes	8,000
Gross purchases should be reported as $_____.	

Exercise 24–13

M. F. Sharp operated a hat shop but had not kept complete business records. The following data were secured from various memoranda and records:

An analysis of canceled checks revealed the following cash expenditures: expenses, $4,800; and accounts payable, $9,200. Sharp stated that money was withdrawn from time to time from the cash register for personal living expenses. These withdrawals were estimated to total $3,600. All other receipts were deposited in the bank.

A list of assets and liabilities that was developed follows:

	January 1, 19A	December 31, 19A
Cash	$ 1,200	$ 900
Accounts receivable	1,000	1,500
Inventories	3,900	4,600
Prepaid expenses	100	60
Equipment (net)	4,200	3,800
	10,400	10,860
Accounts payable	1,100	1,300
Proprietorship	$ 9,300	$ 9,560

Required:

Prepare a worksheet to develop the income statement and balance sheet.

Suggestion: Set up columns for: Balances, January 1, 19A; Interim Entries (Debit and Credit); Income Summary; and Balances, December 31, 19A.

PROBLEMS

PART A
Problems 24–1 to 24–6

Problem 24–1

FR Sales Corporation initiated several accounting changes during the year and discovered some errors. The changes and errors are given below. Assume the current year is 19C and that the accounting period ends December 31. The books have not been adjusted or closed at the end of 19C. Disregard income tax considerations.

a. The merchandise inventory at December 31, 19B, was overstated by $10,000.

b. During January 19A, extraordinary repair on machinery was debited to Repair Expense; the $15,000 should have been debited to Machinery, which is being depreciated 15% per year on cost (no residual value).

c. A patent that cost $9,350 has been amortized (straight line) for the past 7 years (excluding 19C) over its legal life of 17 years. It is now clear that its economic life will not be more than 12 years from acquisition date.

d. At the end of 19B revenue collected in advance of $3,000 was included in revenue. It was earned in 19C.

e. Paid $8,000 during January 19A for ordinary repairs on a machine that was acquired during January 19A. The repairs were erroneously capitalized. The machine has an estimated life of five years and no residual value. Assume straight-line depreciation.

f. The rate for bad debts used has been ½% of credit sales, which has proven to be too low; therefore, for 19C and, thereafter, the rate is to be 1% of credit sales. The amount of the expense recorded per year under the old rate was 19A, $800; and 19B, $1,000 (the amount for 19C has not been entered in the accounts since the adjusting entries have not been made). Sales for 19C exceeded 19B sales by 20%.

g. During January 19A, a five-year insurance premium of $750 was paid, which was debited to Insurance Expense.

h. At the end of 19B, accrued wages payable of $1,800 were not recorded; they were paid early in 19C.

Required:

1. For each of the above situations, identify the type of accounting change or error that was involved and briefly explain how each should be accounted for.
2. Give the appropriate entry to record the change and any subsequent adjusting entry in each instance at the end of 19C. Show computations. If no entry is needed, explain why.

Problem 24–2

On January 3, 19A, CA Sales Company purchased a machine that cost $15,000. Although the machine

has an estimated useful life of ten years and estimated residual value of $3,000, it was debited to expense when acquired. It is now December 19D, and the error has been discovered. The average income tax rate is 45%, and straight-line depreciation is used.

Required:

1. Give the entry to correct the accounts at the end of 19D, assuming the books have not yet been closed for 19D, and a second entry for depreciation for 19D. Assume the income tax return was correct; therefore, disregard income taxes.
2. Assume instead that the income tax return also was incorrect because of this error; therefore, additional taxes must be paid, including an 8% penalty for each year on the amount of the tax underpayments less any overpayments. Give the entry to correct the accounts, including the income tax effects, at the end of 19D, and a second entry for depreciation for 19D. Round amounts to nearest dollar.

Problem 24–3

The accounting department of Virginia Corporation had completed the comparative financial reports for the period ending 19C prior to the initiation of the first audit by an outside certified public accountant. This problem relates specifically to two changes recommended by the CPA after the statements were prepared by the company.

The statements have been summarized for problem purposes; details are provided only in respect to the recommended changes; the statements were as follows:

(Relates to Problem 24-3)

	19A	19B	19C
Balance Sheet:			
Assets:			
Machinery	$ 300,000	$ 300,000	$ 300,000
Accumulated depreciation	(80,000)	(100,000)	(120,000)
Remaining assets	2,280,000	2,290,000	2,420,000
Total	$2,500,000	$2,490,000	$2,600,000
Liabilities	$ 373,000	$ 349,000	$ 410,000
Capital stock (200,000 shares)	2,000,000	2,000,000	2,000,000
Retained earnings	127,000	141,000	190,000
Total	$2,500,000	$2,490,000	$2,600,000
Income Statement:			
Sales (all on credit)	$1,000,000	$1,100,000	$1,200,000
Cost of goods sold	600,000	650,000	700,000
Gross margin	400,000	450,000	500,000
Operating expenses	300,000	330,000	360,000
Income taxes (assume 50%)	50,000	60,000	70,000
Income before extraordinary items	50,000	60,000	70,000
Extraordinary items	10,000	(20,000)	14,000
Less income tax effect	(3,000)	4,000	(5,000)
Net Income	$ 57,000	$ 44,000	$ 79,000
Earnings per share data:			
Income before extraordinary items	$ 0.250	$ 0.300	$ 0.350
Net income	0.285	0.220	0.395
Statement of Retained Earnings:			
Beginning balance	$ 100,000	$ 127,000	$ 141,000
Net income	57,000	44,000	79,000
Dividends	(30,000)	(30,000)	(30,000)
Ending Balance	$ 127,000	$ 141,000	$ 190,000

On the basis of the examination the auditor insisted on the following changes:

1. Starting with 19C, change the expected loss rate on credit sales from ½% to ¼%. This change was dictated by collection experience and losses during the past two years. These analyses indicate a drop in expected bad debt losses. The company has initiated a tight control on credit granting and has also intensified collection efforts.
2. On January 1, 19A, a machine costing $20,000 (ten-year life, no residual value) was inadvertently debited to Operating Expense at that time. The error was discovered by the CPA at the end of 19C; the machine has seven more years of useful life (after 19C). Assume a 6% per annum tax penalty on net tax deficiencies for 19A and 19B only.

Required:

a. Analyze the nature of each item.
b. Determine the effects of implementing the change or error correction, including income tax effects, on the financial statements assuming they are to be reported on comparative statements covering the three years.
c. Give the entry to effect the change including the correction of 19C entries and the related income tax effects. The books for 19C have been adjusted but not closed.
d. Compute the correct amounts for all items on the financial statements that would be affected for each of the three years.

Problem 24-4

Landon Company failed to recognize accruals and deferrals in the accounts. In addition, numerous other errors were made in computing net income. The incomes for the past three years are given below along with a list of the items that were incorrectly recognized in the recordkeeping.

You are to set up a worksheet to correct income for each year. Set up columns for the following: 19A, 19B, 19C, and accounts to be corrected. Key and briefly identify the errors under the "Account" column and enter amounts under the respective years as plus or minus so that the last line will report corrected income.

All items are material. Disregard income tax effects.

		19A	19B	19C
a.	Reported income (loss) ..	$4,000	$(3,500)	$10,000
	Items not recognized correctly at each year-end:			
b.	Accrued expense	400	250	300
c.	Revenue collected in advance	100		200
d.	Prepaid expense	320	410	120
e.	Revenue earned but not collected	170	140	
f.	Annual depreciation overstated (per year)		1,000	1,200
g.	Annual provision for doubtful accounts understated (per year)	170	200	190
h.	Goods purchased on December 31, included in ending inventory; not recorded until following year	460	210	150
i.	Sales on December 31 not recorded until following year; the goods were not included in ending inventory	290	770	390
j.	Ending inventory overstated	130	240	290
k.	Checks written and mailed on December 31 as payment on accounts payable; not recorded until next year	1,100	1,500	1,400
l.	Bad debts that should have been written off to allowance for doubtful accounts by year-end	800	950	1,170

Problem 24–5

R. Waters established a retail business in 19A. Early in 19D Waters entered into negotiations with J. Jones with the intent to form a partnership. You have been asked by Waters and Jones to check Waters' books for the past three years and to compute the correct income for each year.

The profits reported on statements submitted to you were as follows:

	Year Ending 12/31		
	19A	19B	19C
Income	$9,000	$10,109	$8,840

During the examination of the accounts, you found the following:

(Relates to Problem 24–5)

	Year Ending 12/31		
	19A	*19B*	*19C*

Omissions from the books:

A. Accrued expenses at end of year	$2,160	$2,094	$4,624
B. Earned (uncollected) revenue at end of year	200	—	—
C. Prepaid expenses at end of year	902	1,210	1,406
D. Unearned revenue (collected in advance) at end of year	—	610	—

Goods in transit at end of year omitted from inventory:

E. Purchase for which the entry had been made (ownership passed)	—	2,610	—
F. Purchase for which the entry had not been made (ownership not passed)	—		1,710

Other points requiring consideration:

G. Depreciation on equipment had been recorded monthly since acquisition, through 19C, by a debit to expense and a credit to accumulated depreciation account at a blanket rate of 1% of end-of-month balances of equipment account. However, the sale during the early part of December 19B of certain equipment was entered as a debit to Cash and a credit to the asset account for the sale price of .... (This equipment was purchased in July 19A at a cost of $6,000.)	—	5,000	—
H. No allowance had been set up for uncollectible accounts. It is decided to set up an allowance for the estimated probable losses on the outstanding accounts as of December 31, 19C, for:			
19B accounts	—	—	700
19C accounts	—	—	1,500
and to correct the charge against each year so that it will show the losses (actual and estimated) relating to that year's sales. Accounts had been written off to expense as follows:			
19A accounts	1,000	1,200	—
19B accounts	—	400	2,000
19C accounts	—	—	1,600

(AICPA adapted)

Problem 24–6

The records of AB Corporation have never been audited. At the end of 19K, the company prepared the following financial statements (summarized):

Income statement:

Sales and service revenue	$600,000
Expenses:	
Cost of goods sold	(350,000)
Distribution expenses	(120,000)
Administrative expenses	(60,000)
Pretax income	70,000
Income taxes	21,500
Net Income	$ 48,500

Balance Sheet:

Assets:	
Cash	$ 23,000
Accounts receivable (net)	40,000
Inventory (periodic system)	110,000
Property, plant, and equipment (net)	160,000
Patent	8,000
Other assets	9,000
Total Assets	$350,000
Liabilities:	
Accounts payable	$ 80,000
Income taxes payable	15,000
Notes payable, long term (8%)	40,000
Total Liabilities	135,000

Stockholders' Equity:

Common stock, par $10	145,000
Retained earnings (including 19K net income)	80,000
Dividends paid	(10,000)
Total Stockholders' Equity	215,000
Total Liabilities and Stockholders' Equity	$350,000

The company is negotiating a large loan for expansion purposes. The bank has requested that an audit of the company be performed. During the course of the audit, the following facts were determined:

a. The inventory at December 31, 19J, was overstated by $10,000.

b. The inventory at December 31, 19K, was overstated by $20,000.

c. The property, plant, and equipment was underdepreciated in 19J by $9,000 and in 19K by $12,000 (report as a separate expense).

d. A three-year insurance premium of $900 paid on January 3, 19J, was debited to Administrative Expense at that time.

e. Accrued wages (an element of Administrative Expense) were not recorded as follows: 19J, $800; and 19K, $1,000.

f. The patent, which originally cost $17,000, has been amortized to administrative expense over a 17-year life (including 19K). Evidence clearly indicates that its economic life will approximate 14 years from date of acquisition.

g. Service revenues earned but not yet collected were not recognized when earned, as follows: 19J, $5,000; and 19K, $7,500.

h. A delivery truck purchased January 19K, at a cost of $13,000, was debited to Distribution Expense at that time. The truck has an estimated useful life of ten years and an estimated residual value of $2,000. The company uses straight-line depreciation (report depreciation as a Distribution Expense).

i. Bad debts amounting to $7,500 have not been written off.

j. Common stock outstanding, 12,000 shares.

Required:

1. Set up a worksheet to develop corrected amounts for the 19K income statement and balance sheet. Complete the worksheet and key your entries. Assume the income tax expense amount is correct despite the above items. Suggestion: Set up pairs of columns for Trial balance, Entries, Income Summary, Retained Earnings, and Balance sheet. Also, you will need four lines for property, plant,

and equipment; six for retained earnings; and three for administrative expense.

2. Prepare a corrected income statement and balance sheet.

PART B
Problems 24–7 to 24–9

Problem 24–7

Cooper Hat Shop maintained incomplete records. After investigation the following assets and liabilities were identified:

Assets

	January 1, 19A	December 31, 19A
Cash on hand	$ 90	$ 160
Cash in bank	1,250	870
Accounts receivable	6,700	6,830
Inventory	3,100	3,800
Equipment (net of depreciation)	5,200	5,600
Prepaid insurance	120	60
	16,460	17,320

Equities

Accounts payable	1,000	2,200
Bank loan		3,000
Accrued expenses payable	90	50
	1,090	5,250
Owner's Equity	$15,370	$12,070

An analysis of bank deposits and disbursements showed:

Deposits:

Collections from customers	$8,900
Proceeds of bank loan	3,000
Additional investment by proprietor	1,200

Checks and charges:

Payments on account	6,100
Expenses	4,500
Refunds on sales (allowances)	350
Proprietor's withdrawals	1,500
Interest on bank loan	30
Purchase of equipment	1,000

Required:

1. Compute the net income or loss by analyzing the changes in proprietorship.

2. Prepare a detailed income statement, including computation schedules.

Problem 24–8

Harper Company has maintained single-entry records. In applying for a much-needed loan, a set of financial statements was needed. An analysis of the records for 19C provided the following data:

Cash receipts:

Cash sales	$130,000
Collections on credit sales	43,000
Collections on trade notes	1,000
Purchase allowances	1,500
Miscellaneous revenue	250

Cash payments:

Cash purchases	84,500
Payments to trade creditors	34,100
Payment on mortgage on July 1, 19C, plus prepayment of one year's interest of $1,020 to July 1, 19D	4,020
Sales commissions	7,200
Rent expense	2,400
General expenses (including interest)	14,590
Other operating expenses	29,800
Sales returns ($3,000 of which $1,000 was cash)	1,000
Insurance (renewal three-year premium, April 1)	468
Operational assets purchased	1,500

	Balances	
	January 1, 19C	December 31, 19C
Cash	$14,100	$10,172
Accounts receivable	13,000	18,000
Trade notes receivable	2,000	1,500
Inventory	10,000	18,400
Prepaid insurance	39	?
Prepaid interest expense	600	510
Trade accounts payable	26,500	23,800
Income taxes payable		1,984
Accrued operating expenses payable	600	400
Operational assets (net)	35,400	33,290
Other assets	11,861	11,861
Capital stock	40,000	40,000
Mortgage payable (6%, dated July 1, 19A)	20,000	?

No operational assets were sold during the year.

Required:

Prepare a worksheet to provide data for a detailed income statement for 19C and a balance sheet at the end of 19C. Show how the amounts for the various entries were developed. Suggestion: set up columns for Balances, January 1, 19C; Interim entries—debit and credit; Income summary; and Balance sheet, December 31, 19C (use a "debits-over-credits" format).

Problem 24–9

The following data were taken from the records of Baker's Sporting Goods Store:

	Balances	
	January 1, 19A	December 31, 19A
Accounts receivable	$ 2,300	$ 3,900
Notes receivable (trade)	1,500	2,000
Interest receivable	90	70
Prepaid interest on notes payable	75	60
Inventory	9,255	10,400
Prepaid expenses (operating)	100	130
Store equipment (net)	8,500	8,600
Other assets	—	500
Accounts payable	1,700	1,900
Notes payable (trade)	11,000	11,500
Notes payable (equipment)	—	500
Accrued interest payable	40	30
Accrued expenses (operating) payable	170	210
Interest revenue collected in advance	30	40

An analysis of the checkbook, canceled checks, deposit slips, and bank statements provided the following summary for the year:

Balance, January 1, 19A		$4,200
Cash receipts:		
Cash sales	$23,000	
On accounts receivable	7,600	
On notes receivable	1,000	
Interest revenue	160	
Cash disbursements:		
Cash purchases	11,800	
On accounts payable	2,400	
On notes payable (trade)	500	
Interest expense	560	
Operating expenses	14,130	
Miscellaneous nonoperating expenses	970	
Other assets purchased	500	
Withdrawals by H. Baker	2,400	
Balance, December 31, 19A		$2,700

Required:

1. Compute income by analyzing the changes in the proprietorship account.
2. Prepare a detailed income statement with supporting schedules; show computations.

25

Interim Reports, Segment Reporting, and Analysis of Financial Statements

Throughout this book, the focus has been on *annual* financial reporting to *external* parties—stockholders, potential investors, financial analysts, creditors, and the public at large. Two aspects of external financial reporting—interim reports and segment reporting—have been referred to only indirectly. These two types of reporting, designed to help the users of external financial reports, are briefly discussed in this chapter.

Certain analytical techniques which have been developed to meet the special information needs of statement users will be presented. The accountant often is also involved in the analysis, interpretation, and evaluation of financial statements, including the development of related analytical techniques. The latter part of this chapter presents some of the more conventional analytical techniques for interpreting external financial statements. The Appendix to this chapter provides an actual case for study.

INTERIM REPORTING

The focus throughout this book has been on annual financial statements. This focus reflects the time period assumption, discussed in Chapter 2, which is based on investors' need for timely financial information. Actually, annual data are not very timely because investors cannot wait

until shortly after the end of each fiscal year to make all their investment decisions. They need more timely information. Interim data, usually on a quarterly basis, often are presented by companies to help meet this need.

The critical issue in interim reporting may be posed as follows:

> Should each interim period be viewed for reporting purposes as a *discrete* time period unto itself? Or, alternatively, should each interim period be viewed for reporting purposes as an *integral part* of the annual period?

The accounting literature and GAAP strongly imply that investors are primarily interested in annual data, and annual income in particular. On this basis, then, it is not surprising that *APB Opinion No. 28,* "Interim Financial Reporting," focused on attaining more standardization in interim reporting.

The "discrete period" and "integral part" views of interim periods are briefly discussed as background for understanding interim reporting.

The Discrete Period and Integral Part Approaches. An example will illustrate the difference between the discrete period and integral part approaches to interim reporting. Many retailing companies build up their merchandise inventories during the late summer and autumn and make a high proportion of their sales during the months of November, December, and January (many large retailers use fiscal years that end on January 31). Sales volume then declines drastically during the next few months. What income tax rate should these companies use in computing income tax expense for the first quarter report of the new period when sales volume is very low? Assuming pretax income of the first quarter is so low that the tax on that amount of income would be at a relatively low rate (compared to the entire year), the *discrete period approach* would apply the low rate to the first quarter and would apply the higher rates to the pretax incomes of the later quarters. On the other hand, the *integral part approach* would estimate the average income tax rate for the entire year and apply it to the first (and remaining) quarterly income. To derive the estimated average rate, it is necessary to estimate (a) what tax rates will be imposed for the year, (b) what pretax income for the year will be, and (c) the modifications of income taxes that may occur as a result of investment tax credits and other tax-adjusting items. *APB Opinion No. 28* requires use of the integral part approach which has the effect of applying approximately uniform rates to pretax income of each quarter.

APB Opinion No. 28 included the following interim reporting requirements (summarized) for interim financial statements presenting results of operations, financial position, and changes in financial position:

1. Revenues should be recognized in the interim period as earned.
2. Expenses should be divided into two groups:
   a. Expenses that are directly associated with revenue should be recognized when the related revenue is recorded as earned. This reflects the discrete part approach for expenses that are directly associated with revenue.
   b. Expenses not directly associated with revenue should be "charged to income in interim periods as incurred or allocated among interim periods based on an estimate of time expired, benefits received, or activity associated with the (interim) periods." In effect, this rule says to account for expenses not directly associated with revenue of the interim period in the same way such expenses are accounted for on an annual basis. Costs that are capitalized in one year (i.e., prepaid expenses and deferred charges) and amortized over future years should be capitalized in the *interim period* when they are incurred and amortized over future interim periods. Costs that are normally expensed as incurred (i.e., accrued expenses) for annual reporting purposes also should be expensed as incurred for *interim* reporting purposes.

3. Special rules governing accounting for three items included in category 2*(a)* above:
   a. *Lifo* inventory liquidation in an interim period but expected to be replaced before year-end—When a *Lifo* inventory layer is liquidated in an interim period, and is expected to be replaced before year-end, the company should debit cost of goods sold of the interim period of liquidation with the anticipated replacement cost of the number of units (of the *Lifo* layer) liquidated.
   b. Inventory losses from market value declines in an interim period—Such losses should be recognized in the interim period during which they occur, if they are believed to be permanent. If such losses are believed to be temporary (i.e., expected to be recovered later through market value increases before year-end), they "need not be recognized at the interim date since no loss is expected to be incurred in the fiscal year."
   c. Income tax expense for each interim period should be based on an estimate of the income tax rate for the full year to avoid interim period fluctuations in tax amounts which are not warranted in relation to the tax rate for the full year.

Note that the three rules cited above reflect the integral part approach.

4. Special rules governing accounting for three items included in category 2*(b)* above:

a. Unusual, nonrecurring, and extraordinary items, as well as gains and losses on the disposal of a segment of a business, should be reported in the interim period during which they occur.

b. Contingent losses and related liabilities should be reported in the financial statements of the interim period during which they occur and in all subsequent interim and annual financial statements until the contingency is removed.

c. Accounting changes:

   (1) Changes in accounting estimates should be accounted for prospectively, that is, through changes in affected estimated data of the interim period of the change and in the estimated data of all future interim periods affected by the change.

   (2) Changes in accounting principles which require a cumulative "catch-up" adjustment should be reported in accordance with *APB Opinion No. 20* in the financial statements of the interim period of the change. On this point *APB Opinion No. 28*, par. 27, states:

   The cumulative effect of a change in accounting practice or policy should be calculated in an interim period by determining the effect of the change on the amount of retained earnings at the beginning of the annual period in which the interim period falls. The effect of the change from the beginning of the annual period to the period of change should be reported as a determinant of net income in the interim period in which the change is made. When the previously reported interim information is subsequently presented, it should be restated to give effect to the accounting change.

   (3) Changes in accounting reporting entities and changes in accounting principles required in *APB Opinion No. 20* to be reported by retroactively restating prior year financial statements should be accounted for and reported the same way in interim financial statements. That is, retroactively restate, on the new basis, the financial statements of prior interim periods presented in comparative form along with the financial statements of the interim period of change.

Note that the three items (4[*a*], 4[*b*], and 4[*c*]) reflect the discrete period approach inasmuch as the revenue (or gain or credit adjustment) or expense (or loss or debit adjustment) is reported in the interim period during which the item occurred. The revenue or expense is not allocated to other interim periods.

APB Opinion No. 28 requires disclosure of the following items, as a minimum, in interim summary reports other than complete financial statements:

a. Sales, income taxes, and net income.

b. Disposal of a segment of a business and extraordinary, unusual, or infrequently occurring items.

c. Primary and fully diluted earnings per share.

d. Seasonal revenue, costs, or expenses.

e. Significant changes in estimates or provisions for income taxes.

f. Changes in accounting principles or estimates.

g. Contingent items.

h. Significant changes in financial position.

A summary of interim reporting is presented in the illustrative financial statements (Note 11, Quarterly Data) for Peavey Company.

SEGMENT (OR LINE OF BUSINESS) REPORTING

Many large corporations engage in more than one line of business; in fact, even many smaller corporations have diversified their operations into more than one industry. Investors seeking to assess the relative attractiveness of the stock of a diversified company were until recently faced with the difficult task of analyzing the investment from company data which reflected only the aggregate of its operations.

To better understand the problem, suppose you are an investor analyzing General Electric Company (GE). GE produces and sells products ranging from light bulbs to household appliances to aircraft engines. Supply and demand for these three product groups (consumer non-durables, consumer durables, and heavy machinery) react differently during good and bad economic times. For example, consumers will continue to buy light bulbs during depressions as well as during prosperous times. To a lessor extent, consumers must also have kitchen ranges to prepare their meals during hard times; however, they will probably continue to use their old ranges longer than during prosperous times. Thus, demand for kitchen ranges is more elastic than demand for light bulbs. The demand for air travel and the concomitant demand for aircraft engines is even more elastic than the demand for light bulbs. Stated differently, these three industrial groups possess different *risk* characteristics. It is reasonable to suppose that investors who know the relative proportions of company resources committed to operations in specific industries can make more informed decisions than investors who only know the aggregate data of the company.

The above reasoning is the basis for requiring companies to report *segment data*. The basis is supported by the results of a number of empirical research studies which have indicated that hypothetical investment decisions based on segment data turn out better than decisions based on aggregated data.

In recognition of these circumstances, the FASB first issued *FASB Statement No. 14,* "Financial Reporting for Segments of a Business Enterprise" in December 1976. It set out the general principles described above. In November 1977, *FASB Statement No. 18* was issued; it provided that segment information was not required in statements for *interim periods. FASB Statement No. 21,* issued in April 1978, suspended the requirement of reporting segment information by *smaller and closely held* companies and also eliminated reporting of earnings per share by such companies.

In the context of *FASB Statement No. 14,* a *reportable segment* is defined by "(a) identifying the individual products or services from which the enterprise derives its revenue, (b) grouping those products and services by industry lines into industry segments . . . , and (c) selecting those industry segments that are significant with respect to the enterprise as a whole."

A "significant" industry segment is one which meets *any one* of the following criteria:

a. Its revenue is 10% or more of the combined revenue of all segments of the entity.
b. The absolute amount of its operating profit or loss is 10% or more of the greater, in absolute amount, of
   (1) The combined operating *profit* of all industry segments of the entity that did not incur an operating loss, or
   (2) The combined operating *loss* of all industry segments of the entity that did incur an operating loss.
c. Its identifiable assets are 10% or more of the combined identifiable assets of all industry segments (of the entity).

FASB Statement No. 14, as amended by *FASB Statements Nos. 18* and *21,* requires publicly held corporations to report for each *reportable segment* of the entity:

a. Revenues.
b. Operating profit or loss (i.e., revenue less operating expenses).
c. Identifiable assets.
d. Depreciation, depletion, and amortization expense.
e. Capital expenditures.
f. Effects of accounting changes.
g. Equity in net income and net assets of equity method investees whose operations are vertically integrated[1] with the operations of the segment, as well as the geographic areas in which those vertically integrated equity method investees operate.

In addition, *FASB Statement No. 14* requires companies to report the following three items for each *foreign operation,* if either (1) revenue

---

[1] Vertical integration refers to the complementary nature of a parent and its subsidiaries' product lines whereby one supplies inputs to the other. An example of vertical integration would be General Motors and Libbey-Owens-Ford or Fisher Body. Another example would be American Telephone and Telegraph and Western Electric (which builds the telephones).

EXHIBIT 25–1
Segment Reporting

Peavey Company and Subsidiaries Lines of Business
(amounts in thousands)

Net Sales—Year Ended July 31	1973 Amount	%	1974 Amount	%	1975 Amount	%	1976 Amount	%	1977 Amount	%
Agricultural Group.	$ 88,807	27	117,305	25	114,929	25	108,923	22	96,361	20
Industrial Foods Group.	185,808	56	283,793	59	263,856	56	258,034	51	208,787	42
Consumer Foods Group.	18,365	6	25,328	5	26,711	6	30,842	6	41,519	8
Retail Group.	36,662	11	50,481	11	62,116	13	108,023	21	147,639	30
Total before Canadian Operations.	329,642	100	476,907	100	467,612	100	505,822	100	494,306	100
Canadian Operations (Note 1).	34,539		17,831		—		—		—	
Total Net Sales.	$364,181		494,738		467,612		505,822		494,306	

Earnings before Taxes on Income—Year Ended July 31	1973 Amount	%	1974 Amount	%	1975 Amount	%	1976 Amount	%	1977 Amount	%
Agricultural Group.	$ 11,099	61	21,019	69	16,555	60	10,739	33	(3,379)	(18)
Industrial Foods Group.	5,153	29	7,731	25	7,648	28	11,750	36	10,629	58
Consumer Foods Group.	(344)	(2)	(1,573)	(5)	112	—	1,529	5	2,005	11
Retail Group.	2,225	12	3,194	11	3,359	12	8,406	26	9,150	49
Total before Unallocated Items and Canadian Operations.	18,133	100	30,371	100	27,674	100	32,424	100	18,405	100
Canadian Operations (Note 1).	3,126		1,896		—		—		—	
Unallocated Items.	(1,873)		(1,232)		1,329		(3,379)		(5,145)	
Total Earnings before Taxes on Income.	$ 19,386		31,035		29,003		29,045		13,260	

Note 1: Represents operations disposed of in 1974, net of related minority interests.

The chart below graphically indicates progress made over the past five years toward improving the balance of the sources of operating earnings between Peavey's traditional grain and flour milling businesses and the newer activities of consumer foods and specialty retailing.

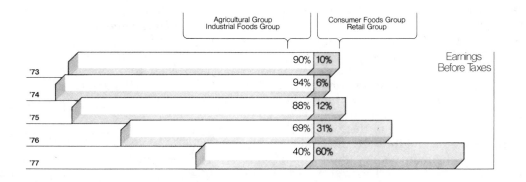

from foreign operations is 10% or more of consolidated revenue or (2) identifiable assets of the entity's foreign operations are 10% or more of consolidated total assets:

a. Revenues.
b. Operating profit or loss.
c. Identifiable assets.

Finally, "if 10% or more of the revenue of an enterprise is derived from sales to any *single customer,* that fact and the amount of revenue from each such customer shall be disclosed." (Emphasis supplied.) Data on these three segment groups—*reportable industry segments, foreign operations,* and *major customers*—are intended to provide investors with the data needed to assess the *relative risks* of diversified companies.

An actual example of segment (line of business) reporting is shown in Exhibit 25–1.

ANALYSIS OF FINANCIAL STATEMENTS

Analysis of financial statements focuses primarily on the data reported in external financial reports plus supplementary information from other sources such as company management, investment advisors, trade associations, business periodicals, government agencies, and other materials distributed by the company. These latter sources are often particularly important because they may disclose useful information on a more timely basis than published financial statements. For example, litigation may threaten the profit potential of a company, and sources such as the *Wall Street Journal* may provide timely disclosure of such events. The analyst can then use this information in evaluating the reported financial statements which are affected by the litigation. One of the primary objectives of financial statement analysis is identification of *major changes* (i.e., turning points) in trends, amounts, and relationships and investigation of the reasons underlying those changes. Often a *turning point* may provide an early warning of a significant change in the future success or failure of the business.

In analyzing and interpreting financial statements, one should recognize that financial statements are *organized summaries* of an extensive mass of detailed financial information. For example, the published financial statements (and notes) of a large corporation, such as General Motors, Exxon, or IBM, usually fill from five to ten printed pages, including the supporting notes. It is difficult to imagine the number of transactions, the critical accounting decisions, and the voluminous detail summarized in these few pages. It is also difficult to perceive, although it is often true, that millions of dollars may be immaterial because they amount to less than 5% of the total base amount of which it is a part. Summarization presents serious communication problems. On the other hand, excessive detail is considered to be undesirable because statement users experience time constraints in analyzing a mass of data.

ANALYTICAL APPROACHES AND TECHNIQUES

The analysis of financial statements is much broader than the mere computation of a few ratios. It involves an organized approach to glean from the totality of the statements selected data relevant to the decision area, analysis of that data, and interpretation of the results of the analysis. Important steps in the evaluation and interpretation of financial statements are as follows:

1. Examine the auditors' report.
2. Analyze the statement of accounting policies included in the notes to the financial statements.
3. Examine the overall financial statements, including notes and supporting schedules.
4. Apply analytical techniques such as
    a. Comparative statements.
    b. Horizontal and vertical percentage analyses.
    c. Ratio analyses.
5. Search for important supplemental information not provided by the financial statements.

EXAMINE THE AUDITORS' REPORT

Expert financial analysts often suggest that in evaluating a financial statement, the first basic step is careful examination of the auditors' report (often called the accountants' report). Of course, this presumes that the financial statements are audited. If they are not, one should usually give very little, if any, credibility to them. The auditors' report is important because it provides the analyst with information concerning the "fairness" of the representations in the financial statements and calls attention to all major concerns of the auditor that came to light as a result of the auditor's intensive examination.

The auditors' report was discussed in Chapter 5, and it would be advisable to restudy that discussion. Examples of unqualified auditors' opinions were given there and at the end of Chapter 4. Also the Appendix to this chapter presents an auditors' report and the statements to which it relates. Of particular importance is the possibility that instead of an *unqualified opinion,* the auditor may give *(a)* a qualified opinion, *(b)* an adverse opinion, or *(c)* a disclaimer of opinion. Each of these three unfavorable opinions must include an explanation by the auditor of the factors underlying the decision to render such an opinion. These unfavorable opinions serve to alert the statement user to major problem areas that should be investigated. An unfavorable auditors' opinion may cause the SEC to stop public trading in the stock of the company which in and of itself is considered serious by investors.

Below is a qualified opinion (and related notes) that illustrates the kind of information frequently cited by an auditor.[2] Observe in this situation that the qualification is related to continuation of the business as a *going concern* because of a critical credit situation. This may be one of the single most important bits of information in the financial statements of this company.

> To the Board of Directors and Stockholders American Motors Corporation, Southfield, Michigan:
>
> We have examined the accompanying consolidated balance sheets of American Motors Corporation and consolidated subsidiaries as of

September 30, 1976 and 1975, and the related statements of operations, additional paid-in capital, earnings retained for use in the business, and changes in financial position for the years then ended. Our examination was made in accordance with generally accepted auditing standards, and accordingly included such tests of the accounting records and such other auditing procedures as we considered necessary in the circumstances.

> As described in Note D, the Company has outstanding short-term notes to various financial institutions at September 30, 1976, pursuant to credit agreements that are renegotiated and renewed each December. The continuity of the business of the Company depends upon the availability of adequate financing as well as an improvement in operating results.
>
> In our opinion, subject to the effects, if any, on the consolidated financial statements of the ultimate resolution of the matters referred to in the preceding paragraph, the aforementioned consolidated financial statements present fairly the financial position of American Motors Corporation and consolidated subsidiaries at September 30, 1976 and 1975, and the results of their operations and changes in their financial position for the years then ended, in conformity with generally accepted accounting principles applied on a consistent basis.

Notes to Financial Statements

Note D: Short-term Bank Borrowings—AM General Corporation, a wholly owned subsidiary, has $35,000,000 outstanding notes at September 30, 1976, with interest at ½ of 1% above the prime rate, pursuant to a Credit Agreement. The assets of AM General are pledged as security for this borrowing, and American Motors Corporation, as guarantor, has agreed to various covenants relating to levels of working capital, net worth, additional indebtedness, and prohibition of cash dividends. In addition, at September 30, 1976, American Motors Corporation had $22,550,000 of notes outstanding with interest at the lenders' prime rate, pursuant to lines of credit.

The above credit facilities annually expire in December, and the Company is negotiating with the lenders for the continued availability of this financing. In the opinion of management, the outstanding credit will be continued, subject to the existing terms and conditions.

Other miscellaneous short-term borrowings at September 30, 1976, were $5,520,000.

---

[2] American Motors Corporation, Annual Report, 1976, Extracted from AICPA *Accounting Trends and Techniques,* 31st ed. (New York, 1977), p. 375.

ANALYZE THE STATEMENT OF ACCOUNTING POLICIES

Accounting is man-made and must accommodate a wide variety of circumstances. Although accounting principles and their implementation are largely prescribed by the *ARBs, APB Opinions, FASB Statements,* and by precedent, there is considerable room for judgment by the reporting entity and by the independent accountant with respect to the accounting treatment to be accorded many items. In numerous areas of accounting, several alternatives are acceptable, such as the completed contract and percentage of completion methods of recognizing revenue on long-term construction contracts (see Chapter 12). The range of judgments and alternatives permitted make it very difficult to analyze financial statements if the major judgments and alternatives used by the company are not clearly communicated.

In response to the *full disclosure* principle, *APB Opinion No. 22* "Disclosure of Accounting Policies," (April 1972) states that "information about the accounting policies adopted by a reporting entity is essential for financial statement users." Accounting policies are the specific accounting principles and methods that have been adopted by a company for preparation of its financial statements. The *Opinion* requires that a statement of these policies be clearly enunciated either in the notes, or preferably "in a separate *Summary of Significant Accounting Policies* preceding the notes to the financial statements or as the initial note." The statement must disclose all important accounting policies including *(a)* selections from acceptable alternatives, *(b)* accounting policies used that are peculiar to the industry, and *(c)* unusual or innovative applications of generally accepted accounting principles. Examples include the basis for consolidated statements, depreciation and amortization methods, inventory pricing, translation of foreign currencies, revenue recognition on long-term construction contracts, franchising, and leasing.

A statement of accounting policies is shown for each of the three companies whose annual financial statements are shown at the end of Chapters 4, 5, and 25.

The information in the statement of accounting policies is fundamental to understanding, interpreting, and evaluating much of the significant information reported in the financial statements. It is particularly useful in evaluating the *credibility and quality of the reported earnings,* and in comparing data across companies and industries.

OVERALL EXAMINATION OF THE FINANCIAL STATEMENTS

Following the examination of the auditors' opinion and analysis of the summary of accounting policies used by the company, the evaluation and interpretive process should continue with a careful examination of the financial statements in their entirety. This phase of the analysis involves study of each statement in order to gain overall perspective and to identify major strengths, weaknesses, and unusual changes, such as *turning points* in the trend of sales, earnings, asset structure, liabilities, capital structure and cash flow.

The overall examination should include careful study of all of the statements included and the *notes* referred to in those statements. Each note should be read and evaluated at the point in the statement where it is referenced. Consideration of the notes as a separate activity is not as fruitful, since a specific note is helpful primarily in the context of the specific statement item to which it is referenced. The official position of the AICPA is that the notes are an integral part of the financial statements.

Concurrent with, or subsequent to, the overall examination of the financial statements under review, application of the analytical techniques discussed in the next section may be quite helpful to the analyst.

APPLICATION OF ANALYTICAL TECHNIQUES

Various approaches are used to enhance effective communication through financial statements, such as ratio analysis, "the president's letter," graphic presentations, special tabulations, earnings per share, subclassifications of information on the statements, comparative statements, and supplementary information in separate schedules and notes to the statements.

Comparative Statements

Comparative statements involve the presentation of financial information for the current and one or more past periods in a way that facilitates comparison by the statement user. Basically, comparative statements are of two types, viz:

1. Presentation of financial reports for *(a)* the current year and *(b)* the immediately preceding year.
2. Presentation of selected financial information for a number of years past (e.g., five or ten years). These are often referred to as *financial* summaries.

Trends in the financial development of a business have particular significance to all users. The comparison of current results with those of one or more prior periods provides an added perspective in evaluating the relationship of current performance with past performance; that is, multiple period results provide one of the useful ways to evaluate progress, improvement, or deterioration. As a result, practically all published financial statements include comparative data for the current and prior year. For example, the actual financial statements presented at the end of Chapters 4 and 5, and in the Appendix to this chapter, are comparative.

For illustrative purposes, the financial statements for WZH Corporation are used throughout this chapter. Exhibits 25–2, 25–3, and 25–4 present the three comparative statements (condensed for discussion purposes). Observe the form: the current year results are in the first column; and single underscores for subtotals facilitate the presentation in a single column for each period. Placing the various items for the two periods in juxtaposition (side by side) in the two columns is preferable to separation.

The *long-term summaries* of selected financial information often included in the annual financial report are especially significant. An actual example of such a summary is presented in the Appendix to this chapter. Observe in par-

EXHIBIT 25–2

WZH CORPORATION
Comparative Income Statements
For the Years Ended December 31, 19B, and 19A

	19B		19A	
	Amount	Percent*	Amount	Percent*
Revenues:				
Sales	$400,000†		$370,000	
Investment revenue	4,500		3,000	
Gain on disposal of investments	500			
Total revenues	405,000	100	373,000	100
Expenses:				
Cost of goods sold	265,000	65	250,000	67
Distribution	67,000	17	61,200	16
General administrative	30,000	7	27,000	7
Interest	7,100	2	6,200	2
Total expenses	369,100	91	344,400	92
Pretax operating income	35,900	9	28,600	8
Income tax expense	16,155	4	12,870	4
Income before extraordinary item	19,745	5		
Extraordinary loss (net of taxes, $3,600)	4,400	1		
Net Income	$ 15,345	4	$ 15,730	4
Earnings per share:				
Income before extraordinary loss	$0.40			
Extraordinary loss	(0.11)			
Net Income‡	$0.29		$0.33	

* For illustrative purposes only; not usually included on published statements.
† Credit sales $345,000.
‡ ($15,345 − $2,500, preferred dividends) ÷ 44,000 = $.29.
   ($15,730 − $2,500, preferred dividends) ÷ 40,000 = $.33.

ticular the nature of the items selected for inclusion in the summary. These measures of the long-term financial performance of the company are particularly relevant for financial statement analysis. The annual financial statements for one year alone present a very narrow view of the successes and failures of the company. In contrast, the long-term summary provides a broad overview of where the company has been (financially) in the past and may provide clues as to where it is apt to go in the future. In this regard, the results of one, or even two, years may give an uninformed view of the potentials of the company. It is for these reasons that analysts are especially interested in the long-term summary.

PERCENTAGE ANALYSIS OF FINANCIAL STATEMENTS

Financial information expressed in absolute amounts is the accepted means of conveying ac-

EXHIBIT 25–3

WZH CORPORATION
Comparative Balance Sheets
At December 31, 19B, and 19A

	19B		19A	
Assets	Amount	Percent*	Amount	Percent*
Current Assets:				
Cash	$ 55,000	12	$ 74,000	16
Investments, short term	4,000	1	10,000	2
Accounts receivable (net of allowance for doubtful accounts)	39,000	8	30,000	6
Inventory (Fifo, lower of cost or market)	95,000	20	80,000	17
Prepaid expenses	200		1,000	
Total Current Assets	193,200	41	195,000	41
Investments, long term	55,000	11	50,000	11
Land, Plant, and Equipment:				
Land	10,000	2	10,000	2
Plant and equipment	315,000	66	290,000	62
Less: Accumulated depreciation	(97,000)	(20)	(77,000)	(16)
Total	228,000	48	223,000	48
Intangible Assets:				
Patent (less amortization)	1,800		2,000	
Total Assets	$478,000	100	$470,000	100
Liabilities				
Current Liabilities:				
Accounts payable	$ 40,000	8	$ 55,000	12
Notes payable, short term	5,000	1	8,000	2
Taxes payable	4,555	1	7,000	1
Total Current Liabilities	49,555	10	70,000	15
Long-Term Liabilities:				
Bonds payable (less unamortized discount)	99,100	21	99,000	21
Total Liabilities	148,655	31	169,000	36
Stockholders' Equity:				
Common stock, par $5, authorized 60,000 shares	220,000	46	200,000	42
Preferred stock, 5%, par $10, authorized 10,000 shares	50,000	10	50,000	11
Contributed capital in excess of par, common stock	14,000	3	12,000	3
Retained earnings	45,345	10	39,000	8
Total Stockholders' Equity	329,345	69	301,000	64
Total Liabilities and Stockholders' Equity	$478,000	100	$470,000	100

* For illustrative purposes only; not usually included on published financial statements.

EXHIBIT 25–4

WZH CORPORATION
Comparative Statements of Changes in Financial Position, Working Capital Basis
For the Years Ended December 31, 19B, and 19A

	19B		19A	
	Amount	Percent*	Amount	Percent*
Sources of working capital:				
Income before extraordinary items	$ 19,745		$15,730	
Add (deduct) items not requiring or generating working capital:				
Depreciation	20,000		18,000	
Amortization of bond discount	100		100	
Amortization of patent	200		200	
Working capital provided by operations	40,045	66	34,030	86
Extraordinary loss (net of tax)	(4,400)	(7)		
Total	35,645	59	34,030	86
Other sources:				
Sale of common stock	22,000	36	5,500	14
Tax refund (from 19X)	3,000	5		
Total from other sources	25,000	41	5,500	14
Total working capital provided	$ 60,645	100	$39,530	100
Uses of working capital:				
Equipment acquired	$ 25,000	59		
Long-term investments	5,000	12	10,000	56
Cash dividends	12,000	29	8,000	44
Total working capital used	$ 42,000	100	$18,000	100
Difference—net increase in working capital	$ 18,645		$21,530	
Summary of changes in components of working capital:				
Increase (decrease) in current asset accounts:				
Cash	$(19,000)		$ (6,070)	
Investments, short term	(6,000)		10,000	
Accounts receivable (net)	9,000		11,000	
Inventory	15,000		12,000	
Prepaid expenses	(800)		600	
Total	(1,800)		27,530	
Increase (decrease) in current liability accounts:				
Accounts payable	15,000		(2,000)	
Notes payable, short term	3,000		(3,000)	
Taxes payable	2,445		(1,000)	
Total	20,445		(6,000)	
Net increase in working capital	$ 18,645		$21,530	

* For illustrative purposes only; not usually included on published financial statements.

counting information. Conversion of absolute amounts to percentages (of some base amount) reveals basic relationships. Thus, the expression of relationships in terms of percentages sometimes may aid in the interpretation of financial information. There are two common forms of percentage analyses used on financial statements—vertical analysis and horizontal analysis.

Vertical analysis involves the expression of each item on a particular financial statement as a percent of one specific item, which is referred to as the *base*. For example, the component items on the income statement may be expressed as a percent of total revenue as shown in Exhibit 25–2. Note that the base amount representing 100% is divided into each component item to derive the component percentages.

In applying vertical analysis, an appropriate base amount must be selected for each statement. Observe on Exhibit 25–3 that the base

EXHIBIT 25-5

WZH CORPORATION
Comparative Income Statements
For the Years Ended December 31, 19B, and 19A
(horizontal analysis)

	Year Ended December 31		Increase (Decrease) 19B over 19A	
	19B	19A	Amount	Percent
Revenues:				
Sales	$400,000	$370,000	$30,000	8
Investment revenue	4,500	3,000	1,500	50
Gain on disposal of investments	500		500	
Total revenues	405,000	373,000	32,000	9
Expenses:				
Cost of goods sold	265,000	250,000	15,000	6
Distribution	67,000	61,200	5,800	9
General administrative	30,000	27,000	3,000	11
Interest	7,100	6,200	900	15
Total expenses	369,100	344,400	24,700	7
Pretax operating income	35,900	28,600	7,300	26
Income tax expense	16,155	12,870	3,285	26
Income before extraordinary item	19,745	15,730	4,015	26
Extraordinary loss (net of taxes)	4,400		4,400	
Net Income	$ 15,345	$ 15,730	$ (385)	(2)
EPS (not illustrated).				

amounts for the balance sheet are total assets, and total liabilities plus stockholders' equity, respectively; and in Exhibit 25–4 the base amounts for the Statement of Changes in Financial Position are total working capital provided and total working capital used, respectively. Financial statements expressed in percentages only are referred to as *common-size* statements.

Horizontal analysis refers to the development of percentages indicating the proportionate change in the same item over *time*. The conversion of absolute amounts of change to percentage changes facilitates interpretation and evaluation of trends. For example, horizontal percentages shown on the income statements in Exhibit 25–5 serve to emphasize the trend of each component.

It should be noted in the examples relating to horizontal analysis that in computing the percentage change from 19A to 19B, as well as the amounts of increase or decrease, the *base year* is the earlier period.

RATIO (PROPORTIONATE) ANALYSIS

The analysis of financial statements generally includes one or more forms of ratio analysis. It involves measurement of the relationship be-

tween two amounts from one statement, such as the income statement, or from two statements, such as the income statement and balance sheet. The amounts may represent the balances of two different accounts, the balance of one account and a classification total (such as total assets), or two classification totals.

The mode of expression of proportionate analysis is quite varied. To illustrate, working capital has been discussed and referred to in a number of preceding chapters. The *current ratio* is the relationship between current assets and current liabilities. Assume the following:

Current assets	$5,000,000
Current liabilities	2,000,000
Difference—working capital	$3,000,000

The amount of working capital, $3,000,000, standing alone is a useful figure; however, proportionate analysis adds insight to this relationship, viz:

Current Ratio (or working capital ratio)
$$= \$5,000,000 \div \$2,000,000 = 2.5$$

Alternatively, this ratio may be expressed as 250%; 2.5 to 1; or for each $2.50 of current assets there is $1 of current liabilities.

Ratio analysis is significant only when the relationship between the selected factors, when expressed as a proportion, sheds additional light on the interpretation of the individual absolute amounts. In view of the large number of ratios that could be computed, it is important to focus on those amounts that are functionally related. For example, the relationship between bad debt expense and credit sales is more meaningful than the relationship between bad debt expense and total sales (including cash sales). In determining significance, consideration must be given to the purposes for which the ratios are to be used. Investors, managers, and creditors have essentially different interests and problems; consequently, they would have somewhat different needs with respect to ratio analysis. Since a complete study of ratio analysis is beyond the scope of this text, only representative ratios having general application are discussed. The analyses selected for discussion will be explained under the following general headings:

1. Ratio measurements of current position.
2. Ratio measurements of equity position.
3. Ratio measurements of operating results.

RATIOS THAT MEASURE
CURRENT POSITION

The ratio measurements in this category focus on working capital; they are supplementary to the statement of changes of financial position, working capital basis. The ratios relate to selected elements of working capital and are designed to assess the short-term liquidity position and the ability of the business to meet its maturing current liabilities. Seven measurements of current position are summarized in Exhibit 25-6. Observe that they are variously expressed as a percent, decimal, fraction, or turnover figure. The analysis of current position involves measures of *(a)* ability to pay short-term obligations and *(b)* movement of current assets.[3]

Working Capital (Current) Ratio

The working capital (or current) ratio has long been recognized as an index of short-term liquidity—the ability of the business to meet the maturing claims of the creditors plus the current operating costs. The amount of working capital and the related ratio have a direct impact on the amount of short-term credit that may be obtained. Traditionally, as a rule of thumb, a working capital ratio of 2 to 1 has been considered adequate. However, analysts in recent years have tended to disavow simplistic decision rules such as this one. The working capital ratio figure is unique to the industry in which the business operates, and even to the business itself in the light of its operating and financial characteristics. For example, a ratio of 2 to 1 may be realistic in one situation, but it may be too low or too high in another situation. The peculiarities of the industry in which the firm operates and other factors, such as methods of financing and seasonal fluctuations, also should be taken into

account in evaluating a working capital ratio.

The working capital ratio is only one measure or index of ability to meet short-term obligations, and it has certain weaknesses. A high working capital ratio may be the result of overstocking of inventory, and it is influenced by the inventory cost flow method used. A business may have a high current ratio although it has a cash deficit. Furthermore, a high current ratio may indicate excess funds which should be invested or otherwise put to use. As with all ratios there is a delicate balance between a ratio that is too high and one that is too low. Determination of the most desirable ratio varies from firm to firm, and determination of the optimum ratio for a particular firm poses a complex problem.

Acid Test Ratio

Cash, accounts receivable, short-term notes receivable, and short-term investments in marketable securities generally represent funds which may be made readily available for paying current obligations. Hence, they are referred to as *quick assets*. Inventories, on the other hand, must be sold and collection made before cash is available for paying obligations. In many cases, particularly where there are raw materials and work in process inventories, the marketability of the inventory involves considerable uncertainty as to its ultimate realization in cash. In view of these considerations the *acid test* or *quick* ratio (quick assets divided by current liabilities) is used as a test of immediate liquidity. Traditionally, an acid test ratio of 1 to 1 (a rule of thumb standard) has been considered desirable. As with the current ratio, the acid test ratio for a particular company must be evaluated in light of industry characteristics and other factors.

Working Capital to Total Assets

The ratio of working capital to total assets is a generalized expression of the distribution and liquidity of the assets employed after current liabilities have been deducted from the current assets. An excessively high ratio might indicate excess cash and/or overstocking of

---

[3] There is no single "generally accepted" method of computing specific ratios or of determining the values to be substituted in the formulas. The computation should be determined by (1) the data available and (2) the use and interpretation expected in the particular situation. The formulas presented reflect a general approach.

EXHIBIT 25–6
Ratios that Measure Current Position

Ratio	Formula for Computation	Significance
Ratios that measure ability to pay short-term obligations:		
1. Working capital (or current) ratio.	Current Assets / Current Liabilities	Test of short-term liquidity. Indicates ability to meet current obligations from current assets as a going concern. Measure of adequacy of working capital.
2. Acid test or quick ratio.	Quick Assets / Current Liabilities	A more severe test of immediate liquidity than the current ratio. Tests ability to meet sudden demands upon liquid current assets.
3. Working capital to total assets.	Working Capital / Total Assets	Indicates relative liquidity of total assets and distribution of resources employed as to liquidity.
Ratios that measure movement of current assets (turnover):		
4. *a.* Receivable turnover.	Net Credit Sales / Average Trade Receivables (net)	Velocity of collection of trade accounts and notes. Test of efficiency of collection.
b. Age of receivables.	365 (days) / Receivable Turnover (computed per [*a*] above)	Number of days to collect average trade receivables.
5. Inventory turnover. *a.* Merchandise turnover (retail firm).	Cost of Goods Sold / Average Merchandise Inventory	Indicates liquidity of inventory. Number of times average inventory "turned over" or was sold during the period. Will indicate possible over- or understocking.
b. Finished goods turnover (manufacturing firm).	Cost of Goods Sold / Average Finished Goods Inventory	Same as 5 *(a).*
c. Raw material turnover.	Cost of Raw Materials Used / Average Raw Materials Inventory	Number of times raw material inventory was "used" on the average during the period.
d. Days' supply in inventory.	365 (days) / Inventory Turnover (computed per [*a*], [*b*], or [*c*] above)	Number of days' supply in the average inventory. Indicates general condition of over- or understocking.
6. Working capital turnover.	Net Sales / Average Working Capital	Indicates the effectiveness with which average working capital was used to generate sales.
7. Percent of each current asset to total current assets.	Each Current Asset / Total Current Assets	Indicates relative investment in each current asset.

inventory, whereas a low ratio may indicate a potential weakness in the current position.

A related analysis involves a *vertical* percentage analysis of current assets employing *total current assets* as the base (100%). This analysis may have some significance in that *(a)* the relative composition of the current asset structure is revealed and *(b)* when compared with similar data from prior periods, important trends may be revealed.

Receivable Turnover

In some businesses cash sales predominate, whereas in others credit sales predominate. In either case the amount of trade receivables on the average should bear some relationship to the credit sales for the period and the terms of credit. The application of the receivable turn-over in these respects may be illustrated by referring to WZH Corporation's financial statements (Exhibits 25–2 and 25–3):

$$\text{Receivable Turnover} = \frac{\text{Credit Sales, \$345,000}}{\text{Average Trade Receivables,}\ \dfrac{\$30,000 + \$39,000}{2}} = 10$$

$$\text{Age of Receivables} = \frac{365\ \text{Days}}{10}$$
$$= 36.5\ (\text{average number of days to collect})$$

If we assume the terms of sale are 1/10, n/30, it appears that collections are lagging terms by six days or more on the average—a suggestion of possible laxity in (a) granting credit and/or (b) making collections.

The above illustration also points up several technical aspects of the computation, viz:

1. Should the total of cash and credit sales, or credit sales only, be used in the computation? A more stable and meaningful ratio will result if credit sales only are used; otherwise a shift in the proportion of cash to credit sales will affect the ratio, although collection experience is unchanged. For internal purposes, credit sales should be used (since the figure is available or may be reconstructed readily); however, for comparison with other firms the total of cash and credit sales generally must be used since published data seldom provide the credit sales amounts for other businesses.

2. Should the ending balance of receivables or average receivables be used? The average *monthly* receivables balance generally should be used in order to smooth out seasonal influences. The average should be determined by adding the 13 monthly balances (January 1, January 31, and through December 31) of trade accounts and trade notes receivable, then dividing by 13. In the absence of monthly balances the average of the annual beginning and ending balance or only the ending balance may be used (with a potentially significant loss of information).

3. Receivables should be net of the allowance for doubtful accounts.

4. Trade notes receivable should be included in averaging receivables.

Whether to express the receivable movement as a "turnover" or as "number of days to collect" is a matter of preference. If the company uses a "natural" business year, the receivables reported on the balance sheet normally will be quite low, which would cause the turnover to look better than is actually the case.

Inventory Turnover

Inventory turnover is the ratio between the cost of goods sold (or used) and the *average* inventory balance. The procedure for determining the average inventory balance is similar to that discussed above for average receivables.

The merchandise inventory turnover may be expressed as a "turnover" or as "days' supply"; the latter appears more often in current usage.[4] The turnover or days' supply figure has significance in that the amount of inventory on hand normally should bear a close relationship to cost of goods sold. The relationship will vary from industry to industry—a grocery store normally should expect a high inventory turnover, whereas an antique dealer may expect a low turnover. Also, the ratio represents an average—a generalization that does not reflect how fast particular items are moving, but rather how fast all items on the average are moving. For example, a grocer may have a turnover of 20, yet may have items on the shelves that have not turned over at all for a three-month period. Furthermore, this ratio is influenced by the inventory cost flow method used, which may affect comparison among firms. For example, when prices are rising, firms using *Lifo* will tend to have higher computed turnover rates than those using other cost flow methods.

Inventory turnover is directly related to profitability. To illustrate, assume that the inventory turnover is 12 (cost of goods sold, $1,200,000; average inventory, $100,000) and that the entrepreneur realizes a profit of $1,000 each time the

---

[4] Some analysts prefer to use 250 (5-day workweek) or 300 (6-day workweek) days, as the case may be, as an approximation of the number of business days in the year.

EXHIBIT 25–7
Ratios that Measure Equity Position

Ratio	Formula for Computation	Significance
Equity ratios:		
1. Owners' equity to total assets.	$\dfrac{\text{Owners' Equity}}{\text{Total Assets}}$	Proportion of assets provided by owners. Reflects financial strength and cushion for creditors.
2. Creditors' equity to total assets.	$\dfrac{\text{Total Liabilities}}{\text{Total Assets}}$	Proportion of assets provided by creditors. Extent of leverage.
3. Total liabilities to owners' equity. (Sometimes computed as owners' equity to total liabilities.)	$\dfrac{\text{Total Liabilities}}{\text{Owners' Equity}}$	Relative amounts of resources provided by creditors and owners. Reflects strengths and weaknesses in basic financing of operations.
Other ratios related to equity position:		
4. Operational assets to owners' equity.	$\dfrac{\text{Operational Assets (net)}}{\text{Owners' Equity}}$	May suggest over- or under-investment by owners.
5. Operational assets to total equities.	$\dfrac{\text{Operational Assets (net)}}{\text{Total Liabilities and Owners' Equity}}$	May suggest over- or under-expansion of plant and equipment.
6. Sales to operational assets (plant turnover).	$\dfrac{\text{Net Sales}}{\text{Operational Assets (net)}}$	Turnover index which tests the efficiency of management in using operational assets to generate sales.
7. Book value per share of common stock.	$\dfrac{\text{Common Stock Equity}}{\text{Number of Outstanding Common Shares}}$	Number of dollars of common equity (at book value) per share of common stock.

$100,000 investment in inventory turns over. A $12,000 profit is indicated. Now assume another firm identical in every respect except that the inventory turnover is 6, indicating a $6,000 profit on a similar $100,000 inventory investment.

Work in process inventory turnover is computed by dividing cost of goods manufactured by the average work in process inventory. With respect to all inventories, turnover computations based on appropriate unit data, when practicable, will provide more reliable results than when based on dollar amount data.

RATIOS THAT MEASURE EQUITY POSITION

The balance sheet reports the two basic sources of funds used by the business: *(a)* owners' equity and *(b)* creditors' equity. The relationships between these two distinctly different equities often are measured because they tend to reflect the financial strengths and weak-nesses of the business; in other words, the long-term solvency of a business and its potential capacity to generate and obtain investment resources. Exhibit 25–7 summarizes seven ratios that are commonly used to measure equity position.

Equity Ratios

These three ratios reflect essentially the same relationship, that is, the proportion of total assets provided by *(a)* the owners and *(b)* the creditors. The three equity ratios for WZH Corporation (Exhibit 25–3) for 19B are as follows:

1. $\dfrac{\text{Owners' Equity, \$329,345}}{\text{Total Assets, \$478,000}}$ = 69% of the assets were provided by owners

2. $\dfrac{\text{Creditors' Equity, \$148,655}}{\text{Total Assets, \$478,000}}$ = 31% of the assets were provided by creditors
$\underline{100\%}$ total assets provided

3. $\dfrac{\text{Creditors' Equity, \$148,655}}{\text{Owners' Equity, \$329,345}}$ = 45% —the creditors' equity is 45% of the owners' equity

Usually only one of the three equity ratios is used because each reflects the same relationship (but in a somewhat different way). The balance between resources provided by debt versus owners' equity is considered critical by analysts. Mathematical models have been constructed to determine optimal capital structure. The most definitive statement to be made from this body of research is that a judicious use of debt financing can increase the value of the firm; however, the incurrence of debt beyond this optimum can lead to higher interest rates at best, and insolvency and bankruptcy at worst. Therefore, there is no rule of thumb that can be pointed to as a guide for evaluation. A company that has 80% debt and 20% owners' equity usually would be considered overborrowed (overextended); interest payments must be made regardless of whether there are profits, and the debts must be paid at the fixed maturity dates. In contrast, if debt and owners' equity are 20% and 80%, respectively, the creditors' position is better and interest payments lower. However, owners' equity usually is more costly than debt from the viewpoints of both the investor and the entity. From the standpoint of the expectations of those providing the investment funds (i.e., the investors), a company heavily financed by *stock* issuances is required by its stockholders to earn more income and have a higher stock value than a company financed by half stock and half debt—because stockholders assume a greater risk from holding their investment than do bondholders. From the point of view of the entity, equity capital (i.e., from the issuance of stock) is more costly than debt capital (i.e., from borrowing) for two reasons: (1) stockholders have higher expectations (because of higher risk) and (2) interest paid on debt is deductible by the entity for income tax purposes, whereas dividends paid to shareholders are not deductible. In effect, the government subsidizes a part of the company's interest on debt but does not subsidize dividends on stock.

Debt financing is, therefore, an important avenue for most businesses because of a favorable effect known as *trading on the equity* or *financial leverage.* These are common terms that refer to the advantage to be gained for the stockholders by borrowing funds, say at 8%, when the business is earning 12% on *total assets.* This topic is discussed later in the chapter in respect to return on investment.

In computing the equity ratios, it is important that all components, such as the appropriated retained earnings and unrealized capital, be included in owners' equity. Some analysts prefer to subtract the carrying value of intangible assets, thereby using *tangible capital* for owners' equity. The authors see no basic reason for this approach, since we assume the intangibles are accounted for properly and, as a consequence, are not carried at more than an appropriate value.

Book Value per Share of Common Stock

Although it is often computed, book value per share of common stock has limited usefulness. It has little, if any, correspondence with the market value per share. Some investors are particularly impressed with stock that has a book value in excess of the market price because this is construed by many to imply a "good" buy; however, under the cost, matching, and conservatism principles, the assets are apt to be carried at amounts significantly less than their market value. In fact, under GAAP, they should rarely be reflected in the accounts at more than their market value on a going-concern basis.

Book value per share is computed by dividing total common stockholders' equity by the number of common shares outstanding. When there is more than one class of stock outstanding, total stockholders' equity must be apportioned among the various classes in accordance with the legal and statutory claims that would be effective in case of liquidation of the company. Since additional classes of stock typically are preferred stock, the usual situation requires allocation based upon the preferential rights of the preferred stock. Liquidation, cumulative, and participating preferences must be included in the computation.

To illustrate a typical allocation, refer to Exhibit 25–3 and assume the *cumulative preferred stock* of WZH Corporation has a liquidation value of $15 per share and that $5,000 of preferred cash dividends were in arrears at December 31, 19B.

Computation of book value per share at December 31, 19B:

Total stockholders' equity..........		$329,345
Allocation to preferred stock:		
Liquidation value—5,000		
shares @ $15	$75,000	
Cumulative dividends in		
arrears	5,000	80,000
Allocation to common		
stock (44,000 shares		
outstanding)		$249,345

Book value per share of common stock:

$$\frac{\$249,345}{44,000} = \$5.67$$

RATIOS THAT MEASURE OPERATING RESULTS

The ability of an entity to earn a satisfactory income and return on investment is often viewed as a more important indicator of good financial "health" than a "solid" balance sheet position. Although ratios relating to income are perhaps of more interest to investors than to creditors, the latter must be concerned about the profitability of their borrowers. A creditor may be unwilling to make loans or grant credit for goods supplied if the prospective borrower has dim profit potentials, even though adequate collateral is available. The principal ratios that measure operating results are summarized in Exhibit 25–8.

Profit Margin

The ratio of net income to net sales, generally referred to as the *profit margin,* is widely used as an index of profitability; however, one significant factor related to profitability—investment—is given no consideration in the ratio. To

EXHIBIT 25–8
Ratios that Measure Operating Results

Ratio	Formula for Computation	Significance
1. Profit margin.	$\dfrac{\text{Net Income}}{\text{Net Sales}}$	Indicates net profitability of each dollar of sales.
2. Return on investment: *a.* On total assets.	$\dfrac{\text{Income Plus Interest Expense*}}{\text{Total Assets}}$	Rate earned on *all resources* used. Measures earnings on all investments provided by owners and creditors.
b. On owners' equity.	$\dfrac{\text{Income}}{\text{Owners' Equity}}$	Rate earned on resources provided by owners (excludes creditors). Measures earnings accruing to the owners.
3. Investment turnover.	$\dfrac{\text{Net Sales}}{\text{Average Total Assets}}$	Indicative of efficiency with which total resources are utilized.
4. Financial leverage	Return on Owners' Equity minus Return on Total Assets	Reflects the advantage gained by borrowing at a rate that is lower than the rate earned on total assets.
5. Earnings per share.	$\dfrac{\text{Income Accruing to Common Stock}}{\text{Common Shares Outstanding}}$	Profit earned on each share of common stock. Indicative of ability to pay dividends and to grow from within. See Chapter 18.
6. Price-earnings ratio (the multiple).	$\dfrac{\text{Market Price per Share}}{\text{Earnings per Share}}$	The number of times EPS that investors are willing to pay for one share of stock.
7. Dividend ratio.	$\dfrac{\text{Dividends per Share}}{\text{Earnings per Share}}$	Measures the proportion of income (before extraordinary items) paid out in dividends.

* Adjusted for tax savings.

illustrate, assume the accounts of Conway Company showed the following data: net income, $20,000; net sales, $2,000,000; and total assets, $100,000. In this case the profit margin appears to be very low at 1%. However, when profit performance is measured by the 20% return on total investment, it appears to be satisfactory. Thus, profit margin considered alone is inadequate as a measure of profitability. The profit margin has value primarily for evaluation of trends and for comparison with industry and competitor statistics.

Return on Investment

Many accountants consider return on investment as the single most important ratio because it incorporates the two fundamental factors that are inherent in measuring profitability: (1) earnings and (2) investment. Fundamentally, return on investment is computed by dividing *income by investment.* Return on investment is referred to variously as capital yield, return on assets employed, return on capital, rate of return, or simply ROI. Return on investment has two important applications in business situations:

1. Evaluating proposed capital additions (not discussed herein).[5]
2. Measuring profitability in relation to investment.

As a measure of profitability, return on investment may be computed on the basis of either:

1. Owners' equity, that is, income divided by owners' equity (ROI_o).
2. Total assets, that is, income (adjusted for interest expense) divided by total assets (ROI_t).

Analysts may compute both ratios and compare them to measure the effect of *financial leverage* (i.e., trading on the equity). The following data are used to illustrate measures of profitability and leverage.

---

[5] For an excellent discussion, see Harold Bierman, Jr. and Seymour Smidt, *The Capital Budgeting Decision* (New York: The Macmillan Co.), or James C. Van Horne, *Financial Management and Policy* (Englewood Cliffs, N.J.: Prentice Hall, Inc.).

XY COMPANY

Balance Sheet Data:

Total assets	$100,000
Total liabilities	40,000
Stockholders' equity	60,000
Total Equities	$100,000

Income Statement Data:

Operating income (before interest expense)...............................	$ 20,000
Interest expense	3,200
Pretax income	16,800
Income taxes ($16,800 × 40%)	6,720
Net Income	$ 10,080

Return on investment for XY Company is computed as follows:

1. Return on owners' equity:

$$ROI_o = \frac{\text{Income*}}{\text{Owners' Equity}} = \frac{\$10,080}{\$60,000} = 16.8\%$$

* Extraordinary items usually are excluded because of their nonrecurring characteristic.

2. Return on total assets (i.e., total investment):

$$ROI_t = \frac{\text{Income} + \text{Interest Expense (net of tax)}}{\text{Total Assets}}$$
$$= \frac{\$10,080 + (\$3,200 - \$1,280)}{\$100,000} = \frac{\$12,000}{\$100,000} = 12.0\%$$

Difference: Financial Leverage .... +4.8%

In computing return on total investment, interest expense (net of income taxes) is added back to income because it is the return paid to creditors of the entity. Since the denominator includes the resources provided by both creditors and owners, the numerator must include the return on both types of equities.

Return on total assets measures the profitability of the total resources available to the business. It indicates the efficiency with which management used the total available resources to earn income.

Return on owners' equity measures the return that accrues to the stockholders *after* the interest payments to the creditors are deducted to derive income. It does not measure the efficiency with which total resources were used, but rather the *residual* return to the owners on their investment in the business.

The difference between these two ratios is one measure of the extent to which the entity borrows at one rate and utilizes its resources to earn at a (hopefully) higher rate.

Return on owners' equity can also be computed using the *market value* of the outstanding stock of the company. This rate of return has the advantage over a rate of return computation based on the book value of owners' equity, that as the market value of the owners' equity is not affected by such things as different accounting methods or changes in accounting methods.

Return on total assets also can be computed on a market value basis by using as the denominator the sum of the market value of the outstanding stock plus the market value of the liabilities (where market prices are quoted for any bonds held), or the book value of the outstanding liabilities.

More on Financial Leverage

Earlier, the concept of financial leverage, sometimes called trading on the equity, was briefly defined. More comprehensively, financial leverage is the effect on return on investment of borrowing versus investment by owners. If the interest rate on debt is lower than the rate earned on total assets, financial leverage will be positive; if the interest rate is higher, financial leverage will be negative. Financial leverage can be measured by subtracting return on total assets (ROI_t) from return on owners' equity (ROI_o), as shown above.

For XY Company, the financial leverage effect (computed above) was (+) 4.8% because the return on owners' equity was greater than the return on total assets. The 4.8% positive effect in favor of owners' equity was due to the fact that the company earned a higher rate of return on total assets than the rate of interest, net of tax, paid for borrowed resources.

Had there been no debt, the rate on total assets and the rate on owners' equity would have been the same. In contrast, however, when there is debt, and the rate on the debt and the rate on total assets are different, there will be a financial leverage effect causing the two ROI percentages to differ.

The analysis of financial statements should include *return on investment* and *financial leverage* evaluations because of their relevance to all statement users. A comparison of the rates of return on owners' equity and total assets provides a measure of the degree and effect of financial leverage. Return on investment has gained wide acceptance as an important tool of managerial control. The measure has the advantage of directing management attention to a combination of the three principal factors affecting profit—sales, expense, and total assets employed.

Investment Turnover

This ratio, also called the asset turnover, is computed by dividing net sales by average total assets for the year. It attempts to measure the effectiveness with which management used the total resources at their disposal. It is similar in concept to inventory turnover. However, a company may have a high asset turnover, viewed as a favorable condition, in the face of a net loss.

Market Ratios

Different market ratios are often used by investors and analysts to measure the relationship between investment by the stockholder (i.e., the market value of the shares) and the return from the shares (i.e., earnings or dividends). Two market ratios are listed in Exhibit 25–8.

1. *Price earnings ratio*—Sometimes called the *multiple,* it is widely used for evaluating stock price because it relates the earnings of the business to the current market price of the stock. For this reason, it is of particular interest to investors. This ratio changes each time the market price of the stock changes. Several years ago, multiples of 20 or more were not unusual; however, multiples in the range of 5 to 10 are currently more common. The multiple generally should be computed on the basis of earnings per share before extraordinary items. To illustrate, assuming

the common stock of WZH Corporation (Exhibits 25–2 and 25–3) is selling at $6.50 per share, on December 31, 19B, the multiple would be as follows:

$$\frac{\text{Market Price per Share, \$6.50}}{\text{EPS (Exhibit 25–2), \$0.40}} = 16$$

(i.e., the stock was selling at approximately 16 times the earnings per share before extraordinary items)

2. *Dividend ratio*—A measure of potential return to the investor since it measures, on the average, the proportion of earnings paid out as dividends. Because dividends and changes in dividend payout ratios have been shown to possess significant information content to investors, and because dividends are construed to be a reliable indicator of management expectations, this ratio has particular significance as an analytical tool.

USE AND INTERPRETATION OF RATIO ANALYSES

Ratio analysis of financial statements is widely used as an adjunct to more sophisticated techniques for making investment and credit decisions because ratios communicate some aspects of the economic situation of an entity better than the absolute amounts reported on the financial statements. Some recent empirical studies have demonstrated that the traditional financial ratios are closely associated with the (unobservable) process by which stock prices are formed. This means that the ratios have information content for investors. As one example, financial ratios were used successfully in prediction models to project whether a business would fail. Thus, it is not surprising that financial and bank lending officers make wide use of ratio analysis in evaluating the future economic prospects of individual companies.

Ratios covering a period of years (as they must to be very useful) represent average conditions; therefore, they must be interpreted in light of the "smoothing" effect inherent in any average. However, when viewed over an extended period of time ratios may signal important *turning points,* either favorable or unfavorable, with respect to the future economic prospects for the business. One writer has suggested that

the idea of their use may be conveyed by a comparison with the interpretation of a thermometer reading by a doctor—beyond a certain range the fever reading indicates *something* is wrong with the patient, but not exactly what it is. An unfavorable ratio can be thought of as a red flag—the matter should be investigated. Additionally, one ratio or even several ratios, whatever their values, may not convey a clear message. Consequently, a primary problem confronting the statement user relates to the evaluation of a ratio. For example, is it good or bad that the inventory turnover for a company is 12? In determining what constitutes an unfavorable or favorable ratio for a particular business the following comparisons are suggested:

1. Comparison of the actual ratios for the current year with those of preceding years for the company. Comparisons of selected ratios for the company over a period of five to ten years often are included in the published financial statements.
2. Comparison of the actual ratios for the company with budgeted or standard ratios developed internally by the company. Unfortunately, this kind of comparison, although relevant, is seldom available to external statement users.
3. Comparison of the company's ratios with those of competitors. The published financial reports of competitors provide information that may make this comparison feasible.
4. Comparison of the company's ratios with ratios for the industry in which the company operates. Industry statistics along these lines may be obtained from the following sources:
   a. Industry trade associations—All major industries support one or more trade associations that generally collect and publish financial statistics relating to the industry.
   b. Bureaus of business research at universities—Most of the major universities collect, analyze, and publish a wide range of regional statistics on the surrounding industries and businesses.
   c. Governmental agencies—Agencies that deal directly with business often publish,

or have available as a matter of public record, financial information relating to industries and individual companies. The more prominent ones are the U.S. Department of Commerce, the U.S. Department of the Treasury, and the Securities and Exchange Commission, Washington, D.C.

d. Commercial publications such as
  (1) Robert Morris Associates.
  (2) Dun & Bradstreet.
  (3) *Almanac of Business and Industrial Ratios,* Leo Troy, Prentice-Hall, Inc., Englewood Cliffs, N.J.

Despite the wide use of ratio analysis, this technique has a number of inherent weaknesses. Because of these limitations, ratios must be carefully evaluated and interpreted. Some of the more important limitations are as follows:

1. Ratios represent average conditions that existed in the *past;* they are historical data that incorporate all of the peculiarities of the past. Also, they are influenced by the latitude available to companies in selecting accounting methods.

2. When the data on which ratios are based are historical book values, they do not reflect either *(a)* price level effects or *(b)* real economic values.

3. Since the method of computing each ratio is not standardized, the computations (and hence, the results) can be influenced by data selection choices. Except for the EPS ratio, they are not subject to audit.

4. The use of various alternative accounting methods may have a significant effect on ratios. For example, the previous chapters have indicated the significant effects on financial statement amounts of such alternatives as *Fifo* versus *Lifo,* straight-line versus accelerated depreciation, and completed contract versus percentage completion on long-term construction contracts.

5. Changes in accounting estimates and principles (such as a change from *Fifo* to *Lifo*) may significantly affect the ratios for the year of change. This possibility suggests the need to remove from the data, or specifically identify the effect of, unusual or nonrecurring items.

6. Comparisons between companies are difficult because of different operating characteristics such as product lines, methods of operation, size, methods of financing, and geographical location.

7. There is an insidious limitation in that those relying on ratio analysis sometimes overlook the fact that all other investors have the same data available and can also compute the same ratios. Studies have shown that the market very quickly absorbs this information and that, as a result, it is extremely difficult to consistently earn above-average returns on stock investments by relying on ratio data only. Thus, *excessive reliance* on ratio analysis, or any analysis that relies on publicly available information, should be practiced with this limitation in mind.

Although the limitations are formidable, ratio analysis is an important technique for financial statement analysis because ratios capitalize on the fundamental relationships in an entity. However, as we have indicated, the results must be used with care.

THE SEARCH FOR ADDITIONAL INFORMATION

An investor should search for information to supplement that provided by the financial statements. Hearsay is hazardous; one should seek objective data concerning the company—its operations, policies, competitive position, the quality of the management, and other nonquantitative information. Brokerage firms and security analysts typically gather and disseminate this type of information. Periodic reports, by listed companies, to the SEC are available; they provide considerable information not included in the published financial statements.

The financial press is a timely source of financial information. Examples of financial publications include *Fortune, Barrons, The Wall Street Journal, Business Week, Forbes,* and various industry publications; such publications are available in most libraries.

The Appendix that follows presents an actual set of financial statements for study of the application of some of the topics discussed in this chapter.

Appendix—Actual Financial Statements
of Peavey Company

PEAVEY COMPANY AND SUBSIDIARIES

Consolidated Statements of Earnings
Years ended July 31, 1977 and 1976

	1977	1976
	(in thousands except per share amounts)	
Net sales.	$494,306	505,822
Costs and expenses:		
Cost of products and services sold, excluding depreciation and amortization.	412,616	418,226
Depreciation and amortization.	6,996	5,572
Selling, general and administrative expense.	56,138	49,180
Interest expense (note 2).	5,226	3,700
Minority interests in earnings of subsidiaries.	70	99
Total costs and expenses.	481,046	476,777
Earnings before taxes on income.	13,260	29,045
Taxes on income (note 3).	3,950	13,400
Net earnings.	$ 9,310	15,645
Net earnings per share of common stock.	$ 1.60	2.73

Consolidated Statements of Earnings Employed in the Business
Years ended July 31, 1977 and 1976

	1977	1976
	(in thousands)	
Balance at beginning of year.	$ 99,274	92,329
Add net earnings.	9,310	15,645
	108,584	107,974
Deduct:		
Cash dividends:		
Preferred stock—$6.00 per share.	218	219
Common stock—$.815 per share in 1977 and $.722 in 1976.	4,639	4,077
Stock split effected in the form of a stock dividend plus cash paid in lieu of fractional shares (note 5).	—	4,404
Total dividends.	4,857	8,700
Balance at end of year.	$103,727	99,274

See accompanying summary of significant accounting policies and notes to consolidated financial statements

Consolidated Balance Sheets
July 31, 1977 and 1976

Assets

	1977	1976
		(in thousands)
Current assets:		
Cash and short-term cash investments....................	$ 1,419	6,773
Segregated funds, principally customer deposits..............	11,215	10,800
Receivables, less allowance for doubtful accounts of $1,042,000 and $1,342,000, respectively...............	48,628	55,575
Inventories:		
Grain, flour and millfeed............................	43,602	68,280
Merchandise......................................	59,591	53,356
Other..	9,882	5,639
Total inventories............................	113,075	127,275
Other current assets.............................	2,121	2,108
Total current assets...........................	176,458	202,531
Property, plant and equipment:		
Land...	4,228	3,525
Buildings and equipment............................	124,813	107,976
Leasehold improvements............................	1,187	1,064
Construction in progress (note 10)...................	17,427	2,647
	147,655	115,212
Less accumulated depreciation and amortization.............	53,406	48,705
Total property, plant and equipment.................	94,249	66,507
Other assets:		
Construction funds held by trustees (note 10).............	21,790	4,103
Investment in and advances to related company..............	164	183
Goodwill, less amortization............................	2,037	2,150
Other..	5,351	2,593
Total other assets............................	29,342	9,029
Total assets................................	$300,049	278,067

See accompanying summary of significant accounting policies and notes to consolidated financial statements.

Liabilities and Stockholders' Equity

	1977	1976
	(in thousands)	
Current liabilities:		
Notes payable.	**$ 40,170**	48.392
Current portion of long-term debt.	**2,338**	1.124
Accounts payable.	**44,704**	53.286
Checks outstanding, net.	**1,150**	—
Customers' margin deposits.	**9,416**	8.440
Accrued expenses.	**9,131**	9.177
Accrued taxes on income.	**1,204**	4.379
Total current liabilities.	**108,113**	124.798
Other liabilities:		
Long-term debt (note 4).	**60,415**	27.834
Deferred income taxes, net.	**5,405**	4.425
Other.	**305**	236
Total other liabilities.	**66,125**	32.495
Total liabilities.	**174,238**	157.293
Minority interests in subsidiaries.	**2,081**	2.323
Stockholders' equity (notes 4, 5 and 6):		
Preferred stock, par value $100.	**5,600**	5.600
Common stock, par value $2.50.	**14,300**	14.300
Additional paid-in capital.	**2,302**	2.205
Earnings employed in the business.	**103,727**	99.274
Deduct treasury stock, at cost.	**(2,199)**	(2.928)
Total stockholders' equity.	**123,730**	118.451
Commitments and contingent liabilities (notes 7, 8, 9 and 10)		
Total liabilities and stockholders' equity.	**$300,049**	278.067

PEAVEY COMPANY AND SUBSIDIARIES

Consolidated Statements of Changes in Financial Position
Years ended July 31, 1977 and 1976

	1977	1976
	(in thousands)	
Working capital provided by:		
Net earnings	$ 9,310	15.645
Items not affecting working capital:		
Depreciation and amortization	6,996	5.572
Deferred income taxes	980	1.907
Equity in earnings of related company	—	(75)
Minority interests in earnings of subsidiaries	70	99
Other	113	(779)
Total from operations	17,469	22.369
New long-term debt	34,559	9.308
Increase in unexpended construction funds held by trustees	(17,687)	(4.103)
Net book value of property, plant and equipment sold or retired	940	720
Sale of common stock upon exercise of options	35	32
Value of common stock issued to employees profit sharing and investment plan	970	1.024
Other	197	123
Total working capital provided	$ 36,483	29.473
Working capital used for:		
Additions to property, plant and equipment	$ 33,765	18.354
Dividends	4,857	4.301
Reduction of long-term debt	2,135	1.808
Purchase of treasury stock and stock warrants	179	1.812
Cost of companies acquired, excluding working capital:		
Net property, plant and equipment	1,913	8.130
Long-term debt	(157)	(2.081)
Other	608	69
Increase in long-term receivables	2,180	—
Other	391	222
Decrease in working capital	(9,388)	(3.142)
Total working capital used	$ 36,483	29.473
Increase (decrease) in working capital:		
Cash and segregated funds	$ (4,939)	(3.797)
Receivables	(6,947)	8.460
Inventories	(14,200)	41.933
Other current assets	13	1.002
Notes payable	8,222	(48.392)
Current portion of long-term debt	(1,214)	(570)
Accounts payable, customer deposits and accrued expenses	6,502	(432)
Accrued taxes on income	3,175	(1.346)
Decrease in working capital	(9,388)	(3.142)
Working capital at beginning of year	77,733	80.875
Working capital at end of year	$ 68,345	77.733

See accompanying summary of significant accounting policies and notes to consolidated financial statements.

Summary of Significant Accounting Policies

The accounting policies followed by Peavey Company are generally accepted accounting principles and conform to common practices of the industries in which it is engaged. In order to more fully inform our stockholders, certain of the Company's accounting policies which affect the more significant elements of the financial statements are described below:

Principles of Consolidation

The accounts of all subsidiaries are fully consolidated with minority interests appropriately reflected in the financial statements. Equity in earnings of a 33-1/3% owned company is reflected in the earnings of the Company with appropriate adjustments to the investment account.

Foreign Currency Translation

The fiscal 1977 financial statements of the Company's foreign subsidiary have been translated in accordance with Statement No. 8 of the Financial Accounting Standards Board. The effect on the current year's earnings is not material. Prior years have not been restated as the effect is not material.

Inventories

Inventories of grain, flour and millfeed are valued at market prices at July 31 and are adjusted to reflect unrealized gains or losses on open purchase and sale contracts. Other inventories are valued substantially at the lower of cost (first-in, first-out) or market.

Property and Depreciation

The cost of buildings and equipment is capitalized and charged to earnings utilizing the straight-line method of depreciation over the estimated useful lives of the assets. Leasehold improvements are amortized over the lesser of the lives of the assets or the terms of the respective leases. The cost of significant improvements to properties is capitalized and similarly depreciated while the costs of repairs and routine maintenance are charged to earnings as incurred. Generally, when items of property are retired or otherwise disposed of, the cost and related accumulated depreciation are removed from the accounts and any resulting gain or loss is reflected in income.

Retirement Plan Provisions

Each year, actuaries determine the contributions necessary to fund the Company's various pension plans. Such contributions, which are charged against earnings, provide for funding of pensions based on current and past employee service.

Income Taxes

Income tax expense is computed based on the elements of income and expense included in the consolidated statements of earnings. Actual income taxes paid or payable for the year will differ from the computed amounts due to temporary differences between reported earnings and taxable earnings. Such differences generally result from differences in timing of deductions such as the Company's use for tax purposes, in some cases, of accelerated depreciation while using the straight-line method for book purposes. Such differences between taxes computed and amounts currently due are reflected in the balance sheet as deferred income tax liability. The investment tax credit is accounted for by the flow-through method.

Grain Sales

Sales of grain and related costs of grain sold are not reflected in the respective classifications in the consolidated statements of earnings. The gross margins earned from such activities are included in net sales.

Earnings Per Share

Net earnings per share have been determined by dividing net earnings, after deduction of preferred stock dividends, by the weighted average number of shares of common stock outstanding during the year without inclusion of shares contingently issuable under terms of stock warrant and option agreements since the effect of their inclusion is not material.

Notes to Consolidated Financial Statements
July 31, 1977 and 1976

NOTE 1
Acquisitions

On November 17, 1975, the Company acquired Wheelers Stores, Inc. for $14,546,000. The Company acquired Home Brands, Inc. on August 2, 1976, and S&S Stores on February 1, 1977. All three acquisitions were made for cash and accounted for as purchases and the consolidated statements of earnings reflect results of operations of the acquired companies from the dates of acquisition. The Company's consolidated results of operations would not have been materially impacted had the acquisitions occurred at the beginning of fiscal year 1976.

NOTE 2
Interest Expense

The Company is a significant borrower of short-term funds both from banks and through issuance of commercial paper. Due principally to the availability of proceeds from the sale, in 1974, of certain Canadian operations and until the acquisition of Wheelers Stores, Inc. (see note 1), funds borrowed occasionally exceeded requirements and the excess borrowed funds earned interest through short-term investments. In addition, the Company received interest from investment of unexpended proceeds from Industrial Revenue Bonds issued to finance construction projects (see note 10). Interest expense is shown net of interest income from such investments of $1,121,000 in 1977 and $1,030,000 in 1976.

NOTE 3
Taxes on Income

Taxes on income consist of the following:

	Federal	Foreign	State and local	Total
			(in thousands)	
Year ended July 31, 1977:				
Current.	$ 4,459	(289)	450	4,620
Investment tax credit.	(1,650)	—	—	(1,650)
Deferred.	961	19	—	980
Total.	$ 3,770	(270)	450	3,950
Year ended July 31, 1976:				
Current.	$10,484	674	1,350	12,508
Investment tax credit.	(1,015)	—	—	(1,015)
Deferred.	1,880	27	—	1,907
Total.	$11,349	701	1,350	13,400

Deferred taxes result from timing differences in the recognition of revenue and expenses for tax and financial statement purposes. The tax effects of these differences are as follows:

	1977	1976
	(in thousands)	
Excess of tax over book depreciation.	$ 795	647
Income deferred for tax purposes by		
Domestic International Sales Corporation.	64	573
Other items, not individually significant.	121	687
	$ 980	1,907

The effective income tax rate is different from the statutory U. S. Federal tax rate for the following reasons:

	1977	1976
U. S. Statutory rate.	48.0%	48.0%
State and local income taxes, net of Federal income tax benefit.	1.8	2.4
Investment tax credit.	(12.4)	(3.5)
Excess accrued taxes of liquidated subsidiary.	(5.3)	—
Other items, not individually significant.	(2.3)	(.8)
Effective income tax rate.	29.8%	46.1%

NOTE 4
Long-Term Debt

Long-term debt consists of the following:

	July 31	
	1977	1976
	(in thousands)	
8.5% promissory notes, due $1,000,000 per year in 1978 through 1987.	$10,000	10,000
3% to 10% mortgage notes due in various amounts to 1995.	3,459	3,554
4.5% to 7.2% Industrial Revenue Bonds, due in various installments to 2006 (includes capitalized lcase obligations of $43,055,000 in 1977 and $10,468,000 in 1976).	45,655	13,168
Other (includes capitalized lease obligations of $2,457,000 in 1977 and $829,000 in 1976).	3,639	2,236
	62,753	28,958
Less amounts due within one year included under current liabilities.	2,338	1,124
	$60,415	27,834

Maturities of long-term debt, including present value of capitalized lease payments (see note 8), for the five years after July 31, 1977 are approximately $2,338,000, $2,230,000, $2,245,000, $3,516,000 and $2,931,000, respectively.

At July 31, 1977, working capital requirements under the Company's long-term debt agreements were met and approximately $37,600,000 of earnings employed in the business were unrestricted as to payment of dividends.

On September 1, 1977 the Company issued 8⅝% promissory notes in the amount of $10,000,000 due in annual installments beginning September 1, 1983 through September 1, 1997. If the agreements relating to these notes had been in effect at July 31, 1977, approximately $6,500,000 of earnings employed in the business would have been unrestricted as to payment of dividends.

NOTE 5
Capital Stock

Preferred stock authorized and issued at July 31, 1977 and 1976 consisted of 24,000 shares of 6% cumulative preferred stock and 32,000 shares of 6% cumulative second preferred stock.

Notes to Consolidated Financial Statements (contd.)

On December 11, 1975, the stockholders approved an increase in the authorized number of common shares from 5,000,000 to 10,000,000, thereby effecting a 3-for-2 stock split in the form of a 50% stock dividend. Common stock issued at July 31, 1977 and 1976 was 5,720,191 shares.

At July 31, 1977 and 1976, 6,257 shares of preferred stock and 13,351 shares of second preferred stock were held in treasury. Common stock held in treasury at July 31, 1977 and 1976 was 21,870 and 70,606 shares, respectively.

During 1976 a warrant, assumed in an acquisition, to purchase the equivalent of 7,500 shares of the Company's common stock was purchased and retired.

Changes in common stock, additional paid-in capital and treasury stock for the two years ended July 31, 1977 are summarized below:

				Treasury Stock	
	Common stock	Additional paid-in capital	Preferred stock	Second preferred stock	Common stock
			(in thousands)		
Balance July 31, 1975.	$ 9,534	2,532	616	1,216	300
3-for-2 stock split, effected in form of 50% stock dividend.	4,766	(367)	—	—	—
Issued to Employees' Profit Sharing and Investment Plan (71,773 shares).	—	110	—	—	(914)
Purchase and retirement of outstanding stock warrants.	—	(65)	—	—	—
Issued upon exercise of stock options (3,000 shares).	—	(5)	—	—	(37)
Stock purchased (122,901 shares).	—	—	—	—	1,747
Balance July 31, 1976.	14,300	2,205	616	1,216	1,096
Issued to Employees' Profit Sharing and Investment Plan (57,854 shares).	—	105	—	—	(865)
Issued upon exercise of stock options (3,000 shares).	—	(8)	—	—	(43)
Stock purchased (12.118 shares).	—	—	—	—	179
Balance July 31, 1977.	$14,300	2,302	616	1,216	367

NOTE 6
Stock Options

Options have been granted to officers and key employees to purchase shares of the Company's common stock at not less than fair market value at dates of grant. Options are exercisable at any time within five years from date of grant. Options have also been assumed in connection with acquisitions. Shares issued upon exercise of stock options have been issued from treasury stock with the difference between the proceeds and the cost being charged to additional paid-in capital. No amounts are charged to net earnings with respect to stock options.

Stock option transactions for the two years ended July 31, 1977 are summarized as follows:

	1977		1976	
	Shares	Option price per share	Shares	Option price per share
Outstanding at beginning of year.	169,600	$10.417-16.00	151,260	$10.417-16.00
Granted during year.	27,000	17.625	131,500	12.167-14.75
Exercised during year.	(3,000)	10.417-12.167	(3,000)	10.417
Cancelled during year.	(17,100)	12.167-16.00	(110,160)	15.00-16.00
Outstanding at end of year.	176,500	10.417-17.625	169,600	10.417-16.00

In addition to shares reserved for outstanding options, 66,500 shares of common stock are reserved for future option grants at July 31, 1977.

The Company and its subsidiaries have several pension plans covering substantially all of their employees. The total pension plan expense was $2,607,000 in 1977 and $1,860,000 in 1976, which includes amortization of prior service costs over periods up to 30 years. The amendments to the plan to comply with the provisions of the Employee Retirement Income Security Act of 1974, plus coverage of additional employees due to acquisitions and expansion, principally accounted for the increase in pension expense. Based on the most recent actuarial determinations, the assets of two plans exceed the vested benefits, while for all other plans the computed value of vested benefits exceed the pension fund assets and balance sheet accruals by approximately $1,800,000. The total unfunded past service costs of the plans was approximately $5,700,000.

All pension plans have been amended to conform with the provisions of the Employee Retirement Income Security Act of 1974.

**NOTE 7
Pension Plans**

Leases entered into during the period January 1, 1977 through July 31, 1977 capitalized in accordance with Statement No. 13 of the Financial Accounting Standards Board, and those leases existing prior to January 1, 1977 capitalized subject to Accounting Principles Board Opinion No. 5 are included in property, plant and equipment and are summarized as follows:

**NOTE 8
Leases**

	July 31	
	1977	1976
	(in thousands)	
Land	$ 579	379
Buildings and equipment	10,436	7,705
Construction in progress	14,604	215
	25,619	8,299
Less accumulated amortization	1,563	1,098
	$24,056	7,201

The following is a schedule by years of future minimum lease payments under capital leases together with the present value of the minimum lease payments included in long-term debt (see note 4) as of July 31, 1977:

Year ending July 31:	(in thousands)
1978	$ 3,640
1979	3,660
1980	3,652
1981	4,856
1982	4,135
Later years	72,790
Total minimum lease payments	92,733
Less amount representing interest	(47,221)
Present value of minimum lease payments	$45,512

Amortization of property under capital leases, included in depreciation and amortization expense, was $471,000 and $321,000 in 1977 and 1976, respectively.

In addition to capital leases, the Company and its subsidiaries, at July 31, 1977, were committed under non-cancellable leases which will require minimum net rentals in future fiscal years as follows:

Notes to Consolidated Financial Statements (contd.)

Fiscal year	Transportation equipment	Real property	Other	Total	Financing leases*
		(in thousands)			
1978.	$3,657	2,971	310	6,938	2,245
1979.	2,567	2,647	141	5,355	1,987
1980.	2,100	2,316	42	4,458	1,791
1981.	1,923	1,844	25	3,792	1,640
1982.	1,770	1,511	10	3,291	1,625
1983-1987.	8,376	5,996	—	14,372	8,076
1988-1992.	8,056	3,964	—	12,020	8,031
1993-1997.	2,430	678	—	3,108	2,430

Non-cancellable leases including financing leases

*Financing leases are those (1) which have terms that, in management's opinion, assure the lessor full recovery of the fair market value of the property at the inception of the lease, plus a reasonable return on investment or (2) whose initial term covers 75% or more of the economic life of the property.

Total rent expense for the years ended July 31, 1977 and 1976 was:

	1977	1976
	(in thousands)	
Financing leases.	$2,488	2,507
Other rentals.	7,149	6,801
	$9,637	9,308

The present value of minimum lease commitments applicable to non-capitalized "financing" leases at July 31, 1977 and 1976 were as follows:

Interest rates used in present value computation

	Weighted average		Range		Present value	
	1977	1976	1977	1976	1977	1976
					(in thousands)	
Transportation equipment	6.6%	6.7%	4.8-12.0%	4.8-12.0%	$16,408	17,426
Real property.	5.5	5.5	5.5	4.0-9.75	429	577
Other.	6.7	8.4	5.0-11.0	5.0-12.0	438	533
Total.					$17,275	18,536

If all non-capitalized "financing" leases had been capitalized, the resulting effect on net income would not have been significant.

NOTE 9
Litigation

In January 1976, a private treble damage action complaint seeking an unstated amount of damages was filed against the Company, a former subsidiary now merged with the Company, and five other corporate defendants alleging certain violations of the Federal antitrust laws in the sale of bakery flour. A similar action commenced in March 1973 was settled on June 28, 1977 and all claims against the Company in that case have been extinguished. A motion to dismiss a third similar action, pending since April 1973, was granted and plaintiff in that case filed a motion for reconsideration requesting the court to vacate the order of dismissal. The Company has denied the allegations of the complaint in the remaining case and intends to vigorously defend that action. Based upon the information presently available, including advice of counsel, management of the Company believes that the liability, if any, of the Company in this action will not have a material adverse effect on the Company.

There are other pending claims and litigation against the Company. The Company has denied the claims. Management believes that these lawsuits will not result in a liability in an amount which will be material in relation to the Company's financial position.

During the years ended July 31, 1977 and 1976, Industrial Revenue Bonds in amounts aggregating $33,000,000 and $9,100,000, respectively, were issued to finance specific construction projects. These funds are deposited with trustees and are used to pay for the projects as they are installed. At July 31, 1977 and 1976, $21,790,000 and $4,103,000, respectively, constituted the unexpended portion of the funds held by trustees. The Company's liability for the revenue bonds has been recorded in the financial statements as capitalized lease obligations and is included in long-term debt.

At July 31, 1977, the cost to complete construction in progress approximated $17,241,000, exclusive of those projects financed by the revenue bonds.

**NOTE 10
Construction Funds and Commitments**

Summarized quarterly data for fiscal years 1977 and 1976 is as follows:

**NOTE 11
Quarterly Data (Unaudited)**

	Three Months Ended			
	October 31	January 31	April 30	July 31
Fiscal 1977	(in thousands except per share and market price amounts)			
Sales	$133,961	115,248	120,386	124,711
Cost of products and services sold, excluding depreciation and amortization	111,300	94,479	103,102	103,735
Net earnings	3,436	2,536	829	2,509
Earnings per share	.60	.43	.14	.43
Dividends per share	.185	.21	.21	.21
Market price of common stock:				
High	18⅝	18½	15⅞	14¾
Low	15¼	15¾	14⅛	13⅝
Fiscal 1976 (a)				
Sales	127,145	124,486	128,724	125,467
Cost of products and services sold, excluding depreciation and amortization	104,378	103,462	106,544	103,842
Net earnings	5,105	3,651	3,596	3,293
Earnings per share	.89	.64	.63	.57
Dividends per share	.167	.185	.185	.185
Market price of common stock:				
High	16	21	20¾	20⅛
Low	11⅞	15	17¾	17⅞

(a) Fiscal 1976 quarterly data were not subject to limited review procedures by the Company's independent certified public accountants.

The Securities and Exchange Commission now requires an estimation of the replacement cost of inventories and productive capacity at the end of the fiscal year, and the approximate effect which replacement cost would have had on the computation of cost of products and services sold and depreciation expense for the fiscal year.

**NOTE 12
Replacement Cost Information (Unaudited)**

The replacement cost of inventories and cost of products and services sold (excluding depreciation) generally approximate the historical costs shown in the financial statements. The current replacement cost of the productive capacity and related depreciation expense are generally higher than the comparable amounts shown in the financial statements.

Quantitative information, including the underlying assumptions used in arriving at replacement cost amounts, is included in the Company's annual report on Form 10-K filed with the Securities and Exchange Commission (a copy of which is available upon request).

Accountants' Report

Ten Year Financial Summary

The Board of Directors
and Stockholders
Peavey Company:

We have examined the
consolidated balance sheets of
Peavey Company and subsidiaries
as of July 31, 1977 and
1976, and the related consolidated
statements of earnings, earnings
employed in the business and
changes in financial position for
the years then ended. Our
examination was made in
accordance with generally
accepted auditing standards, and
accordingly included such tests of
the accounting records and
such other auditing procedures as
we considered necessary in the
circumstances.

In our opinion, the aforementioned
consolidated financial statements
present fairly the financial
position of Peavey Company and
subsidiaries at July 31, 1977
and 1976, and the results of their
operations and the changes
in their financial position for the
years then ended, in conformity
with generally accepted
accounting principles applied on a
consistent basis.

Peat, Marwick, Mitchell & Co.

PEAT, MARWICK, MITCHELL & CO.
Minneapolis, Minnesota
September 22, 1977

Net sales...

Earnings (note 1):

    Before income taxes and extraordinary items..........

    Taxes on income.............................

    Before extraordinary items.....................

    Extraordinary items, net of tax.................

    Net earnings...............................

Per share of common stock (note 1):

    Earnings before extraordinary items..............

    Extraordinary items..........................

    Net earnings...............................

    Dividends.................................

    Book value................................

Average number of shares of common stock outstanding..

Total dividends paid.............................

Working capital................................

Property, plant and equipment, net..................

Gross additions to property, plant and equipment........

Depreciation and amortization.....................

Long-term debt...............................

Stockholders' equity...........................

Number of employees...........................

Number of common stockholders..................

(in thousands except per share amounts and number of employees and stockholders)

1977	1976	1975	1974	1973	1972	1971	1970	1969	1968
$494,306	505.822	467.612	494.738	364.181	290.401	268.789	244.800	218.681	194.462
13,260	29.045	29.003	31.035	19.386	12.359	9.545	5.416	4.540	698
3,950	13.400	13.800	15.543	9.646	5.624	4.684	2.081	1.642	88
9,310	15.645	15.203	15.492	9.740	6.735	4.861	3.335	2.898	610
—	—	—	5.358	232	—	12	15	(4.043)	453
9,310	15.645	15.203	20.850	9.972	6.735	4.873	3.350	(1.145)	1.063
1.60	2.73	2.68	2.72	1.74	1.22	.87	.59	.47	.05
—	—	—	.95	.04	—	—	—	(.75)	.08
1.60	2.73	2.68	3.67	1.78	1.22	.87	.59	(.28)	.13
.81½	.72⅛	.65	.53⅓	.46⅔	.27½	.20	.14⅙	.10	.10
21.07	20.32	18.29	16.30	13.22	12.15	11.21	10.54	10.07	9.82
5,690	5,657	5,591	5,625	5,458	5,302	5,270	5,253	5.600	5,928
4,857	4,301	3,843	3,234	2,612	1,467	1,142	884	727	780
68,345	77,733	80,875	80,203	61,922	53,619	43,699	42,635	41,161	42,704
94,249	66,507	46,315	39,539	44,338	39,943	40.153	38.962	35.484	31,888
33,765	18,354	11,404	8,434	10,608	6,044	6,143	8,777	5,846	5,785
6,996	5,572	4,497	4,056	4,064	2,935	2,861	3,031	2,255	2,980
60,415	27,834	18,253	17,556	25,780	23,017	18,351	21,412	17,340	11,655
123,730	118,451	107,863	95,680	77,808	68,594	63,579	59,755	57,282	62,704
5,010	4,474	3,960	3,665	4,116	3,882	4,081	4,044	3,528	3,712
2,825	2,645	2,762	2,851	2,364	—	—	—	—	—

Notes:
(1) Earnings and earnings per share data for 1974 include the gain on sale of Canadian operations of $5,006,000 ($.89 per share) as extraordinary items.

QUESTIONS

1. Contrast the discrete period and integral part approaches to interim reporting. Toward which approach did *APB Opinion No. 28* lean?

2. How is income tax expense accounted for under the interim reporting rules of *APB Opinion No. 28*? Which approach to interim reporting does this reflect? How are extraordinary items reported? Which approach does this reflect?

3. What critical variable is the focus of segment reporting? That is, about what characteristics of an entity are segment data supposed to inform investors? Why is this variable so important?

4. For which three areas are segment data required to be reported? For what logical reason were these areas identified as segments for separate segment reporting?

5. Why is the past financial track record of a company important to investors? What is meant by a turning point?

6. Explain why financial analysts, in analyzing financial statements, examine the auditors' report and the summary of accounting policies.

7. Explain why the notes to the financial statements should be carefully read in the process of analyzing financial statements. Why are long-term summaries considered important to the statement user?

8. Distinguish between vertical and horizontal analyses. Briefly explain the importance of each.

9. What is meant by ratio analysis? Why is it important in the analysis of financial statements?

10. Distinguish between the current ratio and the quick ratio. What purpose does each serve?

11. Current assets and current liabilities for two companies with the same amount of working capital are summarized below. Evaluate their relative liquidity positions.

	X Company	Y Company
Current assets	$200,000	$900,000
Current liabilities	100,000	800,000
Working capital	$100,000	$100,000

12. X Corporation has an accounts receivable turnover of 15; interpret this figure. What would be the age of the receivables? What does it reveal?

13. Y Corporation has an inventory turnover of 9; interpret this figure. What would be average number of days of supply?

14. Explain and illustrate the effect of leverage.

15. Compute and explain the meaning of the book value per share of common stock of the Pride Manufacturing Company assuming the following data are available:

Preferred stock, 6%, cumulative, non-participating, 200 shares outstanding	$ 20,000
Common stock, par value $10, 10,000 shares outstanding	100,000
Retained earnings	7,000

(Three years dividends in arrears on preferred stock including current year.)

16. Explain the circumstances where a company has debt financing and the leverage factor is (a) positive, (b) negative, and (c) zero.

17. Explain the ROI concept. Why is it a fundamental measure of profitability?

18. What is meant by "the multiple"? Why is it considered important?

19. What are the principal limitations in using ratios?

DECISION CASE 25–1

Scott Corporation needs additional funds for plant expansion. The board of directors is considering obtaining the funds by issuing additional short-term notes, long-term bonds, preferred stock, or common stock.

Required:

1. What primary factors should the board of directors consider in selecting the best method of financing plant expansion?

2. One member of the board of directors suggests that the corporation should maximize the impact of financial leverage by borrowing additional funds.

   a. Explain how financial leverage affects earnings per share of common stock.

   b. Explain how a change in income tax rates affects financial leverage.

   c. Under what circumstances should a corporation seek financial leverage to a substantial degree?

3. Two specific proposals under consideration by the board of directors are the issue of 7% subordinated income bonds (secured only by the general credit of the issuer with interest paid each year only if there is income equal to the interest charge) or 7% cumulative, nonparticipating, nonvoting pre-

ferred stock, callable at par. In discussing the impact of the two alternatives on the debt to stockholders' equity ratio, one member of the board of directors stated that the resulting debt-equity ratio would be the same under either alternative because the income bonds and preferred stock should be reported in the same balance sheet classification. What are the arguments (a) for and (b) against using the same balance sheet classification in reporting the income bonds and preferred stock?

(AICPA adapted)

EXERCISES

Exercise 25–1

Baker Trading Company income statements (condensed) for two quarters are shown below.

	First Quarter	Second Quarter
Gross sales	$221,000	$242,000
Returns	(1,000)	(2,000)
	220,000	240,000
Cost of goods sold	(110,000)	(130,000)
Gross margin	110,000	110,000
Expenses:		
Selling	(62,000)	(63,000)
Administrative (including income taxes)	(30,000)	(31,000)
Financial (net of financial revenue)	(3,000)	2,000
Net income before extraordinary items	15,000	18,000
Extraordinary items, net of tax	5,000	(3,000)
Net Income	$ 20,000	$ 15,000
Shares of common stock outstanding	10,000	10,000

Required:

1. Prepare a multiple-step comparative income statement including a vertical percentage analysis (round to nearest percent). Use net sales as the base amount.
2. Prepare a single-step income statement including horizontal percentage analysis (round to nearest percent).

Exercise 25–2

The following data were taken from the financial statements of the Ralston Company. Based on these data compute (a) the working capital, (b) the current ratio, and (c) the acid test ratio (carry to even percents). Evaluate each change.

	19A	19B
Current Assets:		
Cash	$ 30,000	$ 40,000
Short-term investments	10,000	10,000
Trade accounts receivable (net)	60,000	70,000
Notes receivable	6,000	2,000
Inventory	150,000	170,000
Prepaid expenses	4,000	2,000
Current Liabilities	90,000	120,000

Exercise 25–3

The condensed financial data given below were taken from the annual financial statements of Foster Corporation:

	19A	19B	19C
Current assets (including inventory)	$ 200,000	$ 250,000	$ 270,000
Current liabilities	150,000	180,000	130,000
Cash sales	800,000	780,000	820,000
Credit sales	200,000	280,000	250,000
Cost of goods sold	560,000	600,000	600,000
Inventory	120,000	140,000	100,000
Quick assets	80,000	90,000	85,000
Accounts receivable (net)	60,000	58,000	64,000
Total assets (net)	1,000,000	1,200,000	1,400,000

Required:

1. Based on the above data, calculate the following for 19B and 19C (round to one decimal place):
   a. Current ratio.
   b. Acid test ratio.
   c. Working capital to total assets.
   d. Receivable turnover.
   e. Age of receivables.
   f. Merchandise inventory turnover.
   g. Days' supply in inventory.
   h. Working capital turnover.
2. Evaluate the overall results of the computations including trends. Use 365 days for computation purposes.

Exercise 25–4

The following data were taken from the financial statements of the Action Company:

	19A	19B	19C
Sales—cash	$190,000	$200,000	$220,000
Sales—credit	100,000	120,000	130,000
Average receivables	25,000	34,000	50,000
Average inventory	60,000	70,000	80,000
Cost of goods sold	180,000	190,000	200,000

Required:

What conclusions may be made relative to (a) inventories and (b) receivables? (Use 300 business days in year; credit terms are 90 business days.)

Exercise 25–5

The balance sheets for two similar companies reflected the following:

	Company A	Company B
Current liabilities	$ 30,000	$100,000
Long-term liabilities	70,000	300,000
Stockholders' Equity:		
Common stock, par $5	220,000	46,000
Preferred stock, par $10	100,000	20,000
Contributed capital in		
excess of par, common ...	20,000	4,000
Retained earnings	60,000	30,000
Net Income, included in		
retained earnings		
(less taxes, 45%)	49,500	13,000

Required:

1. Compute the three equity ratios listed in the chapter that measure equity position and the leverage factor for each company.
2. Interpret and evaluate each situation. The average interest rate for both companies is 10% (on total liabilities).

Exercise 25–6

Basey Manufacturing Corporation balance sheet showed the following as of December 31, 19A:

Preferred stock, 7%, par value	
$50 per share	$200,000
Common stock, nopar, 30,000	
shares outstanding	360,000
Contributed capital in excess of par,	
preferred stock	40,000
Retained earnings	80,000

Required:

Compute the book value per share of common stock assuming:

1. None of the preferred shares has been issued.
2. Preferred is noncumulative and nonparticipating; liquidation value of preferred is par.
3. Preferred is cumulative and nonparticipating (three years' dividends in arrears including current year); liquidation value of preferred is par.
4. Preferred has a liquidation value of $60 per share and is noncumulative and nonparticipating.
5. Preferred has a liquidation value of $60 per share and is noncumulative and nonparticipating, and the Retained Earnings account shows a *deficit* of $30,000, instead of the $80,000 credit balance shown above.

Exercise 25–7

The financial statements for Weston Corporation for 19C reported complete comparative statements. The following data were taken therefrom:

	19A	19B	19C
Sales revenue	$12,000,000	$13,000,000	$14,000,000
Net income	100,000	120,000	100,000
Interest expense, net			
of income tax	10,000	12,000	9,000
Stockholders' equity	1,400,000	1,450,000	1,460,000
Shares of common			
stock outstanding	20,000	20,000	24,000
Total assets	3,500,000	3,500,000	3,700,000
Market value per			
share	$66.00	$72.00	$45.00

Required:

1. Based on the above financial data, compute the following ratios for 19B and 19C: *(a)* profit margin; *(b)* return on investment, total assets; *(c)* return on investment, owners' equity; *(d)* the leverage factor; *(e)* earnings per share; and *(f)* price earnings ratio. (Carry computations to two decimal places.)
2. Which ratios would you prefer as a measure of profitability? Why?
3. Explain any significant trends that appear to be developing.

Exercise 25–8

The following data relate to the Wallace Printing Company:

	19A	19B	19C	19D	19E
Net income	$ 12,000	$ 15,000	$ 25,000	$ 30,000	$ 40,000
Interest expense,					
net of tax	1,000	1,200	2,000	2,200	3,000
Sales.............	120,000	140,000	180,000	230,000	260,000
Total assets.......	50,000	72,000	110,000	160,000	190,000
Total liabilities	25,000	30,000	40,000	70,000	80,000

Required:

Evaluate the trend of the company in terms of the *(a)* profit margin, *(b)* ROI, and *(c)* leverage factor. Round to nearest percent.

PROBLEMS

Problem 25–1

Part A:

Raphael Company has engaged you to prepare its interim financial statements for the first, second, and third quarters of its current fiscal year. The complication is that Raphael changed depreciation methods from sum-of-the-years' digits (SYD) to straight line. Although the change was made during the second quarter, its effect was retroactive to become effective January 1 (the beginning date) of the current fiscal year. Summarized data are presented below, on the old (SYD) basis:

	First Quarter	Second Quarter
Income Statement:		
Sales	$100,000	$92,000
Depreciation expense	(3,500)	(3,300)
Other expenses	(91,500)	(89,700)
Net income (loss)	$ 5,000	$ (1,000)
Balance Sheet:		
Operational assets...........	$ 36,750	$36,750
Accumulated depreciation	(14,000)	(17,300)
	$ 22,750	$19,450

Straight-line depreciation on the asset for which the depreciation method was being changed was the following: prior to the current year, (three quarters) $6,000; first quarter of current year, $2,000; and second quarter of current year, $2,000.

Required:

Ignoring income taxes, present the summarized financial statement items shown above as they should appear in the second quarter interim report. Ignore pro forma presentations and footnotes.

Part B:

Summarized data for Raphael Company appear below for the third quarter of the same year. Depreciation expense and accumulated depreciation reflect the (new) straight-line basis adopted during the second quarter of the current year.

	Third Quarter
Income Statement:	
Sales	$89,000
Depreciation expense......................	(2,000)
Other expenses	(86,000)
Net Income	$ 1,000
Balance Sheet:	
Operational assets	$36,750
Less: Accumulated depreciation	(12,000)
	$24,750

Required:

Ignoring income taxes, present comparative, summarized financial statement data for the items shown

above, for interim quarters 1, 2, and 3 of the current year. Ignore pro forma presentations and footnotes.

Problem 25–2

The following data were taken from the annual financial statements of Mason Corporation:

	19A	19B	19C
Current Assets:			
Cash	$ 10,000	$ 5,000	$ 8,000
Trade receivables	180,000	170,000	190,000
Less: Allowance for doubtful accounts	(5,000)	(6,000)	(8,000)
Notes receivable (nontrade)	110,000	125,000	100,000
Short-term investments	45,000	30,000	20,000
Inventories	298,000	355,000	387,000
Prepaid expenses	12,000	11,000	13,000
Total	$ 650,000	$ 690,000	$ 710,000
Current Liabilities:			
Trade payables	$ 70,000	$ 158,000	$ 196,000
Notes payable	90,000	72,000	60,000
Accrued wages payable.....	72,000	46,000	52,000
Income taxes payable	19,000	23,000	24,000
Deferred rent revenue	2,000	2,000	2,000
Accrued liabilities	17,000	19,000	16,000
Total	$ 270,000	$ 320,000	$ 350,000
Additional Data:			
Cash sales	$3,300,000	$3,500,000	$3,200,000
Credit sales	1,500,000	1,700,000	1,800,000
Cost of goods sold	2,500,000	2,900,000	2,800,000
Total assets (net)	6,600,000	7,200,000	7,200,000

Required:

1. Compute the ratios listed in the chapter for each year to measure current position and include a vertical analysis of current assets. Round to nearest percent and ratios to one decimal place.
2. Evaluate the current position as indicated by the statements and the ratios. What additional information would you need to buttress your evaluation?

Problem 25–3

The financial statements of Staley Manufacturing Company for a three-year period showed the following:

	19A	19B	19C
Total assets	$2,000,000	$2,040,000	$1,940,000
Total current assets	368,000	450,000	480,000
Total current liabilities	230,000	150,000	150,000
Operational assets (net)	1,248,000	1,257,600	1,260,000
Total liabilities	1,090,000	1,110,000	900,000
Common stock (par value $100)	600,000	600,000	700,000
Retained earnings	310,000	330,000	340,000
Sales (net)	6,600,000	7,000,000	7,100,000
Net income (after tax)	50,000	70,000	40,000
Interest expense (net of tax)	34,000	38,000	30,000

Required: (Round to nearest percents, or if a decimal, to two places):

1. Based on the above data, calculate the following ratios to measure the current position for each year.
   a. Current ratio.
   b. Working capital turnover.
   Evaluate the current position. What additional information do you need to adequately evaluate the current position? Explain.
2. Based on the above data, calculate the following ratios to measure the equity position:
   a. Creditors' equity to total assets.
   b. Book value per share of common stock.
   Evaluate the equity position. What additional information do you need to adequately evaluate the equity position? Explain.
3. Based on the above data, calculate the following ratios to measure operating results:
   a. Profit margin.
   b. Return on investment on total assets.
   c. Return on investment on owners' equity.
4. Evaluate the operating results. What additional significant information do you need to adequately evaluate operating results? Explain.
5. Evaluate the financial leverage factor.

Problem 25–4

The following annual data were taken from the records of Grant Trading Corporation:

	19A	19B	19C	19D	19E
Sales	$400,000	$420,000	$450,000	$440,000	$490,000
Net income	15,000	16,000	20,000	5,000	40,000
Total assets	200,000	220,000	230,000	240,000	250,000
Owners' equity	100,000	110,000	120,000	115,000	140,000
Market price per share	60	62	55	25	60
Dividends per share	4	4	4	1	5
Capital stock outstanding (shares)	4,000	4,000	4,000	3,900	3,800
Interest expense (net of tax)	4,000	4,500	4,600	5,000	4,100

Required (Round ratios and percents to two decimal places):

1. Compute the ratios listed in the chapter to measure operating results.
2. Compute the price-earnings and dividend ratios.
3. Evaluate the profitability of the company; pinpoint indicated strengths and weaknesses. What additional information do you need? Explain.
4. Compute the financial leverage factor.

Problem 25–5

The following summarized data were taken from the published statements of two companies that are being compared:

	(in thousands)	
	Company A	Company B
Sales	$3,000	$ 9,000
Cost of goods sold	1,900	6,942
Operating expenses	400	1,600
Interest expense (net of tax)	8	108
Extraordinary item (loss), after tax	(22)	550
Income tax (on income before extraordinary item)	240	300
Current assets	1,000	4,000
Operational assets	4,500	19,000
Accumulated depreciation	1,500	7,000
Investments, long term	400	100
Other assets	600	7,900
Current liabilities	900	2,000
Long-term liabilities	100	1,800
Capital stock ($10 par value)	3,000	18,000
Retained earnings	1,000	2,200
Current market value per share	$16.75	$1.50

Compute the one ratio that would best answer each of the following questions (show computations). Justify your choice.

a. Which company probably has the better current position?
b. Which company has the better working capital turnover?
c. Which company is earning the better rate on total resources available to the management? On resources provided by the owners?
d. Which company has the advantage in "trading on the equity"?
e. Which company has the better profit margin?
f. Which company has the higher book value per share of common stock?
g. In your opinion which stock is the better buy?

Problem 25–6

Fulger Corporation is considering building a second plant at a cost of $600,000. The management is considering two alternatives to obtain the funds: (a) sell additional common stock or (b) issue $600,000, five-year bonds payable at 8% interest. The management believes that the bonds can be sold at par (for $600,000) and the stock at $30 per share.

The balance sheet (before the new financing) reflected the following:

Liabilities	None
Common stock, par $10	$200,000
Contributed capital in excess of par	100,000
Retained earnings	120,000
Average income for past several years (net of tax).............................	30,000

The average income tax rate is 45%. Average dividends per share have been $0.50 per share per year. Expected increase in pretax income (excluding interest expense) from the new plant, $100,000 per year.

Required:

1. Prepare an analysis to show *(a)* expected income after the addition, *(b)* cash flows from the company to prospective owners of the new capital, and *(c)* the leverage advantage or disadvantage to the present shareholders of issuing the bonds to obtain the financing.
2. What are the principal arguments for and against issuing the bonds (as opposed to selling the common stock)?

Problem 25–7

This assignment focuses on financial statement analysis, with special emphasis on the disclosure notes to be found in current financial statements. Intermediate accounting typically does not deal comprehensively with note disclosures as a separate topic; instead, the text has listed disclosure requirements of GAAP, and illustrated some, for specific topical areas. This is an opportunity to assess the practical implementation of the full disclosure principle of accounting.

Another important objective of this problem is to familiarize you with actual financial statements and to give you confidence that your knowledge of accounting enables you to understand a major portion of even very complex financial disclosures.

Finally, this provides a comprehensive review of practically everything you have studied in the 25 chapters in this book.

Instructions:

Go to your college library and study the published annual reports of corporations. In particular, read as many annual reports as it takes to locate at least *two* disclosures of each of the 20 types listed below. Some types of disclosures will be contained in almost every financial report you read; others will be hard to find. But don't stop until you have found the 40 required disclosures, or have read a minimum of 12 annual reports, whichever occurs first.

As you study the reports, make notes of *(a)* interesting disclosures and *(b)* questions you may have about the interpretation of specific disclosures. Do not hesitate to be critical of what you find, particularly as to the effectiveness of the notes for communication to statement users (i.e., are they sufficiently clear and understandable as written?). Come to the class meeting for which this problem is assigned prepared to discuss what you have learned and to raise questions. Types of disclosures (find two examples of each):

1. Principles of consolidation.
2. Equity method for long-term investments.
3. Cost (lower of cost or market) for both short-term and long-term investments. Note different ways of accounting for market losses.
4. Market value method for investments. See financial statements of a brokerage firm.
5. Inventory method: *Lifo, Fifo,* weighted average, or other. Also look for the use of lower of cost or market for inventories.
6. Operational assets: useful lives, depreciation method, and amount of depreciation.
7. Long-term debt: interest rates, maturity dates, conversion privileges, call options of issuer, and security agreements.
8. Contingent losses and contingent gains.
9. Income taxes: allocation, and investment tax credit.
10. Leases: capital leases—try airlines because they lease a major portion of their assets; sales type and direct-financing leases—try computer companies; operating leases; and disclosures by both lessor and lessee.
11. Pensions.
12. Treasury stock: cost method, and par value method (you may not be able to locate both of these).
13. Accounting changes: estimate, principle, reporting entity, and error (you may not be able to find all of these).
14. Prior period adjustment—look for restated financial statements of prior year.
15. Appropriations of retained earnings.
16. Stock option plans: compensatory, and noncompensatory.
17. Statement of changes in financial position; working capital basis, cash basis, and cash plus short-term investments basis.
18. Auditors' report—find one with unusual wording (Price Waterhouse's standard format is different, but it does not meet this requirement).
19. Goodwill, including amortization.
20. Extraordinary items.

Problem 25–8 (based on the Appendix)

The chapter Appendix presents a complete set of financial statements for a medium-sized company. This problem focuses on those statements. The objective is to develop an analysis of them.

Required:

1. Examine the auditors' report. What significant information (favorable and unfavorable) is provided?
2. Examine the summary of significant accounting policies. What important information (favorable and unfavorable) is provided?
3. Examine the overall financial report:
   a. What titles are used for the three required statements?
   b. How many notes are included? What is the topic of each?
   c. Is there a statement of retained earnings? What does it report?
   d. Is there a long-term financial summary? How many periods does it encompass? What is its primary purpose.
   e. Income statement—What are the amounts for each year and the changes in net sales, net income, dividends, EPS, extraordinary items, and income tax expense? Did you observe any unusual items? Note all significant changes indicated.
   f. Balance sheet—What are the amounts for each year and the changes for cash, inventories, current assets, operational assets, total assets, current liabilities, long-term debt and stockholders' equity? Do you observe any unusual items on the balance sheet, other than those above? Explain why they are unusual?
   g. Statement of changes in financial position— On what basis was it prepared? What were the two largest sources of funds for each year? What were the two largest uses of funds each year? Did funds increase or decrease during each year? By how much? Did you observe any unusual items? Explain each.
4. What basic groups of data are presented in the long-term financial summary? Evaluate the trend of earnings before extraordinary items versus sales.
5. Analytical—Develop ratios for 1976 and 1977 as follows (show computations and carry to even percents, or if a decimal, to two places):
   Measurements of current position:
   a. Working capital ratio.
   b. Acid test ratio.
   c. Receivables turnover.
   d. Inventory turnover.
   Measurements of equity position:
   e. Creditors' equity to total assets.
   f. Operational assets to total equities.
   g. Book value per share.
   Measurements of operating results:
   h. Profit margin.
   i. Return on total assets.
   j. Return on owners' equity.
   k. Earnings per share (already computed).
   l. Financial leverage.
6. On the basis of your responses to the above requirements:
   a. Evaluate the working capital position.
   b. Evaluate the equity position.
   c. Evaluate the profitability.
   d. Evaluate the leverage effect.
7. Assume you have $50,000 cash to invest and are interested in acquiring common stock. What specific information about this company, other than that reported in the financial statements and your analysis, would you urgently need prior to making a decision to invest, or not invest, in this company?

Index

A

AAA; *see* American Accounting Association
Accountants, independent, 4–5
Accountants' Index, 6
Accountant's report; *see* Auditors' report
Accounting
  accrual basis, 39
  basic objectives, 23–25
  basic principles, 28
  cash basis, 39
  defined, 1
  financial, 2
  historical cost model, 38, 48
  income taxes, 323
  information processing model, 49
  management, defined, 2
  measurement principles, 36
  underlying assumptions, 26
Accounting changes, 34, 494
  accounting principle, 107–8
  currently, 816
  defined, 815
  error correction, 820
  estimates, 107, 815, 818
  interest reporting, 853
  principles, 815–16
  prospectively, 816
  reporting entity, 819
  retroactively, 816
Accounting estimate changes, 818
Accounting models
  comparison, 234, 242–44; *see also*
    Current replacement cost
  current value, 229–30, 233
Accounting policies, 97
  disclosure of, 149
  statement of, 858
Accounting principle change, 816

Accounting principles
  changes, 815
  consistency, 33
  cost, 29
  financial reporting, 34
  matching, 32
  modifying, 35
  objectivity, 33
  revenue, 30
Accounting Principles Board (APB)
    Opinions; see Appendix to Chapter 1
Accounting Principles Board (APB)
    Statements; see Appendix to Chapter 1
Accounting Research Bulletins (ARBs),
    6, 265, 273, 489, 748; *see also Appendix to Chapter 1*
Accounting Research Monograph No. 1,
    456
Accounting Research Studies, 6
Accounting Research Study No. 6, 220
Accounting for Retail Land Sales, 457
Accounting Series Releases (SEC), 8
  No. 163, 457
  No. 190, 220, 244, 369
Accounting Terminology Bulletin No. 1, 481
Accounting Trends and Techniques, 6,
    494, 736
Accounts payable, 310
Accounts receivable; *see* Receivables
Accounts receivable subsidiary ledger,
    65, 69
Accrual basis accounting, 39
Accruals, 28
Accrued expense (for adjustment), 57
Accrued liabilities, 309, 313
Accrued revenue, 58
Acid test ratio, 862

Actuarial gains and losses; *see* Pension
    plans
Actuarial methods; *see* Pension plans
Additional paid-in capital, 144
Adjusting entries
  estimated items, 58
  expenses, 57–58
  revenues, 57–58
Adverse opinion, 152
AICPA; *see* American Institute of Certified Public Accountants
All-inclusive concept of income, 102
All-resources concept, 145; *see also*
    Statement of changes in financial
    position
Allocation of income taxes; *see also*
    Income taxes, allocation
  interperiod, 98
  intraperiod, 98
Allowance for doubtful accounts; *see*
    Receivables
Allowance to reduce investments to
    LCM, 274–75, 279
American Accounting Association
    (AAA), 5, 9–10
    Statement of Basic Accounting Theory, 10
American Institute of Certified Public
    Accountants, 5
Amortization
  bond premium and discount, 690
  defined, 480
  intangible assets, 142
Amount of 1, 180, 182; *see also* Future
    value of 1
Analysis of financial statements, 856,
    861; *see also* Financial statements
Annuities
  defined, 182, 187
  due, 192
  future value of annuity due, 192

Annuities—*Cont.*
  future value of an ordinary annuity, 188
  present value of annuity due, 194
  present value of an ordinary annuity, 190
  rents, 190
  table values, 200–207
Annuities in advance; *see* Annuities, due
Annuities in arrears; *see* Annuities
Antidilution (EPS), 632
Antidilutive securities (EPS), 628; *see also* Earnings per share
APB *Opinions; see Appendix to Chapter 1*
APB *Statements; see Appendix to Chapter 1*
Appropriated retained earnings, 144; *see also* Retained earnings
Appropriations of retained earnings, 323
ARBs; see Accounting Research Bulletins and Appendix to Chapter 1
Arm's-length transaction, 449
Articles of incorporation, 143
ASR; see Accounting Series Releases and Appendix to Chapter 1
ASR No. 190; see Accounting Series Releases, *No. 190 and Appendix to Chapter 1*
Assessments on shareholders, 562
Assets
  current, 138
  defined, 135
Assigned value stock, 552
Auditing, statements on standards, 6
Auditing Standards Executive Committee, 8
Auditors' report, 856
  defined, 151
Audits of Savings and Loan Associations, 457
AudSEC; *see* Auditing Standards Executive Committee
Authorized capital stock, 552
Average cost
  inventory, 386
  investments, 646
  retail inventory, 423

B

Bad debt expense; *see* Receivables
Balance sheet
  classifications, 137
  current replacement cost, 240
  defined, 4, 134
  format, 136
  general price level, 239
  importance, 136
  investment and funds, 141
  liabilities, 143
  owners' equity, 143
  restatement of, 224, 232
Bank reconciliation; *see* Cash, reconciliation
Bargain purchase option; *see* Leases
Base stock (inventory), 394
Basic accounting principles, 28

Basic objectives of accounting, 23–25
Beginning-of-the-period annuities; *see* Annuities, due
Bonds; *see also* Long-term liabilities
  callable, 685, 698
  classification, 685
  convertible, 624, 685, 698
  coupon, 685
  defined, 684
  discount, 180, 689, 695
  effective interest, 686
  income, 685
  indenture, 684
  interest, 687
  issue costs, 697
  municipal, 685
  nonconvertible, 697
  premium, 18, 689, 695
  prices, 687
  redeemable, 685
  refunding, 685, 701
  reporting on financial statements, 691
  serial, 711
  stated interest, 687
Bonus problems, 316
Book value, 135, 141, 450; *see also* Carrying value
  per share of common stock, 866
Boot; *see* Operational assets
Buildings; *see* Operational assets
Business combinations; *see* Consolidated statements, defined

C

Call provision (on debt), 700
Callable bonds, 685, 698
Callable capital stock, 594
Callable preferred stock, 556
Capital
  financial, 234
  physical, 234
  unrealized, 561–62
Capital assets; *see* Operational assets
Capital expenditures, 446
Capital leases; *see* Leases
Capital maintenance, 234
Capital stock, 143; *see also* Corporations *and* Stockholders' equity
  callable, 594
  classes, 552
  common, 554
  convertible, 594
  discount, 560
  dividends, 555
  nature of, 551
  nopar value, 557
  par value, 553, 557
  preferred, 554
  premium, 560
  redeemable, 594
  splits, 669
  subscribed, 558
Carrybacks (income tax), 331
Carrybacks, tax loss, 331–34
Carryforwards (income tax), 331
Carryforwards, tax loss, 331–34
Carrying value, 135; *see also* Book value
Cash
  compensating balances, 264

Cash—*Cont.*
  composition of, 264
  control of, 265
  flow prospects, 3
  overage and shortage, 267
  overdraft, 265
  petty, 265–66
  proof of, 269
  reconciliation, 267, 269
  statement of changes, 783, 798
Cash basis accounting, 39
Cash dividends, 575; *see also* Dividends
Cash flow, *Lifo* inventory, 392
Cash flow statement; *see* Statement of changes in financial position
Cash reconciliation, comprehensive, 269
Cash surrender value, 271, 533–34
Casualty insurance, 528
Casualty losses, 531–33
Catch-up depreciation, 242
CD (Certificate of deposit), 265
Certified management accountants, 5
Certified Public Accountant, 4
Change in accounting estimates, 815
Change in accounting principle, 815–16
Changes in income tax rates, 329–30
Charter (of a corporation), 143
Chicago Board Options Exchange, 618
Clearing (suspense) accounts, 61
Closed corporations, 551
Closing entries, 60
CMA, *see* Certified management accountants
Coinsurance, 529–31
Committee on Accounting Procedure (AICPA), 6
Common stock, 554
Common stock equivalents, 627; *see also* Earnings per share
Comparative financial statements, 148, 859
Comparative statements, restated for price changes, 227
Compensating balances, 264
Compensation cost, 618; *see also* Stock option plans *and* Stock rights
Compensatory stock option plans, 615–16; *see also* Stock rights
Completed contract method (long-term construction), 424, 426
Completed exchange transactions, 92
Complex capital structure, 624; *see also* Earnings per share
Compound interest, 181; *see also* Interest
Concepts, statement of (FASB), 23–25
Concepts of capital maintenance, 234
Conservatism, 36, 356
Consignments, 352
Consistency principle, 33
Consolidated financial statements, 646; *see also* Financial statements
Consolidated statements, defined, 656
Construction in Process (inventory), 425
Construction contracts, 425
  long-term, 817
Consumer Price Index, 216, 221

Contingencies, 319, 322; *see also* Gain contingencies *and* Loss contingencies
  litigation, 321
  loss, 319, 321
Contingency gains, disclosure, 149
Contingency losses, disclosure, 149
Continuity assumption, 26
Contributed capital, 551; *see also* Capital stock; Corporations; *and* Stockholders' equity
Contributed capital in excess of par, defined, 144
Control accounts, 54, 65
Controlling influence; *see* Long-term investments
Controlling interests, 647, 656; *see also* Consolidated statements, defined *and* Long-term investments
Conversion (of bonds), 698
Conversion factor, 227
Conversion fraction (ratio), 221
Convertible bonds, 624, 685, 698
Convertible capital stock, 594
Convertible preferred stock, 556, 624
Convertible securities, 669
Copyrights; *see* Intangible assets
Corporations; *see also* Capital stock
  classification, 551
  formation, 550
  legal capital, 553
Correction of errors, 107–8, 815, 820, 822, 825
Cost, defined, 93
Cost of goods sold, inflation and, 216
Cost Accounting Standards Board (CASB), 11
Cost effectiveness, 38
Cost flow methods (inventory), 396
Cost method, long-term investment, 646–47
Cost method, treasury stock, 589
Cost principle, 29, 318, 384, 447, 481, 498
Cost recovery (revenue recognition), 32
Cost savings
  fictional, 235–36, 240–41
  real, 235–36, 240–41, 243
Counterbalancing errors, 823
Coupon bonds, 685
CPA; *see* Certified Public Accountant
CRC; *see* Current replacement cost
Credit, investment tax, 334
Cross-references, 151
CSE; *see* Common stock equivalents *and* Earnings per share
Cumulative preferred stock, 554
Current accounting changes, 816
Current assets, 138, 265; *see also* Working capital
Current liabilities, 140, 309
Current operating concept, 102
Current ratio, 861–62; *see also* Working capital ratio
Current replacement cost
  accounting model, 232–33
  comparison with historical cost and general price level, 234, 243
  disclosure requirements of SEC, 234, 244–47

Current replacement cost—*Cont.*
  direct pricing, 246
  entries, 237, 240–41
  financial statements, 236–42
  functional pricing, 246
  GPL restatement in, 237
  illustrated, 236
  indexing, 246
  relevance of data, 235
  unit pricing, 246
Current value, 233
Current value accounting models, 231, 233

D

Damaged inventory, 367
Date of grant (stock options), 616, 618
Dollar value *Lifo,* 399–405, 430–33
Domestic corporations, 551
Donated assets, 453
Donated treasury stock, 592
Doubtful accounts; *see* Receivables
Debenture bonds, 685
Debt
  early extinguishment, 700
  modification of terms, 707
  refunding of bonds, 701
  restructuring, 704
Debt securities, 644
Declaration date of dividends, 574
Default on stock subscriptions, 558–59
Deferral method, 497
Deferrals, 28
Deferred charges, 138
  bond issue costs, 367
  defined, 142
  leaseholds, 524
  organization costs, 523
Deferred compensation cost, 620; *see also* Stock option plans
Deferred credits, 138, 143, 313
Deferred income tax, 324–30
  classification of, 327
Deferred items (for adjustment), 57
Deferred taxes, 330
Deficit, 144
Depletion
  defined, 454, 480
  dividends from, 498
  nature of, 497
  percentage, 498
  rates, 498
  statutory, 498
Deposits, returnable, 312
Depreciation, 98
  accelerated methods, 487
  annuity method, 499
  appraisal system, 490
  cash flow, 481
  catch-up, 242
  causes, 482
  changes of, 494
  composite life, 492
  corrections, 494
  current replacement cost, 242
  defined, 480–81
  determination of, 483
  disclosures, 494
  dividends and, 481

Depreciation—*Cont.*
  double-declining balance, 488
  estimates, 482
  expense, 58
  fixed percent on declining base, 488
  fractional period, 489
  group, 491
  idle plant, 482
  inventory system, 490
  investment concepts, 489
  methods, 484, 494
  obsolescence and, 482
  policy, 493
  productive output method, 486
  public utilities, 491, 501
  recording, 483
  reducing charge methods, 487
  replacement system, 491
  residual value, 483, 488
  restated, 226
  retirement system, 491
  rising replacement costs and, 217
  service hours method, 485
  sinking fund method, 499–500
  straight-line, 484, 495
  sum-of-years'-digits, 487, 495
Detachable stock warrants, 697
Development stage companies, 527
Differences, permanent, 326–29
Differences, timing, 326–30
Dilutive common stock equivalents, 627; *see also* Earnings per share
Dilutive securities (EPS), 624
Direct changes, 791, 796; *see also* Statement of changes in financial position
Direct cost (inventory), 395
Direct financing leases; *see* Leases
Disclaimer of opinion, 152
Disclosure; *see also* Full disclosure *and* Notes to the financial statements
  accounting policies, 97, 858
  contingencies, 149
  full defined, 149
  guidelines, 97
  replacement cost (SEC), 369
  subsequent events, 148
  tax allocation, 337
Discontinued operations (of a segment), 105
Discount on bonds, 180, 687; *see also* Bonds
Discount on capital stock, 561
Discounted note, 310
Discounts on purchases, 358
Discovery value, 454, 561–62
Discrete period (interim reporting), 851
Discussion memorandum (FASB), 7; *see also Appendix to Chapter 1*
Disposal of a segment of a business, 105
Distributable income, 235, 243
Dividends, 554, 555; *see also* Retained earnings
  arrears, 580
  cash, 575
  classified, 574
  legality, 582
  liability, 576
  liquidating, 498, 577

Dividends—*Cont.*
  payment, 574–75
  property, 576
  ratio, 870
  stock, 577, 625, 668
  treasury stock, 582
Dividends payable, 312

E

Early extinguishment of debt, 700
Earned surplus, defined, 573
Earnings, defined, 93
Earnings per share, 98, 100
  antidilution, 628, 632
  common stock equivalents, 627
  complex and simple capital structure, 624
  convertible securities, 629
  defined, 622
  dilutive common stock equivalents, 627–28
  dilutive securities, 624
  fully diluted, 630
  primary, 630
  prime rate test, 630
  reporting, 634
  simple capital structure, 624
  stock dividends, 625
  stock options, rights and warrants, 628
  stock splits, 625
  treasury stock method, 628
  weighted number of shares outstanding, 625
Earned surplus; *see* Retained earnings
Economic essence, 28
Economic loss, 702
Effective interest rate, 311–12
Employee Retirement Income Security Act (ERISA), 725, 729, 736
Employee stock options, 615, 618; *see also* Stock rights
End-of-the-period annuities; *see* Annuities, present value of an ordinary
Entries, reversing, 62
Entry value, 233
EPS; *see* Earnings per share
Equipment; *see* Operational assets
Equity method (long-term investments), 646, 650
Equity position, 865; *see also* Ratio analysis
Equity ratios, 865
Equity securities, 644; *see also* Long-term investments
Error correction, 815–16, 820, 822
  prior period adjustment, 824
  worksheet, 825
Errors
  correction of, 107–8
  counterbalancing, 829
  inventory, 353
  noncounterbalancing, 823
Estimated liabilities, 319
Ethics, rule 203, 9
Ex-dividend date, 574
Exit value, 233

Expense
  accrued, 57
  defined, 93
  depreciation, 58
  income tax, 323–37
  prepaid, 57
Ex rights, 613, 670
External index *(Lifo),* 405
Extinguishment of debt, 700
Extraordinary gains and losses
  debt restructure, 710
  early extinguishment of debt, 704
Extraordinary items, 102, 104, 334
Extraordinary repairs, 459

F

FASB; *see* Financial Accounting Standards Board
FICA payroll taxes, 314
Fictional holding gains, 235–36, 240–41
Fifo, 387, 419; *see also* Inventory
  investments, 646
  retail inventory method, 422
  retail method, 422
Financial accounting, effect of income tax, 11
Financial Accounting Standards Board (FASB), 5, 7, 25
  exposure draft "Financial Reporting and Changing Prices," 220
  pronouncements; *see Appendix to Chapter 1*
  Statement of Financial Concepts No. 1, 23
  statements, interpretations, and exposure drafts; *see Appendix to Chapter 1*
Financial Executives Institute (FEI), 11
Financial leverage, 866, 869
Financial position, statement of, 134
Financial position model, 48; *see also* Balance sheet
Financial reporting, objectives, 3
Financial reporting principle, 34
Financial statements, 60; *see also* Consolidated statements, defined
  analysis of, 856
  comparative, 148, 859
  consolidated, 646, 656
  current replacement cost, 236–42
  general purpose, 3
  horizontal analysis, 861
  interim, 851
  Peavey Company, 872
  percentage analysis, 859
  ratio (proportionate) analysis, 861
  single-entry records, 830
  turning points, 858
  vertical analysis, 860
  worksheet to recast, 828
Financing activities, 781; *see also* Statement of changes in financial position
Fire loss, 531
First-in, first-out; *see Fifo*
Fixed assets; *see* Operational assets *and* Property, plant, and equipment

Fixed costs, 395
Fixed liabilities; *see* Long-term liabilities
Flow statement; *see* Statement of changes in financial position
Flow-through method, 496
f.o.b., 352
Fractional share rights, 581, 613; *see also* Stock rights
Franchises; *see* Intangible assets
Freight in (on purchases), 358, 424
Full disclosure, 34–35; *see also* Disclosure
  accounting policies, 858
  defined, 149
Fully diluted earnings per share, 627, 630; *see also* Earnings per share
Funds, special purpose, 671
Funds flow model, 48; *see also* Statement of changes in financial position
Funds statement; *see* Statement of changes in financial position
FUTA payroll taxes, 315
Future losses, 585
Future value, concepts, 180, 182
Future value of annuity due, 192
Future value of 1, 182, 185
Future value of an ordinary annuity of 1, 188

G

GAAP; *see* Generally accepted accounting principles
Gain
  defined, 93
  economic on refunding, 703
Gain contingencies, 32; *see also* Contingency gains, disclosure
General journal, 52
General ledger, 54
General price level (GPL), 219; *see also* General Purchasing Power Restatement
  gain, 231
  restatement, 222
  restatement, illustrated, 229
  restatement, proof of accuracy, 233
  restatements in replacement cost financial statements, 237–38, 240–42
General Purchasing Power Restatement, 219–29
General purpose financial statements, 91
Generally accepted accounting principles, 9–10, 39
GNP Implicit Price Deflator, 216
Going business (incorporation), 562
Going-concern assumption, 26, 857
Going value, 519, 520
Goodwill, 562, 652, 658, 662; *see also* Intangible assets
Government bonds, 685
Gross margin method (inventory), 417, 531
Gross profit; *see* Gross margin method (inventory)

H

Historical cost, compared with restated statements, 242
Historical cost model, 28, 48
Holding gains and losses, 235–36, 240–43
Holding loss, inventory, 361–62
Horizontal analysis, 861

I

Imprest cash; *see* Cash, petty
Issued capital stock, 552
Issue costs (on bonds), 697
Income
  (concept of 1), 91
  defined, 93
  distributable, 235, 243
  pretax, 323
  replacement cost, 235, 240, 241, 243, 244
  taxable, 323
Income bonds, 685
Income statement
  current replacement cost, 240
  defined, 4
  general price level, 239
  multiple step, 96
  restatement of, 227, 232
  single-step, 94
Income taxes, 323–37; *see also* Taxes
  allocation, 98
  carrybacks, 331
  carryforwards, 331
  defined, 324, 327
  effect of legislation, 11
  interperiod tax allocation, 334
  intraperiod allocation, 334
  investment credit, 334
  permanent differences, 326
  refunding of bonds, 703
  timing differences, 326
  withheld, 314
Incomplete records, 830
Indenture (bond), 684
Independent accountants, 4–5
Independent accountants' report; *see* Auditors' report
Index
  external *(Lifo),* 405
  internal *(Lifo),* 405
Indexing *(Lifo),* 405
Industrial bonds, 685
Industry peculiarities, 36
Inflation
  impact on statements, 217
  piecemeal accounting approaches to, 218
Infrequent and unusual items, 105
Installment method, revenue recognition, 32
Insurance, 528
Intangible assets, 142
  amortization, 516
  classification of, 515
  copyrights, 518
  cost, 516
  disposal of, 517
  franchises, 518

Intangible assets—*Cont.*
  goodwill, 519–23
  identifiable, 517
  patents, 518
  reporting, 534
  trademarks, 519
  unidentifiable, 519
Intangibles; *see* Operational assets
Integral part interim reporting, 851
Intercompany profits and losses, 650, 652
Interest
  concept, 181
  effective, 687
  expense, 310
  simple versus compound, 181
  stated rate, 687
Interest-bearing notes, 311
Interest capitalization, 456
Interest method (amortization of bonds), 690
Interim periods, 852
Interim reporting
  accounting changes, 853
  defined, 851
  disclosure, 853
  discrete period and integral part approaches, 851
Internal index *(Lifo),* 405
Interperiod income tax allocation, 98, 324–30, 334
Interpretations of FASB statements, 7; *see also Appendix to Chapter 1*
Intraperiod income tax allocation, 98, 324–30, 334
Investee, 650–51
Investing activities, 781; *see also* Statement of changes in financial position
Inventory
  accounting value, 355
  average cost, 386
  average cost, retail method, 423
  base stock, 394
  classification, 351
  construction in process, 425
  cost flow methods, 384
  cost principle, 384
  damaged and obsolete, 367
  direct cost, 395
  dollar value, *Lifo* retail, 430
  errors, 353
  estimating procedures, 417
  Fifo, 387, 422
  Fifo, retail method, 422
  gross margin method, 417
  holding gains, 235
  holding loss, 361–62
  LCM, allowance method, 362
  LCM, direct reduction, 362
  LCM, retail method, 423
  Lifo complexities, 396
  Lifo liquidation, 852
  Lifo reserves, 405
  liquidation *(Lifo),* 401
  long-term construction contracts, 425
  loss on purchase commitments, 368
  lower-of-cost-or-market, 420
  markdowns, 421

Inventory—*Cont.*
  markups, 418, 421
  moving average cost, 386
  net realizable value, 366
  next-in, first-out, 394
  periodic, 352, 385
  perpetual, 352, 385
  overages and shortage, 352
  relative sales value method, 368
  replacement cost, 366
  repossessions, 367
  retail method, 420, 422
  at selling price, 387
  specific cost identification, 385
  spoilage, 424
  standard cost, 394
  turnover, 864
  variable cost, 395
  weighted average, 386
Inventory cost flow, 396
Investment, return on, 868
Investment tax credit, 334, 496, 817
Investment turnover, 869
Investments, 141, 271, 278, 644; *see also* Long-term investments
  consolidated statements, 656
  controlling interest, 647, 656
  cost method, 646
  equity method, 646, 650–51
  identification of, 278
  goodwill, 652
  holding gains (losses), 276
  investee company, 650–51
  long-term, 271
  long-term defined, 644
  lower-of-cost-or-market example, 278
  market value method, 654
  marketable equity securities, 272
  parent company, 657
  purchase method, 661
  revenue from, 278, 654; *see also* Revenue
  short-term, 271
  short-term defined, 272
  short-term valuation, 272
  special purpose funds, 671
  valuation at cost, 276
  valuation at market, 276
Investments and funds, 141
  bonds, 692

J

Joint cost, 368
Journal, 52
Journal of Accountancy, 6
Journalizing, 52, 60
Journals, 65–66; *see also* Special journals

L

Land; *see* Operational assets
Large stock dividend, 579
Last-in, first-out; *see* Lifo
LCM, 358, 360–61
  direct inventory reduction, 362
  inventory, 420
  inventory allowance method, 362
  long-term investments, 648–49
  retail inventory method, 423

898

Leasehold, 749
Leasehold improvements; *see* Operational assets
Leaseholds; *see* Deferred charges
Leases
  amortization, 749
  bargain purchase option, 748, 757
  bargain renewal option, 748
  capital, 749, 753, 755, 759
  capitalization of, 752
  classification criteria, 753
  defined, 748
  direct financing, 754
  disclosure, 765
  executory costs, 752–53
  inception of, 748
  initial direct costs, 749, 767
  interest rate, 755, 760
  investment credit, 760, 763
  lessee defined, 748
  lessor defined, 748
  leveraged, 766–71
  operating, 749
  prepaid rent, 749
  receivables classification, 766
  sales type, 753–54, 761
  sublease rentals, 765
  termination, 763
Ledger, 53; *see also* Subsidiary ledger
  subscriber, 558
Legal capital, 551, 553
Lessee; *see* Leases
Lessor; *see* Leases
Leverage, financial, 866
Leveraged leases; *see* Leases
Liabilities
  accrued, 313
  classified, 308, 310
  contingent, 319
  current, 140, 309
  defined, 135, 308
  dividends payable, 312
  estimated, 319
  income tax withheld, 314
  litigation, 321
  long-term, 143, 317
  notes, 310
  payroll taxes, 314–15
Liability dividends, 576
Liability insurance, 528
Life insurance, 533
Lifo, 389
  application, 398
  base cost, 397
  cash flow, 392
  complexities, 396
  dollar value, 399
  dollar value retail, 420
  indexing, 405
  initial adoption, 397
  inventory liquidation, 391, 401, 852
  multiple-pools, 398, 401
  quantity of goods method, 398
  reconstructed cost, 404
  recording, 392
  reserves, 405
  single-item approach, 398
  single-pool, 401
  technological changes, 403

Lifo inventory, liquidation, 852
Limited liability (corporations), 550
Line of business reporting; *see* Segment reporting
Liquidating dividends, 577
Liquidation of inventory, *Lifo*, 391
Long-term construction contracts, 32, 425
  percentage completion method, 425
Long-term financial summaries, 859
Long-term investments, 644; *see also* Investments
  classification, 649
  consolidated statements, 656
  controlling interest, 647, 656
  cost method, 647–48
  defined, 644
  equity method, 650
  goodwill, 652, 662
  intercompany profits and losses, 650, 652
  investee company, 650–51
  lower-of-cost-or-market, 648–49
  market value method, 654
  parent company, 657
  pooling of interests, 657–58
  purchase method, 657, 661
  significant influence, 647
  special purpose funds, 671
  stock rights, 670
  stock splits, 669
  subsidiary company, 656
  unrealized gain and losses, 648
Long-term liabilities, 143; *see also* Bonds
  bonds payable, 684, 691
  current maturities, 319
  defined, 143
Loss
  defined, 94
  economic on refunding, 702
  purchase commitments, 368
  reporting future, 585
Loss carrybacks and carryforwards, 331–34
Loss contingencies, 319, 321; *see also* Contingency losses, disclosure
Lower-of-cost-or-market; *see* LCM

M

Management accounting, defined, 2
Manufacturing cost schedule, 96
Manufacturing inventory, 351
Markdowns (inventory), 421
Market gains and losses, 655; *see also* Long-term investments
Market value, 136
Market value method (long-term investments), 646, 654
Marketable equity securities; *see* Investments
Markups (inventory), 418, 421
Matching principle, 32, 313, 356, 384, 447, 480
Materiality, 35
Measurement date (stock options), 617
Measurement principles, 36
Methods of depreciation; *see* Depreciation

Minority interest, 660; *see also* Consolidated statements, defined
Mixed accounts, 54
Models, accounting current value, 233
Modification of terms of debt, 707
Modifying (exception) principle, 35
Monetary assets, 223
Monetary items, 221, 225, 236
Monetary liabilities, 223
Moving average cost (inventory), 386
Multiple-pools approach *(Lifo)*, 398
Multiple-pools *Lifo*, 301
Multiple step income statement, 96
Municipal bonds, 685

N

National Association of Accountants (NAA), 11
Natural business year, 27
Natural resources; *see* Operational assets
Net realizable value, 360, 366
Next-in, first-out, 394
Nominal accounts, 54, 60
Noncompensatory stock option plans, 615, 617; *see also* Stock rights
Nonconvertible bonds, 697
Noncounterbalancing errors, 823
Noncumulative preferred stock, 554
Noninterest bearing notes, 311; *see also* Liabilities *and* Notes
Nonmonetary assets, holding gains, 235
Nonmonetary items, 221, 224, 236
Nonmonetary transactions, 450
Nonqualified stock option plans, 615; *see also* Stock rights
Nopar stock, 553, 557; *see also* Capital stock
Nopar value, treasury stock, 592
Normal operating cycle, 138
Notes
  discounted, 310–11
  long-term, 317
Notes to the financial statements, 97, 149; *see also* Disclosure
  subsequent events, 148
Notes payable, 310, *see also* Liabilities *and* Notes
Notes receivable, 180; *see also* Receivables

O

Objectives of financial statements, 3
Objectivity principle, 33
Obsolete inventory, 367
Oil and gas exploration costs, 526
Open corporations, 551
Operating cycle, normal, 138
Operating results, ratios, 867
Operational assets, 447; *see also* Fixed assets *and* Property, plant, and equipment
  additions, 460
  book value, 450
  boot, 450–51
  buildings, 462
  deferred (installment) payments for, 448

Operational assets—*Cont.*
  defined, 142
  departures from cost, 453
  discounts on, 447
  discovery value, 454
  donated, 453
  exchanged for securities, 449
  exchanges of, 449
  furniture and fixtures, 463
  intangible, 142
  interest during construction, 456
  land, 461
  land improvements, 462
  leasehold improvements, 463
  lump-sum purchase, 452
  machinery, 463
  make-ready costs, 453
  patterns and dies, 463
  rearrangement costs, 461
  repairs and maintenance, 458
  replacements and betterments, 459
  retirement, 461
  returnable containers, 463
  self-constructed, 455
  similar and dissimilar, 450
  tangible, 142
  tools, 463
Opinion, 151; *see also* Auditors' report
  adverse, 152
  disclaimer of, 152
  qualified, 151
  unqualified, 151, 857
Opinions of APB; *see Appendix to Chapter 1*
Options, 618; *see also* Stock option plans *and* Stock rights
Ordinary annuities; *see* Annuities
Ordinary note, 310
Organization costs; *see* Deferred charges
Other assets, 142; *see also* Assets
Outstanding capital stock, 552
Overages, inventory, 353
Owners' equity, 135; *see also* Stockholders' equity

P

Paid-in surplus; *see* Contributed capital in excess of par, defined
Par value method, treasury stock, 590
Par value stock, 552, 557; *see also* Capital stock
Parent company, 657
Participating bonds, 685
Participating preferred stock, 555
Patents; *see* Intangible assets
Payment date of dividends, 575
Payroll taxes, 314–15
Peavey Company (financial statements illustrated), 872
Pension fund, 726
Pension plans
  accrued benefit cost method, 728
  actuarial cost methods, 727–29
  actuarial factors, 725
  actuarial gains and losses, 732–34
  actuarial valuation, 727
  aggregate cost method, 728
  attained age normal method, 728

Pension plans—*Cont.*
  cost amortization, 729–32
  deferred charges, 731–32
  defined benefit, 724
  disclosures, 735–36
  entry age normal method, 728
  funding, 729–32
  income tax requirements, 724
  individual level premium method, 728
  liabilities, 731, 737
  maximum/minimum cost, 734–35
  normal cost, 725, 730–31
  past service cost, 725–26, 729–32
  prior service cost, 727
  projected benefit cost methods, 728
  simple example, 725–27
  statistics concerning, 724
  terminal funding, 726
  termination, 736
  unit credit method, 728
  vesting, 725
Percentage analysis, 859; *see also* Ratio analysis
Percentage-of-completion, long-term construction, 425–26
Periodic inventory, 352, 385, 389; *see also* Inventory
Permanent accounts, 54
Permanent difference (income taxes), 326
Perpetual inventory, 352, 385, 389; *see also* Inventory
Petty cash; *see* Cash, petty
Plant assets; *see* Operational assets
Pollution control, 460
Pooling of interests, 657–58
Portfolio, long-term investments, 648
Post-closing trial balance, 62
Posting entries, 60
Posting to the ledger, 52
Preferred stock, 554; *see also* Capital stock
  callable, 556
  convertible, 556, 624
  cumulative and noncumulative, 554, 625
  nonconvertible, 624
  participating, 555
  redemption, 556
Premium on bonds, 180, 687; *see also* Bonds
Premium on capital stock, 560
Premium, coupons and trading stamps, 320
Prepaid expenses, 57
Present value, 91
  bond prices, 687
  concepts, 180, 182
Present value of annuity due, 194
Present value of 1, 185
Present value of an ordinary annuity, 190
Pretax accounting income, 323
Price changes
  measurement of, 215
Price earnings ratio, 869
Price index
  base year, 216

Price index—*Cont.*
  Consumer Price Index, 216
  defined, 216
  GNP Implicit Deflator, 216
Primary earnings per share, 627, 630; *see also* Earnings per share
Prime rate test (EPS), 630
Principles, full disclosure, 858
Prior period adjustments, 102, 106, 330–31, 495, 824
Private corporations, 551
Product warranties, 320
Productive capacity, 245
Profit defined, 93
Profit margin, 868
Pro forma, 817
Property dividends, 576
Property, plant, and equipment, 142; *see also* Operational assets
Property taxes, 313
Proportionate analysis of financial statements, 86
Pro rata basis, 551
Prospective accounting changes, 816
Public corporations, 551
Public utilities, 457
Purchase commitments, 368
Purchase discount lost, 358
Purchase method (of equity securities), 657, 661; *see also* Long-term investments
Purchase returns, 424
Purchases
  discounts, 358
  freight in, 358
Purchasing power gain (loss), 223–24

Q

Qualified opinion, 151
Qualified stock option plans, 615; *see also* Stock rights
Quantity of good method *(Lifo),* 398
Quasi-reorganizations, 595
Quick ratio, 862

R

Ratio analysis
  of financial statements, 861
  market ratios, 869
  use and interpretation, 876
Raw materials inventory, 351
Real accounts, 54, 60
Real liability gains, 235–36, 240–41, 243
Realization of revenue, 30
Receivable turnover, 863
Receivables
  aging, 283
  assignment, 287
  bad debt expense, 280
  charging off, 282
  collection of previously bad, 283
  credit balances, 284
  defined, 280
  discounting notes, 286
  dishonored notes, 286
  factoring, 289
  notes, 284
  pledging, 289
  sale of, 289

Receivables—*Cont.*
  special, 287
  specific charge off method, 281
  valuation, 280
Reciprocal items; *see* Consolidated
  statements
Reconciliation; *see* Cash, reconciliation
Record date of dividends, 575
Redeemable bonds, 685
Redeemable capital stock, 594
Redemption (preferred stock), 556
Refinancing of short-term obligations,
  704
Refunding bonds, 685, 701
Registered bonds, 685
Regulation S-X (SEC), 8
Relative sales value inventory, 368
Rents (annuities), 190
Repairs and maintenance, 458
Replacement cost, 233–35; *see also* Current
  replacement cost
  disclosure (SEC), 369
  inventory, 366
Replacements and betterments, 459
Reporting
  entity changes, 819
  interim periods, 851
  retained earnings, 585
Reporting principle, 149
Reports, 10–K (SEC), 8
Repossessions (inventory), 367
Reproduction cost, 246
Research and development costs, 149,
  524–26
Reserves, *Lifo,* 405; *see also* Retained
  earnings
Restrictions on retained earnings, 109
Restructuring of troubled debt, 704
Results of operations model, 48; *see also*
  Income statement
Retail inventory method, 420, 422
  dollar value, 420
  LCM, 423
Retained earnings, 144; *see also* Stockholders'
  equity
  appropriated, 323, 583
  classifications, 552
  defined, 144
  reporting, 585
  reserves, 323
  restricted, 144
  restrictions, 109, 593
  statement, 109
Retroactive accounting changes, 816
Return on investment, 868
Return on owners' equity, 868
Return on total assets, 868
Returnable containers; *see* Operational
  assets
Returnable deposits, 312
Revenue
  defined, 30, 92
  investment, 654
  measurement, 30
  sales transactions, 31
  timing recognition, 30
  unearned, 57
Revenue collected in advance, 57; *see
  also* Unearned revenue

Revenue expenditures, 446
Revenue principle, 30, 93
Revenue recognition
  cash approach, 32
  cost recovery, 33
  percentage completion, 32
  production, 32
Reverse stock split, 669
Reversing entries, 62
Rights; *see* Stock rights
Rights on, 613, 670
ROI (return on investment), 868
Rounding of amounts, 148

S

SAB; *see SEC Staff Accounting Bulletins*
Sale and leaseback, 764
Sales returns and allowances, 424
Sales tax, 314
Sales type leases; *see* Leases
SCFP; *see* Statement of changes in financial
  position
SEC, 5, 8, 369; *see also Appendix to
  Chapter 1*
  ASRs, 8
  Regulation S-X, 8
  replacement cost disclosure, 234
  report 10–K, 8
  report 10–Q, 8
  Securities Acts of 1933 and 1934, 8
  Staff Accounting Bulletins (SABs),
    8
Securities, convertible, 669
Securities and Exchange Commission;
  see SEC
Segment of a business, disposal of, 105
Segment reporting
  defined, 853
  definition of a segment, 854
Self-constructed assets, 455
Separate entity assumption, 26
Serial bonds, 685, 711
Service transactions (revenue recognition),
  31; *see also* Revenue
Share rights, 581; *see also* Fractional
  share rights *and* Stock rights
Short-term obligation to be refinanced,
  704
Shortages, inventory, 353
Significant accounting policies; *see* Accounting
  policies
Significant influence, 647; *see also* Long-term
  investments
Simple capital structures, 624; *see also*
  Earnings per share
Simple interest, 181; *see* Interest
  limitations, 838
Single-entry records, 830
  limitations, 838
Single-item approach *(Lifo),* 398
Single-pool *Lifo,* 401
Single step income statement, 94
Small stock dividend, 578
Special journals, 66
  cash payments, 69
  cash receipts, 69
  defined, 52
  merchandise purchases on credit,
    68
  merchandise sales on credit, 67

Special purpose funds, 671
Specific cost (inventory), 385
Spoilage (inventory), 424
Stabilized Accounting, 219
Standard cost (inventory), 394
Stated capital, 551
Stated value stock, 553
Statement of accounting policies, 858
Statement of Basic Accounting Theory
  (AAA), 10
Statement of changes in financial position
  cash basis, 783, 798
  characteristics, 782
  criteria, 785
  defined, 4, 145, 781
  direct exchanges, 791, 796
  working capital basis, 783, 788
Statements of APB; *see Appendix to
  Chapter 1*
Statements on Auditing Standards, 6
Stock; *see* Investments
Stock dividends, 577–78, 625, 668
Stock investments, 444; *see also* Investments
  and Long-term investments
Stock issue costs, 523
Stock option plans, 614; *see also* Stock
  rights
  compensatory, 616
  deferred compensation cost, 620
  measurement date, 617
  noncompensatory, 617
Stock rights, 581; *see also* Fractional
  share rights; Share rights; *and*
  Stock warrants
  compensation cost, 618
  compensatory stock option plans, 615
  defined, 613
  investment shares, 670
  noncompensatory stock option plans,
    615
  options issued to employees, 615
  qualified stock option plans, 615
Stock splits, 578, 625, 669
Stock warrants, 697; *see also* Stock
  rights
Stockholders' equity, 143; *see also* Owners'
  equity *and* Shareholders'
  equity
  capital stock, 143
  contraction and expansion, 587
  contributed capital in excess of par,
    144
Straight-line amortization (bonds), 690
Subscribed stock, 552
Subscriber's ledger, 558
Subscriptions (capital stock), 558
Subsequent events, 148
Subsidiary company, 656; *see also* Long-term
  investments
Subsidiary ledger, 54, 65
  accounts payable, 68
  accounts receivable, 65, 69
  defined, 54, 65
Subsidiary records, 353
Summary of significant accounting policies,
  858
Sunk cost, 32
Surplus; *see* Retained earnings

Surplus reserves; *see* Retained earnings
Suspense (clearing) accounts, 61
Sweeney, Dr. Henry W., 219

T

T-account approach (statement of changes in financial position), 787
Tangible fixed assets, 142; *see also* Operational assets
Tax; *see* Income taxes
Tax allocation (income)
    defined, 324
    disclosure, 337
    intraperiod, 334
Tax and bonus problem, 316
Tax credit, 334
Tax loss carrybacks and carryforwards, 331–34
Tax rates, changes in, 329–30
Taxable income, 323
Taxes, 323; *see also* Income taxes
Technological changes (inventory), 403
Temporary accounts, 54
Terminology, 147; *see also Appendix to Chapter 1*
Time period assumption, 27
Time value of money; *see* Interest
Timing differences (income taxes), 326–30
Trade receivables; *see* Receivables
Trademarks; *see* Intangible assets
Trading on the equity, 866; *see also* Financial leverage

Transaction analysis, 52
Transactions approach, 92
Treasury stock, 552; *see also* Capital stock
    cost method, 589
    defined, 588
    dividends, 582
    donated shares, 592
    nopar value, 593
    par value method, 590
    restriction on retained earnings, 593
    retirement, 592
Treasury stock method (EPS), 628
Trial balance
    post closing, 62
    unadjusted, 54, 62
Troubled debt restructuring, 704
Trustee (bond), 684
Turning points, 858, 870
Turnover
    inventory, 864
    investments, 869
    receivables, 863

U

Unadjusted trial balance, 54
Unappropriated retained earnings; *see* Retained earnings
Uncollectible accounts; *see* Receivables
Unconsolidated subsidiaries, 657; *see also* Long-term investments
Unearned revenue, 57
Unissued capital stock, 552
Unit of measure assumption, 27, 38
Unqualified auditors' opinion, 151, 857

Unrealized capital, 552, 561
    defined, 145
    increment, 454
Unrealized gains and losses, 648
Unusual and infrequent items, 105

V

Value, entry, 233
Value, exit, 233
Variable cost (inventory), 395
Verifiability, 33
Vertical analysis of financial statements, 860

W

Warrants; *see* Stock rights
Weighted average cost (inventory), 386
Weighted shares outstanding, 625; *see also* Earnings per share
Work in process inventory, 351
Working capital
    defined, 141
    statement of changes, 783, 786
Working capital flow statement; *see* Statement of changes in financial position
Working capital ratio, 862; *see also* Current ratio
Worksheets, 55, 59
    correcting errors, 825
    manufacturing company, 71–72
    recasting financial statements, 828
    single entry records, 835
    statement of changes in financial position, 792, 800
    trading company, 56

This book has been set in 9 and 8 point Primer, leaded 2 points. Chapter numbers are 72 point Caslon #540 and chapter titles are 22 point Compano. The overall page size is 37½ by 48 picas.